Contemporary Authors®

NEW REVISION SERIES

ISSN 0275-7176

Contemporary Authors®

**A Bio-Bibliographical Guide to
Current Writers in Fiction, General Nonfiction,
Poetry, Journalism, Drama, Motion Pictures,
Television, and Other Fields**

HAL MAY
JAMES G. LESNIAK
Editors

BRYAN RYAN
Associate Editor

THOMAS WILOCH
Senior Writer

NEW REVISION SERIES *volume* 26

Gale Research Inc. • BOOK TOWER • DETROIT, MICHIGAN 48226

STAFF

Hal May and James G. Lesniak, *Editors, New Revision Series*

Bryan Ryan, *Associate Editor*

Thomas Wiloch, *Senior Writer*

Marilyn K. Basel and Margaret Mazurkiewicz, *Senior Assistant Editors*

Marian Gonsior, Sharon Malinowski, Michael E. Mueller, and Kenneth R. Shepherd, *Assistant Editors and Writers*

Melissa J. Gaiownik, Cheryl Gottler, Kevin S. Hile, Jani Prescott, Diane Telgen, and Michaela Swart Wilson, *Assistant Editors*

Donna Olendorf, Jean W. Ross, and Revan Schendler, *Interviewers*

Joan Goldsworthy, Carolyn Handa, Anne Janette Johnson, Donna Olendorf, Susan Salter, Elizabeth Thomas, and Katherine Wallingford, *Contributing Editors*

Linda Metzger, *Senior Editor, Contemporary Authors*

Mary Rose Bonk, *Research Supervisor*
Alysa I. Hunton, *Research Coordinator*
Jane Cousins-Clegg, *Assistant Research Coordinator*
Reginald A. Carlton, Andrew Guy Malonis, and Norma Sawaya, *Senior Research Assistants*
John P. Dodt, Clare Kinsman, Sharon McGilvray, Shirley Seip, and Tracey Head Turbett, *Research Assistants*

Copyright © 1989 by Gale Research Inc.

Library of Congress Catalog Card Number 81-640179
ISBN 0-8103-1980-2
ISSN 0275-7176

Computerized photocomposition by
Typographics, Incorporated
Kansas City, Missouri

Contents

> **Indexing note:** All *Contemporary Authors New Revision Series* entries are indexed in the *Contemporary Authors* cumulative index, which is bound into the back of even-numbered *Contemporary Authors* original volumes (blue and black cover with orange bands) and available separately as an offprint.

091936

Authors and Media People
Featured in This Volume

Chinua Achebe (Nigerian novelist, essayist, short story writer, and poet)—Achebe has acquired an international following on the basis of such novels as *Things Fall Apart, A Man of the People,* and *Anthills of the Savannah,* and is considered by many to be the finest novelist in Nigeria.

Alice Adams (American short story writer and novelist)—In such fictional works as *To See You Again, Superior Women,* and *Return Trips,* Adams chronicles the lives of well-educated middle-class women searching for love, fulfillment, and self-identity. (Entry contains interview.)

Vicente Aleixandre (Spanish poet who died in 1984)—A member of Spain's poetic Generation of 1927, Aleixandre remained virtually unknown outside his native country until he received the Nobel Prize for literature in 1977. His works in English translation include *Twenty Poems* and *A Longing for the Light.*

Shana Alexander (American journalist and commentator)—A veteran reporter who gained national recognition as a featured commentator on "Sixty Minutes," Alexander analyzes the celebrated trials of Patty Hearst, Jean Harris, Frances Schreuder, and twenty-two Mafia defendants in her books *Anyone's Daughter, Very Much a Lady, Nutcracker,* and *The Pizza Connection.* (Entry contains interview.)

Hannah Arendt (German-born American political philosopher who died in 1975)—Arendt earned a reputation as one of this century's most brilliant and original thinkers through her penetrating analyses of historical and political events. Among her works are *The Origins of Totalitarianism, The Human Condition, Eichmann in Jerusalem: A Report on the Banality of Evil,* and the posthumously published *The Life of the Mind.*

Elizabeth Bishop (American poet, author of nonfiction, and translator who died in 1979)—Considered one of the major poets of the twentieth century, Bishop wrote verse that is characterized by emotional control, technical mastery, and precise use of detail. She received a Pulitzer Prize in 1956 for *Poems: North and South* [and] *A Cold Spring,* a National Book Award in 1970 for *The Complete Poems,* and a National Book Critics Circle Award in 1977 for *Geography III.*

Malcolm Boyd (American Episcopal priest, commentator, and social activist)—Boyd, widely known during the 1960s for his avant-garde method of preaching and his support of the civil rights movement, documents in his autobiographical book *Take off the Masks* both the rewards and costs of openly declaring his homosexuality. (Entry contains interview.)

James Clavell (British-born American novelist and screenwriter)—The blockbuster sagas of the Far East *Tai Pan: A Novel of Hong Kong, Shogun: A Novel of Japan,* and *Noble House: A Novel of Contemporary Hong Kong* have helped make Clavell one of the world's most widely read novelists. An accomplished screenwriter as well, he wrote the filmscripts for the 1958 version of "The Fly," "The Great Escape," and "To Sir with Love."

Henry Steele Commager (American historian)—An eminent scholar who has edited numerous compilations of original source material, Commager seeks to acquaint general readers with the history of the United States in such books as *The Growth of the American Republic, Documents of American History,* and *Our Nation.*

Erica Jong (American novelist and poet)—Jong revolutionized readers' perceptions of female sexuality in her enormously popular novel *Fear of Flying,* the story of Isadora Wing's search for sexual realization. Jong's subsequent books include the sequels *How to Save Your Own Life* and *Parachutes and Kisses,* as well as the picaresque satire *Fanny, Being the True History of the Adventures of Fanny Hackabout-Jones: A Novel.* (Entry contains interview.)

Donald Justice (American poet)—Considered one of America's most elegant and distinctive contemporary poets, Justice has won acclaim for bringing originality to the timeless theme of loss and for demonstrating a remarkable technical prowess. His works include *The Summer Anniversaries, Night Light, Departures,* and the Pulitzer Prize-winning *Selected Poems.* (Entry contains interview.)

Jack Kerouac (American novelist who died in 1969)—Kerouac became the leading spokesman of the Beat Generation through his well-known novel *On the Road,* which countered the prevailing conformism of the 1950s with a vision of freedom, individualism, restless movement, and the renewed possibility of self-transcendence.

Stanley Kunitz (American poet, essayist, and editor)—Kunitz displays in his body of work a stylistic evolution, from highly intricate and intellectually demanding verse forms to simpler, more straightforward constructions. Among his works are the Pulitzer Prize-winning *Selected Poems, 1928-1958* and *Next-to-Last Things: New Poems and Essays.* (Entry contains interview.)

Robert Lowell (American poet and critic who died in 1977)—Noted for the strong images, dense diction, and intense passion that characterize his verse, Lowell pioneered the tradition of autobiographical verse in America and crafted poetry that relied on the past as well. Among his better-known works are *Lord Weary's Castle* and *The Dolphin,* both winners of the Pulitzer Prize.

Joe McGinnis (American author of nonfiction)—McGinnis explores the mass-media marketing of Richard Nixon in his popular account *The Selling of the President, 1968,* and relates the true story of murderer Jeffrey MacDonald in *Fatal Vision.* (Entry contains interview.)

Stephen B. Oates (American historian, educator, and biographer)—Oates is best known for his biographical quartet on the Civil War era and its century-old legacies, *To Purge This Land with Blood: A Biography of John Brown, The Fires of Jubilee: Nat Turner's Fierce Rebellion, With Malice toward None: The Life of Abraham Lincoln,* and *Let the Trumpet Sound: The Life of Martin Luther King, Jr.* (Entry contains interview.)

Robert B. Parker (American author of detective novels)—Called by many the modern successor to Dashiell Hammett and Raymond Chandler, Parker is the creator of Spenser, the tough yet sensitive private eye in a series of novels that includes *The Godwulf Manuscript, Looking for Rachel Wallace,* and *Ceremony.* (Entry contains interview.)

Gordon Parks (American poet, novelist, essayist, photographer, and film director)—In his autobiographical volumes *A Choice of Weapons* and *To Smile in Autumn,* Parks describes how he overcame the difficulties of being black, uneducated, and poor to become the first black photographer at *Life* magazine, a successful composer, and the director of such feature films as "Shaft" and "Leadbelly."

Harold Robbins (American novelist)—The author of such bestsellers as *Never Love a Stranger, The Carpetbaggers,* and *The Betsy,* Robbins has sold more than 250 million copies of novels filled with illicit sex, graphic violence, and powerful conflicts between members of the international jet set.

Mike Royko (American journalist)—Pulitzer Prize-winning columnist Royko uses humor and irony to expose political corruption and modern life's many difficulties in *Boss: Richard J. Daley of Chicago, Sez Who? Sez Me,* and *Like I Was Sayin'.*

Muriel Rukeyser (American poet, social activist, educator, dramatist, and translator who died in 1980)—A poet of social protest, Rukeyser so closely aligned her creative capacities with the current events of her day that many critics believe the history of the United States for several decades can be culled from her powerful verse. Her poetry works include *Theory of Flight, Breaking Open: New Poems, The Gates: Poems,* and *The Collected Poems of Muriel Rukeyser.*

Alan Sillitoe (British novelist, playwright, and poet)—Though he continues to write a variety of books, Sillitoe remains best known for his early novels *Saturday Night and Sunday Morning* and *The Loneliness of the Long Distance Runner.*

Neil Simon (American playwright and screenwriter)—Simon is one of this century's most successful playwrights, having dominated Broadway for three decades with such comedies as "The Odd Couple," "The Sunshine Boys," "Barefoot in the Park," and "Brighton Beach Memoirs." These hits, combined with their film adaptations, have reputedly made him the wealthiest playwright alive.

Judith Viorst (American poet, journalist, and author of nonfiction)—Viorst brings a humorous approach to the problems of everyday life in her *Redbook* column and in the books *It's Hard to Be Hip over Thirty and Other Tragedies of Married Life, How Did I Get to Be Forty and Other Atrocities,* and *When Did I Stop Being Twenty and Other Injustices: Selected Poems from Single to Mid-Life.* (Entry contains interview.)

Margaret Abigail Walker (American poet, novelist, and educator)—A spokeswoman for the rights of blacks and women, Walker is most famous for the title poem in her collection *For My People,* which became a cornerstone of the 1960s black arts movement.

Roger Zelazny (American science fiction writer)—Zelazny's early novels, including *This Immortal, Lord of Light,* and *Creatures of Light and Darkness,* are known for their flamboyant, poetic style and use of ancient mythological stories. His more recent "Amber" series features a world that transcends the limitations of space and time.

Preface

The *Contemporary Authors New Revision Series* provides completely updated information on authors listed in earlier volumes of *Contemporary Authors (CA)*. Entries for active individual authors from *any* volume of *CA* may be included in a volume of the *New Revision Series*. The sketches appearing in *New Revision Series* Volume 26, for example, were selected from more than twenty previously published *CA* volumes.

As always, the most recent *Contemporary Authors* cumulative index continues to be the user's guide to the location of an individual author's listing.

Compilation Methods

The editors make every effort to secure information directly from the authors. Copies of all sketches in selected *CA* volumes published several years ago are routinely sent to the listees at their last-known addresses. Authors mark material to be deleted or changed and insert any new personal data, new affiliations, new writings, new work in progress, new sidelights, and new biographical/critical sources. All returns are assessed, more comprehensive research is done, if necessary, and those sketches requiring significant change are completely updated and published in the *New Revision Series*.

If, however, authors fail to reply or are now deceased, biographical dictionaries are checked for new information (a task made easier through the use of Gale's *Biography and Genealogy Master Index* and other Gale biographical indexes), as are bibliographical sources such as *Cumulative Book Index* and *The National Union Catalog*. Using data from such sources, revision editors select and revise nonrespondents' entries that need substantial updating. Sketches not personally reviewed by the biographees are marked with a dagger (†) to indicate that these listings have been revised from secondary sources believed to be reliable, but they have not been personally reviewed for this edition by the authors sketched.

In addition, reviews and articles in major periodicals, lists of prestigious awards, and, particularly, requests from *CA* users are monitored so that writers on whom new information is in demand can be identified and revised listings prepared promptly.

Format

CA entries provide biographical and bibliographical information in an easy-to-use format. For example, individual paragraphs featuring such rubrics as "Addresses," "Career," and "Awards, Honors" ensure that a reader seeking specific information can quickly focus on the pertinent portion of an entry. In sketch sections headed "Writings," the title of each book, play, and other published or unpublished work appears on a separate line, clearly distinguishing one title from another. This same convenient bibliographical presentation is also featured in the "Biographical/Critical Sources" sections of sketches where individual book and periodical titles are listed on separate lines. *CA* readers can therefore quickly scan these often-lengthy bibliographies to find the titles they need.

Comprehensive Revision

All listings in this volume have been revised and/or augmented in various ways, though the amount and type of change vary with the author. In many instances, sketches are totally rewritten, and the resulting *New Revision Series* entries are often considerably longer than the authors' previous listings. Revised entries include additions of or changes in such information as degrees, mailing addresses, literary agents, career items, career-related and civic activities, memberships, awards, work in progress, and biographical/critical sources. They may also include extensive bibliographical additions and informative new sidelights.

Writers of Special Interest

CA's editors make every effort to include in each *New Revision Series* volume a substantial number of revised entries on active authors and media people of special interest to *CA*'s readers. Since the *New Revision Series* also includes sketches on noteworthy deceased writers, a significant amount of work on the part of *CA*'s editors goes into the revision of entries on important deceased authors. Some of the prominent writers, both living and deceased, whose sketches are contained in this volume are noted in the list on pages vii-viii headed Authors and Media People Featured in This Volume.

Exclusive Interviews

CA provides exclusive, primary information on certain authors in the form of interviews. Prepared specifically for *CA,* the never-before-published conversations presented in the section of the sketch headed "*CA* Interview" give users the opportunity to learn the authors' thoughts, in depth, about their craft. Subjects chosen for interviews are, the editors feel, authors who hold special interest for *CA*'s readers.

Authors and journalists in this volume whose sketches contain exclusive interviews are Alice Adams, Shana Alexander, Malcolm Boyd, Erica Jong, Donald Justice, Stanley Kunitz, Joe McGinnis, Stephen B. Oates, Robert B. Parker, and Judith Viorst.

Contemporary Authors Autobiography Series

Designed to complement the information in *CA* original and revision volumes, the *Contemporary Authors Autobiography Series* provides autobiographical essays written by important current authors. Each volume contains from twenty to thirty specially commissioned autobiographies and is illustrated with numerous personal photographs supplied by the authors. Common topics of discussion for these authors include their motivations for writing, the people and experiences that shaped their careers, the rewards they derive from their work, and their impressions of the current literary scene.

Autobiographies included in the series can be located through both the *CA* cumulative index and the *Contemporary Authors Autobiography Series* cumulative index, which lists not only personal names but also titles of works, geographical names, subjects, and schools of writing.

Contemporary Authors Bibliographical Series

The *Contemporary Authors Bibliographical Series* is a comprehensive survey of writings by and about the most important authors since World War II in the United States and abroad. Each volume concentrates on a specific genre and nationality and features approximately ten major writers. Series entries, which complement the information in other *CA* volumes, consist of three parts: a primary bibliography that lists works written by the author, a secondary bibliography that lists works about the author, and a bibliographical essay that thoroughly analyzes the merits and deficiencies of major critical and scholarly works.

These bibliographies can be located through both the *CA* cumulative index and the *Contemporary Authors Bibliographical Series* cumulative author index. A cumulative critic index, citing critics discussed in the bibliographical essays, also appears in each *Bibliographical Series* volume.

CA Numbering System

Occasionally questions arise about the *CA* numbering system. Despite numbers like "97-100" and "125," the entire *CA* series consists of only 88 physical volumes with the publication of *CA New Revision Series* Volume 26. The following information notes changes in the numbering system, as well as in cover design, to help users better understand the organization of the entire *CA* series.

***CA* First Revisions**	• 1-4R through 41-44R (11 books) *Cover:* Brown with black and gold trim. There will be no further *First Revisions* because revised entries are now being handled exclusively through the more efficient *New Revision Series* mentioned below.
***CA* Original Volumes**	• 45-48 through 97-100 (14 books) *Cover:* Brown with black and gold trim. • 101 through 125 (25 books) *Cover:* Blue and black with orange bands. The same as previous *CA* original volumes but with a new, simplified numbering system and new cover design.

CA New Revision Series	• *CANR*-1 through *CANR*-26 (26 books) *Cover:* Blue and black with green bands. Includes only sketches requiring extensive change; **sketches are taken from any previously published *CA* volume.**
CA Permanent Series	• *CAP*-1 and *CAP*-2 (2 books) *Cover:* Brown with red and gold trim. There will be no further *Permanent Series* volumes because revised entries are now being handled exclusively through the more efficient *New Revision Series* mentioned above.
CA Autobiography Series	• *CAAS*-1 through *CAAS*-8 (8 books) *Cover:* Blue and black with pink and purple bands. Presents specially commissioned autobiographies by leading contemporary writers to complement the information in *CA* original and revision volumes.
CA Bibliographical Series	• *CABS*-1 and *CABS*-2 (2 books) *Cover:* Blue and black with blue bands. Provides comprehensive bibliographical information on published works by and about major modern authors.

Retaining *CA* Volumes

As new volumes in the series are published, users often ask which *CA* volumes, if any, can be discarded. The Volume Update Chart on page xiii is designed to assist users in keeping their collections as complete as possible. All volumes in the left column of the chart should be retained to have the most complete, up-to-date coverage possible; volumes in the right column can be discarded if the appropriate replacements are held.

Cumulative Index Should Always Be Consulted

The key to locating an individual author's listing is the *CA* cumulative index bound into the back of alternate original volumes (and available separately as an offprint). Since the *CA* cumulative index provides access to *all* entries in the *CA* series, the latest cumulative index should always be consulted to find the specific volume containing a listee's original or most recently revised sketch.

Those authors whose entries appear in the *New Revision Series* are listed in the *CA* cumulative index with the designation **CANR-** in front of the specific volume number. For the convenience of those who do not have *New Revision Series* volumes, the cumulative index also notes the specific earlier volumes of *CA* in which the sketch appeared. Below is a sample index citation for an author whose revised entry appears in a *New Revision Series* volume.

Sagan, Carl (Edward) 1934- CANR-11
Earlier sketch in CA 25-28R

For the most recent information on Sagan, users should refer to Volume 11 of the *New Revision Series,* as designated by "CANR-11"; if that volume is unavailable, refer to *CA* 25-28 First Revision, as indicated by "Earlier sketch in CA 25-28R," for his 1977 listing. (And if *CA* 25-28 First Revision is unavailable, refer to *CA* 25-28, published in 1971, for Sagan's original listing.)

Sketches not eligible for inclusion in a *New Revision Series* volume because the biographee or a revision editor has verified that no significant change is required will, of course, be available in previously published *CA* volumes. Users should always consult the most recent *CA* cumulative index to determine the location of these authors' entries.

For the convenience of *CA* users, the *CA* cumulative index also includes references to all entries in these related Gale literary series: *Authors in the News, Children's Literature Review, Concise Dictionary of American Literary Biography, Contemporary Literary Criticism, Dictionary of Literary Biography, Short Story Criticism, Something About the Author, Something About the Author Autobiography Series, Twentieth-Century Literary Criticism,* and *Yesterday's Authors of Books For Children.*

Acknowledgments

The editors wish to thank Judith S. Baughman for her assistance with copyediting.

Suggestions Are Welcome

The editors welcome comments and suggestions from users on any aspect of the *CA* series. If readers would like to suggest authors whose *CA* entries should appear in future volumes of the *New Revision Series,* they are cordially invited to write: The Editors, *Contemporary Authors New Revision Series,* Book Tower, Detroit, MI 48226; or, call toll-free at 1-800-521-0707.

Volume Update Chart

IF YOU HAVE:	YOU MAY DISCARD:
1-4 First Revision (1967)	1 (1962) 2 (1963) 3 (1963) 4 (1963)
5-8 First Revision (1969)	5-6 (1963) 7-8 (1963)
Both 9-12 First Revision (1974) AND *Contemporary Authors Permanent Series,* Volume 1 (1975)	9-10 (1964) 11-12 (1965)
Both 13-16 First Revision (1975) AND *Contemporary Authors Permanent Series,* Volumes 1 and 2 (1975, 1978)	13-14 (1965) 15-16 (1966)
Both 17-20 First Revision (1976) AND *Contemporary Authors Permanent Series,* Volumes 1 and 2 (1975, 1978)	17-18 (1967) 19-20 (1968)
Both 21-24 First Revision (1977) AND *Contemporary Authors Permanent Series,* Volumes 1 and 2 (1975, 1978)	21-22 (1969) 23-24 (1970)
Both 25-28 First Revision (1977) AND *Contemporary Authors Permanent Series,* Volume 2 (1978)	25-28 (1971)
Both 29-32 First Revision (1978) AND *Contemporary Authors Permanent Series,* Volume 2 (1978)	29-32 (1972)
Both 33-36 First Revision (1978) AND *Contemporary Authors Permanent Series,* Volume 2 (1978)	33-36 (1973)
37-40 First Revision (1979)	37-40 (1973)
41-44 First Revision (1979)	41-44 (1974)
45-48 (1974) 49-52 (1975) ↓ ↓ 125 (1989)	NONE: These volumes will not be superseded by corresponding revised volumes. Individual entries from these and all other volumes appearing in the left column of this chart will be revised and included in the *New Revision Series*.
Volumes in the *Contemporary Authors New Revision Series*	NONE: The *New Revision Series* does not replace any single volume of *CA*. All volumes appearing in the left column of this chart must be retained to have information on all authors in the series.

Contemporary Authors

NEW REVISION SERIES

*† Indicates that a listing has been revised from secondary sources believed to be reliable
but has not been personally reviewed for this edition by the author sketched.*

ABRAHAMS, Peter (Henry) 1919-

PERSONAL: Born March 19, 1919, at Vrededorp, near Johannesburg, South Africa; son of James Henry and Angelina (DuPlessis) Abrahams; married Dorothy Pennington, 1942 (marriage dissolved, 1948); married Daphne Elizabeth Miller (an artist), June 1, 1948; children: (second marriage) Anne, Aron, Naomi. *Education:* Attended St. Peter's College and Teacher's Training College.

ADDRESSES: Home—Red Hills, St. Andrew, Jamaica, West Indies. *Agent*—Faber & Faber Ltd., 3 Queen Sq., London WC1N 3AU, England; and 50 Cross St., Winchester, Mass.

CAREER: Began working, as a tinsmith's helper, at the age of nine; attended schools between periods of working at jobs such as kitchen helper, dishwasher, porter, and clerk; failed in his attempt to start a school near Capetown for poor Africans; for a short time worked as an editor in Durban; in 1939, to reach England, he took work as a stoker, and spent two years at sea; correspondent in Kenya and South Africa for the London *Observer* and the *New York Herald Tribune* (New York and Paris), 1952-54; commissioned by British Government in 1955 to write a book on Jamaica; emigrated to Jamaica in 1956; regular radio news commentator in Jamaica, 1957—; editor of the *West Indian Economist*, Jamaica, 1958-62, and radio commentator and controller for the "West Indian News" Program, 1958-62; full-time writer, 1964—. Radio Jamaica chairman, set up a new ownership structure, making major interest groups into shareholders, 1978-80.

MEMBER: International PEN, Society of Authors, Authors League.

WRITINGS:

NOVELS

Song of the City, Dorothy Crisp, 1945.
Mine Boy, Dorothy Crisp, 1946, Knopf, 1955, Collier Books, 1970.
The Path of Thunder, Harper, 1948, Chatham Bookseller, 1975.
Wild Conquest (historical fiction), Harper, 1950, Anchor Books, 1970.
A Wreath for Udomo, Knopf, 1956, Collier Books, 1971.
A Night of Their Own, Knopf, 1965.
This Island Now, Faber, 1966, Knopf, 1967, revised edition, Faber & Faber, 1985.

The View from Coyaba (historical fiction), Faber & Faber, 1985.

OTHER

A Blackman Speaks of Freedom (poetry), Universal Printing Works (Durban, South Africa), 1941.
Dark Testament (short stories), Allen and Unwin, 1942, Kraus Reprint, 1970.
Return to Goli (autobiography), Faber & Faber, 1953.
Tell Freedom (autobiography), Knopf, 1954, published as *Tell Freedom: Memories of Africa,* Knopf, 1969, abridged edition, Macmillan, 1970.
Jamaica: An Island Mosaic (travel), H.M.S.O., 1957.
(And editor) *Souvenir Pictorial Review of the West Indies Federation, 1947-57,* Edna Manley (Kingston, Jamaica), c. 1958.
(With the staff of *Holiday* magazine and others) *The World of Mankind,* Golden Press, 1962.
(With others) *History of the Pan-African Congress,* Hammersmith Bookshop, 1963.

Contributor to *Modern African Prose,* edited by Richard Rive and to *Schwarze Ballade,* edited by Janheinz Jahn. Also author of radio scripts for British Broadcasting Corp. during the 1950s. Contributor to *Holiday* and *Cape Standard.*

MEDIA ADAPTATIONS: Abrahams' novel *Mine Boy* was adapted as a play; the novel *Path of Thunder* was made into a movie and a ballet in the Soviet Union.

SIDELIGHTS: Peter Abrahams, the son of an Ethiopian father and a mother of mixed French and African ancestry, published his first book at a time when nearly all the novelists in South Africa were white. Abrahams himself was considered Colored, a legal designation referring to the descendents from blacks and early white settlers. The Colored people had traditionally remained aloof from blacks, but Abrahams took a unique step by siding with black South Africans. Abrahams also stood apart by being one of South Africa's first non-whites to make a living as a writer. And whether using fiction or autobiography, his focus has remained on the non-whites' struggle for respect and political power. In the book *Peter Abrahams,* Michael Wade writes that "Peter Abrahams is a novelist of ideas. He writes about the machinery of politics and power, but he uses his considerable grasp of this area of activity to serve his central interest, which is the problem of individual freedom in contemporary affairs.''

Abrahams grew up in the slums of Johannesburg, where illiteracy was common. He didn't learn to read until he was nine, but thereafter immersed himself in books. He sought out British classics, including Shakespeare, and found works by black American authors in the local library. At the age of eleven, he started writing short stories. Abrahams left school early and tried to support himself as a journalist, but jobs were hard to find for a non-white; almost every door seemed closed to him. While he considered himself a Marxist, editors sharing his political beliefs found him too restrained, while black editors thought him too left-wing to hire for black newspapers. At twenty, Abrahams decided he had to leave South Africa. In his autobiographical *Return to Goli,* he explains, ''I had to escape or slip into that negative destructiveness that is the offspring of bitterness and frustration.'' He worked his way to England as a ship's stoker, later moving to France, and then to Jamaica, which became his permanent home. After emigrating, he only returned to South Africa as a visitor.

While Abrahams has always felt strongly about the problems of non-whites in Africa, when writing his early works he restrained his anger toward the government. In *Return to Goli,* he explains that he had ''purged himself of hatred,'' since ''art and beauty come of love, not hate.'' Believing that love was necessary to overcome racial prejudice, Abrahams frequently incorporated mixed-race love affairs in his early novels. These relationships and their resulting children represented a new order, where the individual would not be judged by his color. In *An African Treasury,* Abrahams claims that this perception comes from tribal Africa, where ''the attitude to colour is healthy and normal. Colour does not matter. Colour is an act of God that neither confers privileges nor imposes handicaps on a man.... What does matter to the tribal African, what is important, is the complex pattern of his position within his own group and his relations with the other members of the group.... The important things in his life are anything but race and colour—until they are forced on him.''

And yet at the same time, Abrahams felt that the great influence of African tribalism on contemporary blacks was a handicap. He embraced Western culture, because, as he wrote in an issue of *International Affairs,* ''The true motive forces of Western culture are to be found in the first place in the teachings of the Christ who taught a new concept of men's relations with their God and with each other, a concept that cuts across tribal gods and tribal loyalties and embraces all men in all lands offering them a common brotherhood.'' In his novel, *A Night of Their Own,* Abrahams emphasizes the common goals of South African Indians and blacks. Both groups work together to change their tyrannical government. While the setting is fictional, Abrahams tied it to contemporary issues by dedicating the book to imprisoned South African activists Walter Sisulu and Nelson Mandela.

Although critics praise Abrahams' handling of political issues, they often fault his characterization. In the *New York Times Book Review,* Martin Levin says, ''What is rich in this novel is the complexity of its political climate,'' but adds that ''what snarls matters is the author's tendency to spell out his characters' thinking.'' In *The Writing of Peter Abrahams,* Kolawole Ogungbesan voices a similar concern: ''The tone of [*A Night of Their Own*] is uncompromisingly noble and determinedly serious, making the characters' gestures as stagey as their dialogues. But the cumulative effect is powerful.''

In *This Island Now,* Abrahams turns from his early call for a pluralistic society to insisting that blacks first establish their own identity, socially and politically, as free men. He also stops looking to Western civilization for solutions. The plot concerns a left-wing black leader who rises to power on a fictional island. But according to Ogungbesan ''There is no doubt that the physical terrain of *This Island Now* is largely that of Jamaica as described in [Abrahams'] essay, *The Real Jamaica,* ... [with] the political terrain of Haiti.'' *New York Times Book Review* contributor Peter Buitenhuis comments, ''As an analysis of this kind of political process, [*This Island Now*] throws light on the motivations of black leaders who have risen to power in recent years in the Caribbean and elsewhere. Unfortunately [Abrahams'] attempt to make this material into a novel has not been too successful. He has tried to embody each interest—political, journalistic, financial, etc.—in a different character, and as a result, the book is overpopulated and over-schematic.'' But Ogungbesan feels the book's strengths and weaknesses are inseparable, and that it must be regarded as a purely political work. He remarks, ''The book is a serious political novel precisely because it avoids the easy banalities that its theme ... might provoke.... Abrahams is so preoccupied with the political conflict that everything else recedes to the background.''

The View from Coyaba is the work that reflects Abrahams' thorough disenchantment with what he calls ''destructive Westernism.'' Some critics, however, find Abrahams' work closer to a tract or treatise than a novel. While *Times Literary Supplement* contributor David Wright considers the book ''high-minded, sincere, committed,'' he thinks that ''as a philosophic and humane survey of the history of black emancipation since the British abolition of slavery, his book may be recommended; as a novel, not.'' Judith Wilson, writing in the *New York Times Book Review,* agrees in finding *The View from Coyaba* ''unmistakably didactic fiction.'' However, she finds that ''the originality of Mr. Abrahams' message, its global sweep and political urgency exert their own force.... Peter Abrahams challenges us to rethink a large chunk of modern history and to question many of our current ideological assumptions.'' But Andrew Salkey in *World Literature Today* never questions whether the work is a true novel, as Abrahams has produced, he states, ''the most dramatically resonant writing I have read in many years.... It is not only a composite novelistic picture, but also a reverberating metaphor.''

While Abrahams' books may not point to any definite means of eliminating racism, they contain hope that conditions will improve. Ogungbesan affirms, ''Himself such an incurable optimist, all his books are open to the future, based on his belief that change is inevitable, a natural process. This is why the image of the day assumes such symbolic significance in his novels. The implication is that although the black people in South Africa are passing through a long night, their ordeal will not last for ever: after the night inevitably comes the dawn. Abrahams thinks that it will be a glorious dawn if the whites and the blacks can co-operate peacefully to work towards that day.''

AVOCATIONAL INTERESTS: Gardening, tennis, walking, conversation, reading, travel.

BIOGRAPHICAL/CRITICAL SOURCES:

BOOKS

Abrahams, Peter, *Return to Goli,* Faber, 1953.

Barnett, Ursula A., *A Vision of Order: A Study of Black South African Literature in English (1914-1980)*, University of Massachusetts Press, 1983.
Contemporary Literary Criticism, Volume 4, Gale, 1975.
Hughes, Langston, editor, *An African Treasury*, Gollancz, 1961.
Lindfors, Bernth, *Early Nigerian Literature*, Africana Publishing, 1982.
Ogungbesan, Kolawole, *The Writing of Peter Abrahams*, Africana Publishing, 1979.
Tucker, Martin, *Africa in Modern Literature: A Survey of Contemporary Writing in English*, Ungar, 1967.
Wade, Michael, *Peter Abrahams*, Evans Brothers, 1971.

PERIODICALS

Critique, Volume XI, number 1, 1968.
Los Angeles Times Book Review, July 14, 1985.
New Statesman, February 22, 1985.
New Yorker, September 25, 1965.
New York Times Book Review, April 11, 1965, September 24, 1967, April 2, 1972, May 26, 1985.
Observer, February 17, 1985.
Times Literary Supplement, March 25, 1965, October 20, 1966, March 22, 1985.
World Literature Today, fall, 1985.

—*Sketch by Jani Prescott*

*   *   *

ACHEBE, (Albert) Chinua(lumogu) 1930-

PERSONAL: Born November 16, 1930, in Ogidi, Nigeria; son of Isaiah Okafo (a Christian churchman) and Janet N. (Iloegbunam) Achebe; married Christie Chinwe Okoli, September 10, 1961; children: Chinelo (daughter), Ikechukwu (son), Chidi (son), Nwando (daughter). *Education:* Attended Government College, Umuahia, 1944-47; attended University College, Ibadan, 1948-53; London University, B.A., 1953; studied broadcasting at the British Broadcasting Corp., London, 1956.

ADDRESSES: Home—33 Umunkanka St., Nsukka, Anambra State, Nigeria. *Office*—Institute of African Studies, University of Nigeria, Nsukka, Anambra State, Nigeria; and University of Massachusetts, Amherst, Mass. 01003.

CAREER: Writer. Nigerian Broadcasting Corp., Lagos, Nigeria, talks producer, 1954-57, controller of Eastern Region in Enugu, 1958-61, founder, and director of Voice of Nigeria, 1961-66; University of Nigeria, Nsukka, senior research fellow, 1967-72, professor of English, 1976-81, professor emeritus, 1985—; Anambra State University of Technology, Enugu, pro-chancellor and chairman of council, 1986—; University of Massachusetts—Amherst, professor, 1987-88. Served on diplomatic missions for Biafra during the Nigerian Civil War, 1967-69. Visiting professor of English at University of Massachusetts—Amherst, 1972-75, and University of Connecticut, 1975-76. Lecturer at University of California, Los Angeles, and at universities in Nigeria and the United States; speaker at events in numerous countries throughout the world. Chairman, Citadel Books Ltd., Enugu, Nigeria, 1967; director, Heinemann Educational Books Ltd., Ibadan, Nigeria, 1970—; director, Nwamife Publishers Ltd., Enugu, Nigeria, 1970—. Founder, and publisher, *Uwa Ndi Igbo: A Bilingual Journal of Igbo Life and Arts*, 1984—. Governor, Newsconcern International Foundation, 1983. Member, University of Lagos Council, 1966, East Central State Library Board, 1971-72, Anambra State Arts Council, 1977-79, and National Festival Committee, 1983; director, Okike Arts Centre, Nsukka,

1984—. Deputy national president of People's Redemption Party, 1983; president of town union, Ogidi, Nigeria, 1986—.

MEMBER: International Social Prospects Academy (Geneva), Writers and Scholars International (London), Writers and Scholars Educational Trust (London), Commonwealth Arts Organization (member of executive committee, 1981—), Association of Nigerian Authors (founder; president, 1981-86), Ghana Association of Writers (fellow), Royal Society of Literature (London), Modern Language Association of America (honorary fellow), American Academy and Institute of Arts and Letters (honorary member).

AWARDS, HONORS: Margaret Wrong Memorial Prize, 1959, for *Things Fall Apart;* Rockefeller travel fellowship to East and Central Africa, 1960; Nigerian National Trophy, 1961, for *No Longer at Ease;* UNESCO fellowship for creative artists for travel to United States and Brazil, 1963; Jock Campbell/*New Statesman* Award, 1965, for *Arrow of God;* D.Litt., Dartmouth College, 1972, University of Southampton, 1975, University of Ife, 1978, University of Nigeria, Nsukka, 1981, University of Kent, 1982, Mount Allison University, 1984, University of Guelph, 1984, and Franklin Pierce College, 1985; Commonwealth Poetry Prize, 1972, for *Beware, Soul-Brother, and Other Poems;* D.Univ., University of Stirling, 1975; Neil Gunn international fellow, Scottish Arts Council, 1975; Lotus Award for Afro-Asian Writers, 1975; LL.D., University of Prince Edward Island, 1976; D.H.L., University of Massachusetts—Amherst, 1977; Nigerian National Merit Award, 1979; named to the Order of the Federal Republic of Nigeria, 1979; Commonwealth Foundation senior visiting practitioner award, 1984; *A Man of the People* was cited in Anthony Burgess's 1984 book *Ninety-nine Novels: The Best in England since 1939;* Booker Prize nomination, 1987, for *Anthills of the Savannah.*

WRITINGS:

Things Fall Apart (novel), Heinemann, 1958, McDowell Obolensky, 1959, reprinted, Fawcett, 1988.
No Longer at Ease (novel), Heinemann, 1960, Obolensky, 1961, 2nd edition, Fawcett, 1988.
The Sacrificial Egg, and Other Stories, Etudo (Onitsha, Nigeria), 1962.
Arrow of God (novel), Heinemann, 1964, John Day, 1967.
A Man of the People (novel), John Day, 1966, published with an introduction by K.W.J. Post, Doubleday, 1967.
Chike and the River (juvenile), Cambridge University Press, 1966.
Beware, Soul-Brother, and Other Poems, Nwankwo-Ifejika (Enugu, Nigeria), 1971, Doubleday, 1972, revised edition, Heinemann, 1972.
(With John Iroaganachi) *How the Leopard Got His Claws* (juvenile), Nwankwo-Ifejika, 1972, (bound with *Lament of the Deer*, by Christopher Okigbo), Third Press, 1973.
Girls at War (short stories), Heinemann, 1973, reprinted, Fawcett, 1988.
Christmas in Biafra, and Other Poems, Doubleday, 1973.
Morning Yet on Creation Day (essays), Doubleday, 1975.
The Flute (juvenile), Fourth Dimension Publishers (Enugu), 1978.
The Drum (juvenile), Fourth Dimension Publishers, 1978.
(Editor with Dubem Okafor) *Don't Let Him Die: An Anthology of Memorial Poems for Christopher Okigbo*, Fourth Dimension Publishers, 1978.
(Co-editor) *Aka Weta: An Anthology of Igbo Poetry*, Okike (Nsukka, Nigeria), 1982.

The Trouble with Nigeria (essays), Fourth Dimension Publishers, 1983, Heinemann, 1984.

(Editor with C. L. Innes) *African Short Stories,* Heinemann, 1984.

Anthills of the Savannah (novel), Anchor Books, 1988.

Hopes and Impediments (essays), Heinemann, 1988.

CONTRIBUTOR

Ellis Ayitey Komey and Ezekiel Mphahlele, editors, *Modern African Stories,* Faber, 1964.

Neville Denny, compiler, *Pan African Stories,* Nelson, 1966.

Paul Edwards, compiler, *Through African Eyes,* two volumes, Cambridge University Press, 1966.

Mphahlele, editor, *African Writing Today,* Penguin Books (Baltimore), 1967.

Barbara Nolen, editor, *Africa and Its People: Firsthand Accounts from Contemporary Africa,* Dutton, 1967.

Ime Ikiddeh, compiler, *Drum Beats: An Anthology of African Writing,* E. J. Arnold, 1968.

Ulli Beier, editor, *Political Spider: An Anthology of Stories from "Black Orpheus,"* Africana Publishing, 1969.

John P. Berry, editor, *Africa Speaks: A Prose Anthology with Comprehension and Summary Passages,* Evans, 1970.

Joseph Conrad, *Heart of Darkness,* edited by Robert Kimbrough, 3rd edition, Norton, 1987.

OTHER

Founding editor, "African Writers Series," Heinemann, 1962-72. Editor, *Okike: A Nigerian Journal of New Writing,* 1971—; editor, *Nsukkascope,* a campus magazine. *Things Fall Apart* has been translated into forty-five languages.

SIDELIGHTS: Since the 1950s, Nigeria has witnessed "the flourishing of a new literature which has drawn sustenance both from traditional oral literature and from the present and rapidly changing society," writes Margaret Laurence in her book *Long Drums and Cannons: Nigerian Dramatists and Novelists.* Thirty years ago, Chinua Achebe was among the founders of this new literature and over the years many critics have come to consider him the finest of the Nigerian novelists. His achievement has not been limited to his native country or continent, however. As Laurence maintains in her 1968 study of his novels, "Chinua Achebe's careful and confident craftsmanship, his firm grasp of his material and his ability to create memorable and living characters place him among the best novelists now writing in any country in the English language."

Unlike some African writers struggling for acceptance among contemporary English-language novelists, Achebe has been able to avoid imitating the trends in English literature. Rejecting the European notion "that art should be accountable to no one, and [needs] to justify itself to nobody," as he puts it in his book of essays, *Morning Yet on Creation Day,* Achebe has embraced instead the idea at the heart of the African oral tradition: that "art is, and always was, at the service of man. Our ancestors created their myths and legends and told their stories for a human purpose." For this reason, Achebe believes that "any good story, any good novel, should have a message, should have a purpose."

Achebe's feel for the African context has influenced his aesthetic of the novel as well as the technical aspects of his works. As Bruce King comments in *Introduction to Nigerian Literature:* "Achebe was the first Nigerian writer to successfully transmute the conventions of the novel, a European art form, into African literature." In an Achebe novel, King notes, "European character study is subordinated to the portrayal of com-

munal life; European economy of form is replaced by an aesthetic appropriate to the rhythms of traditional tribal life." Kofi Awoonor writes in *The Breast of the Earth* that in wrapping this borrowed literary form in African garb "he created a new novel that possesses its own autonomy and transcends the limits set by both his African and European teachers."

On the level of ideas, Achebe's "prose writing reflects three essential and related concerns," observes G. D. Killam in his book *The Novels of Chinua Achebe,* "first, with the legacy of colonialism at both the individual and societal level; secondly, with the *fact* of English as a language of national and international exchange; thirdly, with the obligations and responsibilities of the writer both to the society in which he lives and to his art." Over the past century, Africa has been caught in a war for its identity between the forces of tradition, colonialism, and independence. This war has prevented many nations from raising themselves above political and social chaos to achieve true independence. "Most of the problems we see in our politics derive from the moment when we lost our initiative to other people, to colonizers," Achebe observes in his book of essays. He goes on to explain: "What I think is the basic problem of a new African country like Nigeria is really what you might call a 'crisis in the soul.' We have been subjected—we have subjected ourselves too—to this period during which we have accepted everything alien as good and practically everything local or native as inferior."

In order to reestablish the virtues of precolonial Nigeria, chronicle the impact of colonialism on native cultures, expose present day corruption, and communicate these to his fellow countrymen and to those outside his country, Achebe must make use of English, the language of colonialism. The ways in which he transforms language to achieve his particular ends distinguishes his writing from the writing of other English-language novelists. To convey the flavor of traditional Nigeria, Achebe translates Ibo proverbs into English and weaves them into his stories. "Among the Ibo the art of conversation is regarded very highly," he writes in his novel *Things Fall Apart,* "and proverbs are the palm-oil with which words are eaten." "Proverbs are cherished by Achebe's people as tribal heirlooms, the treasure boxes of their cultural heritage," explains Adrian A. Roscoe in his book *Mother Is Gold: A Study of West African Literature.* "Through them traditions are received and handed on; and when they disappear or fall into disuse . . . it is a sign that a particular tradition, or indeed a whole way of life, is passing away." Achebe's use of proverbs also has an artistic aim, as Bernth Lindfors suggests in *Folklore in Nigerian Literature.* "Achebe's proverbs can serve as keys to an understanding of his novels," comments the critic, "because he uses them not merely to add touches of local color but to sound and reiterate themes, to sharpen characterization, to clarify conflict, and to focus on the values of the society he is portraying."

To engender an appreciation for African culture in those unfamiliar with it, Achebe alters English to reflect native Nigerian languages in use. "Without seriously distorting the nature of the English," observes Eustace Palmer in *The Growth of the African Novel,* "Achebe deliberately introduces the rhythms, speech patterns, idioms and other verbal nuances of Ibo. . . . The effect of this is that while everyone who knows English will be able to understand the work and find few signs of awkwardness, the reader also has a sense, not just of black men using English, but of black Africans speaking and living in a genuinely black African rural situation." In the opinion of *Busara* contributor R. Angogo, this "ability to shape and mould English to suit character and event and yet still give the impression of an African story is one of the greatest of Achebe's achievements.'' The reason, adds the reviewer, is that ''it puts into the reader a kind of emotive effect, an interest, and a thirst which so to say awakens the reader.''

Finally, Achebe uses language, which he sees as a writer's best resource, to expose and combat the propaganda generated by African politicians to manipulate their own people. ''Language is our tool,'' he told Anthony Appiah in a *Times Literary Supplement* interview, ''and language is the tool of the politicians. We are like two sides in a very hostile game. And I think that the attempt to deceive with words is countered by the efforts of the writer to go behind the words, to show the meaning.''

Faced with his people's growing inferiority complex and his leaders' disregard for the truth, the African writer cannot turn his back on his culture, Achebe believes. ''A writer has a responsibility to try and stop [these damaging trends] because unless our culture begins to take itself seriously it will never . . . get off the ground.'' He states his mission in his essay ''The Novelist as Teacher'': ''Here then is an adequate revolution for me to espouse—to help my society regain belief in itself and to put away the complexes of the years of denigration and self-abasement. And it is essentially a question of education, in the best sense of that word. Here, I think, my aims and the deepest aspirations of society meet.''

Although he has also written poetry, short stories, and essays—both literary and political—Achebe is best known for his novels: *Things Fall Apart, No Longer at Ease, Arrow of God, A Man of the People,* and *Anthills of the Savannah.* Considering Achebe's novels, Anthony Daniels writes in the *Spectator,* ''In spare prose of great elegance, without any technical distraction, he has been able to illuminate two emotionally irreconcilable facets of modern African life: the humiliations visited on Africans by colonialism, and the utter moral worthlessness of what replaced colonial rule.'' Set in this historical context, Achebe's novels develop the theme of ''tradition verses change,'' and offer, as Palmer observes, ''a powerful presentation of the beauty, strength and validity of traditional life and values and the disruptiveness of change.'' Even so, the author does not appeal for a return to the ways of the past. Palmer notes that ''while deploring the imperialists' brutality and condescension, [Achebe] seems to suggest that change is inevitable and wise men . . . reconcile themselves to accommodating change. It is the diehards . . . who resist and are destroyed in the process.''

Two of Achebe's novels—*Things Fall Apart* and *Arrow of God*—focus on Nigeria's early experience with colonialism, from first contact with the British to widespread British administration. ''With remarkable unity of the word with the deed, the character, the time and the place, Chinua Achebe creates in these two novels a coherent picture of coherence being lost, of the tragic consequences of the African-European collision,'' offers Robert McDowell in a special issue of *Studies in Black Literature* dedicated to Achebe's work. ''There is an artistic unity of all things in these books which is rare anywhere in modern English fiction.''

Things Fall Apart, Achebe's first novel, was published in 1958 in the midst of the Nigerian renaissance. Achebe explained his motivation to begin writing at this time in an interview with Lewis Nkosi published in *African Writers Talking: A Collection of Radio Interviews:* ''One of the things that set me thinking [about writing] was Joyce Cary's novel set in Nigeria, *Mr*

Johnson, which was praised so much, and it was clear to me that this was a most superficial picture . . . not only of the country, but even of the Nigerian character. . . . I thought if this was famous, then perhaps someone ought to try and look at this from the inside.'' Charles R. Larson, in his book *The Emergence of African Fiction,* details the success of Achebe's effort, both in investing his novel of Africa with an African sensibility and in making this view available to African readers. ''In 1964, . . . *Things Fall Apart* became the first novel by an African writer to be included in the required syllabus for African secondary school students throughout the English-speaking portions of the continent.'' Later in that decade, it ''became recognized by African and non-African literary critics as the first 'classic' in English from tropical Africa,'' adds Larson.

The novel tells the story of an Ibo village of the late 1800s and one of its great men, Okonkwo. Although the son of a ne'er-do-well, Okonkwo has achieved much in his life. He is a champion wrestler, a wealthy farmer, a husband to three wives, a title-holder among his people, and a member of the select *egwugwu* whose members impersonate ancestral spirits at tribal rituals. ''The most impressive achievement of *Things Fall Apart* . . .,'' maintains David Carroll in his book *Chinua Achebe,* ''is the vivid picture it provides of Ibo society at the end of the nineteenth century.'' He explains: ''Here is a clan in the full vigor of its traditional way of life, unperplexed by the present and without nostalgia for the past. Through its rituals the life of the community and the life of the individual are merged into significance and order.''

This order is disrupted, however, with the appearance of the white man in Africa and with the introduction of his religion. ''The conflict in the novel, vested in Okonkwo, derives from the series of crushing blows which are levelled at traditional values by an alien and more powerful culture causing, in the end, the traditional society to fall apart,'' observes Killam. Okonkwo is unable to adapt to the changes that accompany colonialism. In the end, in frustration, he kills an African employed by the British, and then commits suicide, a sin against the tradition to which he had long clung. The novel thus presents ''two main, closely intertwined tragedies,'' writes Arthur Ravenscroft in his study *Chinua Achebe,* ''the personal tragedy of Okonkwo . . . and the public tragedy of the eclipse of one culture by another.''

Although the author emphasizes the message in his novels, he still receives praise for his artistic achievement. As Palmer comments, ''Chinua Achebe's *Things Fall Apart* . . . demonstrates a mastery of plot and structure, strength of characterization, competence in the manipulation of language and consistency and depth of thematic exploration which is rarely found in a first novel.'' Achebe also achieves balance in recreating the tragic consequences of the clash of two cultures. Killam notes that ''in showing Ibo society before and after the coming of the white man he avoids the temptation to present the past as idealized and the present as ugly and unsatisfactory.'' And, as Killam concludes, Achebe's ''success proceeds from his ability to create a sense of real life and real issues in the book and to see his subject from the point of view which is neither idealistic nor dishonest.''

Arrow of God, the second of Achebe's novels of colonialism, takes place in the 1920s after the British have established a presence in Nigeria. The ''arrow of god'' mentioned in the title is Ezeulu, the chief priest of the god Ulu who is the patron deity of an Ibo village. As chief priest, Ezeulu is responsible for initiating the rituals that structure village life, a position vested with a great deal of power. In fact, the central theme of this novel, as Laurence points out, is power: "Ezeulu's testing of his own power and the power of his god, and his effort to maintain his own and his god's authority in the face of village factions and of the [Christian] mission and the British administration." "This, then, is a political novel in which different systems of power are examined and their dependence upon myth and ritual compared," writes Carroll. "Of necessity it is also a study in the psychology of power."

In Ezeulu, Achebe presents a study of the loss of power. After his village rejects his advice to avoid war with a neighboring village, Ezeulu finds himself at odds with his own people and praised by the British administrators. The British, seeking a candidate to install as village chieftain, make him an offer, which he refuses. Caught in the middle with no allies, Ezeulu slowly loses his grip on reality and slips into senility. "As in Achebe's other novels," observes Gerald Moore in *Seven African Writers*, "it is the strong-willed man of tradition who cannot adapt, and who is crushed by his virtues in the war between the new, more worldly order, and the old, conservative values of an isolated society."

The artistry displayed in *Arrow of God*, Achebe's second portrait of cultures in collision, has drawn a great deal of attention, adding to the esteem in which the writer is held. Charles Miller comments in a *Saturday Review* article that Achebe's "approach to the written word is completely unencumbered with verbiage. He never strives for the exalted phrase, he never once raises his voice; even in the most emotion-charged passages the tone is absolutely unruffled, the control impeccable." Concludes this reviewer, "It is a measure of Achebe's creative gift that he has no need whatever for prose fireworks to light the flame of his intense drama."

Killam recognizes this novel as more than a vehicle for Achebe's commentary on colonialism. He suggests in his study that "Achebe's overall intention is to explore the depths of the human condition and in this other more important sense *Arrow of God* transcends its setting and shows us characters whose values, motivations, actions and qualities are permanent in human kind." Laurence offers this evaluation in her 1968 book: "*Arrow of God*, in which [Achebe] comes into full maturity as a novelist, . . . is probably one of the best novels written anywhere in the past decade."

Achebe's three other novels—*No Longer at Ease, A Man of the People*, and *Anthills of the Savannah*—examine Africa in the era of independence. This is an Africa less and less under direct European administration, yet still deeply affected by it, an Africa struggling to regain its footing in order to stand on its own two feet. Standing in the way of realizing its goal of true independence is the corruption pervasive in modern Africa, an obstacle Achebe scrutinizes in each of these novels.

In *No Longer at Ease*, set in Nigeria just prior to independence, Achebe extends his history of the Okonkwo family. Here the central character is Obi Okonkwo, grandson of the tragic hero of *Things Fall Apart*. This Okonkwo has been raised a Christian and educated at the university in England. Like many of his peers, he has left the bush behind for a position as a civil servant in Lagos, Nigeria's largest city. "*No Longer at Ease* deals with the plight of [this] new generation of Nigerians," observes Palmer, "who, having been exposed to education in the western world and therefore largely cut off from their roots in traditional society, discover, on their return,

that the demands of tradition are still strong, and are hopelessly caught in the clash between the old and the new."

Many, faced with this internal conflict, succumb to corruption. Obi is no exception. "The novel opens with Obi on trial for accepting bribes when a civil servant," notes Killam, "and the book takes the form of a long flashback." "In a world which is the result of the intermingling of Europe and Africa . . . Achebe traces the decline of his hero from brilliant student to civil servant convicted of bribery and corruption," writes Carroll. "It reads like a postscript to the earlier novel [*Things Fall Apart*] because the same forces are at work but in a confused, diluted, and blurred form." In *This Africa: Novels by West Africans in English and French*, Judith Illsley Gleason points out how the imagery of each book depicts the changes in the Okonkwo family and the Nigeria they represent. As she points out, "The career of the grandson Okonkwo ends not with a machet's swing but with a gavel's tap."

Here again in this novel Achebe carefully shapes language, to inform, but also to transport the reader to Africa. "It is through [his characters'] use of language that we are able to enter their world and to share their experiences," writes Shatto Arthur Gakwandi in *The Novel and Contemporary Experience in Africa*. Gakwandi adds: "Through [Achebe's] keen sensitivity to the way people express themselves and his delicate choice of idiom the author illuminates for us the thoughts and attitudes of the whole range of Nigerian social strata." The impact of Achebe's style is such that, as John Coleman observes in the *Spectator*, his "novel moves towards its inevitable catastrophe with classic directness. Nothing is wasted and it is only after the sad, understated close that one realises, once again how much of the Nigerian context has been touched in, from the prejudice and corruption of Lagos to the warm, homiletic simplicities of life."

A Man of the People is "the story of the yokel who visits the sinful city and emerges from it scathed but victorious," writes Martin Tucker in *Africa in Modern Literature*, "while the so-called 'sophisticates' and 'sinners' suffer their just desserts." In this novel, Achebe casts his eye on African politics, taking on, as Moore notes, "the corruption of Nigerians in high places in the central government." The author's eyepiece is the book's narrator Odili, a schoolteacher; the object of his scrutiny is Chief the Honorable M. A. Nanga, Member of Parliament, Odili's former teacher and a popular bush politician who has risen to the post of Minister of Culture in his West African homeland.

At first, Odili is charmed by the politician; but eventually he recognizes the extent of Nanga's abuses and decides to oppose the minister in an election. Odili is beaten, both physically and politically, his appeal to the people heard but ignored. The novel demonstrates, according to Gakwandi, that "the society has been invaded by a wide range of values which have destroyed the traditional balance between the material and the spiritual spheres of life, which has led inevitably to the hypocrisy of double standards." Odili is a victim of these double standards.

Despite his political victory, Nanga, along with the rest of the government, is ousted by a coup. "The novel is a carefully plotted and unified piece of writing," writes Killam. "Achebe achieves balance and proportion in the treatment of his theme of political corruption by evoking both the absurdity of the behavior of the principal characters while at the same time suggesting the serious and destructive consequences of their behavior to the commonwealth." The seriousness of the fictional situation portrayed in *A Man of the People* became real very soon after the novel was first published in 1966 when Nigeria itself was racked by a coup.

Two decades passed between the publications of *A Man of the People* and Achebe's most recent novel, *Anthills of the Savannah*. During this period, the novelist wrote poetry, short stories, and essays. He also became involved in Nigeria's political struggle, a struggle marked by five coups, a civil war, elections marred by violence, and a number of attempts to return to civilian rule. *Anthills of the Savannah* represents Achebe's return to the novel, and as Nadine Gordimer comments in the *New York Times Book Review*, "it is a work in which 22 years of harsh experience, intellectual growth, self-criticism, deepening understanding and mustered discipline of skill open wide a subject to which Mr. Achebe is now magnificently equal." It also represents a return to the themes informing Achebe's earlier novels of independent Africa. "This is a study of how power corrupts itself and by doing so begins to die," writes *Observer* contributor Ben Okri. "It is also about dissent, and love."

Three former schoolmates have risen to positions of power in an imaginary West African nation, Kangan. Ikem is editor of the state-owned newspaper; Chris is the country's minister of information; Sam is a military man become head of state. Sam's quest to have himself voted president for life sends the lives of these three and the lives of all Kangan citizens into turmoil. "In this new novel . . . Chinua Achebe says, with implacable honesty, that Africa itself is to blame," notes Neal Ascherson in the *New York Review of Books*, "and that there is no safety in excuses that place the fault in the colonial past or in the commercial and political manipulations of the First World." Ascherson continues that the novel becomes "a tale about responsibility, and the ways in which men who should know better betray and evade that responsibility."

The turmoil comes to a head in the novel's final pages. All three of the central characters are dead. Ikem, who spoke out against the abuses of the government, is murdered by Sam's secret police. Chris, who flees into the bush to begin a journey of transformation among the people, is shot attempting to stop a rape. Sam is kidnapped and murdered in a coup. "The three murders, senseless as they are, represent the departure of a generation that compromised its own enlightenment for the sake of power," writes Ascherson. And, as Okri observes, "The novel closes with the suggestion that power should reside not within an elite but within the awakened spirit of the people." Here is the hope offered in the novel, hope that is also suggested in its title, as Charles Trueheart relates in the *Washington Post*: "When the brush fires sweep across the savanna, scorching the earth, they leave behind only anthills, and inside the anthills, the surviving memories of the fires and all that came before."

Anthills of the Savannah has been well received and has earned for Achebe a nomination for the Booker Prize. In Larson's estimation, printed in the Chicago *Tribune Books*, "No other novel in many years has bitten to the core, swallowed and regurgitated contemporary Africa's miseries and expectations as profoundly as 'Anthills of the Savannah.'" It has also enhanced Achebe's reputation as an artist; as *New Statesman* contributor Margaret Busby writes, "Reading [this novel] is like watching a master carver skilfully chiselling away from every angle at a solid block of wood: at first there is simply fascination at the sureness with which he works, according to a plan apparent to himself. But the point of all this activity gradually begins to emerge—until at last it is possible to step back and admire the image created."

In his novels, Achebe offers a close and balanced examination of contemporary Africa and the historical forces that have shaped it. "His distinction is to have [looked back] without any trace either of chauvinistic idealism or of neurotic rejection, those twin poles of so much African mythologizing," maintains Moore. "Instead, he has recreated for us a way of life which has almost disappeared, and has done so with understanding, with justice and with realism." And Busby commends the author's achievement in "charting the socio-political development of contemporary Nigeria." However, Achebe's writing reverberates beyond the borders of Nigeria and beyond the arenas of anthropology, sociology, and political science. As literature, it deals with universal qualities. And, as Killam writes in his study: "Achebe's novels offer a vision of life which is essentially tragic, compounded of success and failure, informed by knowledge and understanding, relieved by humour and tempered by sympathy, embued with an awareness of human suffering and the human capacity to endure." Concludes the critic, "Sometimes his characters meet with success, more often with defeat and despair. Through it all the spirit of man and the belief in the possibility of triumph endures."

MEDIA ADAPTATIONS: Things Fall Apart was adapted for the stage and produced by Eldred Fiberesima in Lagos, Nigeria; it was also adapted for radio and produced by the British Broadcasting Corp. in 1983, and for television in English and Igbo and produced by the Nigerian Television Authority in 1985.

AVOCATIONAL INTERESTS: Music.

BIOGRAPHICAL/CRITICAL SOURCES:

BOOKS

Achebe, Chinua, *A Man of the People,* introduction by K.W.J. Post, Doubleday, 1967.

Achebe, Chinua, *Morning Yet on Creation Day,* Doubleday, 1975.

Achebe, Chinua, *Things Fall Apart,* Fawcett, 1977.

Awoonor, Kofi, *The Breast of the Earth,* Doubleday, 1975.

Baldwin, Claudia, *Nigerian Literature: A Bibliography of Criticism,* G. K. Hall, 1980.

Carroll, David, *Chinua Achebe,* Twayne, 1970.

Contemporary Literary Criticism, Gale, Volume 1, 1973, Volume 3, 1975, Volume 5, 1976, Volume 7, 1977, Volume 11, 1979, Volume 26, 1983, Volume 51, 1988.

Duerden, Dennis and Cosmo Pieterse, editors, *African Writers Talking: A Collection of Radio Interviews,* Africana Publishing, 1972.

Gakwandi, Shatto Arthur, *The Novel and Contemporary Experience in Africa,* Africana Publishing, 1977.

Gleason, Judith Illsley, *This Africa: Novels by West Africans in English and French,* Northwestern University Press, 1965.

Killam, G. D., *The Novels of Chinua Achebe,* Africana Publishing, 1969.

King, Bruce, *Introduction to Nigerian Literature,* Africana Publishing, 1972.

King, Bruce, *The New English Literatures: Cultural Nationalism in a Changing World,* Macmillan, 1980.

Larson, Charles R., *The Emergence of African Fiction,* Indiana University Press, 1972.

Laurence, Margaret, *Long Drums and Cannons: Nigerian Dramatists and Novelists*, Praeger, 1968.

Lindfors, Bernth, *Folklore in Nigerian Literature*, Africana Publishing, 1973.

McEwan, Neil, *Africa and the Novel*, Humanities Press, 1983.

Moore, Gerald, *Seven African Writers*, Oxford University Press, 1962.

Njoku, Benedict Chiaka, *The Four Novels of Chinua Achebe: A Critical Study*, Peter Lang, 1984.

Palmer, Eustace, *The Growth of the African Novel*, Heinemann, 1979.

Ravenscroft, Arthur, *Chinua Achebe*, Longmans, Green, for the British Council, 1969.

Roscoe, Adrian A., *Mother Is Gold: A Study of West African Literature*, Cambridge University Press, 1971.

Tucker, Martin, *Africa in Modern Literature*, Ungar, 1967.

Wren, Robert M., *Achebe's World: The Historical and Cultural Context of the Novels*, Three Continents, 1980.

PERIODICALS

Boston Globe, March 9, 1988.
Busara, Volume VII, number 2, 1975.
Commonweal, December 1, 1967.
Economist, October 24, 1987.
English Studies in Africa, September, 1971.
Listener, October 15, 1987.
Lively Arts and Book Review, April 30, 1961.
London Review of Books, August 7, 1986, October 15, 1987.
Los Angeles Times Book Review, February 28, 1988.
Michigan Quarterly Review, fall, 1970.
Nation, October 11, 1965, April 16, 1988.
New Statesman, January 4, 1985, September 25, 1987.
New York Review of Books, March 3, 1988.
New York Times, August 10, 1966, February 16, 1988.
New York Times Book Review, December 17, 1967, May 13, 1973, August 11, 1985, February 21, 1988.
Observer, September 20, 1987.
Saturday Review, January 6, 1968.
Spectator, October 21, 1960, September 26, 1987.
Studies in Black Literature: Special Issue; Chinua Achebe, spring, 1971.
Times Educational Supplement, January 25, 1985.
Times Literary Supplement, February 3, 1966, March 3, 1972, May 4, 1973, February 26, 1982, October 12, 1984, October 9, 1987.
Tribune Books (Chicago), February 21, 1988.
Village Voice, March 15, 1988.
Wall Street Journal, February 23, 1988.
Washington Post, February 16, 1988.
Washington Post Book World, February 7, 1988.
World Literature Today, summer, 1985.
World Literature Written in English, November, 1978.

—Sketch by Bryan Ryan

*   *   *

ADAMS, Alice (Boyd) 1926-

PERSONAL: Born in Fredericksburg, Va., August 14, 1926; daughter of Nicholson (a professor) and Agatha (a writer; maiden name, Boyd); married Mark Linenthal, Jr. (a professor), 1946 (divorced, 1958); children: Peter. *Education:* Radcliffe College, B.A., 1946.

ADDRESSES: *Home*—2661 Clay St., San Francisco, Calif. 94115. *Agent*—Lynn Nesbit, International Creative Management, 40 West 57th St., New York, N.Y. 10019.

CAREER: Writer. Has held various office jobs, including secretary, clerk, and bookkeeper. Instructor at the University of California at Davis, 1980, University of California at Berkley, and at Stanford University.

AWARDS, HONORS: O. Henry Awards, Doubleday & Co., 1971-82 and 1984-88, for short stories; National Book Critics Circle Award nomination, 1975, for *Families and Survivors;* National Endowment for the Arts fiction grant, 1976; Guggenheim fellowship, 1978; O. Henry Special Award for Continuing Achievement, 1982.

WRITINGS:

Careless Love, New American Library, 1966 (published in England as *The Fall of Daisy Duke*, Constable, 1967).
Families and Survivors (novel), Knopf, 1975.
Listening to Billie (novel), Knopf, 1978.
Beautiful Girl (short stories), Knopf, 1979.
Rich Rewards (novel), Knopf, 1980.
To See You Again (short stories), Knopf, 1982.
Molly's Dog (short stories), Ewert, 1983.
Superior Women (novel), Knopf, 1984.
Return Trips (short stories), Knopf, 1985.
Second Chances (novel), Knopf, 1988.

Contributor of short stories to anthologies, including *Best American Short Stories*, 1976, *Prize Stories: The O. Henry Awards*, 1971-82, and 1984-88. Contributor to periodicals, including *New Yorker, Atlantic, Shenandoah, Crosscurrents, Grand Street, Mademoiselle, Virginia Quarterly Review, New York Times Book Review, Vogue, Redbook, McCall's,* and *Paris Review.*

SIDELIGHTS: In many of her short stories and novels, Alice Adams writes about women struggling to find their place in the world. Adams challenges her characters, whether they live alone or attached to a man, to establish meaningful lives, working creatively with both life's blessings and its disappointments. Robert Phillips writes in *Commonweal:* "The usual Adams character does not give in to his or her fate, but attempts to shape it, however misguidedly.... Women become aware not only of missed opportunities, but also of life's endless possibilities." While men occupy important positions in the female characters' lives, Adams's books tend to focus on the women's own struggles with identity. "The conflict—not the outward conflict between men and women, but the private and inward conflict of individual women—runs through all Adams' work," notes Stephen Goodwin in the *Washington Post Book World.* "Her women value men, but prize their own independence." Adams's women generally find true contentment in work and the freedom to make their own choices. According to William L. Stull in the *Dictionary of Literary Biography Yearbook,* "each of her novels concerns a woman's search for satisfying work as a means to economic, artistic, and finally political independence."

And yet the experience of romantic love constantly recurs in Adams's work. Beverly Lowry maintains in the *New York Times Book Review* that "nobody writes better about falling in love than Alice Adams. The protagonists of her stories . . . fall with eyes open, knowing full well that the man in question might be inappropriate. . . . Such women think they should know better. They do know better. That is the glory of an Adams heroine, she is that smart and still goes on. 'Ah,' she says to herself, sighing, 'this again: love.' And plunges in." While the romantic pairings may or may not work out, "Adams' women often learn, in the course of her novels, that the stereotyped 'happy ending' is not feasible and that they must focus on work and on developing a healthy respect for themselves," writes Larry T. Blades in *Critique*. "These are perhaps the ultimate rich rewards."

Beautiful Girl was Adams's first published collection of short stories. Although half of the stories had won the O. Henry Prize, the tales did not fully satisfy *New York Times Book Review* critic Katha Pollitt. While praising Adams's gifts as a storyteller, Pollitt laments the ubiquitous presence of one "recognizable type" of heroine in the collection: "I kept waiting for Miss Adams to flash an ironic smile toward these supremely sheltered, idle, unexamined people.... She never does." *Hudson Review* contributor Dean Flowers believes that in *Beautiful Girl*, Adams portrays difficult problems with too much ease: "At their best these stories explore complex relationships in a quick, deceptively offhand manner. They tend to begin with a tense problem (a wife dying, a divorce impending, a moment of wrath, an anxious move to a new place) and unravel gradually, without much climax except a muted sense of recovered balance and diminished expectation.... One feels neither gladness nor sorrow in such conclusions, but rather an implicit appeal of stylish melancholy." Still, the intensity of her characters' feelings can belie the author's seemingly neat appraisals of their lives. Susan Schindehette comments in her *Saturday Review* appraisal of the stories collected in *Return Trips*, "It is Adams' gift to reveal the tremendous inner workings beneath the apparent tranquility and make characters come to life in her spare, elegant style."

Reviewers frequently praise Adams's concise, understated use of language. "Some writers have such lovely voices they always make you want to hum along. Alice Adams is like that; she is fond of the word 'perfect,' and it suits her," writes Lois Gould in the *New York Times Book Review*. She continues, "For Miss Adams, applying her elegant, rhythmic style to the form, the challenge lies in making it new, fitting it to her own literary place and our time." Adams's sure touch conveys the rough sides of life as well as the tender. Douglas Hill observes in the *Globe and Mail*, "Adams writes decidedly grown-up fiction, though it's by no means X-rated. She uses language almost surgically, and can be quite candid and direct about matters sexual and vulgar. Her characteristic tone is light, even at times airy. But there's always a hint of darkness underneath; for Adams the course of adult affection and love is always at greatest risk when it seems safest and most placid." Critics also like the compactness of Adams's writing and the careful use of detail. "The typical Alice Adams short story announces itself in the very first sentence as a thing of edgy wit and compressed narrative power," says Pollitt. And Phillips in *Commonweal* notes that Adams "suppresses and condenses, allowing the reader to make vital connections between situation and character."

In *Rich Rewards*, Adams focuses on a middle-aged woman who has spent her life in a series of disappointing and often addictive relationships with men. At the novel's beginning the heroine, Daphne, having recently broken off a relationship with an abusive lover, intends to immerse herself in her work as an interior decorator. But the plot carries her to San Francisco and into a friend's troubled marriage. By the book's conclusion, she finds herself unexpectedly reunited with a lover from her youth. According to Blades, "*Rich Rewards* chronicles the maturation of Daphne from a woman who devotes her life to punishing and humiliating sexual encounters into a woman who can establish a productive love relationship because she has first learned to respect herself." In the *New*

York Times Book Review, Anne Tyler says, "This is a marvelously readable book. It's mysterious in the best sense—not a setup, artificial mystery but a real one, in which we wonder along with the heroine just what all the chaotic events are leading up to." *Chicago Tribune Book World* contributor Lynne Sharon Schwartz calls *Rich Rewards* "a stringent story elegantly told, and enhanced by a keen moral judgment.... As in her earlier novels, ... Alice Adams is concerned with the shards of broken families and with the quickly severed ties that spring up in place of families. But in 'Rich Rewards' the harshness latent in such tenuous relations is more overt than before.... It takes a sort of magician to render hope from the brew of pain, muddle, and anomie that Alice Adams has managed charmingly to concoct: Once again she brings it off with panache."

But critics have also faulted the author's "reward" for Daphne, and have called the ending unrealistic compared to the rest of the book. Blades admits that "the novelistic contrivances used to bring the lovers back together also suggest the unrealistic nature of the resolution. There is the sense of enchantment, of a fairy godmother waving her wand and saying, 'Let Daphne and Jean-Paul fall in love again, and let the plot be twisted to accomplish this.'" However, he defends Adams's choice: "Readers who complain about Adams' use of coincidence in *Rich Rewards* have recognized an element conspicuously present in the author's overall purpose. 'This is a novel,' Alice Adams seems to say, 'and since I'm writing it, I can create a happy ending. Real life might end differently.'" Considering Daphne's growth as a character, Tyler writes that the ending fits the story: "If the conclusion seems a bit sudden and easy, lacking the texture of the rest of the story, it is also the 'rich reward' that Daphne deserves. Draw a moral, if you like: Daphne is one of the most admirable female characters in recent fiction."

Adams moved to California in the fifties, and the state and its residents figure prominently in her work. *To See You Again* is a "collection of 19 short stories [that] may surprise readers who have been led to think that all fictional California women are angst-ridden, sex-crazed or mellowed-out," writes Paul Gray in *Time*. Some reviewers have taken issue with the book's even tone. While Benjamin DeMott admires the irony and understatement in the collection, he notes in the *New York Times Book Review:* "Life in this book is indeed lived, ... in easygoing obedience to the key emotional imperative of the age (Change Your Life). None of Miss Adams's people ever tears a passion to tatters.... But these stories do suffer from a lack of tonal variety." Mary Morris, in a *Chicago Tribune Book World* article, says that "[Adams] has spared us the fights, she has spared us the asking of the unaskable, the struggle to love. And in the end she has also spared us what we want most, the drama." Morris claims "the protagonists' inability to achieve involvement" frustrates the reader. Adams's characters in *To See you Again* "don't reach out, they don't fight back. What they do is leave, remember or fantasize." But the strength of the book, Linda Pastan writes in the *American Book Review*, lies in "the cumulative effect" that makes "the reader feel as though he knows the San Francisco of Alice Adams in the special way one knows a place inhabited by friends."

Superior Women concerns the relationship among four young women during their years at Radcliffe and afterwards. The novel has frequently been compared to Mary McCarthy's *The Group*, which describes the lives of eight women who attended Vassar in the thirties. As in *The Group*, *Superior Women* takes its characters through graduation and into the outside world, showing how political and social events affect their lives. This technique has met with some criticism. "The effects of viewing a whole age through gauze in this fashion is pretty deadening," claims Michael Wood in the *London Review of Books*. Jonathan Yardley, a *Washington Post Book World* contributor, states: "What we . . . have is a shopping list of public events, causes and fads. As the women leave Radcliffe and enter the world, Adams dutifully trots them through everything from civil rights to Watergate." And yet other critics found Adams's usual style, allied with a swifter pace, produced a highly satisfactory work. John Updike in the *New Yorker* writes, "The novel . . . reads easily, even breathlessly; one looks forward, in the chain of coincidences, to the next encounter, knowing that this author always comes to the point from an unexpected angle, without fuss." And Barbara Koenig Quart remarks in *Ms.* that Adams's talent holds the reader through any weak points: "Not at all systematically, to be sure, and with fairly thin references to the extraordinary events of those turbulent decades, still, Adams holds us firmly with a lively narrative pace. She creates an almost gossipy interest in what happens to her characters; and she can't write a bad sentence, though hers is the kind of fine unobtrusive style that you notice only if you're looking for it."

Some reviewers have questioned the "superiority" of the young students. Their experiences are similar to other young coeds of the time, and their discussions usually revolve around sex. *West Coast Review of Books* contributor Dorothy Sinclair doubts their credibility: "There is so little that is believable about these young women that one suspects the usually deep and honest Adams of running amuck. Certainly there seems to be nothing 'superior' or original about their endless chatter of 'necking.' (Do they, or don't they 'do it'? They never tell.)" Annabel Edwards in *Books and Bookmen* objects to "the very use of the title *Superior Women* with apparently no ironic overtones at all." Wood, however, feels that the women display an above average concern for each other: "Her characters are genuinely kind and easy, anxious about each other. . . . Certainly Adams's characters, men and women, are nicer than most folks in fiction, or in fact."

Adams earned ample praise with her third collection of stories, *Return Trips*, which "shows a master writer at the height of her powers," says Stull. He relates, "The title is apt in every way, from the dedication [to Adams's son, Peter Adams Linenthal] to the travel motifs that link these fifteen accounts of women recalling or revisiting people and places that shaped their lives." All the stories in the collection depict women struggling along on a physical or spiritual journey. According to Isabel Raphael in the London *Times*: "To make a return trip, [Adams] seems to be saying, you must leave where you are, and there is no guarantee that things will be the same when you come back, or that you yourself will be unaffected by the journey. But with a solid experience of love in your life on which to base a sense of identity, you will not lose your way." And Elaine Kendall concludes in the *Los Angeles Times* that in *Return Trips*, "unburdened by complex rigging, her imagination sails swiftly and gracefully over a sea of contemporary emotional experience, sounding unexpected depths."

Adams's novel *Second Chances* portrays the lives of men and women who face the onset of their sixties and the stigma of "old age." Like Adams's other characters, they worry about relationships and suffer losses, but in this book a marriage dissolving through death forces them to evaluate their own lives. Adams told Mervyn Rothstein in an interview for the *New York Times*: "The novel grew out of the fact I was getting toward being 60 myself. It struck me that 60 is not middle-age. I do not know a lot of people who are 120. . . . I began looking at people who are 10 to 15 years older. The book is for me a kind of exploration." *Second Chances* also gave Adams a chance to speak truthfully about aging. In an interview with Kim Heron for the *New York Times Book Review*, Adams said, "I have the perception that people talk about old age in two ways. One is to focus on the horrors of it, not that they should be underestimated, and the other is to romanticize it."

The book starts with a group of long-term friends, all of them examining changes in their relationships. The scene soon changes to memory, and the reader is filled in on the characters' sometimes highly intricate lives. Barbara Williamson relates in the *Washington Post Book World* that "the backward and forward motion of time in the novel happily captures the way old people tell wistful, probably falsified tales of when they were young and beautiful. And the stories of their youth are the liveliest parts of the novel." But Williamson also finds that the characters' very gracefulness inhibits Adams's attempts to portray old age truthfully: "The picture presented in this novel seems too kind, too pretty. Old age, we suspect, is not a gentle stroll on the beach at twilight with kind and caring friends. Where, we ask, is the 'rage against the dying of the light'?" But *Los Angeles Times Book Review* contributor Joanna Barnes praises the depiction of the pain that exists in all relationships, whether among the young or the old. Barnes writes: "In a larger sense, it is the nature of friendship under Adams' delicate examination here. She re-creates, too, the haunting undertone of the loneliness present in all human intercourse, that separateness which, despite the presence of kindly acquaintances and lovers, can never be bridged nor breached."

Second Chances "is both the richest and the most satisfying novel that Adams . . . has produced," writes Diane Cole in Chicago *Tribune Books*. She adds, "Throughout, Adams demonstrates her gift for capturing the telling detail—the apartment decor, conversation topics, or fears left unsaid—that defines a particular era, setting or social milieu. . . . She has succeeded in painting a moving group portrait of friendship through the ages." *New York Times Book Review* contributor DeMott also feels that *Second Chances* is Adams's strongest work. DeMott believes "the strength flows partly from Ms. Adams's capacity to evoke fellow feeling, kindness and devotion as entirely natural inclinations of the heart. Her people care intensely for one another, and, although not beyond rage, seem beyond meanness. Equally important to the book's success is her grasp of conditions of feeling that are special to the middle classes just now entering their 60's and 70's. . . . [*Second Chances*] is a touching, subtle, truth-filled book."

As Elizabeth Ward observes in the *Washington Post Book World*, "Alice Adams' reputation is as a connoisseur of contemporary American relationships, a specialist in the affairs of white, middle- or upper middle-class, well-educated, well-traveled women." *Washington Post Book World* contributor Goodwin sees in Adams a "worldliness," which is "more than an attitude, a matter of style or sophistication; it amounts to a metaphysics, the wisdom of the world. Adams casts a cold eye on romance, nostalgia, anything that smacks of sentiment. She is staunchly on the side of those who believe that happiness, if it lies anywhere, lies in reality." Adams's future as a writer remains bright, writes Hill in the *Globe and Mail*, since she "is one of a number of productive American writers . . . whose fictional accomplishments are substantial now and will likely loom even larger in years to come."

CA INTERVIEW

CA interviewed Alice Adams by telephone on September 12, 1987, at her home in San Francisco, California.

CA: You started writing early, but success came late, as you've acknowledged yourself. Looking back on the passage of time before you were making your living as a writer, do you feel that it had advantages as well as disadvantages?

ADAMS: I suppose all those silly part-time jobs that I had turned out to be useful in one way or another, and that I learned something about areas I wouldn't normally have.

CA: When did you begin to feel established as a writer—if one ever does?

ADAMS: I still don't! It was quite late when I felt I could make my living as a writer; I was well over forty.

CA: Some of your stories, such as "Roses, Rhododendron," "The Todds" trilogy, "An Unscheduled Stop," and "Berkeley House," are very strongly rooted in autobiography. Were those stories, because of their closeness to you, harder to write than others?

ADAMS: All of those stories you've just mentioned are so different. Once a story is written, it's quite difficult to remember how hard or easy it was to write. The only story I remember as being especially easy is one called "Barcelona," which is a simple story about a bag being snatched in Barcelona. That was as autobiographical as anything I've ever written, but on a very simple level, obviously. "Roses, Rhododendron" was rather hard to write. The *New Yorker* turned it down. I kept rewriting it; I played around with it for a long time. But I rather like doing that, although it became discouraging, because I do think it's a good story.

CA: It's hard to understand the New Yorker's *turning down "Roses, Rhododendron."*

ADAMS: I had a peculiar editor there at that time. It was before I got wonderful Frances Kiernan.

CA: Have you had a sense of needing to work through the personal experiences by dealing with them in fiction?

ADAMS: Of course I have. Some years ago I was, as it were, disinherited. It seems to me I wrote a lot of stories about people not getting houses that they felt they should have. For a Southern person, that's a very shaking experience.

CA: Yes. In fact, it seems to me that it's harder to come to mature terms with a Southern upbringing than with any other kind, but maybe that's because I'm Southern.

ADAMS: I think it is—especially as women. We have all the problems that all women have, only more so.

CA: Do the short stories begin in your mind specifically as short stories rather than ideas for a novel? Is it always clear from the start which form an idea will take?

ADAMS: It really is always clear, except for very recently. I've been playing around with a group of short stories about the same people, and I'm still not sure what that's going to

be. I can't seem to stop writing about these psychiatrists, which is a funny group to be writing about.

CA: It hasn't happened much in your work that you've written about the same people over and over, has it?

ADAMS: No, it hasn't, except in those stories about the people I called the Todds, and that's only three stories.

CA: One of the things you do so well in both the novels and some of the short stories is take your characters—and your readers—across the decades. To me, the emotional climate of the 1950s seems especially real in your work. Was it the most crucial time in your formation as a writer?

ADAMS: It was, as I think back, possibly the worst time for me. I remember the fifties with sheer horror. If I had to live through any decade of my life again, that's the one I would least pick. I was writing only in the most spasmodic, desperate way. I was married and I had a very small child, who is wonderful as an adult, an artist, but was difficult then. I disliked my husband, and we didn't have any money, et cetera. And that was the fifties, when you were supposed to think all those things were quite wonderful.

CA: Did psychoanalysis have discernable effects on the progress of your writing?

ADAMS: This was also in the fifties, and it had a bad effect in that I was going to quite a stupid man who told me that I should stop writing and stay married. But I don't want to come down against analysis, because I don't feel that way. I just happened to pick a lemon. I've had dealings with a much better analyst since, so I know both sides of it.

CA: Friendship is an important theme in your work, not just between females of comparable age and status, but between mothers and daughters, between men and women who may or may not be lovers—in fact, all kinds of friendships. Is it something that you decided quite deliberately to write about, or has the exploration just grown naturally out of your greater concerns?

ADAMS: I was an only child, and I think possibly to us only children friendships are of extreme importance. Our friends *are* our families. Also, friendships last longer than anything else I know about.

CA: In the love relationships you write about, the ones that last are mostly the ones that involve friendship.

ADAMS: In my limited observation, that would appear to be true. I think another reason I like to write about friendship is that it seems to me friendship among women hasn't been written about a lot. I think it's an intensely interesting subject.

CA: And hasn't it changed in good ways over the years?

ADAMS: Yes, hasn't it? In the fifties, it was very hard for women to be, as we say, *honest* with each other. If you hated your husband, you had to pretend you thought he was really swell, because obviously nobody else hated hers. And women were supposed to be natural enemies, a view which, needless to say, men encouraged.

CA: And you've made the point previously that women now can form friendships based on professional ties, which wasn't so true in the past.

ADAMS: Absolutely. I'm going to New York next week, and some people have asked me if it's for business or pleasure. I've said that I can't tell the difference, because most of the people I work with there are close friends, and that's why they *are* my friends.

CA: Do you have favorites among your characters—or, on the other hand, ones that you had a hard time creating or grew rather tired of before you were through with them?

ADAMS: I have a kind of affection for those two young girls in "Roses, Rhododendron." I feel rather impatient with Louisa, who was the heroine of *Families and Survivors;* I thought she could have done a lot more with her life. I rather like Daphne in *Rich Rewards.*

CA: All the reviewers seemed to like Daphne too.

ADAMS: That's one of the advantages of writing in first-person; you can make the heroine rather endearing.

CA: You've been very lucky in your editors, as you've acknowledged in interviews and in book dedications. How most of all do you feel they've helped you?

ADAMS: I think Frances Kiernan at the *New Yorker* and Victoria Wilson at Knopf are the two best editors in New York; I really do. I've been with both of them for a long time now. They're sometimes argumentative, always extremely intelligent. They're quite unlike as people, except they're both brilliant, amazing women. I also have an absolutely first-rate agent, Lynn Nesbit, and I feel extremely lucky with her also. You notice that all these people are women.

CA: Would you like to comment on your relationship with the New Yorker?

ADAMS: It's been very rewarding, especially since Frances has been my editor—which is the last twelve years or so. Before that the relationship with the magazine was a little spotty. Once they turned down two of my stories that I still think are among the best I ever wrote. "Verlie I Say unto You," one of the Todd stories, was turned down. It's an odd magazine from that standpoint. I was once thinking of putting together an anthology of stories that have been turned down by the *New Yorker.* But I enjoy being published in the *New Yorker,* obviously, because everyone reads it. When you're in the so-called women's magazines, even if it's a good story, many people simply don't see it. The *New Yorker* is certainly where I like best to be. And after the recent upheaval surrounding the change of editors, I'm hoping for not much change in the magazine.

CA: I'd imagine that your work is especially comforting to women who have, later rather than sooner, come into their own both economically and emotionally. Do you get a lot of letters from such readers?

ADAMS: Yes. I get extremely gratifying letters from women who sound as if that were the case.

CA: Do you respond to all the letters you get from readers?

ADAMS: I do. It's so kind of people to bother to write, the least I can do is respond. Often I don't write at length; sometimes it's just a postcard saying "Thank you." But I think it's right to do that.

CA: How do you feel about the critical reception of your work, the reviews and reviewers generally?

ADAMS: I think on the whole I've been very generously treated. There is one thing, which I've said on other occasions, that I do object to and that I find happens to other women writers too: often the moral character of the heroine of a novel is reviewed, rather than the book itself. Some reviewer, I can't remember who, talked as though Megan, in *Superior Women,* were a promiscuous, jumping-into-bed kind of woman. I put it out that over forty years she'd had something like four love affairs. If some male writer—many come to mind—writes about the big stud, everyone applauds. There is still that incredible double standard.

CA: Many West Coast writers have complained about neglect of their work or difficulty in getting published and marketed because of their remoteness from New York. How do you feel about San Francisco as a place for a writer to be?

ADAMS: For me it's an ideal place. I don't feel neglected here. That complaint seems to me kind of an excuse. Frankly, I hear it mostly from writers who aren't very good. They may in fact get more attention here than they would there. One of the good things about San Francisco is that there's such a minimal literary life. I would find living in New York very difficult because there's so much going on, and I'm fairly easily distracted. I think carving out a private life, which any writer needs, would be very difficult in New York. It's necessary for me, and important, to see other writers, and there are just enough here to satisfy me.

CA: Travel has obviously contributed a great deal to your writing by way of settings, ideas, opportunities for the sort of looking back and personal assessment that happen especially in the stories in Return Trips. *Is travel always a reliable inspiration for your work, either directly or indirectly?*

ADAMS: I think it is, yes. For a long time, in my broke days— the fifties and most of the sixties—I didn't travel at all, not even to New York. But since I've been able to, I've traveled quite a lot. I do seem always to have written something about it. I go to Mexico usually in January, and that's provided a lot of stories. Other places have too. I like to travel.

CA: You began teaching writing several years ago and seemed to be enjoying it. Are you teaching now?

ADAMS: No, I'm not. I seem to teach seriously about every five years, so it's not time to do that again. I like it a lot, but it does take so much time, and for me it takes almost exactly the same kind of energy that writing does. Also, I think teaching is too easy an ego boost. I used to think, Oh, these kids think I'm wonderful, but they simply don't know any better; they haven't met that many people! I've had to be very careful not to listen to that adulation. I think teaching can be very bad for one's character—but then my father was a professor and so was my former husband, so my view is perhaps sour.

CA: Have television and movie people tried to lure you away from your fiction writing?

ADAMS: Unfortunately, they never have. I'm not sure I would be lured, but it would be nice to be asked.

CA: Would you like to try your hand at that sort of writing, perhaps on one of your own stories or novels?

ADAMS: I don't know. There are some very nice young women in Santa Monica who have optioned an odd story of mine that no one particularly likes except me—and now them. It's a rather long story called "Legends," about an elderly sculptor being interviewed. All her prior interviewers have only wanted to talk about her legendary love affair, but this particular interviewer wanted to talk about her sculpture. These women have had an option on it for years, so I don't know what is going to happen. But, when it comes to my own fiction, I think I'd rather let someone else do the screenwriting.

CA: You have won some fine awards for writing, including, in 1982, a rare O. Henry Special Award for Continuing Achievement. Do you look at the body of your work with a mind to assessing it, acknowledging what you're particularly pleased with and maybe setting goals for the future?

ADAMS: Not really. I don't tend to think in such an overall way. I think in much more immediate terms—what I'm doing now, possibly what I'll do this year.

CA: I've read that you originally wrote poetry, starting when you were very young.

ADAMS: Yes, and by the time I got to college, I realized it was awfully bad and I'd better stop.

CA: And you've never been tempted to go back to it?

ADAMS: Very occasionally. When I finished *Superior Women*—which was so long, and I was so tired of all those words—I wrote haiku for several weeks. That made me very happy. I really enjoyed doing that. Someone pointed out that writing haiku was originally a meditative exercise. It certainly had that effect for me.

CA: What would you like to do that you haven't gotten to yet?

ADAMS: As far as new things go, I suppose poetry is always lurking there somewhere, since you mentioned it. But really I'd just like to get much better. I'd like to write short stories that are unlike the ones I've written. A funny thing has sometimes happened to me: when I've tried to write new kinds of short stories, they've been rejected on the grounds that they don't sound like me. Editors don't encourage writers to try new things. They want you to go on being "you." Occasionally the editors of a small magazine say they'd like a story, and when I send them one, they don't want it—what they meant was a story just like one they saw in the *New Yorker* three years ago. I would like to try doing different stories, and to get better.

BIOGRAPHICAL/CRITICAL SOURCES:

BOOKS

Contemporary Literary Criticism, Gale, Volume 6, 1976, Volume 13, 1980, Volume 46, 1988.
Dictionary of Literary Biography Yearbook: 1986, Gale, 1987.

PERIODICALS

American Book Review, July, 1983.

Booklist, December 15, 1978, January 15, 1982, June 15, 1984, July, 1985.
Books and Bookmen, March, 1985, February, 1986.
Chicago Tribune, September 1, 1985.
Chicago Tribune Book World, September 14, 1980, May 2, 1982.
Christian Science Monitor, February 20, 1975, October 16, 1985.
Commonweal, March 25, 1983.
Critique, summer, 1986.
Globe and Mail (Toronto), November 10, 1984.
Harvard Magazine, February, 1975.
Hudson Review, summer, 1979, spring, 1985.
Listener, January 29, 1976.
London Review of Books, February 21, 1985.
Los Angeles Times, April 13, 1982, August 19, 1985.
Los Angeles Times Book Review, November 16, 1980, May 8, 1988.
Ms., September, 1984.
New England Review, autumn, 1986.
New Leader, March 27, 1978.
New Republic, February 4, 1978.
New Statesman, January 16, 1976.
Newsweek, February 3, 1975.
New Yorker, February 10, 1975, November 5, 1984.
New York Times, January 30, 1975, January 10, 1978, August 21, 1985, May 19, 1988.
New York Times Book Review, March 16, 1975, February 26, 1978, January 14, 1979, September 14, 1980, April 11, 1982, September 23, 1984, September 1, 1985, May 1, 1988.
Observer (London), January 18, 1976.
People, April 3, 1978.
Publishers Weekly, January 16, 1978.
Rolling Stone, April 20, 1978.
San Francisco Review of Books, spring, 1985.
Saturday Review, November-December, 1985.
StoryQuarterly, Number 11, 1980.
Time, December 26, 1977, April 19, 1982.
Times (London), January 9, 1986.
Times Literary Supplement, January 16, 1976, January 31, 1986.
Tribune Books (Chicago), May 1, 1988.
Village Voice, January 9, 1978.
Washington Post Book World, February 23, 1975, January 13, 1978, January 21, 1979, October 12, 1980, May 9, 1982, September 2, 1984, September 15, 1985, May 6, 1988.
West Coast Review of Books, March, 1978, November, 1984.

—*Sketch by Jani Prescott*
—*Interview by Jean W. Ross*

*   *   *

ADAMS, Harrison
[Collective pseudonym]

WRITINGS:

"PIONEER BOYS" SERIES

Pioneer Boys of the Ohio; or, Clearing the Wilderness, Page, 1912.
. . . on the Great Lakes; or, On the Trail of the Iroquois, Page, 1912.
. . . of the Mississippi; or, The Homestead in the Wilderness, Page, 1913.

. . . of the Missouri; or, In the Country of the Sioux, Page, 1914.
. . . of the Yellowstone; or, Lost in the Land of Wonders, Page, 1915.
. . . of the Columbia; or, In the Wilderness of the Great Northwest, Page, 1916.
. . . of the Colorado; or, Braving the Perils of the Grand Canyon Country, Page, 1926.
. . . of Kansas; or, A Prairie Home in Buffalo Land, Page, 1928.

SIDELIGHTS: Stratemeyer Syndicate author St. George Rathborne worked on this series. For more information see the entries for Harriet S. Adams, Edward L. Stratemeyer, and Andrew E. Svenson.

BIOGRAPHICAL/CRITICAL SOURCES:

BOOKS

Johnson, Deidre, editor and compiler, *Stratemeyer Pseudonyms and Series Books: An Annotated Checklist of Stratemeyer and Stratemeyer Syndicate Publications*, Greenwood Press, 1982.

*   *   *

ALEIXANDRE, Vicente   1898-1984

PERSONAL: Born April 26, 1898, in Seville, Spain; died of kidney failure and shock from intestinal hemorrhage, December 14, 1984, in Madrid, Spain; son of Cirilo (an engineer) and Elvira (Merlo) Aleixandre. *Education:* Attended University of Seville; University of Madrid, license in law and diploma in business, both 1919.

ADDRESSES: Home and office—Vicente Aleixandre, 3, 28003 Madrid, Spain.

CAREER: Poet and writer, 1925-84. Central School of Commerce, Madrid, Spain, associate professor, 1919-21; Residencia de Estudiantes, Madrid, teacher of business terminology, 1921; worked for Ferrocarriles andaluces (railroad company), 1921-25. Lecturer at Oxford University and University of London, 1950, and in Morocco, 1953.

MEMBER: Real Academia Espanola, American Association of Teachers of Spanish and Portuguese (honorary fellow), Hispanic Society of America, Monde Latin Academy (Paris); corresponding member of Malaga Arts Academy, Academy of Science and Arts (Puerto Rico), and Hispanic-American Academy (Bogata).

AWARDS, HONORS: National Literary Prize (Spain), 1933, for *La destruccion o el amor;* Spanish Critics' Prize, 1963, 1969, and 1975; Nobel Prize in literature, Swedish Academy, 1977; Grand Cross of the Order of Carlos III, 1977; Gold Medal of the City of Madrid, 1984.

WRITINGS:

IN ENGLISH TRANSLATION; POEMS

La destruccion o el amor, Signo (Madrid), 1935, 2nd edition, 1967, translation by Stephen Kessler of selected poems published as *Destruction or Love: A Selection from La destruccion o el amor of Vicente Aleixandre*, Green Horse Three (Santa Cruz, Calif.), 1976.
Mundo a solas, Clan (Madrid), 1950, translation by Lewis Hyde and David Unger published as *World Alone/Mundo a solas* (bilingual edition), Penmaen Press (Great Barrington, Mass.), 1982.

Poems (bilingual edition), translations by Ben Belitt, Alan Brilliant, and others, Department of English, Ohio University, 1969.
Vicente Aleixandre and Luis Cernuda: Selected Poems (bilingual edition), translations by Linda Lehrer and others, Copper Beach Press (Providence, R.I.), 1974.
The Cave of Night: Poems (bilingual edition), translation by Joeffrey Bartman, Solo Press (San Luis Obispo, Calif.), 1976.
Twenty Poems, edited by Hyde, translations by Hyde and Robert Bly, Seventies Press (Madison, Minn.), 1977.
Poems-Poemas (bilingual edition), Unicorn Press, 1978.
A Longing for the Light: Selected Poems of Vicente Aleixandre, edited by Hyde, translations by Kessler and others, Harper, 1979.
The Crackling Sun: Selected Poems of the Nobel Prize Recipient 1977, translated and introduced by Louis Bourne, Sociedad General Espanola de la Libreria (Madrid), 1981.
A Bird of Paper: Poems of Vicente Aleixandre, translated by Willis Barnstone and David Garrison, Ohio University Press, 1982.

IN SPANISH; POEMS

Ambito (title means "Ambit"), Litoral (Malaga), 1928, reprinted, Raiz (Madrid), 1950.
Espadas como labios (title means "Swords Like Lips"; also see below), Espasa Calpe (Madrid), 1932, reprinted, Losada (Buenos Aires), 1957.
Pasion de la tierra (title means "Passion of the Earth"; also see below), Fabula (Mexico), 1935, revised edition, Adonais (Madrid), 1946, critical edition with notes and commentary by Luis Antonio de Villena, Narceu, 1976.
Sombra del paraiso (title means "Shadow of Paradise"; also see below), Adan (Madrid), 1944, reprinted, Castalia, 1976.
Poemas paradisiacos (title means "Poems of Paradise"; includes selections from *Sombra del paraiso*), [Malaga], 1952, 3rd edition, edited by Jose Luis Cano, Catedra, 1981.
Nacimiento ultimo (title means "Final Birth"), Insula (Madrid), 1953.
Historia del corazon (title means "History of a Heart"), Espasa Calpe, 1954, critical edition with prologue by Cano, 1983.
Antigua casa madrilena (title means "Ancient Madrid House"; also see below), Hermanos Bedia (Santander, Spain), 1961.
Picasso (long poem), [Malaga], 1961.
En un vasto dominio (title means "In a Vast Dominion"; includes *Antigua casa madrilena*), Revista de Occidente, 1962.
Retratos con nombres (title means "Portraits with Names"), El Bardo, 1965.
Poemas de la consumacion (title means "Poems of Consumation"), Plaza y Janes (Barcelona), 1968.
Sonido de la guerra, Fomento de Cultura Ediciones (Valencia), 1972.
Dialogos del conocimiento (title means "Dialogues of Knowledge"), Plaza y Janes, 1974.

OMNIBUS VOLUMES IN SPANISH

Mis poemas mejores (title means "My Best Poems"), Gredos (Madrid), 1956, revised edition, 1976.
Espadas como labios [and] *Pasion de la tierra*, Losada, 1957, critical edition with notes and introduction by Cano, Castalia, 1977.

Poemas amorosos: Antologia (title means "Love Poems: Anthology"), Losada, 1960.

Poesias completas (title means "Complete Poems"), introduction by Carlos Bousono, Aguilar, 1960.

Presencias (title means "Presences"; limited edition), Seix Barral (Barcelona), 1965.

Obras completas (title means "Complete Works"), introduction by Bousono, Aguilar, 1968, revised edition published in two volumes, 1977.

Poesia superrealista (title means "Surrealistic Poetry"), Barral Editores, 1971.

Antologia del mar y de la noche (title means "Anthology of the Sea and the Night"), edited by Javier Lostale, Al-Borak, 1971.

Antologia total (title means "Total Anthology"), compiled by Pere Gimferrer, Seix Barral, 1975.

Antologia poetica (title means "Poetry Anthology"), edited by Leopoldo de Luis, Castalia, 1976.

Aleixandre para ninos (title means "Aleixandre for Children"; juvenile), Ediciones de la Torre (Madrid), 1984.

AUTHOR OF PROLOGUE IN SPANISH

Bousono, *La primavera de la muerte*, Adonais, 1946.

Gregoria Prieto, *Poesia en linea*, Adonais, 1948.

Fernando Charry Lara, *Nocturnos y otros suenos*, [Bogata], 1948.

Adonais: Segunda antologia, Rialp (Madrid), 1962.

CONTRIBUTOR TO ANTHOLOGIES

Eleanor Laurelle Turnbull, editor, *Contemporary Spanish Poetry: Selections from Ten Poets* (bilingual edition), Johns Hopkins University Press, 1945.

Penguin Book of Spanish Verse, Penguin, 1956.

Willis Barnstone, editor, *Modern European Poetry*, Bantam, 1966.

Hardie St. Martin, editor, *Roots and Wings, Poetry from Spain: A Bilingual Anthology*, Harper, 1976.

OTHER

Algunos caracteres de la poesia espanola contemporanea (title means "Some Characteristics of Contemporary Spanish Poetry"; criticism), Imprunta Gongora (Madrid), 1955.

Los encuentros (title means "The Meetings"; critical/biographical sketches), Guadarrama (Madrid), 1958.

(Contributor) Francisco Sabadell Lopez, *Desnudos*, [Valladolid], 1961.

(Author of epilogue) Federico Garcia Lorca, *Obras completas*, Aguilar, 1963.

(Contributor) Jose Angeles, editor, *Estudios sobre Antonio Machado*, Ariel, 1977.

Contributor of poetry and articles to Spanish journals. Co-editor, *Revista de Economia*, 1920-22; staff member, *La Semana Financiera* (financial magazine), ending 1927.

SIDELIGHTS: Poet Vicente Aleixandre was a member of Spain's Generation of 1927, which Manuel Duran described in a *World Literature Today* essay as "perhaps the brightest and most original poetic generation in twentieth-century Western Europe." Along with Aleixandre, the group included many of modern Spain's most influential writers, such as Jorge Guillen, Gerardo Diego, and Rafael Alberti.

Although nearly unknown outside his native country before receiving the Nobel Prize for Literature in 1977, Aleixandre had much in common with the generation's best-known poet, Federico Garcia Lorca. The two men were from the same region in Spain—the southernmost Andalusia—and revealed the same sources of inspiration in their poetry: Spanish writing of the fifteenth and sixteenth centuries, popular folk rhythms of their native Andalusia, and surrealism. But, while Lorca's death at the hands of Franco's forces at the beginning of the Spanish Civil War catapulted him into international recognition, Aleixandre's name was known only in Spanish circles. He survived both having his house nearly destroyed in a Civil War bomb attack—an autographed book of Lorca's was one of the only items recovered from his gutted library—and having his work banned by government censors for nearly five years after the war to become one of Spain's most prominent poets.

Most critics of Aleixandre's work commented on the thematic and stylistic evolution evident in his poetry. In *Contemporary Spanish Poetry (1898-1963)*, for example, Carl W. Cobb noted that in Aleixandre's early poems the poet "rejected the historical and social world around him and created from his elemental passions a vast domain of cosmic and telluric forces anterior to man himself." In contrast, Cobb described the poet's later work as being focused "directly in the historical reality of his *pueblo*, his 'people.'"

Other critics, such as Diana Der Hovanessian, Arthur Terry, and Kessel Schwartz, echoed Cobb's assessment. In the *Christian Science Monitor*, for instance, Der Hovanessian noted: "Some of [Aleixandre's] early poetry might tax a reader with its mysticism and disjointed style. But Aleixandre's poetry loses much of the disconnectedness in later years, and begins to address people directly." Terry similarly stated in the *Times Literary Supplement* that while Aleixandre's early poems were "Surrealist-influenced," in later poems "emphasis shifts to the contemplation of man in his human context." Schwartz described the poet's work in *Vicente Aleixandre* as a movement from "the chaotic maelstrom" of his early work to a new poetry in which Aleixandre "became aware of historical man, the temporal man, that is, man in time and space."

Dario Fernandez-Morera explained the transformation in Aleixandre's poetry in light of the dramatic change in Spanish society following the Civil War. In *Symposium* the critic stated: "Before [the war], poets had lived in an atmosphere of continuity, of relative intellectual security; therefore they could be concerned with their own psyches rather than with the world they lived in.... But the growing turmoil made this attitude no longer feasible."

The selection of Aleixandre as a Nobel laureate was controversial, since the complexity of his surrealistic poetry made it unintelligible to many critics and most readers. A *Washington Post* writer quoted a translated line of poetry from Aleixandre's second book, *Pasion de la tierra* (title means "Passion of the Earth"), as an example of what the reviewer called Aleixandre's "puzzling" verse: "To sleep when my time comes on a conscience without a pillowcase."

G. G. Brown referred to the same book of poetry in *A Literary History of Spain* as "a collection of largely incomprehensible prose-poems, whose private subconscious ramblings Aleixandre tried to excuse later by calling them Freudian." And in *A Longing for the Light: Selected Poems of Vicente Aleixandre*, Lewis Hyde noted that the poems in *Pasion de la tierra* were "written in an almost hermetic dream-language."

According to Hyde, Aleixandre agreed with critics who called *Pasion de la tierra* difficult, but he nevertheless defended the book's worth. Hyde translated the poet's comments: "I have always thought I could see in its chasm-like layers the sudden start of my poetry's evolution, which, from its earliest, has been . . . a longing for the light. This book has therefore produced in me a double, complicated feeling: of aversion, because of its difficulty, which contradicts the call, the appeal it makes to basic levels, common to all of us; and of affection, for the maternal *humus* from which it grew.''

Although Fernandez-Morera pointed out that ''Aleixandre's surrealist phase is perhaps [his] most publicized,'' the poet's Nobel Prize was awarded largely for his later, more accessible, work. This was evident, Pablo Beltran de Heredia observed in the *Texas Quarterly*, ''when [the Swedish Academy] stated, during the award ceremonies, that the work of this Spanish poet 'illuminates the condition of man in the cosmos and in our present-day society.'''

Cobb noted that ''it is perhaps with a feeling of relief that the reader turns from the difficult and turbulent world of Aleixandre's first period . . . to the quieter and simpler but no less moving world of his second phase. . . . His major theme becomes human solidarity, with compassion toward all human beings living in time.'' Cobb singled out *Historia del corazon* (title means ''History of the Heart'') published in 1954 as Aleixandre's first book of this new style of poetry. Abandoning the obscurity of his early poems, Aleixandre came to believe that poetry was essentially communication. In general, the prose-poems gave way to what a *New York Times* writer called ''carefully cadenced free verse.'' The nightmarish images were replaced by portraits of everyday life. According to Duran, ''*Historia del corazon* is basically the story of a love affair, in its daily moments of joy and anguish, and also the story of a growing awareness, a solidarity: the poet realizes that he is only one member of a vast society, the Spanish people, and that ultimately he is a part of mankind.''

Beltran de Heredia pointed out that Aleixandre expressed a fondness for this simpler poetry, preferring *Historia del corazon* among his books and—from that same collection—''En la plaza'' (title means ''On the Square'') among his poems. Both Santiago Daydi-Tolson in *The Post-Civil War Spanish Poets* and Duran emphasized the importance of this same poem. Aleixandre ''uses the image of the public square,'' Daydi-Tolson observed, ''to represent the greatness of human solidarity.'' According to the critic, the plaza, the axis around which society revolves in every Spanish city, is the perfect embodiment of the essence of Spanish life. In the symbol of the public square the poet ''feels and understands this essential communal quality of man's existence.''

Duran saw the poem as an encapsulated portrait of Aleixandre's evolution from personal to communal poet. Duran explained the imagery of the poem: ''After being long confined in his room, the poet goes out into the street, to the square, in order to mingle with other human beings and be part of humanity.'' Duran illustrated his point with a translation from the poem: ''It is a beautiful feeling, beautifully humble and buoyant, life-giving and deep, / to feel yourself beneath the sun among other people.''

Aleixandre is important for his own poetry but also for his influence on the poetry of subsequent generations. As one of the few poets to remain in Spain during the Civil War, he was a symbol of hope to younger poets. In a *New York Times Book Review* essay, Robert Bly suggested that after the war ''the younger writers felt abandoned, dead, in despair. It turned out that Aleixandre's decision to stay helped all that. He represented the wild energy still alive on Spanish soil.''

A London *Times* writer noted that although Aleixandre ''was privately distressed at the low quality of verse of Falangist poets [members of Franco's party], . . . he encouraged them as he encouraged every other poet, seeking with a noble magnanimity of spirit to unify all factions. He worked behind the scenes . . . to obtain the release of imprisoned writers, and was more responsible than any other single person for creating the relaxed [Spanish] censorship of the middle and late 1960s, which led to better things.''

In Aleixandre's prologue to the second edition of *La destruccion o el amor*, the Spaniard summarized his ideas on poets and poetry. The prologue, written in 1944 shortly before the poet began work on *La historia del corazon* and translated by David Pritchard in the *Paris Review*, ends with a short explanation of Aleixandre's poetics. ''Some poets . . . ,'' he wrote, ''are poets 'of the few.' They are artists . . . who address themselves to men by attending, so they say, to exquisite and narrow obsessions. . . . Other poets . . . address themselves to what is permanent in man. Not to the details that set us apart, but to the essence that brings us together. . . . These poets are radical poets and they speak to what is primordial, to what is elemental in humanity. They cannot *feel* themselves to be poets of the few. I am one of these.''

BIOGRAPHICAL/CRITICAL SOURCES:

BOOKS

Aleixandre, Vicente, *Twenty Poems*, edited by Lewis Hyde, Seventies Press, 1977.

Aleixandre, Vicente, *A Longing for the Light: Selected Poems of Vicente Aleixandre*, edited by Lewis Hyde, Copper Canyon Press, 1985.

Alonso, Damaso, *Ensayos sobre poesia espanola*, Revista de Occidente, 1946.

Bousono, Carlos, *La poesia de Vicente Aleixandre*, Insula, 1950, revised edition, 1977.

Brown, G. G., *A Literary History of Spain*, Barnes & Noble, 1972.

Cabrera, Vicente and Harriet Boyer, editors, *Critical Views on Vicente Aleixandre's Poetry*, Society of Spanish and Spanish-American Studies (Lincoln, Neb.), 1979.

Cobb, Carl W., *Contemporary Spanish Poetry (1898-1963)*, Twayne, 1976.

Contemporary Literary Criticism, Gale, Volume IX, 1978, Volume XXXVI, 1986.

Daydi-Tolson, Santiago, editor, *Vicente Aleixandre: A Critical Appraisal*, Bilingual Press, 1981.

Daydi-Tolson, Santiago, *The Post-Civil War Spanish Poets*, Twayne, 1983.

Jimenez, Jose Olivio, *Cinco poetas del tiempo*, Insula, 1964.

Jimenez, Jose Olivio, *Vicente Aleixandre: Una aventura hacia el conocimiento*, Ediciones Jucar (Madrid), 1982.

Ley, Charles David, *Spanish Poetry since 1939*, Catholic University of America Press, 1962.

Morris, C. B., *A Generation of Spanish Poets: 1920-1936*, Cambridge University Press, 1969.

Schwartz, Kessel, *Vicente Aleixandre*, Twayne, 1970.

PERIODICALS

Christian Science Monitor, January 2, 1980.
Hispania, May, 1967.
Hispanic Journal, fall, 1982.
Hudson Review, winter, 1978-79.
Nation, March 4, 1978.
New Republic, December 24-31, 1977.

Newsweek, October 17, 1977.
New York Times, October 7, 1977.
New York Times Book Review, October 30, 1977.
Paris Review, fall, 1978.
Parnassus: Poetry in Review, fall/winter, 1979.
Poetry, April, 1980.
Symposium, summer, 1979.
Texas Quarterly, winter, 1978.
Time, October 17, 1977.
Times (London), December 15, 1984.
Times Literary Supplement, May 17, 1957, November 2, 1958, July 10, 1969, May 23, 1975.
Washington Post, December 15, 1984.
World Literature Today, spring, 1975.

OBITUARIES:

PERIODICALS

AB Bookman's Weekly, January 21, 1985.
Chicago Tribune, December 16, 1984.
Los Angeles Times, December 16, 1984.
Time, December 24, 1984.
Times (London), December 15, 1984.†

—*Sketch by Marian Gonsior*

*   *   *

ALEXANDER, Charles
  See HADFIELD, (Ellis) Charles (Raymond)

*   *   *

ALEXANDER, Shana   1925-

PERSONAL: Born October 6, 1925, in New York, N.Y.; daughter of Milton (a composer) and Cecelia (a film critic; maiden name, Rubenstein) Ager; married Robert Shulman, 1946; married Stephen Alexander, 1951 (divorced); children: Katherine (deceased). *Education:* Vassar College, B.A., 1945.

ADDRESSES: Home—Wainscott, N.Y. *Office*—c/o Joy Harris Lantz Office, 888 Seventh Ave., New York, N.Y. 10106.

CAREER: PM Newspaper, New York City, writer, 1944-46; *Harper's Bazaar*, New York City, writer, 1946-47; *Flair*, New York City, entertainment editor, 1950; *Life* Magazine, member of staff in New York City, 1951-54, on West Coast, 1954-61, staff writer, 1961-64, author of column "The Feminine Eye," 1964-69; *McCall's* Magazine, New York City, editor, 1969-71; Columbia Broadcasting System, New York City, commentator on radio program "Spectrum," 1970-72, regular commentator, "Point-Counterpoint" segment of "Sixty Minutes," 1974-79; vice-president, Norton Simon Communications, Inc., 1971-72; columnist, *Newsweek*, 1972-75; full-time writer, 1979—. Member, New York State Council on the Arts, 1978-80; member of board of directors, American Film Institute, 1978-81.

MEMBER: National Women's Political Caucus (founding member).

AWARDS, HONORS: Sigma Delta Chi award and University of Southern California national journalism award, 1965; named Woman of the Year, *Los Angeles Times*, 1967; Golden Pen Award, American Newspaper Women's Club, 1969; Front Page Award, Newswomen's Club of New York, 1973; Matrix Award, New York Women in Communications, 1973-74; Achievement Award, Women's Division of Albert Einstein College of Medicine, 1976; Edgar Award nominations for best fact crime, Mystery Writers of America, 1980, for *Anyone's Daughter: The Times and Trials of Patty Hearst*, and 1986, for *Nutcracker: Money, Madness, Murder—A Family Album*; Edgar Award for best fact crime, 1984, for *Very Much a Lady: The Untold Story of Jean Harris and Dr. Herman Tarnower*; Creative Arts award, National Women's division of American Jewish Congress.

WRITINGS:

The Feminine Eye, McCall Publishing, 1970.
Shana Alexander's State-by-State Guide to Women's Legal Rights, Wollstonecraft, 1975.
Talking Woman, Delacorte, 1976.
Anyone's Daughter: The Times and Trials of Patty Hearst, Viking, 1979.
Very Much a Lady: The Untold Story of Jean Harris and Dr. Herman Tarnower, Little, Brown, 1983.
Nutcracker: Money, Madness, Murder—A Family Album, Doubleday, 1985.
The Pizza Connection: Lawyers, Money, Drugs, Mafia, Weidenfeld & Nicolson, 1988.

WORK IN PROGRESS: A book on "three American women of high accomplishment brought low by love: Bess Myerson; the Honorable Hortense Gabel; Nancy Capasso," for Random House.

SIDELIGHTS: A college degree in anthropology provided "the ideal subject to train for journalism—the study of exotic people in their native habitats," veteran reporter and commentator Shana Alexander told *Life* magazine. Alexander began working summers as a reporter while in college, and progressed to a career marked with milestones: she was the first female reporter, staff writer, and columnist for *Life;* in 1969 she was named the first female editor of *McCall's;* and she gained national recognition as a featured commentator on the CBS news program "Sixty Minutes." Although Alexander was an experienced writer when she first began working as a columnist, "stepping into the first person for the first time, and talking as myself, was the hardest thing I have ever tried to make myself do," she relates in her collection of essays, *Talking Woman*. Nevertheless, she has won renown with her commentaries; in a *New York Times* review of another collection, *The Feminine Eye*, Anatole Broyard calls Alexander "one of those rare writers who can be witty without ever being cruel; who can be deeply personal without making you feel you opened the wrong door; profound without sounding portentous; emotional without sentimentality. She is a sensible, well-balanced woman raised to the nth power." Despite this success, with the publication of *Anyone's Daughter: The Times and Trials of Patty Hearst* Alexander left mainstream journalism in order to pursue book-writing full time.

When Alexander first heard of the kidnapping of Patty Hearst, whose family owns the Hearst publishing empire, "I thought: This is the story I was made to write, that I was trained for," she told *New York Times Book Review* writer Herbert Mitgang. "It had all the elements that interested me: civil rights, the feminist movement, California, the media itself. The case was a clothesline on which to hang my opinions." Alexander first thought of writing a series of essays on her thoughts about the Hearst case, but instead determined to include Patty Hearst's trial on robbery charges and "cover and write about the event in full," she recounts in the introduction to *Anyone's Daughter*. "The *device* of the trial would enable me to deal with much more than the trial; ordered by a trial's classic unities of time and space, the courtroom doings could serve as a kind of prism through which to refract the whole.''

''What emerges'' from the ensuing account ''is a kind of soap-opera drama of rivalrous lawyers and doctors, and Alexander herself, presented as one of the characters, attempting to account for her strong emotional involvement,'' describes Diane Johnson in the *Washington Post Book World*. ''Yet it is precisely because she uses her feelings that the book takes on a power not earned either by the social analysis or reportage,'' asserts *New York Times Book Review* contributor Richard Kluger. Alexander believes that her strong reaction to the Hearst case is due in part to her identification with Patty Hearst: ''I understood her because in some way she was the girl I had been, and in some way I was also her mother,'' the author writes in her introduction. This attempt to draw parallels between the Hearst case and both personal and universal issues has been criticized by some, however. *New Society* contributor Valerie Miner calls Alexander's writing ''stunted . . . by indulging in the brand of personal journalism which reveals too much about the author and not enough about the subject,'' while Judith Adler Hennessee maintains in the *Village Voice* that ''Alexander tends to get carried away. . . . The parallels are simply not there.'' But Broyard thinks that these same ''feelings about the trial are just what is needed to rescue it from sprawling confusion and to keep reminding us that it is not a 'media event,' but a trial that affects real people,'' the critic observes in his review of *Anyone's Daughter*. ''She is a shrewd Monday morning quarterback who reexamines the evidence for us in a more human light, who humanizes what often comes to resemble . . . 'Theater of Cruelty.' ''

Critics also differ as to the effectiveness of Alexander's reporting; while Johnson believes the characters are described ''a bit too vividly,'' Kluger states that the author ''is especially good at capturing telltale physical detail.'' The critic adds that the book ''is distinguished from the run of courtroom literature by the verve, wit, range and vividness of the author's language.'' In addition, Alexander uses ''a good reporter's sense of pace and detail'' to condense the sheer mass of information produced by an eight-week trial, especially ''the great slag heap of expert testimony,'' as *Newsweek* writer Peter Prescott describes it. Kluger, however, thinks the reporter ''seems swamped'' by the material; an *Atlantic* critic similarly remarks that ''the material almost overwhelms the interpretation.'' This same reviewer, however, admits that ''sometimes floundering, sometimes brilliant, the book throws light into a thousand dark places in American society.'' And Kluger also finds the book similarly insightful: ''At her best, [the author] transcends the literal confines of her subject to produce a kind of charged and resonating journalism that only Norman Mailer, at his best, has managed so well.''

Alexander also uses a broad approach in *Very Much a Lady: The Untold Story of Jean Harris and Dr. Herman Tarnower*, in which she recounts the circumstances surrounding the death of the notorious ''Scarsdale Diet Doctor.'' ''In her book Alexander recounts the familiar events leading up to the doctor's death,'' summarizes Priscilla Johnson McMillan in the *Chicago Tribune Book World*. ''But she does much more. Writing with superb emotional precision, she helps us understand [accused murderer] Jean Harris. Moreover, describing the worlds inhabited by the lovers, she writes brilliantly about social class in America,'' adds the critic. In retracing the events that happened the night Tarnower was shot to death, the author ''has followed every lead back to its source like a thorough lawyer building a case,'' notes *New York Times Book Review* contributor Anne Bernays. This tracing of sources, according to Patricia Blake in *Time*, includes ''lavish[ing] her considerable reportorial skills . . . [in] interviewing hundreds of people who knew the doctor and his lover'' as well as Jean Harris herself. In relating these interviews, ''Alexander has an eye for the telling detail that reveals character and helps to construct a suggestive, flowing narrative,'' observes Bernays. The critic attributes part of this success to Alexander's ability to be ''patient, sensitive, obsessively curious and [to] ask the right questions.'' ''We get a powerful sense of being there,'' states Christopher Lehmann-Haupt of the *New York Times*, ''as well as compelling portraits of the backgrounds of the two principal characters, a dramatic feel for the pressures that were building in them and, at long last, a comprehensible version of the actual shooting.''

Lehmann-Haupt speculates, however, that ''part of the reason Miss Alexander can present such a coherent account is her open sympathy for Jean Harris.'' In Jean Harris's background, Alexander sees her own: ''She reminds me of me. Same hairdo, same shoes, even the same college class,'' the author writes in *Very Much a Lady*, adding that ''we are women of the same era.'' But this sympathy for and identification with Harris gives the book a distinct partiality towards Harris, an approach to journalism that makes many reviewers uncomfortable. In addition, due to a scarcity of ''first-hand documentation, Miss Alexander runs the various risks that inevitably come up whenever nonfiction invades the territory that fiction used to occupy,'' remarks Lehmann-Haupt. ''Yet even when she does document, it is clear enough whose version of events she is depending upon,'' the critic concedes. And Bernays believes that this empathetic approach is acceptable: ''Alexander's bias shows—and why not? No woman, especially one with Mrs. Harris's intelligence, ought to put up with the kind of horror show Dr. Tarnower arranged for her benefit.'' The critic also finds that to ''Alexander's immense credit, you not only want to shake some sense into Mrs. Harris, you also want to put your arm across her shoulder'' and comfort her. ''Despite the author's very strong sympathies for Mrs. Harris,'' asserts Lehmann-Haupt, *Very Much a Lady* ''is probably the most plausible account we have gotten of what happened.''

Nutcracker: Money, Madness, Murder—A Family Album, recounts ''the events leading up to the trial and conviction of Frances Schreuder, a patron of the New York arts who persuaded her 17-year-old son Marc to murder her father, [auto parts millionaire] Franklin Bradshaw,'' summarizes Edwin McDowell in the *New York Times*. Alexander uses an approach to the case comparable to that in *Very Much a Lady;* she concentrates on the character of Frances Schreuder. ''Her book treats the murder less as a 'case' than as a Chekhovian family tragedy,'' describes *Washington Post Book World* contributor John Katzenbach. ''The greatest part of her book focuses on Frances Schreuder and her bizarre, clearly deranged, life. . . . As [her character] takes form, so does the book,'' adds the critic. ''Alexander's compelling narrative builds in intensity around this uniquely twisted woman and the methods she employed to ruin those around her. Alexander's bravura portrayal of this woman makes us shudder at the resourcefulness of the psychological horrors Frances Schreuder performed.'' A key part of this characterization details, as *New York Times Book Review* contributor J. Anthony Lukas describes it, the ''exquisitely byzantine world of ballet'' and how ''Schreuder's campaign to insinuate herself into the confidence'' of the New York City Ballet's leaders motivated the murder.

Although Peter Gorner agrees that the author's greatest strength is that she "dissects the innards of the New York cultural scene," he also comments in the *Chicago Tribune Book World* that her "tone—so seasoned, so sadly knowing—begins to wear early on." Similarly, *Time* writer R. Z. Sheppard thinks *Nutcracker* is characterized by "digressions and cliched prose," while *New York Times* critic John Gross calls much of the writing "mechanical and two-dimensional. . . . It adds to the general sense of slickness, of a mini-series already in the making." Gross admits, however, that Alexander, who he calls "a practiced hand at story telling," has made "an attempt to give her material a satisfactory narrative shape." "In 'Nutcracker' Miss Alexander's skills are on display again," states Lukas. The author "spins this yarn with brio, keeping the narrative rolling along, holding the reader's interest with deft infusions of telling detail." As she has done with her other subjects, Alexander makes the story of *Nutcracker* "uniquely hers, a reflection in part of the empathy she felt for the Bradshaw-Schreuder woman, in part her own fascination with the mental processes that create crime," observes Katzenbach. The critic concludes by calling the book "well written, well researched and well presented," noting that in the depiction of Frances Schreuder, "Alexander is distinctive in her portrayal of madness."

In *The Pizza Connection: Lawyers, Money, Drugs, Mafia* Alexander similarly condenses the story of an extensive seventeen-month trial involving twenty-two Mafia defendants; in the process she has "devoured the dealings among the conspirators, who sometimes conspired against one another, the sleuthing by the F.B.I. and, especially, the trial itself," summarizes Walter Goodman in the *New York Times*. Accused of drug smuggling, money laundering, and conspiracy, each of the defendants had his own lawyer, and the competition between these attorneys provides Alexander with ample occasion for comment on the U.S. judicial system. Calling Alexander "the savviest trial reporter since Dorothy Kilgallen," *New York Post* contributor David Finkle nevertheless notes that "in transcribing this trial with thoroughness only just short of the court stenographer's, [Alexander] has taken the risk . . . of occasionally stretching the patience of curious readers in order to make what is a long and not very encouraging series of points about the state of contemporary criminal justice."

Other critics have also faulted the protracted length of Alexander's account. A *Kirkus Reviews* writer, for example, notes that the author's "sizable cast of characters features precious few good guys, let alone heroes, so there's no real focus to the narrative." George V. Higgins expresses a similar opinion in *Newsday:* "The trouble is that this trial resembles every case that I have ever tried, or observed, myself: There isn't any high drama." The critic adds that while "what goes on outside the trial is at least interesting . . . what leads up to those verdicts is boring." But Goodman believes that "although her book occasionally gets bogged down in the army of witnesses and acres of evidence, Ms. Alexander generally makes a skilled guide, taking us out of the courtroom to dramatize the events on the stand. Her accounts of international smuggling operations, murderous Mafia feuds and long-running police investigations," continues Goodman, ". . .have the appeal of a snappy detective story." "Alexander handles the avalanche of materials that resulted [from the long trial] with great skill and intelligence," maintains *People* contributor Mary Vespa, "juxtaposing flashback scenes with the diary she kept during the trial." Although Vespa acknowledges that the amount of information included may slow some readers,

"the glimpses [Alexander] offers of both Mafia life and the behind-the-scenes maneuvers of defense lawyers and prosecutors are fascinating." "Ms. Alexander notes that not a single juror or alternate stayed awake through the entire ordeal," concludes Goodman. "To her credit, her readers should find it possible to do better."

MEDIA ADAPTATIONS: Nutcracker: Money, Madness, Murder was made into an award-winning mini-series by Warner Bros. TV and broadcast on NBC in 1987.

CA INTERVIEW

CA interviewed Shana Alexander by telephone on December 14, 1987, at her home in Wainscott, New York.

CA: In the introduction to Talking Woman *you described your first assignment as a cub reporter during school vacation, going to interview Gypsy Rose Lee with your questions tucked into the white gloves you were wearing. Was it taken for granted by your writing parents that you would be a writer too, though that might have been secondary to marriage, in their minds?*

ALEXANDER: No. I didn't want to be a writer; it just worked out that way. I wanted to be an anthropologist, and I also wanted to get married. My parents *didn't* want me to get married, so I went ahead and did it, you see. I wish we'd all been smarter. Anthropology was a perfect thing to study. When I was in college, you couldn't be an English major unless you took Latin or Medieval English—that was required. Well, nobody in her right mind took Medieval English at Vassar College. And I had been educated before college at a progressive school which was against Latin and refused to teach it. I've had to teach myself Latin, since I'm a writer and so many of our words come from Latin. I also wish I knew Medieval English. Although I'm radical in some ways, I'm quite conservative about education, and I think Latin should be taught. I think cooking and sewing and shop still should be taught, too.

CA: Life *magazine, where you worked up from researcher to columnist (''The Feminine Eye'') and stayed for eighteen years, was ''a nonstop journalistic carnival,'' you've said, and when* Life *died, you wrote its obituary in your* Newsweek *column. What was* Life*'s greatest legacy to you?*

ALEXANDER: The friendships that I made. It was a lovely place to work. It wouldn't have been near as lovely at *Time* or any of the other magazines, but in the entertainment/show business department of *Life*, we had a kind of father figure, Tom Prideaux, the drama critic; we had a mother figure, who was Mary Leatherbee, the movie editor. And the young reporters had a marvelous time. They've all stayed on in journalism, the ones I knew. One is Clay Felker, who started *New York* magazine. Another is Margaret Williams. Her husband, Bob Ginna, is a superb film producer, and he started *People* magazine. She's running a magazine called *Lear's* that hasn't come out yet. Another was Phil Kunhardt, who was editor of *Life* for many years and now puts out the magnificent *Life* picture books. And I could keep going on and on.

It was extremely congenial, and it wasn't like working. You were well-paid and heavily expense-accounted and had fun. My job was to cover everything that was not movies or theater. That left television and things like ballet and opera. Well, they didn't want to do any stories about television, because television was a competing advertising medium. It was hard to get them to do stories on Howdy Doody or the Army-McCarthy hearings or whatever else was going on in that period, in the 50s. But, on the other hand, I had free tickets every night to the New York City Ballet and the Metropolitan Opera. That was my so-called beat, and it was glorious.

CA: Aside from your parents, were there writers who served as models or inspirations for you when you were starting out?

ALEXANDER: Yes. I would think of the two anthropologists Ruth Benedict and Margaret Mead, whom I read every word of. Then there were some special books. I was raised in hotels, so all our stuff was in storage, including the books. But there was one little bookcase that had four books in it, and much later in my life I realized that everything I knew came out of those four books. One was Carl Sandburg's *The American Songbag*, so I can sing and play virtually anything that's in that book. One was the one-volume edition of *The Golden Bough*. One was *Microbe Hunters* by Paul deKruif, which was a big bestseller in the thirties. It had mini-biographies of four or five people like Louis Pasteur, for example. It was thrilling. I'm having trouble remembering the fourth book. Maybe it was *The Joy of Cooking!* I've still got the 1938 gravy-stained copy.

CA: You seem to have been very happy not only at Life, *but also at* Newsweek, *on the radio show "Spectrum," and opposite Jack Kilpatrick on the Point-Counterpoint segment of CBS's "60 Minutes." Besides having to start at* Life *as a researcher, with a cut in pay from your previous job, how much sexual discrimination have you experienced in the media?*

ALEXANDER: I think there was a lot of it when I was younger, but I wasn't aware of it because it was the accepted way for things to be. I was always the only woman. And I thought, Well, these young men have wives and small children, so they *should* get paid more.

CA: Do you see the roles of women in television reporting changing in positive ways?

ALEXANDER: Yes. There didn't used to be any women, and now the air is twinkling with token women. I don't think there are very many women in the power positions: owners, managers. I'm pretty far away from broadcasting now, so perhaps I'm wrong. But I'm not aware of women owners of newspapers or radio or television stations unless they are the daughters or widows of former owners. But that has nothing to do with sex discrimination. Nobody gives power away. You have to take it away. And I imagine there are women working pretty hard at that right now, but I don't know; I haven't seen any.

CA: When you went to McCall's, *you wanted to produce a magazine for women that didn't condescend to them, didn't assume that their interests were narrowly domestic. Do you feel any of the current magazines aimed primarily at a female audience do a good job of what you had in mind?*

ALEXANDER: No. Maybe *Lear's* will. I haven't seen it. It has the subhead "For the Woman Who Wasn't Born Yesterday." It's coming out in a few months; I don't know exactly when. They asked me to write their theme article. For the first issue, they found fifty women between the ages of forty and sixty, or so—leaders of different kinds in different sorts of communities all over the country. Then they interviewed them

and took photographs. My contribution was to write the tone poem that goes with all this and to make some comments on it.

CA: Would you tell me about your part in founding the National Women's Political Caucus and how you would assess its influence and achievements in women's concerns?

ALEXANDER: The main thing I did was convince them to put Liz Carpenter on the board. She was Mrs. Lyndon Johnson's press secretary at the time. All of us were opposed to Johnson's policy in Vietnam, and several didn't feel at all enthusiastic about taking her on. That was really dumb, because she is a brilliant politician and a politician for women. So we did take her on, and it really helped launch and position the National Women's Political Caucus. Liz has an autobiography out now that she tells some of this in, *Getting Better All the Time*. I really don't know much about the organization now. I retain my warm personal friendship with Betty Friedan, but I resigned from organized female politics in 1972. I jumped ship very early and got back where I feel more comfortable—in a heterosexual world!

CA: You told Holly G. Miller for the Saturday Evening Post *that "the kidnap of Patty Hearst became the rescue of Shana Alexander from the grind of weekly newsmagazine journalism," and that doing the book on her,* Anyone's Daughter, *taught you that you could work without weekly deadlines. Was that a rough transition?*

ALEXANDER: It was tough learning to write at long lengths without being terrified. It took five years to write a normal-size book. In fact, the book is too big. If I had cut it by another third it would be a much better book. But I didn't know what I was doing in the long length. Before that, my pieces were about 5,000 words; the record-breaker was 10,000 words. The columns were about 1,200 words. It's a different kind of stretch. It was hard to put the next piece of paper in the typewriter, to have the confidence to keep going without the reassurance you feel once you see something in print.

CA: In a real way Anyone's Daughter *was a very personal book, examining not only Patty Hearst's relationship with her parents but your own roles as mother and daughter. Was it emotionally wrenching for you?*

ALEXANDER: Yes, it was.

CA: Very Much a Lady, in which you told Jean Harris's story and gave an analysis of how you felt the legal system failed her, was also based on a strong feeling of kinship with your subject. Are you still in touch with Mrs. Harris?

ALEXANDER: Yes. I spoke to her this weekend. We talk almost every weekend. I feel very motherly toward her; I'm very proud of her. She's finished her second book and the publisher likes it very much. It's about the history of women's prisons, and evidently a very remarkable job. I had asked PEN, the writers' organization, to admit her, which would have meant waiving their rule that you have to have two published books before you can be considered a member. She was already working on her second book, and she had special circumstances. I felt that admission to PEN would give her some kind of solidarity with other writers around the world imprisoned for political reasons. At bottom, she is a political prisoner, being punished by the male-dominated power structure, and the male-dominated criminal justice system. For a lot of reasons, this would never have happened to a man. So, just last week we got the notice that they had invited her to join. I'm very pleased about this. You know, it's harder to find a present for somebody in prison than it would be to find one for Donald Trump, somebody very rich—to find something somebody doesn't have and would like.

CA: Very Much a Lady provided a fine study of Mrs. Harris's lover, Scarsdale Diet Dr. Herman Tarnower, as well. Did you find him a hard character to reconstruct in any sense?

ALEXANDER: I had known him, and he wasn't hard to reconstruct—somewhat unpleasant, but not hard. I knew other people like him. I knew his world.

CA: Diana Trilling's Mrs. Harris *came out in 1981, two years before* Very Much a Lady. *Then when your account of the Franklin Bradshaw murder,* Nutcracker, *was published in 1985, so was Jonathan Coleman's competing account,* At Mother's Request. *When did you realize in both cases that someone else was doing an account of the same crime?*

ALEXANDER: On day one. But it didn't bother me. There were thirteen people writing Patty Hearst books and three porno movies. By the time my book on her came out five years later, most of them had fallen by the wayside. A couple had been published, and they were useful to get stuff from that I didn't already know. But Diana Trilling is a woman I've known since my teens and hadn't seen for many years. I wish she hadn't written that book, because it was a lousy book that completely misunderstood Mrs. Harris and did her a great deal of harm by putting forth a wrong view. Diana tore up one book halfway through the trial and started another one. Mrs. Harris was a woman she didn't understand at all. Diana married her childhood sweetheart, a wonderful man who loved her very much. They had a long and happy, rich life until he died. There was nothing in her life that would enable her to understand Mrs. Harris. And she's a professional critic. It was the critical person rather than the human person who looked at the Jean Harris situation—and completely misread it.

CA: Was the "feud" between you and Jonathan Coleman, as Edwin McDowell described it in the New York Times, *blown out of proportion?*

ALEXANDER: There wasn't any feud, and I don't think of Jonathan Coleman as another writer; he just was somebody who found out that Tommy Thompson died and tried to occupy the place that was left. Tommy had started the book on the Bradshaw murder. His publisher had picked me to go on with it—they didn't want Jonathan Coleman—so he decided he would do his own book. That did me a lot of harm, but I don't take it seriously anymore.

CA: The courtroom hours that went into these books must have been as hard for you as they were for the jurors; you had to be there and stay alert to assess the proceedings just as they did. During the Patty Hearst trial there was the crisis with your own daughter as well. How did you keep going?

ALEXANDER: I thought of all the money that I would owe the publishers if I didn't!

CA: You've delved deeply into the psychology of your subjects in these books. Is that a major part of your fascination with them?

ALEXANDER: Yes, that's why I do it. These are twice-told tales. If you'd read your tabloids, you would know that Patty Hearst was kidnapped or that Dr. Tarnower was killed. But what *really* happened is what interests me. I would like to practice the art of nonfiction. I would like it to be considered one of the minor arts, and I would like to get better at it. But after the book I'm finishing now, I don't intend to do any more courtroom books. This current one has twenty-seven lawyers in one trial, including the five prosecutors.

CA: What's the subject of the book?

ALEXANDER: It's about what criminal lawyers really do. It's based on a heroin case. There were twenty-two people accused, and each one had his own lawyer. It went on for seventeen months. It was the longest and biggest criminal trial in the federal system. Everybody got convicted. That was seventeen months of sitting, and there were twenty-four people on the jury—twelve alternates—because of the projected length of the trial. I don't think there will ever be another one like it again. It was known as "The Pizza Connection Case."

BIOGRAPHICAL/CRITICAL SOURCES:

BOOKS

Alexander, Shana, *Talking Woman*, Delacorte, 1976.
Alexander, Shana, *Anyone's Daughter: The Times and Trials of Patty Hearst*, Viking, 1979.
Alexander, Shana, *Very Much a Lady: The Untold Story of Jean Harris and Dr. Herman Tarnower*, Little, Brown, 1983.
Contemporary Issues Criticism, Volume 2, Gale, 1984.

PERIODICALS

Atlantic, July, 1979.
Chicago Tribune Book World, May 20, 1979, April 17, 1983, June 30, 1985.
Detroit News, August 4, 1985.
Kirkus Reviews, July 1, 1988.
Life, October 11, 1963.
Los Angeles Times Book Review, April 10, 1983, July 14, 1985.
Ms., July, 1983.
National Review, September 14, 1979.
Newsday, August 21, 1988.
New Society, October 4, 1979.
Newsweek, April 28, 1969, May 21, 1979, June 17, 1985, August 29, 1988.
New York Post, September 2, 1988.
New York Times, December 14, 1976, May 5, 1979, March 9, 1983, May 19, 1985, May 28, 1985, September 5, 1988.
New York Times Book Review, May 6, 1979, March 27, 1983, June 16, 1985.
People, September 5, 1988.
Publisher's Weekly, April 23, 1979.
Saturday Evening Post, September, 1978.
Time, April 25, 1969, March 21, 1983, June 17, 1985.
Village Voice, May 28, 1979.
Washington Post Book World, May 6, 1979, May 26, 1985.

—*Sketch by Diane Telgen*
—*Interview by Jean W. Ross*

ALI, Schavi M(ali) 1948-
(Schavi M. Diara)

PERSONAL: Name is pronounced Sha-*vee* Ma-*lee* A-*lee*; born April 30, 1948, in Detroit, Mich.; daughter of William Earl (a mechanical engineer) and Margaret Ruis (Walton) Ross; married second husband, Derrick Abdul Raheem Ali (an electrical engineer), April 19, 1986. *Education:* Wayne State University, B.A., 1970, M.A., 1976; University of Michigan, doctoral candidate. *Politics:* "Pan-Africanism." *Religion:* Islam.

ADDRESSES: Residence—Detroit, Mich. *Office*—Center for Black Studies, 586 Student Center, Wayne State University, Detroit, Mich. 48202.

CAREER: High school teacher of English and life science in the public schools of Highland Park, Mich., 1970-71; Wayne State University, Detroit, Mich., instructor in English and social studies, 1971-72; Wayne County Community College, Detroit, instructor in English, 1972-73; Roeper City and Country School, Bloomfield Hills, Mich., teacher of English, 1973-77; Wayne State University, 1977—, began as instructor, currently professor of English and Afro-American studies.

MEMBER: National Council of Teachers of English, Association for Study of Afro-American Life and History, National Council of Black Studies, American Business Women's Association, Phylon Society, Animal Protection Institute of America, Michigan Council of Teachers of English, Phi Delta Kappa.

AWARDS, HONORS: Spirit of Detroit Award, Detroit City Council, 1984; Outstanding Educator, Phi Sigma Fraternity, 1984; Poet of the Year, Afro-American Cultural Society, 1987; Authors' Recognition Award, Wayne State University, 1987, 1988.

WRITINGS:

(Under name Schavi M. Diara) *Growing Together* (poetry), Agascha Productions, 1972.
(With Agadem L. Diara, under name Schavi M. Diara) *Hey! Let a Revolutionary Brother and Sister Come In*, Agascha Productions, 1972.
(Under name Schavi M. Diara) *Song for my Father* (novella), Agascha Productions, 1975.
(Author of introduction, under name Schavi M. Diara) Joseph A. Mills, *Goin' Off* (poetry), Jotarian, 1982.
(Under name Schavi M. Diara) *Zora Neale Huston and Jessie Redmond Fauset: Glistening Reflections from a Bygone Day*, Exposition Press of Florida, 1984.
Moments in Time (poetry), Jotarian, 1987.
(Contributor) *Dictionary of Literary Biography*, Volume 51: *Afro-American Writers from the Harlem Renaissance to 1940*, Gale, 1987.

Contributor to journals, including *Black Books Bulletin, Black American Literature Forum*, and *American Anthology of Verse*.

WORK IN PROGRESS: Legacy, an anthology of poems, essays, and short stories; research on ancient African origins in philosophy and religion.

SIDELIGHTS: Schavi M. Ali told *CA:* "History is a guidepost for future action. It is imperative, therefore, that all people have an accurate understanding of historical events so that they can relate as equals in carrying civilization forward. In this light, it is of particular importance that the African race be given its deserved respect as founders of philosophies of science, literature and art which have aided the human race in its evolution into the modern world. These philosophies began thousands of years ago in Sais, Kuch, and Nubia, known now as Egypt, Ethiopia and Sudan, countries on the continent of Alkebu-lan, known now as Africa. Knowledge of the ancient world will create a new respect for people of African descent."

*   *   *

ALLEN, Captain Quincy
[Collective pseudonym]

WRITINGS:

"OUTDOOR CHUMS" SERIES

The Outdoor Chums; or, The First Tour of the Rod, Gun and Camera Club, Grosset & Dunlap, 1911.
. . . on the Lake; or, Lively Adventures on Wildcat Island, Grosset & Dunlap, 1911.
. . . in the Forest; or, Laying the Ghost of Oak Ridge, Grosset & Dunlap, 1911.
. . . on the Gulf; or, Rescuing the Lost Balloonists, Grosset & Dunlap, 1911.
. . . after Big Game; or, Perilous Adventures in the Wilderness, Grosset & Dunlap, 1911.
. . . on a Houseboat; or, The Rivals of the Mississippi, Grosset & Dunlap, 1913.
. . . in the Big Woods; or, The Rival Hunters of Lumber Run, Grosset & Dunlap, 1915.
. . . at Cabin Point; or, The Golden Cup Mystery, Grosset & Dunlap, 1916.

SIDELIGHTS: Frank Langdon, Jerry Wallington, Bluff Masters, and Will Milton were the "Outdoor Chums." Together they experienced outdoor life in all its variety—camping, fishing, hunting, swimming, and indulging in wildlife photography. St. George Rathborne assisted Edward Stratemeyer with the "Outdoor Chums" series. For more information see the entries for Harriet S. Adams, Edward L. Stratemeyer, and Andrew E. Svenson.

BIOGRAPHICAL/CRITICAL SOURCES:

BOOKS

Johnson, Deidre, editor and compiler, *Stratemeyer Pseudonyms and Series Books: An Annotated Checklist of Stratemeyer and Stratemeyer Syndicate Publications*, Greenwood Press, 1982.

*   *   *

ALLEN, Frank 1939-

PERSONAL: Born March 22, 1939, in Evanston, Ill.; son of William Gordon and Eathal (Wallace) Allen. *Education:* University of Maryland, B.A., 1961, Ph.D., 1969; New York University, M.A., 1963.

ADDRESSES: Home—1546 C-1 Catasauqua Rd., Bethlehem, Pa. 18018.

CAREER: Wilkes College, Wilkes-Barre, Pa., assistant professor of English, 1969-72; free-lance editor, 1972-80; Moravian College, Bethlehem, Pa., adjunct professor of English, 1974-82; Northampton County Area Community College, Bethlehem, adjunct professor of English, 1982; Allentown College of St. Francis de Sales, Allentown, Pa., associate dean of ACCESS, 1983—. Gives poetry readings and workshops;

guest on radio programs. *Military service:* U.S. Army, 1961-67.

WRITINGS:

A Critical Edition of Browning's "Bishop Blougram's Apology," University of Salzburg, 1976.
Magna Mater (poetry chapbook), Cumberland Journal, 1981.
Seeds of Recognition (chapbook), The Friends of H. D., 1984.

Contributor of poems, articles, and reviews to literature journals and literary magazines, including *American Book Review, Axe Factory Review, Common Ground, Creeping Bent, Gargoyle, Iowa Review, Library Journal, Literary Magazine Review, Literature East and West, Menu, National Catholic News Service, North American Mentor Magazine, Painted Bride Quarterly, Parnassus, Poet Lore, Small Press, Small Press Book Review, Stone Country, West Branch,* and *Wind.* Co-editor of *Fusion,* 1976-78; literary editor of *New Valley Press,* 1981-82.

WORK IN PROGRESS: Poetry and criticism.

SIDELIGHTS: Frank Allen told *CA:* "I know of no one journal (*American Book Review, American Poery Review, Library Journal, Parnassus,* university quarterlies and college-associated reviews are excellent), or reviewer-critic (there are many excellent ones), or book series (the University of Michigan's Press's Poets on Poetry is excellent) who is able consistently to assimilate the force and diversity of contemporary international poetry. It takes an academic's scholarship, a critic's willingness to grasp and assess original ideas, a reviewer's taste and command of the recent, and the publicist's willingness to promote and argue for what is good. Such syncretic abilities no longer come into focus with one writer. Men of letters (Matthew Arnold, G. K. Chesterton, T. S. Eliot, Edmund Wilson) were (deliberately?) blind to contemporary poetry of their era.

"It's as though poetic perception is being forced outward from one exploded and exploding center, the now-broken-apart mainstream of American-English poetry, into every corpuscle of American self-consciousness. The American curse is discontinuity; the American blessing is wonder.

"At any regional poetry conference, workshop or creative writing clinic, one meets men and women, old or young, who have never before written poetry but who wish to. Such a desire was perhaps always there, latently, but people either now have the leisure or the word-processing ability to make it a reality. One wonders at the effect of such a continual stream of novices into the pages of 4,400 'markets' listed in the current *International Directory of Little Magazines and Small Presses.*

"The poet's challenge is to write poetry that articulates his or her vision or voice whether flawed or noble. The critic's goal is to discover and remain open to a new truth and yet to explain the new in the context of what has been done, not to confine a current achievement, but to make it whole. A poet blossoms into poetry; a critic is impelled not only by Stevens's aesthetic 'ideas of order' but by a capacity for understanding the moral and psychological dimensions of language.

"A poet (Ralph Robin) once told me that whatever he wrote I would find some earlier parallel for. This is the burden of a knowledge of poetry. It puts things into perspective. Sometimes perspective blinds one to true merit.

"Judgments should open one's view to distant horizons, not constrict or inhibit. There is no way to be a critic and not make judgments, no matter how unwelcome or difficult. A reviewer, always pursued by a 'deadline,' promotes poetry and makes the public aware of what is available. A critic 'places' the work in a manageable or accessible context so that the reader makes a decision, not so much whether to buy a volume, but to incorporate it into his or her experience. (What is the value of inaccessible poetry, no matter how great?) A poet descends into the depths of being; a reviewer ascends into the plateau of awareness; a critic joins the two.

"The critic of contemporary poetry follows the poet down dark roads into an interior landscape of ever-new permutations of language, but, like Theseus, is able to find a way back out of the labyrinth by following a 'thread' of distinctions, dictated, hopefully, by the unpetty, large-minded and humane.

"The American psyche and intellect repel each other. The raw and urgent creative energy of our country has now broken through adopted artistic form and spills forth. Anyone who reads contemporary poetry widely must be amazed at the inchoate ability that is born out of obscurity and that is probably doomed to the college and Y's poetry circuit (Pulitzer Prize winning poets' works sell only in the thousands) because the technological bent that dominates our society in the '80s is afraid to believe in the poet, occasionally with good reason, and because of a fear of recognizing that there is nothing behind a microcomputer screen except silicon chips no bigger than a fingernail.

"Poets, critics, reviewers, academics, editors, agents, publicists and publishers, our literary culture, need each other and need a more resilient, comprehensive language. There should be a dialogue between them, not the keeping of secrets."

BIOGRAPHICAL/CRITICAL SOURCES:

PERIODICALS

Bethlehem Globe Times, March 30, 1974, August 7, 1978, September 7, 1979.
Easton Express, September 3, 1982.
Forbes, August 7, 1978.
Philadelphia Inquirer, September 11, 1982.

*   *   *

ALLEN, Frederick G(arfield)   1936-1986
(Gary Allen)

PERSONAL: Born August 2, 1936, in Glendale, Calif.; died November 29, 1986, of a liver ailment, in Long Beach, Calif.; son of Harold King (a realtor) and Virginia (Campbell) Allen; married Barbara Jean Powers, June 16, 1959; children: Michael, Scott, Bonnie, Cathleen. *Education:* Stanford University, B.A., 1958; California State University, Long Beach, graduate study, 1959-60. *Politics:* "Libertarian."

CAREER: High school teacher of English and history in California, 1959; salesman, 1960-63; writer and lecturer, 1963-86; vice-president and director, '76 Press, Inc., beginning 1975; speechwriter for Governor George Wallace during his presidential campaigns.

AWARDS, HONORS: Patriotism Award, Congress of Freedom, 1967, 1970, 1972, 1973, 1974, and 1975; American Academy of Public Affairs award of merit, 1971.

WRITINGS—Under name Gary Allen:

Communist Revolution in the Streets, Western Islands, 1967.

Richard Nixon: The Man behind the Mask, Western Islands, 1971.

Nixon's Palace Guard, Western Islands, 1971.

(With Larry Abraham) *None Dare Call It Conspiracy,* Concord Press, 1971.

The Rockefeller File, '76 Press, 1976.

Jimmy Carter-Jimmy Carter, '76 Press, 1976.

Kissinger: The Secret Side of the Secretary of State, '76 Press, 1976.

Tax Target: Washington, Concord Press, 1979.

Also author of *Ted Kennedy: In over His Head,* Concord Press.

FILMS AND FILMSTRIPS

"The Berkeley Revolution," Constructive Action, 1960.

"Civil Rights: The Red Reconstruction," B & K Productions, 1961.

"Show Biz in the Streets," John Birch Society, 1967.

"The Great Pretense: How to Finance Communism While Ostensibly Opposing It," John Birch Society, 1968.

"The United Nations: Peace Dove Unmasked," John Birch Society, 1969.

"War on Poverty: Subsidized Revolution," John Birch Society, 1970.

OTHER

Also author of numerous pamphlets published by *American Opinion.* Contributor to *American Opinion* and *Review of the News.* Contributing editor, *Conservative Digest* and *American Opinion.*

SIDELIGHTS: Frederick Allen, known professionally as Gary Allen, was a right-wing investigator of modern political conspiracy who was best known for the controversial bestseller *None Dare Call It Conspiracy.* The book contended that international bankers finance and control the communist movement, which they use as an instrument to establish a world dictatorial government. *None Dare Call It Conspiracy*—described as a "right-wing classic" by George Johnson in his *Architects of Fear: Conspiracy Theories and Paranoia in American Politics*—has sold some six million copies in eight languages. Allen was also a prominent spokesman for the conservative John Birch Society and was a frequent contributor to *American Opinion* and *Review of the News,* the group's official publications.

The John Birch Society is an anticommunist organization founded in 1958 by millionaire candy manufacturer Robert Welch. During its heyday in the 1960s, the group boasted some 600,000 members, operated a nationwide chain of bookstores, and ran a speakers bureau. It was nationally known for its sometimes unusual interpretation of current events. The society believed, for example, that President Dwight D. Eisenhower had been a communist agent and that flouridated water was a communist plot. Such positions alienated the Birchers from more moderate conservatives. In 1965, the prominent conservative magazine *National Review* attacked the John Birch Society as extremists who hurt the conservative cause.

By the late 1960s, the Birchers began to pay less attention to the alleged activities of communists and began to investigate international banks, the United Nations, large corporations, and other business and political groups they believed were collaborating with the communists. These groups, the Birchers came to believe, formed a secret wealthy elite who were using communism as a tool to gain control of the world's economy.

Some Bircher publications hinted that this secret group was descended from the ancient Illuminati, an occult order officially banned in the eighteenth century. Most often, the conspirators were referred to as "the insiders." Insider agents were alleged by the Birchers to control both major political parties, as well as such groups as the Council on Foreign Relations, the Trilateral Commission, the United Nations, and many foundations. As Alan Crawford explained in his *Thunder on the Right: The 'New Right' and the Politics of Resentment,* "Birchers hold that the secret rulers of America are 'the insiders,' a mysterious cabal of rich bankers, including David Rockefeller, who are only using Communism as a means of achieving world domination." Allen was instrumental in formulating the Birchers' political perspective. His many articles for society publications helped to transform the group's members from extreme anticommunists to believers in a secret conspiracy of global proportions. Writing in *The Politics of Unreason: Right-Wing Extremism in America, 1790-1977,* Seymour Martin Lipset and Earl Raab described Allen as "one of the leading theorists of the John Birch Society."

In *None Dare Call It Conspiracy,* published in 1971, Allen presented his controversial theories in great detail, arguing that "what you call 'Communism' is not run from Moscow or Peking, but is an arm of a bigger conspiracy run from New York, London and Paris. . . . Finance capitalism is used as the anvil and Communism as the hammer to conquer the world." Johnson noted that "Allen blamed the Rockefellers for bankrolling the Bolshevik Revolution and postulated that the Students for a Democratic Society, the Black Panthers, and the Yippies were funded by the Rockefeller and Ford foundations to wage a socialist revolution in the United States." Such a revolution would create, Allen believed, a powerful central government that ran the nation's economy on behalf of the bankers. He singled out such prominent banking families as the Rockefellers, Rothschilds, Warburgs, Kuhns, Loebs, Schiffs, and Morgans as the principal members of the conspiracy. As Neal Wilgus pointed out in *The Illuminoids,* what Allen and other rightist conspiracy theorists were "saying is essentially the same as [the arguments of] scholarly leftwingers such as C. Wright Mills and other trackers of the infamous Power Elite, more recently known as the Military-Industrial Complex or The Establishment."

Most commentators dismissed *None Dare Call It Conspiracy* as wild, unfounded speculation. Johnson, for example, called it "the Bible of the paranoid right." Few prominent newspapers or magazines reviewed the book when it first appeared. It has even been banned by the Canadian government. Writing in his introduction to *None Dare Call It Conspiracy,* congressman John G. Schmitz correctly predicted that the book was destined to be "very controversial" and would "not be reviewed in all the 'proper' places or be available on your local bookstand." Allen was obliged to sell his book by mail. He placed notices in far-right publications and relied on word-of-mouth advertising to make the book known. "Those whose plans are exposed in it," Schmitz explained, could not "stop a grass roots book distributing system" from selling *None Dare Call It Conspiracy.* The independent distribution system worked extremely well. In the first year alone, the book sold some four million copies. It has since sold a total of six million copies and is available in several editions from different publishers.

Because of Allen's success at selling *None Dare Call It Conspiracy,* W. Scott Stanley, editor-in-chief of *Conservative Digest,* was quoted in the *Los Angeles Times* as calling Allen "the great popularizer of the conservative cause" and "a pioneer in putting the right message together with the right tool." The *Los Angeles Times* explained that "Allen started and mastered the technique of spreading the conservative message through mail-order books, cassettes and film-strips." Allen's successful book distribution system later assisted other conservatives as well. The *New York Times* reported that "addresses from [Allen's] mail orders were placed on mailing lists, forming an important network for conservative causes and fund raising."

Allen once told *CA* that he was originally "an ADA-type 'liberal' who was challenged to read several anticommunist books by a friend." He read the books with the intention of proving his friend wrong, but Allen became convinced that his friend was correct. His outlook changed. He then, Allen explained, "moved right and became a student of real history and real economics—not the type taught in most classrooms today."

BIOGRAPHICAL/CRITICAL SOURCES:

BOOKS

Allen, Gary and Larry Abraham, *None Dare Call It Conspiracy*, Concord Press, 1971.
Crawford, Alan, *Thunder on the Right: The 'New Right' and the Politics of Resentment*, Pantheon, 1980.
Johnson, George, *Architects of Fear: Conspiracy Theories and Paranoia in American Politics*, J. P. Tarcher, 1983.
Lipset, Seymour Martin and Earl Raab, *The Politics of Unreason: Right-Wing Extremism in America, 1790-1977*, 2nd edition, University of Chicago Press, 1978.
Wilgus, Neal, *The Illuminoids*, Pocket Books, 1979.

PERIODICALS

Best Sellers, November, 1976.
Book List, October 15, 1976.
National Review, October 19, 1965, September 29, 1972, October 29, 1976.

OBITUARIES:

PERIODICALS

Los Angeles Times, November 30, 1986.
New York Times, December 2, 1986.
Washington Post, December 1, 1986.†

—*Sketch by Thomas Wiloch*

*   *   *

**ALLEN, Gary
    See ALLEN, Frederick G(arfield)**

*   *   *

**ALLEN, Samuel W(ashington) 1917-
    (Paul Vesey)**

PERSONAL: Born December 9, 1917, in Columbus, Ohio; son of Alexander Joseph (a clergyman) and Jewett (Washington) Allen; divorced; children: Marie-Christine. *Education:* Fisk University, A.B. (magna cum laude), 1938; Harvard University, J.D., 1941; graduate study at New School for Social Research, 1947-48, and Sorbonne, University of Paris, 1949-50. *Politics:* Democrat. *Religion:* African Methodist Episcopal.

ADDRESSES: Home—145 Cliff Ave., Winthrop, Mass. 02152.

CAREER: Office of District Attorney, Manhattan, N.Y., deputy assistant district attorney, 1946-47; civilian attorney with U.S. Armed Forces in Europe, 1951-55; private practice of law, New York, N.Y., 1956-58; Texas Southern University, Houston, Tex., associate professor of law, 1958-60; U.S. Information Agency, Washington, D.C., assistant general counsel, 1961-64; U.S. Departments of Justice and Commerce, Community Relations Service, Washington, D.C., chief counsel, 1965-68; Tuskegee Institute, Tuskegee Institute, Ala., Avalon Professor of Humanities, 1968-70; Boston University, Boston, Mass., professor of English and Afro-American literature, 1971-81. Visiting professor at Wesleyan University, 1970-71, Duke University, 1972-74, and Rutgers University, 1981; writer in residence at Tuskegee Institute. Member of board of directors, Southern Education Foundation, 1969-76, and New England Museum of Afro-American History; volunteer and member of board of directors, School Volunteers for Boston. *Military service:* U.S. Army, Adjutant Generals Corps, 1942-46; became first lieutenant.

MEMBER: African Studies Association, African Heritage Studies Association, New York Bar Association, New England Poetry Club (member, board of directors).

AWARDS, HONORS: National Endowment for the Arts literature fellow, 1979; Wurlitzer Foundation fellow, 1979, 1980-81; grant from Rockefeller Foundation, 1981.

WRITINGS:

(Under pseudonym Paul Vesey) *Elfenbein Zahne* (title means "Ivory Tusks"; a bilingual edition of poems), translated into German by Janheinz Jahn, Wolfgang Rothe, 1956.
(Translator) Jean Paul Sartre, *Black Orpheus* (translation first published in *Presence Africaine*, 1951), Presence Africaine, 1960.
(Author of introduction) *Pan-Africanism Reconsidered*, University of California Press, 1962.
Ivory Tusks and Other Poems, Poets Press, 1968.
(Author of introduction) Naseer Aruri and Edmund Ghareeb, editors, *Enemy of the Sun: Poetry of the Palestinian Resistance*, Drum & Spear Press, 1970.
(Editor and author of introduction) *Poems from Africa*, Crowell, 1973.
Paul Vesey's Ledger (poetry), Paul Breman, 1975.
Every Round and Other Poems, Lotus Press, 1987.

CONTRIBUTOR

Jacob Drachler, editor, *African Heritage*, Crowell, 1959.
The American Negro Writer and His Roots, American Society of African Culture, 1960.
Africa Seen by American Negro Scholars, American Society of African Culture, 1963.
Arna Bontemps, editor, *American Negro Poetry*, Hill & Wang, 1963.
Langston Hughes, editor, *New Negro Poets: USA*, Indiana University Press, 1964.
Arthur P. Davis and Saunders Redding, editors, *Cavalcade*, Houghton, 1970.
Nathan Wright, Jr., editor, *What Black Educators Are Saying*, Hawthorn, 1970.
Raymond F. Betts, editor, *The Ideology of Blackness*, Heath, 1971.
Ruth Miller, editor, *Background to Black American Literature*, Glencoe Press, 1971.
Stephen Henderson, editor, *Understanding the New Black Poetry: Black Speech and Black Music as Poetic Reference*, Morrow, 1973.

Woodie King, Jr., editor, *The Forerunners: Black Poets in America,* Howard University Press, 1981.

Contributor of poems and essays to numerous other anthologies.

OTHER

Contributor of poems, essays, book reviews, and translations to journals, including *Presence Africaine, Negro Digest, Journal of Afro-American Studies, Black World, Benin Review* (Nigeria), and *Massachusetts Review.*

SIDELIGHTS: Samuel W. Allen "has played a significant role in African and Afro-American criticism as a scholar, reviewer, translator, editor, and lecturer," comments Ruth L. Brittin in a *Dictionary of Literary Biography* essay. While working as a lawyer in France and Germany after World War II, Allen became involved with the negritude movement of poets and from their example was "inspired to write a poetry grounded in the fusion of African and Afro-American culture," describes Brittin. Allen articulates his idea of the role of the black American poet in *The Forerunners: Black Poets in America:* "Black poets are continuing with an increasingly sharpened sense of direction both to define and to vivify the black experience, drawing up and utilizing a more profoundly explored heritage. They listen with new awareness . . . and conjure up from the wellsprings of the creative consciousness an identity both old and new, a vision whole and sufficient."

MEDIA ADAPTATIONS: A reading by Allen of his own poetry was recorded at the Library of Congress in 1972.

BIOGRAPHICAL/CRITICAL SOURCES:

BOOKS

Cooke, M. G., editor, *Modern Black Novelists,* Prentice-Hall, 1971.
Dictionary of Literary Biography, Volume 41: *Afro-American Poets Since 1955,* Gale, 1985.
King, Woodie, Jr., editor, *The Forerunners: Black Poets in America,* Howard University Press, 1981.
Mphahlele, Ezekiel, editor, *Voices in the Whirlwind,* Hill & Wang, 1972.
Redmond, Eugene, editor, *Drumvoices: The Mission of Afro-American Poetry, A Critical History,* Anchor Books, 1976.

PERIODICALS

Black Orpheus, October, 1958.
Rheinische Post, September 14, 1957.

* * *

ANDERSON, Margaret J(ean) 1931-

PERSONAL: Born December 24, 1931, in Gorebridge, Scotland; immigrated to Canada in 1955; came to the United States in 1963; daughter of John A. (a clergyman) and Margaret (Reid) Hall; married Norman H. Anderson (a professor of entomology), September 15, 1956; children: Richard, Judy, Susan, Karen. *Education:* University of Edinburgh, B.Sc. (with honors), 1953. *Religion:* Presbyterian.

ADDRESSES: Home—1930 Northwest 29th Pl., Corvallis, Ore. 97330.

CAREER: Writer. East Malling Research Station, Kent, England, statistician, 1953-55; Canada Department of Agriculture, Summerland, British Columbia, entomologist, 1955-56; Oregon State University, Corvallis, statistician, 1956-57.

MEMBER: Society of Children's Book Writers.

AWARDS, HONORS: Writing competition award from Canadian Entomological Society, 1973, for "Making a Case for the Caddisfly"; *Exploring the Insect World* was named an outstanding science book for children by National Science Teachers Association and Children's Book Council, 1974; *To Nowhere and Back* was named outstanding book of the year by *New York Times Book Review,* 1975.

WRITINGS:

JUVENILES

Exploring the Insect World (nonfiction), McGraw, 1974.
To Nowhere and Back (fiction), Knopf, 1975.
(Contributor) *Medley,* Houghton, 1976.
Exploring City Trees, and the Need for Urban Forest (nonfiction), McGraw, 1976.
In the Keep of Time (fiction; first book in trilogy), Knopf, 1977.
Searching for Shona (fiction), Knopf, 1978.
In the Circle of Time (fiction; second book in trilogy), Knopf, 1979.
(Contributor) *Ranger Rick's Surprise Book,* National Wildlife Federation, 1979.
The Journey of the Shadow Bairns (fiction), Knopf, 1980.
Light in the Mountain (fiction), Knopf, 1982.
The Bride of the Fire God, Knopf, 1982.
The Brain on Quartz Mountain (fiction), Knopf, 1982.
The Mists of Time (fiction; third book in trilogy), Knopf, 1984.
The Druid's Gift, Knopf, 1989.

OTHER

Contributor to magazines, including *Nature and Science, Ranger Rick's Nature Magazine,* and *Instructor.*

SIDELIGHTS: Margaret J. Anderson told *CA:* "I always wanted to write, but thought I first needed to see far away and exciting places to write about. So I set off to see the world. In 1955, I emigrated to Canada from Scotland, and had various jobs, mostly in biology labs. But it has turned out that the far away and exciting places I have found it easiest to write about are the areas of Scotland I knew as a child.

"I now live in Corvallis, Oregon, where my husband, Norman H. Anderson, is an entomology professor. We have four children, and my husband's interest in insects and the outdoors has been shared by the whole family. This led me to write nature articles, and finally my first book, *Exploring the Insect World.*

"During the year 1971-72, we spent a sabbatical leave in Dorset, England, living in a 200-year-old thatched cottage, called Random Cottage. There is a tremendous wealth of history in that area—something I had missed in Oregon. So when I started writing fiction with *To Nowhere and Back,* it was the need for ties with our past that I wanted to convey. I set the story in Random Cottage and the surrounding countryside, and it was from the setting that the story developed. Setting was also important in *In the Keep of Time* and *In the Circle of Time.* Once again, the theme was our commitment to both past and future.

"When my children were young, I used to tell them stories. They were particularly fond of my 'war stories.' I grew up during World War II, but these stories were centered more on my childhood than on the war. So it is with *Searching for Shona.* Although it is a 'war story,' it is also a story about a girl finding out who she is.

"The background of *The Journey of the Shadow Bairns* is based on my husband's family history. His grandfather came to Canada with the Barr colonists in 1903. After he arrived in Saskatchewan, he wrote a long letter to relatives who had stayed in England. The detailed descriptions in this letter gave me the setting for the story, which I peopled with characters from my own imagination. My most recent book is set in New Zealand, where we spent six months in 1979. The forests of the West Coast are so wild and remote that they give you the feeling that you are discovering them for the first time. Out of this feeling grew the story of *The Bride of the Fire God.*

"When I was young (and maybe even still) it always seemed too bad that when we made one choice we ruled out so many other interesting possibilities. Being one person, living in one place and time, seems so restrictive. I have found that by writing, and to a lesser extent by reading, I can change that. I can explore the 'what might have been' and the 'what might be.' But the fantasy life cannot exist without the emotions and experiences of the real life. It can only be an extension of that."

*   *   *

ANDERSON IMBERT, Enrique   1910-

PERSONAL: Born February 12, 1910, in Argentina; son of Jose Enrique and Honorina (Imbert) Anderson; married Margot Di Clerico (a librarian), March 30, 1935; children: Carlos, Anabel (Mrs. Jack Himelblau). *Education:* National University of Buenos Aires, Ph.D., 1946.

ADDRESSES: Home—20 Elizabeth Rd., Belmont, Mass. 02178. *Office*—Harvard University, Cambridge, Mass. 02138.

CAREER: Universidad de Tucuman, Tucuman, Argentina, professor of Spanish literature, 1940-47; University of Michigan, Ann Arbor, assistant professor, 1947-48, associate professor, 1948-51, professor of Spanish literature, 1951-65; Harvard University, Cambridge, Mass., Victor S. Thomas Professor of Hispanic American Literature, 1965—. Visiting associate professor, Princeton University, 1950.

MEMBER: American Academy of Arts and Sciences, Academia Argentina de Letras.

AWARDS, HONORS: Buenos Aires City Hall literary prize, 1934, for manuscript of novel *Vigilia;* Guggenheim fellow, 1954-55.

WRITINGS:

ENGLISH TRANSLATION

Historia de la literatura hispanoamericana, two volumes, Fondo de Cultura Economica (Mexico), 1954-61, 8th edition, 1979, translation of 2nd edition by J. V. Falconieri published in one volume as *Spanish-American Literature: A History,* Wayne State University Press, 1963, revised translation by Elaine Mallery published in two volumes, 1966.

El grimorio, Editorial Losada (Buenos Aires), 1961, translation by Isabel Reade published as *The Other Side of the Mirror,* Southern Illinois University Press, 1966.

Vigilia [and] *Fuga,* Editorial Losada, 1962, translation by Esther Whitmarsh Phillips published as *Fugue,* Coronado Press, 1967.

El gato de cheshire, Editorial Losada, 1965, translation published as *The Cheshire Cat,* Thunder City, 1980.

IN SPANISH

La flecha en el aire, La Vanguardia (Buenos Aires), 1937, reprinted, Editorial Gure (Buenos Aires), 1972.

Tres novelas de Payro con picaros en tres miras, Facultad de Filosofia y Letras, Universidad de Tucuman, 1942.

Ensayos, privately printed, 1946.

Ibsen y su tiempo, Yerba Buena (La Plata), 1946.

Las pruebas el caos, Yerba Buena, 1946.

El arte de la prosa en Juan Montalvo, El Colegio de Mexico, 1948, 2nd edition, Talleres Graficos de Editorial Bedout, 1974.

Estudios sobre escritores de America, Editorial Raigal (Buenos Aires), 1954.

La critica literaria contemporanea, Editorial Platania (Buenos Aires), 1957.

Los grandes libros de Occidente y otros ensayos, Ediciones de Andrea (Mexico), 1957.

Que es la prosa?, Editorial Columba (Buenos Aires), 1958, 4th edition, 1971.

El cuento espanol, Editorial Columba, 1959.

Critica interna, Editorial Taurus (Madrid), 1961.

Los domingos del profesor, Editorial Cultura (Mexico), 1965.

La originalidad de Ruben Dario, Centro Editor de America Latina (Buenos Aires), 1967.

Genio y figura de Sarmiento, Editorial Universitaria (Buenos Aires), 1967.

Analisis de "Tabare," Centro Editor de America Latina, 1968.

Analisis de "Fausto," Centro Editor de America Latina, 1968.

La sandia y otros cuentos, Editorial Galerna (Buenos Aires), 1969.

Una aventura amorosa de Sarmiento, Editorial Losada, 1969.

Metodos de critica literaria, Revista de Occidente (Madrid), 1969, published as *La critica literaria: metodos y problemas,* Alianza Editorial (Madrid), 1984.

(Compiler with Eugenio Florit) *Literatura hispanoamericana,* Holt, 1970.

La locura juega al ajedrez, Siglo XXI Editores (Mexico), 1971.

Estudios sobre letras hispanicas, Editorial Libros de Mexico, 1974.

El arte de la prosa en Juan Montalvo, California State University, Sacramento, 1975.

La botella de Klein, Centro Argentino P.E.N. Club Internacional (Buenos Aires), 1975.

El realismo magico y otros ensayos, Monte Avila (Caracas), 1976.

El leve Pedro (short stories), Alianza Tres (Madrid), 1976.

Cuentos en miniatura (short stories), Equinoccio (Caracas), 1976.

Victoria, Editorial Emece (Buenos Aires), 1977.

Los primeros cuentos del mundo, Ediciones Marymar (Buenos Aires), 1977.

(Contributor) Jorge Lafforgue and Jorge B. Rivera, compilers, *Asesinos de papel,* Calicanto Editorial (Buenos Aires), 1977.

Las comedias de Bernard Shaw, Universidad Nacional Autonoma de Mexico, 1977.

Teoria y tecnica del cuento, Ediciones Marymar, 1979.

En el telar del tiempo, Volume I: *El mentir de las estrellas,* Editorial Emece (Buenos Aires), 1979, Volume II: *El estafador se jubila: la locura juega al ajedrez,* Corregidor (Buenos Aires), 1985, Volume III: *La botella de Klein: dos mujeres y un Julian,* Corregidor, 1980, Volume V: *El tamano de las brujas,* Corregidor, 1986.

La prosa: modalidades y usos, Marymar, 1984.

Paginas selectas de Anderson Imbert, Celtia (Buenos Aires), 1985.
Nuevos estudios sobre letras hispanas, Kapelusz (Buenos Aires), 1986.

WORK IN PROGRESS: El anillo de Mozart, stories; *El pasado por venir,* a novel.

*   *   *

ANTHONY, Evelyn
  See WARD-THOMAS, Evelyn Bridget Patricia Stephens

*   *   *

ARENDT, Hannah   1906-1975

PERSONAL: Born October 14, 1906, in Hannover, Germany; came to the United States, 1941, naturalized, 1950; died December 4, 1975, of an apparent heart attack, in New York, N.Y.; daughter of Paul (an engineer) and Martha (Cohn) Arendt; married Heinrich Bluecher (a professor of philosophy), 1940 (died, 1970). *Education:* Koenigsberg University, B.A., 1924; attended universities at Marburg and Freiburg; Heidelberg University, studied with Karl Jaspers, awarded Ph.D. (philosophy), 1928; Notgemeinschaft der Deutschen Wissenschaft, research fellow, 1931-33. *Politics:* Independent. *Religion:* No religious affiliation.

ADDRESSES: Home—370 Riverside Dr., New York, N.Y. 10025. *Office*—Graduate Faculty of Political and Social Science, New School for Social Research, New York, N.Y.

CAREER: Fled Germany for Paris in 1933; social worker for Youth Aliyah, Paris, France, 1934-40; Conference on Jewish Relations, New York, N.Y., research director, 1944-46; Schocken Books, Inc., New York, N.Y., chief editor, 1946-48; Jewish Cultural Reconstruction, New York, N.Y., executive director, 1949-52; Princeton University, Princeton, N.J., visiting professor of politics (the first woman to be appointed a full professor there), 1959; University of Chicago, Chicago, Ill., professor with committee on social thought, 1963-67; New School for Social Research, Graduate Faculty of Political and Social Science, New York, N.Y., professor, 1967-75. Visiting professor at University of California, Berkeley, 1955, Columbia University, 1960, and at Brooklyn College (now Brooklyn College of the City University of New York). Member of board of directors, Conference on Jewish Relations, Jewish Cultural Reconstruction, and Judah Magnes Foundation.

MEMBER: Institut International de Philosophie Politique, American Academy of Political and Social Science, National Institute of Arts and Letters, American Academy of Arts and Sciences (fellow), American Political Science Association, American Society of Political and Legal Philosophy, Deutsche Akademie fuer Sprache und Dichtung (corresponding member), PEN.

AWARDS, HONORS: Guggenheim fellow, 1952-53; award from National Institute of Arts and Letters, 1954; Rockefeller fellow, 1958-60 and 1969-70; Lessing Preis, Hamburg, 1959; Freud Preis from Deutsche Akademie fur Sprache und Dichtung, 1967; Emerson-Thoreau Medal from American Academy of Arts and Sciences, 1969; M. Cary Thomas Prize from Bryn Mawr College, 1971; Danish Sonning Prize, 1975; honorary degrees from numerous colleges and universities, including

Yale University, 1971, Dartmouth College, 1972, and Princeton University, 1972.

WRITINGS:

Der Liebesbegriff bei Augustin, J. Springer (Berlin), 1929.
Sechs Essays, L. Schneider (Heidelberg), 1948.
(Translator with M. Greenberg) Franz Kafka, *Diaries,* edited by Max Brod, Volume 2, Schocken, 1949.
The Origins of Totalitarianism, Harcourt, 1951 (published in England as *Burden of Our Time,* Secker & Warburg, 1951), new edition, 1966, three volume edition, Volume I: *Totalitarianism,* Volume II: *Imperialism,* Volume III: *Anti-Semitism,* 1968, new edition with added prefaces, 1973.
(Editor and author of introduction) Hermann Broch, *Essays,* Volume I: *Dichten und Erkennen,* Volume II: *Erkennen und Handeln,* Rhein-Verlag (Zurich), 1955.
Fragwuerdige Traditionsbestaende im politischen Denken der Gegenwart: Vier Essays, Europaeische Verlagsanstalt (Frankfurt am Main), 1957.
The Human Condition (lectures delivered under the title "Vita Activa"), University of Chicago Press, 1958, collector's edition, 1969.
Die Krise in der Erziehung, Angelsachsen Verlag (Bremen), 1958.
Rahen Varnhagen: The Life of a Jewess, translation by Richard and Clara Winston, East and West Library for Leo Baeck Institute, 1958, revised edition published as *Rahel Varnhagen: The Life of a Jewish Woman,* Harcourt, 1974, original German text published as *Rahel Varnhagen: Lebensgeschichte einer Deutschen Juedin aus der Romantic,* Piper (Munich), 1959.
Die ungarische Revolution und der totalitaere Imperialismus, Piper, 1958.
Wahrheit, Freiheit, und Friede: Karl Jaspers, Piper, 1958.
Elemente totaler Herrschaft, Europaeische Verlagsanstalt, 1958.
Von der Menschlichkeit in finsteren Zeiten: Rede ueber Lessing, Piper, 1960.
Between Past and Future: Six Exercises in Political Thought, Viking, 1961, enlarged edition published as *Between Past and Future: Eight Exercises in Political Thought,* 1968.
Freedom and Revolution, Connecticut College, 1961.
(Editor) Karl Jaspers, *The Great Philosophers,* translated by Ralph Manheim, Harcourt, Volume I: *The Foundations* (also published as *Kant, Plato and Augustine,* and *Socrates, Buddha, Confucius, Jesus*), 1962, Volume II: *The Original Thinkers,* 1966.
On Revolution, Faber, 1963.
Eichmann in Jerusalem: A Report on the Banality of Evil, Viking, 1963, revised and enlarged edition, 1964.
Men in Dark Times, Harcourt, 1968.
(Editor and author of introduction) Walter Benjamin, *Illuminations: Essays and Reflections,* translated by Harry Zohn, Harcourt, 1968.
Machf und Gewalt, Piper, 1970.
On Violence, Harcourt, 1970.
Crises of the Republic: Lying in Politics, Civil Disobedience, On Violence, Thoughts on Politics and Revolution, Harcourt, 1972.
Wahrheit und Luege in der Politik: Zwei Essays, Piper, 1972.
(Editor) *Spinoza,* translated by Ralph Manheim, Harcourt, 1974.
The Jew as Pariah: Jewish Identity and Politics in the Modern Age, Grove, 1978.
The Life of the Mind, Harcourt, Volume I: *Thinking,* 1978, Volume II: *Willing,* 1978, one-volume edition, 1981.

Lectures on Kant's Political Philosophy, University of Chicago Press, 1983.

CONTRIBUTOR

K. S. Pinson, editor, *Essays on Antisemitism*, 2nd edition, Conference on Jewish Relations, 1946.

William Ebenstein, editor, *Modern Political Thought*, Rinehart, 1954.

Columbia College, *Man in Contemporary Society*, Volume 2, Columbia University Press, 1956.

Carl J. Friedrich, editor, *Authority*, Harvard University Press, 1958.

Robert M. Hutchins and Mortimer J. Adler, editors, *The Great Ideas Today, 1961-1963*, Encyclopaedia Britannica, 1961-1963.

Peter Demetz, editor, *Brecht*, Prentice-Hall, 1962.

Analyse d'un vertige, Societe d'Editions et de Publications, Artistiques et Litteraires, 1968.

Arthur A. Cohn, editor, *Arguments and Doctrines: A Reader of Jewish Thinking in the Aftermath of the Holocaust*, Harper, 1970.

Carl Saner, compiler, *Karl Jaspers in der Diskussion*, Piper, 1973.

OTHER

Contributor to *Contemporary Jewish Record, Review of Politics, New Yorker, New York Review of Books*, and other publications.

SIDELIGHTS: Hannah Arendt earned a reputation as one of the twentieth century's most brilliant and original political thinkers. "Her penetrating analyses of totalitarianism and democracy, the problems of mass society, the reasons for revolution and political image making are widely regarded as required reading for a thorough understanding of modern political history," observed *Washington Post* writer Stephen Klaidman. Arendt studied philosophy at the University of Heidelberg under Karl Jaspers and received her doctorate when she was only twenty-two years old. She was already established as an outstanding essayist in her own country when Hitler's ascent to power in 1933 sent her to Paris. For several years she studied and wrote there; she also was active in a relief agency that found homes in Palestine for the orphaned and homeless children of Europe. Arendt and her husband finally fled for the United States when Nazi troops began to press into France in 1940.

Arendt's first major publication in the United States was a penetrating analysis of the forces that brought Hitler to power, *The Origins of Totalitarianism*. Her contention that anti-Semitism and imperialism were at the root of totalitarianism was disputed by some, but her writing was praised even by those who disagreed with her theories. *New York Times Book Review* contributor E. H. Carr attributed Arendt's emphasis on anti-Semitism to her personal history, but concluded, "Whatever its shortcomings, however, . . . the book is the work of one who has thought as well as suffered. . . . Miss Arendt, her eyes fixed in fascination and repulsion on the horror of Nazi Germany, offers only slender hope for Western civilization to avoid this form of suicide. Yet the reader who shuns this conclusion can still be grateful for a disquieting, moving and thought-provoking book." H. Stuart Hughes believed that Arendt had exaggerated certain facts to prove her point, but he also felt that *The Origins of Totalitarianism* was "a great book. Deeply thought-out and conscientiously documented, [it] will take its place among the major writings of our times. . . . To

the totalitarian threat to change 'human nature' itself she opposes an equally total declaration of human responsibility. Her book is a moving testament of solidarity with all the 'superfluous people' now living out their meaningless days in all the concentration camps of the earth."

Arendt's background led the *New Yorker* magazine to send her to Israel for the trial of Adolf Eichmann, one of Hitler's top bureaucrats. The magazine pieces she wrote from Israel evolved into her most controversial book, *Eichmann in Jerusalem: A Report of the Banality of Evil*. Eichmann was held responsible for the deaths of millions of Jews. Arendt did not excuse him for his part in the Holocaust, but she argued that to hold him personally responsible for so many deaths was to attribute him with a power that was more than any one person could ever embody. She stated that the Nazi leadership had encountered an extraordinary amount of cooperation from all levels of European society, including the Jewish leaders themselves. Her point was that the success of the Nazi regime was attributable to a general moral collapse across Europe. Eichmann she characterized not as a fanatical anti-Semite, but simply an ambitious office worker whose main concern was to provide for his family.

Her subtle arguments provoked highly emotional responses. Many critics wondered if Arendt was defending Eichmann's activities. Her statement that the cooperation of Jewish leaders had led to the deaths of millions who might otherwise have escaped infuriated many Jews; B'nai B'rith pronounced *Eichmann in Jerusalem* an evil distortion of the facts. Arendt herself was suspected of anti-Semitism. Bruno Bettelheim commented in *New Republic* that her analysis was simply too objective for many to accept so soon after the horror of the Holocaust: "The issues are so vast that we do not seem to be able yet to cope with them intellectually. . . . [It is difficult to accept the incongruity] between all the horrors recounted, and this man in the dock, when essentially all he did was talk to people, write memoranda, receive and give orders from behind a desk. It is essentially the incongruity between our conception of life and the bureaucracy of the total state. Our imagination, our frame of reference, even our feelings, are simply not up to it." Bettelheim understood why *Eichmann in Jerusalem* was rejected by so many, but he insisted: "While I would recommend this book for many reasons the most important one is that our best protection against oppressive control and dehumanizing totalitarianism is still a personal understanding of events as they happen. To this end Hannah Arendt has furnished us with a richness of material."

Arendt's later works clarified her position, particularly the collection of essays called *The Jew as Pariah: Jewish Identity and Politics in the Modern Age*. "Readers of this collection will be disabused of the notion that Arendt went to Jerusalem loaded for bear against Zionism, that she was unsympathetic to the Jews, that she reproached them for collaborating and not resisting," wrote Leon Botstein in *New Republic*. "Indeed, I think that if the Eichmann book had been published with several of these essays, Arendt's primary concerns would have been clear from the start." Botstein vigorously defended Arendt against the charges of anti-Semitism that had been levelled at her, declaring: "[Her] analysis of the Jewish dilemma provides an interpretive logic for her whole life's work. [These] essays should stimulate a long overdue rehabilitation of Hannah Arendt in the Jewish community. . . . To [her], being Jewish was the decisive fact of her life as a private person and as a political thinker. It cast the mold for the thinking and willing for which she was, and will be, honored. . . . Apart from its service to the legacy of Hannah Arendt, *The Jew as Pariah* offers brilliance, eloquence, and reasoned committment on issues where clarity and courage are in perpetually short supply.''

Toward the end of her life, Arendt's focus shifted inward. Instead of analyzing political trends, she became increasingly involved in the analysis of thought itself. She planned a three-volume work exploring the three activities of the mind she considered basic—thinking, willing, and judging. She had completed the first volume and part of the second at the time of her death, and these were published posthumously as *The Life of the Mind.* Walter Clemons assessed them in *Newsweek:* ''The Life of the Mind' is a work requiring stubborn application and a readiness to cope with abstractions more elusive than the social and political arguments advanced in 'The Origins of Totalitarianism,' 'The Human Condition,' or 'Eichmann in Jerusalem.' The reward for perseverance is contact with a passionate, humane intelligence addressing itself to the fundamental problem of how the mind operates.'' The ideas examined in the books are complex, Clemons observed, but ''because Arendt was strongly endowed with common sense, her forays into the realm of the unverifiable are as toughly argued as her investigations, in earlier books, of violence and revolution.'' James M. Altman judged *The Life of the Mind* to be Arendt's greatest work, even in its incomplete state. He wrote in *New Republic,* ''Few works of philosophy published today seriously confront the Western philosophical tradition as a whole. *The Life of the Mind* has that bold ambition. At a minimum, it resembles a deep mining operation, which brings to the surface the authentic insights of [the philosophical] tradition which has fragmented and lost its power to guide us. Arendt intentionally preserves those treasures by reflecting upon them anew. At its best, . . . *The Life of the Mind* succeeds in offering us new insights to illuminate our own mental experiences and an integrative vision of their profound meanings.''

BIOGRAPHICAL/CRITICAL SOURCES:

BOOKS

Arendt, Hannah,*On Revolution,* Faber, 1963.
Arendt, Hannah, *On Violence,* Harcourt, 1970.
Canovan, M., *The Political Thought of Hannah Arendt,* Metheun, 1977.
Contemporary Issues Criticism, Volume 1, Gale, 1982.
Essays and Reviews from the Times Literary Supplement, 1964, Oxford University Press, 1965.
Hobsbawm, E. J., *Revolutionaries: Contemporary Essays,* Weidenfeld & Nicolson, 1973.
McCarthy, Mary, *On the Contrary,* Farrar, Straus, 1961.
Podhoretz, Norman, *Doings and Undoings: The Fifties and After in American Writing,* Farrar, Straus, 1964.

PERIODICALS

American Political Science Review, September, 1980.
American Sociological Review, February, 1959.
Atlantic, March, 1963.
Commentary, September, 1963, October, 1963.
Ethics, October, 1962.
Guardian, November 3, 1961.
Nation, March 24, 1951, January 27, 1969, April 6, 1970, November 11, 1978.
New Republic, July 10, 1961, June 15, 1963, January 18, 1969, February 25, 1978, October 21, 1978, August 15, 1983.
Newsweek, March 20, 1978.
New Yorker, July 20, 1963.

New York Review of Books, November 6, 1969, October 26, 1978, February 17, 1983.
New York Times, March 28, 1970, April 3, 1978.
New York Times Book Review, March 25, 1951, May 19, 1963, November 17, 1968, April 12, 1970, May 7, 1972, November 24, 1974, January 21, 1979.
Partisan Review, summer, 1964.
Saturday Review, May 18, 1963.
Social Research, spring, 1977.
Times Literary Supplement, March 26, 1970, July 23, 1970.
Village Voice, January 6, 1975, May 15, 1978.
Washington Post Book World, March 26, 1978.

OBITUARIES:

PERIODICALS

AB Bookman's Weekly, January 1, 1976.
New York Times, December 6, 1975, December 9, 1975.
Publishers Weekly, December 15, 1975.
Time, December 15, 1975.
Washington Post, December 6, 1975.†

—*Sketch by Joan Goldsworthy*

* * *

ASARE, Bediako
  See KONADU, S(amuel) A(sare)

* * *

ASSELINEAU, Roger (Maurice) 1915-
  (Roger Maurice)

PERSONAL: Born March 24, 1915, in Orleans, Loiret, France; son of Maurice Alfred (a postal clerk) and Blanche (Presle) Asselineau; married Paule Maillet (an educator), November 12, 1951; children: Daniel, Jean-Yves, Claire. *Education:* Sorbonne, University of Paris, Licence es Lettres, 1935, Agregation d'anglais, 1938, Doctorat es Lettres, 1953.

ADDRESSES: Home—114 Ave. Leon-Blum, 92160 Antony, France. *Office*—Centre de recherches en litterature et civilisation nord-americaines, Sorbonne, University of Paris, 1 rue Victor-Cousin, 75230 Paris, France.

CAREER: Teacher of English in Le Havre, France, 1938-39, and at various schools in Beauvais, St. Maur, and Paris, France, 1940-45; Harvard University, Cambridge, Mass., researcher, 1945-46, instructor in French, 1946-47, research assistant, 1950-51; Sorbonne, University of Paris, assistant professor of English, 1950-51; University of Clermont-Ferrand, Clermont-Ferrand, France, lecturer in English, 1951-54; University of Lyon, Lyon, France, professor of American literature, 1954-59; Sorbonne, University of Paris, professor of American literature, 1960-83, professor emeritus, 1983—. Visiting professor of American literature at State University of New York, Albany, spring, 1968, University of California, Davis, spring, 1969 and summer, 1972, and New York University, fall, 1978. *Military service:* French Army, Infantry, 1939-44; became second lieutenant.

MEMBER: International Association of University Professors of English, International Federation of Modern Languages and Literatures (vice-president), French Association of American Studies (honorary president), French Society of Men of Letters, French Society of Authors, Composers, and Editors of Music, Societe des anglicistes de l'enseignement superieur,

Modern Language Association of America, Hemingway Society (vice-president).

AWARDS, HONORS: Medaille de la Resistance; Walt Whitman Award from Poetry Society of America, 1961, for *The Evolution of Walt Whitman.*

WRITINGS:

(Under pseudonym Roger Maurice) *Traduit de Moi-Meme* (title means "Translated from Myself"), privately printed, 1949.
L'Evolution de Walt Whitman, Didier, 1954, translation of Part I by Asselineau and Richard P. Adams published as *The Evolution of Walt Whitman: The Creation of a Personality,* Harvard University Press, 1960, translation of Part II by Asselineau and Burton L. Cooper published as *The Evolution of Walt Whitman: The Creation of a Book,* Harvard University Press, 1962.
The Literary Reputation of Mark Twain, 1910-1950, Didier, 1954, reprinted, Greenwood Press, 1971.
Realisme, reve, et expressionnisme dans "Winesburg, Ohio" (title means "Realism, Dream, and Expressionism in 'Winesburg, Ohio'"), Lettres Modernes, 1957.
Poesies incompletes (title means "Incomplete Poems"), Debresse, 1959, translation by Kenneth Christensen published as *The Incomplete Poems of Roger Asselineau,* Cedarshouse Press, 1984.
The Literary Reputation of Hemingway in Europe, New York University Press, 1965.
Edgar Allan Poe, University of Minnesota Press, 1970.
Ernest Hemingway (critical introduction with biobibliographical documents), Seghers, 1972.
The Transcendentalist Constant in American Literature, New York University Press, 1980.
(With Gay Wilson Allen) *St. John de Crevecoeur: The Life of an American Farmer,* Viking, 1987.

EDITOR

Configuration critique de Sherwood Anderson (title means "Critical Profile of Sherwood Anderson"), Lettres Modernes, 1963.
Robert Frost, Seghers, 1964.
Ernest Hemingway, Oeuvres romanesques, poemes de guerre et d'apresguerre, Gallimard, 1966-69.
The Merrill Studies in "The House of the Seven Gables," Merrill, 1970.
(With William White) *Walt Whitman in Europe Today: A Collection of Essays,* Wayne State University Press, 1972.
Washington Irving: Trois Contes (criticism), Aubier, 1979.
E. A. Poe: Histoires Grotesques et Serieuses, Garnier-Flammarion, 1985.

TRANSLATOR

Jorge Guillen, *Fragments d'un cantique,* Seghers, 1956.
Walt Whitman, *Feuilles d'herbe,* Belles Lettres, 1956, revised bilingual edition, Aubier-Flammarion, 1972.
Edgar Allan Poe, *Choix de contes,* Aubier-Flammarion, 1958.

OTHER

Contributor to periodicals, including *Revue de litterature comparee, Etudes anglaises, Walt Whitman Review, Calamus, Forum, Thalia, Europe,* and *Critique.*

WORK IN PROGRESS: Volume two of *Poesies incompletes.*

SIDELIGHTS: One of Roger Asselineau's best-known works, *The Evolution of Walt Whitman* clarifies the relationship between Whitman's life, his search for personal identity, and his poetic achievement. A critic for the *Times Literary Supplement* believes the book "displays scholarship and artistic sensibility, and a keen sense of the significant detail and a broad vision capable of embracing the whole picture and of giving everything its proper place." A reviewer for the *Yale Review* concurs: "[Asselineau's] knowledge of Whitman's book, of the changes it underwent in its continuous revision, and the rest of Whitman's writing, both published and unpublished, gives him a remarkable understanding of the poet's development."

Asselineau told *CA:* "My chief interest is poetry. So, as a critic, I have chiefly written about poets—or about novelists or short-story writers who were also poets, whether they were aware of it or not. I wish I could write more poetry in my own name, but, having to make a living, I spend the greater part of my time commenting on the poetry of others. In the future I intend to introduce a number of contemporary American poets to the French public.

"There are essentially two kinds of poets, those who believe that the writing of a poem is an act of will, and those who believe that a poem is the result of an electric shock which sends a shiver down your spine and makes your skin bristle, so that, like A. E. Housman, you must never allow a line of poetry to stray into your memory while shaving for fear of cutting your face. I belong to the latter category. I never write a poem unless there has been a spark in my mind produced by the clash of two words, or, more often, by my sudden encounter with something unexpected and therefore wonderful in the physical world or in my internal universe. The result in each case is an incomplete poem in which I try to communicate what I have felt with the tom-tom of my words, but it is up to the reader to complete it. This is what I meant by calling my first collection of poems *Poesies incompletes.* But I also meant that *Poesies incompletes* was only the beginning of an endless series of poems which I would go on publishing at irregular intervals. There has been no other volume yet, but there will be sooner or later, for I have accumulated a fairly large number of new poems, some of which appeared for the first time in an English-language version, *The Incomplete Poems of Roger Asselineau.*"

Asselineau added: "As a literary critic, my aim is above all to read texts as intelligently as possible and to make them more intelligible rather than more obscure as is becoming the fashion. I disapprove of the excesses and extravagances of the various French schools of criticism that have sprung up like mushrooms in the last two decades and established beachheads in the United States (notably at Yale and Johns Hopkins). Their ideal is to perform verbal acrobatics around the text (or the subtext) and the result is a parasitical growth that completely hides the authors and their works."

BIOGRAPHICAL/CRITICAL SOURCES:

PERIODICALS

American Literature, January, 1966.
Annales de l'Universite de Paris, January-March, 1961.
Journal of American Studies, April, 1980.
New York Times, September 18, 1987.
New York Times Book Review, September 13, 1987.
Times Literary Supplement, June 7, 1963.
Tribune Books (Chicago), September 8, 1987.
Virginia Quarterly Review, spring, 1963.
Yale Review, March, 1963.

AUBERT, Alvin (Bernard) 1930-

PERSONAL: Born March 12, 1930, in Lutcher, La.; son of Albert (a laborer) and Lucille (Roussel) Aubert; married second wife, Bernadine Tenant (a teacher and librarian), October 29, 1960; children: (first marriage) Stephenie; (second marriage) Miriam, Deborah. *Education:* Southern University, B.A., 1959; University of Michigan, A.M., 1960; further graduate study at University of Illinois, 1963-64, 1966-67.

ADDRESSES: Home—18234 Parkside Ave., Detroit, Mich. 48221. *Office*—Department of English, Wayne State University, Detroit, Mich. 48202.

CAREER: Southern University, Baton Rouge, La., instructor, 1960-62, assistant professor, 1962-65, associate professor of English, 1965-70; State University of New York College at Fredonia, associate professor, 1970-74, professor of English, 1974-79; Wayne State University, Detroit, Mich., professor of English, 1979—. Visiting professor at University of Oregon, summer, 1970. Member of board of directors, Coordinating Council of Literary Magazines, 1982-86. Has given readings of his poems at educational institutions.

MEMBER: Modern Language Association of America, National Council of Teachers of English, African Heritage Studies Association, National Council for Black Studies.

AWARDS, HONORS: Woodrow Wilson fellow, 1959; National Endowment for the Arts grant, 1973, 1981; scholarship for Bread Loaf Writers' Conference, Middlebury, Vt., 1978; Coordinating Council of Literary Magazines Editors fellow, 1979.

WRITINGS:

Against the Blues (poems), Broadside Press, 1972.
Feeling Through (poems), Greenfield Review Press, 1976.
A Noisesome Music (poems), Blackenergy South Press, 1979.
South Louisiana: New and Selected Poems, Lunchroom Press, 1985.
"Home from Harlem" (play; adapted from *The Sport of the Gods* by Paul Laurence Dunbar), first produced in Detroit at the Bonstelle Theatre, January 24, 1986.

CONTRIBUTOR TO ANTHOLOGIES

J. W. Corrington and Miller Williams, editors, *Southern Writing in the Sixties: Poetry*, Volumes I and II, Louisiana State University Press, 1966.
Williams, editor, *Contemporary Poetry in America*, Random House, 1973.
Arnold Adoff, editor, *Celebrations: An Anthology of Black Poetry*, Follett, 1979.
Edward Field, editor, *A Geography of Poets: An Anthology of the New Poetry*, Bantam, 1979.
Guy Owen and Mary C. Williams, editors, *Contemporary Southern Poetry*, Louisiana State University Press, 1979.
Williams, editor, *Patterns of Poetry: An Encyclopedia of Forms*, Louisiana State University Press, 1986.
Leon Stokesburg, editor, *The Made Thing: An Anthology of Contemporary Southern Poetry*, University of Arkansas Press, 1987.

OTHER

Contributor to *Contemporary Novelists*, 1972, and *Writers of the English Language*, 1979. Contributor of poems, articles, and reviews to literary journals, including *Nimrod, Black American Literature Forum, American Poetry Review, Black World, Prairie Schooner, Black Scholar, Iowa Review, Journal of Black Poetry, American Book Review,* and *Epoch.* Book reviewer, *Library Journal,* 1972-74. Advisory editor of *Drama and Theatre,* 1973-75, *Black Box,* 1974—, *Gumbo,* 1976-78, and *Callaloo,* 1977—; founding editor of *Obsidian: Black Literature in Review,* 1975-85.

WORK IN PROGRESS: Poems; a novel, "Port Hudson," set in South Louisiana; a play, "Family Reunion"; several short stories.

SIDELIGHTS: Alvin Aubert wrote: "I grew up in a small Mississippi River town about midway between New Orleans and Baton Rouge, and this locale—particularly the river—and the people, but especially the people, continue to motivate me; not to the extent of my finding out exactly who and what they were (if that were possible), but of initiating and maintaining a spiritual connection. Most representative of this influence are poems of mine such as 'Baptism,' 'Remembrance,' 'Feeling Through,' 'Spring 1937,' 'Father, There,' 'South Louisiana,' 'The Housemovers,' 'All Singing in a Pie,' and 'Fall of '43.' I like to think that all of my writings explore various aspects of the human situation and celebrate human existence at a particular and consequently universal level."

BIOGRAPHICAL/CRITICAL SOURCES:

BOOKS

Dictionary of Literary Biography, Volume 41: *Afro-American Poets since 1955,* Gale, 1985.

PERIODICALS

American Book Review, March, 1987.
Black American Literature Forum, fall, 1987.
Buffalo Courier Express, June 8, 1973.
Kliatt, November, 1972.

*   *   *

AYLESWORTH, Thomas G(ibbons) 1927-

PERSONAL: Born November 5, 1927, in Valparaiso, Ind.; son of Carroll Wells (a salesman) and Ruth (Gibbons) Aylesworth; married Virginia L. Boelter (a teacher), August 13, 1949; children: Carol Jean, Thomas Paul. *Education:* Indiana University, A.B., 1950, M.S., 1953; Ohio State University, Ph.D., 1959.

ADDRESSES: Home—48 Van Rensselaer, Stamford, Conn. 06902.

CAREER: High school teacher in Harvard, Ill., 1951-52; junior high school science teacher in New Albany, Ind., 1952-54; head of science department at a high school in Battle Creek, Mich., 1955-57; Michigan State University, East Lansing, assistant professor of education, 1957-61; Wesleyan University, Middletown, Conn., lecturer in science, 1961-64; Doubleday & Co., Inc., and Natural History Press, New York, N.Y., senior editor, 1964-80; Bison Books, Greenwich, Conn., editor-in-chief, 1980-86. Visiting faculty member at Ohio State University, 1962, and Wisconsin State University (now University of Wisconsin—Whitewater), 1964. *Military service:* U.S. Army, Medical Department, 1946-47.

MEMBER: National Science Teachers Association, National Association of Biology Teachers, National Association for Research in Science Teaching, Central Association of Science and Mathematics Teachers, New York Academy of Sciences, Phi Delta Kappa.

WRITINGS:

Planning for Effective Science Teaching, American Education Publications, 1963.
(With Gerald Reagan) *Teaching for Thinking*, Doubleday, 1969.
America, This Beautiful Land, Bison Books, 1983.
America's National Parks, Bison Books, 1984.
History of Movie Musicals, Bison Books, 1984.
Chicago, Bison Books, 1985.
Indiana, Bison Books, 1985.
Broadway to Hollywood, Bison Books, 1985.
Minnesota, Bison Books, 1986.
Monster and Horror Movies, W. H. Smith, 1986.
The Best of Warner Bros., Gallery Press, 1986.
America's Southwest, Gallery Press, 1986.
Television in America, Exeter Publishing, 1986.
Chicago, the Glamour Years, Bison Books, 1986.
New York, the Glamour Years, W. H. Smith, 1987.
Great Moments in Television, Bookthrift, 1987.
Who's Who in the Movies, World Almanac, 1987.
Hollywood Kids, Dutton, 1987.
The History of the World Series, Bison Books, 1988.

JUVENILES

Our Polluted World, American Education Publications, 1964.
(Editor) *It Works Like This*, Natural History Press, 1968.
This Vital Air, This Vital Water, Rand McNally, 1968, revised edition, 1974.
Into the Mammal's World, Natural History Press, 1970.
Traveling into Tomorrow, World Publishing, 1970.
Servants of the Devil, Addison-Wesley, 1971.
(Editor) *Mysteries from the Past*, Natural History Press, 1971.
Werewolves and Other Monsters, Addison-Wesley, 1972.
Vampires and Other Ghosts, Addison-Wesley, 1972.
Monsters from the Movies, Lippincott, 1973.
Astrology and Foretelling the Future, F. Watts, 1973.
The Alchemists: Magic into Science, Addison-Wesley, 1973.
Who's Out There?, McGraw, 1975.
The World of Microbes, F. Watts, 1975.
ESP, F. Watts, 1975.
Movie Monsters, Lippincott, 1975.
The Search for Life, Rand McNally, 1975.

Cars, Boats, Trains and Planes of Today and Tomorrow, Walker & Co., 1975.
Palmistry, F. Watts, 1976.
Graphology, F. Watts, 1976.
Science at the Ball Game, Walker, 1976.
The Story of Vampires, McGraw, 1977.
Science Update 77, Gaylord, 1977.
The Story of Werewolves, McGraw, 1978.
Science Update 78, Gaylord, 1978.
Geological Disasters: Earthquakes and Volcanoes, F. Watts, 1979.
Understanding Body Talk, F. Watts, 1979.
The Story of Witches, McGraw, 1979.
Storm Alert: Understanding Weather Disasters, Messner, 1980.
The Story of Dragons and Other Monsters, McGraw, 1980.
Spoonbending and Other Impossible Feats, Nutmeg, 1980.
Animal Superstitions, McGraw, 1981.
Science Looks at Mysterious Monsters, Messner, 1982.
The Mount St. Helens Disaster, F. Watts, 1983.
Let's Discover, seventeen volumes, Chelsea House, 1987-88.

OTHER

Senior editor, *Current Science*, 1961-64. Contributor to magazines and newspapers.

SIDELIGHTS: Thomas G. Aylesworth told *CA:* "My first writing job took more out of me than any other job I have ever held. I was editor-in-chief of the unofficial newspaper of Cub Scout Pack 3640 in Chicago. I had just been given a toy typewriter for my tenth birthday and decided to start my scandal sheet ('Merle D. Wormesley of Den 7 has chickenpox'). The problem was that this was in the days before the Xerox machine and I had to make twelve carbons of every page. Now, after more than seventy-five books and hundreds of newspaper and magazine articles, I can say that writing is a great life. It's hard work, but there is nothing more ego-building than seeing your name in print—even if it is on the masthead of Pack 3640's newspaper."

BIOGRAPHICAL/CRITICAL SOURCES:

BOOKS

Children's Literature Review, Volume 6, Gale, 1984.

B

BACKHOUSE, Janet 1938-

PERSONAL: Born February 8, 1938, in Corsham, England; daughter of Joseph Helme and Jessie (Chivers) Backhouse. *Education:* Attended Bedford College, London, 1956-59, and Institute of Historical Research, London, 1959-62.

ADDRESSES: Office—Department of Manuscripts, British Library, Great Russell St., London WC1B 3DG, England.

CAREER: British Museum/Library, London, England, assistant keeper of manuscripts, 1962—.

MEMBER: British Archaeological Association, Henry Bradshaw Society, Bibliographical Society, Society of Art Historians, Society of Antiquarians of London (fellow).

WRITINGS:

John Scottowe's Alphabet Books, Oxford University Press, 1974.
The Madresfield Hours, Oxford University Press, 1975.
The Illuminated Manuscript, Phaidon, 1979.
The Lindisfarne Gospels, Phaidon, 1981.
(Contributor) Helen Wallis, editor, *The Boke of Idrography Presented by Jean Rotz to Henry VIII,* Oxford University Press, 1981.
Books of Hows, British Library Publications, 1985.
(Contributor) Daniel Williams, editor, *England in the Fifteenth Century,* Boydell & Brewer, 1987.
(With Christopher de Hamil) *The Becket Leaves,* British Library Publications, 1988.

Author of exhibition catalogs. Contributor of articles and reviews to library and museum journals and newspapers.

* * *

BAEZ, Joan (Chandos) 1941-

PERSONAL: Born January 9, 1941, in Staten Island, N.Y.; daughter of Albert V. (a physicist) and Joan Chandos (a drama teacher; maiden name, Bridge) Baez; married David Victor Harris, March, 1968 (divorced, 1973); children: Gabriel Earl. *Education:* Studied drama at Boston University Fine Arts School, 1958.

ADDRESSES: Home—Woodside, Calif. *Office*—Diamonds & Rust Productions, Inc., P.O. Box 1026, Menlo Park, Calif. 94026.

CAREER: Learned to play the guitar at age fourteen and sang in a high school choir, Palo Alto, Calif.; first performed in public, playing the guitar and singing folk ballads with other amateurs, at Club 47, a coffee house in Cambridge, Mass., 1958-60; performed regularly in coffee houses around Harvard Square, in Cambridge and Boston, Mass., 1958-60; appeared at The Gate of Horn, a folk-nightclub in Chicago, Ill., 1958, where she was noticed by Bob Gibson and invited to play at the Newport (R.I.) Folk Festival in the summer of 1959; performed again at the Newport Folk Festival in 1960; recordings for Vanguard Records, 1960-72; has toured colleges and concert halls around the United States (first Carnegie Hall concert, 1962), 1961—; numerous concert tours in Europe, 1965—; concert tours in Japan, 1966 and 1982, and Latin America, 1981; extensive television appearances and speaking tours for anti-militarism, United States and Canada, 1967-68; arrested for civil disobedience opposing draft, October and December, 1967; recordings for A & M Records, 1972-76, for Portrait Records, 1977-79, for CBS International, 1980, for Ariola France, 1983, and for Gold Castle Records, 1987. Founded the Institute for the Study of Nonviolence, Palo Alto, Calif. (now the Resource Center for Nonviolence, Santa Cruz, Calif.), 1965; founded Humanitas International, 1979, president, 1979—. Starred with David V. Harris in film "Carry It On" (title song also sung by Baez), New Film Company Production, 1970; also appeared in documentary film "There But for Fortune: Joan Baez in Latin America," 1982, and in a documentary produced for German television, "Music Alone Is Not Enough."

MEMBER: Amnesty International (member of national advisory board, 1973—).

AWARDS, HONORS: Award from Chicago business executives for work for peace, 1971; Thomas Merton Award for commitment to peace, 1975; August 2, 1975, named "Joan Baez Day" in Atlanta, Georgia; public service award for work on behalf of abused children, 1977; Bay Area Music award for top female vocalist in the San Francisco Bay area, 1978 and 1979; Jefferson Award for public service, 1980; award from Americans for Democratic Action, 1982; Lennon Peace Tribute Award, 1982.

WRITINGS:

Daybreak, Dial, 1968.

(With David V. Harris) *Coming Out*, Pocket Books, 1971.
And a Voice to Sing With, Summit Books, 1987.

MUSIC COMPOSITIONS

Joan Baez Songbook, Ryerson Music, 1964.
And Then I Wrote. . . ., Big 3 Music, 1979.

SOUND RECORDINGS

Folksingers 'round Harvard Square, Veritas Recordings, 1959.
Joan Baez, Vanguard, 1960.
Joan Baez, Volume II, Vanguard, 1961.
Joan Baez in Concert, Vanguard, 1962.
Joan Baez in Concert, Part II, Vanguard, 1963.
Joan Baez/5, Vanguard, 1964.
Farewell, Angelina, Vanguard, 1965.
Noel, Vanguard, 1966.
Joan, Vanguard, 1967.
Baptism, Vanguard, 1968.
Any Day Now (songs by Bob Dylan), Vanguard, 1969.
(With Mimi and Richard Farina) *Memories*, Vanguard, 1969.
One Day at a Time, Vanguard, 1969.
David's Album, Vanguard, 1969.
Joan Baez—The First Ten Years, Vanguard, 1970.
Carry It On (sound track), Vanguard, 1970.
Woodstock (sound track), Cotillion, 1970.
Celebration at Big Sur (sound track), Twentieth Century-Fox, 1971.
Celebration, Ode, 1971.
Blessed Are . . ., Vanguard, 1971.
The Joan Baez Ballad Book, Vanguard, 1972.
Big Sur Folk Festival (One Hand Clapping), Columbia, 1972.
Come from the Shadows, A & M Records, 1973.
Hits/Greatest and Others, Vanguard, 1973.
Gracias a La Vida, A & M Records, 1974.
Contemporary Ballad Book, Vanguard, 1974.
Diamonds and Rust, A & M Records, 1975.
From Every Stage, A & M Records, 1976.
Gulf Winds, A & M Records, 1976.
Love Song Album, Vanguard, 1976.
Blowin' Away, Portrait, 1977.
Best of Joan C. Baez, A & M Records, 1977.
Honest Lullaby, Portrait, 1979.
Joan Baez 24 Juglio 1970, Portrait, 1979.
Joan Baez in Italy, Portrait, 1979.
Joan Baez Live in Japan, Portrait, 1979.
Joan Baez—European Tour, CBS International, 1980.
Very Early Joan, Vanguard, 1982.
Recently, Gold Castle Records, 1987.

Other recordings include *Tribute to Woody Guthrie*, Warner Brothers; *Folk Festival at Newport '59*, Vanguard; *Newport Broadside '63*, Vanguard; *The Newport Folk Festival Evening Concerts, Volume I and II*, Vanguard; *The Lucid Interval*, Center for Study of Democratic Institutions; *Earl Scruggs, His Family and Friends*, Columbia; *Save the Children*, Jeffrey Shurtleff/State Farm; and the sound tracks *Sacco and Vanzetti*, RCA; *Silent Running*, Decca; *Metamorphosis*, Sanrio Films; *Renaldo and Clara*, 1978; *Banjo Man*.

SIDELIGHTS: Joan Baez, sometimes known as "Queen of the Folksingers," has gained national attention as much for her political activism as for her music. Baez became aware of social injustice early in life, when the dark skin she inherited from her Mexican father drew racial slurs from her schoolmates. Her commitment to pacifism also originated with her father, a physicist whose belief in nonviolence led him to give

up lucrative work in the defense industry. As Joan Baez writes in *And a Voice to Sing With*, her father's decision meant that she and her sisters "would never have all the fine and useless things little girls want when they are growing up. Instead we would have a father with a clear conscience. Decency would be his legacy to us."

Baez began to develop her singing in childhood, as a way of winning acceptance from her peers. She taught herself to play "House of the Rising Sun" on a guitar from Sears, Roebuck, and practiced her vibrato by tapping on her throat while singing in the shower. When the Baez family moved to Cambridge, Massachusetts, in 1958, Joan found an excellent outlet for her budding talent. Folk music was becoming something of a mass taste at the time and could be heard in many of the area's coffeehouses. Baez began to frequent these, both to listen and to sing. Within a year she made her professional debut in front of thirteen thousand people at the Newport Folk Festival, where she transfixed the crowd with her pure, high soprano and down-to-earth stage presence. Overnight she became a celebrity.

A national tour followed her remarkable appearance at Newport. While on that tour, Baez discovered that blacks were not admitted to her performances at white colleges in the South. To counter this segregation policy, she embarked in 1962 on a tour of all black colleges in Nashville, Atlanta, Mobile, Tuscaloosa and other major Southern cities. In 1963 she refused to perform on the ABC-TV program "Hootenanny" because the network had blacklisted her fellow folksinger, Peter Seeger. The following year she informed the Internal Revenue Service that she would not pay the sixty percent of her taxes destined to be used for defense spending. Actions such as these, combined with her celebrity status, made Joan Baez a national figurehead for the emerging protest movements of the 1960s.

Baez herself considered her work for social change more important than her performing career, and she limited her singing engagements to have more time for civil rights and anti-war demonstrations. Although her pacifism made her a hero to some, Baez's stance drew the ire of political conservatives. The Daughters of the American Revolution refused to let her perform at Constitution Hall in Washington, D.C., due to her "unpatriotic activities." Army bases all over the world banned her albums. She was jailed twice for her part in anti-war demonstrations, and her then-husband, draft resistance leader David Harris, began a three-year jail term just months after their marriage.

To those who supported Baez and her causes, her "remarkably pure voice seemed to stand for the integrity of her generation," writes Margot Hentoff in the *New York Review of Books*. Her popularity assured the success of her first book, *Daybreak*, a brief collection of autobiographical sketches that appeared in 1968. Richard Goldstein discounts *Daybreak* as "at once a poorly written and badly organized book" in the *New York Times Book Review*, although he admits that the book is "not without its charms. . . . As a work of sensitive gossip, delicately phrased, 'Daybreak' can make enchanting filler on an empty afternoon." Other reviewers take Baez's book much more seriously than does Goldstein, however. The *New York Times*'s Christopher Lehmann-Haupt calls *Daybreak* "an impressionistic prose-poem"; he believes that Baez uses an unconventional form in "a bold attempt to describe the growth and beliefs of a profoundly committed advocate of nonviolence." Baez's prose is highly praised by Henry S. Resnik in

Saturday Review. He comments: "In a dozen pages she makes her mother so unforgettably vivid that any novelist could envy the artlessness. She writes about her relationships with her father and with Ira, her closest soulmate, so honestly, so profoundly, that the narrative would be embarrassing if it weren't incredibly delicate. . . . Super patriots will continue to see her as a threat but *Daybreak* is a jewel of American folklore—it captures the America of our dreams."

Baez found her popularity waning in the 1970s, as folk music went out of vogue and the national mood grew more conservative. But even while her career suffered a setback, she remained as strongly dedicated as ever to her ideals. Promoting the cause of Amnesty International, forming the human rights committee Humanitas International, working for nonviolent reform in Central America, and rallying for nuclear disarmament were just a few of her activities in the 1970s and 1980s. Commenting on recent political events to *Chicago Tribune* interviewer Iain Blair, Baez said, "It's very depressing to me that the social and political activism of the '60s has given way to the selfish materialism of the '80s, and for that I blame the [Reagan] administration." Discussing her image with Patrick Connolly in another *Chicago Tribune* interview, Baez laughed and said: "Some people still picture me with a dress made out of hopsack with a peace symbol on it, sitting on railroad tracks with a bucket of organic honey on my lap. . . . That's the stereotype of a dumb nonviolent activist I've spent years trying to do something about." Of her unswerving devotion to pacifism, she told Connolly, "I'm not a utopian fool. I see the world full of conflicts and we have a right to our differences. But we should have a law saying we don't kill over differences. We can't keep giving medals for murder."

In 1985 Joan Baez found herself back in the international spotlight when she was asked to open Live-Aid, a rock concert intended to raise money for famine victims. In 1987 she released her first American album in eight years. It included original compositions, gospel staples, a South African song entitled "Asimbonanga," and cover versions of songs popularized by Dire Straits, U2, and Peter Gabriel. In 1987 she also published a second volume of autobiography, *And a Voice to Sing With*. Stylistically less experimental than *Daybreak*, *And a Voice to Sing With* is called "a frank, open-hearted memoir" by the *New York Times*'s Stephen Holden. While *Daybreak* was an impressionistic portrait of Baez's early life, *And a Voice to Sing With* is a straightforward account of her life as a star and an activist. Todd Gitlin assesses it in the *Los Angeles Times Book Review*: "It is written in a human voice, and if that voice is a gushing and unmodulated one, at least it does not sound manufactured. . . . [Baez] reaches her vivid best when she writes about her visit to Hanoi during Christmas, 1972, when she found herself under the ferocious bombardment that President Nixon had decided upon as an exercise in diplomacy. She starts off self-dramatizing, but her narrative takes on force as she sinks into details, glossing over neither her own fear nor the absurdity of her situation."

Barbara Goldsmith concludes that *And a Voice to Sing With* provides readers with valuable social history as well as a look at the singer's life. "Ms. Baez's 20 year metamorphosis from popular folk singer to 80's survivor provides an instructional tale from which one could extrapolate the changes in values in our society in the past two decades," writes Goldsmith in the *New York Times Book Review*. "She reminds us of who we once were before we replaced hard realities with easily malleable images. But because she is all too human and longs to recapture the success she once enjoyed, she also provides,

perhaps unwittingly, a peculiarly poignant and American story of how an artist addicted to the adoration of the public endeavors to recut her values and become sophisticated, if not cynical, in the manipulation of the media in order to survive. Ms. Baez's voyage to the 80's becomes emblematic of the artist's struggle to accommodate to our present age of celebrity."

BIOGRAPHICAL/CRITICAL SOURCES:

BOOKS

Baez, Joan, *Daybreak*, Dial, 1968.
Baez, Joan, *And a Voice to Sing With*, Summit Books, 1987.
Didion, Joan, *Slouching towards Bethlehem*, Dell, 1968.

PERIODICALS

Atlantic, October, 1968.
Book World, September 8, 1968.
Cambridge 38, April, 1961.
Chicago Tribune, May 30, 1982, June 21, 1987, June 28, 1987.
Christian Century, September 4, 1968.
Christian Science Monitor, October 3, 1968, September 9, 1969.
Detroit Free Press, April 14, 1969, April 4, 1986.
Los Angeles Times, September 14, 1982, June 14, 1987.
Los Angeles Times Book Review, June 21, 1987.
Nation, September 23, 1968.
Newsweek, November 27, 1961, September 2, 1968, March 29, 1971, November 3, 1975, July 20, 1987.
New Yorker, August 23, 1969.
New York Review of Books, November 7, 1968.
New York Times, September 18, 1968, January 26, 1969, June 18, 1972, July 8, 1987.
New York Times Book Review, September 8, 1968, June 21, 1987.
Reporter, January 4, 1962.
Saturday Review, September 7, 1968.
Show Business Illustrated, January 23, 1962.
Time, June 1, 1962, November 23, 1962, April 5, 1968, July 25, 1969, June 15, 1970.
Village Voice, February 22, 1968, July 24, 1969, August 28, 1969.
Washington Post, June 5, 1968, July 5, 1987.
Washington Post Book World, June 7, 1987.

—*Sketch by Joan Goldsworthy*

*   *   *

BANGERTER, Lowell A(llen) 1941-

PERSONAL: Born June 23, 1941, in Ogden, Utah; son of Alma H. (a civil servant) and Helen (Lone) Bangerter; married Judy Lee Pearson, September 16, 1964; children: Grant W., Stephen A., Carl W., Tamara Lynn, Janine Ann. *Education:* Stanford University, B.A., 1966, M.A., 1967; University of Illinois, Ph.D., 1970. *Religion:* Church of Jesus Christ of Latter-day Saints (Mormon).

ADDRESSES: Home—1114 Mitchell, Laramie, Wyo. 82070. *Office*—Department of Modern and Classical Languages, University of Wyoming, Box 3603 University Station, Laramie, Wyo. 82071.

CAREER: University of Wyoming, Laramie, assistant professor, 1970-76, associate professor, 1976-81, professor of German, 1981—, head of department of modern and classical languages, 1981-85.

WRITINGS:

Schiller and Hofmannsthal, Dos Continentes, 1974.
Hugo von Hofmannsthal, Ungar, 1977.
(Contributor of translations of poetry by Johann Wolfgang von Goethe) Frederick Ungar, editor, *The Eternal Feminine*, Ungar, 1980.
The Bourgeois Proletarian: A Study of Anna Seghers, Bouvier, 1980.
Lebensbilder, Stoedtner, 1983.
(Translator) *Austria in Poetry and History*, Ungar, 1984.
Robert Musil, Continuum, 1988.
German Writing since 1945, Continuum, 1988.

Contributor to *Encyclopedia of World Literature in the Twentieth Century*. Contributor of articles and poems to language journals.

WORK IN PROGRESS: Research projects on Walter Kempowski and Hugo von Hofmannsthal.

SIDELIGHTS: Lowell A. Bangerter writes *CA* that his "interest in German language and literature was first aroused during my initial stay in Germany as an American Field Service exchange student in summer, 1958, and further stimulated during thirty months spent in Germany from 1961 to 1964, when I served as a missionary for the Church of Jesus Christ of Latter-day Saints. Language studies include German, French, Old Norse-Icelandic, Modern Danish, and Russian. . . . Most of my own poetry has been stimulated by the experience of the vast panorama of nature in the American West."

*   *   *

BARNARD, Ellsworth   1907-

PERSONAL: Born April 11, 1907, in Shelburne Falls, Mass.; son of David Thompson and Kate (Barnard) Barnard; married Mary Taylor, December 31, 1936. *Education:* University of Massachusetts, B.S., 1928; University of Minnesota, M.A., 1929, Ph.D., 1935. *Politics:* Independent Liberal.

ADDRESSES: Home—86 Leverett Rd., Amherst, Mass. 01002.

CAREER: University of Massachusetts, Amherst, instructor in English, 1930-33; University of Tampa, Tampa, Fla., assistant professor of English, 1936-37; Williams College, Williamstown, Mass., instructor in English, 1937-40; University of Wisconsin, Madison, lecturer in English, 1940-41; Alfred University, Alfred, N.Y., professor of English and head of department, 1941-50; University of Chicago, Chicago, Ill., lecturer in liberal arts, 1952-55; Bowdoin College, Brunswick, Me., visiting lecturer in English, 1955-57; Northern Michigan University, Marquette, associate professor, 1957-62, professor of English, 1962-68; University of Massachusetts, Amherst, visiting professor, 1968-69, professor of English, 1969-73, professor emeritus, 1973—.

MEMBER: Modern Language Association of America (member emeritus), American Association of University Professors (member emeritus).

AWARDS, HONORS: L.H.D., University of Massachusetts, 1969.

WRITINGS:

Shelley's Religion, University of Minnesota Press, 1937.
(Editor) *Shelley: Selected Poems, Essays, and Letters*, Odyssey, 1944.
Edwin Arlington Robinson: A Critical Study, Macmillan, 1952.

Wendell Willkie: Fighter for Freedom, Northern Michigan University Press, 1966.
(Contributor) J. R. Bryer, editor, *Fifteen Modern American Authors*, Duke University Press, 1969, revised edition published as *Sixteen Modern American Authors*, Duke University Press, Norton, 1973, 3rd edition, 1988.
(Editor and contributor) *Edwin Arlington Robinson: Centenary Essays*, University of Georgia Press, 1969.
English for Everybody, Dinosaur Press, 1979.
In Sunshine and in Shadow: A Teacher's Odyssey (autobiography), Dinosaur Press, Volume 1: *A Hill Farm Boyhood*, 1983, Volume 2: *An Academic Apprenticeship*, 1985, Volume 3: *Life in the Ivory Tower*, 1988.

Contributor to *Harper's*, *New York Times Magazine*, *Massachusetts Review*, and several other publications.

WORK IN PROGRESS: Full Circle, concluding volume of *In Sunshhine and Shadow*, an autobiography.

SIDELIGHTS: Ellsworth Barnard told *CA:* "My first love was always teaching and my books were written mostly during summer vacations, or when I was out of a job, or when I took time off (at my own expense) near the end of a project. Not that I wish to downgrade my books. I wrote them because I wanted to, because I cared about the subjects and thought I had something new or significant to say about them. And if you care about the subject, you care—or ought to care—about the style; of which the great virtues, as I say in *English for Everybody*, seem to me to be clarity, naturalness, forcefulness, and beauty. You get a feeling for these through wide reading, especially of the classics of British and American literature. And then you simply work, no matter how long it takes, to get every word and sentence right. I suppose, too, that if over the years you devote your days and nights to helping students to learn to write well, you learn something yourself."

AVOCATIONAL INTERESTS: Nature study, conservation, civil liberties.

*   *   *

BARNES, Clive (Alexander)   1927-

PERSONAL: Born May 13, 1927, in London, England; came to United States, 1965; son of Arthur Lionel (an ambulance driver) and Freda Marguerite (a secretary; maiden name, Garratt) Barnes; married second wife, Patricia Amy Evelyn Winckley, June 26, 1958; children: (second marriage) Christopher John Clive, Joanna Rosemary Maya. *Education:* Attended King's College, London; St. Catherine's College, Oxford, B.A., 1951. *Religion:* Church of England.

ADDRESSES: Office—*New York Post*, 210 South St., New York, N.Y. 10002.

CAREER: Arabesque, Oxford, England, co-editor, 1950; *Dance and Dancers*, London, England, assistant editor, 1950-58, associate editor, 1958-61, executive editor, 1961-65, editor in New York City, 1965—; London County Council, London, administrative officer in town planning, 1952-61; *Times*, London, chief dance critic, 1961-65; *New York Times*, New York City, dance critic, 1965-78, daily drama critic, 1967-78; *New York Post*, New York City, associate editor and chief drama and dance critic, 1978—. Adjunct associate professor of journalism, New York University, 1968-75. *Military service:* Royal Air Force, 1946-48.

MEMBER: Critics Circle London (past secretary, chairperson of ballet section), New York Drama Critics Circle (president, 1973-75), Century (New York).

AWARDS, HONORS: Knight of the Order of Dannebrog (Denmark), 1972; Commander of the British Empire, 1975.

WRITINGS:

Ballet in Britain since the War, C. A. Watts, 1953.
Frederick Ashton and His Ballets, Dance Perspectives Foundation, 1961.
(With A. V. Coton and Frank Jackson) *Ballet Here and Now,* edited by Susan Lester, Dobson, 1961.
(Editor with Horst Koegler) *Ballett 1965: Chronik und Bilanz des Ballettjahres,* Friedrich Verlag, 1965.
(Editor with Koegler) *Ballett 1966: Chronik und Bilanz des Ballettjahres,* Friedrich Verlag, 1966.
(Author of commentary) Jack Mitchell, photographer, *Dance Scene U.S.A.: America's Greatest Ballet and Modern Dance Companies in Photographs,* World Publishing, 1967.
(Editor and author of foreword) *Fifty Best Plays of the American Theatre from 1787 to the Present,* four volumes, Crown, 1969.
(Editor with John Gassner) *Best American Plays: Sixth Series, 1963-1967,* Crown, 1971.
(Author of introduction) *New York Times Directory of the Theatre,* Arno Press, 1973.
(Editor) *Best American Plays: Seventh Series,* Crown, 1975.
Inside American Ballet Theatre, Hawthorn, 1977.
Nureyev, Helene Obolensky, 1982.
(Editor) *Best American Plays: Eighth Series, 1974-1982,* Crown, 1983.

Also author of *Dance as It Happened* and *Dance in the Twentieth Century.* Contributor of articles and reviews to periodicals, including *Dance, Nation, Saturday Review, Holiday, Saturday Evening Post, New Republic, Harper's,* and *Vogue.* Music, dance, drama, and film critic for *Daily Express,* London, 1956-65; dance critic for *Spectator,* London, 1959-65; executive editor of *Plays and Players, Films and Filming,* and *Music and Musicians,* 1961-65.

AVOCATIONAL INTERESTS: Eating, drinking, walking, theatregoing.

BIOGRAPHICAL/CRITICAL SOURCES:

BOOKS

Authors in the News, Volume 2, Gale, 1976.†

*   *   *

BARNES, Elmer Tracey
[Collective pseudonym]

WRITINGS:

"MOTION PICTURE COMRADES" SERIES

The Motion Picture Comrades' Great Venture; or, On the Road with the "Big Round-Top", New York Book, 1917.
The Motion Picture Comrades in African Jungles; or, The Camera Boys in Wild Animal Land, New York Book, 1917, reprinted under title *The Motion Picture Comrades through African Jungles; or, The Camera Boys in Wild Animal Land* by Saalfield.
. . . along the Orinoco; or, Facing Perils in the Tropics, New York Book, 1917.

. . . aboard a Submarine; or, Searching for Treasure under the Sea, New York Book, 1917.
. . . Producing a Success; or, Featuring a Sensation, New York Book, 1917.

SIDELIGHTS: For more information see the entries for Harriet S. Adams, Edward L. Stratemeyer, and Andrew E. Svenson.

BIOGRAPHICAL/CRITICAL SOURCES:

BOOKS

Johnson, Deidre, editor and compiler, *Stratemeyer Pseudonyms and Series Books: An Annotated Checklist of Stratemeyer and Stratemeyer Syndicate Publications,* Greenwood Press, 1982.

*   *   *

BARNUM, Richard
[Collective pseudonym]

WRITINGS:

"KNEETIME ANIMAL STORIES" SERIES

Squinty, the Comical Pig: His Many Adventures, Barse & Hopkins, 1915.
Slicko, the Jumping Squirrel: Her Many Adventures, Barse & Hopkins, 1915.
Mappo, the Merry Monkey: His Many Adventures, Barse & Hopkins, 1915.
Tum Tum, the Jolly Elephant, Barse & Hopkins, 1915.
Don, a Runaway Dog, Barse & Hopkins, 1915.
Dido, the Dancing Bear: His Many Adventures, Barse & Hopkins, 1916.
Blackie, a Lost Cat: Her Many Adventures, Barse & Hopkins, 1916.
Flop Ear, the Funny Rabbit, Barse & Hopkins, 1916.
Tinkle the Trick Pony: His Many Adventures, Barse & Hopkins, 1917.
Lightfoot, the Leaping Goat: His Many Adventures, Barse & Hopkins, 1917.
Chunky, the Happy Hippo, Barse & Hopkins, 1918.
Sharp Eyes, the Silver Fox: His Many Adventures, Barse & Hopkins, 1918.
Nero, the Circus Lion: His Many Adventures, Barse & Hopkins, 1919.
Tamba, the Tame Tiger, Barse & Hopkins, 1919.
Toto, the Bustling Beaver: His Many Adventures, Barse & Hopkins, 1920.
Shaggo, the Mighty Buffalo: His Many Adventures, Barse & Hopkins, 1921.
Winkie, the Wily Woodchuck, Barse & Hopkins, 1922.

SIDELIGHTS: The "Kneetime Animal Stories" series was one of only two Stratemeyer Syndicate series to feature animals rather than people as main characters. These stories were intended for children from 4 to 9 years. For more information see the entries for Harriet S. Adams, Edward L. Stratemeyer, and Andrew E. Svenson.

BIOGRAPHICAL/CRITICAL SOURCES:

BOOKS

Johnson, Deidre, editor and compiler, *Stratemeyer Pseudonyms and Series Books: An Annotated Checklist of Stratemeyer and Stratemeyer Syndicate Publications,* Greenwood Press, 1982.

BARNUM, Vance
[Collective pseudonym]

WRITINGS:

"FRANK AND ANDY" SERIES

Frank and Andy Afloat; or, The Cave on the Island (originally published as *The Racer Boys; or, The Mystery of the Wreck* by Clarence Young, Cupples & Leon, 1912), G. Sully, 1921.
. . . at Boarding School; or, Rivals for Many Honors (originally published as *The Racer Boys at Boarding School; or, Rivals for Many Honors* by Clarence Young, Cupples & Leon, 1912), G. Sully, 1921.
. . . in a Winter Camp; or, The Young Hunters' Strange Discovery (originally published as *The Racer Boys to the Rescue; or, Stirring Days in a Winter Camp* by Clarence Young, Cupples & Leon, 1912), G. Sully, 1921.

"JOE STRONG" SERIES

Joe Strong, the Boy Wizard; or, The Mysteries of Magic Exposed, G. Sully, 1916.
. . . on the Trapeze; or, The Daring Feats of a Young Circus Performer, G. Sully, 1916.
. . . the Boy Fish; or, Marvelous Doings in a Big Tank, G. Sully, 1916.
. . . on the High Wire; or, Motorcycle Perils of the Air, G. Sully, 1916.
. . . and His Wings of Steel; or, A Young Acrobat in the Clouds, G. Sully, 1916.
. . . and His Box of Mystery; or, The Ten Thousand Dollar Prize Trick, G. Sully, 1916.
. . . the Boy Fire Eater; or, The Most Dangerous Performance on Record, G. Sully, 1916.

SIDELIGHTS: For more information see the entries for Harriet S. Adams, Edward L. Stratemeyer, and Andrew E. Svenson.

BIOGRAPHICAL/CRITICAL SOURCES:

BOOKS

Johnson, Deidre, editor and compiler, *Stratemeyer Pseudonyms and Series Books: An Annotated Checklist of Stratemeyer and Stratemeyer Syndicate Publications*, Greenwood Press, 1982.

*   *   *

BARTLETT, Philip A.
[Collective pseudonym]

WRITINGS:

"ROY STOVER" SERIES

The Lakeport Bank Mystery, Barse, 1929.
The Mystery of the Snowbound Express, Barse, 1929.
The Cliff Island Mystery, Barse, 1930.
The Mystery of the Circle of Fire, Grosset & Dunlap, 1934.

SIDELIGHTS: This series, according to Carol Billman in her *The Secret of the Stratemeyer Syndicate: Nancy Drew, the Hardy Boys, and the Million Dollar Fiction Factory*, was an attempt to capitalize on the success of the "Hardy Boys" series. For more information see the entries for Harriet S. Adams, Edward L. Stratemeyer, and Andrew E. Svenson.

BIOGRAPHICAL/CRITICAL SOURCES:

BOOKS

Billman, Carol, *The Secret of the Stratemeyer Syndicate: Nancy Drew, the Hardy Boys, and the Million Dollar Fiction Factory*, Ungar, 1986.
Johnson, Deidre, editor and compiler, *Stratemeyer Pseudonyms and Series Books: An Annotated Checklist of Stratemeyer and Stratemeyer Syndicate Publications*, Greenwood Press, 1982.

*   *   *

BARTON, May Hollis
[Collective pseudonym]

WRITINGS:

(Contributor) *Mystery and Adventure Stories for Girls* (includes *Two Girls and a Mystery;* also see below), Cupples & Leon, 1934.
Favorite Stories for Girls: Four Complete Books in One Volume (contains *Kate Martin's Problem, Charlotte Cross and Aunt Deb, The Girl from the Country,* and *Hazel Hood's Strange Discovery;* also see below), Cupples & Leon, 1937.

"BARTON BOOKS FOR GIRLS"

The Girl from the Country; or, Laura Mayford's City Experiences, Cupples & Leon, 1926.
Three Girl Chums at Laurel Hall; or, The Mystery of the School by the Lake, Cupples & Leon, 1926.
Nell Grayson's Ranching Days; or, A City Girl in the Great West, Cupples & Leon, 1926.
Four Little Women of Roxby; or, The Queer Old Lady Who Lost Her Way, Cupples & Leon, 1926.
Plain Jane and Pretty Betty; or, The Girl Who Won Out, Cupples & Leon, 1926.
Little Miss Sunshine; or, The Old Bachelor's Ward, Cupples & Leon, 1928.
Hazel Hood's Strange Discovery; or, The Old Scientist's Treasure Vault, Cupples & Leon, 1928.
Two Girls and a Mystery; or, The Old House in the Glen, Cupples & Leon, 1928.
The Girls of Lighthouse Island; or, The Strange Sea Chest, Cupples & Leon, 1929.
Kate Martin's Problem; or, Facing the Wide World, Cupples & Leon, 1929.
The Girl in the Top Flat; or, The Daughter of an Artist, Cupples & Leon, 1930.
The Search for Peggy Ann; or, A Mystery of the Flood, Cupples & Leon, 1930.
Sallie's Test of Skill; or, Winning the Trophy, Cupples & Leon, 1931.
Charlotte Cross and Aunt Deb; or, The Queerest Trip on Record, Cupples & Leon, 1931.
Virginia's Venture; or, Strange Business at the Tea House, Cupples & Leon, 1932.

SIDELIGHTS: For more information see the entries for Harriet S. Adams, Edward L. Stratemeyer and Andrew E. Svenson.

BIOGRAPHICAL/CRITICAL SOURCES:

BOOKS

Johnson, Deidre, editor and compiler, *Stratemeyer Pseudonyms and Series Books: An Annotated Checklist of Strat-*

emeyer and Stratemeyer Syndicate Publications, Greenwood Press, 1982.

*   *   *

BAUER, Marion Dane   1938-

PERSONAL: Born November 20, 1938, in Oglesby, Ill.; daughter of Chester (a chemist) and Elsie (a kindergarten teacher; maiden name, Hempstead) Dane; married Ronald Bauer (an Episcopal priest), June 25, 1959 (divorced, December 27, 1987); children: Peter Dane, Elisabeth Alison. *Education:* Student at La Salle-Peru-Oglesby Junior College, 1956-58, and University of Missouri, 1958-59; University of Oklahoma, B.A., 1962. *Politics:* Democrat. *Religion:* Episcopalian.

ADDRESSES: Home—8861 Basswood Rd., Eden Prairie, Minn. 55344.

CAREER: High school English teacher in Waukesha, Wis., 1962-64; Hennepin Technical Center, Minneapolis, Minn., instructor in creative writing for adult education program, 1975-78; instructor at University of Minnesota Continuing Education for Women, 1978-85, and Institute of Children's Literature, 1982-85; Carnival Press, Minneapolis, editor, 1982—.

MEMBER: Authors Guild, Authors League of America, Society of Children's Book Writers.

AWARDS, HONORS: Foster Child was selected as a Golden Kite Honor Book by the Society of Children's Book Writers, 1979; Jane Addams Children's Book Award, Jane Addams Peace Association and Women's International League for Peace and Freedom, 1984, for *Rain of Fire; On My Honor* was named a Newbery Honor Book, 1987.

WRITINGS:

CHILDREN'S NOVELS

Shelter from the Wind, Clarion Books, 1976.
Foster Child, Clarion Books, 1977.
Rain of Fire, Clarion Books, 1983.
Like Mother, Like Daughter, Clarion Books, 1985.
On My Honor, Clarion Books, 1986.
Touch the Moon, Clarion Books, 1987.
A Dream of Kings and Castles, Clarion Books, 1989.

OTHER

Tangled Butterfly (young adult novel), Clarion Books, 1980.

Also author of "God's Tears: A Woman's Journey in Faith," a chancel drama performed as a one-woman show.

SIDELIGHTS: Marion Dane Bauer once told *CA:* "I write for children because there is a child in me who refuses to be subjugated into all the proper forms of adulthood. I write for children because such writing allows me to deal with all my old feeling issues in a context that approximates the original experience. I write for children because I figured, when I began, that if I wrote what was acceptable for children and managed to get published, I would still be acceptable to my parents and to my own children. I write for children because there is something in the inner workings of my brain which returns, always, to origins and to the form underlying form. I write for children because I like children, especially the twelve year olds I return to most often. They are so beautiful in that moment, so knowing and so innocent in the same breath. I write for children because I think children are important, not only for what they will be tomorrow—which is what they are usually trumpeted for—but for what they are today."

Bauer more recently added: "Every one of my books draws from the core of my life and experience though none of them is autobiographical. *On My Honor* is the only one which comes directly from an actual occurrence, but it is based on something which happened to a friend of mine when we were both thirteen. (He and another boy, whom I did not know, went swimming in the Vermillion River near my home in Oglesby, Illinois. The other boy didn't swim, and he suddenly hit deep water and went under. My friend dived for him, repeatedly, but was unable to save him, and he went home afraid to tell anyone what had happened.) This is all I ever knew of the actual event, and from this knowledge come the central facts of the story. And yet the deeper story, the story of questions about responsibility and guilt, comes from a place no more mysterious than my own life and my own experience as a friend, as a parent, as a teacher and editor and writer of books.

"It is the nature of the story to take what we have all lived and to give it significance. Life happens. Story creates meaning. My stories are never an attempt to teach in some kind of literal, absolute sense. In fact, I am mildly distressed by letters from kids which say, 'In *On My Honor* I learned never to swim in rivers . . . or always to obey my parents.' My stories are meant to ask unanswerable questions, to share pain, to test insights, and most of all, to make connections. I am always writing toward that moment when a reader will say, 'But I thought I was the only one who ever felt that, thought that, wanted that'; and when that moment comes, my story has found its reason for being. The more absolutely, uniquely individual the story moment is, the more universal it is as well. And in that moment's connection between story and reader my life takes on flesh and meaning."

*   *   *

BAXTER, Craig   1929-
(David Dunbar)

PERSONAL: Born February 16, 1929, in Elizabeth, N.J.; son of William James (an engineer) and Grace (Craig) Baxter; married Carol Alice Smart, September 17, 1955 (divorced, 1984); married Barbara Townsend Stevens (an attorney), May 28, 1984; children: (first marriage) Craig, Louise Stuart. *Education:* University of Pennsylvania, B.S., 1951, M.A., 1954, Ph.D., 1967; studied Hindi and Urdu at Foreign Service Institute, 1960-61.

ADDRESSES: Office—Department of Political Science, Juniata College, Huntingdon, Pa. 16652.

CAREER: U.S. Department of State, Foreign Service officer, 1956-80, program officer for International Educational Exchange Service, 1956-58, vice-consul in Bombay, India, 1958-60, political officer in New Delhi, India, 1961-64, deputy principal officer and political officer in Lahore, Pakistan, 1965-68, analyst for India, 1968-69, senior political officer for Pakistan and Afghanistan, 1969-71, political counselor in Accra, Ghana, 1974-76, and Dhaka, Bangladesh, 1976-78, officer-in-charge of international scientific relations for the Near East, South Asia, and Africa, 1978-80; United States Military Academy, West Point, N.Y., visiting professor, 1971-74; Mount Vernon College, Washington, D.C., lecturer in South Asian studies, 1981; Juniata College, Huntingdon, Pa., visiting professor of political science and diplomat-in-residence, 1981-82, professor of politics and history, 1982—.

Member of Research Committee on the Punjab, 1965—, National Seminar on Pakistan and Bangladesh, Columbia University, 1969-74, Pakistan Studies Development Committee, 1969-75, 1979—, and Bengal Studies Conference, 1982—; co-chairman of South Asia panel, National Council on Foreign Languages and International Studies, 1980-81; chairman of founding committee, American Institute of Bangladesh Studies, 1983—; trustee and secretary, American Institute of Pakistan Studies, 1988—. Adjunct lecturer in history and international relations, Northern Virginia Center, University of Virginia, 1969-71; lecturer at a number of other universities, including Harvard University, Columbia University, and University of Pennsylvania. Consultant to National Foreign Estimate Center, U.S. Department of State, United States Information Agency, American Institute of Indian Studies, Asia Foundation, and Asia Society. *Military service:* United States Army, 1952-54.

MEMBER: American Foreign Service Association, Association for Asian Studies, Middle East Institute, Asia Society.

WRITINGS:

The Jana Sangh: A Biography of an Indian Political Party, University of Pennsylvania Press, 1969.
District Voting Trends in India: A Research Tool, Columbia University Press, 1969.
Bangladesh, a New Nation in an Old Setting, Westview, 1984.
(With Syed Nur Ahmad) *From Martial Law to Martial Law: Politics in Punjab, 1919-1958,* Westview, 1985.
(Editor and contributor) *Zia's Pakistan: Politics and Stability in a Frontline State,* Westview, 1985.
(With Yogendra K. Malik, Charles H. Kennedy, and Robert C. Oberst) *Government and Politics in South Asia,* Westview, 1987.
(With Syedur Rahman) *Historical Dictionary of Bangladesh,* Scarecrow, in press.

CONTRIBUTOR

Donald E. Smith, editor, *South Asian Politics and Religion,* Princeton University Press, 1966.
John Stoessinger, editor, *Divided Nations in a Divided World,* McKay, 1974.
J. Henry Korson, editor, *Contemporary Problems of Pakistan,* E. J. Brill, 1974.
Maureen Patterson, editor, *South Asian Library Resources in North America,* Inter-Documentation, 1975.
Myron Weiner and John Osgood Field, editors, *Electoral Politics in the Indian States,* Volume IV: *Party Systems and Cleavages,* Manohar (Delhi), 1975.
W. Howard Wriggins, editor, *Pakistan in Transition,* University of Islamabad Press, 1975.
Ralph Braibanti and others, editors, *Pakistan: The Long View,* Duke University Press, 1976.
W. Eric Gustafson, editor, *Pakistan and Bangladesh: Bibliographic Essays in the Social Sciences,* University of Islamabad Press, 1976.
Frederick L. Shiels, editor, *Ethnic Conflict and World Politics,* University Press of America, 1984.
Thomas Naff, editor, *Gulf Security in the Iran-Iraq War,* National Defense University Press, 1985.
Hafeez Malik, editor, *Soviet-American Relations with Pakistan, Iran and Afghanistan,* St. Martin's, 1986.
David H. Partington, editor, *The Middle East Annual: Issues and Events,* G. K. Hall, 1986.

OTHER

Contributor to *Yearbook on International Communist Affairs,* 1973 and 1974, *Encyclopedia of Asian History, World Encyclopedia of Political Systems and Parties,* and *Handbook for Asia and the Pacific.* Also contributor of articles, sometimes under pseudonym David Dunbar, to professional journals, including *Asian Survey, Journal of Asian Studies, World Today, Journal of Asian and African Studies, Current History, Washington Quarterly,* and *Journal of International Affairs.*

WORK IN PROGRESS: Works on South Asian history and politics; editor with Syed Razi Wasti, and contributor, *Pakistan: Emerging Democracy.*

*   *   *

BAYER, Linda 1948-
(Linda Bayer-Berenbaum)

PERSONAL: Born March 8, 1948, in Hartford, Conn.; daughter of Philip (an attorney) and Lillian (a legislative and administrative assistant; maiden name, Siegal) Bayer; married Michael Gary Berenbaum (a professor), August 25, 1968; children: Ilana Beth, Philip Lev. *Education:* Attended New York University, 1968-69; Boston University, B.A., 1969; Clark University, M.A., 1972; attended Study Center in Florence, Florida State University, 1972; Florida State University, Tallahassee, Ph.D., 1976; Harvard University, Ed.D., 1985. *Religion:* Jewish.

ADDRESSES: Home—7606 16th St. N.W., Washington, D.C. 20012. *Office*—Humanities Department, College of Basic Studies, Boston University, Boston, Mass. 02215. *Agent*—Pam Bernstein, William Morris Agency, 1350 Avenue of the Americas, New York, N.Y. 10019.

CAREER: University of New Haven, West Haven, Conn., adjunct lecturer in English, 1973-75; Hartford College for Women, Hartford, Conn., assistant professor of art history, 1976-80; American University, Washington, D.C., assistant professor of art history, literature, and American studies, 1980-82, director of American studies internship program, 1980-81, director of Washington Semester in Arts and Humanities, 1981-82; Boston University, Boston, Mass., assistant professor of humanities, 1982—. Visiting assistant professor at Wesleyan University, Middletown, Conn., 1975-80; Sam and Ayala Zacks Lecturer in Art History and Humanities at Hebrew University of Jerusalem, 1977.

MEMBER: Modern Language Association of America, College Art Association of America.

WRITINGS:

(Under name Linda Bayer-Berenbaum) *The Gothic Imagination,* Fairleigh Dickinson University Press, 1982.
(Under name Linda Bayer-Berenbaum) *Amanoot Ha-Renaissance* (title means "Italian Renaissance Art"), Open University (Tel Aviv, Israel), 1983.
The Blessing and the Curse, Jewish Publication Society, 1988.

Contributor to art, psychology, religion, and literature journals.

WORK IN PROGRESS: An English version of *Italian Renaissance Art.*

SIDELIGHTS: Linda Bayer once told *CA:* "In the academic arena I have taught in interdisciplinary contexts as well as single subject departments. For example, at the Hebrew University in Israel I developed such courses as 'The Absurd in Literature and Art,' 'Violence and Technology in Literature and Art,' 'The Renaissance View of Man in Literature and Art,' and 'Metaphysics and Art: The Locus of Reality in Art,

Literature, and Philosophy.' Likewise, at American University I offered multi-disciplinary courses on the art, architecture, and literature of Washington, D.C., within a historical, socio-political framework, and at Boston University I am teaching in a liberal arts program where my humanities courses are integrated with psychology, the social sciences, and the sciences in a team-teaching arrangement. At American University, as director of the Washington Semester in Arts and Humanities program, I coordinated nine humanities departments, placing interns from these fields in national museums, agencies and organizations, government offices, radio and television stations, social action institutions, and other types of jobs that call upon humanities training. Teaching on both the graduate and undergraduate level, I have specifically taught courses in writing at Wesleyan University (where I developed a writing clinic for the Afro-American Studies Center), at the Hartford College for Women, at the University of New Haven, and at American University.

"My book *The Gothic Imagination* is a study of correspondences between Gothic literature and art, including a detailed examination of five Gothic novels. The Renaissance text for the Open University of Israel (also called Everyman's University) is a pedagogically oriented work for an extensive home-study program. As such, it includes material normally found in a survey text along with the type of presentation that would usually occur in the classroom, including questions and answers.

"In both my teaching and writing I have stressed the common functions of verbal and visual media in interpreting and defining experience. The preface to my Renaissance art text addresses the issue of the purpose and value of the arts, noting: 'Like religion, art recreates our reality so that we can better recognize and evaluate its critical dimensions. Art is one way in which people confront themselves and their gods, leaving their imprint to verify their existence and then returning to that impression to learn what they have thought and felt. Art is humanity's signature. It is how we pronounce our name.'"

Bayer recently added: "My novel, *The Blessing and the Curse*, deals with the possibility of generativity and continuity (historically, biologically, and personally) in light of social disintegration and modern mobility. In the novel, two single women wrestle with the problem of motherhood within their respective religious traditions (Jewish and Catholic) and their family backgrounds. The novel is set at Boston University, although parts also take place in Israel, Connecticut, and Washington."

*   *   *

BAYER-BERENBAUM, Linda
See BAYER, Linda

*   *   *

BEACH, Charles Amory
[Collective pseudonym]

WRITINGS:

"AIR SERVICE BOYS" SERIES

Air Service Boys Flying for France; or, The Young Heroes of the Lafayette Escadrille, G. Sully, 1918.
. . . over the Enemy's Lines; or, The German Spy's Secret, G. Sully, 1918.
. . . over the Rhine; or, Fighting above the Clouds, G. Sully, 1918.

. . . in the Big Battle; or, Silencing the Big Guns, G. Sully, 1919.
. . . Flying for Victory; or, Bombing the Last German Stronghold, G. Sully, 1919.
. . . over the Atlantic; or, The Longest Flight on Record, G. Sully, 1920.

SIDELIGHTS: The "Air Service Boys" were two young Americans who took part in the early air battles of the First World War. For more information see the entries for Harriet S. Adams, Edward L. Stratemeyer, and Andrew E. Svenson.

BIOGRAPHICAL/CRITICAL SOURCES:

BOOKS

Johnson, Deidre, editor and compiler, *Stratemeyer Pseudonyms and Series Books: An Annotated Checklist of Stratemeyer and Stratemeyer Syndicate Publications*, Greenwood Press, 1982.

PERIODICALS

Journal of Popular Culture, winter, 1974.

*   *   *

BECKHAM, Barry (Earl) 1944-

PERSONAL: Born March 19, 1944, in Philadelphia, Pa.; son of Clarence and Mildred (Williams) Beckham; married Betty Louise Hope, February 19, 1966 (divorced, 1977); married Geraldine Lynne Palmer, 1979; children: (first marriage) Brian Elliott, Bonnie Lorine. *Education:* Brown University, A.B., 1966; attended law school at Columbia University. *Religion:* Episcopalian.

ADDRESSES: Home—140 Lancaster St., Providence, R.I. 02906. *Office*—Department of English, Brown University, Brown Station, Providence, R.I. 02912. *Agent*—William Morris Agency, 1350 Ave. of the Americas, New York, N.Y. 10019.

CAREER: Chase Manhattan Bank, New York City, public relations consultant, 1966-67, urban affairs associate, 1969-70; National Council of Young Men's Christian Associations, New York City, public relations associate, 1967-68; Western Electric Co., New York City, public relations associate, 1968-69; Brown University, Providence, R.I., visiting lecturer, 1970-72, assistant professor, 1972-78, associate professor of English, 1979—, director of graduate creative writing program, 1980—. Visiting professor, University of Wyoming, 1972. Member of literature panel, Rhode Island Council on the Arts, 1980—. President, Beckham House Publishers, Inc.

MEMBER: Authors Guild, PEN (member of executive board, American Center, 1970-71).

WRITINGS:

My Main Mother (novel), Walker & Co., 1969 (published in England as *Blues in the Night*, Tandem, 1974).
Runner Mack (novel), Morrow, 1972.
"Garvey Lives!" (play), produced in Providence, R.I., 1972.
Double Dunk (fictionalized biography of Earl Manigault), Holloway House, 1981.
(Editor and contributor) *The Black Student's Guide to College* (nonfiction), Dutton, 1982.

Contributor to *Black Review, Brown Alumni Monthly, Esquire, Intellectual Digest, New York, New York Times, Novel*.

WORK IN PROGRESS: A portrait of Chase Manhattan Bank; another novel.

SIDELIGHTS: Barry Beckham's first novel, *My Main Mother*, won praise as the probing account of a young black man and the events that lead him to the murder of his mother. Narrated by its protagonist, Mitchell Mibbs, the novel is "basically . . . a psychological study of the ruinous effect on a child who is either ignored or tormented by a parent," writes Peter Rowley in the *New York Times Book Review.* Mitchell's beautiful and self-centered mother (Pearl), in delusions of becoming a rich and famous singer, shuns and abandons the already fatherless boy. Mitchell's lone source of support and companionship comes from a kindly uncle, whose death "and the horror of a sordid squabble over his money spur Mitchell into matricide," notes Rowley. A *Times Literary Supplement* contributor observes that "the single act of violence towards which the book works appropriately underlines the particular, personal anxieties which made it, for Mitchell, an inevitability." Less prominently featured, yet as influential as the psychological devastation of Mitchell's upbringing, are the forces of racism in a white dominant society. The *Times Literary Supplement* contributor notes that "the manifestations of racial inequality, when they do appear, have a potency which lies precisely in understatement." Rowley particularly praises the second half of *My Main Mother:* "The scenes of Harlem, of how it feels to be an aged black from Maine getting a flat tire on Times Square, of encountering a homosexual in the Village, of street gangs and boarding houses, of the ironies of racism . . . are fantastically vivid and compelling." Rowley continues: "If Barry Beckham's second book is as brilliant as the second half of his first, he may well become one of the best American novelists of the decade."

In *Runner Mack,* Beckham "move[s] far beyond the boundaries of his first novel," writes Mel Watkins in the *New York Times Book Review.* The story of a naive Southern black man (Henry Adams) who moves to the North to find fortune as a professional baseball player, *Runner Mack* is more directly critical of an American society embedded in racism. "Loosely connected," according to Watkins, by a series of "satirical and burlesque episodes . . . held together by a matter-of-fact prose that belies their nightmarish qualities," the novel takes on a surrealistic quality as Henry is stymied in his attempts to achieve personal fulfillment and identity. En route to a job interview, Henry is hit by a Mack truck and stumbles, bleeding, into the interviewer's office—only to be questioned about his teeth, whether he's had smallpox, or whether he'll "run away" if he "doesn't like the work." He later fails to win a spot on a local professional baseball team, despite outplaying everyone at the tryout. After finding the space and time to have a meaningful conversation with his wife, Henry receives a draft notice saying he must immediately report for military service. He ends up being sent to the front lines of the "Alaskan War," where he meets up with a revolutionary named Runner Mack, who involves Henry in a plot to blow up the White House.

"Its humor and burlesque notwithstanding," writes Watkins, *Runner Mack* ". . . is an unsettling book." Phyllis Rauch Klotman writes in *Another Man Gone: The Black Runner in Contemporary Afro-American Literature* that "each experience in the novel is a kind of education," and notes a disturbing continuity in that "Henry moves from one mad, dehumanizing way of life to another." Watkins views *Runner Mack* as an allegory of Afro-American history, "parallel[ing] black history from slave ship to . . . militant revolutionaries." He continues: "By creating an ironic verbal world, [Beckham] has produced an allegory that both illuminates the despair and

recurring frustration that has characterized blacks' struggle for freedom and brilliantly satirizes the social conditions that perpetuate that frustration." As such, *Runner Mack* has far-reaching implications. "By the novel's midpoint, Beckham has utterly leveled the American Dream of success," notes Joe Weixlmann in *Dictionary of Literary Biography.* "Beckham causes the reader of *Runner Mack* to contemplate what he or she might do to ameliorate the deplorable condition of current-day America. . . . *Runner Mack* is a tightly wrought masterpiece which probes deeply into the American psyche."

MEDIA ADAPTATIONS: The film rights to *My Main Mother* have been acquired by William Castle.

AVOCATIONAL INTERESTS: Photography, chess, film production.

BIOGRAPHICAL/CRITICAL SOURCES:

BOOKS

Beckham, Barry, *Runner Mack,* Morrow, 1972.
Dictionary of Literary Biography, Volume 33: *Afro-American Fiction Writers after 1955,* Gale, 1984.
Klotman, Phyllis Rauch, *Another Man Gone: The Black Runner in Contemporary Afro-American Literature,* Kennikat Press, 1977.

PERIODICALS

Black Images, autumn, 1974.
MELUS, winter, 1981.
Modern Fiction Studies, spring, 1987.
New York Times, October 10, 1982.
New York Times Book Review, November 30, 1969, September 17, 1972.
Studies in Black Literature, winter, 1974.
Times Literary Supplement, February 12, 1971.
Variety, January 14, 1970.†

*   *   *

BEDIAKO, Kwabena Asare
    See KONADU, S(amuel) A(sare)

*   *   *

BELL, Philip W(ilkes)   1924-

PERSONAL: Born October 24, 1924, in New York, N.Y.; son of Samuel Dennis (a physician) and Miriam (Wilkes) Bell; married Virginia Lee Crozier, June 4, 1980; children: Susan, Geoffrey, Mary Ellen, James; stepchildren: Thomas, Steven, Peter. *Education:* Princeton University, A.B., 1947, Ph.D., 1954; University of California, Berkeley, M.A., 1949.

ADDRESSES: Home—2600 Bellefontaine, D22, Houston, Tex. 77025. *Office*—Jones Graduate School of Administration, Rice University, P.O. Box 1892, Houston, Tex. 77251.

CAREER: Council on Foreign Relations, New York, N.Y., research assistant to European aid study group directed by Dwight D. Eisenhower, 1949-50; Princeton University, Princeton, N.J., instructor in economics, 1950-51; Institute for Advanced Study, Princeton, research associate at Institute of International Relations, 1951-52; Haverford College, Haverford, Pa., assistant professor, 1952-56, associate professor of economics, 1956-57; University of California, Berkeley, associate professor of economics, 1957-60; Haverford College, associate professor, 1960-62, professor of economics, 1962-

64; University of East Africa, Makerere University College, Kampala, Uganda, professor of economics and head of department, 1963-65, dean of Social Science faculty, 1964-65; Fisk University, Nashville, Tenn., professor of economics and head of department, 1965-66; Lincoln University, Lincoln University, Pa., professor of economics and head of department, 1966-68; University of California, Santa Cruz, professor of economics, 1968-78, provost of Merrill College, 1968-72; Rice University, Houston, Tex., professor of accounting and economics, 1979—.

Visiting professor of economics at University of Pennsylvania, 1962-63, and University of Nairobi, 1972-74; visiting professor at University Science, Penang, Malaysia, 1976-77, Rice University, 1977, Stanford University, 1978, Norge Handelshoeyskole, Bergen, Norway, 1982, University of Pennsylvania, 1982, and Australian National University, 1988. Lecturer at Salzburg Seminar in American Studies, 1955, University of Waikato, Hamilton, New Zealand, 1981, Australian National University, 1981, University of Bristol, 1984, and University of Lancaster, 1986. Consultant to U.S. Treasury Department, 1961-63, 1965-67, Agency for International Development, 1962-63, Rockefeller Foundation, 1962-63, and U.S. Department of State, 1966-67. *Military service:* U.S. Army Air Forces, 1943-45; became second lieutenant.

MEMBER: American Economic Association, Royal Economic Society.

WRITINGS:

The Sterling Area in the Postwar World, Clarendon Press, 1956.
(With Edgar O. Edwards) *The Theory and Measurement of Business Income*, University of California Press, 1961.
(With Michael P. Todaro) *Economic Theory*, Oxford University Press (Nairobi), 1969.
Industrial Growth and Economic Development in Malaysia, School of Comparative Social Sciences, Universiti Sains Malaysia, 1977.
(With Edwards and L. Todd Johnson) *Accounting for Economic Events*, Scholars Book Co., 1979.
CVA, CCA, and CoCoA: Are There Fundamental Differences? (monograph), Australian Accounting Research Foundation, 1982.
Current Cost/Constant Dollar Accounting and Its Uses in the Managerial Decision-Making Process, University of Arkansas, 1986.

* * *

BELZ, Carl 1937-

PERSONAL: Born September 13, 1937, in Camden, N.J.; son of Irvin Carl (in sales) and Ella (Engler) Belz; married second wife, Barbara Vetter, June 17, 1968; children: (first marriage) Melissa, Gretchen; (second marriage) Portia, Emily. *Education:* Princeton University, B.A., 1959, M.F.A., 1962, Ph.D., 1963.

ADDRESSES: Home—79 Ridge Rd., Waban, Mass. 02168. *Office*—Rose Art Museum, Brandeis University, Waltham, Mass. 02154. *Agent*—Julian Bach, Jr., 3 East 48th St., New York, N.Y. 10017.

CAREER: University of Massachusetts, Amherst, teacher of art history, 1963-65; Mills College, Oakland, Calif., teacher of art history, 1965-68; Brandeis University, Waltham, Mass.,

teacher of art history, 1968-74, director of Rose Art Museum, 1974—.

WRITINGS:

The Story of Rock (on folk art), Oxford University Press, 1969, 2nd edition, 1972.
Cezanne, McGraw, 1974.
Frank Stella: Metallic Reliefs, Rose Art Museum, 1979.
Helen Frankenthaler: The 1950s, Rose Art Museum, 1981.
Charles Garabedian: Twenty Years of Work, Rose Art Museum, 1983.
William Beckman/Gregory Gillespie, Rose Art Museum, 1984.
Katherine Porter, Rose Art Museum, 1985.
Stephen Antonakos, Rose Art Museum, 1986.
Jake Berthot, Rose Art Museum, 1988.

AVOCATIONAL INTERESTS: Tennis.

BIOGRAPHICAL/CRITICAL SOURCES:

PERIODICALS

New York Times Book Review, November 9, 1969.

* * *

BERGER, Arthur Asa 1933-

PERSONAL: Born January 3, 1933, in Boston, Mass.; son of Simon (an owner of a home for the aged) and Frances (Savel) Berger; married Phyllis Wolfson, June 25, 1961; children: Miriam Frances, Gabriel. *Education:* University of Massachusetts—Amherst, B.A., 1954; University of Iowa, M.A., 1956; University of Minnesota, Ph.D., 1965. *Politics:* Democrat. *Religion:* Jewish.

ADDRESSES: Home—118 Peralta Ave., Mill Valley, Calif. 94941. *Office*—Department of Broadcast Communication Arts, San Francisco State University, San Francisco, Calif. 94115.

CAREER: San Francisco State University, San Francisco, Calif., 1965—, began as assistant professor, became associate professor of social sciences, currently professor in the department of broadcast communication arts. Visiting professor, Annenberg School of Communications, University of Southern California, Los Angeles, 1984-85. San Francisco correspondent, *Il Confronto* (Milan, Italy). Former member of board of directors, Committee on Children's Television. *Military service:* U.S. Army, 1956-58.

AWARDS, HONORS: Fulbright fellow at University of Milan, Italy, 1963-64; grant to attend Comparative Popular Culture Research Seminar, East-West Center, 1976.

WRITINGS:

(With S. I. Hayakawa and Arthur Chandler) *Language in Thought and Action*, Harcourt, 1968, 4th edition, 1978.
Li'l Abner: A Study in American Satire, Twayne, 1969.
Pop Culture, Pflaum/Standard, 1973.
The Comic-Stripped American: What Dick Tracy, Blondie, Daddy Warbucks, and Charlie Brown Tell Us about Ourselves, Walker & Co., 1974.
(Editor) *About Man: An Introduction to Anthropology*, Pflaum/Standard, 1974.
The TV-Guided American, Walker & Co., 1976.
Television as an Instrument of Terror, Transaction Books, 1980.
(Editor) *Film in Society*, Transaction Books, 1980.
Media Analysis Techniques, Sage Publications, 1982.
Signs in Contemporary Culture: An Introduction to Semiotics, Annenberg/Longman, 1984.

(Editor) *Television in Society,* Transaction Books, 1986.
(Contributor) Brent D. Ruben, editor, *Information and Behavior,* Transaction Books, 1987.
(Editor) *Media USA: Process and Effect,* Longman, 1988.
Seeing Is Believing: An Introduction to Visual Communication, Mayfield Publishing, in press.
(Editor) *Political Culture and Public Opinion,* Transaction Books, in press.
America as a Sacred Society, Associated University Presses, in press.

Also author of *The Evangelical Hamburger,* 1970. Contributor to *The Semiotic Web: A Yearbook of Semiotics,* 1987. Editor of "Classics in Communications" reprint series, Transaction Books. Television columnist, *Focus.* Contributor of articles to *San Francisco Chronicle, Nation, Journal of Popular Culture, Proteus, International Journal of Visual Sociology,* and other periodicals, and of cartoons to *Army Times* and European publications. Film and television editor, *Society;* editor, *International Series in Visual Sociology;* editor, *American Behavioral Scientist;* consulting editor, *Journal of Communication.*

WORK IN PROGRESS: Anatomy of Humor; Agit-Pop: Political Culture and Mass Media.

SIDELIGHTS: Arthur Asa Berger told *CA:* "I am interested in popular culture (and other kinds of communication), its relation to art and society, our psyches, the political order, etc. Within this broad field I've some special interests: television, humor, terror, and the role language plays in ordering the world for us. I've kept a notebook-journal for over twenty years and hope to use it to do something on journal-writing and creativity. I am also an artist and illustrator."

*   *   *

BERNSTEIN, Seymour

PERSONAL: Born in New Jersey; son of Max (in business) and Nellie (Haberman) Bernstein. *Education:* Studied music with Alexander Brailowsky, Jan Gorbaty, Hans Neumann, and Clifford Curzon; attended Weequahic Hight School and Conservatoire de Fontainebleau.

ADDRESSES: Home—10 West 76th St., New York, N.Y. 10023.

CAREER: Pianist and composer, 1969—. Performer in concert tours in the United States, Canada, Europe, Asia, the Far East, and South America and on television programs. Member of Alsop-Bernstein Trio and New York Philomusica Chamber Ensemble. Lecturer and teacher. *Military service:* U.S. Army, 1950-52.

MEMBER: American Society of Composers, Authors and Publishers (ASCAP), National Association of Music Teachers, National Federation of Music Clubs, Bohemian Club.

AWARDS, HONORS: Griffith Artist Award from Griffith Music Foundation, 1945, for piano performance; Instrumental Award from New York Madrigal Society, 1948, for piano performance; Premiere Prix and Prix Jacques Durand from Fontainebleau, France, 1953, for piano performance; grants from U.S. Department of State for Southeast Asia, the Far East, and South America, 1955, 1960, 1961, and 1967; Martha Baird Rockefeller grants for study with Clifford Curzon and debuts in Europe, 1958, and England, 1959; grant from Beebe Foundation, 1960; award from National Federation of Music Clubs, 1961, for furthering American music abroad; perform-

ance awards from American Society of Composers, Authors and Publishers (ASCAP), 1979, for performances of *BIRDS,* Books 1 and 2, and *New Pictures at an Exhibition,* and 1980 and 1982, for performances of *Tocatta francaise.*

WRITINGS:

With Your Own Two Hands: Self-Discovery Through Music, G. Schirmer, 1981.

COMPOSITIONS

"The Interrupted Waltz," Schroeder & Gunther, 1964.
"The Sad Puppet [and] Korean Bluebird," Seesaw Music, 1967.
"Toccata francaise," Carl Fischer, 1969.
"Birds," Schroeder & Gunther, Book 1, 1972, Book 2, 1973.
"Concerto for Our Time," Schroeder & Gunther, 1972.
"New Pictures at an Exhibition," Hal Leonard Publishing, 1977.
"Insects," Books 1 and 2, Hal Leonard Publishing, 1977.
"Raccoons," Hal Leonard Publishing, Book 1, 1977, Book 2, 1983.
"The Earth Music Series," Books 1 and 2, Hal Leonard Publishing, 1977, Books 3-5, G. Schirmer, 1983.
"One World" (choral work), Hal Leonard Publishing, 1977.
"Moodscapes," Hal Leonard Publishing, 1988.
"Belinda, the Chipmunk," Hal Leonard Publishing, 1988.
"Trees," Hal Leonard Publishing, 1988.
"Koechel and Sheila," Hal Leonard Publishing, 1988.

RECORDINGS

"Sixty Piano Works by American Composers" (includes own compositions), Desto Records, 1972.
"Twenty-six Piano Works by American Composers" (includes own compositions), Desto Records, 1973.
"Three Pieces for Eight [and] Fugue for Trumpet and Piano by Josef Alexander," Serenus Record Editions, 1976.

OTHER

Creator of videotape, "You and the Piano," Hal Leonard Publishing, 1986. Contributor to magazines and to newspapers, including *Newsweek, Music Journal,* and *Keynote.*

WORK IN PROGRESS: A book, *Surviving a Career in Music;* two recordings, "Sonata for Cello and Piano by Ian Hamilton" and "Goethe Cycle for Soprano, Horn and Piano by Meyer Kupferman".

SIDELIGHTS: Seymour Bernstein commented on practicing in *With Your Own Two Hands:* "During the last few years, when I came to understand the real reasons for practicing, I began to hold seminars for teachers and pupils. At the opportune moment, I invariably asked, 'Why do you practice?' The most common responses were: 'I practice to perfect my technique so that I will be able to play more beautifully' or 'I want to make my New York debut and eventually go on tours.' More disturbing was the comment, 'I've never thought about it.' The most encouraging answer was simply: 'I practice because I love music.'

"Naturally, you want to perfect your technique; perhaps you will even make a successful debut one day and eventually go on concert tours. Certainly, it is hard to imagine your doing all this without loving your art. Yet, there is an ultimate goal that transcends all these possible accomplishments: *Productive practicing is a process that promotes self-integration.* It is the kind of practicing that puts you in touch with an all-pervasive order—an order that creates a total synthesis of your emotions, reason, sensory perceptions, and physical coordination. The result is an integration that builds your self-confidence and affirms the unification of you and your talent. You can begin by believing that such an integration is possible, and that through it you can achieve a wholeness that affects your behavior in everything you do. The benefits you can thus bring to the lives of others justify the process of practicing.''

BIOGRAPHICAL/CRITICAL SOURCES:

BOOKS

Bernstein, Seymour, *With Your Own Hands: Self-Discovery Through Music*, G. Schirmer, 1981.

*   *   *

BERNZWEIG, Eli P. 1927-

PERSONAL: Born November 17, 1927, in Hollyood, Fla. *Education:* Rutgers Univesity, B.S., 1950, J.D., 1953.

ADDRESSES: Home—90 Sioux Lane, Los Altos, Calif. 94022.

CAREER: Admitted to Bar of New York State and of U.S. Supreme Court; practicing attorney in Ellenville, N.Y., 1953-57; U.S. Department of Labor, Washington, D.C., staff attorney, 1957-62; U.S. Department of Health, Education, and Welfare, Washington, D.C., chief of health services branch, Office of the General Counsel, 1962-67, legislative planning officer, Bureau of Health Services, 1967-68, legislative attorney, Health Services and Mental Health Administration, 1968-69, special assistant for malpractice research and prevention, Community Health Service, beginning 1969; Argonaut Insurance Co., Menlo Park, Calif., vice president, beginning 1973. Lecturer on medico-legal subjects.

MEMBER: International Association of Insurance Counsel, American Society of Law and Medicine, Society of Hospital Attorneys, National Health Lawyers' Association.

WRITINGS:

Nurse's Liability for Malpractice: A Programmed Course, McGraw, 1969, 4th edition, 1987.
By Accident, Not Design: The Case for Comprehensive Injury Reparations, Praeger, 1980.
The Financial Planner's Legal Guide, Prentice-Hall, 1986.

Author of monographs and manuals for U.S. Public Health Service. Contributor to law and medical journals.†

*   *   *

BESSY, Maurice 1910-

PERSONAL: Born December 4, 1910, in Nice, France; son of Pierre and Emilie (Labiche) Bessy; married Simone Voisin, March 25, 1949. *Education:* Attended Lycee de Nice for seven years.

ADDRESSES: Home—9 Avenue Mozart, Paris 75016, France. *Office*—11 Avenue Victor Hugo, Paris 75116, France.

CAREER: Publisher of motion picture magazines and trade papers, including *Cinemonde*, 1928-66, and *Film Francais*, *Une semaine de Paris*, *Paris-Theatre*, and *Bulletin du Festival de Cannes*, all 1946-66; International Film Festival, Cannes, France, general delegate, 1971—. Founder and president, Prix Louis-Delluc, 1937—; president of board of television, 1960; European general delegate to World Film Festival, Montreal, 1978. Member of consulting commission on cinema, 1958.

MEMBER: Societe des ecrivains du cinema et de television (president, 1958—).

AWARDS, HONORS: Named Officier de la Legion d'honneur.

WRITINGS:

(With Guiseppe Lo Duca) *Georges Melies, mage* (title means ''Georges Melies, Magus), bound with *Mes Memoirs* by Georges Melies, Prisma (Paris), 1945.
(With G. Lo Duca) *Louis Lumiere, inventeur* (title means ''Louis Lumiere, Inventor''), Prisma, 1948.
Le Contre Memorial de Sainte-Helene, Fasquelle, 1949.
Les Truquages au cinema (title means ''Movie Tricks''), preface by Orson Welles, Prisma, 1951.
(With Robert Florey) *Monsieur Chaplin; ou, Le rire dans la nuit* (title means ''Mr. Chaplin; or, Laughter in the Dark''), J. Damase (Paris), 1952.
Imprecis d'erotisme (title means ''Imprecise Eroticism''), J. J. Pauvert, 1961.
Histoire en mille images de la magie, Pont Royal, 1961, translation by Margaret Crosland and Alan Daventry published as *A Pictorial History of Magic and the Supernatural*, Spring Books, 1963.
Histoire en mille images du cinema (title means ''A Pictorial History of Motion Pictures''), Pont Royal, 1962.
Orson Welles, Seghers, 1963, translation by Ciba Vaughan published under same title, Crown, 1971, Pygmalion Press, 1982.
Bilan de la magie (title means ''Magic Schedule''), Albin Michel, 1964.
(With Jean-Louis Chardans) *Dictionnaire du cinema et de la television* (title means ''Dictionary of Motion Pictures and Television''), four volumes, J. J. Pauvert, 1965-71.
Melies, Anthologie du Cinema, 1966.
Walt Disney, Seghers, 1970.
(With Robin Livio) *Charlie Chaplin*, Denoel (Paris), 1972.
Bourvil, Denoel, 1972.
Les Passagers du souvenir, Albin Michel, 1977.
Mort ou est ton visage (photographs of 130 celebrity death masks), Le Rocher, 1982.
Erich von Stroheim, Pygmalion Books, 1984.
Charlie Chaplin, Pygmalion Books, 1984.
(With Raymond Chirat) *Histoire du cinema francais: 1940-1950*, Pygmalion Books, 1986.
(With R. Chirat) *Histoire du cinema francais: 1935-1939*, Pygmalion Books, 1987.
(With R. Chirat) *Histoire du cinema francais: 1929-1934*, Pygmalion, 1988.

NOVELS

Gueule de soleil (title means ''Sunny Mouth''), Fasquelle, 1934.
Sang nouveau (title means ''New Blood''), Fasquelle, 1938.
Buisson ardent (title means ''Burning Bush''), Fasquelle, 1944.
Car c'est Dieu qu'on enterre (title means ''Because God Is Buried''), Albin Michel, 1960.

SCREENPLAYS

''Le Carrefour des enfants perdus'' (title means ''Lost Children Crossroads''), released by M.A.I.C., 1943.
Voici le temps des assassins (title means ''Here Is the Time of Murderers''; released by Filmsonor, 1956), Editions France Empire, 1956.
''Le Diable et les 10 commandements'' (title means ''The Devil and the Ten Commandments''), released by Filmsonor, 1962.

"Le Roi de coeur" (title means "King of Hearts"), released by United Artists, 1966.

OTHER

Also translator of two novels by Orson Welles, *Mr. Arkadin,* 1953, and *V.I.P.,* 1955.

WORK IN PROGRESS: (With Claude Beylie) *Jean Renoir; Les Mysteres de la Chambre Noire; Les Chats du Royaume.*

BIOGRAPHICAL/CRITICAL SOURCES:

PERIODICALS

New York Times, October 5, 1985.

* * *

BETHEL, Dell   1929-

PERSONAL: Born November 22, 1929, in Chicago, Ill.; son of Earl Francis (a sports artist) and Dolly (Bethel) Cowgill; married Pauline Dorothy Halter (a college receptionist), August 30, 1953; children: William Dell. *Education:* University of Minnesota, A.A., 1949; St. Cloud State Teachers College (now St. Cloud State University), B.S., 1955; Central Washington State College (now Central Washington University), M.Ed., 1964, and additional graduate study. *Politics:* Democrat. *Religion:* Lutheran.

CAREER: Profesional baseball player with New York Giants, 1949-53; coach and teacher in Pine City, Minn., Sunnyside, Wash., and Banning, Calif., 1953-66; Olivet College, Olivet, Mich., associate professor of physical education, head of department, and head baseball coach, 1966-71; City College of the City University of New York, New York, N.Y., assistant professor of physical education and head baseball coach, beginning 1971. Has taught baseball and English in Japanese schools. *Military service:* U.S. Army, Infantry, 1951-53; served in Korea; became sergeant; received Bronze Star and Purple Heart.

MEMBER: American Association of Collge Baseball Coaches (member of international committee), Lions Club, Knife and Fork Club.

WRITINGS:

(Contributor) Setphen Jones and Marion Murphy, *Geography and World Affairs,* 2nd edition, Rand McNally, 1962.
Inside Baseball: Tips and Techniques for Coaches and Players, Reilly & Lee, 1969, revised edition, Contemporary Books, 1980.
(Contributor) *The Best in Baseball,* Scholastic Athletic Services, 1970.
The Complete Book of Baseball Instruction, Contemporary Books, 1978.
Coaching Winning Baseball, Contemporary Books, 1979.

Contributor to coaching periodicals.

WORK IN PROGRESS: Baseball with the Pro's; and *Adventure in Living,* a novel.

AVOCATIONAL INTERESTS: Oil painting, chess, fishing, study of great people.†

* * *

BEVILACQUA, Alberto   1934-

PERSONAL: Born June 27, 1934, in Parma, Italy; son of Mario and Giuseppina (Cantadori) Bevilacqua; married Marianna Bucchich (a poet), June 12, 1961. *Education:* University of Parma, law degree, 1956. *Religion:* Catholic.

ADDRESSES: Home—Via Napoleone Colajanni 4, 00191 Rome, Italy.

CAREER: Author, journalist, and film director.

MEMBER: Sindacato Nazionale Scrittori, Comunita Europea Scrittori (both Rome).

AWARDS, HONORS: Prize Libera Stampa, 1955; Premio Campiello, 1966; Premio Strega, 1968, for *L'occhio del gatto;* Premio Banca Rella, 1972, for *Il viaggio misterioso.*

WRITINGS:

La polvere sull'erba (nonfiction), Sciascia, 1955.
L'amicizia perduta (poetry), Sciascia, 1961.
Una citta in amore (novel), Sugar, 1962.
La Califfa (novel), Rizzoli, 1964, translation by Harvey Fergusson II published as *The Califfa,* Atheneum, 1969.
Questa specie d'amore (novel), Rizzoli, 1966.
L'occhio del gatto (novel; title means "Eye of the Cat"), Rizzoli, 1968.
Il viaggio misterioso (novel), Rizzoli, 1972.
L'indignazione (poetry), Rizzoli, 1973.
Umana avventura (novel), Garzanti, 1974.
La crudelta (poetry), Garzanti, 1975.
Una scandalosa giovinczza, Rizzoli, 1978.
La festa parmigiana, Rizzoli, 1980.
Le rose di Danzica, ERI-edizioni RAI, 1981.
Immagine e somiglianza, Rizzoli, 1982.
La mia Parma, Rizzoli, 1982.
Il curioso delle donne, Mondadori, 1983.
La Grande Gio, Mondadori, 1987.

Also author of *Attenti al buffone,* 1975. Adapter and director of screenplays based on his novels *La Califfa,* 1970, *Questa specie d'amore,* 1971, and *Attenti al buffone,* 1975. Writer of film and television scripts. Literary correspondent for *Corriere della sera.*†

* * *

BILLOUT, Guy (Rene)   1941-

PERSONAL: Surname sounds like "be-you"; born July 7, 1941, in Decize, France; came to United States in 1969; son of Rene George (a journalist) and Christiane (a bookseller; maiden name, Vichard) Billout. *Education:* Attended Ecole des Arts appliques de Beaune, France, 1956-60.

ADDRESSES: Home and office—380 Rector Place, 4M, New York, N.Y. 10280-1104.

CAREER: Free-lance illustrator; writer. Publicis (advertising agency), Paris, France, designer, 1962-66; Thibaud-Lintas (advertising agency), Paris, designer, 1966-68.

AWARDS, HONORS: Books listed by *New York Times* as "one of the ten best illustrated children's books" include *Number Twenty-four,* 1973, *By Camel and by Car: A Look at Transportation,* 1979, and *Squid and Spider: A Look at the Animal Kingdom,* 1982; Society of Illustrators gold medal, 1974 and 1988, and silver medal, 1984 and 1985; books selected by American Institute of Graphic Arts include *Stone and Steel: A Look at Engineering,* 1980, *Thunderbolt and Rainbow: A Look at Greek Mythology,* 1981, and *Squid and Spider: A Look at the Animal Kingdom,* 1982.

WRITINGS:

SELF-ILLUSTRATED CHILDREN'S BOOKS

Number Twenty-four, Quist, 1973.
By Camel and by Car: A Look at Transportation, Prentice-Hall, 1979.
Stone and Steel: A Look at Engineering, Prentice-Hall, 1980.
Thunderbolt and Rainbow: A Look at Greek Mythology, Prentice-Hall, 1981.
Squid and Spider: A Look at the Animal Kingdom, Prentice-Hall, 1982.

OTHER

Contributor of feature articles to *Atlantic.*

SIDELIGHTS: Guy Billout told *CA:* "By education and practice, I am used to solving problems for editorial and advertising. [Upon] becoming an author/illustrator I discovered my best capacities, because I was working with a story of my own. For me, so far, the only field allowing such freedom is illustrated books, and illustrated books are mostly made for children. I would like to create picturebooks for adults."

BIOGRAPHICAL/CRITICAL SOURCES:

PERIODICALS

Esquire, November 11, 1987.
New York, December 17, 1973.
New York Times Book Review, November 4, 1973.

*   *   *

BISHOP, Elizabeth   1911-1979

PERSONAL: Born February 8, 1911, in Worcester, Mass; died October 6, 1979, of a cerebral aneurism, in Boston, Mass.; daughter of William Thomas (a builder) and Gertrude (Bulmer) Bishop. *Education:* Vassar College, A.B. (English), 1934.

CAREER: Poet, author of prose, and translator. Library of Congress, Washington, D.C., consultant in poetry, 1949-50, honorary consultant in American Letters, beginning in 1958. Poet in residence, University of Washington, Seattle, 1966; also taught at Harvard University and Massachusetts Institute of Technology.

MEMBER: National Institute of Arts and Letters, Academy of American Poets (chancellor, beginning in 1966).

AWARDS, HONORS: Houghton Mifflin Poetry Award, 1946, for *North & South;* Guggenheim fellowship, 1947; American Academy of Arts and Letters grant, 1951; awarded the first Lucy Martin Donnelly fellowship, Bryn Mawr College, 1951; Shelley Memorial Award, 1952; Academy of American Poets Award, 1955; *Partisan Review* fellowship, 1956; Pulitzer Prize in poetry, 1956, for *Poems: North & South* [and] *A Cold Spring;* Amy Lowell traveling fellowship, 1957; Chapelbrook fellowship, 1962; Academy of American Poets fellowship, 1964; Rockefeller Foundation grant, 1967; Merrill Foundation Award, 1969; National Book Award in poetry, 1970, for *The Complete Poems;* Order Rio Branco (Brazil), 1971; Harriet Monroe Award for Poetry, 1974; Neustadt International Prize for Literature, 1976; National Book Critics Circle Award in poetry, 1977, for *Geography III.* LL.D., Rutgers University and Brown University, both 1972.

WRITINGS:

POETRY

(Contributor) Ann Winslow, editor, *Trial Balances* (anthology of young poets), Macmillan, 1935.
North & South (also see below), Houghton, 1946, reprinted, 1964.
Poems: North & South [and] *A Cold Spring,* Houghton, 1955, abridged edition published as *Poems,* Chatto & Windus, 1956.
Questions of Travel, Farrar, Straus, 1965.
Selected Poems, Chatto & Windus, 1967.
The Ballad of the Burglar of Babylon, Farrar, Straus, 1968.
The Complete Poems, Farrar, Straus, 1969.
Geography III, Farrar, Straus, 1976.
The Complete Poems, 1927-1979, Farrar, Straus, 1983.

Poems anthologized in numerous collections.

PROSE

The Collected Prose, edited and introduced by Robert Giroux, Farrar, Straus, 1984.

OTHER

(Translator from the Portuguese) Alice Brant, *The Diary of "Helena Morley,"* Farrar, Straus, 1957, reprinted, Ecco Press, 1977.
(With the editors of *Life*) *Brazil,* Time, Inc., 1962.
(Editor with Emanuel Brasil) *An Anthology of Twentieth-Century Brazilian Poetry,* Wesleyan University Press, 1972.

Also translator, with others, of *Travelling in the Family* by Carlos Drummond. Contributor of poetry and fiction to periodicals, including *Kenyon Review, New Republic, Partisan Review,* and *Poetry.* Co-founder of *Con Spirito,* Vassar College.

SIDELIGHTS: Elizabeth Bishop's refusal to settle for easy answers to life's problems, her handling of both ordinary and exotic topics, her precise yet relaxed technique, and in particular her extraordinary perception all revealed her supreme control over her craft and marked her poetry as major. Bishop's work has had an extraordinary ability to make the most diverse groups of poets—those who normally disagree over themes, techniques, forms, in short the ideology informing a poem—agree on one point: that she was an artist they could all admire and learn from. As William Meredith put it in his "Invitation to Miss Elizabeth Bishop," reprinted in Lloyd Schwartz and Sybil P. Estess's *Elizabeth Bishop and Her Art:* "[Bishop] will yet civilize and beguile us from our silly schools. The [Charles] Olsons will lie down with the [Richard] Wilburs and the Diane Wakoskis dance quadrilles with the J. V. Cunninghams and the Tooth Mother will suckle the rhymed skunk kittens of [Robert] Lowell."

Only months after Bishop's birth her father died, and her mother suffered a nervous breakdown and never recovered. For her first six years, Bishop lived with her mother's family in Great Village, Nova Scotia, and then moved to the home of her father's parents in Worcester, Massachusetts. The memories of these early traumatic years surface occasionally in poems like "Sestina" or "In the Waiting Room" and the story "In the Village." A lonely child in Great Village and Worcester, a shy orphan with asthma and bronchitis, Bishop found "a much more congenial and sympathetic world for herself in books," according to Anne Stevenson in *Elizabeth Bishop.* In a 1966 *Shenandoah* interview with Ashley Brown, Bishop recollected that while her relatives were not literary, they did own many books, that she started reading poetry when she was eight years old, and that she was also "crazy about fairy tales—Andersen, Grimm, and so on." In "Influences," a memoir published in the *American Poetry Review,* she remembered how old English ballads, nursery rhymes, fairy tales, and riddles affected her as a child and later as a poet. Bishop told Brown during the 1966 interview that when she was thirteen she discovered Walt Whitman; at about the same time, she encountered Emily Dickinson, H. D. (Hilda Doolittle), Joseph Conrad, and Henry James. Soon after she first read some of Gerard Manley Hopkins's poetry, which captivated her. Later at Vassar College she wrote a piece for the *Vassar Review* entitled "Gerard Manley Hopkins: Notes on Timing in His Poetry," and her poem "A Cold Spring," collected in the volume of the same title, begins with an epigraph from Hopkins and is in part a response to Hopkins's perceptions of spring. Bishop also discovered the work of another favorite poet, George Herbert, by the time she was fourteen. Herbert scholar Joseph Summers recalled in the *George Herbert Journal* that when he first met Bishop during the mid-1940s "she knew Herbert's poems better than anyone I had ever met before."

At sixteen, Bishop entered Walnut Hill boarding school in Natick, Massachusetts. Robert Giroux has included the recollection of one of Bishop's schoolmates, Frani Muser, in his introduction to *The Collected Prose:* "When I arrived at the Walnut Hill School in Natick in 1927, I met a most remarkable girl.... She had read more widely and deeply than we had. But she carried her learning lightly. She was very funny. She had a big repertory of stories she could *tell,* not read, and of wonderful songs she could sing, like ballads and sea chanteys. And if some school occasion called for a new song, or a skit, it would appear overnight like magic in her hands. Her name was Elizabeth Bishop. We called her 'Bishop,' spoke of her as 'the Bishop,' and we all knew with no doubt whatsoever that she was a genius." In the interview with Brown, Bishop herself remembered her activities and early work on poetry: "I was on the staff of the literary magazine at school and published some poems there. I had a good Latin teacher and a good English teacher at Walnut Hill.... I now wish I'd studied nothing but Latin and Greek in college. In fact I consider myself badly educated. Writing Latin prose and verse is still probably the best possible exercise for a poet."

Bishop began Vassar with the thought of studying music, but as she told Elizabeth Spires in a *Paris Review* interview, the thought of public piano recitals so terrified her that she changed her major to English. Among Bishop's Vassar classmates were some promising writers: "It was a very literary class. Mary McCarthy was a year ahead of me. Eleanor Clark was in my class. And Muriel Rukeyser, for freshman year. We started a magazine you may have heard of, *Con Spirito.* I think I was a junior then. There were six or seven of us—Mary, Eleanor Clark and her older sister, my friends Margaret Miller and Frani Blough, and a couple of others.... Most of us had submitted things to the *Vassar Review* and they'd been turned down. It was very old-fashioned then.... After [*Con Spirito*'s] third issue the *Vassar Review* came around and a couple of our editors became editors on it and then they published things by us," Bishop told Spires.

The poems "The Flood," "A Word with You," "Hymn to the Virgin," and "Three Sonnets for Eyes" appeared in *Con Spirito,* and "Some Dreams They Forgot," "Valentine," and "Valentine II" were first published in the *Vassar Review;* all of these early works have been collected and reprinted in *The*

Complete Poems 1927-1979. Stevenson has called these poems "exceptionally mature" and technically proficient; Alan Hollinghurst in a 1983 *Poetry Review* article has noted in them "a relished collision of colloquial tone and high formal artifice," finding particularly in "The Flood" an attempt "to create a world free from personalities . . . related to an abiding concern with detachment." Hollinghurst has maintained that this pattern persisted throughout Bishop's work, ultimately forming a body of work "noticeably characterized by its more abstract, questing and, in a way, cerebral poems."

Other readers, however, view "The Flood" in a different relationship to Bishop's canon. Instead of being an early indication of a persistent pattern, the poem, they feel, may present only one segment of a fluctuating tendency to shift between the poles of detachment and involvement, and, in theme, to move increasingly toward the latter position. Robert Lowell sensed that most of the poems in Bishop's first collection *North & South* form a "single symbolic pattern," although one a bit elusive to characterize, as he said in an early *Sewanee Review* assessment; he isolated "two opposing factors," one of which he called "something in motion," and the other "a terminus." More recently, in the *American Poetry Review,* Robert Pinsky has identified what he considers Bishop's great subject: "[The] dual nature of the art [of poetry], its physical reminder of our animal privacy and its formal reminder of our communal dealings. . . . To put the idea a bit differently, her great subject is the contest—or truce, or trade-agreement—between the single human soul on one side and, on the other side, the contingent world of artifacts and other people." And in the 1966 interview with Brown, Bishop herself admitted to the shift between solitary and communal concerns, when she stated that she was "much more interested in social problems and politics now than I was in the '30's."

In many ways poet Marianne Moore was Bishop's mentor. Meeting Bishop while she was still at Vassar, Moore encouraged the younger woman to write, discouraged her from attending medical school, offered editorial and poetic advice during Bishop's early career, and continued a friendship which Bishop recounted with humor and affection both in her poem "Invitation to Miss Marianne Moore," and in her prose piece "Efforts of Affection: A Memoir of Marianne Moore." Throughout their friendship the two poets maintained an active correspondence. They discussed their reading, exchanged books they were eager to have the other read, mailed postcards from exotic places, and sent whimsical little gifts. Bishop solicited Moore's opinions on poems in progress and sometimes mentioned in her letters people or places that later appeared in poems, for instance, the description of a Cuban sitting room that then became part of "Jeronimo's House."

Perhaps because of this friendship and because Moore helped get Bishop's work published in the anthology *Trial Balances,* the introduction of which included Moore's appreciative statements on Bishop, early reviewers continually linked Bishop's poetry with Moore's. They noticed that both poets often described animals and emphasized a visual quality in their work. In a review later collected in *Poetry and the Age,* Randall Jarrell wrote of a poem in *North & South,* "When you read Miss Bishop's 'Florida,' a poem whose first sentence begins, 'The state with the prettiest name,' and whose last sentence begins, 'The alligator, who has five distinct calls:/ friendliness, love, mating, war, and warning,' you don't need to be told that the poetry of Marianne Moore was, in the beginning, an appropriately selected foundation for Miss Bishop's work." Less enthusiastically, Louise Bogan noted in a 1946 *New Yorker* review Bishop's "slight addiction to the poetic methods of Marianne Moore."

Aside from continually invoking Moore, whose influence Bishop increasingly questioned as her own reputation grew, most early reviewers voiced respect or praise. Moore herself, in *The Nation*, emphasized Bishop's tasteful poetics, her tactful handling of material, and finally her uninsistent control of tension and emotion. Bogan declared that the poems of *North & South* "strike no attitudes and have not an ounce of superfluous emotional weight, and they combine an unforced ironic humor with a naturalist's accuracy of observation." In *Pleasure Dome: On Reading Modern Poetry*, Lloyd Frankenberg pointed new readers to the very first poem in *North & South*, "The Map," as a reference point from which to begin reading Bishop's poetry. He felt that this work, as well as the rest of the poetry in the collection, possessed a "surface clarity [which] is deceptive. Its effect is so natural, we are hardly aware how much is being described: the map itself, the seacoast it suggests, and a particular way of seeing and relating both. . . . The method is direct, reticent and gracious." Jarrell found Bishop to be morally attractive because in certain of her poems "she understands so well that the wickedness and confusion of the age can explain and extenuate other people's wickedness and confusion, but not, for you, your own," that individual morality "is usually a small, personal, statistical, but heartbreaking or heartwarming affair of omissions and commissions." Lowell praised Bishop's "unrhetorical, cool, and beautifully thought out poems" and labeled her "one of the best craftsmen alive."

A few reviewers did criticize. Oscar Williams declared in the *New Republic* that Bishop had "possibly overeducated herself in what is, or rather was, going on in the best circles, and hasn't trusted enough in her own psyche. She has listened every once in a while to certain cliques which are trying to palm off academic composition as poetic perception." And in a *Partisan Review* assessment of Bishop's *Poems: North & South* [and] *A Cold Spring*, Edward Honig argued that Bishop's poems "arrest one by their brilliant surfaces and transparency. But underneath is a curious rigidity, a disturbing lack of movement and affective life, betraying a sprained and uneasy patience. [The poems] frequently resemble the fish in her most anthologized poem of that name: caught half-dead, the fight knocked out of it, '. . . a grunting weight, battered and venerable and homely,' achieving in the end, a pyrrhic victory by being thrown back into the sea." Like Frankenberg, Honig regarded "The Map" as emblematic of the volume *North & South*, but unlike Frankenberg, he criticized it and then the volume as "a plan for suppressing rather than compressing contours, dimension, tonality, emotion. A slow hard gaze moves behind the deliberately drawn-out ironies."

The poems of *North & South* may indeed prove unsatisfactory in the several ways Honig mentions, yet such shortcomings must be studied, because they reveal an important pattern in Bishop's canon. While the poems surely function to suppress, as Honig suggests, much feeling and movement do exist beneath their surfaces. The poems suppress emotion, not to stifle it, but to transform it into something shaped and artful, something which both contains and embodies change. While Bishop often gravitated toward comfortably denying change, she also knew she needed to acknowledge and accommodate it in order to continue existing as a person and growing as an artist. Thus she vacillated between the two states throughout her canon.

Bishop's vacillation manifested itself in several ways. She sometimes completely retracted what seemed a decisive judg-

ment, she varied forms and styles, she experimented with tone and diction, and she explored a wide variety of subjects. Inconsistent precisely because it moved back and forth between many different styles ranging from traditional to surreal, *North & South* reflected Bishop's meditation on her own art, her efforts to see what it was, how it affected her, how it would affect her readers. The volume also revealed her questioning how far she should follow already established poetic traditions and how much she should strike out on her own. As a young artist she worried that her comfort with a tradition, with past ideas and forms, might also stifle her own uniqueness. Finding herself breathing what Calvin Bedient has called in a *Parnassus* essay "the awful, sweet ether of tradition," she struggled in her early poetry to find a pure air for nurturing her own style and to change what no longer suited her purpose. *North & South* recorded the beginnings of what would be a life-long effort to merge successfully with a tradition so that her individuality ultimately would shine forth.

North & South was chosen from among 843 manuscripts for the Houghton Mifflin Poetry Award in 1945. In 1949, Bishop was named poetry consultant to the Library of Congress and moved to Washington, D.C. She admitted, however, to both Anne Stevenson and Elizabeth Spires, that she did not enjoy the year: as she told Spires, "There were so many government buildings that looked like Moscow. There was a very nice secretary . . . [who] did most of the work. I'd write something and she'd say, 'Oh, no, that isn't official,' so then she'd rewrite it in gobbledegook. We used to bet on the horses. . . . She and I would sit there reading the *Racing Form* when poets came to call." Still more awards were forthcoming: the American Academy of Arts and Letters Award in 1950, the Lucy Martin Donnelly Fellowship from Bryn Mawr College in 1951, and the Shelley Memorial Award in 1952.

In 1955 Bishop published *Poems*, which contained both her new volume, *A Cold Spring*, and a reprint of the by then out-of-print *North & South*. In a *Hudson Review* assessment, Anthony Hecht praised Bishop's work generally but regarded the poems in *A Cold Spring* as "not quite up to the level of [Bishop's] earlier work; though it is a little hard to say why. . . . Perhaps it is that . . . [her] attitude . . . is distant . . . and uncommitted." Writing in *Dublin Magazine*, Padraic Fallon, also critical, felt that language had "over-awed the person" and that the reader remained unmoved because "in the process of making poetry [Bishop] herself seems to be unmoved." Astutely pointing out that "the rise of the Imagist movement— in England, at least—coincided with the enfranchisement of women," A. Alvarez in the *Kenyon Review* then criticized Bishop for her feminine poetic qualities. Alvarez linked Bishop to Imagism and, like the earlier reviewers of *North & South*, to Marianne Moore's influence. But he ultimately disliked Imagism ("the first full-scale feminist movement in poetry"); he felt Bishop's descriptive powers were overpraised after she wrote *North & South* and considered these powers "little more than an obscure fussiness" conveying a "finicky air" that seemed "improvised and not quite to the point." Alvarez preferred a more masculine style, which he found in "poets— like, say, Richard Eberhart—whose language makes you jump to his meaning . . . [and whose] language has a kind of physical complexity."

Ironically, Eberhart himself also reviewed Bishop's *Poems* in the *New York Times Book Review*, finding the best poems of *A Cold Spring* to be "as good as anything she has done, but with a difference. The difference is that they seem looser-woven, more confessional. . . . [Bishop] has a strong grip on her own realities. She gives the reader a rich world of slow, curious, strong discoveries, uniquely seen and set.'' Still another poet, Howard Nemerou in *Poetry*, praised Bishop's reluctance to moralize openly and singled out ''At the Fishhouses'' as the collection's most beautiful poem: ''its slow-paced and intricate visual development seems justly completed by a serious eloquence. Donald Hall in *The New England Quarterly* correctly observed that Bishop's poems show ''a desperate hanging on to the object as if in refuge from the self,'' a crucial tension reiterated by later critics. Declaring that ''Elizabeth Bishop is a partisan in the world,'' Wallace Fowlie in *Commonweal* contended that ''the observation and the intuition in [the double sonnet ''The Prodigal''] are equivalent to partisan action in the world.'' Fowlie also commented on Bishop's language, calling it ''even more simple and more unmannered than it was in the early poems. It has become more immediate and more direct . . . more aphoristic, more concise, more energetic . . . more serious, more grave.'' Yet as Alan Williamson has shown in an essay collected in *Elizabeth Bishop and Her Art*, Bishop tended in the love poems of *A Cold Spring* to distance emotion because feelings such as despair, loneliness, and apprehension were dialectically uncontrollable through reason or, in poetry, through structure. These poems, for him, ''betray an immense anxiety about the adjustments between inner and outer worlds'' and an obsession with the distance between human beings.

A Cold Spring, in fact, was concerned with growth and with a sort of rebellion against the past. Its title emphasized a specific season—a time of beginnings, of new plant and animal life. Spring also suggests new human life, or at least physical and spiritual renewal. Unlike plants and animals, however, a human being—if she considers—can partially control her life's course. But two things combine with her will to shape her to a certain extent: what happens during her spring, and what happened long before it (established traditions, for example). Thus the adjective in the title, ''cold''—suggesting conditions hostile to growth, suggesting difficulty and stasis as much as ''spring'' implies growth—implicitly reveals the winter's, and by extension the past's, oppressive constriction. This volume's poems, then, explored Bishop's efforts to realize as well as appreciate her own individual self amid such constriction.

One important tension in Bishop's canon emerged clearly in *A Cold Spring*: the fierce need to settle into absolutes—securities—checked by an equally fierce resistance to this need. In other words, Bishop half wished to accept those dogmas, theologies, or poetic schools that had existed as the tradition for many years, but this wish encountered a fierce opponent in her own resistance, stirred mainly by her brutally clear sight. What she saw often rendered tradition unacceptable because, simply, her perceptions offered another story.

Another important tension in *A Cold Spring* occurred between nature and people. Bishop realized early on that separating these two worlds could be disastrous for her. In the earlier poems nature was often more closely associated with the mind, with the imagination, than with human interaction, and Bishop frequently used the lure of nature to signify the lure of the mind and the imagination. In ''The Imaginary Iceberg,'' for example, the title object is an ice mountain of the imagination, a mountain that the poet initially prefers to the ship full of companions in travel. But when she favors nature over society, it becomes siren-like, its chief danger an abstract, romantic self-destruction. For Bishop, withdrawal from people thus signified a tragically empty and impoverished life; she foresaw deadly consequences if at any time she employed nature as a

means of withdrawal from others rather than as a constant reminder of her moral obligation to maintain and nurture connections with those others, despite the pain involved in such connections.

That Bishop had not retreated from contact with the world and its people was shown whenever she visualized nature in images of civilization and people (the birds, for example, moving off ''with humorous elbowings''), and, even more characteristically, when she actively tried to see beyond a surface or through customary descriptions that the influence of the past had trained her mind to see; her efforts to form her own connections with the world were attempts to engage that world dynamically, with not only therapeutic but also aesthetic results. In one poem particularly, ''Over 2000 Illustrations and a Complete Concordance,'' Bishop clearly showed through her careful use of color the difference between visualizing what others had seen before her and seeing on her own; when she saw on her own, the poem's shades turned from the black and white of the Bible's pictures to the brilliant colors of all the sights surrounding her.

Although this volume actually contained no clear ''resolution'' to the split between a self involving nature and people, no one answer for a way to exist, Bishop did hint at what an answer might be. What remained constant through *A Cold Spring* was the tension between the two conditions Bishop had posited as polar opposites. Being a person alive in the world of this volume thus involved the uneasy trading back and forth between poles: trying to control the mind, yet appreciating its imagination; accepting the past and what it offered, yet growing enough oneself to see clearly; accepting the fact that the life human beings see might be ''awful,'' yet having the courage to face it cheerfully. In 1956, the year after its publication, *Poems: North & South* [and] *A Cold Spring* won the Pulitzer Prize for poetry.

In his book, *American Poetry since 1945: A Critical Survey*, Stephen Stepanchev made astute observations about *North & South* and *A Cold Spring* that would apply to the rest of Bishop's canon. Stepanchev declared that Bishop's ''At the Fishhouses'' ''tells brilliantly what Miss Bishop thinks of human knowledge, which is always undermined by time, by change. It is obvious that change is the most disturbing principle of reality for her.'' Bishop was, for him, ''a poet who, early in her career, chose to avoid politics and public issues without, at the same time, abandoning the objective realities that constitute the otherness of the world. She believes in that world, especially when it shocks or baffles her, and she renders it with precision and clarity. By 1955 the interchange between self and scene deepens in her poems, and her love of geography takes her, as tourist and everyman, to many places on many roads.''

Although Stepanchev exaggerated Bishop's avoidance of politics and public issues, he was correct about her feelings for change and about geography taking her on many roads, for in late November 1951, Bishop traveled to South America on a cruise. But then, as Ashley Brown described it in a 1977 *Southern Review* essay, ''Elizabeth ate some item of fruit . . . that disagreed horribly with her; she was laid up for an extended recovery and her ship sailed on without her. But she had friends in Brazil whom she had known in New York during an earlier period; she liked the country, and she stayed.'' One poem from *A Cold Spring*, ''Arrival at Santos,'' then was reprinted in her next collection, *Questions of Travel*, where it fit in more exactly with the rest of the poems.

Ten years passed between the publication of *A Cold Spring* and *Questions of Travel*, a period also marked by the appearance of a pictorial history, *Brazil*, which Bishop wrote with the editors of *Life*. That her perception of herself and her world changed recognizably during these years was clearly influenced by her move to Brazil. There she found a culture that contrasted in values and priorities with the North American culture she had known. It is no wonder that the poems in *Questions of Travel* often explored previously unfelt or rediscovered emotions set vibrating by this exotic, emotional culture. She also began to perceive the flaws of her North American culture and to realize that a kind of provincial blindness as well as emotional paralysis had settled over her.

About *Questions in Travel*, Peter Davison declared in the *Atlantic* that its first section, *Brazil*, qualified Bishop as "the Expatriate, and she writes with an expatriate's feeling of both her homes: the adopted Brazil, and the native Northeast, New England and Nova Scotia." Jean Garrigue in the *New Leader* stated that "In the Village," the short story Bishop included in the center of this volume, "for its intensity and restraint is a masterpiece." Garrigue also maintained that Bishop's fiction presents "a pure emotion of being, of incident given its laden significance because at the back of this richly various Arcady of a Nova Scotian village full of remarkable animals, kind neighbors and customs is a great trouble." Writing about *Questions of Travel* in the *Kenyon Review*, Howard Moss said that Bishop "brings to poetry a new imagination; because of that, she is revolutionary, not 'experimental.' And she is revolutionary in being the first poet successfully to use all the resources of prose." He continued, "But if one tries, say, to write out a Bishop poem as if it were prose, one soon realizes it is impossible to do so. . . . she is a poet pure and simple who has perfect pitch."

In the *New Republic* Frank J. Warnke noted that "*Questions of Travel* is impressively varied in its forms and modes, ranging from the irregular but firmly controlled metrics of many of the Brazilian pieces to such strict forms as the folk ballad ('The Burglar of Babylon') and the sestina." Warnke found "the Brazilian half of the book more exciting," but did point out the technical achievement of "Visits to St. Elizabeths," which concluded the second half and recounted the poet's responses to Ezra Pound who had been confined to the mental hospital for his pro-Mussolini broadcasts during World War II. Irvin Ehrenpreis wrote in the *Virginia Quarterly Review* that in this poem, "one of the masterpieces of this collection, . . . [Bishop's] own presence, on the series of occasions when she saw Pound, is never mentioned; . . . the form is the incremental-refrain structure of 'This is the House that Jack Built.' But by varying or modulating the epithets to reflect with unwavering fidelity the mixture of her feelings toward that great, corrupted poet, she produces a strength of pathos that will make those who read this poem aloud weep."

Remarking, like Howard Moss, on the revolutionary quality of Bishop's verse, Willard Spiegelman in the *Centennial Review* found a "natural hero" in Bishop's work, a hero who "occupies a privileged position which is unattainable by the super—or unnatural—exploits of masculine achievement which the poetry constantly debunks." To illustrate "Bishop's habitual tactic of diminution or undercutting" with which "certain ideas of masculine greatness are filed down or eroded to their essential littleness," Spiegelman cited several poems from this volume, including "'The Burglar of Babylon' [which] deprives its eponymous hero of his glory by recounting, in childlike ballad quatrains, his life as a petty criminal sought

by a whole army of police who finally, and unceremoniously, kill him."

While critics twenty years later would see that Bishop was strongly involved with the world, most contemporary reviewers of *Questions of Travel*, missed this characteristic amid the more spectacularly dramatic political movements and poetry of the time. Peter Michelson declared in the *Chicago Review* that Bishop's poetry, "a poetry of sensibility and sentiment . . . does not involve itself with affairs of the world, either literary or political." And in *Shenandoah* Charles Tomlinson criticized some of the poems for maintaining a distance from their subject matter through form: "The protagonist who wants to be a witchdoctor in 'The Riverman,' the poor people and the criminal in 'The Burglar of Babylon' are primitives seen with an eye for the picturesque so that the true pain of their situation is sedated by 'treatment.' The better-off have always preferred their poor processed by style." Stepanchev, too, felt that "public events, political issues, or socioeconomic ideology" did not inspire Bishop and that her poetry left readers unaware of Hitler and World War II: "Unlike many of her Auden-influenced contemporaries, she distrusts history, with its melodramatic blacks and whites, and prefers geography, with its subtle gradations of color."

In 1985 Robert von Hallberg, however, offered another point of view about two of the poems in *Questions of Travel*, "Arrival at Santos," and "Brazil, January 1, 1502." Writing in *American Poetry and Culture, 1945-1980*, von Hallberg declared the latter a poem "about the Portuguese colonization of Brazil," in that it focused on the way the Portuguese projected the imaginative structures of a Christian, imperialistic ideology onto the foreign landscape they encountered. He felt that Bishop intended to implicate herself in the actions of the Portuguese by setting up these two poems as "the coordinates of Brazilian history. . . . She comes out of a culture that reaches right back to those Christian imperialists. Horrifying as their actions were . . . she can understand their way of seeing." Von Hallberg also argued that as a poet she sensed the attraction of expansion, and because she did, she became critical; implicating herself, she subtly criticized the expansionist, imperialist position.

As a result of Bishop's concern for both the Brazilian people and the several waves of imperialism and foreign expansion Brazil had experienced, three predominant "preoccupations" (to borrow a word from "Sandpiper"), emerged in this volume. The poems treated various attempts at vision, at seeing clearly; they espoused increased feeling—perhaps tenderness—for others; and they attempted to grasp the changes time worked upon a life. When Bishop had begun to see her own and others' lives more clearly, she also had begun to live those lives, as poems like "Twelfth Morning; or What You Will" and "Manuelzinho" quietly showed. But self-love included accepting many unpleasant past occurrences, both personal and national; such poems as "The Burglar of Babylon," "From Trollope's Journal," and "Visits to St. Elizabeths," revealed her tolerance of differences, shortcomings, blindnesses, perhaps insanity. She clearly understood that although she no longer lived in the world of her grandparents, that older world had affected her enormously. Moreover, she saw that love does not necessarily include happiness, but more often sorrow.

Questions of Travel's form openly reflected a point of view hinted at in *North & South* and implied in *A Cold Spring*. The collection's division into two sections, *Brazil* and *Elsewhere*, was more than a convenient sorter for poems about different countries; it reflected the mind organizing the volume. Divisions in all parts of life—between past and present, for instance, or one country and another, even between a person like Bishop and the poorer peasants in Brazil—seemed more pronounced than earlier but reflected a lessening of naivete and idealism and, oddly enough, a trust that change, though difficult, was possible. While both of her previous poetry collections also tended to sift into two styles and subject matters, in her third collection, Bishop found a truer metaphor in her Brazilian experience for the apparently unbridgeable gaps she perceived.

Poet Adrienne Rich has said in the *Boston Review* that at first Bishop's exalted reputation "made her less, rather than more available to me. The infrequency of her public appearances and her geographic remoteness—living for many years in Brazil, with a woman as it happened, but we didn't know that—made her an indistinct and problematic life-model for a woman poet." But, "given the times and customs of the 1940s and 1950s Bishop's work now seems . . . remarkably honest and courageous," embodying her need to come to terms "with a personal past, with family and class and race, with her presence as a poet in cities and landscapes where human suffering is not [simply] a metaphor."

In 1968 Bishop's poem "The Burglar of Babylon" was published as a separate volume, *The Ballad of the Burglar of Babylon*, and in 1969 *The Complete Poems* appeared. Containing all the work from her first three books except the short story "In the Village" from *Questions of Travel, The Complete Poems* also included some of Bishop's translations of Brazilian poetry as well as new and previously uncollected work.

Having returned to the United States from Brazil, by 1976 Bishop no longer treated that country in her poetry. The lush, colorful, and sometimes humorous dimensions that Brazil seemed to inspire in her verse therefore disappeared, and *Geography III*, which was published eleven years after *Questions of Travel*, possessed a much more subdued form, tone, and emphasis. While part of *Questions of Travel*'s thematic preoccupation had been the struggle for vision and its ensuing perceptions, *Geography III* seemed to take that vision for granted and to concentrate instead on observing the world with an unfaltering, unclouded eye. Yet many of this volume's concerns did arise directly from *Questions of Travel*, in particular the willingness to open oneself to the experiences of childhood, a tenderness for others living in the world, and a growing concern over the reason for, even the necessity of, art.

Since *Geography III* was Bishop's fourth book of poetry and followed the premature *The Complete Poems*, which won the National Book Award in 1970, most of her reviewers felt that they now had the perspective to assess *Geography III* in relation to the earlier three books. In *Canto*, J. D. McClatchy, for instance, noted the increasingly autobiographical, intimate quality of the work, an opinion confirmed by Harold Bloom in the *New Republic:* "The poet who gave us meditations like 'The Monument,' 'Roosters,' and 'At the Fishhouses,' comparable to the most memorable poems of [Robert] Frost and [Wallace] Stevens, gives us now work of a curious immediacy, comparable to some of the abrupt lyrics of [Emily] Dickinson, at nearly their most intense. Where the language of personal loss was once barely suggested by Bishop, it now begins to usurp the meditative voice. An oblique power has been displaced by a more direct one, by a controlled pathos all the more deeply moving for having been so long and so nobly

postponed." John Hollander, too, in his *Parnassus* essay, emphasized that *Geography III* expanded on the previous books, calling it "a review of the previous two courses [in geography: *North & South*, and *Questions of Travel*] as well as an advanced text. Like all major poetry, it both demands prerequisites and invites the new student, and each of these to far greater degrees than most of the casual verse we still call poetry can ever do. The important poems here derive their immense power both from the energies of the poet's creative present and from the richness and steadfastness of her created past."

In *Geography III* Bishop focused her art on what it meant to be human, what people felt living on the earth; the physical world more clearly became a metaphor for her self. While she examined the lives and cares of human beings, the poems sometimes revealed her wondering what those lives and cares had, ultimately, to do with such an apparently impractical activity as creating art, with such an apparently useless craft as poetry. This volume recorded her journey as a geographer of the self and her decisions about art's relevance to a life. Loosely outlining an artistic career, *Geography III* suggested that poetry might ultimately offer knowledge useful in alleviating the pain caused by being human but that it should never become the artist's retreat. The volume's first poem, "In the Waiting Room," showed the artistic intuition and the thought processes beginning, as a child considered her part in and her obligation to the world. The next poem, "Crusoe in England," contemplated the advantages of reason versus imagination as well as the effects of solitude upon imagination and the artistic sensibility. Other problems of the poet, especially the twentieth-century poet, emerged: "Night City," for example, showed how the modern landscape, as it reflected reality, also reflected the contemporary poet's problems and fears; and the artistic process itself—or the metaphoric process—along with its "usefulness" were partly the subjects of "12 O'Clock News" and "Poem."

In the villanelle "One Art," perhaps the volume's climax, themes introduced by Bishop elsewhere converged in a perfect lyric indirectly revealing poetry ("Write it!") as one art that could provide some sense of comfort and wholeness in what the collection suggested was a desolate, fragmented, spiritually bankrupt time. But the poems following "One Art" reflected a spirit almost defeated by the world's chaos and cruelty, and Bishop continued musing over her desire to retreat, as in "The End of March" which flirted with her recurring wish to take refuge in a perfect dream house. The final poem, "Five Flights Up," began on a note close to "The End of March," with a mind burdened by consciousness, by time, by the knowledge of what terrible things people can do to each other, but it concluded with the speaker quietly confronting that world, determined to face what she must.

A consistent moral character thus developed in Bishop's poetry, one that faced up to life's difficulties despite its fervent wish to avoid them and always chose to remain involved with a changing world. The constant struggle between Bishop's Dickinsonian wish to withdraw from the world and her desire to confront the world's sorrows and people was apparent early in Bishop's life—if readers take "In the Waiting Room" as any indication—and it certainly showed up in such early works as "The Imaginary Iceberg" or "The Prodigal." Bishop shied from complete connection with others partly because of her acute lifelong awareness that human beings are always eventually faced with their own solitude. Yet she also realized that being human meant making connections between the self and the world; for in the solitude of old age, what mattered were the pacts people had made with life, the treaties they had managed to negotiate in that war between self and world, and the terrain they had been able to map out to help their friends along their ways.

While known mainly for her poetry, Bishop also published in other genres. Preceding her 1962 text for the pictorial history of *Brazil*, Bishop's translation, *The Diary of "Helena Morley,"* an account of a young girl's experiences in a nineteenth-century Brazilian mining town, appeared in 1957. In 1972 Bishop co-edited with Emanuel Brasil *An Anthology of Twentieth-Century Brazilian Poetry*. In their introduction to this volume, Bishop and Brasil noted the esteem that poets and poetry enjoyed in Brazil, discussed the difficulties of Portuguese versification, and also gave brief highlights of Brazilian poetry—shifts in movements and styles—from the nineteenth century to the time of their volume. Bishop also wrote short stories and memoirs, but these remained uncollected, and many of them unpublished, until the 1984 appearance of *The Collected Prose*, edited by Robert Giroux.

Several of Bishop's best readers have lamented the nature of the criticism treating her work. J. D. McClatchy has suggested that because most critics have treated Bishop to "an essentially rhetorical reading" with occasional thematic speculations, their approach is "shortsighted" because "it ignores or distorts or reduces the true power of her work and career." Similarly, in a 1985 *Contemporary Literature* essay, Lee Edelman has noted that many critics "have cited [Bishop's poetry] . . . as exemplary of precise observation and accurate detail, presenting us with an Elizabeth Bishop who seems startingly like some latter-day 'gentle Jane'. . . . Viewing it as a species of moral anecdote, even admirers of Bishop's work have tended to ignore the rigor of her intellect, the range of her allusiveness, the complexity of her tropes." Lynn Keller and Cristanne Miller in a *New England Quarterly* article have observed that the critical tendency to trivialize Bishop's literary contribution represents a failure by many male reviewers to understand that she employed "as a central poetic strategy techniques of indirection available from both literary tradition and women's speech. . . . In [her] work, tools traditionally used by women in speech to control situations without appearing to control, to hide strength while exercising it, complement the more conventional poetic tools that express shades of emotion. . . . Characteristically, in a . . . Bishop poem, subtle manipulations of language create a subtext that contrasts with the direct statement of the poem to reveal a more daring and more intensely personal involvement of the poet with her subject that the surface of the poem suggests or to present a socially disruptive, often feminist, perspective." Moreover, in a *Grand Street* essay, David Kalstone, a longtime friend of Bishop and a major commentator on her work, has persuasively attacked the frequently held assumption that Bishop's work was excessively influenced by Marianne Moore.

Elizabeth Bishop died in 1979, leaving behind an impressive canon of poetry and prose. Among the tributes to Bishop reprinted in *Elizabeth Bishop and Her Art* are those by Richard Wilbur and Frank Bidart. Wilbur recalled, "She attended to her art, but she also attended to other people and to the things of every day. James Merrill put this happily, in a recent reminiscence, when he spoke of her 'life-long impersonation of an ordinary woman.' Well, she was an incomparable poet and a delectable person; we loved her very much." "If the future is smart," Bidard declared, "surely her poems will continue to be read. Great poems don't replace one another; each does

something nothing else does. The pathos and intimacy in her work deepened until the very end of her life. On October 6, 1979, we ran out of luck."

AVOCATIONAL INTERESTS: Travel, sailing.

BIOGRAPHICAL/CRITICAL SOURCES:

BOOKS

Bishop, Elizabeth, *The Collected Prose*, edited and introduced by Robert Giroux, Farrar, Straus, 1984.
Boyers, Robert, editor, *Contemporary Poetry in America*, Schocken, 1974.
Brower, Reuben A., editor, *Twentieth Century Literature in Retrospect*, Harvard University Press, 1971.
Contemporary Authors Bibliographical Series, Volume 2: *American Poets*, Gale, 1986.
Contemporary Literary Criticism, Gale, Volume 1, 1973, Volume 4, 1975, Volume 9, 1978, Volume 13, 1980, Volume 15, 1980, Volume 32, 1985.
Dictionary of Literary Biography, Volume 5: *American Poets since World War II*, Gale, 1980.
Engle, Paul, and Joseph Langland, editors, *Poet's Choice*, Dial, 1962.
Frankenberg, Lloyd, *Pleasure Dome: On Reading Modern Poetry*, Houghton, 1949.
Fussell, Paul, *Abroad: British Literary Travelling between the Wars*, Oxford University Press, 1980.
Jarrell, Randall, *Poetry and the Age*, Random House, 1953.
Jarrell, Randall, *Third Book of Criticism*, Farrar, Straus, 1969.
Kalstone, David, *Five Temperaments: Elizabeth Bishop, Robert Lowell, James Merrill, Adrienne Rich, John Ashbery*, Oxford University Press, 1977.
MacMahon, Candace, compiler, *Elizabeth Bishop: A Bibliography, 1927-1979*, University Press of Virginia, 1980.
Mazzaro, Jerome, *Postmodern American Poetry*, University of Illinois Press, 1980.
Molesworth, Charles, *The Fierce Embrace: A Study of Contemporary American Poetry*, University of Missouri Press, 1979.
Pinsky, Robert, *The Situation of Poetry*, Princeton University Press, 1976.
Rosenthal, M. L., *The Modern Poets*, Oxford University Press, 1960.
Schwartz, Lloyd, and Sybil P. Estess, editors, *Elizabeth Bishop and Her Art*, University of Michigan Press, 1983.
Stepanchev, Stephen, *American Poetry since 1945: A Critical Survey*, Harper, 1965.
Stevenson, Anne, *Elizabeth Bishop*, Twayne, 1966.
Vendler, Helen, *Part of Nature, Part of Us: Modern American Poets*, Harvard University Press, 1980.
von Hallberg, Robert, *American Poetry and Culture, 1945-1980*, Harvard University Press, 1985.
Winslow, Ann, editor, *Trial Balances*, Macmillan, 1935.
Wylie, Diana E., *Elizabeth Bishop and Howard Nemerov: A Reference Guide*, G. K. Hall, 1983.

PERIODICALS

American Literature, March, 1982, October, 1983.
American Poetry Review, March/April, 1978, January/February, 1980, January/February, 1985.
Antaeus, winter/spring, 1981.
Antioch Review, summer, 1981.
Arizona Quarterly, Volume 32, 1976, winter, 1982.
Atlantic, January, 1966.
Books Abroad, winter, 1967.

Book Week, February 20, 1966.
Book World, April 27, 1969.
Boston Review, April, 1983.
Canadian Poetry, fall/winter, 1980.
Canto, winter, 1977.
Centennial Review, winter, 1978, winter, 1981.
Chicago Review, Volume 18, numbers 3-4, 1966.
Chicago Tribune Book World, April 1, 1984.
Christian Science Monitor, January 6, 1966.
College English, February, 1959.
Commonweal, February 15, 1957.
Contemporary Literature, winter, 1971, fall, 1984, summer, 1985.
Dublin Magazine, January-March, 1957.
Encounter, December, 1983.
Field, fall, 1984.
George Herbert Journal, spring, 1982.
Grand Street, autumn, 1983.
Hollins Critic, February, 1977.
Hudson Review, autumn, 1956.
Iowa Review, winter, 1979.
Kenyon Review, Volume 19, number 2, 1957, Volume 28, number 2, 1966.
Life, July 4, 1969.
Listener, November 30, 1967, June 2, 1983.
London Magazine, March 1968.
London Review of Books, May 7, 1984.
Los Angeles Times Book Review, April 17, 1983, February 19, 1984.
Massachusetts Review, autumn, 1970, autumn, 1982, summer, 1983.
Michigan Quarterly Review, winter, 1977.
Modern Poetry Studies, winter, 1975, spring, 1977, winter, 1977.
Nation, September 28, 1946.
New England Quarterly, June, 1956, December, 1984.
New Leader, December 6, 1965.
New Republic, October 21, 1946, April 9, 1966, February 5, 1977, November 10, 1979, April 4, 1983, March 19, 1984.
New Statesman, April 6, 1984.
Newsweek, January 31, 1977, March 14, 1982, February 13, 1984.
New Yorker, October 5, 1946, October 8, 1955, May 29, 1978.
New York Herald Tribune Book Review, September 4, 1955.
New York Review of Books, October 12, 1967, June 9, 1977.
New York Times, January 22, 1977, February 12, 1983, January 5, 1984.
New York Times Book Review, July 17, 1955, May 5, 1968, January 7, 1973, February 6, 1977, December 3, 1978, February 27, 1983, January 15, 1984.
Observer, April 8, 1984.
Paris Review, summer, 1981.
Parnassus, spring/summer, 1973, fall/winter, 1976, spring/summer, 1977.
Partisan Review, winter, 1956, spring, 1970.
Ploughshares, Volume 2, number 4, 1975, Volume 3, numbers 3 and 4, 1977, Volume 5, number 1, 1979, Volume 6, number 2, 1980.
PN Review, February, 1984.
Poetry, December, 1955, March, 1979.
Poetry Review, June, 1983.
Publishers Weekly, July 7, 1945.
Raritan, summer, 1984.

Salmagundi, summer/fall, 1974.
Saturday Review, January 18, 1958.
Sewanee Review, summer, 1947, spring, 1978.
Shenandoah, Volume 17, number 2, 1966, Volume 33, number 1, 1981-82.
South Atlantic Quarterly, summer, 1983.
South Carolina Review, November, 1977.
Southern Review, autumn, 1977.
Times Literary Supplement, November 23, 1967, March 7, 1980, August 28, 1981, June 3, 1983, April 27, 1984.
Twentieth Century Literature, Volume 11, number 4, 1966, Volume 28, number 4, 1982.
Vanity Fair, June, 1983.
Virginia Quarterly Review, spring, 1966, autumn, 1969, spring, 1984.
Washington Post Book World, February 20, 1983.
World Literature Today, winter, 1977.
Young Readers Review, September, 1968.

OBITUARIES:

PERIODICALS

Chicago Tribune, October 9, 1979.
New York Times, October 8, 1979.
Publishers Weekly, October 22, 1979.
Time, October 22, 1979.†

—*Sidelights by Carolyn Handa*

*　　*　　*

BLAIR, Edward P(ayson) 1910-

PERSONAL: Born December 23, 1910, in Woodburn, Ore.; son of Oscar Newton (a minister) and Bertha (Myers) Blair; married Vivian Elizabeth Krisel, 1934; children: Phyllis Marie (Mrs. George W. Belsey III), Sharon Louise (Mrs. Thomas H. Robinson). *Education:* Seattle Pacific College (now University), A.B., 1931; Biblical Seminary in New York (now New York Theological Seminary), S.T.B., 1934; American School of Oriental Research, Jerusalem, graduate study, 1935-36; Yale University, Ph.D., 1939. *Religion:* United Methodist.

ADDRESSES: Home—299 North Heather Dr., Camano Island, Wash. 98292.

CAREER: Seattle Pacific College (now University), Seattle, Wash., professor of Bible and dean of School of Religion, 1939-41; Biblical Seminary in New York (now New York Theological Seminary), New York, N.Y., professor of Old Testament language and literature, 1941-42; Garrett Theological Seminary (now Garrett-Evangelical Theological Seminary), Evanston, Ill., professor, 1942-60, Harry R. Kendall Professor of New Testament Interpretation, 1960-71, adjunct professor of New Testament interpretation, 1971-75, professor emeritus, 1975—. Member of archeological expeditions at Anata, Palestine, 1935, Roman Jericho, 1951, Ostia, Italy, 1965, and Shechem, Israel, 1966 and 1968. Lecturer at conferences.

MEMBER: American Academy of Religion, Society of Biblical Literature, Chicago Society of Biblical Research (president, 1952-53.

AWARDS, HONORS: Citation of appreciation, Laymen's National Bible Committee, 1975, for *The Abingdon Bible Handbook;* named alumnus of the year, Seattle Pacific University, 1981.

WRITINGS:

The Acts and Apocalyptic Literature, Abingdon, 1946.

A Study of the Book of Acts, Abingdon, 1951.
The Bible and You, Abingdon, 1953.
Getting to Know the Bible, Abingdon, 1956.
Jesus in the Gospel of Matthew, Abingdon, 1960.
(Contributor) *Interpreter's Dictionary of the Bible*, Abingdon, 1962.
The Book of Deuteronomy, The Book of Joshua, John Knox, 1964.
(Contributor) *The Layman's Bible Commentary*, John Knox, 1964, revised 2nd edition published as *The Illustrated Bible Handbook*, 1987.
(Contributor) *The Illustrated Family Encyclopedia of the Living Bible*, fourteen volumes, San Francisco Productions, 1967.
Leader's Guide to the Study of the Sermon on the Mount, 1968.
(Contributor) *The Interpreter's One-Volume Commentary on the Bible*, Abingdon, 1971.
The Abingdon Bible Handbook, Abingdon, 1975.
1 and 2 Corinthians, Galations, Ephesians, Graded Press, 1986.
Philippians, Colossians, 1 and 2 Thessalonians, Graded Press, 1988.

* * *

BLAKE, Olive
See SUPRANER, Robyn

* * *

BLAZER, J. S.
See SCOTT, Justin

* * *

BLUMBERG, Rhoda   1917-

PERSONAL: Born December 14, 1917, in New York; daughter of Abraham and Jrena (Fromberg) Shapiro; married Gerald Blumberg (a lawyer), January 7, 1945; children: Lawrence, Rena, Alice, Leda. *Education:* Adelphi College, B.A., 1938.

ADDRESSES: Home—Yorktown Heights, N.Y. *Office*—1 Rockefeller Plaza, New York, N.Y. 10020.

CAREER: Free-lance writer. Member of board of directors of Westchester Jewish Community Services and Federation of Jewish Philanthropy (Westchester County).

MEMBER: Authors Guild, Authors League of America, PEN.

AWARDS, HONORS: Commodore Perry in the Land of the Shogun was named a Newbery Honor Book, a *Boston Globe-Horn Book* Honor Book, and received the Golden Kite Award for best juvenile nonfiction of 1985 from Society of Children's Book Writers, all 1986.

WRITINGS—All for children:

Simon & Schuster Travel Guides, Cornerstone, 1974.
Firefighters, F. Watts, 1975.
Sharks, F. Watts, 1975.
First Ladies, F. Watts, 1977.
Famine, F. Watts, 1978.
Witches, F. Watts, 1979.
Backyard Bestiary, Coward, 1979.
UFO, F. Watts, 1979.
The Truth about Dragons, Four Winds, 1980.
First Travel Guide to the Moon, Four Winds, 1980.

Freaky Facts, Wanderer, 1981.
Southern Africa, F. Watts, 1982.
Devils and Demons, F. Watts, 1982.
(With daughter, Leda Blumberg) *Dictionary of Misinformation*, Wanderer, 1982.
First Travel Guide to the Bottom of the Sea, Lothrop, 1983.
Monsters, F. Watts, 1983.
Commodore Perry in the Land of the Shogun, Lothrop, 1985.
(With L. Blumberg) *Lovebirds, Lizards and Llamas*, Messner, 1986.
The Incredible Journey of Lewis & Clark, Lothrop, 1987.

SIDELIGHTS: Rhoda Blumberg told *CA:* "I love writing for children. What a joy it is to find information about a captivating subject that will eventually intrigue young readers." Referring to herself as "a compulsive researcher, obsessed with and addicted to ferreting out information," Blumberg adds that she is "especially interested in social history, and willingly endure[s] monotonous diaries and poorly written manuscripts when they reward [her] with surprising information about people and events."

Blumberg's award-winning history, *Commodore Perry in the Land of the Shogun*, examines Perry's impact upon Japanese culture in the nineteenth century. Praising the "handsome coffee-tablelike book" in the *Los Angeles Times Book Review*, Kristiana Gregory calls Blumberg's prose "scholarly but not intimidating." Similarly, Michael Dirda of the *Washington Post Book World* describes Blumberg's writing as "clear, crisp and alive with fascinating scraps of information." Blumberg indicates to *CA* that she has now "decided to devote her work to American history."

BIOGRAPHICAL/CRITICAL SOURCES:

PERIODICALS

Los Angeles Times Book Review, May 11, 1986.
Washington Post Book World, July 14, 1985.

* * *

BLY, Carol(yn)   1930-
(Joanna Campbell, Ann Reynolds)

PERSONAL: Born April 16, 1930, in Duluth, Minn.; daughter of C. Russell and Mildred (Washburn) McLean; married Robert Bly (a poet and translator), June 24, 1955 (divorced June, 1979); children: Mary, Bridget, Noah, Micah. *Education:* Wellesley College, B.A., 1951; graduate study at University of Minnesota, 1954-55. *Politics:* Democrat. *Religion:* Episcopalian.

ADDRESSES: Home—Rt. 2, Box 128AA, Sturgeon Lake, Minn. 55783. *Agent*—Georges Borchardt, 136 East 57th St., New York, N.Y. 10022.

CAREER: Fifties (magazine), Madison, Minn., manager, 1958-59; Sixties Press and *Sixties* (magazine), Madison, manager, 1960-70; *Seventies* (magazine), Madison, manager, 1970-71; Custom Crosswords, Sturgeon Lake, Minn., proprietor, 1978—. Humanities consultant and theme developer for American Farm Project, sponsored by National Endowment for the Humanities and National Farmers Union, 1978-81; humanities consultant for Land Stewardship Project, 1982—; project director and writer for "A Lifeline to High School Students," sponsored by Project Impull, 1983. Visiting writer in Basic Arts Program of Duluth, Minn., school system, 1982; COMPAS writer-in-residence of senior writing program, 1982—; associated with University of Minnesota creative writing program, 1986—.

Co-founder of Prairie Arts Center, Madison, 1971. Member of Chamber of Commerce of Madison, 1971-78. County chairperson of Countryside Council, Marshall, Minn., 1975-78. Lay reader in Episcopal Church, 1975-79; member of board of diocesan publications for Episcopal Church, Minn., and of Episcopal City Services, Minneapolis, Minn.

Lecturer at Institute on Man and Science, Renssalaerville, N.Y., and at Rural Institute, Marshall; teacher at The Loft, Minneapolis, 1979-82, Upper Midwest Writers Conference, Bemedji, Minn., 1980 and 1981, Metropolitan University, 1982, Hamline University, 1983, and Summer Arts Program of University of Minnesota, 1983. Lecturer at Carleton College, Mankato State University, University of Minnesota, Minneapolis, Duluth, and Morris, Assumption College, University of Wisconsin, Syracuse University, Indiana University, University of Delaware, University of Iowa, and others; lecturer for Minnesota Council of Teachers of English, Duluth school system, and community organizations.

MEMBER: Minnesota Independent Scholars' Forum (board member, 1982-84).

AWARDS, HONORS: Grant from Minnesota State Arts Board, 1980; Bush Foundation fellowship, 1981.

WRITINGS:

(Translator from Danish) Anders Bodelson, *One Down*, Harper, 1970.
(With Joe Paddock and Nancy Paddock) *Common Ground* (humanities handbook), American Farm Project/National Farmers Union, 1981.
Letters from the Country (essays), Harper, 1981.
Backbone (stories), Milkweed Editions, 1985.
(With J. Paddock and N. Paddock) *Soil and Survival* (essays), Sierra Books, 1986.
Bad Government and Silly Literature, Milkweed Editions, 1986.

Also translator of poems and of story "New Directions," by Eich. Contributor of essays to Minnesota Public Radio's magazine. Contributor of short stories to *New Yorker, American Review, Ploughshares,* and *Twin Cities.* Contributor of poems, under the pseudonyms Joanna Campbell and Ann Reynolds, to *Poetry Northwest* and *Coastlines.*

WORK IN PROGRESS: Collecting a second book of stories.

SIDELIGHTS: Carol Bly, writes Noel Perrin in the *New York Times Book Review,* "wants the farmers and small town merchants of America to live with passion, to have a sense of greatness in their lives, to take themselves as seriously as a Beethoven or a Thoreau." She insists that her peers find and enjoy their individual inner lives in spite of the fact that small-town thinking generally precludes the investigation of personal potential. After living in a rural situation for over twenty-five years, Bly concluded that the sense of community in a small town inhibits people's natural, critical judgments. Suspicious of emotion or argument, the small towner, the author suggests, resembles a "malignant mix of repression and hypocrisy." According to Mark Kramer's *Atlantic* review of Bly's *Letters from the Country,* "Bly develops with keen perception the connections between spiritual malaise and dullness of character and culture. And she delineates, with exquisite accuracy, her neighbors' shared sense of the sacredness of family, of holidays, of country, a sense that seems to paralyze their evaluative instincts."

The lack of critical discussion of important topics, such as the effects of government scandals or even dismissing a preacher,

alarms the author. Townspeople, she believes, bridle their ideas and pen up their frustrations as peacekeeping measures, which is dangerous. Rosellen Brown explains in the *New Republic* that as "residents of an inescapable community, few dare to make the saving distinctions that would allow them to be critical of one another and of their institutions, or of local and national politics, for fear of strewing their dooryards with corpses." According to Bly, unarticulated feelings are explosives while total small talk and perpetual niceties are deadly to man, since he thrives on the thought process and dissenting opinions. "Positive thinking," Bly states, "is [a] kind of naivete. People who practice or commend it are interested in feeling no pain and in preserving a high. Sometimes a whole culture wishes to preserve this high: then its art and doctrines turn not into positive thinking but into positive pretending."

By denying their evaluative instincts, small towners often fail to realize their inner lives, maintains Bly. Recognizing that every individual possesses "an ethical and esthetic nature," the author insists that this inner life be experienced, though it is threatened by the small-town mentality of women's groups and shared opinions. "Few novelists," states Brown, "have distilled as accurately and poignantly as Bly the essences of small-town life—its dense configuration of satisfactions and impoverishments, the contradictory pleasures of community and isolation, and, perhaps the most elusive element, the difficulty of coming to a full exercise of individual capacity without seeming an alien, even a threat, to one's neighbors."

In order to raise rural consciousness, Bly published essays in Minnesota Public Radio's magazine, later collecting the essays in book form. The result, *Letters from the Country,* explores topics such as the ordeal of holidays and family gatherings, artists in small towns, and agrarian literature. Practical suggestions show rural readers how to become energized and aware of their inner selves. For example, Bly suggests the appointment of a "mail order servant" in a small town, a position she once held. As a public employee, the mail order servant peruses reference sources, including *Books in Print,* and orders material for the town's enrichment.

Letters from the Country, says Brown, "is an engaging mixture of specific, practical advice for rural improvement (self- and otherwise) and a sympathetic fiction writer's vision of a diminished sector of American life." "It's a clarion call, fine silver notes, meant to resound along a thousand Main Streets," writes Perrin. And, as Peter J. Prescott remarks in *Newsweek:* "Reading this book, I wish I knew its author; she is, I think, not only a smart woman, but a wise one as well."

Bly has garnered similar praise for her more recent work *Backbone.* "Each of the five stories in this collection has heft to it," notes Tess Gallagher in the *New York Times Book Review.* "With a novel's amplitude, her stories present self-reliant individuals held in a web of communal interdependence. Their very resourcefulness grants them a solitary dignity, even as it holds them captive to the general good. . . . What the reader will remember is Carol Bly's spiritual and moral intelligence as glimpsed through the valor of these vibrant characters."

Bly told *CA:* "I am interested in (and am exploring) the ways in which the new psychology of stage development and moral imagination can be brought to bear in the peace movement. I think writers and nonbehavioristic psychotherapists may link arms in this work. I am organizing conferences and giving talks about this."

MEDIA ADAPTIONS: A film based on three of Bly's short stories, "Rachel River," will be distributed in 1988.

BIOGRAPHICAL/CRITICAL SOURCES:

BOOKS

Lifshin, Lyn, editor, *Ariadne's Thread: A Collection of Contemporary Women's Journals,* Harper, 1982.

PERIODICALS

Atlantic, June, 1981.
Christian Science Monitor, June 3, 1981.
Nation, December 26, 1981.
New Republic, June 20, 1981.
New York Times Book Review, May 24, 1981, January 27, 1985.

*   *   *

BOND, William J(oseph) 1941-

PERSONAL: Born October 23, 1941, in Winchester, Mass.; son of Edmond Charles (a laborer) and Mary Ellen (Costello) Bond; married Janet Lupico (a retailer), November 18, 1967; children: Paul Greg, Marie Christine. *Education:* Burdett College, A.A., 1966; Salem State College, B.S., 1968, M.A.T., 1972.

ADDRESSES: Home and office—67 Melrose Ave., Haverhill, Mass. 01830.

CAREER: Raytheon Co., Andover, Mass., senior analyst, 1968-70; Humphrey Browning McDougall Advertising, Boston, Mass., manager, 1970-74; Newark Boxboard Co., Newark, N.J., controller, 1974-76; Career Publishing/Consulting Co., Haverhill, Mass., president, 1976—; Northern Essex College, Haverhill, instructor in business, 1976-84; American Business Institute, Boston, instructor in business accounting, 1984-86; Bavarian Strudel Shoppe, Salem, N.H., founder and owner, 1986—. Instructor at Middlesex Community College, 1977-81, University of New Hampshire, 1980-82, New Hampshire College, 1982—, and Hesser College, 1982—. Seminar leader and public speaker, guest on radio and television programs. *Military service:* U.S. Army, 1960-62.

MEMBER: American Management Association, Massachusetts Business Educators.

AWARDS, HONORS: Nominated for Gregg Award for outstanding writing and business education scholarship.

WRITINGS:

Secrets to Success in Your Job, Career Publishing, 1977.
1001 Ways to Beat the Time Trap (Fortune Book Club selection), Fell, 1982.
Ten Best Home Businesses, CBI Publishing, 1983.
199 Ways to Build Your Career, New American Library, 1983.
Riding the Success Express at Work, Madonna Publishing, 1983.
Managing Career Skills Successfully, Ashley Books, 1988.
The Joy of Success, Ballantine, 1988.
199 Timewasters and How to Avoid Them, Fell, 1989.

Author of columns, "Time Management Views," in *Executive Review,* 1974, and "Time Means More Money at Work," in *Florida Business Digest.* Contributor to business and accounting journals. Founding editor of newsletter, *New Career Ways.*

WORK IN PROGRESS: A book on success versus expectation.

SIDELIGHTS: William J. Bond told *CA:* "I am interested in helping other people grow in their lives, especially in their jobs and careers. I write about my own experiences in the world of work, and the experiences of others around me. My teaching and writing blend together harmoniously and give me numerous ideas for other books. I run my own seminars on 'time management' and home business at colleges and universities."

He adds: "I feel better about my self and my writing today than ever before in my career. I know how to handle myself, my work, and my publishers now. I handle rejections better, because I send the manuscript right out to another potential buyer. Believe in yourself, believe in what you write, and keep trying. You can succeed, if you think you can. Good luck."

BIOGRAPHICAL/CRITICAL SOURCES:

PERIODICALS

Haverhill Gazette, June 19, 1982.
Lawrence Eagle Tribune, December 28, 1981.
New Jersey Essex Journal, October 14, 1982.

*   *   *

BOULDING, Elise (Biorn-Hansen) 1920-

PERSONAL: Born July 6, 1920, in Oslo, Norway; daughter of Joseph (an engineer) and Birgit (Johnsen) Biorn-Hansen; married Kenneth Ewart Boulding (a professor), August 31, 1941; children: John Russell, Mark David, Christine Ann, Philip Daniel, William Frederick. *Education:* Douglass College, B.A., 1940; Iowa State University, M.S., 1949; University of Michigan, Ph.D., 1969. *Religion:* Society of Friends.

ADDRESSES: Home—624 Pearl St., Boulder, Colo. 80302.

CAREER: University of Michigan, Ann Arbor, research associate at Survey Research Center, 1957-58, secretary for seminar on research development, Center for Research on Conflict Resolution, 1960-63; editor, *International Peace Research Newsletter,* 1963-67; University of Colorado, Boulder, lecturer, 1967-68, assistant professor, 1968-69, associate professor, 1969-73, professor of sociology, 1973-78; Dartmouth College, Hanover, N.H., professor of sociology and chairman of department, 1978-85, professor emerita, 1985—. International chairperson, Women's International League for Peace and Freedom, 1968-70; member of board of directors, Institute for World Order, 1972—; member of Commission on U.S. Peace Academy, 1980-81, United Nations university council, 1980-86, and UNESCO Peace Prize and Peace Education Commission, 1982—.

MEMBER: International Peace Research Association, International Sociological Association, American Association for the Advancement of Science (member of executive committee, 1970-72), American Association of University Professors, American Sociological Association (chairman of committee on status of women in the profession, 1970-72, and committee on sociology of world conflicts, 1972-74; member of council, 1976-79), National Council of Family Relations, World Future Society.

AWARDS, HONORS: Danforth fellow, 1965-67; distinguished alumni award, Douglass College; Ted Lentz Peace Prize, 1976; National Woman of Conscience Award, 1980; Jessie Bernard Award, American Sociological Association, 1981; Athena Award, University of Michigan Alumnae Council, 1983; Women Who Made a Difference Award, National Women's Forum, 1985.

WRITINGS:

My Part in the Quaker Adventure, revised edition, Religious Education Committee, Friends General Conference, 1964.

(With J. Robert Passmore and Robert Scott Gassler) *Bibliography on World Conflict and Peace*, Institute of Behavioral Science, University of Colorado, 1974, 2nd edition, Westview, 1979.

(With Victor Antonio Avila and Jean-Marie Pearse) *From a Monastery Kitchen*, illustrations by Daniel Marshall, Harper, 1976.

(With Shirley Nuss and Dorothy Carson) *Handbook on International Data on Women*, Sage Publications, 1976.

The Underside of History: A View of Women through Time, Westview, 1976.

Women in the Twentieth Century World, Sage Publications, 1977.

Children's Rights and the Wheel of Life, Transaction Press, 1979.

Women: The Fifth World, Foreign Policy Association, 1980.

(With husband, Kenneth E. Boulding, and Guy M. Burgess) *The Social System of the Planet Earth*, Addison-Wesley, 1980.

(With Elizabeth Moen, Jane Lilleydahl, and Rise Palm) *Women and the Social Costs of Development: Two Case Studies*, Westview, 1981.

Building a Global Civic Culture: Education for an Interdependent World, Teachers College Press, 1988.

EDITOR

(With Robert L. Kahn) *Power and Conflict in Organizations*, Basic Books, 1964.

(With Robert Chen and Stephen Schneider) *Social Science Research and Climate*, D. Reidel, 1983.

PAMPHLETS

Children and Solitude, Pendle Hill (Wallingford, Pa.), 1962, reprinted, 1983.

Friends Testimonies in the Home, Friends General Conference, 1964.

Born Remembering, Pendle Hill, 1975.

The Family As a Way into the Future, Pendle Hill, 1978.

CONTRIBUTOR

Reuben Hill, *Families under Stress*, Macmillan, 1949.

M. Schwebel, editor, *Behavioral Science and Human Survival*, Science and Behavior Books, 1965.

Magoroh Maruyama and James A. Dator, editors, *Human Futuristics*, Social Science Research Institute, University of Hawaii, 1971.

Marvin Sussman and Betty Cogswell, editors, *Cross-National Family Research*, E. J. Brill, 1972.

Sylvan Kaplan and Evelyn Kivy-Rosenberg, editors, *Ecology and the Quality of Life*, C. C Thomas, 1973.

Nobuo Shimahara, editor, *Educational Reconstruction: Promise and Challenge*, C. E. Merrill, 1973.

Christoph Wulf, editor, *Handbook on Peace Education*, International Peace Association, 1974.

Robert Bundy, editor, *Images of the Future*, Prometheus Books, 1975.

Shimahara and Adam Scrupski, editors, *Social Forces and Schooling*, McKay, 1975.

Theo F. Lentz, editor, *Humatriotism: Human Interest in Peace and Survival*, Futures Press, 1976.

R. J. Akkerman, P. J. Van Krieken, and C. O. Pannenborg, editors, *Declarations on Principles: A Quest for Universal Peace*, Sijthoff, 1977.

A Critical Economic Balance: Water—Land—Energy—People, Federal Energy Administration, 1977.

William Loehr and John P. Powelson, editors, *Economic Development, Poverty and Income Distribution*, Westview, 1977.

Dennis L. Meadows, editor, *Alternative to Growth I: A Search for Sustainable Futures*, Ballinger, 1977.

Michael Katz, William P. Marsh, and Gail Gordon Thompson, editors, *Earth's Answer: Explorations of Planetary Culture at Lindisfarne Conferences*, Harper, 1978,.

Terrell J. Minger, editor, *The Future of Human Settlements in the Rocky Mountain West*, The Printery, 1978.

Louis Rubin, editor, *Educational Reform for a Changing Society: Anticipating Tomorrow's Schools*, Allyn & Bacon, 1978.

Abdul Azig Said, editor, *Human Rights and World Order*, Transaction Books, 1978.

D. John Grove, editor, *Global Inequality: Politics and Socioeconomics*, Westview, 1979.

Louis Kriesberg, editor, *Research in Social Movements: Conflict or Change*, JAI Press, 1979.

Roslyn Dauber and Melinda Cain, editors, *Impact of Technological Change on Women*, Westview, 1980.

Helen Lopata, editor, *Research in the Interweave of Social Roles*, JAI Press, 1980.

Stein Rokkan, editor, *A Quarter Century of International Social Science*, UNESCO, 1980.

Visions of Desirable Societies, World Futures Federation, 1980.

Violence and Its Causes: Theoretical Methodological Aspects of Recent Research on Violence, UNESCO, 1980.

Magnus Haavelsrud, editor, *Approaching Disarmament Education*, IPC Science and Technology Press, 1981.

Erich Jantsch, editor, *The Evolutionary Vision: Toward a Unifying Paradigm of Physical, Biological and Sociocultural Evolution*, Westview, 1981.

Jerome Perlinski, editor, *The Spirit of Earth: Essays for the Teilhard Centennial*, Seabury Press, 1981.

Proceedings of the Conference on Women in Poverty: What Do We Know?, Johns Hopkins Press, 1982.

Raimo Vayrinen, editor, *Studies on Military Research and Development: The Arms Race and the Scientific Community*, UNESCO, 1983.

Don Carlson and Craig Comstock, editors, *Citizen Summitry: Keeping the Peace When It Matters Too Much To Be Left to Politicians*, Ark Communications Institute, 1986.

Carol Stoneburner and John Stoneburner, editors, *The Influence of Quaker Women on American History*, Edwin Mellen Press, 1986.

Festschrift (for Professor Chikiro Hosoya on retirement from Hitotsubashi University, Japan), Tokyo University Press, 1987.

Saul Mendlovitz and R.B.J. Walker, editors, *Towards a Just World Peace*, Butterworth, 1987.

Raimo Vayrien, editor, *The Quest for Peace: Transcending Collective Violence and War among Societies, Cultures, and States*, Sage Publications, 1987.

Kenneth Berne and Steven Tozer, editors, *Society as Educator in an Age of Transition*, National Society for the Study of Education, in press.

Kai Erickson, editor, *Working*, Yale University Press, in press.

Leonard Kenworthy, editor, *Current Quaker Concerns*, Friends General Conference and Friends United Press, in press.

Ilkka Tarpale and Eva Isaksson, editors, *Women and Militarism*, International Peace Bureau and Peace Union of Finland, in press.

Tom Woodhouse, editor, *Essays on Peace*, Adam Curle Bradford School on Peace Studies, Bradford University, in press.

OTHER

(Translator) Frederik Lodewijk Polak, *The Image of the Future*, two volumes, Oceana, 1961, abridged edition edited by Boulding, Jossey-Bass, 1972.

(Author of introduction) Eric Graham Howe, *War Dance: A Study of the Psychology of War*, Garland Publishing, 1972.

(Author of introduction) Mark May, *A Social Psychology of War and Peace*, Garland Publishing, 1972.

(Author of foreword) Natalie Sokoloff, *Between Money and Love: The Dialectics of Women's Home and Market Work*, Praeger, 1980.

Contributor to annuals and proceedings. Contributor of articles and reviews to *Marriage and Family Living, Human Relations, War/Peace Report, Bulletin of Atomic Scientists, International Social Science Journal, Japan Christian Quarterly, New Era, Journal of World Education, Contemporary Sociology*, and other journals. *International Peace Research Newsletter*, editor, 1963-68, North American editor, 1968-73 and 1984-87; guest editor of *Journal of Social Issues*, January, 1967, and *Journal of Conflict Resolution*, December, 1972; associate editor of *American Sociologist*, 1970-73, and *International Interactions*, 1973—; member of board of editors, *Peace and Change: A Journal of Peace Research*, 1971.

*   *   *

BOULDING, Kenneth E(wart) 1910-

PERSONAL: Born January 18, 1910, in Liverpool, England; came to United States in 1937, naturalized in 1948; son of William Couchman and Elizabeth Ann (Rowe) Boulding; married Elise Biorn-Hansen (a professor), August 31, 1941; children: John Russell, Mark David, Christine Ann, Philip Daniel, William Frederick. *Education:* Liverpool Collegiate School, student, 1923-28; Oxford University, B.A. (first class honors), 1931, M.A., 1939. *Religion:* Society of Friends.

ADDRESSES: Home—624 Pearl St., Boulder, Colo. 80302. *Office*—Institute of Behavioral Science, University of Colorado, Campus Box 484, Boulder, Colo. 80309.

CAREER: University of Edinburgh, Edinburgh, Scotland, assistant in economics, 1934-37; Colgate University, Hamilton, N.Y., instructor, 1937-41; League of Nations, Economic and Financial Section, Princeton, N.J., economist, 1941-42; Fisk University, Nashville, Tenn., professor of economics, 1942-43; Iowa State College (now University), Ames, associate professor, 1943-46, professor of economics, 1947-49; McGill University, Montreal, Quebec, Canada, Angus Professor of Economics and chairman of department, 1946-47; University of Michigan, Ann Arbor, professor of economics, 1949-68, Center for Research on Conflict Resolution, co-director, 1961-64, research director, 1964-65, director, 1965-66; University of Colorado, Boulder, visiting professor, 1967-68, professor of economics, 1968-77, distinguished professor of economics, 1977-80, distinguished professor emeritus, 1980—, project director and research associate with Institute of Behavioral Science, 1967—.

Visiting professor at University College of the West Indies, 1959-60, International Christian University (Japan), 1963-64, University of Natal, 1970, University of Edinburgh, 1972, and Ohio State University, 1981. Andrew D. White Professor-at-large, Cornell University, 1974-79; Barnette Miller Professor, Wellesley College, 1975; Tom Slick Professor, University of Texas, 1976-77; Montgomery Professor, Dartmouth College, 1978; Winegard Professor, University of Guelph, 1981; Downing research fellow, University of Melbourne, 1982. Lecturer in Brazil, 1953; visiting lecturer, Japanese Broadcasting Co., Tokyo, Japan, 1970.

MEMBER: American Economic Association (vice-president, 1958; president, 1968; distinguished fellow, 1969), Society for General Systems Research (president, 1957-59), International Studies Association (vice-president, 1969-70; president, 1974-75), American Academy of Arts and Sciences (fellow), American Association for the Advancement of Science (vice-president and chairman of Section K, 1966-67; president, 1979), American Philosophical Society (fellow), Peace Research Society International (president, 1969-70), Association for the Study of the Grants Economy (president, 1970—), National Academy of Sciences, Academy of Independent Scholars (co-president, 1980-86).

AWARDS, HONORS: Commonwealth fellow, University of Chicago, 1932-34; John Bates Clark Medal, American Economic Association, 1949; Ford Foundation Award for creative scholarship, 1952; fellow, Center for Advanced Study in the Behavioral Sciences, 1954-55; American Council of Learned Societies Prize for Distinguished Scholarship in the Humanities, 1962; nominated for National Book Award, 1970, for *Beyond Economics: Essays on Society, Religion, and Ethics*, and 1979, for *Stable Peace;* Frank E. Seidman Award, 1976; Rufus Jones Award, 1979; has received more than twenty-five honorary degrees from Colgate University, Michigan State University, Loyola University, Pace College, Earlham College, and other schools.

WRITINGS:

Economic Analysis, Harper, 1941, revised edition, 1948, 4th edition published in two volumes, 1966.

There Is a Spirit: The Nayler Sonnets (verse; first published in *Inward Light*, 1944), Fellowship Publications, 1945, reprinted, 1975.

The Economics of Peace, Prentice-Hall, 1945, reprinted, Books for Libraries, 1972.

A Reconstruction of Economics, Wiley, 1950, published with author's "The Fruits of Progress and the Dynamics of Distribution," Science Editions, 1962.

The Organizational Revolution: A Study in the Ethics of Economic Organization, Harper, 1953, reprinted, Greenwood Press, 1984.

The Image: Knowledge in Life and Society, University of Michigan Press, 1956, reprinted, 1977.

Sonnets for Elise (verse), privately printed [Ann Arbor, Mich.], 1957.

The Skills of the Economist, Howard Allen (Cleveland, Ohio), 1958.

Principles of Economic Policy, Prentice-Hall, 1958.

Conflict and Defense: A General Theory, Harper, 1962, reprinted, University Press of America, 1988.

The Meaning of the Twentieth Century: The Great Transition, Harper, 1964, reprinted, University Press of America, 1988.

The Impact of the Social Sciences, Rutgers University Press, 1966.

Beyond Economics: Essays on Society, Religion, and Ethics, University of Michigan Press, 1968.

Economics as a Science, McGraw, 1970, reprinted, University Press of America, 1988.

A Primer on Social Dynamics: History as Dialectics and Development, Free Press, 1970.

The Prospering of Truth (lecture), Friends Home Service Committee (London), 1970.

(With Elvis J. Stahr, Solomon Fabricent, and Martin R. Gainsbrugh) *Economics of Pollution,* New York University Press, 1971.

Collected Papers, Colorado Associated University Press, Volumes 1-2: *Economics,* edited by Fred R. Glahe, 1971, Volume 3: *Political Economy,* edited by Larry D. Singell, 1973, Volume 4: *Toward a General Social Science,* edited by Singell, 1974, Volume 5: *International Systems: Peace, Conflict, Resolution, and Politics,* edited by Singell, 1975, Volume 6: *Toward the Twenty-first Century,* edited by Singell, 1986.

The Appraisal of Change (in Japanese), Japan Broadcast Publishing Co. (Tokyo), 1972.

The Economy of Love and Fear: A Preface to Grants Economics, Wadsworth, 1973, revised edition published as *A Preface to Grants Economics: The Economy of Love and Fear,* Praeger, 1981.

Sonnets from the Interior Life, and Other Autobiographical Verse, Colorado Associated University Press, 1975.

Stable Peace, University of Texas Press, 1978.

Ecodynamics: A New Theory of Societal Evolution, Sage Publications, 1978.

(With Michael Kammen and Seymour Martin Lipset) *From Abundance to Scarcity: Implications for the American Tradition,* Ohio State University Press, 1978.

(With wife, Elise Boulding, and Guy M. Burgess) *The Social System of the Planet Earth,* Addison-Wesley, 1980.

Beasts, Ballads, and Bouldingisms: A Collection of Writings (verse), edited by Richard P. Beilock, Transaction Books, 1980.

Evolutionary Economics, Sage Publications, 1981.

Human Betterment, Sage Publications, 1985.

The World As a Total System, Sage Publications, 1985.

The Anatomy of Power, Sage Publications, in press.

EDITOR

(With W. G. Stigler) *Readings in Price Theory,* Volume 6, Irwin, 1952.

(With W. Allen Spivey, and contributor) *Linear Programming and the Theory of the Firm,* Macmillan, 1960.

(And author of preface with Emile Benoit, and contributor) *Disarmament and the Economy,* Harper, 1963, reprinted, Greenwood Press, 1978.

(Author of introduction, and contributor) *Peace and the War Industry,* Aldine, 1970, 2nd edition with a revised introduction, Transaction Books, 1973, reprinted, 1987.

(With Tapan Mukerjee, contributor with A. H. Gleason, and author of introduction) *Economic Imperialism: A Book of Readings,* University of Michigan Press, 1972.

(And contributor with Martin Pfaff) *Redistribution to the Rich and the Poor: The Grants Economics of Income Distribution,* Wadsworth, 1972.

(With M. Pfaff and Anita Pfaff) *Transfers in an Urbanized Economy: Theories and Effects of the Grants Economy,* Wadsworth, 1973.

(With Thomas Frederick Wilson) *Redistribution through the Financial System: The Grants Economics of Money and Credit,* Praeger, 1978.

(With H. R. Porter) *General Systems,* Society for General Systems Research, 1979.

(With Lawrence Senesh) *The Optimum Utilization of Knowledge: Making Knowledge Serve Human Betterment,* Westview, 1983.

(And contributor) *The Economics of Human Betterment: Proceedings of British Association for the Advancement of Science,* State University of New York Press, 1984.

PAMPHLETS; MONOGRAPHS

Paths of Glory: A New Way with War, Friends Book Centre (London), 1937.

New Nations for Old, Pendle Hill (Wallingford, Pa.), 1942.

The Practice of the Love of God (lecture), Book Committee, Religious Society of Friends (Philadelphia), 1942.

Religious Perspectives of College Teaching in Economics, Edward W. Hazen Foundation (New Haven, Conn.), 1950.

Economic Factors Bearing upon the Maintenance of Peace, Part I: *Perspectives on the Economics of Peace,* Institute for International Order (New York), 1961.

The Evolutionary Potential of Quakerism, Pendle Hill, 1964.

The Parameters of Politics, University of Illinois, 1966.

The Political Consequences of the Social Sciences (lecture), Michigan Center for Education in Politics, Western Michigan University, 1966.

(With Milton Mayer) *The Mayer/Boulding Dialogue on Peace Research,* edited by Cynthia Kerman and Carol Murphy, Pendle Hill, 1967.

Ethical Dilemmas in Religion and Nationalism, Ethical Culture Publications, 1968.

Friends and Social Change, Friends General Conference of the Religious Society of Friends, 1968.

(With Norman Sun) *The Effects of Military Expenditure upon the Economic Growth of Japan* (monograph), International Christian University (Tokyo), 1968.

Profile of the American Economy, U.S. Information Agency (Washington, D.C.), 1968.

The Role of Legitimacy in the Dynamics of Society (lecture), Center for Research, College of Business Administration, Pennsylvania State University, 1969.

The Role of the Church in the Making of Community and Identity (lecture), First Congregational Church (Greeley, Colo.), 1969.

The War Industry and the American Economy (lecture), Department of Economics, Northern Illinois University, 1970.

Toward the Year 2000, Social Science Education Consortium, 1971.

Toward a Pure Theory of Foundations, [Danbury, Conn.], 1972.

(With Alfred Kuhn and Lawrence Senesh) *System Analysis and Its Use in the Classroom,* Social Science Education Consortium, 1973.

Defense against Unwanted Change, Technology and Culture Seminar, Massachusetts Institute of Technology, 1974.

Justification for Inequality: The Contributions of Economic Theory, Technology and Culture Seminar, Massachusetts Institute of Technology, 1975.

Adam Smith As an Institutional Economist, P. K. Seidman Foundation, 1976.

Energy and the Environment, College of Commerce and Industry, University of Wyoming, 1976.

Normative Science and Agricultural Policy, Department of Agricultural Economics, Purdue University, 1978.

Malthus: The Miserific Vision and the Moral Hope, Institute of Nutrition, University of North Carolina, 1979.

The Next 200 Years: Can We Move toward a Sustainable High-Level Society?, Iowa State University, 1979.

CONTRIBUTOR

Economic Theory in Review, Indiana University Publications, 1950.

D. McCord Wright, editor, *The Impact of the Union: Eight Economic Theorists Evaluate the Labor Union Movement,* Harcourt, 1951.

B. Haley, editor, *A Survey of Contemporary Economics,* Volume 2, Irwin, 1952.

Contemporary Economic Problems, Case Institute of Technology, 1953.

Dudley Ward, editor, *Goals of Economic Life,* Harper, 1953.

Lynn White, Jr., editor, *Frontiers of Knowledge in the Study of Man,* Harper, 1956.

The Emerging Environment of Industrial Relations, Michigan State University, 1958.

Erich A. Walter, editor, *Religion and the State University,* University of Michigan Press, 1958.

Leo R. Ward, editor, *Ethics and the Social Sciences,* Notre Dame University Press, 1959.

Lyman Bryson, editor, *An Outline of Man's Knowledge of the Modern World,* McGraw, 1960.

Robert E. Spiller and Eric Larrabee, editors, *American Perspectives,* Harvard University Press, 1961.

Nicholas Spulber, editor, *Study of the Soviet Economy,* Indiana University Publications, 1961.

Richard B. Brandt, editor, *Social Justice,* Prentice-Hall, 1962.

Oscar Handlin and John Burchard, editors, *The Historian and the City,* MIT Press, 1963.

Alfred R. Oxenfeldt, editor, *Models of Markets,* Columbia University Press, 1963.

Robert L. Kahn and Elise Boulding, editors, *Power and Conflict in Organizations,* Basic Books, 1964.

Mihajlo D. Mesarovic, editor, *Views on General Systems Theory,* Wiley, 1964.

Bert F. Hoselitz, editor, *Economics and the Idea of Mankind,* Columbia University Press, 1965.

R. M. Hutchins and M. J. Adler, editors, *The Great Ideas Today,* Encyclopedia Britannica, 1965.

Elton B. McNeil, editor, *The Nature of Human Conflict,* Prentice-Hall, 1965.

Our Working World: Neighbors At Work, Teacher's Resource Unit, Science Research Associates (Chicago), 1965.

Richard Falk and S. Mendlovitz, editors, *The Strategy of World Order,* Volume 1: *Towards a Theory of War Prevention,* Volume 4: *Disarmament and Economic Development,* World Law Fund (New York), 1966.

Human Values on the Spaceship Earth, Council Press (National Council of the Churches of Christ), 1966.

J. D. Jennings and E. A. Hoebel, editors, *Readings in Anthropology,* 2nd edition, McGraw, 1966.

John G. Kirk, editor, *America Now,* Atheneum, 1968.

Gerald P. McCarthy, editor, *Science, Philosophy, Religion,* Air Force Weapons Laboratory, Kirtland Air Force Base (New Mexico), 1968.

The Crisis of Survival, Scott, Foresman, 1970.

Roe L. Johns and others, editors, *Economic Factors Affecting the Financing of Education,* Volume 2, National Educational Finance Project (Gainesville, Fla.), 1970.

The Philosophy of Peace Research, Volume 1: *Philosophy of Peace Research,* Van Gorcum & Company (Assen, Netherlands), 1970.

R. H. Wagenberg, editor, *Canada and the United States in the World of the Seventies,* Simon & Schuster, 1970.

Economic Perspectives of Boulding and Samuelson, Whittemore School of Business and Economics, University of New Hampshire, 1971.

Economics of Pollution (lectures), New York University Press, 1971.

Irving Morrissett and W. W. Stevens, Jr., editors, *Social Science in the Schools,* Holt, Rinehart and Winston, 1971.

The Need for Reform of National Income Statistics, American Statistical Association (Washington, D.C.), 1971.

Reappraisal of the Federal Reserve Discount Mechanism, Volume 2, Board of Governors of the Federal Reserve System (Washington, D.C.), 1971.

John A. Behnke, editor, *Challenging Biological Problems: Directions toward Their Solution,* Oxford University Press, 1972.

(With Martin Pfaff) Gustav Ranis, editor, *The Gap between Rich and Poor Nations,* Macmillan, 1972.

Richard N. Rosecrance, editor, *The Future of the International Strategic System,* Chandler Publishing Company, 1972.

Challenge to Leadership: Managing in a Changing World, Free Press, for the Conference Board, 1973.

Bernard Udis, editor, *The Economic Consequences of Reduced Military Spending,* Heath, 1973.

Philip P. Wiener, editor-in-chief, *Dictionary of the History of Ideas,* Volume II, Scribner's, 1973.

Ronald O. Clarke and Peter List, editors, *Environmental Spectrum: Social and Economic Views on the Quality of Life,* Van Nostrand, 1974.

John Eatweil, Murray Milgate, and Peter Newman, editors, *The New Palgrave: A Dictionary of Economics,* four volumes, Stockton Press, 1987.

Contributor to several other collections of essays, and contributor of occasional papers to numerous collections of proceedings, conferences, and symposia. Contributor to *Encyclopedia Britannica, International Encyclopedia of the Social Sciences,* and to numerous festschrifts, annals, and annual yearbooks.

OTHER

(Author of foreword) T. R. Malthus, *Population, the First Essay,* Ann Arbor Paperbacks, 1959.

(Author of introduction) Clyde Eagleton, *Analysis of the Problem of War,* Garland Publishing, 1972.

(With Harrison Brown, Renee C. Fox, and Edward Edelson) *Science, Development, and Human Values* (sound recording), American Assocation for the Advancement of Science, 1973.

(Author of foreword) Roger M. Downs and David Stea, editors, *Image and Environment: Cognitive Mapping and Spatial Behavior,* Aldine, 1973.

(Author of foreword) Gerhard Hirschfeld, *The People: Growth and Survival,* Aldine for the Council for the Study of Mankind, 1973.

(Author of foreword) Fred Polak, *The Image of the Future,* translated from the Dutch and abridged by Elise Boulding, Jossey Bass/Elsevier, 1973.

(Author of introduction) Richard G. Wilkinson, *Poverty and Progress: An Ecological Perspective on Economic Development,* Praeger, 1973.

(Author of foreword) Cynthia Kerman, *Creative Tension: The Life and Thought of Kenneth Boulding,* University of Michigan Press, 1974.

(Author of foreword) Alfred Kuhn, *The Logic of Social Systems,* Jossey-Bass, 1974.

The Next 200 Years: Can We Move toward a Sustainable High-Level Society? (sound recording), Media Resources Center, Iowa State University, 1976.

Contributor of verse to several books and periodicals, and of reviews and articles to numerous journals, including *Economic Journal, American Friend, Friends Intelligencer, American Economic Review, Nation, Canadian Journal of Economics and Political Science, Christian Century, Social Action, Journal of Higher Education, Michigan Alumnus Quarterly Review, Journal of Religious Thought, American Anthropologist, Daedalus, Contemporary Psychology, New Republic, American Journal of Orthopsychiatry, Monthly Labor Review, Science, Washington Post, New York Review of Books, New York Times Book Review,* and *Saturday Review.* Member of editorial board, *Journal of Conflict Resolution, American Behavioral Scientist, Journal of Business Ethics, Journal of Cultural Economics, Public Choice,* and other publications. Several of Boulding's works have been translated into other languages, including German, French, Spanish, Portuguese, Turkish, Japanese, and Burmese.

SIDELIGHTS: Throughout his long and distinguished career, renowned economist, educator, author, and pacifist Kenneth E. Boulding has sought to synthesize the diversity of economic theory and the social sciences. In an essay in Martin Pfaff's *Frontiers in Social Thought: Essays in Honor of Kenneth E. Boulding,* Cynthia Earl Kerman describes Boulding as "a person who grew up in the poverty-stricken 'inner city' of Liverpool, broke through the class system to achieve an excellent education, had both scientific and literary leanings, became a well-known American economist, then snapped the bonds of economics to extend his thinking into wide-ranging fields—a person who is a religious mystic and a poet as well as a social scientist." In *American Economist,* Boulding explains his efforts to perceive the parts as well as the integrated whole: "My position still is that human knowledge has an essential unity which is, however, characterized by great diversity of methodologies of learning and testing, and that our images of value are just as much part of this unity as our images of which we think of as fact."

"If my life philosophy can be summed up in a sentence," says Boulding, "it is that I believe that there is such a thing as human betterment—a magnificent, multi-dimensional, complex structure—a cathedral of the mind—and I think human decisions should be judged by the extent to which they promote it. This involves seeing the world as a total system." In his *The World As a Total System* and *Human Betterment,* Boulding explains his perception of this system. Wassily Leontief, the 1973 Nobel Prize winner in economics, reviewed these two books for the *New York Times Book Review* and he states: "Boulding's lecturing and writing have clearly expanded rapidly beyond the confines of a single discipline. The thoughts presented in these two books encompass all aspects of the human species." Leontief concludes: "The reader of these volumes will be taken on a well-organized tour of the major problems of the world. He will be introduced to many new ideas and learn many interesting facts that he was ignorant of, and be reminded of many facts and ideas he once knew but had forgotten. He will also enjoy close contact with the unusually lively and imaginative mind of his guide, and turn

the last page comfortably assured that despite all its troubles the human race has a good—though not a 100 percent—chance of becoming better and better, in the future."

Noting that "Boulding's brilliance and manyfold activity in diverse fields have earned him a reputation as one of the outstanding social scientists of our age," Pfaff adds that "perhaps his greatest contribution to human evolution will be found in the effect that his vision of man and society has in raising the level of discourse out of the existing tracks, and in producing a new consciousness on the part of man about his role and ultimate destiny." Kerman maintains that "what we really see in Kenneth Boulding, beyond whatever regularities or truths we may think we discover, is a tremendous unpredictable flow of creative energy that bloweth where it listeth; and most of the time I suspect he does whatever he does just for fun. Fortunately, what is fun for him often turns out to be education, illumination, entertainment or benefit for the rest of us."

BIOGRAPHICAL/CRITICAL SOURCES:

BOOKS

Chisholm, Anne, *Philosophers of the Earth,* Dutton, 1972.

Economics 1973-1974: Text, Dushkin, 1973.

Kerber, Walter, *Die Verteilungstheorie von Kenneth E. Boulding,* Duncker and Humblot, 1966.

Kerman, Cynthia, *Creative Tension: The Life and Thought of Kenneth Boulding,* University of Michigan Press, 1974.

Oltmans, Willem L., editor, *On Growth: The Crisis of Exploding Population and Resource Depletion,* G. P. Putnam's Sons/Capricorn Books, 1974.

Pfaff, Martin, *Frontiers in Social Thought: Essays in Honor of Kenneth E. Boulding,* North-Holland, 1976.

Seligman, Ben B., *Main Currents in Modern Economics,* Free Press of Glencoe, 1962.

Silk, Leonard, *The Economists,* Basic Books, 1976.

PERIODICALS

American Historical Review, December, 1972.
American Journal of Sociology, September, 1969.
American Political Science Review, June, 1972.
American Sociological Review, August, 1971.
British Book News, January, 1985, July, 1985.
Business Week, January 4, 1969.
Challenge, July/August, 1973.
Christian Century, December 13, 1967, February 12, 1969, March 28, 1979.
Commonweal, April 18, 1969.
Economist, July 25, 1970.
Journal of Politics, November, 1971, August, 1979.
Library Journal, May 15, 1970, May 1, 1971.
Los Angeles Times, March 22, 1979.
New York Times, March 19, 1979.
New York Times Book Review, January 12, 1986.
Psychology Today, January, 1973.
Reporter, December 3, 1964.
Saturday Review, December 19, 1964, November 15, 1968.
Social Forces, September, 1971, June, 1979.
Times Literary Supplement, February 17, 1966.
Virginia Quarterly Review, winter, 1965.
Western Humanities Review, autumn, 1967.
World History Review, autumn, 1967.

*   *   *

BOURRICAUD, Francois 1922-

PERSONAL: Born January 28, 1922, in St. Martin du Bois, France; son of Andre R. and Simone (Parraud) Bourricaud.

ADDRESSES: Home—41 Rue des Martyrs, Paris 9, France. *Office*—Department of Sociology, University of Paris, Paris 5, France.

CAREER: Has taught at universities in Paris, Bordeaux, Nanterre, and elsewhere in France; University of Paris, Paris, France, professor of sociology, 1968—.

WRITINGS:

(Editor) *Elements pour une sociologie de Cachon*, Plon, 1955.
Esquisse d'une theorie de l'autorite, Plon, 1961, 2nd edition, 1970.
Changements a Puno: Etude de sociologie andine, Institut des Hautes Etudes de l'Amerique Latine, University of Paris, 1962.
Pouvoir et societe dans le Perou contemporain, A. Colin, 1967, translation by Paul Stevenson published as *Power and Society in Contemporary Peru*, Praeger, 1970.
Universites a la derive, Stock, 1971.
(With others) *Intellectuals and Change*, American Academy of Arts and Sciences, 1972.
L'individualisme institutionnel: essai sur la sociologie de Talcott Parsons, Presses universitaires de France, 1977, translation by Arthur Goldhammer published as *The Sociology of Talcott Parsons*, University of Chicago Press, 1981.
La reforme universitaire en France et ses deboires, Fondation europeenne de la culture, 1977.
Le bricolage ideologique: essai sur les intellectuels et les passions democratiques, Presses universitaires de France, 1980.
Science et theorie de l'opinion publique, Retz, 1981.
(Editor) *Dictionnaire critique de la sociologie*, Presses universitaires de France, 1982.
Le retour de la droite, Calmann-Levy, 1986.†

*   *   *

BOWSER, Eileen   1928-

PERSONAL: Born January 18, 1928, in Columbia Station, Ohio; daughter of Roy and Florence (Doyle) Putt; married William Patton Bowser, June 12, 1950. *Education:* Marietta College, B.A., 1950; University of North Carolina, M.A., 1953.

ADDRESSES: Office—Department of Film, Museum of Modern Art, 11 West 53rd St., New York, N.Y. 10019.

CAREER: Museum of Modern Art, New York, N.Y., member of staff, 1953-55, secretary to curator of film department, 1955-57, research assistant, 1957-59, curatorial assistant, 1959-61, cataloger for D. W. Griffith Collection, 1961, curatorial assistant, 1961-65, assistant curator, 1965-69, curator of film department, 1976—, member of archives advisory committee, 1971—. Curator of film series on David Wark Griffith, 1965 and 1975, Carl-Theodor Dreyer, the art of the twenties, and recent museum acquisitions. Guest lecturer, Columbia University, 1979. Associate, Columbia University Seminars on Cinema and Interdisciplinary Interpretation. Lecturer and participant in national and international symposiums. Chairman, National Education Association panel on film preservation. Member of Exceptional Photoplay Committee of National Board of Review. Reviewer of proposals for National Education Association, National Endowment for the Humanities, and Social Sciences and Humanities Research Council of Canada. Consultant to publishers on cinema projects.

MEMBER: Federation Internationale des Archives du Film (member of executive committee, 1969—; president of documentation commission, 1972-81; vice-president, 1977-85), Film Archives Advisory Committee.

WRITINGS:

Carl Dreyer (monograph), Museum of Modern Art, 1964.
(Author of revision) Iris Barry, *D. W. Griffith: American Film Master* (monograph), Museum of Modern Art, 2nd edition, 1965.
(Editor and contributor) *Film Notes*, Museum of Modern Art, 1969.
(Editor and author of introduction) *Biograph Bulletins, 1908-1912*, Farrar, Straus, 1973.
Harold Lloyd's Short Comedies, for Raymond Borde (monograph), Museum of Modern Art, 1974.
(Contributor) Ted Perry, editor, *Performing Arts Resources*, Volume II, Drama Book Specialists, 1975.
David Wark Griffith, Jugosovenska Kinoteka (Belgrade), 1979.
(Editor with John Kuiper and contributor) *A Handbook for Film Archives*, Federation Internationale des Archives du Film (Brussels), 1980.
(With Richard Griffith and Arthur Mayer) *The Movies*, 3rd edition, 1981.
(Contributor) Roger Holman, editor, *Cinema 1900-1906*, Volume I (proceedings of 1978 Brighton Symposium), Federation Internationale des Archives du Film, 1982.
(Contributor) Susan Swartburg, editor, *Conservation in the Library*, Greenwood Press, 1983.
(Contributor) John Fell, editor, *Film Before Griffith*, University of California Press, 1983.
(Contributor) *David Wark Griffith: Etudes sous la direction de Jean Mottet*, Publications de la Sorbonne (Paris), 1984.
(Contributor and author of introduction) *Circulating Film Library Catalog*, Museum of Modern Art, 1984.
(Contributor) *Les premiers ans du cinema francais*, Actes du V Colloque International de l'Institut Jean Vigo (Perpignan, France), 1985.
(Contributor) Paolo Cherchi Usai, editor, *Vitagraph Co. of America*, Edizioni Studio Tesi (Pordenone, Italy), 1987.
(Editor and contributor) *The Slapstick Symposium*, Film Archives Advisory Committee, 1988.

Contributor to professional journals, including *Griffithiana, Cahiers de la Cinematheque, Bianco e Nero*, and *Cinema Journal*.

WORK IN PROGRESS: Transformation of Cinema: 1907-1915, Volume II of the series edited by Charles Harpole, "The History of American Film," published by Scribners; a revised edition of *A Handbook for Film Archives*.

*   *   *

BOYD, Malcolm   1923-

PERSONAL: Born June 8, 1923, in New York, N.Y.; son of Melville (a financier) and Beatrice (Lowrie) Boyd. *Education:* University of Arizona, B.A. in English, 1944; Divinity School of the Pacific, B.D., 1954; Oxford University, additional study, 1954-55; studied at an ecumenical institute in Geneva, Switzerland; Union Theological Seminary, S.T.M., 1956; member of work-study program at the Taize community in France, 1957.

ADDRESSES: Office—St. Augustine by-the-Sea, 1227 Fourth St., Santa Monica, Calif. 90401.

CAREER: Author, social commentator, and activist. Foote, Cone, & Belding Advertising Agency, Hollywood, Calif., copywriter, 1945-46; director of a homemakers' hour on radio, Hollywood; writer and producer, Republic Pictures and Samuel Goldwyn Productions, 1947-49; Pickford, Rogers, & Boyd, Inc., New York, N.Y., founder with Mary Pickford and Buddy Rogers, 1949, vice-president and general manager, 1949-51. Ordained Episcopal priest, 1955; St. George's Episcopal Church, Indianapolis, Ind., rector, 1957-59; Colorado State University, Fort Collins, Episcopal chaplain, 1959-61; Wayne State University, Detroit, Mich., Protestant chaplain, 1961-64; Grace Episcopal Church, Detroit, assistant priest, 1961-64; Church of the Atonement, Washington, D.C., assistant pastor, 1964-68, on leave as chaplain-at-large to American universities and colleges, beginning 1965; appointed chaplain of Integrity, 1981; St. Augustine by-the-Sea Episcopal Church, Santa Monica, Calif., writer-priest in residence, 1981—. Lecturer, World Council of Churches, 1955, and 1964; national field representative, Episcopal Society for Cultural and Racial Unity, 1965-68. Yale University, Calhoun College, resident fellow, 1968-71, associate fellow, 1971-75; resident guest, Mishkenot Sha'ananim, Jerusalem, 1974. Host of television specials, including "Sex in the Seventies," CBS-TV, 1975. Member, Los Angeles City/County A.I.D.S. Task Force, 1985—.

MEMBER: PEN (president, Los Angeles Center, 1984-87), National Council of Churches (member of film awards committee, 1965), Clergy and Laity Concerned, National Association for the Advancement of Colored People, Episcopal Society for Cultural and Racial Unity.

AWARDS, HONORS: Selected by *Life* magazine as one of the "100 Most Important Young Men and Women in the United States," 1962; Integrity Award, 1978, "for contribution to the gay movement and the gay Christian community"; received award from American Hebrew Congregations, 1980.

WRITINGS:

Crisis in Communication, Doubleday, 1957.
Christ and Celebrity Gods, Seabury, 1958.
Focus: Rethinking the Meaning of Our Evangelism, Morehouse, 1960.
If I Go down to Hell, Morehouse, 1962.
(Contributor) *Christianity and the Contemporary Arts*, Abingdon, 1962.
The Hunger, The Thirst, Morehouse, 1964.
(Editor) *On the Battle Lines* (essays), Morehouse, 1964.
Are You Running with Me, Jesus? (prayers), Holt, 1965.
Free to Live, Free to Die (secular meditations), Holt, 1967.
(Contributor) Edward Fiske, *Witness to a Generation*, Bobbs-Merrill, 1967.
(Editor) *The Underground Church*, Sheed & Ward, 1968.
(Contributor) *You Can't Kill the Dream*, John Knox, 1968.
Malcolm Boyd's Book of Days, Random House, 1968.
The Fantasy Worlds of Peter Stone, and Other Fables, Harper, 1969.
As I Live and Breathe: Stages of an Autobiography, Random House, 1970.
My Fellow Americans, Holt, 1970.
Human Like Me, Jesus, Simon & Schuster, 1971.
The Lover, Word Book, 1972.
(With Paul Conrad) *When in the Course of Human Events*, Sheed & Ward, 1973.
The Runner, Word Books, 1974.
Christian: Its Meanings in an Age of Future Shock, Hawthorn, 1975.

The Alleluia Affair, Word Books, 1975.
Am I Running with You, God?, Doubleday, 1978.
Take off the Masks, Doubleday, 1978, revised edition, New Society, 1984.
Look Back in Joy: Celebration of Gay Lovers, Gay Sunshine, 1981.
Half Laughing/Half Crying: Songs for Myself, St. Martin's, 1986.
Gay Priest: An Inner Journey, St. Martin's, 1986.
(Contributor) Mark Thompson, editor, *Gay Spirit: Myth and Meaning*, St. Martin's, 1987.

Author of plays, all produced in New York City: "They Aren't Real to Me," 1962; "The Job," 1962; "Study in Color," 1962; "Boy" and "The Community," produced on a double bill, 1964. Also co-author of screenplays, including, with Ervin Zavada, "Are You Running with Me, Jesus?," based on Boyd's book of the same name. Also author of weekly column for *Pittsburgh Courier*, 1963-65; motion picture columnist for *Episcopalian*, *United Church Herald*, *Christian Century*, *Presbyterian Survey*, and *Canadian Churchman*; contributing editor, *Renewal and Integrity Forum*; reviewer of devotional books, *Christian Century*, 1974-81; contributor of reviews to *Los Angeles Times Book Review*; occasional contributor of articles to *Ms.*, *New York Times*, *Washington Post*, *Los Angeles Times*, *Parade*, *Advocate*, and many other periodicals.

WORK IN PROGRESS: "A TV screenplay on the winter solstice for Pacen Productions, and two new book projects—one, my dream journal and inner journey; the other, a social history about the centrality of food in human life."

SIDELIGHTS: Malcolm Boyd, the "expresso priest" who moved religion into coffeehouses during the 1960s, believes that writers should get involved in social issues. His own life as a civil rights activist, anti-Vietnam War protester, and gay Episcopalian priest reflects that philosophy—both its rewards and risks. Boyd first became nationally known in the mid-sixties when his avant-garde book of prayers, *Are You Running with Me, Jesus?*, became an unexpected bestseller. But long before that, Boyd had embarked upon a course of social activism that would shape his writing and influence his career. Boyd's willingness to act on his beliefs has often generated controversy. However, as Mark Henry reports in the *Los Angeles Times*, Boyd never went looking for causes. Instead, Boyd told Henry, "I participated in the life of my time."

Boyd did not begin his career as a clergyman. Between the years 1945 and 1951, he worked as a writer and director in the fields of advertising and motion pictures in Hollywood. In 1949, along with Mary Pickford and Buddy Rogers, Boyd formed Pickford, Rogers, & Boyd, Inc., an agency that packaged shows for radio and television. Respect for his reputation in the media field spread throughout Hollywood to the extent that, in 1949, Boyd was elected the first president of the Television Producers Association of Hollywood.

However, in 1951, to the amazement of many of his associates, Boyd gave up his promising career and enrolled in the Divinity School of the Pacific in preparation for a career in the Episcopal ministry. In an interview with Helen Dudar for the *New York Post*, Boyd comments: "It's too complex to explain briefly, but in a somewhat simplified form, this is what happened. I was involved in mass media from a standpoint of taking and exploiting, and I became totally dissatisfied with it. My life had little meaning beyond each day."

After his theological studies, which included a year of training at Oxford University and a year of study under Reinhold Niebuhr at the Union Theological Seminary, Boyd began the first assignment of what many people consider a very controversial religious career and life.

Boyd was assigned to a parish in Indianapolis whose membership was composed of white, middle-class people. He invited a black minister to exchange gatherings with him for one Sunday, and the congregation's angry response introduced Boyd to the power of prejudice in society during this period. This experience might also have been the catalyst that triggered Boyd's later dedication to the civil rights movement.

Boyd's next assignment was at Colorado State University in 1959 where, according to Julius Duscha of the *New York Times,* he "received nationwide attention as well as his first ecclesiastical rebuke when he moved his ministry off the campus into the Golden Grape Coffee House and student beer joints. . . . He ruffled his superiors . . . when he heard confessions in a bar, organized a series of 'expresso nights' in a converted garage and publicly charged Christianity with 'smugness' and 'snobbishness.' "

In 1966 Boyd played a month-long engagement at the 'hungry i' nightclub in San Francisco and donated his salary ($1,000 a week) to civil rights organizations. His act at the club, which followed Dick Gregory's, generally consisted of an hour-long reading from his book of "pop" prayers *Are You Running with Me, Jesus?*

During the next several years Boyd almost totally committed himself to the civil rights movement. His writings reflect this commitment as well as his involvement with such activities as black voter registration in the south and participation in freedom rides from the south to the north.

In 1978, still dissatisfied with the charade he had been living, Boyd dropped the mask that had been hiding his homosexuality and openly declared himself a gay priest. His autobiographical book, *Take off the Masks,* documents the rewards—and costs—of his coming out. "Suddenly, upon announcing that I was gay, I knew that in a strange sense I had lost my life," Boyd wrote, then continued: "But I knew that in the deepest recesses of my soul I had chosen life, with its unpredictable valleys and mountains, its tests and glories, over the plastic death of security, withdrawal, monochrome rigidity, and the refusal to risk." The repercussions of Boyd's decision proved to be deep and long-lasting. There was a backlash from the conservative arm of the Episcopal clergy, and some members demanded his expulsion from the priesthood. Boyd did not leave. Though he never abandoned his ministry, Boyd did sever his ties with organized religion for a time.

Yet the book also received strong support from some quarters. *Christian Century* critic E. J. Curtin applauded *Take off the Masks* as "a testament to truth and courage, an angry, sad, joyful challenge to those who buy the social lie and seek to escape from freedom. Those who seek titillation should look elsewhere. This is a very sensitive story of one man's religious and sexual liberation." *Library Journal* contributor G. M. Gerdes also commended Boyd's honesty and his straightforward approach, which "avoids melodrama, sentimental piety, and defensiveness as he reveals the flesh and soul of a media-myth we thought we knew." Boyd also received scores of letters from readers whose own lives had mirrored his experience in some way.

Even with the support he received, Boyd experienced a personal crisis during the late 1970s and early 1980s. Pulled in conflicting directions, uncertain as to how to support himself

financially, he considered abandoning his ministry to return to motion picture and television work. Instead Boyd decided to work for change from within. "I'm angry toward the Episcopal church for many things, but that [is] all the more reason to remain a priest and work for change," he told Henry. "The people who are going to change anything are the ones who have to be inside it. And they change a lot just being there."

Over time, Boyd has found a niche for himself within the clergy. In 1981, he was invited to be writer-priest in residence at St. Augustine by-the-Sea Episcopal Church in Santa Monica. In addition to preaching every third week, Boyd works to support gay/lesbian causes and to educate the public about AIDS. Still a prolific writer, Boyd served as president of the Los Angeles Center of PEN from 1984 to 1987, in which capacity he developed a special concern for imprisoned writers under authoritarian regimes. As he told *CA:* "I think it's essential to be part of the community of one's time. One has to know what's happened in the world, and one has to feel the pain of it and to cry and to laugh. Unless one is willing and able to do this, art moves into a vacuum."

The Malcolm Boyd Collection and Archives was established at Boston University in 1973.

MEDIA ADAPTATIONS: All of Boyd's plays have appeared on television; film adaptations have been made of "The Job," "Study in Color," and "Boy," and are distributed nationally by the Anti-Defamation League of B'nai B'rith in New York City.

CA INTERVIEW

CA interviewed Malcolm Boyd by telephone on November 17, 1987 at his home in Santa Monica, California.

CA: The last time you spoke to CA, *in November 1980, you were in the midst of a career change and what you described as a "crisis" about the future. What direction has your life taken?*

BOYD: I've become writer-priest in residence at St. Augustine by-the-Sea Episcopal Church in Santa Monica, and I've actually been there now for six years. This has freed me to do my creative work and yet to have a basic place. It's an unusual parish in which I am an openly gay priest and for several years there was also a woman priest there. And there's no subterfuge or hypocrisy about anything. I have also been the president of the Los Angeles Center of PEN for three terms.

CA: Let's focus for a minute on your return to organized religion. Seven years ago you had almost divorced yourself from it, telling CA *"organized religion seems to be anti-God." Now you're affiliated with an Episcopal church. What prompted your return?*

BOYD: I've always had a Virginia Woolf kind of marriage to the Church. I loathe it and also love it. It's such a whore; at the same time it has saintliness. Gay people throughout history have had this very ambiguous relationship to organized religion because, frankly, it was the place where gay people could go. That's why so many so-called celibate priests have been there. There is music, liturgy, drama, color, intellectual life, and theology. So there's always been this ambiguous situation between gay people and the Church. I simply reflected that myself and do.

CA: Did the Church make overtures to you?

BOYD: Yes, I was invited and responded gratefully. But it wasn't black or white. Life is always in the grays, and one is always involved in give and take if one is really open to life. In other words, I've never felt there are good guys and bad guys in anything. You have a mix and you have to find your own space. I think we always have to be evolving and changing. So I didn't "return to the Church" in a Greer Garson dramatic Oscar-winning scene of choosing white over black. I'm a deeply spiritual person, a deeply religious person. I've always cared a great deal about God, about Christ. I'm very open to other spiritual impulses, particularly Buddhism. Something else that has happened to me spiritually is Jungian dream analysis. I've been very deeply involved in that for the past three years: I keep a dream journal; I've been on a shamanic inner journey.

CA: It all seems to fit in with working at the parish?

BOYD: It does, and it also fits under a label of "spiritual" in preference to a label of "religion," because the umbrella is a little more inclusive, I think.

CA: Before you publically acknowledged your homosexuality you predicted that the Church's response would be censure and possible excommunication. What actually happened?

BOYD: Some unfriendly bishops did ask that I be brought to trial and removed from the Church. They felt that my openness about being gay was wrong and the fact that I lived in a relationship openly with another man was a lifestyle that should be censured. But then my bishop, Paul Moore, Jr., the Bishop of New York, along with the standing committee of the diocese refused those demands.

CA: That must have been gratifying for you.

BOYD: Yes, it was, but again we're in grays, not black or white. I have no illusion that I've been accepted by the Church or am loved either in it or by it. Many closeted homosexual bishops and people in high places have made my life quite difficult.

CA: Yet there have also been groups that have made you welcome there.

BOYD: There has been the mix. I think some people couldn't have stood this. They would have had a nervous breakdown or become alcoholic or committed suicide. It really hasn't been easy at all. But it is a joyful story rather than a tragic one. I give myself credit along with other people: I persevered and had faith and had hope and, perhaps, a bit of courage.

CA: Do you think that the organized Church has become more responsive to human needs?

BOYD: I'm not sure. When you look around now at the news about gay people, in parts of the Church you find some very sad stories in terms of repression, nonrecognition, betrayal, cruelty, psychological brutality.

CA: Those are pretty heavy charges.

BOYD: And it's heavy to have it done to you. On the other hand, there are responses, expressions of hope, reaching out in love. And I want to balance my first group of criticisms with an equally strong group of affirmations. I'd say it's up for grabs right now. I don't know what the future will hold. Whether this society will get into scapegoating—and gay men and lesbians may be in the forefront of that—or, if the society is becoming more tolerant of difference, more accepting, more understanding. I would tend to think the latter is true.

CA: You've argued that the Church should accept homosexual behavior as a legitimate alternative that is in every way consistent with the Judeo-Christian ethical tradition. What is your response to those who argue that homosexual behavior contradicts the very doctrines the gay priest is supposed to be teaching?

BOYD: There are several things here. Homosexual behavior is as varied as heterosexual behavior. Obviously there is biblical interpretation. There are those who overlook the overarching themes of the Old Testament, which are justice and deliverance, and the over-arching theme of the New Testament, which is the unconditional love of God in Jesus Christ. There are people who pick out particular references and just keep bringing them up by rote. These people overlook biblical scholarship, which increasingly has offered different interpretations of those traditional texts. So, it does boil down to the question of biblical scholarship and one's interpretation of what scripture is saying.

CA: So there again it seems to be a gray area where there may never be a black or white; it depends on what passages you choose and how you interpret them.

BOYD: I think this will probably always be a gray area with people, presumably sincere, on both sides having different interpretations. Then, another aspect of this is that Jesus never mentioned homosexuality, which I think is major because then how can one say he was opposed to it. Jesus, who lived in a community of men, Jesus, who had a relationship to women that was quite avant-garde for religious men of his period. It may boil down for me to a definition of God. I was recently in a discussion with some rather rigorous biblical fundamentalists who adhered to a traditional view of certain passages of scripture. Period. And I just had to say honestly, "Your God is different from my God. We have different Gods." And that is basic. But my God doesn't happen to run torture chambers and isn't flogging people, and my God is inclusive, not exclusive, is accepting and is loving.

CA: What is your relationship with the more conservative elements in the gay clergy?

BOYD: Well, let's see, do I know any?

CA: I understand there is a group of gay clergy within the Episcopal church who are homosexual but who are working toward reconciling themselves towards either abstinence or heterosexuality.

BOYD: Actually I don't know these people, but I wouldn't call them gay—I would call them homosexual. Homosexual to me is a word like Negro—a white word about black people. Black people have chosen black as a word to describe themselves, and homosexual, in my view relates to one's sexual orientation; gay relates to one's lifestyle and one's life commitment. It is utterly tragic to ask a Jew to become a Christian, to ask someone black to appear to be white, to ask someone homosexual to be heterosexual. Here you get into the situation where well-meaning women sometimes marry these tragically divided men, and their lives are ruined. The dishonesty of this I find extremely offensive. Something very key to me in my coming out—because certain old friends didn't understand why I hadn't been able to come out to them before—was that I couldn't come out until my self-esteem had reached a place where I felt good enough about myself as gay to see it as good news and want to share it. So if I were gay and feeling guilty about it or wanting to become something else, I would find this not only tragic but a denial of spirituality.

CA: And perhaps those homosexuals who are not "gay" have not reached that level of self-acceptance?

BOYD: I don't want to say something judgmental about anyone else. I do want to say something about celibacy, which I consider valid as a calling. I think it's practiced by a very, very small number of people.

CA: And most of them in the Catholic church.

BOYD: I don't think in the Catholic church that many who say they are celibate are celibate at all. A few may be. That's what I'm trying to say. Celibacy has become a label that permitted masturbation, permitted sexual fantasy. I have letters from hundreds of Roman Catholic priests who are very torn because they feel a real calling to love and serve God; yet they are having promiscuous sex because they are not celibate and have very strong needs. They are very confused. For the vast majority of people celibacy is not a valid alternative. And those Roman Catholic priests who have gotten happily married, often to ex-nuns, would understand what I'm talking about.

But this is a question for everyone, not just Roman Catholics. It's based on one's view of sex. If people see sex as dirty or "sinful," then some weird things start happening. I see sex as healthy, God-given, as natural as breathing. Those few people who are legitimately celibate can take that sexual energy and channel it in another way. And I applaud them and support them. For those who cannot, I think it's necessary to come to terms with one's sexual energy. And the Church hasn't been helpful in much of this, particularly when it has denounced "lust," which I can see as a very healthy energy between two people making love.

CA: To what extent do you think a society can tolerate sexual freedom without a collapse of morality?

BOYD: Unless there is authentic sexual freedom, which is responsibility, not license, the society is going to be repressed and the energy that is repressed is going to come out in war, in terror, in very macho attitudes that are dangerous. Incidentally, I want to say about myself that I live in a relationship with another man. It is a monogamous relationship; it is commitment. We own a home together; we are an extended family. He is a writer and an editor.

CA: But certainly that's not the only lifestyle that you tolerate or accept.

BOYD: With AIDS, particularly—which is not a homosexual disease at all, but a medical problem—I think that heterosexuals and gay people alike had better think pretty seriously about promiscuity, about sex with multiple partners, really about anything that is unsafe. We've come to a moment in

history when we have to look at sexuality in a medical way, quite differently than before. I also think that emotionally—and again I'm not doing a prescription for society, that would be very paternalistic—but for myself, the emotional security of a basic partner and a sense of home is awfully helpful in dealing with the kind of future shock world we live in. In Los Angeles this means a seven-point earthquake can hit while you're reading the morning paper. But for all of us it's life in the fast lane now. We're living under a lot of stress.

CA: Does this represent a change from the way the gay movement was when you came out of the closet eleven years ago?

BOYD: The gay movement has undergone an incredible revolution. That time was a little like a speakeasy, flapper era for gays. AIDS has brought a tremendous sense of responsibility, of caring for oneself and for others. Before, the coming out process was seen as coming outside into the world and revealing oneself; what has occurred more recently is a coming out within—a very deep introspection, a look at spiritual values, at what it means to be gay.

CA: And you see this not only within your only life, but within the larger gay community.

BOYD: I'm talking about the movement. And you find it in literature and the arts. And in theater, particularly, one finds the asking of existential questions: Why this identity? What does it mean? What does it mean in relation to the rest of the world? And then, on the part of a growing number of gays, what does it mean in relation to God?

CA: What do you tell people who interpret AIDS as God's punishment for promiscuity?

BOYD: Again, I would almost have to say, You have a different God than I do. My God doesn't give measles, doesn't run concentration camps, doesn't give tuberculosis, doesn't give cancer of the rectum. My God is a healing God. When I'm co-creating with God in the continuing act of creation, I'm involved in holistic things—wholeness, hope, love, support. So I would find that narrow definition of God to be vengeful, self-serving, self-indulgent and really quite dangerous, because the political ramifications of that could be Hitlerian.

CA: Do you think the disease has resulted in a backlash against the gay movement?

BOYD: Since the disease in Africa is basically heterosexual and since the disease in the heterosexual community has a great deal to do with drug users, it isn't a gay disease, but is a medical problem. At the beginning when we were getting used to it and didn't quite know what it was all about, certain political chauvinists and zealots had an opportunity to use it as a political weapon. But increasingly we're understanding that this is a mystery that we're all involved in. Actually, instead of a backlash I see a great deal of compassion. I think there's an awareness on the part of more and more people in relation to multiple issues that John Donne was right: Ask not for whom the bell tolls; it tolls for thee. We are together in this enterprise called life. The arts express this, it comes through in literature and theater and they are quite beautiful.

CA: In Take off the Masks, *published in 1978, you wrote "It seems entirely possible that happier days for gay people lay ahead." Do you still believe this to be the case?*

BOYD: Yes. Personally, I'm happy. I'm not glibly happy. The threads are scarlet and dark as well as light gold in the tapestry. But something I learned a long time ago in the civil rights movement was that it isn't enough to "help others," unless one is working on and with oneself. There are those two commandments: Thou shalt love the Lord thy God with all thy heart and soul and mind, and Thou shalt love thy neighbor as thyself. I've often thought there should be a third commandment: Thou shalt love thyself in an honest, creative way.

A number of do-gooders have traditionally been people who just couldn't deal with themselves. They throw themselves out there to help others and in the process others get burned and hurt. One thing the civil rights movement taught me personally is that part of that energy of helping others had to be directed to open up my own life, to be aware of my shortcomings, and to deal with things within myself that I would project onto others if I didn't deal with them in a positive way.

CA: Do you think your own journey from secrecy to openness has made you more responsive to other people's needs?

BOYD: I do. So many people in the parish affirm that, just the number of people who come to me for counseling who feel I've been through a bit and have an understanding of life that isn't just out of a textbook.

CA: Over the years your ministry has evolved from a traditional parish to more personal and compelling forms of commitment to God and to others. What fuels your sense of mission?

BOYD: With me there has always been a necessity to find meaning—in a situation, in a relationship, in a book I'm writing. I've been offered large amounts of money to do books that have no meaning for me. I just haven't been able to do that, but I look around me at people who do it all the time. They detach themselves and do this work in a craftsmanship way. But meaning has had to be there for me. And then, to reply to your question, it's deeper than meaning; there is the sense of mission. I don't know where that comes from.

CA: Might it come in part from your having been a repressed member of a minority group yourself?

BOYD: I think this is possible. I know that, as a white person discovering and becoming part of the lives of black people, I found meaning in the civil rights movement. It may be the deepest experience of my life. At that time there was such segregation that living in the deep south in small black beleaguered communities, as I did for a while, was like going to Mars. And white friends didn't understand what I was doing and worried about me. I did get scars because I was shut out of one community and couldn't be totally accepted in another—which is very understandable.

CA: Might that experience help you understand how people who are not gay can never be a part of the gay world?

BOYD: Precisely. And I do understand that and without anger, but with a kind of joy that they can do what they can do. We are not robots; we are people. But I've always been deeply concerned about tyranny and unnecessary pain. I stand in awe at the inhumanity projected onto others by human beings. It's something that I don't understand at all.

CA: Sometimes, as with the civil rights movement, it is possible to change laws, but minorities still may face racial harrassment and discrimination.

BOYD: Always. At a very early time in our nation's history Tocqueville pointed out that racism is deeply ingrained in us.

CA: How do you reach people whose minds are closed?

BOYD: The way I try to reach them is not to be dogmatic, not to debate, not to be didactic, but to try—as happened in "To Kill a Mockingbird" where a young child isolated a human being out of a lynch mob—to realize that *this* is a person. And the person is human and there are links between us. What are they? If I can break down someone from an ugly stereotype to a breathing human being, well I'm delighted.

CA: And have you had success in changing people's minds?

BOYD: Yes. My book *Are You Running with Me, Jesus?* changed a lot of people's minds in a useful way. And I hope that others of my books have. I would hope that *Gay Priest* would do that. But *Are You Running with Me, Jesus?* for some reason just reached a mass of people and I still meet them all the time. People who tell me their lives were changed by the book.

CA: What audience are you writing to in your books?

BOYD: I've never written to anyone; I've only tried to be myself and to communicate.

CA: So even now that the content of the books has become more focused on the gay movement, those books are not written exclusively for the gay community.

BOYD: Not at all. As a matter of fact my next book—and I'm not going to get into the specifics of it because I haven't yet completed it—isn't a gay book at all.

CA: Are you pleased with the distribution that your books receive?

BOYD: I've never been awfully pleased with any of that because I find the celebrity problem, for example, a hard one for a creative person. I've seen it destroy a number of awfully good people. We're not permitted a medium success in America; we're either superstars or failures. If you're with a certain kind of publisher the book appears everywhere, then it disappears rather quickly and gets shredded because they have to have other books coming in. It's become such an industry, and the small bookstore is in jeopardy. Even in major cities there are not many of them now, and they're the ones where a book is loved. You can come in and browse. The book remains in print. They don't have to make a big profit.

CA: It sounds like an ideal world.

BOYD: I wish there were a little more of an ideal world and there isn't. I've never been—oh, I guess with a few books I have been satisfied by the books themselves. Usually by the time a book is published it's a year, a-year-and-a-half, away from when I had the sense of necessity to say it. And I run into someone who assumes I'm the person in that book just published. But that's already over for me and I'm concerned about something else. Then, even more complicated, is when someone picks up a paperback of something that's come out four or five years ago, and I'm not there at all.

CA: Your writings reveal both a public and a very private figure. How have you reconciled your opposite needs—the need for public recognition versus private contemplation?

BOYD: I have been able to go public with much of my deeply personal life and feelings; therefore, that has not been a deliberate, thought-out act like opening a door and walking into a room. It's something I've done in the creative process. So I can look over my shoulder at that and not exactly understand it. One reason that, creatively, it was very important to come out is that, both as a priest and a writer, it seemed such a contradiction not to be able to share something this basic. In fact, it seemed a betrayal of the whole creative process. Several reviewers have referred to me as "Holden Caulfield in a collar" or a "balding Holden Caulfield"—they keep bringing Holden into it. And I'm quite aware of Holden in myself.

In a way I'm not an earthling. I'm very detached. I can feel: It's all been a mistake; I don't belong here; I don't understand it at all. Yet I've done the best I could; I've tried very hard and rather successfully to come to terms with the earth and body, mind and soul and who I am. And to communicate. It's important to hear each other. And you can do that if you are able to put the issues away a little bit and say, Here's a person. Who is this person? And also be willing to share something with that person. I've loved having one-on-one encounters with people who, at the outset, seemed to hate me for one reason or another. I observed a lot of hate in the civil rights and peace movement. And when that hate could go, and I changed from pure stereotype into a person in someone else's eyes, then we could laugh, we could eat together, take a walk, focus together on certain things.

CA: It must be very gratifying to see that kind of transformation occur in someone.

BOYD: I consider that one of the most mysterious and beautiful transformations in life.

BIOGRAPHICAL/CRITICAL SOURCES:

BOOKS

Boyd, Malcolm, *As I Live and Breathe: Stages of an Autobiography*, Random House, 1970.
Boyd, Malcolm, *Take off the Masks*, Doubleday, 1978, revised edition, New Society Publishers, 1984.

PERIODICALS

Advocate, September 8, 1976, January 26, 1977, November 30, 1977, March 20, 1978, June 28, 1978, August 7, 1984, December 11, 1984, April 2, 1985, June 11, 1985, July 9, 1985, August 20, 1985, November 12, 1985, January 7, 1986, March 18, 1986, May 27, 1986, November 25, 1986, August 4, 1987, December 22, 1987.
Catholic World, February, 1969.
Christian Century, January 30, 1974, April 10, 1974, June 5, 1974, July 1, 1974, October 2, 1974, December 11, 1974, September 24, 1975, November 26, 1975, December 17, 1975, February 4, 1976, March 3, 1976, April 14, 1976, April 28, 1976, June 23, 1976, November 24, 1976, May 25, 1977, April 19, 1978, June 21, 1978, August 2-9, 1978, November 15, 1978, May 9, 1979, April 2, 1980, October 22, 1980, December 2, 1987.

Christian Science Monitor, July 8, 1966, November 5, 1968, January 22, 1970.
Esquire, July, 1969.
Gay Sunshine, autumn/winter, 1980.
Library Journal, July, 1978.
Los Angeles Reader, April 18, 1986.
Los Angeles Times, January 30, 1966, September 14, 1966, June 8, 1967, May 26, 1968, July 4, 1968, February 27, 1970, July 25, 1971, October 8, 1972, February 18, 1973, December 16, 1973, January 20, 1974, December 25, 1974, June 15, 1975, August 1, 1975, June 10, 1979, October 7, 1979, November 18, 1979, January 20, 1980, May 11, 1980, June 29, 1980, August 29, 1980, October 19, 1980, October 26, 1980, November 16, 1980, February 22, 1981, March 23, 1984, April 3, 1984, April 13, 1984, April 14, 1984, July 21, 1985, October 3, 1985, January 22, 1986, January 26, 1986, February 16, 1987, July 4, 1987, September 11, 1987, December 7, 1987.
McCall's, April, 1972.
Newsday, August 26, 1973, January 18, 1974, December 8, 1974.
Newsweek, May 3, 1965.
New York Post, February 10, 1961.
New York Times, June 7, 1961, August 14, 1964, March 23, 1966, April 9, 1966, September 16, 1966, September 17, 1966, September 18, 1966, November 13, 1966, July 28, 1968, September 8, 1968, June 22, 1969, November 15, 1969, January 11, 1970, June 17, 1970, December 5, 1970, October 24, 1971, December 12, 1971, December 26, 1971, February 17, 1972, August 27, 1972, November 12, 1972, November 21, 1972, February 1, 1973, August 5, 1973, November 2, 1973, December 22, 1973, December 25, 1974, September 1, 1985.
New York Times Book Review, March 26, 1967, September 17, 1967, January 25, 1976, December 20, 1985, October 12, 1986.
Parade, April 12, 1987, July 3, 1988.
San Francisco Sentinel, September 4, 1987.
U.S. Catholic, November, 1969.
Village Voice, November 23, 1967.
Washington Post, March 23, 1965, April 4, 1965, August 10, 1965, May 29, 1966, March 26, 1967, September 24, 1967, June 1, 1968, May 2, 1973, September 9, 1973, January 20, 1974, April 14, 1974.

—*Sketch and interview by Donna Olendorf*

*   *   *

BOYLE, Ann (Peters)   1916-

PERSONAL: Born January 21, 1916, in Independence, Mo.; daughter of Robert Mize (a pharmacist) and Lucy (Conway) Peters; married James Hancock Boyle (a lawyer), December 26, 1938; children: Eleanor Ann (Mrs. Richard Riley), Lucy Charlotte (Mrs. Robert E. Buschmann), Jean Boyle Dannenberg. *Education:* Chevy Chase Junior College, graduate, 1936; University of Kansas City (now University of Missouri—Kansas City), B.A., 1938. *Religion:* Protestant.

CAREER: Writer. Model for various women's clothing shops, Kansas City, Mo., 1936-38; Barstow School, Kansas City, teacher in primary grades, 1938-39.

MEMBER: PEN, (membership vice-president, 1977-78), Association of Junior Leagues of America, California Writers Guild, Long Beach Writers Workshop, Quill Pen (vice-president, 1971; president, 1972), Lambda Beta Writers Workshop.

AWARDS, HONORS: Prize in *Writers' Digest* Short Short Story Contest, 1962, for "The Christmas Eve Surprise"; first and second prizes for short stories in Long Beach Writers Club annual contests.

WRITINGS:

Stormy Slopes (young adult novel), Bouregy, 1971.
Sundown Girl, Bouregy, 1971.
The Well of Three Echoes, Avalon Books, 1972.
Rim of Forever, Avalon Books, 1973.
One Golden Earring, Avalon Books, 1974.
Dark Mountain, Avalon Books, 1975.
Beyond the Wall, Avalon Books, 1976.
The Snowy Hills of Innocence, Avalon Books, 1977.
Veil of Sand, Avalon Books, 1977.
Moon Shadows, Woodhill, 1978.
Never Say Never, Ace Books, 1984.

Contributor of short stories and serials to *Jack and Jill, Wee Wisdom, Children's Activities, Highlights for Children,* and other juvenile magazines.

WORK IN PROGRESS: Untitled teenage book; untitled adult Gothic.

SIDELIGHTS: Ann Boyle once wrote *CA:* "For all its hard work and frequent frustrations, writing gives me great pleasure and is important to my personal life. Since I believe that the background or setting must be an integral, working part of a story, like another character, I fictionalize and use experiences from our own recreational activities as backgrounds for my novels and short stories. My husband and I spend much of our free time hiking, backpacking, and cross-country skiing in the mountains and deserts of the west, and these activities and settings play an important role in most of my fiction. My husband is patient when I stop on the trail to jot down an idea in my miniature notebook, but when I delay us too long, he sometimes says, 'If you stop to write the whole book, we'll never make it to the mountain's summit.'

"But there is also research, not only to check the accuracy and feasibility of the situations I create, but also the fields that are new to me. One of the reasons I like to write is that there are so many things I would like to do if I had time. By researching subjects that interest me and weaving them into the background of the story, I feel almost as if I had actually designed and cast jewelry by the lost wax method, as a character in *Beyond the Wall* did, or had actually spent a summer as a lookout with Charlie in *Sundown Girl*, in one of the fire towers we have visited in the wilderness. So, writing has given me a second, if vicarious, life and enabled me to enjoy twice as many experiences as could be packed into one lifetime."

AVOCATIONAL INTERESTS: Skiing, hiking, swimming, travel, sewing, music, art, collecting antiques.†

* * *

BRADLEY, David (Henry, Jr.) 1950-

PERSONAL: Born September 7, 1950, in Bedford, Pa.; son of David Henry (a minister and historian) and Harriette M. (maiden name, Jackson) Bradley. *Education:* University of Pennsylvania, B.A. (summa cum laude), 1972; attended Institute for United States Studies, London; King's College, London, M.A., 1974.

ADDRESSES: Home—433270 Viamarin, La Jolla, Calif. 92024. *Office*—Department of English, Temple University, Philadel-phia, Pa. 19122. *Agent*—Wendy Weil Literary Agency, Inc., 747 Third Ave., New York, N.Y. 10017.

CAREER: Educational Testing Service, Princeton, N.J., research assistant with Office of Data Analysis and Research, 1971; J. B. Lippincott Co. (publisher), Philadelphia, Pa., assistant editor in Philadelphia and New York, N.Y., 1974-76; Temple University, Philadelphia, visiting instructor, 1976-77, assistant professor, 1977-81, associate professor of English, 1981—. Guest lecturer at University of Warwick, University of Nottingham, and University of Edinburgh, 1972-73; visiting lecturer at University of Pennsylvania, 1975, and San Diego State University, 1980-81. Member of board of directors of Bradley, Burr & Sherman, 1977-79.

MEMBER: Authors Guild, Authors League of America, PEN, National Book Critics Circle.

AWARDS, HONORS: PEN/Faulkner Award, American Academy and Institute of Arts and Letters award for literature, and *New York Times Book Review* "Editors' Choice" citation, all 1982, all for *The Chaneysville Incident*.

WRITINGS:

South Street (novel), Viking, 1975, reprinted, Scribner's, 1986.
The Chaneysville Incident (novel; Book-of-the-Month Club alternate selection), Harper, 1981.

Contributor of articles, stories, and reviews to magazines and newspapers, including *Signature, Savvy, Tracks, Quest, New York Arts Journal, Esquire, New York Times Magazine, Philadelphia Magazine, Southern Review, New York Times Book Review, Los Angeles Times Book Review, Washington Post Book World,* and *Philadelphia Inquirer Magazine.*

WORK IN PROGRESS: A nonfiction book on race in America.

SIDELIGHTS: David Bradley has reaped considerable critical acclaim for his novels *South Street* and *The Chaneysville Incident*, both published before he turned thirty-five. *Dictionary of Literary Biography* contributor Valerie Smith ranks Bradley "among the most sophisticated literary stylists of his generation," a fiction writer whose works "present subtle and original perspectives on issues that traditionally have concerned significant Afro-American writers: the meaning of community, the effects of racism, the shape and substance of history." Indeed, *The Chaneysville Incident*, winner of the 1982 PEN/Faulkner Award, blends historical fact and fiction in its representation of a rural Pennsylvania community through which the Underground Railroad once ran. Acclaimed "by fiction writers and by popular and scholarly writers alike," notes Smith, the work has "placed Bradley in the vanguard of contemporary novelists." A professor of English at Philadelphia's Temple University, Bradley is a self-styled perfectionist who can work many years crafting a novel. He also writes nonfiction articles for magazines and newspapers, including *Esquire* and the *New York Times Book Review*, and is a member of the National Book Critics Circle.

Geographically, the city of Philadelphia is less than three hundred miles from Bradley's home town of Bedford, Pennsylvania. As Bradley notes in a *New York Times Book Review* profile, however, the region that formed his authorial sensibility was starkly different from the urban area in which he now lives. "The town of Bedford is perilously close to the Mason-Dixon line," he said. ". . . It was not that hospitable for blacks—or that comfortable." Bradley grew up among a community of about one hundred blacks in a county with a scattered population of 30,000; his experiences in that environment imbued him with skepticism toward the Black Power movement that was gaining momentum as he entered college. "I had grown up in a rural white society," he said, "and I knew damn well we [blacks] had no power." Although an honors student at the University of Pennsylvania, Bradley felt alienated from his peers because of his rural background; as an undergraduate he discovered a group of compatriots in an unlikely setting—a bar on Philadelphia's South Street. "I really enjoyed that place," he recollected. ". . . My experiences there confirmed my impression that the things I saw in the blacks at the university, my contemporaries, were as artificial as everything else. The people on South Street were totally without power. Their lives were terrible—they just lived with the situation and made the best of it."

Bradley's first novel—written while he was still an undergraduate—was inspired by his visits to the South Street bar. The book, *South Street,* "is not simply another grim, naturalistic litany of the anguish of the downtrodden," notes Mel Watkins in the *New York Times.* "Without blunting the pathos of this tale, Mr. Bradley has infused what could have been a standard story and stock characters with new vigor. Probing beneath the sociological stereotypes, he portrays his characters with a fullness that amplifies much of the lusty irony of ghetto life. . . . It is Bradley's unerring depiction of the vitality that rears itself even within this despairing setting that distinguishes this novel." The work centers on Adlai Stevenson Brown, a young poet who begins to frequent Lightnin' Ed's Bar. There he talks to patrons and listens to their stories; this plot structure provides for vignettes recounted by other characters. "The novel is really about the street itself, as Bradley's energetic and shifting narrative makes clear," Smith writes. ". . . These frequent changes in perspective illustrate various ways in which individuals confront the turbulence of ghetto life. Furthermore, the shifts imitate the vibrancy and the multifariousness of the world the author explores."

Bradley began to conceive *The Chaneysville Incident* while he was in college, too, but he spent nearly a decade reworking four different drafts of the story before arriving at the final manuscript. The author had grown up hearing stories about the Underground Railroad in Bedford County. But in 1969, Bradley's mother told him a story he had not heard before, about thirteen runaway slaves who, upon the point of recapture in Bedford County, had chosen death over a return to slavery. The slaves were buried in thirteen unmarked graves in a family burial plot on a nearby farm. Bradley told the *New York Times Book Review:* "I knew my second novel would be about those 13 runaway slaves. And in writing about them I wanted to use material that had been glossed over, material that had been mined for descriptions of the horror of slavery without bringing along any understanding of how the system came about."

The Chaneysville Incident is the story of a young man's confrontation with his personal past, his family history, and the living legacies of racism and slavery. The protagonist, a history professor, returns to his hometown in western Pennsylvania to visit the deathbed of a man who helped to raise him. With the aid of his dying mentor, the professor begins to explore his father's mysterious death in the mountains outside Bedford—and this exploration leads, in time, to a reconstruction of one telling moment in the history of American blacks. Smith contends that the novel "is somewhat reminiscent of a musical composition in which the different movements represent variations on a common theme." Smith also notes that the varieties of narrative—the protagonist's pedantic lectures and increasingly emotional flashbacks, his old friend's tales

of bootlegging and lynchings—"all exemplify the kinds of physical and emotional cruelty that are commonplace within a racist culture."

In addition to the prestigious PEN/Faulkner Award, *The Chaneysville Incident* won an American Academy and Institute of Arts and Letters grant for literature, and it was cited by the editors of the *New York Times Book Review* as one of the best novels of 1981. *Los Angeles Times* book editor Art Seidenbaum calls the book "the most significant work by a new male black author since James Baldwin," and *Christian Science Monitor* contributor Bruce Allen finds it "the best novel about the black experience in America since Ellison's 'Invisible Man' nearly 30 years ago." Vance Bourjaily offers similar praise in the *New York Times Book Review.* "Whatever else may be said," Bourjaily claims, ". . . [Bradley's] a writer. What he can do, at a pretty high level of energy, is synchronize five different kinds of rhetoric, control a complicated plot, manage a good-sized cast of characters, convey a lot of information, handle an intricate time scheme, pull off a couple of final tricks that dramatize provocative ideas, and generally keep things going for 200,000 words." The critic concludes that *The Chaneysville Incident* "deserves what it seems pretty sure to get: a lot of interested and challenged readers."

Bradley commented: "I think of myself as an 'old-fashioned' writer, primarily because my fictional models are 'old-fashioned.' Like the Victorians, I am interested in the basics of plot and character, less concerned with abstract ideas. It is my belief that writers of novels should have no belief, that the idea of what is true is something that emerges from the writing, rather than being placed into it. Ultimately, I believe that if I cannot create a character who holds an idea, write a conversation (as opposed to a speech) that expresses it, or work out a plot that exemplifies it, there is something wrong either with my understanding of the idea or with the idea itself. In either case it has no place in my writing.

"I must frankly say that I do not love many 'contemporary' novels. For the most part they seem to me self-absorbed, self-indulgent, derivative, and basically lacking truth. Our technique has become an end rather than a means, primarily, I think, because we writers have been led to believe that truth does not sell. If we would write well, we are told, we will be obscure. Obscurity, then, becomes the measure of writing well. I do not believe this. I have faith in the ability of people to respond to a story that treats them with kindness, honesty, dignity, and understanding. I put my faith not in publishers, and certainly not in reviewers and/or critics, but in those who read."

BIOGRAPHICAL/CRITICAL SOURCES:

BOOKS

Contemporary Literary Criticism, Volume 23, Gale, 1983.
Dictionary of Literary Biography, Volume 33: *Afro-American Fiction Writers after 1955,* Gale, 1984.

PERIODICALS

America, May 30, 1981.
Atlantic, May, 1981.
Christian Science Monitor, May 20, 1981.
Los Angeles Times, April 8, 1981.
New York Times, October 4, 1975, May 12, 1981.
New York Times Book Review, September 28, 1975, April 19, 1981.
Publishers Weekly, April 10, 1981.

Saturday Review, July, 1981.
Times Literary Supplement, January 16, 1987.
Washington Post, April 12, 1982.
Washington Post Book World, April 12, 1981.

* * *

BRAILSFORD, Frances
See WOSMEK, Frances

* * *

BRAMS, Steven J(ohn)   1940-

PERSONAL: Born November 28, 1940, in Concord, N.H.; son of Nathan (a shoe clerk) and Isabelle (Tryman) Brams; married Eva Floderer (a writer), November 12, 1971; children: Julie, Michael. *Education:* Massachusetts Institute of Technology, S.B., 1962; Northwestern University, Ph.D., 1966.

ADDRESSES: Home—4 Washington Square Village, Apt. 2N, New York, N.Y. 10012. *Office*—Department of Politics, New York University, 25 Waverly Pl., New York, N.Y. 10003.

CAREER: National Institutes of Health, Office of the Director, Bethesda, Md., program analyst, summer, 1962; Office of the Secretary of Defense, Washington, D.C., executive trainee, summer, 1963; Institute for Defense Analyses, Arlington, Va., research associate, 1965-67; Syracuse University, Syracuse, N.Y., assistant professor of political science, 1967-69; New York University, New York, N.Y., assistant professor, 1969-73, associate professor, 1973-76, professor of politics, 1976—. Visiting lecturer at University of Michigan, 1969-70, and University of Pennsylvania, spring, 1972, fall, 1977, fall, 1978; visiting professor at University of Rochester, spring, 1967, 1968-69, fall, 1971, 1972-73, Yale University, spring, 1977, fall, 1981, Institute for Advanced Studies, Vienna, 1978, University of California, Irvine, 1979, University of Haifa, 1984. Modules and Monographs in Undergraduate Mathematics and Its Applications project, national steering committee member, 1976-80, consortium council member, 1980-83.

MEMBER: American Association for the Advancement of Science, American Political Science Association, International Studies Association, Public Choice Society, Policy Studies Organization, Peace Science Society (International), Peace Research Society, Society for Judgment and Decision Making.

AWARDS, HONORS: National Science Foundation grants, 1968-70, 1970-71, 1974-75, 1980-83, 1984-85, 1986-87; Ford Foundation grant, 1984-85; Sloan Foundation grant, 1985-86; United States-Israel Binational Science Foundation Grant, 1985-88; Guggenheim fellowship, 1986-87.

WRITINGS:

Game Theory and Politics, Free Press, 1975.
Paradoxes in Politics: An Introduction to the Nonobvious in Political Science, Free Press, 1976.
The Presidential Election Game, Yale University Press, 1978.
(Editor with A. Schotter and G. Schwodiaver and contributor) *Applied Game Theory: Proceedings of a Conference, Vienna, 1978*, Physica-Verlag, 1979.
Biblical Games: A Strategic Analysis of Stories in the Old Testament, MIT Press, 1980.
(Editor and contributor with William F. Lucas and Philip D. Straffin, Jr.) *Modules in Applied Mathematics: Political and Related Models*, Volume 2, Springer-Verlag, 1983.
(With Peter C. Fishburn) *Approval Voting*, Birkhaeuser, 1983.

Superior Beings: If They Exist, How Would We Know? Game-Theoretic Implications of Omniscience, Omnipotence, Immortality, and Incomprehensibility, Springer-Verlag, 1983.
Superpower Games: Applying Game Theory to Superpower Conflict, Yale University Press, 1985.
Rational Politics: Decision, Games, and Strategy, CO Press, 1985.
(With D. Marc Kilgour) *Game Theory and National Security*, Basil Blackwell, 1988.

CONTRIBUTOR

Roderick Bell, David V. Edwards, and R. Harrison Wagner, editors, *Political Power: A Reader in Theory and Research*, Free Press, 1969.
James N. Rosenau, editor, *International Politics and Foreign Policy: A Reader in Research and Theory*, 2nd revised edition, Free Press, 1969.
Clifford D. Stewart and others, editors, *Computer/Architecture Programs*, Center for Environmental Research, 1970.
James F. Herndon and Joseph L. Bernd, editors, *Mathematical Applications in Political Science, VI*, University Press of Virginia, 1972.
Richard G. Niemi and Herbert F. Weisberg, editors, *Probability Models of Collective Decision-Making*, C. E. Merrill, 1972.
Cornelius P. Cotter, editor, *Political Science Annual IV: An International Review*, Bobbs-Merrill, 1973.
Barbara W. Hinckley, editor, *Coalitions and Time: Cross-Disciplinary Studies*, Sage Publications, 1976.
Lawrence M. Friedman and Stewart Macauley, editors, *Law and the Behavioral Sciences*, 2nd edition, Bobbs-Merrill, 1977.
R. Henn and O. Moeschlin, editors, *Mathematical Economics and Game Theory: Essays in Honor of Oskar Morgenstern*, Springer-Verlag, 1977.
John V. Gillespie and Dina A. Zinnes, editors, *Mathematical Systems in International Relations Research*, Praeger, 1977.
Peter C. Ordeshook, editor, *Game Theory and Political Science*, New York University Press, 1978.
Stuart Langton, editor, *Citizen Participation Perspectives: Proceedings of the National Conference on Citizen Participation*, Lincoln Filene Center for Citizenship and Public Affairs, 1979.
Michael Bradie and Kenneth Sayre, editors, *Reason and Decision*, Volume 3, Bowling Green Studies in Applied Philosophy, 1982.
Robert S. Hirschfield, editor, *Selection/Election: A Forum on the American Presidency*, Aldine, 1982.
Bernard Grofman, Arend Lijphart, Robert McKay, and Howard Scarrow, editors, *Representation and Redistricting Issues of the 1980s*, Lexington Books, 1982.
Ordeshook and Kenneth A. Shepsle, editors, *Political Equilibrium*, Kluwer-Nijhoff, 1982.
Manfred J. Holler, editor, *Power, Voting, and Voting Power*, Physica-Verlag, 1982.
(With Fishburn) Lijphart and Grofman, editors, *Choosing an Electoral System: Issues and Alternatives*, Praeger, 1984.
(With Kilgour) Ellen Frankel Paul and others, editors, *Nuclear Right/Nuclear Wrongs*, Basil Blackwell, 1985.
(With Kilgour) Newton Garver and Peter H. Hare, editors, *Naturalism and Rationality*, Prometheus, 1985.
(With Kilgour) Urs Luterbacher and Michael D. Ward, editors, *Dynamic Models of International Conflict*, Lynne Rienner, 1985.

(With Kilgour) Rudolf Avenhaus, Reiner K. Huber, and John D. Kettelle, editors, *Modelling and Analysis in Arms Control,* Springer-Verlag, 1986.

(With Dan S. Felsenthal and Zeev Maoz) Andreas Diekmann and Peter Mitter, editors, *Paradoxical Effects of Social Behavior: Essays in Honor of Anatol Rapoport,* Physica-Verlag, 1986.

(With Morton D. Davis) Claudio Cioffi-Revella, Richard L. Merritt, and Zinnes, editors, *Interaction and Communication in Global Politics,* Sage Publications, 1987.

(With Kilgour) Jacek Kugler and Frank C. Zagare, editors, *Exploring the Stability of Deterrence,* Lynne Rienner, 1987.

(With Kilgour) Allan M. Din, editor, *Arms and Artificial Intelligence,* Oxford University Press, 1987.

(With Felsenthal and Maoz) Gerald Eberlein and Hal Berghel, editors, *Theory and Decision: Essays in Honor of Werner Leinfellner,* D. Reidel, 1987.

OTHER

Contributor to journals in his field. Member of editorial boards of *Journal of Politics,* 1968-73, 1978-82, *Behavioral Science,* 1972—, *Theory and Decision,* 1972—, *Public Choice,* 1973—, *American Political Science Review,* 1978-82, *Monograph Series in World Affairs,* 1979—, *Mathematical Social Sciences,* 1980—, *Journal of Behavioral Decision Making,* 1987—, and *Journal of Theoretical Politics,* 1987—.

SIDELIGHTS: In a *Science '81* review of Steven J. Brams's *Biblical Games: A Strategic Analysis of Stories in the Old Testament,* Jake Page remarks: "This curiously compelling book is likely to irritate humanists, enrage theologians, and dissatisfy certain mathematicians—wherein, of course, lies its charm and perhaps its ultimate effectiveness. The author is a political scientist who has taken it into his head to apply modern game theory to the enduringly fascinating and therefore unquestionably important stories of the Old Testament." Leonard Silk states in the *New York Times:* "Marvel of marvels, the mathematical theory of games appears to predict correctly the strategic choices of God and the human characters in the Bible, as well as the outcome of the conflicts between them." *Biblical Games,* Silk continues, "is neither religious nor sacrilegious; it is logical and deeply rooted in its sources." And a reviewer for the *Los Angeles Times* suggests that the reader of this book does not "have to agree with the author's rationale to be stimulated by his unusual approach."

BIOGRAPHICAL/CRITICAL SOURCES:

PERIODICALS

Choice, January, 1979.
Los Angeles Times, July 24, 1980.
New York Times, September 7, 1981.
Science '81, January/February, 1981.
Times Literary Supplement, November 30, 1979.

*   *   *

BRATHWAITE, Edward (Kamau) 1930-

PERSONAL: Born May 11, 1930, in Bridgetown, Barbados; son of Hilton Edward and Beryl (Gill) Brathwaite; married Doris Monica Welcome (a teacher and librarian), March 26, 1960; children: Michael. *Education:* Attended Harrison College, Barbados; Pembroke College, Cambridge, B.A. (honors in history), 1953, Diploma of Education, 1954; University of Sussex, D.Phil., 1968.

ADDRESSES: Office—Department of History, University of the West Indies, Mona, Kingston 7, Jamaica.

CAREER: Writer, poet, playwright, and editor. Education officer with Ministry of Education of Ghana, 1955-62; University of the West Indies, Kingston, Jamaica, tutor in Department of Extra Mural Studies assigned to island of Saint Lucia, 1962-63, university lecturer, 1963-72, senior lecturer in history, 1972-76, reader, 1976-83, professor of social and cultural history, 1982—. Plebiscite Office for the United Nations in the Trans-Volta Togoland, 1956-57.

MEMBER: Caribbean Artists Movement (founding secretary, 1966—).

AWARDS, HONORS: Arts Council of Great Britain bursary, 1967; Camden Arts Festival prize, 1967; Cholmondeley Award, 1970, for *Islands;* Guggenheim fellowship, 1972; City of Nairobi fellowship, 1972; Bussa Award, 1973; Casa de las Americas Prize for Poetry, 1976; Fulbright fellow, 1982; Institute of Jamaica Musgrave Medal, 1983.

WRITINGS:

The People Who Came, three volumes, Longman, 1968-72.
Folk Culture of the Slaves in Jamaica, New Beacon, 1970, revised edition, 1981.
The Development of Creole Society in Jamaica, 1770-1820, Clarendon Press, 1971.
Caribbean Man in Space and Time, Savacou Publications, 1974.
Contradictory Omens: Cultural Diversity and Integration in the Caribbean, Savacou Publications, 1974.
Our Ancestral Heritage: A Bibliography of the Roots of Culture in the English-Speaking Caribbean, Literary Committee of Carifesta, 1976.
Wars of Respect: Nanny, Sam Sharpe, and the Struggle for People's Liberation, API, 1977.
The Colonial Encounter: Language, University of Mysore, 1984.
History of the Voice: The Development of Nation Language in Angolophone Caribbean Poetry, New Beacon, 1984.

POETRY

Rights of Passage (also see below), Oxford University Press, 1967.
Masks (also see below), Oxford University Press, 1968.
Islands (also see below), Oxford University Press, 1969.
Panda No. 349, Roy Institute for the Blind, 1969.
The Arrivants: A New World Trilogy (contains *Rights of Passage, Masks,* and *Islands*), Oxford University Press, 1973.
Days and Nights, Caldwell Press, 1975.
Other Exiles, Oxford University Press, 1975.
Black and Blues, Casa de las Americas, 1976.
Mother Poem, Oxford University Press, 1977.
Word Making Man: A Poem for Nicolas Guillen, Savacou Publications, 1979.
Sun Poem, Oxford University Press, 1982.
Third World Poems, Longman, 1983.
X/Self, Oxford University Press, 1987.

PLAYS

Four Plays for Primary Schools (first produced in Saltpond, Ghana, 1961), Longmans, Green, 1964.
Odale's Choice (first produced in Saltpond, Ghana, 1962), Evans Brothers, 1967.

EDITOR

Iouanaloa: Recent Writing from St. Lucia, Department of Extra Mural Studies, University of West Indies, 1963.
Barbados Poetry, 1661-1979, Savacou Publications, 1979.
New Poets from Jamaica (anthology), Savacou Publications, 1979.

RECORDINGS

The Poet Speaks 10, Argo, 1968.
Rights of Passage, Argo, 1969.
Masks, Argo, 1972.
Islands, Argo, 1973.
The Poetry of Edward Kamau Brathwaite, Casa de las Americas, 1976.
Poemas, Casa de las Americas, 1976.

OTHER

Contributor to *Bim* and other periodicals. Editor, *Savacou* (magazine), 1970—.

SIDELIGHTS: Edward Brathwaite is generally regarded as one of the West Indies' most prolific and talented writers. More well known for his poetry, most of Brathwaite's writings seek to explore his past and present self while examining his identity as a black person living in the Caribbean. Andrew Motion writes in the *Times Literary Supplement* that "throughout his career Brathwaite has been concerned to define his identity as a West Indian."

It was the publication of *Rights of Passage* in 1967, *Masks* in 1968, and *Islands* in 1969, that brought Brathwaite to the attention of a larger group of critics and readers. These three books of poetry constitute an autobiographical trilogy collectively entitled *The Arrivants: A New World Trilogy* that examines a Caribbean man's search for identity. The volumes trace Brathwaite's initial encounter with white culture, his journey to Africa in search of a racial self-image, and his eventual return to his Caribbean homeland. Laurence Lieberman writes in *Poetry*: "[Brathwaite] has been able to invent a hybrid prosody which, combining jazz/folk rhythms with English-speaking meters, captures the authenticity of primitive African rituals." "In general," writes Hayden Carruth in the *Hudson Review*, "[Brathwaite] has been remarkably successful in reproducing black speech patterns, both African and Caribbean, in English syntax, using the standard techniques of contemporary poetry, and he has been equally successful in suggesting to an international audience the cultural identities and attitudes of his own people."

In 1977 Brathwaite released *Mother Poem*, the first book in a proposed second trilogy. The second book of the trilogy, *Sun Poem*, was published in 1982. As in Brathwaite's first trilogy, *Mother Poem* and *Sun Poem* continue Brathwaite's exploration of his selfhood. As Andrew Motion explains in the *Times Literary Supplement*: "In *Mother Poem*, [Brathwaite] provides another detailed account of his home [in the West Indies]. But in addition to exploring his complex relationship with the place, he also recounts its own efforts to find an independent and homogeneous character." David Dorsey remarks in *World Literature Today*: "Brathwaite is particularly ingenious in achieving semantic complexity through his use of assonance, enjambment, word divisions, grammatical and lexical ambiguity, puns and neologisms. This *joie d'esprit* occurs within a rhythm always obedient to the emphases and feelings intended. The style paradoxically reveals the author's sober, passionate and lucid perception on the beauty and pain black Barbadians are heir to."

In a *World Literature Today* review of *Sun Poem* Andrew Salkey comments that "Brathwaite writes 'performance,' 'rituals' and 'illuminations' which result in conflated portraits of persons, places and events recalled through a filter of sequential evocative poems—no ordinary creative accomplishment."

BIOGRAPHICAL/CRITICAL SOURCES:

BOOKS

Authors and Areas of the West Indies, Steck-Vaughn, 1970.
Caribbean Writers, Three Continents, 1979.
Contemporary Literary Criticism, Volume 11, Gale, 1979.
West Indian Literature, Archon Books, 1979.

PERIODICALS

Books, January, 1970.
Books and Bookmen, May, 1967.
Book World, November 3, 1968.
Caribbean Quarterly, June, 1973.
Caribbean Studies, January, 1971.
Choice, June, 1976.
Critical Quarterly, summer, 1970.
Hudson Review, summer, 1974.
Library Journal, March 15, 1970.
New Statesman, April 7, 1967.
Poetry, April, 1969, May, 1971.
Saturday Review, October 14, 1967.
Times Literary Supplement, February 16, 1967, August 15, 1968, January 28, 1972, June 30, 1972, November 14, 1975, Janaury 20, 1978, February 18, 1983.
Virginia Quarterly Review, autumn, 1963, autumn, 1968, spring, 1970.
World Literature Today, winter, 1977, summer, 1978, summer, 1983.†

* * *

BROWN, Margery (Wheeler)

PERSONAL: Born in Durham, N.C.; daughter of John Leonidas and Margaret (Hervey) Wheeler; married Richard E. Brown, December 22, 1936 (deceased); children: Janice (Mrs. Jan E. Carden). *Education:* Spelman College, B.A.; Ohio State University, art studies, 1932-34. *Religion:* Presbyterian.

ADDRESSES: *Home*—245 Reynolds Terrace, Orange, N.J. 07050.

CAREER: Art teacher in Newark, N.J., 1948-74; writer.

WRITINGS:

JUVENILES

That Ruby (self-illustrated), Reilly & Lee, 1969.
Animals Made by Me (self-illustrated), Putnam, 1970.
The Second Stone, Putnam, 1974.
Yesterday I Climbed a Mountain, Putnam, 1976.
No Jon, No Jon, No!, Houghton, 1981.

ILLUSTRATOR

G. Allred, *Old Crackfoot*, Obolensky, 1965.
I'm Glad I'm Me, Putnam, 1971.

OTHER

Contributor to *Life* and *School Arts.*

WORK IN PROGRESS: Stories for and about inner city children.

* * *

BROWN, Sterling Allen 1901-

PERSONAL: Born May 1, 1901, in Washington, D.C.; son of Sterling Nelson (a writer and professor of religion at Howard University) and Adelaide Allen Brown; married Daisy Turnbull, September, 1927; children: John L. Dennis. *Education:* Williams College, A.B., 1922; Harvard University, A.M., 1923, graduate study, 1930-31.

ADDRESSES: c/o John L. Dennis, 9704 Saxony Rd., Silver Spring, Md. 20910.

CAREER: Virginia Seminary and College, Lynchburg, Va., English teacher, 1923-26; also worked as a teacher at Lincoln University in Jefferson City, Mo., 1926-28, and at Fisk University, 1928-29; Howard University, Washington, D.C., professor of English, 1929-69. Visiting professor at University of Illinois, University of Minnesota, New York University, New School for Social Research, Sarah Lawrence College, and Vassar College. Editor on Negro Affairs, Federal Writers' Project, 1936-39, and staff member of Carnegie-Myrdal Study of the Negro, 1939.

MEMBER: Phi Beta Kappa.

AWARDS, HONORS: Guggenheim fellowship for creative writing, 1937; honorary doctorates from Howard University, 1971, University of Massachusetts, 1971, Northwestern University, 1973, Williams College and Boston University, both 1974, Brown University and Lewis and Clark College, both 1975, Harvard University, Yale University, University of Maryland, Baltimore County, Lincoln University (Pennsylvania), and University of Pennsylvania; Lenore Marshall Poetry Prize, 1982, for *The Collected Poems of Sterling A. Brown;* named poet laureate of District of Columbia, 1984.

WRITINGS:

POETRY

Southern Road, Harcourt, 1932, revised edition, Beacon Press, 1974.
The Last Ride of Wild Bill, and Eleven Narrative Poems, Broadside Press, 1975.
The Collected Poems of Sterling A. Brown, selected by Michael S. Harper, Harper, 1980.

NONFICTION

The Negro in American Fiction (also see below), Associates in Negro Folk Education, 1937, Argosy-Antiquarian, 1969.
Negro Poetry and Drama (also see below), Associates in Negro Folk Education, 1937, revised edition, Atheneum, 1969.
(Editor with Arthur P. Davis and Ulysses Lee, and contributor) *The Negro Caravan,* Dryden, 1941, revised edition, Arno, 1970.
Negro Poetry and Drama [and] *The Negro in American Fiction,* Ayer, 1969.
(With George E. Haynes) *The Negro Newcomers in Detroit* [and] *The Negro in Washington,* Arno, 1970.

CONTRIBUTOR

Benjamin A. Botkin, editor, *Folk-Say,* University of Oklahoma Press, 1930.
American Stuff: An Anthology of Prose and Verse by Members of the Federal Writers' Project, with Sixteen Prints by the Federal Arts Project, U.S. Government Printing Office, 1937.
Washington City and Capital, U.S. Government Printing Office, 1937.
The Integration of the Negro into American Society, Howard University Press, 1951.
Lillian D. Hornstein, G. D. Percy, and others, editors, *The Reader's Companion to World Literature,* New American Library, 1956.
Langston Hughes and Arna Bontemps, editors, *The Book of Negro Folklore,* Dodd, Mead, 1958.
John Henrik Clarke, editor, *American Negro Short Stories,* Hill & Wang, 1966.

OTHER

Sixteen Poems by Sterling Brown (sound recording), Folkway Records, 1973.

Also author of *Outline for the Study of the Poetry of American Negroes,* 1930, and contributor to *What the Negro Wants,* 1948. Contributor of poetry and articles to anthologies and journals, including *Crisis, Contempo, Nation, New Republic,* and *Journal of Negro Education.* Contributor of column, "The Literary Scene: Chronicle and Comment" to *Opportunity,* beginning 1931.

SIDELIGHTS: Sterling Allen Brown has devoted his life to the development of an authentic black folk literature. A poet, critic, and teacher at Howard University for 40 years, Brown was one of the first people to identify folklore as a vital component of the black aesthetic and to recognize its validity as a form of artistic expression. He has worked to legitimatize this genre in several ways. As a critic, he has exposed the shortcomings of white literature that stereotypes blacks and demonstrated why black authors are best suited to describe the negro experience. As a poet, he has mined the rich vein of black Southern culture, replacing primitive or sentimental caricatures with authentic folk heroes drawn from Afro-American sources. As a teacher, Brown has encouraged self-confidence among his students, urging them to find their own literary voices and to educate themselves to be an audience worthy of receiving the special gifts of black literature. Overall, Brown's influence in the field of Afro-American literature has been so great that scholar Darwin T. Turner told *Ebony* magazine: "I discovered that all trails led, at some point, to Sterling Brown. His *Negro Caravan* was *the* anthology of Afro-American literature. His unpublished study of Afro-American theater was *the* major work in the field. His study of images of Afro-Americans in American literature was a pioneer work. His essays on folk literature and folklore were preeminent. He was not always the best critic . . . but Brown was and is the literary historian who wrote the Bible for the study of Afro-American literature."

Brown's dedication to his field has been unflinching, but it was not until he was in his late sixties that the author received widespread public acclaim. Before then, he labored in obscurity on the campus of Howard University. His fortune improved in 1968 when the Black Consciousness movement revived an interest in his work. In 1969, two of his most important books of criticism, *Negro Poetry and Drama* and *The Negro* in *American Fiction*, were reprinted by Argosy; five years later, in 1974, Beacon Press reissued *Southern Road*, his first book of poems. These reprintings stimulated a reconsideration of the author, which culminated in the publication of *The Collected Poems of Sterling A. Brown* in 1980. More than any other single publication, it is this title, which won the 1982 Lenore Marshall Poetry prize, that has brought Brown the widespread recognition that he deserves.

Because he had largely stopped writing poetry by the end of the 1940s, most of *Collected Poems* is comprised of Brown's early verse. Yet the collection is not the work of an apprentice, but rather "reveals Brown as a master and presence indeed . . . ," in the view of a *Virginia Quarterly Review* critic. While acknowledging that "his effective range is narrow," the critic calls Brown "a first-rate narrative poet, an eloquent prophet of the folk, and certainly our finest author of Afro-American dialect." *New York Times Book Review* contributor Henry Louis Gates appreciates that in *Collected Poems* "Brown never lapses into bathos or sentimentality. His characters confront catastrophe with all of the irony and stoicism of the blues and of black folklore. What's more, he is able to realize such splendid results in a variety of forms, including the classic and standard blues, the ballad, the sonnet and free verse." Despite Brown's relatively small poetic output, *Washington Post* critic Joseph McClellen believes this collection "is enough to establish the poet as one of our best."

While the book will help insure that Brown is not forgotten, some believe it serves as a painful reminder of a great talent that was stunted because it was ignored. Brown encountered inexplicable resistance to his poetry in the mid-1930s. Even though *Southern Road* had been heralded by critics as the work of a major talent, Brown could not find a publisher for his second volume of poetry. (Titled *No Hiding Place* the work has yet to be published separately though it was included in *Collected Poems*.) Nor was resistance from his publishers the only source of Brown's obscurity. Another part stemmed from Brown's lifelong dedication to Howard University. Offered a full-time teaching position at Vassar College in 1945—an offer so extraordinary for a black man at the time that it made national news—Brown politely declined. "I am devoted to Howard," he explained to *Ebony* some twenty-four years later. "These are my people and if I had anything to give they would need it more.'

Brown's connection with the university dates back to his birth. He was born in a house that has since become part of the Howard campus. His father, a minister at the Lincoln Congregational Church, was a professor of religion at Howard and a one-time member of the District of Columbia Board of Education. Because of his father's position, young Brown came into contact with some of the most important black leaders of the day. Sociologist and writer W.E.B. DuBois, cultural philosopher and critic Alain Locke, and social historian Kelly Miller were but three of the important personages he came to know while growing up at Howard. Important as these figures were, however, "the person who most encouraged Brown's admiration for literature and the cultural heritage of black people was his mother," according to Joanne V. Gabbin in Volume 51 of the *Dictionary of Literary Biography*.

Adelaide Allen was valedictorian of her graduating class at Fisk University. A poetry lover who read verse aloud, Adelaide introduced her son to the works of Henry Wadsworth Longfellow, Robert Burns, and black poet and family friend Paul Laurence Dunbar. In a 1973 interview with Stephen Jones

quoted in Gabbin's article, Brown recalled of his mother: "I remember even now her stopping her sweeping . . . now standing over that broom and reading poetry to me, and she was a good reader, great sense of rhythm." The high school Brown attended further developed his gifts. Dunbar High School (named to honor the poet) was then considered one of the best black schools in the country. Brown had history classes taught by Haley Douglass, Frederick Douglass's grandson, and Neville Thomas, president of the Washington Branch of the NAACP. Among his other teachers were Angelina Weld Grimke and Jessie Redmond Fauset, "artists in their own right," who "taught him a strict sense of academic discipline," according to Gabbin.

After high school, Brown won a scholarship to the predominantly white, ivy league institution, Williams College. There he first began writing poetry. While other young poets his age were imitating T. S. Eliot, Ezra Pound, and other high modernists, Brown was not impressed with their "puzzle poetry."Instead, he turned for his models to the narrative versifiers, poets such as Edward Arlington Robinson, who captured the tragic drama of ordinary lives, and Robert Frost, who used terse vernacular that sounded like real people talking. At Williams, Brown studied literature with George Dutton, a critical realist who would exert a lasting influence. "Dutton was teaching Joseph Conrad," Brown recalled, as reported in the *New Republic*. "He said Joseph Conrad was being lionized in England . . . [but] Conrad was sitting over in the corner, quiet, not participating. Dutton said he was brooding and probably thinking about his native Poland and the plight of his people. He looked straight at me. I don't know what he meant, but I think he meant, and this is symbolic to me, I think he meant don't get fooled by any lionizing, don't get fooled by being here at Williams with a selective clientele. There is business out there that you have to take care of. Your people, too, are in a plight. I've never forgotten it."

Brown came to believe that one way to help his people was through his writing. "When Carl Sandburg said 'yes' to the American people, I wanted to say 'yes' to my people," Brown recalled in *New Directions: The Howard University Magazine*. In 1923, after receiving his Masters degree from Harvard, Brown embarked on a series of teaching jobs that would help him determine what form that "yes" should assume. He moved south and began to teach among the common people. As an instructor, he gained a reputation as a "red ink man," because he covered his students' papers with corrections. But as a poet, he was learning important lessons from students about black Southern life. Attracted by his openness and easygoing manner, they invited him into their homes to hear worksongs, ballads, and the colorful tales of local lore. He met ex-coal-miner Calvin "Big Boy" Davis, who became the inspiration for Brown's "Odyssey of Big Boy" and "Long Gone," as well as singer Luke Johnson, whom he paid a quarter for each song Luke wrote down. As Brown began to amass his own folklore collection, "he realized that worksongs, ballads, blues, and spirituals were, at their best, poetical expressions of Afro-American life," writes Robert O'Meally in the *New Republic*. "And he became increasingly aware of black language as often ironic, understated and double-edged."

At this time many black writers were moving away from using dialect in literature. White abuse of the black idiom had reduced it to a simplistic cliche, which writer James Weldon Johnson believed was capable of only two full stops: humor and pathos. His criticism was largely a reaction against white plantation literature that ridiculed black speech, nonetheless, it was a powerful incentive to negro poets to use traditional English. Against this backdrop, Brown made a decision to explore the potential of folk language. As O'Meally explains, Brown made a commitment "to render black experience as he knew it, using the speech of the people. He would not, because of white stereotyping, avoid phonetical spellings. . . . His goal was not to run from the stereotype, but to celebrate the human complexity behind the now grinning, now teary-eyed mask."

In 1929, the same year his father died, Brown returned to Howard University, where he would remain for the rest of his career. Three years later, Harcourt, Brace published *Southern Road*, a first book of poems, drawn primarily from material he had gathered during his travels south. The book was heralded as a breakthrough for black poetry. Alain Locke, one of the chief proponents of what was then called the New Negro Movement, acknowledged the importance of the work in an essay collected in *Negro Anthology*. After explaining that the primary objective of Negro poetry should be "the poetic portrayal of Negro folk-life . . . true in both letter and spirit to the idiom of the folk's own way of feeling and thinking," he declared that with the appearance of *Southern Road*, it could be said "that here for the first time is that much-desired and long-awaited acme attained or brought within actual reach."

James Weldon Johnson was so moved by the work that he provided a glowing introduction in which he reconsidered his earlier objections to black dialect: "Brown's work is not only fine, it is also unique. He began writing just after the Negro poets had generally discarded conventionalized dialect, with its minstrel traditions of Negro life. . . . He infused his poetry with genuine characteristic flavor by adopting as his medium the common, racy, living speech of the Negro in certain phases of *real* life. For his raw material he dug down into the deep mine of Negro folk poetry." As Sterling Stuckey observes in his introduction to the *Collected Poems*, "it was a remarkable achievement for a young poet: not one of the major reviewers hailed Brown as a poet of promise, as a talented young man awaiting creative maturity; on the contrary, he was regarded as a poet of uncommon sophistication, of demonstrated brilliance whose work had placed him in the front rank of working poets here and elsewhere."

The success of *Southern Road* did not insure Brown's future as a publishing poet. Not only did Harcourt, Brace reject *No Hiding Place* when Brown submitted the manuscript a few years later, they also declined to issue a second printing of *Southern Road*, because they did not think it would be profitable. These decisions had a devastating impact upon Brown's poetic reputation. Because no new poems appeared, many of his admirers assumed he had stopped writing. "That assumption," writes Sterling Stuckey, "together with sadly deficient criticism from some quarters, helped to fix his place in time—as a not very important poet of the past."

Discouraged over the reception of his poems, Brown shifted his energies to other arenas; he continued teaching, but also produced a steady stream of book reviews, essays, and sketches about black life. He argued critically for many of the same goals he had pursued in verse: recognition of a black aesthetic, accurate depiction of the black experience, and the development of a literature worthy of his people's past. One of his most influential forums for dissemination of his ideas was a regular column he wrote for *Opportunity* magazine. There "Brown argued for realism as a mode in literature and against such romantic interpretations of the South as the ones presented in *I'll Take My Stand* (1930), the manifesto of Southern

agrarianism produced by contributors to the *Fugitive*, including John Crowe Ransom, Allen Tate, and Robert Penn Warren," writes R.V. Burnette in Volume 63 of the *Dictionary of Literary Biography*. "Although he praised the efforts of white writers like Howard Odum ('he is a poetic craftsman as well as a social observer'), he was relentless in his criticism of popular works that distorted black life and character."

Brown did not limit his writing to periodicals, but also produced several major books on Afro-American studies. His 1938 works, *Negro Poetry and Drama* and *The Negro in American Fiction*, are seminal studies of black literary history. The former shows the growth of black artists within the context of American literature and delineates a black aesthetic; the latter examines what has been written about the black man in American fiction since his first appearance in obscure novels of the 1700s. A pioneering work that depicts how the prejudice facing blacks in real life is duplicated in their stereotyped treatment in literature, *The Negro in American Fiction* differs "from the usual academic survey by giving a penetrating analysis of the social factors and attitudes behind the various schools and periods considered," Alain Locke believes, as quoted in Volume 63 of the *Dictionary of Literary Biography*.

In 1941, Brown and two colleagues Arthur P. Davis and Ulysses S. Lee edited *The Negro Caravan*, a book that "defined the field of Afro-American literature as a scholarly and academic discipline," according to *Ebony*. In this anthology, Brown demonstrates how black writers have been influenced by the same literary currents that have shaped the consciousness of all American writers—"puritan didacticism, sentimental humanitarianism, local color, regionalism, realism, naturalism, and experimentalism"—and thus are not exclusively bound by strictures of race. The work has timeless merit, according to Julius Lester, who writes in the introduction to the 1970 revised edition that "it comes as close today as it did in 1941 to being the most important single volume of black writing ever published."

As a writer, Brown's first twelve years at Howard were his most productive. By the mid-1940s, he had completed the major works on which his reputation as an essayist, critic, and poet rests. But even his national reputation as a writer did little to secure his stature in the English department at Howard, where colleagues scoffed at his "lowbrow" interest in jazz and the blues. For decades, Brown paid no mind to this lack of recognition and simply went about his work. When he wanted to give poetry readings, he gave them as a guest lecturer at other campuses. Ultimately his "nonconformity cost him more than he realized," reports Michael Winston in the *Dictionary of Literary Biography*, Volume 51. Shunned by many of Howard's more conservative professors, Brown (who never completed his doctoral degree) began to suffer long periods of depression, sometimes so severe that he required hospitalization. The situation was partially rectified in the late 1960s when students participating in the Black Arts movement demanded that he receive the attention he deserved. In 1971, he was awarded an honorary doctorate from Howard (the first of many he would eventually garner), and several of his most important books were reprinted in the mid-seventies.

In summing up his impact on black literature of the twentieth century, *New Republic* contributor John F. Callahan observes: "It is his achievement to have fulfilled the complex double purpose of writing poetry worthy of a great audience and of helping to shape that diverse, responsive, critical, and inclusive audience through his essays and criticism." Concludes

Henry Louis Gates, Jr., in the *New York Times Book Review:* "Such a prolific output in a life that spans the era of Booker T. Washington and the era of Black Power makes him not only the bridge between 19th and 20th-century black literature, but also the last of the great 'race men,' the Afro-American men of letters, a tradition best epitomized by W.E.B. DuBois. A self-styled 'Old Negro,' Sterling Brown is not only the Afro-American Poet Laureate, he is a great poet.''

BIOGRAPHICAL/CRITICAL SOURCES:

BOOKS

Brown, Sterling A., Arthur P. Davis and Ulysses Lee, *The Negro Caravan*, Dryden, 1941, revised editon, Arno, 1970.
Brown, Sterling A., *The Collected Poems of Sterling A. Brown*, selected by Michael S. Harper, Harper, 1980.
Contemporary Literary Criticism, Gale, Volume 1, 1973, Volume 23, 1983.
Cunard, Nancy, editor, *Negro Anthology*, Wishart Co., 1934.
Davis, Arthur P., *From the Dark Tower: Afro-American Writers, 1900-1960*, Howard University Press, 1974.
Dictionary of Literary Biography, Gale, Volume 48: *American Poets, 1880-1945*, Second Series, 1986, Volume 51: *Afro-American Writers from the Harlem Renaissance to 1940*, 1987, Volume 63: *Modern American Critics, 1920-1955*, 1988.
Gayle, Addison, Jr., editor, *Black Expression: Essays by and About Black Americans in the Creative Arts*, Weybright & Talley, 1969.
Mangione, Jerre, *The Dream and the Deal: The Federal Writers' Project, 1935-1943*, Little, Brown, 1972.
Wagner, Jean, *Black Poets of the United States: From Paul Laurence Dunbar to Langston Hughes*, translated by Kenneth Douglas, University of Illinois Press, 1973.

PERIODICALS

Black American Literature Forum, spring, 1980.
Callaloo: A Black South Journal of Arts and Letters, February-May, 1982.
Ebony, October, 1976.
Los Angeles Times Book Review, August 3, 1980.
New Directions: The Howard University Magazine, winter, 1974.
New Republic, February 11, 1978, December 20, 1982.
New York Times, May 15, 1932.
New York Times Book Review, November 30, 1969, January 11, 1981.
Studies in the Literary Imagination, fall, 1974.
Village Voice, January 14, 1981.
Virginia Quarterly Review, winter, 1981.
Washington Post, November 16, 1969, May 2, 1979, September 4, 1980, May 12, 1984.

—*Sketch by Donna Olendorf*

*   *   *

BRUNVAND, Jan Harold   1933-

PERSONAL: Born March 23, 1933, in Cadillac, Mich.; son of Harold N. (a civil engineer) and Ruth (Jorgensen) Brunvand; married Judith Darlene Ast (a librarian and archivist), June 10, 1956; children: Erik, Amy, Dana, Karen. *Education:* Michigan State University, B.A., 1955, M.A., 1957; attended University of Oslo, 1956-57; Indiana University, Ph.D., 1961.

ADDRESSES: Home—1031 1st Ave., Salt Lake City, Utah 84103. *Office*—Department of English, University of Utah, Salt Lake City, Utah 84112.

CAREER: University of Idaho, Moscow, assistant professor of English, 1961-65; Southern Illinois University at Edwardsville, associate professor of English, 1965-66; University of Utah, Salt Lake City, associate professor, 1966-71, professor of English and folklore, 1971—. Visiting assistant professor at Indiana University, summer, 1965. Member of Utah Folk Arts Advisory Panel, 1976—. Has appeared on talk shows, including "David Letterman" and morning programs. *Military service:* U.S. Army, Signal Corps, 1962-63.

MEMBER: American Association of University Professors, American Folklore Society (fellow), California Folklore Society.

AWARDS, HONORS: Fulbright scholar in Norway, 1956-57, grant for Romania, 1970-71; Guggenheim fellow, 1970-71; fellow of International Research and Exchanges Board in Romania, 1973-74, 1981.

WRITINGS:

A Dictionary of Proverbs and Proverbial Phrases from Books Published by Indiana Authors before 1890, Indiana University Press, 1961.
The Study of American Folklore (instructor's manual available), Norton, 1968, 3rd edition, 1986.
A Guide for Collectors of Folklore in Utah, University of Utah Press, 1971.
Norwegian Settlers in Alberta, Canadian Centre for Folk Cultural Studies, 1974.
Folklore: A Study and Research Guide, St. Martin's, 1976.
Readings in American Folklore, Norton, 1979.
The Vanishing Hitchhiker: American Urban Legends and Their Meanings, Norton, 1981.
The Choking Doberman and Other "New" Urban Legends, Norton, 1984.
The Mexican Pet: More "New" Urban Legends and Some Old Favorites, Norton, 1986.

CONTRIBUTOR

Austin E. Fife and J. Golden Taylor, editors, *The Western Folklore Conference: Selected Papers* (monograph), Utah State University Press, 1964.
A. E. Fife, Alta Fife, and Henry H. Glassie, editors, *Forms upon the Frontier* (monograph), Utah State University Press, 1969.
Ray B. Browne and Ronald J. Ambrosetti, editors, *Popular Culture and Curricula*, Bowling Green University, 1970.
Wayland D. Hand, editor, *American Folk Legend: A Symposium*, University of California Press, 1971.
Glassie, Linda Degh, and Felix J. Oinas, editors, *Folklore Today: Festschrift for Richard W. Dorson*, Indiana University Press, 1976.
Paul Eschholz and Alfred Rosa, editors, *Subject and Strategy: A Rhetoric Reader*, 2nd edition (Brunvand was not included in 1st edition), St. Martin's, 1981.

RECORDINGS

(Co-editor) "The New Beehive Songster" (album; two volumes), Okedokee Records, 1976-77.
"Folktale" (tape), Everett/Edwards, 1979.
"School Folklore" (tape), Everett/Edwards, 1979.

OTHER

Author of column "Urban Legends," distributed by United

Features Syndicate, 1987—. Contributor of over a hundred articles and reviews to folklore journals and to newspapers. Assistant editor of *Midwest Folklore*, 1959-60, book review editor, 1961-64; associate editor of *Journal of American Folklore*, 1963-67, and 1973-76, book review editor, 1967-73, editor, 1976-80.

WORK IN PROGRESS: Fourth book of urban legends, *Curses, Broiled Again!*, for Norton.

SIDELIGHTS: Jan Harold Brunvand, professor of English and folklore at the University of Utah, has written three books to date on what he calls the "urban legend," and a fourth is said to be on the way. Urban legends, though often sworn to be true by their tellers, are largely unverifiable modern-day stories which criss-cross the globe mainly by word of mouth. Have you heard the one about the woman tourist in Mexico who, upon finding a cute little dog, sneaks the dog back to the States only to discover from her veterinarian that the dog is actually a sewer rat? Or maybe the one about the cat who exploded after being placed in the microwave oven as a means of drying it off? According to Brunvand, some of these legends are grounded in the past and they often take slightly different forms as they move from region to region, but no matter what their origin or form, they are pure myth. However, it is not uncommon for these stories to be picked up by the media and printed or reported as truth, making them seem all the more valid.

Brunvand's three books on urban legends—*The Vanishing Hitchhiker, The Choking Doberman and Other "New" Urban Legends,* and *The Mexican Pet*—relate the plots of many known urban legends and, without getting too deep into analysis, provide some explanation as to what they mean and why they have arisen. In a conversation with *U.S. News and World Report* contributor Alvin P. Sanoff, Brunvand maintains that "urban legends fill a need people have to tell each other stories, to know the latest that's going on. . . . These stories are the folklore of the mostly educated, white middle class. . . . In an urbanized society, these stories provide a common bond. They are a means by which strangers can easily communicate with one another." Additionally, in a *Time* review, Donald Morrison responds: "Why do such stories survive, even flourish, in an age of science and cynicism? Many of them, says Brunvand, serve as cautionary tales, sermonettes on the evils of, say, parking in deserted lanes or buying cheap imported goods. Others are inspired by suspicion of change—of microwave ovens or fast-food restaurants. Writes Brunvand: 'Whatever is new and puzzling or scary, but which eventually becomes familiar, may turn up in modern folklore.'" Some of these legends are even viewed as part of ongoing racial or cultural stereotyping, like the ones about Southeast Asian immigrants to the United States capturing and eating people's pets.

Most reviewers find Brunvand's three books entertaining. Although *Times Literary Supplement* critic Mark Abley feels that Brunvand's first collection, *The Vanishing Hitchhiker*, is weak in terms of explaining the implications and the significance of urban legends, *New York Times* reviewer Christopher Lehmann-Haupt claims Brunvand's third collection, *The Mexican Pet*, "offers enough material to suggest a number of conclusions." According to Lehmann-Haupt, in *The Mexican Pet* "Brunvand includes new versions of beliefs and stories discussed in his earlier books, so that we may judge for ourselves how apocryphal stories evolve. He also attempts here to establish the provenance of several legends, particularly those

that have been circulated by the media. . . . 'The Mexican Pet' is enlightening in several respects. By seeing new permutations of old stories, we become convinced that what we once took as gospel is indeed nothing more than plausible fabrication."

BIOGRAPHICAL/CRITICAL SOURCES:

BOOKS

Brunvand, Jan Harold, *The Vanishing Hitchhiker: American Urban Legnds and Their Meanings,* Norton, 1981.

PERIODICALS

Chicago Tribune Book World, July 17, 1986.
Choice, May, 1969, May, 1982.
Columbia Journalism Review, March, 1982.
Detroit Free Press, July 6, 1984.
Journal of American Folklore, January, 1969, July, 1978, October, 1978.
New York Times, July 21, 1986.
New York Times Book Review, July 6, 1986.
Time, November 9, 1981.
Times Literary Supplement, August 13, 1982.
U.S. News and World Report, September 22, 1986.

*   *   *

BRYAN, Ashley F. 1923-

PERSONAL: Born July 13, 1923, in New York, N.Y. *Education:* Attended Cooper Union and Columbia University.

ADDRESSES: Office—Department of Art, Dartmouth College, Hanover, N.H. 03755.

CAREER: Author and illustrator of books for children; professor emeritus of art and visual studies at Dartmouth College.

AWARDS, HONORS: American Library Association, Social Responsibilities Round Table, Coretta Scott King Award, 1980, for illustrating *Beat the Story-Drum, Pum-Pum*, 1986, for writing *Lion and the Ostrich Chicks and Other African Folk Tales*, and Coretta Scott King Honor Award, 1988, for illustrating *What a Morning! The Christmas Story in Black Spirituals*.

WRITINGS:

JUVENILES; SELF-ILLUSTRATED

The Ox of the Wonderful Horns and Other African Folktales, Atheneum, 1971.
The Adventures of Aku; or, How It Came about That We Shall Always See Okra the Cat Lying on a Velvet Cushion while Okraman the Dog Sleeps among the Ashes, Atheneum, 1976.
The Dancing Granny, Macmillan, 1977.
Beat the Story-Drum, Pum-Pum (Nigerian folk tales), Atheneum, 1980.
The Cat's Drum, Atheneum, 1985.
Lion and the Ostrich Chicks and Other African Folk Tales, Atheneum, 1986.

ILLUSTRATOR

Rabindranath Tagore, *Moon, for What Do You Wait?* (poems), edited by Richard Lewis, Atheneum, 1967.
Mari Evans, *Jim Flying High* (juvenile), Doubleday, 1979.
Susan Cooper, *Jethro and the Jumbie* (juvenile), Atheneum, 1979.
John Langstaff, editor, *What a Morning! The Christmas Story in Black Spirituals*, Macmillan, 1987.

OTHER

(Compiler) *Black American Spirituals,* Volume I: *Walk Together Children* (self-illustrated), Atheneum, 1974, Volume II: *I'm Going to Sing* (self-illustrated), Macmillan, 1982.
(Compiler and author of introduction) Paul Laurence Dunbar, *I Greet the Dawn: Poems,* Atheneum, 1978.

SIDELIGHTS: As a folklorist, Ashley Bryan works to preserve African traditions in America. For example, his collection of the spirituals of American slaves *Walk Together Children* records "the brave and lonely cries of men and women forced to trust in heaven because they had no hope on earth," remarks Neil Millar in the *Christian Science Monitor.* The subject of bondage set to native African rhythms produced songs such as "Go Down Moses," "Deep River," "Mary Had a Baby," "Go Tell It on the Mountain," "Nobody Knows the Trouble I Seen," "Walk Together Children," "O Freedom," "Little David," and "Swing Low, Sweet Chariot." "With Ashley Bryan's collection," writes Virginia Hamilton of the *New York Times Book Review,* "the tradition of preserving the spiritual through teaching the young is surely enriched."

Several of the folklorist's collections contain stories that explain why certain animals became natural enemies. In *The Adventures of Aku* Bryan recounts the day that the enmity between dogs and cats began. This "is a long involved magic tale that has echoes of Aladdin's lamp and Jack and the Beanstalk to mention just two familiar stories with similar motifs," says the *New York Times Book Review*'s Jane Yolen. It utilizes a magic ring, a stupid son, a heroic quest, and Ananse, the standard trickster figure in African folklore, to capsulize the Ashanti proverb stating, "No one knows the story of tomorrow's dawn."

The Nigerian folktales in *Beat the Story-Drum, Pum-Pum* also reveal the origins of hostilities between animals, such as that between the snake and the frog or the bush cow and the elephant. These "retellings make the stories unique, offering insight into the heart of a culture," notes M. M. Burns in *Horn Book.* Each story, the reviewer adds, "has a style and beat appropriate to the subject, the overall effect being one of musical composition with dexterously designed variations and movements."

Like *The Adventures of Aku, The Dancing Granny* continues the saga of the trickster Ananse. Originally titled "He Sings to Make the Old Woman Dance," this folktale recounts the day when a little old lady, who danced continually, foiled the Spider Ananse's plan to eat all of her food. While Granny worked, Ananse sang so that she might dance. Then, when she danced away, the spider would eat up her corn. This went on four times until Granny took Ananse to be her partner and danced him away, too.

For all of his work, Bryan creates block prints, paintings and drawings which, according to a *Horn Book* reviewer, "add flavor and authenticity" to the books.

MEDIA ADAPTATIONS: Ashley Bryan recorded *The Dancing Granny and Other African Tales* for Caedmon.

BIOGRAPHICAL/CRITICAL SOURCES:

PERIODICALS

Christian Science Monitor, November 6, 1974, November 3, 1976, August 2, 1985.
Commonweal, November 22, 1974.

Horn Book, February, 1977, April, 1981, February, 1983, May, 1985.
Language Arts, March, 1977, February, 1978, March, 1984, October, 1985.
Ms., December, 1974.
New York Times Book Review, November 3, 1974, October 10, 1976.
Scientific American, December, 1980.
Washington Post Book World, November 7, 1971, December 12, 1976.
Wilson Library Bulletin, February, 1986.

*   *   *

BUESCHEL, Richard M.   1926-

PERSONAL: Surname is pronounced Bush-ell; born December 26, 1926, in Chicago, Ill.; son of Martin W. and Helen (Kernacs) Bueschel; married Helen Snyder, November 24, 1951; children: Stacey Brooks, Megan Conley. *Education:* Wright Junior College, Chicago, Ill., A.Sc., 1949; Illinois College, Jacksonville, B.A., 1951.

ADDRESSES: Home—414 North Prospect Manor, Mount Prospect, Ill. 60056. *Office*—c/o Zylke & Associates, Inc., 215 Revere Dr., Northbrook, Ill. 60062.

CAREER: Wilson Sporting Goods, Chicago, Ill., advertising assistant, 1951-52; Wallace, Ferry, Hanly & Co. (advertising), Chicago, copy-contact, 1952-54; Erwin Wasey & Co. (advertising), Chicago, copywriter, 1954-57; Erwin Wasey, Ruthrauff & Ryan, Chicago, account executive, 1957-58; Waldie & Briggs, Inc. (advertising), Chicago, 1959-75, president, 1967-75; Ladd/Wells/Presba Advertising, Inc., senior vice-president and creative director, 1975-79; Zylke & Associates, Inc., Northbrook, Ill., account supervisor, 1979—. Consultant on Oriental aviation to Twentieth Century-Fox, and on popular culture and coin machines to Smithsonian Institution. *Military service:* U.S. Army Air Forces, Ninth Air Force Aviation Engineers, 1945-46.

MEMBER: Business and Professional Advertising Association (president of Chicago chapter, 1968-69), Authors Guild.

WRITINGS:

Japanese Aircraft Camouflage and Markings, Aero, 1966.
Japanese Code Names, Aero, 1966.
Communist Chinese Airpower, Praeger, 1968.
Aircam Japanese Fighters, eight volumes, Osprey, 1970-71.
Aircam Japanese Bombers, four volumes, Osprey, 1972-73.
Japanese Army Aircraft, AeroFile, 1976.
Japanese Army and Navy Aircraft, AeroFile, 1976.
Guide to Collectible Slot Machines, Coin Slot Books, five volumes, 1978-89.
Guide to Collectible Trade Stimulators, Coin Slot Books, three volumes, 1979-88.
Coin Slot Guide, Coin Slot Books, forty volumes, 1979-83.
Pinball 1, Hoflin Publishing, 1988.
Jennings Slot Machines, Hoflin Publishing, 1988.
International Slot Machines, Hoflin Publishing, 1989.
(With Steve Gronowski) *Arcade 1,* Coin Slot Books, 1989.

Historical editor, *Coin Slot Magazine,* 1974—. Consultant on Oriental aviation to *American Heritage,* 1966-74.

WORK IN PROGRESS: Japanese Aircraft in Color; Lemons, Cherries, and Bell-Fruit Gum; Peck & Snyder Amusements; Coin-Operated Scales; Rolling Mountain, a history of the Ferris wheel; research on the battle of El Caney of the Spanish-American War.

SIDELIGHTS: Richard M. Bueschel told *CA:* "To find the unfindable, and to publish the forgotten—that's the direction of my research and writing. The search is the thing, and the ability to share these findings with a ready reading audience is a joy unto itself. My areas are popular culture and American industrial growth. Both are subjects for which the surface has barely been tapped. Yet all are of unusual and general interest. And there's room for as many writers as are interested. We can't really understand our present if we don't know our past. It's fun to find out, and exciting to share."

*   *   *

BULLOUGH, Vern (LeRoy) 1928-

PERSONAL: Born July 24, 1928, in Salt Lake City, Utah; son of David Vernon (a tool and die maker) and Augusta (Rueckert) Bullough; married Bonnie Uckerman (a nurse and teacher), August 2, 1947; children: David (deceased), James, Steven, Susan, Robert, Michael. *Education:* University of Utah, B.A., 1951; University of Chicago, M.A., 1951, Ph.D., 1954; California State University, Long Beach, R.N., 1980.

ADDRESSES: Home—590 Le Brun Rd., Amherst, N.Y. 14226. *Office*—State University of New York College at Buffalo, 1300 Elmwood Ave., Buffalo, N.Y. 14222.

CAREER: Youngstown University, Youngstown, Ohio, associate professor of history, 1954-59; California State University, Northridge, 1959-80, began as assistant professor, became professor of history; State University of New York College at Buffalo, dean of natural and social sciences, 1980—. Lecturer, California College of Medicine, Los Angeles; visiting lecturer, School of Public Health, University of California, Los Angeles, and University of Southern California; Morris Fishbein Lecturer, University of Chicago, 1970; Beaumont Lecturer, University of Vermont, 1975; adjunct professor of nursing and history, State University of New York at Buffalo. Member of southern California board, American Civil Liberties Union; member of Los Angeles Building Commission, 1975-78; member of Housing Opportunities Made Equal, 1981-87. *Military service:* U.S. Army, Army Security Agency, 1946-48.

MEMBER: International Society for Comparative Study of Civilizations, American Historical Association, American Association for Advancement of Science, Mediaeval Academy, Renaissance Society, American Association for History of Medicine, American Association for History of Nursing, American Nurses Association, History of Technology Society, Society for Study of Social Problems, History of Science Society, Society for the Scientific Study of Sex (fellow, 1981; president, 1981-83).

AWARDS, HONORS: Newberry fellowship; Huntington Library fellowship; Fulbright exchange scholar; recipient of grants from American Philosophical Society, National Science Foundation, Rockefeller Foundation, American Council of Learned Societies, U.S. Department of Education, and Erickson Educational Foundation; named outstanding professor, California State Universities and Colleges, 1969; President's Award, California State University, 1978; Distinguished Humanist Award, 1979; Founders Award, Center for Sex Research, 1980; Lau-

reate, Humanist Academy, 1984; named State University ofNew York Distinguished Professor, 1987; Garrison Lecturer, American Association for History of Medicine, 1988.

WRITINGS:

The History of Prostitution, University Books, 1964.
The Development of Medicine as a Profession: The Contribution of the Medieval University to Modern Medicine, S. Karger, 1966.
Man in Western Civilization, Holt, 1970.
The Scientific Revolution, Holt, 1970.
(With Raoul Naroll and Frada Naroll) *Military Deterrence in History: A Statistical Survey*, State University of New York Press, 1971.
Sex, Society, and History, Neale Watson, 1976.
Sexual Variance in Society and History, Wiley, 1976.
(With others) *Annotated Bibliography of Homosexuality*, Garland Publishing, 1977.
(With Barett Elcano) *Bibliography of Prostitution*, Garland Publishing, 1978.
Homosexuality: A History, New American Library, 1979.
(Editor) *The Frontiers of Sex Research*, Prometheus Books, 1979.
(With James Brundage) *Sexual Practice and the Medieval Church*, Prometheus Books, 1982.
(With Olga Church and Alice Stein) *Amerian Nursing: A Biographical Dictionary*, Garland Publishing, 1988.
(With Brenda Shelton and Sarah Slavin) *Subordinated Sex*, University of Georgia, 1988.

WITH WIFE, BONNIE BULLOUGH

What Color Are Your Germs? (pamphlet), Committee to End Discrimination in Chicago Medical Institutions, 1954.
The Emergence of Modern Nursing, Macmillan, 1964, 2nd edition, 1969.
(Editors) *Issues in Nursing*, Springer Publishing Co., 1966.
(Editors) *New Directions for Nurses*, Springer Publishing Co., 1971.
Poverty, Ethnic Identity, and Health Care, Appleton-Century-Crofts, 1972.
(Editors) *The Subordinate Sex: A History of Attitudes toward Women*, University of Illinois Press, 1973.
Sin, Sickness, and Sanity: A History of Sexual Attitudes, New American Library, 1977.
(Editors) *Expanding Horizons in Nursing*, Springer Publishing Co., 1977.
Prostitution: An Illustrated Social History, Crown, 1978.
The Care of the Sick, Neale Watson, 1978.
Nursing: An Historical Bibliography, Garland Publishing, 1981.
Health Care for the Other Americans, Appleton-Century-Crofts, 1982.
(Editors with Mary Claire Soukup) *Nursing Issues and Strategies for the Eighties*, Springer Publishing Co., 1983.
History and Politics of Nursing, Appleton-Century-Crofts, 1984.
(Co-editors with Jane Garvey and Karen Miller Allen) *Issues Nursing*, Garland Publishing, 1985.
Prostitution and Society, Prometheus, 1987.

OTHER

Contributor of chapters to about twenty-five books. Contributor of articles to *Nation, Saturday Review, Progressive, New Leader, Free Inquiry, Skeptical Inquirer*, and numerous other publications.

WORK IN PROGRESS: With wife, Bonnie Bullough, *Community Health Nursing;* with Fang Fu Ruan, *Sex in China;* books on achievement, sex research, and biohistory.

BURMEISTER, Edwin 1939-

PERSONAL: Born November 30, 1939, in Chicago, Ill.; son of Edwin Carl and Dorothy (Braithwaite) Burmeister. *Education:* Cornell University, B.A., 1961, M.A., 1962; Massachusetts Institute of Technology, Ph.D., 1965.

ADDRESSES: Home—P.O. Box 149, Ivy, Va. 22945. *Office*—Department of Economics, 114 Rouss Hall, University of Virginia, Charlottesville, Va. 22901.

CAREER: University of Pennsylvania, Wharton School, Philadelphia, assistant professor, 1965-68, associate professor, 1968-71, professor of economics, 1972-76; University of Virginia, Charlottesville, professor of economics and member of Center for Advanced Studies, 1976-79, Commonwealth Professor of Economics, 1979—. Professor of economics and finance, University of Illinois, 1982. Visiting professor at Duke University, Durham, N.C., 1971-72 and University of Chicago, 1980; visiting research professor, Australian National University, Canberra, Australia, 1974-75.

MEMBER: American Association of University Professors, American Economics Association, American Finance Association, Royal Economic Society, American Statistical Association, Econometric Society (fellow), Western Economic Association, Southern Economic Association, Canadian Economic Society.

AWARDS, HONORS: Woodrow Wilson fellowship, 1961-62; National Science Foundation research grants, 1967-68, 1968-70, 1970-72, 1972-75, 1976-78, 1979-81, 1983—; John Simon Guggenheim Memorial fellowship, 1974-75.

WRITINGS:

(Contributor) Peter Newman, editor, *Readings in Mathematical Economics,* Volume I, Johns Hopkins Press, 1968.
(With A. Rodney Dobell) *Mathematical Theories of Economic Growth,* Macmillan, 1970.
(Contributor) Paul Kay, editor, *Explorations in Mathematical Anthropology,* M.I.T. Press, 1971.
(With Ngo Van Long) *On Some Unresolved Questions in Capital Theory,* Australian National University, 1975.
(Editor with Lawrence R. Klein) *Econometric Model Performance: Comparative Simulation Studies of the U.S. Economy,* University of Pennsylvania Press, 1976.
Capital Theory and Dynamics, Cambridge University Press, 1980.
Nurse Little, Dorrance, 1984.

Contributor to economics journals. *International Economic Review,* acting editor, 1970-71, editor, 1971-76, associate editor, 1976—.†

*   *   *

BURMEISTER, Lou E(lla) 1928-

PERSONAL: Born April 7, 1928, in Milwaukee, Wis.; daughter of Marvin Robert and Myrtle (Smith) Burmeister. *Education:* University of Wisconsin—Madison, M.S., 1951, Ph.D., 1966; summer study at University of Colorado, 1956, Syracuse University, 1961, and University of Geneva, 1962. *Religion:* Christian Scientist.

ADDRESSES: Home—6008 Torrey Pines Dr., El Paso, Tex. 79912. *Office*—College of Education, University of Texas, El Paso, Tex. 79968.

CAREER: High school teacher of reading in Milwaukee, Wis., 1950-52, and in Thiensville, Wis., 1961-64; University of Wisconsin—Milwaukee, instructor, 1952-61; University of Wisconsin—Madison, assistant professor of education, 1966-68; University of Texas at El Paso, professor of curriculum and instruction, 1968-88, professor emerita, 1988—. Visiting professor at Syracuse University, 1968.

MEMBER: International Reading Association (president of Southwest special interest group, 1972-74; member of board of directors, 1976-79), National Council of Teachers of English, American Educational Research Association, Wisconsin State Reading Association (president, 1964-65), Texas Education Association, Milwaukee Area Reading Association (president, 1955-57), Pi Lambda Theta, Phi Kappa Phi.

WRITINGS:

(Editor) James Hilton, *Good-bye, Mr. Chips,* Riverside Press, 1964.
(With Theodore L. Clymer and T. C. Barrett) *Ginn Word Enrichment Program,* Ginn, 1969, 2nd revised edition, 1985.
Reading Strategies for Middle and Secondary School Teachers, Addison-Wesley, 1974, 2nd edition, 1978.
Words—From Print to Meaning, Addison-Wesley, 1975.
Foundations and Strategies for Teaching Children to Read, Addison-Wesley, 1983.

Contributor to numerous anthologies and to journals, including *Reading Teacher, Journal of Reading, Reading Research Quarterly,* and *Journal of the Reading Specialist.*

*   *   *

BURNS, Robert I(gnatius) 1921-

PERSONAL: Born August 16, 1921, in San Francisco, Calif.; son of Harry (a railroad engineer) and Viola (Whearty) Burns. *Education:* Attended University of San Francisco, 1939-40, and University of Santa Clara; Gonzaga University, B.A. (with honors), 1945, M.A. (philosophy) and Phil.Lic., 1947; Fordham University, M.A. (history), 1949; Jesuit Faculty of Theology, S.Th.B. and S.Th.Lic., 1953; graduate study at Villa Machiavelli, Florence, Italy, 1953-54, Gregorian University, Rome, Italy, 1954-55, and Campion Hall, Oxford, 1955-56; Johns Hopkins University, Ph.D. (with honors), 1958; University of Fribourg, Doc. es Sc. Hist. (double summa cum laude), 1961.

ADDRESSES: Home—Xavier Hall, 7101 West 80th St., Los Angeles, Calif. 90045. *Office*—Department of History, Graduate School, University of California, Los Angeles, Calif. 90024.

CAREER: Entered Society of Jesus (Jesuits), 1940, ordained Roman Catholic priest, 1952. Jesuit Historical Archives, Spokane, Wash., assistant archivist, 1946-47; University of San Francisco, San Francisco, Calif., instructor, 1947-48, assistant professor, 1958-63, associate professor, 1963-66, professor of history, 1967-76; University of California, Los Angeles, senior professor of history, 1976—, member of staff of Near Eastern Center and of Center for Medieval and Renaissance Studies, 1977—. Visiting professor of history at College of Notre Dame, Belmont, Calif., 1963—; visiting James Chair Professor, Brown University, 1970; member of faculty, Institute for Advanced Study, Princeton University, 1972; visiting lecturer at universities in United States, Italy, Spain, Germany, Israel, and Canada. Director, Institute of Medieval Mediterranean Spain, 1976—; member of executive committee, Hill Monastic Library, 1977-81. Has conducted research in Europe, Near East, and North Africa. Member of international advisory board of American Bibliographical Center, 1982—, University of California Press, 1985—, and Patronato Nacional del "Misteri de Elche" [government of Spain], 1986—. Served briefly as civilian relief chaplain to U.S. Air Force near Casablanca and in pastoral work during study periods in England and Italy.

MEMBER: North American Catalan Society (member of board of directors, 1978—), American Historical Association (Pacific Coast branch vice-president, 1978; president, 1979-80), American Society of Church History (Pacific Coast branch vice-president, 1962), American Catholic Historical Association (life member; vice-president, 1974; president, 1975), Society for Spanish and Portuguese Historical Studies, Academy of Research Historians on Medieval Spain (president, 1976-78), Medieval Academy of America, Conference on Peace Research in History, Medieval Association of the Pacific.

AWARDS, HONORS: Guggenheim fellowship to Spain, 1963-64; Pierre Charles Award of Mission Institute, 1966; John Gilmary Shea Prize from American Catholic Historical Society, 1966, for *The Jesuits and the Indian Wars of the Northwest,* and 1968, for *The Crusader Kingdom of Valencia: Reconstruction on a Thirteenth-Century Frontier;* American Association for State and Local History award, 1967; Pacific Coast of American Historical Association award, 1968, for *The Crusader Kingdom of Valencia: Reconstruction on a Thirteenth-Century Frontier;* D.Litt. from Gonzaga University, 1968, Marquette University, 1977, Loyola University of Chicago, 1978, Boston College, 1982, University of San Francisco, 1983, Fordham University, 1984, and Universidad de Valencia, Spain, 1985; National Endowment for the Humanities fellowships, 1971, 1973-82; American Council of Learned Societies fellowship, 1972; Catholic Press Association of the United States and Canada book award, 1975, for *Islam under the Crusaders: Colonialism in the Thirteenth-Century Kingdom of Valencia;* Phi Alpha Theta book award, 1976, for *Medieval Colonialism: Postcrusade Exploitation of Islamic Valencia;* Haskins Gold Medal from Medieval Academy of America, 1976; Medieval Academy of America elected fellow, 1978; Accio Cultural del Pais Valencia, 1979; Premi de la Critica "Serra d'Or," 1982; Premi Catalonia from Institut d'Estudis Catalans, 1982; Hispanic Society of America elected fellow, 1985; Celtic Foundation award, 1985; grants from Ford Foundation, Guggenheim Foundation, and Robb Foundation.

WRITINGS:

(Contributor) *I Lift My Lamp,* Newman Press, 1955.
The Jesuits and the Indian Wars of the Northwest, Yale University Press, 1966, reprint, University of Idaho Press, 1986.

The Crusader Kingdom of Valencia: Reconstruction on a Thirteenth-Century Frontier, two volumes, Harvard University Press, 1967.
Islam under the Crusaders: Colonial Survival in the Thirteenth-Century Kingdom of Valencia, Princeton University Press, 1974.
Medieval Colonialism: Postcrusade Exploitation of Islamic Valencia, Princeton University Press, 1975.
(Co-author) *Islam and Cultural Change in the Middle Ages,* University of California Press, 1975.
(Co-author) *Contributions to Mediterranean Studies,* Royal University of Malta Press, 1977.
Moors and Crusaders in Mediterranean Spain, Variorum Reprints (London), 1978.
(Co-author) *Islamic Middle Ages, 700-1900,* Darwin Press, 1981.
Jaume I i els Valencians del segle XIII, [Valencia], 1981.
Muslims, Christians, and Jews in the Crusader Kingdom of Valencia: Societies in Symbiosis (essays), Cambridge University Press, 1984, 2nd edition, 1986.
Diplomatarium Regni Valentiae, Volume I: *Society and Documentation in Crusader Valencia,* Princeton University Press, 1985.
(Editor) *The Worlds of Alfonso the Learned and James the Conqueror: Intellect and Force in the Middle Ages,* Princeton University Press, 1985.
(Editor) *Alfonso X the Learned: Emperor of Culture,* Fordham University Press, 1985.

Also associate editor of *Encyclopedia of Iberia in the Middle Ages,* Garland Publishing. Contributor of more than one hundred articles on Spain to encyclopedias; also contributor to proceedings of international historical congresses. Contributor of about seventy articles to periodicals and history journals, including *Speculum, Mid-America, Anuario de estudios medievales,* and *American Historical Review.* Regular abstracter for *Historical Abstracts* and *America: History and Life.* Editor, *Viator,* 1980—; member of board of editors, *Trends in History,* 1978—, *Anuario de Estudios Medievales* (Spain), 1985—, and *Bulletin of the Society of Cantigueiros,* 1986—.

WORK IN PROGRESS: Five additional volumes of *Diplomatarium Regni Valentiae,* for Princeton University Press; *Regnante Jacobo I Ejus Conquistatoris,* in six volumes, for Princeton University Press.

SIDELIGHTS: The library of the University of California, Los Angeles, maintains a permanent deposit for Robert I. Burns's manuscript drafts and correspondence in its special collection. Burns reads Italian, French, German, Spanish, Catalan, Latin, and Greek.

BIOGRAPHICAL/CRITICAL SOURCES:

PERIODICALS

Times Literary Supplement, December 1, 1966, January 17, 1975, April 4, 1986, July 18, 1986.

C

CAMPBELL, Edward D(unscomb) C(hristian), Jr. 1946-

PERSONAL: Born October 24, 1946, in Richmond, Va.; son of Edward Dunscomb Christian (a realtor) and Jane (Robertson) Campbell. *Education:* Virginia Polytechnic Institute and State University, B.A., 1970, M.A., 1973; University of South Carolina, Ph.D, 1979.

ADDRESSES: Home—1811 Hanover Ave., Richmond, Va. 23220. *Office—Virginia Calvalcade,* Virginia State Library, Eleventh St. at Capitol Square, Richmond, Va. 23219.

CAREER: United Virginia Bank, Richmond, portfolio analyst, 1972-73; University of South Carolina, Columbia, instructor in history, 1975-78; Museum of the Confederacy, Richmond, director, 1978-83; Virginia Historical Society, Richmond, director of development, 1983-84; *Virginia Calvalcade,* Virginia State Library, Richmond, editor, 1985—. Member of adjunct faculty, departments of English and history, Virginia Commonwealth University, 1979-83. Consultant to television series, "Life and Leisure in the Old South," National Endowment for the Humanities, 1976. Co-director of film/lecture series, "Images of the South in History, Fiction, and Film," Virginia Foundation for the Humanities and Public Policy, 1980. Conducted lecture series to accompany exhibition, "Painting in the South," Virginia Museum of Fine Arts, 1983; member of planning committee for exhibition, "Is It True What They Say about Dixie," Tennessee State Museum, 1984; project consultant to exhibition, "Victory and Defeat: Jefferson Davis and the Lost Cause," Museum of the Confederacy, 1984-85. Member of advisory board, Historic Lexington Foundation, 1981—; board member, Historic Richmond Foundation, 1985—. Member of advisory board, Tompkins-McGraw Library Archives and Museum, Medical College of Virginia, 1982. Reader of grant proposals, Institute of Museum Services, U.S. Department of Education, 1980-82. Chairman of attractions committee, Richmond Convention and Visitors Bureau, 1979-80.

MEMBER: American Historical Association, Organization of American Historians, American Association for State and Local History (member of project and publications awards committee, 1982-84), American Association of Museums, American Film Institute, Association for the Study of Afro-American Life, Victorian Society in America, Southern Historical Association, Virginia Historical Society, Virginia Association of Museums (member of board of directors and treasurer, 1980-84), Association for the Preservation of Virginia Antiquities (secretary of William Byrd Branch, Richmond, 1986), Phi Alpha Theta.

AWARDS, HONORS: "Outstanding Academic Book" citation, *Choice,* 1982, for *The Celluloid South.*

WRITINGS:

The Celluloid South: Hollywood and the Southern Myth, University of Tennessee Press, 1981.
(Contributor) Walter J. Fraser and Winfred B. Moore, editors, *From the Old South to the New: Essays on the Transitional South,* Greenwood Press, 1981.
(Contributor) Warren French, editor, *The South and Film,* University Press of Mississippi, 1981.
(Contributor) Richard B. Harwell, editor, *Gone with the Wind as Book and Film,* University of South Carolina Press, 1983.
(Contributor) Robert Toplin, editor, *Using Films in the Classroom: An OAH Guide,* Organization of American Historians, 1983.
(With Patricia R. Loughride) *Women in Mourning* (catalogue to accompany exhibition, "Life after Death: Mourning in the Old South and the Confederacy"), Museum of the Confederacy, 1986.

Also contributor to *The Dictionary of Afro-American Slavery,* edited by Randall M. Miller; to *The Encyclopedia of Southern Culture,* edited by Charles R. Wilson and William Ferris; to *The American Past through Film,* edited by Robert Brent Toplin. Also author of program notes for exhibition, "Is it True What They Say about the South?" Contributor of numerous articles and reviews to periodicals, including *Journal of American History* and *Journal of Southern History.*

WORK IN PROGRESS: Fields of Film and Fire: Hollywood and the Civil War, for "American Military History" series, University of South Carolina Press; *The Youngest Slaves: Black Children on the Eve of Emancipation.*

*   *   *

**CAMPBELL, Joanna
See BLY, Carol(yn)**

CAMPBELL, Rita Ricardo
  See RICARDO-CAMPBELL, Rita

*   *   *

CAMPOLO, Anthony, Jr.   1935-

PERSONAL: Born February 25, 1935, in Philadelphia, Pa.; son of Anthony (a radio repairman) and Mary (Piccirelli) Campolo; married Margaret Davidson, June 7, 1958; children: Lisa Davidson, Bart Anthony. *Education:* Eastern Baptist College (now Eastern College), B.A., 1956; University of Pennsylvania, graduate study, 1958-59; Eastern Baptist Theological Seminary, Th.M. and B.D., both 1960; Temple University, Ph.D., 1968.

ADDRESSES: Office—Department of Sociology, Eastern College, St. Davids, Pa. 19087.

CAREER: Ordained Baptist minister, 1959. Pastor of Baptist Churches in Jacobstown and Chesterfield, N.J., 1957-61, and of American Baptist church in King of Prussia, Pa., 1961-65; Eastern College, St. Davids, Pa., associate professor, 1965-73, professor of sociology, 1973—, chairman of department, 1966—, chairman of youth ministries, 1982—. Visiting associate professor at University of Pennsylvania, 1966-75; visiting lecturer at Eastern Baptist Theological Seminary, 1968-73. Executive director of Youth Guidance of Southeastern Pennsylvania. Staff member of WCAU-Television; host of television programs; has appeared on "Good Morning America." Democratic candidate for U.S. Congress, 1976.

MEMBER: American Baptist Sociological Association, Evangelical Association for the Promotion of Education (founder and president).

WRITINGS:

A Denomination Looks at Itself, Judson, 1971.
The Success Fantasy, Victor Books, 1982.
A Reasonable Faith: Responding to Secularism, Word Books, 1983.
The Power Delusion, Victor Books, 1983.
Ideas for Social Action, Youth Specialities, 1983.
It's Friday, but Sunday's Comin', Word Books, 1984.
Partly Right, Word Books, 1985.
Who Switched the Price Tags, Word Books, 1986.
Seven Deadly Sins, Word Books, 1987.

Contributor to periodicals, including *Watchman-Examiner,* *Foundations,* and *Observer.*

WORK IN PROGRESS: Intellectuals Christians Must Take Seriously, for Word Books.

SIDELIGHTS: "The most important aspect of my ministry is the challenging of young people to participate in missionary work for Jesus Christ," Anthony Campolo told *CA.* "Much of this is done by encouraging their participation in the projects of the Evangelical Association for the Promotion of Education, which operates out of my offices at Eastern College. Many Eastern students are directly involved in missions in Third World countries and in the city of Philadelphia. Other volunteers are recruited when I travel to churches, and to other colleges and seminary campuses across the country."

CARDENAS, Daniel N(egrete)   1917-

PERSONAL: Born July 21, 1917, in Williams, Ariz.; son of Jose Hipolito (a millwright) and Juanita (Negrete) Cardenas; married E. Florence Gustaw, January 25, 1942 (divorced, 1977); married Dorothy K. Booth, January 12, 1979; children: (first marriage) Donal Sean, Dana Maria, Teresa Eileen. *Education:* Park College, B.A., 1941; Columbia University, M.A., 1947, Ph.D., 1953.

ADDRESSES: Home—4924 Icaria Way, Ocean Hills, Calif. 92056. *Office*—Department of Spanish and Portuguese, California State University, 1250 Bellflower Blvd., Long Beach, Calif. 90840.

CAREER: Columbia University, New York, N.Y., lecturer in Spanish, 1947-48; University of Oklahoma, Norman, instructor, 1948-53, assistant professor of Spanish, 1953-57; University of Chicago, Chicago, Ill., assistant professor, 1957-62, associate professor of Spanish, 1962-70; California State University, Long Beach, professor of Spanish, 1970-85, professor emeritus, 1985—, chairman of department, 1970-73 and 1976-78. Visiting professor at Columbia University, summer, 1950, University of Colorado, summer, 1957, and Pennsylvania State University, spring, 1968; Fulbright lecturer, University of Madrid, 1961-62. Consultant for Coronet Instructional Films, 1962-63, and Lingua Film, Inc. *Military service:* U.S. Army, 1941-45.

MEMBER: International Linguistic Association, American Association of Teachers of Spanish and Portuguese, American Dialect Society (member of executive council, 1973-76), La Real Academia Espanola (corresponding member).

AWARDS, HONORS: U.S. Department of State travel grant for research in Mexico, 1949-50; Ford Foundation fellow, 1955-56; named academic de numero, Academia Norte-americana de la Lengua Espanola.

WRITINGS:

Introduccion a una comparacion fonologica del espanol y del ingles, Center for Applied Linguistics, 1960.
(With Simon Belasco) *Applied Linguistics—Spanish: A Guide for Teachers,* Heath, 1961.
El Espanol de Jalisco, Consejo Superior de Investigaciones Cientificas (Madrid), 1967.
(Contributor) *Essays in Romance Philology,* University of Chicago, 1968.
Dominant Spanish Dialects Spoken in the United States (monograph), Center for Applied Linguistics, 1970.
Otra interpretacion de Romance sonambulo, Explicacion de Textos, 1973.
El arbol de Maria Bombal, Kanina, 1980.

Contributor of articles and more than forty reviews to language journals and to *Books Abroad* and *American Anthropologist.* Associate editor, *Hispania,* 1969-78.

WORK IN PROGRESS: Introduccion a una comparacion linguistica del espanol y del ingles; Introduccion a la interpretacion y analisis literario; Negative Force Equals Positive Energy, an autobiography; writing on the phonological development of Spanish in America and on the acoustic vowel loops of Spanish-American dialects.

CARR, Annie Roe
[Collective pseudonym]

WRITINGS:

"NAN SHERWOOD" SERIES

Nan Sherwood at Pine Camp; or, The Old Lumberman's Secret, G. Sully, 1916.
. . . at Lakeview Hall; or, The Mystery of the Haunted Boathouse, G. Sully, 1916.
Nan Sherwood's Winter Holidays; or, Rescuing the Runaways, G. Sully, 1916.
. . . at Rose Ranch; or, The Old Mexican's Treasure, G. Sully, 1919.
. . . at Palm Beach; or, Strange Adventures among the Orange Groves, G. Sully, 1921.
Nan Sherwood's Summer Holidays, World, 1937.
. . . on the Mexican Border, World, 1937.

SIDELIGHTS: For more information see the entries for Harriet S. Adams, Edward L. Stratemeyer, and Andrew E. Svenson.

BIOGRAPHICAL/CRITICAL SOURCES:

BOOKS

Johnson, Deidre, editor and compiler, *Stratemeyer Pseudonyms and Series Books: An Annotated Checklist of Stratemeyer and Stratemeyer Syndicate Publications*, Greenwood Press, 1982.

*   *   *

CARSON, Captain James
[Collective pseudonym]

WRITINGS:

"SADDLE BOYS" SERIES

The Saddle Boys of the Rockies; or, Lost on Thunder Mountain, Cupples & Leon, 1913.
. . . in the Grand Canyon; or, The Hermit of the Cave, Cupples & Leon, 1913.
. . . on the Plains; or, After a Treasure of Gold, Cupples & Leon, 1913.
. . . at Circle Ranch; or, In at the Grand Round-up, Cupples & Leon, 1913.
. . . on Mexican Trails; or, In the Hands of the Enemy, Cupples & Leon, 1915.

SIDELIGHTS: For more information see the entries for Harriet S. Adams, Edward L. Stratemeyer, and Andrew E. Svenson.

BIOGRAPHICAL/CRITICAL SOURCES:

BOOKS

Johnson, Deidre, editor and compiler, *Stratemeyer Pseudonyms and Series Books: An Annotated Checklist of Stratemeyer and Stratemeyer Syndicate Publications*, Greenwood Press, 1982.

*   *   *

CHANDOR, (Peter John) Anthony   1932-

PERSONAL: Born November 9, 1932, in Moshi, Tanzania (then Tanganyika); son of Peter France (an author) and Eileen (Hives) Chandor; married Maryanne Bankes (an editor), September 6, 1958; children: Sarah Jane Murray, Nicholas Anthony Bankes. *Education:* Attended Epsom College, Surrey, England, 1946-51; New College, Oxford, B.A. (honors), 1956, M.A., 1967. *Politics:* Conservative. *Religion:* Church of England.

ADDRESSES: Home—Blackdown Border, Haslemere, Surrey, England.

CAREER: Benn Brothers Ltd. (publishers), London, England, editor, 1956-58; International Computers Ltd., London, executive, 1958-75; National Computing Centre, London, director, 1975—. United Nations specialist in electronic data processing in Czechoslovakia, 1969-71, and in Malaysia, 1972. *Military service:* British Army, Royal Artillery, 1951-53; became lieutenant.

MEMBER: British Computer Society (fellow; member of council), English-Speaking Union.

WRITINGS:

A Short Introduction to Computers, Arthur Barker, 1968.
(Editor) *A Dictionary of Computers*, Penguin, 1970, 3rd edition (with John Graham and Robin Williamson) published as *The Penguin Dictionary of Computers*, 1985.
(With Graham and Williamson) *Practical Systems Analysis*, Hart-Davis, 1970, Putnam, 1971.
Computers as a Career, Hart-Davis, 1970.
Choosing and Keeping Computer Staff: Recruitment, Selection and Development of Computer Personnel, Allen & Unwin, 1976.
The Facts on File Dictionary of Micro-Computers, Facts on File, 1981.
The Penguin Dictionary of Microprocessors, Penguin, 1981.

SIDELIGHTS: "I believe that, as well as being a good deal easier to manufacture, people are a great deal more important than computers," Anthony Chandor once wrote *CA*. "This is not always recognized in the computer field, especially by computers, and my books attempt to emphasize it. The only computer to have read a book by me, however, seemed to remain unmoved." Chandor goes on to write: "It is also true that while my books have been translated into Japanese, Italian, Hungarian, Slovak, Swedish, Spanish, and Portuguese, none has yet appeared in COBOL, FORTRAN, or any other computer languages."†

*   *   *

CHAPMAN, Colin   1937-

PERSONAL: Born March 17, 1937, in Croydon, England; son of Norman Charles and Marjorie (Wakefield) Chapman; married Susan Dorothy Grice. *Education:* Attended school in London, England, 1946-53. *Politics:* "Unattached." *Religion:* None.

ADDRESSES: Home—85 Andrewes House, Barbican, London EC2 8AY, England. *Agent*—Carol Smith Agency, 25 Hornton Court, Kensington High St., London W8, England.

CAREER: Times, London, England, staff writer, 1962-65; *Sunday Times*, London, education correspondent, 1965-67, foreign news editor, 1967-69; affiliated with British Broadcasting Corp., London, 1969-72; *Observer*, London, industrial editor, 1973-76; British Broadcasting Corp., economics correspondent, 1975-79; *Australian*, Sydney, deputy editor, 1980-82; Australian Broadcasting Corp., Sydney, executive producer, 1982-84; Financial Television Ltd., London, managing director, 1984—.

AWARDS, HONORS: Young British Journalist Award from National Council for Training of Journalists, 1963; Winston Churchill fellow, 1966.

WRITINGS:

August 21: The Rape of Czechoslovakia, Lippincott, 1968.
How the New York Stock Exchange Works, Hutchinson Business, 1986, 2nd edition, 1988.

* * *

CHAPMAN, G(eorge) W(arren) Vernon 1925-
(Vernon Warren)

PERSONAL: Born June 30, 1925, in London, England; married, 1953; wife's name, Margaret; children: Carol, Robert. *Education:* Educated in London, England.

ADDRESSES: Home—Edmonton, Alberta, Canada.

CAREER: Osler, Hammond & Nanton Insurance Ltd., Edmonton, Alberta, assistant manager, beginning 1959. *Military service:* Royal Air Force Volunteer Reserve.

MEMBER: Rotary Club of West Edmonton (secretary).

WRITINGS—Under pseudonym Vernon Warren:

Brandon Takes Over, Gifford, 1953.
The Blue Mauritius, Gifford, 1954.
Brandon Returns, Gifford, 1954.
Bullets for Brandon, Gifford, 1955.
No Bouquets for Brandon, Gifford, 1955.
Appointment in Hell, Gifford, 1955.
Stop-Over Danger, Gifford, 1955.
By Fair Means or Foul, Gifford, 1956.
Back-Lash, Gifford, 1960.
Farewell by Death, Gifford, 1961.
Invitation to Kill, Gifford, 1963.
Mister Violence, Gifford, 1964.

WORK IN PROGRESS: Another thriller; a long-term work on the Spanish invasion of Peru.

AVOCATIONAL INTERESTS: World War I aviation and vintage aircraft.†

* * *

CHESHAM, Sallie

PERSONAL: Born in Detroit, Mich.; daughter of Robert Henry and Margaret (Ebsary) Keeler; married Howard Chesham (director of Eastern Territory finance department and national treasurer of the Salvation Army); children: David Howard, Julie Margaret (Mrs. Alan Kennedy). *Education:* Studied journalism at Northwestern University.

ADDRESSES: Home—145 Claremont Ave., Mount Vernon, N.Y. 10550.

CAREER: Ordained minister of the Salvation Army (third generation Salvationist), with current rank of colonel; certified social worker; Salvation Army, Central Territory Headquarters, Chicago, Ill., former member of editorial department, head of historical research section, and director of "Old Hat" Inner City coffee house program, Eastern Territory Headquarters, New York, N.Y., head of special services section (creative writing and public speaking), 1971—.

MEMBER: Society of Midland Authors, Women's Press Club (London, England; honorary member).

AWARDS, HONORS: Chicago Poetry Award, 1970, for *Walking with the Wind;* Chicago Publishers Award, 1973, for *Trouble Doesn't Happen Next Tuesday.*

WRITINGS:

Born to Battle, Rand McNally, 1965.
Walking with the Wind, Word Books, 1969.
(Editor) *Today Is Yours,* Word Books, 1972.
Trouble Doesn't Happen Next Tuesday, Word Books, 1972.
One Hand Upon Another, Salvation Army, 1978.
Peace Like a River, Salvation Army, 1981.
Preaching Ladies, Salvation Army, 1983.
Wind Chimes, Salvation Army, 1983.

Also author of Salvation Army booklets and published reports include *The Contender,* 1958, *It Isn't So,* 1960, *Creators All,* 1960, *Plus and Minus,* 1963, *Combat Songs,* 1965, and *One Hand Upon Another,* 1976. Writer and producer of "Marching On," the Salvation Army 75th anniversary pageant, and the centennial pageant; also writer of more than 400 feature stories, short stories, serials, and poems.

WORK IN PROGRESS: A play, "Evangeline"; two musicals, "Jehovah," and "Combat," the story of the first five years of struggle by the Salvation Army.†

* * *

CHOLDIN, Marianna Tax 1942-

PERSONAL: Born February 26, 1942, in Chicago, Ill.; daughter of Sol (a professor) and Gertrude (Katz) Tax; married Harvey M. Choldin (a professor); children: Mary, Kate. *Education:* University of Chicago, B.A., 1962, M.A., 1967, Ph.D., 1979. *Religion:* Jewish.

ADDRESSES: Home—1111 South Pine St., Champaign, Ill. 61820. *Office*—Slavic and East European Library, University of Illinois, Urbana, Ill. 61801.

CAREER: Michigan State University, East Lansing, Slavic bibliographer at library, 1967-69; University of Illinois, Urbana, Slavic bibliographer, 1969—, research director at Russian and East European Center, 1980—, director, 1987—, head of Slavic and East European Library, 1982—. Member of two U.S.-Soviet commissions in the social sciences and humanities.

MEMBER: American Library Association, American Association for the Advancement of Slavic Studies (chairperson of bibliography and documentation committee, 1978-83; member of board of directors, 1987—), Phi Beta Kappa, Nu Pi Sigma.

WRITINGS:

(Editor) *Access to Information in the Eighties,* Russica Publishers, 1982.
A Fence around the Empire: Russian Censorship of Western Ideas under the Tsars, Duke University Press, 1985.
(Editor) *Books, Libraries and Information in Slavic and East European Studies,* Russica Publishers, 1986.
(Editor with Maurice Friedberg) *The Red Pencil: Artists, Scholars, and Censors in the USSR,* Allen & Unwin, in press.

Also contributor to *Encyclopedia of Library and Information Science.* Contributor to library and Slavic studies journals.

WORK IN PROGRESS: A book on Soviet censorship of foreign publications.

SIDELIGHTS: Marianna Tax Choldin told *CA:* "As a librarian I am interested in the flow of information between countries. As a Russian specialist I cannot help but be aware of serious obstructions to that flow, especially from other countries into the Soviet Union. Before the revolution, censorship was openly acknowledged in Russia, and I was able to find ample material describing the operation of the system controlling Western publications entering the empire. Now censorship is no longer acknowledged, and it is much more difficult to describe the system, which creates a great challenge for the writer. I am interested in finding the continuities between the Russian and Soviet systems, and in exploring the changes which have taken place. In general, I think it is very important that we strive to understand the nature of obstructions to the flow of information. Such obstructions do no one any good in the long run, and it will be to the mutual benefit of the United States and the Soviet Union if we can find ways to remove the obstructions."

*   *   *

CLARE, Ellen
See SINCLAIR, Olga

*   *   *

CLAVELL, James (duMaresq)   1925-

PERSONAL: Born October 10, 1925, in Australia; came to the United States, 1953; naturalized, 1963; son of Richard Charles (a captain in the British Royal Navy) and Eileen Clavell; married April Stride, February 20, 1951; children: Michaela, Holly. *Education:* Attended University of Birmingham, 1946-47.

ADDRESSES: Agent—Foreign Rights, Inc., 400 East 58th St., #17D, New York, N.Y. 10022.

CAREER: Worked as a carpenter, 1953; screenwriter, director, and producer, 1954—, director of television programs, 1958—, novelist, 1962—. *Military service:* Served as captain with the Royal Artillery, 1940-46.

MEMBER: Writers Guild, Authors League of America, Producers Guild, Dramatists Guild, Directors Guild.

AWARDS, HONORS: Writers Guild Best Screenplay Award, 1964, for "The Great Escape"; honorary doctorates from the University of Maryland and the University of Bradford.

WRITINGS:

NOVELS

King Rat, Little, Brown, 1962, reprinted as *James Clavell's "King Rat,"* Delacorte, 1983.
Tai-Pan: A Novel of Hong Kong, Atheneum, 1966, reprinted, Delacorte, 1983.
Shogun: A Novel of Japan, Atheneum, 1975.
Noble House: A Novel of Contemporary Hong Kong, Delacorte, 1981.
The Children's Story, Delacorte, 1981.
James Clavell's "Whirlwind," William Morrow, 1986.
James Clavell's "Thrump-o-moto" (juvenile), illustrated by George Sharp, Delacorte, 1986.

SCREENPLAYS

"The Fly," Twentieth Century-Fox, 1958.
"Watusi," Metro-Goldwyn-Mayer, 1959.

(Also producer and director) "Five Gates to Hell," Twentieth Century-Fox, 1959.
"Walk Like a Dragon," Paramount, 1960.
"The Great Escape," United Artists, 1963.
"633 Squadron," United Artists, 1964.
"The Satan Bug," United Artists, 1965.
"Where's Jack?," Paramount, 1968.
(Also producer and director) "To Sir with Love," Columbia, 1969.
(Also producer and director) "The Last Valley," ABC Pictures, 1969.

OTHER

"Countdown to Armageddon: $E = mc^2$" (play), first produced in Vancouver, British Columbia by Vancouver Playhouse Theatre, November, 1966.
(Author of introduction) *The Making of James Clavell's "Shogun,"* Dell, 1980.
(Editor) *Sun Tzu, The Art of War,* Delacorte, 1983.

Also author of poetry ("published and paid, by God").

WORK IN PROGRESS: A sequel to *Whirlwind.*

SIDELIGHTS: James Clavell, who calls himself an "old-fashioned storyteller," is one of this century's most widely read novelists. His sagas of the Far East—*Tai-Pan: A Novel of Hong Kong, Shogun: A Novel of Japan,* and *Noble House: A Novel of Contemporary Hong Kong,* have each sold millions of copies and dominated bestseller lists for months, while his Iran-based adventure, *James Clavell's "Whirlwind,"* commanded a record-setting $5,000,000 advance from its publisher. An industry insider told the *Los Angeles Times* that Clavell is "one of the very few writers . . . whose names have marquee value. Clavell's name on the cover sells enormous quantities of books." The reason for Clavell's popularity is quite simple. As James Vesely notes in the *Detroit News,* the author "always does one thing right: he is never boring." Indeed, Clavell combines action, intrigue, cultural conflicts, and romance to produce "event-packed books with the addictive appeal of popcorn," to quote *Detroit News* correspondent Helen Dudar. Although critics agree that Clavell's blockbusters never aspire to literary greatness, they also concur that his works possess the sort of research and detail rarely found in so-called "popular novels." In the *National Review,* Terry Teachout calls Clavell a "first-rate novelist of the second rank," the kind of writer "who provides genuinely stimulating literary entertainment without insulting the sensibilities."

Washington Post contributor Cynthia Gorney describes the main theme of Clavell's novels; namely, "the enormous gulf between Asian and Occidental views of the world." Against exotic backgrounds, the books explore the powerful human obsession with waging war, cornering power, or forming giant corporations. International espionage, skullduggery, and forbidden romance often round out the picture. "Each of [Clavell's] novels involves an enormous amount of research and enough plot for a dozen books," writes Ann Marie Cunningham in the *Los Angeles Times.* "All describe strategic thinking during wartime: Teams of tough British boys try to extract themselves from tight spots, . . . often in parts of the former empire." According to Webster Schott in the *New York Times Book Review,* Clavell is "neither literary psychoanalyst nor philosophizing intellectual. He reports the world as he sees people—in terms of power, control, strength. . . . He writes in the oldest and grandest tradition that fiction knows." Likewise, *Chicago Tribune* correspondent Harrison E. Salisbury claims that the author "gives you your money's worth if you like suspense, blood, thunder, romance, intrigue, lust, greed, dirty work—you name it—and pages. He is a generous man." Clavell has "sprayed his prose in machine-gun fashion, strafing targets the size of billboards," notes Paul King in *Maclean's*. "Still, he has learned the art of structuring convoluted plots that would have dazzled even Dickens. Above all, with lengthy tales of gut wrenching suspense, Clavell has mastered the technique of keeping readers turning pages until dawn."

"The people I write about are mostly doers," Clavell told the *Washington Post*. "They're not people who sit on their tails in New York, who are concerned about their place in life or should they get a divorce." His epics, he told *Publishers Weekly*, concern "ordinary people placed in extraordinary circumstances and exposed to danger. They have to do something to extract themselves from this situation, and what you have, then, are heroics and a good read." In the *New York Times Magazine*, Paul Bernstein compares Clavell's characters to those of Charles Dickens. "Dickens's big-hearted orphans become Clavell's larger-than-life men of action," writes Bernstein, "Dickens's hard-hearted villains, Clavell's hard-hearted business or political adversaries. The social commentary of Dickens becomes in Clavell cross-cultural education and reactionary political warnings." Schott admits in the *Washington Post Book World* that some of Clavell's characters are romantic stereotypes. The critic adds, however, that "others are troubled outsiders, wondering who they are and what their lives mean. Some of his villains and contemporary courtesans have distant cousins in Marvel Comics. But others are men and women painfully compromised into evil because they do not know how to fight evil without becoming it." Elsewhere in the same review, Schott offers further praise for Clavell: "The riches of his imagination and the reach of his authority are only the start. James Clavell tells his stories so well . . . that it's possible to miss the tough-minded intelligence at work. . . . Clavell knows people and what motivates them. He understands systems and how they work and fail. He remembers history and sees what technology has wrought. . . . James Clavell does more than entertain. He transports us into worlds we've not known, stimulating, educating, questioning almost simultaneously."

Clavell's life has been almost as eventful as one of his books. He was born in Australia in 1924, the son of a British Royal Navy captain who travelled to ports all over the world. As a child, Clavell relished the swashbuckling sea tales—most of them fictional—recounted by his father and grandfather, both career military men. A career in the service seemed a natural choice for Clavell, too, and after his secondary schooling was completed, he joined the Royal Artillery in 1940. A year later, he was sent to fight in the Far East and was wounded by machine gun fire in the jungles of Malaysia. For several months he hid in a Malay village, but he was eventually captured by the Japanese and sent to the notorious Changi prison near Singapore. The conditions at Changi were so severe that only 10,000 of its 150,000 inmates survived incarceration—and Calvell was there three and a half years. He told the *Guardian*: "Changi was a school for survivors. It gave me a strength most people don't have. I have an awareness of life others lack. Changi was my university. . . . Those who were supposed to survive didn't." The experience invested Clavell with some of the same verve that characterizes his fictional protagonists. Calling Changi "the rock" on which he put his life, he said: "So long as I remember Changi, I know I'm living forty borrowed lifetimes."

Released from captivity afer the war, Clavell returned to Great Britain to continue his military career. A motorcycle accident left him lame in one leg, however, and he was discharged in 1946. He attended Birmingham University briefly, considering law or engineering as a profession, but when he began to visit movie sets with his future wife—an aspiring actress—he became fascinated with directing and writing for films. He entered the movie industry on the ground floor as a distributor, gradually moving into production work. In 1953 he and his wife emigrated to the United States, where, after a period of television production in New York, they moved to Hollywood. There Clavell bluffed his way into a screenwriting contract ("They liked my accent, I suppose," he told the *Washington Post*) and set to work in the field that would bring him his first success. His first produced screenplay, "The Fly," was based on a science fiction story about an atomic scientist whose experiments cause an exchange of heads with a housefly. The movie made $4,000,000 profit in two years and has since become a classic genre film in its own right and the source of several sequels and remakes. Clavell won a Writers Guild Best Screenplay Award for the 1963 film "The Great Escape," also a box office success. The author is best remembered, though, for the films he produced, directed, *and* wrote—most notably the 1969 hit "To Sir with Love." Made with a budget of $625,000, the movie about a black teacher's efforts to mould a class of tough British delinquents grossed $15,000,000. Both Clavell and star Sidney Poitier had contracted for percentages of the profits, so the project proved lucrative indeed.

A Hollywood screeenwriters' strike brought a fortuitous change to Clavell's career in 1960. Simultaneously sidelined from his regular employment and haunted by returning memories of Changi, he began to work on a novel about his prison experiences. The process of writing unbottled many suppressed emotions; in twelve weeks he had completed the first draft of *King Rat*. Set in Changi, the novel follows the fortunes of an English prisoner of war and his ruthless American comrade in their struggles to survive the brutal conditions. *New York Times Book Review* contributor Martin Levin notes: "All personal relationships [in the work] pale beside the impersonal, soul-disintegrating evil of Changi itself which Mr. Clavell, himself a Japanese P.O.W. for three years, renders with stunning authority." Some critics have maintained that the book loses some impact because it is aimed at the popular audience, but Paul King calls it the work of "a sensitive craftsman." A *New York Herald Tribune Books* reviewer concludes that *King Rat* is "at once fascinating in narrative detail, penetrating in observation of human nature under survival stress, and provoking in its analysis of right and wrong." In the *Christian Science Monitor*, R. R. Bruun also observes that by virtue of his careful plotting, "Mr. Clavell manages to keep the tension wound up to the snapping point through much of the book." *King Rat* was a bestseller, and it was also adapted for film in 1965.

Clavell was still primarily a screenwriter when he penned *Tai-Pan*, a sweeping fictional account of the founding of Hong Kong. A historical novel set in 1841, the story recounts the adventures of Dirk Struan, first tai-pan (merchant overlord) of the Noble House trading company. Struan builds his empire on the nearly deserted peninsula of Hong Kong, convinced that a British colony there would provide a power base for the growing empire. *New York Times* reviewer Orville Prescott claims that in *Tai-Pan*, Clavell "holds attention with a relentless grip. 'Tai-Pan' frequently is crude. It is grossly exaggerated much of the time. But seldom does a novel appear so stuffed with imaginative invention, so packed with melodramatic action, so gaudy and flamboyant with blood and sin, treachery and conspiracy, sex and murder.'' A *Time* critic calls the work ''a belly-gutting, god-rotting typhoon of a book'' and adds: ''Its narrative pace is numbing, its style deafening, its language penny dreadful. . . . It isn't art and it isn't truth. But its very energy and scope command the eye.'' *Tai-Pan* has certainly commanded the eyes of many readers. Since its publication in 1966, and its forty-four-week stay on the best-seller lists, it has sold more than two million copies. It too has been made into a motion picture that was released in 1986.

According to Gorney, Clavell's best-known novel, *Shogun,* had an inauspicious beginning in the author's mind. She writes: ''James Clavell, his imagination awash with plans for the modern-day Asian chronicle that was to be his third novel, picked up one of his 9-year-old daughter's school books one afternoon in London, and came upon an intriguing bit of history.'' He read the following sentence from the text: ''In 1600, an Englishman went to Japan and became a Samurai.'' Fascinated by that possibility, Clavell began to read everything he could find about medieval Japan and Will Adams, the historical figure in question. The research led Clavell into the story of *Shogun,* but it also gave him a new understanding of the culture that had kept him in captivity during the Second World War. ''I started reading about Japan's history and characteristics,'' he told the *New York Times,* ''and then the way the Japanese treated me and my brothers became clearer to me.'' After a year of research in the British Museum and several visits to Japan, Clavell created the tale of John Blackthorne, an Elizabethan sailor cast upon the shores of Japan during a period of internal conflict between rival warlords. Spanning all the elements of seventeenth-century Japanese society, the adventure recounts Blackthorne's transformation from a European ''barbarian'' into a trusted advisor to the powerful Shogun Toranaga.

Most critics have praised *Shogun* for its historical detail as well as for its riveting plot. ''Clavell offers a wide-ranging view of feudal Japan at a time of crisis,'' states Bruce Cook in the *Washington Post Book World.* Elsewhere Cook notes: ''Scene after scene is given, conversation after conversation reported, with the point not merely of advancing the narrative (which does somehow grind inexorably forward), but also of imparting to us the peculiar flavor of life in feudal Japan and the unique code of conduct (*bushido*) which dominated life there and then.'' Other reviewers have cited the story itself as the source of *Shogun*'s appeal. Gorney calls it ''one of those books that blots up vacations and imperils marriages, because it simply will not let the reader go,'' and *Library Journal* contributor Mitsu Yamamoto deems it ''a wonderful churning brew of adventure, intrigue, love, philosophy, and history.'' ''Clavell has a gift,'' contends Schott in the *New York Times Book Review.* ''It may be something that cannot be taught or earned. He breathes narrative. It's almost impossible not to continue to read 'Shogun' once having opened it. The imagination is possessed by Blackthorne, Toranaga and medieval Japan. Clavell creates a world: people, customs, settings, needs and desires all become so enveloping that you forget who and where you are.''

Praise has also been forthcoming for *Noble House,* Clavell's 1981 bestseller. *Washington Post* correspondent Sandy Rovner notes that the novel about financial power struggles in modern Hong Kong is ''1,207 pages long, 2½ inches (not counting covers) thick and 3 pounds and 13 ounces to drag around because you can't put it down.'' Henry S. Hayward offers a similar opinion in the *Christian Science Monitor.* ''James Clavell

is a master yarn-spinner and an expert on detail,'' Hayward writes. ''Indeed, one sometimes feels overwhelmed with the masses of information and wishes a firmer editing pencil had been applied. But the author, nevertheless, is in a class with James Michener and Robert Elegant in his ability to handle a massive cast and hold your attention through the intricacies of a 1,200 page plot.'' Teachout notes that one ''races through *Noble House* like a fire engine, torn between savoring each tasty bit of local color and wanting to find out as soon as possible what new outrage [the hero] will put down next.'' In the *New York Times Book Review,* Schott concludes that the novel ''isn't primarily about any particular story or character or set of characters. It's about a condition that's a place, Hong Kong. Mr. Clavell perceives that city to be a unique setting for extremes of greed and vengefulness, international intrigue and silky romance.'' Commenting on Clavell's plotting, *New York Times* columnist Christopher Lehmann-Haupt observes: ''Curiously enough, its staggering complexity is one of the things that the novel has going for it. Not only is 'Noble House' as long as life, it's also as rich with possibilities. . . . There are so many irons in the fire that almost anything can plausibly happen.''

Clavell's successes with his novels have not been limited to the sales of books. As Teachout notes, ''even non-readers have gotten pleasure out of his lucrative knack for telling an appealing story.'' Through movies and mini-series television dramas, Clavell's works have reached audiences estimated in the hundreds of millions. The best known of these efforts are ''King Rat,'' a film produced in 1965, ''Shogun,'' which aired on television in 1980, ''Tai-Pan,'' a 1986 movie, and ''James Clavell's 'Noble House,''' a 1988 mini-series. Clavell, who has served as executive producer for the ''Shogun'' and ''Noble House'' mini-series programs, expresses great approval for the use of his work in that medium. ''Television keeps you current, and so do movies,'' he told *Publishers Weekly.* ''People are seeing your name regularly enough that they remember you. . . . In a way, it makes me almost a brand name.''

The publishing industry seems to concur that Clavell's name alone is quite appealing to book buyers. An auction of his 1986 novel *Whirlwind* brought Clavell an unprecedented $5,000,000 advance from the William Morrow Company, which had based its bid on a preview of only 10 percent of the manuscript. Morrow also ordered a first printing of 950,000 hardcover copies, another unprecedented move. Set in Iran during the hectic weeks after the overthrow of the Shah, *Whirlwind* charts the activities of a group of helicopter pilots trying to move their precious machinery out of the country before the government can seize it. Dorothy Allison describes the work as ''1147 pages of violence, passion, cutthroat business, religious obsession, and martyrdom—exactly what his readers expect and want along with their exotic settings.'' Although the book has received mixed reviews, it was also a bestseller; a mini-series based on it has been planned.

In various interviews, Clavell has discussed both his aims as a writer and his methods of putting a book together. He told the *Los Angeles Times* that when he starts a novel, he doesn't have a detailed plan in his mind. ''I look at storytelling in picture form,'' he said. ''I watch the story happen, and I describe what I see. When you write a screenplay, you write only what you can photograph and what you can hear. As a result, my books have no fat, no purple prose, and they're very visual.'' Writing a lengthy novel, he told the *Washington Post,* ''is pertinacity, you know, grim determination. And a marvelous selfishness to finish, to exclude everything. I begrudge the time spent away from my novel. . . . I've got this need to finish, to find the last page.'' Clavell said in the *National Review* that his basic goal is entertainment—for himself as well as his readers. ''I'm not a novelist, I'm a storyteller,'' he contended. ''I'm not a literary figure at all. I work very hard and try to do the best I can; and I try and write for myself, thinking that what I like, other people may like. My attitude is perhaps more romantic than psychiatric. I've never been trained as a writer, either. I stumbled into it in a funny way; I do not know how it works; and I'm petrified that it will vanish as easily as it came!'' Clavell concluded his remarks in the *National Review* with comments about why he keeps writing: ''My concern is with the people who read my books for pleasure; hopefully, I can entertain them; hopefully, I can pass on a little information which I find interesting. And hopefully—perhaps—I can be a bridge between East and West.''

MEDIA ADAPTATIONS: Movies—''King Rat'' was produced by Columbia in 1965; ''Tai-Pan'' was produced by De-Laurentiis Entertainment Group, 1986. *Television*—''Shogun'' was produced as a mini-series in 1980 (Clavell was executive producer); ''The Children's Story'' was produced as a Mobile Showcase special in 1982; *Noble House* was produced as a mini-series entitled ''James Clavell's 'Noble House''' in 1988; a mini-series based on *King Rat* and one based on *Whirlwind* are planned.

AVOCATIONAL INTERESTS: Sailing, flying helicopters.

BIOGRAPHICAL/CRITICAL SOURCES:

BOOKS

Contemporary Literary Criticism, Gale, Volume 6, 1976, Volume 25, 1983.
The Making of James Clavell's ''Shogun,'' Dell, 1980.

PERIODICALS

Best Sellers, July 15, 1966, October, 1981.
Chicago Tribune, April 12, 1981, February 18, 1982, November 21, 1986.
Christian Science Monitor, August 9, 1962, June 24, 1981.
Detroit News, May 3, 1981.
Globe & Mail (Toronto), January 4, 1986.
Guardian, October 4, 1975.
Los Angeles Times, November 7, 1986, December 11, 1986.
Maclean's, May 11, 1981, November 24, 1986.
National Review, November 12, 1982.
New Republic, July 4, 1981.
New Statesman, November 21, 1975.
Newsweek, November 10, 1986.
New York Herald Tribune Books, August 5, 1962.
New York Review of Books, September 18, 1975, December 18, 1986.
New York Times, May 4, 1966, April 28, 1981, May 17, 1981, February 18, 1982, December 28, 1985, January 7, 1986, January 11, 1986, November 1, 1986, November 7, 1986, November 17, 1986.
New York Times Book Review, August 12, 1962, May 22, 1966, June 22, 1975, May 3, 1981.
New York Times Magazine, September 13, 1981.
Publishers Weekly, October 24, 1986.
Saturday Review, August 11, 1962.
Time, June 17, 1966, July 7, 1975, July 6, 1981.
Times Literary Supplement, December 5, 1986, December 26, 1986.
Village Voice, September 2, 1981, December 16, 1986.

Washington Post, February 4, 1979, May 5, 1981, November 11, 1986.
Washington Post Book World, July 13, 1975, October 26, 1986, December 7, 1986.

—*Sketch by Anne Janette Johnson*

*　　*　　*

CLEARY, Jon 1917-

PERSONAL: Born November 22, 1917, in Sydney, New South Wales, Australia; son of Matthew and Ida (Brown) Cleary; married Constantine Joy Lucas, September 6, 1946; children: Catherine, Jane. *Education:* Left school at end of second year of high school in Sydney, Australia.

ADDRESSES: Home—71 Upper Pitt St., Kirribilli, New South Wales, Australia. *Agent*—John Farquharson Ltd., 162-168 Regent St., London W1R 5TB, England.

CAREER: Prior to World War II worked at ''too many jobs to be listed,'' including commercial artist, salesman, delivery man, laundry worker, bush worker, and sign painter; full-time writer, 1945—, except for a year in London, England, as journalist with Australian Government Bureau, and two years in New York, N.Y., with the Australian Bureau. *Military service:* Australian Army, 1940-45; served in Middle East, New Guinea, and New Britain campaigns; became lieutenant.

AWARDS, HONORS: Co-winner of first prize, National Play Award, Australian Broadcasting Commission, 1944; second prize, National Novel Contest, *Sydney Morning Herald*, 1946; Crouch gold medal for best Australian novel of 1950; Edgar Allan Poe award, Mystery Writers of America, 1974, for *Peter's Pence;* co-winner of Australian section, World Story Contest, *New York Herald Tribune.*

WRITINGS:

These Small Glories, Angus & Robertson, 1946.
You Can't See around Corners, Scribner, 1947, 4th edition, Horwitz, 1965.
The Long Shadow, Laurie, 1950, reprinted, Severn House, 1976.
Just Let Me Be, Laurie, 1951.
The Sundowners, Scribner, 1952, reprinted, 1984.
The Climate of Courage, Collins, 1954, reprinted, Magna Print Books, 1980.
Justin Bayard, Morrow, 1955.
The Green Helmet, Morrow, 1958, reprinted, Collins, 1983.
Back of Sunset, Morrow, 1959, reprinted, Ulverscroft Large Print Books, 1978.
North from Thursday, Morrow, 1961.
The Country of Marriage, Morrow, 1962.
Forests of the Night, Morrow, 1963.
A Flight of Chariots, Morrow, 1963.
The Fall of an Eagle, Morrow, 1964, reprinted, Collins, 1983.
The Pulse of Danger, Morrow, 1966.
The High Commissioner, Morrow, 1966.
The Long Pursuit, Morrow, 1967.
Season of Doubt, Morrow, 1968.
Remember Jack Hoxie, Morrow, 1969.
Helga's Web, Morrow, 1970.
The Liberators, Morrow, 1971 (published in England as *Mask of the Andes*, Collins, 1971).
The Ninth Marquess, Morrow, 1972 (published in England as *Man's Estate*, Collins, 1972).
Ransom, Morrow, 1973.

Peter's Pence, Morrow, 1974.
"Sidecar Racers" (screenplay), Universal, 1975.
The Safe House, Morrow, 1975.
A Sound of Lightning, Collins, 1975, Morrow, 1976.
High Road to China, Morrow, 1977.
Vortex, Collins, 1977, Morrow, 1978.
The Beaufort Sisters, Morrow, 1979.
A Very Private War, Morrow, 1980.
The Golden Sabre, Morrow, 1981.
The Faraway Drums, Collins, 1981, Morrow, 1982.
Spearfield's Daughter, Collins, 1982, Morrow, 1983.
The Phoenix Tree, Collins, 1984.
City of Fading Light, Collins, 1985, Morrow, 1986.
Dragons at the Party, Morrow, 1988.

Also author of film scripts for Warner Brothers, Inc., Metro-Goldwyn-Mayer, Inc., Paramount Pictures Corp., and Ealing Films. Author of television scripts for programs in the United States and England.

SIDELIGHTS: Author of over thirty-five novels, Jon Cleary considers himself to be "the biggest earner in Australia, in large part because I write popular entertainment." Nevertheless, Cleary is "primarily a storyteller," as he told Wayne Warga in the *Los Angeles Times.* "I'm interested in telling a story and entertaining people, and also communicating something about the place where the story takes place." Although his permanent home is in Australia, Cleary and his family spend more than half their time traveling. "I don't write about a place I haven't visited," he told Varga, and since Cleary has traveled through six continents, he has had a wide variety of settings from which to choose. It is because of this variety that Cleary feels he has been so successful: "I do well. I sell well. . . . My agents and publishers and I think it's because I never write the same book in succession. I can't be categorized."

MEDIA ADAPTATIONS: The films "The Sundowners," produced by Warner Bros. in 1960, "The Green Helmet," produced by Metro-Goldwyn-Mayer in 1961, "The High Commissioner," produced by Rank in 1968, and "High Road to China," produced by Warner Bros. in 1984, were all based on Cleary's novels with the same titles. "You Can't See 'round Corners," based on his novel *You Can't See around Corners,* was produced by Universal in 1969; "Scobie Malone," based on his novel *Helga's Web,* was produced by Kingscroft in 1975. A screen adaptation of *Justin Bayard* was produced by Southern Pacific in 1958. Television adaptations were produced of *Ransom,* by Kokusai Hoei (Japan) in 1981, and of *Spearfield's Daughter,* by Metromedia (United States) in 1986.

AVOCATIONAL INTERESTS: Cricket, tennis.

BIOGRAPHICAL/CRITICAL SOURCES:

PERIODICALS

Los Angeles Times, July 4, 1980.
Los Angeles Times Book Review, March 20, 1983.
New York Times Book Review, July 9, 1967, July 7, 1968, September 14, 1969, June 2, 1974.
Times Literary Supplement, July 17, 1969, March 16, 1973.
Tribune Books, January 31, 1988.

*   *   *

CLEMENT, Hal
  See STUBBS, Harry C(lement)

CNUDDE, Charles F(rancis)   1938-

PERSONAL: Surname pronounced Ka-*noo*-dee; born February 12, 1938, in Fraser, Mich.; son of Francis Alva and Lucille Frances (Neering) Cnudde; married Susan H. Beamer, June 19, 1961; children: Katherine H., Emily M. *Education:* University of Michigan, A.B., 1960; attended Wayne State University, 1961-63; University of North Carolina, Ph.D., 1967.

ADDRESSES: Office—College of Social Sciences, Florida State University, Tallahassee, Fla. 32306.

CAREER: University of California, Irvine, assistant professor of political science, 1966-68; University of Wisconsin—Madison, visiting lecturer, 1967, assistant professor, 1968-70, associate professor of political science, 1970-73; Michigan State University, East Lansing, professor of political science and chairman of department, 1973-81, co-director of Social Science Research Bureau, 1976-77; University of Texas at Austin, chairman of government department, 1980-87; Florida State University, Tallahasse, Fla., dean of College of Social Sciences, 1987—. Visiting senior lecturer, University of Essex, 1970-71; distinguished visiting professor, University of Arizona, 1979. California election analyst, Institute for Social Science Research, University of North Carolina, 1968; member of executive committee, Inter-University Consortium for Political Research, Ann Arbor, Mich., 1968-69. Member of Michigan Task Force on Higher Education Enrollments, 1977—; member of Michigan Internship Advisory Board, 1977—.

MEMBER: American Political Science Association, American Association for Public Opinion Research, American Society of Public Administration, Midwest Political Science Association.

WRITINGS:

(Contributor) Robert E. Crew, Jr., editor, *State Politics: A Behavioral Reader,* Wadsworth, 1968.
(Editor with Deane E. Neubauer and contributor) *Empirical Democratic Theory,* Markham, 1969.
Democracy in the American South, Markham, 1970.
The Public Administration of the Public Schools, Center for Political Studies, 1977.
(With Robert E. Crew, Jr.) *Constitutional Democracy in Texas,* West Publishing, in press.

Articles written for *American Political Science Review* have been reprinted in four books; contributor of articles and reviews to other professional journals.

WORK IN PROGRESS: Research on theories and measures of power and influence and on application of econometric methods to political data; an analysis of presidential power and leadership.

*   *   *

COLLINS, David R(aymond)   1940-

PERSONAL: Born February 29, 1940, in Marshalltown, Iowa; son of Raymond A. (an educator) and Mary Elizabeth (Brecht) Collins. *Education:* Western Illinois University, B.S., 1962, M.S., 1966. *Politics:* Democrat. *Religion:* Roman Catholic.

ADDRESSES: Home—3403 45th St., Moline, Ill. 61265. *Office*—Department of English, Moline Senior High School, 3600 23rd Ave., Moline, Ill. 61265.

CAREER: Teacher of English in Moline, Ill., at Woodrow Wilson Junior High School, 1962-83, and Moline Senior High

School, 1983—. President of Friends of the Moline Public Library, 1965-67.

MEMBER: National Education Association (life member), Children's Reading Roundtable, Society of Children's Book Writers, Authors Guild, Authors League of America, Juvenile Forum (president, 1975—), Writers' Studio (president, 1968-72), Mississippi Valley Writers Conference (founder; director, 1974—), Illinois Education Association, Illinois Congress of Parents and Teachers (life member), Illinois State Historical Society (life member), Blackhawk Division of Teachers of English (president, 1967-68), Quad City Writers Club, Quad City Arts Council, Phi Delta Kappa, Kappa Delta Pi, Delta Sigma Pi.

AWARDS, HONORS: Outstanding Juvenile Writer Award, Indiana University, 1970; Judson College Writing Award, 1971; Writer of the Year Awards, Writers' Studio, 1971, and Quad City Writers Club, 1972; Western Illinois University Alumni Achievement Award, 1973; Outstanding Illinois Educator Award, 1976; Junior Literary Guild Award, 1981; Midwest Writing Award, 1982; Gold Key Award, 1983; Catholic Press Writing Award, 1983; National Catholic Book Award, 1984, for *Thomas Merton: Monk with a Mission;* Veterans of Foreign Wars Teacher of the Year Award, 1987-88.

WRITINGS:

JUVENILES

Kim Soo and His Tortoise, Lion Press, 1970.
Great American Nurses, Messner, 1971.
Walt Disney's Surprise Christmas Present, Broadman, 1971.
Linda Richards: First American Trained Nurse, Garrard, 1973.
Harry S. Truman: People's President, Garrard, 1975.
Football Running Backs: Three Ground Gainers, Garrard, 1976.
Abraham Lincoln, Mott Media, 1976.
Illinois Women: Born to Serve, DeSaulniers, 1976.
Joshua Poole Hated School, Broadman, 1976.
George Washington Carver, Mott Media, 1977.
A Spirit of Giving, Broadman, 1978.
Charles Lindbergh: Hero Pilot, Garrard, 1978.
If I Could, I Would, Garrard, 1979.
Joshua Poole and Sunrise, Broadman, 1980.
The Wonderful Story of Jesus, Concordia, 1980.
The One Bad Thing about Birthdays, Harcourt, 1981.
Joshua Poole and the Special Flowers, Broadman, 1981.
George Meany: Mr. Labor, St. Anthony Messenger Press, 1981.
Dorothy Day: Catholic Worker, St. Anthony Messenger Press, 1981.
Thomas Merton: Monk with a Mission, St. Anthony Messenger Press, 1982.
Francis Scott Key, Mott Media, 1982.
(With Evelyn Witter) *Notable Illinois Women,* Quest Publishing, 1982.
Johnny Appleseed, Mott Media, 1983.
Florence Nightingale, Mott Media, 1983.
The Special Guest, Broadman, 1984.
The Long-legged Schoolteacher, Eakin Press, 1985.
Not Only Dreamers, Brethren Press, 1986.
Ride a Red Dinosaur, Milliken Press, 1987.
Probo's Amazing Trunk, Modern Curriculum Press, 1987.
Ara's Amazing Spinning Wheel, Modern Curriculum Press, 1987.
Ursi's Amazing Fur Coat, Modern Curriculum Press, 1987.
Leo's Amazing Paws and Jaws, Modern Curriculum Press, 1987.

Ceb's Amazing Tail, Modern Curriculum Press, 1987.
Hali's Amazing Wings, Modern Curriculum Press, 1987.
The Wisest Answer, Milliken Press, 1988.
Grandfather Woo Comes to School, Milliken Press, 1988.
Country Artist: The Story of Beatrix Potter, Carolrhoda, 1988.
To the Point: The Story of E. B. White, Carolrhoda, 1988.
Harry S Truman: Our 33rd President, Garrett Educational, 1988.
Grover Cleveland: Our 22nd and 24th President, Garrett Educational, 1988.
Woodrow Wilson: Our 28th President, Garrett Educational, 1989.
Zachary Taylor: Our 12th President, Garrett Educational, 1989.
Noah Webster—God's Master of Words, Mott Media, 1989.
Jane Addams, Warner Press, 1989.
Clara Barton, Warner Press, 1989.

OTHER

Contributor to periodicals, including *Plays, Modern Woodman, Junior Discoveries, Catholic Boy, Vista,* and *Catholic Miss.*

WORK IN PROGRESS: Numerous biographies for youth.

SIDELIGHTS: David R. Collins told *CA* this about writing for children: "Children are curious, their minds open and flexible. A child is eager to enjoy new adventures. Anyone choosing to write for young readers faces an exciting challenge and a great responsibility. He must remember that his words and ideas may have a lasting effect on his reader's imagination, personality, even his entire character. Young readers deserve the best in reading.

"Why did I decide to write for children? Probably because some of my best childhood adventures were discovered in books. . . . I owe a tremendous debt to the realm of children's literature. Perhaps if I can offer something worthwhile to young readers, part of that debt will be repaid."

*   *   *

COMMAGER, Henry Steele 1902-

PERSONAL: Born October 25, 1902, in Pittsburgh, Pa.; son of James Williams and Anna Elizabeth (Dan) Commager; married Evan Carroll, July 3, 1928; married Mary E. Powlesland, July 14, 1979; children: (first marriage) Henry Steele (deceased), Nellie Thomas McColl, Elisabeth Carroll. *Education:* University of Chicago, Ph.B., 1923, M.A., 1924, Ph.D., 1928; attended University of Copenhagen, Cambridge University, M.A.; Oxford University, M.A. *Politics:* Independent Democrat.

ADDRESSES: Home—405 South Pleasant St., Amherst, Mass. 01002. *Office*—Department of History, Amherst College, Amherst, Mass. 01002.

CAREER: New York University, New York, N.Y., instructor in history, 1926-29, assistant professor, 1929-30, associate professor, 1930-31, professor, 1931-38; Columbia University, New York, N.Y., professor of American history, 1939-56, adjunct professor, 1956-59, Sperenza Lecturer, 1960; Amherst College, Amherst, Mass., Smith Professor of History, 1956-72, Simpson Lecturer, 1972—. Pitt Professor of American History, Cambridge University, 1941, 1947-48; Bacon Lecturer, Boston University, 1943; Richards Lecturer, University of Virginia, 1944; Harmsworth Professor of American History, Oxford University, 1952-53; Gottesman Lecturer, Uppsala University, 1953; Ziskind Professor, Brandeis University, 1955; Commonwealth Lecturer, University of London, 1963; Harris Lecturer, Northwestern University, 1964; Patton Lecturer, Indiana University, 1977. Visiting professor or lecturer at Duke University, Harvard University, University of Chicago, and University of California, 1926-38, University of Copenhagen, 1956, University of Aix-en-Provence, 1957, University of Jerusalem, 1958, University of Mexico, 1965, New York University, and Massachusetts Institute of Technology, 1975; lecturer for the Department of State at universities in Germany, 1954, Israel and Italy, 1955, Trinidad, 1959, Italy, spring, 1960, Chile, 1963, Mexico, 1964, and Japan, 1975. Member of War Department Commission on History of the War; travelled to Britain for War Department, Office of War Information, summer, 1943, and to France and Belgium, 1945. *Military service:* Served with U.S. Army Information and Education Division, 1945.

MEMBER: American Academy of Arts and Letters, American Scandinavian Society (fellow), American Antiquarian Society, Massachusetts Historical Society, Phi Beta Kappa, Century Association, St. Botolph's (Boston), Athenaeum Club (London).

AWARDS, HONORS: Herbert B. Adams Award of the American Historical Association, 1929; special award from Hillman Foundation, 1954, for *Freedom, Loyalty, Dissent;* Guggenheim fellowship, 1960-61; Gold Medal Award from American Academy and Institute of Arts and Letters, 1972, for history; Sarah Josepha Hale Award, 1973; decorated Knight, Order of Dannebrog. Honorary degrees from numerous colleges and universities, including Washington College (Maryland) and Ohio Wesleyan University, both 1958; Monmouth College, 1959; Brandeis University and Michigan State University, both 1960; Franklin and Marshall College, Alfred University, University of Hartford, and Cambridge University, all 1962; University of Puget Sound, 1963; Merrimack University and Carleton College, both 1966; Dickinson College, 1967; Columbia University, 1969; Ohio State University, University of Pittsburgh, Marietta College, Hampshire College, Wilson College, University of Virginia, and Maryville College, all 1970; University of Massachusetts, 1972.

WRITINGS:

The Literature of the Pioneer West, [Saint Paul], 1927.
(With Samuel Eliot Morison) *The Growth of the American Republic,* Oxford University Press, 1931, 7th edition, 1980, abbreviated and newly revised edition published as *A Concise History of the American Republic,* 1977.
Our Nation's Development, Harper, 1934.
Theodore Parker, Little, Brown, 1936, reissued with a new introduction, Beacon Press, 1960.
(With Allan Nevins) *America: The Story of a Free People,* Little, Brown, 1942, Oxford University Press, 1976, reissued in paperback as *The Pocket History of the United States,* Pocket Books, 1943, revised edition, 1982.
Majority Rule and Minority Rights, Oxford University Press, 1943.
(With Nevins) *A Short History of the United States,* Modern Library, 1945, 6th edition, Knopf, 1976.
The American Mind: An Interpretation of American Thought and Character Since the 1880's, Yale University Press, 1950.
(With others) *Civil Liberties under Attack,* University of Pennsylvania Press, 1951.
(Contributor) Courtlandt Canby, editor, *The World of History,* New American Library, 1954.

(With Geoffrey Brunn) *Europe and America since 1492,* Houghton, 1954.
Freedom, Loyalty, Dissent, Oxford University Press, 1954.
Federal Centralization and the Press, University of Minnesota, 1956.
(Contributor) *Conference on the American High School,* University of Chicago Press, 1958.
(With Robert W. McEwen and Brand Blanshard) *Education in a Free Society,* University of Pittsburgh Press, 1961.
The Nature and the Study of History, C. E. Merrill, 1965.
The Role of Scholarship in an Age of Science, Laramie, 1965.
Freedom and Order: A Commentary on the American Political Scene, Braziller, 1966.
The Study of History, C. E. Merrill, 1966.
(With Elmo Giordonetti) *Was America a Mistake?: An Eighteenth Century Controversy,* Harper, 1967.
The Search for a Usable Past, and Other Essays in Historiography, Knopf, 1967.
(With Richard B. Morris) *Colonies in Transition,* Harper, 1968.
The Commonwealth of Learning, Harper, 1968.
The Defeat of America: Presidential Power and the National Character, Simon & Schuster, 1974.
Britain through American Eyes, McGraw, 1974.
Jefferson, Nationalism, and the Enlightment, Braziller, 1974.
The Empire of Reason: How Europe Imagined and America Realized the Enlightenment, Doubleday, 1977.
(Author of text) *Mort Kuenstler's 50 Epic Paintings of America,* Abbeville Press, 1979.
(With Raymond H. Muessig) *The Study and Teaching of History,* Merrill, 1980.
(Author of introduction) *The Civil War Almanac,* Facts on File, 1983.
(Author of introduction) *Of America East and West: From the Writings of Paul Horgan,* Farrar, Straus, 1984.

EDITOR

Documents of American History (Volume I, to 1898; Volume II, from 1865), F. S. Crofts, 1934, 9th edition, 1973.
(With Nevins) *The Heritage of America,* Little, Brown, 1939, revised and enlarged edition, 1949.
(And author of historical narrative) *The Story of the Second World War,* Little, Brown, 1945.
(And author of introduction and notes) *America in Perspective: The United States through Foreign Eyes,* Random House, 1947, abridged edition, New American Library, 1959.
Alexis de Tocqueville, *Democracy in America,* translated by Henry Reeve, Oxford University Press, 1947.
Selections from "The Federalist," Appleton, 1949.
(With others) *Years of the Modern: An American Appraisal,* Longmans, Green, 1949.
The Blue and the Gray: The Story of the Civil War as Told by Participants, two volumes, Bobbs-Merrill, 1950, reprinted, Fairfax Press, 1982.
William Dean Howells, *Selected Writings,* Random House, 1950.
(And author of commentary) *Living Ideas in America,* Harper, 1951, enlarged edition, 1967.
(With Morris) *The Spirit of 'Seventy-Six: The Story of the American Revolution as Told by the Participants,* two volumes, Bobbs-Merrill, 1958, bicentennial edition, Harper, 1975, reprinted, Bonanza Books, 1983.
Official Atlas of the Civil War, Yoseloff, 1958.
Living Documents of American History, [Washington], 1960.
The Era of Reform, 1830-1860, Van Nostrand, 1960, reprinted, Krieger, 1982.

Theodore Parker: An Anthology, Beacon Press, 1960.

James Bryce, *Reflections on American Institutions: Selections from "The American Commonwealth,"* Fawcett, 1961.

Immigration and American History: Essays in Honor of Theodore C. Blegen, University of Minnesota Press, 1961.

Chester Bowles, *The Conscience of a Liberal*, Harper, 1962.

Winston Churchill, *History of the English-Speaking Peoples* (one volume of a four volume series), Bantam, 1963.

Noah Webster's American Spelling Book, Teachers College Press, 1963.

The Defeat of the Confederacy: A Documentary Survey, Van Nostrand, 1964.

Fifty Basic Civil War Documents, Van Nostrand, 1965, reprinted, Krieger, 1982.

(Consulting editor) *Encyclopedia of American History*, Harper, 1965.

Lester Ward and the Welfare State, Bobbs-Merrill, 1966.

The Struggle for Racial Equality: A Documentary Record, Harper, 1967.

Churchill, *Marlborough: His Life and Times*, Scribner, 1968.

(And author of introduction and commentary) *Britain through American Eyes*, Bodley Head, 1974.

(With others) *The West: An Illustrated History*, Promotory Press, 1976.

Edward M. Kennedy, *Our Day and Generation: The Words of Edward M. Kennedy*, Simon & Schuster, 1979.

(With others) *Illustrated History of the American Civil War*, Orbis, 1979.

Also editor with Morris of the "New American Nation" series, published by Harper; editor-in-chief of *The American Destiny: An Illustrated Bicentennial History of the United States*, twenty volumes, published by Danbury Press.

JUVENILES

(With Eugene Campbell Barker) *Our Nation*, Row, Peterson, 1941.

(Editor) *St. Nicholas Anthology*, Random House, 1948.

(Editor) *Second St. Nicholas Anthology*, Random House, 1950.

America's Robert E. Lee, Houghton, 1951.

Chestnut Squirrel, Houghton, 1952.

The First Book of American History, illustrated by Leonard Everett Fisher, F. Watts, 1957.

The Great Declaration, Bobbs-Merrill, 1958.

A Picture History of the United States of America, F. Watts, 1958.

The Great Proclamation, Bobbs-Merrill, 1960, reprinted, 1977.

The Great Constitution, Bobbs-Merrill, 1961.

Crusaders for Freedom, Doubleday, 1962.

OTHER

Contributor of essays to scholarly and popular journals, including *Book Week*, *New York Times Book Review*, *New Republic*, *Saturday Review*, *New York Review of Books*, and *American Scholar*.

WORK IN PROGRESS: Editing "The Rise of the American Nation," a projected fifty-volume series.

SIDELIGHTS: Henry Steele Commager has been one of America's preeminent historians for more than half a century. His writings include textbooks for children and college students, edited compilations of historical source material, original studies of the nature of American democracy, and biographies of prominent Americans. As Lawrence Wells Cobb explains in the *Dictionary of Literary Biography*, Commager "has devoted his energies to making it easier for scholars and lay readers both to 'get at' the sources of the American historical record and to understand their heritage more fully. He has undertaken these tasks so that his readers might become more informed and responsible participants in the great experiment launched in the eighteenth century to make a free, democratic, and bountiful society a reality on the North American continent." *New Republic* contributor Alexander R. Butler calls Commager "one of America's most distinguished historians," a scholar whose "excellent reputation" stems from his "simple, straightforward, and assertive" style. Behind that style lies serious conviction, however. Butler notes that Commager is "convinced that the reader can learn from history" and profit from the lessons of the usable past. Cobb likewise observes that in his writings the historian demands "that Americans live responsibly and prove worthy of their heritage. . . . His sprightly style, his eye for the illuminating vignette, his catholic knowledge, and his optimistic perspective have served him well in bringing his insights to generations of readers."

Commager's best known book is *The Growth of the American Republic*, a title he co-authored with Samuel Eliot Morison. First published in 1931, the work is still in print and is still used as a standard text in undergraduate history courses. According to *New York Times Book Review* correspondent Esmond Wright, the "limpidly clear style and the easy marshaling of arguments . . . have made 'The Growth of the American Republic' one of the most unusual and certainly one of the most readable of textbooks." Commager's other books for lay readers include a 1941 title *Our Nation* for high school students, and a 1942 popular study *America: The Story of a Free People*, co-authored by Allan Nevins. Commager's aim, in Cobb's words, has been "always to provide the facts within the matrix of an unobtrusive liberal interpretation and to provoke thought on the part of the reader." As early as 1934 Commager also began the editing duties for which he has become well known; his *Documents of American History* collects in two volumes the important primary sources on the creation and development of the United States. Cobb calls the work "the best single-volume source book in its field." Throughout the following forty years Commager continued to publish anthologies of historical source material; his efforts have produced, among others, *The Blue and the Gray: The Story of the Civil War as Told by Participants*, *The Era of Reform, 1830-1860*, and *The Struggle for Racial Equality: A Documentary History*. Cobb claims that such collections are "intended to put the words and ideas that shaped America within easy reach of both the generalist and interested layman." In the *New York Herald Tribune Book Review*, Bernard DeVoto contends that these books provide "a way of experiencing the nation's most tremendous experience. No one can read [them] without being impelled to think searchingly about the American people, the American nation, the American past and future."

As a scholar Commager has sought to define the strengths of democracy. Cobb suggests that the historian's theses "always revolved around Jeffersonian liberalism: give the public the maximum amount of information and the people can be trusted to make the right decisions in the long run." Such a view stresses the importance of education as well as the necessity for free speech and dissent, so Commager became one of the strongest opponents of the 1950s' communist-fearing conformity. His comment in the 1951 volume *Civil Liberties under Attack* has since become famous: "The great danger that threatens us is neither heterodox thought nor orthodox thought, but the absence of thought." Commager continued to argue for the preservation of free speech and inquiry as the Vietnam War escalated in the 1960s. According to Cobb, the historian "reminded visitors, distressed to see all the unrest in America, . . . that the idealism of the 1960s was a reassertion, not a repudiation, of our Revolutionary ideals of liberty and equality." Since then, in such essentially optimistic books as *Jefferson, Nationalism, and the Enlightenment* and *The Empire of Reason: How Europe Imagined and America Realized the Enlightenment,* Commager has maintained that America is an ongoing experiment in the practical implementation of philosophy; the nation's continued strength depends on its forging a link with the ideals of the founding generation. As Cobb puts it, history is "definitely a usable past for citizens of the United States, and this history [is] also a living proof to all the people of the world that such 'good things' as continental self-government and socio-economic mobility [are] possible."

Commager's committment to educating the public has not led him to adopt the pose of a judge. Rather, he offers readers a spectrum of facts which they can judge themselves. Critics such as *New York Times* columnist Herbert Mitgang note, however, that Commager's very enthusiasm for history and the "crystalline clarity of the writing" he produces cause "explosions in the reader's mind." Mitgang concludes: "Here is history to be pondered and cherished." Cobb sees Commager as an author who has "kindled a love for the spectacle of history and personality in thousands of young minds" through his juvenile literature and his many source books. *Atlantic* contributor C. J. Rolo also contends that Commager's value as a writer "is that he combines an exhilarating enthusiasm for his subject with a keenly critical viewpoint and an absence of cant that is becoming increasingly rare." Amherst College's Simpson Lecturer is continuing to edit and compile historical texts that reveal both the benefits and the challenges of democratic government. In the *New York Times Book Review,* Arthur Schlesinger, Jr. concludes that in Henry Steele Commager, "learning and reason are at the service of a mind whose understanding of democracy gains brilliance and power from a passion for democratic freedom."

BIOGRAPHICAL/CRITICAL SOURCES:

BOOKS

Civil Liberties under Attack, University of Pennsylvania Press, 1951.
Dictionary of Literary Biography, Volume 17: *Twentieth Century American Historians,* Gale, 1983.
Garraty, John, *Interpreting American History: Conversations with Historians,* Macmillan, 1970.
Hyman, Harold M. and Leonard W. Levy, editors, *Freedom and Reform: Essays in Honor of Henry Steele Commager,* Harper, 1967.

PERIODICALS

Atlantic, May, 1950.
Christian Century, July 5, 1950, October 24, 1962.
Christian Science Monitor, April 6, 1936, March 18, 1950.
Commonweal, May 5, 1950.
Nation, April 22, 1950, December 23, 1950.
New Republic, April 24, 1950, May 24, 1954, May 20, 1967, December 21, 1974.
New Statesman, June 2, 1967.
Newsweek, November 15, 1948.
New York Herald Tribune Book Review, March 12, 1950, November 19, 1950, May 30, 1954.

New York Times, March 12, 1950, November 12, 1950, June 7, 1977.
New York Times Book Review, March 12, 1950, October 23, 1966, June 25, 1967, November 26, 1967, August 14, 1977, November 4, 1979, April 8, 1984.
San Francisco Chronicle, March 24, 1950, November 26, 1950.
Saturday Review, March 11, 1950, December 2, 1950, May 1, 1954, January 28, 1967, May 14, 1977.
Survey, April, 1950.
Time, December 11, 1950.
Times Literary Supplement, November 17, 1950, July 23, 1954, September 27, 1974, August 4, 1978.
Yale Review, summer, 1950.†

—*Sketch by Anne Janette Johnson*

* * *

COOPER, I(rving) S(pencer) 1922-1985

PERSONAL: Born July 15, 1922, in Atlantic City, N.J.; died of cancer October 30, 1985, in Naples, Fla.; son of David (a salesman) and Eleanor (Cooper) Cooper; married Mary Dan Frost, December 15, 1944 (died, 1968); married Sissel Holn Svenningsen, January 31, 1970; children: Daniel Alan, Douglas Paul, Lisa Frost, David Erik Louis, Eric Holm, Charles Spencer. *Education:* George Washington University, B.A., 1942, M.D. 1945; University of Minnesota, M.S. and Ph.D., both 1951.

ADDRESSES: Home—3753 Fort Charles Dr., Port Royal Club, Naples, Fla. 33940. *Agent*—Russell & Volkening, Inc., 551 Fifth Ave., New York, N.Y. 10017.

CAREER: U.S. Naval Hospital, St. Albans, N.Y., intern, 1945-46; Mayo Foundation, Rochester, Minn., resident in neurosurgery, 1948-51; New York University, New York City, assistant professor, 1951-57, professor of neurosurgery at Bellevue Medical Center, 1957-66, associate attending neurosurgeon at university hospital, 1951-66; New York Medical College, New York City, research professor of neuroanatomy, beginning 1966, professor of physiologic neurosurgery, beginning 1978. Director of department of neurosurgery at St. Barnabas Hospital, 1953-77. Diplomate of American Board of Psychiatry and Neurology, 1951, and American Board of Neurological Surgery, 1953. Eliza Savage Visiting Professor in Australia, 1962; visiting professor at Mayo Foundation and University of London, both 1974. President and member of board of trustees, Naples Institute for Medicine and Humanities, beginning 1976. *Military service:* U.S. Naval Reserve, active duty in Medical Corps, 1946-48; became lieutenant junior grade.

MEMBER: American College of Surgeons (fellow), American Association for Neurological Surgery, American Medical Association, Neurosurgical Society of America, American Academy of Neurology, American Geriatric Society (fellow), American Federation of Clinical Research, American Congress of Physical Medicine and Rehabilitation, Pan American Society of the United States, Harvey Cushing Neurosurgical Society, Society of Cryobiology (governor), Society of Cryosurgery (president), Medical Honor Society, Luther Rice Society, Royal Academy of Medicine (Madrid; foreign academic correspondent), Scandinavian Neurosurgical Society, Czechoslovak Neurosurgical Society, Neurological Society of Czechoslovakia, Neurological and Neurosurgical Society of Argentina, Society for Neurology and Neurosurgery (Cuba), Egyptian Neurosurgical Society, New York Academy of Medicine (fellow), New York Academy of Science (fellow), Sigma Xi, Alpha Omega Alpha.

AWARDS, HONORS: Neurosurgical fellowship, Mayo Clinic, 1948-51; Hektoen Bronze Medal from American Medical Association, 1957, 1958, certificate of merit, 1961; Lewis Harvey Taylor Award from American Therapeutic Society, 1957; award from New York Philanthropic League, 1960; civic award in medicine from Bronx Board of Trade, 1961; award from National Cystic Fibrosis Foundation, 1962; humanitarian merit award from Chicago National Parkinson Foundation, 1962, and United Parkinson Fund, 1965; Henderson Lecture Award from American Geriatric Society, 1967; gold medal from Worshipful Society of Apothecaries (London), 1967; bronze award from American Congress of Rehabilitation Medicine, 1967; Comenius Medal from University of Bratislava, 1971; D.Sc. from Trinity University, Hartford, Conn. and Fordham University, both 1974; Golden Plate Award, American Academy of Achievement, 1983.

WRITINGS:

The Neurosurgical Alleviation of Parkinsonism, C. C Thomas, 1956.
Parkinsonism: Its Medical and Surgical Therapy, C. C Thomas, 1961.
Involuntary Movement Disorders, Hoeber, 1969.
The Victim Is Always the Same (autobiographical), Harper, 1973.
It's Hard to Leave While the Music's Playing, Norton, 1977.
The Vital Probe: My Life as a Brain Surgeon, Norton, 1981.

Contributor to medical journals.

SIDELIGHTS: During his four decades as a neurosurgeon, I. S. Cooper gained international acclaim as the developer of a revolutionary procedure for treating Parkinson's disease. Cooper's treatment, which involved freezing affected areas of the brain, helped to relieve symptoms like uncontrollable shaking, without causing further damage. Some years after his discovery, Cooper surprised the medical community and society at large by cancelling further scheduled operations and endorsing another doctor's treatment—in this case, George Cotzias' drug L-Dopa, which could treat the Parkinson's symptoms without surgery.

Cooper, who also taught neurosurgery at New York University from 1951 to 1966, was the author of several medical texts. In 1981, though, he caught the reading public's attention with an autobiography, *The Vital Probe: My Life as a Brain Surgeon.* As *Los Angeles Times Book Review* critic Elaine Kendall saw it, the volume presents a doctor "whose work has aroused passionate controversy among colleagues and rivals, roused reverence from the thousands of people he has helped. When we do meet him, ready for vanity, arrogance, egocentricity, ready for anything, we find imagination and courage, brilliance, compassion and terror, a set of traits that should be the sine qua non of neurosurgery and all medicine.''

Within the text of *The Vital Probe,* the author described a trait among his peers that some critics found disturbing, but not surprising: that a breakthrough such as Cooper's caused a virtual tidal wave of professional jealousy and rumor-mongering. The reason, as Kendall described, is that "a truly revolutionary innovation can totally obliterate another man's career, make his life's work meaningless, his skills superfluous and deprive him of his livelihood. Medical competition is merciless. 'The Vital Probe' makes this stunningly and finally clear.''

P. B. Medawar, writing in a *New York Review of Books* piece, took a similar tack. Noting that Cooper was not only a surgeon and professor, but also a diplomate of the American Board of Psychiatry and Neurology, he added that even these qualifications "were not high enough, unfortunately, to protect him from the campaign of depreciation amounting sometimes to vilification of which [Cooper] became the victim. It is as true in the world of medicine and science as it is in the world of letters that any very notable accomplishment by a young man—particularly if there is a suspicion that it is due to a real superiority of hand or mind—arouses an extreme envy or resentment.''

The Vital Probe earned praise from Medawar and from Walter Clemons. Clemons, reviewing the work in *Newsweek,* found Cooper "an excellent writer, able to describe intricate surgical procedures with clarity and suspenseful excitement. But the main interest of his autobiography is personal. He [was] a lively, touchy, vulnerable and quarrelsome human being.'' And to Medawar, the book "is both stirring and informative. We learn from it much about the surgeon and the brain and much about people, and most rewardingly about Cooper himself, a man very well worth getting to know.''

BIOGRAPHICAL/CRITICAL SOURCES:

BOOKS

Cooper, I. S., *The Victim Is Always the Same,* Harper, 1973.
Cooper, I. S., *The Vital Probe: My Life as a Brain Surgeon,* Norton, 1981.

PERIODICALS

Los Angeles Times Book Review, October 25, 1981.
Newsweek, February 8, 1982.
New York Review of Books, January 21, 1982.

OBITUARIES:

PERIODICALS

Detroit Free Press, November 5, 1985.
New York Times, November 4, 1985.
Nyack Rockland Journal-News, November 6, 1985.
White Plains Reporter-Dispatch, November 6, 1985.†

*   *   *

COOPER, James A.
[Collective pseudonym]

WRITINGS:

Cap'n Abe, Storekeeper; A Story of Cape Cod, Sully & Kleinteich, 1917.
Cap'n Jonah's Fortune; A Story of Cape Cod (also see below), G. Sully, 1919.
Sheila of Big Wreck Cove; A Story of Cape Cod, G. Sully, 1922.
Tobias o' the Light; A Story of Cape Cod (also see below), G. Sully, 1920.

"HEROINE" SERIES

Tobias o' the Light; A Story of Cape Cod, World, 1933.
Cap'n Jonah's Fortune; A Story of Cape Cod, World, 1933.

SIDELIGHTS: For more information see the entries for Harriet S. Adams, Edward L. Stratemeyer, and Andrew E. Svenson.

BIOGRAPHICAL/CRITICAL SOURCES:

BOOKS

Johnson, Deidre, editor and compiler, *Stratemeyer Pseudonyms and Series Books: An Annotated Checklist of Stratemeyer and Stratemeyer Syndicate Publications*, Greenwood Press, 1982.

*   *   *

COOPER, Parley J(oseph) 1937-
(Dorothy Dawes, Joseph Freytag, Josephine Freytag, Jack Mayfield, D. J. McKinney, Alex Nebrensky)

PERSONAL: Born June 8, 1937, in Glendale, Ore.; son of Howard (a lumberman) and Dorothy (McKinney) Cooper. *Education:* Attended Santa Monica City College, 1956-57, University of Hawaii, 1959-60, and University of California, Berkeley, 1961-63. *Religion:* Christian.

ADDRESSES: Home—Medford, Ore. *Agent*—Jay Garon, Jay Garon-Brooke Associates, Inc., 415 Central Park W., New York, N.Y. 10025.

CAREER: Writer. Worked in New York City and Washington, D.C., 1963-65; associate editor and business manager of *Diplomat* (magazine), 1965-67; David L. Wolper Productions, Hollywood, Calif., business manager, 1967-68. *Military service:* U.S. Navy, 1955-56.

WRITINGS:

NOVELS

The Feminists, Pinnacle Books, 1971.
The Devil's Child, Pocket Books, 1972.
Marianne's Kingdom, Pocket Books, 1972.
The Inheritance, Popular Library, 1972.
A Reunion of Strangers, Berkley Publishing, 1973.
My Lady Evil, Simon & Schuster, 1974.
The Shuddering Fair One, Pocket Books, 1974.
Moonblood, Pocket Books, 1975.
The Studio, Ace Books, 1975.
The Scapegraces, Pyramid, 1975.
Reverend Mama, Pocket Books, 1975.
Dark Desires, Pocket Books, 1976.
Wreck!, Ace Books, 1977.
San Francisco, Pocket Books, 1977.
Restaurant, Macmillan, 1979.
(Under pseudonym Jack Mayfield) *The Magnate*, New American Library, 1980.
Golden Fever, Pocket Books, 1981.
(Under pseudonym Jack Mayfield) *The Appraiser*, Ace Books, 1982.
(Under pseudonym D. J. McKinney) *Secret Lives*, Ace Books, 1982.
(Under pseudonym Alex Nebrensky) *The Unholy*, New American Library, 1982.
The Wives, Pocket Books, 1987.
Grand Deception, PaperJacks, 1987.
Conspiracy, Worldwide Library, 1988.

Also author, under several pseudonyms (including Dorothy Dawes, Joseph Freytag, and Josephine Freytag), of a number of other novels.

OTHER

Contributor of stories to magazines.

WORK IN PROGRESS: Soul Mate, an occult thriller; *Fatal Friends*, a novel of a serial killer; *Targets*, a thriller.

SIDELIGHTS: Parley J. Cooper's novel *The Feminists* has been translated into Spanish.

*   *   *

COREY, Dorothy

PERSONAL: Born in Rush Lake, Saskatchewan, Canada; married Edward Corey (an engineer; deceased); children: Richard, Jan Sebastian. *Education:* Attended school in Nebraska.

ADDRESSES: Home—16654 Parthenia St., Sepulveda, Calif. 91343.

CAREER: Writer. Active in a cooperative nursery school, Parent/Teacher Association; leader in Girl Scouts of America.

MEMBER: Society of Children's Book Writers (charter member).

AWARDS, HONORS: New Shoes!, New Shoes! was listed on a Bank Street List of Best Books, 1985.

WRITINGS:

BOOKS FOR CHILDREN

You Go Away, Albert Whitman, 1975.
No Company Was Coming to Samuel's House/No llegaban invitados a la casa de Samuel (in English and Spanish; translation by Marguerite Arguedas Baker), Blaine Ethridge, 1976.
Tomorrow You Can, Albert Whitman, 1977.
Pepe's Private Christmas, Parents Magazine Press, 1978.
Everybody Takes Turns, Albert Whitman, 1980.
We All Share, Albert Whitman, 1980.
New Shoes!, New Shoes!, Albert Whitman, 1985.
Will It Ever Be My Birthday?, Albert Whitman, 1986.
A Shot for Baby Bear, Albert Whitman, 1988.

Also author of *You Can Depend on Santa*. Contributor of short stories to numerous magazines, including *Humpty Dumpty*.

WORK IN PROGRESS: Writing an orthodontic narrative for middle-aged children.

SIDELIGHTS: Dorothy Corey wrote *CA:* "I made my first sale when I was ten years old. A large garage in Omaha was having a slogan contest. I entered and won fourth prize—a generous two hundred-fifty dollars worth of parts and labor at the garage!

"I wrote many extra-curricular skits during the seventh and eighth grades and I sometimes think I did my best writing in the eighth grade. I didn't write again until, as a teen-ager, I published some verse and Rebecca Caudill encouraged me to continue my writing.

"When I read to my first child I decided to write for children. I made a brief start. Then I moved to the country and had so much outdoor work and another child that I didn't get back to juvenile manuscripts for many years.

"In the meantime I fell into the clutches of the local Parent/Teacher Association and I spent years preparing skits and programs for them (they always needed one more) when I could have had books of my own. After all, memories are not very permanent.

"I wish I could say that I was imaginative enough to make up plots and situations, but all my manuscripts, published and unpublished, grew out of things that really happened. My child left the door open for Santa Claus so I wrote *Pepe's Private Christmas*. My niece received a bike with one wheel so I wrote *You Can Depend on Santa*.

"My concept books grow from my own experiences and the suggestions of a panel of nursery school teachers I am fortunate to have as friends. A bilingual teacher told me there was no material about a Spanish Thanksgiving. Everything was American turkey and her pupils could not relate to it. So I wrote the bilingual *No Company Was Coming to Samuel's House*.

"In nursery school we used to tell the children that 'maybe tomorrow' they would be able to go down the slide and do all kinds of grown-up things, so I wrote *Tomorrow You Can. You Go Away* was inspired by seeing Glo Coalson's 'On Mother's Lap,' but it drew upon many departures. Nursery school teachers have found *You Go Away* especially useful."

AVOCATIONAL INTERESTS: Music.

*   *   *

COSGROVE, Carol Ann
See TWITCHETT, Carol Cosgrove

*   *   *

COTES, Peter 1912-
(Peter Northcote)

PERSONAL: Original name, Sydney Arthur Boulting; born March 19, 1912, in Maidenhead, Berkshire, England; son of Arthur and Rose (Bennett) Boulting; maried Myfanwy Jones, 1938 (marriage dissolved); married Joan Miller, May 19, 1948. *Education:* Educated in private schools and by tutor. *Politics:* Liberal Democrat. *Religion:* Humanist.

ADDRESSES: Office—c/o Pinar Harman, Cotes Logan Productions, 53 Chancery Lane, London WC2, England.

CAREER: Began as juvenile actor, appearing in numerous plays and films; became play producer, theatre owner, film and television drama director. Artistic director in association with Arts Council of Great Britain at Library Theatre, Manchester, England, 1948-49, produced such plays as "John Gabriel Borkman" and "Anna Christie," 1948, "Miss Julie," 1949; drama director, Associated Rediffusion Ltd., 1955-58, produced and directed such television productions as "Woman in a Dressing Gown," "The Young and the Guilty," "The Right Person," "The Hungry God," "Look in Any Window," and "The Two Letters"; senior drama director, Associated British Picture Corp., 1959-61; supervising producer of drama for Channel 7, Melbourne, Australia, 1961; story consultant and director for Anglia Television Ltd., 1964. Has also produced "The Master Builder," "The Biggest Thief in Town," "Candida," and "The Father," in London's West End, "A Pin to See the Peepshow" in London and on Broadway, "Epitaph for George Dillon" in Holland, "Hidden Stranger" on Broadway, and directed "The Impossible Years," Cambridge Theatre, London, 1966-67. Founder of New Lindsey Theatre Club, 1946, and New Boltons Theatre, 1951.

MEMBER: Theatrical Managers Association, Society of Authors, Medico-Legal Society, Our Society, Guild of Drama Adjudicators, Savage Club (London).

AWARDS, HONORS: Fellow, Royal Society of Authors; Knight of Mark Twain; award as best director in British theatre, 1951,

for such productions as "The Biggest Thief in Town" at Duchess Theatre, "Pick Up Girl" at Prince of Wales Theatre.

WRITINGS:

No Star Nonsense, Rockliff, 1949.
(With Thelma Niklaus) *The Little Fellow: The Life and Work of Charles Spencer Chaplin*, Bodley Head, 1951, revised edition, J. Lane, 1952.
A Handbook for Amateur Theatre, Oldbourne, 1957.
George Robey: The Darling of the Halls, Cassell, 1972.
(Editor, and author of introduction) *Trial of Elvira Barney*, David & Charles, 1976.
(With Rupert Croft-Cooke) *Circus: A World History*, Macmillan, 1977.
J. P.—the Man Called Mitch: A Memoir, Paul Elek, 1978.
(With Harold Atkins) *The Barbirollis: A Musical Marriage*, Robson, 1983.

Adapter of plays for television and radio, and screenwriter. Author of George Robey centenary tribute, "Omnibus" series, BBC-TV, 1969, and "One Pair of Eyes," which he also directed for BBC-TV, 1970. Has also written and narrated many productions for radio, including "Back into the Light," "The Prime Minister of Mirth," and "Mervyn Peake." Also author of radio series "Old Stagers" for British Broadcasting Corporation, 1984. Contributor of film and stage criticism to British periodicals including, *Queen Magazine, Film Weekly, Stage, New Theatre, Films and Filming, Plays and Players, Guardian, News Chronicle*, and *Daily Herald* under pseudonym Peter Northcote.

WORK IN PROGRESS: Autobiography tentatively entitled *This Is How It Was*.

AVOCATIONAL INTERESTS: Walking, writing letters, criminology.

*   *   *

COULSON, Juanita (Ruth) 1933-
(John Jay Wells, a joint pseudonym)

PERSONAL: Surname is pronounced *Col*-son; born February 12, 1933, in Anderson, Ind.; daughter of Grant Elmer (a tool and die maker) and Ruth Margaret (Oemler) Wellons; married Robert Stratton Coulson (a writer), August 21, 1954; children: Bruce Edward. *Education:* Ball State University, B.S., 1954, M.A., 1961. *Politics:* Independent. *Religion:* Unitarian Universalist.

ADDRESSES: Home—2677W-500N, Hartford City, Ind. 47348. *Agent*—Jim Allen, Virginia Kidd Literary Agency, 538 East Harford St., Milford, Pa. 18337.

CAREER: Writer; art editor and publisher of *Yandro* (science fiction magazine), 1953—. Elementary school teacher, 1954-55; collator, Heckman's Bookbindery, North Manchester, Ind., 1955-57.

MEMBER: Science Fiction Writers of America.

AWARDS, HONORS: Joint nominee with husband, Robert S. Coulson, for Hugo Award, World Science Fiction Convention, 1960-64, 1966-67, for best amateur science fiction magazine, *Yandro;* joint winner with R. S. Coulson, Hugo Award, 1965, for *Yandro;* Ralph Holland Memorial Award, Fan Art Show, 20th World Science Fiction Convention, 1962; co-Fan Guest of Honor, with R. S. Coulson, 30th World Science Fiction Convention, 1972.

WRITINGS:

Crisis on Cheiron, Ace Books, 1967.
The Singing Stones, Ace Books, 1968.
The Secret of Seven Oaks, Berkley Publishing, 1972.
Door into Terror, Berkley Publishing, 1972.
(Contributor) Richard A. Lupoff and Don Thompson, editors,
    The Comic-Book Book, Arlington House, 1973.
Stone of Blood, Ballantine, 1975.
Unto the Last Generation, Laser Books, 1975.
Space Trap, Laser Books, 1976.
Fear Stalks the Bayou, Ballantine, 1976.
(Contributor) Sandra Marshak and Myrna Culbreath, editors,
    Star Trek: The New Voyages, Bantam, 1976.
Dark Priestess, Ballantine, 1977.
Web of Wizardry, Del Rey Books, 1978.
Fire of the Andes, Ballantine, 1979.
The Death God's Citadel, Del Rey Books, 1980.
(Contributor) Peter Wilfert, editor, *Goldmann Fantasy Foliant
    III*, Wilhelm Goldmann Verlag, 1985.
Hostage to Magic, Del Rey Books, in press.
Jewel of Darkness, Del Rey Books, in press.
Sorcery's Crown, Del Rey Books, in press.

*"CHILDREN OF THE STARS" SERIES; PUBLISHED BY DEL REY
    BOOKS*

Tomorrow's Heritage, 1981.
Outward Bound, 1982.
Legacy of Earth, in press.
The Past of Forever, in press.

OTHER

Also contributor to Andre Norton, editor, *Tales of Witch World
IV;* also contributor to *If, Fantastic*, and, with Marion Zimmer
Bradley under joint pseudonym John Jay Wells, to *Fantasy
and Science Fiction.* Art editor and publisher of Science Fiction Writers of America's *Forum* magazine, 1971-72.

SIDELIGHTS: Juanita and Robert S. Coulson's publication,
Yandro, is referred to as a "fanzine" by science fiction enthusiasts. Although it is one of the longest-running large fan-
zines, *Yandro* is only one of many published throughout the
world. A fanzine is an amateur science fiction magazine published by those interested in the genre.

Juanita Coulson adds: "In recent years, our amateur publication *Yandro* has virtually ceased publication, due to increasing
pressure of free-lance writing. Originally, *Yandro* served as
our forum, and that of our fellow science fiction and fantasy
enthusiasts. Now we have acquired broader outlets—not to say
considerably more profitable ones. My husband's interest in
reviewing has been transferred to several professional periodicals, and I have been able to concentrate my creative focus
on the writing of novels.

"Prior to the '80s, my work lay in the fields of women's
genre, action/adventure-oriented SF and fantasy. When I was
commissioned to write the 'Children of the Stars' series for
Del Rey Books, I was forced into a very different mode. Following the dictum of 'stick to what you know—or can extrapolate from what you know,' I had never attempted even the
fringes of so-called 'hard science' fiction. My degrees are in
the 'soft sciences,' not astrophysics and computer technology,
etc. However, I was able to pick the brains of a number of
highly-trained friends employed in those fields. The results
apparently are satisfactory; numerous readers, also qualified
in high-tech industries, have complimented me not only on the

characters and stories I have created but on the technological
'scenery' in the backgrounds of those books. It has certainly
been the most challenging task of my writing career—to date.

"Now I would like to make the swing back to the quite different genre of fantasy adventure. Style and background re-
quirements vary enormously in the science fiction and fantasy
specialties, but the basics of solid characterizations and a narrative the reader can become involved in are constants. In *that*
regard, I've found that storytelling in novel form really is the
same; and I hope it continues to be indefinitely, for *my* enjoyment as well as the reader's."

Several of her books have been translated into German.

BIOGRAPHICAL/CRITICAL SOURCES:

PERIODICALS

Science Fiction Review, November, 1981.

*   *   *

COURTER, Gay   1944-

PERSONAL: Born October 1, 1944, in Pittsburgh, Pa.; daugh-
ter of Leonard M. (an international businessman) and Elsie
(Spector) Weisman; married Philip Courter (a film director),
August 18, 1968; children: Blake Zachary, Joshua Forrest.
Education: Antioch College, B.A., 1966.

ADDRESSES: Home and office—Courter Film & Associates,
121 Northwest Crystal St., Crystal River, Fla. 32629. *Agent*—
Sterling Lord Literary Agency, Inc., 1 Madison Ave., New
York, N.Y. 10021.

CAREER: Free-lance film writer and producer, 1969—; novelist. Childbirth and Parent Education of New Jersey, member
of board of directors, 1973, vice-president, 1975.

MEMBER: International Childbirth Education Association,
Authors Guild, Authors League of America.

AWARDS, HONORS: "Reflections in Space" was chosen most
honored film by *Business Screen*, 1970; first prize from Amer-
ican Film Festival, 1974, for "Handy-Dandy-Do-It-Yourself
Filmmaker's Series"; Cine Golden Eagle Awards for films
"Reflections in Space," "Gristmiller," "The Bonding Birth
Experience," and four fire fighter training films: "Structural
Fire Attack," "Breathing Apparatus: Why?," "Basic Search
and Rescue," and "The Foam Film"; White House Confer-
ence Awards for films "Child's Eye View," "Take a Running
Start," "Hey, Look at Me!," and "Children Make Films:
The Young Art"; blue ribbon from Educational Film Library
Association for "Handy-Dandy-Do-It-Yourself Filmmaker's
Series."

WRITINGS:

The Beansprout Book (nonfiction), Simon & Schuster, 1973.
(With husband, Philip Courter) *The Filmmaker's Craft* (text-
    book), Van Nostrand, 1976.
The Midwife (novel), Houghton, 1981.
River of Dreams (historical romance; Book-of-the-Month Club
    alternate selection), Houghton, 1984.
Code Ezra (spy novel; Literary Guild selection), Houghton,
    1986.

Also writer and/or producer with P. Courter of the following
films: "Child's Eye View," 1967, "Take a Running Start,"
1969, "Hey, Look at Me!," 1969, "Reflections in Space,"
1970, "Children Make Films: The Young Art," 1972, "Along

the Way'' (three films), 1973, "Learning about Solar Energy," 1974, "Learning about Water," 1974, "Handy-Dandy-Do-It-Yourself Filmmaker's Series" (three films), 1974, "Gristmiller," 1976, "Cidermaker," 1976, "Are You Ready for the Postpartum Experience?," 1976, "The Cesarean Birth Experience," 1977, "The Bonding Birth Experience," 1977, four fire fighter training films—"Structural Fire Attack," "Breathing Apparatus: Why?," "Basic Search and Rescue," and "The Foam Film"—1977-78, "The Breastfeeding Experience," 1978, "Caring and Coping," 1980, "The Teenage Pregnancy Experience," 1981, "Saturday's Children," 1982, "Family-Centered Cesareans," 1983, "The Mysterious Manatee," 1983, "Don't Risk Your Child's Life," 1983, "Tender Loving Care: Parenting the Newborn," 1984, "Incident Command Series" (three films), 1986-87, "Healthy Mothers, Healthy Babies," "Buckle Up and Do It Right," "The Florida Water Story" (three films), and "My Child Is Deaf, My Child Is Blind." Contributor to periodicals, including *Publishers Weekly*.

SIDELIGHTS: Gay Courter told *Library Journal* that she wrote *The Midwife* because she thought that "by writing about one midwife, I could explain much about birth that science ignores. After all[,] fiction is about feelings, and emotions motivate change." She found writing this novel "exhilarating. Eight thousand hours later I knew that writing fiction was the way I most wanted to spend my days." In a review of *The Midwife* for the *Washington Post,* Carol Eisen Rinzler states: "Courter, to use a time-tested phrase, knows how to tell a story." Although finding fault with the novel's characterizations and too-intrusive research, Rinzler believes that "frequently Courter does manage to create a scene that is alive and arresting."

When Courter's spy novel *Code Ezra* was first published, Alice Hornbaker wrote in the *Cincinnati Enquirer:* "Don't let 605 pages scare you away from one of this year's best spy novels. . . . *Code Ezra* is more than a story of betrayal within the most secret of spy agencies in the world—Israel's Mossad. It's alive with multiple love stories, revenge, intrigue and . . . many world locations. . . . Anyone who thinks the life of a spy is glamorous should read *Code Ezra*." According to Courter, *Code Ezra* is a "concerted mingling of fact and fiction," quotes Kathleen Ovack in the *St. Petersburg Times.* For the novel, Courter interviewed several individuals in Israel, Egypt, France, and Britain who had previously worked as undercover agents for Israel's secret service. As recorded by Ovack, Courter claimed: "I didn't have problems getting people to speak with me, because I made it clear I was writing fiction and I didn't care about who they really were or when things happened. . . . I wanted to know about the essence of spycraft, the historical background, the technicalities . . . not the make-believe world of James Bond." Courter went so far as learning how to fly so that she could provide authentic flying scenes in her work.

Code Ezra's time span covers the four decades that Mossad has been in existence, with special emphasis on those members who make up the (fictitious) Ezra team: three female spies and their leader, Eli Katzar. The novel's intrigue revolves around the discovery of betrayal within the Ezra group. "On the surface . . . ," writes Leola Floren for the *Detroit News,* "Courter's *Code Ezra* smacks of a kosher *Charlie's Angels* . . . [but] it doesn't take too many pages for Courter, an able spinner of novel adventure, to rise above the cliches and weave a captivating story of four Jews who pool their talents in order to preserve their homeland." Floren also finds that the developing friendships among the Ezra members, as well as the

assignments they fulfill over the years, makes for entertaining reading. As for *New York Times Book Review* critic Elizabeth Fishel, although she believes Courter's drive for authenticity weighs the novel down and that the denouement is weak, she nevertheless finds the story absorbing. Finally, in terms of the book's political stance, Ovack notes: "Some readers have told Courter that although they expected to get a pro-Israel point of view from her book, they came away from it with a sympathy for the Palestinians. But Courter says that while she is pro-Israel, she wrote her book without bias to present several points of view. 'I am inherently a pacifist,' Courter says."

BIOGRAPHICAL/CRITICAL SOURCES:

PERIODICALS

Cincinnati Enquirer, May 25, 1986.
Detroit News, April 27, 1986.
Florida Times-Union, September 7, 1986.
Library Journal, February 1, 1981.
New York Times Book Review, May 25, 1986.
St. Petersburg Times, June 30, 1986.
Washington Post, March 12, 1981, April 30, 1984.

*   *   *

CRAIG, M. F.
    See CRAIG, Mary (Francis) S(hura)

*   *   *

CRAIG, M. S.
    See CRAIG, Mary (Francis) S(hura)

*   *   *

CRAIG, Mary
    See CRAIG, Mary (Francis) S(hura)

*   *   *

CRAIG, Mary (Francis) S(hura)   1923-
(M. F. Craig, M. S. Craig, Mary Craig, Mary Shura Craig, Mary Francis Shura; pseudonyms: Alexis Hill, Meredith Hill)

PERSONAL: Born February 27, 1923, in Pratt, Kan.; daughter of Jack Fant and Mary (Milstead) Young; married Daniel C. Shura, October 24, 1943 (died June 13, 1959); married Raymond Craig, December 8, 1961 (divorced, 1984); children: (first marriage) Marianne Francis Shura Sprague, Daniel Charles, Alice Barrett Craig Stout; (second marriage) Mary Forsha. *Education:* Attended Maryville State College, 1940-43.

ADDRESSES: Home—301 Lake Hinsdale Dr., No. 112, Clarendon Hills, Ill. 60514. *Agent*—(juvenile books) Dorothy Markinko, McIntosh & Otis, 310 Madison Ave., New York, N.Y. 10017; (adult books) Roslyn Targ Literary Agency, 105 West 13th St., Suite 15E, New York, N.Y. 10011.

CAREER: Free-lance writer. Public relations director, Girl Scouts of America, 1960-61. Creative writing teacher at various universities, including University of Kansas and California State University; lecturer and participant in workshops, including Mystery Writers Workshops, 1986-88. Had weekly book review program, WOI-TV, Ames, Iowa, 1976.

MEMBER: Authors League of America, Authors Guild, Mystery Writers of America (Midwest regional vice-president, 1983-

84; general awards chairman, 1988; member, national board of directors), Women in Communication, Children's Book Writers of America, Crime Writers of Great Britain, Children's Reading Round Table (Chicago).

AWARDS, HONORS: Simple Spigott was named to the *World Book Encyclopedia* 100 Best list, 1960; *The Nearsighted Knight* was named to the *New York Times* best books list, 1963; citation for outstanding contribution to children's literature, Central Missouri State University, 1974; Lillian Steinhauer Award, New York Poetry Forum, 1976; Pinetree Award, 1983, for *Chester;* Carl Sandburg Award, Friends of the Chicago Public Library, 1985, for *The Search for Grissi.*

WRITINGS:

ADULT FICTION

(Under name Mary Francis Shura) *The Shop on Threnody Street,* Grosset, 1972.
(Under name Mary Craig) *A Candle for the Dragon,* Dell, 1973.
(Under name Mary Craig) *Ten Thousand Several Doors,* Hawthorn, 1973, published as *Mistress of Lost River,* Manor Books, 1976.
(Under name Mary Craig) *The Cranes of Ibycus,* Hawthorn, 1974, published as *Shadows of the Past,* Manor Books, 1976.
(Under name Mary Craig) *Were He a Stranger,* Dodd, 1978.
(Under pseudonym Alexis Hill) *Passion's Slave,* Jove, 1979.
(Under pseudonym Alexis Hill) *The Untamed Heart,* Jove, 1980.
(Under name M. S. Craig) *The Chicagoans: Dust to Diamonds,* Jove, 1981.
(Under name M. S. Craig) *To Play the Fox,* Dodd, 1982.
Lyon's Pride, Jove, 1983.
Pirate's Landing, Jove, 1983.
(Under name M. S. Craig) *Gillian's Chain,* Dodd, 1983.
(Under name M. S. Craig) *The Third Blonde,* Dodd, 1985.
The Chicagoans: Fortune's Destiny, Ace Books, 1986.
Dark Paradise, Warner Books, 1986.
(Under name M. S. Craig) *Flash Point,* Dodd, 1987.

JUVENILE FICTION; UNDER NAME MARY FRANCIS SHURA

Simple Spigott, Knopf, 1960.
The Garret of Greta McGraw, Knopf, 1961.
Mary's Marvelous Mouse, Knopf, 1962.
The Nearsighted Knight, Knopf, 1964.
Run Away Home, Knopf, 1965.
A Shoefull of Shamrock, Atheneum, 1965.
A Tale of Middle Length, Atheneum, 1966.
Backwards for Luck, Knopf, 1967.
Audhumla and the Blue Valley, Lothrop, 1969, published as *The Valley of the Forest Giants,* 1971.
Pornado, Atheneum, 1970.
The Seven Stone, Holiday House, 1972.
Topcat of Tam, Holiday House, 1972.
The Riddle of Raven's Gulch, Dodd, 1975, published as *The Riddle of Raven's Hollow,* Scholastic Books Services, 1976.
A Season of Silence, Atheneum, 1976.
The Gray Ghosts of Taylor Ridge, Dodd, 1978.
Mister Wolf and Me, Dodd, 1979.
The Barkley Street Six-Pack, Dodd, 1979.
Chester (Junior Literary Guild selection), Dodd, 1980.
Happles and Cinnamunger, Dodd, 1981.
My Friend Natalie, Scholastic, Inc., 1982.
Eleanor (Junior Literary Guild selection), Dodd, 1983.

Jefferson (Junior Literary Guild selection), Dodd, 1984.
Jessica, Scholastic, Inc., 1984.
Marilee, Scholastic, Inc., 1985.
Tales from Dickens, Scholastic, Inc., 1985.
The Search for Grissi (Junior Literary Guild selection), Dodd, 1985.
The Josie Gambit (Junior Literary Guild selection), Dodd, 1986.
Don't Call Me Toad! (Junior Literary Guild selection), Dodd, 1987.
Gabrielle, Scholastic, Inc., 1987.
The Sunday Doll (Junior Literary Guild selection), Dodd, 1988.
Diana, Scholastic, Inc., 1988.
Darcy, Scholastic, Inc., 1989.

OTHER

(Under pseudonym Meredith Hill) *The Silent Witness* (juvenile), Scholastic, Inc., 1983.
(Under name M. F. Craig) *The Mystery at Peacock Place* (juvenile), Scholastic, Inc., 1986.
(Contributor under name M. S. Craig) Marilyn Wallace, editor, *Sisters in Crime* (anthology), Jove, 1989.
(Contributor under name Mary Shura Craig) Phillip L. Berman, editor, *The Courage to Grow Old,* Ballantine, 1989.

Author of column "Scrapbook from Shura 'Nuff Farm," 1959-64. Contributor of short stories and poetry to periodicals. Book reviewer, *Independent Journal* (San Rafael, Calif.), 1973-77.

SIDELIGHTS: Mary S. Craig told *CA:* "Having passed the twenty-fifth anniversary of the publication of my first book, I am astonished to find that my feeling about my work has undergone so little change. If pressed to tack a moral on this I would suggest that time alone does not transform a storyteller into a philosopher. . . .

"Admitting myself to be a writer obsessed with the desire to create some rational order for the chaos of life, I have certainly been provided (by this particular period of time) with an abundance of the raw material of chaos.

"Yet even as the drumbeat has changed, the march continues the same. Humans still yearn and love and will take great risks to achieve what they yearn for or protect what they cherish. They continue to inflict pain where they intend pleasure and stumble when they have all the feathers glued on for flight. They still chuckle at the pompous and support their companions whose masks slip to reveal weakness. And whatever the floods have swept away, they still rise, as Millay so poignantly put it, 'with twisted face and pocketful of seeds.'

"And storytellers are still invited close to the hearth for tales of love and pain and prevailing. They also carry on long irrelevant conversations with their own characters while they are punching down French bread and laugh and cry when they read their own galleys.

"If anyone asks what kind of a life that is, the answer is, simply, 'marvelous.'"

A Mary Craig Collection was established at the Acquisitions Library of the University of Oregon in 1968.

BIOGRAPHICAL/CRITICAL SOURCES:

PERIODICALS

America, November 4, 1967.
Chicago Tribune Book World, May 30, 1982, February 13, 1983, September 25, 1983.
Christian Science Monitor, May 12, 1976.

Los Angeles Times Book Review, January 2, 1983.
New York Times Book Review, September 25, 1966, September 7, 1975, January 16, 1983.
Saturday Review, December 16, 1967.
Times Literary Supplement, December 9, 1965.
Tribune Books (Chicago), February 22, 1987.

*   *   *

CRAIG, Mary Shura
    See CRAIG, Mary (Francis) S(hura)

*   *   *

CROSS, Aleene (Ann)   1922-

PERSONAL: Born January 19, 1922, in Ocilla, Ga.; daughter of John Gordon and Mae (Baker) Cross. *Education:* Georgia State College for Women (now Georgia College), B.S.H.E., 1943; University of Georgia, M.Ed., 1952; Columbia University, Ed.D., 1959. *Politics:* Democratic. *Religion:* Methodist.

ADDRESSES: Home—320 South Pope, Athens, Ga. 30605. *Office*—University of Georgia, Aderhold Hall, Athens, Ga. 30602.

CAREER: Teacher of home economics at high schools in Nashville, Ga., Fitzgerald, Ga., and College Park, Ga., 1943-54; University of Georgia, Athens, instructor in home economics, 1954-57, professor of home economics education and head of department, 1959—. Visiting instructor, Columbia University, 1958.

MEMBER: American Vocational Association (vice-president of home economics division, 1967-71; president of home economics division, 1972-73; past president, 1973-74), American Home Economics Association (member of accreditation committee, 1968-70), Phi Delta Kappa, Kappa Delta Pi, Omicron Nu, Pi Lambda Theta, Phi Upsilon Omicron.

AWARDS, HONORS: Teacher Education Award from Kappa Delta Phi, 1968. Future Homemakers of America Award, 1969.

WRITINGS:

Suggestions for Teaching Foods and Nutrition, Department of Homemaking Education, University of Georgia, 1958, revised edition, 1965.
(Project director) *A Post-High School Program in Child Care Services and Food Services,* Department of Home Economics Education, University of Georgia, 1966.
Enjoying Family Living, Lippincott, 1967, revised edition, 1973.
Introduction to Homemaking, Lippincott, 1970.
(Contributor) *The Individual and His Education,* American Vocational Association, 1972.
Home Economics Evaluation, C. E. Merrill, 1973.
Family Living, Lippincott, 1973.
(Editor) *Vocational Instruction,* American Vocational Association, 1979.†

D

DANIELS, Olga
See SINCLAIR, Olga

       *   *   *

DATHORNE, O(scar) R(onald)   1934-

PERSONAL: Born November 19, 1934, in Georgetown, British Guiana (now Guyana); son of Oscar Robertson and Rosalie Belona (Peazer) Dathorne; married Hildegard Ostermaier, 1959; children: Shade Cecily and Alexander Franz Keith. *Education:* University of Sheffield, B.A. (honors), 1958, M.A., 1960, Ph.D., 1966; University of London, Grad. Cert. in Ed., 1959, Diploma in Ed., 1967; University of Miami, M.B.A., M.P.A., 1984.

ADDRESSES: Home—8904 Friedberg bei Augsburg, Luberstrasse 2, Germany. *Office*—Department of English, University of Miami, Coral Gables, Fla. 33124.

CAREER: Ahmadu Bello University, Zaria, Nigeria, lecturer in English, 1959-63; University of Ibadan, Ibadan, Nigeria, lecturer in English, 1963-66; U.N.E.S.C.O., Paris, France, adviser to Government of Sierra Leone, 1967-68; University of Sierra Leone, Njala University College, Freetown, professor of English and chairman of department, 1968-70; professor of Afro-American studies at Howard University, Washington, D.C. and University of Wisconsin, Madison, 1970-71; Ohio State University, Columbus, professor of English and black studies, 1971-74, 1975-77; visiting professor of literature, Florida International University, 1974-75; University of Miami, Coral Gables, Fla., professor of English and director of American Studies, 1977—. Has given radio lectures and poetry readings for Nigerian Broadcasting Corp., B.B.C. (London), and several university-owned radio stations. Part-time teacher at Western Nigerian Training College, 1963-66, University of Sierra Leone, 1967-68; visiting professor at Yale University, 1970.

WRITINGS:

Dumplings in the Soup (novel), Cassell, 1963.
The Scholar-Man (novel), Cassell, 1964.
The Black Mind: A History of African Literature, University of Minnesota Press, 1974, abridged edition published as *African Literature in the Twentieth Century*, 1976.
Kelly Poems (verse), privately printed, 1977.

Dark Ancestor: The Literature of the Black Man in the Caribbean, Louisiana State University Press, 1981.
Dele's Child (novel), Three Continents, 1986.

EDITOR

(And author of introduction) *Caribbean Narrative: An Anthology of West Indian Writing*, Heinemann, 1966.
(And author of introduction) *Caribbean Verse: An Anthology*, Heinemann, 1967.
(With Willfried Feuser) *Africa in Prose*, Penguin, 1969.
(And author of introduction) *African Poetry for Schools and Colleges*, Macmillan, 1969.
Derek Walcott, *Selected Poems*, Heinemann, 1977.
Afro World: Adventures in Ideas, University of Wisconsin Press, 1984.
(With others) *Four Way Dictionary*, Cassell, in press.

CONTRIBUTOR

P. L. Brent, editor, *Young Commonwealth Poets '65*, Heinemann, 1965.
Andrew Salkey, editor, *Stories from the Caribbean*, Elek, 1965, published as *Island Voices*, Liveright, 1970.
Howard Sergeant, editor, *Commonwealth Poets of Today*, J. Murray, 1967.
Sergeant, editor, *New Voices of the Commonwealth*, Evans Brothers, 1968.
D. R. Dudley and D. M. Lang, editors, *Penguin Companion to Literature: Part IV*, Penguin, 1969.
Political Spider, Heinemann, 1969.
David Lowenthal and Lambros Comitas, editors, *West Indian Societies*, Doubleday, 1973.

OTHER

(Author of introduction) Donald St. John-Parsons, compiler, *Our Poets Speak*, University of London Press, 1966.
(Author of introduction) Mongo Beti, *King Lazarus*, Collier-Macmillan, 1971.

Editor, *Journal of Caribbean Studies.* Contributor of verse to *Black Orpheus, Transition, Outposts,* and *Presence Africaine;* contributor of stories to *Nigerian Radio Times*, Ibadan, 1967; contributor of critical articles to *Journal of Commonwealth Literature, Times Literary Supplement, New African, Phylon, London Magazine,* and others.

WORK IN PROGRESS: A-Z of African Literature; translating Aime-Cesaire's *Et les chiens se taissaient;* a novel, *Granman* (tentative title); and poetry, *Songs from a New World.*

BIOGRAPHICAL/CRITICAL SOURCES:

PERIODICALS

Choice, October, 1986.
New Yorker, February 28, 1970.
Times Literary Supplement, July 28, 1966, April 2, 1982.
World Literature Today, winter, 1965, autumn, 1965, spring, 1977, winter, 1987.

* * *

DAVENPORT, Spencer
[Collective pseudonym]

WRITINGS:

"RUSHTON BOYS" SERIES

The Rushton Boys at Rally Hall; or, Great Days in School and Out, Hearst's International Library, 1916.
. . . at Treasure Cove; or, The Missing Oaken Chest, Hearst's International Library, 1916.
. . . in the Saddle; or, The Ghost of the Plains, Hearst's International Library, 1916.

SIDELIGHTS: For more information see the entries for Harriet S. Adams, Edward L. Stratemeyer, and Andrew E. Svenson.

BIOGRAPHICAL/CRITICAL SOURCES:

BOOKS

Johnson, Deidre, editor and compiler, *Stratemeyer Pseudonyms and Series Books: An Annotated Checklist of Stratemeyer and Stratemeyer Syndicate Publications,* Greenwood Press, 1982.

* * *

DAVIDSON, Avram 1923-
(Ellery Queen, a house pseudonym)

PERSONAL: Born April 23, 1923, in Yonkers, N.Y.; son of Harry Jonas and Lillian (Adler) Davidson; married Grania Kaiman (a writer; divorced); children: Ethan Michael Anders. *Education:* Attended New York University, 1940-42, Yeshiva University, 1947-48, and Pierce College, 1950-51. *Politics:* None. *Religion:* Tenrikyo.

CAREER: Magazine of Fantasy and Science Fiction, executive editor, 1961-64; free-lance writer, 1964—. *Military service:* U.S. Navy, 1942-46; served with Hospital Corps in Okinawa and China; served with Israeli Army in the Arab-Israeli War, 1948-49.

MEMBER: Science Fiction Writers of America, Serendipitous Order of Beavers, Order of Ailing Cockroaches, Berkeley Circle.

AWARDS, HONORS: Ellery Queen Award, *Ellery Queen's Mystery Magazine,* 1958, for short story "The Necessity of His Condition"; Hugo Award, World Science Fiction Convention, 1958, for short story "Or All the Seas with Oysters," and 1963, for editing *Magazine of Fantasy and Science Fiction;* Edgar Allan Poe Award, Mystery Writers of America, 1962, for short story "The Affair at the Lahore Cantonment"; World Fantasy Award, World Fantasy Convention, 1975, for

collection *The Enquiries of Dr. Eszterhazy,* 1978, for short fiction "Naples," and 1986, for lifetime achievement.

WRITINGS:

SCIENCE FICTION NOVELS

(With Ward Moore) *Joyleg,* Pyramid, 1962.
Mutiny in Space, Pyramid, 1964.
Masters of the Maze, Pyramid, 1965.
Rogue Dragon (also see below), Ace, 1965.
Rork!, Berkley, 1965.
Clash of Star-Kings, Ace, 1966.
The Enemy of My Enemy, Berkley, 1966.
The Kar-chee Reign (also see below), Ace, 1966.
The Kar-chee Reign [and] *Rogue Dragon,* Ace, 1979.

FANTASY NOVELS

The Island under the Earth, Ace, 1969.
The Phoenix and the Mirror; or, The Enigmatic Speculum, Doubleday, 1969.
Peregrine: Primus, Walker, 1971.
Ursus of Ultima Thule, Avon, 1973.
Peregrine: Secundus, Berkley, 1981.
Vergil in Averno, Doubleday, 1987.
(With Grania Davis) *Marco Polo and the Sleeping Beauty,* Baen Books, 1988.

SHORT STORIES

Or All the Seas with Oysters, Berkley, 1962.
What Strange Stars and Skies, Ace, 1965.
Strange Seas and Shores, Doubleday, 1971.
The Enquiries of Doctor Eszterhazy, Warner Books, 1975.
The Redward Edward Papers, Doubleday, 1978.
The Best of Avram Davidson, edited by Michael Kurland, Doubleday, 1979.
The Collected Fantasies of Avram Davidson, edited by John Silbersack, Berkley, 1982.

UNDER PSEUDONYM ELLERY QUEEN; MYSTERY NOVELS

And on the Eighth Day, Random House, 1964.
The Fourth Side of the Triangle, Random House, 1965.

CONTRIBUTOR TO ANTHOLOGIES

The Playboy Book of Science Fiction, Playboy Press, 1960.
Judith Merril, editor, *The 5th Annual of the Year's Best S-F,* Simon & Schuster, 1960.
(With Morton Klass) Groff Conklin, editor, *13 Above the Night,* Dell, 1965.
Terry Carr, editor, *New Worlds of Fantasy 1,* Ace, 1967.
Carr and Donald A. Wollheim, editors, *World's Best Science Fiction, 1967,* Ace, 1967.
Damon Knight, editor, *Orbit 5,* Putnam, 1969.
Carr, editor, *New Worlds of Fantasy 2,* Ace, 1970.
Anne McCaffrey, editor, *Alchemy and Academe,* Doubleday, 1970.
Knight, editor, *Orbit 6,* Putnam, 1970.
Playboy's Short Shorts, Playboy Press, 1970.
Knight, editor, *Orbit 8,* Putnam, 1971.
Edward L. Ferman, editor, *The Best from Fantasy and Science Fiction 19,* Doubleday, 1971.
Samuel R. Delany and Marilyn Hacker, editors, *Quark 4,* Paperback Library, 1971.
Sandra Ley, editor, *Beyond Time,* Pocket Books, 1976.
Gerald Page, editor, *The Year's Best Horror Stories 4,* DAW Books, 1976.
Lin Carter, editor, *Flashing Swords! 3,* Doubleday, 1976.

Charles L. Grant, editor, *Shadows 1*, Doubleday, 1978.
(With Grania Davis) Ursula K. Le Guin and Virginia Kidd, editors, *Interfaces*, Ace, 1980.
Le Guin and Kidd, editors, *Edges*, Pocket Books, 1980.
Roy Torgeson, editor, *Other Worlds 2*, Zebra, 1980.

OTHER

Crimes and Chaos (articles), Regency, 1962.
(Editor) *The Best from Fantasy and Science Fiction*, Doubleday, twelfth series, 1963, thirteenth series, 1964, fourteenth series, 1964.
(Editor) *Magic for Sale*, Ace, 1983.

Also author of stories for television, including "The Ikon of Elijah" and "Thou Still Unravished Bride" for "Alfred Hitchcock Presents." Contributor of short stories to magazines, including *Amazing, Analog, Ellery Queen's Mystery Magazine, Magazine of Fantasy and Science Fiction, Galaxy, Harlequin,* and *Twilight Zone.*

SIDELIGHTS: Avram Davidson "should be counted among the 20th century's ironic fantasists," says a reviewer for the *Washington Post Book World,* "the latest in a line that extends from Saki and Kipling through Chesterton and John Collier." Characterized by poetic diction and ironic plots, Davidson's fiction, according to Kevin Mulcahy in the *Dictionary of Literary Biography,* reveals "an observant eye, a keen ear, and the ability to create subtle irony, broad comedy, the bizarre, and the terrifying.... Instead of returning again and again to one theme or gimmick, he experiments with plot, characterization, and style and frequently succeeds in reinvigorating a worn-out device."

Davidson's stories, says Mulcahy, are marked by "humor (at times sinister), a vivid sense of place (he is a master of accumulating details to create moods), or a sharp parody of science-fiction cliches." Examples of these types include "The Golem," a story with a variation on the Frankenstein motif—a monster which threatens an elderly Jewish couple is subdued by the husband slapping it into submission—and "The House the Blakeneys Built," a version of the lost space colony theme. In these stories, Mulcahy indicates, Davidson patterns "the intersection of the strange and the familiar, [in order to] produce comic or terrifying results," and the contributor celebrates the way in which Davidson "takes a standard science-fiction device . . . and gives it a unique and refreshing expression." Other stories, Mulcahy continues, show the development of a social conscience "before the heyday of the civil rights movement." "Or the Grasses Grow," for instance, depicts the consequence of the Americans breaking their last treaty with the Indians.

Besides his short fiction, Davidson has also received acclaim for his fantasy novels. Two of the most popular of these are *The Phoenix and the Mirror; or, The Enigmatic Speculum* and *Vergil in Averno.* Both are based on the tradition of legends which surround Vergil, the Roman poet and author of *The Aeneid, The Georgics,* and *The Eclogues.* The medieval world believed him to be a magician as well as a poet, who was supposed to have lived in a spinning castle and to have performed many strange and wonderful feats of magic; the Italian poet Petrarch and humanist writer Boccaccio both mention these stories. "These legends," states Gregory Feeley of the *Washington Post Book World,* "project the medieval universe back upon the ancient world, strangely conceiving 1st-century Rome by the lights of the Holy Roman Empire. It is this never-existent world that Avram Davidson has taken as the setting for his series of novels, a world whose anachronisms, like the knights and tourneys of Chaucer's Trojan War, create a peculiar and complex beauty of their own."

The Phoenix and the Mirror, characterized by Algis Budrys in the *Magazine of Fantasy and Science Fiction* as "an almost legendary" novel, traces the adventures of Vergil as he struggles to create a virgin mirror, one whose surface has never yet seen light, in order to scry the whereabouts of the bride-to-be of the Duke of Naples. In the process, he travels across the Mediterranean world to collect the extremely pure materials he needs for the work. The journey, in Feeley's words, furnishes Davidson with the chance to "display the full range of his erudition and stylistic virtuosity," adding to the novel's impact. "His world is peopled with real sailors and soldiers as well as real alchemists and magi," say Marshall B. Tymn, Kenneth J. Zahorski and Richard H. Boyer in *Fantasy Literature: A Core Collection and Reference Guide;* "It is a world that tantalizes and satisfies, capitalizing on familiarity with medieval accounts and reflecting a firm knowledge of the first century B.C."

Vergil in Averno is "another of Davidson's wry and profound explorations of human perversity," in the opinion of Adrian de Wit of *Fantasy Review;* it is one which takes place years before the events of *The Phoenix and the Mirror.* Much of the action occurs in The Very Rich City of Averno, a great center of industry inhabited by merchants and manufacturers who have gained their wealth by exploiting the volcanic heat and gases beneath their town to make large quantities of cheap goods. Vergil, a young man, is employed by the city to discover why its power sources move erratically from one place to another, and, if possible, to locate the ultimate origin of the gases. His answer to the city's predicament is to conserve their natural resources by a system of pipes which would deliver heat to any desired location, but the local dignitaries prefer a simpler solution; they tap directly into the center chamber, which they call the father-fire, and in the process destroy the city. "Note, please, that it's characteristic of Davidson to have given us a simple, rueful point to his homily," declares Budrys. "All of Davidson's work with the manuscript is ultimately intended to permit him to dance up on us with a story—a dramatic observation—on something we have previously found ways to soothe."

Many critics feel that Davidson's command of language adds greatly to the impact of this fantasy. "What distinguishes *Vergil in Averno,*" remarks Feeley, "is Davidson's voice. He adopts a faintly archaic diction and large vocabulary of half-familiar terms to evoke the romance of an ancient world, and succeeds without sounding affected or obscure." *Analog Science Fiction/Science Fact* reviewer Tom Easton adds, "There is plot, character, climax, anticlimax [in the book], but Davidson is far more remarkable as a stylist. [He] loves the language, and he plays with it. He also plays with his intimate knowledge of Classical times, and with various rational anachronisms, while he spins a narrative thread that twists and turns. . . ." Budrys declares, "The joy, the almost unique joy of reading Avram Davidson's work, is that it evidences his infectuous delight in making the language dance. He has other fine qualities as a writer, [but] in this one he is without peer among us. . . . The deployment of words is not, to Davidson, a utilitarian skill, or a love of words as isolated things, or a process of linear construction as taught in academies of journalism. The words in a Davidson sentence are chosen flowers in a garland, so twined that one can scarcely tell where the stem of one leaves off."

Mulcahy suggests that Davidson's fascination with ancient times, which he explores in *The Phoenix and the Mirror* and *Vergil in Averno*, "set in a past created partly out of history and partly out of history reimagined," has steered the author away from science fiction. "Almost by definition, most science fiction is future oriented—concerned with technology or its ethical, political, military, social, or economic impact," Mulcahy states. Much of Davidson's fiction, he continues, takes place in "a past in which technology plays little role," perhaps reflecting the author's distrust of the future. "It is perhaps revealing," Mulcahy concludes, "that *The Enquiries of Dr. Eszterhazy*, which is largely a cheerful book set in a pleasant past world, ends on a somber note as Eszterhazy broods over an ominous future."

BIOGRAPHICAL/CRITICAL SOURCES:

BOOKS

Dictionary of Literary Biography, Volume 8: *Twentieth Century American Science Fiction Writers*, Gale, 1981.
Searles, Baird, Beth Meacham, and Michael Franklin, *A Reader's Guide to Fantasy*, Avon, 1982.
Searles, Baird, Beth Meacham, Michael Franklin, and Martin Last, *A Reader's Guide to Science Fiction*, Avon, 1979.
Tymn, Marshall B., Kenneth J. Zahorski, and Richard Boyer, *Fantasy Literature: A Core Collection and Reference Guide*, R. R. Bowker, 1979.

PERIODICALS

Analog Science Fiction/Science Fact, August, 1987.
Fantasy Review, April, 1987.
Magazine of Fantasy and Science Fiction, December, 1971, July, 1972, September, 1976, March, 1979, April, 1987.
New York Times Book Review, July 25, 1971.
Science Fiction Chronicle, May, 1987.
Times Literary Supplement, October 14, 1965, March 10, 1966, August 15, 1968.
Washington Post Book World, August 30, 1981, Janaury 25, 1987.

—*Sketch by Kenneth R. Shepherd*

* * *

DAVIES, Ruth A(nn) 1915-

PERSONAL: Born June 28, 1915, in Pittsburgh, Pa.; daughter of William Tarleton (a locomotive engineer) and Ruth Ann (Crawford) Davies. *Education:* Pennsylvania College for Women, B.A., 1939; University of Pittsburgh, M.Litt., 1940; Carnegie Institute of Technology (now Carnegie-Mellon University), B.S.L.S., 1941.

ADDRESSES: Home—156 McIntyre Rd., Pittsburgh, Pa. 15237.

CAREER: Carnegie Institute of Technology (now Carnegie-Mellon University), Pittsburgh, Pa., instructor in library science, 1947-62; University of Pittsburgh, Pittsburgh, department of education, member of research staff, 1956-58, Graduate School of Library Science, instructor, 1963-78. North Hills School District, Pittsburgh, coordinator of library services, 1950-78. Chairman of advisory committee, Pennsylvania Department of Public Instruction. Member of Pittsburgh North Side Redevelopment Council, 1956-57.

MEMBER: American Association of School Librarians (member of federal legislative committee, 1960-71; member of standards revision committee, 1969-70), American Library Association (chairman of standards implementation program for Pennsylvania), National Education Association, Association for Supervision and Curriculum Development, Pennsylvania Library Association, Pennsylvania School Library Association, Pennsylvania State Education Association.

AWARDS, HONORS: Received citation from Pennsylvania Department of Public Instruction, 1964; Pennsylvania Library Association, award of merit, 1968, distinguished service award, 1975; Outstanding Alumnus Award, University of Pittsburgh School of Library Science, 1970; Citation of Merit, Pennsylvania School Librarians Association, 1970; Outstanding Contributors Award, Pennsylvania School Library Association, 1977; citation of merit from Pennsylvania House of Representatives and Pennsylvania Senate, both 1977.

WRITINGS:

Revitalizing American History through Primary Sources: Bibliography, Pennsylvania Department of Public Instruction, 1968.
The School Library: A Force for Educational Excellence, Bowker, 1969, 2nd edition published as *The School Library Media Center: A Force for Educational Excellence*, 1973, 3rd edition published as *The School Library Media Program: Instructional Force for Excellence*, 1979.
(With Corinne P. Clendening) *Creating Programs for the Gifted: A Guide for Teachers, Librarians, and Students*, Bowker, 1980.
(Editor with Clendening) *Challenging the Gifted: Curriculum Enrichment and Acceleration Models*, Bowker, 1983.

Contributor to *World Book Encyclopedia, Encyclopedia of Library and Information Science*, and numerous library journals. Member of editorial staff, *School Instructional Materials Center*, Pennsylvania Department of Public Instruction, 1963.

* * *

DAVIS, David Brion 1927-

PERSONAL: Born February 16, 1927, in Denver, Colo.; son of Clyde Brion (a writer) and Martha (a writer and painter; maiden name, Wirt) Davis; married Frances Warner, October 22, 1948 (divorced, 1971); married Toni Hahn (an attorney), September 9, 1971; children: (first marriage) Jeremiah, Martha, Sarah; (second marriage) Adam, Noah. *Education:* Dartmouth College, A.B., 1950; Harvard University, A.M., 1953, Ph.D., 1956. *Politics:* Democrat.

ADDRESSES: Home—733 Lambert Rd., Orange, Conn. 06477. *Office*—Hall of Graduate Studies, Yale University, New Haven, Conn. 06520.

CAREER: Dartmouth College, Hanover, N.H., instructor in history and Fund for the Advancement of Education intern, 1953-54; Cornell University, Ithaca, N.Y., assistant professor, 1955-58, associate professor, 1958-63, Ernest I. White Professor of History, 1963-69; Yale University, New Haven, Conn., professor of history, 1969-72, Farnham Professor of History, 1972-78, Sterling Professor of History, 1978—. Fulbright lecturer in India, 1967, and at universities in Guyana and the West Indies, 1974; Harold Vyvyan Harmsworth Professor of American History, Oxford University, 1969-70; lecturer at fourth International Symposium, Smithsonian Institution, 1970; Benjamin Rush Lecturer, American Psychiatric Association, 1976; lecturer at George Washington University, 1977, and at University of Wyoming and Center for Study of Southern Culture and Religion, Tallahassee, Fla., 1979; Pierce Lecturer, Oberlin College, 1979; French-American Foundation Chair in American Civilization, Ecole des Hautes Etudes en Sciences Sociales, Paris, 1980-81; Patten Foundation Lecturer, Indiana University, 1981; Hanes Foundation Lecturer, University of North Carolina, 1982; C. Mildred Thompson Lecturer, Vassar College, 1983; Fortenbaugh Memorial Lecturer, Gettysburg College, 1983; distinguished scholar in residence, Kentucky State University, 1984, and Westminster College of Salt Lake City, 1985; Phi Beta Kappa visiting lecturer, 1984-85; Gilbert Osofsky Memorial Lecturer, University of Illinois at Chicago Circle, 1986; Arnold Shankman Memorial Lecturer, Winthrop College, 1987; public lecturer at Universities of Paris, Leiden, Amsterdam, Utrecht, Tel Aviv, and Beer Shiva, and at Hebrew University, Jerusalem, and the University of the West Indies, Kingston; has presented papers to professional conferences and learned societies, including an international conference on slavery, Bellagio, Italy, 1984, and the Conference on Northwest Ordinances, Indiana University, 1987. Commissioner, Orange, Conn., Public Library Commission, 1974-75; associate director, National Humanities Institute, Yale University, 1975. *Military service:* U.S. Army, 1945-46.

MEMBER: American Historical Association (member of Pulitzer Prize and Beveridge Prize committees), Organization of American Historians (president-elect, 1987-88; president, 1988-89), Society of American Historians, American Antiquarian Society, Institute of Early American History and Culture (member of council), American Academy of Arts and Sciences, Phi Beta Kappa.

AWARDS, HONORS: Guggenheim fellow, 1958-59; Anisfield-Wolf Award, 1967; Pulitzer Prize, 1967, for *The Problem of Slavery in Western Culture;* National Mass Media Award from National Conference of Christians and Jews, 1967; Center for Advanced Study in the Behavioral Sciences fellow, 1972-73; Beveridge Prize from American Historical Association, 1975; National Book Award for history, 1976, for *The Problem of Slavery in the Age of Revolution, 1770-1823;* Bancroft Prize, 1976; Huntington Library fellow, 1976; Litt.D., Dartmouth College, 1977; National Endowment for the Humanities, research grants, 1980 and 1981, and fellowship for independent study and research, 1983-84; Fulbright traveling fellow, 1980-81; L.H.D., University of New Haven, 1986.

WRITINGS:

Homicide in American Fiction, 1798-1860: A Study in Social Values, Cornell University Press, 1957.
The Problem of Slavery in Western Culture, Cornell University Press, 1967.
(Editor) *Ante-bellum Reform,* Harper, 1967.
The Slave Power Conspiracy and the Paranoid Style, Louisiana State University Press, 1969.
Was Thomas Jefferson an Authentic Enemy of Slavery?, Clarendon Press, 1970.
(Editor) *The Fear of Conspiracy: Images of Un-American Subversion from the Revolution to the Present,* Cornell University Press, 1971.
The Problem of Slavery in the Age of Revolution, 1770-1823, Cornell University Press, 1975.
(With others) *The Great Republic: A History of the American People,* Little, Brown, 1977, revised edition, 1985.
(Editor) *Antebellum American Culture: An Interpretive Anthology,* Heath, 1979.
The Emancipation Moment (pamphlet), [Gettysburg], 1984.
Slavery and Human Progress, Oxford University Press, 1984.

From Homicide to Slavery: Studies in American Culture, Oxford University Press, 1986.

CONTRIBUTOR

Alfred Kazin and Charles Shapiro, editors, *The Stature of Theodore Dreiser,* Indiana University Press, 1955.
Shapiro, editor, *Twelve Original Essays on Great American Novels,* Wayne State University Press, 1958.
Martin Duberman, editor, *The Antislavery Vanguard,* Princeton University Press, 1965.
C. Vann Woodward, editor, *The Comparability of American History,* Basic Books, 1967.
Samuel Klausner, editor, *Why Man Takes Chances,* Anchor Books, 1968.
Richard Blum, editor, *Surveillance and Espionage in a Free Society,* Praeger, 1972.
Sidney Mintz, editor, *Slavery, Colonialism, and Racism,* Norton, 1974.
Harry Owens, editor, *Perspectives and Irony in American Slavery,* University of Mississippi Press, 1976.
David Reiss, editor, *The American Family,* Plenum, 1979.
Max Skidmore, editor, *Viewpoints, U.S.A.,* Heinemann (New Delhi), 1979.
Christine Bolt and Seymour Drescher, editors, *Religion, Anti-Slavery, and Reform,* Dawson, 1980.
Erich Angermann and Marie-Luise Frings, editors, *Oceans Apart?: Comparing Germany and the United States,* Klett Cotta (Stuttgart), 1981.

OTHER

Contributor to professional journals and other periodicals, including *New York Times Book Review, Times Literary Supplement, New York Review of Books, New Republic, American Historical Review, Journal of American History, New England Quarterly, Yale Review,* and *Reviews in American History.*

WORK IN PROGRESS: The Problem of Slavery in the Age of Emancipation, 1815-1890, for Oxford University Press.

SIDELIGHTS: "David Brion Davis ranks high among the elite historians of New World slavery," remarks M. I. Finley in the *New York Times Book Review.* Davis's series, "The Problem of Slavery," has won numerous awards, including a Pulitzer Prize and a National Book Award. His books on slavery have been praised for their scholarship, lucidity, and especially for their new insights into a much-analyzed institution.

In a *New York Times Book Review* article, J. H. Plumb calls the Pulitzer Prize-winning *The Problem of Slavery in Western Culture* "one of the most scholarly and penetrating studies of slavery" and says that here Davis displays "his mastery not only of a vast source of material, but also of the highly complex, frequently contradictory factors that influenced opinion on slavery." In this book, according to George M. Fredrickson in the *New York Review of Books,* Davis is concerned "mainly with the changes that had to occur in Western views of the nature of man and his relationship to society and authority before antislavery ideas could emerge." For example, he discusses "the role of original sin as a justification for slavery and how the modification and dilution of this traditional Christian doctrine in the eighteenth century had raised troublesome questions about black servitude."

In *The Problem of Slavery in the Age of Revolution, 1770-1823,* Davis continues this analysis with, Fredrickson writes, a study of "how ideas antithetical to slavery could win acceptance and become the basis of practical policies that served the broader needs of dominant groups." To do this, Davis compares the American antislavery movement with that in Great Britain and other countries at the same time. Fredrickson feels that it is clear from Davis's account "that the British antislavery movement had much greater success in this period than the American, even though both countries legislated against the international slave trade in the same year (1807)." To account for this dichotomy, "Davis undertakes a detailed analysis of the relationship of antislavery to dominant ideologies in both the United States and Great Britain." The result, according to Plumb is "a rich and powerful book [that] will, I am sure, stand the test of time—scholarly, brilliant in analysis, beautifully written."

Slavery and Human Progress approaches the issues of slavery from a perspective different from that of the author's previous work. "The most striking characteristic of this richly learned book is Davis's sensitivity to ambiguities and ambivalences," writes William H. McNeill in the *Washington Post Book World*. The work explores one particular issue, the similarity in rhetoric and reasoning of both the pro- and anti-slavery forces. "The scope of the study is awe-inspiring," comments *Los Angeles Times Book Review* contributor Larry May, covering "slavery in the Western world from biblical times to the present." Finley finds this scope somewhat limiting: "From this reading [Davis] has distilled a lively but superficial account of the rhetoric. . . . The account is superficial because genuine explanation is persistently avoided and often even the importance or typicality of the people he cites is not discussed." J. Morgan Kousser, writing in the *Times Literary Supplement*, echoes this assessment, commenting that the book lacks "a straight-forward discussion of the ideas of progress and slavery." Nevertheless, the critic finds that "as perceptive as he is learned and diligent, [Davis] offers illuminating comments on a whole range of topics."

BIOGRAPHICAL/CRITICAL SOURCES:

PERIODICALS

Los Angeles Times Book Review, November 25, 1984.
Nation, April 26, 1975.
New York Review of Books, October 16, 1975.
New York Times Book Review, February 9, 1975, February 3, 1985, October 5, 1986.
Times (London), January 24, 1985.
Times Literary Supplement, February 1, 1985.
Washington Post Book World, October 21, 1984.

*   *   *

DAVIS, Ossie 1917-

PERSONAL: Born December 18, 1917, in Cogdell, Ga.; son of Kince Charles (a railway construction worker) and Laura (Cooper) Davis; married Ruby Ann Wallace (an actress; professional name Ruby Dee), December 9, 1948; children: Nora, Guy, La Verne. *Education:* Attended Howard University, 1935-39, and Columbia University, 1948.

ADDRESSES: Agent—Artists Agency, 10000 Santa Monica Blvd., Suite 305, Los Angeles, Calif. 90067.

CAREER: Actor, playwright, screenwriter, and director and producer of stage productions and motion pictures. Worked as janitor, shipping clerk, and stock clerk in New York, N.Y, 1938-41. Actor in numerous stage productions, including "Joy Exceeding Glory," 1941, "Jeb," 1946, "No Time for Sergeants," 1957, and "A Raisin in the Sun," 1959. Actor in

motion pictures and teleplays, including "The Joe Louis Story," 1953, "The Emperor Jones," 1955, "The Cardinal," 1963, "Man Called Adam," 1966, "Teacher, Teacher," 1969, and "Let's Do It Again," 1976. Director of motion pictures, including "Black Girl," 1972, and "Gordon's War," 1973. Cohost of radio program "Ossie Davis and Ruby Dee Story Hour," 1974-78, and of television series "With Ossie and Ruby," Public Broadcasting System (PBS-TV), 1981. Co-producer of stage production "Ballad for Bimshire," 1963. Founder, Institute of Cinema Artists, 1973. Performer on recordings for Caedmon and Folkways Records. Civil rights activist. *Military service:* U.S Army, 1942-45; served as surgical technician in Liberia, West Africa, and with Special Services Department.

AWARDS, HONORS: Emmy Award nomination for outstanding single performance by an actor in a leading role, Academy of Television Arts and Sciences, 1969, for "Teacher, Teacher"; with wife Ruby Dee, Frederick Douglass Award from New York Urban League, 1970.

WRITINGS:

PLAYS

(And director) "Goldbrickers of 1944," first produced in Liberia, West Africa, 1944.
"Alice in Wonder," one-act; first produced in New York at Elks Community Theatre, September 15, 1952; revised and expanded version produced as "The Big Deal" in New York at New Playwrights Theatre, March 7, 1953.
Purlie Victorious (first produced in New York at Cort Theatre, September 28, 1961; also see below), French, 1961.
Curtain Call, Mr. Aldridge, Sir (first produced in Santa Barbara at the University of California, summer, 1968), published in *The Black Teacher and the Dramatic Arts: A Dialogue, Bibliography, and Anthology*, edited by William R. Reardon and Thomas D. Pawley, Negro Universities Press, 1970.
(With Philip Rose, Peter Udell, and Gary Geld) *Purlie* (adaptation of *Purlie Victorious;* first produced on Broadway at Broadway Theatre, March 15, 1970), French, 1971.
Escape to Freedom: A Play about Young Frederick Douglass (first produced in New York at the Town Hall, March 8, 1976), Viking, 1978.
Langston: A Play, Delacorte, 1982.

Also author of "Last Dance for Sybil."

SCREENPLAYS AND TELEPLAYS

"Gone Are the Days" (adaptation of Davis's *Purlie Victorious;* also released as "Purlie Victorious" and "The Man from C.O.T.T.O.N."), Trans Lux, 1963.
(With Arnold Perl, and director) "Cotton Comes to Harlem," United Artists, 1970.
(And director) "Kongi's Harvest" (adapted from work by Wole Soyinka), Calpenny Films Nigeria Ltd., 1970.
"Today Is Ours," Columbia Broadcasting System (CBS-TV), 1974.

Also author of teleplay "Just Say the Word," 1969, and author and director of screenplay "Countdown at Krisni," 1976. Also author of scripts for television series, including "Bonanza" and "N.Y.P.D."

OTHER

(Contributor) Herbert Hill, editor, *Anger, and Beyond: The Negro Writer in the United States*, Harper, 1966.

(Contributor) Hill, editor, *Soon, One Morning: New Writing by American Negroes, 1940-1962*, Knopf, 1968.
(Contributor) Ruby Dee, editor, *Glowchild, and Other Poems*, Third Press, 1972.
(With others) "The Black Cinema: Foremost Representatives of the Black Film World Air Their Views" (sound recording), Center for Cassette Studies 30983, 1975.
(Author with Hy Gilbert of book, and director) "Bingo" (baseball musical based on novel *The Bingo Long Traveling All-Stars and Motor Kings* by William Brashler), first produced in New York at AMAS Repertory Theater, November, 1985.

Contributor to journals and periodicals, including *Negro History Bulletin*, *Negro Digest*, and *Freedomways*.

SIDELIGHTS: "Ossie Davis is best known as an actor, but his accomplishments extend well beyond the stage," writes Michael E. Green in the *Dictionary of Literary Biography*. "In the theater, in motion pictures, and in television he has won praise both for his individual performances and those he has given with his wife, Ruby Dee. He has, however, also been a writer, director, producer, social activist, and community leader."

He began his career after enrolling at Howard University, where Alain Locke, a drama critic and professor of philosophy, spurred Davis's budding interest in the theatre. On Locke's counseling, Davis became involved in several facets of stage life, including maintenance and set construction, while biding time as an actor. He first appeared on the stage as a member of Harlem's Ross McClendon Players in a 1941 production of "Joy Exceeding Glory." Few offers followed, however, and Davis was reduced to sleeping in parks and scrounging for food.

In 1942 Davis was inducted into the army, where he served as a medical technician in Liberia, West Africa. After his transfer to Special Services, he began writing and producing stage works to entertain military personnel. Upon discharge, though, Davis returned to his native Georgia. There he was reached by McClendon director Richard Campbell, who encouraged Davis to return to New York City and audition for Robert Ardrey's "Jeb." Davis accepted Campbell's encouragement and eventually secured the title role in Ardrey's work. The play, which concerns a physically debilitated veteran's attempt to succeed as an adding machine operator in racist Louisiana, was poorly received, but Davis was exempted for his compelling performance.

Davis married fellow "Jeb" performer Ruby Dee in 1948 after they completed a stint with the touring company of "Anna Lucasta." The pace of his acting career then accelerated as Davis performed admirably in works such as "Stevedore," in which he played a servant who assumes a misplaced worldliness following a visit to Paris, and "The Green Pastures," in which he played one of several angels in a black-populated Heaven.

While acting, Davis also continued to devote attention to his writing. "As a playwright Davis was committed to creating works that would truthfully portray the black man's experience," says Jayne F. Mulvaney in a *Dictionary of Literary Biography* essay. In 1953, his play "Alice in Wonder," which re-created McCarthy-era action, was dimly received in Harlem; however, his 1961 opus *Purlie Victorious* generated a more favorable response. Mulvaney describes the play as a comedy about the schemes of an eloquent itinerant preacher

who returns to his Georgia home with hopes of buying the old barn that once served as a black church, and establishing an integrated one. To realize his plan, he must secure the inheritance of his deceased aunt, a former slave, whose daughter has also died. Because Captain Cotchipee, the play's antagonist and holder of the inheritance, is unaware of the death of Purlie's cousin, Purlie plans to have a pretty young black girl impersonate his cousin so that he can claim the inheritance to finance the church of his dreams. "The action of the play involves the hilarious efforts of Purlie, his family, and the captain's liberal son, Charlie, to outwit the captain," says Mulvaney; and critics were especially pleased with Davis's humorous portrayal of the black preacher's efforts to swipe the five-hundred-dollar inheritance from the white plantation owner.

Greene calls *Purlie Victorious* a "Southern fable of right against wrong, with Purlie's faith in the cause of equality triumphing over the bigotry of Ol' Cap'n Cotchipee, the local redneck aristocrat." Considering the comedy's brilliance to derive "chiefly from how cliches and stereotypes are blown out of proportion," Mulvaney suggests that "*Purlie Victorious* is satire which proceeds toward reconciliation rather than bitterness. Its invective is not venomous." "Unfortunately, despite the reviews, the endorsement of the National Association for the Advancement of Colored People, and the play's seven-and-a-half month run, neither playwright nor producer made money," says Mulvaney. "The financial support of the black community was not enough; the white audiences did not come." Greene suggests that the play would have been considerably more successful had it been written either ten years before or after it was; "Davis himself recognized that his handling of stereotypes, black and white, would have been offensive had a white writer created them." Also, Greene writes that Davis "argues that one of his purposes in the play was to present justice as an ideal, as something that is not always the same as traditional law-and-order, which allows the Ol' Cap'ns of American society to win too often."

Purlie Victorious was adapted by Davis as the motion picture "Gone Are the Days." A. H. Weiler, writing in the *New York Times*, complained that the film rarely availed itself of cinematic techniques, but added that the work "is still speaking out against injustice in low, broad, comic fashion." Weiler praised the performances of Davis, who played the preacher Purlie Victorious, and Ruby Dee, Purlie's lover.

In 1970 Davis collaborated with the songwriting team of Peter Udell and Gary Geld on "Purlie," a musical adaptation of the play. The *New York Times*'s Clive Barnes called the new version "so strong, . . . so magnificent" that audiences would respond by shouting "Hallelujah!" in praise. He deemed it "by far the most successful and richest of all black musicals" and attributed its prominence to "the depth of the characterization and the salty wit of the dialogue." For Davis, "Purlie" was not just another success—it was an experience in self-discovery. "Purlie told me," he wrote, "I would never find my manhood by asking the white man to define it for me. That I would never become a man until I stopped measuring my black self by white standards."

The careers of Dee and Davis have been intertwined throughout the 1970s and 1980s. They have performed together in stage productions, films, and recordings and shared duties as hosts/performers on the brief PBS-TV series "With Ossie and Ruby." Dee and Davis have also been active in the civil rights movement, participating in marches and hearings and sponsoring showings before hospital, church, and prison groups. *Ebony* called their marriage "a living argument against the popular notion that the theater is bound to wreck the homes of those couples who choose it as a profession."

BIOGRAPHICAL/CRITICAL SOURCES:

BOOKS

Abramson, Doris E., *Negro Playwrights in the American Theatre, 1925-1959*, Columbia University Press, 1969.
Dictionary of Literary Biography, Gale, Volume 7: *Twentieth-Century American Dramatists*, 1981, Volume 38: *Afro-American Writers after 1955: Dramatists and Prose Writers*, 1985.
Funke, Lewis, *The Curtain Rises—The Story of Ossie Davis*, Grosset & Dunlap, 1971.
Patterson, Lindsay, editor, *Anthology of the American Negro in the Theatre*, Association for the Study of Life and History/Publishers Company, 1967.

PERIODICALS

Detroit Free Press, November 11, 1983.
Ebony, February, 1961, December, 1979.
Freedomways, spring, 1962, summer, 1965, summer, 1968.
Nation, April 6, 1970.
National Observer, March 22, 1970.
Negro Digest, February, 1966, April, 1966.
Negro History Bulletin, April, 1967.
Newsweek, March 30, 1970.
New York, April, 1970.
New Yorker, October 7, 1961.
New York Times, September 24, 1963, May 5, 1968, October 12, 1969, March 10, 1970, November 11, 1985.
Variety, March 5, 1969, January 28, 1970, March 28, 1970.†

*   *   *

DAVIS, Richard

PERSONAL: Born in London, England; married Patricia Green, 1984; children: David William. *Education:* Educated in England.

ADDRESSES: Home—40 Eagle House Gardens, Blandford, Dorset DT11 7BS, England. *Agent*—MBA Literary Agents, Ltd., 45 Fitzroy St., London W1P 5HR, England.

CAREER: Writer, film producer, and editor. Story editor, British Broadcasting Corp.-Television, London, 1966-68.

WRITINGS:

Spies and Spying, Macmillan, 1986.
Monsters, Macmillan, 1987.

"SPACE" SERIES

Space One, Abelard, 1973.
. . . Two, Abelard, 1974.
. . . Three, Abelard, 1974.
. . . Four, Abelard, 1975.
. . . Five, Abelard, 1976.
. . . Six, Hutchinson, 1978.
. . . Seven, Hutchinson, 1980.
. . . Eight, Hutchinson, 1982.
. . . Nine, Hutchinson, 1984.

"SPECTRE" SERIES

Spectre One, Abelard, 1973.
. . . Two, Abelard, 1974.

. . . Three, Abelard, 1974.
. . . Four, Abelard, 1977.

"SCIENCE FICTION" SERIES

Science Fiction One, Armada, 1975.
. . . Two, Armada, 1975.
. . . Three, Armada, 1976.
. . . Four, Armada, 1976.

EDITOR

(And contributor) *Tandem Horror Two*, Tandem Press, 1968.
(And contributor) *Tandem Horror Three*, Tandem Press, 1969.
Year's Best Horror Stories, Sphere Books, 1971.
Year's Best Horror Stories Two, Sphere Books, 1972, DAW Books, 1974.
Year's Best Horror Stories Three, Sphere Books, 1973, DAW Books, 1975.
Jon Pertwee Book of Monsters, Methuen, 1978.
I've Seen a Ghost: True Stories from Show Business, Hutchinson, 1979.
(With Vincent Price) *Price of Fear*, Everest Books, 1979.
Animal Ghosts, Hutchinson, 1980.
Encyclopedia of Horror, Octopus Books, 1981.
Spies One, Hutchinson, 1982.

Also editor of *Orbit Book of Horror Stories One*, 1976.

CONTRIBUTOR

Harbert van Thal, editor, *Fourth Pan Book of Horror Stories*, Pan Books, 1963.
Frederick Pickersgill, editor, *Graves Give up Their Dead*, Corgi Books, 1964.
Pickersgill, editor, *No Such Thing as a Vampire*, Corgi Books, 1965.
Pickersgill, editor, *Horror Seven*, Corgi Books, 1965.
van Thal, editor, *Sixth Pan Book of Horror Stories*, Pan Books, 1965.
Rosemary Timperley, editor, *Fifth Ghost Book*, Barrie & Jenkins, 1969.
Timperley, editor, *Sixth Ghost Book*, Barrie & Jenkins, 1970.
David Sutton, editor, *New Writing in Horror and Fantasy*, Sphere Books, 1971.
You Always Remember the First Time, Alison & Busby, 1975.
A Chill to the Sunlight, Kimber, 1979.

OTHER

Author and producer of film, "Viola," 1968; story editor of BBC-TV dramas "Thirteen against Fate" and "Late Night Horror"; contributor to BBC-Radio series "Price of Fear." Critic and columnist, *Films and Filming*, 1964-71.

*   *   *

DAWES, Dorothy
See COOPER, Parley J(oseph)

*   *   *

DAWKINS, Richard   1941-

PERSONAL: Born March 26, 1941, in Nairobi, Kenya; brought to England in 1949; son of Clinton John (a farmer) and Jean Mary Vyvyan (Ladner) Dawkins; married Marian Stamp, August 19, 1967 (divorced, 1984); married Eve Barham, June 1, 1984; children: Juliet Emma. *Education:* Balliol College, Oxford, B.A., 1962, M.A., 1966, D.Phil., 1966. *Religion:* None.

ADDRESSES: Home—74 Hawkswell Gardens, Oxford OX2 7JW, England. *Office*—Department of Zoology, New College, Oxford University, Oxford OX1 3BN, England.

CAREER: University of California, Berkeley, assistant professor of zoology, 1967-69; Oxford University, Oxford, England, lecturer in zoology and fellow of New College, 1970—.

AWARDS, HONORS: Los Angeles Times Book Prize in current interest, 1987, for *The Blind Watchmaker: Why the Evidence of Evolution Reveals a Universe Without Design.*

WRITINGS:

The Selfish Gene, Oxford University Press, 1976.
The Extended Phenotype: The Gene as the Unit of Selection, W. H. Freeman, 1982.
(Editor) *Oxford Surveys in Evolutionary Biology 1984,* two volumes, Oxford University Press, 1985.
The Blind Watchmaker: Why the Evidence of Evolution Reveals a Universe Without Design, Norton, 1986.

Honorary editor of *Animal Behaviour,* 1974—.

SIDELIGHTS: A zoologist at Oxford University, Richard Dawkins "has already established himself as a biological guru" with the publication of three books detailing and expanding upon Darwinian theory, according to *Times Literary Supplement* contributor Stephen R. L. Clark. Seeing a decline in the popular acceptance of Darwin's theories, Dawkins "has been concerned to convince the literate public that they must now take evolutionary theory seriously as the context within which to think about ourselves and the world," writes Clark. Although his theoretical explanations are often very technical and involved, Dawkins is able to bring his theories to an audience of lay readers through comprehensible analogies and clear writing.

In *The Selfish Gene,* Dawkins "gently and expertly debunks some of the favourite illusions of social biology about altruism," writes Peter Medawar in *Spectator.* The critic also remarks that the work is "a most skilful reformulation of the central problems of social biology in terms of the genetical theory of natural selection." "Building on a beautifully chosen set of analogies," describes Douglas R. Hofstadter in the *Washington Post Book World,* ". . . Dawkins shows how, in the end, spectacularly complex organizations can have the properties we attribute to ourselves, all as a consequence of aimless chemical reactions. This is one of the coldest, most inhuman and disorienting views of human beings I have ever heard," continues Hofstadter, "and yet I love it! It is so deep an insight, to bridge the gap between the lifeless and the living, the chemical and the biological, the random and the teleological, the physical and the spiritual."

In contrast, John Pfeiffer finds the significance of Dawkins's evolutionary theories somewhat elusive: "Dawkins is somewhat ambiguous when it comes to considering how all this applies to human beings," he writes in the *New York Times Book Review.* "[He is] perhaps swayed by his own eloquence." *New York Times* critic Christopher Lehmann-Haupt, however, finds Dawkins's writing more than adequate to his task: "It is not the theory of 'The Selfish Gene' that is so arresting as the marvelous lucidity with which Mr. Dawkins applies it to various behavior mechanisms that have hitherto been misunderstood." And Pfeiffer also admits that Dawkins "demonstrates a rare and welcome ability to make formidably technical findings come alive." A *New Yorker* reviewer expresses a similar opinion: "What makes [*The Selfish Gene*]

accessible is the brilliance and wit of Mr. Dawkins' style. It is a splendid example of how difficult scientific ideas can be explained by someone who understands them and is willing to take the trouble."

The Extended Phenotype: The Gene as the Unit of Selection, another exploration of Darwinian theory, "is in large part a reply to critics of *The Selfish Gene,*" which had an "often hostile" reception from Dawkins's professional colleagues, observes David Papineau in the *Times Literary Supplement.* One of these colleagues, Stephen Rose, writes in the *New Statesman* that Dawkins's "determinist" theories are paradoxical and contradictory. "The odd thing is that, having built his—false—case with customary clarity, elegance, and forcefulness, Dawkins then uses the remaining four chapters of the book to self-destruct it. . . . His critics have accused him of reductionism and biological determinism. Dawkins denies these charges and in almost the same breath recommits the same errors," remarks Rose. While Papineau does not find *The Extended Phenotype* to be completely determinist, he does fault some of the author's arguments as being incomplete or inconsistent. Nevertheless, the critic says that even if the work "is still saddled with some of Dawkins's earlier confusions, its virtues far exceed its vices." Dawkins "is an extremely gifted expositor," continues Papineau, "and with the help of the useful glossary he includes most lay readers should be able to enjoy the book."

Dawkins once again investigates aspects of Darwinian theory in *The Blind Watchmaker: Why the Evidence of Evolution Reveals a Universe Without Design.* Lee Dembart of the *Los Angeles Times* calls the work "a clear, logical, rational book that is the antidote to silliness. . . . [The book] cuts through the nonsense about the origin and development of life and leaves it for dead," continues Dembart. "He demonstrates beyond a shadow of a doubt that evolution is the only possible explanation for the world we see around us." In this work, Dawkins refutes the argument that the complexity of life cannot be random, thus implying a designer or creator. The author uses Darwin's idea of small mutational variation to "demonstrate that it (and it alone) is competent to explain the enormous diversity of living things in all their extremes of complexity and specialization," writes David Jones in the London *Times.* Like the author's previous work, Jones finds that *The Blind Watchmaker* "is brilliant exposition, tightly argued but kept readable by plentiful recourse to analogies and examples."

Because of its controversial topic and method of exposition, this book has inevitably drawn its share of criticism. Rose, writing in the *New Statesman,* once again finds the author's work self-contradictory: "There is much which is good and not merely clever about this book. But Dawkins' greatest problem is his continual tendency to allow himself to be dragged over the top by the very vigour of his own writing." While Dawkins "provides an excellent account of why and how reductionism fails," remarks Rose, ". . . he can't resist beginning a chapter . . . [with] beautiful and fallacious writing, not only profoundly reductionist, but, as he would himself put it, 'deeply superficial.'" Clark not only disputes Dawkins's methods, he argues against his theory as well, claiming that the work lacks "any argument for the claim that the god of hard metaphysical theism either is or ought to be conceived as something inordinately complex." The critic continues: "Dawkins cannot simply ignore theological and philosophical discussion of what it would mean to speak of God's design, or God's existence."

While Clark disagrees with many of Dawkins's theories and faults the author for omitting what he feels are important considerations, he still thinks the book works on a specific level. "What Dawkins does successfully is very good: *The Blind Watchmaker* is as clear, as enthralling, as convincing an account of neo-Darwinian theory as I have read.... His opposition to dogmatic vivisectionists and his appreciation of the marvellous diversity and ingenuity of the world are very welcome." Dembart summarizes his own impression of the work: "The book is beautifully and superbly written. It is completely understandable, but it has the cadence of impassioned speech. Every page rings of truth," continues the critic. "It is one of the best science books—one of the best any books—I have ever read." Explaining the origin of this "passion" for truth, Dawkins remarked that his "early interest in evolution was really as a sort of alternative to religion, and an explanation for the way things are," the author remarked to Sarah Duncan in the London *Times.* While "other biologists start out as bird watchers or bug hunters," said Dawkins, "I started with a curiosity about why things exist."

AVOCATIONAL INTERESTS: Computer programming.

BIOGRAPHICAL/CRITICAL SOURCES:

PERIODICALS

Chicago Tribune, November 20, 1986.
Los Angeles Times, November 25, 1986.
Los Angeles Times Book Review, December 28, 1986, October 25, 1987.
New Statesman, November 19, 1976, April 16, 1982, November 14, 1986.
New Yorker, April 11, 1977.
New York Times, March 17, 1977.
New York Times Book Review, February 27, 1977, December 14, 1986.
Saturday Review, February 19, 1977.
Science, May 13, 1977, December 10, 1982.
Spectator, January 15, 1977.
Times (London), October 3, 1986, December 11, 1986.
Times Literary Supplement, February 4, 1977, July 20, 1984, September 26, 1986.
Washington Post Book World, December 2, 1979.†

—*Sketch by Diane Telgen*

*   *   *

DEAN, Karen Strickler 1923-

PERSONAL: Born November 24, 1923, in Los Angeles, Calif.; daughter of R. V. (a commercial artist and watercolor painter) and Laura (a teacher; maiden name, Ness) Strickler; married Ervin S. Dean, Jr. (an engineer), June 16, 1947; children: Pamela, Nathan C., Lucie Signa, Thomas S. *Education:* University of California, Los Angeles, B.A., 1946; San Jose State University, elementary teaching credential, 1973, specialist teaching credential, 1976, M.A., 1979.

ADDRESSES: Home—Palo Alto, Calif.

CAREER: Highland-Park News Herald, Los Angeles, Calif., reporter and society editor, 1943-45; Cutter Laboratories, Berkeley, Calif., advertising and publicity copywriter, 1946-47; University of California Press, Berkeley, publicity and book jacket copywriter, 1947-49; Palo Alto Unified Schools, Palo Alto, Calif., instructional aide, 1974-76, volunteer creative writing teacher, 1975; Morland School District, San Jose, Calif., teacher of learning-disabled children, 1976-77; New Haven Unified School District, Union City, Calif., teacher of learning-disabled children at Alvarado Middle School, 1977-82, creative writing teacher and school newspaper sponsor, 1979-81; writer, 1982—. Speaker at writing classes for children. Home teacher in Whisman School District, Mountain View, Calif., 1974-77.

MEMBER: Authors Guild, Authors League of America, Society of Children's Book Writers, California Writers.

AWARDS, HONORS: Winner of numerous prizes in local writing competitions, including Christmas short story contest in *Peninsula Living,* 1973, for "How Silently, How Silently"; Member of the Year, Society of Children's Book Writers, 1987.

WRITINGS:

(Contributor) *Sullivan Reading Comprehension,* Books 5-20, Behavioral Research Labs, 1973.
(Contributor) Joanne Robinson Mitchell and Anne Libby Pyle, editors, *Prisms,* Heath, 1975.
(Contributor) *Independent Reading Skills Laboratory,* Educational Progress, 1976.

YOUNG ADULT FICTION

Maggie Adams, Dancer, Avon, 1980.
Mariana, Avon, 1981.
Between Dances: Maggie Adams' Eighteenth Summer, Avon, 1982.
A Time to Dance, Scholastic, 1985.
Stay on Your Toes, Maggie Adams!, Avon, 1986.
Cammy Takes a Bow, Avon, 1988.

OTHER

Also contributor to *Salt Lake Tribune, Society of Children's Book Writers Bulletin, Norseman, Motorland,* and religious magazines. Editor of monthly newsletter for Parents' Alliance for the Mentally Ill; editor of *Bay Area Kite,* a bi-yearly newsletter.

WORK IN PROGRESS: Research for a young adult historical novel; a children's novel for ages eight to twelve; a young adult psychological novel.

SIDELIGHTS: For several years, Karen Strickler Dean combined writing and teaching children with learning disabilities. In an *Argus* interview, Dean told Joette Dignan Weir that at the time her writing was limted to "about two hours, two or three times a week" and "about four hours on weekends." Summers, Weir relates, had "become a writing marathon" for Dean. The dual career, however, also had its benefits; Dean's students provided experiences that enriched her characterizations. Dean commented, "The characters in my next three books are not based on one recognizable person, but a composite." Dean's writing method begins, she told Weir, with "a detailed history of each character and a brief outline of my idea." This preparation allows her to work "completely off the outline."

Dean's first novel, *Maggie Adams, Dancer,* details a year in the life of a fourteen-year old ballet student who encounters problems in balancing a demanding class and rehearsal schedule with parental expectations and typical teenage distractions. Among the difficulties Maggie encounters are an impatient boyfriend, a father who wants her to study something practical, and a dance teacher who is less than encouraging. Dean illustrates some very unromantic aspects of ballet in the novel: the physical rigors, a dominating "stage mother" involved in troupe politics, and a girl who becomes anorexic by attempting to maintain a dancer's body. All ends well for Maggie, however. She receives a full scholarship to the City Ballet, and wins the approval of both her parents and her teacher.

In a *Peninsula Times Tribune* article by Angelika von der Assen, Dean calls *Maggie Adams* "a realistic—unrealistic story. All the obstacles in a young dancer's way do exist—but successful girls like Maggie are hard to find." Critics centered their praise on the nonfictional aspects of Maggie's life. Barbara Karlin relates in the *Los Angeles Times* that "Dean has shown how tough, how demanding a life devoted to dance can be, and . . . points out the importance of family and friends." Similarly, Beverly Kobrin in a *Palo Alto Weekly* critique, finds that "Dean hasn't given us another Cinderella story. . . . She has written a realistic, insightful, and engaging story about an aspiring young dancer, her family and friends, and the disappointments and pleasures that accompany the growth of a performing artist."

Dean explains her reasons for choosing to write about ballet in a *Galleys* article: "Ballet is one of the passions of my life. I studied ballet for seven years." She continues that editors "believe that young girls like to read about ballet," and that, in addition to describing the lives of young dancers, "the books also express a lot of other concerns. The world of ballet becomes a microcosm of the larger world."

AVOCATIONAL INTERESTS: Reading, Mexican-American culture, skiing, swimming, ballet (studied with Branislava and Irina Nijinska and the San Francisco Ballet School).

BIOGRAPHICAL/CRITICAL SOURCES:

PERIODICALS

Argus, June 8, 1980.
Galleys: A Newsletter for Children's Writers and Illustrators, May, 1986.
Los Angeles Times, July 13, 1980.
Palo Alto Weekly, December 4, 1980.
Peninsula Times-Tribune, July 11, 1980, April 26, 1986.
State-ment, July/August, 1986.
Voice of Youth Advocates, August/October, 1986.

*   *   *

DeBOER, John C(harles)   1923-

PERSONAL: Born May 23, 1923, in Kodaikanal, India; son of John (a clergyman, educator, and missionary) and Erma Elizabeth (Eardley) DeBoer; married Clara L. Merritt (a professor of history), April 29, 1944; children: John L., Katharine L., David C. *Education:* University of Michigan, B.S., 1944; New Brunswick Theological Seminary, B.D., 1950; Drew University, S.T.M., 1954.

ADDRESSES: Office—475 Riverside Dr., New York, N.Y. 10027.

CAREER: Clergyman of United Church of Christ; Grumman Aircraft Co., Bethpage, N.Y., flight test engineer, 1944-47; minister of Congregational churches in Union, N.J., 1949-53, and Maple Shade, N.J., 1953-59; Vermont Congregational Conference, Burlington, associate minister, 1959-65; United Church of Christ Board for Homeland Ministries, New York City, national secretary to church extension, 1965-77; Joint Strategy and Action Committee, Inc., New York City, executive director, 1977-88. Vice-president, Boston Seamen's Friend

Society, 1963-65. Founder and secretary of Cornucopia Network of New Jersey, Inc., 1983-85.

MEMBER: Sigma Xi, Tau Beta Pi, Phi Kappa Phi.

WRITINGS:

Discovering Our Mission, United Church Board for Homeland Ministries, 1966, revised edition, 1969.
Let's Plan: A Guide to the Planning Process for Voluntary Organizations, Pilgrim Press, 1970.
How to Succeed in the Organization Jungle without Losing Your Religion, Pilgrim Press, 1972.
(Co-editor with Alexander Greendale) *Are New Towns for Lower Income Americans, Too?,* Praeger, 1974.
Energy Conservation Manual for Congregations, Joint Strategy and Action Committee, Inc., 1980.

Also author of *Primer on Food Fellowship,* 1982. Contributor to church periodicals.

*   *   *

DEE, Ruby
   See WALLACE, Ruby Ann

*   *   *

DEKOVIC, Gene   1922-

PERSONAL: Born June 9, 1922, in Chicago, Ill.; son of Charles W. (a teamster) and Lillian (a secretary; maiden name, Hill) Dekovic; married Margery Jean Walker (a secretary), July 14, 1945; children: Barry Walker. *Education:* Attended Northwestern University, 1940-42, Institute of Design, 1946-48, and University of Chicago, 1955-59.

ADDRESSES: Home—P.O. Box 126, 1451 Library Ln., Saint Helena, Calif. 94574.

CAREER: R. R. Donnelley & Sons, Chicago, Ill., photographer, 1945-46; Schnell Mills, Inc. (advertising agency), Chicago, production manager, 1946-48; Gaylord Productions, Chicago, assistant advertising manager, 1948-49; Warren, Wetherell & Associates, Chicago, salesman, 1949-51; Dekovic-Smith Design Organization, Chicago, partner and business manager, 1951-57; Gene Dekovic (communications research planning), Chicago, owner, 1957-74. Teacher of business communication at Western Electric Graduate Training Center, 1958, and University of Chicago, 1958-59; Columbia College, Chicago, teacher of mass communication media, 1963-71, trustee, 1965-71. Special researcher on educational efficiency textbooks. Consultant to publishers of elementary and high school textbooks. *Military service:* U.S. Army Air Forces, 1942-46, navigator; German prisoner of war.

MEMBER: Society of Typographic Arts (fellow; president, 1964-65), Mensa.

WRITINGS:

(Editor and photographer) *Self Reliance,* Funk, 1975.
Au tu per tu: Contemporary Italy as Seen through Actual Interviews, National Textbook Co., 1978.
Vita italiana, National Textbook Co., 1979.
This Blessed Land, Illuminations, 1980.

"LOOKING AT SPAIN" SERIES

Looking at Spanish Cities, National Textbook Co., 1988.
Looking at Spanish Food, National Textbook Co., 1988.

Looking at Spanish Signs, National Textbook Co., 1988.
Looking at a Spanish Village, National Textbook Co., 1988.
Looking at Spanish History, National Textbook Co., in press.

Also author of *En directo desde Espana.*

WORK IN PROGRESS: Editing and photography for books; *Exposures,* a book of photographs and writings on human communication; editing publications for wineries.

SIDELIGHTS: Called "a clever concept, and a well-executed one too," *This Blessed Land* is a photo-journalistic essay on wine making at the Robert Mondavi Winery from the planting to the drinking stages. The wineries of the Napa Valley are the number two tourist attraction in California, so Gene Dekovic's book offers wine lore, technology, and advice for a large audience. "Perhaps the refreshing thing about this book," praised a *Wine Spectator* reviewer, "is that it is written from the perspective of a man who does not write about wine for a living—it's a perspective that consumers and people in the business can enjoy on equal terms."

Many critics commented on the quality of the photographs in *This Blessed Land.* The pictures, according to Robert Goerner's *Performing Arts*'s review, are "poetry in a picture." Ken Forrester, writing in the *Arkansas Gazette,* noted that the color photos "range from superb to dazzling," and Peter Kroon's *Standard Times* critique submitted that "the photography alone is worth the price of this tasteful publication."

In a similar vein, Dekovic's *Vita italiana,* a treatise combining photography and prose to describe Italy for second-year students, inspired Jack Shreve to comment in the *Modern Language Journal,* "What truly excel, however, are Dekovic's shots of people...." Shreve observes that "the text itself reads too much like a tourist brochure," yet concludes, "The novelty of its photojournalistic approach is sure to be welcomed by certain teachers in special instructional situations."

Dekovic told *CA:* "In doing research for educational publishing, it became quite clear that the visual content of textbooks played a much greater part than was indicated by the term 'visual aids' or than was ever revealed in conventional subject exams. Filmmakers know this very well as do television producers. However, I refuse to give up on print as a primary medium of communication. It has yet to achieve its potential for achieving effective communication of the kinds of subjects that need to be disseminated in a democratic society. We have to go beyond pretty pictures or shocking pictures and learn to use visual information and verbal presentations welded together in new ways, ways that stimulate more comprehensive understandings. Our students, our citizens deserve no less. That is what I am working toward whether it is a foreign-language text or a wine book. There is a long way to go, and I don't think I have enough time left to get there."

BIOGRAPHICAL/CRITICAL SOURCES:

PERIODICALS

Arkansas Gazette, May 2, 1982.
Modern Language Journal, summer, 1986.
Performing Arts, June, 1982.
Standard Times (Bedford, Mass.), June 13, 1982.
Wine Spectator, June 16-30, 1982.

*　　*　　*

DEMPSEY, Hugh Aylmer 1929-

PERSONAL: Born November 7, 1929, in Edgerton, Alberta, Canada; son of Otto L. and Lily (Sharp) Dempsey; married Pauline S. Gladstone, September 30, 1953; children: L. James, Louise, John, Leah, Lois. *Education:* Educated in primary and secondary schools in Edmonton, Alberta. *Religion:* Anglican.

ADDRESSES: Home—95 Holmwood Ave. N.W., Calgary, Alberta, Canada T2K 2G7. *Office*—Glenbow Museum, 130 Ninth Ave. S.E., Calgary, Alberta, Canada T2G 0P3.

CAREER: Edmonton Bulletin, Edmonton, Alberta, reporter and editor, 1949-51; Government of Alberta, Edmonton, publicity writer, 1951-56; Glenbow Foundation, Calgary, Alberta, archivist, 1956-67; Glenbow-Alberta Institute, Calgary, technical director, 1967-70, director of history, 1970-80; Glenbow Museum, Calgary, assistant director, 1980-86, associate director of collections, 1986—. Lecturer at Canadian universities. Associate director of Calgary Exhibition and Stampede, 1958—; member of Alberta Records Publication Board, 1981—.

MEMBER: Canadian Historical Association (chairperson of archives section, 1961-62), Canadian Museums Association (executive member, 1968-70), Indian-Eskimo Association of Canada (executive member, 1960-65), Champlain Society (member of council, 1972-74), Historical Society of Alberta (executive member, 1952—; vice-president, 1955-56; president, 1956-57), Indian Association of Alberta, Fort Calgary Preservation Society (executive member, 1969-75), Kainai Chieftainship.

AWARDS, HONORS: Annual award from Historical Society of Alberta, 1963; Alberta Achievement Award, 1974, 1975; L.L.D. from University of Calgary, 1974; Order of Canada, 1975; Alberta Non-Fiction Award, 1975, for *The Best of Bob Edwards.*

WRITINGS:

Historic Sites of Alberta, Government of Alberta, 1952.
(Editor) *The Big Chief of the Prairies* (on Father Lacombe), Palm Publishers, 1953.
(Editor) Thomas Edmund Wilson, *Trailblazer of the Canadian Rockies,* Glenbow-Alberta Institute, 1972.
Crawfoot: Chief of the Blackfeet, University of Oklahoma Press, 1972.
A History of Rocky Mountain House, Department of Indian Affairs and Northern Development (Ottawa), 1973.
William Parker, Mounted Policeman, Hurtig, 1973.
(Editor) *A Winter at Fort Macleod,* McClelland & Stewart, 1974.
(Editor) *Men in Scarlet,* McClelland & Stewart, 1974.
(Editor) *The Best of Bob Edwards,* Hurtig, 1975.
(Editor) *The Wit and Wisdom of Bob Edwards,* Hurtig, 1976.
(Editor) Robert Terrill Rundle, *The Rundle Journals, 1840-1848,* Historical Society of Alberta, 1977.
Charcoal's World, Western Producer Prairie Books, 1978.
Indian Tribes of Alberta (monograph), Glenbow-Alberta Institute, 1978.
Hutterites: The Hutterite Diamond Jubilee, Glenbow-Alberta Institute, 1978.
(Editor and author of introduction) *My Tribe, the Crees,* Glenbow Museum, 1979.
Red Crow, Warrior Chief, University of Nebraska Press, 1980.
(Editor) *The Best from Alberta History,* Western Producer Prairie Books, 1981.
Christmas in the West, Western Producer Prairie Books, 1982.
History in Their Blood, Douglas & McIntyre, 1982.
(Editor) *The CPR West,* Douglas & McIntyre, 1984.
Big Bear: The End of Freedom, Douglas & McIntyre, 1984.

The Gentle Persuader: James Gladstone, Western Producer Prairie Books, 1986.
Treaty Seven, Indian and Northern Affairs, 1987.

Former author of column "Tawasi," in the daily *Edmonton Bulletin.* Contributor to national and international journals, including *Journal of American Folklore, Plains Anthropologist,* and *Journal of the Washington Academy of Science.* Editor of *Canadian Archivist,* 1963-66; associate editor of *Alberta History,* 1953-58, editor, 1958—; Northern and Canadian editor of *Montana Magazine of History.*

WORK IN PROGRESS: Tom Three Persons.

SIDELIGHTS: While associated with the Government of Alberta, Hugh Aylmer Dempsey was responsible for historical work, including a historic highway sign program and historic sites research. His interest in history developed alongside his work with and research on Canadian Indians. His wife is a Blood Indian and in 1967 Dempsey was made an honorary Blood chief. Beginning with work for the Indian Association of Alberta, he assisted attempts to organize locals on Blackfoot and Peigan Reserves. Much of his writing concerns the Indian tribes of Alberta. He directed the documentary film "Okan, Sun Dance of the Blackfoot" and served as consultant for "West to the Mountains."

*   *   *

DENMARK, Harrison
See ZELAZNY, Roger (Joseph)

*   *   *

de REGNIERS, Beatrice Schenk (Freedman)   1914-
(Tamara Kitt)

PERSONAL: Surname is pronounced "drain-yay"; born August 16, 1914, in Lafayette, Ind.; daughter of Harry and Sophia Freedman; married Francis de Regniers (an airline shipping manager), 1953. *Education:* Attended University of Illinois, 1931-33; University of Chicago, Ph.B., 1935, graduate study, 1936-37; Winnetka Graduate Teachers College, M.Ed., 1941.

ADDRESSES: Home—180 West 58th St., New York, N.Y. 10019. *Agent*—A. E. Suter, Gotham Art & Literary Agency, 25 Tudor Pl., Suite 1504, New York, N.Y. 10017.

CAREER: Writer of juvenile books. Eloise Moore Dance Group, Chicago, Ill., member, 1942-43; Scott, Foresman & Co., Chicago, copywriter, 1943-44; United Nations Relief and Rehabilitation Administration, Egypt, welfare officer, 1944-46; American Book Co., New York City, copywriter, 1948-49; American Heart Association, New York City, director of educational materials, 1949-61; Scholastic Book Services, New York City, editor of Lucky Book Club, 1961-81.

MEMBER: Authors Guild, Authors League of America, Society of Children's Book Writers, Dramatists Guild, PEN.

AWARDS, HONORS: Children's Spring Book Festival honor book, *New York Herald Tribune,* 1958, for *Cats Cats Cats Cats Cats;* Boys' Clubs Junior Book Award, 1960, for *The Snow Party;* Indiana Authors Day Award, honorable mention, 1961, for *The Shadow Book;* Caldecott Award, 1965, for *May I Bring a Friend?;* certificate of excellence, American Institute of Graphic Arts, for communicating with children; Brooklyn Art Books for Children citation, 1973, for *Red Riding Hood: Retold in Verse for Boys and Girls to Read Themselves.*

WRITINGS—All juveniles:

The Giant Story, illustrations by Maurice Sendak, Harper, 1953.
A Little House of Your Own, illustrations by Irene Haas, Harcourt, 1954, reprinted, 1987.
What Can You Do with a Shoe?, illustrations by Sendak, Harper, 1955.
Was It a Good Trade? (verse), illustrations by Haas, Harcourt, 1956.
A Child's Book of Dreams, illustrations by Bill Sokol, Harcourt, 1957.
Something Special (poems), illustrations by Haas, Harcourt, 1958.
Cats Cats Cats Cats Cats (poems), illustrations by Sokol, Pantheon, 1958.
The Snow Party, illustrations by Reiner Zimnik, Pantheon, 1959.
What Happens Next?: Adventures of a Hero, illustrations by Remo, Macmillan, 1959.
The Shadow Book, illustrations by Isabel Gordon, Harcourt, 1960.
Who Likes the Sun?, illustrations by Leona Pierce, Harcourt, 1961.
(Self-illustrated) *The Little Book,* Walck, 1961, published as *Going for a Walk,* Harper, 1982.
The Little Girl and Her Mother, illustrations by Esther Gilman, Vanguard, 1963.
May I Bring a Friend?, illustrations by Beni Montresor, Atheneum, 1964.
How Joe the Bear and Sam the Mouse Got Together, illustrations by Brinton Turkle, Parents' Magazine Press, 1965.
The Abraham Lincoln Joke Book, illustrations by William Lahey Cummings, Random House, 1965.
David and Goliath, illustrations by Richard M. Powers, Viking, 1965.
(With Marvin Bileck) *Penny,* Viking, 1966, revised and reillustrated edition, Lothrop, 1987.
Circus, photographs by Al Giese, Viking, 1966.
The Giant Book, illustrations by Cummings, Atheneum, 1966.
The Day Everybody Cried, illustrations by Nonny Hogrogian, Viking, 1967.
Willy O'Dwyer Jumped in the Fire: Variations on a Folk Rhyme, illustrations by Montresor, Atheneum, 1968.
(Compiler with Eva Moore and Mary Michaels White) *Poems Children Will Sit Still For: A Selection for the Primary Grades,* Citation, 1969.
Catch a Little Fox: Variations on a Folk Rhyme, illustrations by Turkle, Seabury, 1970.
The Boy, the Rat, and the Butterfly, illustrations by Haig and Regina Shekerjian, Atheneum, 1971.
Red Riding Hood: Retold in Verse for Boys and Girls to Read Themselves, illustrations by Edward Gorey, Atheneum, 1972.
It Does Not Say Meow, and Other Animal Riddle Rhymes, illustrations by Paul Galdone, Seabury, 1972.
The Enchanted Forest, from a Story by La Contesse de Segur, illustrations from old prints by Gustave Dore and others, Atheneum, 1974.
Little Sister and the Month Brothers, illustrations by Margot Tomes, Seabury, 1976.
A Bunch of Poems and Verses, illustrations by Mary Jane Dunton, Seabury, 1977.
Laura's Story, illustrations by Jack Kent, Atheneum, 1979.
Everyone Is Good for Something, illustrations by Tomes, Houghton, 1980.

Picture Book Theater: The Mysterious Stranger, the Magic Spell, illustrations by Cummings, Clarion Books, 1982.
Waiting for Mama, Clarion Books, 1984.
So Many Cats, Clarion Books, 1985.
This Big Cat and Other Cats I've Known, Crown, 1985.
Jack and the Beanstalk Retold in Verse, Atheneum, 1985.
(Author of script and lyrics) "Everyone Is Good for Something" (musical based on de Regnier's book of same title), first produced in Louisville, Kentucky, at Stage One, 1986.
A Week in the Life of Best Friends and Other Poems of Friendship, Athentum, 1986.
Jack the Giant-Killer Retold in Verse and Other Useful Information about Giants, Atheneum, 1987.
The Way I Feel, Sometimes (poems), Clarion Books, 1988.

UNDER PSEUDONYM TAMARA KITT

The Adventures of Silly Billy, illustrations by Jill Elgin, Grosset & Dunlap, 1961.
Billy Brown: The Baby Sitter, illustrations by Rosalind Welcher, Grosset & Dunlap, 1962.
A Special Birthday Party for Someone Very Special, illustrations by Turkle, Norton, 1966.
Sam and the Impossible Thing, illustrations by Turkle, Norton, 1967.
Jake, illustrations by Turkle, Abelard-Schuman, 1969.

Also author of *The Surprising Pets of Billy Brown,* 1962.

WORK IN PROGRESS: Opera based on her book *Little Sister and the Month Brothers.*

SIDELIGHTS: Beatrice Schenk de Regniers writes: "I think of writing—particularly of writing picture books—as a kind of choreography. A picture book must have pace and movement and pattern. Pictures and text should, together, create the pattern, rather than simply run parallel."

De Regniers's books have been translated into French, German, Japanese, and Swedish.

BIOGRAPHICAL/CRITICAL SOURCES:

BOOKS

Arbuthnot, May Hill, *Children and Books,* 3rd edition, Scott, Foresman, 1964.
Hopkins, Lee Bennett, *Books Are by People,* Citation, 1969.

PERIODICALS

New York Times Book Review, March 3, 1985.

*   *   *

De VEAUX, Alexis   1948-

PERSONAL: Born September 24, 1948, in New York, N.Y.; daughter of Richard Hill and Mae De Veaux. *Education:* State University of New York Empire State College, B.A., 1976.

ADDRESSES: Home—135 Eastern Parkway, Suite 8K, Brooklyn, N.Y. 11238.

CAREER: Writer and illustrator. New York Urban League, New York, N.Y., assistant instructor in English for WIN Program, 1969-71; Frederick Douglass Creative Arts Center, New York City, instructor in creative writing, 1971-72; Bronx Office of Probations, New York City, community worker, 1972-73; Project Create, New York City, instructor in reading and creative writing, 1973-74. Intern for Roundabout Theatre/Stage

One, 1974; cultural coordinator of Black Expo for the Black Coalition of Greater New Haven, 1975. Poetry editor, *Essence* magazine. Has given readings at colleges, churches, and theaters; has appeared on radio and television programs in New York City, Washington, D.C., and New Haven, Conn. Artist and co-founder of Coeur de l'Unicorne Gallery, 1975—.

MEMBER: Screen Writers Guild of America (East), Poets and Writers, Inc., American Theatre Association, Black Theatre Alliance, Afro-American Cultural Center (Yale University).

AWARDS, HONORS: First prize from Black Creation, 1972, for short story; best production award from Westchester Community College Drama Festival, 1973, for "Circles"; Art Books for Children awards from Brooklyn Museum, 1974 and 1975, for *Na-ni; Don't Explain: A Song of Billie Holiday* appeared on the American Library Association's Best Books for Young Adults list in 1981; Coretta Scott King Honor Award, 1988, for *An Enchanted Hair Tale.*

WRITINGS:

(And illustrator) *Na-ni* (juvenile), Harper, 1973.
(And illustrator) *Spirits in the Street* (novel), Doubleday, 1973.
Li Chen/Second Daughter First Son (prose poem), Ba Tone Press, 1975.
Don't Explain: A Song of Billie Holiday, Harper, 1980.
An Enchanted Hair Tale (juvenile), Harper, 1987.

Also author of *Blue Heat* and *Adventures of the Dread Sisters.*

PLAYS

"Circles" (one-act), first produced in New York, N.Y., at Frederick Douglass Creative Arts Center, March, 1973.
"The Tapestry," first broadcast on KCET-TV (PBS), March, 1976, produced in New York at Harlem Performance Center, May, 1976.
"A Season to Unravel," first produced Off-Broadway at St. Mark's Playhouse, January 27, 1979.

OTHER

Contributor of poems and stories to *Sunbury II, Encore, Black Creation,* and *New Haven Advocate.*

WORK IN PROGRESS: This Handed/That Handed (tentative title), for children; "Fox Street War" (tentative title), a play; research on the life of Lorraine Hansberry.

SIDELIGHTS: Writer and illustrator Alexis De Veaux believes that "art should confront head-on the racial and economic inequities in American life," writes *Dictionary of Literary Biography* contributor Priscilla R. Ramsey. In her self-illustrated children's story *Na-ni,* for example, De Veaux writes about a poor Harlem child, Na-ni, whose dream of a new bicycle goes unfulfilled when the family's welfare check is stolen. Reviews of *Na-ni* praised both the storyline and illustrations. "The style is spare, poetic—a performance startlingly personal and alive," Margaret F. O'Connell writes in the *New York Times Book Review.* A *Library Journal* contributor comments, "this is a unique, poignant, and poetic book, illustrated with line drawings of haunting power." Concludes a *Horn Book* reviewer: "Powerful and stark, the text itself has such a poetic quality that the reader is simultaneously aware of the tragedy and the beauty in Na-ni's life."

De Veaux also has a particular interest in addressing the image of the black woman in her work. Ramsey relates that De Veaux once stated: "In all of the work I've done, there is a certain and deliberate care I've taken with laying out the image of the black woman as I have seen or experienced her, which indicates that there is a clear and conscious desire to address myself to her.'' In *Don't Explain: A Song of Billie Holiday* De Veaux recreates, in lyric form, the life of the renowned jazz singer. *Ms.* contributor June Jordan writes: ''De Veaux gives you the life of Billie Holiday fitted into its time, the music of Billie Holiday traced back to its source, the voice of Billie Holiday fathomed for its meaning.'' *Don't Explain* is written for young adults, and reviewers note that the book will enlighten this audience in several ways. A *Publishers Weekly* contributor believes that *Don't Explain* ''can help young people understand inequity and iniquity and arm themselves against the deadly lure of drugs.'' Mary Laka Cannella concludes in *Best Sellers:* ''[*Don't Explain*] is melodic, gripping and emotional. It could turn on some young readers to poetry.''

AVOCATIONAL INTERESTS: Studying Egyptian mythology and ancient culture, astrology, art history, ''development of a new language composed of musical sounds and derived from African, Haitian, American Black, and neo-sexual sources.''

BIOGRAPHICAL/CRITICAL SOURCES:

BOOKS

Dictionary of Literary Biography, Volume 38: *Afro-American Writers after 1955: Dramatists and Prose Writers,* Gale, 1985.

PERIODICALS

Best Sellers, October, 1980.
Booklist, May 15, 1980.
Children's Literature in Education, winter, 1986.
Essence, June, 1981.
Horn Book, June, 1973.
Library Journal, May 15, 1973.
Ms., June, 1980.
New York Times, January 26, 1979.
New York Times Book Review, April 1, 1973.
Publishers Weekly, February 5, 1973, May 30, 1980.
School Library Journal, August, 1980.†

* * *

DeVORKIN, David H(yam) 1944-

PERSONAL: Born January 6, 1944, in Los Angeles, Calif.; son of Howard (a chemical engineer) and Judith (a teacher; maiden name, Schoenberg) DeVorkin; married Kunie Fujiki (a systems analyst), June 2, 1970; children: Hannah Fujiki. *Education:* University of California, Los Angeles, A.B., 1966; San Diego State College (now University), M.S., 1968; Yale University, M.Phil., 1970; University of Leicester, Ph.D., 1978.

ADDRESSES: Office—Department of Space Science, National Air and Space Museum, Smithsonian Institution, Washington, D.C. 20560.

CAREER: Central Connecticut State College, New Britain, assistant professor of astronomy, 1970-76; American Institute of Physics Center for History of Physics, consultant research associate, 1977-78; Central Connecticut State College, associate professor of astronomy, 1979; National Air and Space Museum, Washington, D.C., associate curator, 1980-84, curator, 1984—, Space Science and Exploration Department chairman, 1984-86.

MEMBER: History of Science Society, International Astronomical Union, American Astronomical Society, Royal Astronomical Society, Astronomical Society of the Pacific.

WRITINGS:

(Editor with A.G.D. Philip) *In Memory of Helen Norris Russell,* Dudley Observatory, 1977.
The History of Modern Astronomy and Astrophysics: A Selected, Annotated Bibliography, Garland Publishing, 1982.
Practical Astronomy: Lectures on Time, Place, and Space, Smithsonian Institution Press, 1986.
Stratospheric Science: Manned Scientific Ballooning in the United States, Springer-Verlag, 1989.
Science with a Vengeance: The Origins of American Space Science, Springer-Verlag, in press.

WORK IN PROGRESS: Henry Norris Russell and Modern Stellar Astronomy.

SIDELIGHTS: David H. DeVorkin told *CA:* ''My early interest in astronomy was stimulated by my father, who worked on rocket propulsion chemistry after World War II and often talked about astronomy, rockets (especially V2 rockets), and science fiction with me. I became an amateur astronomer and telescope builder and worked through UCLA as a research assistant, planetarium guide and lecturer, and guitar instructor. I became interested in the history of modern astronomy while an observer at Lick and Yerkes observatories and especially after graduate work at Yale. I switched formally to history in 1974 while teaching astronomy at CCSC, and completed a thesis on the symbiotic relationship of schemes of spectral classification and stellar evolution in the late nineteenth and twentieth centuries. My interests have always been on the history of recent astrophysics, and coming to the National Air and Space Museum has given me a chance to study what science has done with captured German V2 rockets. The 'V' stands for 'vengeance weapon,' and so it is a study of 'science with a vengeance.' ''

* * *

de VRIES, Jan 1943-

PERSONAL: Born November 14, 1943, in the Netherlands; came to United States in 1948, naturalized in 1954; son of Cornelius (a construction worker) and Elly (a sales clerk; maiden name, van Konynenburg) de Vries; married Jeannie Grace Green, September 25, 1968; children: Nicholas, Saskia. *Education:* Columbia University, A.B., 1965; Yale University, Ph.D., 1970. *Religion:* Protestant.

ADDRESSES: Home—1701 La Vereda Rd., Berkeley, Calif. 94709. *Office*—Department of History, University of California, Berkeley, Calif. 94720.

CAREER: Michigan State University, East Lansing, assistant professor of history, 1970-73; University of California, Berkeley, associate professor, 1973-77, professor of history, 1977—. Visiting assistant professor at Yale University, 1972.

MEMBER: American History Association, Economic History Association, Agricultural History Association.

AWARDS, HONORS: Netherlands Institute for Advanced Study fellow, 1975; Guggenheim fellow, 1979.

WRITINGS:

The Dutch Rural Economy in the Golden Age, 1500-1700, Yale University Press, 1974.
The Economy of Europe in an Age of Crisis, 1600-1750, Cambridge University Press, 1976.

Barges and Capitalism: Passenger Transportation in the Dutch Economy, 1632-1839, Hes (Netherlands), 1978, John Benjamins, 1981.
European Urbanization 1500-1800, Harvard University Press, 1984.

SIDELIGHTS: Jan de Vries wrote to *CA:* "My chief interest is long-term economic history and the blending of the New Economic History with the 'Annales School.'"

BIOGRAPHICAL/CRITICAL SOURCES:

PERIODICALS

Times Literary Supplement, March 15, 1985.†

*   *   *

DEYNEKA, Anita 1943-
(Ada Millington)

PERSONAL: Born July 7, 1943, in Seattle, Wash.; daughter of Frank Howard and Ada (McIntosh) Marson; married Peter Deyneka, Jr. (a director of a mission organization), June 15, 1968. *Education:* Attended Wenatchee Valley College, 1961-63; Seattle Pacific College, B.A. (summa cum laude), 1966; Mundelein College, M.A., 1982. *Religion:* Evangelical Protestant.

ADDRESSES: Home—47 Venetian Way, Wheaton, Ill. 60187. Office—Slavic Gospel Association, P.O. Box 1122, Wheaton, Ill. 60187.

CAREER: Overseas Radio and Television, Taipei, Taiwan, missionary, spring, 1966; high school English teacher in Wenatchee, Wash., 1966-68; Slavic Gospel Association, Wheaton, Ill., publications administrator, 1968—. Instructor, Institute of Soviet and East European Studies, 1980—. Adjunct faculty member of graduate school, Wheaton College, 1983—. Clerk-typist for U.S. Forest Service, 1963-67.

MEMBER: National Association of Evangelicals, American Association for the Advancement of Slavic Studies, Institute for the Study of Christianity and Marxism (member of advisory committee), Coalition for Solidarity with Christians in the U.S.S.R. (member of steering committee), Evangelical Press Association, Outstanding Young Women of America.

WRITINGS:

BOOKS FOR CHILDREN

Tanya and the Borderguard, David Cook, 1973.
Fire!, David Cook, 1974.
Alexi's Secret Mission, David Cook, 1975.
Alexi and the Mountain Treasure, David Cook, 1979.
(Under pseudonym Ada Millington) *I Know His Touch,* Crossway Books, 1984.

BOOKS FOR ADULTS

(With husband, Peter Deyneka, Jr.) *Christians in the Shadow of the Kremlin,* David Cook, 1974.
A Song in Siberia, David Cook, 1977.

OTHER

Contributor to religious periodicals, including *New Oxford Review, Christianity Today, Christian Herald, Moody Monthly, Sparks, Eternity, Interlit, Catholic Digest,* and *Pulse.*

SIDELIGHTS: Anita Deyneka's travels have taken her to the Far East, South America, Central America, the Soviet Union, and eastern and western Europe. Many of her books have been translated into foreign languages, including German, Spanish, Finnish, Dutch, and Norwegian.

*   *   *

DIARA, Schavi M.
See ALI, Schavi M(ali)

*   *   *

DIXON, Bernard 1938-

PERSONAL: Born July 17, 1938, in Darlington, England; son of Ronald and Grace (Peirson) Dixon; married Margaret Helena Charlton, 1963 (marriage ended, 1987); children: two sons, one daughter. *Education:* King's College, Durham, B.Sc., 1961; University of Newcastle-upon-Tyne, Ph.D., 1964.

ADDRESSES: Home—7 Warburton Ct., Victoria Rd., Ruislip Manor, Middlesex HA4 0AN, England. Office—Institute for Scientific Information, 132 High St., Oxbridge, Middlesex UB8 1DP, England.

CAREER: University of Newcastle-upon-Tyne, Newcastle-upon-Tyne, England, research microbiologist, 1961-65; *World Medicine,* London, England, assistant editor, 1965-66, deputy editor, 1966-68; *New Scientist,* London, deputy editor, 1968-69, editor, 1969-79; *Omni* magazine, London, European editor, 1979-82; *Science 80 Magazine,* London, editor, 1980-86; European editor for *Scientist* newspaper, 1986—.

MEMBER: British Association for the Advancement of Science (council member), Association of British Science Writers (member of committee, 1969—; chairman, 1971-72), Society for General Microbiology, Institute of Biology (fellow), Institute of Biotechnology (fellow, 1987).

AWARDS, HONORS: Luccock Research Fund fellowship, 1961-64, Frank Schon fellowship from Marchon Products, 1964-65; special award from the Medical Journalists' Association, 1978; Glaxo travelling fellowship, 1980.

WRITINGS:

(Editor) *Journeys in Belief,* Allen & Unwin, 1968.
What Is Science For?, Harper, 1973.
Magnificent Microbes, Atheneum, 1976 (published in England as *Invisible Allies: Microbes and Man's Future,* Temple Smith, 1976).
Beyond the Magic Bullet, Harper, 1978.
Medicine and Care, Heinemann, 1981.
(With Geoffrey Holister) *The Ideas of Science,* Basil Blackwell, 1986.
Genetically Engineered Organisms in the Environment: Scientific Issues, American Society for Microbiology, 1986.
Health and the Human Body, Perseus Press, 1987.

CONTRIBUTOR

David Patessa and Richard Ryder, *Animal Rights,* Centaur, 1979.
David Wallechinsky and others, editors, *The Book of Predictions,* Morrow, 1980.
James D. Watson and John Tooze, editors, *The DNA Story,* W. H. Freeman, 1981.
Colette Kinnon, editor, *From Biology to Biotechnology,* UNESCO, 1982.

Also contributor to *Development of Science Publishing in Europe,* 1980.

OTHER

Correspondent for *World Medicine*, 1968-83; science correspondent for *Spectator*, 1971-79; correspondent for *British Medical Journal*, 1985—, for *Tiede* (Finland), 1985—, for *Biotec* (Italy), 1985—, and the *Observer*, 1987—. Contributor to scientific and popular journals.

SIDELIGHTS: In his book *What Is Science For?*, Bernard Dixon explores the scientific research process, including such subjects as the education of scientists, the financial factors, the outside pressures for results in research, and the internal competition. Dixon also examines how these elements affect the final scientific result.

In a review of *What Is Science For?*, a critic for the *Times Literary Supplement* remarks that "scientifically educated, [Dixon] is gifted with an admirable sense of history. He writes most readably, drawing on an abundance of recent illustration; and he deals with a complex subject both in depth and in extent in a way seldom achieved in a book of this modest length." Roger Williams writes in *Encounter*: "Dixon does a convincing job of showing how more than most things science manages to be 'all things to all men,' from deadly genie to rescuing angel, from the purely utilitarian to the purely cultural. And his prescription for restoring a symbiosis between science and society is something one can only applaud."

In a later book *Beyond the Magic Bullet*, Dixon explains his ideas concerning the medical concept of etiology, which is the theory that specific germs cause specific diseases. According to Harold M. Schmeck, Jr., writing in the *New York Times*, Dixon believes that this hypothesis has "outlived much of its usefulness.... He insists that the 'specific cause' idea tells far less than the whole story and, in any case, is largely irrelevant to some of the most important public-health problems of the late twentieth century." Schmeck reports that Dixon "says that too slavish an adherence to the science of specific etiology has spawned a monstrous overuse of antibiotic drugs; the public perception that there must be an available cure for every human ill, real or imagined, and the spending of many hundreds of millions of American dollars in a war against cancer that has yet to conquer anything."

In a *Best Sellers* review of *Beyond the Magic Bullet*, R. H. Knight states: "This is a book a concerned citizen should read. It is a book a thoughtful layman should read. It is a book that anyone who has not had the chance to take a good course in the history of science and medicine should read."

BIOGRAPHICAL/CRITICAL SOURCES:

PERIODICALS

Economist, May 15, 1976.
Encounter, January, 1974.
New Statesman, October 26, 1973.
Newsweek, August 2, 1976.
New York Times, January 9, 1979, May 1, 1979.
Times Literary Supplement, October 12, 1973.

* * *

DMYTRYSHYN, Basil   1925-

PERSONAL: Born January 14, 1925, in Poland; naturalized U.S. citizen; married Virginia Roehl, July 16, 1949; children: Sonia, Tania. *Education:* University of Arkansas, B.A. 1950, M.A., 1951; University of California, Berkeley, Ph.D., 1955. *Politics:* Democrat.

ADDRESSES: Home—11300 Southwest 92nd Ave., Portland, Ore. 97223. *Office*—Department of History, Portland State University, Portland, Ore. 97207.

CAREER: University of California, Berkeley, research associate, 1955-56; Portland State University, Portland, Ore., assistant professor, 1956-59, associate professor, 1959-64, professor of history, 1964—. Visiting professor at University of Illinois, 1964-65, Harvard University, summer, 1971, University of Hawaii, summer, 1976, and Hokkaido University, Japan, 1978-79. Conductor of college credit course in history on both Oregon educational television and commercial television.

MEMBER: American Historical Association, American Association for the Advancement of Slavic Studies, Canadian Association of Slavicists, Kennan Institute for Advanced Russian Studies (fellow), Oregon Historical Society, World Affairs Council of Oregon, National Geographic Society.

AWARDS, HONORS: John Mosser Award for teaching excellence, 1966, 1967; Fulbright fellowship for research in Germany, 1967-68; Branford P. Millar Award for faculty excellence, 1985.

WRITINGS:

Moscow and the Ukraine, 1918-53, Bookman Associates, 1956.
(Translator with John M. Letiche and Richard Pierce) *A History of Russian Economic Thought*, University of California Press, 1964.
USSR: A Concise History, Scribner, 1965, 4th edition, 1984.
(Editor) *Medieval Russia: A Source Book, 900-1700*, Holt, 1967, 2nd edition, Dryden, 1973.
(Editor) *Imperial Russia: A Source Book, 1700-1917*, Holt, 1967, 2nd edition, Dryden, 1974.
(Author of introduction) Fedir Savchenko, *Zabrona ukrainstva tysiacha visimsot simdesiat shostyi r* (title means "The Suppression of the Ukrainian Activities in 1876"), W. Fink (Munich), 1970.
(Editor) *Modernization of Russia under Peter I and Catherine II*, Wiley, 1974.
(Translator with E.A.P. Crownhart-Vaughan) *Colonial Russian America, 1817-1832*, Oregon Historical Society, 1976.
A History of Russia, Prentice-Hall, 1977.
(Editor with Crownhart-Vaughan) *The End of Russian America: Captain P. N. Golovin's Last Report, 1862*, Oregon Historical Society, 1979.
(Translator with Crownhart-Vaughan) *Civil and Savage Encounters: The Worldly Travel Letters of an Imperial Russian Naval Officer, Pavel N. Golovin*, Oregon Historical Society, 1983.
(Editor and translator with Crownhart-Vaughan and Thomas Vaughan) *Russian Conquest of Siberia: A Documentary Record, 1558-1700*, Oregon Historical Society, 1985.
(Translator with John M. Letiche) *Russian Statecraft: The Politika of Iurii Krizhanich*, Basil Blackwell, 1985.
(Editor and translator with Frederick J. Cox) *The Soviet Union and the Middle East: A Documentary Record of Afghanistan, Iran, and Turkey, 1917-1985*, Kingston, 1987.
(Editor and translator with Crownhart-Vaughan and T. Vaughan) *Russian Penetration of the North Pacific Ocean: A Documentary Record, 1700-1799*, Oregon Historical Society, 1988.

Contributor to professional journals in the United States, Canada, Germany, France, England, Italy, Yugoslavia, Japan, and Korea.

WORK IN PROGRESS: Research in Russian expansion to the Pacific, mercantilist thought, and the impact of Adam Smith on Russia.

SIDELIGHTS: Basil Dmytryshyn told *CA:* "I have researched and published for three principal reasons: as a sign of respect for and tribute to my profession, my former mentors, my family, and my students; because I feel that research and publishing compel a person to organize his/her thoughts, enrich his/her knowledge, and make him/her a more informed teacher; and because anyone in the teaching profession who is not involved in research and publishing will fall so far behind that he/she will perish academically and intellectually."

Dmytryshyn speaks German, Russian, Czechoslovak, Ukrainian, Polish, and Serbo-Croatian. He also reads French and Church Slavonic.

*   *   *

DOMINI, Rey
    See LORDE, Audre (Geraldine)

*   *   *

DOUGLAS, Carole Nelson   1944-

PERSONAL: Born November 5, 1944, in Everett, Wash.; daughter of Arnold Peter (a salmon fisherman) and Agnes (a teacher; maiden name, Lovchik) Nelson; married Sam Scott Douglas (an artist), November 25, 1967. *Education:* College of St. Catherine, B.A., 1966.

ADDRESSES: Home—3920 Singleleaf Lane, Fort Worth, Tex. 76133. *Agent*—Howard Morhaim Literary Agency, 501 Fifth Ave., New York, N.Y. 10017.

CAREER: St. Paul Pioneer Press and *St. Paul Dispatch,* St. Paul, Minn., reporter and feature writer, 1967-83, part-time Sunday and daily section editor, 1980-83, copy and layout editor and occasional editorialist for Opinion Pages, 1983-84; full-time writer, 1984—. Member of board of directors of Newspaper Guild of the Twin Cities, 1970-72; member of honorary committee of St. Paul Library's centennial fund drive and celebration, 1982.

MEMBER: Newspaper Guild, Authors Guild, Authors League of America, Science Fiction Writers of America, Romance Writers of America.

AWARDS, HONORS: Finalist in *Vogue* Prix de Paris Writing competition for college seniors, 1966; Page One awards from the Newspaper Guild of the Twin Cities, 1969, 1971, 1972, 1973, 1974, and 1975; Catherine L. O'Brien Award honorable mention for outstanding achievement in women's interest newspaper reporting from Stanley Home Products, Inc., and second place newswriting award from the Minnesota Associated Press, both 1975, both for an article on destitute elderly; president's citation from the American Society of Interior Designers (Minnesota chapter), 1980, for design and home furnishing reporting; Silver Medal for best historical romance from *West Coast Review of Books,* 1982, for *Fair Wind, Fiery Star;* finalists for Golden Medallion Awards from Romance Writers of America include *Fair Wind, Fiery Star,* 1982, *In Her Prime,* 1983, *Lady Rogue,* 1984, and *The Exclusive,* 1987; Science Fiction-Fantasy Award from *Romantic Times,* 1984; Science Fiction Award from *Romantic Times,* 1986, for *Probe.*

WRITINGS:

NOVELS

Amberleigh (historical), Jove, 1980.
Fair Wind, Fiery Star (historical), Jove, 1981.
In Her Prime, Ballantine, 1982.
Her Own Person, Ballantine, 1982.
The Best Man, Ballantine, 1983.
Lady Rogue (historical), Ballantine, 1983.
Azure Days, Quicksilver Nights (romance), Bantam, 1985.
Probe (science fiction), Tor Books, 1985.
The Exclusive, Ballantine, 1986.
Counterprobe (science fiction; sequel to *Probe*), Tor Books, 1988.

FANTASY SERIES

Six of Swords, Del Rey, 1982.
Exiles of the Rynth, Del Rey, 1984.
Keepers of Edanvant, Tor Books, 1987.
Heir of Rengarth, Tor Books, 1988.
The Seventh Sword, Tor Books, in press.

SIDELIGHTS: Carole Nelson Douglas told *CA:* "From 1967 to 1983 I worked as a reporter and feature writer, covering social changes, particularly as they apply to women and family life, and the spectrum of the arts—performing, visual, and literary. Our society has weathered major political, moral, and philosophical watersheds during my years as a reporter, and in 1976 I began to explore, in fiction, these contemporary issues—particularly as they affect past, current, and potential attitudes toward women.

"My first novel, *Amberleigh,* was my Victorian-set update of what has been a model for so-called women's fiction since *Jane Eyre*—the Gothic. I call mine a 'feminist' Gothic. Submitting *Amberleigh* to publishers unsolicited resulted in getting it returned unread (because it was considered 'off market'—no sex) until playwright-author Garson Kanin volunteered to take it to his publisher. I interviewed Kanin on two separate occasions, and it was his enduring enthusiasm for my writing style that was the key to opening the door to publishing for me.

"Although fiction directed at a woman's audience is extremely lucrative to publishers right now, this very popularity, I discovered, hampers writers who want to expand on the publishers' current limitations of formula. Frustrated by the fact that 'transcending a genre,' as my books do, is considered a handicap rather than an advantage, I turned to applying my same themes in a more veiled and symbolic manner with *Six of Swords,* a fantasy which showed up on national science fiction/fantasy top-ten-bestseller lists its first week out and is now in its twelfth printing. . . . I've also written two mainstream science fiction novels, *Probe* and *Counterprobe.* I find [that] both fantasy and science fiction encourage originality and imagination, while so much of commercial fiction does not.

"Because of my undergraduate major in theatre, I'm especially interested in fiction that captures and affects an audience with the immediacy of a stage play. For this reason, I prefer working in 'popular' fiction forms and find nothing unusual in the idea of fiction being 'entertaining' as well as enlightening. After all, that is precisely what Dickens, Scott, Austen, and Dumas did for their audiences. I like to say that what I write is principally entertainment, but that the best entertainment always has principles.

"Like most writers, my constant battle is to write what I want to write, the way I want to write it, and get someone else to publish it. It's unfortunate that most new writers today face a publishing world that more and more can only afford to print established 'brand names' in hardcover fiction, and yet nothing has been done to enhance the reputation of softcover publishing. More serious, thorough review of paperback fiction, like that done by *West Coast Review of Books* and *Rave Reviews,* is vital. The few review channels that occasionally look at paperbacks are basically contemptuous of them and stick to reviewing the major lead titles the publishers are pushing. Often the better paperback originals are behind the upfront purveyors of sex and mayhem. Those who fight for quality in this field—writers and editors—are few, far between, and mostly engaged in rolling rocks uphill in Hades.

"In effect, I write on a fine line between 'serious' fiction on one hand and sneered-at 'popular' fiction on the other. It is not a particularly comfortable position, but somebody has to do it; otherwise, we will hve nothing but serious writers that nobody knows how to read and popular writers that nobody ought to read.

"As for 'illuminating personal data,' I suffer the reporter's malady of a general interest in almost every subject. My strongest interests are history, art and design, theatre, natural history, and literature. I collect vintage clothing and jewelry, ranging from 1850 to 1959, which I've sometimes integrated into my historical novels. A European tour during the summer of 1965 provided the Irish background for *Amberleigh.* Between the ages of fifteen and twenty-five I acted extensively in school and community theatre productions, a factor that has influenced the immediacy and empathy of my writing style. In theatre I never could decide whether I wanted most to act, direct, or design the production. Now, writing permits me to satisfy all disciplines at once and, furthermore, gives me control over the weather, which even David Belasco [American playwright and producer], the super realist, had to forego."

AVOCATIONAL INTERESTS: Graphic design, design and execution of silversmithed and strung jewelry, collecting fashion prints.

BIOGRAPHICAL/CRITICAL SOURCES:

PERIODICALS

Locus, August, 1982.
Minneapolis/St. Paul Magazine, November, 1981.
St. Paul Sunday Pioneer Press, September 14, 1980.
West Coast Review of Books, December, 1981.

*   *   *

DOWN, Goldie (Malvern) 1918-

PERSONAL: Born June 26, 1918, in Sydney, Australia; daughter of Herbert William (an insurance inspector) and Violet Marion (Knox) Scarr; married David Kyrle Down (a clergyman), September 8, 1946; children: Kendall, Glenda, Michele, Teddy, Richley, another daughter (adopted). *Education:* Attended Avondale College (New South Wales, Australia), 1940-42.

ADDRESSES: Home—2 Neridah Ave., Mount Colah 2079, Australia.

CAREER: Secretary in Australia, 1943-44; Seventh-Day Adventist missionary with her husband, in India, 1953-73; teacher of creative writing to adult students, principally at government evening colleges, 1976—; free-lance writer.

AWARDS, HONORS: Second prize in *Write Now* competition, Review & Herald, for *Fear Was the Pursuer.*

WRITINGS:

Missionary to Calcutta, Review and Herald, 1958.
Twenty-One Thousand Miles of Adventure, Southern Publishing, 1964.
God Plucked a Violet, Southern Publishing, 1968.
If I Have Twelve Sons, Southern Publishing, 1968.
Their Kind of Courage, Review and Herald, 1973.
No Forty Hour Week, Southern Publishing, 1977.
Kerri and Company, Review and Herald, 1978.
More Lives Than a Cat, Southern Publishing, 1979.
You Never Can Tell When You May Meet a Leopard, Review and Herald, 1980.
Fear Was the Pursuer, Review and Herald, 1981.
Missionaries Don't Cry, Review and Herald, 1981.
Like Fire in His Veins, Review and Herald, 1982.
We Gotta Tell Them, Edie Review and Herald, 1982.
Saga of an Ordinary Man, Pacific Press, 1984.
Feed Me Well, Ilona, Pacific Press, 1985.
Work for Your Dreams, Pacific Press, 1988.

Also author of *The Smiley Man* and *Paper in the Mud.* Contributor of numerous stories and articles to church and health periodicals.

WORK IN PROGRESS: A book on the customs of ancient Egypt, *Dead Men Do Tell Tales; There's No Magic Formula.*

SIDELIGHTS: Goldie Down told *CA* that three of the five Down children completed their entire twelve years of schooling in India by correspondence, with her help, before they returned to Australia to do college work. Three times the entire family travelled overland by jeep and trailer from India through the Middle East, and twice on to Europe and England. In addition to their own five children, the Downs have an adopted Indian daughter. Down claims to be a compulsive writer and writes solely for her own pleasure, hoping that those who read her writings may also be entertained, instructed, or amused by her efforts. She explained that her writings are all truth, not fiction.

*   *   *

DOWNIE, John 1931-

PERSONAL: Born December 12, 1931, in Glasgow, Scotland; naturalized Canadian citizen; married Mary Alice Dawe Hunter (a writer), June 27, 1959; children: Christine, Jocelyn, Alexandra. *Education:* University of Glasgow, B.Sc., 1953; University of Toronto, M.A.Sc., 1956, Ph.D., 1959.

ADDRESSES: Home—190 Union St., Kingston, Ontario, Canada K7L 2P6. *Office*—Department of Chemical Engineering, Queen's University, Kingston, Ontario, Canada K7L 3N6.

CAREER: Research engineer at Gulf Research & Development Co., 1959-62; Queen's University, Kingston, Ontario, 1962—, began as assistant professor, became associate professor, currently professor of chemical engineering, 1971—.

MEMBER: Chemical Institute of Canada, Canadian Society of Chemical Engineering.

AWARDS, HONORS: Second prize, children's section (with wife, Mary Alice Downie), 4th CBC Literary Competition, 1982, for "Bright Paddles."

WRITINGS:

FOR YOUNG PEOPLE

(With wife, Mary Alice Downie) *Honor Bound,* illustrated by Joan Huffman, Oxford University Press, 1971.
(Contributor with M. A. Downie) *Inside Outside,* Holt, 1978.
(Contributor with M. A. Downie) *Measure Me Sky,* Ginn & Co., 1979.
(With M. A. Downie) *Alison's Ghosts,* illustrated by Paul McCusker, Thomas Nelson, 1984.
(Contributor with M. A. Downie) *Thread the Needle,* Holt, 1987.

*   *   *

DOWNIE, Mary Alice (Dawe) 1934-

PERSONAL: Born February 12, 1934, in Alton, Ill.; daughter of Robert Grant and Doris Mary (Rogers) Hunter; married John Downie (a professor of chemical engineering and a writer), June 27, 1959; children: Christine, Jocelyn, Alexandra. *Education:* University of Toronto, B.A. (with honors), 1955. *Religion:* Anglican.

ADDRESSES: Home—190 Union St., Kingston, Ontario, Canada K7L 2P6.

CAREER: Reporter, *Marketing Magazine,* 1955-56; editorial assistant, *Canadian Medical Association Journal,* 1956-57; Oxford University Press, Canadian Branch, Toronto, Ontario, publicity manager, 1958-59; free-lance writer, 1959—; *Kingston Whig-Standard,* Kingston, Ontario, book review editor, 1973-78.

MEMBER: PEN, Writers Union of Canada (chairman of membership committee, 1986-87), Canadian Society of Children's Authors, Illustrators, and Performers (CANSCAIP).

AWARDS, HONORS: Ontario Council for the Arts awards, 1970, 1975, 1978, 1981, and 1987; Canada Council Arts awards, 1972-73 and 1981-82; Exploration Grant, 1984; second prize, children's section (with husband, John Downie), 4th CBC Literary Competition, 1982, for "Bright Paddles."

WRITINGS:

FOR YOUNG PEOPLE

(Compiler with Barbara Robertson) *The Wind Has Wings: Poems from Canada,* illustrated by Elizabeth Cleaver, Oxford University Press, 1968, revised edition, 1984.
(With husband, John Downie) *Honor Bound,* illustrated by Joan Huffman, Oxford University Press, 1971.
Scared Sarah, illustrated by Laszlo Gal, Thomas Nelson, 1974.
The Magical Adventures of Pierre, illustrated by Yuksel Hassan, Thomas Nelson, 1974.
Dragon on Parade, illustrated by Mary Lynn Baker, PMA Books, 1974.
The Witch of the North: Folktales from French Canada, illustrated by Cleaver, Oberon, 1975.
(Contributor with J. Downie) *Inside Outside,* Holt, 1978.
(Contributor with J. Downie) *Measure Me Sky,* Ginn & Co., 1979.
(Contributor) *Crossroads I,* Van Nostrand Reinhold, 1979.
The King's Loon, illustrated by Ron Berg, Kids Can Press, 1979.
(Contributor) *Storytellers Rendezvous,* Canadian Library Association, 1980.
The Last Ship, illustrated by Lissa Calvert, PMA Books, 1980.

(Compiler with Mary Hamilton) *And Some Brought Flowers: Plants in a New World,* illustrated by John Revell, University of Toronto Press, 1980.
(Contributor) *Out and About,* Academic Press, 1981.
(With George Rawlyk) *A Proper Acadian,* illustrated by Berg, Kids Can Press, 1981.
(With Jillian Gilliland) *Seeds and Weeds: A Book of Country Crafts,* Four Winds Press, 1981.
Jenny Greenteeth, illustrated by Anne Powell, Rhino Books, 1981.
The Wicked Fairy-Wife, illustrated by Kim Price, Kids Can Press, 1983.
(With J. Downie) *Alison's Ghost,* illustrated by Paul McCusker, Thomas Nelson, 1984.
(With Gilliland) *Stones and Cones,* Scholastic, Inc., 1984.
(Contributor) *All in Good Time,* McGraw-Hill, 1985.
(With Elizabeth Greene and M. A. Thompson) *The Window of Dreams: New Canadian Writing for Children,* Methuen, 1986.
(Contributor with J. Downie) *Thread the Needle,* Holt, 1987.
(Contributor) *Winter Welcomes,* Thomas Nelson, 1987.
(With Robertson) *The Well-Filled Cupboard: Everyday Pleasures of Home and Garden,* Lester & Orpen Dennys, 1987.
(With Gilliland) *How the Devil Got His Cat,* Quarry Press, 1988.

OTHER

Founding editor, "Northern Lights" series, Clarke Irwin, and "Kids Canada" series, Kids Canada Press. Also contributor to *Canadian Children's Annual,* 1978, 1979, and 1987. Contributor of articles to *Horn Book, Pittsburgh Press, Kingston Whig-Standard Magazine, Ottawa Citizen, Globe and Mail* (Toronto), *United Church Observer, OWL, Chickadee,* and *Crackers.*

SIDELIGHTS: Mary Alice Downie once told *CA:* "I write different books for different reasons. The anthologies and folktales are a kind of literary archeology, rescuing neglected materials from obscure journals and university stacks, finding and sharing lost treasures. The historical books are written for a range of ages and are meant to involve Canadian children with their country's past. The other stories are just for fun although they probably convey a quaintly old-fashioned belief in the strength and importance of the family."

*   *   *

DOYLE, Charles (Desmond) 1928-
(Mike Doyle)

PERSONAL: Born October 18, 1928, in Birmingham, England; son of Charles and Mary (Carroll) Doyle; married Helen Merlyn Lopdell, November 26, 1952 (deceased); married Doran Ross Smithells, July 28, 1959; children: (second marriage) Aaron William, Patrick Haakon, Kegan Ross, Mary Elizabeth Katharine. *Education:* Victoria University College, University of New Zealand (now Victoria University of Wellington), B.A., 1956, M.A. (honors), 1958; Wellington Teachers' College, Diploma of Teaching, 1955; University of Auckland, Ph.D., 1968. *Politics:* "Socialist anarchist." *Religion:* Catholic.

ADDRESSES: Home—759 Helvetia Crescent, Victoria, British Columbia, Canada. *Office*—Department of English, University of Victoria, Victoria, British Columbia, Canada.

CAREER: University of Auckland, Auckland, New Zealand, lecturer, 1961-66, senior lecturer in English and American literature, 1966-68; University of Victoria, Victoria, British Columbia, associate professor, 1968-76, professor of English and American literature, 1976—. Visiting fellow in American studies, Yale University, 1967-68. *Military service:* Royal Navy.

MEMBER: League of Canadian Poets, Canadian Union of Writers, Canadian Association of University Teachers.

AWARDS, HONORS: UNESCO creative artist's fellowship, 1959; American Council of Learned Societies fellow at Yale University, 1967-68; Canada Council grants, 1971, 1972, fellowship, 1974-75; Social Sciences and Humanities Research Council of Canada fellowship, 1982-83.

WRITINGS:

POETRY

A Splinter of Glass: Poems, 1951-56, Pegasus, 1956.
(With James K. Baxter, Louis Johnson, and Kendrick Smithyman) *The Night Shift: Poems on Aspects of Love*, Capricorn Press, 1957.
Distances: Poems, 1956-61, Paul's Book Arcade (Auckland), 1963.
Messages for Herod, Collins, 1965.
A Sense of Place, Wai-te-Ata Press, 1965.
Earth Meditations: 2, Alldritt, 1968.
Noah, Soft Press, 1970.
(Under pseudonym Mike Doyle) *Abandoned Sofa*, Soft Press, 1971.
(Under pseudonym Mike Doyle) *Earth Meditations: One to Five*, Coach House Press, 1971.
(Under pseudonym Mike Doyle) *Earth Shot*, Exeter Books, 1972.
(Under pseudonym Mike Doyle) *Preparing for the Ark*, Weed/Flower Press, 1973.
(Under pseudonym Mike Doyle) *Planes*, Seripress, 1975.
(Under pseudonym Mike Doyle) *Stone-dancer*, Oxford University Press, 1976.
(Under pseudonym Mike Doyle) *A Steady Hand*, Porcupine's Quill, 1983.

NONFICTION

(Editor) *Recent Poetry in New Zealand*, Collins, 1965.
R.A.K. Mason, Twayne, 1970.
James K. Baxter, Twayne, 1976.
(Editor) *William Carlos Williams: The Critical Heritage*, Routledge & Kegan Paul, 1980.
William Carlos Williams and the American Poem, Macmillan, 1982.
(Co-editor) *The New Reality: The Politics of Restraint in British Columbia*, New Star, 1984.
(Editor) *Wallace Stevens: The Critical Heritage*, Routledge & Kegan Paul, 1985.
(Co-editor) *After Bennett: A New Politics for British Columbia*, New Star, 1986.
Richard Aldington: A Biography, Macmillan, in press.

CONTRIBUTOR TO ANTHOLOGIES

Twentieth Century New Zealand Poetry, edited by Vincent O'Sullivan, Oxford University Press, 1970.
Contemporary Poetry of British Columbia, edited by J. M. Yates, Sono Nis, 1970.
New Zealand Poetry: An Introduction, edited by F. M. McKay, New Zealand University Press, 1970.

OTHER

Contributor of poetry to periodicals, and critical essays to professional journals.

SIDELIGHTS: Charles Doyle wrote *CA:* "There has to be a new politics, decentralized, energized from the grass-roots, a new economic structure world-wide and the struggle for a just peace and multilateral control of armaments must continue."

AVOCATIONAL INTERESTS: Taoism, T'ai Chi, tennis, open form poetry, and the music of Hayden, Mozart, and C.P.E. Bach.

*　　　*　　　*

DOYLE, Denis P. 1940-

PERSONAL: Born April 22, 1940, in Chicago, Ill.; son of Phil A. and Alyce D. Doyle; married Gloria Revilla; children: Alicia, Christopher. *Education:* University of California, Berkeley, A.B., 1962, M.A., 1964.

ADDRESSES: Home—110 Summerfield Rd., Chevy Chase, Md. 20815. *Office*—Hudson Institute, 4401 Ford Ave., Suite 200, Alexandria, Va. 22302.

CAREER: Sequoia Institute, Sacramento, Calif., president, 1968-72; U.S. Office of Economic Opportunity, Washington, D.C., director of Voucher Project, 1972-73; National Institute of Education, Washington, D.C., assistant director of education finance, 1973-79; Brookings Institution, Washington, D.C., federal executive fellow, 1979-80; American Enterprise Institute for Public Policy Research, Washington, D.C., director of education policy studies, 1981-86; Hudson Institute, Alexandria, Va., senior research fellow, 1986—. Member of board of directors of Sequoia Institute.

MEMBER: American Educational Research Association.

WRITINGS:

Debating National Education Policy: The Question of Standards, American Enterprise Institute for Public Policy Research, 1981.
(Co-author) *Excellence in Education: The States Take Charge*, American Enterprise Institute for Public Policy Research, 1985.
(Co-author) *Investing in Our Children: Business and the Public Schools*, Committee for Economic Development, 1985.
(With David T. Kearns) *Winning the Brain Race: A Bold Plan to Make Our Schools Competitive*, ICS Press, 1988.

CONTRIBUTOR

Paul A. Olsen and others, editors, *Education for 1984*, University of Nebraska Press, 1971.
Joel Bergsman and Howard L. Wiener, editors, *Urban Problems Public Policy Choice*, Praeger, 1975.
Lawrence Chickering, editor, *Parents, Teachers, and Children: Prospects for Choice in American Education*, ICS Press, 1977.
Susan Abramowitz, editor, *The Private High School Today: A Survey of Private School Heads*, U.S. Government Printing Office, 1981.
Edward McGlynn Gaffney, editor, *Private Schools and the Public Good: Alternatives for the Eighties*, University of Notre Dame Press, 1981.
Jack A. Meyer, editor, *Meeting Human Needs: Toward a New Public Philosophy*, American Enterprise Institute for Public Policy Research, 1982.

OTHER

Also contributor to *Standard Education Almanac* and *International Encyclopedia of Education*. Contributor of nearly fifty articles to education journals, popular magazines, and newspapers, including *California Journal* and *New Republic*. Member of board of editorial consultants, *Phi Delta Kappan*.

SIDELIGHTS: Denis P. Doyle told *CA:* "At an early age my father told me, 'If you can't put it in writing, you don't know what you're thinking.' The comment has never left me. My field is public policy analysis, and because I am convinced that much public policy is only weakly supported by evidence, my role is constructive critic. I write, then, to test my own ideas and to reach opinion makers, those who eventually establish public policy. I balance my work between professional journals and mass publications to keep my research and analytic skills sharpened as I satisfy the stylistic demands of different publications."

*　　*　　*

DOYLE, Mike
    See DOYLE, Charles (Desmond)

*　　*　　*

DUNBAR, David
    See BAXTER, Craig

*　　*　　*

DUNDES, Alan   **1934-**

PERSONAL: Surname is pronounced *Dun*-deez; born September 8, 1934, in New York, N.Y.; son of Maurice (an attorney) and Helen (Rothschild) Dundes; married Carolyn Browne, September 8, 1958; children: Alison, Lauren, David. *Education:* Yale University, B.A., 1955, M.A.T., 1958; Indiana University, Ph.D., 1962.

ADDRESSES: Home—1590 La Vereda, Berkeley, Calif. 94708. *Office*—Department of Anthropology, University of California, Berkeley, Calif. 94720.

CAREER: University of Kansas, Lawrence, instructor in English, 1962-63; University of California, Berkeley, assistant professor of anthropology, 1963-65, associate professor, 1965-68, professor of anthropology and folklore, 1968—. *Military service:* U.S. Navy, 1955-57; became lieutenant.

MEMBER: American Folklore Society, American Anthropological Association, California Folklore Society.

AWARDS, HONORS: Second place in Chicago Folklore Prize competition for *The Morphology of North American Indian Folktales;* Guggenheim fellowship, 1966-67; senior fellowship, National Endowment for the Humanities, 1972-73.

WRITINGS:

The Morphology of North American Indian Folktales, Academic Scientarium Fennica, 1964.
(Editor) *The Study of Folklore*, Prentice-Hall, 1965.
(Editor) *Every Man His Way: Readings in Cultural Anthropology*, Prentice-Hall, 1968.
(Editor) *Mother Wit from the Laughing Barrel: Readings in the Interpretation of Afro-American Folklore*, Prentice-Hall, 1973.
(With Alessandro Falassi) *La Terra in Piazza: An Interpretation of the Palio of Siena*, University of California Press, 1975.

(With Carl R. Pagter) *Urban Folklore from the Paperwork Empire*, American Folklore Society, 1975.
Analytic Essays in Folklore, Mouton, 1975.
(Compiler) *Folklore Theses and Dissertations in the United States*, University of Texas Press, 1976.
Interpreting Folklore, Indiana University Press, 1980.
(Editor) *The Evil Eye: A Folklore Casebook*, Garland Publishing, 1981.
(Editor with Wolfgang Mieder) *The Wisdom of Many: Essays on the Proverb*, Garland Publishing, 1981.
(With Claudia A. Stibbe) *The Art of Mixing Metaphors: A Folkloristic Interpretation of the "Netherlands Proverbs," by Pieter Bruegel the Elder*, Academia Scientiarum Fennica, 1981.
(Editor) *Cinderella: A Folklore Casebook*, Garland Publishing, 1982.
(Editor with Lowell Edmunds) *Oedipus: A Folklore Casebook*, Garland Publishing, 1983.
Life Is Like a Chicken Coop Ladder: A Portrait of German Culture through Folklore, Columbia University Press, 1984.
(Editor) *Sacred Narrative: Readings in the Theory of Myth*, University of California Press, 1984.
(With C. Banc) *First Prize: Fifteen Years! An Annotated Collection of Romanian Political Jokes*, Associated University Presses, 1986.
(Editor with Galit Hasan-Rokem) *The Wandering Jew: Essays in the Interpretation of a Christian Legend*, Indiana University Press, 1986.
(With Carl R. Pagter) *When You're Up to Your Ass in Alligators: More Urban Folklore from the Paperwork Empire*, Wayne State University Press, 1987.
Cracking Jokes: Studies of Sick Humor Cycles and Stereotypes, Ten Speed Press, 1987.
Parsing through Customs: Essays by a Freudian Folklorist, University of Wisconsin Press, 1987.

Contributor to professional journals.

SIDELIGHTS: Folklorist Alan Dundes writes about a wide range of sometimes unconventional material, from traditional fables to xeroxed office memos. *Cinderella: A Folklore Casebook* interprets the familiar story from several academic viewpoints. *Times Literary Supplement* contributor T. A. Shippey praises Dundes' even selection of essays by "structuralists, Jungians, anthroposophists *et al.*" He continues, "the main message of this collection is 'armchair critics should at least review the literature': and every facility is offered for that in future, with long bibliographies and masterly introductions by Dundes to each of the essays selected." *Cracking Jokes: Studies of Sick Humor Cycles and Stereotypes* ties jokes with the often sexual or racial message they offhandedly convey. According to Dundes, jokes are "effective as socially sanctioned outlets for expressing taboo ideas and subject." In *Chicago Tribune Books*, Clarence Petersen notes that Dundes "knows why jokes are funny, as well as to whom and under what circumstances. Because he knows, too, that brevity is the soul of wit, he does not analyze jokes to death." *When You're Up to Your Ass in Alligators* also looks at common modern communication not always termed as folklore. "What others dismiss as dirty jokes, pranks and low-brow humor, Dundes defends as genuine American folklore," states Jeff Kunerth in the *Chicago Tribune*. He continues that Dundes' book "includes examples of phony correspondence, fake business cards, parodied poems, nonsensical instructions and satirical memos. Much of it reveals a cynical disgust with bureaucracy and incompetence.'' Most of the book's examples were initially transmitted through office photocopiers. ''Not everyone can tell a joke,'' Dundes explains. ''But anyone can operate a Xerox machine.''

BIOGRAPHICAL/CRITICAL SOURCES:

BOOKS

Dundes, Alan, and Carl R. Pagter, *When You're Up to Your Ass in Alligators: More Urban Folklore from the Paperwork Empire,* Wayne State University Press, 1987.

PERIODICALS

California Monthly, Volume 74, number 1, October, 1965.
Chicago Tribune, February 5, 1988.
Los Angeles Times Book Review, July 7, 1985.
New York Times Book Review, January 24, 1988.
Times Literary Supplement, July 22, 1983.
Tribune Books (Chicago), May 3, 1987.

E

EBAN, Abba (Solomon) 1915-
(Aubrey Eban)

PERSONAL: Surname originally Solomon; later adopted step-father's name, Eban; born February 2, 1915, in Cape Town, South Africa; emigrated to England, 1915; son of Abraham Meir Solomon and Alida (Sachs) Solomon Eban; married Susan Ambache, March 18, 1945; children: Eli, Gila. *Education:* Queen's College, Cambridge, B.A., 1931, M.A. (triple first class honors), 1938. *Religion:* Jewish.

ADDRESSES: Office—The Knesset, Jerusalem, Israel.

CAREER: Cambridge University, Pembroke College, Cambridge, England, research fellow and tutor in Oriental languages, 1939; Allied Headquarters, Jerusalem, Palestine (now Israel), liaison officer to Jewish population, 1942-44; Middle East Arab Centre, Jerusalem, chief instructor, 1944-46; Jewish Agency for Palestine, Political Department, Jerusalem, member of staff, 1946-47, liaison officer to United Nations, 1947; appointed representative of provisional government of Israel to United Nations, 1948; head of Israeli mission to United Nations, 1948-53, also serving as vice-president of U.N. General Assembly, 1953; Israeli ambassador to United States, 1950-59; elected to Israel's Knesset, 1959, serving as Minister without Portfolio, 1959-60, and Minister of Education and Culture, 1960-63; Deputy Prime Minister of Israel, 1963-66, Minister of Foreign Affairs, 1966-74; member of foreign affairs and security commission of Knesset, 1974—.

President of Weizmann Institute of Science, 1958-66; vice-president of United Nations Conference on Science and Technology in Advancement of New States, 1963; head of Israeli delegation to United Nations General Assembly, 1964; member of United Nations Advisory Committee on Science and Technology for Development. Visiting professor, Columbia University, 1974, and Institute of Advanced Study, Princeton University, 1978. Host of Public Broadcasting Corporation series, "Heritage: Civilization and the Jews," 1984. *Military service:* British Army, 1939-46; became major; served in Middle East.

MEMBER: World Academy of Arts and Sciences (fellow), American Academy of Arts and Sciences (foreign member).

AWARDS, HONORS: Honorary degrees from New York University, Boston University, University of Maryland, University of Cincinnati, Lehigh University, Brandeis University, Dropsie College, Yeshiva University, Temple University, Chicago Institute of Jewish Studies, Hebrew Union College, Jewish Theological Seminary, Tel Aviv University.

WRITINGS:

(Translator and editor under name Aubrey Eban) Leo Pinsker, *Auto-Emancipation,* Federation of Zionist Youth (London), 1939.

The Modern Literary Movement in Egypt, [London], 1946.

(Translator from the Arabic under name Aubrey Eban) Tawfiq al-Hakim, *The Maze of Justice* (novel), Harvill Press, 1947.

Social and Cultural Problems in the Middle East, [London], 1947.

The Toynbee Heresy, Israel Office of Information (New York), 1955.

Voice of Israel, Horizon Press, 1957, revised edition, 1969.

The Tide of Nationalism, Horizon Press, 1959.

Chaim Weizman: A Collective Biography, Weidenfeld & Nicolson, 1962.

Israel in the World (transcript of two television interviews), W. H. Allen, 1966.

My People: The Story of the Jews, Behrman House, 1968.

(Author of foreword) Avigdor Dagan, *Moscow and Jerusalem,* Abelard, 1971.

My Country: The Story of Modern Israel, Random House, 1972.

Abba Eban: An Autobiography, Random House, 1977.

Promised Land, illustrated by Gordon Wetmore, Thomas Nelson, 1978.

The New Diplomacy: International Affairs in the Modern Age, Random House, 1983.

Heritage: Civilization and the Jews (companion volume to Public Broadcasting Corporation series of the same title), Summit Books, 1984.

Israel: The First Forty Years, Scribner, 1987.

Also author of *Reality and Vision in the Middle East,* 1965. Contributor to learned journals in English, French, Hebrew, and Arabic.

SIDELIGHTS: Diplomat, gifted orator, and scholar, Abba Eban represented the emerging nation of Israel in the international arena for nearly thirty years. Alfred Friendly states in the

Washington Post Book World that no single man in Israel's short national history "ever projected to the world [Israel's] essence and its anguish, its vision and its spirit, in nobler and more exalted terms or won more credit in doing it." Since 1947 Eban has served as a vocal proponent of Israel's interests, first in the United Nations from 1947 until 1959, then as Israeli ambassador to the United States from 1950 to 1959, and then in a variety of prominent political posts in Israel itself, including Deputy Prime Minister and Minister of Foreign Affairs. As Seymour Siegel notes in the *Saturday Review*, Eban's long career "has projected him onto the stage of world politics, where his superb command of the language, his controlled yet effective passion have made him the best-known Jewish voice of our time." A master of more than a half-dozen European and Middle Eastern languages, and a Cambridge University-educated academician, Eban has authored a number of well-received books about the Jews' place in history and about Israel's turbulent birth as a modern Jewish homeland. Critics of works such as *My People: The Story of the Jews, Abba Eban: An Autobiography, The New Diplomacy: International Affairs in the Modern Age,* and *Heritage: Civilization and the Jews,* consistently cite Eban for his accessible descriptions of highly complex events. Toronto *Globe and Mail* contributor John Gellner calls Eban "the archetype of a highly gifted person who has made the best of his native endowment." Gellner adds: "If anybody is qualified to evaluate diplomacy in our age, it is Abba Eban, scholar and political practitioner. He has yet another qualification: his writing is mellifluent, yet wonderfully clear."

Eban was born in South Africa, but his parents moved to England while he was still an infant. Shortly thereafter, his father died; the surname Eban comes from a stepfather. As a youngster growing up in one of London's poorer districts, Eban concentrated on his education seven days per week—he went to public school and learned Hebrew on weekends. His achievements earned him a scholarship to Queen's College, Cambridge, where he excelled in debates and languages, especially Arabic and Persian. After receiving his Bachelor's degree in 1931, he went on to study for a Master's, and earned it with triple first class honors in 1938. By that year he had become quite active in the Zionist movement in London, and the ensuing events of World War II only strengthened his dedication to the notion of a Jewish nation in Palestine. He served in the British army in the Middle East during the war, staying in Jerusalem when a restoration of peace revealed the extent of devastation wreaked on European Jewry by Nazi Germany.

Eban was thirty-two when he was named to the United Nations Special Commission on Palestine. According to Gellner, the young diplomat "helped to bring about the partition of what was then a territory under British mandate, which led to the establishment of the State of Israel." In 1948 Eban began to represent the new country in the United Nations, and he quickly gained a reputation as an eloquent and impassioned orator. "Anyone who has ever heard Abba Eban deliver a speech before the United Nations will remember forever the occasion, the man, and the acerbic style of classical rhetoric," contends Dan Isaac in the *Saturday Review*. Eban dedicated himself to the task of recruiting public and international support for Israel; particularly in America, he was very successful. *Commentary* reviewer Ben Halpern writes that Eban "attributes his own achievements as much to the cultivation of public opinion as to the persuasive and reasonable argument with policy-makers. And indeed, Mr. Eban was taken to the heart of the American public. Diaspora Jewry in particular saw him as its own

fair-haired boy." The Israeli government, grateful to have found such a charismatic spokesman, made Eban ambassador to the United States in 1950, a post he held until 1959.

Eban returned to Israel in 1959 and was promptly elected to the Knesset. The 1960s saw his political power wax to its highest point as he served as Minister of Education and Culture from 1960-63, Deputy Prime Minister from 1963-66, and Minister of Foreign Affairs from 1966-74. The scope of his experience and his central diplomatic role during such events as the 1967 Six Day War and the 1973 Yom Kippur War made Eban "a valuable witness to all the vicissitudes of Israel," according to a *Choice* reviewer. As Friendly observes, however, Eban was denied the highest position in Israel—Prime Minister—probably because his tasks kept him abroad much of the time. "He can take small comfort from being the central figure in a piece of irony," Friendly writes. "He worked for Israel's interests as valiantly and successfully abroad as anyone at home; but just as a prophet is without honor in his own country, so is a politician when he is *not* in his country."

Eban's books are acclaimed for their intellect and for their penetrating analyses of current affairs. In the *New York Times Book Review*, Nelson Glueck comments that in works by Eban, "Everything is seen through the prism of his own tremendous knowledge and deeply reflective and sensitive personality." *Times Literary Supplement* contributor Adam Watson writes: "Dedicated Israeli as he is, [Eban] retains an urbane and quizzical English style which was already evident in his Cambridge days. These two qualities make his books at once authoritative and readable." Indeed, Eban writes in English, often for British or American publishing houses, and his works command a wide audience of intellectuals and general readers alike. A *Times Literary Supplement* reviewer observes that Eban's "eloquence as the spokesman of Israel . . . never wearies. He is a master of the soothing and pathetic, and also of the devastating, phrase." In 1984 Eban broadened his audience even further when he hosted a Public Broadcasting System series entitled "Heritage: Civilization and the Jews." The companion volume to the shows, also entitled *Heritage: Civilization and the Jews,* was a bestseller; it explores the long and dramatic history of the Jewish people and their contributions to human advancement. Commenting on his own feelings of achievement in his 1977 title *Abba Eban: An Autobiography,* the author writes: "My main satisfaction is that many people across the world may have learned from me that the Israel story, with its culmination in Israel's statehood, is a brave and noble adventure."

Kenneth Lindsay notes in *Spectator* that after more than forty years of "breathless activity," Eban is "still striding the corridors of power, urbane, self-controlled and dedicated." Since 1974, he has served as a member of the Knesset's foreign affairs and security commission, counselling Labor party leaders on foreign policy positions. Eban also continues to write about Israel from his unique position among its most erudite founding fathers. In *My People: The Story of the Jews* he claims: "A special role was thrust upon me at an early public age and has clung to me ever since. My vocation has been to explain the Jewish people to a confused and often uncomprehending world. The central fact in modern Jewish experience has been the renewal of Israel's statehood." Glueck feels that as an author, Eban "has brilliantly measured up to the demands of his compelling subject." In Eban's hands, Glueck concludes, the stories of Jewish history become a "deeply personal and moving psalm of glorious quality on the theme of miraculous rebirth, indomitable vitality and enduring significance of Israel.''

BIOGRAPHICAL/CRITICAL SOURCES:

BOOKS

Eban, Abba, *My People: The Story of the Jews,* Behrman House, 1968.
Eban, Abba, *Abba Eban: An Autobiography,* Random House, 1977.

PERIODICALS

Choice, May, 1978.
Christian Science Monitor, May 9, 1957.
Commentary, May, 1978.
Contemporary Review, March, 1984.
Globe and Mail (Toronto), March 24, 1984.
Los Angeles Times Book Review, October 9, 1983, November 6, 1983.
Newsweek, January 16, 1978.
New Yorker, December 19, 1977.
New York Herald Tribune Book Review, June 2, 1957.
New York Times, December 14, 1968.
New York Times Book Review, May 5, 1957, September 6, 1959, January 12, 1969, March 16, 1969, December 18, 1977, November 6, 1983.
Saturday Review, June 1, 1957, February 1, 1969, December 10, 1977.
Spectator, February 18, 1978.
Times Literary Supplement, November 10, 1966, October 30, 1969, May 25, 1973, June 29, 1984.
Washington Post Book World, December 18, 1977, November 20, 1983.†

—Sketch by Anne Janette Johnson

*   *   *

EBAN, Aubrey
    See EBAN, Abba (Solomon)

*   *   *

EDBERG, Rolf   1912-

PERSONAL: Born March 14, 1912, in Lysvik, Sweden; married Astrid Persson, 1937; children: Joergen, Ranveig Jacobsson, Birgitta.

ADDRESSES: Home—Hagtornsgatan 3, 652 30 Karlstad, Sweden.

CAREER: Oskarshamns Nyheter, Oskarshamm, Sweden, chief editor, 1934-37; *Oestgoeten,* Linkoeping, Sweden, chief editor, 1938-44; *Ny Tid,* Gothenburg, Sweden, chief editor, 1945-56; Swedish ambassador to Norway, 1956-67; governor of Swedish province of Vaermland, 1967-77. Member of Swedish Parliament, 1940-44 and 1948-56. Delegate to Council of Europe, 1949-52, United Nations, 1952-55, 1957, 1960-61, Northern Council, 1953-56, and Disarmament Conference, 1961-65.

MEMBER: Swedish Press Club (president, 1951-53), Swedish Association of Writers, Pen Club, Swedish Association of Biologists, Swedish Royal Academy of Sciences, Swedish Society for Anthropology and Geography.

AWARDS, HONORS: Socrates Prize, 1972, from School of Adult Education; gold medal, 1974, from Royal Swedish Academy of Science; Doctor Honoris Causa, 1974, from University of Gothenburg; gold medal, 1976, from Geographical-Anthropological Society; Selma Lagerloef's Prize, 1976; Dag Hammarskjoeld Medal, 1978; King's Medal, 1981; gold medal from government of Sweden, 1984; Nordic Environmental Prize, 1984; Let Live! Award, 1985; Premio Mondiale delle Cultura, 1985; Natur och Kultur's Cultural Prize, 1987.

WRITINGS:

Nansen, european: En studie i vilja och god-vilja (title means ''Nansen, the European: A Study in Will and Good Will''), Tiden, 1961.
Spillran av ett moln, Norstedt, 1966, translation by Sven Aahman published as *On the Shred of a Cloud: Notes in a Travel Book,* University of Alabama Press, 1969, same translation published as *On the Shred of a Cloud: Reflections on Man and His Environment,* Harper, 1971.
Vid traedets fot, Norstedt, 1971, translation by David Mel Paul and Margareta Paul published as *At the Foot of the Tree: A Wanderer's Musings before the Fall,* University of Alabama Press, 1974.
Brev till Columbus (title means ''Letters to Columbus''), Norstedt, 1973.
Ett hus i kosmos (title means ''A House in the Cosmos''), Esselte Studium, 1974.
Dalens Ande, Norstedt, 1976, translation by Keith Bradfield published as *The Dream of Kilimanjaro,* Pantheon, 1979.
Skuggor oever Savannen (title means ''Shadows across the Savannah''), Bra Boecker & Trevi, 1977.
De glittrande vattnens land (title means ''The Land of Glittering Waters''), Bra Boecker & Norstedts, 1980.
(Editor) *Haer aer vi hemma* (title means ''This Is Our Home''), Bra Boecker & Norstedts, 1982.
(Editor) *Vaart hotade hem* (title means ''Our Threatened Home''), Bra Boecker & Norstedts, 1983.
Droppar av vatten, droppar av act (title means ''Drops of Water, Drops of Years''), Bra Boecker & Norstedts, 1984.
. . . och de seglade staendigt (title means ''. . . and They Always Sailed''), Norstedts, 1986.
Aarsbarn med Plejaderna (title means ''Born with the Pleiades''), Norstedts, 1987.
(With Alexey Yablokov) *Soendag aer foer sent* (title means ''Sunday Is Too Late''), Norstedts, 1988.

Also author of *Ge dem en chans* (title means ''Give Them a Chance''), 1939, *I morgon Norden* (title means ''Tomorrow Nordic''), 1944, *Demokratisk linje* (title means ''Democratic Line''), 1948, *Femte etappen* (title means ''The Fifth Stage''), 1949, *Oeppna grindarna* (title means ''Open the Gates''), 1952, and *Paa jordens villkor* (title means ''On Earth's Terms''), 1974.

SIDELIGHTS: Rolf Edberg writes to *CA:* ''I grew up in a fresh and beautiful countryside and very early I got in contact with the science of evolution, which started a lifelong interest in natural sciences. The first book about man's condition was created in order to disentangle my own meditating threads and to put man's moment on earth in a bigger continuity. We have in our constantly greedy searching acquired an ever increasing richness in knowledge of details and have been forced into an even harder specialization. However, nature is interaction, not separation. What we have to do today is to place our varying knowledge under a unifying comprehensive view giving us a vision of our destiny. My ambition as a layman has been to arrive at such a comprehensive view.

"The scientific literature—especially in the environmental field—published in the United States has given me great inspiration in my work. Europe has a lot to learn from the American research which is the most advanced in the world. But I believe that America, highly urbanized, has some to learn from the Scandinavian people with their natural love of nature.

"And that is the way it ought to be: that we learn from each other's research, thinking, and experience."

MEDIA ADAPTATIONS: Dalens Ande was adapted as a symphony by the Finnish composer, Henrik Otto Donner.

BIOGRAPHICAL/CRITICAL SOURCES:

PERIODICALS

Chicago Tribune Book World, May 20, 1979.

* * *

EDMONDSON, G. C.   1922-
(Garry C. Edmondson; pseudonyms: Kelly P. Gast, J. B. Masterson, Mario Murphy)

PERSONAL: Original name, Jose Mario Garry Ordonez Edmondson y Cotton; born October 11, 1922, in the United States (some biographical sources cite birthplace as Hermosa de Rascuachitlan, Tabasco, Mexico); son of William J. Edmondson and Edith Cotton; married Carmen Medrano Paez; children: two sons, two daughters. *Education:* "Damn little; Percussion U."

ADDRESSES: Home—12328 Rockcrest, Lakeside, Calif. 92040. *Agent*—Robert P. Mills, Ltd., 333 Fifth Ave., New York, N.Y. 10016.

CAREER: Writer. Blacksmith and weapons maker. *Military service:* U.S. Marine Corps, 1942-46.

MEMBER: Science Fiction Writers of America, Western Writers of America.

WRITINGS:

The Ship That Sailed the Time Stream [and] *Stranger Than You Think* (novels), Ace Books, 1965.
Chapayeca (novel), Doubleday, 1971, published as *Blue Face,* Daw Books, 1972.
T.H.E.M. (novel), Doubleday, 1974.
The Aluminum Man (novel), Berkley, 1975.
(Under name Garry C. Edmondson; with Leroy A. Scheck) *Practical Welding* (nonfiction), Bruce, 1976.
Le Livre noir d'haute cuisine (dictionary), Bookmaker, 1977.
(With T. J. Roybal) *The Basic Book of Home Maintenance and Repair* (nonfiction), American Technical Society, 1979.
(Under name Garry C. Edmondson; with Richard Little) *Diesel Mechanics: An Introduction* (nonfiction), Wadsworth, 1982.
(With C. M. Kotlan) *The Takeover* (novel), Ace Books, 1984.
(With Kotlan) *The Black Magician* (novel), Ballantine, 1986.
(With Kotlan) *Maximum Effort* (novel), Ballantine, 1987.

UNDER PSEUDONYM KELLY P. GAST; WESTERN NOVELS

Dil Dies Hard, Doubleday, 1975.
Murphy's Trail, Doubleday, 1976.
The Long North Trail, Doubleday, 1976.
Last Stage from Opal, Doubleday, 1978.
Murder at Magpie Flats, Doubleday, 1978.

OTHER

(Under pseudonym J. B. Masterson) *Rudge* (novel), Doubleday, 1979.

Also author of *The Man Who Corrupted the Earth* and *To Sail the Century Sea,* both for Ace Books; (with Kotlan) of *Cunningham Equations;* of forty other novels under various pseudonyms including Mario Murphy.

WORK IN PROGRESS: A historical novel set in Ireland, Iceland, and Finland ca. 1000 A.D.; a western novel and a science fiction novel.

SIDELIGHTS: G. C. Edmondson is one of the few remaining blacksmiths in the United States. He speaks Spanish, Portuguese, Italian, French, and German "in descending scale of fluency."

* * *

EDMONDSON, Garry C.
See EDMONDSON, G. C.

* * *

EHRMAN, John (Patrick William)   1920-

PERSONAL: Born March 17, 1920, in London, England; son of Albert and Rina (Bendit) Ehrman; married Elizabeth Susan Anne Blake, July 1, 1948; children: William Hugh, Richard, Thomas. *Education:* Trinity College, Cambridge, M.A., 1945. *Religion:* Church of England.

ADDRESSES: Home—The Mead Barns, Taynton, Burford, Oxfordshire, England.

CAREER: Cambridge University, Trinity College, Cambridge, England, fellow, 1947-52; Cabinet Office, London, England, member of historical section, 1948-56; Cambridge University, Trinity College, Lees Knowles Lecturer, 1957-58; currently full-time writer. James Ford Special Lecturer, Oxford University, 1976-77. Member of reviewing committee on the export of works of art, 1970-76; member, Royal Commission on Historical Manuscripts, 1973—; chairman of advisory comittee, British Library Reference Division, 1975-84. Trustee, National Portrait Gallery, 1971-85. *Military service:* Royal Naval Volunteer Reserve, 1940-45; became lieutenant.

MEMBER: Friends of the National Libraries (honorary secretary, 1949-55; honorary treasurer, 1960-77), Society of Antiquaries (fellow), Royal Historical Society (fellow), Navy Records Society (vice-president, 1968-70, 1974-76), Army and Navy Club, Beefsteak Club, Garrick Club.

WRITINGS:

The Navy in the War of William III, Cambridge University Press, 1953.
Grand Strategy, Volume V: *August 1943-September 1944,* Volume VI: *October 1944-August 1945,* H.M.S.O., 1956.
Cabinet Government and War, 1890-1940, Cambridge University Press, 1958.
The British Government and Commercial Negotiations with Europe, 1783-1793, Cambridge University Press, 1962.
The Younger Pitt, Volume I: *The Years of Acclaim,* Dutton, 1969, Volume II: *The Reluctant Transition,* Stanford University Press, 1983.
Stephen Roskill: 1903-82, Longwood, 1985.

BIOGRAPHICAL/CRITICAL SOURCES:

PERIODICALS

New Republic, January 31, 1970.
Newsweek, December 1, 1969.
New York Review, May 9, 1970.
New York Review of Books, April 9, 1970.
New York Times, December 9, 1969.
Spectator, November 9, 1969, June 25, 1983.
Times (London), October 6, 1983.
Times Literary Supplement, January 8, 1970, June 24, 1983.

* * *

EL-BAZ, Farouk 1938-

PERSONAL: Born January 1, 1938, in Zagazig, Egypt; son of El-Sayed (an educator) and Zahia (Hammouda) El-Baz; married Catherine Patricia O'Leary; children: Monira, Soraya, Karima, Fairouz. *Education:* Ain Shams University, B.S., 1958; University of Assiut, graduate study, 1958-60; University of Missouri School of Mines and Metallurgy (now University of Missouri—Rolla), M.S., 1961, Ph.D., 1964; Massachusetts Institute of Technology, graduate study, 1962-63. *Religion:* Muslim.

ADDRESSES: *Home*—213 Silver Hill Rd., Concord, Mass. 01742. *Office*—Center for Remote Sensing, Boston University, 725 Commonwealth Ave., Boston, Mass. 02215.

CAREER: University of Assiut, Assiut, Egypt, instructor in geology, 1958-60; University of Missouri—Rolla, instructor in geology, 1963-64; University of Heidelberg, Institute of Mineralogy and Petrography, Heidelberg, West Germany, instructor in mineralogy, 1964-65; Pan American-UAR Oil Co., Cairo, Egypt, exploration geologist, 1966-67; Bellcomm, Inc., Washington, D.C., member of technical staff, 1967-69, supervisor of lunar exploration, 1969-72; Smithsonian Institution, National Air and Space Museum, Washington, D.C., director of Center for Earth and Planetary Studies, 1973-82; Litton Industries, Itek Optical Systems, Lexington, Mass., vice-president for international development, 1982-86; Boston University, Boston, Mass., director of Center for Remote Sensing, 1986—. Consultant to Dover Publications, Time-Life Books, and National Geographic Society.

MEMBER: International Association of Sedimentology, International Association of Geochemistry and Cosmochemistry, International Association of Stereology, International Astronomical Union, American Association for the Advancement of Science, Geological Society of America, Mineralogical Society of America, American Geophysical Union, Society of Economic Paleontologists and Mineralogists, Geochemical Society, Deutsche Mineralogische Gesellschaft, Geologische Vereinigung, Missouri Academy of Science, Sigma Xi.

WRITINGS:

Say It in Arabic, Dover, 1968.
(With Walter Haentzschel and G. C. Amstutz) *Coprolites: An Annotated Bibliography,* Geological Society, 1968.
(With L. J. Kosofsky) *The Moon as Viewed by Lunar Orbiter,* National Aeronautics and Space Administration, 1970.
(With Amstutz and others) *Glossary of Mining Geology,* Springer Verlag, 1970.
Astronaut Observations from the Apollo-Soyuz Mission, Smithsonian Institution, 1977.

(With H. Masursky and G. W. Colton) *Apollo over the Moon: A View from Orbit,* National Aeronautics and Space Administration, 1978.
Egypt as Seen by Landsat, Dar Al-Maaref (Cairo), 1978.
(With D. M. Warner) *Apollo-Soyuz Test Project Summary Science Report,* Volume II: *Earth Observations and Photography,* National Aeronautics and Space Administration, 1979.
(With T. A. Maxwell) *Desert Landforms of Southwest Egypt: A Basis for Comparison with Mars,* National Aeronautics and Space Administration, 1982.
(Editor with M. H. Hassan) *Physics of Desertification,* Martinus Nijhoff, 1986.

Also author of *Deserts and Arid Lands,* 1984, and compiler of *Geology of Egypt: An Annotated Bibliography,* 1984. Contributor to magazines and journals, including *National Geographic, Explorers Journal,* and *Smithsonian.*

WORK IN PROGRESS: *Remote Sensing of Natural Resources,* proceedings of an international workshop; *Khufu's Second Boat,* a study of a disassembled boat in a chamber at the base of the Great Pyramid; *Where on the Moon,* a study of landing site selection for the Apollo missions; *Naming the Moon,* an explanation of how surface features on the Moon acquired their names; *The Desert,* a study of the origins and evolution of desert landscapes.

SIDELIGHTS: Farouk El-Baz told *CA* that he involves the space program in his writing because he believes in its value and long-term benefits. To El-Baz, "observations from space, particularly photography, will help us better utilize the Earth for the benefit of mankind, especially in deserts and semiarid lands."

* * *

El MUHAJIR 1944-
(Marvin X, Nazzam Al Fitnah Muhajir)

PERSONAL: Original name, Marvin Ellis Jackmon; born May 29, 1944, in Fowler, Calif.; son of Owendell and Marian Jackmon; married; five children. *Education:* Oakland City College (now Merritt College), A.A., 1964; additional study at San Francisco State College (now University), 1964-66, 1974.

CAREER: Poet, playwright, editor, and lecturer. Founder with Ed Bullins of Black Arts/West Theatre, San Francisco, Calif., 1966, and with Bullins and Eldridge Cleaver of Black House (political-cultural center), San Francisco, 1967; founder of Al Kitab Sudan Publishing Co., San Francisco, 1967; founder and director of Your Black Educational Theatre, Inc., San Francisco, beginning 1971. Teacher of black studies courses at California State University at Fresno, 1969, University of California, Berkeley, 1972, and Mills College, 1973; has given lectures or poetry readings at numerous universities and colleges, including Stanford University, Cornell University, Loyola University of Chicago, University of Toronto, University of California, Davis, University of California, Los Angeles, and University of Oklahoma.

AWARDS, HONORS: Writing grants totaling $8,000 from Columbia University, 1969, and National Endowment for the Arts, 1972; on-the-job training grant of $36,000 for Your Black Educational Theatre, 1971-72.

WRITINGS:

Sudan Rajuli Samia (poems), Al Kitab Sudan Publishing, 1967.

Black Dialectic (proverbs), Al Kitab Sudan Publishing, 1967.

(Under name Marvin X) *Fly to Allah: Poems*, Al Kitab Sudan Publishing, 1969.

(Under name Marvin X) *The Son of Man*, Al Kitab Sudan Publishing, 1969.

(Under name Marvin X) *Black Man Listen: Poems and Proverbs*, Broadside Press, 1969.

Black Bird (parable), Al Kitab Sudan Publishing, 1972.

Woman—Man's Best Friend (also see below), Al Kitab Sudan Publishing, 1973.

Selected Poems, Al Kitab Sudan Publishing, 1979.

(Under name Marvin X) *Confession of a Wife Beater and Other Poems*, Al Kitab Sudan Publishing, 1981.

Liberation Poems for North American Africans, Al Kitab Sudan Publishing, 1982.

PLAYS

"Flowers for the Trashman" (one-act), first produced in San Francisco at San Francisco State College, 1965, musical version produced as "Take Care of Business," in Fresno, Calif. at Your Black Educational Theatre, 1971.

"Come Next Summer," first produced in San Francisco at Black Arts/West Theatre, 1966.

"The Trial," first produced in New York City at Afro-American Studio for Acting and Speech, 1970.

"Resurrection of the Dead" (ritual dance drama), first produced in San Francisco at Your Black Educational Theatre, 1972.

"Woman—Man's Best Friend" (musical dance drama; based on author's book of same title), first produced in Oakland, Calif. at Mills College, 1973.

"In the Name of Love," first produced in Oakland at Laney College Theatre, 1981.

CONTRIBUTOR TO ANTHOLOGIES

Black Fire: An Anthology of Afro-American Writing, edited by Amiri Baraka and Larry Neal, Morrow, 1968.

New Plays from the Black Theatre, edited by Ed Bullins, Bantam, 1969.

Black Arts: An Anthology of Black Creations, edited by Ahmed Alhamisi and Haroun Kofi Wangara, Black Arts Publications, 1969.

Vietnam and Black America, edited by Clyde Taylor, Doubleday, 1973.

You Better Believe It, edited by Paul Breman, Penguin, 1973.

OTHER

Contributor to *Soul Book, Encore, Black World, Black Scholar*, and other magazines and newspapers. Fiction editor, *Black Dialogue*, 1965—; contributing editor, *Journal of Black Poetry*, 1965—; associate editor, *Black Theatre*, 1968; foreign editor, *Muhammad Speaks*, 1970.

WORK IN PROGRESS: An elementary Arabic textbook; *Black Man in the Americas*, a series of conversations with black writers, artists, historians, musicians, and politicians; *Handbook of Black Theatre*, a world guide; *Bibliography for the Proper Understanding of Black People*.

BIOGRAPHICAL/CRITICAL SOURCES:

BOOKS

Dictionary of Literary Biography, Volume 38: *Afro-American Writers after 1955*, Gale, 1985.†

ELSEN, Albert E(dward) 1927-

PERSONAL: Born October 11, 1927, in New York, N.Y.; son of Albert (a lawyer) and Julia (a teacher; maiden name, Huseman) Elsen; married Patricia Morgan Kline, July 7, 1951; children: Matthew, Nancy, Katherine. *Education:* Columbia University, B.A. (with distinction), 1949, M.A., 1951, Ph.D., 1955. *Politics:* Democratic.

ADDRESSES: Home—10 Peter Coutts Cir., Stanford, Calif. 94305. *Office*—Department of Art, Stanford University, Stanford, Calif. 94305.

CAREER: Carleton College, Northfield, Minn., 1952-58, began as instructor, became assistant professor of history of art; Indiana University at Bloomington, associate professor, 1958-63, professor of history of art, 1964-68; Stanford University, Stanford, Calif., professor of art history, beginning 1968, Walter A. Haas Professor of Art History, 1975—. Cooperating professor of art law, Stanford Law School, Stanford University. Brandeis Poses Lecturer; lecturer on art at various institutions, including Metropolitan Museum of Art, Museum of Modern Art, Philadelphia Museum of Art, S. R. Guggenheim Museum, Cambridge University, and Courtauld Institute of Art, University of London. Taught educational television program, "Images of Man in Modern Art," 1958; art commentator for television station KQED in San Francisco, Calif. Helped organize art exhibitions for Museum of Modern Art, 1963, Baltimore Museum, 1969, Guggenheim Museum, 1972, London's Hayward Gallery, 1973, and National Gallery of Art, 1981. Member of committee on advanced placement in art history, Educational Testing Service; founder of committee for the development of art in negro colleges, 1963-66. Consultant to U.S. Office of Education, 1965-66; adviser to Kinsey Institute for Sex Research, 1966-68. *Military service:* U.S. Army, 1946-47; 752nd Tank Batallion in Italy; became sergeant major.

MEMBER: American Association of University Professors, College Art Association of America (member of board of directors, 1966-70; secretary and chairman of committee on public policy, 1970-72; vice-president and chairman of professional practices committee, beginning 1972; president, 1974-76), Authors Guild, Authors League of America.

AWARDS, HONORS: Fulbright fellow, 1949-50; grant-in-aid for research on Rodin from American Council of Learned Societies, 1952 and 1960; Clark Foundation research grant for work on second Rodin book, and to assist in assembling Rodin show, 1962; Guggenheim fellowship for research in the origins and development of modern sculpture, 1966-67; National Endowment for the Humanities, senior fellow, 1973-74; Honorary Doctorate of Fine Arts, Dickinson College, 1980.

WRITINGS:

Rodin's Gates of Hell, University of Minnesota Press, 1960.

Purposes of Art: An Introduction to the History and Appreciation of Art, Holt, 1962, 4th edition, 1981.

Rodin, Museum of Modern Art, 1963.

(Editor) *Auguste Rodin: Readings on His Life and Work*, Prentice-Hall, 1965.

The Partial Figure in Modern Sculpture, from Rodin to 1969, Baltimore Museum, 1969.

Seymour Lipton, Abrams, 1970.

(With J. Kirk T. Varnedoe) *The Drawings of Rodin*, Praeger, 1971.

The Sculpture of Henri Matisse, Abrams, c. 1972.

Paul Jenkins, Abrams, 1973.

Pioneers of Modern Sculpture: Catalogue of an Exhibition Held at the Hayward Gallery, London, 20 July-23 September, 1973, Arts Council of Great Britain, 1973.

Rodin's "Balzac," Cantor Fitzgerald, 1973.

Origins of Modern Sculpture: Pioneers and Premises, Braziller, 1974.

(With John Henry Merryman) *Law, Ethics, and the Visual Arts*, Matthew Bender, 1979, 2nd edition, University of Pennsylvania Press, 1987.

Other Realities: Modern European Sculpture, 1918-1945, Braziller, 1979.

In Rodin's Studio: A Photographic Record of Sculpture in the Making, Cornell University Press, 1980.

(Editor) *Rodin Rediscovered*, New York Graphic Society, 1981.

"The Gates of Hell" by Auguste Rodin, Stanford University Press, 1985.

Rodin's "Thinker" and the Dilemmas of Modern Public Sculpture, Yale University Press, 1986.

Also editor of *Handbook for the Development of Art in Small Colleges*. Contributor of articles on art to various magazines, including *Magazine of Art, Art Journal, Burlington Magazine, Art International, Art Forum, Studio International, Art History, Arts,* and *Artnews*. Contributing editor, *Artnews*, 1975—.

WORK IN PROGRESS: A history of artists' freedom from ancient times, a chapter of which, "The Oldest Artist's Right?" appeared in *Art History*, June, 1988.

SIDELIGHTS: Art historian Albert E. Elsen told *CA* that the most important influence on his career was a doctoral study with Meyer Schapiro at Columbia University. "His writings as well as those of Sidney Geist and Leo Steinberg have been crucial to my own," he said. Elsen calls his text *Purposes of Art: An Introduction to the History and Appreciation of Art* "a topical approach to art history, meant to counter the linear chronological approach prevalent in this country." His research in modern sculpture, as seen in *The Partial Figure in Modern Sculpture, from Rodin to 1969* deals with what he calls "ideas and premises of modern art rather than styles, movements and national groupings."

In his 1974 publication *The Origins of Modern Sculpture*, Elsen gives readers "a rigorous critical account of the development of modern European sculpture during the crucial years 1890-1918," the *Times Literary Supplement* reviewer reports, adding that "not the least of the merits of Elsen's book is his refusal to accept glib generalizations." *Times Literary Supplement* contributor Tim Hilton considers Elsen one of the "most practised Rodin scholars of our time." He continues, "during the last two decades, in a series of articles and exhibitions [Elsen and scholar Kirk Varnedoe have] introduced the sculptor to a new generation." In the *New York Times Book Review*, Raymond A. Sokolov praises Elsen's 1980 publication *In Rodin's Studio: A Photographic Record of Sculpture in the Making:* "Elsen, a Rodin specialist at Stanford University, edited this quite fabulous album and shows . . . how the pictures relate to Rodin's life and to the creation of the statues they depict." *Rodin's "Thinker" and the Dilemmas of Modern Public Sculpture* discusses the current need for outdoor sculpture that is smaller in scale and that restores "a human scale to our built environment," as well as relating the history of the famous statue. Hilton commends "Elsen's genial and learned approach to a most familiar sculpture," which, according to the author, has rarely been "closely and rightly read." However, Jonathan Kirsch writes in the *Los Angeles Times Book Review* that Elsen "gives us precisely such a read-

ing of 'The Thinker'" in *Rodin's "Thinker" and the Dilemmas of Modern Public Sculpture*.

BIOGRAPHICAL/CRITICAL SOURCES:

BOOKS

Rodin's "Thinker" and the Dilemmas of Modern Public Sculpture, Yale University Press, 1986.

PERIODICALS

Los Angeles Times Book Review, February 9, 1986.
New York Times Book Review, May 18, 1980.
Times Literary Supplement, March 23, 1973, April 25, 1975, November 14, 1980, March 28, 1986.

*   *   *

ELSON, R. N.
    See NELSON, R(adell) Faraday

*   *   *

ENDICOTT, Ruth Belmore
[Collective pseudonym]

WRITINGS:

"CAROLYN" SERIES

Carolyn of the Corners, Dodd, Mead, 1918.
Carolyn of the Sunny Heart, Dodd, Mead, 1919.

SIDELIGHTS: For more information see the entries for Harriet S. Adams, Edward L. Stratemeyer, and Andrew E. Svenson.

BIOGRAPHICAL/CRITICAL SOURCES:

BOOKS

Johnson, Deidre, editor and compiler, *Stratemeyer Pseudonyms and Series Books: An Annotated Checklist of Stratemeyer and Stratemeyer Syndicate Publications*, Greenwood Press, 1982.

*   *   *

ESEKI, Bruno
    See MPHAHLELE, Ezekiel

*   *   *

ESLER, Anthony (James)   1934-

PERSONAL: Born February 20, 1934, in New London, Conn.; son of James Arthur (an artist, sheetmetal worker, and shipfitter) and Helen (a teacher; maiden name, Kreamer) Esler; married Carol Clemeau (a college professor and novelist), 1961; children: Kenneth Campbell, David Douglas. *Education:* University of Arizona, B.A., 1956; Duke University, M.A., 1958, Ph.D., 1961; University of London, postdoctoral study, 1961-62.

ADDRESSES: Office—Department of History, College of William and Mary, Williamsburg, Va. 23185.

CAREER: College of William and Mary, Williamsburg, Va., assistant professor, 1962-67, associate professor, 1967-72, professor of history, 1972—. Visiting associate professor, Northwestern University, 1968-69. American Council of Learned Societies research fellow, Chicago, 1969-70; College of William and Mary research fellow, 1975-76.

MEMBER: Amnesty International, American Historical Association, Authors Guild, Authors League of America.

AWARDS, HONORS: Fulbright scholar in London, 1961-62; Fulbright scholar in Tanzania, 1984.

WRITINGS:

The Aspiring Mind of the Elizabethan Younger Generation, Duke University Press, 1966.
Bombs, Beards and Barricades, Stein & Day, 1971.
The Youth Revolution: The Conflict of Generations in Modern History, Heath, 1974.
The Blade of Castlemayne, Morrow, 1974.
Hellbane, Morrow, 1975.
Lord Libertine, Morrow, 1976.
Forbidden City, Morrow, 1977.
The Freebooters, Futura (London), 1978, revised edition published as *Pirate,* Morrow, 1979.
Generational Studies: A Basic Bibliography, privately printed, 1979.
Babylon, Morrow, 1980.
Bastion, Jade Books (London), 1981, Critics Choice, 1987.
Generations in History: An Introduction to the Concept, privately printed, 1981.
The Generation Gap in Society and History: A Select Bibliography, two volumes, Vance, 1983.
The Human Venture, Volume I: *The Great Enterprise—A World History,* Volume II: *The Globe Encompassed—A World History since 1500,* Prentice-Hall, 1986.

WORK IN PROGRESS: Phoenix: A History of the Western World, two volumes, for Prentice-Hall; *Liberation,* a novel.

SIDELIGHTS: Anthony Esler told *CA:* "As a novelist and historian, I have always wanted to lead vicariously—through writing—as wide a variety of interesting lives as I could find or invent. Every book I do is therefore a new challenge. A new subject, of course, new characters, a new setting in time and space, and a new story—true or fictional—to tell. But also and every bit as important, new themes, new formal problems to solve, new genres to explore.

"I have thus written about political revolutionaries and religious zealots, about romantic young men and women and cynical older ones, about people in love with power, in love with ideas, in love with money, in love with love. I have set these stories—and found these histories—in the Americas, in Europe, in the Near and Far East, from the sixth century B.C. to the 1960s A.D. And I have presented this gallery of human lives in what seemed to me to be an appropriate range of literary forms: in romantic and ironic adventure, stark tragedy, picaresque comedy, monographic and semi-popular history.

"There have of course been underlying continuities. Perennials like love and death, faith and fanaticism, and the eternal conflicts of cultures, social types, and generations have permeated almost all my writing. But mostly it is the variety that fascinates me when I sit down to meditate on ancient Mesopotamia or ask myself what the *last* President of the United States might be like. I write for the same reason that I travel: to see what I can of the world we all live in—a village-eye view of East Africa, a spiritual seeker's vision of the Ganges, or Moscow through the eyes of a young Russian woman who set out to be a mathematician and got lost along the way.

"Infinite variety within the bounds of one man's finite life is the point of writing for me."

AVOCATIONAL INTERESTS: Drawing, travel, islands and mountains, sea-beaches, ruins, serious talk, and a very few people.

*   *   *

EVELYN, Anthony
    See WARD-THOMAS, Evelyn Bridget Patricia
    Stephens

*   *   *

EVEREST, Allan S(eymour)   1913-

PERSONAL: Born October 9, 1913, in South Shaftsbury, Vt.; son of Charles Seymour (a merchant) and Clara (Hawkins) Everest; married Elsie Hathaway Lewis, October 10, 1942; children: Martha Everest Lockwood. *Education:* University of Vermont, Ph.B., 1936; Columbia University, M.A., 1937, Ph.D., 1948.

ADDRESSES: Home—26 South Catherine St., Plattsburgh, N.Y. 12901. *Office*—Department of History, State University of New York College, Plattsburgh, N.Y. 12901.

CAREER: Green Mountain Junior College, Poultney, Vt., instructor in social science, 1938-41; State University of New York College at Plattsburgh, professor of American history, 1947-83, professor emeritus, 1983—. *Military service:* U.S. Army Air Forces, 1941-46; became captain.

MEMBER: New York State Historical Association, Vermont Historical Society, Clinton County Historical Association (former president), Phi Beta Kappa, Pi Gamma Mu.

WRITINGS:

Morgenthau, the New Deal and Silver: A Story of Pressure Politics, King's Crown Press, 1950, reprinted, Da Capo Press, 1973.
British Objectives at the Battle of Plattsburgh, Moorsfield Press, 1960.
(Editor) David Sherwood Kellogg, *Recollections of Clinton County and the Battle of Plattsburgh, 1800-1840,* Clinton County Historical Association, 1964.
Pioneer Homes of Clinton County, 1790-1820, Clinton County Historical Association, 1966.
(Editor) Kellogg, *A Doctor at All Hours: A Private Journal of a Small-Town Doctor's Varied Life, 1886-1909,* Greene, 1970.
Change in the Provinces: The Seventeenth Century, Leicester University Press, 1970.
Our North Country Heritage: Architecture Worth Saving in Clinton and Essex Counties, Tundra Books, 1972.
(Editor) Charles Carroll, *The Journal of Charles Carroll of Carrollton,* Champlain-Upper Hudson Bicentennial Committee, 1976.
Moses Hazen and the Canadian Refugees in the American Revolution, Syracuse University Press, 1976.
Run across the Border: The Prohibition Era in Northern New York, Syracuse University Press, 1978.
Henry Delord and His Family, George Little Press, 1979.
The War of 1812 in the Champlain Valley, Syracuse University Press, 1981.
Briefly Told: Plattsburgh, New York, 1784-1984, Clinton County Historical Association, 1984.

SIDELIGHTS: Allan S. Everest has traveled extensively in the British Isles, Western Europe, and Canada and has twice taught at English universities.

F

FAINLIGHT, Ruth (Esther) 1931-

PERSONAL: Born May 2, 1931, in New York, N.Y.; daughter of Leslie Alexander and Fanny (Nimhauser) Fainlight; married Alan Sillitoe (a writer), November 19, 1959; children: David Nimrod, Susan (adopted). *Education:* Attended schools in United States and England until the age of sixteen, then studied two years at Birmingham and Brighton Colleges of Arts and Crafts, England.

ADDRESSES: Home—14 Ladbroke Ter., London W11 3PG, England.

CAREER: Poet, writer, and translator. Vanderbilt University, Nashville, Tenn., poet in residence, 1985.

WRITINGS:

A Forecast, a Fable (poems), Outposts Publications, 1958.
Cages (poems), Macmillan (London), 1966, Dufour, 1967.
18 Poems from 1966, Turret Books, 1967.
To See the Matter Clearly (poems), Macmillan (London), 1968, Dufour, 1969.
(Translator and adapter with husband, Alan Sillitoe) Lope de Vega, *All Citizens Are Soldiers* (two-act play; first produced at Theatre Royal, Stratford, London, 1967), Macmillan (London), 1969, Dufour, 1970.
(Contributor) *Poems* [by] *Ruth Fainlight, Ted Hughes, Alan Sillitoe,* Rainbow Press, 1971.
Daylife and Nightlife (short stories), Deutsch, 1971.
The Region's Violence (poems), Hutchinson, 1973.
21 Poems, Turret Books, 1973.
Another Full Moon (poems), Hutchinson, 1976.
Sibyls and Others (poems), Hutchinson, 1980.
Climates (poems), Bloodaxe Books, 1983.
Fifteen to Infinity (poems), Hutchinson, 1983.
Selected Poems, Hutchinson, 1983.
(Translator) Sophia de Mello Breyner, *Marine Rose* (poems), Black Swan Books, 1987.

CONTRIBUTOR TO POETRY ANTHOLOGIES

E. Lucie-Smith, editor, *Holding Your Eight Hands,* Doubleday, 1969.
D. Abse, editor, *Poetry Dimension Number 2,* Abacus, 1974.
T. Kneale, editor, *Contemporary Women Poets,* Rondo, 1975.
H. Sergeant, editor, *New Poems 76-77* (PEN anthology), Hutchinson, 1976.

K. Crossley-Holland and P. Beer, editors, *New Poetry 2,* Arts Council, 1976.
A. Brownjohn and M. Duffy, editors, *New Poetry 3,* Arts Council, 1977.
D. Abse, editor, *Poetry Dimension Number 5,* Robson Books, 1978.
Daryl Hine and J. Parisi, editors, *The Poetry Anthology,* Houghton, 1978.
P. Redgrove and J. Silkin, editors, *New Poetry 5,* Arts Council, 1979.
H. Schwartz and A. Rudolf, editors, *Voices within the Ark,* Avon, 1980.
Sergeant, editor, *How Strong the Roots,* M. Evans, 1981.
Diana Scott, editor, *Bread and Roses,* Virago, 1982.
J. Couzyn, editor, *The Bloodaxe Book of Contemporary Women Poets,* Bloodaxe Books, 1985.
D. Abse and J. Abse, editors, *Voices in the Gallery,* Tate Gallery, 1986.

CONTRIBUTOR TO SHORT STORY ANTHOLOGIES

Judith Burnley, editor, *Penguin Modern Stories,* Volume IX, Penguin, 1971.
Emma Tennant, editor, *Bananas,* Quartet, 1977.
D. Val Baker, editor, *Stories by Famous Women Writers,* W. H. Allen, 1978.
E. Feinstein and F. Weldon, editors, *New Stories 4* (Arts Council Anthology), Hutchinson, 1979.

CONTRIBUTOR OF TRANSLATIONS TO ANTHOLOGIES

Bankier, Cosman, Earnshaw, Keefe, Lashgari, and Weaver, editors, *The Other Voice,* Norton, 1976.
D. Junkins, editor, *The Contemporary World Poets,* Harcourt, 1976.
H. Macedo and E. M. Melo e Castro, editors, *Contemporary Portugese Poetry,* Carcanet, 1978.
W. Carrier and B. Neumann, editors, *Literature from the World,* Scribner, 1981.

WORK IN PROGRESS: A new collection of poems.

SIDELIGHTS: Ruth Fainlight told *CA:* "I enjoy slow travel, by which I mean going somewhere and living there a while. So far I have only done this in France, Spain, Morocco, Israel, and England. . . . My main interests apart from literature are in the fields of sociology, psychology, anthropology, religion, history, animal behaviour, biology, cosmology—in fact, every area of science I am capable of understanding, having had no scientific education at all.''

BIOGRAPHICAL/CRITICAL SOURCES:

BOOKS

Couzyn, J., editor, *The Bloodaxe Book of Contemporary Women Poets*, Bloodaxe Books, 1985.

PERIODICALS

London Review of Books, February 2, 1984.
New Statesman, March 12, 1976, May 9, 1980.
Poetry, February, 1978.
Times Literary Supplement, April 8, 1977, May 23, 1980, April 13, 1984.

*   *   *

FARRER, Claire R(afferty) 1936-

PERSONAL: Born December 26, 1936, in New York, N.Y.; daughter of Francis Michael (a welder) and Clara Anna (a nurse; maiden name, Guerra) Rafferty; married Donald Nathanael Farrer (a psychologist), February 2, 1957 (divorced, 1973); children: Suzanne Claire. *Education:* University of California, B.A., 1970; University of Texas, M.A., 1974, Ph.D., 1977. *Politics:* Democrat. *Religion:* Quaker.

ADDRESSES: Office—California State University, Chico, Calif. 95929.

CAREER: San Jose State University, San Jose, Calif., worked in personnel office, 1956; International Business Machines Corp. (IBM), San Jose, statistical analyst, 1956-57; Jennings Radio Manufacturing Co., San Jose, statistical consultant, executive secretary, 1957-58; Washington State University, Pullman, clerk, 1958-59, executive secretary, 1959-61; *Otero County Star*, Alamogordo, N.M., columnist, 1963-65; Unitarian Universalist Fellowship, Alamogordo, founder, administrator, 1964-71; Zia School, Alamogordo, curriculum consultant and teacher, 1966-68, 1970-71; Smithsonian Institution, Washington, D.C., conducted survey, 1973-74; ethnographic analyst, Texas Joint Senate-House Committee on Prison Reform, 1974; ethnographic researcher, Mescalero Apache Indian Reservation, 1974-75; National Endowment for the Arts, Washington, D.C., administrator of Folk Arts program, 1976-77; School of American Research, Santa Fe, N.M., resident scholar, 1977-78; University of Illinois at Urbana-Champaign, assistant professor of anthropology, 1978-85; California State University, Chico, associate professor of anthropology and coordinator of Applied Anthropology Program, 1985—.

Field research at Mescalero Apache Indian Reservation, 1972-75, 1977, 1978—. Has presented papers at professional meetings. Fund raiser for Otero County Child Care Center, 1967-71; member of Interdisciplinary Committee on Folk Curriculum, University of Illinois, 1978-85. Consultant on several advisory boards; consultant on film ''Geronimo's Children,'' broadcast by the British Broadcasting Corp., 1976.

MEMBER: American Anthropological Association (fellow), American Ethnological Society, American Folklore Society, American Society for Ethnohistory, Society for the Anthropology of Visual Communication, Association for the Anthropological Study of Play (fellow), Southwestern Anthropological Association, California Scholastic Federation, Phi Kappa Phi, Sigma Xi.

AWARDS, HONORS: Whitney M. Young, Jr., memorial fellowship, 1974-75; Weatherhead resident fellowship, School of American Research, 1977-78; University of Illinois grants, 1979; American Philosophical Society grant, 1983; American Council of Learned Societies grants, 1984, 1987.

WRITINGS:

(Editor) *Women and Folklore*, University of Texas Press, 1976, revised edition, Waveland Press, 1986.
(Contributor) David F. Lancy and B. Allan Tindall, editors, *The Anthropological Study of Play: Problems and Prospects*, Leisure Press, 1976.
(Editor with Edward Norbeck) *Forms of Play of Native North Americans*, West Publishing, 1979.
(Contributor) Charlotte J. Frisbie, editor, *Southwestern Indian Ritual Drama*, University of New Mexico Press, 1980.
(Contributor) Alyce T. Cheska, editor, *Play and Context*, Leisure Press, 1981.
(Contributor with Bernard Second) Ray A. Williamson, editor, *Archaeoastronomy in the Americas*, Ballena, 1981.
(Contributor) Louise Carus Mahdi, Steven Foster, and Meredith Little, editors, *Betwixt and Between: Patterns of Masculine and Feminine Initiation*, Open Court, 1987.
(Editor with Ray A. Williamson) *Earth and Sky: Visions of the Cosmos in Native American Folklore*, University of New Mexico Press, in press.
(Contributor) Thomas A. Green and Paul Smith, editors, *Folk Drama: Contemporary Perspectives*, Sheffield Academic Press, in press.
(Contributor) Von Del Chamberlain, M. Jane Young, and John B. Carlson, editors, *Ethnoastronomy: Indigenous Astronomical and Cosmological Traditions of the World*, Slo'w Press, in press.
(Contributor) Anthony F. Aveni, editor, *World Archaeoastronomy*, Cambridge University Press, in press.
(Contributor) Helen Tierney, editor, *Women's Studies Encyclopedia*, Garland Publishing, in press.

Also author of ''Graded Supplementary Reading Materials for the Children of the Bent-Mescalero School'' (twenty-four stories concerning Mescalero Apache history).

Western Folklore, book review editor, 1985—, and author of quarterly column, ''New and Noteworthy.'' Contributor of articles to journals, including *Parabola*, *The World and I*, *Archaeoastronomy*, and *Canadian Journal of Native Studies*. Co-founder and co-editor of first issue, *Folklore Feminists Communication*; editor of *Women and Folklore*, special issue of *Journal of American Folklore*; reader for several refereed journals.

WORK IN PROGRESS: Further research on Mescalero Apache society and culture, folklore of women and children, and cross-cultural aesthetics; *Living Life's Circle: Mescalero Apache Cosmovision.*

SIDELIGHTS: Claire Farrer told *CA:* ''I am an old-fashioned cultural anthropologist interested in ethnography and folklore, in its widest sense. I am particularly attracted to desert and maritime people as well as expressive behavior—the latter especially of women and children. I am led by serendipity oftentimes—a quixotic but fascinating guide.''

*   *   *

FERLITA, Ernest (Charles) 1927-

PERSONAL: Born December 1, 1927, in Tampa, Fla.; son of

Giuseppe R. (a macaroni manufacturer) and Vincenta (Ficarrotta) Ferlita. *Education:* Spring Hill College, B.S., 1950; St. Louis University, M.A., 1964; Yale University, D.F.A., 1969.

ADDRESSES: Home and office—Department of Drama and Speech, Loyola University, New Orleans, La. 70118.

CAREER: Entered Order of Society of Jesus (Jesuits), 1950, ordained Roman Catholic priest, 1962; high school teacher in New Orleans, La., 1956-59; Spring Hill College, Mobile, Ala., instructor in English and speech, 1964-65; Loyola University, New Orleans, La., professor of drama, 1969—, chairman of department of drama and speech, 1970-88. Fulbright traveling scholar to Brazil, 1980. Member of board of directors, Loyola University, 1970-75, 1984-88, chairman of board, 1972-75. *Military service:* U.S. Army, Medical Corps, 1946-47.

AWARDS, HONORS: American Radio Theatre Award, 1985, for "The City of Seven Rivers"; Miller Drama Award, 1986, for *The Truth of the Matter.*

WRITINGS:

"The Ballad of John Ogilvie" (three-act play), first produced Off-Broadway at Blackfriars' Theatre, October 9, 1968.
The Theatre of Pilgrimage, Sheed & Ward, 1971.
(With John R. May) *Film Odyssey,* Paulist/Newman, 1976.
(With May) *The Parables of Lina Wertmuller,* Paulist/Newman, 1977.
The Way of the River: A Book of Scriptural Meditations, Paulist/Newman, 1977.
"The Obelisk," first produced in New York City at Fordham College at Lincoln Center, 1982.
(With May and others) *Religion in Film,* University of Tennessee, 1983.
Gospel Journey, Winston Press, 1983.
The City of the Seven Rivers (play), American Radio Theatre, 1986.
"Black Medea," first produced in New York City at Actor's Outlet, 1987.
"The Mask of Hiroshima," first produced at Actor's Outlet, 1988.
(Contributor) *Best Short Plays of 1989,* Applause Theatre Books, 1989.

Also contributor to *Drama Critique* and *New Orleans Review.*

SIDELIGHTS: Ernest Ferlita told *CA,* "Every scribe trained for the truth 'brings out of his treasure what is new and what is old' (Matthew 13:51). I like to think that I'm such a scribe when I tell an old story in another time and place, always with the hope that the truth will appear and be seen afresh."

*   *   *

FIELDS, Julia 1938-

PERSONAL: Born January, 1938, in Perry County, Ala.; daughter of Winston and Maggie Fields. *Education:* Knoxville College, B.S., 1961; Bread Loaf School of English, M.A., 1972; further study at University of Edinburgh, 1963.

ADDRESSES: Home—Box 209, Scotland Neck, N.C. 27874.

CAREER: Poet and author of short stories. Has worked as a high school teacher in Birmingham, Ala., and as poet-in-residence, lecturer, or instructor at several universities and colleges, including Miles College, Hampton Institute, St. Au-

gustine College, East Carolina University, Howard University, North Carolina State University, and University of the District of Columbia. Founder and consultant to the Learning School of the American Language, 1979.

AWARDS, HONORS: National Endowment for the Arts grant, 1967; Seventh Conrad Kent Rivers Memorial Fund Award, 1973.

WRITINGS:

I Heard A Young Man Saying, Broadside Press, 1967.
Poems, Poets Press, 1968.
East of Moonlight, Red Clay Books, 1973.
A Summoning, A Shining, Scotland Neck, 1976.
Slow Coins, Three Continents Press, 1981.
The Green Lion of Zion Street, Macmillan, 1988.

PLAYS

"All Day Tomorrow," produced in Knoxville, Tenn. at the Knoxville College Drama Workshop, 1966.

CONTRIBUTOR TO ANTHOLOGIES

New Negro Poets: U.S.A., edited by Langston Hughes, Indiana University Press, 1964.
Kaleidoscope, edited by Robert Hayden, Harcourt, 1967.
Black Fire, edited by LeRoi Jones and Larry Neal, Morrow, 1968.
Nine Black Poets, edited by R. Baird Shuman, Moore, 1968.
The Poetry of the Negro, 1746-1970, edited by Hughes and Arna Bontemps, Doubleday, 1970.
The Poetry of Black America, edited by Arnold Adoff, Harper, 1972.

OTHER

Contributor of poetry and short stories to *Massachusetts Review, Black World, Callaloo, First World, Essence, Negro Digest,* and other periodicals.

SIDELIGHTS: In a biographical entry published in *Dictionary of Literary Biography* Mary Williams Burger writes that Julia Fields "is an important representative of the cultural and artistic renaissance that gave birth to her writings, not only because her poems and short stories probe the political, social, and moral status of black people, but because they are saturated with their authentic language, sensibilities, values, rituals, and myths." Burger continues to state that "against a background of surging and resurging black consciousness and aesthetics, her works capture and reflect the folk spirit in black life, shatter the illusions of history, and demystify sacred areas of Southern life and black experience; she liberates, therefore, the feelings, mind, and spirit of her readers and audiences."

BIOGRAPHICAL/CRITICAL SOURCES:

BOOKS

Dictionary of Literary Biography, Volume 41: *Afro-American Poets Since 1955,* Gale, 1985.

PERIODICALS

Los Angeles Times Book Review, May 22, 1988.

*   *   *

FINLEY, Glenna
See WITTE, Glenna Finley

FISHER, Robert (Tempest) 1943-

PERSONAL: Born August 2, 1943, in Perivale, England; son of John Tempest (a civil servant) and Doris (an antique dealer; maiden name, Hiscock) Fisher; married Celia Margaret Fulton (an editor), April 13, 1969; children: Jacob Alexander, Thomas Gabriel. *Education:* Goldsmiths College, London, B.A. (with honors), 1976.

ADDRESSES: Home—7 Maze Rd., Kew, Surrey TW9 3DA, England.

CAREER: Teacher at primary schools in London, England, 1964-66 and 1969-72, and Addis Ababa, Ethiopia, 1966-69; Beacon Hill School (primary school), Hong Kong, deputy principal, 1972-74; St. Mary's Primary School, Twickenham, England, deputy headmaster, 1974-82; Archdeacon Cambridge School, Twickenham, head teacher, 1983-87; West London Institute of Higher Education, London, England, senior lecturer of higher education, 1988—.

MEMBER: National Association of Primary Education, Thinking Skills Network.

AWARDS, HONORS: Research grant from Schools Curriculum Development Council (U.K.), 1985-86, for setting up a program to teach thinking skills to three- to eleven-year-olds.

WRITINGS:

Together Today: Themes and Stories for Assembly (for teachers), Evans Brothers, 1981.
(Editor) *Amazing Monsters: Verses to Chill and Thrill* (for children), Faber, 1982.
Together With Infants: Themes and Stories for Assembly (for teachers), Evans Brothers, 1982.
(Editor) *Ghosts Galore: Haunting Verse* (for children), Faber, 1983.
The Assembly Year (for teachers), Collins, 1985.
(Editor) *Funny Folk: Poems about People* (for children), Faber, 1986.
Religions (reference for children), Macdonald, 1987.
(Editor) *Witch Words: Poems of Magic and Mystery* (for children), Faber, 1987.
Problem Solving in Primary Schools, Basil Blackwell, 1987.
Investigating Mathematics, Basil Blackwell, 1988.
Pet Poems, Faber, in press.
Teaching Children to Think, Basil Blackwell, in press.

Contributor to education journals. Consultant to *Pictorial Education*, 1980-81; editorial consultant to educational publishers, 1981—.

SIDELIGHTS: Robert Fisher told *CA:* "I have taught in the United Kingdom, Ethiopia, and Hong Kong, at all age levels from preschool to adult. I write books for teachers to foster a creative and integrative approach to education. In my poetry books for children, my aim is to freshen and stimulate the imagination, whether the child is eight or eighty. The distinction between child and adult is often a false one. Poetry is one aspect of creative education which can reach both the mind of the child and the child within the adult. My recent research is into teaching children thinking and problem solving skills. I would welcome contacts with people working in this field, or in the field of children's poetry."

AVOCATIONAL INTERESTS: Creating educational games for children and adults, reviewing books, lecturing on educational topics.

FLACK, Audrey L. 1931-

PERSONAL: Born May 30, 1931, in Brooklyn, N.Y.; daughter of Morris and Jeanette Flack; married H. Robert Marcus, June 7, 1970; children: Melissa, Hannah. *Education:* Cooper Union, graduated, 1951; attended Cranbrook Academy of Art; Yale University, B.F.A., 1952; attended New York University, 1953.

ADDRESSES: Home—110 Riverside Dr., New York, N.Y. 10024. *Agent*—Louis K. Meisel Gallery, 141 Prince St., New York, N.Y. 10012.

CAREER: New York University, New York City, instructor in anatomy, 1960-68; Pratt Institute, Brooklyn, N.Y., instructor in drawing and painting, 1960-68; School of Visual Arts, New York City, instructor in drawing and painting, 1970-74; University of Bridgeport, Bridgeport, Conn., Albert Dorne Professorship, 1975; Cooper Union, New York City, Mellon Professor of Anatomy, 1982. Work exhibited in solo shows at Roko Gallery and Louis K. Meisel Gallery, in group exhibitions at Whitney Museum of American Art, 1970, 1972, 1978, and 1986, Wadsworth Athenaeum, Tokyo Metropolitan Art Museum, 1974 and 1981, Toledo Museum of Art, 1975, National Gallery of Art, 1980, and in permanent collections at Museum of Modern Art, Guggenheim Museum, Smithsonian Institute, St. Louis Museum, and National Gallery of Australia. Member of advisory board of Women's Caucus for Art and of Visual Artists and Galleries Association (VAGA). Visiting professor and lecturer at national and international universities and museums.

AWARDS, HONORS: National Award of Merit from national exhibit of paintings at Butler Institute of American Art, 1974; honorary doctorate from Cooper Union, 1977; St. Gaudens Medal, Cooper Union, 1982.

WRITINGS:

(Contributor of illustrations) *Yanitas* (exhibit catalogue), Louis K. Meisel Gallery, 1978.
(Contributor of illustrations) *Super Realism*, Phaidon, 1979.
Audrey Flack on Painting, self-illustrated, Abrams, 1981.
Art and Soul: Notes on Creating (self-illustrated), Dutton, 1986.

Contributor of illustrations, *Tokyo Biennale* (catalogue), 1974. Contributor of illustrations to magazines, including *Time, Art News, Art in America,* and *Arts,* and to newspapers.

WORK IN PROGRESS: A book, *The Artist's Second Book of Notes.*

SIDELIGHTS: Audrey Flack, who has taught anatomy, drawing, and painting, is also "one of the foremost photorealist artists," writes a *Booklist* contributor. A painter working in the photorealistic style uses a hard-edged clarity to give his work a photographic look. Flack's paintings plus bits of conversations with artists, reminiscences, and observations appear in her book, *Art and Soul: Notes on Creating.* In putting the book together, Flack intended to "identify and record the shared but often unspoken knowledge among artists." The *Booklist* contributor, while remarking that some of the pieces are "sentimental and trite," continues that "the majority of them are engrossing and lively." And *Los Angeles Times Book Review* contributor Jonathan Kirsch believes *Art and Soul* "is a book whose insights will be useful and even inspiring, not only to the aspiring visual artist but to the earnest practitioner in any creative endeavor."

BIOGRAPHICAL/CRITICAL SOURCES:

BOOKS

Coke, Van Deren, *The Painter and the Photograph,* University of New Mexico Press, 1972.
Flack, Audrey, *Art and Soul: Notes on Creating,* Dutton, 1986.
Kultermann, Udo, *New Realism,* New Yale Graphic Society, 1972.
Meisel, Louis K., *Photorealism,* Abrams, 1980.
Nemser, Cindy, *Art Talk,* Scribner, 1975.

PERIODICALS

Booklist, September 1, 1986.
Library Journal, December, 1986.
Los Angeles Times Book Review, November 16, 1986.

* * *

FLORES, Janis 1946-

PERSONAL: Born January 12, 1946, in Fort Benton, Mont.; daughter of J. Eldon (an airline dispatcher) and Dorothea (a legal secretary; maiden name, Dickens) Overholser; married Raynaldo G. Flores (a horseshoer), January 13, 1968. *Education:* Immaculate Heart College, Los Angeles, Calif., B.A., 1967; St. Luke Hospital, Pasadena, Calif., license in medical technology, 1969.

ADDRESSES: Home—Sebastopol, Calif. *Agent*—Emilie Jacobson, Curtis Brown Ltd., Ten Astor St., New York, N.Y. 10003.

CAREER: Live Oak Laboratory, Arcadia, Calif., medical technologist, 1969-72; Biskind Laboratory, Santa Rosa, Calif., supervisor, 1972-76; Empire Laboratory, Santa Rosa, supervisor, 1976—.

MEMBER: American Society of Clinical Pathologists, National Mustang Association, Defenders of Wildlife, Fund for Animals, California Writers Club, Redwood Writers Club.

WRITINGS:

NOVELS

Hawkshead, Doubleday, 1976.
Peregrine House, Doubleday, 1977.
Gyrfalcon Hall, Ace Books, 1977.
Bittersweet, Bantam, 1978.
Cynara, Ace Books, 1979.
High Dominion, Signet, 1981.
Loving Ties, Fawcett, 1986.
Running in Place, Fawcett, 1987.
Divided Loyalties, Fawcett, 1988.

Also author of various contemporary romances, 1981-88.

WORK IN PROGRESS: Women's contemporary fiction and medical/suspense.

AVOCATIONAL INTERESTS: Animals (especially horses—she owns three—and endangered species); piano, gardening, sewing.

* * *

FORBES, Calvin 1945-

PERSONAL: Born May 6, 1945, in Newark, N.J.; son of Jacob and Mary (Short) Forbes. *Education:* Attended New School for Social Research and Rutgers University; Brown University, M.F.A., 1978.

ADDRESSES: Home—Washington, D.C. *Office*—73 Arsdale Terrace, East Orange, N.J. 07018.

CAREER: Emerson College, Boston, Mass., assistant professor of English, 1969-73; Tufts University, Medford, Mass., assistant professor of English, 1973-74, 1975-77; Howard University, Washington, D.C., writer in residence; Washington College, Chestertown, Md., assistant professor of creative writing, 1988-89. Fulbright lecturer in Denmark, France, and England, 1974-75; guest lecturer at University of the West Indies, 1982-83.

MEMBER: Modern Language Association, College Language Association.

AWARDS, HONORS: Breadloaf Writers Conference fellowship in poetry, summer, 1973; summer residency at Yaddo, 1976-77; National Endowment for the Arts fellowship, 1982-83; D.C. Commission on the Arts fellowship, 1984; New Jersey State Council on the Arts fellowship.

WRITINGS:

POETRY

Blue Monday, Wesleyan University Press, 1974.
From the Book of Shine, Burning Deck Press, 1979.

CONTRIBUTOR

Arnold Adoff, editor, *The Poetry of Black America: Anthology of the Twentieth Century,* Harper, 1972.
Abraham Chapman, editor, *New Black Voices,* New American Library, 1972.
X. J. Kennedy, editor, *Messages: A Thematic Anthology of Poetry,* Little, Brown, 1973.
Daryl Hine and Joseph Parisi, editors, *The Poetry Anthology, 1912-1977,* Houghton, 1978.
Frank Stewart and John Unterecker, editors, *Poetry Hawaii: A Contemporary Anthology,* University Press of Hawaii, 1979.
Keith Waldrop and Rosemarie Waldrop, editors, *A Century in Two Decades: A Burning Deck Anthology, 1961-1981,* Burning Deck Press, 1982.

Also contributor to *The Morrow Anthology of Younger American Poets,* 1985.

WORK IN PROGRESS: A novel.

SIDELIGHTS: Poet Calvin Forbes is "one of the prominent black voices to develop out of the 1970s. . . . He communicates a . . . highly moral philosophy as well as the thoughts and emotions of a writer whose artistic ability and vision are still expanding," states *Dictionary of Literary Biography* essayist Robert A. Coles. An important part of the poet's development as a writer were the years he spent hitchhiking around the United States, notes Coles. The poet's early education also included an association with poet Jose Garcia Villa at the New School for Social Research, and intense study of John Donne, Gwendolyn Brooks, and Philip Larkin. Like these poets, Forbes writes in a complex, controlled style.

His subjects vary from the lives of street people to the origin of the artistic impulse, but in all his work, observes Coles, "Forbes is skillful in the way he suggests double, and sometimes, triple layered meanings through tight control over simile and metaphor, both of which spark clear, powerful phrases and images." For an example, writes Joseph Parisi in *Poetry* magazine, one only has to consider the title of Forbes's first volume, *Blue Monday:* "Both in subjects and style the analogy to the bittersweet blues is particularly apt in describing these poems, whose plangent phrases wander as digressive variations sprung out from, around, and back again to their central themes. The pains of, for the most part, love mingle with despair over the dreadful past and for the doubtful future; yet the burnt-out if not consuming feelings following failure aren't vented in rage but released in the tenderness of a sensuous lyrical mode.''

BIOGRAPHICAL/CRITICAL SOURCES:

BOOKS

Dictionary of Literary Biography, Volume 41: *Afro-American Poets since 1955,* Gale, 1985.

PERIODICALS

Poetry, July, 1975.†

*   *   *

FOSTER, Paul 1931-

PERSONAL: Born October 15, 1931, in Salem, N.J.; son of Eldridge M. and Mary (Manning) Foster. *Education:* Rutgers University, B.A., 1954; St. John's University, Jamaica, N.Y., LL.B., 1958. *Religion:* Protestant.

ADDRESSES: Home—242 East Fifth St., New York, N.Y. 10003.

CAREER: Playwright. La Mama Experimental Theatre Club, New York, N.Y., president and co-founder, 1962—. Foreign lecturer on American theater for Department of State in Europe and South America, 1978, 1980. Taught dramatic writing at University of California, San Diego, 1981, and at New York University, 1982. *Military service:* U.S. Naval Reserve, Judge's Advocate General Corps, 1955-57.

MEMBER: PEN, Dramatists Guild, Authors League of America, Societe des Auteurs et Compositeurs (Paris), Eugene O'Neill Theatre Foundation, New Dramatists, Players Club.

AWARDS, HONORS: Rockefeller Foundation fellowship for playwriting, 1967, 1968; New York Drama Critics Award, 1968, for "Tom Paine"; Tony Award nomination, 1972, for "Elizabeth I"; Creative Artists Public Service grants, 1972, 1974; National Endowment for the Arts fellowship, 1973, 1975; British Arts Council award, 1973, for *Elizabeth I;* Guggenheim literature fellowship, 1974; Theatre Heute award, 1977.

WRITINGS:

Minnie the Whore, The Birthday, and Other Stories, Ediciones Zodiaco (Caracas), 1962.
The Buddhist Influence in T. S. Eliot's "Four Quartets," Haag und Hergen, 1977.
(Translator with others) Odon von Horvath, *Odon von Horvath: Kasimir and Karoline; Faith, Hope, and Charity; Figaro Gets a Divorce; Judgement Day,* PAJ Publications, 1986.

PLAYS

Hurrah for the Bridge (also see below; one-act; first produced Off-Off Broadway at Caffe Cino, 1963), Canal Ramirez, 1963.
Balls and Other Plays (contains: "Hurrah for the Bridge"; "The Recluse," first produced Off-Off Broadway at Cafe La Mama, 1964; "Balls," one-act, first produced Off-Off Off Broadway at Cafe La Mama, November, 1964;

"The Hessian Corporal," first produced Off-Off Broadway at Cafe La Mama, 1966), Calder & Boyars, 1967, Samuel French, 1968.
Tom Paine (full-length; first produced Off-Off Broadway at Cafe La Mama, May 15, 1967; produced on the West End at the Vaudeville Theatre, 1967; produced Off-Off-Broadway at Stage 73, March 25, 1968), Calder & Boyars, 1967, Grove Press, 1968.
The Madonna in the Orchard (also see below; full-length; first produced Off-Off Broadway at Cafe La Mama, 1965), Breakthrough Press, 1971.
"Satyricon" (also see below; first produced Off-Broadway at La Mama Theatre, 1972), published in *The Off-Off Broadway Book,* edited by Bruce Mailman and Albert Poland, Bobbs-Merrill, 1972.
Elizabeth I (also see below; first produced on Broadway at the Lyceum Theatre, 1972), Samuel French, 1972.
Elizabeth I and Other Plays (contains "The Madonna in the Orchard," "Elizabeth I," and "Satyricon"), Calder & Boyars, 1973.
"Rags to Riches to Rags," first produced Off-Broadway at La Mama Theatre, December, 1974.
(With John Braden) *Silver Queen Saloon* (also see below; musical; first produced Off-Broadway at La Mama Theatre, 1973), Samuel French, 1975.
Marcus Brutus (also see below; first produced at Stage West, Springfield, Mass., January 11, 1975), Calder & Boyars, 1975.
Marcus Brutus [and] *Silver Queen Saloon,* Calder & Boyars, 1977.
"A Kiss Is Just a Kiss," first produced Off-Broadway at Manhattan Punchline Theatre, June 6, 1983.
"The Dark and Mr. Stone," first produced Off-Broadway at La Mama Theatre, October 23, 1985.
"The Dark and Mr. Stone: Murder in the Magnolias," first produced Off-Broadway at La Mama Theatre, December, 1985.
"The Dark and Mr. Stone III: Murder in the Mummy's Tomb," first produced Off-Broadway at La Mama Theatre, November 5, 1986.

Also author of "The House on Lake Geneva," as yet neither published nor produced.

OTHER

Heimskringla; or, The Stoned Angels (teleplay; produced by National Education Television for "Theatre America" series, 1969), Calder & Boyars, 1970, Samuel French, 1971.
"Mellon" (filmscript), produced by Francis Thompson, Inc. for Exxon Corp., 1981.
"The Cop and the Anthem" (filmscript), produced by Learning Corp. of America, 1982.

Also author of "The Tragedy of the Commons," 1979, and "The Vampyre and Dr. Frankenstein," 1980, both teleplays. Author of filmscripts "Smile," 1983, "Cinderella Story," 1984, and "Home Port," 1984.

SIDELIGHTS: Playwright Paul Foster "writes plays that try genuinely to extend the range of the theater," observes Clive Barnes in a *New York Times* review of "Marcus Brutus." "More than most of his colleagues, he wants to push theater beyond its conventionally realistic bounds, and to use it as an arena for philosophic and, almost more interestingly, historic thought." "Marcus Brutus" presents the story of "a playwright going mad, obsessed with the creatures of his own creation," describes Barnes. Because the protagonist is often unable to distinguish between objective existence and his work, the play contains "curious levels of fantasy and reality," comments the critic. Barnes does find that "the mechanics of the play—where does fantasy fade into reality—are never quite clear"; nevertheless, he admits that "as always with Mr. Foster, the proposition is dramatically interesting."

In "A Kiss Is Just a Kiss," Foster again presents a character's skewed view of reality, this time using the daydreams of a Humphrey Bogart film buff as his focus. The play "is a kind of Walter Mitty adventure . . . mixed in with the story of Bogart's actual life, his marriages, his career," describes Richard F. Shepard in the *New York Times*. "Done with high good humor," remarks Shepard, ". . . it all slips back and forth between life and film unreality—crazily, but intelligibly and most wittily." Concludes the critic: "As humor should be, ['A Kiss Is Just a Kiss'] says no more than it needs to say to make its point."

BIOGRAPHICAL/CRITICAL SOURCES:

PERIODICALS

Boston Advocate, January 12, 1975.
Hudson Review, summer, 1968.
Long Island Press, April 6, 1972.
Newsweek, April 8, 1968.
New Yorker, April 6, 1978.
New York Times, January 19, 1975, June 24, 1978, June 18, 1985, November 18, 1985, December 2, 1985, November 10, 1986.
Village Voice, March, 1968.†

*   *   *

FOX-GENOVESE, Elizabeth 1941-

PERSONAL: Born May 28, 1941, in Boston, Mass.; daughter of Edward Whiting (a professor of history) and Elizabeth (Simon) Fox; married Eugene Dominick Genovese (a professor of history), June 6, 1969. *Education:* Bryn Mawr College, A.B., 1963; Harvard University, A.M., 1966, Ph.D., 1974.

ADDRESSES: Home—1487 Sheridan Walk, Atlanta, Ga. 30324. *Office*—Department of Women's Studies, 210 Physics, Emory University, Atlanta, Ga. 30322.

CAREER: Harvard University, Cambridge, Mass., teaching fellow, 1965-69; Houghton Mifflin Co., Boston, Mass., assistant editor in history, 1966-67; Prentice-Hall, New York City, picture researcher, 1971-72; University of Rochester, Rochester, N.Y., assistant professor of history and liberal arts, 1973-76, associate professor of history, 1976-80; State University of New York at Binghamton, professor of history, 1980-86; Emory University, Atlanta, Ga., professor of history and director of women's studies, 1986—, Eleanor Raoul Professor of the Humanities, 1988—. Instructor, Newberry Library, 1980; directeur d'etudes associe, Ecole des Hautes Studes en Sciences Sociales, Paris, 1982. Lecturer; has presented scholarly papers at academic meetings and served on several university committees; research associate, Organization of American Historians; director, project on Integrating Materials on Women into Traditional Survey Courses. Developer and chairperson, Cluster on Interdisciplinary Study of Women in Culture and Society, 1978-80. Consultant for Women's History, UNESCO, 1980, University of Maine at Orono and Canisius College, both 1982, and William Patterson College and Grinnell College, both 1987.

MEMBER: American Historical Association, Society for French Historical Studies (member of program committee, 1975-76), American Studies Association (program committee, 1985-87), Social Science History Association (program committee, 1985-86; executive council, 1986-88), Modern Language Association of America, Southern Association of Women Historians, Southern Historical Association, Societe des Etudes Robespierristes, Berkshire Conference of Women Historians.

AWARDS, HONORS: Grants from Eleutherian Mills-Hagley Foundation, 1972-73, and University of Rochester, 1975; fellowships from University of Rochester, 1975, 1978, National Endowment for the Humanities, 1976-77, New York Institute for the Humanities, 1978-79, Newberry Library, 1979, Rockefeller Foundation, 1979-80, American Council of Learned Societies and the Ford Foundation, 1984, and National Humanities Center, 1984-85; Fund for the Improvement of Postsecondary Education grant, 1979-80 and Lilly Endowment, 1982-83, both for research project, "Integrating Materials on Women into Traditional Survey Courses."

WRITINGS:

The Origins of Physiocracy: Economic Revolution and Social Order in Eighteenth-Century France, Cornell University Press, 1976.
(Author of introduction) *The Economic and Political Writings of Pierre Samuel Du Pont De Nemours*, Kto Press, 1980.
(Contributor) *Girondins et Montagnards*, Clavreuil (Paris), 1982.
(With husband, Eugene D. Genovese) *Fruits of Merchant Capital: Slavery and Bourgeois Property in the Rise and Expansion of Capitalism*, Oxford University Press, 1983.
(Translator and author of introduction) *The Autobiography of Pierre Samuel Du Pont De Nemours*, Scholarly Resources, 1983.
Within the Plantation Household: Black and White Women of the Old South, University of North Carolina Press, 1988.

Contributor to journals, including *Nation, New Left Review, Journal of American History, Antioch Review, Partisan Review*, and *New Republic*. Editor for international affairs, *Marxist Perspectives*, 1977-80; *Partisan Review*, assistant editor, 1978-82, contributing editor, 1982—. Member of publications committee, American Studies Association, 1980—; member of advisory board, *Women and History*.

WORK IN PROGRESS: Research on "the fashionable woman," feminist theory, women and individualism, and, with husband, Eugene D. Genovese, the slave-holding class of the antebellum South.

SIDELIGHTS: Elizabeth Fox-Genovese told *CA:* "Through the years, writing becomes an ever greater source of pleasure for me. As craft, writing gives me a sense of power—the power that derives from the ability to shape and to choose. Increasingly, I strive for clarity and simplicity. Increasingly, I am conscious of wanting to write to be understood. My greatest joy has been the discovery that it is possible to write of intellectual—even academic—subjects in my own voice. In this sense writing has become an important way of taking possession of my own life and of communicating my particular vision. And the pleasures of writing rank high among the things that I try to teach my students."

*   *   *

FRANKLIN, John Hope 1915-

PERSONAL: Born January 2, 1915, in Rentiesville, Okla.; son of Buck Colbert (an attorney; also the first Negro judge to sit in chancery in Oklahoma district court) and Mollie (Parker) Franklin; married Aurelia E. Whittington, June 11, 1940; children: John Whittington. *Education:* Fisk University, A.B., 1935; Harvard University, A.M., 1936, Ph.D., 1941.

ADDRESSES: Home—208 Pineview Rd., Durham, N.C. 27707. *Office*—Department of History, Duke University, Durham, N.C. 27708.

CAREER: Fisk University, Nashville, Tenn., instructor in history, 1936-37; St. Augustine's College, Raleigh, N.C., instructor in history, 1938-43; North Carolina College (now North Carolina Central University), Durham, instructor in history, 1943-47; Howard University, Washington, D.C., professor of history, 1947-56; Brooklyn College of the City University of New York, Brooklyn, professor of history and chairman of department, 1956-64; University of Chicago, Chicago, Ill., professor of history, 1964-82, John Matthews Manly Distinguished Service Professor, 1969-82, chairman of history department, 1967-70; Duke University, Durham, James B. Duke Professor of History, 1982-85, professor emeritus, 1985—. Visiting professor at University of California, Harvard University, University of Wisconsin, Cornell University, University of Hawaii, Australia National University, Salzburg (Austria) Seminar, and other institutions; Pitt Professor of American History and Institutions, Cambridge University, 1962-63. Board of Foreign Scholarships, member, 1962-69, chairman, 1966-69. Member of board of trustees, Fisk University, 1947-84, and De Sable Museum, Chicago.

MEMBER: American Historical Association (member of executive council, 1959-62; president, 1979), Organization of American Historians (president, 1975), Association for Study of Negro Life and History, NAACP (member of board of directors, Legal Defense and Education Fund), American Association of University Professors, American Philosophical Society, American Studies Association, Southern Historical Association (life member; president, 1970), Phi Beta Kappa (president, 1973-76), Phi Alpha Theta.

AWARDS, HONORS: Guggenheim fellowships, 1950-51, 1973-74; LL.D. from Morgan State University, 1960, Lincoln University, 1961, Virginia State College, 1961, Hamline University, 1965, Lincoln College, 1965, Fisk University, 1965, Columbia University, 1969, University of Notre Dame, 1970, and Harvard University, 1981; A.M., Cambridge University, 1962; L.H.D., Long Island University, 1964, University of Massachusetts, 1964, and Yale University, 1977; Litt.D., Princeton University, 1972; Clarence L. Holte Literary Award, 1986, for *George Washington Williams: A Biography.*

WRITINGS:

The Free Negro in North Carolina, 1790-1860, University of North Carolina Press, 1943, reprinted, Russell, 1969.
From Slavery to Freedom: A History of Negro Americans, Knopf, 1947, 6th edition (with Alfred A. Moss, Jr.), 1987.
The Militant South, 1800-1860, Belknap Press, 1956, revised edition, 1970.
Reconstruction after the Civil War, University of Chicago Press, 1961.
The Emancipation Proclamation, Doubleday, 1963.
(With John W. Caughey and Ernest R. May) *Land of the Free: A History of the United States*, Benziger, 1965, teacher's edition, 1971.
(With the editors of Time-Life Books) *Illustrated History of Black Americans*, Time-Life, 1970.

Racial Equality in America, University of Chicago Press, 1976.
A Southern Odyssey: Travelers in the Antebellum North, Louisiana State University Press, 1976.
George Washington Williams: The Massachusetts Years, American Antiquarian, 1983.
George Washington Williams: A Biography, University of Chicago Press, 1985.

EDITOR

The Civil War Diary of J. T. Ayers, Illinois State Historical Society, 1947.
Albion Tourgee, *A Fool's Errand*, Belknap Press, 1961.
T. W. Higginson, *Army Life in a Black Regiment*, Beacon Press, 1962.
Three Negro Classics, Avon, 1965.
(With Isadore Starr) *The Negro in Twentieth Century America: A Reader on the Struggle for Civil Rights*, Vintage Books, 1967.
Color and Race, Houghton, 1968.
W.E.B. Du Bois, *The Suppression of the African Slave Trade*, Louisiana State University Press, 1969.
John R. Lynch, *Reminiscences of an Active Life: The Autobiography of John R. Lynch*, University of Chicago Press, 1970.
Eugene Levy, *James Weldon Johnson: Black Leader, Black Voice*, University of Chicago Press, 1973.
(With August Meier) *Black Leaders of the Twentieth Century*, University of Illinois Press, 1982.

CONTRIBUTOR

Arthur S. Link and Richard Leopold, editors, *Problems in American History*, Prentice-Hall, 1952, 2nd revised edition, 1966.
Rayford W. Logan, editor, *The Negro Thirty Years Afterward*, Howard University Press, 1955.
The Americans: Ways of Life and Thought, Cohen & West, 1956.
Charles Frankel, editor, *Issues in University Education*, Harper, 1959.
Ralph Newman, editor, *Lincoln for the Ages*, Doubleday, 1960.
Charles G. Sellars, Jr., editor, *The Southerner as American*, University of North Carolina Press, 1960.
Abraham Seldin Eisenstadt, editor, *American History: Recent Interpretations*, Crowell, 1962.
Herbert Hill, editor, *Soon One Morning*, Knopf, 1963.
H. V. Hodson, editor, *The Atlantic Future*, Longmans, Green, 1964.
John C. McKinney and Edgar T. Thompson, editors, *The South in Continuity and Change*, Duke University Press, 1965.
John P. Davis, editor, *The American Negro Reference Book*, Prentice-Hall, 1966.
Harold Hyman, editor, *New Frontiers of the American Reconstruction*, University of Illinois Press, 1966.
Kenneth Clark and Talcott Parsons, editors, *The Negro American*, Houghton, 1966.
Daniel J. Boorstin, editor, *The American Primer*, University of Chicago Press, 1966.
C. Vann Woodward, editor, *The Comparative Approach to American History*, Basic Books, 1968.
William Edward Farrison, editor, *William Wells Brown: Author and Reformer*, University of Chicago Press, 1969.
Marcia M. Mathews, *Henry Ossawa Tanner, American Artist*, University of Chicago Press, 1969.

Also contributor to *Crusade for Justice: The Autobiography of Ida B. Wells*, edited by Alfreda M. Duster, 1970.

OTHER

Also author of pamphlets for U.S. Information Service. Contributor of articles to numerous journals and periodicals. Coeditor of series in American history for Crowell and AHM Publishing, 1964—; general editor of "Zenith Book" series on secondary education, Doubleday, 1965—; general editor of "Negro American Biographies and Autobiographies" series, Univeristy of Chicago Press, 1969; editor, with Eisenstadt, of "American History Series," Harlan Davidson, Inc., 1985—. Contributor of articles to numerous journals and periodicals.

WORK IN PROGRESS: A book on runaway slaves; a collection of essays; editing the autobiography of his father, Buck Colbert Franklin.

SIDELIGHTS: Author of the critically acclaimed *George Washington Williams: A Biography,* John Hope Franklin "has long been a leader in the study of Afro-American life," writes Ira Berlin in the *New York Times Book Review.* For over four decades, the distinguished Franklin has pioneered a number of historical studies; included among his books are *Reconstruction after the Civil War, The Emancipation Proclamation,* and *Racial Equality in America,* an examination of the egalitarian principles of America's founding fathers. Furthermore, his general history entitled *From Slavery to Freedom: A History of Negro Americans*—its sixth edition published in 1987—is considered by many to be the standard text on Afro-American history. Franklin's overall contributions to the field of Afro-American history prompted Roy Wilkins in the *New Republic* to remark: "John Hope Franklin is an uncommon historian who has consistently corrected in eloquent language the misrecording of this country's rich heritage."

In 1985, Franklin won recognition for *George Washington Williams: A Biography,* which represents forty years of Franklin's research into the life and achievements of the nineteenth century black historian. "Beginning in 1945 with less than a dozen letters and a hasty reading of Williams' African diary, which has since disappeared," remarks Louis R. Harlan in the *Washington Post Book World,* "Franklin has painstakingly gathered the pieces of evidence from three continents and, like an archaeologist, reconstructed a mosaic that is astonishingly life-like." Soldier, journalist, public speaker, historian—among other roles—the multi-faceted Williams was the author in 1883 of *History of the Negro Race in America from 1619 to 1880,* a two-volume history which represents one of the first scholarly treatments of the black experience in America. "Williams's sources and methods qualify him as a pioneer in the transformation of American historical scholarship from panegyrics to professionalism," Berlin states. "One of the most significant achievements of Mr. Franklin's biography is that it restores Williams to his proper place in the development of an American historiography." Robert A. Hill likewise praises Franklin's illuminating assessment of Williams's achievements: "On the basis of the evidence here presented, it becomes clear that Williams is entitled, by his virtuosity, erudition, and contribution to the fields of history and African protest, to a place among the most notable public figures of America's Gilded Age, and this in an era truly rich in its profusion of outstanding personalities."

An aspect of *George Washington Williams* that reviewers found particularly interesting was the insight offered into Franklin's own life as an Afro-American historian. "Stalking George Washington Williams," the title of the book's opening chapter, "offers a unique view of the historian as detective as well as scholar," notes Berlin: "Beginning in 1945 when the author—who had never taken a course in Afro-American history—first considered writing a general history of black Americans, he sensed the connection between his own pioneering work and that of Williams. Through the next four decades he stalked his subject from Williams's origins in a small Pennsylvania town, across North America, to Mexico, to Europe, to central Africa, to Egypt and finally to England where Williams died. 'George Washington Williams' is thus part autobiography and part general history—a mixture that makes for fascinating and engaging reading." James Olney similarly comments in the *Southern Review:* "The major interest of the book is that the life of John Hope Franklin is fully present in the (re)creation of the life of George Washington Williams, his predcecessor, his forefather, perhaps his alter ego."

In 1975, thirty years into his study of Williams, Franklin discovered that the historian's burial place was an unmarked grave in a cemetery near the center of Blackpool, England. Accompanied by his wife, two reporters, and a photographer, Franklin laid a wreath at the site—now marked by a tablet that reads, "George Washington Williams, Afro-American Historian, 1849-1891."Olney draws a comparison to author Alice Walker's discovery of the unmarked grave of author Zora Neale Hurston, commenting on the particular importance of Franklin's work in Afro-American history: "Just as Afro-American literary history is a matter of recovering predecessors, of reviving and revising, of crossing and combining ancestral figures, so also Afro-American history, in the person and present moment of John Hope Franklin, devotes itself to recovering and resuscitating the ancestral past and to rescuing its own particular progenitors and predecessors from the obscurity that has been so often their fate in this country."

AVOCATIONAL INTERESTS: Fishing, growing orchids.

BIOGRAPHICAL/CRITICAL SOURCES:

BOOKS

Franklin, John Hope, *George Washington Williams: A Biography,* University of Chicago Press, 1985.

PERIODICALS

American Historical Review, April, 1962.
Chicago Tribune Book World, November 24, 1985.
Christian Science Monitor, September 22, 1947.
Commonweal, July 16, 1943, October 31, 1947, March 8, 1963.
Journal of American History, September, 1986.
New Republic, January 22, 1977.
New York Herald Tribune Book Review, December 14, 1947, September 23, 1956.
New York Times, October 12, 1947, September 23, 1956.
New York Times Book Review, April 7, 1963, December 10, 1967, November 17, 1985.
Saturday Review, December 22, 1956.
Saturday Review of Literature, June 19, 1943, November 8, 1947.
Southern Review, spring, 1986.
Times Literary Supplement, July 19, 1963.
Washington Post Book World, January 11, 1986, May 25, 1986.
Yale Review, winter, 1957.

*   *   *

FRANKLIN, Linda Campbell 1941-

PERSONAL: Born February 4, 1941, in Memphis, Tenn.;

daughter of Robert Dumont (a writer and librarian) and Mary Mac (a writer and librarian; maiden name, Wilson) Franklin. *Education:* Attended University of Colorado, 1958-60; University of Toledo, B.A., 1962.

ADDRESSES: Home—P.O. Box 383, Murray Hill Station, New York, N.Y. 10156.

CAREER: Worked as waitress and museum librarian in Memphis, Tenn., as bookstore manager at Jewish Museum, as manager of bicycle shop, and as bookkeeper of a film company, all in New York City, 1965-70; free-lance writer, editor, and illustrator, 1970-76; Tree Communications, Inc., New York City, editor, 1976-81, senior editor, 1981-84. Illustrator for filmstrip "A Turn of the Phrase" for Westinghouse Learning Corp., New York City, 1973. Resident at Ossabaw Island Project, an artists' colony in Ossabaw, Ga., 1981.

MEMBER: Ephemera Society of America, Early American Industries Association.

WRITINGS:

From Hearth to Cookstove: An American Domestic History of Gadgets and Utensils Made or Used in America From 1700 to 1930, House of Collectibles, 1976, 2nd edition, 1979.
Antiques and Collectibles: A Bibliography of Works in English, Sixteenth Century to 1976, Scarecrow, 1978.
Library Display Ideas, McFarland & Co., 1980.
300 Years of Kitchen Collectibles, Books Americana, 1981, 2nd edition, 1984.
Breads and Biscuits, Tree Communications, 1981.
Our Christmas Book, Tree Communications, 1981.
(Editor) *Birthday Book,* Tree Communications, 1981.
Classroom Display Ideas, McFarland & Co., 1982.
Publicity and Display Ideas, McFarland & Co., 1985.

Editor/author of *Our Old-Fashioned Country Diary,* 1980—, *Ephemera News,* 1982-83, and *Show Forth: Library Publicity and Display,* 1982-84. Publisher/author of *Kitchen Collectibles News,* 1984-86.

WORK IN PROGRESS: A third enlarged edition of *300 Years of Kitchen Collectibles,* and a collectors' bibliography and price guide on cookbooks, both for Books Americana.

SIDELIGHTS: Linda Campbell Franklin's *From Hearth to Cookstove* is a history, and *Three Hundred Years of Kitchen Collectibles* is an identification and price guide to antique kitchen implements and utensils. Franklin gathers information from her experience as a collector and from antique cookbooks and trade catalogues. The books contain many engravings, drawings, and photographs as well as some recipes and anecdotes.

Antiques and Collectibles is an annotated list of 10,000 books located in the major public and private libraries of English-speaking countries. This bibliography contains a coding system to aid the reader in his search for books. Called "very worthwhile" by a *Wilson Library Bulletin* contributor, *Antiques and Collectibles* covers over two hundred subjects, including bottle tickets, fire fighting equipment, barbed wire, games and toys, shaving mugs, baskets, and Wedgwood pottery. Critically acclaimed, the book, said a *RQ* reviewer, "offers surprises in the serendipitous sense for both browser and peruser."

Unlike the above-mentioned books, *Library Display Ideas* and *Publicity and Display Ideas* are handbooks for school librarians who require new and innovative ideas for display case

and bulletin board designs. The books provide librarians with themes, samples, instructions and manufacturers, and *Publicity and Display Ideas* contains a chapter on newsletters.

Franklin told *CA:* "Both my parents are librarians, writers, and lovers of books, and my slightly younger brother (who claims *I* taught him to read) is a publisher. So it seems that I was born in the right cradle of civilization. It remains to be seen whether certain happy confluences of soft water, Mississippi River beats, heat and high humidity, plus plenty of sunlight for seven of my formative years, have created a recognizably Southern novelist, because my first novel remains undone.

"In the last *Sidelights* I listed a few books read to me and my brother, that I thought had probably influenced my young mind, and therefore my adult writing. *Water Babies,* was one, especially for the ominous sooty buildings and mysterious *aqua vitae* drowned-but-alive babies. Lewis Carroll's works—in particular Alice's spectacular fall down the hole—are still visceral experiences. I loved fairy tales and myths, the stranger the better. 'Rumplestiltskin' seems to me now to have been my favorite. Simpler influences, read to me closer to bedtime, were *The Poky Little Puppy,* published in 1942, and all the Curious George and Babar stories. Obviously, I admired stubbornness in adventure stories.

"Reading adds immensely to my store of ideas and understanding, and often stimulates a state of dual consciousness, during which a lot of daydreaming and ten-second fantasies coexist with the actual words I'm reading. A sort of syncopated drumming, during which I often stop to make quick notes to myself. I get immense pleasure from science books and from fiction, but suspect that because I like only a tiny percentage of what I try to read, and that I see only a tiny percentage of what's published, that there is much I might like that is left undiscovered by me or some publisher.

"I don't like short stories, not that I don't appreciate the form or even envy the discipline of a condensed viewpoint, but I just prefer more complex plots that unfold over several months to two or three years, and hence enjoy novellas or novels. I relish freakish characters, singular occurrances, and peculiar details that complement mundane but structurally important details. I especially like the kind of realistic fantasy found in some twentieth century South American, German, and Czechoslovakian books, and in some science fiction.

"I do not like intellectual works whose main purpose is to exercise the virtuosity of the writer or to intimidate the reader. I want a good readable story, but I do want writing rules to be broken. Give me made-up words, sentences and paragraphs of greatly variable length, incomplete sentences. Don't give me dangling participles or casual or no punctuation. Give me the English language used imaginatively and with individual style. I love how our language is so continuously refreshed and sustained by foreign and invented words, by metaphors coming from specialized vocabularies, and by the words and cadence of dialect and slang.

"Five books I recommend are *Three Serious Ladies,* by Jane Bowles; *Widows,* by Ariel Dorfman; *Tristram Shandy,* by Laurence Sterne; *The Tin Drum,* by Gunther Grass; and *Leaf Storm,* by Gabriel Garcia-Marquez.

"Recurrent themes in my own work, and in the books I admire, are: variable perceptions of the passage of time; evidence, tracks, spoor, skeletons, visions, shadows and reflections in water and mirrors; appearances as clues to the past, present and future; accumulation of evidence by design, accident and invention; and acts of collecting and sorting or dividing. All are the stuff of detection, archaeology and time travel, which would be naturals for plot structures for me . . . I guess. The most difficult thing about writing fiction, for me, is recognizing a plot when I see one, knowing its boundaries, beginning and ending. I'm great on bits and pieces of dialogue, description and connective tissue, but poor at plot. In the next two years I am going to try to concentrate on seeking structure in events and characters, and to learn the mechanics of plotting, which requires analytical thought. A friend and I had an interesting conversation recently during which he revealed that while he was growing up his family spent dinnertime talking about motivation—why certain people they knew did what. My family's dinner table was the scene of make-believe, with stories and songs. He grew up with the habit of analyzing; I grew up synthesizing.

"I have spent too much precious time writing nonfiction books, and this has led to a dangerous sense of security because I can earn my living that way. Pain and torment aren't necessary for creativity, but a few timely howls from even timid wolves at the door might get me to struggle harder. My plan for 1987 and 1988 is to complete the nonfiction books I've agreed to do and to work regularly on fiction, also.

"In the last quarter of 1986, I joined a small group of neighborhood writers in New York City. It meets once a week, very informally, and we discuss craft topics such as point of view or editing, but we also read short selections from completed works and works in progress. This has stimulated me because I feel challenged to surpass the expectations of my peers and to try to surprise them. I like their useful criticisms of my work, and think that my analyzing skills are sharpened by trying to put into words exactly what I like or don't like about the work of others. Finally, I am very happy to have found a sort of writing family available in person and frequently. Writing isn't so much a lonely profession as a solitary one. I love New York for the constant activity and opportunity to meet people of all kinds, but the city's demands for attention get in the way of hard work sometimes. Not only would I like to write fiction in the next few years, I'd like to find a writing and thinking retreat, with real grass and trees and my own front porch to sweep. A little mud, a little heat, a bit of rain and a sort of Northern Southern beat.''

BIOGRAPHICAL/CRITICAL SOURCES:

PERIODICALS

American Reference Books Annual, 1979.
Christian Science Monitor, April 28, 1977.
Hobbies, December, 1976.
Museum News, November, 1979.
RQ, spring, 1979.
Washington Post Book World, December 5, 1976.
Wilson Library Bulletin, December, 1978, June, 1981.

* * *

FRANKLIN, S(amuel) Harvey 1928-

PERSONAL: Born in 1928, in Birmingham, England; son of Samuel (a molder) and Isabel (a clerk; maiden name, Latimer) Franklin; married Sonya Coleman (a legal executive), November 28, 1953; children: Michael, Margot, Robert. *Education:* University of Birmingham, B.Com. (with honors) and M.A.

ADDRESSES: Home—143 Glenmore St., Wellington, New Zealand. *Office*—Department of Geography, Victoria University of Wellington, Private Bag, Wellington, New Zealand.

CAREER: Victoria University of Wellington, Wellington, New Zealand, member of faculty, 1951-67, professor of geography, 1967—. Consultant to government and business.

AWARDS, HONORS: Lit.D., University of Birmingham, 1973; New Zealand Book Award from Arts Council and Literary Fund, 1979, for *Trade, Growth, and Anxiety.*

WRITINGS:

The European Peasantry, Methuen, 1969.
Rural Societies, Macmillan, 1971.
Trade, Growth, and Anxiety: New Zealand Beyond the Welfare State, Methuen, 1978.
(Contributor) J. Blum, editor, *Our Forgotten Past*, Thames & Hudson, 1982.
Cul de Sac: The Question of New Zealand's Future, Allen & Unwin, 1985.
(Contributor) F. Slater, editor, *People and Environments*, Collins, 1986.

Also contributor to academic journals and local magazines. Founding editor of *Pacific Viewpoint*, 1960—.

WORK IN PROGRESS: Inferior Goods: Consumption, Social Change, and Industrial Restructuring in C. 20th.

AVOCATIONAL INTERESTS: Skiing.

SIDELIGHTS: S. Harvey Franklin writes: "My interest is absorbed by places rather than people. The incongruities of places reveal as much, maybe more, about life, than the incompleteness of personalities; which perhaps explains why I am a geographer first, and as my colleagues put it, a 'closet historian' second. As Rebecca West wrote—and I admire her writing—'I [have] never used my writing to make a continuous disclosure of my own personality to others, but to discover for my own edification what I know about various subjects which I found to be important to me.'

"But I am equally absorbed by language and therefore tend to talk about my writing rather than my research—a revealing distinction. I hope eventually to produce a book of short stories called *Mistaken Journies*, in which I examine people through places.''

* * *

FREEMAN, Eugene 1906-

PERSONAL: Born February 16, 1906, in New York, N.Y.; son of Alexander Samuel (a designer and worker in ornamental iron) and Rose (Farkas) Freeman; married Ann Sternberg (an editor), November 30, 1930; children: James Montague, Thomas Parry. *Education:* University of California, Los Angeles, A.B., 1926; University of Chicago, fellow, 1928-31, Ph.D, 1937; Northern Illinois College of Optometry, O.D., 1934.

ADDRESSES: Home and office—15401 Blackberry Hill Rd., Los Gatos, Calif. 95030; and P.O. Box 1908, Los Gatos, Calif. 95030.

CAREER: Northern Illinois College of Optometry, Chicago, assistant professor, 1933-36, associate professor, 1936-39, professor of physiologic optics and professional ethics, 1939-43; Illinois Institute of Technology, Chicago, assistant professor of philosophy, 1947-53; Chicago College of Optometry,

Chicago, professor of ethics and vice-president, 1949-56; free-lance writer and editor, 1956-59; Open Court Publishing Co., La Salle, Ill., editor-in-chief, 1959-65, editor of *Monist*, 1959-73; editor emeritus, 1973—, director of philosophy division, 1973—, also has served as editor of scholarly books division; San Jose State University, San Jose, Calif., associate professor, 1965-67, professor of philosophy, 1967-73, professor emeritus, 1973—, chairman of department, 1966-69.

MEMBER: American Philosophical Association, Charles S. Peirce Society, Metaphysical Society of America.

AWARDS, HONORS: D.O.S., Chicago College of Optometry, 1949; other awards for contributions to optometric education include Distinguished Service Foundation Award, Omega Epsilon Phi Award, and Gold Medal of Beta Sigma Kappa.

WRITINGS:

The Categories of Charles Peirce, Open Court, 1934.
(With I. M. Borish) *Manual of Accreditation*, American Optometric Association, 1942.
(Editor with David Appel) *The Great Ideas of Plato*, Lantern Press, 1952, reissued as *The Wisdom and Ideas of Plato*, Fawcett, 1956, 6th edition, 1969.
(Editor with William L. Reese and contributor) *Process and Divinity: The Hartshorne Festschrift*, Open Court, 1967.
(Editor with Joseph Owens) *The Wisdom and Ideas of St. Thomas Aquinas*, Fawcett, 1968.
(Editor with Wilfrid Sellars) *Basic Issues in the Philosophy of Time*, Open Court, 1971.
(Editor with Maurice Mandelbaum) *Spinoza: Essays in Interpretation*, Open Court, 1975.
The Abdication of Philosophy; Philosophy and the Public Good: Essays in Honor of Paul Schlipp, Open Court, 1976.
(Editor) *The Relevance of Charles Peirce*, Hegeles Institute (La Salle, Ill.), 1983.

Also editor of *Spirit, Being, and Self: Studies in Indian Thought*, 1981; also editor of and contributor to the Popper and Blanshard volumes in "Library of Living Philosophers" series, Open Court. Contributor to *Yale Review, Monist,* and optometry journals. Editor of "Monist Library of Philosophy" series, Open Court, three volumes published; member of editorial advisory board to "Library of Living Philosophers." Member of editorial advisory board to journals, including *Folia Humanistica* (Barcelona), *Studi Internazionali di Filosofia* (Turin), and *Rassegna Internazionale di Logica* (Bologna).

*   *   *

FREEMAN, Roger A(nthony Wilson)   1928-

PERSONAL: Born May 11, 1928, in Ipswich, England; married Jean Margaret Blain; children: Sarah, Emma, Daniel. *Education:* Educated in high school in Colchester, England. *Religion:* Church of England.

ADDRESSES: Home—Mays Barn, Dedham, Colchester, Essex, England.

CAREER: Farmer; F.F.C. Freeman & Sons (family enterprise), Colchester, Essex, England, partner, 1959—.

WRITINGS:

NONFICTION

(With others) *U.S. Army and Air Force Fighters*, Harleyford, 1961.
Consolidated B-24 H & J Liberator (monograph), Profile, 1969.

The Mighty Eighth, Doubleday, 1970.
Republic Thunderbolt, Ducimus, 1970.
American Bombers, Volume I, Profile Publications, 1972.
Boeing B-17G Fortress (monograph), Profile, 1972.
Republic P-47N Thunderbolt (monograph), Profile, 1974.
Mustang at War, Doubleday, 1974.
The U.S. Strategic Bomber, Macdonald & Jane's, 1975.
Camouflage and Markings: U.S.A.A.F., Ducimus, 1975.
B-17 Fortress at War, Scribner, 1977.
Airfields of the Eighth: Then and Now, Battle of Britain Prints, 1978.
Thunderbolt: A Documentary History, Scribner, 1978.
B-26 Marauder at War, Ian Allan, 1978.
Mighty Eighth War Diary, Macdonald & Jane's, 1981.
B-24 Liberator at War, Ian Allan, 1983.
B-17 Flying Fortress, Jane's Publishing, 1983.
Mighty Eighth War Manual, Jane's Publishing, 1984.
Combat Profile: Merlin Mustang, Ian Allan, 1988.
The Hub: Fighter Leader, Airlife, 1988.

Also author of twelve monographs on U.S. Army Air Force aircraft markings during World War II, Ducimus, 1971-73.

OTHER

(Under name Roger Anthony Freeman) *I Mind the Time* (fiction), Cassell, 1988.

Also author of television documentaries. Contributor to magazines.

WORK IN PROGRESS: Three books of nonfiction, one book of fiction.

*   *   *

FREYTAG, Joseph
See COOPER, Parley J(oseph)

*   *   *

FREYTAG, Josephine
See COOPER, Parley J(oseph)

*   *   *

FRINGS, Manfred S.   1925-

PERSONAL: Surname rhymes with "rings"; born February 27, 1925, in Cologne, Germany (now West Germany); U.S. citizen; son of Gottfried (a teacher) and Maria (Over) Frings; married Karin Muckes, 1985; children: one. *Education:* University of Cologne, Ph.D., 1953, and staatsexamen in English and Philosophy, State Teacher Training Diploma, postdoctoral study, 1953-55. *Religion:* Roman Catholic.

ADDRESSES: Office—Department of Philosophy, DePaul University, 2322 North Kenmore, Chicago, Ill. 60614.

CAREER: University of Detroit, Detroit, Mich., assistant professor of philosophy, 1958-61; Gymnasium of Monchen-Gladbach, Monchen-Gladbach, Germany, school master, 1961-63; Duquesne University, Pittsburgh, Pa., associate professor of philosophy, 1963-66; DePaul University, Chicago, Ill., associate professor, 1966-68, professor of philosophy, 1968—. Founder of Heidegger Conference, 1966—.

MEMBER: American Association of University Professors, American Philosophical Association, Husserl Society (secretary, 1971-72).

AWARDS, HONORS: Fulbright grant, 1958-59; American Council of Learned Societies grant, 1973; Deutsche Forschungsgemeinschaft research grant, 1979-80, 1987-88.

WRITINGS:

(Editor) *Readings in the Philosophy of Science*, University of Detroit Press, 1960.
Max Scheler: A Concise Introduction into the World of a Great Thinker, Duquesne University Press, 1965.
Person und Dasein: Zur Frage der Ontologie des Wertseins, Nijhoff, 1969.
Zur Phaenomenologie der Lebensgemeinschaft, Anton Hain, 1970.
(Contributor) *Linguistic Analysis and Phenomenology*, Macmillan, 1972.
(Co-translator) Max Scheler, *Formalism in Ethics and Non-Formal Ethics of Values*, Northwestern University, 1973.
(Contributor) *Grundprobleme der Grossen Philosophen*, Vandenhoeck & Ruprecht, 1973.
(Translator) Scheler, *Problems of a Sociology of Knowledge*, Routledge & Kegan Paul, 1980.
(Editor) Martin Heidegger, *Parmenides*, Klostermann, 1982.
(Editor) Scheler, *Politisch-paedagogische Schriften*, Francke, 1982.
Philosophy of Prediction and Capitalism, Nijhoff, 1987.
(Translator) Scheler, *Person and Self-Value*, Nijhoff, 1987.

Also editor of *The German Collected Works of Max Scheler*, and co-editor of *The German Collected Works of M. Heidegger*. Contributor to numerous international journals.

SIDELIGHTS: "I believe that writing a book should be a creative process coming from one's own imagination, preferably from the spur of the moment," Manfred S. Frings told *CA.* "Having been born with perfect pitch, I am at heart a musician. I improvised and created music (piano) from my fourth year of life. I am completely self-taught, playing almost exclusively Chopin. I have tried to convey creating music to writing. At times it works, but only for a short while. I feel that at those moments I might have reached the essence of writing which I hold should have only a minimum of planning ahead. In philosophy this is very difficult to do and yields mostly fragments or jottings."

Frings received a private audience with Pope John Paul II on March 6, 1980.

*   *   *

FROMMER, Harvey 1937-

PERSONAL: Born October 10, 1937, in Brooklyn, N.Y.; son of Max and Fannie (Wechsler) Frommer; married Myrna Katz (a writer, teacher, and free-lance editor), January 23, 1960; children: Jennifer, Freddy, Jan. *Education:* New York University, B.S., 1957, M.A., 1961, Ph.D., 1974. *Religion:* Jewish.

ADDRESSES: Home—791 Oakleigh Rd., North Woodmere, N.Y. 11581.

CAREER: United Press International (UPI), Chicago, Ill., sportswriter, 1957-58; New York public schools, New York City, high school English teacher, 1960-70; City University of New York, New York City Technical College, professor of writing and speech, 1970—. As a sports nostalgia and trivia expert, has appeared on television and radio talk shows. *Military service:* U.S. Army, 1958-59.

MEMBER: Association of American University Professors.

AWARDS, HONORS: Salute to Scholars Award, City University of New York, 1984; *Olympic Controversies* was nominated by the U.S. Olympic Committee for "Olympic Book of the Year."

WRITINGS:

A Baseball Century: The First 100 Years of the National League, Macmillan, 1976.
A Sailing Primer, Atheneum, 1977.
The Martial Arts: Judo and Karate, Atheneum, 1978.
Sports Lingo: A Dictionary of the Language of Sports, Atheneum, 1979.
Sports Roots: How Nicknames, Namesakes, Trophies, Competitions, and Expressions Came to Be in the World of Sports, Atheneum, 1979.
The Great American Soccer Book, Atheneum, 1980.
New York City Baseball: The Last Golden Age, 1947-1957, Macmillan, 1980.
The Sports Dates Book, Grosset, 1981.
Rickey and Robinson: A Dual Biography, Macmillan, 1982.
(With Nancy Lieberman) *Basketball My Way*, Scribner, 1982.
Baseball's Greatest Rivalry: The New York Yankees vs. the Boston Red Sox, Atheneum, 1982.
Baseball's Greatest Records, Streaks, and Feats, Atheneum, 1983.
Jackie Robinson (juvenile), F. Watts, 1984.
(Editor with wife, Myrna Frommer) *The Games of the Twenty-Third Olympiad: Los Angeles 1984 Commemorative Book*, International Sport Publications, 1984.
Baseball's Hall of Fame (juvenile), F. Watts, 1985.
Baseball's Greatest Managers, F. Watts, 1985.
City Tech: The First Forty Years, Technical College Press, 1986.
Olympic Controversies (juvenile), F. Watts, 1987.
(With Red Holzman) *Red on Red* (autobiography), Bantam, 1987.
Primitive Baseball: The First Quarter-Century of the National Pastime, Atheneum, 1988.
(With Nolan Ryan) *Throwing Heat: The Autobiography of Nolan Ryan*, Doubleday, 1988.
150th Anniversary Album of Baseball, F. Watts, 1988.
Holzman on Hoops, Lynx, in press.
Little League Baseball: The First Fifty Years, Pharos, in press.

Contributor of articles and reviews to professional journals and periodicals, including *New York Times, New York Daily News, Los Angeles Times, Yankees Magazine, United Features, Library Journal, Golf Digest, St. Louis Post-Dispatch, Queens Magazine*, and *Newsday.*

SIDELIGHTS: In 1974 Harvey Frommer wrote his doctoral dissertation in English on the influence of sports on television and of television on sports. His efforts to have the work published resulted in the opportunity to write *A Baseball Century*, the official centennial history of the National League.

Frommer told *CA:* "Sports and work and writing fascinate me; gardening acts as a release. I am involved all the time with one of these or another. I have written almost twenty-five books on sports in a decade and look forward to doing many more. I also have hopes of expanding my writing into other fields—gardening, travel, and institutional history. In 1986 *City Tech: The First Forty Years* was published. I spent three years on the project—the story of New York City Technical College of the City University of New York, an educational, cultural history.

"I enjoy my dual careers—as professor of writing and speech and as sports author and lecturer. My family functions as support and critic. My wife Myrna is at times my co-author and always my editor; my daughter and two sons are involved in the world of sports, and we are able to share anecdotes and good times playing and viewing games—especially baseball. I still find myself anchored in my own childhood world of games and fanhood. Perhaps that is what inspired *New York City Baseball* and *Rickey and Robinson*—both books deal with the golden heroes of my growing up years, when the world we all knew was very different.

"I received the 'Salute to Scholars Award' from the Chancellor of the City University of New York in 1984 and was invited by the government of Mexico in 1983 to tour that nation and write about its sports. Together with my wife Myrna, I have expanded my publications to include travel writing. We have been guests of the governments of Greece, Jamaica, and Finland in 1987 and 1988.

"It was my *Contemporary Authors* listing that was of critical help in my being selected in a national search of 500 sports authors to be the editor and major author of the Official Olympic Book in 1984. So far that has been the crown jewel of my career.

"I take great satisfaction when I realize how far a poor kid from a seedy neighborhood in Brooklyn came in the United States of America. I dream now of other journeys, other accomplishments, other big and significant books for the future—in sports, in other areas."

BIOGRAPHICAL/CRITICAL SOURCES:

PERIODICALS

Chicago Tribune Book World, June 6, 1982.
Los Angeles Times Book Review, May 23, 1982, October 2, 1983, May 12, 1985.
New York Times, April 13, 1980.
New York Times Book Review, June 15, 1980, February 15, 1988, May 8, 1988.
Washington Post Book World, July 18, 1982.

*   *   *

FROST, Erica
    See SUPRANER, Robyn

*   *   *

FROST, Lawrence A(ugust)   1907-

PERSONAL: Born May 1, 1907, in Ann Arbor, Mich.; son of Elvin Rinehart (a podiatrist) and Selema (a musician; maiden name, Teufel) Frost; married Ethel Duby, September 1, 1932; children: Jill Thel (Mrs. William Merke). *Education:* Attended Illinois College of Podiatry and University of Toledo; Ohio College of Podiatric Medicine, D.P.M., 1929. *Religion:* Presbyterian.

ADDRESSES: Home—211 Cranbrook Blvd., Monroe, Mich. 48161.

CAREER: Podiatrist in Monroe, Mich., 1929-79. Diplomate

of American Board of Foot Surgery; president of Michigan Board of Registration in Podiatry, 1944-50. Member of Advisory Committee, Center for the History of Foot Care, Pennsylvania College of Podiatric Medicine. Instructor of postgraduate foot surgery at Ohio College of Podiatric Medicine and the Illinois College of Podiatry. Member of Monroe City Commission, 1956-57; vice-president of Michigan Municipal League, 1960; mayor of Monroe, 1960-64; vice-chairman of Monroe County Board of Supervisors, 1962; member of Monroe County Planning Commission, 1964-75 (chairman, 1972-75), and Monroe County Historical Commission (Custer curator, 1950-75; chairman, 1967-69; Custer curator emeritus, 1981).

MEMBER: American Podiatry Association (historian), American College of Foot Surgeons (fellow; president, 1950-52), Company of Military Historians (fellow), Council on America's Military Past (member of board of directors, 1974-77), First Cavalry Division Association (life member), Little Big Horn Associates (member of board of directors, 1967—), Michigan State Podiatry Association (president, 1935-37), Michigan State Historical Society (member of board of trustees, 1950-52), Monroe County Historical Society (president, 1948-50, 1966, 1973).

AWARDS, HONORS: Gran Prix diploma and medal from City of Paris, France, in international foot research competition, 1952, for a new surgical technique for in-grown toenails; D.Litt. from Ohio College of Podiatric Medicine, 1968; Ohioana Book Award from Ohioana Library Association, 1970, for *The Thomas A. Edison Album;* Liberty Bell Award, Monroe County Bar Association, 1981; Literary Award, Little Big Horn Associates, 1984, for *The Custer Album* and *General Custer's Libbie,* and 1987, for *Custer's 7th Cavalry and the Campaign of '73;* Distinguished Alumnus Award, Ohio College of Podiatric Medicine, 1984.

WRITINGS:

The Custer Album, Superior, 1964.
The U. S. Grant Album, Superior, 1966.
The Phil Sheridan Album, Superior, 1968.
The Court-Martial of General George Armstrong Custer, University of Oklahoma Press, 1968.
The Thomas A. Edison Album, Superior, 1969.
General Custer's Libbie, Superior, 1976.
(Editor with John M. Carroll) *Private Theodore Ewert's Diary of the Black Hills Expedition of 1874*, CRI, Books, 1976.
With Custer in '74, Brigham Young University Press, 1979.
Addressing the Custer Story, Gary Owen Publishers, 1980.
Some Observations on the Yellowstone Expedition of 1873, Arthur H. Clark, 1981.
Custer Legends, Bowling Green University Press, 1981.
Boy General in Bronze: Custer, Michigan's Hero on Horseback, Arthur H. Clark, 1985.
General Custer's Thoroughbreds, Carroll & Co., 1986.
Custer's 7th Cavalry and the Campaign of '73, Upton & Sons, 1986.

WORK IN PROGRESS: It Can't Be Coincidence; Lucky Cuss; Burnside's Slim Buttes Journal.

SIDELIGHTS: Lawrence A. Frost's *The Custer Album* has been translated into Italian. He writes *CA:* "It has been my fate to live in a town steeped in Custer lore. Since Monroe is General Custer's hometown, it abounds with Custer legends. Here, as elsewhere, people delight in repeating and believing the sensational stories about him. Though many of these legends are based on the truth, a great number are exaggerations or untruths. Others are figments of the imagination. Many wonder why I concentrate my writing and research on the life of a soldier when there is so much source material about statesmen like Lincoln. I have a ready answer. Lincoln didn't live here.

"I have always been a hero worshiper. George Washington, Thomas Jefferson, Abe Lincoln, Thomas Edison, Babe Ruth and Jack Dempsey are a few of our country's heroes that have made me proud I am an American. Most of our heroes have feet of clay but it is their accomplishments that provide us with inspiration and this feeling of pride. Here in Monroe I discovered a hero—as American as apple pie—who was being denigrated and besmirched by crepe hangers and followers of our national guilt corps. Americans usually support the side of the underdog. I choose to follow the same path."

G

GALLIX, Francois 1939-

PERSONAL: Born March 1, 1939, in Paris, France; son of Pierre Vincent (an insurance executive) and Andree (a secretary; maiden name, Mouchard) Gallix; married Carolyn Wanless, March 2, 1963 (divorced December 19, 1967); children: Andrew, Sophie, Delphine. *Education:* Faculte de Droit de Paris, licence, 1962; Sorbonne, University of Paris, licence, 1969, maitrise, 1970, agregation, 1972, doctorat d'etat, 1984.

ADDRESSES: Home—9 rue de Douai, 75009 Paris, France. *Office*—Sorbonne 1, rue Victor Cousin, 75230 Paris, France. *Agent*—David Higham, 5 Lower John St., London W1R 4HA, England.

CAREER: Teacher of English in secondary schools, 1964-72; Karaouigine University, Fez, Morocco, teacher of English, 1965 and 1967; Sorbonne, University of Paris, Paris, France, 1972—, began as assistant lecturer, now senior lecturer in English. Has been interviewed on "Bookshelf" and "The Matter of Britain," both produced by the British Broadcasting Corp. (BBC-Radio).

MEMBER: Association of International American Universities, Society of Agreges.

AWARDS, HONORS: Fulbright Awards, 1978 and 1982.

WRITINGS:

(Editor and author of introduction) *T. H. White: Letters to a Friend: The Correspondence between T. H. White and L. J. Potts*, Putnam, 1982, revised edition, Berkley Publishing, 1984.
(Author of introduction) T. H. White, *The Book of Beasts*, Sutton Publishing, 1984.
(Compiler) *T. H. White: An Annotated Bibliography*, Garland, 1986.
(Translator and author of introduction) T. H. White, *Contes etranges et histoires fantastiques*, Publications de la Sorbonne, 1987.

Contributor of articles to periodicals, including *Mosaic, Cerli, Etudes Anglaises*, and *Stoic;* contributor of articles on films and literature to newspapers; contributor of translation of White's "The Troll" to *Nouvelles Nouvelles*, 1987.

WORK IN PROGRESS: Researching two articles, one on the influence of the Stowe school on White's *Mistress Masham's Repose*, the other on the friendship between T. H. White and David Garnett; translating some of White's works into French, including *The Goshawk*.

SIDELIGHTS: T. H. White, the renowned author of *The Once and Future King* and many other highly respected works, maintained a nearly life-long correspondence with his teacher and friend, L. J. Potts. Many of White's letters to Potts, as well as some to Potts's wife, are reproduced by Francois Gallix in *Letters to a Friend*. The letters include criticism of Potts's poetry, insights into his own work, and reflections of White's personal life.

Gallix once told *CA:* "During my research on T. H. White, I met several of his friends, including Mary Potts, who asked me to edit White's letters to herself and her husband, who was White's tutor at Queen's College, Cambridge. I recorded most of my interviews on cassettes. I went to see White's biographer, Sylvia Townsend Warner, several times in Dorset and we exchanged many letters. I also visited the author David Garnett and we corresponded about White's works and his own. I am now extremely interested in the novels of Sylvia Townsend Warner and David Garnett.

"I also interviewed the author Sir John Verney, the actor Michael Trubshawe, and many of White's friends in England and on the Channel island of Alderney, where White lived from 1946 until his death in 1964. I have a lot of White's unpublished material and letters, and have collected most of his first editions, as well as those of David Garnett and Sylvia Townsend Warner.

"Twice, in June, 1978, and in July, 1982, I went to Austin, Texas, on Fulbright Awards and was able to work on the White Collection at the Humanities Research Center."

BIOGRAPHICAL/CRITICAL SOURCES:

PERIODICALS

New York Times, September 10, 1982.
Times Literary Supplement, October 19, 1984.

*   *   *

GALVIN, James 1951-

PERSONAL: Born May 8, 1951, in Chicago, Ill.; son of James

A. (a physician) and Ruth (an educator; maiden name, Stalter) Galvin. *Education:* Antioch College, B.A., 1974; University of Iowa, M.F.A., 1977.

ADDRESSES: Home—P.O. Box 94, Tie Siding, Wyo. 82084.

CAREER: Murray State University, Murray, Ky., assistant professor of English, 1977-79; Humboldt State University, Arcata, Calif., assistant professor of English, 1979-83; University of Iowa, Iowa City, assistant professor, 1983-87, associate professor of English and creative writing, 1987—.

AWARDS, HONORS: Discovery Award from *Nation* and Young Men's Hebrew Association, 1977, for poetry; fellow at Writer's Workshop, University of Iowa, 1977; grant from National Endowment for the Arts, 1978; Ingram Merrill grant from Ingram Merrill Foundation, 1982; co-winner, National Poetry Series Open Competition, 1984; National Endowment for the Arts creative writing fellowship in poetry, 1986.

WRITINGS:

Imaginary Timber (poems), Doubleday, 1980.
God's Mistress (poems), Harper, 1984.
Elements, Copper Canyon Press, 1988.

Contributor of poems to magazines, including *New Yorker, Nation, Antioch Review, Poetry Now, Antaeus,* and *Sewanee Review.* Editor of *Crazyhorse,* 1979-81.

WORK IN PROGRESS: Another book of poems.

BIOGRAPHICAL/CRITICAL SOURCES:

BOOKS

Contemporary Literary Criticism, Volume 38, Gale, 1986.

PERIODICALS

Los Angeles Times Book Review, September 23, 1984.
Nation, October 13, 1984.
Ontario Review, fall/winter, 1981/82.
Southwest Review, summer, 1982.

*   *   *

GANNON, Thomas M(ichael) 1936-

PERSONAL: Born October 19, 1936, in Chicago, Ill.; son of Thomas M. (a district sales manager) and Bernice D. (Pouk) Gannon. *Education:* Loyola University of Chicago, B.A., 1959, Ph.L. and M.A., both 1961; Jesuit School of Theology, Chicago, Ill., S.T.L., 1968; University of Chicago, Ph.D., 1972.

ADDRESSES: Office—Department of Sociology, Loyola University, 2058 North Clark St., Chicago, Ill. 60614.

CAREER: Entered Societas Jesu (Society of Jesus; Jesuits; S.J.), 1954, ordained Roman Catholic priest, 1967; St. Ignatius High School, Cleveland, Ohio, instructor, 1961-64; Loyola University, Chicago, Ill., lecturer, 1966-68, assistant professor, 1971-73, associate professor, 1974-77, professor of sociology, 1978—, chairman of department, 1972-82. Professor of sociology and director of Woodstock Theological Center at Georgetown University, 1983-86; visiting professor and fellow, St. Edmund's College, Cambridge, 1987-88. Director of professional and graduate studies for Chicago Province of Society of Jesus, 1970-80. Consultant to New York City Youth Board, Federal Poverty Program, and Chicago Commission on Youth Welfare.

MEMBER: International Conference for the Sociology of Religion, International Sociological Association (U.S. secretary,

1971-89), Religious Research Association (president, 1970-73), Association for the Sociology of Religion (president, 1977-78), American Sociological Association, Society for the Scientific Study of Religion (member of executive council, 1985-88).

AWARDS, HONORS: Fellow of Japan Society for the Promotion of Science, 1981; fellow of St. Edmunds House, Cambridge University, 1982; named faculty member of the year by Loyola University of Chicago, 1983.

WRITINGS:

(Contributor) George A. Lane, editor, *Christian Spirituality,* Argus Communications, 1968.
(With George W. Traub) *The Desert and the City: An Interpretation of the History of Christian Spirituality,* Macmillan, 1969, 2nd edition, Loyola University Press, 1984.
General Survey of the Society of Jesus: North America, five volumes, Argus Communications, 1970-71.
(Editor) *Military Ethics and Civilian Control,* Sage Publications, 1976.
(Editor) *The Catholic Challenge to the American Economy,* Macmillan, 1987.
(Editor) *World Catholicism in Transition,* Macmillan, 1988.

Also contributor of more than fifty articles to sociology journals.

WORK IN PROGRESS: Research on religious and social change, and on the culture of unbelief.

SIDELIGHTS: Thomas M. Gannon told *CA:* "People today, everywhere on the globe, are involved as never before in a quest for meaning in their lives and for their identity in a rapidly-changing world. In reality, human beings have always sought such knowledge, but rarely with such urgency or with so tormenting a sense of loss. At the same time, people also search—often secretly and unconsciously—for the identity of God and God's meaning in their lives. Here too, men and women struggle with a numbing sense of lost awareness. I believe that these two identities—human beings' and God's—are found together or not at all: that only in knowing God can people come to know themselves, and in knowing themselves they know God.

"Most of what I have written is an attempt to explore how people have pursued this double quest. I use an approach that emphasizes social-cultural analysis, though at times my methods are more theological. Regardless of approach, it has been to better comprehend this quest that I undertook a study of the history of Christian spirituality and, later, edited a collection of essays on military ethics. It is this same concern that, ultimately, underlies my other writings as well, coupled with an abiding passion for promoting justice and moral solidarity."

BIOGRAPHICAL/CRITICAL SOURCES:

PERIODICALS

Choice, September, 1987.
Christian Century, June 17, 1987.
Commonweal, February 26, 1988.
Kirkus Reviews, December 15, 1986.
Los Angeles Times Book Review, February 22, 1987.

*   *   *

GAST, Kelly P.
See EDMONDSON, G. C.

GERBER, Merrill Joan 1938-

PERSONAL: Born March 15, 1938, in Brooklyn, N.Y.; daughter of William (an antique dealer) and Jessie (Sorblum) Gerber; married Joseph Spiro (a college teacher), June 23, 1960; children: Becky Ann, Joanna Emily, Susanna Willa. *Education:* Attended University of Miami, 1955; University of Florida, B.A., 1959; Brandeis University, graduate study, 1959-60, M.A., 1981. *Religion:* Jewish.

ADDRESSES: Home—542 Santa Anita Ct., Sierra Madre, Calif. 91024.

CAREER: Former editor, Houghton Mifflin Co., Boston, Mass. Lecturer at many writers' conferences, including those at University of California, University of Florida, and Pasadena City College; has taught creative writing at California State University, Los Angeles and University of Redlands; currently teaches fiction writing at Pasadena City College, Pasadena, Calif.

AWARDS, HONORS: Stanford University creative writing fellowship, 1962-63; residency grant, Yaddo Writers' Colony, 1981; Andrew Lytle Fiction Prize, *Sewanee Review*, 1985, for "At the Fence"; short fiction award, *Fiction Network*, 1985, for "Hairdos"; O. Henry Award, Doubleday and Co., Inc., 1986, for "I Don't Believe This."

WRITINGS:

NOVELS

An Antique Man, Houghton, 1967.
Now Molly Knows, Arbor House, 1974.
The Lady with the Moving Parts, Arbor House, 1978.

FOR YOUNG ADULTS

Please Don't Kiss Me Now, Dial, 1981.
Name a Star for Me, Viking, 1983.
I'm Kissing as Fast as I Can, Fawcett, 1985.
The Summer of My Indian Prince, Fawcett, 1986.
Also Known as Sadzia! The Belly Dancer!, Harper, 1987.
Marry Me Tomorrow, Fawcett, 1987.
Even Pretty Girls Cry at Night, Crosswinds, 1988.
I'd Rather Think About Robby, Harper, 1988.

OTHER

Stop Here, My Friend (short stories), Houghton, 1965.
Honeymoon (short stories), University of Illinois Press, 1985.
(Contributor) *Prize Stories: The O. Henry Awards 1986*, William Abrahams, editor, Doubleday, 1986.

Contributor of short stories to *Mademoiselle, New Yorker, Redbook, Sewanee Review, McCall's, Ladies' Home Journal, Woman's Day, Family Circle*, and other periodicals. Contributor of articles on writing to *The Writer* and *Writer's Digest*.

WORK IN PROGRESS: King of the World, a novel.

SIDELIGHTS: Merrill Joan Gerber has published more short stories in *Redbook* (thirty-eight and counting) than any other contributor.

BIOGRAPHICAL/CRITICAL SOURCES:

PERIODICALS

Los Angeles Times, May 7, 1988.
Los Angeles Times Book Review, December 18, 1985.
New York Times Book Review, December 15, 1985.
Washington Post Book World, November 17, 1985.

GHOSH, Arun Kumar 1930-

PERSONAL: First "h" of surname is pronounced; born February 1, 1930, in Burdwan, West Bengal, India; son of Ashutosh (a lawyer in District Judge's Court, Burdwan) and Induprova (Roy Mitter) Ghosh; married Krishna Datta, 1986. *Education:* Vidyasagar College, B.A. (with honors in economics), 1948; University of Calcutta, M.A., 1950. *Politics:* Former radical humanist; "at present, a leftist and a democrat, and believer in wider democratic movement." *Religion:* "Hindu by birth, but accept some of its cultural aspects only; accept the role of religion in life, in some form or other."

ADDRESSES: Home—72 One B.C. Rd., Burdwan 713101, West Bengal, India; and 170 Walden Way, Imperial, Pa. 15127. *Office*—Institute of Cost and Works Accountants of India, 12, Sudder St., Calcutta, India.

CAREER: Burdwan Town School, Burdwan, West Bengal, India, assistant teacher of civics and English, 1950-51; University of Calcutta, Calcutta, India, postgraduate research fellow in economics, 1952-55; Seth Anandaram Jaipuria College, Calcutta, lecturer in economics and commerce, 1955-56; University of Calcutta, examiner and scrutineer of intermediate and bachelor examinations, 1955-74; Calcutta University, Calcutta, research assistant in industrial finance, department of economics, 1956-66; Institute of Cost and Works Accountants of India, Calcutta, part-time tutor, 1965-70, assistant director of research, 1970-85, part-time lecturer, 1971-72, assistant director of examinations, 1985—; International Institute of Management Sciences, Calcutta, member of faculty, 1984—, chairman of examinations committee, 1984-86. Visiting professor, Indian Institute of Management, 1973.

MEMBER: Indian Economic Association, Bardhaman Sahitya Sabha (literary society of Burdwan; member of executive committee, 1956-76), Mukta Mela (cultural society), AUC Jazz Club of Calcutta, Cine Club of Calcutta.

AWARDS, HONORS: Banco Behari Banerjee Gold Medal, 1950, and Beereshwar Mitter Gold Medal, 1966, both from University of Calcutta.

WRITINGS:

Fiscal Problem of Growth with Stability (monograph), Calcutta University Press, 1959.
Fiscal Policy and Economic Growth: A Cross-Section Study (monograph), Calcutta University Press, Part I, 1962, Part II, 1963.
(Contributor) *Monetary Policy of the Reserve Bank of India*, Popular Prakasan (Bombay), 1963.
Cost Accounting in Commercial Banking Industry, Institute of Cost and Works Accountants of India, 1979.
(With C. R. Sengupta) *Bank Finance Criteria and the Tandon Committee Report*, Jamshedpur Chapter of Cost Accountants of India, 1975.
Management Accountant's Role in Monitoring Bank Financing, Institute of Cost and Works Accountants of India, 1982.
Introduction to Cost Accounting in Commercial Banking Industry, Institute of Cost and Works Accountants of India, 1983.

Also author of *Fiscal Policy, Stability, and Growth: The Experience and Problems of the Underdeveloped Economies, 1929-1939 and 1945-1965, Capital Market in a Developing Econ-*

omy, with *Special Reference to India, Cost and Output in Banking, Inflation and Price Control,* and *Cost Accounting and Farm Product Costing.* Frequent contributor to *Radical Humanist,* 1954-57, to *Calcutta Review, Indian Economic Journal,* and other professional journals in India. Founder and editor of *Research Bulletin of the Institute of Cost and Works Accountants of India.*

WORK IN PROGRESS: Investigating fiscal problems of the underdeveloped economies of Latin America, Middle East and Africa, and Asia and the Far East, 1929-39, 1945-65; collecting material for an industrial economics textbook; *Rate Fixation in Public Utilities; Inflation, Price Management and Cost Accounting; Programme Budgeting and Fiscal Management.*

SIDELIGHTS: Arun Kumar Ghosh once wrote *CA:* "An important motivating factor in my life, both in my social existence and while writing, has been that whatever I do besides my personal existence must have some social impact. I joined the political and philosophical movement spearheaded by the late M. N. Roy, a great humanist in his later life and a world famous Marxist and Communist in his earlier life, with the same objective in view. Even while writing technical, intellectual discourses on specific matters, I consider that the objective should not merely be writing a good book, well appreciated by its readership, but also—and more important—that the book should have some impact on the society.

"Another thing I very much wish to stress, that is, in research activities and writing books and articles which form part of our knowledge and experience, nothing is more important than native intelligence. Moreover, the connecting link should be the basic curiosity of life itself. I am a voracious reader of mystery and detective stories and my favourite authors are Ellery Queen, Dorothy Sayers, Agatha Christie, John Dickson Carr, Sir Arthur Conan Doyle and G. K. Chesterton. They stimulate me to looking into the 'whys' and the 'hows' of phenomena.

"Films by such eminent film-makers as Orson Welles, Andrejed Wasda, Roman Polanski, Christof Zanusci, Ingmar Bergman, Francois Truffaut, and Jean Luc Goddard, and many others, inspire me a lot, making me conscious of my individual and social existence and the associated responsibilities and problems. I spend my evening hours, after hard days of labour, listening to music and viewing films."

AVOCATIONAL INTERESTS: Debate, sports (was a chief scorer of University of Calcutta's Post-Graduate Athletic Club), architecture, sculpture, painting, and music.

* * *

GILCHRIST, Andrew (Graham)   1910-

PERSONAL: Born April 19, 1910, in Scotland; son of James Graham (a farmer) and Jane Ann (Hepburn) Gilchrist; married Freda Grace Slack, 1946; children: Christopher, Jeremy, Janet Gilchrist Rayner. *Education:* Attended Oxford University.

ADDRESSES: Home—Arthur's Crag, Hazelbank, by Lanark, Scotland.

CAREER: British Foreign Service, London, England, numerous diplomatic appointments, including ambassador to Iceland, Indonesia, and Ireland, 1933-70; writer, 1970—. Chairman of Scottish Highlands and Islands Development Board, 1965-71. *Military service:* British Army, 1943-46, mentioned in dispatches.

AWARDS, HONORS: Knight Commander of St. Michael and St. George.

WRITINGS:

Bangkok Top Secret: Being the Experiences of a British Officer in the Siam Country Section of Force 136 (memoirs), Hutchinson, 1970.
Cod Wars and How to Lose Them, Canongate Publishing (Edinburgh), 1978.
The Russian Professor, R. Hale, 1984.
Watercress File, R. Hale, 1985.
Ultimate Hostage, R. Hale, 1986.

Also author of *South of Three Pagodas* and *Death of an Admiral,* both published by R. Hale, and *Lafest.*

WORK IN PROGRESS: An autobiography; a political novel set in Scotland.

SIDELIGHTS: Andrew Gilchrist told *CA:* "Back in 1960, the *Chicago Tribune* asked me to review one or two books. I obliged and threw in a few poems for free. This is what really got me hooked on writing.

"*Bangkok Top Secret* was a success but not quite sufficiently so to justify a reprint. It is about secret military operations and intelligence contacts behind the Japanese lines in Southeast Asia from 1944 to 1946, all entirely authentic.

"*Cod Wars and How to Lose Them* is an account of the 'cod wars' between Britain and Iceland, in which the Icelanders were victorious and drove British fishermen out of their waters, despite the attempted interference of the Royal Navy. The political background is fully set out (after all, I was the British ambassador at the time). The book sold very well in Iceland, but not so well in Britain.

"After that I moved into fiction, with two light-hearted spy stories, followed by a kidnap thriller and a romantic novel set in the Thai jungles. *Lafest* (1988) is a historical novel about the great British naval disaster near Singapore which came just after Pearl Harbor.

"If I am ever going to write a best-seller I shall have to hurry along, bearing in mind that I was born in the reign of King Edward VII!"

* * *

GILDER, George F.   1939-

PERSONAL: Born November 29, 1939, in New York, N.Y.; son of Richard Watson and Anne (Alsop) Gilder; married Cornelia Brooke (an historic preservationist), 1976; children: Louisa Ludlow, Mary Ellen Tiffany, Richard Brooke, Cornelia Chapin. *Education:* Harvard University, A.B., 1962. *Politics:* Republican.

ADDRESSES: Home—The Red House, Tyringham, Mass. 01264.

CAREER: Advance (magazine), editor and co-founder, Cambridge, Mass., 1961-62, and Washington, D.C., 1962-64; *New Leader,* New York City, associate editor, beginning 1965; legislative assistant to Senator Charles McC. Mathias, Washington, D.C., 1968-70; Manhattan Institute for Policy Research, New York City, program director, 1981—. Speech writer for Nelson A. Rockefeller, 1964, Richard M. Nixon, 1968, Ben C. Toledano, 1972, and Robert Dole, 1976. *Military service:* U.S. Marine Corps Reserve, 1958-64.

AWARDS, HONORS: Kennedy Institute of Politics fellow, Harvard University, 1971-72; White House Special Presidential Award for "entrepreneurial excellence," 1986, for *The Spirit of Enterprise*.

WRITINGS:

(With Bruce K. Chapman) *The Party That Lost Its Head*, Knopf, 1966.
Sexual Suicide, Quadrangle, 1973, revised and expanded edition published as *Men and Marriage*, Pelican Publishing, 1986.
Naked Nomads: Unmarried Men in America, Quadrangle, 1974.
Visible Man, Basic Books, 1978.
Wealth and Poverty, Basic Books, 1981.
The Spirit of Enterprise, Simon & Schuster, 1985.
Microcosm, Simon & Schuster, 1988.

Contributor to *National Review, American Spectator, Commentary, Forbes, Wall Street Journal*, and other periodicals. Editor, *Ripon Forum*, 1971-72; semiconductors editor, *RELease 1.0*, 1983.

SIDELIGHTS: George F. Gilder has created controversy with his conservative commentary on everything from the biological basis of women's roles as housewives to the moral basis of the capitalist system. For example, he was named "the nation's leading male-chauvinist-pig author" by *Time* magazine in 1974, and M. J. Sobran of the *National Review* says he is "a man of free and fresh mind and genial temper whose ideas have a way of making people want to scratch his eyes out." Probably best known for his views on the women's movement and on supply-side economics, Gilder has appeared on numerous television talk shows and at public lectures to discuss his unique brand of social philosophy and economic theory.

Gilder's book *Sexual Suicide* concerns the biological and anthropological bases of sexual behavior in our culture, and how, in his view, contemporary American society is courting cultural disaster by its deviation from the norms established by primitive man. In using the term "sexual suicide," Gilder claims that every impulse we have as social animals is tied closely to our sexual instincts; behaviors that depart from the norm, including homosexuality, the enjoyment of pornography, and promiscuity, are all "indices of sexual frustration." In fact, Gilder continues in the book, these types of behavior "all disclose a failure to achieve profound and loving sexuality. When a society deliberately affirms these failures—contemplates legislation of homosexual marriage, celebrates the women who denounce the family, and indulges pornography as a manifestation of sexual health," the author suggests, ". . . [then] the culture is promoting a form of erotic suicide. For it is destroying the cultural preconditions of profound love and sexuality: the durable heterosexual relationships necessary to a community of emotional investments."

The "women who denounce the family"—or feminists—says Gilder, are collectively "promoting in the United States an epidemic of erotic and social disorders." The author reasons that by attempting to make marriage and sexuality more "open," feminists, along with sexologists and pornographers, are "subverting and stifling real sexuality and love, and are undermining civilized society." In an interview with Richard K. Rein in *People* magazine, Gilder reemphasizes his stance against the feminist movement. "All the cliches about oppressed women are baloney," he says. "Women have the opportunity of motherhood, time to be creative and be individuals, and less pressure to submit their lives to a wretched career. You read these feminist books and you'd think every man is a U.S. senator. The fact is most men work for other men."

"The beauty of Gilder's reasoning" in *Sexual Suicide*, says Isa Kapp in the *New Leader*, "is that it is so persevering and complete. Yet it rests on the somewhat questionable first premise that because woman's responsibility in procreation is more important and more sensuously satisfying than man's, men feel emotionally deprived. To compensate for this male disadvantage, women must hew to their role and reinforce men in theirs; if they falter, we tumble into social disarray." Kapp disputes this conclusion, remarking that "in real life, few males minimize their part in conceiving babies, and most seem content to remain fond spectators in the process of bearing and nursing them. That men feel in any way inferior is not clear."

"One reads this elaborate, Freud-haunted apology for patriarchy with a depressing sense of deja vu," says Judith Adler Hennessee in the *New York Times Book Review*. "Whether men invent a mythology that makes women superior or inferior, the end result is likely to be the same—women belong in the home." Hennessee also remarks that there are "dozens of statements in this book that are preposterous, as well as over-simple generalizations that contain a germ of truth but veer off wildly into fantasy. One searches in vain for some understanding of the individual need for self-fulfillment."

National Review contributor Morton A. Kaplan, however, feels that Gilder's book presents "an interesting and provocative thesis. As a counterpoint to the unisex myth and the belief that biology does not matter either in personal relationships or in the cementing of society, it almost surely points in the direction of truth." While the critic finds that Gilder's "insights are often profound, his apothegms often brilliant, and his flair for argument strong," he also criticizes the author for his authoritative and impassioned style. "As with the feminists he attacks, one senses a desire to convert the reader rather than to engage his intellect," comments Kaplan. In addition, "where Mr. Gilder does marshal evidence, he shows that he can read better and think more clearly than most of his opponents; on the whole, however, we are left more with Mr. Gilder's conclusions than with the analysis that produced them." Overall, Kaplan finds that "as a provocative polemic, designed to stimulate debate, Mr. Gilder's book is effective, and as social commentary its insights touch deep wounds in our society."

In 1986, Gilder authored a revised edition of *Sexual Suicide* entitled *Men and Marriage*, in part to expand upon his theories and in part to replace the original work, which had been removed from print shortly after it first appeared. Even though Gilder's recent works had been best sellers, he found it difficult to find a publisher for the revision; eventually he found a small Louisiana press to print it. In this new edition, according to M. D. Aeschliman in the *National Review*, Gilder "tries to do in expository prose what no major novelist since Tolstoi has succeeded in doing: to paint the virtues and joys of pious and civilized marriage. Gilder has a social imagination, not in the sense of conceiving fictions, but in his capacity for understanding the real implications of individual acts and habits." But Barbara Ehrenreich, writing in the *Los Angeles Times Book Review*, finds the work "no less floridly idiosyncratic than the original," criticizing the author's theories and style. In addition, the reviewer accuses Gilder of adjusting historical facts to fit his ideas; speaking of "the pact between the sexes" where women let men rule in order to compensate for their loss of freedom, Ehrenreich finds that "the odd society that doesn't fit the pattern (such as the Trobianders) is dismissed by Gilder as 'perverse' and even 'retarded.'" In contrast, Aeschliman remarks that the author "never simply opines or asserts; the wealth of statistical documentation he brings to bear is enormously impressive."

Writing in *Commentary*, Terry Teachout expresses a more moderate opinion; while frustrated by the author's outbreaks of "purple" prose, Teachout observes that "the insights on which Gilder's sexual myth are built are genuinely compelling. Time and again one encounters striking passages that are rooted in cool observation rather than in some fantastic construct of a fevered imagination." Nevertheless, the critic feels that the book is made less effective by Gilder's style: "Gilder is no crank, and had he tempered his rhetoric and written *Men and Marriage* with the skeptical reader firmly in mind, he might well have" convinced the skeptic. Instead, Teachout comments, "Gilder has insisted . . . on preaching only to the converted."

In his 1981 book, *Wealth and Poverty*, which he calls a "theology" for capitalism, Gilder attempts to establish a moral basis for the capitalist system, using examples from the economies of primitive tribal societies to illustrate the relationship between gift-giving and the spirit of capitalism. In an article in the *Washington Post Book World* on *Wealth and Poverty*, James K. Glassman says, "If you don't understand the wave of new conservative ideas that has swept this country during the past four or five years—or if you consider those ideas window dressing for jingoism and bigotry—then this is the book to read." *Wealth and Poverty* has been publicly endorsed by President Ronald Reagan and proclaimed "Promethean in its vision" by Reagan's former budget adviser David Stockman, as quoted in a *New York Times* article.

"The ultimate strength and crucial weakness of both capitalism and democracy are their reliance on individual creativity and courage, leadership and morality, intuition and faith," writes Gilder in *Wealth and Poverty*. "Capitalist production entails faith—in one's neighbors, in one's society, and in the compensatory logic of the cosmos. Search and you shall find, give and you will be given unto, supply creates its own demand. It is this cosmology, this sequential logic, that essentially distinguishes the free from the socialist economy."

In the *National Review*, conservative critic Irving Kristol, writing of Gilder's belief in the fundamental morality of capitalism, disagrees with what he calls Gilder's "pseudo-anthropological analysis of economic activity as inherently and ineluctably giving birth to a viable morality." Kristol feels that successful commercial activity "[does] not add up to a complete moral code that a society can base itself on." Similarly, Andrew Klaven, discussing *Wealth and Poverty* in the *Saturday Review*, claims that the book "is rendered nonsensical not by its methodical defense of what is known as conservative, supply-side economics, but by the moral hogwash on which that defense is based." Gilder's particular brand of economics, says Ann Crittenden in the *New York Times*, "comes in an ideological fruitcake that many find hard to swallow."

New York Times Book Review contributor Roger Starr, however, finds that *Wealth and Poverty* "offers a creed for capitalism worthy of intelligent people. Mr. Gilder has written the kind of good book that alternately astonishes the reader with new and rather daring insights into familiar problems and bores him with long, tract-like passages to support them." Although the critic is not entirely convinced by Gilder's theories, he admits that "the book stands as an eloquent defense of the capitalist high ground and the human values that capitalists, despite their bad manners and admitted defects, managed to embody to the benefit of their fellows." And Adam Meyerson, writing in *Commentary*, feels that "despite its flaws . . . *Wealth and Poverty* remains one of the most significant, and gracefully written, works of political economy in years." Concludes the critic: "Hardly a page fails to provoke thought or to challenge some conventional assumption."

Gilder focuses on the role of the entrepreneur in capitalist society in his 1984 book *The Spirit of Enterprise*. Reprising several themes from *Wealth and Poverty*, the book "celebrates the entrepreneur, that wellspring of progress, the hero, who undertakes enormous risks in the face of impossible odds and brings forth benefits to mankind that far exceed the rise in his personal net worth," summarizes Paul Craig Roberts in the *Washington Post Book World*. Detailing the stories of several successful enterprisers, Gilder's book explores the backgrounds of these successes and how they demonstrate the productive capacity of the capitalist system. As Roberts describes him, "Gilder is a person who drives economists up the wall. The reason is that he writes about their subject with far more lucidity, insight, enthusiasm, and verve than they do." Other critics object to this "enthusiasm," however, describing it as "evangelism" instead. Eliot Janeway, for example, writes in the *New York Times Book Review* that "Gilder is an economic evangelist, and evangelists of every persuasion habitually simplify their struggles and glorify their goals."

Los Angeles Times Book Review contributor Donald G. Campbell, however, thinks that Gilder presents a thorough picture of the role of entrepreneurship: "Gilder is a sprightly writer and storyteller with provocative ideas. Those ideas, admittedly, lean heavily to supply-side economics and may dismay some readers, but those ideas still refuse to go away."

For all the controversy and opposition his work has invited, Gilder is still praised by some critics for his social vision. "For all his inflammatory generalizations . . . and intellectual U-turns," comments Hazlitt, Gilder "is a writer with a fine sense of what America has become—and what it still might be." Similarly, Sobran maintains that Gilder is a "dauntlessly original thinker, who is unbiased at reaching traditional conclusions. He says things that were never before necessary to say, and it may be a long time before anyone else says them as well."

BIOGRAPHICAL/CRITICAL SOURCES:

BOOKS

Authors in the News, Volume 1, Gale, 1976.
Contemporary Issues Criticism, Volume 1, Gale, 1982.
Gilder, George, *Sexual Suicide*, Quadrangle, 1973.
Gilder, George, *Wealth and Poverty*, Basic Books, 1981.

PERIODICALS

American Anthropologist, Number 4, 1976.
Commentary, July, 1981, April, 1987.
Commonweal, December 4, 1981.
Contemporary Sociology, September, 1974.
Los Angeles Times Book Review, April 19, 1981, December 12, 1984, October 5, 1986.
Nation, February 26, 1983.
National Review, December 21, 1973, May 9, 1975, August 18, 1978, April 17, 1981, February 27, 1987.
New Leader, December 10, 1973.
Newsweek, February 16, 1981.

New York Times, April 26, 1981, May 16, 1981, November 8, 1986.
New York Times Book Review, December 9, 1973, February 1, 1981, October 21, 1984.
People, May 18, 1981.
Playboy, October, 1977.
Saturday Review, January, 1981.
Time, December 9, 1974.
Times Literary Supplement, September 13, 1985.
Washington Post Book World, February 8, 1981, October 7, 1984.
Washington Star-News, December 13, 1974.

* * *

GOINS, Ellen H(aynes)   1927-1979

PERSONAL: Born May 4, 1927, in Amarillo, Tex.; died September 12, 1979; daughter of Eugene B. (a construction engineer) and Bess (Bennett) Haynes; married Otto Goins (a territorial sales manager), August 2, 1946; children: Ellen, Richard Greg, Laura Gail. *Education:* Attended Northeast Louisiana University, 1944-46; American Academy of Art, diploma, 1950.

ADDRESSES: Home—Houston, Tex. *Office*—Steck-Vaughn Co., P.O. Box 2028, Austin, Tex. 78767.

CAREER: Hoskinson-Rohloff Studios, Chicago, Ill., artist, 1950-55; portrait painter and free-lance artist, 1955-79; Steck-Vaughn Co., Austin, Tex., textbook artist, beginning 1968.

MEMBER: Houston Writers Workshop, Houston Watercolor Art Society.

WRITINGS:

Omar the Undercover Cat (self-illustrated), Steck-Vaughn, 1968.
Horror at Hinklemeyer House, Follett, 1971.
She Was Scared Silly (self-illustrated), Steck-Vaughn, 1971.
David's Pockets (self-illustrated), Steck-Vaughn, 1972.
Big Diamond's Boy (novel; self-illustrated), Thomas Nelson, 1977.
The Long Winter Sleep: The Story of Mammal Hibernation, McKay, 1978.
(With John L. Tveton) *Treasures of the Nest: Bird Eggs* (illustrated with drawings by Goins and photographs by Tveton), McKay, 1978.

ILLUSTRATOR

Frances Williams, *Red Mouse,* Steck-Vaughn, 1967.
V. Clyde Arnspringer, James A. Brill, and W. Ray Rucker, *Our Values,* Steck-Vaughn, 1969.
The Human Values Series Teaching Pictures, Steck-Vaughn, 1969.
Myself, Steck-Vaughn, 1970.
Myself and Others, Steck-Vaughn, 1970.

OTHER

Contributor of writings and art to periodicals.†

[Death date provided by husband, Otto Goins]

* * *

GOLDBERG, E(lliott) Marshall   1930-

PERSONAL: Born December 19, 1930, in North Adams, Mass.; son of Jack and Ida (Lenhoff) Goldberg; children: five. *Edu-*cation: University of Rochester, A.B. (with high honors), 1952; Tufts University, M.D., 1956.

ADDRESSES: Office—Hurley Medical Center, Flint, Mich. 48502. *Agent*—Mel Berger, William Morris Agency, 1350 Avenue of the Americas, New York, N.Y. 10019.

CAREER: District of Columbia Hospital, Washington, intern, 1956-57; Memorial Hospital, Worcester, Mass., resident, 1960-61; University Hospitals, Madison, Wis., resident, 1962-63; Wayne State University, Detroit, Mich., assistant professor of medicine, 1964-65; Michigan State University, East Lansing, assistant professor, 1966-68, associate professor, 1968, professor of medicine, 1973—; Hurley Hospital, Flint, Mich., chief of medicine 1970—. Visiting professor of humanities, Medical College of Pennsylvania, 1986-87. Research associate in endocrinology at St. Vincent's Hospital, Worcester, Mass., 1960; endocrine fellow at University of Wisconsin, 1961-62; cancer research, in collaboration with Wistar Institute, Philadelphia, Pa., 1981—. Diplomate of American Board of Internal Medicine; licensed in Massachusetts, Wisconsin, and Michigan. Book editor for Physicians' Radio Network; health expert for "Canada A.M." on Canadian Television (CTV); medical correspondent and chief medical consultant, "World News Tonight" (ABC), 1981-83; host, "The Medical Agenda" (Health Television Corporation and UTV Cable Network); co-host, with Dr. Robert Moser, of "The World of Medicine," MacNeil-Lehrer Production Company, for PBS. Member of board of directors of Medgar Evers Foundation. *Military service:* U.S. Army, Medical Corps, 1957-59; served in France; became captain.

MEMBER: American College of Physicians (fellow; professional and public communications committee, and telecommunications committee, 1981-83; public information officer, Michigan Chapter, 1981—), Endocrine Society, American Federation of Clinical Research, American Diabetes Association, Royal College of Physicians (associate), Massachusetts Medical Society, Michigan Medical Society, Michigan Association for Medical Education (president, 1972-75), Genesee County Medical Society.

AWARDS, HONORS: National Institutes of Health research grant, 1963-64; Humanitarian Award from National Association for the Advancement of Colored People, 1974.

WRITINGS:

NOVELS

The Karamanov Equations, World Publishing Co., 1972.
The Anatomy Lesson, Putnam, 1974.
Critical List (also see below), Bantam, 1978.
Skeletons (also see below), Bantam, 1979.
(With Kenneth Kay) *Disposable People,* Tower, 1979.
Nerve, Coward, 1981.
Natural Killers, Dorchester Publishing, 1986.
Intelligence, Dorchester Publishing, 1986.

NONFICTION

Cell Wars: The Immune System's Weapons Against Cancer, Farrar, Straus, 1988.

SCREENPLAY ADAPTATIONS

"Critical List," National Broadcasting Company, Inc., 1978.
"Skeletons," National Broadcasting Company, Inc., 1978.

OTHER

Contributor of articles to medical journals and popular magazines, including *Ladies Home Journal, Parade, TV Guide, Detroit,* and *Medical World News.*

WORK IN PROGRESS: Death of a Hospital; Virus-Hunter: The Biography of Dr. Robert Gallo, M.D.

SIDELIGHTS: E. Marshall Goldberg served as host and interviewer in the American College of Physicians videotape series, "Leaders in American Medicine" in collaboration with the National Library of Medicine, made during the years from 1984 to 1988.

*　　*　　*

GOLDSTEIN, Donald M(aurice) 1932-

PERSONAL: Born December 15, 1932, in New York, N.Y.; son of Max A. and Jean M. Goldstein; married Mariann Norma Zinck, August 5, 1963 (separated); children: Tammie, Timmie, Tommie, Teri. *Education:* University of Maryland, B.A., 1954, M.A., 1962; Georgetown University, M.S., 1963; graduated from U.S. Air Force Air Command and Staff College, 1965; George Washington University, M.B.A., 1965; University of Denver, Ph.D., 1970; graduated from U.S. Air Force War College, 1973. *Religion:* Roman Catholic.

ADDRESSES: Home—2146 Meadowmont Dr., Upper St. Clair Twp., Pittsburgh, Pa. *Office*—Office of the Dean, University of Pittsburgh, 3G32 Forbes Quadrangle, Pittsburgh, Pa. 15260.

CAREER: University of Maryland, College Park, assistant track coach and head freshman track coach, 1955; U.S. Air Force, career officer, 1955-71, squadron adjutant at Robins Air Force Base, Fla., 1955-58, coach of Air Force Track Team, 1957-59, radar-missiles site commander in Pescadore Islands, Taiwan, 1960-61, instructor at Tactical Air Command Missile School, Orlando, Fla., 1960-61, operations officer in U.S. Strike Command, 1961-64, associate professor of history and counselor at U.S. Air Force Academy, Colorado Springs, Colo., 1965-71, assistant track coach at academy, 1967-71, school secretary at U.S. Tactical Missile School, Orlando, 1968-70, retiring as lieutenant colonel; Air Command and Staff College, Maxwell Air Force Base, Ala., instructor in history, 1971-73, military historian, 1971-74, wing chief, 1973-74; University of Pittsburgh, Pittsburgh, Pa., research associate, 1974-75, professor of aerospace studies, 1975-77, associate professor of public and international affairs, 1975—, director of placement and alumni affairs, 1977-85, associate dean, 1986—, director of international security program and Asian study program. Assistant professor at Troy State University, 1971-74; high school cross-country track coach in Montgomery, Ala., 1972-73.

MEMBER: International Studies Association, American Historical Association, American Society of Public Administrators, American Political Science Association, Air Force Association, Omicron Delta Kappa, Phi Kappa Phi, Phi Alpha Theta, Sigma Nu, Toastmasters Club.

WRITINGS:

(Editor with Katherine V. Dillon) Gordon W. Prange, *At Dawn We Slept: The Untold Story of Pearl Harbor,* McGraw, 1981.
(Editor with Dillon) Prange, *Miracle at Midway,* McGraw, 1982.
(Editor with Dillon) Prange, *Target Tokyo: The Story of the Sorge Spy Ring,* McGraw, 1984.

(Editor with Dillon) Prange, *Pearl Harbor: The Verdict of History* (sequel to *At Dawn We Slept: The Untold Story of Pearl Harbor*), McGraw, 1987.
December 7, 1941, McGraw, 1988.
God's Samurai, McGraw, 1988.
Amelia Earhart, McGraw, in press.
Seaweeds of History: The Story of Admiral M. Urgaki, McGraw, in press.

Author of unpublished manuscripts "Adolph Hitler in the Perspective of the American Press," 1961, "Adolph Hitler: Administrator of a Society," 1965, and "Ennis C. Whithead: Aerospace Commander." Assistant editor of papers on foreign policy for U.S. House of Representatives Committee on International Affairs, 1947-54. Contributor to military and political science journals.

WORK IN PROGRESS: A Pictorial History of Pearl Harbor, "a book with over four hundred photos of the attack, most of which have never been published."

SIDELIGHTS: At the time of Gordon W. Prange's death in May, 1980, *At Dawn We Slept: The Untold Story of Pearl Harbor* remained unfinished. Donald M. Goldstein and another former student of Prange's, Katherine V. Dillon, edited thirty-seven-years-worth of Prange's research and completed the book. In the years that followed, Goldstein and Dillon collaborated on three additional books based on Prange's research.

Goldstein commented to *CA:* "To all aspiring authors—hang in there. You will get the break you need if you don't quit. Don't despair, that best seller may be right around the corner."

BIOGRAPHICAL/CRITICAL SOURCES:

PERIODICALS

Los Angeles Times Book Review, February 7, 1982, March 27, 1983, November 11, 1984.
New Yorker, September 12, 1983, April 14, 1986.
New York Times Book Review, January 5, 1986.
Washington Post Book World, Janaury 16, 1983, November 11, 1984, January 19, 1986.

*　　*　　*

GORDON, Frederick [Collective pseudonym]

WRITINGS:

"UP AND DOING" SERIES

The Young Crusoes of Pine Island; or, The Wreck of the Puff (also see below), Graham & Matlack, 1912.
Sammy Brown's Treasure Hunt; or, Lost in the Mountains (also see below), Graham & Matlack, 1912.
Bob Bouncer's School Days; or, The Doings of a Real, Live, Everyday Boy (also see below), Graham & Matlack, 1912.

"FAIRVIEW BOYS" SERIES

The Fairview Boys Afloat and Ashore; or, The Young Crusoes of Pine Island (originally published as *The Young Crusoes of Pine Island; or, The Wreck of the Puff*), Graham & Matlack, 1914.
. . . on Eagle Mountain; or, Sammy Brown's Treasure Hunt (originally published as *Sammy Brown's Treasure Hunt; or, Lost in the Mountains*), Graham & Matlack, 1914.

... *and Their Rivals; or, Bob Bouncer's School Days* (originally published as *Bob Bouncer's School Days; or, The Doings of a Real, Live, Everyday Boy*), Graham & Matlack, 1914.

... *at Camp Mystery; or, The Old Hermit and His Secret*, Graham & Matlack, 1914.

... *at Lighthouse Cove; or, Carried out to Sea*, Graham & Matlack, 1914.

... *on a Ranch; or, Riding with the Cowboys*, Graham, 1917.

SIDELIGHTS: For more information see the entries for Harriet S. Adams, Edward L. Stratemeyer, and Andrew E. Svenson.

BIOGRAPHICAL/CRITICAL SOURCES:

BOOKS

Johnson, Deidre, editor and compiler, *Stratemeyer Pseudonyms and Series Books: An Annotated Checklist of Stratemeyer and Stratemeyer Syndicate Publications*, Greenwood Press, 1982.

*   *   *

GORDON, Ira J(ay)   1923-1978

PERSONAL: Born January 15, 1923, in New York, N.Y.; died September 7, 1978; son of Herman Paul and Esther (Feltenstein) Gordon; married Esther Goldberg, August 4, 1949; children: Gary David, Bonnie Debra. *Education:* City College (now of the City University of New York), B.B.A. (cum laude), 1943; Columbia University, M.A., 1947, Ed.D., 1950. *Religion:* Jewish.

ADDRESSES: Home—1600 Halifax Rd., Chapel Hill, N.C. 27514.

CAREER: City College (now of the City University of New York), New York City, director of Lamport House (student activity center), 1946-48; Kansas State College of Agriculture and Applied Science (now Kansas State University), Manhattan, assistant professor of psychology, 1948-49, associate professor of psychology and counseling, 1949-51; University of Maryland, College Park, assistant professor at Institute for Child Study, 1951-54, associate professor of psychology, 1954-56; University of Florida, Gainesville, associate professor, 1956-60, professor, 1960-71, graduate research professor of education, 1971-77, chairman of department of foundations of education, 1964-67, director of Institute for Development of Human Resources, 1966-77; University of North Carolina at Chapel Hill, Kenan Professor of Education and dean of School of Education, both beginning 1977. Director of University of Maryland Institute for Child Study Summer Workshop, 1956; visiting professor at University of Illinois, 1960, Rutgers University, 1962, University of New Hampshire, 1969, 1970, 1973, and University of North Carolina at Chapel Hill, 1976; visiting scholar at University of London Institute of Education, 1973-74. Member of Gainesville City Planning Board, 1972-73, 1975-77, chairman, 1975-76. Adviser, Department of Health, Education, and Welfare, 1972-75. Consultant, U.S. Air Force Human Resources Research Laboratories, 1952-54. *Military service:* U.S. Army, 1943-46; became second lieutenant, U.S. Army Reserve, 1946-51.

MEMBER: Association for Childhood Education International, American Psychological Association (fellow; member of executive committee, 1970-73), Association for Supervision and Curriculum Development, National Association for Education of Young Children, National Society for the Study of Education, American Educational Research Association, American Personnel and Guidance Association, Beta Gamma Sigma, Phi Delta Kappa, Kappa Delta Pi, Alpha Phi Omega.

AWARDS, HONORS: Achievement award from Bernard M. Baruch Alumni Society, School of Business and Public Administration, City College (now of the City University of New York), 1968.

WRITINGS:

How to Be a Good Discusser (pamphlet), B'nai B'rith Youth Organization, 1951, revised and enlarged edition, 1952.
The Teacher as a Guidance Worker, Harper, 1956.
Children's Views of Themselves (pamphlet), Association for Childhood Education International, 1959, revised edition, 1972.
Human Development: A Transactional Approach, Harper, 1962, 3rd edition, 1975.
Changing View of Childhood (pamphlet), Florida Association for Supervision and Curriculum Development, 1964.
(Editor) *Human Development: Readings in Research*, Scott, Foresman, 1965.
Studying the Child in School, Wiley, 1966.
(With J. R. Lally) *Intellectual Stimulation for Infants and Toddlers*, Institute for the Development of Human Resources, University of Florida Press, 1967.
(Editor) *Criteria for Theories of Instruction* (pamphlet), Association for Supervision and Curriculum Development, 1968.
A Test Manual for the "How I See Myself Scale" (monograph), Educational Research and Development Council, University of Florida Press, 1968.
Reaching the Child through Parent Education: The Florida Approach (monograph), Institute for the Development of Human Resources, University of Florida Press, 1969.
Baby Learning through Baby Play: A Parent's Guide for the First Two Years, St. Martin's, 1970.
Parent Involvement in Compensatory Education, University of Illinois Press, 1970.
(Editor) *Reading in Research in Developmental Psychology*, Scott, Foresman, 1971.
On Early Learning: The Modifiability of Human Potential (monograph), Association for Supervision and Curriculum Development, 1971.
(With Barry J. Guinagh and R. E. Jester) *Child Learning through Child Play: Learning Activities for Two- and Three-Year Olds*, St. Martin's, 1972.
(Editor and contributor) *Early Childhood Education: 1972 National Society for the Study of Education Yearbook*, University of Chicago Press, 1972.
(With Guinagh) *A Home Learning Center Approach to Early Stimulation*, Institute for Development of Human Resources, University of Florida Press, 1974.
(With others) *The Florida Parent Education Follow-through Program*, Institute for Development of Human Resources, University of Florida Press, 1974.
The Florida Parent Education Early Intervention Projects: A Longitudinal Look, University of Illinois Press, 1975.
The Infant Experience, C. E. Merrill, 1975.
(With others) *Research Report of Parent Oriented Home-Based Early Childhood Education Program*, Institute for Development of Human Resources, University of Florida Press, 1975.
On the Continuity of Development, Association for Childhood Education International, 1976.

(Editor with W. F. Breivogel, and contributor) *Building Effective Home-School Relationships*, Allyn & Bacon, 1976.

(Editor with Breivogel and Michael L. Hanes, and contributor) *Update: The First Ten Years of Life—Proceedings of a Conference Held March 29, 30, 31, 1976*, Division of Continuing Education, University of Florida Press, 1977.

Baby to Parent, Parent to Baby: A Guide to Developing Parent-Child Interaction in the First Twelve Months, illustrated by Ethel Gold, St. Martin's, 1977.

(With Lally) *Learning Games for Infants and Toddlers: A Playtime Handbook*, Institute for Development of Human Resources, University of Florida Press, 1977.

CONTRIBUTOR

Portfolio of College Teaching Techniques, A. C. Croft, 1951.

S. Farwell and H. Peters, editors, *Readings in Guidance*, Rand McNally, 1960.

Peters and others, editors, *Guidance in the Elementary School: A Book of Readings*, Macmillan, 1963.

Changes in Teacher Education: An Appraisal, National Commission on Teacher Education and Professional Standards, National Education Association, 1964.

P. F. Regan and E. G. Pattishall, editors, *Behavioral Science Contributions to Psychiatry*, Little, Brown, 1965.

W. B. Waetjen, editor, *Learning and Mental Health in the School*, Association for Supervision and Curriculum Development, 1966.

M. R. Smith, editor, *Guidance-Personnel Work: Future Tense*, Bureau of Publications, Teachers College, Columbia University, 1966.

Ralph Ojemann and Karen Pritchett, editors, *Giving Emphasis to Guided Learning*, Education Research Council of Greater Cleveland, 1966.

J. L. Frost, editor, *Early Childhood Education Rediscovered*, Holt, 1968.

D. C. Dinkmeyer, editor, *Guidance and Counseling in the Elementary School*, Holt, 1968.

Education and the City Child: Some New Approaches, Day Care Council of New York, 1969.

E. Grotberg, editor, *Critical Issues in Research Related to Disadvantaged Children*, Educational Testing Service, 1969.

N. J. Vigilante, editor, *Mathematics in Elementary Education: Selected Readings*, Macmillan, 1969.

W. R. Baller, editor, *Readings in the Psychology of Human Growth and Development*, 2nd edition, Holt, 1969.

Pupil Personnel Services: Where Are We? Where Are We Going?, University Press at Buffalo, 1970.

Needs of Elementary and Secondary Education of the Seventies, Committee on Education and Labor, House of Representatives, 1970.

H. F. Cottingham, editor, *Elementary School Guidance: Conceptual Beginnings and Initial Approaches*, American Personnel and Guidance Association, 1970.

I. D. Welch, F. Richards, and A. C. Richards, editors, *Education Accountability: A Humanistic Perspective*, Shield Publishing Co., 1973.

P. Satz and J. Ross, editors, *The Disabled Learner*, Rotterdam University Press, 1973.

G. Hass, editor, *Curriculum Planning: A New Approach*, Allyn & Bacon, 1974.

E. G. Boyer, A. Simon, and G. Karafin, editors, *Measures of Maturation: An Anthology of Early Childhood Observation Instruments*, Volume II, Research for Better Schools, 1974.

Frost, editor, *Understanding and Nurturing Infant Development*, Association for Childhood Education International, 1976.

M. C. Day and R. K. Parker, editors, *The Preschool in Action: Exploring Early Childhood Programs*, Allyn & Bacon, 1977.

OTHER

Contributor to *Encyclopedia of Education Research* and *Handbook of Research on Teaching*. Contributor of approximately one hundred articles and reviews to scholarly journals, including *Adult Education Bulletin, Personnel and Guidance Journal, Contemporary Psychology, Science, Childhood Education, Educational Theory, Educational Leadership*, and *Journal of Medical Education*. Consulting editor, *American Journal of Mental Deficiency*, 1971-73, and *American Educational Research Journal*, 1976; national adviser, *Children's.*

SIDELIGHTS: Ira J. Gordon once wrote to *CA:* "My wife was most instrumental in educating me about the capabilities of infants and the importance of parenting. She taught me, more than twenty-five years ago, to 'father.' The research and field work in parent education is thus an outgrowth of her efforts."

A number of Gordon's books are available in German, Italian, Japanese, and Spanish.†

*   *   *

GOWIN, D(ixie) Bob 1925-

PERSONAL: Born December 11, 1925, in West Palm Beach, Fla.; son of Lafayette (a horse breeder) and Marie (Betts) Gowin; married, 1950 (divorced, 1972); children: Sarah Gowin Gifford, Robert Bancroft, John Frederic. *Education:* University of Texas, B.A., 1948; Stanford University, M.A., 1951; Yale University, Ph.D., 1956.

ADDRESSES: Home—1030 Cayuga Heights Rd., Ithaca, N.Y. 14850. *Office*—Graduate Field of Education, Roberts Hall, Cornell University, Ithaca, N.Y. 14853.

CAREER: University of Bridgeport, Bridgeport, Conn., assistant professor of philosophy of education, 1956-58; University of Chicago, Chicago, Ill., assistant professor of education, 1958-61; Cornell University, Ithaca, N.Y., assistant professor, 1961-63, associate professor, 1963-70, professor of philosophy of education, 1970—. Visiting associate professor at Stanford University, 1968-69. *Military service:* U.S. Navy, 1944-46.

MEMBER: American Philosophical Association (fellow), Philosophy of Education Society (president, 1969-70), Metaphysical Society of America, American Educational Research Association, John Dewey Society (chairperson of lecture commission).

AWARDS, HONORS: Postdoctoral fellow at Yale University, 1958; fellow of U.S. Office of Education at Stanford University, 1967-68.

WRITINGS:

(Editor with L. G. Thomas and Harold Dunkel, and contributor) *Philosophical Redirection of Educational Research*, National Society for Studies in Education, 1972.

(With Jason Millman) *Appraising Educational Research*, Prentice-Hall, 1974.

Educating, Cornell University Press, 1981, revised edition, 1987.

(With Joseph J. Novak) *Learning How to Learn*, Cambridge University Press, 1984.

(Author of foreword) James Gouinlock, *Excellence in Public Discourse: J. S. Mill and J. Dewey*, Teachers College Press, Columbia University, 1984.

(Author of foreword) Elsie Baulding, *Building a World Civic Culture*, Teachers College Press, Columbia University, 1988.

(Author of foreword) Maxine Greene, *The Dialectic of Freedom*, Teachers College Press, Columbia University, 1988.

Member of editorial board, *Studies in Philosophy of Education*, 1962-70, and *Social Epistemology*, 1988.

WORK IN PROGRESS: Concept Mapping in Educating, with Joseph Novak; *Professors' Ways of Knowing*.

SIDELIGHTS: D. Bob Gowin told *CA:* "All writing is difficult, and rewriting is always necessary. Yet there are times when it flows and flows. My special purpose has been to write theory so it means something in itself and to engage in practice so it has a point for theory. I fully believe that educating changes the meaning of human experience.

"In my book *Educating*, I generate a comprehensive theory that brings together four components: teaching, curriculum, learning, and governance—each of equal weight and none to be reduced to any of the others. My theory is grounded in an event epistemology that conceives of educating as an eventful process rather than an end product. The purpose is to add meaning to experience and value to facts. Of all the promising possibilities for combating boredom in school and life, my first choice would be to capture an event sense of educating. The end of educating is self-educating, where we are empowered to take charge of our lives by creating our own scripts of meaning. On the way, we need help from teachers (teaching is defined as the achievement of shared meaning), help from primary and secondary sources whose codes we must learn to crack, and from a humane social milieu that encourages equality of initial opportunity to an education, that stimulates simultaneously both freedom and authority, and that works toward mutuality of purpose and resource.

"Educating is not, as it is so often thought to be, behavior modification, indoctrination, or socialization, which may shape a person but not educate. I believe the conventional views are moribund; they cannot, by their own principles and methods, advance our understanding. That is why I developed a new set of terms and distinctions and put them to use. Over two dozen completed doctoral dissertations use these ideas in the actual context of educative events.

"Educating is not a mystery but a clearly reasoned process with clearly attainable goals. But a new justification for schooling is sorely needed; it is to make schools and universities places where boredom is reduced, living enhanced, and the meaning of human experience changed."

Educating has been translated into Spanish, and *Learning How to Learn* has been translated into Italian and Thai.

*   *   *

GRAHAM, (Roger) Neill   1941-

PERSONAL: Born February 21, 1941, in Augusta, Ga.; son of Roger Neill (a sales representative) and Charlie Mae (a teacher; maiden name, Scattergood) Graham. *Education:* Attended Augusta College, 1959-61; Valdosta State College, B.S., 1963; University of North Carolina, Ph.D., 1971.

ADDRESSES: Home—913 Papaya St., Augusta, Ga. 30904.

CAREER: Concord College, Athens, W.Va., assistant professor, 1968-76, associate professor of physics, 1976-78; freelance writer, 1978—.

MEMBER: Association for Computing Machinery, I.E.E.E. Computer Society, Sigma Xi.

WRITINGS:

(Editor with Bryce S. Dewitt) *The Many Worlds Interpretation of Quantum Mechanics*, Princeton University Press, 1973.

The Mind Tool, West Publishing, 1976, 5th edition, 1989.

Microprocessor Programming for Computer Hobbyists, TAB Books, 1977.

Artificial Intelligence, TAB Books, 1979.

Introduction to Computer Science, West Publishing, 1979, 4th edition, 1988.

Introduction to Pascal, West Publishing, 1980, 3rd edition, 1988.

Computers and Computing, West Publishing, 1982.

Programming the IBM Personal Computer: BASIC, Holt, 1982.

Programming the IBM Personal Computer: Pascal, Holt, 1983.

Programming the IBM Personal Computer: COBOL, Holt, 1984.

Programming the IBM Personal Computer: Fundamentals of BASIC, Holt, 1984.

WORK IN PROGRESS: College textbooks on computers and computing.

SIDELIGHTS: Neill Graham commented: "As a youngster, I was interested in science and science fiction. My interest in science led to my studies of mathematics, physics, and computer science. My interest in science fiction led me first to the science fiction of Isaac Asimov, then to his science popularizations, which I greatly admired and which inspired me to write about science. When the opportunity to write about computer science arose, I grasped it eagerly and soon put aside my teaching and other scientific endeavors to devote my full time to writing."

*   *   *

GRAVES, Richard Perceval   1945-

PERSONAL: Born December 21, 1945, in Brighton, England; son of John Tiarks Ranke (a teacher) and Mary (a teacher; maiden name, Wickens) Graves; married Anne Katharine Fortescue, April 4, 1970 (separated May, 1987); children: David John Perceval, Philip Macartney, Lucia Mary. *Education:* St. John's College, Oxford, B.A., 1968, M.A., 1972. *Politics:* Social Democrat. *Religion:* Church of England.

ADDRESSES: Home—Rosehill, 12 Betton St., Belle Vue, Shrewsbury, Salop SY3 7NY, England. *Agent*—Andrew Best, Curtis Brown, 162-168 Regent St., London W1R 5TA, England.

CAREER: Writer. Teacher of English, history, and Latin at private schools in England, 1968-73; Whittington parish councillor, 1973-76; chairman of Whittington Youth Club, 1974-79, Oswestry borough councillor, 1977-83.

MEMBER: Society of Authors.

WRITINGS:

Lawrence of Arabia and His World, Scribner, 1976.

A. E. Housman: The Scholar-Poet, Routledge & Kegan Paul, 1979, Scribner, 1980.

The Brothers Powys, Scribner, 1983.
Robert Graves: The Assault Heroic, 1895-1926, Weidenfeld & Nicolson, 1986, Viking, 1987.

Editor of *Housman Society Journal,* 1977-80.

WORK IN PROGRESS: Volume two of a biography of Robert Graves and an authorized biography of Richard Hughes, both for Weidenfeld & Nicolson; annotated edition of Robert Graves's *Goodbye to All That,* for Cassell; a historical novel about William Rufus.

SIDELIGHTS: English biographer Richard Perceval Graves's book *A. E. Housman: The Scholar-Poet* is especially commended for bringing Housman the man into the forefront. According to William Pratt in *World Literature Today,* "Housman is a stern test for the biographer, and Graves has met it handsomely, constructing an honest and good-humored portrait of an exceedingly reticent and aloof figure, whose own family could never fathom him." Similarly, Joseph Parisi comments in the *Chicago Tribune Book World* that Graves's text on Housman "presents a portrait of not only the sad artist and acerbic scholar, but what Housman's contemporaries were prevented from seeing: the kind, sensuous, many-sided human being."

At the same time that reviewers praise Graves for success in this regard, criticisms arise concerning, among other things, Graves's analysis of Housman's poetry. Whereas James Atlas maintains in the *New York Times Book Review* that the author's estimate of Housman's poetry "seems to me just right," others, like Molly Tibbs in *Contemporary Review,* express some reservations. In the opinion of Tibbs, "the essay on Housman's achievements as a classical scholar . . . is neat, compendious and useful. One is, however, somewhat taken aback by . . . Graves'[s] apologetic attitude to the poetry. He begins his discussion thereof with the discouraging comment that there is much that is morbid and self-pitying. . . . [Graves] expressly wishes to introduce a new generation to the neglected beauties of Housman's poetry, and this cannot be the way to do it." As for Pratt, "it has to be said that if Graves adds much to the understanding of Housman's mind and character, he adds little to the appreciation of his art. In fact, he dismisses some of Housman's finest lyrics as 'inferior work.'" Nevertheless, according to a *New Yorker* reviewer, "[Graves's] realistic, honest, admiring approach is the best thing that could have happened to Housman's reputation."

Several years later, Graves published the first volume in a proposed multi-volume study of his uncle, poet and novelist Robert Graves. A detailed examination of the elder writer's early years, *Robert Graves: The Assault Heroic, 1895-1926,* has received extensive critical attention, particularly regarding the family connection between the biographer and his subject. Opinions are divided as to the effect this relationship has on the book. Commenting in the *New York Review of Books,* for example, John Wain states that the Graves biography "is very much a family job, and none the worse for a certain old-fashioned sense of family loyalty that peeps through its pages. He inherited a vast amount of manuscript material, and . . . it would have been a waste for him not to use it." John Gross concurs; according to his *New York Times* contribution, "one . . . enjoys the advantages of intimate family knowledge and access to previously unexplored family papers." In turn, Martin Seymour-Smith, who was once a tutor to Robert Graves's son and who had written the first biography of the poet in 1956, presents his view of the newer study in the *London Review of Books:* "The virtue of this account of Graves's life . . . is its

meticulous Victorian charm. The author has relied on the diaries of his grandfather, Alfred Percevel, to a large degree. . . . What we have here is the first-hand account of a wayward genius from the viewpoint of one who 'loves' him—'loves' in that somewhat distant, uncarnal, strictly family sense—but cannot possibly even begin to understand him. . . . So although I have to say that this book does seem to me to be awful and misleading as an account of the processes of mind of Robert Graves between his birth and 1926, I can also say that it is a perfect family record: something that I should have thought, until I read it, impossible of achievement at this over-sophisticated instant in history. Readers who want to know what Graves grew out of and away from will find it laid out here in an astonishingly pure form."

In contrast to these viewpoints, some critics think there might be too much of a family orientation in *Robert Graves: The Assault Heroic.* According to London *Times* commentator Peter Ackroyd, "this particular volume takes some 328 pages to complete a period of Robert Graves's history which, in Martin Seymour-Smith's own . . . biographical account, needed only 130. It is easy to see why Graves's nephew has included so much material—he happens to have it at his disposal, and the fact that most of it was unpublished proved too great a temptation to resist. But the recital of family memories does not necessarily make for interesting reading. . . . And there are times when this biography recalls the worst moments of the photograph album brought out at tea-time." *Books and Bookmen* contributor Paul O'Prey shares this opinion: "We get rather bogged down in the minutiae of events . . . , while the seemingly endless list of relatives we meet can only be of limited interest to those outside the clan. This concentration on the family seriously unbalances the book. . . . Robert's friendships with . . . Siegfried Sassoon, T. E. Lawrence and Basanta Mallik, which were more important for him after he reached a certain age than were his relationships with his parents, and which are surely more important for us, receive a relatively superficial treatment."

Though the assessment of *Robert Graves: The Assault Heroic* is divided on the matter of how much family detail the author should have included in his study, there is much agreement concerning the book's lucidity and its devotion to honest revelation. "His truth of tone and his respectfulness," notes Peter Levi in the *Spectator,* "have produced a full and clear picture with many currents under its surface." Levi ultimately judges the work a "wonderful and deeply stirring biography." According to Gross, "[Richard Perceval] Graves tells his story straightforwardly and unaffectedly; there is no doubt a cleverer book on [Robert] Graves waiting to be written, but it is hard to imagine one that enters into his spirit with keener sympathy or more intuitive understanding." Samuel Hynes, commenting in the *New Republic,* describes *Robert Graves: The Assault Heroic* as "a promising beginning of what may well become the standard life of Graves. . . . It provides a full and sympathetic account of Graves's early worlds, told by an intelligent and informed observer." "Richard Graves is a good writer and a conscientious historian," concludes an *Atlantic* reviewer. "This is the first volume of what promises to be a splendid biography."

BIOGRAPHICAL/CRITICAL SOURCES:

BOOKS

Contemporary Literary Criticism, Volume XLIV, Gale, 1987.

PERIODICALS

Atlantic, April, 1987.
Books and Bookmen, November, 1986.
Chicago Tribune Book World, June 15, 1980.
Contemporary Review, February, 1980, April, 1983.
London Review of Books, October 9, 1986.
New Republic, June 28, 1980, March 30, 1987.
New Yorker, August 18, 1980.
New York Review of Books, June 25, 1987.
New York Times, March 6, 1987.
New York Times Book Review, May 25, 1980.
Observer (London), September 21, 1986.
Spectator, March 19, 1983, September 27, 1986.
Time, July 28, 1980, September 11, 1986.
Times (London), April 4, 1981.

Times Literary Supplement, December 21, 1979, November 21, 1986.
Washington Post Book World, June 29, 1980, March 15, 1987.
World Literature Today, spring, 1981.

—*Sketch by Cheryl Gottler*

*   *   *

GREGORY, J. Dennis
   See WILLIAMS, John A(lfred)

*   *   *

GRESHAM, Anthony
   See RUSSELL, Roy

H

HADFIELD, Alice M(ary) 1908-
(Alice M. Smyth)

PERSONAL: Born December 14, 1908, in South Cerney, England; daughter of Henry (an army officer) and Alice Mary (a secretary; maiden name, Goodwin) Smyth; married Peter Miller, April 27, 1935 (died May 20, 1940); married Charles Hadfield (a writer), October 20, 1945; children: Laura Langley, Alexander, Caroline Switek. *Education:* St. Hilda's College, Oxford, B.A., 1931; Mount Holyoke College, A.M., 1932. *Religion:* Church of England.

ADDRESSES: Home—13 Meadow Way, South Cerney, Cirencester, Gloucestershire GL7 6HY, England. *Agent*—David Higham Associates Ltd., 5-8 Lower John St., Golden Sq., London W1R 4HA, England.

CAREER: Oxford University Press, London, England, librarian, 1933-38; Admiralty House, Bermuda, cipher assistant, 1940-41; writer, 1941—. Founder of South Cerney Trust, 1962, chairman until 1972.

MEMBER: Charles Williams Society (co-founder).

WRITINGS:

(Editor) *The Oxford Dictionary of Quotations,* Oxford University Press, 1941.
What Happens Next? (novel), Falcon Press, 1950.
King Arthur and the Round Table, Dutton, 1953.
An Introduction to Charles Williams, R. Hale, 1959.
Time to Finish the Game, Phoenix House, 1964.
Williver's Luck, Chatto & Windus, 1964.
Williver's Quest, Chatto & Windus, 1965.
(With husband, Charles Hadfield) *The Cotswolds,* Batsford, 1966.
Williver's Return, Chatto & Windus, 1967.
The Chartist Land Company, David & Charles, 1970.
(Editor with C. Hadfield) *The Cotswolds: A New Study,* David & Charles, 1973.
(With C. Hadfield) *Introducing the Cotswolds,* David & Charles, 1976.
(With C. Hadfield) *Afloat in America,* David & Charles, 1979.
Charles Williams: An Explanation of His Life and Work, Oxford University Press, 1983.
(Editor) Charles Williams, *Outlines of Romantic Theology,* Eerdmans, 1988.

(Editor and author of introduction) *Religion and Love in Dante,* Eerdmans, 1988.

UNDER NAME ALICE M. SMYTH

Clarendon High School History of England, Clarendon Press, 1935.
The Story of Peter (juvenile), Oxford University Press, 1936.
A Book of Fabulous Beasts (juvenile), Oxford University Press, 1939.
A Book of Famous Pirates (juvenile), illustrations by C. Walter Hodges, Oxford University Press, 1940.
St. Peter (juvenile), Oxford University Press, 1947.
The Adventures of Peter (juvenile), Oxford University Press, 1948.

SIDELIGHTS: Alice M. Hadfield told *CA:* "My main interests are church membership, writing, local village affairs, poetry, and theology."

BIOGRAPHICAL/CRITICAL SOURCES:

PERIODICALS

Times Literary Supplement, February 19, 1984, March 2, 1984.

*   *   *

HADFIELD, (Ellis) Charles (Raymond) 1909-
(E. C. R. Hadfield; pseudonym, Charles Alexander)

PERSONAL: Born August 5, 1909, in Pietersburg, South Africa; son of Alexander Charles and Marion Francis (Fulford) Hadfield; married Alice Mary Smyth (a writer), October 20, 1945; children: Alexander, John, Caroline; Laura (stepdaughter). *Education:* Attended Blundell's School and St. Edmund Hall, Oxford. *Religion:* Church of England.

ADDRESSES: Home and office—13 Meadow Way, South Cerney, Cirencester, Gloucestershire GLY 6HY, England. *Agent*—David Higham Associates Ltd., 5-8 Lower John St., Golden Square, London W1R 4HA, England.

CAREER: Oxford University Press, London, England, editor, 1936-38, chief editor of juvenile books, 1938-39, 1945-46; Central Office of Information, London, director of publications, 1946-48, overseas controller, 1948-62; David & Charles (publishers), Newton Abbot, England, director, 1960-64.

Councillor, Paddington Borough Council, 1924-35; part-time member, British Waterways Board, 1962-66.

MEMBER: Railway and Canal Historical Society (president, 1960-63), Inland Waterways Association (vice-president), Newcomen Society.

AWARDS, HONORS: Companion of Order of St. Michael and St. George, 1954.

WRITINGS:

(With Frank Eyre) *English Rivers and Canals*, World Publishing, 1945.
British Canals: An Illustrated History, Phoenix House, 1950, 7th edition, David & Charles, 1984.
(Under pseudonym Charles Alexander) *The Church's Year*, Oxford University Press, 1950.
Introducing Canals, Benn, 1955.
The Canals of Southern England, Phoenix House, 1955, augmented excerpts published as *The Canals of South West England*, David & Charles, 1967, 2nd edition, 1985, and *The Canals of South and South East England*, David & Charles, 1969.
The Canals of South Wales and the Border, University of Wales Press, 1960, 2nd edition, David & Charles, 1967.
(With John Norris) *Waterways to Stratford*, David & Charles, 1962, 2nd edition, 1968.
Canals of the World, Basil Blackwell, 1964.
The Canals of the West Midlands, 1966, 3rd edition, David & Charles, 1985.
The Canals of the East Midlands, David & Charles, 1966, 2nd edition, 1970.
Canals and Waterways, Raleigh Press, 1966.
(With wife, Alice Mary Hadfield) *The Cotswolds*, Batsford, 1966.
Atmospheric Railways: A Victorian Venture in Silent Speed, David & Charles, 1967, 2nd edition, Alan Sutton, 1985.
(With Michael Streat) *Holiday Cruising on Inland Waterways*, David & Charles, 1968, 2nd edition, 1971.
The Canal Age, David & Charles, 1968, Praeger, 1969, 2nd edition, David & Charles, 1981.
(With Gordon Biddle) *The Canals of North West England*, David & Charles, 1970.
(Editor) *Canal Enthusiasts' Handbook, 1970-1971*, David & Charles, 1970.
The Canals of Yorkshire and North East England, David & Charles, 1972-73.
(Editor) *Canal Enthusiasts' Handbook Number 2*, David & Charles, 1973.
(Editor with A. M. Hadfield, and contributor) *The Cotswolds: A New Study*, David & Charles, 1973.
Waterways Sights to See, David & Charles, 1976.
(With A. M. Hadfield) *Introducing the Cotswolds*, David & Charles, 1976.
Inland Waterways, David & Charles, 1978.
(With A. M. Hadfield) *Afloat in America*, David & Charles, 1979.
(With A. W. Skempton) *William Jessop, Engineer*, David & Charles, 1979.
World Canals: Inland Navigation Past and Present, David & Charles, 1986.

UNDER NAME E. C. R. HADFIELD

(Editor) *Book of Sea Verse*, Oxford University Press, 1940.
Civilian Fire Fighter, English Universities Press, 1941.

(Compiler) *Book of Animal Verse*, Oxford University Press, 1943.
(With James E. MacColl) *Pilot Guide to Political London*, Pilot Press, 1945.
(With MacColl) *British Local Government*, Hutchinson University Library, 1948.

CHILDREN'S BOOKS; UNDER NAME E. C. R. HADFIELD

(With C. H. Ellis) *Young Collector's Handbook*, Oxford University Press, 1940.
(With Alexander D'Agapeyeff) *Maps*, Oxford University Press, 1942, 2nd edition, 1950.
Fire Service To-day, Oxford University Press, 1944, 2nd edition, 1953.

OTHER

Contributor of articles on canals to journals. Editor, *Quaker Monthly*, 1963-69.

WORK IN PROGRESS: An Inquiry into the Working Relationship between Two Engineers, William Jessop and Thomas Telford.

BIOGRAPHICAL/CRITICAL SOURCES:

BOOKS

Baldwin, Mark, and Anthony Burton, editors, *Canals, A New Look: Studies in Honour of Charles Hadfield*, Phillimore, 1984.

*   *   *

HADFIELD, E. C. R.
  See HADFIELD, (Ellis) Charles (Raymond)

*   *   *

HALLIN, Emily Watson
  (Elaine Harper)

PERSONAL: Born in Fort Smith, Ark.; married Clark Ossell Hallin (a pilot), August 16, 1952 (lost on a flight in West Africa, 1969); children: Daniel, Diane, Brian. *Education:* University of Missouri—Kansas City, A.B. (cum laude). *Religion:* Protestant.

ADDRESSES: Home—13861 Cicerone Ln., Los Altos Hills, Calif. 94022.

CAREER: Publicist and industrial editor for Pratt & Whitney Aircraft and for Chance Vought Aircraft, 1942-52; free-lance writer, 1952—; Stanford University, Stanford, Calif., administrator of International Relations Program, 1967—.

AWARDS, HONORS: Teen Novel Award, Popular Fiction Day (New York), 1984; Jack London Award, California Writers Convention, 1987.

WRITINGS:

Wild White Wings (juvenile), McKay, 1965.
Follow the Honey Bird (juvenile), McKay, 1967.
Moya and the Flamingoes (juvenile), McKay, 1969.
The Bird of Paradise, Crosswinds, 1988.
No Easy Answers, Crosswinds, 1988.
Wanted: Tony Roston, Crosswinds, 1988.
Dark Horse, Crosswinds, 1988.
Queen Bee, Crosswinds, 1988.

YOUNG ADULT NOVELS; PUBLISHED BY SIMON & SCHUSTER

Love at First Sight, 1981.
We Belong Together, 1982.
Be My Valentine, 1983.
Light of My Life, 1983.
The Mystery Kiss, 1983.
Short Stop to Romance, 1984.
Fireworks, 1984.
Turkey Trot, 1984.
Christmas Date, 1984.
Ghost of Gamma Rho, 1985.
Lover's Lake, 1985.
Janine, 1985.
The Phantom Skateboard, 1985.
Orinoco Adventure, 1986.
Homecoming, 1986.
Coral Island, 1987.

OTHER

Contributor to aviation and trade magazines and newspapers and periodicals, including *Coronet, Sunset,* and *American Illustrated.*

SIDELIGHTS: Emily Watson Hallin has lived in Japan and Saudi Arabia and traveled in Europe, the Near East, and Africa. She knows French, Spanish, Portuguese, Arabic, and some Japanese and Russian. She told *CA* that her work as an administrator of the International Relations Program at Stanford University has brought her into contact with hundreds of young people and led to her interest in writing young adult novels, commenting "When a teen-ager writes to me that my work has sparked her interest in reading books, that's the ultimate fulfillment for me."

Hallin's work has appeared in several foreign languages.

AVOCATIONAL INTERESTS: Birdwatching (has traveled to the New Guinea highlands to view the birds of paradise, to the Australian rain forests and the Great Barrier Reef, the Galapagos Islands, and the rain forests of Peru and Ecuador).

*   *   *

HAMILTON, Richard F(rederick) 1930-

PERSONAL: Born January 18, 1930, in Kenmore, N.Y.; son of Delmer Vernon (a carpenter) and Ethelwyn Gertrude (Stevenson) Hamilton; married Irene Maria Elisabeth Wagner, August 12, 1957; children: Carl Thomas, Tilman Michael. *Education:* Attended University of Michigan, 1947-48; University of Chicago, B.A., 1950; Columbia University, M.A., 1953, Ph.D., 1963.

ADDRESSES: Home—1354 London Dr., Columbus, Ohio 43211. *Office*—Sociology Department, Ohio State University, 392 Bricken Hall, 190 North Oval Mall, Columbus, Ohio 43210.

CAREER: Skidmore College, Saratoga Springs, N.Y., instructor in sociology, 1957-59; Harpur College (now State University of New York at Binghamton), Binghamton, N.Y., instructor in sociology, 1959-64; Princeton University, Princeton, N.J., assistant professor of sociology, 1964-66; University of Wisconsin—Madison, associate professor, 1966-69, professor of sociology, 1969-70; McGill University, Montreal, Quebec, Canada, professor of sociology, 1970-86; Ohio State University, Columbus, professor of sociology and political science, 1986—. Member of council of Inter-University Consortium for Political and Social Research, 1975-79; member of steering committee of Council for European Studies, 1975-78. *Military service:* U.S. Army, 1954-56.

WRITINGS:

Affluence and the French Worker in the Fourth Republic, Princeton University Press, 1967.
Class and Politics in the United States, Wiley, 1972.
Restraining Myths: Critical Studies of U.S. Social Structure and Politics, Halsted, 1975.
Who Voted for Hitler?, Princeton University Press, 1982.
(With James Wright) *The State of the Masses,* Aldine, 1986.

Contributor to scholarly journals, including *American Journal of Sociology, Canadian Journal of Political Science,* and *Geschichte und Gesellschaft.*

WORK IN PROGRESS: Revolution in Germany, 1848—History, Theory and Political Practice, an analysis of Frederick Engels's treatment of the 1848 revolution in Germany; *Intellectuals, History, and Society,* an analysis of Marxism in the German context.

SIDELIGHTS: Richard F. Hamilton's *Who Voted for Hitler?* takes issue with the accepted explanation of who voted Nazi in the 1933 German elections. According to Hamilton's analysis, based on urban election returns, Nazi support did not spring from the lower middle classes, as is widely believed; instead, it was concentrated in areas of upper-middle-class background. Hamilton, says Jeremy Noakes in the *Times Literary Supplement,* "provides a subtle and perceptive analysis of the political attitudes and behaviour of urban white-collar workers," and he has "clearly proved his main point." *New York Times Book Review* contributor Walter Laqueur disagrees with some of Hamilton's findings, but concedes that "Hamilton should be congratulated for having demolished some old shibboleths and having asked important questions."

BIOGRAPHICAL/CRITICAL SOURCES:

PERIODICALS

New York Times Book Review, June 20, 1982.
Times Literary Supplement, September 21, 1984.

*   *   *

HAMILTON, Robert W.
[Collective pseudonym]

WRITINGS:

Belinda of the Red Cross, Sully & Kleinteich, 1917.

SIDELIGHTS: For more information see the entries for Harriet S. Adams, Edward L. Stratemeyer, and Andrew E. Svenson.

BIOGRAPHICAL/CRITICAL SOURCES:

BOOKS

Johnson, Deidre, editor and compiler, *Stratemeyer Pseudonyms and Series Books: An Annotated Checklist of Stratemeyer and Stratemeyer Syndicate Publications,* Greenwood Press, 1982.

*   *   *

HAMLEY, Dennis 1935-

PERSONAL: Born October 14, 1935, in Crockham Hill, Kent, England; son of Charles Richard (a post office engineer) and

Doris May (Payne) Hamley; married Agnes Moylan (a nurse), August 6, 1965; children: Peter Richard John, Mary Elizabeth Carmel. *Education:* Jesus College, Cambridge, M.A., 1959; University of Bristol, P.G.C.E., 1960; University of Manchester, diploma in advanced studies in education, 1965; University of Leicester, Ph.D., 1980. *Politics:* "Generally leftward inclined. But hating Communism, despairing of Labour Party and not impressed with Social Democratic Party, wondering how one can take the political process seriously anymore." *Religion:* "Lapsed Anglican, but still with Christian belief."

ADDRESSES: Home—"Hillside," 2 King's Rd., Hertfordshire SG13 7EY, England. *Office*—Education Department, County Hall, Hertfordshire SG13 8DF, England.

CAREER: English master at grammar and secondary modern schools in England, 1960-67; Milton Keynes College of Education, Bletchley, Milton Keynes, England, lecturer, 1967-69, senior lecturer in English, 1969-78; Hertfordshire Local Education Authority, Hertfordshire, England, county adviser for English and drama, 1978—. Counselor and tutor for Open University, 1971-78. Member of literature panel, Eastern Arts Association, 1984—; conductor of residential writing workshop for children. *Military service:* Royal Air Force, 1954-56.

MEMBER: Society of Authors (chairman, educational writers group, 1982-83), National Association of Educational Inspectors and Advisers.

WRITINGS:

JUVENILES

Pageants of Despair (novel; also see below), S. G. Phillips, 1974.
Very Far from Here (novel), Deutsch, 1976.
Landings (novel), Deutsch, 1979.
The Fourth Plane at the Flypast (novel), Deutsch, 1985.
Haunted United (novel), Deutsch, 1986.
Dangleboots (novel), Deutsch, 1987.
Tigger and Friends (picture book), illustrated by Meg Rutherford, Deutsch, 1988, Lothrop, 1989.
Hare's Choice (novel), illustrated by Rutherford, Deutsch, 1988.

CONTRIBUTOR OF SHORT STORIES

Jean Russell, editor, *The Methuen Book of Sinister Stories*, Methuen, 1982.
Bryan Newton, editor, *Choices*, Collins Educational, 1984.
Newton, editor, *Aliens*, Collins, 1985.
Dennis Pepper, editor, *An Oxford Book of Christmas Stories*, Oxford University Press, 1986.
Mick Gowar, editor, *Twisted Circuits*, Century Hutchinson, 1987.
Gowar, editor, *Electric Heroes*, Bodley Head, 1988.
Jim Sweetman, editor, *Collins English Project*, Collins Educational, 1988.
Oranges and Lemons, Basil Blackwell, 1988.

OTHER

Three Townley Plays (adapted into modern English), Heinemann, 1963.
(With Colin Field) *Fiction in the Middle School*, Batsford, 1975.
"Pageants of Despair" (radio play; based on novel of the same title), British Broadcasting Corporation, 1979.
"Court Jester" (radio play), BBC, 1979.

(Adaptor into English) Gian Paolo Ceserani, *The Travels of Columbus*, Kestrel, 1979.
(Adaptor into English) Ceserani, *The Travels of Livingstone*, Kestrel, 1979.
(Adaptor into English) Ceserani, *The Travels of Marco Polo*, Kestrel, 1980.
(Adaptor into English) Ceserani, *The Travels of Captain Cook*, Kestrel, 1980.
"Julius Caesar" (study guide and cassette), Argo Records, 1980.

Reviewer for *School Librarian.*

WORK IN PROGRESS: Janine (juvenile novel); *Coded Signals* (short stories).

SIDELIGHTS: Dennis Hamley writes that he has "always loved the art of narrative, but for many years as a listener, not a teller—until I started to write for myself, when I discovered that the end of a story is implicit in its beginning. If you begin it, you will end it. You don't always see the destination at the start of the journey, but you'll get there all right. This to me is now a simple fact which only writing as a sort of act of faith taught me. Not realizing it delayed my start as a writer of stories for many years because, try as I would—and I thought one had to—I could never work out a story before I started writing it.

"My own children, Peter and Mary, have always been helpful and assiduous critics. They've given advice I ignore at my peril, suggestions I always use, on occasions have changed the course of stories for me—always correctly. They—and a marvelous editor at Andre Deutsch—have been very good for me."

AVOCATIONAL INTERESTS: Music, railways, watching football, drama, camping, motoring.

* * *

HAMMOND, Ralph
    See HAMMOND INNES, Ralph

* * *

HAMMOND INNES, Ralph   1913-
    (Ralph Hammond, Hammond Innes)

PERSONAL: Indexed in some sources under Innes; born July 15, 1913, in Horsham, England; son of William and Dora Beatrice (Crisford) Hammond Innes; married Dorothy Mary Lang (an actress, playwright, and author), 1937. *Education:* Educated in England.

ADDRESSES: Home—Ayres End, Kersey, Suffolk, England. *Agent*—Curtis Brown, 162-168 Regent St., London W1R 5TA, England.

CAREER: Member of staff, *Financial News*, 1934-40; freelance writer, 1946—. *Military service:* British Army, Royal Artillery, 1940-46; served with Eighth Army in Sicily landings; became major.

MEMBER: Society of Authors, PEN, Royal Ocean Racing Club, Royal Cruising Club, Royal Yacht Squadron, and other charitable and nautical organizations.

AWARDS, HONORS: Named Commander of the British Empire, 1978; has received honorary degrees.

WRITINGS:

NOVELS; UNDER PSEUDONYM HAMMOND INNES

The Doppelganger, Jenkins, 1937.
Air Disaster, Jenkins, 1937.
Sabotage Broadcast, Jenkins, 1938.
All Roads Lead to Friday, Jenkins, 1939.
Trapped, Putnam, 1940 (published in England as *Wreckers Must Breathe,* Collins, 1940).
The Trojan Horse, Collins, 1940, reprinted, 1974.
Attack Alarm, Collins, 1941, Macmillan, 1942, reprinted, Fontana, 1969.
Dead and Alive, Collins, 1946, reprinted, Fontana, 1970.
The Killer Mine, Harper, 1947, reprinted, Collins, 1973, published as *Run by Night,* Bantam, 1951.
Fire in the Snow, Harper, 1947, reprinted, 1985 (published in England as *The Lonely Skier,* Collins, 1947).
Gale Warning, Harper, 1948 (published in England as *Maddon's Rock,* Collins, 1948, reprinted, Fontana, 1970).
The Blue Ice, Harper, 1948, reprinted, 1985.
The White South (Book Society selection), Collins, 1949, published as *The Survivors,* Harper, 1950, reprinted, 1985.
The Angry Mountain, Collins, 1950, Harper, 1951, reprinted, Avon, 1980.
Air Bridge, Collins, 1951, Knopf, 1952.
Campbell's Kingdom (also see below; Book Society selection), Knopf, 1952, reprinted, Carroll & Graf, 1986.
The Naked Land, Knopf, 1954, reprinted, Carroll & Graf, 1986 (published in England as *The Strange Land,* Collins, 1954).
The Wreck of the "Mary Deare" (Literary Guild selection), Knopf, 1956, reprinted, Carroll & Graf, 1985 (published as *The "Mary Deare"* [Book Society selection], Collins, 1956).
The Land God Gave to Cain, Knopf, 1958, reprinted, Carroll & Graf, 1985.
The Doomed Oasis (Literary Guild selection), Knopf, 1960, reprinted, Carroll & Graf, 1986.
Atlantic Fury, Knopf, 1962, reprinted, Carroll & Graf, 1985.
The Strode Venturer, Knopf, 1965.
Lekvas Man, Knopf, 1971.
Golden Soak, Knopf, 1973.
North Star, Collins, 1974, Knopf, 1975.
The Big Footprints, Knopf, 1977.
Solomon's Seal, Knopf, 1980.
The Black Tide, Collins, 1982, Doubleday, 1983.
High Stand, Collins, 1985, Atheneum, 1986.

OTHER; UNDER PSEUDONYM HAMMOND INNES

(Editor) Richard Keverne, *Tales of Old Inns,* 2nd edition, Collins, 1947.
(With Robin Estridge) "Campbell's Kingdom" (screenplay; based on the novel of same title), Rank, 1957.
Harvest of Journeys (travel), Knopf, 1960.
(With the editors of *Life*) *Scandanavia* (travel), Time-Life Books, 1963.
Sea and Islands (travel), Knopf, 1967.
The Conquistadors (history), Knopf, 1969, reprinted, Collins, 1986.
Hammond Innes Introduces Australia, edited by Clive Turnbull, McGraw, 1971.
The Last Voyage: Captain Cook's Lost Diary, Collins, 1978, Knopf, 1979.
Hammond Innes' East Anglia, Hodder & Stoughton, 1986.

Also author of television play, "The Story of Captain James Cook," 1975. Contributor to *Saturday Evening Post* and *Holiday.*

JUVENILES; UNDER PSEUDONYM RALPH HAMMOND

Cocos Gold, Harper, 1950.
Isle of Strangers, Collins, 1951, published as *Island of Peril,* Westminster, 1953.
Cruise of Danger, Westminster, 1952 (published in England as *Saracen's Tower,* Collins, 1952).
Black Gold on the Double Diamond, Collins, 1953.

SIDELIGHTS: Ralph Hammond Innes draws upon his many years as a seafaring yachtsman and world traveler to write highly-acclaimed adventure novels set on the high seas or in exotic foreign locales. He normally spends six months each year travelling with his wife and six months writing at his fourteenth-century home in the Suffolk countryside. His adventure novels have been set in East Africa, the Antarctic, the Canadian Northwest, Morocco, and the South Pacific—all places Hammond Innes himself has visited. "I seldom make notes on these trips," he tells Alan Bestic of the *Radio Times.* "I'm like a sponge, absorbing people, atmospheres." The resulting novels are as often praised for their vividly recreated settings as for their exciting plots. "It is the authenticity of [Hammond Innes's] background," Ernle Bradford writes in the *New York Times Book Review,* "which provides the frame of reality for his tales of his adventure." Hammond Innes "has taken his readers," a *Newsday* reviewer writes, "from the Outer Hebrides to the Maldive Islands and from Labrador . . . to the Empty Quarter of Arabia. Any follower of [his] . . . winds up a world traveler by proxy if not in fact." Hammond Innes is now one of the most popular adventure writers in the world; some forty million copies of his books have been sold in over fifty different languages.

Hammond Innes's success as a writer came after a grueling apprenticeship. His first four novels, published in the 1930s, earned him a total of 120 English pounds. He was obliged to work on the staff of the *Financial News,* a daily newspaper for the banking industry, to support himself. But with *Attack Alarm,* published in 1941, Hammond Innes began to receive critical recognition for his work. Set in London during the early years of the Second World War, the novel was written while Hammond Innes was serving as a gunner during the Battle of Britain, a period when the Nazis made nightly bombing raids over England. His description of those harrowing nights has been critically praised. David Tilden of *Books,* for example, claims that *Attack Alarm* "contains pages of some of the most convincing and graphic descriptions of air raids, air fighting and bombing, especially of the work of anti-aircraft, yet to come out of the war, and all in human and story terms." "The description of daily life at the station," the reviewer for the *Times Literary Supplement* believes, "and the almost terrifyingly graphic picture of a dive-bombing attack on the aerodome bear the imprint of truth."

After his stint in the British Army, Hammond Innes embarked on a free-lance writing career in 1946. Since then, he has turned out an average of one book per year, "all of them bestsellers in the most extravagant sense of the term," as William Green maintains in the *Telegraph Sunday Magazine.* Although the novels do not follow a predictable formula, there are qualities they all share. Roger Baker of *Books and Bookmen* finds that all of Hammond Innes's work is characterized by "a narrative that possesses . . . pace, excitement, theatrical set-pieces and open-air drama." Green reports that "familiar elements recur in every story—the first person narrator and the lone girl he falls for; the half-legendary father-figure; the sense of quest. But they are only a kind of jumping-off point." Hammond Innes explains to Green: "If I wrote to a formula, I would have got bored long ago, and so would the reader."

Among Hammond Innes's most successful novels is *The Blue Ice,* an adventure story set in the rugged Norwegian mountains. It tells of the hunt for an escaped criminal who knows the location of a valuable mine. But "the plot," writes Anthony Boucher of the *New York Times,* "is merely a just-strong-enough thread to hold together a series of descriptions . . . as breathtaking as anything you'll find in contemporary adventure literature, fact or fiction." R. W. Henderson of *Library Journal* describes *The Blue Ice* as "a typical Innes thriller, packed with suspense, mystery, horror, murder and surprises."

Another critically-acclaimed novel, *The Doomed Oasis,* is set in Arabia where a young Englishman has gone to work in the oilfields. There he meets his long-lost father and gets entangled in the dangerous machinations of Arab chieftains and British oil tycoons. According to Rex Stout, in his appraisal for the *New York Times Book Review, The Doomed Oasis* "is the best tale of adventure I have read in many desert moons, and I thank Mr. Innes warmly, and salute him." Taliaferro Boatwright of the *New York Herald Tribune Book Review* calls the novel "bloody, exotic, colorful, and completely plausible. . . . [It] is an adult adventure story complex and involute, solidly anchored to today's headlines and yet adequately escapist, entertaining but nonetheless engaging to the mind. This is the way adventure stories ought to be written."

Perhaps Hammond Innes's most popular novel has been *The Wreck of the "Mary Deare,"* the story of a sea captain who struggles to save his ship when it runs aground on a treacherous reef in the English Channel. A best-seller in several countries and adapted as a successful film, *The Wreck of the "Mary Deare"* has also garnered critical acclaim as one of the finest sea adventures of recent times. "I have been reading sea stories for more than half a century," Gene Markey maintains in the *Chicago Sunday Tribune,* "and this is the most exciting one I've read." Although she has some reservations about the quality of the prose, Isabel Quigly of the *Spectator* calls *The Wreck of the "Mary Deare"* "first-rate and the climax one of the most thrilling, in the old danger-and-endurance tradition, that I remember meeting." Several critics especially praise the portrait of the ship's captain in his struggle with the sea. The *New Yorker* critic believes that "the characterization of Patch, master of the Mary Deare, is expertly done." G. H. Favre of the *Christian Science Monitor* believes that the novel is "dominated by the bold figures of a man and a ship, both equally scarred by the vicissitudes of a hard life and seafaring."

The novel was so popular that Hammond Innes named his own boat, a ten-ton yacht, the *Mary Deare.* For over ten years he and his wife used it to explore the European coastline from Scandinavia to Turkey. His travels have made him sensitive to the ecological damage that man has caused in all parts of the world. Several of his books focus on environmental issues: *The Big Footprints* concerns the dwindling herds of African elephants; *The Black Tide,* the damaging spills from huge oil tankers; and *High Stand,* the destruction of irreplaceable forestland.

Hammond Innes has been involved with reforesting projects for over twenty-five years. During that time he has, Bestic reports, "planted a million trees." He also owns four forest areas in England and Wales, and has devoted so much of his time to forestry that he was obliged in the late 1970s to give up, sailing the *Mary Deare.* Speaking of his reforesting projects to Bestic, Hammond Innes explains: "I'm replacing some of the timber used up by my books." In *High Stand,* "an old-fashioned tale of intrigue and treachery," as *Maclean's* describes it, Hammond Innes builds his plot around efforts to preserve a forest of red cedars from some unscrupulous loggers. But the plot is almost incidental to the novel. Hammond Innes is more concerned with the forest setting of the story than with its characters and their actions. There are "lovely descriptive passages" of the forest, Jack Sullivan writes in the *New York Times Book Review.* But ultimately, *High Stand* is "a book where the nonhuman world is depicted," Sullivan writes, "as more admirable and more alive, than the human."

Hammond Innes is usually described as a master storyteller whose novels are invariably exciting, entertaining, and believable. "There is no one in our time," D. B. Hughes writes in *Book Week,* "who can compare with him in creating the saga of man against the elements." William Hogan of the *San Francisco Chronicle* calls him "a born story-teller," while T. J. Binyon of the *Times Literary Supplement* finds that he "always spins a good solid yarn." Edwin Fadiman, Jr., believes that Hammond Innes is part of an important literary tradition. "Hammond Innes," Fadiman explains in the *Saturday Review,* "belongs to a group of British writers whose artistic heritage derives from such craftsmen as Somerset Maugham. To these men, novel writing represents an opportunity to serve the reader, to entertain, to amuse and, occasionally, to educate him—unobtrusively." Hammond Innes's own evaluation of his work is modest. "I write by the seat of my pants," he tells Green. "I don't know where the story comes from, and I never know quite how it will turn out. . . . I rely on what I know I can do well—tell a story." Speaking to Green of his life as a free-lance writer, Innes remarks: "I am a novelist. I am one of the self-employed. I have to rely on myself."

MEDIA ADAPTATIONS: Fire in the Snow was filmed as "Snowbound," RKO, 1948; *The White South* was filmed by Columbia, 1953; *Campbell's Kingdom* was filmed by Rank, 1957; *The Wreck of the "Mary Deare"* was filmed by Metro-Goldwyn-Mayer, 1959; *Golden Soak* and *Levkas Man* were adapted for television; *The Doomed Oasis* was adapted by the British Broadcast Corporation.

AVOCATIONAL INTERESTS: Traveling, forestry, ocean racing and cruising.

BIOGRAPHICAL/CRITICAL SOURCES:

BOOKS

Innes, Hammond, *Harvest of Journeys,* Knopf, 1960.
Innes, Hammond, *Sea and Islands,* Knopf, 1967.

PERIODICALS

Atlantic, June, 1971, April, 1979.
Best Sellers, November 15, 1967.
Books, April 12, 1942.
Books and Bookmen, March, 1971.
Book Week, November 21, 1965.
Book World, January 21, 1968, June 29, 1971.
Chicago Sunday Tribune, October 21, 1956.
Christian Science Monitor, November 8, 1956, April 22, 1968.
Globe & Mail (Toronto), November 15, 1985.
Harper's, May, 1971.

Library Journal, July, 1949.
Los Angeles Times Book Review, September 15, 1981, March 27, 1983.
Maclean's, October 21, 1985.
National Observer, December 15, 1969.
Newsday, May 22, 1971.
New Yorker, October 27, 1956.
New York Herald Tribune Book Review, October 21, 1956, November 25, 1956, November 13, 1960.
New York Times, March 8, 1942, August 14, 1949, October 21, 1956, May 26, 1977.
New York Times Book Review, November 25, 1956, November 13, 1960, December 24, 1967, December 7, 1969, April 14, 1974, February 8, 1981, June 21, 1985, December 21, 1986.
Observer Review, August 6, 1967.
Radio Times, August 18-24, 1984.
San Francisco Chronicle, October 21, 1956.
Saturday Review, July 3, 1971, April 28, 1979.
Spectator, July 13, 1956, February 19, 1977.
Telegraph Sunday Magazines, August 10, 1980.
Times (London), September 26, 1985.
Times Literary Supplement, October 25, 1941, May 28, 1970, March 4, 1977.
Village Voice, August 6, 1979.
Washington Post Book World, July 22, 1979, December 27, 1980, April 3, 1983, October 20, 1985.
Wilson Library Bulletin, September, 1954.
World Literature Today, winter, 1979.
Writer, March, 1970.

—*Sketch by Thomas Wiloch*

*   *   *

HARDY, Alice Dale
[Collective pseudonym]

WRITINGS:

"FLYAWAYS" SERIES

The Flyaways and Cinderella, Grosset & Dunlap, 1925.
. . . and Little Red Riding Hood, Grosset & Dunlap, 1925.
. . . and Goldilocks, Grosset & Dunlap, 1925.

"RIDDLE CLUB" SERIES

The Riddle Club at Home: How the Club Was Formed, What Riddles Were Asked, and How the Members Solved a Mystery, Grosset & Dunlap, 1924.
. . . in Camp: How They Journeyed to the Lake, What Happened around the Campfire, and How a Forgotten Name Was Recalled, Grosset & Dunlap, 1924.
. . . through the Holidays: The Club and Its Doings, How the Riddles Were Solved, and What the Snowman Revealed, Grosset & Dunlap, 1924.
. . . at Sunrise Beach: How They Toured to the Shore, What Happened on the Sand, and How They Solved the Mystery of Rattlesnake Island, Grosset & Dunlap, 1925.
. . . at Shadybrook: Why They Went There, What Happened on the Way, and What Occurred during Their Absence from Home, Grosset & Dunlap, 1926.
. . . at Rocky Falls: How They Went up the River, What Adventures They Had in the Woods, and How They Solved the Mystery of the Deserted Hotel, Grosset & Dunlap, 1929.

SIDELIGHTS: Alice Dale Hardy was the pseudonym used by the Stratemeyer Syndicate for some of its series for little children. The "Flyaways" books featured adventures with characters from classic fairytales, and was the only Stratemeyer fantasy series to feature human characters. The "Riddle Club" was formed by three boys and three girls; the books chronicled the adventures of the members. For more information see the entries for Harriet S. Adams, Edward L. Stratemeyer, and Andrew E. Svenson.

BIOGRAPHICAL/CRITICAL SOURCES:

BOOKS

Johnson, Deidre, editor and compiler, *Stratemeyer Pseudonyms and Series Books: An Annotated Checklist of Stratemeyer and Stratemeyer Syndicate Publications*, Greenwood Press, 1982.

*   *   *

HARPER, Elaine
See HALLIN, Emily Watson

*   *   *

HARRIGAN, Kathryn Rudie   1951-

PERSONAL: Born March 15, 1951, in Minneapolis, Minn.; daughter of Norbert J. and Florence G. (Gelking) Rudie; married Richard Scott Harrigan (deceased). *Education:* Macalester College, B.A., 1972; University of Texas at Austin, M.B.A., 1976; Harvard University, D.B.A., 1979.

ADDRESSES: Home—400 West 119th St., Apt. 11J, New York, N.Y. 10027. *Office*—Graduate School of Business, 716 Uris Hall, Columbia University, New York, N.Y. 10027.

CAREER: Minneapolis Institute of Art, Children's Theatre Company, Minneapolis, Minn., apprentice, 1966-67; North Hennipen Young People's Theatre, Minneapolis, business manager, 1967-69; artistic director and designer of stage productions throughout the Midwest, 1973-75; Babson College, Babson Park, Mass., assistant professor of business and management, 1977-79; University of Texas at Dallas, assistant professor of business administration, 1979-81; Columbia University, New York, N.Y., assistant professor, 1981-83, associate professor, 1983-87, professor of business and director of Strategy Research Center, 1987—.

MEMBER: Academy of International Business, Institute of Management Science, National Academy of Management (member of executive committee of Business Policy and Planning Division, 1983-85; member of board of governors, 1986-88), Strategic Management Society, Beta Gamma Sigma (Alpha chapter).

AWARDS, HONORS: General Electric Award for Outstanding Research in Strategic Management from National Academy of Management, 1979, for *Strategies for Declining Businesses;* Glueck Best Paper Award from National Academy of Management, 1983, for *Strategies for Vertical Integration;* Schoenheimer Award for research excellence from Columbia University, 1987, for *Managing for Joint Venture Success.*

WRITINGS:

Strategies for Declining Businesses, Lexington Books, 1980.
Strategies for Vertical Integration, Lexington Books, 1983.
Strategies for Joint Ventures, Lexington Books, 1985.

Strategic Flexibility: A Management Guide for Changing Times, Lexington Books, 1985.
Managing for Joint Venture Success, Lexington Books, 1986.
Managing Maturing Businesses: Restructuring Declining Industries and Revitalizing Troubled Operations, Lexington Books, 1988.

CONTRIBUTOR

C. Roland Christensen, editor, *Teaching by the Case Method*, Division of Research, Business School, Harvard University, 1981.

J. Ronald Fox, editor, *Managing Business-Government Relations*, Irwin, 1982.

M. E. Porter, editor, *Cases in Competitive Strategy*, Free Press, 1982.

Robert Lamb, editor, *Advances in Strategic Management*, JAI Press, Volume 1, 1983, Volume 2, 1984.

Lamb, editor, *Competitive Advances in Strategic Management*, Prentice-Hall, 1984.

W. F. Glueck and L. R. Jauch, *Business Policy and Strategic Management*, 4th edition, McGraw, 1984.

L. G. Thomas, editor, *Proceedings: Joel Dean Consortium on the Economics of Strategic Planning*, Lexington Books, 1985.

Wolfgang Schurer, editor, *The Spirit of Competition: Choice, Challenge, Commitment*, St. Gallen International Management Foundation (Switzerland), 1986.

A Pettrigrew, editor, *The Management of Strategic Change*, Basil Blackwell, 1987.

F. Corno, editor, *Prevenzione e Terapia della Crisi d'Impresa*, Centro Studi d'Impresa (Italy), 1987.

C. Baden-Fuller, editor, *Management of Excess Capacity in the European Environment*, Basil Blackwell, 1988.

P. Lorange and F. Contractor, editors, *Cooperative Strategies in International Business*, Lexington Books, 1988.

OTHER

Author of computer software educational simulation programs, including "Simmons Simulator Inc.," 1985, revised in 1986, "Trintex Corporation," 1985, revised in 1986, and "Note on the Mainframe Computer Industry," 1986, revised in 1987. Author of education videos, including "Zenith Radio Corporation: Videodisc," 1983, "Zenith Data Systems: Strategies for Settings of Rapid Technological Change," 1983, revised as "Apple Computer" in 1985, "Union Carbide Corporation: Genetic Engineering," 1983, revised in 1986, "SmithKline Beckman Corporation: Strategies for Innovation in the Ethical Pharmaceutical Industry," 1983, revised in 1986, "The Financial Securities Industry," 1983, revised in 1987, "Note on the Personal Computer Software Industry," 1984, revised in 1986, "Note on the U.S. Chain Saws Industry in 1984," 1984, revised in 1986, "Esmark-Norton Simon-Beatrice Companies," 1986, revised in 1987, and "General Electric Corporation," 1986, revised in 1987. Contributor of articles and reviews to business journals, such as *Strategic Management Journal*, *Academy of Management Journal*, *Planning Review*, and *Journal of Business Strategy*. Member of editorial board, *Academy of Management Journal*, 1981-87, *Journal of Business Strategy*, 1982-87, *Strategic Management Journal*, 1983—, and *Academy of Management Executive*, 1987; consulting editor, *Academy of Management Review*, 1987—.

WORK IN PROGRESS: *Strategies for Synergy*, for Lexington Books.

SIDELIGHTS: Kathryn Rudie Harrigan told *CA*: "I first became involved in theatre when I met the members of a touring company of the Tyrone Guthrie Theatre backstage at my high school. It seemed to be a good occupation for a female during the 1960s (merit overcomes gender, like in athletics) and seemed more interesting than secretarial work. The vast interest in theatre in the Minneapolis-St. Paul community enabled me to earn enough cash to finance my education. (I also sorted mail with the Minneapolis Postal Service to finance my schooling.)

"I changed from theatre to management because I was interested in the chief executive function. As a director, designer, and producer, I was responsible for the same duties as the president of a small business. It became attractive to take an M.B.A. to manage other types of businesses.

"My limited acting experiences helped me to procure a teaching position to finance my doctorate. I continue to enjoy my classroom experiences, although my primary activities are research and consulting.

"*Strategies for Declining Businesses* addresses the problem of declining demand—how to rationalize industry capacity without inciting competitive bloodshed. Since this study of decline and exit barriers, many subsequent doctoral dissertations have been written on the problems of divestiture, and management consulting firms have added these concepts to the range of services they offer. Because I am a scholar, I can examine the patterns of strategic behavior in many industries and generalize concerning the efficacy of various generic strategies firms might undertake. Most corporations cannot afford the time needed to make such empirical studies. The insights I can offer prove beneficial."

Harrigan's *Strategies for Vertical Integration* has been translated into Japanese; *Managing for Joint Venture Success* has been translated into Japanese and Italian.

BIOGRAPHICAL/CRITICAL SOURCES:

PERIODICALS

Business Week, July 21, 1986.
Forbes, July 13, 1987, August 24, 1987.

*   *   *

HARRIS, Fred (Roy)   1930-

PERSONAL: Born November 13, 1930, in Walters, Okla.; son of Fred B. (a farmer) and Alene (Person) Harris; married LaDonna Crawford (an administrator), April 8, 1949 (divorced, 1981); married Margaret S. Elliston, September 7, 1982; children: (first marriage) Kathryn Tijerina, Byron, Laura. *Education:* University of Oklahoma, B.A., 1952, J.D., 1954. *Politics:* Democrat.

ADDRESSES: *Home*—P.O. Box 1203, Corrales, N.M. 87048. *Office*—Department of Political Science, University of New Mexico, Albuquerque, N.M. 87131.

CAREER: Admitted to Oklahoma Bar, 1954; Harris, Newcomre, Redman & Doolin, Lawton, Okla., founder and senior partner, 1954-64; member of Oklahoma Senate, 1956-64; member of U.S. Senate from Oklahoma, 1964-73; Peoples Policy Center (public interest and research organization), Washington, D.C., president, 1973-75; campaigned for Democratic U.S. presidential nomination, 1975-76; University of New Mexico, Albuquerque, professor of political science, 1976—. Member of National Advisory Commission on Civil

Disorders, 1967-68. Chairperson of Democratic National Committee, 1969-70. Adjunct professor of government, American University, 1973-75.

MEMBER: Phi Beta Kappa.

WRITINGS:

NONFICTION

Alarms and Hopes, Harper, 1967.
Now Is the Time, McGraw, 1971.
The New Populism, Saturday Review Press, 1973.
Potomac Fever, Norton, 1977.
America's Democracy: The Ideal and the Reality, Scott, Foresman, 1980, 2nd edition, 1983.
(With Paul L. Hain) *America's Legislative Processes: Congress and the States,* Scott, Foresman, 1983.

SIDELIGHTS: Harris, the ''neo-populist'' candidate for president in 1976, was the emotional, if not the practical, favorite of Democratic liberals, as several political commentators have noted. Harris's neopopulism was described in a *New Republic* review by Philip Terzian as ''a spellbinding combination of affirmative action, Naderism, youthophilia, elitist-baiting, and good old fashioned legislative know-how.'' Although Harris began his career as a moderate Democratic senator from Oklahoma, during the late 1960s he drifted leftward politically and became known as a critic of the country's maldistribution of wealth.

Harris's presidential campaign was predicated, Jules Witcover relates in *Progressive,* ''on a perception of an electorate that is tired of old trappings, that yearns for a new kind of open, straightforward candidate and politics, but that is justifiably suspicious of anyone who projects himself as different from the pack of old jacks.'' In a 1974 memo outlining his campaign plans, Harris wrote about himself as candidate: ''The candidate must be plain-spoken, candid, open. He must demonstrate, from the very first and even in little things, that he will tell the people the truth. None of this 'people are asking me to run' business. No coy 'non-candidate' status. . . . The candidate must articulate in blunt language the real frustrations that people rightly feel because of elitism, privilege, bigness, and concentrated power. No twelve-point programs and new bureaucracies, but common sense steps to diffuse economic and political power more widely.''

The style of Harris's campaign was in accordance with his political stance. He ran what Witcover termed a ''guerilla-type campaign,'' crossing the country with his family in their camper, sponsoring $4.76 a plate fund-raising dinners, and generally conducting the campaign in a manner that made ''Jimmy Carter look like John Connally,'' to quote Jeff Greenfield's piece in the *New York Times Book Review.*

Many Democrats likened Harris to George McGovern and avoided supporting him for that reason. They feared that if Harris became the Democratic nominee, he would be defeated in the national election, like McGovern, because he was perceived by the electorate as a ''radical.'' Harris explained the difference between himself and McGovern to *Time* magazine correspondent Stanley Cloud: ''I never tell people that they ought to do something because it's morally right. I show how it's in their own self-interest. My dad used to listen to McGovern and then say, 'Well, it sounds fine, but when's he gonna start talking to me?' Dad was right, and that's what I try to do—talk a language that ordinary people can understand.''

After bowing out of the race for the presidential nomination, Harris wrote his political memoirs. In the book *Potomac Fever,* he discussed his own case of ''Potomac Fever'': Harris felt that he concerned himself more with Washington and neglected his home state of Oklahoma. Colman McCarthy of the *Washington Post Book World* thought that Harris misdiagnosed his affliction—that instead Harris was suffering from ''Potomac Blahs.'' Harris's problem, according to McCarthy, ''was in believing that he, the mighty liberal and champion of the little guy, could bring on reforms quickly. He couldn't, and he got the Potomac Blahs. . . . The value of Harris's book is what it says about one person's failure to deal with the frustrations of reform.''

In a *Progressive* review of the book, Les Whitten describes Harris's image during the campaign: ''With his penultimate shirt button open, flesh showing through the gap, a suit too small, a 1930's hairstyle, he was a portrait in noble disorganization—caused by doing too much for others, his wife, LaDonna, and himself, in that order. Sometimes, he was a sudden dry handful of Dust Bowl wit in our surprised faces.'' On the other hand, complains Whitten, ''*That* vivid Harris isn't enough in evidence in this book, and it is badly flawed thereby. . . . We hear too much about Harris's 'deeply seated concern with the issues,' and far too little about how, imaginatively, often bumblingly, always humanly, he tried to deal with the issues.'' Although Harris's book contains disappointments, they are not, according to Whitten, ''fatal ones.'' He continues, ''Lumpy as the book is, it still flashes with the precursors of the better, more anecdotal book Harris has inside him.''

Philip Terzian, writing in the *New Republic,* says he was also drawn to the anecdotal humor of the book. He comments: ''If Hollywood had any imagination, it would buy the rights for this book of Fred Harris's memoirs and film it as a political *Pilgrim's Progress* of the past two decades. Except, of course, it would require a script writer with more humor than Bunyan to bring the tale off, because Fred Harris's career has not only been instructive, but funny.''

Harris told *CA:* ''In Moscow once, the Soviet Union's Americanologist chief, Georgi Arbatov, and I were talking, and I mentioned that I was at a disadvantage in commenting on the Soviet economic and political system, as compared to his ability to comment on ours, because the Soviet system was not open to outside researchers. 'That's no disadvantage for you,' he replied. 'We study your system, but we still cannot understand it.'

''The American system looks simple, but it is a labyrinth of complexity. I enjoy writing about it, to make it more understandable—not just *how* a bill goes through Congress, but also *why,* for example—to point the way for citizen participation and suggest ways to make participation opportunities better.''

BIOGRAPHICAL/CRITICAL SOURCES:

BOOKS

MacPherson, Myra, *Power Lovers,* Putnam, 1975.

PERIODICALS

Best Sellers, June 15, 1968, July, 1977.
Nation, February 8, 1975.
New Republic, August 7, 1971, September 8, 1973, May 21, 1977.
Newsweek, November 3, 1975, December 22, 1975, January 12, 1976.

New Yorker, August 24, 1968, August 13, 1973.
New York Times Book Review, June 5, 1977.
Progressive, January, 1976, July, 1977.
Time, December 22, 1975.
U.S. News & World Report, December 1, 1975.
Washington Post Book World, May 15, 1977.

*   *   *

HARRIS, Warren G(ene)   1936-

PERSONAL: Born January 29, 1936, in Newark, N.J.; son of Frank G. (an aviation executive) and Maude (Friedman) Harris. *Education:* Queens College (now Queens College of the City University of New York), B.A., 1957.

ADDRESSES: Home—205 West 57th St., New York, N.Y. 10019. *Agent*—William Morris Agency, 1350 Avenue of the Americas, New York, N.Y. 10019.

CAREER: Quigley Publications, New York City, reporter and film reviewer for *Motion Picture Daily* and *Motion Picture Herald*, 1957-59; Paramount Pictures, New York City, publicity executive, 1959-69; unit publicist for motion pictures in New York City and Europe, 1970-72; writer, 1972—.

WRITINGS:

Gable and Lombard, Simon & Schuster, 1974.
(With Eddie Fisher) *Eddie Fisher: My Life, My Loves*, Harper, 1981.
The Other Marilyn: A Biography of Marilyn Miller, Arbor House, 1985.
Cary Grant: A Touch of Elegance, Doubleday, 1987.

Contributor to film journals.

*   *   *

HAUSMAN, Patricia   1953-

PERSONAL: Born December 17, 1953, in Philadelphia, Pa.; daughter of Melvin Burton (a pharmacist) and Ruth Gilda (a pharmacist; maiden name, Weinstock) Hausman. *Education:* Kirkland College (now Hamilton College), B.A., 1975; University of Maryland, M.S., 1977.

ADDRESSES: Office—NutriProse, P.O. Box 3235, Silver Spring, Md. 20901-0235. *Agent*—Sterling Lord Literary Agency, Inc., 1 Madison Ave., New York, N.Y. 10021.

CAREER: Center for Science in the Public Interest, Washington, D.C., research associate, 1974-76, editor of *Nutrition Action*, 1976-78, staff nutritionist, 1978-81; currently president of NutriProse, Silver Spring, Md.; writer and consulting nutritionist.

MEMBER: Authors Guild, Authors League of America, American Society of Journalists and Authors, American Nutritionists Association (executive vice-president).

WRITINGS:

Jack Sprat's Legacy: The Science and Politics of Fat and Cholesterol, Richard Marek, 1981.
Foods That Fight Cancer, Rawson Associates, 1984.
At-a-Glance Nutrition Counter, Ballantine, 1985.
The Calcium Bible: How to Have Better Bones All Your Life, Rawson Associates, 1985.
The Right Dose: How to Take Vitamins and Minerals Safely, Rodale Press, 1987.

Contributor to *FIT*, *Washington Post*, *McCall's*, *Nutrition Action*, and *Runner's World*.

WORK IN PROGRESS: Various writings on nutrition.

SIDELIGHTS: Patricia Hausman's *Jack Sprat's Legacy: The Science and Politics of Fat and Cholesterol* is deemed "readable and engaging" by a reviewer for the *Journal of the American Dietetic Association*. In the book, Hausman, who has a master's degree in nutrition from the University of Maryland, asserts that traditionally accepted foods, such as eggs, milk, and meat, are promoting heart disease and cancer in Americans, a proven fact she believes the United States Government is suppressing. According to Hausman, the Wisconsin chapter of the American Heart Association publishes little information on the dangers of high fat diets, a condition Hausman says is due to submission to the Wisconsin dairy industry. She also charges the American Cancer Society with slighting the relation between fat and cancer. "The [American] Cancer Society just hasn't been progressive," she told the *Baltimore Evening Sun*; "it's stuck on smoking and [finding a cancer] cure and hardly does anything with diet." *Washington Post*'s Jean Carper writes: "Even though one may not agree absolutely with Hausman, she is an author to be trusted and listened to. Few who read her book can still think it is anything but lunacy to put a high premium on fat in a nation where fat-laden products pose a major health problem."

Hausman told *CA*: "In *Jack Sprat's Legacy*, I propose that the controversy about diet and heart disease is the predictable component of a scientific revolution now underway in the field of nutrition. Throughout its history, the science of nutrition has been concerned almost exclusively with essential nutrients and deficiency diseases; meat, milk fat, and egg yolk were long ago dubbed 'protective foods' in recognition of their protein, vitamin, and mineral value. This view, however, is challenged by the vast body of scientific research linking the saturated fat and cholesterol of such foods to coronary heart disease. I believe that the controversy surrounding this research results not from inconclusive or equivocal data but rather from the inability of some scientists to part with long-time notions that deemed high-fat, high-cholesterol foods to be the most nutritious. Thomas Kuhn's book *The Structure of Scientific Revolutions* strongly influenced the view that I present in *Jack Sprat's Legacy*."

Foods That Fight Cancer is Hausman's book of practical advice regarding the much-publicized topic of diet and cancer. Hausman comes at her topic from two angles by pointing out nutrients and foods that promote cancer and those that may prevent it. In *Interview* magazine, Hausman tells Mark Matousek: "It's only a slight exaggeration to say that there are carcinogens in virtually every food—from mushrooms to steaks to oranges—some of them very weak, some of them very potent. It's impossible to avoid all of these chemicals because they're everywhere. I've started telling people to stop trying to avoid all of these foods and to concentrate on eating other foods that provide the protective substances that counteract them. . . . People have been hearing for so long that food causes cancer. . . . If they'd open [my] book, they'd find out that they can stop worrying about how food is going to hurt them and learn how it can help." Although the link between fat and cancer has been much touted, Hausman points to four seemingly protective nutrients and foods: vitamin A, vitamin C, whole-grain fiber, and the "inhibitors" known as indoles found in vegetables of the cabbage family. Hausman says medical research indicates that "better nutrition could reduce colon cancer by 90 percent, breast cancer by 50 percent and lung cancer by 20 percent. Total reduction might reach 35 percent. That translates into about 150,000 lives a year, and that's a lot of people," records Peggy Brawley for *People*.

Hausman stepped onto controversial ground with two succeeding books which advocate the necessity of vitamin and mineral supplementation. While researching for *The Calcium Bible: How to Have Better Bones All Your Life*, Hausman came to the conclusion that calcium supplementation for women who were not getting sufficient calcium in their diets made better sense than pushing a greater intake of calcium-rich but high-fat dairy products. The message of Hausman's *The Right Dose: How to Take Vitamins and Minerals Safely* is at odds with national nutrition organizations, like the American Dietetic Association and the American Society for Clinical Nutrition. Whereas these organizations urge people to get their nutrients from foods rather than from pills since, among other things, there is the potential for toxicity from pills, Chicago *Tribune Books* contributor Barbara Sullivan records Hausman's stance: "Frankly, it is embarrassing to me that members of my profession exaggerate so the dangers of [vitamin and mineral] supplements. . . . 'Whereas it might be possible to get all of the nutrients you need from food, it would be utopian. . . .' Supplements 'can help make up for shortcomings in your diet. There is no doubt in my mind that an inadequate diet plus a safe supplement program is certainly better than an inadequate diet alone.'" Hausman claims documentation of the dangers of supplementation is just not prevalent in the medical research. In *The Right Dose*, Hausman recommends safe dosage levels and provides information on the general roles of vitamins and minerals, food sources in which they can be found, useful recipes, current scientific literature and medical case studies regarding toxicity, and more. According to *Baltimore Evening Sun* reviewer Linell Smith, Hausman professes: "Electricity can kill you, but you don't ban electricity. What most of my colleagues are saying is 'Don't take any Vitamin D because it can be toxic.' I think my job is to tell people how to take vitamins safely, not to tell them 'Don't touch them!'"

AVOCATIONAL INTERESTS: Cooking, refinishing antiques, reading, ballroom dancing.

BIOGRAPHICAL/CRITICAL SOURCES:

BOOKS

Hausman, Patricia, *The Right Dose: How to Take Vitamins and Minerals Safely*, Rodale Press, 1987.

PERIODICALS

Baltimore Evening Sun, May 18, 1981, July 1, 1987.
Glamour, February, 1986.
Interview, April, 1985.
Journal of Nutrition Education, December, 1981.
Journal of the American Dietetic Association, April, 1982.
Milwaukee Journal, August 12, 1981.
New England Journal of Medicine, September 10, 1981, December 10, 1981.
People, March 12, 1984.
Tribune Books (Chicago), May 7, 1987.
Washington Post, August 20, 1981.

*   *   *

HAUSMANN, Winifred 1922-
(Winifred Wilkinson)

PERSONAL: Born September 1, 1922, in Atlanta, Ga.; daugh-

ter of Boyce Taylor (an insurance representative) and Ruby (a voice teacher; maiden name, Gaffney) Wilkinson; married George Rowe Hausmann (a Unity minister), December 19, 1965 (died, December 31, 1985). *Education:* Agnes Scott College, B.A. 1946; Unity Training School, Lee's Summit, Mo., graduate, 1958.

ADDRESSES: Home—327 Katey Rose Lane, Cleveland, Ohio 44143-2429.

CAREER: Ordained Unity minister, 1959; Unity Church, Little Rock, Ark., minister, 1957-58; United Center of Cleveland, Cleveland Heights, Ohio, minister, 1958-66, co-minister with husband, George Rowe Hausmann, 1966-85, minister, 1985-88, minister emeritus, 1988—. Secretary, Great Lakes Unity Regional Conference, 1966-67. Affiliated with U.S. Office of Censorship and U.S. Army Signal Corps, 1941-44; publicity and promotion worker for *Atlanta Journal* and International News Service, 1946-48. Writer and narrator of "Focus on Living" (five-minute weekday radio program), WCLV-FM, 1964-68, WBKC-AM, 1969-70, and WABQ-AM, 1979-82.

MEMBER: Association of Unity Churches (member of board of directors).

WRITINGS:

(Under name Winifred Wilkinson) *Focus on Living*, Unity Books, 1967.
(Under name Winifred Wilkinson) *Miracle Power for Today*, Doubleday, 1969.
Your God-Given Potential, Unity Books, 1978.
How to Live Life Victoriously, Unity Books, 1982.
Dealing with Stress through Spiritual Methods, Spiritual Resources Foundation, 1985.
A Guide to Love-Powered Living, DeVorss, 1986.

SIDELIGHTS: Winifred Hausmann wrote *CA:* "All of my books have been an outgrowth and extension of my ministry. They are designed to enable individuals to improve every department of their lives by using spiritual principles. Each book not only outlines universal laws of mind and matter, but also details ways in which the principles can be applied to solving the challenges of daily living and to improving the quality of life in general. Examples are drawn from my own experience and the experiences of those with whom I have counselled and prayed in more than thirty years in the ministry. Each book was written to fulfill a particular need. For instance, while I had seen many books on the subject of mental and physical methods for dealing with stress, I had not seen books presenting spiritual laws as a means of coping with stress. So I wrote one. Now that I have retired after more than thirty years as a full time Unity minister, I plan to continue my ministry through my writing and speaking."

*   *   *

HAWLEY, Mabel C.
[Collective pseudonym]

WRITINGS:

"FOUR LITTLE BLOSSOMS" SERIES

Four Little Blossoms at Brookside Farm, G. Sully, 1920, reprinted, Saalfield Publishing, 1938.
. . . at Oak Hill School, G. Sully, 1920, reprinted, Saalfield Publishing, 1938.

. . . and Their Winter Fun, G. Sully, 1920, reprinted, Saalfield Publishing, 1938.
. . . on Appletree Island, G. Sully, 1921, reprinted, Saalfield Publishing, 1938.
. . . through the Holidays, G. Sully, 1922.
. . . at Sunrise Beach, Cupples & Leon, 1929.
. . . Indoors and Out, Cupples & Leon, 1930.

SIDELIGHTS: The Blossom siblings, Bobby, Meg, and the twins Twaddles and Dot, were the featured characters in this series for young children. For more information see the entries for Harriet S. Adams, Edward L. Stratemeyer, and Andrew E. Svenson.

BIOGRAPHICAL/CRITICAL SOURCES:

BOOKS

Johnson, Deidre, editor and compiler, *Stratemeyer Pseud-onyms and Series Books: An Annotated Checklist of Strat-emeyer and Stratemeyer Syndicate Publications,* Greenwood Press, 1982.

*   *   *

HELLER, Michael (David)   1937-

PERSONAL: Born May 11, 1937, in New York, N.Y.; son of Peter Frank (a publicist) and Martha (Rosenthal) Heller; married Doris C. Whytal, June 10, 1962 (divorced, March 23, 1978); married Jane Augustine (writer), March 5, 1979; children: (first marriage) Nicholas Solomon. *Education:* Rensselaer Polytechnic Institute, B.S. Eng., 1959; New York University, M.A., 1986; graduate study at New School for Social Research.

ADDRESSES: Home—P.O. Box 981, Stuyvesant Station, New York, N.Y. 10009. *Office*—American Language Institute, New York University, New York, N.Y. 10003.

CAREER: Norelco, New York City, chief technical writer, 1963-65; private teacher of English in Spain, 1965-66; free-lance industrial and advertising writer, 1966-67; New York University, American Language Institute and Washington Square College, New York City, master teacher in English, 1967—. Lecturer, New York City Community College, 1973. Curator, "Poetry—An Exhibition," City University of New York, 1977. Has lectured on poetry for New York Sculpture Symposium and has given readings; participant in Poetry-in-the-School programs in New York and Wyoming; member of advisory panel, New York Poetry-in-the-Schools, 1970—.

MEMBER: PEN International, Poetry Society of America, Poets and Writers, Modern Language Association, New York State Poets in Public Service.

AWARDS, HONORS: Poetry fellowship from New York State Creative Artists Public Service, 1975; grants from National Endowment for the Humanities, 1979, 1986; Alice Fay di Castagnola Award from Poetry Society of America, 1980.

WRITINGS:

Conviction's Net of Branches: Essays on the Objectivist Poets and Poetry, Southern Illinois University Press, 1984.

POETRY

Two Poems, Perishable Press, 1970.
Accidental Center, Sumac Press, 1972.
Figures of Speaking, Perishable Press, 1977.
Knowledge, SUN, 1979.

Marginalia in a Desperate Hand, Staple Diet Pig Press, 1985.
In the Builded Place, Coffee House Press, 1989.

CONTRIBUTOR

Richard Kostelanetz, editor, *The Young American Writers,* Funk, 1967.
Kostelanetz, editor, *Imaged Word-Worded Image,* Outerbridge & Dienstfrey, 1970.
Robert Vas Dias, editor, *Inside Outer Space,* Doubleday, 1970.
Clayton Eshleman, editor, *Caterpillar Anthology,* Doubleday, 1971.
George Quasha and Ronald Gross, editors, *Open Poetry,* Simon & Schuster, 1973.
Robert Long, editor, *Long Island Poets,* Permanent Press, 1986.

OTHER

Contributor of articles and poems to literary journals and national publications, including *Nation, Caterpillar, Sumac, Paris Review, Extensions, Ohio Review, Ironwood,* and *Parnassus: Poetry in Review.* U.S. editor, *Origin;* contributing editor, *Montemora.*

WORK IN PROGRESS: Europe of the Last, a novel; editor of *Carl Rakosi: Man and Poet,* National Poetry Foundation.

SIDELIGHTS: Michael Heller told *CA:* "My formal education has been in science and engineering, and recently, in philosophy, interests which continually play a great part in my thinking and writing. Science, thought—these later gods—deny the comforts of the old animisms; they too, however, are in need of demystification, not because they are wrong, but because they are not sufficient. I try to pose something as language which gives more force to a human argument of the world. Nevertheless, I would not want to call it a 'fine art.'"

*   *   *

HELYAR, Jane Penelope Josephine   1933-   (Josephine Poole)

PERSONAL: Born February 12, 1933, in London, England; daughter of Charles Graham (a managing director of engineering firm) and Astrid (an artist; maiden name, Walford) Cumpston; married Timothy Ruscombe Poole (a driving instructor), July 14, 1956; married second husband, Vincent J. H. Helyar (a farmer), August 29, 1975; children: (first marriage) Theodora Mary, Emily Josephine, Katherine Virginia, Isabel Beatrice; (second marriage) Charlotte Mary, Vincent Graham. *Education:* Attended schools in Cumberland and London, England. *Religion:* Roman Catholic.

ADDRESSES: Home—Poundisford Lodge, Poundisford, Taunton, Somerset TA3 7AE, England. *Agent*—A. P. Watt Ltd., 26-28 Bedford Row, London WC1R 4HL, England.

CAREER: Employed as solicitors' secretary in Portugal, Spain, Italy, and Belgium, 1950-54; British Broadcasting Corp., London, England, secretary in features department, 1954-56; free-lance writer.

WRITINGS—Under name Josephine Poole:

FOR YOUNG ADULTS

A Dream in the House, Hutchinson, 1961.
Moon Eyes, Hutchinson, 1965, Little, Brown, 1967.
Catch as Catch Can, Hutchinson, 1969, Harper, 1970.
The Visitor, Harper, 1972 (published in England as *Billy Buck,* Hutchinson, 1972).

Touch and Go, Harper, 1976.
When Fishes Flew, Benn, 1978.
The Open Grave, Benn, 1979.
The Forbidden Room, Benn, 1979.
Hannah Chance, Hutchinson, 1980.
Diamond Jack, Hutchinson, 1983.
Three for Luck, Hutchinson, 1985.
The Loving Ghosts, Hutchinson, 1988.
Puss in Boots, Hutchinson, 1988.

TELEVISION SCRIPTS

"The Harbourer," British Broadcasting Corp. (BBC-TV), 1975.
"The Sabbatical," BBC-TV, 1981.
"The Breakdown," BBC-TV, 1981.
"Miss Constantine," BBC-TV, 1982.
"The Animal Lover," BBC-TV, 1982.
"Ring a Ring a Rosie" (episode of "West Country Story" series), BBC-TV, 1982.
"With Love, Belinda" (episode of "West Country Story" series), BBC-TV, 1982.
"The Wit to Woo" (episode of "West Country Story" series), BBC-TV, 1983.

Also author of "Fox," "Buzzard," and "Dartmoor Pony," all for "Three in the Wild" series, 1984.

OTHER

The Lilywhite Boys (adult novel), Hart-Davis, 1968.
Yokeham (adult novel), J. Murray, 1970.
(Contributor) *West Country Stories*, Webb & Bower, 1981.
Wildlife Tales (short stories), Hutchinson, 1986.

Also author of *The Country Diary Companion*, a complement to the Central Television production of "The Country Diary of an Edwardian Lady," 1983.

SIDELIGHTS: According to Anne Carter in the *Times Literary Supplement*, Josephine Poole's favorite theme can best be described as a "matter of menace lurking in a smiling countryside." In her gripping tales of suspense and the supernatural, Poole seeks to terrify her readers while demonstrating the ultimate triumph of good over evil. Though she writes primarily for young adults, she avoids "talking down" to her audience. In *Moon Eyes*, for instance, the story of two children who must fight to overcome the mysterious powers of a sinister relative, "it's clear [from the plot] the author isn't fooling," points out Jean C. Thompson in the *New York Times Book Review*. "The book's gratifying frights . . . ," adds Thompson, "entrap the reader himself in an uncertain world." The *Saturday Review*'s Zena Sutherland likes "the creeping aura of suspense and horror" in Poole's "smoothly written tale," while a *Times Literary Supplement* critic observes that there is "a real study of the nature of good and evil" in Poole's book. There is "no pandering to the young reader, . . . either in the excellent writing or the events of the story, and this makes it a good book as well as a most unusual one."

Commenting on *Catch as Catch Can*, another story of children whose lives are threatened by menacing adults, a writer for *Kirkus Reviews* notes that it is "a slow sizzler that makes most juvenile mysteries look like comic strips. . . . [It is] convincingly peopled and detailed so that there's *real* life in danger." A *Times Literary Supplement* critic is not quite sure what makes the book "remarkable" but speculates that it has something to do with "the quality of the writing itself, and the subtle buildup of tension to a pitch of sustained menace." In short, says Pamela Marsh in the *Christian Science Monitor*, Jose-

phine Poole has a talent for "surrounding the terrifying with the everyday and making both routine and terror convincing."

Poole herself reports that "inspiration for my children's books begins with my own childhood: a close—sometimes too close—family life, side by side with fear; of the dark, of the huge old house where we lived with its woods, attics, and imagined ghosts, of my mother's bad health, and of the war, which though remote, colored everything. . . . I [try] to remember the kind of book that gripped me most as a child, the kind of situations I found most tense, and put them in. . . . I am convinced of the strength of goodness against the lure of evil."

AVOCATIONAL INTERESTS: Traveling, history, arts in general.

BIOGRAPHICAL/CRITICAL SOURCES:

BOOKS

Contemporary Literary Criticism, Volume 17, Gale, 1981.

PERIODICALS

Bulletin of the Center for Children's Books, September, 1976.
Children's Book Review, February, 1973.
Christian Science Monitor, November 12, 1970.
Growing Point, November, 1976.
Horn Book, April, 1967.
Junior Bookshelf, August, 1967, April, 1977.
Kirkus Reviews, October 1, 1970, October 1, 1972.
New York Times Book Review, May 7, 1967, November 8, 1970.
Saturday Review, May 13, 1967, February 20, 1971.
School Librarian, March, 1970, March, 1973.
Times Literary Supplement, December 9, 1965, February 6, 1969, December 4, 1969, November 3, 1972, December 10, 1976, September 19, 1980.

*   *   *

HENDERLEY, Brooks
[Collective pseudonym]

WRITINGS:

"Y.M.C.A. BOYS" SERIES

The Y.M.C.A. Boys of Cliffwood; or, The Struggle for the Holwell Prize, Cupples & Leon, 1916.
. . . on Bass Island; or, The Mystery of Russabaga Camp, Cupples & Leon, 1916.
. . . at Football; or, Lively Doings on and off the Gridiron, Cupples & Leon, 1917.

SIDELIGHTS: The first volume of this series told the story of a group of boys who, after a Halloween escapade, were reformed by the creation of a boys' branch at the local Y.M.C.A. Cupples & Leon described this series as "full of good times and every-day practical Christianity." For more information see the entries for Harriet S. Adams, Edward L. Stratemeyer, and Andrew E. Svenson.

BIOGRAPHICAL/CRITICAL SOURCES:

BOOKS

Johnson, Deidre, editor and compiler, *Stratemeyer Pseudonyms and Series Books: An Annotated Checklist of Stratemeyer and Stratemeyer Syndicate Publications*, Greenwood Press, 1982.

HERNTON, Calvin C(oolidge) 1934-

PERSONAL: Born April 28, 1934, in Chattanooga, Tenn.; son of Magnolia Jackson; married Mildred Webster, May 28, 1958; children: Antone. *Education:* Talladega College, B.A., 1954; Fisk University, M.A., 1956; attended Columbia University, 1961.

ADDRESSES: Office—Department of Black Studies, Oberlin College, Rice Hall, Oberlin, Ohio 44074. *Agent*—Marie Brown Associates, 412 West 154 St., New York, N.Y. 10032.

CAREER: Writer. Benedict College, Columbia, S.C., instructor in history and sociology, 1957-58; Alabama Agricultural and Mechanical College (now University), Normal, instructor in social sciences, 1958-59; Edward Waters College, Jacksonville, Fla., instructor in sociology, 1959-60; Southern University and Agricultural and Mechanical College, Baton Rouge, La., instructor in sociology, 1960-61; New York State Department of Welfare, New York City, social worker, 1961-62; *Umbra* (magazine), New York City, co-founder, 1963; London Institute of Phenomenological Studies, London, England, research fellow, 1965-69; Oberlin College, Oberlin, Ohio, writer in residence, 1970-72, professor of black studies and creative writing, 1973—. Poet in residence, Central State University, Wilberforce, Ohio, 1970.

WRITINGS:

(Contributor) Rosey E. Pool, editor, *Beyond the Blues: New Poems by American Negroes,* Hand & Flower Press, 1962.
The Coming of Chronos to the House of Nightsong: An Epical Narrative of the South (poetry), Interim, 1963.
Sex and Racism in America, Doubleday, 1965 (revised edition published in England as *Sex and Racism,* Deutsch, 1969).
White Papers for White Americans, Doubleday, 1966, reprinted, Greenwood Press, 1982.
(Contributor) LeRoi Jones and Larry Neal, editors, *Black Fire: An Anthology of Afro-American Writing,* Morrow, 1969.
Coming Together: Black Power, White Hatred, and Sexual Hangups, Random House, 1971.
(Contributor) D. L. Grummon and A. M. Barclay, editors, *Sexuality: A Search for Perspective,* Van Nostrand, 1971.
Scarecrow (novel), Doubleday, 1974.
(With Joseph Berke) *The Cannabis Experience: The Study of the Effects of Marijuana and Hashish,* Humanities, 1974.
Medicine Man (poetry), Reed, Cannon, & Johnson, 1976.
Sexual Mountains and Black Women Writers: Adventure in Sex, Literature, and Real Life, Doubleday, 1987.

Also author of plays "Glad to Be Dead," 1958, "Flame," 1958, and "The Place," 1972. Contributor to *Negro Digest, Freedomways,* and other periodicals.

SIDELIGHTS: A poet, scholar, and novelist, Calvin C. Hernton utilizes various literary forms to express his theories concerning sexism and racism. Hernton believes that "racism is inextricably related to sex and that the two have served to polarize America for centuries," relates Anthony S. Magistrale in a *Dictionary of Literary Biography* essay. Magistrale believes that this theme can be found throughout all of Hernton's work: "it remains the ascendant concept unifying his literary and scholarly activities."

Because of his familiarity with both verse and prose forms, Hernton's writing contains an interesting blend of the two. Speaking of *Coming Together: Social Struggle and Sexual Crisis,* Carol Eckberg Wadsworth in *Library Journal* says that Hernton is "more a poet than a theorist . . . [and] he seems to delve deeper than many writers on race and/or sex." Hernton's "style of writing is seldom jargonistic or academic sounding; instead, it is often passionate and highly personal," comments Magistrale. "Hernton's fiction and nonfiction thus represent an interesting blend of his roles as poet and social scientist."

White Papers for White Americans, for example, a series of essays on American culture and racism, "represent the best study on America's race problem that has come out in years," says Edward Margolies in a 1966 *Library Journal* review. "It is virtually impossible to bring something new to the area of race," writes Brooks Johnson in *Negro Digest,* "but, infrequently, the very gifted see and are able to express the centuried problems with something that approaches creativity because of the sensitivity and forcefulness with which they relate the old truths. Calvin C. Hernton's work is an example of such a process." Johnson believes that in *White Papers* Hernton demonstrates "the ability to tell, narrate, and explain, which he does at varying tempos and moods—in the manner of a good, highly polished jazz group. I don't mean to imply that his technique is slick—it isn't. Mr. Hernton is smooth because he is a man who knows his subject matter and has mastered the delicate balance between what observation and honesty dictate and what natural talent makes possible." The critic concludes that the result "is a book that knows no time."

Hernton's book *Sex and Racism in America* has been translated into Spanish, Japanese, Swedish, and French.

BIOGRAPHICAL/CRITICAL SOURCES:

BOOKS

Dictionary of Literary Biography, Volume 38: *Afro-American Writers after 1955: Dramatists and Prose Writers,* Gale, 1985.

PERIODICALS

Library Journal, March 1, 1966, May 15, 1971.
Negro Digest, May, 1967.
Publishers Weekly, January 10, 1966.
Saturday Review, February 12, 1966.

*   *   *

HICKMAN, Martha Whitmore 1925-

PERSONAL: Born December 9, 1925, in Holyoke, Mass.; daughter of George Deming (a lawyer) and Ruth Olive (Carr) Whitmore; married Hoyt Leon Hickman (a minister of United Methodist Church), December 16, 1950; children: Peter Carr, John Whitmore, Stephen Hoyt, Mary Esther. *Education:* Mount Holyoke College, B.A. (cum laude), 1947. *Politics:* Democrat. *Religion:* United Methodist.

ADDRESSES: Home—2034 Castleman Dr., Nashville, Tenn. 37215.

CAREER: Writer. American Baptist Convention, Philadelphia, Pa., assistant editor, 1947-50; nursery school teacher in New Haven, Conn., 1951-52. Consultant, Information Services, Nashville, 1974-80.

MEMBER: Authors Guild, Authors League of America, Society of Children's Book Writers, Mount Holyoke College Alumnae Association, Nashville Writers Alliance, Phi Beta Kappa.

AWARDS, HONORS: Friends of American Writers award in Juvenile Division, 1976, for *I'm Moving;* Golden Kite nomination, 1987, for *Lost and Found.*

WRITINGS:

(Contributor) *Days of Grass* (anthology), Channel Press, 1965.
How to Marry a Minister, Lippincott, 1968.
Love Speaks Its Voice, Word, Inc., 1976, paperback edition published as *The Growing Season*, Upper Room, 1980.
(Contributor) *Images: Women in Transition*, Upper Room, 1976.
I Will Not Leave You Desolate: Some Thoughts for Grieving Parents, Upper Room, 1982.
Waiting and Loving: Thoughts Occasioned by the Illness and Death of a Parent, Upper Room, 1984.

PUBLISHED BY ABINGDON

I'm Moving, 1975.
My Friend William Moved Away, 1979.
The Reason I'm Not Quite Finished Tying My Shoes, 1981.
When Can Daddy Come Home?, 1983.
Eeps Creeps, It's My Room, 1984.
Last Week My Brother Anthony Died, 1984.
With Crown: Good Manners for Girls and Boys, 1985.
When James Allen Whitaker's Grandfather Came to Stay, 1985.
When Our Church Building Burned Down, 1986.
Lost and Found, 1987.

OTHER

Contributor of articles and fiction to periodicals, including *Good Housekeeping, Christian Science Monitor, Pastoral Psychology, Presbyterian Life, Christian Herald, Creative Years*, and *Weavings*.

WORK IN PROGRESS: A novel; a nonfiction book for teachers, for publication by Abingdon.

AVOCATIONAL INTERESTS: Painting, drawing, swimming, travel.

*　　　*　　　*

HILL, Alexis
See CRAIG, Mary (Francis) S(hura)

*　　　*　　　*

HILL, Errol Gaston 1921-

PERSONAL: Born August 5, 1921, in Trinidad, West Indies; son of Thomas David (an accountant) and Lydia (Gibson) Hill; married Grace Hope (a teacher), August 12, 1956; children: Da'aga, Claudia, Melina, Aaron. *Education:* Royal Academy of Dramatic Art (England), graduate diploma, 1951; University of London, diploma in drama, 1951; Yale University, B.A., 1962, M.F.A., 1962, D.F.A., 1966.

ADDRESSES: Office—Department of Drama, Dartmouth College, Hanover, N.H. 03755. *Agent*—Lucy Kroll Agency, 390 West End Ave., New York, N.Y. 10024.

CAREER: British Broadcasting Corp., London, England, announcer and actor, 1951-52; University of the West Indies, Kingston, Jamaica, and Port-of-Spain, Trinidad, creative arts tutor, 1953-58, 1962-65; University of Ibadan, Ibadan, Nigeria, teaching fellow in drama, 1965-67; City University of New York, College of Staten Island, associate professor of drama, 1967-68; Dartmouth College, Hanover, N.H., professor of drama, 1968—, John D. Willard Professor of Drama and Oratory, 1976, head of department, 1970-73, 1976-79. Evaluator, National Association of Schools Theatre; consultant, National Humanities Faculty, 1971-80. *Military service:* U.S. military engineer, Trinidad, 1941-43.

MEMBER: American Society for Theatre Research, Association for Commonwealth Language and Literature Studies.

AWARDS, HONORS: British Council Scholar, 1949-51; Rockefeller Foundation fellow, 1958-60; Theatre Guild of America playwriting fellow, 1961-62; Hummingbird Gold Medal, governments of Trinidad and Tobago, 1973; Guggenheim fellow, 1985-86; Barnard Hewitt Award for theatre history research, and Bertram Joseph Award for Shakespeare studies, both 1985; Fulbright fellow, 1988.

WRITINGS:

(Editor) *Caribbean Plays*, Extramural Department, University of West Indies, Volume I, 1958, Volume II, 1965.
(Editor and contributor) *The Artist in West Indian Society*, Extramural Department, University of West Indies, 1964.
The Trinidad Carnival: Mandate for a National Theatre, University of Texas Press, 1972.
(Contributor) *Resource Development in the Caribbean*, McGill University, 1972.
(With Peter Greer) *Why Pretend?* (a dialogue on the arts in education), Chandler, 1973.
(Editor) *A Time . . . and a Season: Eight Caribbean Plays*, Extramural Department, University of the West Indies, 1976.
(Editor) *Three Caribbean Plays for Secondary Schools*, Longman, 1979.
(Editor) *The Theatre of Black Americans: A Collection of Critical Essays*, two volumes, Prentice-Hall, 1980.
Shakespeare in Sable: A History of Black Shakespearean Actors, foreword by John Houseman, University of Massachusetts Press, 1984.
(Editor) *Plays for Today*, Longman, 1985.

PLAYS

The Ping-Pong (one-act), Extramural Department, University of the West Indies, 1958.
"Man Better Man" (three-act folk musical; first produced on Broadway at St. Mark's Playhouse, July 2, 1969), in John Gassner, editor, *Three Plays from the Yale School of Drama*, Dutton, 1964.
Dance Bongo (one-act), Extramural Department, University of the West Indies, 1965.
Oily Portraits (one-act), Extramural Department, University of the West Indies, 1966.
Square Peg (one-act), Extramural Department, University of the West Indies, 1966.
Dilemma (one-act), Extramural Department, University of the West Indies, 1966.
Strictly Matrimony (one-act), Extramural Deparment, University of the West Indies, 1966.
Wey-Wey (one-act), Extramural Department, University of the West Indies, 1966.

Also author of "Broken Melody," 1954. Plays anthologized in *Caribbean Literature*, edited by G. R. Coulthard, University of London Press, 1966, and *Black Drama Anthology*, edited by Woody King and Ron Milner, Signet, 1971.

OTHER

Contributor to *West Indian Review, Caribbean, Trinidad Guardian, Ethnomusicology, Cutures, Caribbean Quarterly*, and other West Indian periodicals, and to *Theatre Survey, Black American Literature Forum*, and *Theatre Journal*. Editor, *Bulletin of Black Theatre* (of the American Theatre Association), 1971-78.

WORK IN PROGRESS: Thespis in Jamaica: Profile of a Colonial Theatre; History of the Afro-American Drama and Theatre.

SIDELIGHTS: Errol Gaston Hill's book *Shakespeare in Sable: A History of Black Shakespearean Actors* ''[documents] a long and often distinguished history of black actors who, while struggling against great adversity, made their mark on classical theatre,'' writes Robin Breon in the Toronto *Globe and Mail.* Covering the years from the 1820s through the 1970s, *Shakespeare in Sable* is the first book to describe how difficult it was, and sometimes still is, for even the most highly skilled black actors and actresses to secure roles in Shakespearean productions. *Shakespeare in Sable* is, therefore, ''a story of courage to the point of heroism, persistence on to madness, and dreaming without hope,'' concludes James V. Hatch in *Black American Literature Forum.*

BIOGRAPHICAL/CRITICAL SOURCES:

PERIODICALS

American Anthropologist, August, 1973.
American Historical Review, June, 1985.
Black American Literature Forum, summer, 1985.
Comparative Drama, spring, 1986.
Globe and Mail (Toronto), February 9, 1985.
Journal of American Folklore, April, 1975.
Shakespeare Quarterly, summer, 1986.
Spotlight (Jamaica), October, 1958.
Theatre Journal, October, 1985.
Urbanite, March, 1961.

*   *   *

HILL, Grace Brooks
[Collective pseudonym]

WRITINGS:

"CORNER HOUSE GIRLS" SERIES

The Corner House Girls: How They Moved to Milton, What They Found, and What They Did, Barse & Hopkins, 1915.
. . . at School: How They Entered, Whom They Met, and What They Did, Barse & Hopkins, 1915.
. . . under Canvas: How They Reached Pleasant Cove and What Happened Afterward, Barse & Hopkins, 1915.
. . . in a Play: How They Rehearsed, How They Acted, and What the Play Brought In, Barse & Hopkins, 1916.
The Corner House Girls' Odd Find: Where They Made It, and What the Strange Discovery Led To, Barse & Hopkins, 1916.
. . . on a Tour: Where They Went, What They Saw, and What They Found, Barse & Hopkins, 1917.
. . . Growing Up: What Happened First, What Came Next, and How It Ended, Barse & Hopkins, 1918.
. . . Snowbound: How They Went Away, What They Discovered, and How It Ended, Barse & Hopkins, 1919.
. . . on a Houseboat: How They Sailed Away, What Happened on the Voyage, and What They Discovered, Barse & Hopkins, 1920.
. . . among the Gypsies: How They Met, What Happened, and How It Ended, Barse & Hopkins, 1921.
. . . on Palm Island: Looking for Adventure, How They Found It, and What Happened, Barse & Hopkins, 1922.
. . . Solve a Mystery: What It Was, Where It Was, and Who Found It, Barse & Hopkins, 1923.
. . . Facing the World: Why They Had to, How They Did It, and What Came of It, Barse & Hopkins, 1926.

SIDELIGHTS: The Corner House Girls were four girls, aged eight to fourteen years, who were left an old house by a rich bachelor uncle. The books chronicled their adventures after they moved into the place. For more information see the entries for Harriet S. Adams, Edward L. Stratemeyer, and Andrew E. Svenson.

BIOGRAPHICAL/CRITICAL SOURCES:

BOOKS

Johnson, Deidre, editor and compiler, *Stratemeyer Pseudonyms and Series Books: An Annotated Checklist of Stratemeyer and Stratemeyer Syndicate Publications,* Greenwood Press, 1982.

*   *   *

HILL, Meredith
  See CRAIG, Mary (Francis) S(hura)

*   *   *

HINGORANI, R(up) C.   1925-

PERSONAL: Born September 10, 1925; son of Chandumal Nanikram (an advocate) and Savitri Hingorani; married wife, Kamla, December, 1959; children: Mohan (son), Chitra (daughter). *Education:* Bombay University, LL.B., 1945; Delhi University, LL.M., 1949; Yale University, J.S.D., 1955.

ADDRESSES: Home—Rani Ghat, Patna-6, India. *Office*—Law Department, Patna University, Patna-6, India.

CAREER: Instructor of law in Universities of Agra, Lucknow, and Gorakhpur, India, 1951-63; Delhi University, Delhi, India, reader, 1963-64; Patna University, Patna, India, professor of international law and dean of law department, 1964—, dean of faculty of law.

MEMBER: International Law Association, World Association of Law Professors (member of executive committee), International Institute of Human Rights, International Institute of Humanitarian Law (member of scientific committee), World Peace Through Law Center, Indian Law Institute, Association of Law Teachers and Schools in Southeast Asia.

WRITINGS:

Prisoners of War, N. M. Tripathi (Bombay), 1963, revised edition, Oceana, 1982.
Indian Extradition Law, Asia Publishing House (Bombay), 1969.
(Editor) *International Law through the United Nations,* N. M. Tripathi, 1972.
Modern International Law, Oceana, 1979, 2nd edition, 1984.
Studies in International Law, Oceana, 1981.
Human Rights in India, Oxford & IBH (New Delhi), 1985.

Editor-in-chief of *Journal* of All India Law Teachers Association, 1969-70.†

*   *   *

HOLDER, Bob N.
  See MULLARKY, Taylor

*   *   *

HOLLI, Melvin G(eorge)   1933-

PERSONAL: Born February 22, 1933, in Ishpeming, Mich.;

son of Walfred M. (a welder) and Sylvia (Erickson) Holli; married Betsy Biggar (a clinic dietitian), August 12, 1961; children: Susan J., Steven E. *Education:* Northern Michigan University, B.A., 1957; University of Michigan, M.A., 1958, Ph.D., 1966. *Religion:* Lutheran.

ADDRESSES: Home—1311 Ashland Ave., River Forest, Ill. 60305. *Office*—Department of History, University of Illinois at Chicago Circle, Chicago, Ill. 60680.

CAREER: University of Michigan, Ann Arbor, curator of historical collections, 1963-64; University of Illinois at Chicago Circle, Chicago, associate professor, 1965-76, professor of history, 1976—.

MEMBER: American Historical Association, Organization of American Historians.

AWARDS, HONORS: Woodrow Wilson fellowship, 1957-58; National Endowment for the Humanities fellowship, 1969-70; Society of Midland Authors prize for best history, 1981, for *Ethnic Chicago.*

WRITINGS:

Reform in Detroit: Hazen S. Pingree and Urban Politics, Oxford University Press, 1969.
(Author of new introduction) Tom L. Johnson, *My Story,* University of Washington Press, 1971.
Detroit: Fur Trading Post to Industrial Metropolis, 1701-1976, New Viewpoints, 1976.
(With P. Jones) *Ethnic Frontier,* Eerdmans, 1977.
Ethnic Chicago, Eerdmans, 1981, revised edition, 1984.
(Editor with Jones) *Biographical Dictionary of American Mayors, 1820-1980,* Greenwood Press, 1982.
The Making of the Mayor of Chicago, 1983, Eerdmans, 1984.
(With Paul M. Green) *The Mayors: The Chicago Political Tradition,* Southern Illinois University Press, 1987.

WORK IN PROGRESS: A study of political decision-making in the American city, 1865-1920.

* * *

HOLMES, Thomas K.
[Collective pseudonym]

WRITINGS:

The Man from Tall Timber, G. Sully, 1919.
The Heart of Canyon Pass, G. Sully, 1921.

SIDELIGHTS: For more information see the entries for Harriet S. Adams, Edward L. Stratemeyer, and Andrew E. Svenson.

BIOGRAPHICAL/CRITICAL SOURCES:

BOOKS

Johnson, Deidre, editor and compiler, *Stratemeyer Pseudonyms and Series Books: An Annotated Checklist of Stratemeyer and Stratemeyer Syndicate Publications,* Greenwood Press, 1982.

* * *

HOM, Ken 1949-

PERSONAL: Born May 3, 1949, in Tucson, Ariz.; son of J. Thomas and Fong (Ying) Hom. *Education:* Attended Roosevelt University, 1968-69, University of California, Berkeley, 1971-74, and University of Aix-Marseille, 1973-74.

ADDRESSES: Home—Berkeley, Calif. *Office*—P.O. Box 4303, Berkeley, Calif. 94704. *Agent*—Martha Sternberg, 1263 12th Ave., San Francisco, Calif. 94122.

CAREER: Free-lance photographer in France, 1971-74; KQED-TV (public television), San Francisco, Calif., production assistant and free-lance producer, 1975-76; Ken Hom Cooking School, Berkeley, Calif., founder and owner, 1976-79; California Culinary Academy, San Francisco, member of faculty, 1979—. Guest on radio and television programs; gives cooking demonstrations.

AWARDS, HONORS: Nominated for Emmy Award from Academy of Television Arts and Sciences, 1976, for film "The Long March"; second place award from Tastemaker, 1982, for *Chinese Technique;* runner-up for Andre Simon Memorial Fund Book Award, 1987, for *Ken Hom's East Meets West Cuisine.*

WRITINGS:

Chinese Technique (cookbook), Simon & Schuster, 1981.
Ken Hom's Chinese Cookery (cookbook), Harper & Row, 1985.
Ken Hom's East Meets West Cuisine (cookbook), Simon & Schuster, 1987.
Asian Vegetarian Feast (cookbook), Morrow, 1988.
The Fragrant Harbor Cuisine: The New Chinese Cooking of Hong Kong, Simon & Schuster, in press.
Quick and Easy Cooking, BBC Books, in press.

Contributor to periodicals, including *Taste, A La Carte, New York Times Magazine, Bon Appetit, Gourmet Traveller, Vogue* (Australia), and *Cuisine* (New Zealand).

WORK IN PROGRESS: Cooking for One or Two, for Macmillan (London); *Taste of China,* for Pavilion Books.

SIDELIGHTS: About *Ken Hom's East Meets West Cuisine,* Linda Greider comments in the *Washington Post* that Hom "has done the best that inventors can do: He's produced the truly new flavors that are not only truly 'interesting' . . . but also taste good." She also admires "the ease with which most of the recipes are prepared."

BIOGRAPHICAL/CRITICAL SOURCES:

PERIODICALS

Bon Appetit, April, 1980.
Chicago Sun-Times, December 3, 1981.
Chicago Tribune, December 10, 1987.
Cuisine, February, 1982.
House and Garden, July, 1982.
Newsweek, June 7, 1982.
New York Times, February 4, 1981.
Seattle Post-Intelligencer, March 24, 1982.
South China Morning Post, April 25, 1982.
Washington Post, October 14, 1987.
Washington Post Book World, December 13, 1981.

* * *

HOOD, William (Joseph) 1920-

PERSONAL: Born April 19, 1920, in Waterville, Me.; son of Walter J. (a musician) and Berthina (Hutchins) Hood; married Cordelia Dodson, 1951 (divorced, 1975); married Mary Carr Thomas (an editor), June, 1976. *Eduction:* Attended University of Southern Maine, 1939-40, and George Washington University, 1950.

ADDRESSES: Home—55 Spurwink Road, Scarborough, Me. 04074. *Office*—158 East 82nd St., New York, N.Y. 10028. *Agent*—Harold Ober Associates, Inc., 40 East 49th St., New York, N.Y. 10017.

CAREER: Portland Press Herald, Portland, Me., reporter, 1939-40; Central Intelligence Agency (CIA), Washington, D.C., senior official in operational component stationed in Austria, Germany, Switzerland, France, and England, 1945-75; writer, 1975—. *Military service:* U.S. Army, 1941-45, served in Armored Force and with Office of Strategic Services (OSS) as special agent; became master sergeant.

MEMBER: Special Forces Club (London), The Players (New York), Waistcoat Club (Switzerland), The Beefsteak (Vienna).

WRITINGS:

Mole (nonfiction), Norton, 1982.
Spy Wednesday (novel), Norton, 1986.
Cry Spy (novel), Norton, 1988.

Contributor of reviews and articles to newspapers and magazines, including *Midstream, Portland Sunday Telegram,* and *Foreign Intelligence Literary Scene.*

WORK IN PROGRESS: Under contract to Norton for a biography of James Angleton, a former CIA officer.

SIDELIGHTS: William Hood describes a Russian spy's association with the Central Intelligence Agency in the book *Mole.* Pyotr Popov, a major in the Soviet military intelligence wing (GRU), agreed to spy for the United States in 1952. Working from Vienna and Berlin under the guise of a loyal GRU officer, Popov provided the names of Russian operatives in Europe and the United States and details of his country's military command to CIA "handlers" for the next six years. Major Popov was exposed in 1958, arrested by the Soviets, and later shot for treason.

Hood, who worked within the CIA and its World War II predecessor, the OSS, for nearly thirty-five years, was operations chief of the agency station in Vienna when Popov decided to switch sides, and he helped establish the agent in the American intelligence network. In *Mole,* his agency-approved memoir which illustrates Popov's day-to-day relationship with the organization and concludes with speculation on how the agent might have been discovered, Hood uses pseudonyms to protect himself and other CIA officials involved in the case.

In a *Washington Post Book World* review, Robert G. Kaiser found Hood's version of the Popov story "a good yarn, ably recounted" and deemed *Mole* "a wonderful book for the beach and a must for the aficionado." Phillip Taubman concurred, declaring in the *New York Times Book Review* that Hood "is surprisingly skilled at telling the story. The book moves along crisply and builds to a dramatic conclusion with the kind of mounting tension one would expect to find in the best novels about espionage." Walter Laqueur of the *Times Literary Supplement* proclaimed Hood's *Mole* "an authentic story told in convincing detail."

Hood told *CA:* "There has been so much outright nonsense written about espionage that I thought it past time for someone to give a more realistic picture of what is involved in handling an important spy. The Popov story is an interesting one—he had been given the best the U.S.S.R. had to offer, but rejected the system and, on his own, decided to fight against it. Along with telling a true spy story, I hoped to give Popov a small footnote in history."

Hood tries his hand at the fictional depiction of spies in *Spy Wednesday,* his first novel. Jack Sullivan, writing in the *New York Times Book Review,* states, "The characters in this exceptionally intelligent spy novel exist somewhere between the suave C.I.A. operatives of William F. Buckley Jr. and the hard-boiled antiheroes of John Le Carre." A reviewer for the *New Yorker* praises the book, saying, "Mr. Hood has reinvented a not unfamiliar plot and molded it into a novel of unusual distinction." Sullivan echoes this assessment, declaring, "'Spy Wednesday' is a quiet, even austere novel, but with a powerful charge of electricity and danger. I suspect this is how the racket really is. Mr. Hood certainly makes us feel so."

BIOGRAPHICAL/CRITICAL SOURCES:

PERIODICALS

Business Week, July 5, 1982.
Christian Science Monitor, July 28, 1982.
New Yorker, November 17, 1986.
New York Times Book Review, May 23, 1982, February 9, 1986.
Times Literary Supplement, February 11, 1983.
Virginia Quarterly Review, autumn, 1982.
Washington Post Book World, July 27, 1982.

* * *

HOPES, David Brendan 1953-

PERSONAL: Born September 1, 1953, in Akron, Ohio; son of Eugene David (an accountant) and Marion (Summers) Hopes. *Education:* Hiram College, B.A., 1972; attended Johns Hopkins University, 1972-73; Syracuse University, M.A., 1976, Ph.D., 1980. *Politics:* Democrat. *Religion:* Anglo-Catholic.

ADDRESSES: Home and office—One University Heights, Asheville, N.C. 28804. *Agent*—Janet Manus, 370 Lexington Ave., New York, N.Y. 10017.

CAREER: City of Akron, Ohio, naturalist in department of parks and recreation, 1970-72; Koinonia Foundation, Baltimore, Md., resident naturalist, 1973; Syracuse University, Syracuse, N.Y., instructor in English, 1979-81; Hiram College, Hiram, Ohio, visiting assistant professor, 1982-83; University of North Carolina at Asheville, associate professor of literature, 1983—.

MEMBER: Dramatists Guild, Poets and Writers, National Audubon Society, Phi Beta Kappa.

AWARDS, HONORS: Juniper Prize, University of Massachusetts Press, 1981, for *The Glacier's Daughters;* Creative Artists Public Service grant, 1981; Saxifrage Prize, University of North Carolina, 1982, for *The Glacier's Daughters;* Southern Playwrights Award, Playwrights Fund of North Carolina, 1986, for *Timothy Liberty,* and 1987, for "Phantom of the Blue Letters."

WRITINGS:

Shadow Mass (poems), Hiram Press, 1972.
The Basswood Tree (poems), Climate Books, 1979.
The Glacier's Daughters (poems), University of Massachusetts Press, 1981.
A Sense of the Morning (nonfiction), Dodd, 1988.
Timothy Liberty (drama), Playwrights Fund of North Carolina, 1988.

Also author of play, "Phantom of the Blue Letters."

Work represented in anthologies, including *Seventy-Three Ohio Poets, Men on Men II,* and *On Turtle's Back.* Contributor of more than two hundred poems, stories, reviews, and articles to magazines, including *New Yorker, Audubon, Kansas Quarterly, Salmagundi,* and *Poetry Northwest.* Associate editor of *Porto de Contacto,* 1976-77, and *Hiram Poetry Review.*

WORK IN PROGRESS: The Age of Silver, a novel; *A Dream of Adonis,* poetry; *All the Tired Horses,* a novel; *Men's Lives,* nonfiction.

SIDELIGHTS: Along with fiction, drama, and nonfiction, David Brendan Hopes writes poetry that embraces both the natural and spiritual worlds. Writing about the collection *The Glacier's Daughters* in *New England Review and Bread Loaf Quarterly,* Andrew Higgins says that in Hopes' best work, "the drive is toward mystical union with nature in a oneness beyond expression." Hopes describes himself to *CA* as both "a voluptuary and a religious fanatic," and tells audiences at readings that his poetry arises from an "implicit tension." He adds, "reviews of and commentaries on my work have tended to define me as a poet of nature and a poet of Christianity, both accusations of which I initially found surprising, but to which I am becoming reconciled." Andrews thinks that "nothing is harder to write well than poetry of joy and celebration, and Hopes, when everything pulls together, can do it. That alone is enough to put him in a league by himself."

Hopes also wrote *CA,* "My refusal to acknowledge a division between the 'traditional' and the 'contemporary' strikes some reviewers as effete and others as medicinal.

"Readers of my short fiction and novels have observed that they see two nearly opposite writers, a Dionysian poet and an Apollonian fiction writer, an extreme romantic and a limpid classicist. I have no explanation for this.

"Voice is foremost in my craft, in both fiction and poetry, and it is no accident that I am a singer and actor as well as a writer and academic. In my reviews of the work of other writers, I have praised what I hope to achieve in my own work: spiritual ambition, music, accessibility. My work possesses both the defects and the merits of these qualities. To some

ears my desire to take heaven by storm sounds like mere chest-thumping; to some my musicality seems derivative or overdone; some fear that my anxiety for accessibility leads me close to the line where the poetic sensibility dissolves altogether, and only the subject matter remains."

BIOGRAPHICAL/CRITICAL SOURCES:

PERIODICALS

New England Review and Bread Loaf Quarterly, summer, 1986.

*   *   *

**HUNT, Francis
[Collective pseudonym]**

WRITINGS:

"MARY AND JERRY MYSTERY STORIES"

The Messenger Dog's Secret, Grosset & Dunlap, 1935.
The Mystery of the Toy Bank, Grosset & Dunlap, 1935.
The Story the Parrot Told, Grosset & Dunlap, 1935.
The Secret of the Missing Clown, Grosset & Dunlap, 1936.
The Mystery of the Crooked Tree, Grosset & Dunlap, 1937.

SIDELIGHTS: Mary and Jerry Denton solved mysteries during school and on weekends. For more information see the entries for Harriet S. Adams, Edward L. Stratemeyer, and Andrew E. Svenson.

BIOGRAPHICAL/CRITICAL SOURCES:

BOOKS

Johnson, Deidre, editor and compiler, *Stratemeyer Pseudonyms and Series Books: An Annotated Checklist of Stratemeyer and Stratemeyer Syndicate Publications,* Greenwood Press, 1982.

*   *   *

**HUNT, Nan
See RAY, N(ancy) L(ouise)**

I

INCOGNITEAU, Jean-Louis
See KEROUAC, Jean-Louis Lebrid de

*   *   *

INNES, Hammond
See HAMMOND INNES, Ralph

*   *   *

INNES, Ralph Hammond
See HAMMOND INNES, Ralph

*   *   *

IQBAL, Afzal   1919-

PERSONAL: Born August 14, 1919, in Lahore, Pakistan. *Education:* Government College, Lahore, Pakistan, B.A. (with honors), 1939; University of the Punjab, M.A., 1941.

ADDRESSES: Office—13 A Satellite Town, Rawalpindi, Pakistan.

CAREER: Ministry of Foreign Affairs, Islamabad, Pakistan, 1950—, served as second secretary at embassies in Iran, 1950, Burma, 1952, first secretary in Spain, 1955-57, England, 1957-58, as deputy secretary for external publicity, 1959-61, served at embassies in Thailand, 1961-63, and Syria, 1963-64, deputy high commissioner at embassy in India, 1964-66, minister in London, England, 1966-69, ambassaor to Switzerland and the Holy See, 1969-71, to Brazil, Bolivia, Colombia, and Paraguay, 1971-73, ambassador to Sweden and Norway, 1973-76, ambassador to Canada, Guyana, Trinidad, and Tobago, 1976-79. Has lectured at Universities of London, Durham, Manchester, Geneva, Berne, Rio de Janeiro, Sao Paulo, Bangkok, Stockholm, Uppsala, Oslo, Ankara, Istanbul, Konya, and Azamgarh, and at Oxford and Cambridge Universities.

AWARDS, HONORS: Decorated by Order of Istihquq (Syrian Arab Republic), Order of Humayun and order of Sipas (both Iran), order of Pius IX (Holy See), and Order of the Grand Cruz do Sul (Brazil); elected fellow, Royal Society of Arts, 1957; University of the Punjab, Ph.D., 1970.

WRITINGS:

(Editor) *My Life: A Fragment* (on the life of Mohamed Ali, leader of the Khilafat Movement of the 1920s), Muhammad Ashraf, 1942, 4th edition, 1966.

(Editor) *Select Writings and Speeches of Maulana Mohamed Ali,* two volumes, Muhammad Ashraf, 1944, 3rd edition, 1969.

The Life and Work of Maulana Jalaluddin Rumi, Institute of Islamic Culture (Lahore), 1956, 5th revised edition, Octagon Press (London), 1983.

Diplomacy in Islam, Institute of Islamic Culture, 1961, 2nd edition, 1965.

The Culture of Islam, Institute of Islamic Culture, 1967, 3rd revised edition, 1981.

The Life and Times of Maulana Mohamed Ali, Institute of Islamic Culture, 1974, 2nd edition, 1979.

The Impact of Maulana Jalaluddin Rumi on Islamic Culture, Regional Cultural Institute (Tehran), 1975.

The Prophet's Diplomacy, Claude Stark, Inc., 1975.

Circumstances Leading to the First Afghan War, Research Society of Pakistan and University of the Punjab, 1975, 2nd edition, 1975.

(Translator) Albert Camus, *Ajnabi* (Urdu translation of *L'Etranger*), Ayeena-i-adab, 1975.

Contemporary Muslim World, Hurriyet, 1983.

Islamisation of Pakistan, [Delhi], 1984, Vanguard Books, 1986.

Dimensions of Islam, [Delhi], 1986.

Diplomacy in Islam: The First Forty Years, Institute of Islamic Culture, 1988.

Contributor to magazines and newspapers.

SIDELIGHTS: Afzal Iqbal is an authority on Islam in general and on Maulana Jalaluddin and Mohamed Ali of the Khilafat movement in particular. *The Life and Work of Maulana Jalaluddin Rumi* has been translated into Urdu and Turkish. Other works have been published in the United States, the United Kingdom, Iran, Turkey, India, and Pakistan.

J

JEAN-LOUIS
See KEROUAC, Jean-Louis Lebrid de

*   *   *

JONES, Cranston E(dward)   1918-

PERSONAL: Born March 12, 1918, in Albany, N.Y.; son of Edward Thomas and Katharine Phoebe (Lamson) Jones; married Jean Campbell, 1949; children: Abigail Ainsworth, Baird. *Education:* Phillips Academy, Andover, 1936; Harvard University, B.S., 1940.

ADDRESSES: Home—8 East 96th St., New York, N.Y. 10028. *Office*—Time-Life Building, New York, N.Y. 10020.

CAREER: Time-Life, New York City, correspondent in San Francisco, Calif., London, England, and Paris, France, 1946-52, bureau chief, Rio de Janeiro, Brazil, 1952-55; *Time* magazine, staff member, 1955-69; *Travel & Camera,* editor in chief, 1969-70, and *Travel & Leisure,* New York City, 1970-71; *Atlas* magazine, executive director, 1971-73, senior editor, 1973-74; *People* magazine, New York City, senior editor, 1974-88. Executive vice-president, U.S. Camera Publications Corp., 1969-71; member of board of directors, Bear Run Foundation. *Military service:* U.S. Navy, 1940-45; became lieutenant, commanding officer, U.S.S. *Crouter.*

MEMBER: Municipal Art Society, Society of Architectural Historians, Society of Mayflower Descendants, Century Club, Edgartown Yacht Club.

AWARDS, HONORS: Received awards for excellence in architectural journalism, American Institute of Architects, 1956, 1958, 1959, and 1960.

WRITINGS:

Architecture Today and Tomorrow, McGraw, 1961.
(Editor) *Walking Tours of New York,* Museum of Modern Art, 1961.
Homes of the American Presidents, McGraw, 1962.
Marcel Breuer: Buildings and Projects, 1921-1961, Praeger, 1963.
(Editor) *The Best of People: The First Decade,* Fawcett Columbine/Ballantine, 1984.

Contributor of articles on art and architecture to *Fortune, Life, Sports Illustrated, Horizon,* and other magazines; television writer.

SIDELIGHTS: Cranston E. Jones organized "Form Givers at Mid-Century," an exhibit of thirteen architects, for the American Federation of Arts, 1958-60.

*   *   *

JONES, Diana Wynne   1934-

PERSONAL: Born August 16, 1934, in London, England; daughter of Richard Aneurin (an educator) and Marjorie (an educator; maiden name, Jackson) Jones; married John A. Burrow (a university professor), December 23, 1956; children: Richard, Michael, Colin. *Education:* St. Anne's College, Oxford, B.A., 1956.

ADDRESSES: Home—9 The Polygon, Clifton, Bristol BS8 4PW, England. *Agent*—Laura Cecil, 17 Alwyne Villas, London N1 2HG, England.

CAREER: Writer, 1965—.

AWARDS, HONORS: Guardian Award, 1977, for *Charmed Life; Boston Globe—Horn Book* Honor Book Award, 1984, for *Archer's Goon; Horn Book* Honor List, 1984, for *Fire and Hemlock; Horn Book* Fanfare List, 1987, for *Howl's Moving Castle.*

WRITINGS:

JUVENILES

Wilkins' Tooth, Macmillan (London), 1973, published as *Witch's Business,* Dutton, 1974.
The Ogre Downstairs, Macmillan, 1974.
Eight Days of Luke, Macmillan, 1974.
Dogsbody, Macmillan, 1975, Greenwillow, 1977.
Power of Three, Macmillan, 1976, Greenwillow, 1978.
Who Got Rid of Angus Flint?, Evans Brothers, 1978.
The Four Grannies, Hamish Hamilton, 1980.
The Homeward Bounders, Greenwillow, 1981.
The Time of the Ghost, Macmillan, 1981.
The Skiver's Guide, Knight Books, 1984.
Warlock at the Wheel and Other Stories, Greenwillow, 1984.
Archer's Goon, Greenwillow, 1984.

Fire and Hemlock, Greenwillow, 1985.
Howl's Moving Castle, Greenwillow, 1986.
A Tale of Time City, Greenwillow, 1987.

"CHRESTOMANCI" CYCLE; JUVENILES

Charmed Life, Macmillan, 1977, Greenwillow, 1979.
The Magicians of Caprona, Greenwillow, 1980.
Witch Week, Greenwillow, 1982.
The Lives of Christopher Chant, Greenwillow, 1988.

"DALEMARK" CYCLE; JUVENILES

Cart and Cwidder, Macmillan, 1975, Atheneum, 1977.
Drowned Ammet, Macmillan, 1977, Atheneum, 1978.
The Spellcoats, Atheneum, 1979.

JUVENILE PLAYS

"The Batterpool Business," first produced in London at Arts Theatre, October, 1968.
"The King's Things," first produced in London at Arts Theatre, February, 1970.
"The Terrible Fisk Machine," first produced in London at Arts Theatre, January, 1971.

OTHER

Changeover (adult novel), Macmillan (London), 1970.
(Contributor) *The Cat-Flap and the Apple Pie*, W. H. Allen, 1979.
(Contributor) *Hecate's Cauldron*, DAW Books, 1981.
(Contributor) *Hundreds and Hundreds*, Puffin, 1984.
(Contributor) *Dragons and Dreams*, Harper, 1986.
(Contributor) *Guardian Angels*, Viking Kestrel, 1987.

WORK IN PROGRESS: Five short books about a wizard, for younger children.

SIDELIGHTS: Diana Wynne Jones, states Jane Yolen in the *Washington Post Book World*, "is one of those English wonders who can combine wit with wisdom. Her sense of humor weaves in and out of the most absurd plots and twists around outrageous situations with a deftness any vaudevillian would envy." With a power of imagination sometimes compared to that of the early twentieth-century children's writer E. Nesbit, Wynne Jones uses traditional fantasy themes in a highly comic way to examine the problems facing her protagonists. Critics celebrate her highly original treatment of witches, ghosts, mound-fairies, enchanted animals, and characters from Greek, Celtic, and Norse mythologies. She "has a remarkable ability to grasp the basic elements of myth or fairytale, twist them sharply, then fit them without undue strain into patterns of her own making," says *Times Literary Supplement* contributor Penelope Farmer.

Representative of the originality in Jones's work is the novel *The Homeward Bounders*, in which "she postulates a fantasy War Game that applies to all worlds and times," says Sarah Hayes in the *Times Literary Supplement*. A fantasy novel with elements of science fiction, "the book contains terror, humour, adventure, everyday problems of survival and references to mythical characters," according to *Times Literary Supplement* contributor Judith Elkin. Elkin calls this book "a complex story with many different threads running through it," and Hayes echoes this assessment, saying that "pace and cerebral fibrillation are maintained marvelously right to the end of this fascinating novel." The story follows the adventures of Jamie, a teenager who accidentally witnesses the process by which the worlds are run: mysterious figures known only as "Them" play a game that controls the destinies of a number of worlds. Jamie, having watched "Them" play, "must be 'discarded' to the 'Bounds' between the worlds," says Elkin; "He has become a 'Homeward bounder.'" He moves in a random fashion from one world to the next. Although he makes friends—including the Flying Dutchman, Ahasuerus the Wandering Jew, Prometheus chained to a rock, and several children, all of whom become his friends—he is unable to return home unless he arrives there by accident.

Jones's use of mythic figures in new contexts lends depth to her treatment of characters, critics contend. "At times Jamie seems, simply, the questing, questioning spirit of Man, and this is confirmed by his bitterly real dealings with the Promethean sufferer who encourages his independence of mind: at other times he is simply a boy driven by gigantic, inexplicable forces," remarks Margery Fisher in *Growing Point*. Jamie must develop in order to free Prometheus; he must cast aside all hope of ever returning home before "They" can be defeated, says Elkin. Furthermore, he must sacrifice himself in order to keep the worlds secure from "Them." He must continue to walk the bounds, "alone on his travels, as the anchor who holds all the worlds in place," states Marcus Crouch in a *Junior Bookshelf* review.

Diana Wynne Jones wrote *CA:* "When I write for children, my first aim is to make a story—as amusing and exciting as possible—such as I wished I could have read as a child. My second aim is equally important. It is to give children—without presuming to instruct them—the benefit of my greater experience. I like to explore the private terrors and troubles which beset children, because they can thereby be shown they are not unique in misery. Children create about a third of their misery themselves. The other two-thirds is causd by adults—inconsiderate, mysterious, and often downright frightening adults. I put adults like this in my stories, in some firmly contemporary situation beset with very real problems, and explore the implications by means of magic and old myths. What I am after is an exciting—and exacting—wisdom, in which contemporary life and potent myth are intricately involved and superimposed. I would like children to discover that potent old truths are as much part of everyone's daily life as are—say—the days of the week."

BIOGRAPHICAL/CRITICAL SOURCES:

BOOKS

Contemporary Literary Criticism, Volume 26, Gale, 1983.

PERIODICALS

Book Window, spring, 1978.
Bulletin of the Center for Children's Books, July-August, 1975.
Chicago Tribune Book World, November 4, 1982.
Globe and Mail (Toronto), July 12, 1986.
Growing Point, May, 1974, April, 1975, October, 1975, December, 1975, March, 1978, May, 1981, January, 1982, November, 1982.
Horn Book, August, 1980.
Junior Bookshelf, August 1979, August, 1980, October, 1981, February, 1982, December, 1982.
Los Angeles Times, January 31, 1987.
New Statesman, May 24, 1974, May 20, 1977.
New York Times Book Review, May 5, 1974.
School Librarian, June, 1978, December, 1982.
School Library Journal, April, 1974, April, 1978.
Spectator, June 30, 1979.
Times (London), May 1, 1986.

Times Educational Supplement, November 18, 1977, November 30, 1979, April 18, 1980, November 23, 1984.

Times Literary Supplement, March 12, 1970, April 6, 1973, July 5, 1974, April 4, 1975, July 11, 1975, April 2, 1976, March 25, 1977, April 7, 1978, March 28, 1980, September 19, 1980, March 25, 1981, March 27, 1981, November 20, 1981, July 23, 1982, October 19, 1984, November 29, 1985, January 31, 1986, December 12, 1986, November 20-26, 1987.

Washington Post Book World, May 13, 1984, May 12, 1985, May 11, 1986, June 14, 1987, November 8, 1987.

World of Children's Books, spring, 1978.

*   *   *

JONES, Linda Phillips
See PHILLIPS-JONES, Linda

*   *   *

JONG, Erica 1942-

PERSONAL: Born March 26, 1942, in New York, New York; daughter of Seymour (an importer) and Eda (a painter and designer; maiden name, Mirsky) Mann; married Michael Werthman (divorced); married Allan Jong, 1966 (a child psychiatrist; divorced September 16, 1975); married Jonathan Fast, 1977 (a writer; divorced, 1983); children: (third marriage) Molly Miranda. *Education:* Barnard College, B.A., 1963; Columbia University, M.A., 1965; post-graduate study at Columbia School of Fine Arts, 1969-70. *Politics:* "Left-leaning feminist." *Religion:* "Devout pagan."

ADDRESSES: Agent—Morton L. Janklow Associates, Inc., 598 Madison Ave., New York, N.Y. 10022.

CAREER: Writer. Member of English faculty, City College of the City University of New York, 1964-65, 1969-70; member of faculty, University of Maryland, Overseas Division, Heidelberg, West Germany, 1966-69; instructor in English, Manhattan Community College, 1969-70; instructor in poetry, YM-YWCA Poetry Center, New York, N.Y., 1971—; lecturer. Member, New York State Council on the Arts, 1972-74.

MEMBER: PEN, Authors League of America, Authors Guild, Dramatists Guild of America, Writers Guild of America, Poetry Society of America, Poets and Writers, Phi Beta Kappa.

AWARDS, HONORS: American Academy of Poets Award, 1963; New York State Council on the Arts grant, 1971; Borestone Mountain Award in poetry, 1971; Bess Hokin prize, *Poetry* magazine, 1971; Madeline Sadin Award, *New York Quarterly,* 1972; Alice Faye di Castagnolia Award, Poetry Society of America, 1972; Creative Artists Public Service (CAPS) award, 1973, for *Half-Lives;* National Endowment for the Arts fellowship, 1973-74; Premio International Sigmund Freud, 1979.

WRITINGS:

NOVELS

Fear of Flying: A Novel (Book of the Month Club alternate selection; also see below), Holt, 1973.

How to Save Your Own Life: A Novel, Holt, 1977.

Fanny, Being the True History of the Adventures of Fanny Hackabout-Jones: A Novel, New American Library, 1980.

Parachutes and Kisses, New American Library, 1984.

Serenissima: A Novel of Venice, Houghton, 1987.

POETRY

Fruits & Vegetables: Poems, Holt, 1971.

Half-Lives, Holt, 1973.

Loveroot, Holt, 1975.

Here Comes and Other Poems, New American Library, 1975.

The Poetry of Erica Jong, 3 volumes, Holt, 1976.

Selected Poetry, Granada, 1977.

The Poetry Suit, Konglomerati Press, 1978.

At the Edge of the Body, Holt, 1979.

Ordinary Miracles: New Poems, New American Library, 1983.

OTHER

Fear of Flying (sound recording; includes selections from poetry and from the novel of the same title; read by the author), Spoken Arts, 1976.

(Contributor) *Four Visions of America,* Capra Press, 1977.

Witches (miscellany), illustrated by Joseph A. Smith, H. A. Abrams, 1981.

Megan's Book of Divorce: A Kid's Book for Adults, illustrated by Freya Tanz, New American Library, 1984.

Serenissima (sound recording of the novel of the same title; read by the author), Brilliance Corp./Houghton Mifflin, 1987.

Also author of introduction to the Book-of-the-Month Club Facsimile first edition of Vladimir Nabokov's *Lolita,* 1988, and author, with Jonathan Fast, of screenplay "Love Al Dente." Contributor of poems and articles to periodicals, including *Esquire, Ladies Home Journal, Ms., Nation, Vogue, Poetry,* and *Redbook;* contributor to *New York Times Book Review, Los Angeles Times, New Republic, New York, Expressen* (Sweden), *Corriere della Sera* (Italy), *News Day, New Yorker,* and many others.

WORK IN PROGRESS: "Currently developing *Fanny* as a Broadway musical."

SIDELIGHTS: "Although Erica Jong is a versatile poet, a novelist and a social critic," states *Interview* magazine contributor Karen Burke, "her fame from the enormous success of *Fear of Flying* has overshadowed these accomplishments." The story of Isadora Wing's escapades in search of sexual realization won Jong "a special place in woman's literary history," in the opinion of *Ms.* reviewer Karen Fitzgerald. "Jong was the first woman to write in such a daring and humorous way about sex," Fitzgerald declares. "She popularized the idea of a woman's ultimate sexual fantasy . . . sex for the sake of sex."

Dictionary of Literary Biography contributor Benjamin Franklin V points out that the success of Jong's novels has "tended to obscure the fact that she is a popular and good poet." Jong was a poet before she became a novelist—her first collection, *Fruits & Vegetables,* appeared two years before the first of her novels—and her early work was generally well received by critics. "Welcome Erica Jong," announces *Saturday Review* contributor James Whitehead, reviewing *Fruits & Vegetables,* "and welcome the sensuality she has so carefully worked over in this wonderful book . . . clearly she has worked hard to gain this splendid and various and serious comic vision." "Too frequently commercial success comes to poets of little ability," says Franklin. "Such is not the case with Jong. In deft verse she addresses life's difficulties with ever-increasing maturity. As a poet of substance, she speaks to the human condition."

Jong's poetry, remarks Douglas Dunn in *Encounter,* is written in the confessional mode, the "crazed exposure of the American ego,'' and resembles the work of Sylvia Plath and Anne Sexton, confessional poets who wrote extensively on existential despair and the relations between men and women, and who both committed suicide. Unlike them, Jong's intent is encouraging. She chooses to affirm life, and, according to Franklin, her work is "generally positive and optimistic about the human condition.'' John Ditsky, writing for the *Ontario Review,* explains that Jong is "a Sexton determined to survive,'' and sees the influence of Walt Whitman, another sensualist, in her poems. Above all, says Franklin, "her own work illustrates women's victory and that instead of flaunting their success and subduing men, women and men should work together and bolster each other.''

Isadora Zelda White Stollerman Wing, a poet and writer like her creator, is a woman "unblushingly preoccupied with her own libido,'' according to Elizabeth Peer of *Newsweek. Fear of Flying* tells the story of Isadora's adventures in search of her ideal sexual experience. On her way to a congress of psychoanalysts in Vienna with her Chinese-American Freudian analyst husband Bennett, she meets Adrian Goodlove, an English analyst and self-proclaimed free spirit. He coaxes her to leave her husband and run off with him on an existential holiday across Europe, to gratify sexual appetites without guilt and remorse. In the course of her sensual odyssey, Isadora realizes that Adrian, who epitomized sex-for-the-sake-of-sex to her, is in fact impotent, and that the freedom she sought in the encounter is false; as Carol Johnson writes in the *Dictionary of Literary Biography,* Isadora finds Adrian's "promised 'liberation' to be simply a new style of confinement.'' After two weeks he deserts her to keep a planned rendezvous with his own family, leaving Isadora to return to her husband unrepentant, if unfulfilled.

While sex plays a major role in *Fear of Flying,* it is only one of the themes Jong explores in the book. Johnson remarks that the story "revolves around themes of feminism and guilt, creativity and sex,'' and indeed, Jong tells Burke that *Fear of Flying* is "not an endorsement of promiscuity at all. It [is] about a young woman growing up and finding her own independence and finding the right to think her own thoughts, to fantasize.'' Emily Toth points out in the *Dictionary of Literary Biography* that "*Fear of Flying* is essentially a literary novel, a Bildungsroman with strong parallels to the *Odyssey,* Dante's *Inferno,* and the myths of Daedalus and Icarus.'' Parts of the book may be regarded as satirical: Johnson states that Jong's most erotic scenes "are parodies of contemporary pornography, her liberated woman [is] openly thwarted and unfulfilled.'' Other aspects of the novel, according to an *Atlantic* magazine contributor, include a "diatribe against marriage—against the dread dullness of habitual, connubial sex, against the paucity of means of reconciling the desire for freedom and the need for closeness, against childbearing,'' and a search for personal creativity.

Fear of Flying was a smashing popular success, selling more than two million paperback copies in its first two years. Whether read for its graphic eroticism, for its wry humor, or for its portrayal of women as people with a right to sexual expression, it revolutionized readers' perceptions of female sexuality with its depiction of Isadora's passions. *Detroit Free Press* contributor Donna Olendorf explains, "By granting Isadora Wing, her irrepressible heroine, the same liberties that men have typically taken for granted, Jong touched a responsive chord with women all over the world.'' Jong's work declared to a generation of women that they need not be ashamed of their own sensuality. In an interview with Cynthia Wolfson in the *Chi-*

cago Tribune Magazine, Jong declared, "My spirit and the world's spirit happened to be in the same place at the same time, and I was the mouth.'' As Isa Kapp put it in the *Washington Post Book World,* the women of America "had been endowed with freedoms even the women's liberation movement was afraid to ask for and did not know it wanted: to bathe in steamy fantasies of seduction by strangers, and to turn the tables on men and treat them as sex objects.''

Critical reaction to the novel varied. John Updike, writing for the *New Yorker,* found Jong's work had "class and sass, brightness and bite.'' He compared the author to Chaucer and Isadora to the Wife of Bath in the *Canterbury Tales,* and found parallels between *Fear of Flying* and both J. D. Salinger's *Catcher in the Rye* and Philip Roth's *Portnoy's Complaint.* Christopher Lehmann-Haupt of the *New York Times* praised Jong's characterization of Isadora, saying, "I can't remember ever before feeling quite so free to identify my own feelings with those of a female protagonist.'' He concluded that "Isadora Wing, with her unfettered yearnings for sexual satisfaction and her touching struggle for identity and self-confidence, is really more of a person than a woman (which isn't to deny in the least Mrs. Jong's underlying point that it's harder to become a person if you're a woman than it is if you're a man).'' In a *New York Times* appraisal, Henry Miller compared *Fear of Flying* to his own *Tropic of Cancer,* only "not as bitter and much funnier,'' and predicted that "this book will make literary history, that because of it women are going to find their own voice and give us great sagas of sex, life, joy, and adventure.''

Other reviewers were not so enthusiastic. *New Statesman* contributor Paul Theroux accused the novel of "misusing vulgarity to the point where it becomes purely foolish, picturing woman as a hapless organ animated by the simplest ridicule, and devaluing imagination in every line,'' and concluded that it "represents everything that is to be loathed in American fiction today.'' Jonathan Raban in *Encounter,* while comparing a reading of the book to "being locked in a lift with a woman who tells you her life story twice over, rapes you, and stops you reaching for the Emergency button,'' did admit that Isadora "has a crude genius for reality. . . . She persuades one of her existence by brute force, and she will not be budged.'' However, he asserted, Jong's heroine is "botheringly close to the insatiably willing dream-girl of male fantasies and male fiction.'' Although Michael Wood of the *New York Review of Books* felt that the novel "has far too much maudlin or portentous self-examination which it seems we are to take seriously,'' and that "the wit often seems to be working harder than it ought to be,'' he concluded, "Nevertheless, or even partly because of all this, the book has a helplessness, a vulnerability that makes it very likable, and in some backhanded way successful.''

Later books continue Isadora's story. In *How to Save Your Own Life* Isadora, now the successful author of the very daring and very explicit novel *Candida Confesses,* strikes out on her own. Her marriage and her life have become stultifying: husband Bennett confesses that he had an affair with another woman early in their marriage. "Despite herb tea and sympathy'' from various female friends, says Kapp, "her frame of mind is gloomy. Sex palls, fame galls, and her spirits do not lift. . . .'' Her sexual experiments continue, he adds, and include "a Lesbian episode justified as research, and an orgy itemized like the instructions for stuffing a holiday turkey.'' Finally, she leaves Bennett and travels to California to visit the movie producer who wants to film her book. There she meets Josh

Ace, an aspiring screenwriter some years younger than herself, and falls in love with him. Convinced that she has found her ideal man, she prepares to settle down.

Some seven years later even that relationship has soured, and Isadora, pushing forty and the mother of a three-year-old girl, is deserted by Josh. *Parachutes and Kisses* tells of her attempt to reexamine her identity, to cope with the pressures and problems of being single with children, of approaching middle age, and of supporting a household on a writer's income. In an interview with Gil Pyrah of the London *Times,* Jong describes what she tries to do in this novel: "It is about having it all in the 1980s. Isadora exemplified the 1970s woman and now, in the 1980s, we are trying to be single parents, breadwinners and feminine at the same time." In the course of her journey toward self-realization Isadora makes a tour of Russia, partly in search of her roots and partly to honor her recently deceased grandfather. She has a number of sexual adventures on the way, eventually finding contentment of sorts with a young actor named Bean.

New York Review of Books contributor Diane Johnson likes *How to Save Your Own Life,* calling it "a plain, wholesome American story, containing as it does that peculiarly American and purely literary substance Fulfillment, modern equivalent of fairy gold." However, John Leonard, writing in the *New York Times Book Review,* finds the novel lacking in the "energy and irreverence of 'Fear of Flying,' the Huck Finnishness, the cheerful vulgarity, the eye for social detail." "Whereas the author of 'Fear of Flying' was looking inside her own head, shuffling her fantasies, and with a manic gusto playing out her hand," he concludes that "the author of 'How to Save Your Own Life' is looking over her shoulder, afraid that the critics might be gaining on her." *Parachutes and Kisses,* on the other hand, "is funny and searching enough to suggest that *How to Save Your Own Life* was Jong's sophomoric jinx," says *Washington Post Book World* reviewer Grace Lichtenstein.

Many people confuse Isadora with Jong herself; the author and her protagonist come from similar backgrounds and have led similar lives. Both are New York born, were educated at Barnard and Columbia, have Jewish origins, and have published poetry. Jong herself is somewhat ambivalent about the sources she uses for these books; as Peer says: "There are days when Erica Jong flies into a fit at the suggestion that 'Fear of Flying' is autobiographical. 'It's not true,' she protests. 'I resent that question.' There are other days when Jong, with a buoyant giggle, admits, 'I cannibalized real life.'" Jong has also used her readers' confusion in the further adventures of Isadora. Lehmann-Haupt points out in another *New York Times* article that the main character of Isadora's novel *Candida Confesses,* in *How to Save Your Own Life,* is a promiscuous woman whom her readers insist on confusing with her, "much to her distress, because everyone ought to know the difference between fiction and autobiography." The distinction is very clear in Jong's mind; in a *Publishers Weekly* interview with Barbara A. Bannon, she maintains that "the sophisticated reader who has read Colette, Proust, Henry Miller knows that what I am writing is a mock memoir, allowing for a complete range of interpretations in between fact and fancy." Lehmann-Haupt concludes, finally, that "though 'Fear of Flying' isn't meant to be an autobiography, it certainly has the ring of candid confession."

Fanny, Being the True History of the Adventures of Fanny Hackabout-Jones: A Novel is "a picaresque of intelligence, buoyant invention and wonderful Rabelaisian energy" in the opinion of *New York Times Book Review* contributor Michael

Malone. According to Judy Klemesrud in the *New York Times,* it is also "a radical departure from the so-called confessional style of her first two novels." A longtime student of the eighteenth-century English novels of Lawrence Sterne, Henry Fielding, and John Cleland, Jong designed *Fanny* as "a cross between *Tom Jones* and *Moll Flanders,* with a wink at *Fanny Hill,*" according to Julia M. Klein in the *New Republic.* Like the fiction it resembles, *Fanny* is filled with adventures in the picaresque tradition: "ripped bodices, witchcraft, piracy, torture, murder, suicide, highway robbery, execution at the yardarm, madness, nay cruelty to horses," says *Times Literary Supplement* reviewer Pat Rogers.

But *Fanny* resembles its predecessors in more than plot. Jong adopts archaic language, spelling and diction, as *Washington Post Book World* contributor Judith Martin illustrates: "She also hath this funny Way with Words that can drive the faithful Reader nuts in the extream, but 'tis a pleasant Prose when once the Reader hath accustom'd herself to't." The author, says Anatole Broyard of the *New York Times,* embellishes her work with "didactic reflections in the 18th-century manner, and with the rather emphatic humor that made Henry Fielding and Laurence Sterne popular." However, he adds, the story also exhibits "the bad habits of the 18th-century novel: the inert moralizing, the strenuous diction, the relentless archness, the picaresque construction, which E. M. Forster described as 'and then, and then.'"

In other ways, however, the author's work is more contemporary; notes Toth, "Jong uses the eighteenth-century novel form to satirize both Fanny's century and her own." "At heart," comments *Chicago Tribune Book World* contributor James Goldman, "this novel is a vehicle for Jong's ideas about Woman and Womanhood." Still, Fanny remains a woman of her times; as Alan Friedman in the *New York Times Book Review* says, "It would be naive to insist that an 18th-century heroine who is in confident command of the entire arsenal of 20th-century feminism is a heroine who defies belief." Essentially, he concludes, Fanny is "a contemporary heroine chained to a romantic sage with neoclassical links."

Jong explores a history different from that of eighteenth-century England in *Serenissima: A Novel of Venice,* described by Olendorf as "another carefully blended concoction of eroticism, feminism and poetry." This novel relates the story of Jessica Pruitt, a much-married and much-divorced actress, who has come to Venice ostensibly to judge a film festival, but also to come to terms with her mother's suicide which took place in Venice years before, with her own middle age, and with the lack of direction in her life. She falls ill and, either in the delirium of her fever or through the use of a magic ring given her by a witchlike silent film star, finds herself in the sixteenth century. There she meets William Shakespeare, on tour with his patron and lover, the Earl of Southampton, and becomes the inspiration for the Dark Lady of his sonnets and for Jessica, daughter of Shylock in *The Merchant of Venice.*

Although replete with sexual overtones and local imagery, *Serenissima* expands the genre of the historical novel not through its use of these, but through its doubling of characters and its disregard for a linear sequence of time. In her *CA* interview, Jong states, "[*Serenissima*] was a book that owed its inspiration to [Virginia Woolf's] *Orlando* in the sense that I tried to abolish linear time and say that time is a fiction we invent to please ourselves." Jessica is a twentieth-century actress, but, as Jong tells Burke, she is at the same time a woman of the sixteenth century. "This is a novel full of masks, actors, costumes, performances,'' declares *Times Literary Supplement* contributor Valentine Cunningham. "Persons and personae converge, intersect, get confused at every turn on and off stage, in public and private, in brothels, at balls, in the here and now, back then,'' Cunningham explains.

Critics praise the novel for its evocation of the atmosphere of Venice; says Olendorf, "[Jong's] evocation of the city is especially beautiful, fairly shimmering with liquid imagery,'' and Joan Aiken, writing for the *Washington Post Book World*, lauds the author's descriptive prowess: "the Adriatic, the shimmer of Venice—Jong's control of narrative is beautiful, floating, hypnotic.'' Burke states, "Jong's novel captures for her readers the time-warped, haunted magic of this city of love and death.'' At the same time, however, other reviewers find her use of sixteenth-century literature overdone and disappointing. For instance, Shakespeare talks in quotes from his as yet unwritten work, "Southampton reels off sonnets, [and] Shylock wails in passages from 'Lear,''' explains Malone. Notes Susan Jacoby in *Tribune Books*, "This would have been a good joke if it were used sparingly, but repetition makes it truly tedious.'' Malone concludes, "The Renaissance has not served [the author] as well as did the eighteenth century.''

While Jong's Jessica resembles the author's other heroines in some ways, her differences are more apparent. Jessica is older than Fanny and Isadora, and many of her problems are rooted in her occupation. As Cunningham explains, Jessica is "approaching middle age in a male-directed celluloid world where the starlets must never droop or wrinkle.'' In her *CA* interview Jong calls her "the girl who starts out to be a Shakespearean actress and somehow winds up in Hollywood, wondering how she got there,'' unlike Isadora, "the smart Jewish kid on the couch,'' or Fanny, who is "fearless. . . . She surrenders to her fate, and her fate never disappoints her.''

Burke indicates that Erica Jong's books all involve "women who are in an ambiguous position, philosophically confused, emotionally overwrought,'' and the author uses these women to create "a realistic collage of the woman's situation today.'' Jong agrees; at the time *Fear of Flying* was published, she tells Burke, there was a void in literature about women: "Nobody was writing honestly about women and the variousness of their experience.'' What was missing from the American literary scene, she concludes, was "a thinking woman who also had a sexual life,'' a woman who could be just as much a hero as any man. As Peer observes, Jong's protagonists make it clear "that women and men are less different than literature has led us to believe. With a courage that ranges from deeply serious to devil-may-care, Jong . . . [has] stripped off the pretty masks that women traditionally wear, exposing them as vulgar, lecherous and greedy, frightened and flawed—in short, as bewilderingly human. Sort of like men.''

MEDIA ADAPTATIONS: Fear of Flying was optioned for film by Columbia Pictures, but never produced.

CA INTERVIEW

CA interviewed Erica Jong by telephone on September 30, 1987, at her home in New York, New York.

CA: In your new novel, Serenissima, *set in Venice, Jessica Pruitt goes back in time to have an affair with William Shakespeare, but without giving up her contemporary self. Do you see Jessica as a version of the heroine you've been developing from* Fear of Flying *on, or as a completely separate creation?*

JONG: There are obviously similarities amongst my heroines, just as there are similarities between the heroes of most major writers' books. I think you can find, if you look in Saul Bellow's books, that there's a pretty straight line from *Dangling Man* to *The Dean's December*. There are similarities because of the consciousness of the creator, and the heroes in Bellow's books or in Isaac Bashevis Singer's books or in Philip Roth's books are always some version of the consciousness of the authors. I think it's probably true of my heroines in that they tend to be very bright and bookish, and they tend to be eager to reconcile the demands of the body with the demands of the mind. The whore/Madonna split persists in our culture, and persists in a way that is very deleterious to women. My heroines are always looking for wholeness and integration in a society where women are not allowed to be bodies and brains both. Certainly that was Isadora, certainly that is Fanny, certainly that is Jessica, and it's true of me.

What's interesting are the differences. Isadora is the smart Jewish kid on the couch, as I think John Updike said. She's a female Holden Caulfield or Henry Miller. Jessica is the WASP aristocrat, very well educated, literarily educated, the girl who starts out to be a Shakespearean actress and somehow winds up in Hollywood, wondering how she got there. If I had to tell you who my favorite heroine was, I would say Fanny, still, because she has the most joie de vivre, and because she is the most heroic. She is the heroine I wish I totally were, and interestingly enough, she is the heroine I am coming to be in my life. She is fearless. She truly knows that her life is guided by a higher power. She surrenders to her fate, and her fate never disappoints her. Insofar as I learn to be more that way myself, my life gets happier and happier. I think Fanny is pointing the way for me. When I wrote her, I was not quite there yet, but my life has imitated my books at times. My books point to ways I want to go in my life.

CA: In a talk with Karen Burke published in Interview, *you described* Serenissima's *progression from notes in a journal to "What if?" to book. Tell me about the research. You must have had to immerse yourself not only in Shakespeare, but in Venetian history and Jewish history as well.*

JONG: I read everything I could lay my hands on about the history of the ghetto of Venice and the Jews of Venice, which I found was a great education, and which I adored. It taught me a lot about my own heritage. It taught me why Jewish mothers wanted their sons to be doctors: doctors were the only ones who could leave the ghetto at night without wearing a red hat; those mothers wanted their sons to be free. I read lots and lots of Elizabethan stuff that I had read in graduate school and much that I had not. I read many biographies of Shakespeare. I read biographies of the Earl of Southampton, Christopher Marlowe, Queen Elizabeth I; studies of Elizabethan England and street life in Elizabethan England, studies of daily life in sixteenth-century Venice. I listened constantly to John Gielgud's recording of the sonnets to get the sound of Elizabethan English in my ears. I listened to the Royal Shakespeare Company's recordings of *The Merchant of Venice* and other of the Italian plays of Shakespeare. I listened to Monteverdi at times during the writing.

I wrote much of the book in Venice, in a friend's sixteenth-century house, in fact in the room described in the last chapter of *Serenissima*, the room that looks out on the little canal and the French Embassy, the room in which Jessica wakes up. Every time I would get stuck on the story, I would fly back to Venice and let the stones dictate it to me.

The book was written in a kind of hallucinatory state, as was *Fanny*, a state in which I was searching back to past lives or searching ahead to future lives. It was a book that owed its inspiration to *Orlando* in the sense that I tried to abolish linear time and say that time is a fiction we invent to please ourselves. I don't believe time really exists, and I'm not saying that as hyperbole—I literally believe that times does not exist in the unconscious. I believe that Einsteinian physics proves that time is circular and that we can drop into it at any moment. We live at any moment in our lives in past, present, and future, remembering a childhood memory; whether it's biting into a madeleine or watching our own child having her first horseback lesson, we're constantly in our own childhoods simultaneously in the present and in the future. Every time I walk my daughter to school, I am remembering myself as a nine-year-old going to school, and I am experiencing her life and my life and simultaneously future lives.

I have tried as a novelist to mirror in *Serenissima* that doubleness and tripleness of vision with which we see the world. Virginia Woolf said it appalled her that contemporary novelists were not trying to show time as we actually experience it. They were sticking to the nineteenth-century way of writing novels. Back in the '20s and '30s she wondered why people were not breaking out of the parameters of that old novel form. She tried to in *Orlando* and in *The Waves* and, I think, succeeded very well. It's interesting that most British and American novelists have abandoned all experimentation with linear time, and I wonder why. Both Virginia Woolf and James Joyce were interested in such experimentation. Certainly it's a very rich field for exploration, and I think I may deal more and more with it in my new novel as well.

CA: You had art training and artists in your family as well as a background and interest in literature. Was the choice between painting and writing a difficult one to make?

JONG: Not at all. There were so many talented painters in my family that I just wanted out of the competition. I abandoned painting when I was eighteen or nineteen and turned to poetry. I had always written, but I had gone to art school throughout my teenage years and had attended the High School of Music and Art and was a pretty good painter. I think I retain a terrifically visual sense of the world. I think you can see the traces of the painting in my poetry.

CA: Yes. I've thought there was a connection between the painting and the imagery of the poetry.

JONG: I think it's there from *Fruits & Vegetables* to *Ordinary Miracles,* and it's certainly there in all my novels. My apprehension of the physical world is very visual. It's not rare, you know, for poets to be painters—E. E. Cummings, Alexander Pope, many poets have been painters throughout the history of English literature. In my case, I think the visual sense is very much there in my books. The *Fruits & Vegetables* poems certainly show it, and also the later poems.

I also think there's a frustrated travel writer in me longing to get out. You could almost make a compendium of travel writings out of my various novels. There are large sections in all five of them that deal with a sense of place: Wiltshire and Oxfordshire in *Fanny*, Connecticut in *Parachutes and Kisses*, Vienna and Heidelberg in *Fear of Flying*, Venice in *Serenissima*, California and New York in *How To Save Your Own Life*. There's a great visual connection there, and I see it looking back on my own work. The painter in me is not dead, but she took another form.

CA: In "A Note from the Author" in Ordinary Miracles, *you said that the poem is "as much a container of energy as the unsplit atom. Speaking the poem aloud should activate the energy in much the same way as splitting the atom activates nuclear force." Is speaking the poem aloud, hearing it as you make it, a central part of the writing?*

JONG: After I've written a first draft of a poem, I read it aloud to myself as one of my ways of reworking it. I like giving public readings of my work, and I've just recorded all of *Serenissima* on cassettes. When I read a poem aloud to an audience, I feel I'm re-experiencing the creation of the poem. I am very aural, and the sound of a poem is very important to me. There are whole sections of my prose works also that scan in iambic meter. If you read aloud, as I often do when I go to universities, the section of *Fanny* in which Fanny is describing her pregnancy, you will find that it could be set as blank verse. I'm very aware of the rhythms of the writing. I think in *Serenissima* I succeeded better than in any other book in mingling the poet and the novelist completely. The rhythms of the language are of great importance to me.

CA: Do you think of yourself as a poet and a novelist equally?

JONG: I think of myself as a poet who stumbled into the habit of writing novels. But they use different muscles, really.

CA: Fear of Flying *came out in 1973 and fell in perfectly with the burgeoning women's liberation movement. At the last count I saw—long ago—it had sold more than six million copies. Does it continue to attract new readers?*

JONG: Yes. Teenagers all over the world read me. That book sold six million in the U.S. in the paperback version, and about ten million total around the world. This was not just a book, but a phenomenon, a force. It sold 600,000 copies in Italy alone and about the same in Japan. And these are little book markets. It really was an extraordinary best-seller, and it's been a kind of curse for me. It made me a household name in much of the world—including China and Russia, where the books aren't published!—and also typecast me in a way that I've been trying to get free of ever since. I'm enormously grateful to it, and yet very eager to be seen as a woman of letters and not just Erica "Zipless" Jong.

CA: Karen FitzGerald, writing for Ms., *said, "As a member of a generation fed on the melodramatic and farfetched plots of blockbuster miniseries and evening soaps, I find this is all pretty tame stuff and I wonder what all the fuss was about back in 1973." How do you feel about* Fear of Flying *in that sense, looking back on it almost fifteen years later?*

JONG: I forced myself to read the first three chapters not long ago. (It's very hard for me to reread my books, because I rework them so endlessly and read them aloud to myself and edit and revise so much that when I'm done, I don't want to see the damn things again.) I think that judgment is wrong. Reading those few chapters again recently, I was struck by their incredible chutzpah, by the fearlessness of a woman absolutely putting down the contents of her brain. It was *not* the sex that was so fearless; it was her telling the truth about men. It's what Muriel Rukeyser said in one of her poems: if one woman were to tell the truth about her life, the world would split open. That's what was radical about *Fear of Flying*. It was a woman giving a no-holds-barred description of what was going on in her mind with relation to husbands, lovers, fathers, mothers; and it still is shocking, even to me. When I read it a few days ago, I thought, What a ballsy kid I was. How did I *dare*? One of the reasons, I think, is that I didn't realize how cruel the world was. I was very naive. I was fresh out of graduate school and I believed that the word could change the world. I believed that books were instruments of social change. I still do. And I wrote as if it was going to be overheard, seen through a keyhole. I try always to write that way. I try never to think of the marketplace or the audience, because I think the only value of being a writer is to tell the truth. I think we live in a society where there's a mass conspiracy for hypocrisy, where no one tells the truth. Politicians don't. People in corporations *can't*—they'll lose their jobs. Most people are bound to the system in one way or another, so they self-censor because they're afraid for their jobs, for their marriages, for their children. If writers don't tell the truth, no one does.

CA: As reported by Publishers Weekly, *you said at a National Book Critics panel discussion entitled "A Decade of Change in American Letters" that you saw a "greater emotional openness" and "more openness to writing by women." Maybe the word has helped to change the world. Don't you feel that* Fear of Flying *played a role in greater openness?*

JONG: I think it made a tremendous difference. I think it opened doors for women writers, and it opened doors for men writers. It opened doors for people writing movies. I believe we accept a level of intimacy in writing now that we never accepted before. It's still very hard to write honestly and gutsily about your life. It doesn't get easier. What happens is that you develop a new form; you have the woman's confessional novel. And it's possible to do it honestly or to do it in a canned way. The most important thing about a book is whether or not it has the gift of life. Does it seem real? Does it seem like life, not literature? What was good about *Fear of Flying*, I think, was that it seemed like life, not like a book. That was why all the criticism it got, which was primarily that it was confessional, was almost a compliment.

CA: Will we see Isadora White Wing again?

JONG: She's fighting her way back through my unconscious, wrestling me to the ground. She's creeping into the book I'm writing now, as a minor character. She will not be ignored. I want no part of her—she's trouble—but she's going to get in there somehow. She's very difficult for me, because every time I publish an Isadora book, I get holy hell from everybody. It's a real gauntlet I have to run. But she is determined to come back, and I think she is stronger than I am.

CA: Fanny *was a brave undertaking, using the form of the eighteenth-century picaresque novel. What were the toughest challenges?*

JONG: The question was, could I get the language? Could I create a language that wasn't Fielding or Swift or Smollett, that had its own sound and evoked the eighteenth century and the balance and antithesis of the sentences. Those writers were all trained on Latin, so their sentences were Latinate. We've abandoned that in the last two hundred and fifty years. We write Hemingway sentences now. I had to go back to that rhythm of language, of a generation trained on the classics,

on Horace and Catullus, and find a sentence that sounded eighteenth-century and yet was not a turn-off for the modern reader, that was fun to read and pulled you along. That was a terrific challenge. If I had done it in a dry-as-dust academic way, who would have read it but eighteenth-century scholars?

The form of the novel was clear. It was a picaresque, and an eighteenth-century picaresque has all its parameters given to you: the hero is an orphan who goes through the trials and tribulations of the Road of Life and tests herself or himself and winds up an heir to a great country house. The form is given. But I was both using the form and spoofing the form, and I was using the form in order to comment on the plight of women then and now. It was great fun. I never had more fun writing any book.

CA: Did the nonfiction book Witches *grow directly from your research for the witches segment in* Fanny?

JONG: Absolutely. I was left with all this fascination with that world, and I also had come, during the process of writing *Fanny*, to be a pagan. I had come to be a mother-goddess worshipper. And I had become a mother. I had become interested in matriarchal religion, and it had become absolutely clear to me that what was known as witchcraft in a pejorative sense was probably midwifery, white magic, herbal lore, and very healing pagan arts that were carried along in the countryside by women and passed from mother to daughter underneath a patriarchal culture. I still believe that—I believe it more than I did when I wrote *Witches*—and I wanted to write a book that would rehabilitate the witch. That book has had a kind of cult following. It's been reprinted, and it sells out every new printing. Every Halloween they repromote it. Although it was never promoted in a kind of best-seller fashion because it was published by an art-books publisher, and there were people who didn't even know it existed, it keeps on going. And I get very interesting mail about it, including letters from people who want to ban it as anti-Christian. Last year a school library in the Northeast took it off the shelves, and the Freedom to Read Committee of PEN took up the cause.

CA: You've become at least an unofficial spokesperson for women's concerns. How would you assess the progress of the current feminist movement, and what are your main worries for us?

JONG: I think we have an incomplete revolution. We have made things better for women in certain superficial ways, but we haven't changed the culture at its root. We have women editors-in-chief in publishing houses, we have women in movie studios—we have women in the communications industry with more clout than they ever had when I was in college or graduate school, or when I was starting out as a writer. We don't have women running Exxon, we don't have women enough in the Senate, and we are not near having a woman president in America. The real power is still the big bad boys. Even where women have entered the culture in middle management, and in upper management in the communications industry, we have women mimicking the male model in the boardroom—in other words, pretending that they don't have breasts and uteruses, dressing like men, behaving and acting on the male model. I think this is a mistake. What we need is women breast-feeding in the corporations. This will make people scream and say, "That's what we always suspected they wanted—breast-feeding in the boardroom!" But I mean it as a metaphor for feminizing our culture. For women to copy all that is the worst of the white male culture is no liberation. Interestingly enough, our culture is a de facto matriarchy and becoming more so, and one in which women and children are being penalized and impoverished by the white male culture. The nuclear family no longer exists in any great numbers. There are great numbers of single mothers raising children, and these mothers and children are sliding into poverty at an alarming rate. We have to go back to feminism and be more radical in the sense of looking at the roots of our culture and changing things there. I don't think that's being done.

CA: Don't you think many younger women are complacent about it all because they didn't have to fight for much of it?

JONG: They are complacent, but women get more radical with age. And until you're thirty-five and you have two babies and a husband who just left you for a twenty-five-year-old and is not paying child support, you're not truly radical *yet.* At that point, you get radical fast. That is going to happen to the Yuppie generation. They haven't hit it yet; they haven't hit the tough stuff.

CA: Now you're putting your art background to use in the novel in progress, according to the interview with Karen Burke. Can you talk about it?

JONG: The new novel is in a state of creative chaos at the moment. It is about an artist, the artist I might have become had I become an artist. But that's all I can say, because the more I talk about a book, the less I'm able to write it. Somehow, one defeats the other.

BIOGRAPHICAL/CRITICAL SOURCES:

BOOKS

Authors in the News, Volume 1, Gale, 1976.
Contemporary Literary Criticism, Gale, Volume 4, 1975, Volume 6, 1976, Volume 8, 1978, Volume 18, 1981.
Dictionary of Literary Biography, Gale, Volume 2: *American Novelists since World War II,* 1978, Volume 5: *American Poets since World War II,* 1980, Volume 28: *Twentieth-Century Jewish-American Fiction Writers,* 1984.
Jong, Erica, *Ordinary Miracles: New Poems,* New American Library, 1983.

PERIODICALS

Atlantic, December, 1973, April, 1977, November, 1981.
Books of the Times, November, 1980.
Chicago Tribune Book World, June 10, 1979, August 10, 1980, April 5, 1981, October 14, 1984.
Chicago Tribune Magazine, December 12, 1982.
Courier-Journal and Times (Louisville, Ky.), October 13, 1974.
Detroit Free Press, May 17, 1987.
Encounter, July, 1974, December, 1974.
Globe and Mail (Toronto), November 24, 1984, November 21, 1987.
Harpers Bazaar, August, 1984.
Hudson Review, summer, 1974.
Interview, July, 1987.
Listener, May 2, 1974.
Los Angeles Times, November 4, 1981, May 16, 1987, May 18, 1987.
Los Angeles Times Book Review, August 17, 1980, June 24, 1984, November 11, 1984.
Moons and Lion Tailes, Volume II, number 1, 1976.
Ms., November, 1980, July, 1981, July, 1986, June, 1987.

Nation, January 12, 1974.
National Review, May 24, 1974, April 29, 1977.
New Republic, February 2, 1974, September 20, 1980.
New Review, May, 1974.
New Statesman, April 19, 1974.
Newsweek, November 12, 1973, May 5, 1975, March 28, 1977, November 5, 1984.
New Yorker, December 17, 1973, April 4, 1977, October 13, 1980, November 19, 1984.
New York Review of Books, March 21, 1974, April 28, 1977, November 6, 1980.
New York Times, August 25, 1973, November 6, 1973, September 7, 1974, June 11, 1975, March 11, 1977, August 4, 1980, August 28, 1980, March 8, 1984, October 10, 1984.
New York Times Book Review, August 12, 1973, November 11, 1973, September 7, 1975, March 20, 1977, March 5, 1978, September 2, 1979, August 17, 1980, April 12, 1981, October 31, 1982, July 1, 1984, October 21, 1984, April 19, 1987, June 5, 1988.
North American Review, summer, 1975.
Ontario Review, fall/winter, 1975-76.
Parnassus: Poetry in Review, spring/summer, 1974.
People, May 25, 1987.
Poetry, March, 1974.
Publishers Weekly, February 14, 1977, January 4, 1985, February 22, 1985.
Saturday Review, December 18, 1971, April 30, 1977, August, 1980, November, 1981, December, 1981.
Time, March 14, 1977, June 22, 1987.
Times (London), November 2, 1984.
Times Literary Supplement, April 27, 1973, July 26, 1974, May 6, 1977, October 24, 1980, September 18-24, 1987.
Tribune Books (Chicago), April 5, 1987.
Virginia Quarterly Review, summer, 1979.
Washington Post Book World, December 19, 1971, July 6, 1975, March 20, 1977, August 17, 1980, October 21, 1984, April 19, 1987.
Washington Star-News, January 2, 1974.

—*Sketch by Kenneth R. Shepherd*
—*Interview by Jean W. Ross*

* * *

JUSTICE, Donald (Rodney) 1925-

PERSONAL: Born August 12, 1925, in Miami, Fla.; son of Vasco J. (a carpenter) and Mary Ethel (Cook) Justice; married Jean Catherine Ross, August 22, 1947; children: Nathaniel Ross. *Education:* University of Miami, Fla., B.A., 1945; University of North Carolina, M.A., 1947; attended Stanford University, 1947-48; State University of Iowa (now University of Iowa), Ph.D., 1954.

ADDRESSES: Home—2717 S.W. 5th Place, Gainesville, Fla. 32607.

CAREER: University of Missouri, Columbia, visiting assistant professor of English, 1955-56; Hamline University, St. Paul, Minn., assistant professor of English, 1956-57; State University of Iowa, Iowa City, visiting lecturer, 1957-59, assistant professor of English, 1959-63, associate professor of English, 1963-66; Syracuse University, Syracuse, N.Y., associate professor, 1966-67, professor of English, 1967-70; University of California—Irvine, visiting professor of English, 1970-71; University of Iowa, professor of English, 1971-82; University of Florida, professor of English, 1982—. Bain-Swiggett Lecturer, Princeton University, 1976; visiting professor, University of Virginia, Charlotte, 1980.

AWARDS, HONORS: University of Iowa, Rockefeller Foundation fellow in poetry, 1954-55; *The Summer Anniversaries* was the Lamont Poetry Selection of the Academy of American Poets, 1959; Inez Boulton Prize, *Poetry* Magazine, 1960; Ford Foundation fellowship in theater, 1964-65; National Council on the Arts grant, 1967-68, 1973, and 1979-80; National Book Award nomination, 1973, for *Departures;* Guggenheim fellowship in poetry, 1976-77; Pulitzer Prize in poetry, 1979, for *Selected Poems;* Harriet Monroe Award, University of Chicago, 1984; National Book Critics Circle Award nomination, 1988, for *The Sunset Maker: Poems/Stories/A Memoir.*

WRITINGS:

The Summer Anniversaries (poems), Wesleyan University Press, 1960.
(Editor) *The Collected Poems of Weldon Kees,* Stone Wall Press, 1960, revised edition, University of Nebraska Press, 1975.
(Assistant editor) *Midland,* Random, 1961.
A Local Storm (poems), Stone Wall Press, 1963.
(Contributor) Paul Engle, editor, *On Creative Writing,* Dutton, 1964.
(Editor with Alexander Aspel) *Contemporary French Poetry,* University of Michigan Press, 1965.
Night Light (poems), Wesleyan University Press, 1967.
(With Tom McAfee, Donald Drummond, and R. P. Dickey) *Four Poets,* Central College of Pella (Iowa), 1968.
(Editor) *Syracuse Poems,* Syracuse University Department of English, 1968.
Sixteen Poems, Stone Wall Press, 1970.
From a Notebook, Seamark Press, 1971.
(Translator) Guillevic, *L'Homme qui se ferme/The Man Closing Up,* Stone Wall Press, 1973.
Departures, Atheneum, 1973.
Selected Poems, Atheneum, 1979.
Platonic Scripts (prose), University of Michigan Press, 1984.
Tremayne, Windhover Press, 1984.
The Sunset Maker: Poems/Stories/A Memoir, Atheneum, 1987.
The Death of Lincoln (libretto), A. Thomas Taylor, 1988.

Works represented in numerous anthologies, including *New Poets of England and America,* Conrad Aiken's *Twentieth Century American Poetry,* A. J. Poulin's *Contemporary American Poetry,* Robert Richman's *The Direction of Poetry,* Donald Hall's *Contemporary American Poetry* and *The Structure of Verse.* Contributor to literary journals such as *Poetry, Antaeus, New Yorker, The New Criterion,* and other magazines.

WORK IN PROGRESS: An edition of *G. M. Hopkins* for the Essential Poets Series of Ecco Press.

SIDELIGHTS: "Those in a position to appreciate craft" in poetry have long admired Donald Justice, Cathrael Kazin says in the *Dictionary of Literary Biography Yearbook 1983.* "His first book, *The Summer Anniversaries,* was the Lamont Poetry Selection for 1959; *Departures* . . . was nominated for the 1973 National Book Award"; and furthermore, she reports, since his *Selected Poems* won the Pulitzer Prize in 1979, "Justice has come to be recognized not only as one of America's most elegant and distinctive contemporary poets but also as one of its most significant." His credentials are a relatively small number of poems that focus on the theme of loss and reflect a remarkable mastery of prosody, or poetic technique.

Even so, technical prowess "never calls attention to itself in Justice's understated work," claims *Southern Review* contributor Dana Gioia. The poet's presence is implied by his control of form, say reviewers, but otherwise Justice uses the poems to efface the self rather than to vaunt it. Because one way of diminishing the self is to relax its control over form, Justice has sometimes used chance methods (such as shuffling word cards together) to compose poems. Thus, writes Gioia, "Justice has published very little, but he has also distilled a decade of writing and experimentation in each new volume."

The Summer Anniversaries established Justice's reputation for attention to craft. The book, relates Greg Simon in the *American Poetry Review,* "consists of flawless poems, moving as inexorably as glaciers toward beautiful comprehension and immersion in reality." Writing in the *Washington Post Book World,* Doug Lang suggests, "Justice's concern for form is really a concern with experience" that seeks to be conveyed in "an appropriate arrangement of words." In his essay on Justice in *Contemporary American Poetry,* A. J. Poulin calls Justice "a master of what might be called sparse elegance. . . . [His] poems are moving because of his consummate linguistic, tonal, and formal exactitude." But less attention to form may have improved the poems in this first book, some readers suggest; *New York Times Book Review* contributor Charles Molesworth explains, "What some might see as proper formality might strike others as unnecessary stiffness." Looking back on these poems himself in a poem from his next book, *Night Light,* Justice reflects, "How fashionably sad those early poems are! / On their clipped lawns and hedges the snows fall."

As one would expect after this self-criticism, *Night Light* presents poems that "are not so tame, not so manicured as those in *The Summer Anniversaries,*" notes Joel O. Conarroe in a *Shenandoah* review. But reviewers hear the same tone in both books, and conclude that understatement is another Justice hallmark. According to Molesworth, for instance, poems "of small scale dooms and dim light" in the first book are followed by verses that depict a "twilight perspective verging on total darkness" in the second. For Alan Hollinghurst of the *New Statesman,* the poems seem to suffer from a "lack of color and surprise," or seem haunted "by a weary passivity, a lack of vitality that is unsupported by fastidious formal elegance." Others see the poetry's muted tones in a more favorable light. Offers Molesworth, "If you are the sort of reader who occasionally suspects too much of poetry's grandeur is 'prerecorded,' then the whisper of Donald Justice may be music to your ears."

Conarroe relates Justice's tone to his subject matter: "Justice brings a controlled, urbane intensity to his Chekovian descriptions of loss and of the unlived life, of the solitary, empty 'sad' world of those who receive no mail, have no urgent hungers—who, in short, lead their lives but do not own them." As a *Times Literary Supplement* reviewer phrases it, "People who fascinate [Justice] are elegiacally evoked by a handful of quiet images, and made fascinating to us. The poet conveys these remarkably suggestive images through a select troupe of words varied and repeated in a sustained, low-keyed music." The same reviewer defends the tone of a later book, *Departures:* "Poems draw our attention to the minute effects of language. In them we discover connexions of syntax to meaning that invite a second and third review. Truth, wisdom, drama become deeper, stronger, more genuine than ordinary speech can make them. . . . [*Departures*] reflects a familiarity with such standards and an acceptance of them."

Many critics note that if Justice sustains his mastery of craft from book to book, in *Departures* he achieves a command of poetic technique that surpasses nearly all earlier works. Remaining unsurpassed, feels Simon, is "the core of the book[,] . . . the absolutely indispensable *Sixteen Poems* that Justice published in a limited edition in 1970." Of these and the others in *Departures,* Simon comments: "The new Justice poem is no longer a set piece or still life, forced into shape, but vigorous and rhythmical composition, prosody at the limit of its kinetic potential. This remarkable new intention in Justice's work accounts for the fact that the forms of the best poems in *Departures* are invisible architecture. . . . It is intoxicating to see Justice now unfettered by the forms that circumscribed and dictated the action in his early poems; and to see him working with sources that are not only naturally energetic and new, but demanding in conception and daring in stance."

In the later books, for example, Justice proves himself "equally as willing to give a new twist to an old form . . . as he is to find a new form to fit the materials at hand," Lang observes. For Justice, this involves experimenting with deliberate "mistranslations" of poems in other languages, or with methods of composition that combine words at random until they suggest a statement or a form. These methods help the poet to focus more on his materials than on his conscious control over them. Paul Ramsey, writing in the *Sewanee Review,* comments that Justice's poems composed in this way are prone "to fragmentation, to deconstructive poetics, to wandered and incompleted narrative. Yet his poetic integrity . . . bears Justice safely by such swamps and murmured gleams. His fragments sound completed. . . . His gift for order is an irresistible gift."

Lang relates that "some of the forms [Justice] finds are very direct and simple," while others are more complex, coming from the poet's sensitivity to patterns of sound. "Justice gives each poem structure according to its own weight and he shows great versatility in the process." Thomas Swiss remarks in *Modern Poetry Studies* that, as a result, "the reader feels the poet performing with a great sense of confidence, clearing a path for himself between the radical and the conservative." These claims are supported by the poem "Counting the Mad," says Robert Peters in the *American Book Review.* It is, he relates, "an echoing of one of the most famous of all children's poems, 'This little pig went to market.' But there are startling differences. . . . These people never get out to go to market. What the mad retain is the power to cry NO NO NO NO (all the way home) against their keepers' brutalizations and the horrors rampant within their own psyches. This is a stunning use of a simple form for complex purposes."

Gioia suggests that no other American poet has perfected as many poetic styles. "At times," he says, ". . . *Selected Poems* reads almost like an anthology of the possibilities of contemporary poetry. There are sestinas, villanelles and ballads rubbing shoulders with aleatory poems [composed using chance methods], surreal odes, and . . . free verse. . . . A new technique is often developed, mastered, and exhausted in one unprecedented and unrepeatable poem." During the selection process credited in the title, Justice rewrote some poems and gave them a new sequence to make this "nearly perfect volume," writes Gioia, who finds "almost no bad poems . . . and quite a few perfect ones" in the book. In a *Parnassus* review, Vernon Young concurs, "I doubt if there are six poems in [*Selected Poems*] which could be claimed for the public sensibility. But Justice has written a dozen lyrics I'd call virtually incomparable."

The little autobiography to be found in Justice's oeuvre must be gleaned despite the poet's refusal to let his personality dominate his writing. "The principles of composition . . . really occupy him, not his own life," concludes *Yale Review* contributor Richard Wertime after reading the essays in *Platonic Scripts.* Swiss makes a similar observation, maintaining that Justice brings images of mirrors into the poems not, as some reviewers have seen it, to indulge a narcissistic impulse, but rather to point out how language and art can render, at best, only distorted images of the self. Citing the series of unanswered questions in the poem "Fragment: To a Mirror," Simon comments, "We confront the reticence of Justice, the obvious scarcity of lies . . . , the fact that Justice has produced fewer lines and fewer poems in twenty years than others . . . are able to publish in two. But reticence is an attitude toward writing that Justice has assumed with malice of forethought."

Particularly in "Poem," Swiss relates, "Justice speaks about the effacement of self" with an "agnostic and stoic" attitude: "You have begun to vanish. And it does not matter. / The poem will go on without you." In other poems, the speaker reports himself to authorities as a missing person, or views his own corpse from a distance. Thus, observes Jerome McGann in *Poetry* magazine, "His interior poems are not confessions. . . . Justice is too busy attending to the needs of his audience and his subjects ever to get preoccupied with himself." He rarely wanders from an abstract perspective, "and the result is a series of splendid labyrinths" and still points, devoid of comforting self-deceptions, McGann continues. "Given the air of remoteness so often hovering around them," notes Anthony Ostroff in the *Western Humanities Review,* "these poems bring us into a peculiarly intimate relationship with themselves." In the *New American Review,* Richard Howard also muses on the paradoxical strength Justice achieves by exercising restraint: "Here is a poet who perpetuates his powers by taking leave of them, 'patient,' as he says, 'and, if anything, somewhat reluctant to continue.'"

That Justice does continue to write is due to his belief that art is a hedge against death and loss. In his essay "Meters and Memory," reprinted in *Platonic Scripts,* he explains how writing about loss enables him to endure it: "To remember an event is almost to begin to control it, as well as to approach an understanding of it; incapable of recurring now, it is only to be contemplated rather than acted on or reacted to. . . . The terror or beauty or, for that matter, the plain ordinariness of the original event, being transformed, is fixed and thereby made more tolerable. That the event can recur only in its new context, the context of art, sheers it of some risks, the chief of which may anyhow have been its transitory character." Submitting his materials to metrical structures is part of this process: "The meters . . . may be . . . some psychological compulsion, a sort of counting on the fingers or stepping on cracks, magic to keep an unpredictable world under control." Furthermore, as Peters notes, because "art endures while life is brief," Justice's elegies mitigate the total loss of death. Observes Kazin, "In the guise of lamenting a loss, [the poems] perform acts of preservation"; resurrected by memory and ensconced in art, the lost friends of childhood, suicides, and other casualties gain an extended life. Because Justice succeeds, says Edward Hirsch in the *New York Times Book Review,* because "he counters our inevitable human losses with an unforgettable and permanent music," Justice, who is "the resident genius of nostalgia in the ever-expanding house of American poetry," deserves to be called "an elegiac poet of the first order."

Piano lessons Justice enjoyed as a child provide the central motif of *The Sunset Maker: Poems/Stories/A Memoir*, which seems like a "complex piece of music" dedicated to the working out of a single theme, "the pain and beauty of memory and loss," as Frances Ruhlen McConnel of the *Los Angeles Times* sees it. "Justice shows you how closely related to the pleasures of music are the pleasures of poetry" in its elegies and memoirs, some written in verse, some in prose. These come together most powerfully, she feels, in the book's final poem, which calls up from the past the six notes Justice can recall of a musical piece for cello and piano. These notes—because they are here written down—constitute the immortality of the musician who had composed the piece, Justice suggests. "On the whole," Bruce Bawer comments in the *Washington Post Book World*, "*The Sunset Maker* is a deeply affecting volume—a beautiful, powerful meditation by a modern master upon the themes of aging, lost innocence, and the unalterable, terrifying pastness of the past."

Of Justice's works as a whole, Gioia reflects, "There are no long poems in his canon, no epics, no dramas, none of those ambitious single poems on which most contemporary reputations are founded." Instead, says Poulin, Justice has eloquently chronicled "the depth of loneliness, the isolation, and the spiritual desolation at the heart of the twentieth century experience." Due to his penchant for "Mordancies of the Armchair," as Justice calls them in a later poem, the Pulitzer Prize-winner has produced, says Howard, "some of the most assured, elegant and heartbreaking . . . verse in our literature so far." To a *Times Literary Supplement* reviewer, this achievement seems more remarkable because Justice works with themes that are timeless: "If the large themes of love, heroism and death are to be handled, only a profoundly gifted poet will discover images that are not second-hand. Mr. Justice has this power." Howard observes, "There is a deep committed reverence about the way Justice celebrates . . . madness, love, old age, death. . . . But given such a burden altogether, and such a resonance, . . . the wonder is not that Donald Justice has written [so few poems] . . . , but that we have an elegant monument of fifty such poems [at least] to testify to his doomed transactions with life."

More importantly, perhaps the key to Justice's distinction as poet and critic is his love for "the cooler technical brilliancies" and "mysterious precisions" of classical metrics, as he calls them in *Platonic Scripts*. Proposing "that the anticlassical movement in current poetry is dead," to cite Wertime's paraphrase, Justice ventures: "A tradition could be put back together starting with not much more than this. Not forgetting rhythm; not forgetting truth."

A collection of Justice's manuscripts is housed at the University of Delaware Library in Dover, Delaware.

AVOCATIONAL INTERESTS: Composition in music, drawing and painting.

CA INTERVIEW

CA interviewed Donald Justice by telephone on September 8, 1987, at his home in Gainesville, Florida.

CA: You studied music seriously before you decided on writing as a life's work: piano, clarinet, and composition.

JUSTICE: Yes. Composition was what I was really most interested in.

CA: Did you have to make a definite decision, a hard choice, between music and writing as a life's work?

JUSTICE: It felt that way at a certain moment, when I was about eighteen. It seemed fairly dramatic to me at the time. I decided—and I'm sure I was right—that I didn't have enough specific musical talent to go on with it. That was my own decision. I pondered it very seriously for most of one summer and decided that I was never going to be able to compose as well as I wanted to.

CA: In some of your poems you've experimented with adapting musical forms to poetry. Are there more general ways in which you feel the study of music has lent something to the writing?

JUSTICE: I don't know of any, no. I'm not sure the study of music ever would connect with writing directly. A *love* of music might. I have a kind of general theory that anybody with a love of one art and some practice in it may have a natural inclination to love and practice one of the other arts. In that way, I think, the arts may all be connected by way of the sensibility. But beyond that I don't think there is anything much in the association.

CA: Reviewing Night Light *for the* Saturday Review, *Lewis Turco said, "Mr. Justice writes a spare line, and he writes by the line, painstakingly." Would you talk about the process of writing a poem, how it works for you?*

JUSTICE: I suppose I must always have written by the word or the phrase or the line: small piece by small piece. That may be one of the reasons I've written slowly. To talk about the process of writing in general terms comes hard for me, though.

CA: Does a poem usually come to you as a whole idea, or must you piece it out?

JUSTICE: Mostly I have to piece it out, little by little; but at some point, fairly early, I'm usually able to define for myself what the overall form is likely to turn out to be. In the last few years, among other things, I've written several sonnets, or near-sonnets—not necessarily having a sonnet in mind from the beginning. After a few lines I might think, Well, this begins to look as if it might turn out to be a sonnet, if I let it. In a couple of cases I intended to write a sonnet and found that my idea was not taking that shape, so I backed off and let it develop differently. It almost always has been, for me, a question of feeling out where I wanted to go, what sort of formal treatment seemed right for each poem.

CA: Do you feel that the formal bounds in poetry are somehow freeing for the writer?

JUSTICE: They are for me at times. I don't think it's true for many people, but for some writers I think it always has been so. It depends on attitude, on the writer's experience and temperament. Some of us have temperaments suited to writing in one form or another, and some don't seem to have either the temperament or the conviction or the ability. For me certain forms are invigorating and enlivening and, to some degree, liberating.

CA: At one period you wrote some "chance" poems involving a method of writing words on cards, which you would then shuffle and deal to yourself. My description is greatly oversimplified, obviously. Do you feel that this experimentation made any kind of general change in your writing or your approach to writing?

JUSTICE: Well, I think the "chance" method was, in its way, a formal approach, too. It did of course lead to changes in the poems I attempted to write using those "play" methods, but beyond that, I wouldn't like to guess. I thought for a while that it had allowed me to see images a little differently, but beyond that, who knows?

CA: You've been asked a lot in earlier interviews about the business of taking the self out of poetry, and you've spoken about not wanting to manipulate the reader emotionally. But there is a great deal of nostalgia in your poems, and in your stories too. Does the experience begin to get de-emotionalized for you before you start putting it on paper?

JUSTICE: Yes, somewhat. And while I'm writing, it seems to get cooled down a little more. I believe strongly in the power of what used to be called aesthetic distance. I want to believe that there is always a certain distance between me and what I'm writing about, and that for the reader, likewise, there exists a similar distance.

CA: What happens to a memory so that it inspires a piece of writing? Does it resurface unbidden at just the right time?

JUSTICE: Sometimes. In the last five or ten years I have written a great deal about and from memory, and more than once I have consciously sought out something from memory to dwell on, perhaps to write about. Sometimes a memory has simply risen to the surface unbidden and taken hold. That's the more common case. I'd remember a bit of something perhaps and gradually a whole host of other details would gather about the thing remembered. I don't think this sort of experience is in itself in any way extraordinary.

CA: Is the passage of time usually a necessary element in shaping the experience into writing?

JUSTICE: For me it always has been, partly because my ways are slow, but partly, too, because the passage of time colors and does a sort of honor to the old experience, allows it to be understood. That's what I would like to believe, anyhow.

CA: I know you write far more poems than stories, but I wonder if it's ever unclear at the beginning whether an idea will become a poem or a story?

JUSTICE: It hasn't ever been for me, but in my new book, *The Sunset Maker*, I did turn one of the two stories into a poem, just to see if it could really be done; done well, that is. The title poem is a version in verse of a short story, also included in the book, so that others may see and judge for themselves, you might say.

CA: What do you hope readers will find in your work—if you think in such terms at all when you're writing?

JUSTICE: I don't think about it much—I don't put the question that way, anyhow. Once asked the question, I would probably have to answer something large and grand like *the truth.*

CA: Did the 1980 Pulitzer Prize for Selected Poems *bring new kinds of readers?*

JUSTICE: Let me be a little ironical. Possibly more of my colleagues looked at my work then because of the prize. Writers in universities often feel, and rightly, that their colleagues have no interest at all in what they're writing, and a prize like the Pulitzer may grab the attention of a few.

CA: I wonder how many people pick up poetry to read just because they like it. But it does seem that a Pulitzer Prize would attract a few, at least.

JUSTICE: Maybe, but I think the number would rarely be very large. There are three ways that poets attract readers in our culture. One is by public readings. Another is by teaching, in a school regularly or in short stints in workshops and conferences. The third is through anthologies. Anthologies strike me as absolutely crucial. Otherwise I think our readers are likely to remain sparse and scattered.

CA: Do you do readings?

JUSTICE: I do a few, not nearly as many as some do; it would take too much out of me. But I do six or eight readings a year.

CA: You have been both a student and a teacher at the Iowa Writers' Workshop. How do you feel now about the workshop or writing school? Is it the best way for most aspiring writers to work toward a career?

JUSTICE: Fifteen years ago I could have answered that more positively, but now I don't know. Things have changed as I've been around writing programs, and I'm less sanguine now about what goes on in them than I once was. When there were not many workshops, not many writing programs, and not many poets involved in them, the chances were much better that something good might come of it all. I'm afraid I believe now that the whole thing has become something like an industry or factory, just as the opponents of writing programs *always* claimed, mistakenly, for workshops were really not always like what they have now evolved into. Frankly, I'm discouraged.

CA: Do you see promising writers among the students you teach?

JUSTICE: Oh yes. I've had some great students.

CA: Do they bring with them, generally, a good strong background in literature? Have they read? Or is there ever a budding writer who is better off for not *having read the work of other writers?*

JUSTICE: I've never seen a student who was better off for not having read; no exceptions. Either young writers have read a lot or they get started reading. In my experience, for the ones who are good or who are on their way, reading becomes an absolutely essential part of developing the personal talent. Off and on all through my life I've heard young writers say, "I don't dare read that stuff. It might influence me." And I think, You should be so lucky. The good young writer seeks out what is going to help him or her in the work of others and is passionately enthusiastic about it.

CA: How do you feel about American poetry being written today? Is it in a healthy state?

JUSTICE: I don't think so, not at all. But I'd rather not name names! I think a lot of American poetry now is mindless and formless, endless—terribly longwinded. I add that those are emphatically not virtues, for there are those who seem to believe otherwise. By form, by the way, I don't mean just the traditional forms; I mean *any* sense of form at all.

CA: You've been interested in writing plays from time to time.

JUSTICE: And I continue to be, but I have no luck at it. My plays are not good. I wish I could write plays. I have one about half done now that I wish I could finish, but I'm not sure I ever will.

CA: Your wife also writes, under the name Jean Ross. Do the two of you ever act as sounding boards for each other, or as editors?

JUSTICE: Sometimes she will allow me to try out something new on her, but she doesn't show me what she's written. I have to wait until it's published, and then I get to see it, like anybody else.

CA: Is your traveling usually connected with your writing?

JUSTICE: Not really. Normally the trips I take have to do with a short teaching job or a reading.

CA: In an interview in the Ohio Review, *you said of the stages of your work, ''There's a way in which, since it's mine, I like it all.'' Twelve years later, can you say what you're happiest about in the work?*

JUSTICE: There's a handful of poems over the years that I think is better than the rest. I especially like the ones in my new book. Of course, most people do tend to like their most recent work best, whether they're right about that or not. But, yes, it's still true that most of what I've published I'm fond of in one way or other, just as I said back then.

CA: Is there anything new you would wish for in your writing—besides a play?

JUSTICE: I *would* like to finish a good play. And I'd like to write some more stories. At the moment I feel that I've written all the poems I want to write for a while; I'm thinking of other things, other forms. What I would like is for everyone who reads poetry with interest and affection to read my work. Well, of course, I am always astonished when anyone who professes to like poetry hasn't read my work, but of course it happens all the time. Probably all poets, even the ones who are terribly popular—within the limits of popularity in poetry—wish they had more sympathetic readers; or simply *more* readers. There's a sort of network of poets in this country, but even so we'd never make up more than a small town even if, god forbid, we could all be brought together somehow; and sometimes you feel pretty isolated, as if you were writing for yourself and a very small band of others. There are worse ways to be left feeling, of course.

BIOGRAPHICAL/CRITICAL SOURCES:

BOOKS

Contemporary Literary Criticism, Gale, Volume 6, 1976, Volume 19, 1981.

Dictionary of Literary Biography Yearbook 1983, Gale, 1984.
Fussell, Paul, *Poetic Meter and Poetic Form*, Random House, 1965, revised edition, 1979.
Howard, Richard, *Alone with America*, Atheneum, 1969, revised edition, 1980.
Justice, Donald, *The Summer Anniversaries*, Wesleyan University Press, 1960.
Justice, Donald, *Night Light*, Wesleyan University Press, 1967.
Justice, Donald, *Departures*, Atheneum, 1973.
Justice, Donald, *Selected Poems*, Atheneum, 1979.
Justice, Donald, *Platonic Scripts*, University of Michigan Press, 1984.
Justice, Donald, *The Sunset Maker: Poems/Stories/A Memoir*, Atheneum, 1987.
Poulin, A. J., editor, *Contemporary American Poetry*, 4th edition, Houghton, 1985.
Rubin, Louis D., *The History of Southern Literature*, Louisiana State University Press, 1985.

PERIODICALS

American Book Review, January, 1982.
American Poetry Review, Volume 5, number 2, March/April, 1976.
Antaeus, spring/summer, 1982.
Antioch Review, winter, 1988.
Boston Review, June, 1987.
Hudson Review, Volume 27, number 1, spring, 1974.
Iowa Review, spring/summer, 1980.
Library Journal, February 1, 1967.
Los Angeles Times, August 12, 1987.
Missouri Review, fall, 1980.
Modern Language Studies, Volume 9, number 1, winter, 1978-79.
Modern Poetry Studies, Volume 10, number 1, spring, 1980.
New England Review and Breadloaf Quarterly, winter, 1984.
New Statesman, August 22, 1980.
New York Herald Tribune Books, September 4, 1960.
New York Review of Books, October 16, 1975.
New York Times Book Review, February 19, 1961, March 9, 1980, August 23, 1987.
North American Review, spring, 1974.
Ohio Review, spring, 1975.
Parnassus, fall/winter, 1979.
Partisan Review, Volume 47, number 4, 1980.
Perspective, spring, 1962.
Poetry, October, 1974.
Prairie Schooner, Volume 47, 1973.
Saturday Review, October 14, 1967.
Sewanee Review, spring, 1974, summer, 1980, fall, 1980.
Shenandoah, summer, 1967.
Southern Review, summer, 1981.
Southwest Review, spring, 1980.
Times Literary Supplement, May 18, 1967, March 29, 1974, April 16, 1976, May 30, 1980, April 15-21, 1988.
Tribune Books (Chicago), June 21, 1987.
Washington Post Book World, February 10, 1980, January 3, 1988.
Western Humanities Review, summer, 1974.
Yale Review, June, 1960, summer, 1985, spring, 1988.

—*Sketch by Marilyn K. Basel*

—*Interview by Jean W. Ross*

K

KELSEY, Morton T(rippe) 1917-

PERSONAL: Born January 12, 1917, in Depue, Ill.; son of Weston Maynard and Myra Etta (Trippe) Kelsey; married Barbara Jones, February 11, 1944; children: Myra Louise (Mrs. Stephen Allan Johnson), Morton Trippe, Jr., John Colburn. *Education:* Washington and Lee University, B.A. (summa cum laude), 1938; Episcopal Theological Seminary, B.D., 1943; additional study at Princeton University, 1939, Pomona College, 1956, and C. G. Jung Institute, Zurich, Switzerland, 1958.

ADDRESSES: *Office*—P.O. Box 617, Gualala, Calif. 95445.

CAREER: Episcopal clergyman. Emmanuel Church, East Syracuse, N.Y., priest-in-charge, 1943-46; Trinity Cathedral, Phoenix, Ariz., assistant to dean, 1946-49, canon, 1949-50; St. Luke's Episcopal Church, Monrovia, Calif., rector, 1950-70; University of Notre Dame, Notre Dame, Ind., professor of theology, 1969-78, professor emeritus, 1978—. Extension lecturer at University of California, Los Angeles, 1963, 1964; adjunct professor at San Francisco Theological Seminary, San Anselmo, Calif., 1982. Marriage, family, and child counselor.

WRITINGS:

Tongue Speaking: An Experiment in Spiritual Experience, foreword by Upton Sinclair, Doubleday, 1964.
Dreams: The Dark Speech of the Spirit, Doubleday, 1968.
Encounter with God, Bethany Fellowship, 1972.
Healing and Christianity, Harper, 1973.
Myth, History, and Faith, Paulist/Newman, 1974.
God, Dreams, and Revelation, Augsburg, 1974.
The Christian and the Supernatural, Augsburg, 1976.
The Other Side of Silence, Paulist Press, 1977.
Can Christians Be Educated?, Paulist Press, 1977.
The Cross, Paulist Press, 1977.
Discernment, Paulist Press, 1978.
Dreams: A Way to Listen to God, Paulist Press, 1978.
The Age of Miracles, Ave Maria Press, 1979.
Adventure Inward, Augsburg, 1980.
Reaching for the Real, Dove, 1981.
Caring, Paulist Press, 1981.
Prophetic Ministry, Paulist Press, 1982.
Companions on the Inner Way, Crossroads, 1982.
Christo-Psychology, Augsburg, 1984.
Resurrection, Paulist Press, 1985.

Christianity as Psychology, Augsburg, 1986.
(With Barbara Kelsey) *Sacrament of Sexuality*, Amity House, 1986.

Contributor to religious journals.

WORK IN PROGRESS: *The Fulfilled Life.*

* * *

KEMERER, Frank R(obert) 1940-

PERSONAL: Born October 22, 1940, in Minneapolis, Minn.; son of Robert W. (a business executive) and Marion (Nordin) Kemerer; married Barbara Kellner, May 7, 1971; children: Ann Elizabeth, Jennifer Lynn. *Education:* Stanford University, A.B. (history) and A.B. (political science), both 1963, M.A., 1968, Ph.D., 1975; University of Minnesota Law School, graduate study, 1963-64. *Politics:* Democrat.

ADDRESSES: *Home*—27 Timbergreen, Denton, Tex. 76205. *Office*—College of Education, North Texas State University, Denton, Tex. 76203.

CAREER: Blake School, Minneapolis, Minn., teacher of history, speech, and journalism, and counselor, 1964-67, 1968-69; Stanford University, Stanford, Calif., admissions officer, 1967-68; Latin School of Chicago, Chicago, Ill., instructor and assistant headmaster, director of studies and counseling, 1969-72; Lick-Wilmerding School, San Francisco, Calif., instructor and director, 1973-75; Stanford University, senior research associate, 1973-75; State University of New York College at Geneseo, College of Arts and Science, lecturer in political science, assistant to president, and director of college enrollment management, 1975-78; North Texas State University, Denton, professor of education law and administration, 1978—. Guest lecturer at colleges and universities, including State University of New York College at Brockport, Indiana University of Pennsylvania, Harvard University, and Stanford University; speaker at numerous national and regional conferences; chairman of various committees at North Texas State University, 1980—. Member of State University of New York negotiations advisory committee, 1975-78; consultant on education and management at universities.

MEMBER: National Organization on Legal Problems of Education, American Association of University Administrators (member of board of directors, 1981-82), Phi Kappa Delta, Kappa Delta Pi.

AWARDS, HONORS: Excellence in Governmental/Legislature Relations Award, State University of New York College and University Relations Council, 1976.

WRITINGS:

(With J. Victor Baldridge) *Unions on Campus: A National Study of the Consequences of Faculty Bargaining,* Jossey-Bass, 1975.
Understanding Faculty Unions and Collective Bargaining (monograph), National Association of Independent Schools, 1976.
(Contributor) Baldridge and Gary Lee Riley, *Governing Academic Organizations: New Issues, New Perspectives,* McCutchan, 1977.
(With Ronald P. Satryb) *Facing Financial Exigency: Strategies for Educational Administrators,* Lexington Books, 1978.
(With Kenneth L. Deutsch) *Constitutional Rights and Student Life,* with textbook supplement and instructor's manual, West Publishing, 1979.
(With Baldridge) *Assessing the Impact of Faculty Collective Bargaining,* American Association for Higher Education, 1981.
Texas Teachers' Guide to School Law, University of Texas Press, 1982.
(With Baldridge and Kenneth C. Green) *The Enrollment Crisis: Factors, Actors, and Impact,* American Association for Higher Eduction, 1982.
(With Baldridge and Green) *Strategies for Effective Enrollment Management,* American Association of State Colleges and Universities, 1982.
The Educator's Guide to Texas School Law, University of Texas Press, 1986.
A Judge Named Justice: A Biography of William Wayne Justice, University of Texas Press, in press.

Also author of research reports and discussion papers. Contributor to journals, including *Journal of Higher Education, Educational Forum, Independent School,* and *Journal of Law and Education.*

SIDELIGHTS: Frank R. Kemperer writes that he is "concerned about the lack of knowledge by administrators about the law as it applies to the world of education. I hope through research, teaching, and writing to promote a better understanding of this subject and a more rational approach in general to assisting professionals conduct educational activities."

*   *   *

KENNEDY, Adrienne (Lita) 1931-

PERSONAL: Born September 13, 1931, in Pittsburgh, Pa.; daughter of Cornell Wallace and Etta (Haugabook) Hawkins; married Joseph C. Kennedy, May 15, 1953; children: Joseph C., Adam. *Education:* Ohio State University, B.A.,1952; graduate study at Columbia University, 1954-56; also studied at New School for Social Research, American Theatre Wing, Circle in the Square Theatre School, and Edward Albee's workshop.

ADDRESSES: Office—Department of Afro-American Studies, Princeton University, Princeton, N.J. 08544. *Agent*—Bridget Aschenberg, 40 West 57th St., New York, N.Y. 10019.

CAREER: Playwright. Lecturer, Yale University, 1972-74, Princeton University, 1977; visiting associate professor, Brown University, 1979-80. International Theatre Institute representative, Budapest, 1978. Member of playwriting unit, Actors Studio, New York, N.Y. 1962-65.

MEMBER: PEN (member of board of directors, 1976-77).

AWARDS, HONORS: Obie Award from *Village Voice,* 1964, for "Funnyhouse of a Negro"; Guggenheim memorial fellowship, 1967; Rockefeller grants, 1967-69, 1974, 1976; National Endowment for the Arts grant, 1973; CBS fellow, School of Drama, 1973; Creative Artists Public Service grant, 1974; Yale fellow, 1974-75; Stanley award for play writing; New England Theatre Conference grant.

WRITINGS:

People Who Led to My Plays (memoir), Knopf, 1987.

PLAYS

Funnyhouse of a Negro (one-act; first produced Off-Broadway at Circle in the Square Theatre, 1962), Samuel French, 1969.
"The Owl Answers" (one-act; also see below), first produced in Westport, Conn., at White Barn Theatre, 1963, produced Off-Broadway at Public Theatre, January 12, 1969.
"A Lesson in a Dead Language" (also see below), first produced in 1964.
"A Rat's Mass" (also see below), first produced in Boston, Mass., by the Theatre Company, April, 1966, produced Off-Broadway at La Mama Experimental Theatre Club, November, 1969.
"A Beast's Story" (one-act; also see below), first produced in 1966, produced Off-Broadway at Public Theatre, January 12, 1969.
(With John Lennon and Victor Spinetti) *The Lennon Play: In His Own Write* (adapted from Lennon's books *In His Own Write* and *A Spaniard in the Works;* first produced in London by National Theatre, 1967; produced in Albany, N.Y., at Arena Summer Theatre, August, 1969), Simon & Schuster, 1969.
"Sun: A Poem for Malcolm X Inspired by His Murder" (also see below), first produced on the West End, London, at Royal Court Theatre, 1968, produced in New York at La Mama Experimental Theatre Club, 1970.
Cities in Bezique (contains "The Owl Answers" and "A Beast Story"; first produced in New York at Shakespeare Festival, 1969), Samuel French, 1969.
"Boats," first produced in Los Angeles at the Forum, 1969.
"An Evening With Dead Essex," first produced in New York by American Place Theatre Workshop, 1973.
"A Movie Star Has to Star in Black and White" (also see below), first produced in New York by Public Theatre Workshop, 1976.
"A Lancashire Lad" (for children), first produced in Albany, N.Y., at Governor Nelson A. Rockefeller Empire State Plaza Performing Arts Center, May, 1980.
"Orestes and Electra," first produced in New York at Julliard School of Music, 1980.
"Black Children's Day," first produced in Providence, R.I., at Brown University, November, 1980.
"Solo Voyages" (contains excerpts from "The Owl Answers," "A Rat's Mass," and "A Movie Star Has to Star in Black and White"), first produced in New York at Interart Center, 1985.

CONTRIBUTOR

William M. Hoffman, editor, *New American Plays,* Hill & Wang, 1968.

Edward Parone, editor, *Collision Course* (includes "A Lesson in a Dead Language"), Random House, 1968.

William Couch, Jr., editor, *New Black Playwrights* (includes "A Rat's Mass"), Louisiana State University Press, 1968.

Rochelle Owens, editor, *Spontaneous Combustion* (includes "Sun: A Poem for Malcolm X Inspired by His Murder"), Winter House, 1972.

Paul C. Harrison, editor, *Kuntu Drama* (includes "A Beast's Story" and "The Owl Answers"), Grove Press, 1974.

Wordplay 3 (includes "A Movie Star Has to Star in Black and White"), Performing Arts Journal Publications, 1984.

OTHER

Contributor of plays to periodicals, including *Scripts 1.*

SIDELIGHTS: "While almost every black playwright in the country is fundamentally concerned with realism... Miss [Adrienne] Kennedy is weaving some kind of dramatic fabric of poetry," Clive Barnes comments in the *New York Times.* "What she writes is a mosaic of feeling, with each tiny stone stained with the blood of the gray experience. Of all our black writers, Miss Kennedy is most concerned with white, with white relationship, with white blood. She thinks black, but she remembers white. It gives her work an eddying ambiguity."

In her complex and introspective plays, Martin Duberman remarks in *Partisan Review,* Kennedy is "absorbed by her private fantasies, her interior world. She disdains narrative, 'everyday' language and human interaction; the dream, the myth, the poem are her domain." James Hatch and Ted Shine also note that "in a tradition in which the major style has long been realism, Adrienne Kennedy has done what few black playwrights have attempted: used form to project an interior reality and thereby created a rich and demanding theatrical style."

Kennedy's first play, "Funnyhouse of a Negro," examines the psychological problems of Sarah, a young mulatto woman who lives with a Jewish poet in a boarding house run by a white landlady. Dealing with the last moments before Sarah's suicide, the play consists of scenes of the young woman's struggle with herself. Tortured by an identity crisis, Sarah is "lost in a nightmare world where black is evil and white is good, where various personages, including Queen Victoria, Patrice Lumumba, and Jesus Himself, materialize to mock her," says *New Yorker*'s Edith Oliver. "Funnyhouse of a Negro" earned Kennedy an Obie award, and, notes a *Variety* reviewer, a reputation as "a gifted writer with a distinctive dramatic imagination."

Oliver described "The Owl Answers" as another fantasy of "a forbidden and glorious white world, viewed with a passion and frustration that shred the spirit and nerves and mind of the dispossessed heroine." The illegitimate child of a black cook and the wealthiest white man in Georgia, the heroine is riding on a New York subway. The subway doors become the doors to the chapel of the Tower of London through which appear masked historical characters, including Chaucer, Shakespeare, Anne Boleyn, and the Virgin Mary, who at times unmask to become other characters, such as the heroine's mother and father.

"A Beast's Story," produced with "The Owl Answers" under the title "Cities in Bezique," was described as more elaborate, hallucinatory and obscure than the first play. It draws analo-

gies, says Steve Tennen in *Show Business,* "between inhuman beings and man's bestial tendencies." Kennedy's later play, "A Rat's Mass," staged as a parody mass, is also abstract, centering around the relationship between a black brother and sister and their childhood involvement with the white girl next door.

In all of these plays, Kennedy's writing is poetic and symbolic; plot and dialogue are secondary to effect. Her reliance on such devices as masks, characters who become other characters, characters played by more than one actor, and Christian symbolism makes her work difficult to understand, and her plays have been seen as both nightmarish rituals and poetic dances. Marilyn Stasio explains in *Cue:* "Kennedy is a poet, working with disjointed time sequences, evocative images, internalized half-thoughts, and incantatory language to create a netherworld of submerged emotions surfacing only in fragments. Events are crucial only for the articulated feelings they evoke."

During 1971, Kennedy joined five other women playwrights to found the Women's Theatre Council, a theatre cooperative devoted to producing the works of women playwrights and providing opportunities for women in other aspects of the theatre, such as directing and acting. Mel Gussow of the *New York Times* notes that the council's "founding sisters all come from Off Off Broadway, are exceeding prolific, have had their plays staged throughout the United States and in many foreign countries and feel neglected by the New York commercial theater. Each has a distinctive voice, but their work is related in being largely non-realistic and experimental. The women feel unified as innovators and by their artistic consciousness."

Kennedy branched out into juvenile theatre in 1980 after being commissioned by the Empire State Youth Theatre Institute. "A Lancashire Lad," her first play for children, is a fictionalized version of Charles Chaplin's childhood. Narrated by the hero, the play traces his life growing up in Dickensian England and beginning his career in the British music halls. Although an entertaining musical, the show confronts the poverty and pain of Chaplin's youth. Praising Kennedy's language for achieving "powerful emotional effects with the sparest of means," *New York Times* reviewer Frank Rich concludes: "The difference between 'The Lancashire Lad' and an adult play is, perhaps, the intellectual simplicity of its ambitions. Yet that simplicity can also be theater magic in its purest and most eloquent form."

BIOGRAPHICAL/CRITICAL SOURCES:

BOOKS

Abramson, Doris E., *Negro Playwrights in the American Theatre, 1925-1959,* Columbia University Press, 1969.

Betsko, Kathleen, and Rachel Koenig, *Interviews with Contemporary Women Playwrights,* Beech Tree Books, 1987.

Cohn, Ruby, *New American Dramatists: 1960-1980,* Grove Press, 1982.

Dictionary of Literary Biography, Volume XXXVIII: *Afro-American Writers after 1955; Dramatists and Prose Writers,* Gale, 1985.

Harrison, Paul Carter, *The Drama of Nommo,* Grove Press, 1972.

Hatch, James V., and Ted Shine, editors, *Black Theater U.S.A.,* Free Press, 1974.

Mitchell, Loften, *Black Drama,* Hawthorne Books, 1967.

Oliver, Clinton, and Stephanie Sills, *Contemporary Black Drama,* Scribners, 1971.

PERIODICALS

City Arts Monthly, February, 1982.
CLA Journal, December, 1976.
Cue, January 18, 1969, October 4, 1969.
Drama Review, December, 1977.
International Times, September 22, 1968.
Los Angeles Times Book Review, July 12, 1987.
Ms., June, 1987.
New Yorker, January 25, 1964, January 25, 1969.
New York Times, January 15, 1964, June 20, 1968, July 9, 1968, January 13, 1969, January 19, 1969, November 1, 1969, February 22, 1972, May 21, 1980, February 15, 1981, September 11, 1985, September 20, 1985.
Observer Review, June 23, 1968.
Partisan Review, Number 3, 1969.
Show Business, January 25, 1969, October 4, 1969.
Studies in Black Literature, summer, 1975.
Variety, January 29, 1969.
Village Voice, August 14, 1969, September 25, 1969.†

*   *   *

KENNEDY, (Jerome) Richard 1932-

PERSONAL: Born December 23, 1932, in Jefferson City, Mo.; son of Donald and Mary Louise (O'Keefe) Kennedy; married Lillian Nance, 1960 (divorced); children: Joseph Troy, Matthew Cook. *Education:* Portland State University, B.S. (with honors), 1958; Oregon State University, graduate study, 1964-65. *Politics:* "Innocent Bystander." *Religion:* "Bound for Glory."

ADDRESSES: Home—415 West Olive, Newport, Ore. 97365.

CAREER: Writer. Fifth-grade teacher in Harrisburg, Ore., and Dayton, Ore., 1968-69; currently custodian, Oregon State Univesity, Marine Science Center, Newport, Ore. Has worked as out-of-print and rare book dealer, woodcutter, cab driver, archivist, fisherman, plant worker, deckhand, and fireman. *Military service:* U.S. Air Force, 1951-54; became staff sergeant.

AWARDS, HONORS: American Library Association Notable Book Award, 1976, for *The Blue Stone,* and 1978, for *The Dark Princess;* Pacific Northwest Booksellers' Award, 1976, for *The Blue Stone* and *The Porcelain Man;* Association of Logos Bookstores Award, 1985, and Pied Piper Prize, Hameln, Germany, 1988, both for *Amy's Eyes.*

WRITINGS:

JUVENILES

The Parrot and the Thief (also see below), illustrated by Marcia Sewall, Atlantic-Little, Brown, 1974.
The Contests at Cowlick (also see below), illustrated by March Simont, Atlantic-Little, Brown, 1976.
The Porcelain Man (also see below), illustrated by Sewall, Atlantic-Little, Brown, 1976.
Come Again in the Spring (also see below), illustrated by Sewall, Harper, 1976.
The Blue Stone (also see below), illustrated by Ronald Himler, Holiday House, 1976.
Oliver Hyde's Dishcloth Concert (also see below), illustrated by Robert A. Parker, Atlantic-Little, Brown, 1977.
The Dark Princess (also see below), illustrated by Donna Diamond, Holiday House, 1978.
The Rise and Fall of Ben Gizzard (also see below), illustrated by Sewall, Atlantic-Little, Brown, 1978.

The Mouse God (also see below), Atlantic-Little, Brown, 1979.
Delta Baby and Two Sea Songs (also see below), illustrated by Lydia Dabcovich and Charles Mikolaycak, Addison-Wesley, 1979.
The Lost Kingdom of Karnica (also see below), illustrated by Uri Shulevitz, Sierra Club/Scribner, 1979.
The Leprechaun's Story (also see below), illustrated by Sewall, Dutton, 1979.
Inside My Feet: The Story of a Giant (also see below), illustrated by Himler, Harper, 1979.
Crazy in Love (also see below), Dutton, 1980.
The Song of the Horse (also see below), Dutton, 1981.
The Boxcar at the Center of the Universe, Harper, 1982.
Amy's Eyes, illustrated by Richard Egielski, Harper, 1985.
Richard Kennedy: Collected Stories (contains *The Parrot and the Thief, The Contests at Cowlick, The Porcelain Man, Come Again in the Spring, The Blue Stone, Oliver Hyde's Dishcloth Concert, The Dark Princess, The Rise and Fall of Ben Gizzard, The Mouse God, Delta Baby and Two Sea Songs, The Lost Kingdom of Karnica, The Leprechaun's Story, Inside My Feet: The Story of a Giant, Crazy in Love,* and *The Song of the Horse*), Harper, 1987.

OTHER

Also author of two musicals with Mark Lambert, "The Snow Queen," 1985, and "What a Woman Wants," 1986. Contributor of poems to periodicals.

SIDELIGHTS: Called "one of the few distinctive male voices in contemporary American children's books" by Michael Patrick Hearn of the *New York Times Book Review,* Richard Kennedy is noted for his poetic style and a sure, confident narrative. His stories possess "the same timelessness as classic fairy tales," according to Faith McNulty of the *New Yorker,* while Barbara Karlin of the *Los Angeles Times Book Review* judges Kennedy to be a "masterful storyteller." After writing a score of successful children's books, Kennedy published his most ambitious work in 1985, *Amy's Eyes,* a 500-page novel about a little girl who turns into a doll and embarks on a quest for pirate treasure with a shipload of colorful companions. This book won him widespread critical acclaim and—together with *Richard Kennedy: Collected Stories,* a volume containing fifteen of his picture books—constitutes his most important work.

"In most of his best books," writes Karla Kuskin of the *New York Times Book Review,* Kennedy "uses the language of folk narratives, simple and conversational, full of singing rhythms and repetitions and decorated with sudden, vivid images. He must have been born a storyteller, because he speaks this language like a native." This high regard for Kennedy's style is shared by other reviewers as well. Speaking of *The Boxcar at the Center of the Universe,* the story of a young boy on a journey of self discovery, Marilyn Kaye of the *New York Times Book Review* remarks that it is "a strange, mystical narrative, a free-floating fantasy of sorts that combines the elements of a wise man's parable with the ramblings of an old bum. . . . There is also some very fine writing, with sentences chockfull of unpretentious imagery." Selma Lanes of *Publishers Weekly* notes that with his very first children's book, *The Parrot and the Thief,* Kennedy "revealed a sure narrative voice, resonant with experience, yet with no taint of cynicism. There is as well in all his work a quiet undercurrent of melancholy. This is refreshing, both because such a tone is infrequently rung in children's books, and because it lends reality to the events in his tales."

Although he has enjoyed great success as a children's writer, Kennedy admits that he only entered the field by chance. After a brief stint as a teacher, a career he found did not suit him, Kennedy tried a number of different jobs, including book store employee, cabdriver, and archivist. After turning to writing, Kennedy tells *CA* that he kept a journal, one "of dark meditations the shades of Kafka, Lagerkvist, Nitezsche, Camus, Dostoevsky, Kierkegaard, Rimbaud, Sartre, Baudelaire, and other inner demons, while far in the background laughed Benchley, Thurber, George Ade, E. B. White, S. J. Perelman, Max Schulman, Mark Twain, Stephen Leacock, and other inner clowns. One night I burned the journal, with the prayer that all its disasters of heart and mind would work together and make children's books have some hope and humor yet, and so God bless us everyone." After telling Lanes of the disparate authors who influenced him, Kennedy remarks: "How this background worked its way to children's books, I wouldn't know."

In 1985, having already published sixteen children's books, Kennedy wrote the longest book of his career, *Amy's Eyes.* Lanes notes that this one novel is "nearly as long as the total of Kennedy's previous books." It tells the story of Amy, a little girl who makes her cherished sailor doll come to life by reading and talking to him. Later, when Amy is deprived of her father's love and attention, she transforms into a doll. Her now-living sailor friend takes her aboard his ship, convinced that he can make Amy a girl again by reading and talking to her. Most of the novel follows the pair's journey aboard the ship Ariel in search of pirate treasure. The ship's crew consists of former stuffed animals come-to-life, an animated suit of long underwear who quotes the Bible and serves as deckhand, and a troublesome duck who betrays the ship to the evil villains who plot to steal the treasure for themselves. In the course of this adventure the sailor comes to realize that one needs a purpose in life, a task to perform, in order to feel worthwhile. As Edwin J. Kenney, Jr., notes in the *New York Times Book Review, Amy's Eyes* "is primarily an old-fashioned sea adventure about a dangerous quest for gold treasure that ends in a discovery of personal destiny."

Amy's Eyes, Kennedy reveals to Lanes, "started as a story of maybe 30 pages, but it just kept going on and on." Indeed, Amy's many adventures include a stay in an orphanage, a battle on the high seas, and the loss of her button eyes to a hungry fish. In relating her exploits, Kennedy comments on such subjects as friendship, numerology, and the nature of evil. Sandra Martin, writing in the Toronto *Globe and Mail,* calls *Amy's Eyes* "an exciting, imaginative novel, an adventure story for all ages, burbling and seething with allusions (not to mention illusions), a book crammed with insights and perceptive statements about life and death and the power of love."

Some critics feel that *Amy's Eyes,* although an admirable work of the imagination, fails to achieve the greatness it promises. Michael Dirda of the *Washington Post Book World,* for example, calls the novel "an impressive book, [which] may become a classic. But I still wish Amy and the Captain didn't pale next to the novel's haunting villains." Martin, too, sees flaws in the book, claiming that the story grows "becalmed and befuddled. . . . As a result, the last third of the book clouds the brilliance of Kennedy's vision."

But most commentators praise the novel's power to entertain its readers at the same time it confronts important philosophical questions. Lanes describes *Amy's Eyes* as "a masterpiece full of wise commentary on life that also offers one of the chief pleasures of children's books—the promise that, against all odds, good is going to triumph in the end." Holly Sanhuber of *School Library Journal* finds that "the grave, measured tone, the deft use of foreshadowing to create suspense, the gentle, philosophical asides to readers, the compact wisdom of pithy phrases and the generous use of the art of description remind one of the great fantasists of the late Victorian period. . . . Emotionally moving, enjoying a deceptive ease of presentation and masterly command of the nuances of language, this richly textured fantasy lingers in the mind long after the last page has been turned." Noted children's writer Lloyd Alexander is quoted by Lanes as claiming that, with *Amy's Eyes,* "Richard Kennedy sets a new high standard for all of us concerned with quality in literature for young people."

BIOGRAPHICAL/CRITICAL SOURCES:

PERIODICALS

Globe and Mail (Toronto), August 10, 1985.
Los Angeles Times Book Review, December 28, 1980.
New Yorker, November 30, 1987.
New York Times Book Review, November 9, 1980, January 31, 1982, September 5, 1982, June 9, 1985, February 21, 1988.
Observer, November 30, 1986.
Publishers Weekly, February 22, 1985.
School Library Journal, May, 1985.
Washington Post Book World, July 14, 1985.

—*Sketch by Thomas Wiloch*

*   *   *

KENNY, James Andrew 1933-

PERSONAL: Born October 12, 1933, in Evanston, Ill.; son of James Valentine (a lawyer) and Ann Freda (Filz) Kenny; married Mary Jane Nelsen (a writer), January 26, 1957; children: Joseph, Christopher, Theresa, Michael, John Paul, Thomas, Peter, Ann, Elizabeth, Robert, Sharon, Matthew. *Education:* Maryknoll College, B.A., 1954; Loyola University, Chicago, Ill., M.S.W., 1957; University of Mainz, Ph.D. (psychology; cum laude), 1962; Indiana University, M.A., 1971, Ph.D. (anthropology), 1974.

ADDRESSES: Home—623 Milroy, Rensselaer, Ind. 47978. *Office*—Clinic of Family Medicine, Rensselaer, Ind. 47978.

CAREER: Chicago Department of Welfare, Chicago, Ill., social caseworker, 1955; Cook County Department of Welfare, Chicago, social caseworker, 1956; St. Joseph's College, Rensselaer, Ind., associate professor, 1964-72, professor of psychology, 1972-75, chairman of department, 1968-75, clinical psychologist, 1964-75; Jasper-Newton Mental Health Center, Rensselaer, director and clinical psychologist, 1975-82. Clinic of Family Medicine, Rensselaer, private practice of clinical psychology, 1973-75, 1982—. Associate professor of anthropology at Indiana University, 1975-76; visiting professor at St. Joseph's College, 1975—. *Military service:* U.S. Air Force, psychiatric social worker at Eglin Air Force Base, 1957-60, and at U.S. Air Force hospital in Wiesbaden, West Germany, 1960-62, clinical child psychologist and director of Child Guidance Clinic in Wiesbaden, 1962-64; became captain.

MEMBER: American Psychological Association, Academy of Certified Social Workers, National Association of Social Workers, American Anthropological Association (fellow),

Midwestern Psychological Association, Indiana Psychological Association.

AWARDS, HONORS: Edwin G. Kaiser Faculty Scholar Award from St. Joseph's College, 1973; distinguished service award from Indiana Commission on Mental Health, 1977; "Family Talk" was named best syndicated column of 1982 and 1983 by Catholic Press Association.

WRITINGS:

The CHAP Guide to Facilities in Europe, U.S. Air Force in Europe, 1963.
(With wife, Mary Kenny) *When Your Marriage Goes Stale*, Abbey Press, 1979.
(With M. Kenny) *Making the Family Matter*, St. Anthony Messenger Press, 1980.
(Co-author) "Families Doing Things Together" (cassette series), Abbey Press, 1980.
(With M. Kenny) *Happy Parenting!*, St. Anthony Messenger Press, 1982.
(With M. Kenny) *Whole-Life Parenting*, Crossroad/Continuum, 1982.
(With S. Spicer) *Caring for Your Aging Parent*, St. Anthony Messenger Press, 1984.
(Co-author) "Caring for the Elderly" (cassette series), Abbey Press, 1986.
(Co-author) "Helping Children Handle Divorce" (cassette series), St. Anthony Messenger Press, 1987.
(With Ron Miller) *Fireball and the Lotus: Emerging Spirituality from Ancient Roots*, Bear & Co., 1987.

Co-author of "Family Talk," a weekly column syndicated by National Catholic News Service, 1976—. Contributor of nearly fifty articles to professional journals and popular magazines, including *Marriage*, *Our Family*, *Columbia*, *Catholic Digest*, *Today's Family*, and *Family Digest*, and newspapers.

SIDELIGHTS: "Everything I had learned in school seemed so far-removed and academic when we had to spend an all-nighter with a sick child or confront a growing adolescent who had had too much to drink. Bit by bit, incident by incident, we put together a childrearing philosophy that is practical, positive, developmental, and above all, effective. I write to stay sane and to find the humor that underlies all great endeavors. Our book *Whole-Life Parenting* gives our thoughts on raising children learned through mistakes, hammered out on the anvil of everyday demands, salted by education, and tempered by the reality of raising twelve children. The book is dedicated to our children, who have taught us most of what we know and in some cases more than we wanted to learn."

AVOCATIONAL INTERESTS: "We lived in Europe for five years, during which time I visited Russia and the Middle East. After returning to the United States, we bought an old school bus which we outfitted with hammocks to sleep twelve, and were frequent campers. I have been a swim coach for several years. I jog-run four miles daily and enjoy road races, which help me keep one step ahead of our twelve children."

*   *   *

KENT, Cromwell
   See SPARSHOTT, Francis (Edward)

*   *   *

KERIN, Roger A(nthony) 1947-

PERSONAL: Born April 19, 1947, in Duluth, Minn.; son of

Joseph and Mary (Mlikota) Kerin; married Shirley Goldman, June 22, 1979; children: Suzanne. *Education:* University of Minnesota, Duluth, B.A., 1969; University of Minnesota, Minneapolis, M.B.A., 1970, Ph.D., 1973.

ADDRESSES: Office—Edwin L. Cox School of Business, Southern Methodist University, Dallas, Tex. 75275.

CAREER: Southern Methodist University, Dallas, Tex., assistant professor, 1973-76, associate professor, 1977-80, professor of marketing, 1980—. Visiting professor of marketing at University of Texas at Austin, 1976-77.

MEMBER: American Marketing Association, American Psychological Association, Decision Sciences Institute.

WRITINGS:

Strategic Marketing Problems: Cases and Comments, Allyn & Bacon, 1978, 5th edition, in press.
Perspectives on Strategic Marketing Management, Allyn & Bacon, 1980, 2nd edition, 1983.
Marketing, Times Mirror/Mosby, 1986, 2nd edition, 1989.
Contemporary Perspectives for Strategic Market Planning, Business Publications, Inc., 1989.

Contributor to marketing journals.

WORK IN PROGRESS: Research on strategic issues in marketing, improving data collection procedures in marketing research, and the impact of product and process innovation on marketing performance.

*   *   *

KERMAN, Sheppard 1928-

PERSONAL: Born August 26, 1928, in Brooklyn, N.Y.; son of Louis (a businessman) and Leila (a poet; maiden name, Benowitz) Kerman; married Ilona Murai (a ballet teacher), January 19, 1957; children: Christina. *Education:* City College (now of the City University of New York), B.S.S., 1950.

ADDRESSES: Home—41B Dunes Lane, Port Washington, N.Y. 11050. *Office*—Affman-Sheral International, 135 West 26th St., New York, N.Y. 10001.

CAREER: Kenyon & Eckhardt Advertising, New York City, writer and producer, 1964-69; Charisma Organization, New York City, writer and producer, 1969-71; Stage Right (multimedia producers), New York City, creative director, 1971-72; In-Perspective Communications, Inc., New York City, president and creative director, 1973-82; Affman-Sheral International, Inc., New York City, president and creative director, 1983—. Actor in films, including "Boss Tweed," and industrial and army training films, and in Broadway plays, including "All for Love," 1950-51, "The Prescott Proposals," 1953, "Tonight in Samarkand," 1954, "The Great Sebastians," 1956, and "The Sound of Music," 1959-63; producer and director of "Mr. Simian," 1963-64; narrator of television commercials. Creator of multi-media works for industry, including speeches, motivational pieces, and musicals such as "Seesaw," Broadway production, 1973, "Beatlemania," Winter Garden Theatre and touring company, 1977, and "Platinum," Broadway production, 1978. Currently on the faculty of Parsons School of Design and Long Island University, teaching courses in multi-media design and broadcast communications.

MEMBER: New Dramatists, American Federation of Television and Radio Artists, American Society of Composers, Authors and Publishers, Dramatists Guild, Screen Actors Guild, Actors' Equity Association, Players Club.

AWARDS, HONORS: Best radio play, WNYC students awards, 1946, for "Jacob Rils"; best actor award, *Show Business,* 1950, as Everyman in "Everyman," and 1951, as Marc Antony in "All for Love"; Obie award, 1964, for "Mr. Simian"; Los Angeles Drama Critics Circle award, 1978, for overall visual design concept in "Beatlemania"; Grand Award, International Film and Television Festival of New York, 1982, for writing and direction of "Opportunity Unlimited."

WRITINGS:

PLAYS

"The Dark and the Day" (three-act), first produced in New York City at New Dramatists Committee, 1952.
"Bilby's Doll" (two-act), first produced in New York City at New Dramatists Committee, 1953.
Cut of the Axe (two-act; first produced on Broadway at Ambassador Theatre, February 1, 1960), Samuel French, 1961.
"Players on a Beach" (one-act), first produced in New York City at Masters' Institute Theatre, 1961.
"The Accused" (one-act opera), first produced on CBS Camera 3, 1961.
"Mr. Simian" (three-act), first produced Off-Broadway at Astor Place Playhouse, October, 1963.
"The Tune of the Time" (two-act), first produced in Atlanta at Civic Theatre, October, 1969.
"Funny Business" (one-act musical), first produced in New York City at Players' Club, June, 1983.

Also author of "Nine Rebels" (two-act), 1962, and "The Husband-In-Law" (three-act), 1968; author of one-act musicals "Orgy on Park Avenue," "Roast," "Mamma," "The Mood Synthesizer," and "Lady Collona," all between 1977-82. Author of multi-media musical "Distant Relations," 1981, with music by Ralph Affoumado.

OTHER

Author of television scripts for *Danger, Studio One, Camera Three, Philco Playhouse,* and *Kraft Playhouse,* all for CBS-TV, and *Matinee Theatre.* Author of television script "Opportunity Unlimited," produced by Avon. Author of radio play "Jacob Rils," produced by WNYC, 1946. Lyricist for songwriters Marvin Hamlisch, Lee Pockriss, John Strauss, and Ralph Affoumado. Author of unpublished volume of poetry, *The Candy Man.*

WORK IN PROGRESS: "Peter, Paul, and the Piper," a play; musical adaptation of *The Picture of Dorian Gray,* with James Hammerstein.

SIDELIGHTS: Sheppard Kerman commented: "My plays, poems, operas, and television scripts have somehow placed emphasis on the survival of the individual in a world of contradictory philosophies. Today my primary work is in the area of mixed and multi-media presentations for industry and theatre. My unique background as writer, lyricist, director, and producer has been the source of my own creative survival and has fortunately led me into a new art form in which the disciplines of the media I previously performed in, wrote for, and directed, still apply. It has allowed me to innovate and set a standard in visual projections for the theatre. (At least, that has been the attempt since "Seesaw," in 1973, through "Beatlemania," in 1977, and "Platinum," in 1978.)

"The writer draws images in words. I am now able to draw words, characters, and emotions in images—images that can

perform in harmony with all aspects of a staged performance and can communicate deeper aspects of character and theatricality. If survival—coping—has, and continues to be the thread that runs through my written work, the visual media has become both needle and fabric."

In the Broadway musical "Seesaw" the effects were achieved by projecting pictures onto tall vertical panels on stage. The projection of the pictures had to be precisely coordinated with the movement of the screens from backstage. Kerman and his crew took over three thousand pictures for the play, including night panoramas, double exposures, and dissolves, of which 158 were used in "Seesaw."

BIOGRAPHICAL/CRITICAL SOURCES:

PERIODICALS

Atlantic City Sunday Press, June 10, 1973.
Back Stage, November 17, 1978.

*   *   *

KEROUAC, Jack
    See KEROUAC, Jean-Louis Lebrid de

*   *   *

KEROUAC, Jean-Louis Lebrid de   1922-1969
    (Jean-Louis, Jean-Louis Incogniteau, Jack
    Kerouac, John Kerouac)

PERSONAL: Born March 12, 1922, in Lowell, Mass.; died October 21, 1969, of a stomach hemorrhage in St. Petersburg, Fla.; buried in Lowell, Mass.; son of Leo Alcide (a job printer) and Gabrielle-Ange (a shoe-factory worker; maiden name, Levesque) Kerouac; married Frankie Edith Parker, August 22, 1944 (marriage annulled, 1945); married Joan Haverty, November 17, 1950 (divorced); married Stella Sampas, November 18, 1966; children: (second marriage) Jan Michele Hackett. *Education:* Attended Horace Mann School for Boys, New York, N.Y.; attended Columbia College, 1940-42; attended New School for Social Research, 1948-49. *Religion:* Roman Catholic.

CAREER: Writer. Worked at odd jobs in garages and as a sports reporter for the Lowell (Mass.) *Sun,* 1942; was a railroad brakeman with the Southern Pacific Railroad, San Francisco, Calif., 1952-53; traveled around the United States and Mexico; was a fire lookout for the U.S. Agriculture Service in northwest Washington, 1956. *Military service:* U.S. Merchant Marine, 1942 and 1943. U.S. Navy, 1943.

MEMBER: Authors Guild, Authors League of America.

AWARDS, HONORS: American Academy of Arts and Sciences grant, 1955.

WRITINGS:

(Under name John Kerouac) *The Town and the City,* Harcourt, 1950, reprinted under name Jack Kerouac, Grosset, 1960, reprinted, Harcourt, 1978.
(Under name John Kerouac) *Visions of Gerard* (also see below), Farrar, Straus, 1963, reprinted under name Jack Kerouac, McGraw, 1976.

Contributor to *Columbia Review* (under pseudonym Jean-Louis Incogniteau) and to *New World Writing* (under pseudonym Jean-Louis).

NOVELS; UNDER NAME JACK KEROUAC

On the Road, Viking, 1957, critical edition with notes by Scott Donaldson published as *On the Road: Text and Criticism,* Penguin, 1979.

The Dharma Bums, Viking, 1958.

The Subterraneans (also see below), Grove, 1958, 2nd edition, 1981.

Doctor Sax: Faust Part Three, Grove, 1959, reprinted, McGraw, 1976.

Maggie Cassidy: A Love Story, Avon, 1959, reprinted, McGraw, 1978.

Excerpts from Visions of Cody, New Directions, 1959, enlarged edition published as *Visions of Cody,* McGraw, 1972.

Tristessa, Avon, 1960 (published in England with *Visions of Gerard,* Deutsch, 1964), reprinted, McGraw, 1978.

Big Sur, Farrar, Straus, 1962, reprinted, Harcourt, 1978.

Desolation Angels, Coward, 1965.

Satori in Paris (also see below), Grove, 1966.

Vanity of Duluoz: An Adventurous Education, 1935-46, Coward, 1968.

Pic, Grove, 1971 (published in England with *The Subterraneans* as *Two Novels,* Deutsch, 1973; published with *Satori in Paris,* Grove, 1986).

Also author, with William S. Burroughs, of unpublished novel "And the Hippos Were Boiled in Their Tanks," and of unpublished novels "The Sea Is My Brother," "Buddha Tells Us," and "Secret Mullings about Bill."

POETRY; UNDER NAME JACK KEROUAC

Mexico City Blues, Grove, 1959, reprinted, 1981.

Hugo Weber, Portents, 1967.

Someday You'll Be Lying, privately printed, 1968.

A Last Haiku, privately printed, 1969.

Scattered Poems, City Lights, 1971.

(With Albert Saijo and Lew Welch) *Trip Trap: Haiku along the Road from San Francisco to New York, 1959,* Grey Fox, 1973.

Heaven and Other Poems, Grey Fox, 1977.

San Francisco Blues, Beat Books, 1983.

Hymn: God Pray for Me, Caliban, 1985.

American Haikus, Caliban, 1986.

SOUND RECORDINGS; UNDER NAME JACK KEROUAC

"Jack Kerouac Steve Allen Poetry for the Beat Generation," Hanover, 1959.

"Jack Kerouac Blues and Haikus," Hanover, 1959.

"Readings by Jack Kerouac on the Beat Generation," Verve, 1959.

OTHER; UNDER NAME JACK KEROUAC

(Contributor) *January 1st 1959: Fidel Castro,* Totem, 1959.

Rimbaud, City Lights, 1959.

The Scripture of the Golden Eternity (philosophy and religion), Corinth Books, 1960, new edition, 1970.

Book of Dreams, City Lights, 1961.

(Author of introduction) *The Americans,* photographs by Robert Frank, Grove, 1960, revised and enlarged edition, 1978.

Lonesome Traveler (autobiography), McGraw, 1960.

(Ad lib narrator) *Pull My Daisy* (screenplay), Grove, 1961.

A Pun for Al Gelpi (broadside), [Cambridge], 1966.

A Memoir in which Is Revealed Secret Lives and West Coast Whispers, Giligia, 1970.

Two Early Stories, Aloe Editions, 1973.

Home at Christmas, Oliphant, 1973.

Old Angel Midnight, Unicorn Bookshop, 1976.

(With Allen Ginsberg) *Take Care of My Ghost, Ghost* (letters), Ghost Press, 1977.

Une veille de Noel, Knight, 1980.

(With Carolyn Cassady) *Dear Carolyn: Letters to Carolyn Cassady,* Unspeakable Visions, 1983.

Also author of *Before the Road: Young Cody and the Birth of Hippie,* and of *Not Long Ago Joy Abounded at Christmas,* 1972. Author of pamphlet, "Nosferatu (Dracula)," New York Film Society, 1960. Contributor to periodicals, including *Ark-Moby, Paris Review, Evergreen Review, Big Table, Black Mountain Review,* and *Chicago Review.* Contributor of regular column, "The Last Word," to *Escapade,* 1959-61.

SIDELIGHTS: Jean-Louis Lebrid de Kerouac became famous as Jack Kerouac, author of *On the Road,* the novel that is considered the quintessential statement of the 1950s literary movement known as the Beat Generation. *On the Road* described the growing friendship of two men, Sal Paradise and Dean Moriarty, and their criss-crossing journeys over the American continent. On a deeper level, it was the story of the narrator's search for religious truth and for values more profound than those embraced by most of mid-twentieth-century America. In both form and subject *On the Road* was completely unlike the formal, elitist fiction that dominated the era, and it was ridiculed accordingly by Kerouac's contemporaries in the literary establishment, who viewed it as "an insane parody of the mobility of automotive America," wrote Dennis McNally in *Desolate Angel: Jack Kerouac, the Beat Generation, and America.* The book spoke to many readers, however, expressing their own unarticulated dissatisfaction with the repressive climate of the United States after World War II. "It is difficult, separated as we are by time and temper from that period, to convey the liberating effect that *On the Road* had on young people all over America," wrote Bruce Cook in *The Beat Generation.* "There was a sort of instantaneous flash of recognition that seemed to send thousands of them out into the streets, proclaiming that Kerouac had written their story, that *On the Road* was their book." More and more people took their cue from Kerouac's novel and adopted a lifestyle that emphasized personal freedom over social conformity, expanded consciousness over material wealth. The mass media jokingly referred to these modern Bohemians as "beatniks" and portrayed Kerouac as their leader. In this position he achieved a celebrity status uncommon for a novelist, but it was an uncomfortable role for Kerouac, a shy, insecure man ill-equipped to deal with fame. As the scattered beat scene evolved into the hippie counterculture of the 1960s, Kerouac continued to be named the progenitor of it all, but by that time he had withdrawn from public life, frustrated by critics' continuing attacks on his work. It was not until several years after his death that Kerouac began to be recognized as an important artist, one who, according to *Midwest Quarterly* contributor Carole Gottlieb Vopat, has "provided an enduring portrait of the national psyche; like Fitzgerald, he has defined America and delineated American life for his generation."

Kerouac was born to French-Canadian parents in the working-class "Little Canada" neighborhood of Lowell, Massachusetts, a mill town some thirty miles northwest of Boston. He spoke only French until the age of seven, and his French-Canadian heritage, along with the Roman Catholic faith in which he was raised, strongly influenced him throughout his life. He was a highly imaginative child who created a private world of racing stables and sports teams, then wrote his own newspapers to report their performances. Diaries, radio plays, and a novel entitled "Jack Kerouac Explores the Merrimack" were some of his other childhood writing projects. He was an excellent student, and by the time he entered Lowell High School, he was also developing into a gifted athlete. It was his performance on the high school football team that provided his ticket out of Lowell: he was offered a football scholarship to Columbia University. New York City was a world away from Lowell. Forty percent of Kerouac's home town received some form of public assistance, but at the Horace Mann School (where he spent a year preparing for Columbia's Ivy League standards), his classmates were the heirs to Manhattan's fortunes. Kerouac seemed amusingly rustic to them, but he was well-liked, and his new friends guided his explorations of the city. He found its vibrance and diversity inspirational.

He had a checkered career at Columbia. A broken leg kept him from playing much football in 1940, and his 1941 season was marked by disagreements with his coach. Furthermore, Kerouac was beginning to feel deeply troubled by the great shift in morals brought about by the Second World War. A whole way of life seemed to be vanishing, and as McNally observed, "Studying and practicing seemed trivial exercises in an apocalyptic world." Late in 1941 Kerouac left the university for a hitch in the Merchant Marine. In his off-duty hours he read the works of Thomas Wolfe and worked on a novel he called "The Sea Is My Brother." He returned briefly to Columbia in 1942, left to join the Navy, then found himself unable to submit to the military discipline of that service. This earned him some time in the psychiatric ward of Bethesda Naval Hospital, but he eventually received an honorable discharge for "indifferent character." Kerouac reentered the less-regimented Merchant Marine for some time before returning to New York City, although not to Columbia. It was at this time that he began to meet the people who would profoundly influence the rest of his life and his work—the people who would in fact be the core of the Beat Generation.

"Cutting away the amateurs, the opportunists, and the figures whose generational identification was fleeting or less than wholehearted on their own part, the Beat Generation—as a literary school—pretty much amounts to Kerouac and his friends William Burroughs and Allen Ginsberg," suggested Barry Gifford and Lawrence Lee in *Jack's Book: An Oral Biography of Jack Kerouac.* Allen Ginsberg was a seventeen-year-old Columbia freshman when he and Kerouac first met. Later he would write the most famous Beat poem, "Howl." The two became like brothers, excitedly discussing their literary and philosophical ideas. Several years older than Kerouac, William Burroughs was a shadowy figure who had worked as an adman, a detective, an exterminator, and a bartender. He would eventually publish the novels *Junky* and *Naked Lunch.* Now he served as Kerouac's tutor, introducing him to the works of Spengler, Nietzsche, and Celine. He also provided an intimate introduction to the underground society of Times Square, to morphine, and to amphetemines.

Though very different in temperament and experience, these three men were alike in their detachment from the values that characterized most of the United States in the 1940s. They regarded with suspicion the rapid growth of bureaucracy and technocracy, which most Americans considered proof of their country's global supremacy. McNally related that when Hiroshima and Nagasaki were destroyed by atomic bombs, "two million hysterical New Yorkers surged into Times Square drunk with joy," but Kerouac and his friends were less enthusiastic about the awesome new bomb. In fact, Burroughs symboli-

cally dressed himself in a crimson devil's suit to join the celebrating crowd in Times Square. "Seen in the blinding glare of the mushroom cloud, this new nation *was* hell as far as [Kerouac] was concerned," wrote McNally. "The war had left the federal government tripled in size and corporate assets doubled, with an accompanying increase in 'efficiency' and a decrease in the visionary and human qualities that Jack prized." Rejecting the blind patriotism of the moment, the three men groped for what Ginsberg called the "New Vision," a set of values that would make sense to them in the post-atomic world. McNally stated that "their tutors [were] the renegades of high culture like Yeats, Rimbaud, and Baudelaire—[men who] had abandoned politics and religion for beauty."

In 1945 their intense talk, the mood of nihilistic despair, and Kerouac's heavy use of benzedrine took their toll. Thrombophlebitis made his legs swell painfully, and he was confined to a hospital bed. His father and mother had come to New York in search of factory work two years earlier; now Leo Kerouac began to die a painful death of stomach cancer. Released from the hospital, Jack returned not to his intellectual friends in the city, but to his parents' shabby home in Ozone Park. For many months he cared for his father, who berated his son for his aimless life, his worthless friends and his foolish artistic aspirations. On his deathbed Leo repeatedly made Jack swear to support his mother, and Jack promised that he would.

It was in the hope of fulfilling that promise that he returned to his mother's home after Leo's burial and began working on a new novel, an idealized autobiography that would be published in 1950 as *The Town and the City.* This book "reflected his return to family, replacing the New Vision aura of symbolic decadence with the style of his first love, Thomas Wolfe," remarked McNally. "The work was underlaid not only with his new insight into death but with the idealism of Goethe's autobiography *Dichtung und Wahrheit (Poetry and Truth),* Kerouac's main reading matter that summer and fall.... Goethe calmly rejected satire and preached an affirmative love of life, and more, told Jack that all of his work was merely 'fragments of a great confession'.... Jack worked at his own confession... for two years, grimly struggling from morning until late at night to recite the history of the Kerouacs and America."

Stretches of work on *The Town and the City* were broken by occasional visits to friends in New York, and on one such trip, Kerouac met the man who would inspire some of his best work. Neal Cassady was the motherless son of a derelict from Denver, Colorado. Cassady grew up in a series of skid row hotels, eating in missions, begging quarters for his father, and avoiding his brutal older brothers. He had been born in an automobile, and he was fourteen years old when he stole his first car. Cassady quickly became addicted to the feeling of freedom he experienced behind the wheel. By the time he was twenty-one, he'd stolen five hundred cars, been arrested ten times, convicted six times, and spent fifteen months in jail. Nightmares of his father's wasted life tormented Cassady in prison, but he found relief by reading philosophy. In 1947 he arrived in New York City, hungry for knowledge and hoping to enter Columbia. Cassady's nervous energy generated an almost constant stream of ideas, talk, and action. Kerouac admired him because he'd retained his tremendous enthusiasm for living in spite of his deprived childhood, and found his openness refreshing "after seven years of cynical East Coast sophistication," commented McNally. "Twenty-year-old Neal swept into [Kerouac's] life like a Wild West siren singing freedom, kicks, a 'wild yea-saying overburst of American joy,' as Jack characterized him, enthusiastically flying after food and sex like a holy primitive, a 'natural man'; he was the embodiment of Jack's American dream."

The two men quickly developed an intense friendship, but when Cassady's plan to enter Columbia collapsed, he returned to Denver. Four months later, Kerouac took a break from his work on *The Town and the City* to hitchhike west and join his friend. Once there, he found Cassady preoccupied by his love affairs with his mistress, his estranged fifteen-year-old wife, and Allen Ginsberg, so Kerouac continued on to San Francisco alone, then returned to New York by bus. This first of many restless journeys around the United States provided Kerouac with the ending he needed for *The Town and the City*. The finished book opened with a lyrical re-creation of a New England childhood, featuring a large, happy family with strong foundations. War scatters the family, however, and eventually even its anchor, the father, must tear up his roots and move to the city. His death there symbolized the final destruction of the idyllic way of life evoked in the novel's first half. In a final scene which prefigured the *On the Road* story, the most promising son turned his back on conventional success and took to the open road in search of a new way of life. *The Town and the City* was cordially reviewed upon its publication in 1950. Although there were objections to the message implied in the novel's closing scene, most critics noted the book's vitality and praised its style as powerful and evocative.

Kerouac was elated to be a published novelist, but by the time *The Town and the City* appeared he was struggling with his next book. Its subject was Neal Cassady. Kerouac wanted this new novel to reflect the fevered pace of modern life; the gracious prose he'd used in *The Town and the City* was inappropriate for that purpose. After several false starts, Kerouac found the inspiration for a new style in the letters he received from Cassady. Kerouac remembered them in a *Paris Review* interview with Ted Berrigan as "all first person, fast, mad, confessional, completely serious, all detailed." In one 40,000-word letter, Cassady described his seduction of a woman he met on a bus. It read "with spew and rush, without halt, all unified and molten flow; no boring moments, everything significant and interesting, sometimes breathtaking in speed and brilliance," as McNally quoted Ginsberg. Kerouac decided to model his book about Cassady on the style of these letters. Instead of revising, he would let the story assume its own shape, allowing details and impressions to accumulate as they do in life. Threading a long roll of paper through his typewriter so he would not have to pause at the end of each page, Kerouac sat down in April, 1951, to pour out the story of his friendship with Cassady. In twenty days he had completed a 175,000-word, single-spaced paragraph that was the first version of *On the Road*. McNally assessed the author's output: "The sentences were short and tight, clickety-pop word bursts that caught the rhythm of the high-speed road life as no author before him ever had.... [The book was] bursting with energy, with a feeling of life struggling inside a deathly society, energy burning bright before the laws of entropy and the nation caught up."

"Spontaneous prose" was Kerouac's name for the high-speed writing method he was developing. *Dictionary of Literary Biography* contributor George Dardess explained what this style symbolized to the author: "'Spontaneous prose' was the way by which the inner mind, trapped as Kerouac finally felt it to be by social, psychological, and grammatical restrictions, could free itself from its muteness and take verbal shape in the outside world. The result of this liberation would not be chaotic, however, since the inner mind was innately shapely and would

cause the words with which it expressed itself to be shapely.... 'Spontaneous prose' became a metaphor for the paradoxes of the human condition as Kerouac, the Roman Catholic, conceived it: hopelessly corrupted and compromised, yet somehow, in ways only indirectly glimpsed and never fully understood, redeemable, even in the midst of its sin." Spontaneous prose had contemporary parallels in music and the visual arts, noted McNally: "At roughly the same time and place and in response to the same stimuli—a world at once accelerating and constricting—the painter Jackson Pollock and the musician Charlie Parker had accomplished similar revolutions in their own art forms.... All three men were working-class sons of matrifocal families who refused to 'adjust' to the conformist society of mid-century or the accepted styles of their disciplines, and for their efforts were labeled psychopaths and falsely associated with violence. Each ignored the critical authorities in their field and stood emotionally naked before their audiences, spewing words, notes, or paintdrops that were like the fiery rain of a volcano: The rain captured the passing moment in a luminous veil of particulars that depicted the universal as an expression of the artist's own self.... [Parker] played with the raw energy of a high-power line, and it was that stabbing electricity that Jack had attempted to put into *On the Road*, that mortal sense that the candle *must* burn furiously, else the times will surely snuff it out."

After retyping his giant roll of manuscript, Kerouac confidently submitted it to Robert Giroux, the editor who had handled *The Town and the City*. Giroux rejected it, becoming the first of many editors to do so. Part of the problem was the experimental prose, but even after Kerouac had reluctantly revised the manuscript to read in a more conventional style, he was unable to sell *On the Road*. The greatest barrier to its acceptance was the author's empathy with social outcasts. Kerouac wrote of the dignity and spirituality of blacks, Mexicans, hobos, and even drug addicts. His attitudes denied "complacency and middle-class notions of propriety and status"; they "seemed incomprehensible in 1957," wrote John Tytell in *Naked Angels: The Lives and Literature of the Beat Generation*. "One of the readers for Viking Press, for example, while appreciating Kerouac's lavish power, was dismayed by the raw sociology of the book, finding in it the quintessence of 'everything that is bad and horrible about this otherwise wonderful age we live in.' The characters were irredeemable psychopaths and hopeless neurotics who lived exclusively for sensation. This judgment, delivered prior to publication, can stand as a sign of how those born before the war would see the book."

On the Road was apparently unpublishable, but Kerouac remained passionately committed to his confessional style. In fact, the six years between *On the Road*'s completion and its publication were the most productive of the author's life. He began a series of novels which he thought of as one vast story, in the tradition of Proust's *Remembrance of Things Past*. As he moved between New York, San Francisco, and Mexico City, Kerouac paused for intense writing sessions that yielded more than eight books, including *Tristessa*, *Doctor Sax: Faust Part Three*, and *Visions of Cody*. In them he told the stories of his family and friends, striving to do so with complete emotional honesty. His approach could be exhausting. For example, he wrote *The Subterraneans* in response to his breakup with a woman he called "Mardou Fox" in his book. On the day Kerouac realized their affair was over, he swallowed some benzedrine, inserted a roll of teletype paper in his typewriter, and in three days produced what is considered one of his best novels. Kerouac characterized that effort to Berrigan as "really a fantastic athletic feat as well as mental.... After I was done . . . I was pale as a sheet and had lost fifteen pounds and looked strange in the mirror." Kerouac was able to maintain unswerving faith in the value of his own writing, but he was tormented by the fact that no publisher would accept his work during those years. In 1954 he found a measure of relief from his frustration in his study of Buddhist texts. "It does not seem difficult to explain Kerouac's attraction to Buddhism," mused Dardess. "Torn as he often was by the paradox of God's seemingly simultaneous presence and absence in the world he saw, Kerouac could seize with relief on Buddhism's annihilation of the paradox." Through his later novels, the author was one of the first people to introduce the concepts of Buddhism to the American public.

While Kerouac remained largely anonymous, some of his friends were becoming well known. In 1952 John Clellon Holmes published an article entitled "This Is the Beat Generation," using a term Kerouac had offhandedly coined to compare modern feelings of disillusionment with those of the Lost Generation writers. In 1955 Allen Ginsberg and other poets gave an influential reading at the Six Gallery in San Francisco, and were subsequently featured in a widely-read issue of *Evergreen Review*. Ginsberg's "Howl" was the subject of a highly-publicized obscenity trial in 1956. By that year there was sufficient public awareness of the emerging Beat writers for Viking Press to risk purchasing *On the Road*, after Kerouac agreed to extensive cuts, revisions, and name changes (Kerouac is "Sal Paradise" in the novel and Neal Cassady is "Dean Moriarty.") Its 1957 publication was hailed as "a historic occasion" in the *New York Times* by Gilbert Millstein, the editor who had earlier commissioned Holmes's "This Is the Beat Generation" article. He wrote: "'On the Road' is the most beautifully executed, the clearest and most important utterance yet made by the generation Kerouac himself named years ago as 'beat,' and whose principal avatar he is. Just as, more than any other novel of the Twenties, 'The Sun Also Rises' came to be regarded as the testament of the 'Lost Generation,' so it seems certain that 'On the Road' will come to be known as that of the 'Beat Generation'.... There are sections ... in which the writing is of a beauty almost breathtaking. There is a description of a cross-country automobile ride fully the equal, for example, of the train ride told by Thomas Wolfe in 'Of Time and the River.' There are details of a trip to Mexico ... that are, by turns, awesome, tender and funny.... 'On the Road' is a major novel."

Most critics perceived the book in a different light, however. McNally summarized: "The *Times Book Review* waffled, first praising the book as 'enormously readable and entertaining,' then dismissing it as 'a sideshow—the freaks are fascinating although they are hardly part of our lives'.... It was 'verbal goofballs' to *Saturday Review*, 'infantile, perversely negative' to the *Herald Tribune*, 'lack[ed] . . . seriousness' to *Commonweal*, 'like a slob running a temperature' to the *Hudson Review*, and a 'series of Neanderthal grunts' to *Encounter*. The *New Yorker* labeled Dean Moriarty 'a wild and incomprehensible ex-convict'; the *Atlantic* thought him 'more convincing as an eccentric than as a representative of any segment of humanity,' and *Time* diagnosed him as a victim of the Ganser Syndrome, whereby people weren't really mad—they only seemed to be." McNally concluded: "To understand *On the Road* one somehow needed an affinity for the intuitive and the sensual, for the romantic quest as opposed to the generally analytic realm of the critics. Since most critics had never experienced anything like the *Road*, they denied its existence as

art and proclaimed it a 'Beat Generation' tract of rebellion, then pilloried it as immoral." "According to the critics who wrote these reviews, ecstasy, when it occurred in a noninstitutional setting like the backseat of a car, was indistinguishable from mental and physical illness, filth, incoherence, deceit, criminal violence, degeneracy, and mindless folly," concurred Dardess. "This assumption said much, for those who had ears to hear it, about the depth of those critics' fears of their emotions and of their pride in the narrow limits of their intellects. But it did not say much of anything about *On the Road*."

Readers ignored the critics' negative appraisal of Kerouac and made *On the Road* a best seller for many weeks. The book came "at just the right time" to trigger a powerful response, William Burroughs told *Washington Post* interviewer Henry Allen. "The alienation, restlessness and dissatisfaction were already there," and *On the Road* offered a rallying point for the discontented; the book became a symbol for a rapidly evolving social movement. Kerouac was suddenly a celebrity, faced with many offers to explain the beat phenomenon in lecture halls, on radio, and on television. Public speaking was a nerve-wracking ordeal for him, but he did his best to publicize his novel. Unfortunately, these engagements often ended with Kerouac "uselessly trying to explain mystical poetry to pragmatic reporters who wanted nothing from him but hot copy," suggested McNally. The adulation of his fans proved even harder for him to cope with than the hostility of his critics. More than once, the writer was mobbed by crowds who came to hear him read. "Abuse he could comprehend, but not the blankness of an image-blinded fan," observed McNally. Kerouac began drinking heavily, and "the private person inside him began to crumble.... Even immersed in his booze, 'my liquid suit of armor, my shield which not even Flash Gordon's super ray gun could penetrate,' it was difficult for him to talk with people. Hungover and trembling, he groaned to John Holmes, 'I can't stand to meet anybody anymore. They talk to me like I wasn't me.' The fans wanted Jack to be Dean Moriarty, the free American cowboy, the limitless man who lived on life's mental frontiers. What no one beyond friends knew was that *On the Road* was six years old and superseded by a body of work Jack considered superior. Worse still, the Great God Public had condemned Jack to the easy-to-catalogue stereotype role of the bohemian novelist; evermore, he would be the King of the Beats."

Kerouac's stack of unpublished manuscripts ranged from the tender memories of a brother who died in childhood, simply expressed in *Visions of Gerard*, to the baroque surrealism of *Doctor Sax: Faust Part Three*, a novel of guilt and shadows. All of it was deemed unpublishable by *On the Road*'s editor. "Viking was not interested in bringing out a quirky legend, merely books," observed Gifford and Lee. Kerouac responded to the demand for a saleable manuscript with ten days of writing that produced *The Dharma Bums*. According to Gifford and Lee, *The Dharma Bums* was written "with an air of patient explanation, as though addressed to a book editor." Just as *On the Road* focused on Neal Cassady, *The Dharma Bums* provided a portrait of Gary Snyder, a poet and student of Oriental religions who had become Kerouac's friend in 1955. Viking again insisted that names be changed to avoid possible lawsuits, so Kerouac appeared as "Ray Smith," Snyder as "Japhy Ryder." *The Dharma Bums* characterized Ray and Japhy as modern religious wanderers in search of *dharma*, or truth. It is especially notable for Japhy Ryder's speech describing his vision of "a great rucksack revolution" of millions of young Americans, all becoming "Dharma Bums refusing to subscribe to the general demand that they consume . . . all that crap they didn't really want anyway such as refrigerators, TV sets, . . . certain hair oils and deodorants and general junk you finally always see a week later in the garbage anyway.'' It was an accurate prophecy of the hippies of the next decade.

The rest of Kerouac's work was published piecemeal, and never appeared as the interconnected series of novels he envisioned. *The Subterraneans, Doctor Sax: Faust Part Three, Maggie Cassidy: A Love Story, Mexico City Blues, Tristessa,* and *Lonesome Traveler* all came out within two years, most of them as inexpensive paperbacks. "Despite the fact that these titles included some of his strongest and most original spontaneous extended narrative, especially *Doctor Sax,* . . . the critics paid less and less attention to [Kerouac] as a serious writer in the furor over the emergence of the beat generation [as a social phenomenon]," wrote Ann Charters in the *Dictionary of Literary Biography.* Alfred Kazin's comments on *The Dharma Bums* typify most critics' dismissal of Kerouac as an artist. Kazin wrote in *Harper's*: "It is ridiculous that novels can now be sent off as quickly as they are written and published immediately afterwards in order to satisfy the hopped-up taste of people who, when they open a novel, want to feel that they are not missing a thing. The sluttishness of a society whose mass ideal seems to be unlimited consumption of all possible goods and services is the reason for the 'success' of writers [like Kerouac]."

Kerouac was unable to finish any writing projects for almost four years after completing *The Dharma Bums* late in 1958. He made several false starts, but even in his mother's house, his privacy was invaded by reporters and teenaged admirers who slipped through his bedroom window to steal his journals. By 1960, "the words had stopped," wrote Gifford and Lee. His subject had always been his own life, but "Jack found himself unable to translate what had happened to him since *On the Road* was published into a novel. . . . If he remained true to his aim of 'one vast book,' he would have to tell the story of a man incapable of dealing with his own success, unable to begin a family of his own, to find peace, to tend his art." Kerouac retreated to the tranquillity of a friend's cabin in California's remote Big Sur region, but once there he suffered a serious alcoholic breakdown, including a series of terrifying hallucinations of himself as a prize in a war between angels and devils. It took him a year to recuperate from the experience, but it provided him with the material for what Gifford and Lee referred to as "his capstone novel," *Big Sur,* "his single book dealing with the effects of the fame which had destroyed him." Ironically, when *Big Sur* was published in 1962 "it received excellent reviews, perhaps because it portrayed the 'King of the Beats' brought low, perhaps because of its frightening honesty."

But the joy had gone out of writing for Kerouac, as he told Ted Berrigan in a *Paris Review* interview: "I had a ritual once of lighting a candle and writing by its light and blowing it out when I was done for the night . . . also kneeling and praying before starting . . . but now I simply hate to write. . . . Frankly I do feel my mind is going. So another 'ritual' as you call it, is to pray to Jesus to preserve my sanity and my energy so I can help my family: That being my paralyzed mother, and my wife, and the ever-present kitties. . . . What I do now is write something like an average of 8,000 words a sitting, in the middle of the night, and another about a week later, resting and sighing in between. I really hate to write." Kerouac be-

came increasingly reclusive throughout the 1960s, and in 1969, he died of a stomach hemorrhage caused by chronic alcoholism.

Several years after Kerouac's death, his book *Visions of Cody* was published. Like *On the Road, Visions of Cody* was a prolonged meditation on Neal Cassady. In fact, the opening section was one of the false starts Kerouac made on the story that eventually became *On the Road. Visions of Cody* covered the same events as Kerouac's most famous book, but it was written in a style so unusual that he'd only been able to publish excerpts of it during his lifetime. When printed in its entirety in 1973, the book prompted *New York Times* reviewer Anatole Broyard to "propose, once and for all, a pox on 'spontaneity' in fiction. Spontaneity is a psychological, not a literary, quality. . . . The notion that what comes naturally is naturally welcome is one of the great idiocies of our age. What is 'Visions of Cody' about? Well, I've read it and I'm damned if I know.'' But while reviews like Broyard's echoed the hostility of Kerouac's original critics, more of them reflected a growing respect for the author's work. Aaron Latham's *New York Times Book Review* assessment of *Visions of Cody* began by stating that "'On the Road' was the 'Huckleberry Finn' of the mid-20th century," and went on to compare Kerouac to Thomas Wolfe, Louis-Ferdinand Celine, Mark Twain, and Jean Genet. "You will find some of Kerouac's very best writing in this book," summarized Latham. "It is funny. It is serious. It is eloquent. To read 'On the Road' but not 'Visions of Cody' is to take a nice sightseeing tour but to forgo the spectacular rapids of Jack Kerouac's wildest writing." Numerous biographies and scholarly works on Kerouac began appearing in the late 1970s, indicating that a complete reassessment of his literary output was taking place.

"Probably no famous American writer has been so mishandled by critics, who with few exceptions ignored the larger design in Kerouac's books, the integrity of his theme of individualism, his romantic optimism and his reverence for life, as well as the remarkable energy and humor of his novels, the originality of his prose method and the religious context of all his writing," declared Ann Charters in the *Dictionary of Literary Biography.* Kerouac's early detractors often referred to both his plots and his narrative voice as monotonous, but Charters challenged that judgement, calling his body of work "one of the most ambitious projects conceived by any modern writer in its scope, depth, and variety." Tytell commented similarly: "In so many ways there is something essentially American about Kerouac's writing; his restless energies could never settle for a final form, and each of his novels demonstrates an eager variety in their differences from each other, and from conventional expectations of what novels should be like."

Kerouac is now ranked among America's most important novelists by many commentators. Seymour Krim told the *National Observer,* "The only way you can understand Kerouac is as an *American* phenomenon. He is in the great American tradition of fiction from Thomas Wolfe right back through Mark Twain to Herman Melville. He did a lot to bring our fiction back home. His wild enthusiasm for all that is right and wrong with the country is really unique." Latham also emphasized Kerouac's role in revitalizing twentieth-century American prose: "When an effete literary language . . . threatened to silence all other voices, Kerouac . . . discovered the vernacular."

Kerouac's freedom with language is generally acknowledged as a liberating influence on many writers who came after him, including Ken Kesey, Charles Bukowski, Tom Robbins, and Richard Brautigan, as well as songwriter Bob Dylan. His nakedly confessional style led to the subjective reportage or "New Journalism" of Hunter S. Thompson and Tom Wolfe. Latham related that "when 'On the Road' made Jack Kerouac famous, [Truman] Capote delivered his famous one-liner: 'That's not writing, it's just typewriting.' But would he have written 'In Cold Blood' as a non-fiction novel if Jack Kerouac had not helped to make the form respectable?"

Finally, although Kerouac came to bitterly resent being cast as a social figurehead, his novels did make a significant impact on the lives of many who read them. According to Tytell, "*On the Road* still has a large and growing audience. For many, it was *the book* that most motivated dissatisfaction with the atmosphere of unquestioning acceptance that stifled the fifties; remarkably, despite the passage of time and its relative unpopularity among older university instructors, its audience grows, and young people especially gravitate to a force in it." Charters concluded: "What has been increasingly clear in the last twenty years is that the fabric of American culture has never been the same since 'Sal Paradise' and 'Dean Moriarty' went on the road. As Burroughs said, 'Kerouac opened a million coffee bars and sold a trillion Levis to both sexes. . . . Woodstock rises from his pages.'"

There is no major collection of Kerouac's papers in any university library. One notebook is at the University of Texas, Austin; five notebooks and a typescript are in the Berg Collection of the New York Public Library; some of his correspondence with Allen Ginsberg is at the Butler Library of Columbia University; other letters are in the Gary Snyder Archives at the library of the University of California, Davis. Ginsberg and other poets created the Jack Kerouac School of Disembodied Poetics at the Naropa Institute in Boulder, Colorado. *Moody Street Irregulars: A Jack Kerouac Newsletter*, edited by Joy Walsh and Michael Basinski, was established in 1978.

AVOCATIONAL INTERESTS: Reading, walking, late TV movies, and tape-recording FM musical programs.

MEDIA ADAPTATIONS: The Subterraneans was adapted as a film of the same title by Metro-Goldwyn-Mayer in 1960, starring George Peppard and Leslie Caron. A play based on Kerouac's life and works was produced in New York in 1976.

BIOGRAPHICAL/CRITICAL SOURCES:

BOOKS

Authors in the News, Volume 1, Gale, 1976.
Balakian, Nona, and Charles Simmons, *The Creative Present: Notes on Contemporary American Fiction*, Doubleday, 1963.
Cassady, Carolyn, *Heart Beat: My Life with Jack and Neal*, Creative Arts Book Co., 1977.
Challis, Chris, *Quest for Kerouac*, Faber, 1984.
Charters, Ann, *Kerouac: A Biography*, Straight Arrow, 1973.
Charters, *A Bibliography of Works by Jack Kerouac, 1939-1975*, Phoenix Book Shop, 1975.
Clark, Tom, *Jack Kerouac*, Harcourt, 1984.
Concise Dictionary of American Literary Biography, Volume 1: *The New Consciousness, 1941-1968*, Gale, 1987.
Contemporary Literary Criticism, Gale, Volume 1, 1973, Volume 2, 1974, Volume 3, 1975, Volume 5, 1976, Volume 14, 1980, Volume 29, 1984.
Cook, Bruce, *The Beat Generation*, Scribner, 1971.
Dictionary of Literary Biography, Gale, Volume 2: *American Novelists since World War II*, 1978, Volume 16: *The Beats: Literary Bohemians in Postwar America*, Gale, 1983.

Dictionary of Literary Biography Documentary Series, Volume 3, Gale, 1983.
Donaldson, Scott, editor, *On the Road: Text and Criticism*, Viking, 1979.
Feied, Frederick, *No Pie in the Sky: The Hobo as American Culture Hero in the Works of Jack London, John Dos Passos, and Jack Kerouac*, Citadel, 1964.
Fiedler, Leslie, *Waiting for the End*, Stein & Day, 1964.
French, Warren, editor, *The Fifties: Fiction, Poetry, Drama*, Everett/Edwards, 1970.
French, *Jack Kerouac*, Twayne, 1986.
Fuller, Edmund, *Man in Modern Fiction: Some Minority Opinions on Contemporary American Writings*, Random House, 1958.
Gaffie, Luc, *Jack Kerouac: The New Picaroon*, Postillion Press, 1977.
Gifford, Barry, *Kerouac's Town*, Capra, 1973, revised edition, Creative Arts Book Co., 1977.
Gifford and Lawrence Lee, *Jack's Book: An Oral Biography of Jack Kerouac*, St. Martin's, 1978.
Ginsberg, Allen, *Allen Verbatim: Lectures on Poetry, Politics, Consciousness*, McGraw, 1974.
Hipkiss, Robert A., *Jack Kerouac: Prophet of the New Romanticism*, University of Kansas Press, 1977.
Holmes, John Clellon, *Nothing More to Declare*, Dutton, 1967.
Huebel, Harry Russell, *Jack Kerouac*, Boise State University, 1979.
Hunt, Tim, *Kerouac's Crooked Road: Development of a Fiction*, Archon Books, 1981.
Jarvis, Charles E., *Visions of Kerouac*, Ithaca Press, 1973.
Jones, Granville H., *Lectures on Modern Novelists*, Carnegie Institute, 1963.
Kerouac, Jack, *Lonesome Traveler*, McGraw, 1960.
Kerouac and Allen Ginsberg, *Take Care of My Ghost, Ghost*, Ghost Press, 1977.
Kerouac and Carolyn Cassady, *Dear Carolyn: Letters to Carolyn Cassady*, Unspeakable Visions, 1983.
Lindberg, Gary, *The Confidence Man in American Literature*, Oxford University Press, 1982.
McNally, Dennis, *Desolate Angel: Jack Kerouac, the Beat Generation, and America*, McGraw, 1979.
Milewski, Robert J., *Jack Kerouac: An Annotated Bibliography of Secondary Sources, 1944-1979*, Scarecrow, 1981.
Montgomery, John, *The Kerouac We Knew: Unposed Portraits: Action Shots*, Fels & Firn, 1982.
Moore, Harry T., editor, *Contemporary American Novelists*, Southern Illinois University Press, 1964.
Nicosia, Gerald, *Memory Babe: A Critical Biography of Jack Kerouac*, Grove, 1983.
Nisonger, T. E., *Jack Kerouac: A Bibliography of Biographical and Critical Material, 1950-1979*, Bull Bibliography, 1980.
Parkinson, Thomas, editor, *A Casebook on the Beat*, Crowell, 1961.
Podhoretz, Norman, *Doings and Undoings*, Farrar, Straus, 1964.
Tanner, Tony, *City of Words*, Harper, 1971.
Tytell, John, *Naked Angels: The Lives and Literature of the Beat Generation*, McGraw, 1976.
Waldmeir, Joseph J., editor, *Recent American Fiction*, Houghton, 1963.

PERIODICALS

American Literature, May, 1974.
Atlantic, July, 1965.
Best Sellers, February 15, 1968.

Books, December, 1966.
Books Abroad, summer, 1967.
Books and Bookmen, May, 1969.
Chicago Review, winter-spring, 1959.
Chicago Tribune, August 22, 1986.
Commonweal, February 2, 1959.
Contemporary Literature, summer, 1974.
Critique: Studies in Modern Fiction, Volume XIV, number 3, 1973.
Detroit Free Press, November 13, 1986.
Evergreen Review, summer, 1958, spring, 1959.
Harper's, October, 1959.
Hudson Review, winter, 1959-60, spring, 1967.
Listener, June 27, 1968.
Los Angeles Times, September 19, 1986, September 20, 1986.
Midwest Quarterly, summer, 1973.
National Observer, February 5, 1968, December 9, 1968.
New Statesman, November 23, 1973.
Newsweek, December 19, 1960.
New York Post, March 10, 1959.
New York Review of Books, May 20, 1965, April 11, 1968.
New York Times, September 5, 1957, May 4, 1965, June 8, 1965, January 9, 1973, April 16, 1986.
New York Times Book Review, May 2, 1965, February 26, 1967, February 18, 1968, January 28, 1973.
Observer, November 19, 1967.
Observer Review, November 19, 1967.
Paris Review, summer, 1968.
Partisan Review, Volume XL, number 2, 1973.
Playboy, June, 1959.
Prairie Schooner, spring, 1974.
Reporter, April 3, 1958.
Review of Contemporary Fiction, Volume III, number 2, 1983.
Saturday Review, January 11, 1958, May 2, 1959, June 12, 1965, December 2, 1972.
Small Press Review, March, 1983.
South Atlantic Quarterly, autumn, 1974.
Spectator, November 24, 1967, March 28, 1969, August 10, 1974, August 24, 1974.
Stand, Volume XVI, number 2, 1975.
Tamarack Review, spring, 1959.
Time, February 23, 1968.
Times Literary Supplement, May 26, 1966, February 1, 1968, March 27, 1969, April 6, 1973, November 2, 1973, September 13, 1974, April 22, 1977.
Village Voice, September 18, 1957, November 12, 1958.
Virginia Quarterly Review, spring, 1973.
Washington Post, October 22, 1969, August 2, 1982.
Washington Post Book World, April 8, 1973.

OTHER

"What Happened to Kerouac?" (documentary film), produced by Richard Lerner, 1986.

OBITUARIES:

PERIODICALS

Detroit Free Press, October 22, 1969.
L'Express, October 27-November 2, 1969.
Newsweek, November 3, 1969.
New York Times, October 22, 1969.
Publishers Weekly, November 3, 1969.
Rolling Stone, November 29, 1969.
Time, October 31, 1969.
Variety, October 29, 1969.
Village Voice, October 30, 1969, November 28, 1969.

Washington Post, October 22, 1969.†

—*Sketch by Joan Goldsworthy*

*   *   *

KEROUAC, John
See KEROUAC, Jean-Louis Lebrid de

*   *   *

KESLER, Jay 1935-

PERSONAL: Born September 15, 1935, in Barnes, Wis.; son of Herbert E. and Elsie (Campbell) Kesler; married Jane Smith, June 7, 1957; children: Laura, Bruce, Terri. *Education:* Attended Ball State University, 1953-54; Taylor University, B.A., 1958.

ADDRESSES: Home—711 Reade Ave., Upland, Ind. 46989. *Office*—Taylor University, Reade Ave., Upland, Ind. 46989.

CAREER: Youth for Christ International, Wheaton, Ill., director of Marion, Ind. branch, 1955-58, crusade staff evangelist, 1959-60, director of Illinois-Indiana region, 1960-62, director of college recruitment, 1962-63, vice-president for personnel, 1963-68, vice-president for field coordination, 1968-73, president, 1973-85, and current member of board of directors; Taylor University, Upland, Ind., president, 1985—. Chief executive officer, Youth for Christ International's interdenominational ministry to high school students throughout the United States. Co-pastor, First Baptist Church of Geneva, Geneva, Ill., 1972-85. Faculty member, Billy Graham Schools of Evangelism. Lecturer, Staley Distinguished Christian Scholar lecture program. Speaker on daily radio broadcast "Family Forum." Member of board of directors, Brotherhood Mutual Insurance Co.

MEMBER: Christian Educators Association International, International Council on Biblical Inerrancy (member of advisory board), Prison Fellowship International (member of board of directors), Venture Middle East (member of advisory board), National Association of Evangelicals Board of Administration (member of board of directors), National Educators Fellowship, Christianity Today (member of board of directors), Evangelical Council for Financial Accountability (member of board of directors), Christian Camps, Inc., Christian College Coalition, Christian Bible Society (member of advisory board), Discovery Network, Inc. (member of advisory board), Evangelicals for Social Action (member of advisory board), Project Partner, Independent Colleges and Universities of Indiana (member of board of directors).

AWARDS, HONORS: D.D., Barrington College, 1977, Asbury Theological Seminary, 1984; L.H.D., Taylor University, 1982, John Brown University, 1987; H.H.D., Huntington College, 1983; Angel Award, Religion in Media, 1985.

WRITINGS:

Let's Succeed with Our Teenagers, David Cook, 1973.
I Never Promised You a Disneyland, Word, Inc., 1975.
The Strong Weak People, Victor Books, 1976.
Outside Disneyland, Word, Inc., 1977.
I Want a Home with No Problems, Word, Inc., 1977.
Growing Places, Revell, 1978.
Too Big to Spank, Regal Books, 1978.
Breakthrough, Zondervan, 1981.
Family Forum, Victor Books, 1984.
Parents and Teenagers, Victor Books, 1984.

Making Life Make Sense, Tyndale, 1986.
Parents and Children, Victor Books, 1986.

Contributor to numerous evangelical publications, including *Christianity Today, Christian Herald, Partnership, Focus on the Family*, and *Today's Christian Woman*. Also author of column, "I Never Promised You a Disneyland," *Campus Life* (magazine), 1974-75. Member of editorial review committee for *New King James Bible;* member of advisory committee, *Campus Life*.

*   *   *

KEYES, Daniel   1927-

PERSONAL: Born August 9, 1927, in Brooklyn, N.Y.; son of William and Betty (Alicke) Keyes; married Aurea Vazquez (a fashion stylist, photographer, and artist), October 14, 1952; children: Hillary Ann, Leslie Joan. *Education:* Brooklyn College (now Brooklyn College of the City University of New York), A.B., 1950, A.M., 1961.

ADDRESSES: Home—Athens, Ohio. *Office*—Department of English, Ohio University, Athens, Ohio 45701. *Agent*—Ned Leavitt, William Morris Agency, 1350 Avenue of the Americas, New York, N.Y. 10019.

CAREER: Stadium Publishing Co., New York City, associate fiction editor, 1951-52; Fenko & Keyes Photography, Inc., New York City, co-owner, 1953; high school teacher of English, Brooklyn, N.Y., 1954-55, 1957-62; Wayne State University, Detroit, Mich., instructor in English, 1962-66; Ohio University, Athens, lecturer, 1966-72, professor of English, 1972—, director of creative writing center, 1973-74, 1977-78. *Wartime service:* U.S. Maritime Service, senior assistant purser, 1945-47.

MEMBER: Associated Writers Program, Authors Guild, Authors League of America, P.E.N., Dramatists Guild.

AWARDS, HONORS: Hugo Award, World Science Fiction Convention, 1959, for "Flowers for Algernon" (short story); Nebula Award, Science Fiction Writers of America, 1966, for *Flowers for Algernon* (novel); special award, Mystery Writers of America, 1981, for *The Minds of Billy Milligan;* Kurd Lasswitz Award for best book by a foreign author, 1986, for German translation of *The Minds of Billy Milligan;* Edgar Allan Poe Award nomination, Mystery Writers of America, 1986, for *Unveiling Claudia: A True Story of a Serial Murder;* individual artists fellowship, Ohio Arts Council, 1986-87; Baker Fund Award, Ohio University, 1986-87.

WRITINGS:

NOVELS

Flowers for Algernon, Harcourt, 1966 (several foreign editions published as *Charly;* published as *I.Q. 185* by Vitgeverij Born NV [Amsterdam]).
The Touch, Harcourt, 1968 (published in England as *The Contaminated Man*, Mayflower, 1973).
The Fifth Sally, Houghton, 1980.

NONFICTION

The Minds of Billy Milligan (Book-of-the-Month Club selection), Random House, 1981, revised edition, with afterword, Bantam, 1982.
Unveiling Claudia: A True Story of a Serial Murder, Bantam, 1986.

OTHER

(Contributor) David A. Sohn, editor, *Ten Top Stories*, Bantam, 1964.

Also contributor to numerous anthologies. Contributor of fiction to periodicals. Associate editor, *Marvel Science Fiction*, 1951.

WORK IN PROGRESS: The Sunshine Executioner, a novel.

SIDELIGHTS: The author of several books focusing on psychological themes, Daniel Keyes told *CA* that he is "fascinated by the complexities of the human mind." Keyes is perhaps best known for his novel *Flowers for Algernon*, the story of Charlie, a mentally retarded man who is transformed into a genius by psychosurgery, only to eventually regress. *Flowers for Algernon*, which originally appeared as a short story in *Magazine of Fantasy and Science Fiction*, is viewed by a *Times Literary Supplement* contributor as "a good example of that kind of science fiction which uses a persuasive hypothesis to explore emotional and moral issues. . . . In its ideas, especially in its speculations about the relationship between I.Q. and maturity, this is a far more intelligent book than the vast majority of 'straight' novels. . . . Charlie's hopeless knowledge that he is destined to end in a home for the feeble-minded, a moron who knows that he is a moron, is painful, and Mr. Keyes has the technical equipment to prevent us from shrugging off the pain."

Two of Keyes's books, *The Fifth Sally* and *The Minds of Billy Milligan*, deal with the subject of multiple personalities and are dramatic recreations of factual cases. The title character of *The Fifth Sally* is Sally Porter, a woman who harbors four personalities that embody her emotional states: Nola, an intellectual artist; Derry, a free-spirited tomboy; Bella, a promiscuous woman; and Jinx, a murderous personality. The novel examines the efforts of Sally and her doctor to fuse the four beings into one complete person. "This is an intriguing story," writes mel Gilden in the *Los Angeles Times*, "but the reader is able to remain an observer rather than becoming emotionally involved. . . . Despite the intellectual distance maintained between Sally and reader, the book will reward almost anyone who reads it."

The Minds of Billy Milligan is based on the case of Billy Milligan, who was arrested on rape charges in Ohio in 1977 and who later became the first person in U.S. history to be acquitted of a major felony by reason of multiple personality. At the time of his arrest, Billy Milligan was found to possess no fewer than twenty-four personalities—three of them female—ages ranging from three to twenty-four years old. Among Milligan's dominant personalities were Arthur, a Britisher in charge of all the others; Ragen, a violent Yugoslav who acted as physical protector; and Adalana, a nineteen-year-old lesbian who confessed to instituting the three rapes with which Milligan was charged. According to Keyes, these personalities, along with all the rest, would share "the spot"—control of Milligan's consciousness—whenever their distinctive qualities were needed.

The circumstances under which Keyes was contracted to write Milligan's story proved unusual: It was only after several of Milligan's selves read *Flowers for Algernon* that they agreed among themselves to work with the author. In *The Minds of Billy Milligan*, Keyes writes of a personality known as "The Teacher." The Teacher kept the memory of all the other beings in Milligan and provided much of the book's background information. Through the different personas, the author describes the life of a young man who had suffered years of mental and physical abuse at the hands of his stepfather, and how he had sought solace and protection from the various people existing in him.

After Milligan was arrested and sent to a correctional institution for observation, debate surfaced as to how to best classify his mental state. According to Robert Coles in the *New York Times Book Review*, "Keyes makes quite evident in 'The Minds of Billy Milligan,' [that] historical tensions within the [medical] profession have yet to be resolved, and have, in fact, been given new expression in this instance. . . . Even as the Ohio prosecuting attorneys were quite rightfully arguing that Mr. Milligan should be jailed, a number of Ohio doctors, nurses, and psychologists . . . were wrangling strenuously over precisely where and how such a person should be locked up. When he was found 'insane,' needless to say, the arguments did not by any means abate. Was he a 'sociopath'—a liar, an impostor?. . . Was he a severely disturbed and dangerous 'psychotic' who required careful watching, lots of medication, maybe a course or two of electric shock treatment?"

Coles ultimately commends Keyes for telling "this complicated story well. It reads like a play: Billy's 'personalities' come onstage, leave to be replaced by others and then reappear." Peter Gorner finds this distracting; in a *Chicago Tribune* review of the book, he states that the author "interviews everybody, reconstructs, flashes back, and confuses the story in a chatty, conversational style. The alter egos seem to dance before our eyes like a stroboscope." However, in the opinion of David Johnston in the *Los Angeles Times*, "telling the stories of twenty-four different personalities would be a difficult task for any writer. To tell of two dozen personalities in one human body is an extremely complex task. Keyes, on balance, carries it off quite well. While it shortchanges the reader by limiting explanation of motives almost exclusively to Milligan's personalities, [*The Minds of Billy Milligan*] is nonetheless a fascinating work." Finally, *Washington Post Book World*, reviewer Joseph McLellan points out that "complexity is . . . the keynote of the Billy phenomenon and equally of its treatment by Daniel Keyes. The challenge of first unearthing this story . . . and then telling it intelligibly was a daunting one. He has carried it off brilliantly, bringing to the assignment not only a fine clarity but a special warmth, and empathy for the victim of circumstances and mental failings that made *Flowers for Algernon* one of the most memorable novels of the 1960s."

As in his two previous works, Keyes unravels the bizarre incidents in a mentally ill person's life in *Unveiling Claudia: A True Story of a Serial Murder*. Claudia Elaine Yasko, having known both the victims and the murderers in three Ohio killings in the late 1970s, fantasized herself as the murderer. She confessed to the homicides in 1978 but the charges were dropped once the real killers were accidentally discovered. Keyes's book records the evolving incidents and attempts to explain why Yasko knew so much about the killings. Writes Gregor A. Preston in the *Library Journal*, "while not as intriguing as *Billy Milligan*, this is a masterfully told, absorbing story."

MEDIA ADAPTATIONS: Television play "The Two Worlds of Charlie Gordon," based on the short story "Flowers for Algernon," CBS Playhouse, February 22, 1961; feature film "Charly," based on the novel *Flowers for Algernon*, starring Cliff Robertson, winner of an Academy Award for this role, Cinerama, 1968; two-act play "Flowers for Algernon," adapted by David Rogers, Dramatic Publishing, 1969; dramatic musical "Charlie and Algernon," first produced at Citadel The-

ater, Alberta, Canada, December 21, 1978, produced at Queens Theater, London, England, June 14, 1979, first produced in the United States at Terrace Theater, Kennedy Center, Washington, D.C., March 8, 1980, produced on Broadway at Helen Hayes Theater, September 4, 1980; other adaptions of *Flowers for Algernon* include: French stage play, first produced at Theater Espace Massalia, Marseille, France, October 11, 1982; Irish radio monodrama, first broadcast by Radio Telefis Eireann, Dublin, Ireland, October 25, 1983; Australian stageplay, produced by Jigsaw Theater Company, March, 1984; Polish stage play, adapted by Jerzy Gudejka, first produced at W. Horzyca Memorial Theater of Torun, Torun, Poland, March 3, 1985; and Japanese stage play, first produced at Kinokuniya Theater, Tokyo, Japan, January 20, 1987.

BIOGRAPHICAL/CRITICAL SOURCES:

BOOKS

Scholes, Robert, *Structural Fabulation*, University of Notre Dame Press, 1975.

PERIODICALS

Chicago Tribune, November 11, 1981.
Library Journal, July, 1986.
Los Angeles Times, December 12, 1980.
Los Angeles Times Book Review, January 3, 1982.
New York Times Book Review, November 15, 1981, August 24, 1986.
Saturday Review, March 26, 1966.
Times Literary Suppplement, July 21, 1966.
Village Voice Literary Supplement, October, 1981.
Washington Post Book World, November 29, 1981.

*   *   *

KILLENS, John Oliver   1916-1987

PERSONAL: Born January 14, 1916, in Macon, Ga.; died of cancer, October 27, 1987, in Brooklyn, N.Y.; son of Charles Myles, Sr., and Willie Lee (Coleman) Killens; married Grace Ward Jones; children: Jon Charles, Barbara Ellen Rivera. *Education:* Attended Edward Waters College, Morris Brown College, Atlanta University, Howard University, Robert H. Terrell Law School, Columbia University, and New York University.

ADDRESSES: Home—1392 Union St., Brooklyn, N.Y. 11212.

CAREER: Member of staff, National Labor Relations Board, 1936-42, and 1946; free-lance writer, 1954-87. Writer in residence, Fisk University, 1965-68, Columbia University, 1970-73, Howard University, 1971-72, Bronx Community College, 1979-81, and Medgar Evers College of the City University of New York, 1981-87. Former lecturer and teacher of creative writing at New School for Social Research, and lecturer at several other colleges and universities, including Southern University, Cornell University, Rutgers University, University of California, Los Angeles, Tufts University, Brandeis College (now Brandeis University), Springfield College, Western Michigan University, Savannah State College, and Trinity College. Co-founder and past chairperson, Harlem Writers Guild, 1952. *Military service:* U.S. Army, Pacific Amphibian Forces, 1942-45.

MEMBER: PEN, American Poets, Playwrights, Editors, Essayists, and Novelists (former member of executive board), Black Academy of Arts and Letters (former vice-president),

National Center of Afro-American Artists (former member of executive board).

AWARDS, HONORS: Afro Art Theatre Cultural Award, 1955; Literary Arts Award, National Association for the Advancement of Colored People (Brooklyn), 1957; Culture, Human Relations Award, Climbers Business Club; citation from Empire State Federation of Women; cultural award, New York State Fraternal Order of Elks; Charles Chesnut Award, Brooklyn Association for the Study of Negro Life and History; *And Then We Heard the Thunder* was nominated for a Pulitzer Prize, 1962; Rabinowitz Foundation grant, 1964; *The Cotillion; or, One Good Bull Is Half the Herd* was nominated for a Pulitzer Prize, 1971; Harlem Writers Guild award, 1978; National Endowment for the Arts fellowship, 1980; Lifetime Achievement Award, Before Columbus Foundation, 1986; elected to Black Filmmaker's Hall of Fame.

WRITINGS:

FICTION

Youngblood, Dial, 1954, published with foreword by Addison Gayle, University of Georgia Press, 1982.
And Then We Heard the Thunder, Knopf, 1962, reprinted, Howard University Press, 1983.
'Sippi, Trident Press, 1967, reprinted, Thunder's Mouth Press, 1988.
Slaves, Pyramid, 1969.
The Cotillion; or, One Good Bull Is Half the Herd (also see below), Trident Press, 1971, reprinted, Ballantine, 1988.
Great Gittin' Up Morning: A Biography of Denmark Vesey (young adult), Doubleday, 1972.
A Man Ain't Nothin' but a Man: The Adventures of John Henry (young adult), Little, Brown, 1975.
The Great Black Russian: A Novel on the Life and Times of Alexander Pushkin, Wayne State University Press, 1988.

Also author of *The Minister Primarily.*

PLAYS

(With Loften Mitchell) "Ballad of the Winter Soldier," first produced in Washington, D.C., at Philharmonic Hall, Lincoln Center, September 28, 1964.
"Lower Than the Angels," first produced in New York City, at American Place Theatre, January, 1965.
"Cotillion" (based on Killens's novel of same title, with music by Smokey Robinson and Willie Hutch), first produced in New York City at New Federal Theatre, July, 1975.

SCREENPLAYS

(With Nelson Gidding) "Odds Against Tomorrow," Belafonte Productions/United Artists, 1959.
(With Herbert J. Biberman and Alida Sherman) "Slaves," Theatre Guild-Walter Reade/Continental, 1969.

WORK REPRESENTED IN ANTHOLOGIES

David Boroff, *The State of the Nation,* Prentice-Hall, 1966.
John Henrik Clarke, editor, *American Negro Short Stories,* Hill & Wang, 1966.
Langston Hughes, editor, *The Best Short Stories by Negro Writers: An Anthology from 1899 to the Present,* Little, Brown, 1967.
Harlem, New American Library, 1970.
Raman K. Singh and Peter Fellowes, editors, *Voices from the Soul of Black America,* Crowell, 1970.

Nick Aaron, editor, *Black Insights: Significant Literature by Black Americans, 1760 to the Present,* Ginn, 1971.
Patricia L. Brown, Don L. Lee, and Francis Ward, editors, *To Gwen with Love: An Anthology Dedicated to Gwendolyn Brooks,* Johnson, 1971.
Addison Gayle, Jr., editor, *The Black Aesthetic,* Doubleday, 1971.
John A. Williams and Charles F. Harris, editors, *Amistad 2,* Vintage Books, 1971.
William H. Robinson, editor, *Nommo: An Anthology of Modern African and Black American Literature,* Macmillan, 1972.

OTHER

Black Man's Burden (essays), Trident Press, 1965.
(Author of prologue) Fred Halstead, *Harlem Stirs,* photographs by Don Hogan Charles and Anthony Aviles, Marzani & Munsell, 1966.
(Contributor) John Henrik Clarke, editor, *William Styron's Nat Turner: Ten Black Writers Respond,* Beacon, 1968.
(Editor and author of foreword) *Trial Record of Denmark Vesey,* Beacon, 1970.
(Author of introduction) Woodie King, editor, *Black Short Story Anthology,* Columbia University Press, 1972.
"John O. Killens on Alexander Pushkin" (audio cassette), Institute of Afro-American Affaris (New York), 1976.
"John Oliver Killens" (audio cassette), Tapes for Readers (Washington, D.C.), 1978.

Also author of *Write On!: Notes from a Writers Workshop.* Contributor to periodicals, including *Ebony, Black World, Black Aesthetic, African Forum, Library Journal, Nation, Saturday Evening Post, Black Scholar, Freedomways, Redbook,* and *Arts in Society.*

SIDELIGHTS: "Ever since I can remember, I have always been a sucker for a well-told tale, and the more outlandish and outrageous, the better, as far as I was concerned," John Oliver Killens wrote in his autobiographical essay in *Contemporary Authors Autobiography Series,* "The Half Ain't Never Been Told." Killens credited his beloved paternal great-grandmother for his decision to become a writer. Seven years old when slavery was abolished, she had regaled Killens in his youth with memorable stories about those days: "Puffing on her corncob pipe, speaking in the mellifluous voice, enriched by age.... She seemed to encompass within herself all the wisdom of the ages. Sometimes at the end of each tale, she would shake her head, all white with age, the skin of her face unwrinkled and tight as a newborn baby's backside, stretchd tautly over high cheekbones. And she'd say, 'Aaah Lord, Honey, THE HALF AIN'T NEVER BEEN TOLD!'" And challenged to tell at least part of that untold half, Killens remarked, "I felt I owed that much to Granny."

Killens also indicated in his autobiographical essay that he had been a voracious reader as a child, taking his cherished library books to bed with him to read by flashlight. During his teenage years, his early dreams of becoming a physician, though, were replaced with those of becoming a lawyer. And despite years of studying law by night and working by day at the Negro Labor Relations Board, he decided during a stint with the U.S. Army in the South Pacific that he would not return to law school, but would become a writer instead. "One evening in the early fifties or late forties, I gathered with seven others up above a store front on 125th Street in Harlem and, in a very trembly voice, read the first chapter of *Youngblood,*" wrote Killens in his autobiographical essay. This early group of young, black, and soon-to-be prominent writers, formed the nucleus of the distinguished and prolific Harlem Writers Guild; and Killens's first book, *Youngblood*, was the first novel to be published from it.

Youngblood is about a Southern black family's struggle for survival. Through the characters of the parents and their two children, Killens "exposes his readers to what life was like for Afro-Americans living in the American South during the first third of this century," wrote William H. Wiggins, Jr. in the *Dictionary of Literary Biography*. "The novel demonstrates how these four characters band together to overcome the economic, educational, social, and religious manifestations of Jim Crow life in their hometown of Crossroads, Georgia." Called a "fine novel, vivid, readable," by Ann Petry in the *New York Herald Tribune Book Review*, *Youngblood* is described by Granville Hicks in the *New York Times* as "a record of petty, mean-spirited, wanton discrimination." And although Hicks found it "didactic" at times, he also found it to have "the power of the author's passion" and declared that "the novel of social protest, which survives precariously today, justifies itself when it is as moving as 'Youngblood' and deals with so gross an evil."

Killens's second novel, *And Then We Heard the Thunder*, is based on his own experience with segregation and racism in the military during the Second World War. According to Martin Levin in the *New York Times Book Review*, the novel's black protagonist, who wishes only to be "the best damn soldier," is forced instead "to make common cause with his race rather than with his army." Although critics tended to fault the style of the novel, they nonetheless responded well to its message. While Nelson Algren suggested in the *New York Herald Tribune Book Review* that the book "lacked the passion of men at war," J. H. Griffin in the *Saturday Review* found the battle scenes in particular filled with "hallucinatory power," and declared that the reader who has not experienced racial discrimination, "living all the indignities of the Negro soldier, sees clearly how it looked from the other side of the color line." Griffin concludes that "this novel magnificently illumines the reasons why" the wounds remain despite discrimination having been eliminated from the armed forces.

Killens's *'Sippi* "reflects his new militancy," wrote Wiggins, indicating that the title originates from a "civil rights protest joke" in which a black man informs his white landlord that he will no longer include mister or miss when addressing others, including the state of Mississippi, "It's just plan 'Sippi from now on!" The novel concerns the struggles over voting rights during the 1960s and Wiggins added that Killens "recounts in vivid detail the bombings, shootings, and other acts of terror and intimidation endured by the courageous students and local blacks who dare stand up and push for voter registration." Wiggins reported that there was a lack of a critical middle ground regarding the novel—critics either did or did not like it. Acknowledging in his autobiographical essay that the novel "was a critical bust," Killens added, "I heartily disagreed with the critics, naturally. Or else why would I have written it?"

Killens's *The Cotillion; or One Good Bull Is Half the Herd* is a satire about an annual ball held by an exclusive black women's club in Brooklyn. "Through hyperbole and cutting social and political commentary, Killens's novel becomes a biting didactic piece of Afro-American literature, written in the tradition of verbal contests known as the dozens to many Afro-Americans," explained Wiggins. "The object of the game is

to unsettle one's verbal opponent with exaggerated statements of personal insults." Noting that "this is precisely the plot" of *The Cotillion*, Wiggins wrote that by the end of the novel, "Killens has reduced this sedate group of society matrons to a confused and disorganized group of babbling black women who have been verbally stripped of their veneer of white middle-class values and exposed for what they truly are: comically tragic Afro-Americans who are out of touch with their cultural heritage." Calling its language "Afro-Americanese," George Davis commented in *Black World* that *The Cotillion* "signifies and lies and intrudes on itself whenever it sees fit. It dances around while it is talking and comes all out of itself to make sure you get the point that it is making. It starts to exaggerate and keeps on exaggerating even though it knows that you know that the truth is being stretched out of shape." Leonard Fleischer observed in *Saturday Review* that "in a prose often buoyantly evocative and musical, Killens caricatures some of the more egregious foibles of black and white society." Moreover, continued Fleischer, while making use of stereotyped blacks to satirically reveal a "willing acceptance of the standards of white culture," Killens is simultaneously "mocking the rage for instant blackness."

"Killens's major themes evolve around social protest and cultural affirmation," wrote Wiggins, who felt that Killens "fashioned his career in the protest mold of Richard Wright. For both of these writers the primary purpose of art is to attack and ultimately change society for the better." Although recognized and praised for his novels, Killens also achieved distinction for his essays on the quality of black life in America. Wiggins wrote that Killens's collection of political essays, *Black Man's Burden*, "demonstrates the shift in Killens's philosophy" away from the nonviolence espoused by Martin Luther King, Jr., and toward the more militant views of his friend, Malcolm X: "In the series of essays on such subjects as white paternalism, black manhood, unions, sit-ins, boycotts, religion, black nationalism, Africa, nonviolence, and the right of self-defense, Killens argued that passive acceptance of racial oppression only encourages more racial violence. Killens believed that the only way blacks could break the vicious cycle of racial violence would be to respond to white violence with black violence." In an *America* review of the collection, John Hattman stated that "Killens writes in rough strong language, but it is a language well suited to carry the author's harsh message." And in the *Saturday Review*, Frank M. Cordasco observed that Killens had assembled "a pastiche of perceptive, sharply delineated vignettes animated by the twin engines of hate and despair."

Killens's work is internationally known, having been translated into more than a dozen languages. In his autobiographical essay, he wrote that when he travelled to Africa in 1961 to do research for a British Broadcasting Corp. script, he viewed a screening of his own motion picture, "Odds Against Tomorrow," with French subtitles. And when the author journeyed to China in 1973 with a group of writers and teachers, he learned that he and Ernest Hemingway were "two of the most widely read writers there." Killens's travels also took him to the Soviet Union. In 1968 and 1970, he attended a festival in the Soviet Union where "writers and artists are invited . . . from all over the world to celebrate the life of Alexander Sergeievich Pushkin," the subject of a novel on which he had worked since the middle 1960s. Killens indicated in his autobiographical essay that he had also completed a comedic novel entitled *The Minister Primarily*, and a book about the art and craft of creative writing entitled *Write On!: Notes from a Writers Workshop*. As a prominent novelist, playwright, essayist, and teacher, Killens "strove in all his work to distill and express the black experience in this country," wrote Richard Pearson in the *Washington Post*. "In doing so he reached an audience that transcended boundaries of race or color to express common denominators in human nature."

BIOGRAPHICAL/CRITICAL SOURCES:

BOOKS

Contemporary Authors Autobiography Series, Volume 2, Gale, 1985.
Contemporary Literary Criticism, Volume 10, Gale, 1979.
Dictionary of Literary Biography, Volume 33: Afro-American Fiction Writers after 1955, Gale, 1984.
Gayle, Addison, Jr., *The Way of the World: The Black Novel in America*, Anchor Press/Doubleday, 1975.
Littlejohn, David, *Black on White: A Critical Survey of Writing by American Negroes*, Viking Penguin, 1966.
Williams, John A., and Charles F. Harris, editors, *Amistad 2*, Random House, 1971.

PERIODICALS

Atlantic, February, 1971.
Best Sellers, February 1, 1963, October 1, 1965, March 15, 1972.
Black Scholar, November, 1971.
Black World, June, 1971.
Christian Science Monitor, May 4, 1972.
Crisis, October, 1954, April, 1965.
Freedomways, 1971.
Keystone Folklore Quarterly, fall, 1972.
Midwest Journal, summer, 1954.
Nation, August 21, 1954.
National Observer, July 15, 1968.
Negro Digest, November, 1967.
Newsweek, May 26, 1969.
New York Herald Tribune Book Review, July 11, 1954, April 14, 1963.
New York Review of Books, April 20, 1972.
New York Times, June 6, 1954, March 2, 1969, March 28, 1969, March 27, 1970, May 29, 1972.
New York Times Book Review, February 27, 1966, January 17, 1971, April 30, 1972, August 10, 1975.
Saturday Review, January 26, 1963, March 12, 1966, March 6, 1971.
Time, October 26, 1959.
Washington Post Book World, May 29, 1988.

OBITUARIES:

PERIODICALS

Jet, November 16, 1987.
Los Angeles Times, October 31, 1987.
New York Times, October 30, 1987.
Washington Post, November 3, 1987.†

—*Sketch by Sharon Malinowski*

*   *   *

KIMBALL, Stanley B(uchholz)   1926-

PERSONAL: Born November 25, 1926, in Farmington, Utah; son of Richard H. and Vontella (Hess) Kimball; married Violet Tew, June 27, 1953; children: Chase, Hope, Vontella Kay, April. *Education:* University of Denver, B.A., 1948, M.A.,

1952; Columbia University, Ph.D. and Certificate, Program on East Central Europe, 1959. *Religion:* Mormon.

ADDRESSES: Home—745 Saddle Dr., Florissant, Mo. 63033. *Office*—Department of History, Southern Illinois University at Edwardsville, Edwardsville, Ill. 62026.

CAREER: Worker for Mormon Church in Prague, Czechoslovakia, 1948-50; Arts Council, Inc., Winston-Salem, N.C., director, 1952-55; City College (now City College of the City University of New York), New York City, instructor, 1956-59; Columbia University, New York City, instructor, 1958-59; Southern Illinois University at Edwardsville, assistant professor, 1959-64, associate professor, 1964-69, professor of European history, 1969—. Historian, Mormon Pioneer Trail Foundation, 1969—; vice-chairman of advisory board, Mormon Pioneer National Historic Trail, 1981—. *Military service:* U.S. Army Air Forces, 1945.

MEMBER: American Historical Association, American Association for the Advancement of Slavic Studies, Society of Mormon Historians, Czechoslovak Society of Arts and Sciences in America, Conference for Central European Affairs, Society of Czechoslovak Historians, Mormon History Association, Santa Fe Trail Association, Rocky Mountain Slavic Congress, Oregon-California Trails Association.

AWARDS, HONORS: Rockefeller grant, 1974, for study of Slavic societies in Utah; Outdoor Recreation Award, U.S. Department of the Interior, 1974, and special commendation from U.S. National Park Service, 1982, both for research on the Mormon Trail; award for best book in Mormon history, Mormon History Association, 1982, for *Heber C. Kimball: Mormon Patriarch and Pioneer;* Outstanding Service Award, Slavic and East European Friends Association, 1983.

WRITINGS:

Czech Nationalism: A Study of the National Theatre Movement, 1845-1883, University of Illinois Press, 1964.
The Sources of Mormon History in Illinois, 1839-1848: An Annotated Catalogue of the Microfilm Collection at Southern Illinois University, Southern Illinois University Press, 1964, revised edition, 1966.
(With R. Don Oscarson and Leslie F. Medley) *The Travelers' Guide to Historic Mormon America*, Bookcraft, 1965.
Slavic-American Imprints, Southern Illinois University Press, 1972, supplement, 1979.
The Austro-Slav Revival: A Study of Nineteenth-Century Literary Foundations, American Philosophical Society, 1973.
Discovering Mormon Trails, Deseret, 1979.
One Hundred Eleven Days to Zion, Deseret, 1979.
(Author of introduction) Joseph E. Brown and Dan Guravich, *The Mormon Trek West: The Journey of American Exiles*, Doubleday, 1980.
East European in Southwestern Illinois: The Ethnic Experience in Historical Perspective, Southern Illinois University Press, 1981.
Heber C. Kimball: Mormon Patriarch and Pioneer, University of Illinois Press, 1981.
The Latter-Day Saints' Emigrants' Guide, Patrice Press, 1983.
Historic Sites and Markers along Great Western Trails, University of Illinois Press, 1988.

Contributor to journals. Member of editorial baord, *Dialogue: A Journal of Mormon Thought*, 1966-70, and *Journal of Mormon History*, 1981—.

WORK IN PROGRESS: Villages on Wheels: The Mormon Migration, a Social History.

SIDELIGHTS: Stanley B. Kimball speaks French and German, and can do research in most of the Slavic languages. He has traveled behind the Iron Curtain in the Soviet Union, Poland, East Germany, Czechoslovakia, Hungary, and Yugoslavia.

AVOCATIONAL INTERESTS: "Especially interested in preserving our western trails heritage. We live in a renaissance of such interest and, with care, we can yet save important parts of some of the most famous trails."

* * *

KING, Preston (Theodore) 1936-

PERSONAL: Born March 3, 1936, in Albany, Ga.; son of Clennon Washington and Margaret (Slater) King; children: one son, one daughter. *Education:* Fisk University, B.A. (magna cum laude), 1956; London School of Economics and Political Science, M.Sc. (with distinction), 1958, Ph.D., 1966; additional study at University of Vienna, University of Paris, and University of Strasbourg.

ADDRESSES: Office—Department of Politics, University of Lancaster, Lancaster LA1 4YF, England.

CAREER: University of London, London School of Economics and Political Science, London, England, tutor in political philosophy and government, 1958-60; conducted lecture tour of United States, speaking on African politics, winter, 1961; lecturer in philosophy at University of Maryland Overseas, England, summer, 1961, and at University of Keele, Keele, England, 1961-63; University of Ghana, Accra, lecturer in political philosophy, 1963-66; University of Sheffield, Sheffield, England, lecturer in political philosophy, 1966-69; University of Nairobi, Nairobi, Kenya, university reader, 1969-70; deputy director of the Study of Toleration Project of the Acton Society, 1970-72; University of Nairobi, professor of government and head of department, 1972-76; University of New South Wales, Kensington, Sydney, Australia, professor of political science, 1976-86; University of Lancaster, Lancaster, England, professor of politics, 1986—.

MEMBER: Phi Beta Kappa.

WRITINGS:

Fear of Power: An Analysis of Anti-Statism in Three French Writers, Humanities, 1967.
(Editor with B. C. Parekh) *Politics and Experience: Essays Presented to Professor Michael Oakeshott on the Occasion of His Retirement,* Cambridge University Press, 1968.
The Ideology of Order: A Comparative Analysis of Jean Bodin and Thomas Hobbes, Barnes & Noble, 1974.
Toleration, St. Martin's, 1976.
(Editor) *The Study of Politics: A Collection of Inaugural Lectures,* Cass & Co., 1978.
Federalism and Federation, Johns Hopkins University Press, 1982.
The History of Ideas, Barnes & Noble, 1983.
An African Winter, Viking/Penguin Books, 1986.

Contributor to periodicals and newspapers, including *Political Quarterly, Books and Bookmen, Presence Africaine, African Review, Guardian, Observer,* and *African Digest.*

WORK IN PROGRESS: Research on political identities.

KITCHEN, Martin 1936-

PERSONAL: Born December 21, 1936, in Nottingham, England; son of John Sutherland (an insurance manager) and Margaret (Pearson) Kitchen; married Brigitte Meyer (a social worker), March 13, 1960 (divorced); children: Corinna, Susan. *Education:* Attended Magdalen College, Oxford, 1957-59; University of London, B.A. (with honors), 1963, Ph.D., 1966. *Politics:* Social Democrat. *Religion:* Roman Catholic.

ADDRESSES: Home—7321 Celista Dr., Vancouver, British Columbia, Canada V5S 4A1. *Office*—Department of History, Simon Fraser University, Burnaby, British Columbia, Canada.

CAREER: Simon Fraser University, Burnaby, British Columbia, assistant professor, 1966-69, associate professor, 1969-74, professor of history, 1974—. *Military service:* British Army, 1955-57; became lieutenant.

WRITINGS:

The German Officer Corps, 1890-1914, Clarendon Press, 1968.
A Military History of Germany, Weidenfeld & Nicolson, 1975.
Fascism, Macmillan, 1976.
The Silent Dictatorship: The Politics of the German High Command under Hindenburg and Ludendorff, Croom Helm, 1976.
The Political Economy of Germany, 1815-1914, Croom Helm, 1978.
The Coming of Austrian Fascism, Croom Helm, 1980.
(Editor with Volker R. Berghahn) *Germany in the Age of Total War,* Croom Helm, 1981.
British Policy towards the Soviet Union during the Second World War, Macmillan, 1986.
Europe between the Wars, Longman, 1988.
(With Laurence Aronsen) *The Origins of the Cold War in Comparative Perspective,* Macmillan, 1988.

WORK IN PROGRESS: "Responses to the Inter-War Crisis."

SIDELIGHTS: Martin Kitchen writes that his work "concentrates on militarism which I examine in terms of the relationships between the army and society, and of the social origins of extreme right wing movements."

BIOGRAPHICAL/CRITICAL SOURCES:

PERIODICALS

Times Literary Supplement, August 1, 1980, June 26, 1981.

* * *

KITT, Tamara
See de REGNIERS, Beatrice Schenk (Freedman)

* * *

KLAASSEN, Leo(nardus) H(endrik) 1920-

PERSONAL: Born June 21, 1920, in Rotterdam, Netherlands; son of Cornelis Hendrik Leonardus (an administrator) and Alida (Bakker) Klaassen; married Annemarie Ablinger, June 19, 1957; children: Marianne Elizabeth, Hendrik Leonardus. *Education:* Netherlands School of Economics, M.A., 1946, Ph.D., 1959.

ADDRESSES: Home—Joost Banckertsplaats 133, Rotterdam, Netherlands. *Office*—Netherlands Economic Institute, Pieter de Hoochweg 118, Rotterdam, Netherlands.

CAREER: Economic Technological Institute, Rotterdam, Netherlands, research fellow, 1943-45; Netherlands Economic Institute, Rotterdam, research fellow, 1945-51, chief of research, 1951-60, director, 1960-68, president, 1968-85, economic advisor, 1985—; Erasmus University, Netherlands School of Economics, Rotterdam, lecturer, 1951-59, professor, 1959-85, professor emeritus, 1985—. Visiting professor, University of California, Los Angeles, 1962, 1966. Faculty member, World University, Cambridge, Mass., 1973. Advisor to the Government of the City of Rotterdam, 1986—.

Supervisor of studies on economic development of Curacao, 1960-68, on the economic consequences of the Euphrates Dam in Syria, 1964, on mineral development possibilities in Turkey, 1964, on economic evaluation of the Jordan Valley irrigation project in Jordan, 1967-68, on national transportation in the Netherlands, 1967—, on regional development in Algecia, Spain, on the industry in the Ruhr Area, 1969—, and on the national accounts and the administrative structure of the Netherlands Antilles, 1973—; member of transportation or survey teams in Niger and Dahomey (now Republic of Benin), 1961-62, Finland, 1964-65, Korea, 1965-68 and 1968-70, Cameroon and Central African Republic, 1967-69, Nigeria, 1970, and Iran, 1971; trustee for regional development study of Malaysia, 1967-69; director of study on the development potentials of Clyde area in Scotland, 1971-73. Member of Common Market Committee on Capital-coefficients and Investment Forecasts, and of Government of Netherlands Committee on the Profitability of Infrastructural Investments. Member of selection committee of the August Loesch Honour Ring, 1982. Member of Board of Governors, International Land Development Institute, Munich, 1980. President, Board of Supervisory Directors for Holland (a dredging company).

Consultant to World Bank on transport study in Zambia, 1964, to NEDECO transportation mission to Brazil, 1965-67, to Iranian Government on city planning of Tehran, 1967-68, to Portuguese Government on industrialization policies and on amenity planning, 1968—, to Spanish government, 1973-74, to Planning Office, Paramaribo, Surinam, 1982, to Institute of Land Reform, Wageningen, to Economic-Technological Institute, Maastricht, and to Netherlands Ministries of Transport, Agriculture, Communication, Health and Environment, Foreign Affairs, and Finance. Member of honorary advisory board, American Biographical Institute.

MEMBER: International Association for Regional and Urban Statistics (president, 1984), World Academy of Art and Science (fellow; executive committee, 1979), American Geographic Society (fellow), Econometric Society, Society for Statistics, International Association for Regional and Urban Statistics, Polish Academy of Sciences, Netherlands Demographic Association, Regional Science Association (vice-president of Philadelphia branch, 1972, president-elect, 1976, president, 1977), World Society of Skippers of the Flying Dutchman.

AWARDS, HONORS: Medal of honor, University of Gdansk, 1976, Instytut Morski, Sopot, 1976; medals from University of Katowice, City of Seoul, City of Incheon (Korea), 35th Anniversary of the University of Lodz, 10th Anniversary of the University of Gdansk, City of Lodz, University of Ghent, Erasmus University of Rotterdam, Port of Gydnia, and 50th Anniversary Academy of Economics Katowice; honorary doctorate, University of Poznan, University of Lodz, University of Ghent, and University of Gdansk; Knight of the Order of the Dutch Lion; Golden Badge of the Order of Merit, Polish People's Republic; Golden Badge of the Senate of the University of Katowice; Boleslaw Kasprowicz Medal of the Polish Nautological Society; August Loesch Honour Ring, Heidenheim an der Brenz; Van Oldenbarnevelt medal, City of Rotterdam, 1985; Fontes Medal, Erasmus University, 1985; Baltona medal, 1987; honorary citizen of Baltimore, Md., and Lodz.

WRITINGS:

(With D. H. van Dongen Torman and L. M. Koyck) *Hoofdlijnen van de Sociaal-Economische Ontwikkeling der Gemunte Amersfoort van 1900-1970* (title means "The Development of the City of Amersfoort 1900-1970"), H. E. Stenfert Kroese, 1949.

(With J. Tinbergen and E. H. Mulder) *Observations on the Planned Provision of Nitrogen Fertilizers for the World,* H. E. Stenfert Kroese, 1956.

(With A. de Klerk) *De Verwarming van de Volkswoning* (title means "Heating of Low Rent Houses"), H. E. Stenfert Kroese, 1959.

(With W. C. Kroft, W. M. van Liefland, and D. Zuiderhoek) *Deventer, Stad van 250,000 inwoners* (title means "Deventer, City of 250,000"), A. E. Kluwer, 1959.

Richtlijnen voor het toegepast economisch onderzoek (title means "Principles of Economic Research"), H. E. Stenfert Kroese, 1959.

(With E. H. van den Poll) *Economische Aspecten van de Wegenbouw* (title means "Economic Aspects of Road Construction"), Het Nederlandse Wegencongres, 1960.

(Contributor) J. L. Mey, editor, *Depreciation and Replacement Policy,* North-Holland Publishing, 1961.

(With others) *Capital Formation for Housing in Latin America,* Pan American Union, 1963.

(With others) *Area Redevelopment Policy in Great Britain and the Countries of the Common Market,* U.S. Department of Commerce, 1965.

Area Economic and Social Redevelopment, Organization for Economic Co-operation and Development, 1965.

(With R. Iwema, de Klerk, and J. W. Meijer) *Energie in Perspectief* (title means "Energy in Perspective"), Steenkolen Handels-Vereniging, 1966.

Kurzfristige Sozialloesungen contra langfristige Regionalpolitik (title means "Short-term Social Solutions and Long-run Regional Policy") [Hamburg], 1966.

Methods of Selecting Industries for Depressed Areas: An Introduction to Feasibliity Studies, Organization for Economic Co-operation and Development, 1967.

Social Amenities in Area Economic Growth: An Analysis of Methods of Defining Needs for Local Social Amenities, Organization for Economic Co-operation and Development, 1968.

(With van den Poll) *Lineamenti della politica economica nei Paesi Bassi* (title means "Economic Policy in the Netherlands"), Instituto per gli Studi Sullo Sviluppo Economico e il Progresso Tecnico, [Rome], 1968.

(With others) *Theory and Practice in Transport Economics,* European Conference of Ministers of Transport, 1969.

(With E. Bloembergen, E. D. Kruijtbosch and M. C. Verburg) *Spatial Planning,* The Hague, 1969.

(With others) *The Future of European Ports,* College of Europe, 1970.

(Co-author and editor) *Regionale economie* (title means "Regional Economics"), Noordhoff, 1972.

(With others) *Growth Poles,* United National Research Institute for Social Development, 1972.

The Impact of Changes in Society on the Demand for Passenger and Freight Transport, European Conference of Ministers of Transport, 1973.

(Editor with J. R. Zuidema) *Economie dezer dagen* (title means "Economics of These Days"), University Press of Rotterdam, 1973.

(With Paul Drewe) *Migration Policy in Europe: A Comparative Study*, Lexington Books, 1973.

(With G. Rehn and A. Bernfeld) *Manpower Policy in Germany*, Organization for Economic Co-operation and Development, 1974.

(With Jean J. P. Paelinck) *Integration of Socio-Economic and Physical Planning*, Rotterdam University Press, 1974.

(With A.C.P. Verster and T. H. Botterweg) *Kosten-Baten-analyse in Regionaal Perspectief* (title means "Cost Benefit Analysis in Regional Perspective"), H. D. Tjeenk Willink, 1974.

(With J.A.M. Heijke and C. J. Offereins) *Naar een arbeidmarktmodel* (title means "Toward a Labor Market Model"), H. D. Tjeenk Willink, 1975.

(With J. A. Bourdrez and G. Billet) *Transport Policy in Western Europe*, Ministry of Public Works (Madrid), 1976.

Integrated Planning Systems in Western Europe, Wroclaw-Warszawa-Krakow-Gdansk, 1977.

(With Paelinck) *Spatial Econometrics*, Saxon House, 1979.

(With Paelinck and S. Wagenaar) *Spatial Systems: A General Introduction*, Saxon House, 1979.

(With Norbert Vanhove) *Regional Policy: A European Approach*, Allanheld, Osmun, 1980, 2nd edition, Gower, 1987.

(Editor with W.T.M. Molle and Paelinck) *The Dynamics of Urban Development: Proceedings of an International Conference Held on the Occasion of the Fiftieth Anniversary of the Netherlands Economic Institute in Rotterdam, September 4, 1979*, St. Martin's, 1981, Gower, 1981.

(With Bourdrez and J. Volmuller) *Transport and Reurbanization*, Lexington Books, 1981.

(Co-editor and co-author) *Dynamics of Urban Development*, Gower, 1981.

(With others) *Urban Europe: A Study of Growth and Decline*, Pergamon, 1982.

(Co-editor and co-author) *Industrial Mobility and Migration in the European Community*, Gower, 1983.

(Co-editor and co-author) *Spatial Cycles*, Gower, 1987.

CONTRIBUTOR

H.J.E. Beth, *Inleiding tot de differentiaal—en integraalrekening*, Groningen-Batavia, 1948.

Regionale Economie, Gent, 1955.

De economische positie van de baksteenindustrie, Leiden, 1955.

Inter-firm Comparison, [Paris], 1956.

Regionale structuur en interregionale functie, Utrecht, 1957.

Wiskundige propadeuse voor economisten, Utrecht, 1957.

(And co-editor) *Jan Tinbergen, Selected Papers*, [Amsterdam], 1959.

Problemen van economische ontwikkeling, Gent, 1961.

Capital Formation for Housing in Latin America, Union Panamericana (Washington), 1963.

Bedeutung und Anwendung oekonometrischer Methoden in der agrarwirtschaflichen Forschung, Hiltrup, 1963.

Area Redevelopment Policy in Great Britain and the Countries of the Common Market, U.S. Department of Commerce, 1965.

Essays in Urban Land Economics, [Los Angeles], 1966.

Polis und Regio, [Basel/Tuebingen], 1967.

Towards a Strategy for Development Cooperation, [Rotterdam], 1967.

Espace et les poles de croissance, [Paris], 1968.

De functie van Twente in de Nederlandse economie, [Rotterdam], 1968.

Ruimtelijke ordening, Lustrumcongres Academy of Architecture, 1968.

Towards Balanced International Growth, [Amsterdam/London], 1969.

The Urban Transportation Planning Process, Organization for Economic Cooperation and Development, 1969.

The Future of European Ports, College of Europe, 1970.

The Influence of Centralism on the Future, [Edinburgh], 1970.

De tertiaire sector in de economische groei, Gent, 1970.

Amenity and Recreation in High Density Zones, [Rotterdam], 1971.

Growth Poles and Regional Policies, United National Research Institute for Social Development, 1972.

Desarrollo regional, Universidad Comercial de DUESTO, 1972.

Energy Conservation: Ways and Means, [The Hague], 1974.

Planowie Rozwoju Regionalnego w swietle Doswiadczen Miedzynarodwych, [Warsaw], 1974.

Beslissen, [Deventer], 1974.

Environment, Regional Science and Interregional Modeling, [Berlin, Heidelberg, New York], 1976.

Environmental Economics, Leiden, 1976.

Product Range Policy in Retailing and Cooperation with Manufacturers, Breukelen, 1976.

The European Economy beyond the Crisis: From Stabilization to Structural Change, College of Europe, 1977.

Social Issues in Regional Policy and Regional Planning, [The Hague], 1977.

Economia Regional, Belo Horizonte, 1977.

The Contribution of Economic Research to Transport Policy Decisions, European Conference of Ministers of Transport, 1977.

Problemy i metody ekonomiki regionalnej, [Warsaw], 1978.

Regional Dynamics of Socio-Economic Change, Tampere (Finland), 1979.

Spatial Inequalities and Regional Development, Martinus Nijhoff, 1979.

Urban Transport and the Environment, Organization for Economic Cooperation and Development, 1979.

Transport and Regional Development, An International Handbook, Saxon House, 1979.

Changes in the Field of Transport Studies, Martinus Nijhoff, 1979.

Metropolitan Planning: Issues and Politics, Korea Research Institute for Human Settlements, 1979.

Handlexicon fuer Handel und Absatz, Verlag Moderne Industrie, 1979.

Economic-Environmental-Energy Interactions, Martinus Nijhoff, 1980.

Problemy planowania i polityki spoleczno-gospodarczej, Polskie Towarzystwo Ekonomiczne, 1980.

P. Nijkamp and P. Rietveld, editors, *Cities in Transition: Problems and Policies*, Alphen aan den Rijn (Rockville, Maryland), 1981.

Vervoers—en haveneconomie; tussen actie en abstractie, Stenfert Kroese, 1981.

On Self-Sufficiency, Gaia Institute for the Study of Natural Resources, 1982.

The Future Use of the Car, European Conference of Ministers of Transport, 1982.

Zielsetzung und methoden zur Erarbeitung eines Gesamtverkehrskonzeptes, Oesterreichische Verkehrswissenschaftliche Gesellschaft, 1982.

Decentralisatie van rijkstaken: Verkeer en vervoer, Raad voor het Binnenlands Bestuur, 1982.

Regional Development Modelling: Theory and Practice, North Holland, 1982.

A. Kuklinski and J. G. Lambooij, editors, *Dilemmas in Regional Policy,* [Berlin/New York/Amsterdam], 1983.

Probleme der Ordnungs—und Strukturpolitik, Goettingen, 1984.

Spatial, Environmental and Resource Policy in the Developing Countries, Gower, 1984.

The Modelling of Socio-Economic Planning Processes, Gower, 1984.

Theorie und Praxis der Kosten-Nutzen Analyse im Verkehrswesen, Universitaet Zurich, Institut fuer Verkehrsplanung und Transporttechnik, 1984.

Financement des transports urbains, Laboratoire d'Economie des Transports, 1985.

The Future of Urban Form: The Impact of New Technology, Nichols Publishing, 1985.

Verkehr im laendlichen Raum, Oesterreichische Verkehrswissenschaftliche Gesellschaft, 1985.

Transportation and Mobility in an Era of Transition, North Holland, 1985.

Kingsley E. Haynes, Antoni Kuklinski and Olli Kultalahti, editors, *Pathologies of Urban Processes,* Finn Publishers, 1985.

Rotterdam bouwt een metro, Betonvereniging, 1986.

Genpachiro Konno and Yukihide Okano, editors, *Papers of the Fourth International Transport Conference,* [Tokyo], 1986.

Rolf A. Funck and Kulinski, editors, *Space-structure-economy,* Karlsruhe, 1986.

Huidige en toekomstige betekenis van de Benelux Zeehavens, Gent-Louvain-la-Neuve-Rotterdam, 1986.

Lloyd Rodwin, editor, *Shelter, Settlement and Development,* Allen and Unwin, 1987.

H. G. Wind, editor, *Impact of Sea Level Rise on Society,* A. A. Balke, 1987.

Special Issue Workshop on High Speed Rail Transportation, Martinus Nijhoff, 1987.

L. van den Berg, editor, *Stedelijke vernieuwing,* Den Haag, 1987.

OTHER

Also author of *Urban Europe, Exercises in Spatial Thinking, The City: Engine behind Economic Recovery?,* and numerous books and pamphlets on economy, regional development, and society, in Russian, German, Dutch, French, Italian, Spanish, and Polish. Contributor of more than eighty articles to the "Foundations of Empirical Economic Research" series. Contributor of more than two hundred articles to professional and business journals in Europe and the United States, including *Econometrica, Economie, Ifo Studien, Regional and Urban Economics,* and *Urban Studies.* Member of editorial board, *European Economic Review,* the Groupement Interuniversitaire des Economistes des Transports (Brussels), *Planning in the Netherlands, Revue d'Economie Regionale et Urbaine* (Paris), *Studies in Applied Regional Science, Transport Reviews* (England), the Dutch *Economist,* and *Regional Studies,* 1987—; chairman of editorial board, *Economisch Statistische Berichten,* 1986—; member of board of associate editors of *Man, Space, Environment and Time.*

BIOGRAPHICAL/CRITICAL SOURCES:

BOOKS

Paelinck, Jean H. P., editor, *Human Behaviour in Geographical Space: Essays in Honour of Leo H. Klaassen,* Gower, 1986.

*   *   *

KNOKE, David (Harmon) 1947-

PERSONAL: Born March 4, 1947, in Philadelphia, Pa.; son of Donald Glenn (a carpenter) and Frances (a school teacher; maiden name, Dunn) Knoke; married Joann Margaret Robar, August 29, 1970; children: Margaret Frances. *Education:* University of Michigan, B.A., 1969, M.S.W., 1971, Ph.D., 1972; University of Chicago, M.A., 1970. *Politics:* "Passive observer of the parade." *Religion:* Unitarian Universalist.

ADDRESSES: Home—7305 Wooddale, Edina, Minn. 55435. *Office*—University of Minnesota, Minneapolis, Minn. 55455.

CAREER: Indiana University at Bloomington, assistant professor, 1972-75, associate professor, 1975-81, professor of sociology, 1981-85; University of Minnesota, Minneapolis, professor of sociology, 1985—, chairperson of department, 1989-92. Member of sociology program review board, National Science Foundation, 1981-83. Member of advisory committee of National Opinion Research Center's general social survey, 1976—.

MEMBER: International Network for Social Network Analysis, American Sociological Association, Sociological Research Association, Phi Beta Kappa.

AWARDS, HONORS: National Science Foundation fellowship, 1969-70; research scientist development award, National Institute of Mental Health, 1977-82; principal investigator on five National Science Foundation grants.

WRITINGS:

Change and Continuity in American Politics, Johns Hopkins University Press, 1976.

(With Peter J. Burke) *Log-Linear Models,* Sage Publications, 1980.

(With James R. Wood) *Organized for Action,* Rutgers University Press, 1981.

(With James H. Kuklinski) *Network Analysis,* Sage Publications, 1982.

(With George W. Bohrnstedt) *Statistics for Social Data Analysis,* F. E. Peacock, 1982, 2nd edition, 1987.

(With Edward O. Laumann) *The Organizational State,* University of Wisconsin Press, 1987.

Contributor to social science journals.

WORK IN PROGRESS: Research, with Franz U. Pappi, on American and German labor policy networks, funded by the National Science Foundation and the Volkswagen Foundation, with a monograph expected to result.

SIDELIGHTS: David Knoke told *CA:* "My writing increasingly reflects the interplay between abstract theorizing and empirical data analysis, to the extent that where one breaks off and the other begins is obscure. Showing students how to break into this continuous process has been a major challenge in recent years."

AVOCATIONAL INTERESTS: Running, reading.

KONADU, Asare
    See KONADU, S(amuel) A(sare)

*   *   *

KONADU, S(amuel) A(sare)   1932-
    (Asare Konadu; pseudonyms: Bediako Asare,
    Kwabena Asare Bediako)

PERSONAL: Born January 18, 1932, in Asamang, Ghana; son of Kofi (a farmer) and Abena (Anowuo) Konadu; married Alice Dede, February 26, 1958; children: Samuel Asare, Jr., Cecilia, Lucy, Frederick, Birago, Yamoah. *Education:* Attended Abuakwa State College, Kibi, Ghana, 1948-51, Polytechnic, London, England, 1956-58, and University of Strasbourg, 1958. *Religion:* Seventh-day Adventist.

ADDRESSES: Home—100 Aburaso St., Asamang, Ashanti, Ghana. *Office*—2R McCarthy Hill, Box 3918, Accra, Ghana.

CAREER: Ghana Information Services, Accra, junior reporter, 1952-56, journalist, 1956-58; Ghana News Agency, Accra, editor, 1958-60, chief editor, 1961-63; full-time writer, 1963—. Publisher and director, Anowuo Educational Publishers.

MEMBER: Ghana Writers Club, Ghana Journalists Association.

AWARDS, HONORS: University of Strasbourg fellowship for research in history of the Ghanaian press, 1959.

WRITINGS:

Wizard of Asamang, Waterville Publishing, 1962.
The Lawyer Who Bungled His Life, Waterville Publishing, 1965.
Night Watchers of Korlebu, Anowuo Educational Publishers, 1967, Humanities Press, 1969.
Come Back Dora, Humanities Press, 1969.

UNDER NAME ASARE KONADU

Shadow of Wealth, Anowuo Educational Publishers, 1966.
A Woman in Her Prime, Heinemann, 1967, Humanities Press, 1969.
Ordained by the Oracle, Heinemann, 1968, Humanities Press, 1969.
Vanishing Shadows, Anowuo Educational Publishers, 1987.
Reconciliation, Anowuo Educational Publishers, 1988.

UNDER PSEUDONYM BEDIAKO ASARE

Rebel, Heinemann Educational, 1969.
Majuto, East African Literature Bureau, 1975.
The Stubborn, East African Literature Bureau, 1976.

UNDER PSEUDONYM KWABENA ASARE BEDIAKO

Don't Leave Me Mercy, Anowuo Educational Publishers, 1966.
A Husband for Esi Ellua, Anowuo Educational Publishers, 1967, Humanities Press, 1969.
Return of Mercy, Anowuo Educational Publishers, 1987.
The Koala Called Too Late, Anowuo Educational Publishers, 1988.

WORK IN PROGRESS: Research into traditional healing and Ghanaian customs.

SIDELIGHTS: In 1961 S. A. Konadu toured the Soviet Union with Kwame Nkrumah, ex-president of Ghana, visiting all of its states. He traveled in Europe in 1958 and 1962, and in the Congo, Rwanda, and Burundi, 1963. In 1968 Konadu was the guest of the U.S. State Department and spent ninety days on a publishing tour of eleven states.

KORTEPETER, C(arl) Max   1928-

PERSONAL: Born May 27, 1928, in Indianapolis, Ind.; son of Carl F. (a civil engineer) and Olive (Derbyshire) Kortepeter; married Cynthia King, April 7, 1957; children: four sons, two daughters. *Education:* Harvard University, A.B., 1950; McGill University, M.A., 1954; University of Michigan, graduate study, 1956-57; School of Oriental and African Studies, Ph.D., 1962; Rutgers University, M.S., 1985.

ADDRESSES: Home—32 Oxford Circle, Skillman, N.J. 08558. *Office*—Kevorkian Center of Near Eastern Studies, New York University, Washington Square, New York, N.Y. 10003.

CAREER: Robert College, Istanbul, Turkey, instructor in biology, 1950-53; University of Toronto, Toronto, Ontario, lecturer, 1961-63, assistant professor, 1963-66, associate professor of Islamic history, 1966-67, member of faculty council, 1964-66; New York University, New York, N.Y., associate professor of Near East history, 1967—, acting chairman of department of Near Eastern languages and literatures, 1968-70, acting director of Center for Near Eastern Studies, 1969-70. Visiting professor at Princeton University, 1969-70, and New Brunswick Dutch Reformed Seminary, 1975-76; special lecturer on Middle East, U.S. Department of State, 1976-78. Co-founder and secretary-treasurer, Kingston Press, Inc., 1981—. Member of board of directors, Center for Slavonic and East European Studies (Toronto), 1963-66; secretary and member of board of directors, American Research Institute in Turkey, 1964-74; founder and director, Princeton Middle East Systems (consulting firm), 1976—. Consultant on subjects about the Middle East to television and radio. Member of Griggstown Voluntary Fire Co., 1967-81; member of board of directors, Mercer County Youth Orchestra Association, 1976-78. Member of Vietnamese Refugee Settlement Committee of Montgomery Township, 1980-81. *Military service:* U.S. Marine Corps Reserve, 1947-54; became first lieutenant. U.S. Army Reserve, 1954-57; intelligence analyst in Germany and lecturer in Russian history for University of Maryland in Heidelberg, 1954-56; became master sergeant.

MEMBER: Middle East Institute, Middle East Studies Association (member of committee on research, 1969-71), American Association of University Professors (vice-president of humanities division, New York University chapter, 1972-73), Turkish Studies Association, American Historical Association, Association of Russian-American Scholars, Americans for Middle East Understanding (secretary, 1972, 1973-76).

AWARDS, HONORS: Institute of Islamic Studies grant, McGill University, 1953; travel grant to Istanbul from School of Oriental and African Studies, 1960; American Research Institute in Turkey senior fellow, 1966-67; commendation from National Security Council of the United States, 1969; IREX travel grant, American Council of Learned Societies, 1973; senior fellow, American Research Center in Egypt, 1978-79.

WRITINGS:

(Contributor) R. Schoeck, editor, *Editing Sixteenth Century Texts,* University of Toronto Press, 1967.
(Contributor) R. B. Winder, editor, *The New York University Round Table,* [New York], 1969.
(Editor) Judith M. Spiegelman, *Ali of Turkey,* Messner, 1969.
(Editor and contributor) *Modern Near East: Literature and Society,* Center for Near Eastern Studies, New York University, 1972.

Ottoman Imperialism during the Reformation: Europe and the Caucasus, New York University Press, 1972.

(Contributor) Kemel Karpat, editor, *Institutions of the Ottoman Empire,* [Leiden], 1975.

(Contributor) *International Symposium on the Reforms of Atatuerk,* [Istanbul], 1975.

(Contributor) Donald Little, editor, *Essays on Islamic Civilization Presented to Niyazi Berkes,* [Leiden], 1976.

(With Mounir Farah and Andrea Berens Karl) *The Human Experience: A World History* (textbook), C. E. Merrill, 1985.

(Editor with Guensel Renda) *The Transformation of Turkish Culture: The Atatuerk Legacy,* Kingston, 1986.

Consulting editor, United Nations children's series on the Middle East, 1968-69; history editor, "All-Color" series, 32 volumes, Grosset, 1968-72; editor, "Leaders, Politics and Social Change in the Islamic World" Middle East series, Kingston, 1982—. Contributor to *Proceedings of Association of Russian-American Scholars,* 1973, *New World Encyclopedia,* and *Encyclopedia of Islam.* Contributor of articles and reviews to journals, including *Journal of the American Oriental Society, Middle East Journal,* and *Journal of the American Institute for the Study of Middle East Civilizations.*

WORK IN PROGRESS: Two Centuries of American Experience in the Middle East, 1776-1976; A History of the Arabian Peninsula.

AVOCATIONAL INTERESTS: Athletics, folk dancing.

*   *   *

KUNITZ, Stanley (Jasspon) 1905-

PERSONAL: Born July 29, 1905, in Worcester, Mass.; son of Solomon Z. (a manufacturer) and Yetta Helen (Jasspon) Kunitz; married Helen Pearce, 1930 (divorced, 1937); married Eleanor Evans, November 21, 1939 (divorced, 1958); married Elise Asher (an artist), June 21, 1958; children: (second marriage) Gretchen. *Education:* Harvard University, A.B. (summa cum laude), 1926, A.M., 1927.

ADDRESSES: Home—37 West 12th St., New York, N.Y. 10011.

CAREER: Poet. *Wilson Library Bulletin,* New York City, editor, 1928-42; Bennington College, Bennington, Vt., professor of English, 1946-49; Potsdam State Teachers College (now State University of New York College at Potsdam), Potsdam, N.Y., professor of English, 1949-50; New School for Social Research, New York City, lecturer in English, 1950-58; Poetry Center of the Young Men's Hebrew Association, New York City, director of poetry workshop, 1958-62; Columbia University, New York City, lecturer, 1963-66, adjunct professor of writing in School of the Arts, 1967-85. Member of staff of writing division, Fine Arts Work Center in Provincetown, 1968—. Fellow, Yale University, 1969—; visiting senior fellow, Council of the Humanities, and Old Dominion Fellow in creative writing, Princeton University, 1978-79. Director of seminar, Potsdam Summer Workshop in Creative Arts, 1949-53; poet in residence, University of Washington, 1955-56, Queens College (now Queens College of the City University of New York), 1956-57, Brandeis University, 1958-59, and Princeton University, 1979. Danforth Visiting Lecturer at colleges and universities in the United States, 1961-63; visiting professor, Yale University, 1972, and Rutgers University, 1974. Lectured and gave poetry readings under

cultural exchange program in USSR and Poland, 1967, in Senegal and Ghana, 1976, and in Israel and Egypt, 1980. Library of Congress, Washington, D.C., consultant on poetry, 1974-76, honorary consultant in American letters, 1976-83. *Military service:* U.S. Army, Air Transport Command, 1943-45; became staff sergeant.

MEMBER: American Academy and Institute of Arts and Letters, Academy of American Poets (chancellor, 1970—), Phi Beta Kappa.

AWARDS, HONORS: Oscar Blumenthal Prize, 1941; John Simon Guggenheim Memorial fellowship, 1945-46; Amy Lowell travelling fellowship, 1953-54; Levinson Prize, *Poetry* magazine, 1956; *Saturday Review* award, 1957; Ford Foundation grant, 1958-59; Harriet Monroe Poetry Award, University of Chicago, 1958; National Institute of Arts and Letters award, 1959; Pulitzer Prize, 1959, for *Selected Poems, 1928-1958;* Litt.D., Clark University, 1961, Anna Maria College, 1977; Brandeis University creative arts award medal, 1965; Academy of American Poets fellowship, 1968; New England Poetry Club Golden Rose Trophy, 1970; American Library Association notable book citation, 1979, for *The Poems of Stanley Kunitz, 1928-1978;* L.H.D., Worcester State College, 1980; Lenore Marshall Award for Poetry, 1980; National Endowment for the Arts senior fellowship, 1984; Bollingen Prize in Poetry, Yale University Library, 1987; Walt Whitman Award citation of merit, with designation as State Poet of New York, 1987.

WRITINGS:

Intellectual Things (verse), Doubleday, Doran, 1930.
Passport to the War: A Selection of Poems, Holt, 1944.
Selected Poems, 1928-1958, Atlantic-Little, Brown, 1958.
The Testing-Tree: Poems, Atlantic-Little, Brown, 1971.
(Translator with Max Hayward) *Poems of Anna Akhmatova,* Atlantic-Little, Brown, 1973.
The Terrible Threshold: Selected Poems, 1940-70, Secker & Warburg, 1974.
The Coat without a Seam: Sixty Poems, 1930-1972, Gehenna Press, 1974.
(Translator) Andrei Voznesensky, *Story under Full Sail,* Doubleday, 1974.
Robert Lowell: Poet of Terribilita, Pierpont Morgan Library, 1974.
A Kind of Order, a Kind of Folly: Essays and Conversations, Atlantic-Little, Brown, 1975.
(Editor and author of introduction) Ivan Drach, *Orchard Lamps,* Sheep Meadow Press, 1978.
The Lincoln Relics (verse), Graywolf Press, 1978.
Poems of Stanley Kunitz: 1928-1978, Atlantic-Little, Brown, 1979.
The Wellfleet Whale and Companion Poems, Sheep Meadow Press, 1983.
Next-to-Last Things: New Poems and Essays, Atlantic Monthly Press, 1985.

EDITOR

Living Authors: A Book of Biographies, H. W. Wilson, 1931.
(With Howard Haycraft) *Authors Today and Yesterday: A Companion Volume to "Living Authors,"* H. W. Wilson, 1933.
(With Haycraft) *The Junior Book of Authors: An Introduction to the Lives of Writers and Illustrators for Younger Readers,* H. W. Wilson, 1934, 2nd revised edition, 1951.

(With Haycraft) *British Authors of the Nineteenth Century*, H. W. Wilson, 1936.

(With Haycraft) *American Authors, 1600-1900: A Biographical Dictionary of American Literature*, H. W. Wilson, 1938, 8th edition, 1971.

(With Haycraft) *Twentieth Century Authors: A Biographical Dictionary*, H. W. Wilson, 1942, first supplement, 1955.

(With Haycraft) *British Authors before 1800: A Biographical Dictionary*, H. W. Wilson, 1952.

Poems of John Keats, Crowell, 1964.

(With Vineta Colby) *European Authors, 1000-1900: A Biographical Dictionary of European Literature*, H. W. Wilson, 1967.

(Editor) *Selections: University and College Poetry Prizes, 1973-78*, Academy of American Poets, 1980. (And author of introduction) *The Essential Blake*, Ecco Press, 1987.

CONTRIBUTOR

John Fischer and Robert B. Silvers, editors, *Writing in America*, Rutgers University Press, 1960.

Anthony J. Ostroff, editor, *The Contemporary Poet as Artist and Critic*, Little, Brown, 1964.

Vineta Colby, editor, *American Culture in the Sixties*, H. W. Wilson, 1964.

(Of translations) Andrei Voznesensky, *Antiworlds*, Basic Books, 1966.

(Of translations) Voznesensky, *Antiworlds* [and] *The Fifth Ace*, Anchor Books, 1967.

Robert Lowell and others, editors, *Randall Jarrell, 1914-1965*, Farrar, Straus, 1967.

(Of translations) Yevgeny Yevtushenko, *Stolen Apples*, Doubleday, 1971.

CONTRIBUTOR TO POETRY ANTHOLOGIES

Oscar Williams, editor, *War Poets: An Anthology of the War Poetry of the 20th Century*, John Day, 1945.

W. H. Auden, editor, *The Criterion Book of Modern American Verse*, Criterion, 1956.

John Ciardi, editor, *How Does a Poem Mean?*, Houghton, 1959.

Louis Untermeyer, editor, *Modern American Poetry*, Harcourt, 1962.

Paul Engle and Joseph Langland, editors, *Poet's Choice*, Dial, 1962.

John Wain, editor, *Anthology of Modern Poetry*, Hutchinson, 1963.

John Malcolm Brinnin and Bill Read, *The Modern Poets*, McGraw, 1963.

Elder Olson, editor, *American Lyric Poems: From Colonial Times to the Present*, Appleton, 1964.

William J. Martz, editor, *The Distinctive Voice*, Scott, Foresman, 1966.

Walter Lowenfels, editor, *Where Is Vietnam?: American Poets Respond*, Doubleday-Anchor, 1967.

Richard Ellmann and Robert O'Clair, editors, *Norton Anthology of Modern Poetry*, Norton, 1973.

Daryl Hine and Joseph Parisi, editors, *Poetry Anthology 1912-1977: Sixty-five Years of America's Most Distinguished Verse Magazine*, Houghton, 1978.

Fifty Years of American Poetry: Anniversary Volume for the Academy of American Poets, Abrams, 1984.

A. Poulin, Jr., editor, *Contemporary American Poetry*, Houghton, 4th edition, 1985.

OTHER

General editor, "Yale Series of Younger Poets," Yale University Press, 1969-77. Contributor to many periodicals, including *Atlantic, New Republic, New Yorker, Antaeus, New York Review of Books, American Poetry Review*, and *Harper's*.

SIDELIGHTS: Poet Stanley Kunitz "has always been a fine and quiet singer," writes James Whitehead in *Saturday Review*. A published poet for nearly sixty years, Kunitz has exerted a subtle influence on such major poets as Theodore Roethke and Robert Lowell, and has provided encouragement to hundreds of younger poets as well. His output has been modest but enduring: since 1930 he has published ten volumes of poetry. Conceding that he has never been a prolific poet, Kunitz comments in *Publishers Weekly:* "I think that explains why I am able to continue as a poet into my late years. If I hadn't had an urgent impulse, if the poem didn't seem to me terribly important, I never wanted to write it and didn't. And that's persisted." While the highly-crafted nature of Kunitz's initial works delayed critical attention, in 1959 Kunitz was awarded the Pulitzer Prize in poetry for his *Selected Poems, 1928-1958*. Critical opinion suggests that in the years since, Kunitz's poetry has steadily increased in quality. *Virginia Quarterly Review* contributor Jay Parini, for instance, observes: "The restraints of [Kunitz's] art combine with a fierce dedication to clarity and intellectual grace to assure him of a place among the essential poets of his generation, which includes Roethke, Lowell, Auden, and Eberhart."

Kunitz's early poetry collections, *Intellectual Things* and *Passport to the War*, earned him a reputation as an intellectual poet. Reflecting Kunitz's admiration for the English metaphysical poets like John Donne and William Blake, these intricate poems, rich in metaphor and allusion, were recognized more for their craft than their substance. Thus, they were somewhat slow to garner widespread critical attention. As *New York Review of Books* contributor Vernon Young observes, Kunitz "is notable for his intelligence, and intelligence tends to wait a longer time for recognition or acquires it within a relatively limited circle." Kunitz insists, however, that his motive in writing those early poems was not "merely to be clever and to juggle ideas and ironies," he states in the *Washington Post*. "I was, even in those very earliest poems, really trying to find out who I am, where I am going, why I am here. I still ask the same questions."

Kunitz followed his Pulitzer Prize-winning work with *The Testing-Tree*. Published thirteen years after *Selected Poems, 1928-1958*, *The Testing-Tree* represents a significant stylistic departure, according to critics. Robert Lowell, for example, comments in the *New York Times Book Review* that the two volumes "are landmarks of the old and the new style. The smoke has blown off. The old Delphic voice has learned to speak 'words that cats and dogs can understand.'" *Dictionary of Literary Biography* contributor Marie Henault concurs: "*The Testing-Tree* [reveals] a new, freer poetry, looser forms, shorter lines, lowercase line beginnings. . . . Overall the Kunitz of this book is a 'new' Kunitz, one who has grown and changed in the thirteen years since *Selected Poems*."

Kunitz comments on these two styles in *Publishers Weekly:* "My early poems were very intricate, dense and formal. . . . They were written in conventional metrics and had a very strong beat to the line. . . . In my late poems I've learned to depend on a simplicity that seems almost nonpoetic on the surface, but has reverberations within that keep it intense and alive. . . . I think that as a young poet I looked for what Keats called 'a fine excess,' but as an old poet I look for spareness and rigor and a world of compassion." Gregory Orr offers this view in *American Poetry Review:* "There *is* a stylistic shift, but more deeply than that there is a fundamental shift in Kunitz's relation to the world and to his life. If the earlier poems were often structured as intense, lyricized metaphysical and intellectual allegories whose discoveries and dramas involved transcending the physical world, then the later work is marked by a deep shift toward acceptance of the physical world and the existence of others. The intensity of many early Kunitz poems is the intensity of passionate intellect, but later work opens itself to a new world of feeling."

While Kunitz's style may have changed over the years, his themes have not. One of Kunitz's most pervasive themes concerns the simultaneity of life and death. Kunitz comments in the *New York Times:* "The deepest thing I know is that I am living and dying at once, and my conviction is to report that dialogue. It is a rather terrifying thought that is at the root of much of my poetry." Other themes concern "rebirth, the quest, and the night journey (or descent into the underworld)," explains Kunitz in *Poetry.*

Kunitz's willingness to explore such grave themes has prompted critics to applaud his courage, and to describe him as a risk taker. Analyzing one of Kunitz's better known poems, "King of the River," a selection from *The Testing-Tree, New York Times Book Review* contributor Robert B. Shaw writes: "This poem is emblematic in more ways than one: Kunitz's willingness to risk bombast, platitude or bathos in his contemplation of what he calls 'mystery' is evident in it. Mystery—of the self, of time, of change and fate—is not facilely dispelled but approached with imaginative awe in his work; in our rationalistic century this is swimming against the stream. This is a form of artistic heroism; and when Kunitz's scorning of safety meshes firmly with his technical skills, the outcome is poetry of unusual power and depth." Mary Oliver similarly observes in *Kenyon Review* that "what is revealed, then, is courage. Not the courage of words only, but the intellectual courage that insists on the truth, which is never simple."

A *Poetry* critic believes that "the risks [Kunitz] has taken have ever sprung from inner necessity; they have the stamp of personal rightness upon them." Some critics speculate that Kunitz's thematic concerns stem from the trauma associated with the suicide of his father prior to Kunitz's birth. Orr writes: "To read Kunitz rightly we must accept that there is a hurt, a negation, at the beginning of Kunitz's life that resonates and persists through the whole life and that affects all the important aspects of his life. This negation is not only the primary negation of death (his father's suicide and the early death of a beloved stepfather telescoped together), but the secondary negation of the mother's unwillingness or inability to 'forgive.'"

In *The Testing-Tree* Kunitz "ruthlessly prods [these] wounds," writes Stanley Moss in the *Nation.* "His primordial curse is the suicide of his father before his birth. The poems take us into the sacred woods and houses of his 66 years, illuminate the images that have haunted him. . . . Kunitz . . . searches for secret reality and the meaning of the unknown father. He moves from the known to the unknown to the unknowable—not necessarily in that order." Lowell comments: "One reads [*The Testing-Tree*] from cover to cover with the ease of reading good prose fiction. . . . I don't know of another in prose or verse that gives in a few pages the impression of a large autobiography." Writes a *Yale Review* critic: "*The Testing-Tree,* Kunitz's first book in the thirteen years since the publication of . . . *Selected Poems,* resounds with the upheaval of a spiritual recluse coming back to the world, to voice, after a long

self-banishment: the voice surprised at its own return from muteness with intense shocks of awakening like those of a body amazed to have exhumed itself from a premature burial." Concludes Moss: "At a time when literature seems to edge us toward suicide, or lead us into hell, Kunitz stands with Roethke on 'the terrible threshold' and says, 'I dance for the joy of surviving.'"

Kunitz's essential optimism is revealed further in his celebration of rural life, *Next-to-Last Things: New Poems and Essays,* published in 1985. *New York Times Book Review* contributor R. W. Flint observes: "The sharp and seasoned good humor Stanley Kunitz brings to the poems, essays, interviews and aphorisms in 'Next-to-Last Things' is a tonic in our literary life. . . . Paradox and complication entice him, and he now cheerfully discusses a body of poetry, his own, that he rightly finds to have been 'essentially dark and grieving—elegiac.'"

Kunitz reflects on similar themes in *Next-to-Last Things,* but critics note that both his perception of these themes and his style have undergone further transitions. Oliver writes: "Here Kunitz reveals himself personally and professionally in considerable detail. His early life—the fatherlessness which plays an important role in his work—is discussed with candor as though, after years of dealing physically with this fact, the potency and perhaps some of the sorrow too have been erased." *Chicago Tribune Book World* contributor James Idema notes that Kunitz's poetry has become yet more austere: "The poems that open the book are leaner than those from the early and middle years, narrower on their pages. . . . Some of them are serene and melancholy, as you might expect. Most reflect the sky-and-weather environment of his Provincetown summer home, where he is most comfortable confronting 'the great simplicities.' But the best ones are full of action and vivid imagery.'"

Parini concludes: "We may be grateful for this poet who has paid his dues. He has erred in the directions of intellect and heart, but he has learned from his errors and managed, poem by poem, to snatch from the ineluctable sea of experience a few prize words; his best work feels beyond language itself to the mysterious and 'delicate engine' of life which is, always, before mere words themselves."

CA INTERVIEW

CA interviewed Stanley Kunitz on April 4, 1987, in New York, New York.

CA: You appear to work a good deal of your personal experience into your poetry. How much effort do you put into transforming that experience, or do you find that it transforms itself as you write?

KUNITZ: By its nature poetry is an intimate medium, the most self-revelatory of the arts. Perhaps that's why it is so dangerously seductive to the creative spirit. The transformation of individual experience—the transpersonalization of the persona, if you will—is work that the imagination has to do, its obligatory task. One of the problems with so much of what was called, in the '60s, confessional poetry was that it relied excessively on the exploitation of self, on the shock effect of raw experience. My conviction is that poetry is a legendary, not an anecdotal, art.

CA: Do you tend to choose certain elements of your experience over others?

KUNITZ: As I say in one of my poems ["King of the River"], "I did not choose the way, the way chose me." Some of the materials of the life want to be transformed, while others resist. You can shape a poem, but you can't will it into existence.

CA: How has this changed as you've grown older, or hasn't it?

KUNITZ: In my youth, as might be expected, I had little knowledge of the world to draw on. But I had fallen in love with language and was excited by ideas, including the idea of being a poet. Early poetry is much more likely to be abstract because of the poverty of experience.

CA: Were you conscious of that poverty?

KUNITZ: I was really an innocent—daring to speculate without trepidation about grand abstractions like love and death and immortality. They are still my themes. Only I address them now through particulars of experience.

CA: In your essay "Poet and State," you write that the poet is in some respects freer than the novelist or playwright because he is not obligated to entertain. Did you feel that freedom when you began to write poetry?

KUNITZ: Freedom and poetry have always been associated in my mind. The main point of the passage you quote was that since poetry is practically worthless as a commodity in our market-oriented society, the poet is not only privileged to say what he pleases, but also free to aspire to the purity and perfection of an absolute art.

CA: Your poetry seems to have become freer, stylistically, over the years.

KUNITZ: I began as a rather formal poet in the tradition of the period.

CA: Do certain structures suggest themselves to you as appropriate to your different themes, or can't you generalize?

KUNITZ: I don't try to preordain the form of a poem. There's a good deal of automatism in the beginning, as I try to give the poem its head. Most of all I am looking for a distinctive rhythm. Once the rhythm asserts itself, I feel I can ride on it as far as the original impulse will carry me. I want the poem to grow out of its own materials, to develop organically. I haven't written in set patterns, such as the sonnet or villanelle, since my youth, but who knows?—I may be tempted to tinker with them again, to see how much disorder I can introduce into them without breaking the mold.

CA: How do you feel about being named New York's first official state poet?

KUNITZ: It's something of an anomaly. I'm not prepared to think of myself as any kind of official poet.

CA: Were you amused?

KUNITZ: A little amused, a little embarrassed, and a little proud.

CA: I'm struck by your suite of poems "Words for the Unknown Makers," especially "A Blessing of Women." There's a good deal of compassion in the poem. Isn't it true that your irony is directed at male oppressors?

KUNITZ: I admit to being a feminist.

CA: In what way do you identify with the makers of quilts and samplers, the obscure craftswomen whom you apostrophize in your poem?

KUNITZ: I tend to gravitate toward all the lost and oppressed—a category into which women historically fall. Perhaps the circumstances of my childhood have some relevance here. I was brought up in a family of females, and my mother was a professional needleworker, a dress designer. It seems to me that I've always felt close to women and to their sensibility. Poetry isn't for me a macho art.

CA: Can you tell me about your love for gardening?

KUNITZ: When you say gardening, I think of my work, sunlight, beauty, meditation, happiness. All my life I've enjoyed working with my hands. I need a sense of physical activity. When I was a boy, during World War I, I had a Victory Garden. I didn't really understand why it was called that, because I thought it was a victory every time you made anything grow. I used to explore the woods behind our house in Worcester, Massachusetts, and hunt for arrowheads and other Indian traces. I've never felt completely right in an urban environment: I need some green. In 1930, shortly after I'd come to New York, I found a farmhouse in Connecticut that I acquired for five hundred dollars down, and ever since I've managed to keep some foothold in the country, some place where I can make things grow.

CA: In much of your poetry, I'm thinking particularly of "The Mulch," you dramatize the tension between the creative and destructive forces of nature. Is that tension a compelling one for you?

KUNITZ: It's the way things are: death and life inextricably bound to each other. One of my feelings about working the land is that I am celebrating a ritual of death and resurrection. Every spring I feel that. I am never closer to the miraculous than when I am grubbing in the soil.

CA: There's a certain melancholy tone in "The Mulch."

KUNITZ: But also joy. One of the tests of the poetic imagination is its ability to hold contradictory feelings in suspension. That's what complicates the interpretation of a poem.

CA: Do you find the meanings of your own poems shift as you look at them in different ways?

KUNITZ: I never inquire what the meanings of my poems are. I know fairly well what the meanings of my life are, and I trust that those meanings diffuse themselves through the poems. It is the poems as a collective whole that I think of with respect to meaning rather than individual poems, which I prefer not to question too closely.

CA: Other than as a visual construct, what function does the image serve in the writing of a poem?

KUNITZ: The physicality of a poem is largely concentrated in its images. These are points of tension and resistance, little whirlpools of energy in the midst of the word-flow. When language is deprived of concrete sensory details, it tends to vaporize, is in danger of blowing away. Images help you nail your poem to the wall—that is, to reality.

CA: Are you ever offended when critics assign certain meanings to your poems?

KUNITZ: I don't pay much attention to criticism of my work—that goes for praise as well as blame.

CA: Your own criticism is nearly always sympathetic.

KUNITZ: Poetry that's worth writing about, I feel, deserves a sympathetic reading. If my response to a work is negative, I leave it alone.

CA: What do you think about poetry that is inspired by other arts, painting, for example?

KUNITZ: It isn't fair to generalize, but I have to say that most poems based on other arts strike me as secondhand or warmed-over stuff. They have the air of being composed at an extra remove—a polite distance—from what Yeats called the mire of existence. Painting is the other art I care most about—I am, in fact, married into the world of painting, and I have written a number of essays on the visual arts—but I don't feel any particular need to convert paintings into poems.

CA: Do you ever research material for your poems, or do you incorporate into them things you've already read?

KUNITZ: I am not likely to do organized research in advance, but my random reading—particularly in the sciences—is a fortuitous source of information and metaphor. Back in 1966 I had a traumatic encounter with a leviathan that had beached itself near my summer place on Cape Cod. For years after I read everything about whales that I could lay my hands on. Eventually, when I began the actual writing of "The Wellfleet Whale," all the lore I had accumulated fed my imagination. In an earlier poem, "The Science of the Night," the image of two souls "flying fast apart" dissolved into the concept of the expanding universe and led me to allude—reputedly for the first time in poetry—to the spectroscopic phenomenon of the red shift. In the same poem, when I wrote about "the calcium snows of sleep," I thought that the image, which both pleased and baffled me, was of spontaneous origin. It was only by chance, some time later, that I discovered an old notation in my journal that there is a measurable precipitation of calcium in the brain during sleep. You might say that this sort of creative luck, the inadvertent conversion of fact into metaphor, depends on a passionate curiosity about the exotic details of a life. That's the kind of research I'm happiest about.

CA: You feel that poetry should be read aloud. I'm sure you recognize that much of your own audience reads you silently.

KUNITZ: It's true that I write my poems for the ear. In fact, my method of writing a poem is to say it. The pitch and tempo and tonalities of a poem are elements of its organic life. A poem is as much a voice as it is a system of verbal signs. I realize that ultimately the poet departs from the scene, and the poems that he abandons to the printed page must speak for themselves. But I can't help wondering about the influence on posterity of the technical revolution that will enable them to see and hear, on film and tape, the poets of our century. Suppose we had videotapes of Keats reading his ode "To Au-

tumn" or Blake declaiming "The Marriage of Heaven and Hell"!

CA: Do you feel when you're reading a poem aloud that your voice is able to capture the poem's original sound?

KUNITZ: That's exactly what I try to do—to recapture the way the poem sounded to me at the time of its making. In its public aspect, poetry is one of the performing arts. I am perplexed at the number of poets who have never even bothered to learn how to project their voice—an elementary lesson. If we want audiences, we need to work seriously at the mastery of an appropriate reading style.

CA: You have translated a good deal of Russian poetry. Can you describe some of the challenges you have had to face, and your personal response to creating a new poem out of an old one?

KUNITZ: I've written at some length on that subject in my prefatory note to *Poems of Akhmatova*. The challenges I have had to face are not peculiar to my individual circumstances. As I point out, the poet as translator is pulled in opposite directions. One voice enjoins him, "Be faithful to the text!" The other demands, "Make it new!" The tension between these contradictory imperatives is precisely what causes a translation to come alive. We all know that poetry is a marriage of sound and sense; yet every time we translate a poem, we begin by wrenching sound and sense apart. The pedantic insistence on literal translation is an egregious fallacy, because each language is an independent system and makes a different music. There is a reasonable argument to be made that poetry is untranslatable, but I cannot think of any poets who would choose to listen. This is, in fact, one of the great ages of translation. All literatures, however minor or esoteric, are at the point of becoming world literature.

CA: Each of your translations bears your own unique mark, in your choice and positioning of words. Is the process of transforming a poem from one language to another as compelling to you as creating your own?

KUNITZ: Translation is one of the things I do as a poet, and enjoy doing, but it's not my central involvement. The reason I gave up the violin at an early age was that I didn't want to spend my life playing someone else's music.

CA: Are you still teaching?

KUNITZ: Last year I resigned from the writing program at Columbia, but I'm still a pilgrim on the roads, giving readings and seminars. I'm not ready to give that up.

CA: You find it invigorating?

KUNITZ: I do. Wonderful things can happen in a classroom. I've had tremendous luck with some of my students.

CA: What do you feel about poets learning their trade in an academic environment?

KUNITZ: It has never happened before, on such a scale, in any country on earth. And the irony is that it is happening in a culture that has little love or respect for poetry. I belong to the last generation of self-taught poets in America. Up to now poetry has survived through all the vicissitudes of history as a passionate and solitary enterprise, the most indelible testimony we have of the adventures of the human spirit in the dominions of the sacred and profane. How much of that can be taught as an academic discipline? Poetry workshops are designed to teach what is teachable—that is, the craft of verse. Despite the affirmative feelings I have expressed about my experience as a teacher, I worry that, by and large, we are developing a new breed of graduate poets, certified Masters of the Fine Arts, who have earned their degree as verbal technicians, experts in word-play, makers of publishable poems. Our writing programs are producing more poets per annum than great civilizations of the past generated in a century. You have to ask yourself, is it for real? I do not pretend to know the answer.

BIOGRAPHICAL/CRITICAL SOURCES:

BOOKS

A Celebration for Stanley Kunitz on His 80th Birthday, Sheep Meadow Press, 1986.

Contemporary Literary Criticism, Gale, Volume 6, 1976, Volume 11, 1979, Volume 14, 1980.

Dictionary of Literary Biography, Volume 48: *American Poets, 1880-1945*, second series, Gale, 1986.

Henault, Marie, *Stanley Kunitz*, Twayne, 1980.

Hungerford, Edward, editor, *Poets in Progress*, Northwestern University Press, 1962, revised edition, 1967.

Mills, Ralph J., Jr., *Contemporary American Poetry*, Random, 1965.

Orr, Gregory, *Stanley Kunitz: An Introduction to the Poetry*, Columbia University Press, 1985.

Ostroff, Anthony J., editor, *The Contemporary Poet as a Critic and Artist*, Little, Brown, 1964.

Rodman, Selden, *Tongues of Fallen Angels*, New Directions, 1974.

Rosenthal, M. L., *The Modern Poets: A Critical Introduction*, Oxford University Press, 1960.

PERIODICALS

American Poetry Review, March/April, 1976, July, 1980, September/October, 1985.

Chicago Tribune Book World, December 22, 1985.

Contemporary Literature, winter, 1974.

Harper's, February, 1986.

Iowa Review, spring, 1974.

Kenyon Review, summer, 1986.

Nation, September 20, 1971.

New York Quarterly, fall, 1970.

New York Review of Books, November 22, 1979.

New York Times, July 7, 1979, March 11, 1987.

New York Times Book Review, November 11, 1965, March 21, 1971, July 22, 1979.

Paris Review, spring, 1982.

Poetry, September, 1980.

Prairie Schooner, summer, 1980.

Publishers Weekly, December 20, 1985.

Saturday Review, September 27, 1958, December 18, 1971.

Times Literary Supplement, May 30, 1980.

Virginia Quarterly Review, spring, 1980.

Washington Post, May 12, 1987.

Washington Post Book World, September 30, 1979.

Yale Literary Magazine, May, 1968.

Yale Review, autumn, 1971.

—*Sketch by Melissa Gaiownik*

—*Interview by Revan Schendler*

L

LAMMING, George (William) 1927-

PERSONAL: Born June 8, 1927, in Barbados; emigrated to England, 1950. *Education:* Attended Combermere High School in Barbados.

ADDRESSES: Home—14-A Highbury Place, London N 5, England.

CAREER: Writer. Worked as schoolmaster in Trinidad, 1946-50; factory worker in England, 1950; broadcaster for British Broadcasting Corp. (BBC) Colonial Service, 1951. Writer-in-residence and lecturer in Creative Arts Centre and Department of Education, University of West Indies, Mona, Jamaica, 1967-68; visiting professor at University of Texas at Austin, 1977, and at University of Pennsylvania. Lecturer in Denmark, Tanzania, and Australia.

AWARDS, HONORS: Kenyon Review fellowship, 1954; Guggenheim Fellowship, 1955; Somerset Maugham Award, 1957; Canada Council fellowship, 1962; Commonwealth Foundation grant, 1976; Association of Commonwealth Literature Writers Award; D.Litt., University of West Indies.

WRITINGS:

NOVELS

In the Castle of My Skin, with introduction by Richard Wright, McGraw, 1953, with a new introduction by the author, Schocken, 1983.
The Emigrants, M. Joseph, 1954, McGraw, 1955, reprinted, Allison & Busby, 1980.
Of Age and Innocence, M. Joseph, 1958, reprinted, Allison & Busby, 1981.
Season of Adventure, M. Joseph, 1960, reprinted, Allison & Busby, 1979.
Water With Berries, Holt, 1972.
Natives of My Person, Holt, 1972.

CONTRIBUTOR OF POETRY TO ANTHOLOGIES

Peter Brent, editor, *Young Commonwealth Poets '65,* Heinemann, 1965.
John Figueroa, editor, *Caribbean Voices,* two volumes, Evans, 1966.
O. R. Dathorne, editor, *Caribbean Verse,* Heinemann, 1968.

CONTRIBUTOR OF SHORT FICTION TO ANTHOLOGIES

Andrew Salkey, editor, *West Indian Stories,* Faber, 1960.
Salkey, editor, *Stories from the Caribbean,* Dufour, 1965, published as *Island Voices,* Liveright, 1970.
O. R. Dathorne, editor, *Caribbean Narrative,* Heinemann, 1966.
Barbara Howes, editor, *From the Green Antilles,* Macmillan, 1966.
Salkey, editor, *Caribbean Prose,* Evans, 1967.
James T. Livingston, editor, *Caribbean Rhythms,* Pocket Books, 1974.

OTHER

The Pleasures of Exile (essays and autobiographical observations), M. Joseph, 1960, reprinted, Allison & Busby, 1984.
(With Henry Bangou and Rene Depestre) *Influencia del Africa en las literaturas antillanas* (title means "The Influence of Africa on the Antillian Literatures"), I. L. A. C. (Montevideo, Uruguay), 1972.
(Editor) *Cannon Shot and Glass Beads: Modern Black Writing,* Pan Books, 1974.

Co-editor of Barbados and Guyana independence issues of *New World Quarterly* (Kingston), 1965 and 1967. Contributor to journals, including *Bim* (Barbados), *Savacou, New World Quarterly, Caribbean Quarterly,* and *Casa de las Americas* (Cuba).

SIDELIGHTS: Barbadian writer "George Lamming is not so much a novelist," asserts *New York Times Book Review* contributor Jan Carew, "as a chronicler of secret journeys to the innermost regions of the West Indian psyche." George Davis, however, believes Carew's assessment does not go far enough. Davis notes in his own *New York Times Book Review* critique, "I can think of very few writers who make better use of the fictional moments of their stories to explore the souls of any of us—West Indian or not."

In Lamming's essay, "The Negro Writer in His World," the West Indian explains the universality on which Davis comments. In the essay Lamming maintains that black writers are the same as all other writers who use writing as a method of self-discovery. According to Carolyn T. Brown in *World Literature Today,* in Lamming's opinion, "the contemporary human condition . . . involves a 'universal sense of separation

228

and abandonment, frustration and loss, and above all, of man's direct inner experience of something missing.''

In Lamming's work the ''something missing'' is a true cultural identity for the West Indian. This lack of identity is, according to Lamming, a direct result of the long history of colonial rule in the region. Caribbean-born writer V. S. Naipaul explains the importance of this idea in his *New Statesman* review of Lamming's novel, *Of Age and Innocence:* ''Unless one understands the West Indian's search for identity, [the novel] is almost meaningless. It is not fully realised how completely the West Indian Negro identifies himself with England. . . . For the West Indian intellectual, speaking no language but English, educated in an English way, the experience of England is really traumatic. The foundations of his life are removed.''

James Ngugi makes a similar observation in his *Pan-Africanist* review of the same novel. ''For Lamming,'' Ngugi writes, ''a sense of exile must lead to action and through action to identity. The West Indian's alienation springs . . . from his colonial relationship to England.''

Lamming's first four novels explore the West Indian search for identity, a search which often leads to a flight to England followed by, for some, a return to their Caribbean roots. His first novel, *In the Castle of My Skin,* which is nearly universally acclaimed by critics, is a quasi-autobiographical look at childhood and adolescence on Lamming's fictional Caribbean island, San Cristobal. The book ''is generally regarded,'' notes Michael Gilkes in *The West Indian Novel,* ''as a 'classic' of West Indian fiction. It is one of the earliest novels of any substance to convey, with real assurance, the life of ordinary village folk within a genuinely realized, native landscape: a 'peasant novel' . . . written with deep insight and considerable technical skill.''

Several reviewers compare Lamming's prose style in the book to poetry. In *New Statesman and Nation* Pritchett describes Lamming's prose as ''something between garrulous realism and popular poetry, and . . . quite delightful''; while in the *San Francisco Chronicle* J. H. Jackson says Lamming ''is a poet and a human being who approaches a question vital to him, humanly and poetically.'' A *Time* contributor finds the book ''a curious mixture of autobiography and a poetic evocation of a native life. . . . It is one of the few authentically rich and constantly readable books produced [thus far] by a West Indian.''

Lamming's next novel, *The Emigrants,* follows a group of West Indians who—like Lamming, himself—leave their native islands for exile in England, while the two novels that follow, *Of Age and Innocence* and *Season of Adventure,* feature a return to San Cristobal. According to Carew, these last two novels also have a bit of autobiography in them because through their action it seems ''as though Lamming [is] attempting to rediscover a history of himself by himself.''

In Lamming's novels, as critics note, self-discovery is often achieved through an inquiry into his characters' pasts. For example, while *Yale Review* contributor Michael Cook quotes Lamming's *Of Age and Innocence* description of San Cristobal—''an old land inhabiting new forms of men who can never resurrect their roots and do not know their nature,'' the reviewer comments that ''it is obvious'' that in ''*Season of Adventure* . . . [Lamming] is committed to his characters' at least trying to discover their roots and their natures.'' Details of the plot seem to verify Cook's assessment for the novel traces

Fola Piggott's quest to discover whether her father was European or African.

According to Kenneth Ramchand in *The West Indian Novel and Its Background,* ''*Season of Adventure* is the most significant of the West Indian novels invoking Africa.'' In the novel, Ramchand maintains, Lamming invokes ''the African heritage not to make statements about Africa but to explore the troubled components of West Indian culture and nationhood.'' Lamming accomplishes ''this without preventing us from seeing that Fola's special circumstances . . . are only a manifestation . . . of every man's need to take the past into account with humility, fearlessness, and receptivity.''

After a silence of over a decade Lamming published two new novels almost simultaneously: *Water with Berries* and *Natives of My Person.* Again, his fiction focuses on the effects of history on the present. In both books Lamming uses symbolism to tell his story. In *Water with Berries* Lamming uses a theme previously dealt with in his nonfiction work *The Pleasures of Exile.* A *Times Literary Supplement* reviewer quotes from Lamming's collection of essays: ''My subject is the migration of the West Indian writer, as colonial and exile, from his native kingdom, once inhabited by Caliban, to the tempestuous island of Prospero's and his language.'' Caliban and Prospero are both characters from Shakespeare's *The Tempest,* Caliban being the deformed slave of Prospero, ruler of an enchanted island. According to the *Times Literary Supplement* contributor, Lamming also refers to himself in the same book as an ''exiled descendent of Caliban.''

In *Water with Berries* Lamming uses the plot of *The Tempest* to symbolize the various ills of West Indian society, but critics are divided on the success of the novel. In *World Literature in English* Anthony Boxill notes that Lamming uses *The Tempest* to ''help put across his points about disintegration of personality . . . , especially in people who are products of a colonial past. . . . However, the *Tempest* pattern which might have been the strength of this novel proves its undoing. . . . In his unrelenting faithfulness to this . . . pattern Lamming loses touch with the characters he is creating; they cease to be credible.'' A *Times Literary Supplement* contributor similarly states, ''Lamming writes very well, but *Water with Berries* does not entirely convince either as a study of the pains of exile, or as an allegory of colonialism. . . . [And,] as for the melodrama of . . . Lamming's *Tempest* myth, it tells us nothing new.''

Other critics praise Lamming's novel and disregard its connections to *The Tempest.* Paul Theroux and George Davis, for instance, find the work a very compelling statement on the effects of colonialism. In *Encounter* Theroux claims, ''the poetic prose of the narrative has a perfect dazzle. . . . When expatriation is defined and dramatised . . . *Water with Berries* takes on a life of its own, for . . . Lamming is meticulous in diagnosing the condition of estrangement.'' *New York Times Book Review* contributor Davis writes: ''This is an effectively written fictional work. Lamming brings his characters . . . into the same nightmare of arson, perversity, suicide and murder, which, we are forced to feel, is the legacy of the colonial experience.''

Natives of My Person, according to Gilkes, ''is an exceedingly complex work, full of allegorical and historical meanings and echoes. It is an embodiment of all [Lamming's] themes: a kind of *reviewing* process in which he appears to take stock of things.'' Boxill notes that the novel ''provides richly complex insights into human personality and the history of colonialism.'' It tells the story of the sixteenth-century voyage of the ship *Reconnaissance* from Europe to America by way of Africa. The chief goal of the ship's Commandant is the establishment of a slave-free settlement on the island of San Cristobal, but he is killed by two of the ship's officers before he can accomplish his mission.

Some critics find that Lamming's prose detracts from the novel. In *Book World* Theroux calls Lamming "a marvelously skillful writer" but also refers to the novel's "shadowy action and vaguely poetical momentousness." A *Times Literary Supplement* reviewer complains that Lamming writes "a prose of discovery which is effortful, uncolloquial, and almost always mannered."

While Thomas R. Edwards and Carew also regret the complexity of Lamming's prose they are able to find redeeming qualities in the novel. "Lamming's prose is portentous," Edwards notes in the *New York Review of Books*, "hooked on simile, and anxious to suggest more than it says, inviting questions thestory never answers. . . . Yet if reading *Natives of My Person* is a voyage into frustration and annoyance, Lamming's story survives and grows in the mind afterward. . . . This imagined history reveals itself as a version of significances that 'real' history is itself only a version of."

Carew similarly comments on the book's difficult prose but calls the work "undoubtedly . . . Lamming's finest novel." In the book, according to Carew's assessment, Lamming expresses better than in any of his other novels his concerns about the effects of colonization on the West Indies and its people. In *Natives of My Person*, Carew maintains, Lamming "succeeds in illuminating new areas of darkness in the colonial past that the colonizer has so far not dealt with; and in this sense it is a profoundly revolutionary and original work."

BIOGRAPHICAL/CRITICAL SOURCES:

BOOKS

Baugh, Edward, editor, *Homecoming: Essays on African and Caribbean Literature, Culture and Politics*, Laurence Hill, 1972.
Contemporary Literary Criticism, Gale, Volume 2, 1974, Volume 4, 1975.
Cooke, Michael G., editor, *Modern Black Novelists: A Collection of Critical Essays*, Prentice-Hall, 1971.
Gilkes, Michael, *The West Indian Novel*, Twayne, 1981.
Lamming, George, *In the Castle of My Skin*, McGraw, 1954.
Lamming, George, *Of Age and Innocence*, M. Joseph, 1958.
Lamming, George, *The Pleasures of Exile*, M. Joseph, 1960.
Massa, Daniel, editor, *Individual and Community in Commonwealth Literature*, University Press (Malta), 1979.
Paquet, Sandra Pouchet, *The Novels of George Lamming*, Heinemann, 1982.
Ramchand, Kenneth, *The West Indian Novel and Its Background*, Faber, 1970.

PERIODICALS

Book World, January 23, 1972.
Canadian Literature, winter, 1982.
Caribbean Quarterly, February, 1958.
Encounter, May, 1972.
New Statesman, December 6, 1958, January 28, 1972, December 19, 1980.
New Statesman and Nation, April 18, 1953.
New Yorker, December 5, 1953, May 28, 1955, April 29, 1972.
New York Herald Tribune Book Review, July 17, 1955.
New York Review of Books, March 9, 1972.
New York Times, November 1, 1953, July 24, 1955, January 15, 1972.
New York Times Book Review, February 27, 1972, June 4, 1972, October 15, 1972, December 3, 1972.
Observer, October 8, 1972.
Pan-Africanist, March, 1971.
Punch, August 19, 1981.
San Francisco Chronicle, November 17, 1953, June 24, 1955.
Saturday Review, December 5, 1953, May 28, 1955.
Studies in Black Literature, spring, 1973.
Time, November 9, 1953, April 25, 1955.
Times Literary Supplement, March 27, 1953, February 11, 1972, December 15, 1972, September 4, 1981, October 24, 1986.
World Literature Today, winter, 1983, spring, 1985.
World Literature Written in English, November, 1971, April, 1973, November, 1979.
Yale Review, autumn, 1953, summer, 1973.†

—*Sketch by Marian Gonsior*

*   *   *

LANSKY, Vicki 1942-

PERSONAL: Born January 6, 1942, in Louisville, Ky.; daughter of Arthur (an executive in the men's ready-to-wear business) and Mary (Kaplan) Rogosin; married Bruce Lansky (a publisher and literary agent), June 13, 1967 (divorced, 1983); children: Douglas, Dana. *Education:* Connecticut College, B.A., 1963.

ADDRESSES: Home—3342 Robinson Bay Rd., Deephaven, Minn. 55391. *Office—Practical Parenting*, 18326B Minnetonka Blvd., Deephaven, Minn. 55391.

CAREER: Lord & Taylor and Mercantile Stores, New York, N.Y., sportswear buyer, 1965-69; free-lance photographer, 1968-72; Childbirth Education Association, Minneapolis, Minn., teaching assistant, 1971-74; Meadowbrook Press, Wayzata, Minn., founder, treasurer and executive vice-president in charge of operations, beginning 1975; *Practical Parenting* (newsletter), Deephaven, Minn., editor and publisher, 1979—; The Book Peddlers (publisher and literary agency), Deephaven, Minn., owner, 1983—; writer. Daily radio commentator, Associated Press Broadcast Features; has appeared on a number of television programs, including "Donahue" and the "Today" show. Former member, Pillsbury/Green Giant Consumer Advisory Panel.

WRITINGS:

(With others) *Feed Me! I'm Yours*, Meadowbrook Press, 1974.
The Taming of the C.A.N.D.Y. Monster, Meadowbrook Press, 1978.
(Editor with Bruce Lansky) *The Best Baby Name Book in the Whole World*, Meadowbrook Press, 1979.
(Editor with B. Lansky) *Watch Me Grow: The Baby Memory and Record Book*, Meadowbrook Press, 1979.
Vicki Lansky's Best Practical Parenting Tips, edited by Kathe Grooms, Meadowbrook Press, 1980, revised edition published as *Vicki Lansky's Practical Parenting Tips*, edited by Kathryn Ring, 1982.
(Editor with others) *Free Stuff for Parents* (catalog), Meadowbrook Press, 1981.
Dear Babysitter, edited by Ring, Meadowbrook Press, 1982.
Practical Parenting Tips, Meadowbrook Press, 1982.
Toilet Training, Bantam, 1984.

Welcoming Your Second Baby, Bantam, 1984, revised, 1987.
Practical Parenting Tips for the School Age Years, Bantam, 1985.
Traveling with Your Baby, Bantam, 1985.
Getting Your Baby to Sleep (and Back to Sleep), Bantam, 1985.
Birthday Parties, Bantam, 1986.
Koko Bear's New Potty (juvenile), Bantam, 1986.
The Best of Vicki Lansky's Practical Parenting, Book Peddlers, 1987.
Fat-Proofing Your Kids, Bantam, 1987, reprinted as *Fat-Proofing Your Children . . . So That They Never Become Diet-Addicted Adults*, 1988.
Koko Bear's New Babysitter (juvenile), Bantam, 1987.
A New Baby at Koko Bear's House (juvenile), Bantam, 1987.
Vicki Lansky's Kids Cooking (juvenile), Scholastic, Inc., 1987.
Koko Bear's Big Earache (juvenile), Bantam, 1988.

Sunday newspaper columnist, Minneapolis *Star and Tribune*.

SIDELIGHTS: What do you do when you have important ideas to communicate to the American public, but publishers show no interest in your book? Vicki Lansky faced this dilemma in 1974 when she and several other mothers from a local Childbirth Education Association chapter wrote a baby food cookbook for new mothers. Undaunted, Lansky and her husband turned their back porch into their own publishing company and began producing *Feed Me! I'm Yours* for commercial distribution. Their creative promotional efforts and appearances on television talk shows made *Feed Me! I'm Yours* America's best selling baby food and toddler cookbook.

As her children grew older, Lansky found the struggle to maintain good nutritional habits intensifying. Saturday morning television commercials for junk food permeated her children's minds along with their fare of cartoons, and she perceived the need to counter this offensive with tasty alternative recipes for young children. In *The Taming of the C.A.N.D.Y. Monster* she sought to provide parents with practical ideas to improve their children's eating habits. The book rose quickly to the number one spot on the *New York Times* Trade Paperback Bestseller list, and Meadowbrook Press is struggling to meet the demand for it.

When an interviewer for *Us* magazine asked Lansky how she had broken her own children of the sugar habit, she replied: "I don't know if I have, but if I have cured them, it's because they didn't have any choice; I don't keep any sugar around the house. That makes it easier to say no to the kids without fear of repercussions. They're not going to move out. I told them: 'I don't want you to have it because I want you to grow up to be strong and healthy, and all this sugar is not going to help you. I'm not doing this to punish you, I'm doing it because I love you.' I think that kids are willing to accept that.'' Her idea of a good diet involves "a greater emphasis on vegetables and fruits, . . . a switch from meats into poultry and fish . . . less emphasis on the simple carbohydrates, the sugars and flours, and more on the complex carbohydrates, the whole grains and rices," but she admitted: "It's going to be a long time before Americans can achieve this diet. I'm not into supernutrition or supervitamins, just eating better with what we've got."

In 1979, Lansky began publishing *Practical Parenting*, a bimonthly newsletter consisting of articles and tips on different issues of childrearing. The newsletter has grown into a nationally syndicated radio feature and a series of "Practical Parenting" books. Lansky designs each book to cover a single topic, providing a quick and easy source of information for inexperienced parents. As Sue MacDonald reports in the *Cincinnati Enquirer:* Lansky says "'a lot of these books [are] a replacement for the support group,' . . . pointing out that many new parents have no family or close friends in whom to confide—or feel too stupid to ask their own mothers for advice.''

AVOCATIONAL INTERESTS: Tending plants and children, swimming, windsurfing, photography.

BIOGRAPHICAL/CRITICAL SOURCES:

PERIODICALS

Cincinnati Enquirer, August 3, 1984.
Los Angeles Times Book Review, July 25, 1982.
New York Times Book Review, April 2, 1978.
Us, June 27, 1978.

* * *

LAQUIAN, Aprodicio A(rcilla) 1935-

PERSONAL: Born March 23, 1935, in Pampanga, Philippines; son of Narciso Cruz (a tailor) and Crisanta (Arcilla) Laquian; married Eleanor del Rio (a journalist), October 24, 1962; children: George Edwardo R., Agnes Helen R. *Education:* University of the Philippines, B.A. (cum laude), 1959; Massachusetts Institute of Technology, Ph.D., 1965. *Religion:* Roman Catholic.

ADDRESSES: c/o Regional Director, International Development Research Centre, P.O. Box 30677, Nairobi, Kenya.

CAREER: Associate professor of political science, University of the Philippines, Manila; University of Hawaii, East-West Center, Honolulu, senior specialist, 1968-69; International Association for Metropolitan Research and Development, Toronto, Ontario, director of research, beginning 1969. Lecturer, Faculty of Environmental Studies, York University, beginning 1970. Consultant, United Nations, 1970.

MEMBER: Society for Public Administration of the Philippines, American Association for the Advancement of Science, American Society for Public Administration, American Political Science Association, Canadian Association for Asian Studies, Canadian Association for African Studies, Asia Society, Phi Kappa Phi.

WRITINGS:

The City in Nation-Building: Politics and Administration in Metropolitan Manila, School of Public Administration, University of the Philippines, 1966.
Slums Are for People: The Barrio Magsaysay Pilot Project in Urban Community Development, College of Public Administration, University of the Philippines, 1968, 2nd edition, 1969, revised edition, East-West Center, 1971.
(Editor) *Rural-Urban Migrants and Metropolitan Development*, Intermet, 1971.
Administrative Aspects of Urbanization, United Nations, 1971.
Slums and Squatters in Six Philippine Cities, International Development Research Centre (Ottawa), 1972.
(With Alan B. Simmons and Sergio Diaz-Briquets) *Social Change and Internal Migration: A Review of Research Findings from Africa, Asia, and Latin America*, International Development Research Centre, 1977.
(Editor with Stephen H. Yeh) *Housing Asia's Millions: Problems, Policies, and Prospects for Low-Cost Housing in Southeast Asia*, Unipub, 1979.

Basic Housing: Policies for Urban Sites, Services, and Shelter in Developing Countries, International Development Research Centre, 1983, Unipub, 1984.

Managing editor, *Philippine Journal of Public Administration*, 1962-64; editor-in-chief, *Local Government Bulletin*, 1965-68.

SIDELIGHTS: Aprodicio Laquian told *CA:* "My interest in slums and squatters in developing countries is rooted in the fact that until I was twenty-five years old, I lived in the slums of Manila. . . . To me, slums and squatter areas are necessary parts of urbanization—they make it possible for many migrants from the countryside to live in the city and find their place in society."†

*   *   *

LAWSON, Don(ald Elmer) 1917-

PERSONAL: Born May 20, 1917, in Chicago, Ill.; son of Elmer Daniel and Christina (Grass) Lawson; married Beatrice M. Yates, March 30, 1945. *Education:* Cornell College, Mt. Vernon, Iowa, B.A., 1939; attended University of Iowa Writers' Workshop, 1939-40. *Religion:* Methodist.

ADDRESSES: Home—1122 Lunt Ave., No. 7B, Chicago, Ill. 60626. *Office*—United Educators, Inc., Green Bay Rd., Lake Bluff, Ill. 60044. *Agent*—Schaffner Agency, Inc., 264 Fifth Ave., New York, N.Y. 10001.

CAREER: Nora Springs Advertiser, Nora Springs, Iowa, editor, 1940-41; F. E. Compton, Chicago, Ill., member of staff of *Compton's Encyclopedia*, 1946-73, managing editor, 1960-65, editor-in-cief, 1965-72, vice-president and editor-in-chief of *Compton's Encyclopedia-Encyclopaedia Britannica*, 1972-73; United Educators, Inc., Lake Bluff, Ill., executive editor, 1973-75, editor-in-chief, 1975—. Member of board of directors, Marcy-Newberry Association Settlement Houses. *Military service:* U.S. Army Air Forces, 1941-45; served with Counterintelligence in European Theater; awarded Silver Battle Star.

MEMBER: Authors Guild, Society of Midland Authors, Chicago Literary Club, Chicago Book Clinic International Platform Association, Cliff Dwellers, Chicago Press Club, Phi Beta Kappa.

AWARDS, HONORS: First prize, *Story* magazine's Armed Forces contest, World War II; Litt.D., Cornell College (Iowa), 1970.

WRITINGS:

A Brand for the Burning (adult), Abelard-Schuman, 1961.

JUVENILES

Young People in the White House, Abelard-Schuman, 1961, revised edition, 1970.
The United States in World War I, Abelard-Schuman, 1963.
The United States in World War II, Abelard-Schuman, 1963.
The United States in the Korean War, Abelard-Schuman, 1964.
Famous American Political Families, Abelard-Schuman, 1965.
The War of 1812, Abelard-Schuman, 1966.
Frances Perkins: First Lady of the Cabinet, Abelard-Schuman, 1966.
(Editor) *Great Air Battles of World Wars I and II*, Lothrop, 1968.
The Lion and the Rock: The Story of the Rock of Gibraltar, Abelard-Schuman, 1969.

(Editor) *Youth and War*, Lothrop, 1969.
(Editor) *Ten Fighters for Peace*, Lothrop, 1971.
The Colonial Wars, Abelard-Schuman, 1972.
The American Revolution, Abelard-Schuman, 1974.
The United States in the Indian Wars, Abelard-Schuman, 1975.
The United States in the Spanish American War, Abelard-Schuman, 1976.
The United States in the Mexican War, Abelard-Schuman, 1976.
The United States in the Civil War, Abelard-Schuman, 1977.
Democracy, F. Watts, 1978.
Education Careers, F. Watts, 1978.
The Secret World War II, F. Watts, 1978.
Morocco, Algeria, Tunisia, and Libya, F. Watts, 1978.
The Changing Face of the Constitution, F. Watts, 1979.
FDR's New Deal, Crowell Junior Books, 1979.
An Album of World War II Homefronts, F. Watts, 1980.
The Picture Life of Ronald Reagan, F. Watts, 1981, revised edition, 1985.
The United States in the Vietnam War, Crowell Junior Books, 1981.
The War in Vietnam, F. Watts, 1981.
Libya and Qaddafi, F. Watts, 1982, revised edition, 1987.
The Long March: Red China under Chairman Mao, Crowell Junior Books, 1983.
The KGB, Messner, 1984.
Marcos and the Philippines, F. Watts, 1984, revised edition published as *The New Philippines*, 1986.
The Pacific States, F. Watts, 1984.
The French Resistance, Wanderer Books, 1984.
The Eagle and the Dragon: The History of U.S.-China Relations, Crowell Junior Books, 1985.
Geraldine Ferraro: The Woman Who Changed American Politics, Messner, 1985.
An Album of the Vietnam War, F. Watts, 1986.
South Africa, F. Watts, 1986.
The C.I.A., Pan Books, 1986.
Landmark Supreme Court Cases, Enslow Publishers, 1987.
The Abraham Lincoln Brigade, Crowell Junior Books, 1989.
Presidential Scandals, Enslow Publishers, 1989.

OTHER

Contributor of short stories to numerous magazines in the United States and abroad.

SIDELIGHTS: Don Lawson writes: "Of my some forty books, half deal with wars in which the United States has taken part. In fact, eleven of the titles comprise a complete history of all of America's wars. This series is the only one of its kind ever published so far as I know.

"Naturally, I am often asked why I seem to be so overwhelmingly preoccupied with war and especially in books for young people. My answer is purely and simply that young people, and especially boys, are eternally interested in books about war, and since they are they should be given a true picture of what war is like. I'm not too sure that it is possible to end wars, but obviously we must do so, and in order to do so young people are going to have to learn how terrible human conflict is by reading and hearing about it rather than experiencing it.

"I am also often asked how I happened to want to become a writer and when I started to write. I don't know how. It seems to me I always wanted to be an author and that authors just *are* the way some animals are cats and some are men and women. One writes because one must, just as one must breathe. I started to write in grade school with an essay entitled 'Our

Trip to the Circus' which was printed in the home-town newspaper in Downers Grove, Ill. From that point on, I couldn't quit. I had stories published in the high school magazine in Downers Grove and in the college magazine at Cornell College in Iowa. The first story I sold was to *Story* magazine during World War II, which I supect was the brightest day of my life—except perhaps for the sale of my first book which came some years later.

"My advice to young writers is to write. It doesn't do any good to wait until the muse comes. One must plant his seat in a seat at a desk or before a typewriter regularly no matter how one feels and *write*. Nothing much may come out right at first, but it will if you keep at it. If you can't follow that sort of regimen, then you are simply not a writer. And nobody can help you do it. It's just you and that blank sheet of paper, and you're the one who must put the words on it—just you and nobody else. It's a lonely, lonely business, but a wonderfully rewarding one—if not in money, certainly in personal satisfaction."

"What children will learn from reading Don Lawson's book [*The United States in the Vietnam War*]," notes *New York Times Book Review* contributor C.D.B. Bryan, "is how and why the Vietnam War began and how and why it ended. They will learn who made the decisions that committed an increasing number of America's young men to fight. . . . They will learn why Vietnam was more a political conflict than a military one and how our failure to understand that caused us to lose." The critic adds, "The children will get all this and more," in a book marked with "intellectual and moral courage."

BIOGRAPHICAL/CRITICAL SOURCES:

PERIODICALS

New York Times Book Review, May 7, 1967, May 5, 1968, November 9, 1969, April 26, 1981.
Times Literary Supplement, September 9, 1965.
Washington Post Book World, November 23, 1969.

*   *   *

LEES, Richard 1948-

PERSONAL: Born October 21, 1948, in Ann Arbor, Mich.; married wife, Carol (a film composer), September 6, 1970. *Education:* Attended Stanford University, 1966-67; University of Michigan, B.A., 1970; Yale University, M.F.A., 1975.

ADDRESSES: Home—Los Angeles, Calif. *Agent*—Melinda Jason, 1900 Avenue of the Stars, Suite 2375, Los Angeles, Calif. 90067.

CAREER: Playwright, 1969—. Playwright in residence with Ensemble Company for the Performing Arts, New Haven, Conn, 1974, the O'Neill Center, Waterford, Conn, 1977, Guthrie Theatre, Minneapolis, Minn, 1979, Playwrights Horizons, New York, N.Y., 1981.

AWARDS, HONORS: Avery Hopwood Award from University of Michigan, 1970, for "Arrival"; CBS Foundation Award in Playwriting, 1975, for "Out of Sync"; award from National Playwright's Conference, 1977, for "At the End of Long Island"; grants from Rockefeller Foundation, 1979, and National Endowment for the Arts, 1981.

WRITINGS:

PLAYS

"Arrival" (one-act), first produced in Ann Arbor, Mich, at Arena Theatre, December, 1969.
"Shoppin'" (two-act), first produced in Ann Arbor at Trueblood Auditorium, March, 1970.
"Scenes in Isolation" (one-act), first produced in Ann Arbor at Ann Arbor Drama Festival, January, 1971.
"Alma's Rules" (one-act), first produced in New Haven, Conn, at Yale Repertory Theatre, February, 1973.
"Seth" (one-act), first produced in New Haven at Yale Studio, May, 1973.
"Land's End" (two-act; original title "At the End of Long Island"), first produced in Waterford, Conn., at O'Neill Center, August, 1977.
"Right of Way" (two-act), first produced in Minneapolis, Minn., at Guthrie Theatre, June, 1979.

Also author of plays "Apres Ski," 1982, and "Murders Rising," 1984. Author of unproduced plays "Out of Sync" (two-act) and "Ophelia Kline" (two-act).

SCREENPLAYS

"Right of Way" (made-for-television film), first broadcast on Home Box Office, spring, 1983.

NOVELS

Out of Sync, PAJ Publications, 1988.
Parachute, Bantam, 1988.

BIOGRAPHICAL/CRITICAL SOURCES:

PERIODICALS

Los Angeles Times, April 11, 1988.

*   *   *

LEHANE, Brendan 1936-

PERSONAL: Born May 17, 1936, in London, England; son of Christopher (a teacher) and Honor (Millar) Lehane. *Education:* Attended King's College, Cambridge, 1957-60.

ADDRESSES: Home—Hey Farm Cottage, Winsham, Chard, Somerset, England.

CAREER: Writer. Formerly a private tutor; *About Town*, London, England, features editor, 1961-62; Rupert Hart-Davis Ltd. (publishers), London, assistant editor, 1962. *Military service:* British Army, National Service, 1955-57; became second lieutenant.

AWARDS, HONORS: Arts Council Award, 1967, for *The Quest of Three Abbots.*

WRITINGS:

Natural History, M. Joseph, 1967.
The Quest of Three Abbots, Viking, 1968.
The Compleat Flea, Viking, 1969.
The Companion Guide to Ireland, Collins, 1972, 2nd edition, 1985.
The Power of Plants, McGraw, 1977.
Dublin, Time-Life, 1978.
The Northwest Passage, Time-Life, 1981.
Wizards and Witches, Time-life, 1984.
Legends of Valor, Time-Life, 1985.
The Book of Christmas, Time-Life, 1986.

A Walk down the Thames, Barrie & Jenkins, 1988.

Contributor to numerous periodicals, including the *Telegraph Sunday Magazine.*

WORK IN PROGRESS: A history of the Anglo-Irish, for Macmillan.

AVOCATIONAL INTERESTS: Ireland, travel (has been in most countries of Europe, around Africa, and parts of the Middle East, with brief visits in United States, Canada, and the Bahamas).

* * *

LEMARCHAND, Elizabeth (Wharton) 1906-

PERSONAL: Born in 1906; daughter of a country doctor in Devonshire, England. *Education:* University of London, M.A., 1929. *Politics:* Liberal. *Religion:* Church of England.

ADDRESSES: Home—36A The Strand, Topsham, Exeter, England. *Agent*—Watson, Little Ltd., Suite 8, 26 Charing Cross Rd., London WC2H 0DG, England.

CAREER: Took up writing as a hobby after poor health forced her retirement as headmistress of a girls' public school in England.

MEMBER: National Trust, Crime Writers Association, Westcountry Writers, Devonshire Association, Dartmoor Preservation Association, Devon and Exeter Institution.

WRITINGS:

DETECTIVE NOVELS

Death of an Old Girl, Hart-Davis, 1967, Walker & Co., 1986.
The Affacombe Affair, Hart-Davis, 1968, State Mutual Book, 1985.
Alibi for a Corpse, Hart-Davis, 1969, Walker & Co., 1986.
Death on Doomsday, MacGibbon & Kee, 1971, Walker & Co., 1975.
Cyanide with Compliments, MacGibbon & Kee, 1972, Walker & Co., 1973.
Let or Hindrance, Hart-Davis, 1973, published as *No Vacation from Murder,* Walker & Co., 1974.
Buried in the Past, Hart-Davis, 1973, Walker & Co., 1976.
Step in the Dark, Hart-Davis, 1976.
Unhappy Returns, Hart-Davis, 1977, Walker & Co., 1978.
Suddenly While Gardening, Hart-Davis, 1978, Walker & Co., 1979.
Change for the Worse, Walker & Co., 1980.
Nothing to Do with the Case, Walker & Co., 1981.
Troubled Waters, Walker & Co., 1982, revised edition, 1985.
The Wheel Turns, Piatkus, 1983, Walker & Co., 1984.
Light through the Glass, Piatkus, 1984, Walker & Co., 1986.
Who Goes Home?, Piatkus, 1986, Walker & Co., 1987.
The Glade Manor Murder, Piatkus, 1988.

Contributor of short stories to *Argosy, Good Housekeeping, Woman's Journal,* and other magazines.

SIDELIGHTS: "Elizabeth Lemarchand always has had a sprightly way with the traditional British mystery," writes Jean M. White in *Washington Post Book World.* Though she writes quickly, averaging a book a year and adhering to a standard format, Lemarchand is never dull. Careful plotting and scrupulous attention to details of atmosphere and character keep her mysteries lively. "She has a deft writing style; and in her quiet, efficient way she manages to make her characters

live and breathe," Newgate Callendar observes in the *New York Times Book Review.*

BIOGRAPHICAL/CRITICAL SOURCES:

PERIODICALS

New York Times Book Review, July 29, 1973, March 10, 1974, March 23, 1975, April 10, 1977.
Washington Post Book World, February 24, 1974, September 21, 1975, May 15, 1977, January 21, 1979, November 15, 1981.

* * *

LERNER, Gerda 1920-

PERSONAL: Born April 30, 1920, in Vienna, Austria; came to the United States in 1939; naturalized in 1943; daughter of Robert and Ilona (Neumann) Kronstein; married Carl Lerner (a film maker), 1941 (died, 1973); children: Stephanie, Daniel. *Education:* New School for Social Research, B.A., 1963; Columbia University, M.A., 1965, Ph.D., 1966.

ADDRESSES: Office—5123 Humanities Building, University of Wisconsin, Madison, Wis. 53706.

CAREER: Professional writer and translator, 1941—; New School for Social Research, New York, N.Y., lecturer and historian, 1963-65; Long Island University, Brooklyn, N.Y., assistant professor, 1965-67, associate professor of American history, 1967-68; Sarah Lawrence College, Bronxville, N.Y., member of history faculty, 1968-80, director of graduate program in women's history, 1972-76, 1978-79; University of Wisconsin—Madison, Robinson-Edwards Professor of History, 1980—. Radio lecturer for "Forgotten Women in American History" on WBAI, 1963. Member of Columbia University seminar in American civilization, and seminar on women and society, 1972. Educational director, summer institutes in women's history, Sarah Lawrence College, 1976 and 1979.

MEMBER: Organization of American Historians (president, 1981-82), American Historical Association, American Association of University Professors, PEN, Authors League.

AWARDS, HONORS: National Endowment for the Humanities fellow, 1976; Ford Foundation fellow, 1978-79; Lilly Foundation fellow, 1979; Guggenheim fellow, 1980-81; Organization of American Historians grant, 1980-83; Litt.D., Colby-Sawyer College, 1981; D.Letters, Bucknell University, 1982, New School for Social Relations, 1985; Senior Distinguished Research Professor, University of Wisconsin—Madison Alumni Research Foundation, 1984.

WRITINGS:

No Farewell (novel), Associated Authors (New York), 1955.
(With husband, Carl Lerner) "Black Like Me" (screenplay; based on book of same title by John Howard Griffin), Walter Reade Distributors, 1964.
The Grimke Sisters from South Carolina: Rebels Against Slavery, Houghton, 1967.
The Woman in American History (textbook), Addison-Wesley, 1971.
Black Women in White America: A Documentary History, Pantheon, 1972.
Women Are History: A Bibliography in the History of American Women, Sarah Lawrence College, 1975, 4th revised edition (with Marie Laberge), University of Wisconsin—Madison, 1986.

(Editor) *The Female Experience: An American Documentary,* Bobbs-Merrill, 1976.
A Death of One's Own, Simon & Schuster, 1978.
The Majority Finds Its Past: Placing Women in History, Oxford Univeristy Press, 1979.
Teaching Women's History, American Historical Association, 1981.
Women and History, Volume 1: *The Creation of Patriarchy,* Oxford University Press, 1986.

Author of "Dorothea Dix" and "Elizabeth Cady Stanton and Susan B. Anthony," sound recordings, Pacifica Tape Library. Contributor of short stories to little literary magazines, and of articles and reviews to professional journals. Author of numerous professional translations.

SIDELIGHTS: A pioneer in the field of women's studies, Gerda Lerner has written extensively about the role of women in history and how traditional histories have failed to address specifically female issues. Using extensive sources, Lerner frequently compares issues of race and class with gender issues in her studies of women. Believed to have taught the first postwar college course in women's history, she has also helped establish several graduate programs in the field. As Elizabeth Fox-Genovese describes her in the *New Republic,* Lerner "has played a unique role in making women's history the thriving field it has become; she has delineated its appropriate contours; searched for a method and a theory appropriate to its practice; unearthed the sources necessary to its writing; insisted not merely on its autonomy and integrity, but on its inescapable centrality to any worthy history of humankind."

After writing a history of two abolitionist sisters whose work led them to become feminists, Lerner applied her talents to writing more broad-based histories of women. *Black Women in White America: A Documentary History* chronicles 350 years of suffering by individuals who were often considered property not only by reason of their race but of their gender. Written in 1972, reviewer Joyce Jenkins comments in *Saturday Review* that this "superb" book is "the first, to my knowledge, to treat in depth the grossly neglected segment of American history staked out by the book's title." Lerner uses numerous documents as well as newspaper items to report the troubles of these women from their own perspective, not that of a distanced observer. While Jenkins disputes some of the author's assertions, such as the supposedly recurrent theme of racial solidarity, she remarks that overall it "displays sharp insight into the long-range effects of this slave past."

Although as a white historian Lerner was "scrupulously restrained in her theorizing," in *Black Women in White America* she provides "a thorough historical framework in which the documents could be read and interpreted," observes Adrienne Rich in the *New York Times Book Review.* It is an "indispensable complement" to her next work, *The Female Experience: An American Documentary,* which Rich says "expands her vision of history, while keeping the form begun earlier." As with *Black Women in White America,* the book presents letters, diaries, newspaper clips, speeches, and other documents that had not been published previously. "More than any other compilation," remarks Eve Merriam in *Ms.,* "... all the many strands needed for comprehending the female experience are successfully interwoven." More notable, however, is the author's presentation of her material; instead of following traditional divisions of history, which she claims do not represent important milestones for women, Lerner attempts to establish an historical order according to women's issues known as

"historical periodization." As Rich describes, the author recognizes that "periods of history regarded as progressive for men have often been regressive for women. . . . 'Progress' has been defined from a male point of view." "Gerda Lerner has gone indeed toward the essence," says Merriam. "Hers is the impulse of creation combined with exemplary scholarship. In *The Female Experience,* Lerner has lifted history out of its iron rigidity, out of its chronological framework—what a daring concept and how inexorable it seems now that she has done so."

The Majority Finds Its Past: Placing Women in History compiles many of Lerner's essays and speeches into one book, including those of her theories of historical periodization. "By bringing these pieces together," comments June Sochen in the *Washington Post Book World,* "Lerner gives us a good opportunity to see the development of her thought as she participated in the shaping of the discipline." Sochen criticizes some of Lerner's ideas, however, such as her tendency to see women's history and culture as independent of mainstream events: "Does the existence of a female culture operate outside history? Don't women, like men, live in multiple cultures and play various roles within their lives every day of the week? . . . The temptation of some women historians to portray all examples of female culture as subversive, alternative value-systems is questionable at best." Fox-Genovese, while she praises Lerner's work as ground-breaking, still faults the author's failure to consider religious and class issues as influences in women's history. These reservations aside, the critic finds that "committed to recreating the female perspective, Lerner nonetheless never sacrifices the specificities of income and race to an all-inclusive feminism."

In *The Creation of Patriarchy,* Lerner ventures into prehistory, attempting to trace the roots of patriarchal dominance. In doing so, Elizabeth Kamarck Minnich claims in *Ms.* that Lerner "gives us a grand historical framework that was impossible even to imagine before the enlightenment about women's place in the world provided by her earlier work." In the work, Lerner cites "historical, archeological, literary, and artistic evidence for the idea that patriarchy is a cultural invention," describes Glenn Collins in the *New York Times.* Although the author herself acknowledges that this kind of evidence is "fragile," Sarah B. Pomeroy still criticizes her use of these sources. "To construct a grandiose paradigm demonstrating the continually deteriorating position of women," the critic writes in the *New York Times Book Review,* "Mrs. Lerner considers societies as different as the Sumerians, Babylonians, . . . Hebrews, and Greeks as though they existed on a historical continuum and evolved directly from one another." This kind of evidence, remarks Pomeroy, "does not permit definitive conclusions." Contrarily, Minnich finds that Lerner uses "careful scholarship and ever more carefully refined theoretical concepts" to present her ideas about women and the evolution of patriarchy.

Although it is a personal narrative rather than a historical study, *A Death of One's Own* contains the same humanist perspective and development of ideas as the rest of Lerner's work. Written six years after her husband's death, the work recounts Gerda and Carl Lerner's attempts to deal with the knowledge that Carl was dying of a brain tumor. The two decide on a policy of openness and honesty, sharing their feelings as the cancer progresses, even if this policy conflicts with their individual needs. "There's little melodrama or self-pity in this," observes Alex Raksin in the *Los Angeles Times Book Review,* ". . . only an extraordinarily personal evocation of [Lerner's] struggle to achieve peace of mind through realism rather than nihilism.''

In writing the book, Lerner takes an approach similar to that of her other work; she uses various sources, such as diary entries, poems, and straight narrative to present her story. ''In her deeply moving book,'' comments Joan Kron in *Ms.*, Lerner ''has woven a tapestry: recollections of Carl's illness, her conflicting diary entries from the same period, and 'fragments' of her life in Europe before she became a refugee from the Nazis.'' In doing so, she ''strives to connect past and present, living and dead in a continuum of meaning,'' says Helen Yglesias in the *New York Times Book Review*.

Many reviewers express similar praises for *A Death of One's Own*. Yglesias comments that it is ''a book that heartens and breaks the heart at the same time,'' even though Lerner ''. . . is no sentimentalist, and does not sensationally display the grim details.'' ''Gerda Lerner's simple ability to cope—her endurance, her strength, her willingness to fight whenever fighting will help—is admirable,'' writes *Washington Post Book World* contributor Anne Tyler. ''But what I found awe-inspiring is the fact that through it all, she never loses the capacity to feel.'' Tyler also finds the book to be a ''page-turner,'' and Kron similarly thinks it involving. ''When Carl Lerner finally dies,'' the critic writes, ''one not only weeps for him, but for *oneself* with envy for such a relationship.''

In *A Death of One's Own*, Lerner's ''search to extract meaning . . . glows with the humanist energy of an honest yet consoling and inspiring vision,'' writes Yglesias. The same search for meaning and humanist vision characterize all of Lerner's scholarly work as well. Through the perspective of her literary and scholarly career, Lerner ''can be seen as a worthy,'' writes Fox-Genovese. ''An historian to be sure, the most active and politically astute of the opening phase of the new women's history, but also a specially talented writer, an inspiring and demanding teacher, a model as well as a companion to younger female scholars, a forceful presence in her chosen profession.''

AVOCATIONAL INTERESTS: Music, gardening, backpacking.

BIOGRAPHICAL/CRITICAL SOURCES:

BOOKS

Lerner, Gerda, *A Death of One's Own*, Simon & Schuster, 1978.

PERIODICALS

Life, May 5, 1972.
Los Angeles Times Book Review, November 17, 1985.
Ms., May, 1977, October, 1978, September, 1980, May, 1986.
New Republic, December 1, 1979.
New Yorker, March 25, 1972.
New York Times, April 28, 1986.
New York Times Book Review, March 20, 1977, August 6, 1978, April 20, 1986.
Saturday Review, May 6, 1972.
Washington Post Book World, August 13, 1978, January 27, 1980.

—*Sketch by Diane Telgen*

* * *

LESTER, Andrew D(ouglas) 1939-

PERSONAL: Born August 8, 1939, in Coral Gables, Fla.; son of Andrew R. and Dorothy V. (Atkinson) Lester; married Ju-

dith A. Laesser (a marriage and family therapist), September 8, 1960; children: Scott, Denise. *Education:* Mississippi College, B.A., 1961; Southern Baptist Theological Seminary, B.D., 1964, Ph.D., 1968. *Religion:* Baptist.

ADDRESSES: Home—1907 Lonlipman Court, Louisville, Ky. 40207. *Office*—Box 1918, Lexington Rd., Louisville, Ky. 40280.

CAREER: Youth minister at Baptist churches in Memphis, Tenn., 1960, Washington, Miss., 1960-61, Jackson, Miss., 1961-62, and Louisville, Ky., 1966-67; ordained as Southern Baptist minister in 1962; pastor of Baptist church in Bryantsville, Ky., 1962-66; Southern Baptist Theological Seminary, Louisville, Ky., special instructor in psychology and religion, 1967-69; North Carolina Baptist Hospital, Winston-Salem, N.C., assistant director of department of pastoral care, 1969-70, director of counseling services, 1970-71, director of School of Pastoral Care, 1971-77; Southern Baptist Theological Seminary, associate professor, 1977-82, professor of psychology of religion, 1982—. Pastoral counselor at Personal Counseling Service, Jeffersonville, Ind., 1965-69 and 1977-86. Visiting professor at Southeastern Baptist Theological Seminary and visitng lecturer at Wake Forest University, both 1972-77.

MEMBER: Association of Clinical Pastoral Education (chaplain supervisor), American Association of Pastoral Counselors (diplomate), American Protestant Hospital Association (fellow of College of Chaplains), American Association of Marriage and Family Therapists (clinical member).

WRITINGS:

(Editor with Wayne E. Oates) *Pastoral Care in Crucial Human Situations*, Judson, 1969.
Sex Is More Than a Word, Broadman, 1973.
It Hurts So Bad, Lord!: The Christian Encounters Crisis, Broadman, 1976.
(With wife, Judith L. Lester) *Understanding Aging Parents*, Westminster, 1980.
Coping With Your Anger: A Christian Guide, Westminster, 1983.
Pastoral Care with Children in Crisis, Westminster, 1985.
(Editor with Gerald L. Borchert) *Spiritual Dimensions of Pastoral Care: Witness to the Ministry of Wayne E. Oates*, Westminster, 1985.
(Editor) *When Children Suffer: A Sourcebook for Ministry with Children in Crisis*, Westminster, 1987.
The Place of Hope in Pastoral Care, Westminser, 1989.

Contributor to church magazines.

SIDELIGHTS: Andrew D. Lester told *CA:* ''I have always been interested in what psychology and theology can teach each other. My basic purpose for writing is to introduce laypersons to some of the insights of psychology of religion and pastoral theology. Popular ideas about the Christian faith are often destructive of personhood. *Coping With Your Anger*, for instance, is an attempt to help Christians understand that the capacity for anger is part of the creation and not the result of sin. *Sex Is More Than a Word* has the same goal, to help Christians recognize that sex is one of God's gifts rather than some demonic aspect of selfhood. Both anger and sex can help fulfill life and add to love and intimacy if handled ethically.''

* * *

LEVENSON, Sam(uel) 1911-1980

PERSONAL: Born December 28, 1911, in New York, N.Y.;

died August 27, 1980, in New York, N.Y., of a heart attack; son of Hyman (a tailor) and Rebecca (Fishelman) Levenson; married Esther Levine, December 27, 1936; children: Conrad Lee, Emily Sue. *Education:* Brooklyn College (now of the City University of New York), B.A., 1934; Columbia University, M.A., 1938. *Religion:* Jewish.

ADDRESSES: Agent—Peter Matson, Harold Matson Co., Inc., 276 Fifth Ave., New York, N.Y. 10001.

CAREER: Teacher of Spanish at public high schools in Brooklyn, N.Y., 1934-46; worked as part-time entertainer, master of ceremonies, and folk-humorist, 1940-46; became full-time entertainer and appeared on radio and television programs, including "Cavalcade of Stars" and "The Milton Berle Show," 1949, "Toast of the Town," 1949-50; regular panelist on "This Is Show Business," 1951-54; host of CBS program "The Sam Levenson Show," 1951-52; appeared on "Two for the Money," 1955-56; lecturer and night club performer, 1957-58; regular panelist on "Masquerade Party," 1959-60, "To Tell the Truth," 1961-63, and "The Match Game," 1965; had made guest appearances on "The Jack Paar Show," "The Ed Sullivan Show," and other television and radio programs. Member of board of directors, League School for Seriously Disturbed Children, and New York Clinic for Mental Health; honorary president, Citizen's Scholarship Program; president, Rockaway Music and Arts Council.

MEMBER: American Federation of Television and Radio Artists, American Guild of Variety Artists, Actors Equity Association, Screen Actors Guild, B'nai B'rith—Anti-Defamation League (member of district board of governors), Friends of Music of New York City, Brooklyn College Alumni Association.

AWARDS, HONORS: Brooklyn College Alumnus Award, 1956; D.Lett., St. Francis College, 1973; D.Humane Letters, Brooklyn College of the City University of New York, 1976.

WRITINGS:

Meet the Folks: A Session of American-Jewish Humor, Citadel Press, 1948.
Everything But Money, Simon & Schuster, 1966.
Sex and the Single Child, Simon & Schuster, 1969, published as *A Time for Innocence:A Kid's-Eye View of the Facts of Life,* 1977.
In One Era and Out the Other, Simon & Schuster, 1973.
You Can Say That Again Sam, Simon & Schuster, 1975.
You Don't Have to Be in Who's Who to Know What's What, G. K. Hall, 1979.

Contributor of articles to magazines, including *Ladies' Home Journal, McCall's,* and other popular periodicals.

SIDELIGHTS: Sam Levenson was a high-school Spanish teacher when he got the opportunity to perform stand-up comedy around his native New York City. His big break came in 1949, when he appeared on Ed Sullivan's "Toast of the Town"—an experience he remembered in a *Detroit News* interview: "[Television] was a frightening new medium. That night I walked out and there were these monstrous cameras and people who looked like men from Mars giving signals. They told me to look at whichever camera had red lights on. I did that and then the lights would go out and I'd think, 'Did I blow a fuse?'

"It was a terror. They gave me six minutes and 30 seconds and of course it was a live audience—today they put the laughs on tape. I'd tell a joke and it was a dead audience. No laughs. You could hear the air hum."

However, far from being a failure, Levenson got a contract with CBS television and eventually parlayed his success into several well-received books, which were mostly memoirs of "growing up poor, Jewish and funny in New York tenements," as Diana McLellan put it in a *Washington Star-News* interview. In that same article, Levenson demonstrated his own brand of "kosher philosophy," telling McLellan his thoughts of the day's big problems: "People think they're entitled to happiness, as though it had a *daily minimum requirement,* like vitamins. . . . That's not what the Founding Fathers guaranteed. They talked about the right to pursue happiness. That's completely different. Like my Uncle Benny on the farm says, 'It's not the sugar that makes the tea sweet, it's stirring.'"

BIOGRAPHICAL/CRITICAL SOURCES:

BOOKS

Authors in the News, Volume I, Gale, 1975.
Levenson, Sam, *Everything But Money,* Simon & Schuster, 1966.
Levenson, Sam, *In One Era and Out the Other,* Simon & Schuster, 1973.
Levenson, Sam, *You Don't Have to Be in Who's Who to Know What's What,* G. K. Hall, 1979.

PERIODICALS

Detroit News, November 24, 1974.
Washington Star-News, December 16, 1974.

OBITUARIES:

PERIODICALS

Los Angeles Times, August 28, 1980.
Newsweek, September 8, 1980.
New York Times, August 29, 1980.
Publishers Weekly, September 19, 1980.
Time, September 8, 1980.
Washington Post, August 29, 1980.†

*   *   *

LEVIN, Jenifer   1955-

PERSONAL: Born October 31, 1955, in New York, N.Y.; daughter of Sherman and Florence (Rosenfeld) Levin. *Education:* University of Michigan, B.A., 1973.

ADDRESSES: Agent—Wendy Weil, Julian Bach Literary Agency, 747 Third Ave., New York, N.Y. 10017.

CAREER: Writer. Also worked as bartender, cook, waitress, secretary, life guard, factory electrician in Israel, and agricultural laborer.

MEMBER: Phi Beta Kappa.

AWARDS, HONORS: Jule and Avery Hopwood Award from University of Michigan, 1973, for essay "Love, Light, and Language: Shakespeare's Comedies," 1975, for short story "Skint on Saturday," and 1977, for novelette "Cripples."

WRITINGS:

(Contributor) *Avon Nine,* Street Fiction Press, 1975.
Water Dancer (novel), Poseidon Press, 1982.
Snow (novel), Poseidon Press, 1984.
Shimoni's Lover, Harcourt, 1987.

Contributor to anthologies; contributor to *Mademoiselle, Ms., New York Times,* and *Rolling Stone.*

WORK IN PROGRESS: A novel; a short-short story collection.

SIDELIGHTS: "I've always been impressed by grandeur," Jenifer Levin stated in *Library Journal.* "I like big things, big ideas, pursuits requiring endurance, and long books. In *Moby Dick,* Melville wrote that 'to produce a mighty book, you must choose a mighty theme,' and I believe that wholeheartedly."

In her first novel, *Water Dancer,* Levin explores the mighty theme of survival. In it, she tells the story of a marathon swimmer, Dorey Thomas, who trains to cross the freezing, turbulent waters of the San Antonio Strait. Her pursuit of this single goal touches the lives of several people, including her coach and his wife, who lost their son in this same pursuit. "It is refreshing to read a story about simple human strengths," writes Sharon Dirlam in the *Los Angeles Times.* Although the novel deals with "human strength," Dirlam observes that the story is told "in a form more for poetry lovers than sports fans. It swims with water metaphors—they are everywhere." *New York Times Book Review* contributor Brina Caplan, although she finds the sports setting "attractive," criticizes the novel's plotting and style: "Unfortunately, the characters never manage to sort out their problems.... Miss Levin's prose acquires knots as well; labored generalities and overwrought images further obscure her characters' inner lives." Dirlam, however, characterizes Levins' work as well written: "The writing has a sensual rhythm.... When the swimming and the primary relationships might become too murky and heavy, the cast of characters expands to let in new points of view." The critic summarizes by calling the novel "a beautiful exploration of strength and femaleness and the endurance of the human spirit."

In *Snow,* her second novel, Levin is "indebted to Herman Melville for the central metaphor," writes Carol Verderese in the *New York Times Book Review.* The novel relates the story of the chemical defoliation of a rebellious island nation. "Snow" refers to both the defoliant and the "White Goddess" who is the head of and symbol for the rebel resistance. Verderese finds this metaphor too pronounced, remarking that "the White Goddess is more a cliche than the powerful symbol she is intended to be." *Los Angeles Times* critic Carolyn See expresses similar reservations: "Somewhere in this hodgepodge of literary derivations and mythical foundations to a structure that never gets to stand up by itself, there is a story—that's what's so infuriating about this novel." See comments, however, that "there's much to be said for this novel. Levin's heart is in the right place and her ambitions were vast, too vast, but still commendable."

In her third novel, *Shimoni's Lover,* Levin draws upon her own visits to Israel to create "a tale of many characters, rich in incident, alive with the tensions Israelis breathe every day," remarks Anne Roiphe in the *Washington Post.* "It is at once a political allegory and a troubling story of men and violence and the disastrous effect of that violence on women and children." The novel relates the story of an Israeli family and the influence the death of Shimoni, the eldest son, has upon them and the way they deal with their world. Although the novel follows a singular family, it also describes the larger issues of war. Comments *New York Times Book Review* contributor Joan Silber, "it is pleasurable to read a novel whose scope is beyond the purely personal and in which the action has real excitement. The kibbutz scenes are especially well handled, full of texture and bright detail," continues the critic. Elaine Kendall, however, feels this broader scope makes the work preceptive; the critic writes in the *Los Angeles Times* that the work "remains essentially didactic despite richness of incident, complexity of plot, and Jenifer Levin's sophisticated technique." Because the author uses flashbacks to show the various sides to each issue, the novel "tends to separate into set pieces," observes Kendall. "These vignettes not only supply essential background but often compete with the story. Like the songs in a musical drama, they're 'liftable,'" continues the critic, "remembered long after the twists and turn of plot have slipped away."

Whether focusing on the specific problems of her characters or the more general problems of Israelis, Levin demonstrates a talent for realistic description. Roiphe remarks that the author "describes the Israeli landscape with perfect detail and precision. She is not a contemporary novelist who tells as little as possible but one who fills her story with sight and smell and touch." Speaking of the book's opening sequence, a recounting of Israeli army basic training, Silber finds it "depicted with considerable vividness" while Kendall writes that Levin's description "reduces most other literature on this subject to Pabulum." "Against this background what lingers most strongly is the catalogue of dead and maimed warriors in an ordinary Israeli family," comments Silber. "In the end we are given a convincing picture of an Israel in which the cost of a continual war in lives and in the shaping of personalities is tragic." "By the end of this thoughtful and probing novel," concludes Kendall, the "purposes" of war have been "questioned and confronted as directly as the fictional framework permits. Levin meets her urgent issues head on, never flinching from the moral and political implications of her theme." The critic continues: "She has done exactly what she promised in the opening chapters—stripped away all the layers to reveal a core of 'something' we immediately recognize as empirical truth."

Levin remarked to *CA:* "While I'm still impressed by grandeur and big things, I am more impressed with those rare and all-too-overlooked moments of human compassion, tenderness, and love—the things that sometimes exist so close to the ground that we tend to step right over them in our daily existence. *Moby Dick* is still my favorite novel, and I add to that list of favorites *David Copperfield, Daniel Deronda,* and *The Magic Mountain;* lest anyone think that my literary taste is firmly entrenched in the last century, I'll add Paul Scott's extraordinary third book of 'The Raj Quartet'—*The Towers of Silence*—to the list. These were all authors who dealt as honestly as possible with the themes of human birth and death and spiritual evolution, pain, quest for truths, and the frailty and glory of love—which, after all, is the fiber that connects all life in the universe. And which, after all, may be the most difficult thing of all to write about."

AVOCATIONAL INTERESTS: Travel (England, France, Ireland, Italy, Greece, Spain, the Middle East), playing classical guitar, physical fitness (swimming, running, weight lifting), anthropology, theater.

BIOGRAPHICAL/CRITICAL SOURCES:

PERIODICALS

Library Journal, June 15, 1982.
Los Angeles Times, December 2, 1982, March 20, 1984, October 2, 1987.
New York Times Book Review, November 28, 1982, March 11, 1984, November 29, 1987.
Voice Literary Supplement, November, 1982.
Washington Post, September 18, 1982, October 20, 1987.

LEVINSON, Henry Samuel 1948-

PERSONAL: Born February 11, 1948, in Cincinnati, Ohio; son of Joseph E. (a physician) and Mimi F. Levinson; married Catherine Kaplan (a university librarian), August 30, 1969; children: Molly, Sarah. *Education:* Stanford University, B.A. (with honors), 1970; Princeton University, Ph.D., 1976.

ADDRESSES: Home—Greensboro, N.C. *Office*—Dean of the College of Arts and Sciences, University of North Carolina—Greensboro, Greensboro, N.C. 27412.

CAREER: Stanford University, Stanford, Calif., assistant to the provost, 1970-72, assistant professor of religious studies, 1975-82; University of North Carolina, Greensboro, assistant professor, 1982-85, associate professor, 1985—, associate dean of College of Arts and Sciences, 1987—. Andrew J. Mellon Foundation faculty fellow, Harvard University, 1982-83.

MEMBER: American Academy of Religion, American Studies Association, Charles S. Peirce Society, Phi Beta Kappa.

AWARDS, HONORS: National Endowment for the Humanities grant, 1979; National Humanities Center fellowship, and National Endowment for the Humanities independent fellow, both 1985-86.

WRITINGS:

Science, Metaphysics and the Chance of Salvation, Scholars Press, 1978.
The Religious Investigations of William James, University of North Carolina Press, 1981.
(Contributor) Richard J. Payne, general editor, *World Spirituality: An Encyclopedia of the Religious Quest,* Volume 22: *Modern Secular Spirituality,* edited by Langdon Gilkey, Crossroad Publishing, 1984.

WORK IN PROGRESS: Research on George Santayana.

*   *   *

LEVY, Emanuel 1947-

PERSONAL: Born February 4, 1947, in Sophia, Bulgaria; came to the United States in 1973, became permanent resident, 1979; son of Abraham (an architect) and Matilda Levy. *Education:* Tel-Aviv University, B.A., 1971, M.A., 1973; Columbia University, M.Phil., 1975, Ph.D., 1978.

ADDRESSES: Home—11 Riverside Dr., Apt. 17PW, New York, N.Y. 10023. *Office*—Department of Sociology, Wellesley College, Wellesley, Mass. 02181.

CAREER: Tel-Aviv University, Tel-Aviv, Israel, instructor in sociology, 1970-73; Hunter College of the City University of New York, New York City, instructor in sociology, 1977-79; Queens College of the City University of New York, Flushing, N.Y., assistant professor of sociology, 1979-81; Yeshiva University, New York City, assistant professor of sociology, 1981-87; Wellesley College, Wellesley, Mass., associate professor of sociology, 1987—. Visiting associate professor, Columbia University, 1983—.

MEMBER: American Sociological Association, Society for the Study of Social Problems, American Association for Public Opinion Research, American Society for Theater Research, American Film Institute.

AWARDS, HONORS: National Jewish Book Award from Jewish Book Council, 1980, for *The Habima: Israel's National Theater, 1917-1977; A Study in Cultural Nationalism.*

WRITINGS:

The Habima: Israel's National Theater, 1917-1977; A Study in Cultural Nationalism, Columbia University Press, 1979.
The History of the Israeli National Theater, Eked Publishers, 1981.
And the Winner Is: The History and Politics of the Oscar Award, Ungar, 1987.
John Wayne: Prophet of the American Way of Life, Scarecrow, 1988.
From John Doe to Peggy Sue: Small Town America on the Screen, Ungar, 1989.

WORK IN PROGRESS: Hollywood's New Leading Ladies—Women in Film; The Vietnam War and American Culture.

SIDELIGHTS: Emanuel Levy told *CA:* "Studying film and theatre from a sociological perspective is an intellectual challenge, as the sociology of art and culture has been one of the least developed areas of specialization within the discipline of sociology."

Levy explores the world of film awards in his *And the Winner Is: The History and Politics of the Oscar Award.* Of it, *Los Angeles Times Book Review* contributor Hal Kanter states: "Emanuel Levy, no ponderous pedant, offers logical explanations and valid theories as to Oscar's global impact on society and why the awards show brings Americans together on a Monday night each year."

Levy continued, "My book on the Oscar Awards, *And the Winner Is,* was prompted by an interest in the popularity and tremendous impact of the awards on the winners' careers and on the film world in general. The book raises questions that are pertinent to the acting profession, one of the most popular and 'glamorous' but least studied professions.

"The books on John Wayne and the Western film attempt to understand the creation of a movie star and a film genre that were uniquely American and have had significance as American myths and legends."

AVOCATIONAL INTERESTS: Politics, art, popular culture.

BIOGRAPHICAL/CRITICAL SOURCES:

PERIODICALS

Los Angeles Times Book Review, March 29, 1987.

*   *   *

LIPPMAN, Peter J. 1936-

PERSONAL: Born May 19, 1936, in Flushing, N.Y. *Education:* Columbia University, B.A., 1957, M.Arch., 1960; further study at Art Students League.

ADDRESSES: Home—Montgomery Hollow, Roxbury, N.Y. 12474.

CAREER: Author and illustrator of books for children. Early in career worked briefly for an architect. *Military service:* U.S. Army.

MEMBER: National Wildlife Federation, Audubon Society, Sierra Club.

AWARDS, HONORS: Plunkety Plunk was chosen by *New York Times* as one of the ten best illustrated children's books of the year, 1963; Children's Book of the Year Award, Child Study Association of America, 1972, for *Science Experiments You Can Eat*, and 1975, for *Supersuits*.

WRITINGS:

SELF-ILLUSTRATED JUVENILES

Plunkety Plunk, Ariel Books, 1963.
New at the Zoo, Harper, 1969.
The Little Riddle Book, Harper, 1972.
Busy Wheels, Random House, 1973.
The Great Escape: or, The Sewer Story, Golden Press, 1973.
Ingrid Our Turtle, Golden Press, 1973.
The Mix or Match Storybook: 2,097,152 Silly Stories, Random House, 1974.
Archibald; or, I Was Very Shy, Windmill Books, 1975.
From Here to There, Bookstore Press, 1975.
Animals! Animals!, Golden Press, 1976.
Busy Boats, Random House, 1977.
Peter Lippman's One and Only Wacky Wordbook, Golden Press, 1979.
Peter Lippman's Great Mix or Match Book, Random House, 1980.
Busy Trains, Random House, 1981.
Mix or Match Mysteries: Carstairs Cat Solves Millions of Cases, Random House, 1982.
Trucks, Trucks, Trucks, Doubleday, 1984.
Peter Lippman's America, Crown, 1985.
Peter Lippman's Opposites, Grosset & Dunlap, 1988.
Peter Lippman's Numbers, Grosset & Dunlap, 1988.

ILLUSTRATOR; JUVENILES

George Selden (pseudonym of George Selden Thompson), *Sparrow Socks*, Harper, 1965.
Selden, *Oscar Lobster's Fair Exchange*, Harper, 1966.
Selden, *The Dunkard*, Harper, 1968.
Bill Martin, Jr., *The Haunted House*, Holt, 1970.
Vicki Cobb, *Science Experiments You Can Eat*, Lippincott, 1972.
Cobb, *Arts and Crafts You Can Eat*, Lippincott, 1974.
Supersuits, Lippincott, 1975.
Noodles, *This Little Thing*, Holt, 1979.
Jovial Bob Stine, *The Pigs' Book of World Records*, Random House, 1980.
Stine, *Gnasty Gnomes*, Random House, 1981.
John Archambault, *Allafred the Anteater*, DLM Teaching Resources, 1987.
Martin and Archambault, *The Bugs, the Goats, and the Little Pink Pigs*, DLM Teaching Resources, 1987.

"THE KNOW-IT-ALLS" SERIES; PUBLISHED BY RANDOM HOUSE

The Know-It-Alls Help Out, 1982.
. . . Take a Winter Vacation, 1982.
. . . Mind the Store, 1982.
. . . Go to Sea, 1982.

OTHER

Contributor of articles on the history of architecture to periodicals, and of illustrations to magazines, including *New Yorker, Town and Country, National Wildlife, Harper's*, and *Reader's Digest*.

AVOCATIONAL INTERESTS: Collecting nineteenth-century illustrated children's books; kayaking, telemark skiing.

LOCKE, Clinton W.
[Collective pseudonym]

WRITINGS:

"PERRY PIERCE MYSTERY STORIES"

Who Closed the Door; or, Perry Pierce and the Old Storehouse Mystery, Henry Altemus, 1931.
Who Opened the Safe; or, Perry Pierce and the Secret Cipher Mystery, Henry Altemus, 1931.
Who Hid the Key; or, Perry Pierce Tracing the Counterfeit Money, Henry Altemus, 1932.
Who Took the Papers; or, Perry Pierce Gathering the Printed Clues, Henry Altemus, 1934.

SIDELIGHTS: Perry Pierce was the leader of the Skull Mystery Club, whose members had to solve at least one mystery a year to retain their membership. For more information, see the entries for Harriet S. Adams, Edward L. Stratemeyer, and Andrew E. Svenson.

BIOGRAPHICAL/CRITICAL SOURCES:

BOOKS

Johnson, Deidre, editor and compiler, *Stratemeyer Pseudonyms and Series Books: An Annotated Checklist of Stratemeyer and Stratemeyer Syndicate Publications*, Greenwood Press, 1982.

*   *   *

LOCKE, Elsie   1912-

PERSONAL: Born August 17, 1912, in Hamilton, New Zealand; daughter of William John (a builder) and Ellen (Bryan) Farrelly; married John Gibson Locke (a meat worker); children: Donald Bryan, Keith James, Maire Frances, Alison Gwyneth. *Education:* University of Auckland, B.A., 1932. *Politics:* No political affiliation. *Religion:* Agnostic-humanist.

ADDRESSES: Home—392 Oxford Ter., Christchurch 1, New Zealand.

CAREER: Has worked in libraries in New Zealand and in a number of other occupations; began to write "seriously and systematically" only after her children were grown enough to allow her the time and freedom from distractions.

AWARDS, HONORS: Katherine Mansfield Award, 1959, for essay "Looking for Answers," published in *Landfall*, December, 1958; D.Litt., University of Canterbury, Christchurch, 1987, for work in children's literature and history.

WRITINGS:

The Runaway Settlers (juvenile historical novel), J. Cape, 1965, Dutton, 1966.
The End of the Harbour (juvenile historical novel), J. Cape, 1968.
Maori King and British Queen, Hulton Educational, Round the World Histories, 1974.
Look under the Leaves (juvenile ecological picture book), Pumpkin Press (Christchurch, New Zealand), 1975.
Moko's Hideout (New Zealand animal stories), Whitcoulls (Christchurch), 1976.
(With Ken Dawson) *The Boy with the Snowgrass Hair* (juvenile adventure novel), Whitcoulls, 1976, Price Milburn, 1983.
Explorer Zach (juvenile novel), Pumpkin Press, 1978.

The Gaoler (adult history), Dunmore Press, 1978.
(Contributor) Dorothy Butler, editor, *The Magpies Said* (juvenile anthology), Kestrel, 1980.
Student at the Gates (personal experience), Whitcoulls, 1981.
Journey under Warning (juvenile historical novel), Oxford University Press, 1983.
The Kauri and the Willow, Government Printer (New Zealand), 1984.
A Canoe in the Mist (juvenile historical novel), J. Cape, 1984.
Two Peoples, One Land (a junior history of Aotearoa/New Zealand), Government Printer, 1988.

Also author of radio scripts, articles, and poems.

SIDELIGHTS: Of European descent from early New Zealand settlers on both sides of her family, Elsie Locke told *CA* that she is "also very interested in the Maori (Polynesian) side of New Zealand life, and the human relationship with the earth and all it bears." She adds: "Children are to be enjoyed, their individuality respected, their imaginations cherished; and writing for them is a privilege and a pleasure. To defend their world from the threat of nuclear and/or ecological disaster, and to secure a fully human life for those now deprived, are aims I share with millions of others; but I am optimistic and not solemn in my writings. I would like all children to enjoy their childhood as much as I did mine."

* * *

LONG, Helen Beecher
[Collective pseudonym]

WRITINGS:

The Girl He Left Behind, G. Sully, 1918.

"DO SOMETHING" SERIES

Janice Day at Poketown, Sully & Kleinteich, 1914.
The Testing of Janice Day, Sully & Kleinteich, 1915.
How Janice Day Won, Sully & Kleinteich, 1916.
The Mission of Janice Day, Sully & Kleinteich, 1917.
Janice Day, the Young Homemaker, G. Sully, 1919.

SIDELIGHTS: For more information see the entries for Harriet S. Adams, Edward L. Stratemeyer, and Andrew E. Svenson.

BIOGRAPHICAL/CRITICAL SOURCES:

BOOKS

Johnson, Deidre, editor and compiler, *Stratemeyer Pseudonyms and Series Books: An Annotated Checklist of Stratemeyer and Stratemeyer Syndicate Publications*, Greenwood Press, 1982.

* * *

LOOS, Anita   1893(?)-1981

PERSONAL: Born April 26, 1893(?), in Sisson (now Mt. Shasta), Calif.; died August 18, 1981, of a heart attack in New York City; daughter of Richard Beers (a theatrical producer and newspaper editor) and Minnie Ellen (Smith) Loos; married Frank Palma, Jr., June, 1915 (marriage annulled one day later); married John Emerson (an actor, director, and playwright), 1919 (died March 8, 1956); children: one adopted daughter. *Education:* Attended high school in San Francisco, Calif.

CAREER: Writer, 1912-1981.

MEMBER: Dramatists Guild.

AWARDS, HONORS: Vanity Fair magazine award for "Red-Headed Woman."

WRITINGS:

(With husband, John Emerson) *How to Write Photoplays*, McCann, 1920.
(With Emerson) *Breaking into the Movies*, McCann, 1921.
"Gentlemen Prefer Blondes": The Illuminating Diary of a Professional Lady (also see below; story collection), Boni & Liveright, 1925, reprinted, Telegraph Books, 1986.
"But Gentlemen Marry Brunettes" (story collection), Boni & Liveright, 1928.
A Mouse Is Born (novel), Doubleday, 1951.
No Mother to Guide Her (novel), McGraw, 1961.
A Girl Like I (autobiography), Viking, 1966.
(Author of foreword) Dody Goodman, *Women, Women, Women*, Dutton, 1966.
(Translator and adaptor) Jean Canolle, *The King's Mare* (also see below), Evans Brothers, 1967.
(With Helen Hayes) *Twice Over Lightly: New York Then and Now*, Harcourt, 1972.
Kiss Hollywood Good-by (autobiography), Viking, 1974.
Cast of Thousands (autobiography), Grosset & Dunlap, 1977.
The Talmadge Girls: A Memoir, Viking, 1978.
San Francisco: A Screenplay (also see below), edited by Matthew J. Bruccoli, Southern Illinois University Press, 1979.
Fate Keeps On Happening: Adventures of Lorelei Lee and Other Writings, Dodd, 1984.

Contributor to *Reader's Digest, New York Times Magazine, Woman's Home Companion, Saturday Review*, and *Harper's*.

PLAYS

(With Emerson) "The Whole Town's Talking," first produced on Broadway at the Bijou Theatre, August 29, 1923.
(With Emerson) "The Fall of Eve," first produced on Broadway at the Booth Theatre, August 31, 1925.
(With Emerson) "Gentlemen Prefer Blondes" (based on their book of the same title), first produced in New York at the Times Square Theatre, September 28, 1926, musical adaptation (with Joseph Fields), first produced on Broadway at the Ziegfeld Theatre, December 8, 1949.
(With Emerson) "The Social Register," first produced in New York at the Fulton Theatre, November 9, 1931.
Happy Birthday (first produced on Broadway at the Broadhurst Theatre, October 31, 1946), Samuel French, 1948.
Gigi (based on the novel by Colette; first produced in New York at the Fulton Theatre, November 24, 1951), Random House, 1952, revised edition, 1956.
"Cheri" (based on the novels *Cheri* and *The End of Cheri* by Colette), first produced on Broadway at the Morosco Theatre, October 12, 1959.

LIBRETTOS

"The Amazing Adele" (based on the play by Pierre Barrillet and Jean-Pierre Gredy), first produced in Philadelphia at the Shubert Theatre, December 26, 1955.
"Gogo Loves You," first produced in New York at the Theatre de Lys, October 9, 1964.
"Something about Anne" (based on the play "The King's Mare" by Jean Canolle), first produced in London, November, 1966.

SCENARIOS FOR SILENT FILMS

"The New York Hat," American Biograph, 1913.

"The Power of the Camera," American Biograph, 1913.
"A Horse on Bill," American Biograph, 1913.
"A Hicksville Epicure," American Biograph, 1913.
"Highbrow Love," American Biograph, 1913.
"A Hicksville Romance," American Biograph, 1913.
"A Fallen Hero," American Biograph, 1913.
"A Fireman's Love," American Biograph, 1913.
"A Cure for Suffragettes," American Biograph, 1913.
"The Suicide Pact," American Biograph, 1913.
"Bink's Vacation," American Biograph, 1913.
"How the Day Was Saved," American Biograph, 1913.
"Fall of Hicksville's Finest," American Biograph, 1913.
"The Wedding Gown," American Biograph, 1913.
"Yiddish Love," American Biograph, 1913.
"Gentlemen and Thieves," American Biograph, 1913.
"Pa Says," American Biograph, 1913.
"The Widow's Kids," American Biograph, 1913.
"The Lady in Black," American Biograph, 1913.
"His Hoodoo," American Biograph, 1913.
"The Deacon's Whiskers," Reliance Mutual, 1913.
"His Awful Vengeance," Reliance Mutual, 1913.
"All for Mabel," Reliance Mutual, 1913.
"The Fatal Deception," Reliance Mutual, 1913.
"For Her Father's Sins," Reliance Mutual, 1913.
"Unlucky Jim," Kornick, 1913.
"All on Account of a Cold," Kornick, 1913.
"The Saving Grace," Cinemacolor, 1913.
"A Narrow Escape," Cinemacolor, 1913.
"Two Women," Cinemacolor, 1913.
"The Wall Flower," Lubin, 1913.
"A Bunch of Flowers," American Biograph, 1914.
"When a Woman Guides," American Biograph, 1914.
"The Road to Plaindale," American Biograph, 1914.
"The Meal Ticket," American Biograph, 1914.
"The Saving Presence," American Biograph, 1914.
"The Suffering of Susan," American Biograph, 1914.
"Where the Roads Part," American Film Manufacturing, 1914.
"His Rival," American Film Manufacturing, 1914.
"The Chieftain's Daughter (Some Bull's Daughter)," Reliance Mutual, 1914.
"The Fatal Dress Suit," Reliance Mutual, 1914.
"The Girl in the Shack," Reliance Mutual, 1914.
"His Hated Rival," Reliance Mutual, 1914.
"A Corner in Hats," Reliance Mutual, 1914.
"Nearly a Burglar's Bride," Reliance Mutual, 1914.
"The Fatal Curve," Reliance Mutual, 1914.
"The Million-Dollar Bride," Reliance Mutual, 1914.
"A Flurry in Art," Reliance Mutual, 1914.
"Nellie, the Female Villain," Reliance Mutual, 1914.
"The Gangsters of New York," Reliance Mutual, 1914.
"The Tear on the Page," American Biograph, 1915.
"The Cost of a Bargain," American Biograph, 1915.
"Pennington's Choice," Metro Pictures, 1915.
"Sympathy Sal," Reliance Mutual, 1915.
"Mixed Values," Reliance Mutual, 1915.
"A Corner in Cotton," Quality Pictures, 1916.
"Wild Girl of the Sierras," Fine Arts-Triangle, 1916.
"Calico Vampire," Fine Arts-Triangle, 1916.
"Laundry Liz," Fine Arts-Triangle, 1916.
"French Milliner," Fine Arts-Triangle, 1916.
"The Wharf Rat," Fine Arts-Triangle, 1916.
"The Little Liar," Fine Arts-Triangle, 1916.
"Stranded," Fine Arts-Triangle, 1916, also released by Sterling Pictures, 1927.

"The Social Secretary," Fine Arts-Triangle, 1916, also released by Tri-Stone Pictures, 1924.
"His Picture in the Papers," Fine Arts-Triangle, 1916.
"The Half-Breed," Fine Arts-Triangle, 1916.
"American Aristocracy," Fine Arts-Triangle, 1916.
"Manhattan Madness," Fine Arts-Triangle, 1916.
"The Matrimaniac," Fine Arts-Triangle, 1916.
"The Americano," Fine Arts-Triangle, 1917.
"In Again, Out Again," Artcraft Pictures, 1917.
"Wild and Wooly" (based on a story by H. B. Carpenter), Artcraft Pictures, 1917.
"Down to Earth" (based on a story by Douglas Fairbanks), Artcraft Pictures, 1917.
(With Emerson) "Reaching for the Moon," Artcraft Pictures, 1917.
(With Emerson) "Let's Get a Divorce" (based on the play "Divorcons" by Victorien Sardou), Famous Players-Lasky, 1918.
(With Emerson) "Hit-the-Trail Holiday" (based on the play by George M. Cohan), Famous Players-Lasky, 1918.
(With Emerson) "Come On In," Famous Players-Lasky, 1918.
(With Emerson) "Good-Bye, Bill," Famous Players-Lasky, 1918.
(With Emerson) "Oh, You Women!," Famous Players-Lasky, 1919.
(With Emerson) "Getting Mary Married," Marion Davis Film Co., 1919.
(With Emerson) "A Temperamental Wife," Constance Talmadge Film Co., 1919.
(With Emerson) "A Virtuous Vamp" (based on the play "The Bachelor" by Clyde Fitch), Joseph M. Schenck, 1919.
(With Emerson) "Isle of Conquest" (based on the novel *By Right of Conquest* by Arthur Hornblow), Select Pictures, 1919.
(With Emerson) "In Search of a Sinner," Joseph M. Schenck, 1920.
(With Emerson) "The Love Expert," Joseph M. Schenck, 1920.
(With Emerson) "The Branded Woman" (based on the play "Branded" by Oliver D. Bailey), Joseph M. Schenck, 1920.
(With Emerson) "The Perfect Woman," First National, 1920.
(With Emerson) "Two Weeks" (based on the play "At the Barn" by Anthony Wharton), First National, 1920.
(With Emerson) "Dangerous Business," First National, 1921.
(With Emerson) "Mama's Affair" (based on the play by Rachel Barton Butler), First National, 1921.
(With Emerson) "Woman's Place," Joseph M. Schenck, 1921.
(With Emerson) "Red Hot Romance," Joseph M. Schenck, 1922.
(With Emerson) "Polly of the Follies," First National, 1922.
(With Emerson) "Dulcy" (based on the play by George S. Kaufman and Marc Connelly), Joseph M. Schenck, 1923.
(With Emerson) "Three Miles Out" (based on a story by Neysa McMein), Kenma, 1924.
(With Emerson) "Learning to Love," First National, 1925.
"Publicity Madness," Fox Film, 1927.
(With Emerson) "Gentlemen Prefer Blondes" (based on the play by Loos), Paramount, 1928.

UNPRODUCED SCENARIOS FOR SILENT FILMS

"He Was a College Boy," "Queen of the Carnival," "The Mayor-Elect," "The Making of a Masher," "Path of True Love," "A Girl like Mother," "The Mother," "The Great Motor Race," "A No Bull Spy," "A Balked Heredity," "A

Blasted Romance," "Mortimer's Millions," "A Life and Death Affair," "The Sensible Girl," "At the Tunnel's End," and "How to Keep a Husband," all for American Biograph; "The Deadly Glass of Beer," "The Stolen Masterpiece," "The Last Drink of Whisky," "Nell's Eugenic Wedding," "The School of Acting," "A Hicksville Reformer," "The White Slave Catchers," "The Style Accustomed," "The Deceiver," "How They Met," "The Burlesque," "The Fatal Fourth," "The Fatal Fingerprints," and "Wards of Fate," all for Reliance Mutual; "The Earl and the Tomboy," for Lubin; "Heart that Truly Loved," for Pictorial Review; "Mountain Bred," for Mabel Normand; also author of "The Telephone Girl and the Lady."

Also author of title cards for the silent films "Macbeth," Lucky Film Producers, 1916, and "Intolerance," D. W. Griffith, 1916.

SCREENPLAYS

(With Emerson) "The Struggle," United Artists, 1931.
"Red-Headed Woman" (based on the novel by Katherine Brush), Metro-Goldwyn-Mayer, 1932.
(With Elmer Harris) "The Barbarian" (based on the story by Edgar Selwyn), MGM, 1933.
(With Howard Emmett Rogers) "Hold Your Man," MGM, 1933.
(With Emerson) "The Girl from Missouri," MGM, 1934, released in England as "100 Per Cent Pure."
"Biography of a Bachelor Girl," MGM, 1935.
(With Frances Marion and H. W. Haneman) "Riffraff," MGM, 1935.
"San Francisco" (based on a story by Robert Hopkins), MGM, 1936.
"Mama Steps Out," MGM, 1937.
(With Robert Hopkins) "Saratoga," MGM, 1937.
(With Jane Murfin) "The Women" (based on the play by Clare Booth), MGM, 1939.
"Susan and God" (based on the play by Rachel Crothers), MGM, 1940, released in England as "The Gay Mrs. Trexel."
(With Edwin Justin Mayer and Leon Gordon) "They Met in Bombay" (based on a story by Franz Kafka), MGM, 1941.
"Blossoms in the Dust" (based on a story by Ralph Wheelwright), MGM, 1941.
(With S. K. Lauren) "When Ladies Meet" (based on the play by R. Crothers), MGM, 1941.
"I Married an Angel" (based on the musical by Vaszary Janos, Lorenz Hart, and Richard Rodgers), MGM, 1942.
(With others) "The Pirate," MGM, 1948.

Also author of unproduced screenplays, "The Great Canadian" and "Alaska," for MGM; also author of dialogue for "Blondie of the Follies," MGM, 1932.

SIDELIGHTS: "I really never consider myself as a writer," Anita Loos once commented to Matthew J. Bruccoli in *Conversations with Writers II.* "I'm just a girl out there trying to get a fast buck." In a career spanning some six decades, Loos wrote over 150 screenplays and scenarios, as well as popular Broadway plays and books of memoirs. But she was always "indissolubly linked" with her bestselling story collection *"Gentlemen Prefer Blondes": The Illuminating Diary of a Professional Lady,* as Alden Whitman noted in the *New York Times.* Adapted as a play, two musicals, and two movies, and translated into fourteen languages, *"Gentlemen Prefer Blondes"* established Loos's reputation as a writer of sparkling satire. Asked by Roy Newquist of *Palm Springs Life* whether she

minded "being so closely identified" with the one book, Loos replied: "Heavens no, not as long as those lovely royalty checks keep coming in."

Loos began her career as a child actress in her father's theatrical company in San Francisco. By the time she was ten years old, her stage earnings were a vital cash source for her financially unstable family. Loos admitted on several occasions that her father's business often kept him away from home for long periods, usually in the company of other women. John Fitzgerald of the *Detroit News* quoted Loos explaining: "My mother was refined . . . my father was a charming tramp."

While still in her teens, Loos became interested in the then-new medium of silent films, which were at first shown in between live acts at local theatres. Believing that she could write a silent film as good as the ones shown in her father's theatre, Loos submitted the scenario for "The New York Hat" to D. W. Griffith's American Biograph Company. She took the company's address off a film cannister. Griffith accepted the scenario and Loos received twenty-five dollars for her work. The resulting film featured Lillian and Dorothy Gish, Mary Pickford, and Lionel Barrymore.

Between 1912 and 1916, Loos wrote at least 100 scenarios for the silent films, usually for American Biograph but, when a particular idea did not seem strong enough to Griffith, for other film companies as well. The exact number of Loos silent films, the years they were released, and the production companies that made them, are questions that will never be answered definitively. Few records were kept by those in the business, many films, particularly the very short films, were never registered for copyright, and others were later lost either through haphazard storage or deliberate destruction for the silver nitrate content in the film itself. And to many people in the silent film world, the business was nothing but a transitory craze not to be taken too seriously. "We . . . looked on them as a fad that would soon lose public interest," Whitman quoted Loos explaining.

Specializing in writing "slapstick comedies and romantic melodramas," as Thomas Grant noted in the *Dictionary of Literary Biography,* Loos emerged as one of the luminaries of the silent film world. She wrote for such stars as Mabel Normand, Mae Marsh, Marian Davies, Francis X. Bushman, Constance and Norma Talmadge, and Douglas Fairbanks, and worked with the legendary director D. W. Griffith. She also wrote the title cards for Griffith's "Intolerance," one of the silent screen's classic films. Yet, despite her position in the industry, Loos never went to see any of her films. She told Bruccoli: "I never paid any attention to any of them. They were a job and I'd get them done."

In 1916, Loos became the sole writer for Douglas Fairbanks after the success of the satirical film "His Picture in the Papers." The film introduced a new element to the silent film genre: satirical title cards which were meant to contrast ironically with the action on the screen. Together with her future husband, director John Emerson, Loos and Fairbanks shaped the Fairbanks screen persona into one of the most popular and lucrative characters in the cinema industry. Speaking of Loos's writing for these early films, Joanne Yeck of the *Dictionary of Literary Biography* reported that she "introduced satire to the silent film. Her dialogue cards were bright with sharp wit, exposing her real talent for verbal comedy."

In 1919 Loos married Emerson and the two went on to collaborate on a number of films and plays. It was only years later, in her autobiography *Kiss Hollywood Good-by*, that Loos confessed that her husband's "'collaboration' consisted of glancing over my morning's work while he was eating breakfast in bed." By the late 1920s the couple had done well enough to leave screenwriting and move to Europe. Loos's movie fame allowed her entrance to European high society, and she was soon a regular at the country houses of royalty. Numbered among her friends were Ernest Hemingway, Gertrude Stein, Aldous Huxley, H. G. Wells, and F. Scott Fitzgerald. But Loos's lifestyle came to an abrupt end with the stock market crash of 1929; Emerson had invested the couple's money in the market and lost it all. In 1931, Loos returned to the United States to become a screenwriter with Metro-Goldwyn-Mayer at a salary of $3,500 a week.

During the 1930s Loos worked with Irving Thalberg, the head of MGM studios and the man Loos later claimed taught her all about the "talkies." Her first film for the studio was "Red-Headed Woman," the story of a young vamp who breaks up a marriage. Thalberg had already had several writers try their hand at the script—including F. Scott Fitzgerald—but not one had been able to render the story in the ironic manner Thalberg wanted. He thought that Loos might be able to treat the story's sexual slant humorously. Loos did. The resulting script catapulted lead actress Jean Harlow to instant fame. But the film, because of "its lighthearted view of sex," as Yeck reported, also ran afoul of the religious community. "Red-Headed Woman," Yeck wrote, "started the national protest of women's clubs and church groups that eventually culminated in the formation of the Breen Office," a censorship group that was to set the "acceptable" standards for the film industry for years to come. Writing in *Kiss Hollywood Good-by*, Loos noted that the film outraged many people because "our heroine, the bad girl of whom all good husbands dream, ended her career as many such scalawags do, rich, happy, and respected, without ever having paid for her sins."

In 1936, Loos wrote "San Francisco" for MGM, a film inspired by her close friend Wilson Mizner. Loos and Robert Hopkins, who wrote the original story for the film, had known Mizner for many years. Mizner had worked in gambling houses, sold nonexistent Florida real estate, and engaged in a score of other fraudulent operations before finally opening a legitimate business—the Brown Derby Restaurant in Hollywood. His notorious past, colorful anecdotes, off-color remarks, and unfailing charm made Mizner a favorite with many among the Hollywood set, including W. C. Fields. After Mizner's death in 1933, Loos and Hopkins wrote "San Francisco," as Loos explained in *Kiss Hollywood Good-by*, "to the glory of Wilson Mizner and the Frisco all three of us knew when we were kids." In the film, Blackie Norton, played by Clark Gable, is a Barbary Coast gambler in the San Francisco of the turn of the century who is inspired to go straight after the great earthquake of 1906. The story is partly based on Mizner's own career as a gambling house operator. "San Francisco," Yeck reported, was "by far the most commercially successful film Thalberg ever produced." Loos admitted in *Kiss Hollywood Good-by* that "it became one of MGM's most durable hits."

Although she enjoyed great success as a writer for Hollywood films, Loos is best known for "Gentlemen Prefer Blondes," a book she later adapted as a play, a musical, and for the screen. The story of an uneducated and naive young flapper who uses her charms to coax expensive gifts from her "gentlemen friends," the idea for "Gentlemen Prefer Blondes" apparently came to Loos during a cross-country train ride in the early 1920s. One of her fellow passengers was a blond

Broadway actress on her way to Hollywood for a screen test. Over the course of the journey, the men on the train fawned over her while Loos, a brunette, steamed. Her resentment took shape as a series of loosely-linked satirical short stories written in diary form. But on other occasions Loos claimed that she wrote "Gentlemen Prefer Blondes" because her friend H. L. Mencken had been infatuated with a particularly brainless blond and she wanted to show him his mistake.

Whatever the source of "Gentlemen Prefer Blondes"—Whitman maintained that "Loos seldom permitted precise facts to spoil a good story, so the true origins of her book are in doubt"—the stories were first published in *Harper's Bazaar* and immediately caused sales of the magazine to quadruple. The story proved popular when published in book form in 1925; since its first appearance there have been some 85 editions of "Gentlemen Prefer Blondes" and the book has even been translated into Chinese.

The book follows beautiful Lorelei Lee on a tour of Europe with her friend Dorothy. Lorelei's innane observations about European society and culture, and her frankly materialistic attitude toward sexual relations, form the basis of the comedy. "As a fictional character," Grant wrote, "Lorelei harks back to an earlier comic stereotype, the malaprop-inclined, misspelling rustic busybody." Fitzgerald noted that Loos "gave the world neither blonds nor gentlemen but managed to make both shimmer through the eyes of one diamond-loving Lorelei Lee." Perhaps the book's most famous line is Lorelei's observation that "kissing your hand may make you feel very good but a diamond lasts forever." In the course of her European tour Lorelei acquires a number of both kisses and diamonds, including a $7,500 tiara from an English nobleman. She ends the book safely ensconced on Park Avenue, the wife of a wealthy man. "Lorelei's stunning progress from small-town girl to metropolitan socialite," Grant remarked, "makes her story seem like an urban version of the familiar American tall tale, a delightfully improbable yarn perfectly suited to the 1920s era of excess."

Critical response to "Gentlemen Prefer Blondes" was enormously favorable. George Santayana once remarked with tongue in cheek that he thought the book "the best philosophical work by an American." William Faulkner, James Joyce, Edith Wharton, and Aldous Huxley were among those who recommended it. H. L. Mencken reportedly told Loos: "Young woman, do you realize you are the first American writer to ever make fun of sex?" Years later, Peter S. Prescott of *Newsweek* could still note that "Gentlemen Prefer Blondes" "remains one of the great American comic novels."

The adaptations of the book also proved successful. Loos's stage version of 1926 ran on Broadway for 201 performances. A 1949 musical version enjoyed a run of 740 performances and launched the career of actress Carol Channing. The popular song "Diamonds Are a Girl's Best Friend" is from this play. In 1974, yet another Broadway adaptation appeared under the title of "Lorelie." Loos also wrote a silent film version of "Gentlemen Prefer Blondes" which was produced in 1928; a later film, featuring Marilyn Monroe as Lorelei, appeared in 1953.

Loos followed "Gentlemen Prefer Blondes" with a sequel, "But Gentlemen Marry Brunettes," recounting the romantic misadventures of Lorelei's girlfriend Dorothy. Lorelei, who has married successfully, assists Dorothy in her quest to enter Manhattan society. But Dorothy's eventual marriage to a rich polo player comes only after a series of trials, including a marriage to a cocaine addict who is killed by mobsters. One of the novel's high points, according to Grant, is a scene in which the two women visit the Algonquin Hotel and acidly comment on the circle of writers and journalists who frequented the hotel bar in the early 1920s. "Loos's portrayal of the Algonquin wits," Grant wrote, "has become established wisdom. She was one of their first critics, and one of the most accurate." Other reviewers, such as the *New Republic* critic, found that, like its predecessor, *"But Gentlemen Marry Brunettes"* contains "that wonderful mixture of canned, naive sentiment and equally naive, but extremely business-like gold-digging."

In 1946, Loos returned to the Broadway stage with "Happy Birthday," a comedy set in a Newark saloon and starring her old friend Helen Hayes. Revolving around an inhibited librarian who finally opens up after a few drinks at the local tavern, "Happy Birthday" ran for 564 performances on Broadway. Speaking to Bruccoli about the play, Loos explained the basis of its plot: "I had this old maid go into a bar and get tight, and in the process of getting tight she regenerates her whole life." Later Loos stage efforts included two popular adaptations of novels by the French writer Colette: "Gigi," in 1951, and "Cheri," in 1959.

Beginning in the 1960s, Loos began to publish a series of memoirs about her long career as a writer for Hollywood and Broadway. Written in a chatty, informal style, these books are peppered with lively anecdotes and reminiscences about the many famous people she knew. Grant explained that Loos's memoirs chronicled "her own long, lucrative career and the dazzling times in which she worked." In her review of *A Girl Like I*, Sister M. Gregory of *Best Sellers* found that the "book is more than an autobiography; it is an intriguing bit of Americana that mirrors the brash confidence, rugged independence and changing mores of a rapidly growing, prosperous country." Speaking of *Kiss Hollywood Good-by*, Joel Sayre of the *New York Times Book Review* remarked that if the book reached the bestseller lists, it would be because of Loos's "marvelous, casual putting forth of bizarre doings and sayings." Writing in the *Christian Science Monitor*, Guernsey Le Pelley called the same book "a jolly adventure in trivia. . . . But along with all the flotsam are many delectable and interesting tidbits, which make the book bouncy and largely enjoyable. Also [the book] holds up a mirror of unintended satire to that demi-Disneyland called Hollywood." In similar terms, Richard Lingeman of the *New York Times*, reviewing *Cast of Thousands*, warned that "one should not regard [Loos's] witty, determinedly surface view of life as the sign of a superficial mind. Actually, Miss Loos is a sharp-eyed chatterbox, who lets fly some quick cynical shafts."

Despite the many successes of her long career, Loos always maintained a cavalier attitude towards her work. She told Fitzgerald: "I did it for the money and it was the easiest money I ever made." When questioned by Bruccoli about whether *"Gentlemen Prefer Blondes"* had obscured "the range of your other work," Loos replied: "I think *Gentlemen Prefer Blondes* is the range of my work. I think everything else I do is just earning a living." Perhaps one reason for her adamant refusal to place much value on her writings is revealed in a remark Loos made to Fitzgerald in the last interview she gave. "It was all so easy," she said. "It didn't seem to mean anything."

Critical evaluations of Loos's career usually stress the impressive range of genres in which she excelled. Her silent film work includes some of that genre's finest examples and intro-

duced depth and subtlety to the medium. Her later films and plays feature sparkling, witty dialogue that ensures their lasting humor and audience appeal. And her character Lorelei Lee is, Grant believed, "a true American original. . . . So memorable [that she] ought to earn her inventor a place as one of the important minor figures among twentieth-century American humorists." Enid Nemy of the *New York Times Book Review* summed up Loos in this way: "The keenness of her eye never faltered, and for something like six decades she sliced neatly through the gauze that surrounds glamour and fame."

MEDIA ADAPTATIONS: "Gentlemen Prefer Blondes" was filmed by 20th Century-Fox in 1953 and was adapted as a musical entitled "Lorelei" in 1974; "But Gentlemen Marry Brunettes" was filmed as "Gentlemen Marry Brunettes" by United Artists in 1955; *Happy Birthday* was adapted for television in Italy and the United States.

BIOGRAPHICAL/CRITICAL SOURCES:

BOOKS

Authors in the News, Gale, Volume 1, 1976.
Conversations with Writers II, Gale, 1978.
Dictionary of Literary Biography, Gale, Volume 11: *American Humorists, 1800-1950*, 1982, Volume 26: *American Screenwriters*, 1984.
Dictionary of Literary Biography Yearbook, 1981, Gale, 1982.
Loos, Anita, *A Girl Like I*, Viking, 1966.
Loos, Anita, *Kiss Hollywood Good-by*, Viking, 1974.
Loos, Anita, *Cast of Thousands*, Grosset & Dunlap, 1977.

PERIODICALS

Akron Beacon Journal, September 8, 1974.
Atlantic, October, 1960.
Best Sellers, October 1, 1966.
Boston Transcript, November 25, 1925.
Canadian Review of American Studies, spring, 1976.
Chicago Tribune, August 2, 1961.
Chicago Tribune Book World, November 26, 1978.
Christian Science Monitor, September 18, 1974.
Detroit News, August 30, 1981.
Literary Review, November 21, 1925.
New Republic, June 13, 1928, August 10, 1974.
New Statesman, May 19, 1928.
Newsweek, December 17, 1984.
New York Times, April 29, 1918, September 23, 1918, October 27, 1919, January 23, 1922, February 23, 1925, December 27, 1925, January 16, 1928, May 20, 1928, December 11, 1935, March 2, 1935, January 13, 1936, June 27, 1936, July 23, 1937, September 22, 1939, July 12, 1940, June 27, 1941, July 4, 1941, September 5, 1941, July 10, 1942.
New York Times Book Review, May 6, 1951, August 18, 1974, March 23, 1977, November 27, 1984, December 30, 1984.
New York Tribune, December 27, 1925.
Palm Springs Life, October, 1974.
Saturday Review, June 9, 1928, September 24, 1966.
Times Literary Supplement, February 23, 1967.

OBITUARIES:

PERIODICALS

AB Bookman's Weekly, September 14, 1981.
Chicago Tribune, August 20, 1981.
Newsweek, August 31, 1981.
New York Times, August 19, 1981.

Publishers Weekly, September 4, 1981.
Time, August 31, 1981.†

—*Sketch by Thomas Wiloch*

*   *   *

LORD, Jeffrey
See NELSON, R(adell) Faraday

*   *   *

LORDE, Audre (Geraldine) 1934-
(Rey Domini)

PERSONAL: Born February 18, 1934, in New York, N.Y.; daughter of Frederic Byron (a real estate broker) and Linda (Belmar) Lorde; married Edwon Ashley Rollins (an attorney), March 31, 1962 (divorced, 1970); children: Elizabeth, Jonathan. *Education:* Attended National University of Mexico, 1954; Hunter College (now Hunter College of the City University of New York), B.A., 1959; Columbia University, M.L.S., 1961. *Politics:* Radical. *Religion:* Quaker.

ADDRESSES: Home—AZ Judith's Fancy, Christiansted, St. Croix 00820, U.S. Virgin Islands. *Office*—Department of English, Hunter College of the City University of New York, 695 Park Ave., New York, N.Y. 10019.

CAREER: Mount Vernon Public Library, Mount Vernon, N.Y., librarian, 1961-63; Town School Library, New York City, head librarian, 1966-68; City University of New York, New York City, lecturer in creative writing at City College, 1968, lecturer in education department at Herbert H. Lehman College, 1969-70, associate professor of English at John Jay College of Criminal Justice, beginning 1970, professor of English at Hunter College, 1980—, Thomas Hunter Professor, 1987—. Distinguished visiting professor, Atlanta University, 1968; poet in residence, Tougaloo College, 1968. Lecturer throughout the United States.

MEMBER: American Association of University Professors, Harlem Writers Guild.

AWARDS, HONORS: National Endowment for the Arts grants, 1968 and 1981; Creative Artists Public Service grants, 1972 and 1976; National Book Award nominee for poetry, 1974, for *From a Land Where Other People Live;* Borough of Manhattan President's Award for literary excellence, 1987.

WRITINGS:

The Cancer Journals (nonfiction), Spinsters Ink, 1980.
Zami: A New Spelling of My Name (fiction), Crossing Press, 1982.
Sister Outsider (nonfiction), Crossing Press, 1984.
Burst of Light, Firebrand Books, 1988.

POETRY

The First Cities, introduction by Diane di Prima, Poets Press, 1968.
Cables to Rage, Broadside Press, 1970.
From a Land Where Other People Live, Broadside Press, 1973.
The New York Head Shop and Museum, Broadside Press, 1974.
Coal, Norton, 1976.
Between Our Selves, Eidolon, 1976.
The Black Unicorn, Norton, 1978.
Chosen Poems Old and New, Norton, 1982.
Our Dead Behind Us, Norton, 1986.

CONTRIBUTOR OF POETRY TO ANTHOLOGIES

Langston Hughes, editor, *New Negro Poets, USA,* University of Indiana Press, 1962.
P. Breman, editor, *Sixes and Sevens,* Breman Ltd. (London), 1963.
R. Pool, editor, *Beyond the Blues,* Hand & Flower Press (Amsterdam), 1964.
G. Menarini, editor, *I Negri: Poesie E Canti,* Edizioni Academia (Rome), 1969.
C. Major, editor, *New Black Poetry,* International Press, 1969.
T. Wilentz, editor, *Natural Process,* Hill & Wang, 1970.
T. Cade, editor, *The Black Woman,* American Library Publishing, 1970.

Contributor of poetry to other anthologies, including *Soul-Script,* edited by J. Meyer, Simon & Schuster.

OTHER

Contributor of poetry to periodicals, including *Iowa Review, Black Scholar, Chrysalis, Black World, Journal of Black Poetry, Transatlantic Review, Massachusetts Review, Pound, Harlem Writers' Quarterly, Freedomways, Seventeen,* and *Women: A Journal of Liberation;* contributor of fiction, under pseudonym Rey Domini to *Venture* magazine. Editor, *Pound* magazine (Tougaloo, Miss.), 1968; poetry editor, *Chrysalis* and *Amazon Quarterly.*

WORK IN PROGRESS: Poetry and collected essays.

SIDELIGHTS: Audre Lorde's poetry and "indeed all of her writing," according to contributor Joan Martin in *Black Women Writers (1950-1980): A Critical Evaluation,* "rings with passion, sincerity, perception, and depth of feeling." Her first poem to be published was accepted by *Seventeen* magazine when she was still in high school. The poem had been rejected by her school paper, Lorde explains in *Black Women Writers,* because her "English teachers . . . said [it] was much too romantic." Her mature poetry, published in volumes including *New York Head Shop and Museum, Coal,* and *The Black Unicorn,* is sometimes romantic also. Often dealing with her lesbian relationships, her love poems have nevertheless been judged accessible to all by many critics. In Martin's words, "one doesn't have to profess heterosexuality, homosexuality, or asexuality to react to her poems. . . . Anyone who has ever been in love can respond to the straightforward passion and pain sometimes one and the same, in Lorde's poems."

As Jerome Brooks reports in *Black Women Writers (1950-1980): A Critical Evaluation,* however, "Lorde's poetry of anger is perhaps her best-known work." In her poem "The American Cancer Society Or There Is More Than One Way to Skin a Coon," she protests against white America thrusting its unnatural culture on blacks; in "The Brown Menace or Poem to the Survival of Roaches," she likens blacks to cockroaches, hated, feared, and poisoned by whites. *Poetry* critic Sandra M. Gilbert remarks that "it's not surprising that Lorde occasionally seems to be choking on her own anger . . . [and] when her fury vibrates through taut cables from head to heart to page, Lorde is capable of rare and, paradoxically, loving jeremiads." Her anger does not confine itself to racial injustice but extends to feminist issues as well, and occasionally she criticizes black men for their role in the perpetuating of sex discrimination: "As Black people, we cannot begin our dialogue by denying the oppressive nature of *male privilege,*" Lorde states in *Black Women Writers.* "And if Black males choose to assume that privilege, for whatever reason, raping, brutalizing, and killing women, then we cannot ignore Black male oppression. One oppression does not justify another.''

Of her poetic beginnings Lorde comments in *Black Women Writers:* ''I used to speak in poetry. I would read poems, and I would memorize them. People would say, well what do you think, Audre. What happened to you yesterday? And I would recite a poem and somewhere in that poem would be a line or a feeling I would be sharing. In other words, I literally communicated through poetry. And when I couldn't find the poems to express the things I was feeling, that's what started me writing poetry, and that was when I was twelve or thirteen.'' As an adult, her primary poetic goal is still communication. ''I have a duty,'' she states later in the same publication, ''to speak the truth as I see it and to share not just my triumphs, not just the things that felt good, but the pain, the intense, often unmitigating pain.'' As a mature poet, however, rather than relying solely on poetry as a means of self-expression Lorde often extracts poems from her personal journals. Explaining the genesis of ''Power,'' a poem about the police shooting of a ten-year-old black child, Lorde discusses her feelings when she learned that the officer involved had been acquitted: ''A kind of fury rose up in me; the sky turned red. I felt so sick. I felt as if I would drive this car into a wall, into the next person I saw. So I pulled over. I took out my journal just to air some of my fury, to get it out of my fingertips. Those expressed feelings are that poem.''

In addition to race problems and love affairs, another important theme that runs through many of Lorde's volumes of poetry is the parent-child relationship. Brooks sees a deep concern with the image of her deceased father in Lorde's ''Father, Son, and Holy Ghost'' which carries over to poems dealing with Africa in *The Black Unicorn.* According to Brooks, ''the contact with Africa is the contact with the father who is revealed in a wealth of mythological symbols. . . . The fundamental image of the unicorn indicates that the poet is aware that Africa is for her a fatherland, a phallic terrain.'' Martin, however, takes a different view: ''Audre Lorde is a rare creature. . . . She is the Black Unicorn: magical and mysterious bearer of fantasy draped in truth and beauty.'' Further, Martin finds the poet's feelings about her mother to be more vital to an understanding of her works. In many of Lorde's poems, the figure of her mother is one of a woman who resents her daughter, tries to repress her child's unique personality so that she conforms with the rest of the world, and withholds the emotional nourishment of parental love. For example, Lorde tells us in *Coal*'s ''Story Books on a Kitchen Table'': ''Out of her womb of pain my mother spat me / into her ill-fitting harness of despair / into her deceits / where anger reconceived me.'' In *The Black Unicorn*'s ''From the House of Yemanja,'' the mother's efforts to shape the speaker into something she is not do not quench the speaker's desire for the mother's love: ''Mother I need / mother I need / . . . I am / the sun and moon and forever hungry.'' ''Ballad From Childhood'' in *The New York Head Shop and Museum* is Lorde's depiction of the ways in which a child's hopes and dreams are crushed by a restrictive mother. After the mother has made withering replies to her child's queries about planting a tree to give some beauty to their wasteland surroundings, the child gives up in defeat, saying: ''Please mommy do not beat me so! / yes I will learn to love the snow! / yes I want neither seed nor tree! / yes ice is quite enough for me! / who knows what trouble-leaves might grow!''

As Martin notes, however, Lorde's ambivalent feelings about her mother ''did not make [her] bitter against her own children

when circumstances changed her role from that of child to mother.'' *Coal* includes the poem ''Now That I Am Forever with Child,'' which discusses the birth of Lorde's daughter. ''I bore you one morning just before spring,'' she recounts, ''my legs were towers between which / A new world was passing. / Since then / I can only distinguish / one thread within runnings hours / You, flowing through selves / toward You.''

Lorde is also famed for writing the courageous account of her agonizing struggle to overcome breast cancer and mastectomy, *The Cancer Journals.* Her first major prose work, the *Journals* discuss Lorde's feelings about facing the possibility of death. Beyond death, Martin asserts, Lorde feared ''she should die without having said the things she as a woman and an artist needed to say in order that her pain and subsequent loss might not have occurred in vain.'' The book also explains Lorde's decision not to wear a prosthesis after her breast was removed. As Brooks points out, ''she does not suggest [her decision] for others, but . . . she uses [it] to expose some of the hypocrisies of the medical profession.'' Lorde summarizes her attitude on the issue thus in the *Journals:* ''Prosthesis offers the empty comfort of 'Nobody will know the difference.' But it is that very difference which I wish to affirm, because I have lived it, and survived it, and wish to share that strength with other women. If we are to translate the silence surrounding breast cancer into language and action against this scourge, then the first step is that women with mastectomies must become visible to each other.'' Martin concludes: ''*The Cancer Journals* affords all women who wish to read it the opportunity to look at the life experience of one very brave woman who bared her wounds without shame, in order that we might gain some strength from sharing in her pain.''

Lorde's 1982 novel, *Zami: A New Spelling of My Name,* is described by its publishers as a ''biomythography, combining elements of history, biography and myth,'' and Rosemary Daniell, in the *New York Times Book Review,* considers the work ''excellent and evocative. . . . Among the elements that make the book so good are its personal honesty and lack of pretentiousness, characteristics that shine through the writing, bespeaking the evolution of a strong and remarkable character.'' Daniell says that, throughout the book, Lorde's ''experiences are painted with exquisite imagery. Indeed, her West Indian heritage shows through most clearly in her use of word pictures that are sensual, steamy, at times near-tropical, evoking the colors, smells—repeatedly, the smells—shapes, textures that are her life.''

BIOGRAPHICAL/CRITICAL SOURCES:

BOOKS

Addison, Gayle, editor, *Black Expression,* Weybright & Talley, 1969.

Bigsby, C. W. E., editor, *The Black American Writer,* Penguin, 1969.

Christian, Barbara, editor, *Black Feminist Criticism: Perspectives on Black Women Writers,* Pergamon, 1985.

Contemporary Literary Criticism, Volume 18, Gale, 1981.

Evans, Mari, editor, *Black Women Writers (1950-1980): A Critical Evaluation,* Doubleday, 1984.

Lorde, Audre, *The New York Head Shop and Museum,* Broadside Press, 1974.

Lorde, Audre, *Coal,* Norton, 1976.

Lorde, Audre, *The Black Unicorn,* Norton, 1978.

Lorde, Audre, *The Cancer Journals,* Spinsters Ink, 1980.

Tate, Claudia, editor, *Black Women Writers at Work,* Continuum, 1984.

PERIODICALS

Callaloo, Volume 9, number 4, 1987.
Essence, January, 1988.
Ms., September, 1974.
Negro Digest, September, 1968.
New York Times Book Review, December 19, 1982.
Poetry, February, 1977.

—*Sketch by Elizabeth Thomas*

*   *   *

LOWELL, Robert (Traill Spence, Jr.)   1917-1977

PERSONAL: Born March 1, 1917, in Boston, Mass.; died of congestive heart failure, September 12, 1977, in New York, N.Y.; buried in Dumbarton, N.H.; son of Robert Traill Spence (a naval officer) and Charlotte (Winslow) Lowell; married Jean Stafford (a writer), April 2, 1940 (divorced June, 1948); married Elizabeth Hardwick (a writer), July 28, 1949 (divorced, 1972); married Caroline Blackwood (a writer), 1972; children: (second marriage) Harriet Winslow; (third marriage) Robert Sheridan. *Education:* Attended St. Marks School; attended Harvard University, 1935-37; Kenyon College, A.B. (summa cum laude), 1940; additional study at Louisiana State University, 1940-41.

ADDRESSES: Home—Neilgate Park, Bearsted, Maidstone, Kent, England.

CAREER: Writer, poet. Sheed & Ward, New York, N.Y., editorial assistant, 1941-42; Library of Congress, Washington, D.C., consultant in poetry, 1947-48. Taught at State University of Iowa (now Iowa State University), 1950 and 1953, Kenyon School of Letters, 1950 and 1953, Salzburg Seminar on American Studies (Salzburg, Austria), 1952, University of Cincinnati, 1954, Boston University, 1956, Harvard University, 1958, 1963-70, 1975, and 1977, New School for Social Research, 1961-62, University of Essex (Wivenhoe, Colchester, England), 1970-72, and Kent University (Canterbury, England), 1970-75. Writer in residence, Yale University, 1967. Visiting fellow, All Souls College, Oxford, 1970. *Wartime activity:* Conscientious objector, World War II; served a prison term as a result, 1943-44.

MEMBER: National Academy and Institute of Arts and Letters, American Academy of Arts and Letters, Phi Beta Kappa.

AWARDS, HONORS: National Institute of Arts and Letters Award, 1947; Guggenheim fellowship, 1947; Pulitzer Prize, 1947, for *Lord Weary's Castle;* Harriet Monroe Poetry Award, University of Chicago, 1952; Guinness Poetry Award (Ireland; shared with W. H. Auden, Edith Sitwell, and Edwin Muir), 1959, for "Skunk Hour"; National Book Award, 1960, for *Life Studies;* Boston Arts Festival Poet, 1960; Harriet Monroe Memorial Prize, *Poetry,* 1961; Bollingen Prize in Poetry for translation, Yale University Library, 1962, for *Imitations;* Levinson Prize, *Poetry,* 1963; Golden Rose Trophy, New England Poetry Club, 1964; Obie Award for best new play, *Village Voice,* 1965, for "The Old Glory"; Sarah Josepha Hale Award, Friends of the Richards Library, 1966; National Council on the Arts grant, 1967, to produce "Prometheus Bound"; Copernicus Award, Academy of American Poets, 1974; Pulitzer Prize, 1974, for *The Dolphin;* National Medal for Literature, National Academy and Institute of Arts and Letters, 1977; National Book Critics Circle Award, 1978, for *Day by Day,* and posthumous nomination (in criticism), 1987, for *Col-*

lected Prose. Litt.D., Williams College, 1965, and Yale University, 1968; honorary degree, Columbia University, 1969.

WRITINGS:

POETRY

Land of Unlikeness, introduction by Allen Tate, Cummington Press (Cummington, Mass.), 1944, reprinted, University Microfilms (Ann Arbor, Mich.), 1971.
Lord Weary's Castle (also see below), Harcourt, 1946, reprinted, 1985.
Poems, 1938-1949, Faber, 1950, reprinted, 1987.
The Mills of the Kavanaughs (also see below), Harcourt, 1951.
Life Studies (also see below), Farrar, Straus & Cudahy, 1959, 2nd edition published with prose memoir "91 Revere Street," Faber, 1968.
Lord Weary's Castle [and] *The Mills of the Kavanaughs,* Meridian Books, 1961, reprinted, Harcourt, 1979.
For the Union Dead (also see below), Farrar, Straus, 1964.
Nathaniel Hawthorne, 1804-1864 (limited edition keepsake of centenary commemoration of Hawthorne's death), Ohio State University Press, 1964.
Selected Poems, Faber, 1965, reprinted, 1986.
The Achievement of Robert Lowell: A Comprehensive Selection of His Poems, edited and introduced by William J. Martz, Scott, Foresman, 1966.
Life Studies [and] *For the Union Dead,* Noonday, 1967.
Near the Ocean (also see below), drawings by Sidney Nolan, Farrar, Straus, 1967.
4, privately printed limited edition by Laurence Scott (Cambridge, Mass.), 1969.
R.F.K., 1925-1968, privately printed limited edition, 1969.
Notebook 1967-68, Farrar, Straus, 1969, 3rd edition revised and expanded as *Notebook,* 1970.
Fuer die Toten der Union (English with German translations; contains poetry from *Life Studies, Near the Ocean,* and *For the Union Dead*), Suhrkamp (Frankfort on the Main), 1969.
Poems de Robert Lowell (English with Spanish translations), Editorial Sudamericana (Buenos Aires), 1969.
Poesie, 1940-1970 (English with Italian translations), Longanesi (Milan), 1972.
History (also see below), Farrar, Straus, 1973.
For Lizzie and Harriet (also see below), Farrar, Straus, 1973.
The Dolphin (also see below), Farrar, Straus, 1973.
Robert Lowell's Poems: A Selection, edited and introduced, with notes, by Jonathan Raban, Faber, 1974.
Selected Poems, Farrar, Straus, 1976, revised edition, Noonday, 1977.
Ein Fischnetz aus teerigem Garn zu knuepfen: Robert Lowell (English with German translations; contains poems from *Lord Weary's Castle, Life Studies, For the Union Dead, Near the Ocean, History, The Dolphin,* and *For Lizzie and Harriet*), Verlag Volk und Welt (Berlin), 1976.
Day by Day, Farrar, Straus, 1977.
A Poem, Menhaden Press (Vermillion, S.D.), 1980.

DRAMA

The Old Glory (theatre trilogy; contains "Endecott and the Red Cross" [also see below] and "My Kinsman, Major Molineux," both based on short stories by Nathaniel Hawthorne, and "Benito Cereno" [also see below], based on a novella by Herman Melville; first produced Off-Broadway at the American Place Theatre, November 1, 1964), introduction by Robert Brustein, director's note by Jonathan Miller, Farrar, Straus, 1965, revised edition, 1968.

Prometheus Bound: Derived from Aeschylus (first produced by Yale School of Drama, May 9, 1967; produced Off-Broadway at Mermaid Theatre, June 24, 1971), Farrar, Straus, 1969, reprinted, 1987.

Endecott and the Red Cross (revised and expanded version of one-act play of the same title; first produced in New York City by the American Place Theatre at St. Clements Episcopal Church, May, 1968), American Place Theatre, 1968.

Benito Cereno (English with Italian translation), edited and introduced by Rolando Anzilotti, All'insegna del pesce d'oro (Milan), 1969.

TRANSLATOR

Eugenio Montale, *Poesie de Montale*, Laterna (Bologna), 1960.

(And editor) *Imitations* (versions of poems by Homer, Sappho, Rainer Maria Rilke, Francois Villon, Stephane Mallarme, Charles-Pierre Baudelaire, and others; mimeographed typescript entitled *Imitations: A Book of Free Translations by Robert Lowell for Elizabeth Bishop* privately circulated before publication, c. 1960), Farrar, Straus & Cudahy, 1961.

(With Jacques Barzun) Jean Baptiste Racine and Pierre Beaumarchais, *Phaedra and Figaro* (also see below; Beaumarchais's *Figaro* translated by Barzun; Racine's *Phedra* translated by Lowell), Farrar, Straus & Cudahy, 1961.

Phaedra, Faber, 1963, Octagon Books, 1971.

The Voyage, and Other Versions of Poems by Baudelaire, illustrations by Sidney Nolan, Farrar, Straus, 1968.

The Oresteia of Aeschylus (contains "Agamemnon," "Orestes," and "The Furies"), Farrar, Straus, 1978.

CONTRIBUTOR

Gerard Manley Hopkins by the Kenyon Critics (essays), New Directions, 1945.

Louis Untermeyer, editor, *Modern American Poetry*, Harcourt, 1950.

W. H. Auden, editor, *Criterion Book of Modern American Verse*, Criterion, 1956.

Alfred Kazin, editor, *The Open Form: Essays for Our Time*, Harcourt, 1961.

George Plimpton, editor, *Writers at Work: "Paris Review" Interviews*, 2nd series, Viking, 1963.

Anthony Ostroff, editor, *Contemporary Poet as Artist and Critic* (essays), Little, Brown, 1964.

Walter Lowenfels and Nan Braymer, editors, *Where Is Vietnam?: American Poets Respond*, Doubleday-Anchor, 1967.

Contemporary Poetry in America, Salmagundi (Saratoga Springs, N.Y.), 1973.

Works also represented in numerous other anthologies.

OTHER

(Author of introduction) Nathaniel Hawthorne, *Pegasus, the Winged Horse*, Macmillan, 1963.

(Author of introductions with Kenneth Rexroth) Ford Madox Ford, *Buckshee* (poems), Pym-Randall Press, 1966.

(Author of appreciation) Randall Jarrell, *The Lost World*, Collier, 1966.

(Editor with Peter Taylor and Robert Penn Warren) *Randall Jarrell, 1914-1965* (essays), Farrar, Straus, 1967, reprinted, Noonday, 1985.

The Poetry of Robert Lowell (sound recording of reading at Y.M.-Y.W.H.A. Poetry Center in New York City, 1968), Jeffrey Norton, 1974.

Robert Lowell: A Reading (sound recording of reading at Poetry Center of the 92nd Street "Y" in New York City, December 8, 1976), Caedmon, 1978.

Robert Lowell Reading His Own Poems (sound recording of Twentieth-Century Poetry in English series), Library of Congress, 1978.

Collected Prose, edited and introduced by Robert Giroux, Farrar, Straus, 1987.

Contributor to periodicals, including *Kenyon Review, New Republic, New World Writing, New York Review of Books, Observer, Partisan Review, Salmagundi*, and *Sewanee Review*.

SIDELIGHTS: Robert Lowell is best known for his volume *Life Studies*, but his true greatness as an American poet lies in the astonishing variety of his work. In the 1940s he wrote intricate and tightly patterned poems that incorporated traditional meter and rhyme; in the late 1950s when he published *Life Studies*, he began to write startlingly original personal or "confessional" poetry in much looser forms and meters; in the 1960s he wrote increasingly public poetry; and finally in the 1970s he created poems that incorporated and extended elements of all the earlier poetry. Meanwhile he also produced a volume of translations he called "imitations" and wrote or translated several plays. Lowell had a profound interest in history and politics; in his poetry he juxtaposed self and history in ways that illuminated both. His art and his life were inseparably intertwined, and he believed firmly in the identity of self and language.

In "After Enjoying Six or Seven Essays on Me," a 1977 *Salmagundi* essay, Lowell wrote that "looking over my *Selected Poems*, about thirty years of writing, my impression is that the thread that strings it together is my autobiography." His poetry and "91 Revere Street," the prose sketch that forms an important part of *Life Studies*, give glimpse after glimpse into the world of his childhood. He was born on March 1, 1917, into a home dominated by the incessant tension between his ineffectual father and his imperious mother. His father was a member of the famous Lowell family of Massachusetts, and his mother's prominent family, the Winslows, dated, like the Lowells, back to the early days of New England. The young Lowell felt acutely the strains of his childhood, and both his immediate family and his Puritan forebears would figure largely in his poetry.

In "91 Revere Street," Lowell described his experiences at the Brimmer Street School in Boston; he later attended preparatory school at St. Mark's in Southborough, Massachusetts, and then, briefly, Harvard University. But while he was a student at Harvard in 1937, he had a fight with his father and left home, a rebellion that had serious consequences for his life and his poetry. Lowell went south to the Tennessee home of poet Allen Tate, who proved to be an important influence on the young writer; in a 1961 *Paris Review* interview with Frederick Seidel, Lowell gave this account of his arrival at the Tate home: "Mrs. Tate . . . had three guests and her own family, and was doing the cooking and writing a novel. And this young man arrived, quite ardent and eccentric. I think I suggested that maybe I'd stay with them. And they said, 'We really haven't any room, you'd have to pitch a tent on the lawn.' So I went to Sears Roebuck and got a tent and rigged it on their lawn. The Tates were too polite to tell me that what they'd said had been just a figure of speech. I stayed two months in my tent and ate with the Tates."

Lowell crammed much activity into the next few years. He followed Tate to Kenyon College in Ohio; received a degree in classics, summa cum laude; met Randall Jarrell and Peter Taylor, two writers who would remain his lifelong friends; converted to Roman Catholicism; married the fiction writer Jean Stafford; refused induction into the armed forces; and served five months in jail as a conscientious objector. And during all this time, Lowell was working on the poems that would be published in *Land of Unlikeness* and *Lord Weary's Castle.*

The title of *Land of Unlikeness,* as Jerome Mazzaro points out in *The Poetic Themes of Robert Lowell,* is taken from a quotation of Saint Bernard and refers to the human soul's unlikeness to God and unlikeness to its own past self. In this volume, according to Hugh B. Staples in *Robert Lowell: The First Twenty Years,* the poet "appears so horrified by the spectacle of contemporary chaos that he can scarcely bring himself to comment on it in realistic terms. Cut off from the sight of God, modern man wanders about in his Land of Unlikeness, driven by greed and cruelty." But, as Mazzaro shows, some images of salvation also operate in these poems, images usually based on the figure of Mary or related in some other way to Roman Catholic beliefs.

Many of the poems in *Land of Unlikeness* appear as well in Lowell's second volume, *Lord Weary's Castle,* and the two books address the same concerns. Staples says that in these poems "the conflicts . . . remain unresolved, and the theme of rebellion remains dominant." Randall Jarrell declares in an essay collected in *Poetry and the Age* that these poems "understand the world as a sort of conflict of opposites. In this struggle one opposite is that cake of custom in which all of us lie embedded. . . . Into this realm of necessity the poems push everything that is closed, turned inward, incestuous, that blinds or binds: the Old Law, imperialism, militarism, capitalism, Calvinism, Authority, the Father, the 'proper Bostonians,' the rich who will 'do everything for the poor except get off their backs.' But struggling within this like leaven, falling to it like light, is everything that is free or open, that grows or is willing to change: . . . this is the realm of freedom, of the Grace that has replaced the Law, of the perfect liberator whom the poet calls Christ."

Lord Weary's Castle, with its blending of oppositions to war, to the Puritan ethic, and to materialism and greed, is Lowell's finest early volume, one that earned him the Pulitzer Prize in 1947. But his next book, *The Mills of the Kavanaughs,* was less successful. By the time of its publication in 1951, Lowell had been divorced from Jean Stafford, had left the Roman Catholic church, had suffered the first serious attack of the manic-depressive illness that was to plague him throughout his life, and had married the writer Elizabeth Hardwick. *The Mills of the Kavanaughs,* which consists of a series of dramatic monologues, reflects, like the other volumes, the turbulence of its writer's life.

Between the publication of *The Mills of the Kavanaughs* and the publication in 1959 of *Life Studies,* Lowell taught at several universities and made a speaking tour of the west coast, where he encountered the thematically and stylistically revolutionary poetry of Allen Ginsberg and the other "Beat" writers. He continued the friendship he had earlier begun with the poet William Carlos Williams, who as an innovator in language and forms began to have an important influence on his work. Lowell and Hardwick lived primarily in Boston during this time; the poet taught for several years at Boston University, and their daughter Harriet was born in 1957. During this period, Lowell continued to suffer attacks of mania and depres-

sion, and for a while found it difficult to write. "When I was working on *Life Studies,*" he revealed in his *Salmagundi* essay, "I found I had no language or meter that would allow me to approximate what I saw or remembered. Yet in prose I had already found what I wanted, the conventional style of autobiography and reminiscence. So I wrote my autobiographical poetry in a style I thought I had discovered in [French novelist Gustave] Flaubert, one that used images and ironic or amusing particulars. I did all kinds of tricks with meter and the avoidance of meter. . . . I didn't have to bang words into rhyme and count."

In an essay appearing in *Next-to-Last Things: New Poems and Essays,* Stanley Kunitz has called *Life Studies,* which won the 1960 National Book Award, "perhaps the most influential book of modern verse since [T. S. Eliot's] *The Waste Land.*" There is no question but that its so-called "confessional" poetry was something radically new in American literature. As Marjorie Perloff declares in *The Poetic Art of Robert Lowell,* this new poetry "is informal and autobiographical; its diction is casual and colloquial, its sound patterns tend to be almost prosaic." Discussing the important poem "Skunk Hour," Perloff says that the "One dark night" of that poem—"the painful moment of terror and anxiety that leads to a renewal of self-insight and understanding—this is the central experience that Lowell's self undergoes." Some readers were troubled by the personal nature of many of the poems in this volume; several of the works deal with Lowell's reminiscences of childhood and include often unflattering portraits of his parents and grandparents, while others deal with his marriage, his illness, and other aspects of his adult life. But *Life Studies,* very different from both his own earlier work and most of the verse being written in English by anyone else, had an enormous influence on the future of poetry in the United States.

In 1960, Lowell moved to New York, where he was to live for the next ten years; beginning in 1963 he commuted on a more or less regular basis to Harvard, where he taught intermittently until his death in 1977. In 1961, Lowell published two volumes, a verse translation called *Phaedra* of Racine's tragedy, and *Imitations,* a collection of loose translations of poems by writers from Homer to the contemporary Italian, Eugenio Montale. Although these volumes might appear to be a radical change from the personal poetry of *Life Studies,* Irvin Ehrenpreis says in an essay appearing in *American Poetry* that in *Imitations* Lowell "is legitimizing his progeny, replacing the Lowells and Winslows by [the poets Charles-Pierre] Baudelaire, [Arthur] Rimbaud, and [Rainer Maria] Rilke. In drawing up such a genealogical tree, Lowell . . . implies that he has found his essential identity not in a social class or in a religious communion but in his character as a writer."

With the publication in the mid-1960s of *The Old Glory* and *For the Union Dead,* Lowell returned to a consideration of the individual's relation to history, both in its personal and in its public dimensions. *The Old Glory* consists of three plays: "Endecott and the Red Cross" and "My Kinsman, Major Molineux," both adapted from short stories by Nathaniel Hawthorne, and "Benito Cereno," adapted from a novella by Herman Melville. In his introduction to the plays, Robert Brustein says that "Mr. Lowell feels the past working in his very bones. And it is his subtle achievement not only to have evoked this past, but also to have superimposed the present upon it, so that the plays manage to look forward and backward at the same time." All the plays incorporate some aspect of conflict between individuals and authority and thus look back to Lowell's earlier poetry, as well as outward to the political turmoil of the 1960s.

In a *Salmagundi* essay Thomas Parkinson declares, "The person in history is the main subject" of *For the Union Dead,* "and it is good to see poetry treating the moment where person and history meet." In an essay collected in Jonathan Price's *Critics on Robert Lowell,* Richard Poirier agrees: "It is nearly impossible in Lowell's poetry to separate personal breakdown from the poet's visions of public or historical decline. . . . The assurance that the poet's most private experiences simply *are* of historical, even mythical, importance" gives this poetry "an extraordinary air of personal authority." Many of these poems are as personal as the works in *Life Studies,* but here they are anchored more firmly in the world outside the family, the world of history and myth. "More than any contemporary writer, poet or novelist," Poirier asserts, "Lowell has created the language, cool and violent all at once, of contemporary introspection. He is our truest historian."

Of *For the Union Dead,* Lowell said in "After Reading Six or Seven Essays on Me" that "free verse subjects seemed to melt away, and I found myself back in strict meter, yet tried to avoid the symbols and heroics of my first books." In his next collection, *Near the Ocean,* he wrote a long sequence in eight-line four-foot couplet stanzas, a form he borrowed from the seventeenth-century English poet Andrew Marvell; "God knows why, except that it seemed fit to handle national events," Lowell remarked in the same essay. The publication of *Near the Ocean* coincided with the period of Lowell's most active involvement in national events. He protested against United States involvement in Vietnam, and in fact appears as a character in Norman Mailer's *The Armies of the Night,* an account of the historic protest march on the Pentagon in 1967.

Besides his books of poetry, Lowell continued in the late 1960s to write for the theater. The revised edition of *The Old Glory* was published in 1968, with most of the revisions appearing in "Endecott and the Red Cross." "What I have added are mostly Indians," Lowell said, only partly in jest, in his note on the revised edition. "It has been lengthened to give it substance," and "innumerable lines have been 'improved' to be stronger, to be quieter, less in character, more in character." His translation of Aeschylus's *Prometheus Bound* also appeared during this period; Lowell's is a prose version of the myth of this famous rebel.

In 1969 Lowell also published the first of what would become a series of volumes of sonnets. "For six years I wrote unrhymed blank verse sonnets," he recalled in his *Salmagundi* essay. "They had the eloquence at best of iambic pentameter, and often the structure and climaxes of sonnets. . . . I had a chance such as I had never had before, or probably will again, to snatch up and verse the marvelous varieties of the moment." Lowell's plan, says Steven Gould Axelrod in *Robert Lowell: Life and Art,* was "to achieve the balance of freedom and order, discontinuty and continuity, that he observed in [Wallace] Stevens's late long poems and in John Berryman's *Dream Songs,* then nearing completion. He hoped that his form . . . would enable him 'to describe the immediate instant,' an instant in which political and personal happenings interacted with a lifetime's accumulation of memories, dreams, and knowledge. In his 'jagged' yet unified poem Lowell sought to create nothing less than an epic of his own consciousness."

In his "Afterthought" to *Notebook 1967-68,* the first version of this epic, Lowell explained that "the poems in this book are written as one poem." The plot, he said, "rolls with the

seasons": "The time is a summer, an autumn, a winter, a spring, another summer; here the poem ends, except for turned-back bits of fall and winter 1968. I have flashbacks to what I remember, and notes on old history." Axelrod, who sees Lowell's political activism as the "motive and thematic center" for this volume, suggests that the "real subject" of the volume is "the human lust for violence and the moral horror of violence, a polarity Lowell has long detected in his own character and which he now discerns on a massive scale throughout human history." In the course of the volume, Axelrod continues, Lowell "obsessively exposes the violent acts of 'the great,' among them Caligula, Mohammed, Henry VIII, Marie Antoinette, Napoleon, Frederick the Great, the Russian Czars, Lenin, Stalin, Mao, the Indian killers, Andrew Jackson, Truman, an unnamed 'leader of the left,' and the book's darkest villain, Adolf Hitler."

But these sonnets are full of personal history as well, and this history is equally bleak. Axelrod suggests that in the next volume of sonnets, *Notebook,* which consists largely of revised and rearranged versions of the poems in *Notebook 1967-68,* "the theme of Lowell's increasingly troubled domestic life" comes to the fore, while the political emphasis is somewhat muted. He continues to juxtapose personal and public history, however, and jumbles together in the volume and in individual poems his friends, his family, historical figures, writers, artists, and characters from literature and myth. In the eight sonnets that make up the "Charles River" sequence, for example, he refers, among other subjects, to his parents, his first love, M.I.T., Harvard, industrial pollution, Milton's "Lycidas," the *Anschluss,* Nero, Christ, French painter Claude Lorrain, miscellaneous Greeks, aqueducts and arches, a snow-yellow knife with eleven blades, and plowshares beaten into swords. He conflates the particular and the general, the fresh and the hackneyed, the present and the past into an amalgam of poetry that ranges in quality from outstanding to outrageous.

In 1970 Lowell moved to England, where he spent most of his next six years; for two of these years he taught at Essex University, although he also returned to Harvard for one semester each year. The British had been favorably disposed to Lowell's poetry from the beginning; indeed, the British publisher Faber & Faber brought out editions of Lowell's poetry throughout his career, and in 1962 had published Staples's *Robert Lowell,* the first important critical book on the poet. Lowell's move to England was in part a result of continuing personal and domestic turmoil; in 1972 he was divorced from Elizabeth Hardwick and married to the British writer Caroline Blackwood, with whom he had a son, Robert Sheridan Lowell.

Among the three volumes of poetry published by Lowell in 1973, two are made up primarily of poems from *Notebook. For Lizzie and Harriet* is a slender volume reprinting *Notebook* sonnets that deal with Lowell's personal life, while *History,* as its title suggests, is more ambitious in scope. For *History,* Lowell added some new sonnets and revised and rearranged the old ones; the result is a much more coherent volume, arranged in the chronology of historical time. In this book, Axelrod says, Lowell downplays the once-dominant theme of political revolt and "expunges the theme of married love from the poem entirely. Instead, he expands upon two of the minor themes of the preceding volumes, making them central to his new conception"—the theme of death and the theme of art. "Art, the triumph of consciousness, counters death, the cessation of consciousness," Axelrod declares, but, as the critic notes, "Lowell suffers from no illusion that art affords immortality; rather he views art as proof of existence and means of creating identity. Throughout his career he has struggled to close the gap between life and artwork, and in *History* the two have finally joined.'' This volume, says Axelrod, ''seeks to reveal not the truth of the past but the truth of Lowell's mind as it meditates upon the past in terms of its inmost concerns.''

Although *The Dolphin*, the third volume of Lowell's poetry published in 1973, was like the others in that it consisted of a series of sonnets, these sonnets were all new. In *Robert Lowell: An Introduction to the Poetry,* Mark Rudman observes that this book ''charts a year, from summer to summer. The plot, such as it is, revolves around the breakup with his wife, Elizabeth Hardwick, and his relationship with Caroline Blackwood.'' Calling the volume ''half memoir'' and ''half fiction,'' Axelrod says that ''it is a book of changes, not only of 'changing marriages' but of changing minds (Lowell's, Caroline's, Lizzie's) and changing lives. On this level *The Dolphin* is about human freedom and growth. And it is supremely a poem about love, love that makes freedom meaningful, love that allows for human growth. The figure of love in the poem is Caroline, the dolphin and mermaid. . . . In the largest sense Caroline as dolphin stands for Lowell's loving relationship to the universe. His opening himself to her represents his opening to the world outside himself; his physical and spiritual union with her represents his union with his world. His love for the dolphin brings him to earth and rescues his life.''

Critical reception of *The Dolphin* was mixed, with some readers objecting strenuously to Lowell's use of language taken directly from the personal letters of Elizabeth Hardwick. But the volume is not simply a collection of poems about family turmoil; Axelrod finds a second subject of *The Dolphin* to be ''the process of the poem itself. As Lowell tells his love story, he simultaneously meditates upon his consciousness, which through invention and intense perception becomes imagination, which in turn through inspired craft becomes art. On this level the poem explores the interrelationship of being, consciousness, and art.'' Although some critics found the poetry unsatisfying, *The Dolphin* was awarded the 1974 Pulitzer Prize for poetry.

After the flurry of sonnets that culminated in the publication of the three 1973 volumes, collections of Lowell's poems appeared in England (*Robert Lowell's Poems: A Selection*) and in the United States (*Selected Poems*). Lowell's translation of *The Oresteia of Aeschylus* would not be published until 1978, but his last volume of new poetry, *Day by Day,* appeared shortly before he died on September 12, 1977. With this volume, Lowell abandoned the sonnet form and returned to free verse. He returned as well for a last look at many of the situations and people whom he had incorporated into his earlier poetry. *Day by Day,* which won the National Book Critics Circle Award in 1978, is an elegiac and deeply personal volume that discusses Lowell's family and friends, his wives and children, the horrors of his illness and the joys of his recoveries. As J. D. McClatchy observes in the *American Poetry Review,* the poems are like a series of snapshots—quick glimpses of past and present moments.

In a note prefacing his *Selected Poems,* Lowell remarked that ''my verse autobiography sometimes fictionalizes plot and particular''; by labeling his poems ''verse autobiography,'' he called attention to the inseparable relation between his life and his art. At the end of his life he left England and Caroline Blackwood and returned to the United States and Elizabeth Hardwick. After his death from congestive heart failure his funeral was held at the Episcopal Church of the Advent on Brimmer Street, in Boston, near where he had lived and gone to school as a child; he was buried in the cemetery where generations of his family had been buried. Thus he returned to his beginnings in his life as well as in his poetry.

Lowell said in the ''Afterthought'' to *Notebook 1967-68* that ''in truth I seem to have felt mostly the joys of living; in remembering, in recording, thanks to the gift of the Muse, it is the pain.'' A poetry of scrupulous self-examination, Lowell's work, as Vereen M. Bell declares in *Robert Lowell: Nihilist as Hero,* ''is identifiable by nothing so much as its chronic and eventually systematic pessimism''; indeed, says Bell, ''whatever spirit of affirmation that we think we perceive in Lowell's work we must always suspect ourselves of projecting upon it.'' Furthermore, in *Pity the Monsters: The Political Vision of Robert Lowell,* Alan Williamson observes that ''Lowell's vision of civilization—being a product both of the man he is and of the time he lives in—is particular, painful, and dark. It is redeemed neither by . . . faith that an adequate, if authoritarian, utopia may have existed in the past, nor by a revolutionary's faith that one can be abstractly yet accurately designed for the future. Consequently, Lowell must necessarily leave more questions of value, of cause and responsibility, of fundamental 'human nature' open to poetic inquiry than did his nearest predecessors. But it is this very appalling fundamentalness of Lowell's questions, combined with his honesty about historical terror, that make him a modern epic poet.''

Lowell was an epic poet as well in the scope and greatness of his poetry. He addressed large questions, and he used a multiplicity of forms and styles in his continuing quest, which his friend Peter Taylor describes in a 1979 *Ploughshares* essay as a search for ''a oneness in himself and a oneness in the world.'' ''This is how he must always be remembered,'' Taylor says, ''one moment playful to the point of violent provocation, the next in profound contemplation of the great mystery: What does life mean? What is it all about?''

BIOGRAPHICAL/CRITICAL SOURCES:

BOOKS

Anzilotti, Rolando, editor, *Robert Lowell: A Tribute,* Nistri-Lischi Editori (Pisa), 1979.
Axelrod, Steven Gould, *Robert Lowell: Life and Art,* Princeton University Press, 1978.
Alexrod, and Helen Deese, editors, *Robert Lowell: A Reference Guide,* G. K. Hall, 1982.
Axelrod and Deese, editors, *Robert Lowell: Essays on the Poetry,* Cambridge University Press, 1986.
Bell, Vereen M., *Robert Lowell: Nihilist as Hero,* Harvard University Press, 1983.
Berryman, John, *The Freedom of the Poet,* Farrar, Straus, 1976.
Bogan, Louise, *Selected Criticism: Prose and Poetry,* Noonday, 1955.
Breslin, James E. B., *From Modern to Contemporary: American Poetry, 1945-1965,* University of Chicago Press, 1984.
Brooks, Cleanth, and Robert Penn Warren, editors, *Conversations on the Craft of Poetry,* Holt, 1961.
Brustein, Robert, *Seasons of Discontent: Dramatic Opinions, 1959-1965,* Simon & Schuster, 1967.
Cambon, Glauco, *The Inclusive Flame: Studies in Modern American Poetry,* Indiana University Press, 1963.
Clurman, Harold, *The Naked Image: Observations on the Modern Theatre,* Macmillan, 1966.
Contemporary Authors Bibliographical Series, Volume 2: *American Poets,* Gale, 1986.

Contemporary Literary Criticism, Gale, Volume 1, 1973, Volume 2, 1974, Volume 3, 1975, Volume 4, 1975, Volume 5, 1976, Volume 8, 1978, Volume 9, 1978, Volume 11, 1979, Volume 15, 1980, Volume 37, 1986.

Cooper, Philip, *The Autobiographical Myth of Robert Lowell*, University of North Carolina Press, 1970.

Cosgrave, Patrick, *The Public Poetry of Robert Lowell*, Gollancz, 1970, Taplinger, 1972.

Crick, John, *Robert Lowell*, Oliver & Boyd, 1974.

Deutsch, Babette, *Poetry in Our Time*, Holt, 1952, revised edition, Doubleday, 1963.

Dictionary of Literary Biography, Volume 5: *American Poets since World War II*, Gale, 1980.

Dillard, R. H. W., George Garrett, and John Rees Moore, editors, *The Sounder Few: Essays from the Hollins Critic*, University of Georgia Press, 1971.

Donoghue, Denis, *Connoisseurs of Chaos: Ideas of Order in American Poetry*, Macmillan, 1965.

Ehrenpreis, Irvin, editor, *American Poetry*, St. Martin's, 1965.

Fein, Richard J., *Robert Lowell*, Twayne, 1970, 2nd edition, 1979.

Frankenberg, Lloyd, *Pleasure Dome: On Reading Modern Poetry*, Houghton, 1949.

Hamilton, Ian, *Robert Lowell: A Biography*, Random House, 1982.

Heymann, C. David, *American Aristocracy: The Lives and Times of James Russell, Amy, and Robert Lowell*, Dodd, 1980.

Hungerford, Edward, editor, *Poets in Progress*, Northwestern University Press, 1962, new edition, 1967.

Jarrell, Randall, *Poetry and the Age*, Knopf, 1953, reprinted, Vintage, 1959.

Jarrell, *The Third Book of Criticism*, Farrar, Straus, 1969.

Kalstone, David, *Five Temperaments: Elizabeth Bishop, Robert Lowell, James Merrill, Adrienne Rich, John Ashbery*, Oxford University Prses, 1977.

Kazin, Alfred, *Contemporaries*, Little, Brown, 1962.

Kazin, *New York Jew*, Knopf, 1978.

Kostelanetz, Richard, *On Contemporary Literature: An Anthology of Critical Essays on the Major Movements and Writers of Contemporary Literature*, Avon, 1964.

Kunitz, Stanley, *Next-to-Last Things: New Poems and Essays*, Atlantic Monthly, 1985.

London, Michael, and Robert Boyars, editors, *Robert Lowell: A Portrait of the Artist in His Time*, David Lewis, 1970.

Lowell, Robert, *Land of Unlikeness*, Cummington Press, 1944, reprinted, University Microfilms, 1971.

Lowell, *Lord Weary's Castle*, Harcourt, 1946, reprinted, 1985.

Lowell, *The Mills of the Kavanaughs*, Harcourt, 1951.

Lowell, *Life Studies*, Farrar, Straus & Cudahy, 1959, 2nd edition, Faber, 1968.

Lowell, *For the Union Dead*, Farrar, Straus, 1964.

Lowell, *Selected Poems*, Faber, 1965, reprinted, 1986.

Lowell, *The Old Glory*, introduction by Robert Brustein, Farrar, Straus, 1965, revised edition, 1968.

Lowell, *Near the Ocean*, Farrar, Straus, 1967.

Lowell, *Notebook 1967-68*, Farrar, Straus, 1969, 3rd edition revised and expanded as *Notebook*, 1970.

Lowell, *History*, Farrar, Straus, 1973.

Lowell, *For Lizzie and Harriet*, Farrar, Straus, 1973.

Lowell, *The Dolphin*, Farrar, Straus, 1973.

Lowell, *Robert Lowell's Poems: A Selection*, Faber, 1974.

Lowell, *Selected Poems*, Farrar, Straus, 1976, revised edition, 1977.

Lowell, *Day by Day*, Farrar, Straus, 1977.

Mailer, Norman, *The Armies of the Night*, New American Library, 1968.

Martin, Jay, *Robert Lowell*, University of Minnesota Press, 1970.

Mazzaro, Jerome, *The Achievement of Robert Lowell: 1939-1959*, University of Detroit Press, 1960.

Mazzaro, *The Poetic Themes of Robert Lowell*, University of Michigan Press, 1965.

Mazzaro, editor, *Profile of Robert Lowell*, Merrill, 1971.

Meiners, R. K., *Everything to Be Endured: An Essay on Robert Lowell and Modern Poetry*, University of Missouri Press, 1970.

Meyers, Jeffrey, editor, *Robert Lowell: Interviews and Memoirs*, University of Michigan Press, 1988.

Mills, Ralph J., *Cry of the Human: Essays on Contemporary Poetry*, University of Illinois Press, 1975.

Ostroff, Anthony, editor, *The Contemporary Poet as Artist and Critic*, Little, Brown, 1964.

Parkinson, Thomas Francis, editor, *Robert Lowell: A Collection of Critical Essays*, Prentice-Hall, 1968.

Perloff, Marjorie, *The Poetic Art of Robert Lowell*, Cornell University Press, 1973.

Plimpton, George, editor, *Writers at Work: "Paris Review" Interviews*, 2nd series, Viking, 1963.

Price, Jonathan, editor, *Critics on Robert Lowell*, University of Miami Press, 1972.

Procopiow, Norma, *Robert Lowell: The Poet and His Critics*, American Library Association, 1984.

Raffel, Burton, *Robert Lowell*, Ungar, 1981.

Rosenthal, M. L., *The Modern Poets: A Critical Introduction*, Oxford University Press, 1960.

Rosenthal, *The New Poets: American and British Poetry since World War II*, Oxford University Press, 1967.

Rudman, Mark, *Robert Lowell: An Introduction to the Poetry*, Columbia University Press, 1983.

Sexton, Anne, *Anne Sexton: A Self-Portrait in Letters*, edited by Linda Gray Sexton and Lois Ames, Houghton, 1977.

Simpson, Eileen, *Poets in Their Youth: A Memoir*, Random House, 1982.

Smith, Vivian, *The Poetry of Robert Lowell*, Sydney University Press, 1974.

Staples, Hugh B., *Robert Lowell: The First Twenty Years*, Faber, 1962, Farrar, Straus, 1962.

Stein, Jean, and George Plimpton, editors, *American Journey: The Times of Robert Kennedy*, Harcourt, 1970.

Steiner, George, *Language and Silence: Essays on Language, Literature, and the Inhuman*, Atheneum, 1967.

Stepanchev, Stephen, *American Poetry since 1945*, Harper, 1965.

Untermeyer, Louis, *Lives of the Poets: The Story of 1000 Years of English and American Poetry*, Simon & Schuster, 1959.

von Hallberg, Robert, *American Poetry and Culture: 1945-1980*, Harvard University Press, 1985.

Weatherhead, A. Kingsley, *The Edge of the Image*, University of Washington Press, 1967.

Williamson, Alan, *Pity the Monsters: The Political Vision of Robert Lowell*, Yale University Press, 1974.

Yenser, Stephen, *Circle to Circle: The Poetry of Robert Lowell*, University of California Press, 1975.

PERIODICALS

Agenda (special Lowell issue), autumn, 1980.
American Book Review, December, 1978-January, 1979.
American Literature, March, 1980.

American Poetry Review, Volume 7, number 5, 1978.
American Quarterly, fall, 1967, winter, 1970.
Antioch Review, spring, 1985.
Ariel, January, 1981.
Atlantic, January, 1952, July, 1959, July, 1982, June, 1983.
Book Week, October 11, 1964, February 20, 1966, January 29, 1967.
Book World, May 11, 1969.
Boundary 2, fall, 1972.
Christian Science Monitor, October 15, 1964, December 16, 1965, January 26, 1967, September 21, 1977.
Classical and Modern Literature, winter, 1981.
Commonweal, May 12, 1961, May 12, 1967, October 17, 1969.
Contemporary Literature, Volume 23, number 4, 1982.
Critic, April, 1966.
Criticism, winter, 1969.
Dissent, November/December, 1969.
Encounter, October, 1973, August, 1978, July, 1987.
English Language Notes, March, 1974.
English Literary History, winter, 1978.
Esquire, September, 1969.
Essays in Criticism, January, 1979.
Georgia Review, spring, 1971, summer, 1973.
Harvard Advocate (special Lowell issues), November, 1961, November, 1979.
Journal of Modern Literature, September, 1979.
Life, February 17, 1967.
Literary Review, spring, 1980.
London Review of Books, September 17, 1987.
Los Angeles Times Book Review, February 2, 1986.
Modern Drama, March, 1973.
Nation, January 18, 1947, September 19, 1959, October 26, 1964, January 24, 1966, December 23, 1968, July 7, 1969, May 19, 1979, April 11, 1987.
National Review, February 17, 1978, March 13, 1987, August 14, 1987.
New England Quarterly, March, 1971, December, 1972.
New Republic, June 8, 1959, October 17, 1964, July 7-14, 1973, July 17, 1976, November 20, 1976, November 26, 1977, June 30, 1979, March 30, 1987.
New Statesman, August 31, 1973, March 10, 1978, June 15, 1979.
Newsweek, October 12, 1964, September 6, 1976, September 5, 1977, April 27, 1987.
New York, July 7, 1969.
New Yorker, November 30, 1946, June 9, 1951.
New York Herald Tribune, February 7, 1966, February 9, 1966.
New York Herald Tribune Book Review, April 22, 1951, February 4, 1962.
New York Review of Books, November 23, 1967, October 28, 1976, October 27, 1977, February 9, 1978, March 8, 1979, March 3, 1988.
New York Times, November 3, 1946, April 22, 1951, May 3, 1959, April 4, 1976, July 18, 1976, July 7, 1987.
New York Times Book Review, May 28, 1961, October 4, 1964, January 15, 1967, September 3, 1967, June 15, 1969, April 4, 1971, July 18, 1976, August 14, 1977, October 16, 1977, December 3, 1978, April 8, 1979, July 12, 1987.
Observer, July 14, 1987.
Paris Review, Volume 25, 1961.
Partisan Review, fall, 1967, summer, 1968.
Philological Quarterly, spring, 1983.
Ploughshares, Volume 5, number 2, 1979.

PMLA, January, 1975.
Poetry, October, 1959, April, 1962, June, 1966, September, 1967, December, 1971, May, 1978.
Prose, Volume 6, 1973.
Review, Volume 20, 1969.
Salmagundi (special Lowell issues), fall/winter, 1966-1967, spring, 1977.
Saturday Review, September 2, 1967, May 3, 1969, September 6, 1969.
Saturday Review of Literature, November 16, 1946.
Sewanee Review, winter, 1978.
Spectator, July 18, 1987.
Texas Studies in Language and Literature, summer, 1973, winter, 1976.
Time, April 28, 1961, November 3, 1961, October 16, 1964, June 2, 1967, September 15, 1967, June 6, 1969, August 29, 1977.
Times (London), June 15, 1962, April 25, 1985.
Times Literary Supplement, August 3, 1967, December 25, 1970, August 10, 1973, January 25, 1980, July 10, 1987.
Tulane Drama Review, summer, 1967.
Twentieth Century Literature, October, 1971, spring, 1985.
Virginia Quarterly Review, summer, 1967, spring, 1968.
Washington Post Book World, January 28, 1979, August 2, 1987.
Weekly Book Review, November 24, 1946.
Yale Review, December, 1959, March, 1962, December, 1964, June, 1967, December, 1969.

OTHER

Lieberson, Goddard, *Benito Cereno by Robert Lowell* (recorded interview), Columbia Records, 1965.
Robert Lowell (filmed interview), National Educational Television, 1964.

OBITUARIES:

PERIODICALS

AB Bookman's Weekly, November 7, 1977.
New York Times, September 13-14, 1977.
Observer, September 18, 1977.
Washington Post, September 14, 1977.†

—*Sidelights by Katharine Wallingford*

*   *   *

LYALL, Gavin (Tudor) 1932-

PERSONAL: Born May 9, 1932, in Birmingham, England; son of Joseph Tudor (an accountant) and Ann (Hodgkiss) Lyall; married Katharine Whitehorn (a columnist), January 4, 1958; children: two sons. *Education:* Pembroke College, Cambridge, B.A. (with honors). *Religion:* Quaker.

ADDRESSES: Home—14 Provost Rd., London NW3, England. *Agent*—A. D. Peters & Co., 10 Buckingham St., London WC2N 6BU, England.

CAREER: Free-lance writer, 1963—. *Picture Post*, London, England, journalist, 1956-57; British Broadcasting Corp., London, television film director, 1958; *Sunday Times*, London, 1959-63, began as journalist, became aviation editor. Lyall has travelled as a staff journalist in Europe, the United States, Libya, India, Pakistan, Nepal, and Australia. *Military service:* Royal Air Force, 1951-53; became pilot officer.

MEMBER: Crime Writers' Association, Detection Club, Royal Air Force Club, Groucho Club.

WRITINGS:

ADVENTURE NOVELS

The Wrong Side of the Sky, Scribner, 1961.
The Most Dangerous Game, Scribner, 1963.
Midnight Plus One, Scribner, 1965.
Shooting Script, Scribner, 1966.
Venus with Pistol, Scribner, 1969.
Blame the Dead, Viking, 1973.
Judas Country, Viking, 1975.

"MAJOR MAXIM" SPY NOVEL SERIES

The Secret Servant, Viking, 1980.
The Conduct of Major Maxim, Hodder & Stoughton, 1982, Viking, 1983.
The Crocus List, Hodder & Stoughton, 1985, Viking, 1986.

OTHER

(Editor) *The War in the Air, 1939-1945: An Anthology of Personal Experience*, Hutchinson, 1968, published as *The War in the Air: The Royal Air Force in World War II*, Morrow, 1969.

WORK IN PROGRESS: A crime thriller; research on the history of military aviation.

SIDELIGHTS: Gavin Lyall's adventure thriller entitled *Venus with Pistol* received generally favorable reviews. Peter Parley of *Spectator* offers "all praise" for the book and recommends it "for those with a thirst for the find in the attic and a bottle of scotch in the third drawer down." Maurice Prior of *Books* comments that while the theme is "not . . . outrageously original," Lyall possesses a "nice lucid smooth style." Prior further notes that "any thinness in story-content" is offset by "effortless and studious" narration and concludes that *Venus with Pistol*, with Lyall's "inimitable stamp," is "cogent, neatly devised, with nicely-contrived denouement."

After having written several well-received adventure thrillers, Lyall moved into the genre of espionage with his book *The Secret Servant*. In the opinion of a London *Times* critic, *The Secret Servant* is "the richest [of all Lyall's books] yet, a new departure that has paid off handsomely." Although noting that the book lacks "steel-compressed intensity," this same reviewer applauds the book's "splendid readability" and proposes that it is "Le Carre made easy." Also pleased with Lyall's departure is *New York Times Book Review* contributor Peter Andrews. Andrews describes *The Secret Servant* as "neat, literate and deliciously cynical. . . . Lyall . . . knows how to lash a narrative from chapter to chapter pausing only for some judicious bloodletting along the way. . . . 'The Secret Servant' is a first-class piece of work." However, *Times Literary Supplement* reviewer T. J. Binyon found Lyall's change of genre disconcerting: "Anything by Gavin Lyall is bound to be original, intelligent and well-written. *The Secret Servant* is certainly all these things. . . . But with the move into the field of Deighton and le Carre has come the use of their kind of oblique, allusive dialogue, their kind of jargon. . . . *The Secret Servant* is exciting, very readable, and far better than most of its kind, but one still wishes that Gavin Lyall had stuck to his guns."

The Secret Servant evolved into a spy novel series with the reappearance of its trigger-happy protagonist British Army Major Harry Maxim, first in *The Conduct of Major Maxim* and then in *The Crocus List*. In two succeeding *Times Literary Supplement* reviews, Binyon concedes that the quality of *The Conduct of Major Maxim* will silence any doubts about Lyall's

genre switch and maintains that *The Crocus List* "is undoubtedly the best Harry Maxim yet. Brilliantly engineered and written with . . . elegance, it moves forward with the irresistible power of a Tiger tank." A few reviewers mention that *The Crocus List* starts off slow but that its pace quickens. The novel's opening scene describes a failed assassination attempt made on the President of the United States in Britain, the details of which Maxim must untangle. According to *Spectator* critic Harriet Waugh, "This is an exciting and well-plotted story and Harry Maxim is an odd, almost interesting hero—an honourable man who gets a kick out of killing."

AVOCATIONAL INTERESTS: Aviation, firearms, cats.

BIOGRAPHICAL/CRITICAL SOURCES:

PERIODICALS

Books, January, 1970.
Globe and Mail (Toronto), November 15, 1986.
New York Times Book Review, November 16, 1980, February 9, 1986.
Spectator, November 22, 1969, August 17, 1985.
Times (London), June 19, 1980.
Times Literary Supplement, June 20, 1980, December 31, 1982, June 21, 1985.
Washington Post Book World, March 2, 1986.

* * *

LYSTAD, Mary (Hanemann) 1928-

PERSONAL: Born April 11, 1928, in New Orleans, La.; daughter of James and Mary (Douglass) Hanemann; married Robert Lystad, June 20, 1953; children: Lisa Douglass, Anne Hanemann, Mary Lunde, Robert Douglass, James Hanemann. *Education:* Newcomb College, A.B. (cum laude), 1949; Columbia University, M.A., 1951; Tulane University of Louisiana, Ph.D., 1955.

ADDRESSES: Home—4900 Scarsdale Rd., Washington, D.C. 20016. *Office*—National Institute of Mental Health, 5600 Fishers Lane, Rockville, Md. 20857.

CAREER: Southeast Louisiana Hospital, Mandeville, fellow in social psychology, 1955-57; conducted field research in social psychology in Ghana, 1957-58; Charity Hospital of Louisiana, New Orleans, chief psychologist on collaborative child development project, 1958-61; American University, Washington, D.C., consultant to special operations research office, 1962; Voice of America, Washington, D.C., feature writer for African division, 1964-73; National Institute of Mental Health, Rockville, Md., 1973—, began as special assistant to director of special mental health programs, became chief of Center for Mental Health Studies of Emergencies, currently chief of Emergency Services Branch. Consultant to White House national goals research staff on youth, 1969-70.

AWARDS, HONORS: Children's book of the year awards, Child Study Association of America, 1968, for *Millicent the Monster*, 1972, for *James the Jaguar*, and 1973, for *Halloween Parade*.

WRITINGS:

Social Aspects of Alienation, U.S. Public Health Service, 1969.
As They See It: Changing Values of College Youth, Schenkman, 1973.
A Child's World as Seen in His Stories and Drawings, U.S. Department of Health, Education and Welfare, 1974.

Violence at Home, U.S. Department of Health, Education and Welfare, 1974.

From Dr. Mather to Dr. Seuss: 200 Years of American Books for Children, Schenkman, 1980.

At Home in America, Schenkman, 1983.

(Editor) *Innovations in Mental Health Services to Disaster Victims*, U.S. Department of Health and Human Services, 1985.

(Editor) *Violence in the Home: Interdisciplinary Perspectives*, Brunner/Mazel, 1986.

(Editor) *Mental Health Response to Mass Emergencies: Theory and Practice*, Brunner/Mazel, 1988.

JUVENILES; WITH SOCIAL PSYCHOLOGICAL THEMES

Millicent the Monster, Harlin Quist, 1968.

Jennifer Takes Over P.S. 94, Putnam, 1972.

James the Jaguar (Weekly Reader Book Club selection), Putnam, 1972.

That New Boy, Crown, 1973.

The Halloween Parade, Putnam, 1973.

OTHER

Contributor to academic journals.

SIDELIGHTS: Millicent the Monster has been published in French, German, and Danish.

M

MABEY, Richard (Thomas) 1941-

PERSONAL: Born February 20, 1941, in Berkhamsted, England; son of Thomas Gustavus (a bank official) and Nelly (Moore) Mabey. *Education:* St. Catherine's College, Oxford, B.A. (with honors), 1963, M.A., 1971. *Politics:* "Green."

ADDRESSES: Home—10 Cedar Rd., Berkhamsted, Hertfordshire, England. *Agent*—Richard Simon, 32 College Cross, London N.1, England.

CAREER: Dacorum College of Further Education, Hemel Hempstead, Hertfordshire, England, lecturer in social studies, 1963-65; Penguin Books Ltd., Education Division, Harmondsworth, Middlesex, England, senior editor, 1966-73; free-lance writer and broadcaster, 1973—. Visiting associate, St. Catherine's College, Oxford, 1982-86.

MEMBER: London Wildlife Trust (president), Nature Conservancy Council, Green Alliance.

AWARDS, HONORS: Information Book Award, *Times Educational Supplement,* 1977, for *Street Flowers;* Leverhulme research fellowship, 1983-84; Children's Science Book Award (younger category), New York Academy of Sciences, 1985, for *Oak and Company;* Whitbread Literary Award in biography, Booksellers Association of Great Britain, 1986, for *Gilbert White: A Biography of the Author of the Natural History of Selborne.*

WRITINGS:

(Editor) *Class: A Symposium,* Anthony Blond, 1967, Dufour, 1969.
Behind the Scene, Penguin, 1968.
The Pop Process, Hutchinson, 1969.
Food for Free: Guide to Edible Wild Plants of Britain, drawings by Marjorie Blamey, Collins, 1972.
Connexions: A Series of Topic Books for Students in Schools and Colleges of Further Education, Penguin, 1972.
Children in Primary School: The Learning Experience, Penguin, 1972.
The Unofficial Countryside, Collins, 1973.
The Roadside Wildlife Book, David & Charles, 1974.
The Pollution Handbook: The ACE-"Sunday Times" Clean Air and Water Surveys, Penguin, 1974.
Street Flowers (illustrated by Sarah Kensington), Kestrel, 1976.

(Editor and author of introduction) Gilbert White, *The Natural History of Selborne,* Penguin, 1977.
Plants with a Purpose: A Guide to the Everyday Uses of Wild Plants (drawings by Marjorie Blamey), Collins, 1977.
(With David Mabey) *In Search of Food: Traditional Eating and Drinking in Britain,* Macdonald & Jane's, 1978.
The Common Ground: A Place for Nature in Britain's Future?, Hutchinson, 1980.
(With Tony Evans) *The Flowering of Britain,* Hutchinson, 1980.
(With Francesca Greenoak) *Back to the Roots,* Arrow, 1983.
(Compiler) *Cold Comforts: An Almanack of the Best and Worst of Britain's Weather,* Hutchinson, 1983.
In a Green Shade: Essays on Landscape, 1970-1983, Hutchinson, 1983.
Oak and Company (illustrated by Clare Roberts), Greenwillow Books, 1983.
(Editor and author of introduction) Richard Jefferies, *Landscape with Figures: An Anthology of Prose,* Penguin, 1983.
Nature in Your Basket: Wild Plants That You Can Pick and Eat, Reader's Digest (London), 1984.
(Editor with Susan Clifford and Angela King) *Second Nature,* Cape, 1984.
The Frampton Flora, Century, 1985, Prentice Hall, 1986.
Gilbert White: A Biography of the Author of the Natural History of Selborne, Century, 1986.
(Editor and author of introduction) Thomas Hill, *The Gardener's Labyrinth: The First English Gardening Book,* Oxford University Press, 1987.

Also author of numerous broadcasts for British Broadcasting Corp. (BBC-TV). Contributor to numerous periodicals, including *Country Living, Good Housekeeping, Harper's and Queen, Independent, Listener, Nature, New Scientist, New Society, Times* (London), and *Vole.*

WORK IN PROGRESS: A history of botanical illustration at Kew Gardens; an autobiographical/historical study of love of place, tentatively entitled *Home Country;* editing, with Greenoak, the journals of Gilbert White.

SIDELIGHTS: Richard Mabey is regarded as one of Great Britain's foremost nature writers. Over the last fifteen years he has authored a number of books which, according to Colin Ward in *Times Educational Supplement,* rank him "as quite the best of our 'country writers,' enthusiastic and informative on flora and fauna, delighting in the natural world, and anxious to share it with his fellow citizens.'' Reviewers have praised Mabey's works for being both informative and engaging. His 1973 *The Unofficial Countryside*, an account of wildlife in unlikely urban environments, ''is a discursive, pleasing and very personal book by a committed naturalist,'' writes a reviewer for the *Times Literary Supplement*. John Fowles adds in the *New Statesman* that ''Mabey writes with a sympathetic blend of self-humour, poetry and science about his own sharp-eyed finds in and around London.'' Similarly, Mabey's books display a combined respect, enthusiasm, and knowledge regarding things of nature. In *The Flowering of Britain*, Mabey has an ability to ''communicate his feelings to the reader, making us share his wonder, for example, at the indestructibility of our wild plants,'' writes Ruth Isabel Ross in the *Times Literary Supplement*. Andrew Clements in *New Statesman* praises the same book for being ''as much a work of enthusiasm as it is an ecological study or a conservationist's manifesto. . . . Scientific learning is worn lightly in this lucid history; botanical facts are interwoven with folklore and legend in its portrait of woodland and field, mountain and wasteland.''

Mabey's knowledge and enthusiasm regarding the natural world is also easily adapted to younger audiences, as demonstrated in his books *Street Flowers* and *Oak and Company*. The former possesses, according to a reviewer in *Growing Point*, ''the essential qualities of a good information book for the young. . . . It is lucid; it is easy in manner and accurate and selective in detail; it is elegantly and usefully illustrated; above all, it has a *voice*.'' Regarding *Oak and Company*, which traces the life of a 283-year-old oak tree, Cynthia Marquand writes in the *Christian Science Monitor* that Mabey has told ''a superb story for budding naturalists'' and that ''the exquisite array of colorful drawings makes it all the more enjoyable.'' A reviewer in *Scientific American* comments that ''in this beautifully illustrated book young readers will share the long, slow story of an oak'' at a pace, appropriately, ''slow and majestic.''

Mabey's *In a Green Shade: Essays on Landscape, 1970-1983* brought together over a decade of his writings, most of which had previously been published in periodicals. Stephen Mills of the *Times Literary Supplement* comments that the collection includes ''erudite little reappraisals of [naturalists] Richard Jefferies and Gilbert White, portraits of favourite landscapes colourfully dotted with local history and anecdote, and samples, twelve years old now, of [Mabey's] own pioneering investigations into the natural history of factory waste grounds.'' Ward adds that unlike some writers on country landscapes, Mabey avoids ''a self-indulgent nostalgia for a make-believe rural past. . . . There is no corrupt grief or phoney nostalgia in his collection of occasional pieces, the very slightest of which are full of rare common sense, elegantly and wittily expressed.'' Neil Philip in the *Times Education Supplement* concludes that Mabey ''writes lucidly and to the point'' in his essays, and that ''each piece looks from its different angle at the same question: what is man's relationship to landscape, and what should it be?''

Mabey's more recent *Gilbert White: A Biography of the Author of the Natural History of Selborne* has been praised as an insightful portrayal of the influential eighteenth-century naturalist and clergyman. According to David Allen in the *London Review of Books*, Mabey's book ''is all that we would expect of natural history's leading contemporary stylist: an admirable well-written study which is full of original insights born of a profound familiarity with country things.'' Fiona MacCarthy concurs in the London *Times*, writing that Mabey ''has had a

deep rapport with White the man and with White's countryside. He has done his fieldwork with a manic assiduity, trampling Selborne's sunken lanes, and exploring in great detail White's dense, luxuriant, and *muddled* English landscape.'' Oliver Rackham concludes in *Spectator* that ''Mabey himself shares [the] qualities of his hero: he is one of the most vivid ecological writers of our time, and he still has a sense of wonder and delight.''

BIOGRAPHICAL/CRITICAL SOURCES:

PERIODICALS

Christian Science Monitor, October 7, 1983.
Growing Point, January, 1977, May, 1983.
Listener, September 4, 1980, January 19, 1984, July 4, 1985.
London Review of Books, January 22, 1987.
New Statesman, December 14, 1973, July 30, 1982.
New Yorker, September 22, 1986.
Scientific American, December, 1983.
Spectator, July 19, 1986.
Times (London), November 27, 1986.
Times Educational Supplement, July 13, 1984, January 25, 1985, September 6, 1985.
Times Literary Supplement, December 15, 1972, March 15, 1974, March 25, 1977, December 12, 1980, October 26, 1984, December 18-24, 1987.

*   *   *

MALPEDE, Karen (Sophia)   1945- (Karen Taylor)

PERSONAL: Born June 29, 1945, in Wichita Falls, Tex.; daughter of Joseph James Malpede (a certified accountant) and Doris Jane (Liebschultz) Malpede Isrig; children: Carrie Sophia. *Education:* University of Wisconsin, B.S. (with honors), 1967; Columbia University, M.F.A., 1971. *Politics:* Anarchist. *Religion:* ''Nonviolence.''

ADDRESSES: Home—160 Washington Park, Brooklyn, N.Y. 11205.

CAREER: Writer and editor. New Cycle Theater, Brooklyn, N.Y., co-founder and resident playwright, 1976-85. Member of field faculty, Norwich University, 1979—; visiting lecturer, Smith College, 1982-86; adjunct faculty, Tisch School of the Arts, New York University, 1986—; conductor of playwriting workshops, 1986—; lecturer, School of Continuing Education, New York University, 1988. Has given lectures and readings at universities, festivals, and conventions across the United States.

MEMBER: PEN American Center, Dramatists Guild.

AWARDS, HONORS: Production grants, Windward Foundation, 1976, 1977; PEN Writers Grant, 1981; Creative Artists Public Service grant, 1982-83; Smith College travel grant, 1984; finalist, Broadcloth Series of New Plays, At the Foot of the Mountain, 1984; Harnish Fund for Visiting Artists, Smith College, 1985; Ludwig Vogelstein Foundation Writer's Grant, 1987.

WRITINGS:

(Under name Karen Taylor) *People's Theater in Amerika*, Drama Book Publishers, 1972.
(Editor with Joseph Chaikin) *Three Works by the Open Theater*, Drama Book Specialists, 1974.
(Editor) *Women in Theater: Compassion and Hope*, Drama Book Specialists, 1983.

PLAYS

"A Lament for Three Women" (also see below), first produced in Cummington, Mass., 1974, produced in Brooklyn, N.Y., at the New Cycle Theater, 1977.

Rebeccah (first produced by Playwrights Horizons, 1974), New Cycle Theater, 1975.

The End of War (also see below; first produced in Dallas at Richland College, April, 1976, produced in Brooklyn at the Arts at St. Ann's, June, 1982), privately printed, 1977.

"Making Peace: A Fantasy," first produced in Brooklyn at the New Cycle Theater, 1979.

(Contributor) Rachel France, editor, *A Century of Plays by American Women* (contains "A Lament for Three Women"), Richards Rosen, 1979.

"A Monster Has Stolen the Sun" (also see below), first produced in part in Brooklyn at the Arts at St. Ann's, January, 1981, first produced in its entirety in Trenton, N.J., at the Passage Theater, 1988.

"Sappho and Aphrodite" (also see below), first produced in Northampton, Mass., at Smith College, summer, 1984, produced in New York at the Perry Street Theater, December, 1984, produced in London at The Oval House, October 16, 1987.

"Us," first produced in New York at the Theater for the New City, December 17, 1987.

A Monster Has Stolen the Sun and Other Plays (contains "A Monster has Stolen the Sun," "Sappho and Aphrodite," and "The End of War"), Marlboro, 1987.

OTHER

Contributor of articles and reviews to professional journals.

SIDELIGHTS: Karen Malpede "is a poet, and a politically committed person," commented stage producer Judith Malina to *New York Times* contributor Rosette C. Lamont. "She's not afraid to write the kind of words which are not usually heard on the stage, words most people dare not voice to themselves, even on the psychiatrist's couch." Much of Malpede's work is avant-garde and surreal; as she remarked in *Interviews with Contemporary Women Playwrights,* "What interested me most as a potential playwright (I didn't dare know I was a playwright yet) about the work I researched for *People's Theatre* [*in Amerika*] was that the prevalent form of American theater, realism, seemed so completely inadequate for expressing the highest aspirations of people. I was interested in how the realistic form was being stretched or even discarded because I felt that here was the real area of exploration if one wanted to make a theater which would reveal the divine in us." This "theater of the divine" was the tradition upon which Malpede first drew in her own writing; a tradition, she comments, that was somewhat paradoxical for her as a woman. If theater's purpose, as a friend once defined for her, is to reveal "man's" divinity, this purpose contained an "inherent contradiction, because in order for me to reveal the divine in 'man' I had to come to feminism," she recalled in her interview. "There was no other way, I had to come to an understanding of the divine in women. Now I can truly be one within a long tradition of people who believe that theater is a way to reveal the spirit, the deep essence, the unrealized desires, the true holiness of humankind."

Commenting in *Interviews* on the role of women in contemporary theater, Malpede said: "It's not until very recently that women have had a collective sense of being history makers. It's not until faced with nuclear disaster that the relationships between the sexes have seemed so inadequate to our future as a race that women in large numbers, and feelingful men as well, have had to break with history and assert ourselves as individuals and as culturally responsible people." The playwright continues: "At this moment, of course, you have an explosion of women working in the theater, because the theater is that place where a society in crisis asserts itself and explores new values."

BIOGRAPHICAL/CRITICAL SOURCES:

BOOKS

Barolini, Helen, editor, *The Dream Book: An Anthology of Writings by Italian American Women,* Schocken, 1985.
Betsko, Kathleen, and Rachel Koenig, editors, *Interviews with Contemporary Women Playwrights,* Beech Tree Books, 1987.
Chinoy, Helen Krich, and Linda Walsh Jenkins, editors, *Women in American Theater,* Crown, 1981.

PERIODICALS

New York Times, December 13, 1987, December 28, 1987.
Washington Post Book World, September 2, 1973.

*   *   *

MANO, D. Keith   1942-

PERSONAL: Born February 12, 1942, in New York, N.Y.; son of William Franz (a business executive) and Marion Elizabeth (Minor) Mano; married Jo Margaret McArthur, August 3, 1964 (divorced, 1979); married Laurie E. Kennedy (an actress), July 18, 1980; children: (first marriage) Roderick Keith, Christopher Carey. *Education:* Columbia University, B.A. (summa cum laude), 1963. *Politics:* Conservative. *Religion:* Eastern Orthodox.

ADDRESSES: Home—392 Central Park West, Apt. 6P, New York, N.Y. 11025.

CAREER: Writer. X-Pando Corp. (building materials manufacturer), Long Island City, N.Y., vice-president, 1965-86. Actor with Marlowe Society in England, 1963-64, and with National Shakespeare Company, 1964-65.

AWARDS, HONORS: Kellet Fellow, Clare College, Cambridge, 1963-64; Woodrow Wilson fellowship, 1965-66; *Bishop's Progress* named one of year's ten best novels, 1968, by *Time;* Modern Language Association award, 1969, for *Bishop's Progress; Playboy* nonfiction award, 1977.

WRITINGS:

NOVELS

Bishop's Progress, Houghton, 1968.
Horn, Houghton, 1969.
War Is Heaven!, Doubleday, 1970.
The Death and Life of Harry Goth, Knopf, 1971.
The Proselytizer, Knopf, 1972.
The Bridge, Knopf, 1973.
Take Five, Doubleday, 1982.

OTHER

"Resistance," first produced in New York at the Judith Anderson Theater, June 2, 1988.

Also author of scripts for "St. Elsewhere" television series. Contributor to *People, Esquire, Sports Illustrated, Playboy, New York Times Book Review,* and other publications. Contributing editor and author of column, "The Gimlet Eye,"

National Review, 1972—; former film reviewer and contributing editor, *Oui.*

SIDELIGHTS: D. Keith Mano is a novelist whose books are inventive, satirical, and extravagant. "He is," Joan Reardon explains in the *Los Angeles Times,* "a razzle-dazzle kind of writer—a Renaissance man reincarnated as a magical word processor." "Just a little too much is just enough for Mr. Mano," claims Geoffrey Wolff of the *New York Times Book Review.* "Not for him peace and quiet, the ordinary. He cherishes crisis, calamity and farce; he drives at full throttle, straight pipes howling." Underneath the surface turmoil, however, his stories speak of religious salvation in a society lacking moral values. "As a novelist," Mano writes in his article for the *Contemporary Authors Autobiography Series,* "I am a conservative, committed to Western traditions. I consider myself a Christian writer, though some reviewers have called me a Christian pornographer. . . . In my novels I have tried to relate traditional Christianity to the concerns of the modern world."

Between 1968 and 1973, Mano published six novels in quick succession. These books established his reputation as what Peter S. Prescott of *Newsweek* calls "one of our most exciting younger writers." His first novel, *Bishop's Progress,* the story of an ailing bishop's spiritual rebirth during a twelve-day stay in a hospital, won two major awards and moved R. V. Cassill, writing in the *New York Times Book Review,* to remark that "the luminous talents of D. Keith Mano have produced a work which is, at the same time, witty, disturbing, entertaining, grave, full of suspense, and a prolonged meditation on the riddle of faith in our epoch." But the novel also contains some humor which several reviewers found distasteful. Gillian Tindall of the *New Statesman* believes that "instead of revealing the true predicament of his central character . . . Mr. Mano obscures it with the purely gruesome [such as] a sadistic doctor [who] botches injections and enemas." But Barry H. Leeds, in an article for *Saturday Review,* finds that *Bishop's Progress* sets the pattern for the serious concerns of Mano's later fiction. The novel, "which recounted the pilgrimage of a spiritually lazy bishop from imminent damnation to salvation through suffering and a new recognition of his own mortality," Leeds writes, "forms the keystone of a carefully structured body of work."

Horn, Mano's second novel, also concerns a clergyman. In this story an Episcopal priest is sent to a church in Harlem, where he encounters and tries to accomodate Horn, the leader of a black power group. The priest's efforts to make peace with Horn lead him to a better understanding of racial tensions. As Arthur Curley writes in *Library Journal,* "black-white (as well as black-black and white-white) differences and relationships emerge as complex and subtle matters which can never be understood in terms of social cliches, either pernicious or well-intentioned in nature." Despite the differences between the two men, they develop an admiration and respect for each other. Although Shane Stevens of *Book World* complains that "the usual fare of racist rallies, sex orgy and firebombings" can be found in *Horn,* Stephen F. Caldwell of the *New York Times Book Review* finds the novel to be "a fine young writer's tale about two men who might reasonably expect to find the worst in the other but instead find the best."

Mano turned to the subject of war in *War Is Heaven!,* a look at a U.S. military intervention in a Central American conflict. "As were Mano's first two books, . . ." remarks Caldwell, "'War Is Heaven!' is about the complexity and ambiguity of good and evil." The story focuses on two soldiers who rep-

resent opposing views of religious belief. Sergeant Clarence Hook has a strong faith, while Corpsman Andrew Jones is a sour nonbeliever. Their conversations about their roles in the war reveal the tensions and paradoxes of the situation. L. J. Davis of *Book World* calls *War Is Heaven!* "disturbing, powerful, and often downright irritating. . . . Mano's book, nevertheless, remains a work of considerable imaginative power."

The Death and Life of Harry Goth is a black comedy in which Harry Goth, an industrial sanitation supply salesman, learns that he is dying of leukemia. This discovery paradoxically gives him a renewed energy for life. In the course of the story most of Harry's eccentric family is killed, he gets bloated and bald from a quack cancer cure, and, following the advice of his hermit brother, he hides away in his house, refusing to confront the world. "Mano," Tom McHale writes in the *New York Times Book Review,* "is a gutsy writer with an extravagant vision of the universe. His real genius . . . is in somehow keeping a funeral ship, heavily laden with pathos and parable, afloat, while it is buffeted by howling gales of laughter." Frank Day, writing in the *Dictionary of Literary Biography,* calls the novel "talented black humor, deft and wicked, reminiscent of Evelyn Waugh."

In *The Proselytizer,* Mano tells the story of television evangelist Kris Lane, an excessive and perverse man whose sexual exploits are fully depicted in the course of the novel. "There is no note of hope, no celebration of indomitable spirit," Leeds maintains. "Instead, there is compassion in this black humor and real wisdom. This is not as enjoyable a book as *Bishop's Progress* or *Harry Goth,* nor is it as well balanced between high seriousness and humor; yet it takes Mano's vision a step farther than those books did. And it may be more difficult to forget." But other critics found fault with *The Proselytizer.* Writing in the *New York Times Book Review,* Geoffrey Wolff admits that Mano "manages some startling scenes. He pushes the vocabulary of sexual congress beyond its previous boundaries. . . . But he has left out whatever it is that translates little losers like Harry Goth into great fictional characters." Prescott, too, was disappointed by the book. "A miss for Mano this time," he comments, "but like most misses by really good authors, it makes better reading than most bland successes."

In 1973, Mano published *The Bridge,* a novel set in the distant future in a world free of all forms of environmental pollution. The cost for such a clean environment, however, has been high. Plant, animal, and insect life flourish everywhere, nearly overrunning human life. Strict governmental prohibitions prevent many kinds of activity. Those who ate meat have been put to death. One character, Dominick Priest, comes to learn of Christianity and converts. But his knowledge of the religion is incomplete, and the manner in which he practices his faith includes the cannibalistic slaughter of primitives. The novel's disturbing subject matter bothered some critics. J. F. Cotter of *America,* for example, maintains: "I cannot remember reading a more repellent novel. . . . I would never read a book like this of my own sweet will." But R. V. Williams of *Best Sellers* claims that "Mano's striking imagery, his slashing irreverence, the savagery of his satire, and the never-ceasing drive of his imagination make the reading of this book a provocative and deeply troubling experience."

It was not until 1982 that Mano published his next novel, *Take Five.* The idea for the book took hold of him shortly after writing *The Bridge,* but writing it took some nine years. "I'm very proud of myself for having hung in all those years," Mano tells C. H. Simonds of *National Review.* He adds, "There were times when I could have just given up, times when I couldn't even remember who the characters were.''

Mano did a tremendous volume of work for magazines during the years he spent writing *Take Five*, including articles for *Playboy*, *Oui*, and other men's magazines. In his article for the *Contemporary Authors Autobiography Series*, Mano notes the many unusual experiences he underwent to produce these stories: ''I lived as a transvestite; had my skeleton bent by Rolfers; sank, glub, underwater in a rebirthing tank. I met incestuous fathers and people who knew all about cannibalism. I gave blood; pretended I was a wino; went under hypnosis; had myself put away in a goofy garage.'' These experiences were relayed in what Mano describes as his ''side-of-the-mouth, attention-hooking voice. . . . When your prose is in direct visual competition with soft, nubile young women all set for some antic hay, you better talk *loud*, brother.''

Some of the extravagance of Mano's nonfiction reappears in *Take Five*, ''a picaresque epic which satirizes contemporary politics, sexuality and religion,'' according to Jack Sullivan of the *Washington Post*. It is, Sullivan believes, ''full of energy, invention and great gusts of hot air.'' John Leonard of the *New York Times* explains that *Take Five* ''is long enough for three ordinary novels.'' Because the protagonist, Simon Lynxx, is an unappealing, obnoxious character, the novel proved a challenge for some reviewers to evaluate. As Sullivan remarks, ''It is difficult to convey in a short review the full unpleasantness and tedium of [Simon's] ugly tantrums.''

Take Five traces the story of filmmaker Simon Lynxx as he tries to raise money for his latest project, a film entitled ''Jesus 2001''. During the course of the novel, which is told in Joycean verbal pyrotechnics and is loaded with wild humor, Simon loses his physical senses one by one, ending up completely cut off from the world around him. It is at this point that Simon attains spiritual salvation. ''No man,'' Hugh Kenner comments in the *National Review*, ''has ever found a crazier way to write a book about the Christian faith.''

Simon Lynxx attracts the most comments from reviewers, primarily because of his outspoken opinions on sexual and racial questions. He is, V. D. Balitas notes in *America*, ''a boisterous, obscene (his language wearies as it combines a pseudo-Wildean wit, the raunchiness of the legendary longshoreman and an exaggerated bigotry reminiscent of Bunker and Rickles), egotistical young film maker.'' Through this character, Mano comments satirically on a number of topics. ''More than half of 'Take Five' is hilarious, even when it is vile,'' notes Leonard. ''Mr. Mano speaks in many tongues, all of them vipers. What he tells us about Hollywood, the art world, Episcopalianism, homosexuality, Jewish motherhood, black huckstering, Eastern religion, Queens night life, Freud . . . and white dwarves is savage, but it is also very, very funny. You will laugh, and then feel guilty about it.'' Some critics were harsh on Mano for creating a character like Simon. Writing in *Nation*, Gerald Jay Goldberg finds Simon to be a ''sexist, racist, bigot and bully, with an ego the size of Quasimodo's hump.''

The novel itself had its share of criticism as well. Sullivan complains that *Take Five* ''is clever, even virtuosic, but it is ultimately only an intellectual good-old-boy novel.'' Robert M. Adams, in an article for the *New York Review of Books*, finds that Simon's conversion at novel's end is unconvincing. ''Simon the capering, obnoxious punchinello is the mainspring

of the action; at least some of the pieties that he joyfully desecrates deserve the vigorous boot he gives them,'' Adams writes. ''That pious ending seems to leave the door uncomfortably open to cheap edification.''

But many critics find much to praise in *Take Five*. Leonard calls it ''a novel about 300 years of American history, a low-budget movie singing the song of assimilation. It is a novel about art, especially modernist art; its many parodies, puns and anagrams serve as a thesis on the nature of metaphor and play.'' Leonard sees Simon's ultimate salvation to be well handled by Mano: ''The last 40 pages . . . depict salvation as persuasively as Joyce did damnation in 'Portrait of the Artist as a Young Man.''' Reardon concludes that *Take Five* ''challenges a reader's better judgement; its hero makes Prometheus look like a pussy cat, and its sheer verbal pushiness cowers an audience into attention. Simon Lynxx said it best: 'Only outrages—howls—get any air time in this society.'''

Writing in his contribution to the *Contemporary Authors Autobiography Series*, Mano explains how he reconciles the sometimes offensive material found in his novels with his basically Christian message. ''In a profane age,'' he states, ''the profane must be taken unawares and in their own tongue. . . . You might say that the end, doubtful as it is, cannot justify the means. But the Flood was a means. Saint Paul's blindness. And the crucifixion. God does not go gently into our self-imposed night.''

BIOGRAPHICAL/CRITICAL SOURCES:

BOOKS

Contemporary Authors Autobiography Series, Volume 6, Gale, 1988.
Contemporary Literary Criticism, Gale, Volume 2, 1974, Volume 10, 1979.
Dictionary of Literary Biography, Volume 6: *American Novelists since World War II*, second series, Gale, 1980.
Mano, D. Keith, *Take Five*, Doubleday, 1982.

PERIODICALS

America, October 27, 1973, August 7-14, 1982.
Best Sellers, September 15, 1973.
Book World, March 23, 1969, May 10, 1970.
Christianity and Literature, spring, 1979.
Hudson Review, autumn, 1972.
Library Journal, April 1, 1969.
Los Angeles Times, July 15, 1982.
Nation, June 26, 1982.
National Review, August 11, 1970, June 11, 1982, May 27, 1983.
New Statesman, February 7, 1969.
Newsweek, April 5, 1971, March 27, 1972.
New Yorker, April 8, 1972.
New York Review of Books, June 10, 1982.
New York Times, April 30, 1982, June 8, 1988.
New York Times Book Review, February 18, 1968, March 9, 1969, June 21, 1970, March 14, 1971, April 23, 1972, May 23, 1982.
Prairie Schooner, winter, 1968-69.
Saturday Review, July 15, 1972.
Time, April 18, 1969, April 20, 1970, September 10, 1973.
Times Literary Supplement, June 11, 1970.
Washington Post, July 17, 1982.

—*Sketch by Thomas Wiloch*

MARLOWE, Amy Bell
[Collective pseudonym]

WRITINGS:

"AMY BELL MARLOWE'S BOOKS FOR GIRLS"

The Oldest of Four; or, Natalie's Way Out, Grosset & Dunlap, 1914.

The Girls of Hillcrest Farm; or, The Secret of the Rocks, Grosset & Dunlap, 1914.

A Little Miss Nobody; or, With the Girls of Pinewood Hall, Grosset & Dunlap, 1914.

The Girl from Sunset Ranch; or, Alone in a Great City, Grosset & Dunlap, 1914.

Wyn's Camping Days; or, The Outing of the Go-Ahead Club, Grosset & Dunlap, 1914.

Frances of the Ranges; or, The Old Ranchman's Treasure, Grosset & Dunlap, 1915.

The Girls of Rivercliff School; or, Beth Baldwin's Resolve (also see below), Grosset & Dunlap, 1916.

Sunset Ranch, Grosset & Dunlap, 1933.

"ORIOLE" SERIES

When Oriole Came to Harbor Light (also see below), Grosset & Dunlap, 1920.

When Oriole Travelled Westward (also see below), Grosset & Dunlap, 1921.

When Oriole Went to Boarding School (also see below), Grosset & Dunlap, 1927.

Oriole's Adventures: Four Complete Adventure Books for Girls in One Big Volume (contains *When Oriole Came to Harbor Light, When Oriole Travelled Westward, When Oriole Went to Boarding School*, and *The Girls of Rivercliff School*), Grosset & Dunlap, 1933.

SIDELIGHTS: The "Amy Bell Marlowe Books for Girls" series did not share the same characters or focus on a single theme, but were advertised by Grosset & Dunlap as a series. The publishers also described them as "somewhat of the style of Miss [Louisa May] Alcott," but brought up to date. For more information see the entries for Harriet S. Adams, Edward L. Stratemeyer, and Andrew E. Svenson.

BIOGRAPHICAL/CRITICAL SOURCES:

BOOKS

Johnson, Deidre, editor and compiler, *Stratemeyer Pseudonyms and Series Books: An Annotated Checklist of Stratemeyer and Stratemeyer Syndicate Publications*, Greenwood Press, 1982.

*   *   *

MARROW, Stanley B.   1931-

PERSONAL: Born February 10, 1931, in Baghdad, Iraq; son of Behjet J. and Victoria (Korkis) Marrow. *Education:* Boston College, A.B., 1954, A.M., 1955, Ph.L., 1955, S.T.L., 1962; Pontifical Biblical Institute, Rome, S.S.L., 1964; Pontifical Gregorian University, Rome, S.T.D., 1966.

ADDRESSES: Home and office—Weston College School of Theology, 3 Phillips Pl., Cambridge, Mass. 02138.

CAREER: Roman Catholic priest of Society of Jesus (Jesuits), Al-Hikma University, Baghdad, Iraq, chairman of theology department, 1966-68; Pontifical Biblical Institute, Rome, Italy, associate professor, 1968-71; Weston College School of Theology, Cambridge, Mass., 1971—, began as associate professor, currently professor of New Testament.

MEMBER: Catholic Biblical Association of America, American Academy of Religion, Society for Biblical Literature, Society of New Testament Studies.

WRITINGS:

(With Wilhelm Kutsch) *Commentary on Aristotle's Peri Hermeneias (De Interpretatione)*, Imprimerie Catholique (Beirut), 1958.

The Christ in Jesus, Paulist Press, 1968.

(Contributor) R. J. Clifford and G. W. MacRae, editors, *The Word in the World*, Weston College Press, 1973.

Basic Tools of Biblical Exegesis, Biblical Institute Press, 1978.

The Words of Jesus in Our Gospels, Paulist Press, 1979.

Speaking the Word Fearlessly: Boldness in the New Testament, Paulist Press, 1982.

Paul: His Letters and His Theology, Paulist Press, 1986.

(Editor with D. J. Harrington) MacRae, *Studies in the New Testament and Gnosticism*, Michael Glazier, 1987.

(Contributor) L. Richard, editor, *Vatican II: The Unfinished Agenda*, Paulist Press, 1987.

Compiler of index to *Biblica*, Volumes XXVI-L, 1945-1969. Also contributor to *New Catholic Encyclopedia*. Associate editor of *New Testament Abstracts*, 1972—, and *Catholic Biblical Quarterly*, 1980-87.

*   *   *

MARSH, Mary Val   1925-

PERSONAL: Born April 28, 1925, in Uniontown, Pa.; daughter of Roy William (an osteopathic physician) and Mary (a teacher; maiden name, Hickman) Marsh; married Dwight Ellsworth Twist (a school superintendent), August 4, 1962; stepchildren: Barbara (Mrs. Roger A. Williams), Charles Russell. *Education:* University of California, Los Angeles, B.A., 1946; Claremont Graduate School, M.A., 1953. *Politics:* Republican. *Religion:* Presbyterian.

ADDRESSES: Home—879 Rosecrans St., San Diego, Calif. 92106.

CAREER: Elementary school teacher in Redlands, Calif., 1946-48; San Bernadino County Department of Education, San Bernadino, Calif., curriculum consultant, 1948-52, music coordinator, 1952-59; music supervisor for public schools in Beverly Hills, Calif., 1959-62; San Diego State University, San Diego, Calif., part-time lecturer in music education, 1963-73; free-lance writer, music arranger, and consultant in music education, 1973—. Faculty member at University of Redlands, Claremont Graduate School and University Center, and Idyllwild School of Music and the Arts; director of music education workshops in the United States and Canada. Member of Music Educators National Conference-Ford Foundation "Contemporary Music Project" Committee, San Diego, 1963-65; supervisor of local "Opera Participation Project for Youth," 1971-75; member of board of directors of Civic Youth Orchestra, 1976—.

MEMBER: International Society for Music Education, Music Educators National Conference (life member), California Music Educators Association (life member), Sigma Alpha Iota, Delta Kappa Gamma, Pi Lambda Theta, P.E.O. Sisterhood.

WRITINGS:

Choruses and Carols (for unchanged voices), Summy-Birchard, 1964.

Here a Song, There a Song (for elementary and junior high school choruses), Shawnee Press, 1969.

Explore and Discover Music: Creative Approaches to Music Education in Elementary, Middle, and Junior High Schools, Macmillan, 1970.

(With Carroll Rinehart and Edith Savage) *The Spectrum of Music* (textbook series for elementary and junior high school), Macmillan, 1974-75, 1978, 1980, 1983.

(With Carroll Rinehart) *Wish I Had a Song: Music for Today's Children* (with record or cassette), Alfred Publishing, 1987.

CHORAL COMPOSITIONS AND ARRANGEMENTS

Aardvarks on the Ark, Alfred Publishing, 1978.
Singin' a Song, Alfred Publishing, 1980.
Watah Come a Me Eye, Alfred Publishing, 1982.
I'd Rather Be Sailing, Alfred Publishing, 1982.
Linstead Market, Alfred Publishing, 1983.
Sing for America, Alfred Publishing, 1984.
The Yellow Sun, Alfred Publishing, 1985.
Christmas Time, Alfred Publishing, 1988.
I Have Music, Alfred Publishing, 1988.

OTHER

Contributor to *Music Educators Journal.* Editor, *CMEA News,* 1978-82, and *Soundings,* 1982-86.

WORK IN PROGRESS: Choral arranging and composing; additional music textbook materials; *Wish I Had Another Song.*

SIDELIGHTS: Mary Val Marsh writes *CA:* "I am committed to the belief that arts education is essential to improving the quality of life for all, and that without a commitment to the arts, a culture will gradually deteriorate. Only as children and youth encounter the arts in meaningful situations will they develop aesthetic sensitivity. As a specialist in music education, I believe that *creating music* is one of the most effective means of learning about music and of developing a continuing interest in it. This belief led me a number of years ago to organize an experimental creative music class, which subsequently led to my writing of *Explore and Discover Music.*"

*   *   *

MARTIN, Eugene
[Collective pseudonym]

WRITINGS:

"SKY FLYERS" SERIES

Randy Starr after an Air Prize; or, The Sky Flyers in a Dash down the States, Henry Altemus, 1931.

. . . above Stormy Seas; or, The Sky Flyers on a Perilous Journey, Henry Altemus, 1931.

. . . Leading the Air Circus; or, The Sky Flyers in a Daring Stunt, Henry Altemus, 1932.

. . . Tracing the Air Spy; or, The Sky Flyers Seeking the Stolen Plane, Henry Altemus, 1933.

SIDELIGHTS: The "Sky Flyers" books told the story of Randy Starr, a boy who "yearns for what nearly every American boy does—a pilot's license," according to the Henry Altemus Company series advertisements. The series chronicled his adventures in winning his wings. For additional information see the entries for Harriet S. Adams, Edward L. Stratemeyer, and Andrew E. Svenson.

BIOGRAPHICAL/CRITICAL SOURCES:

BOOKS

Johnson, Deidre, editor and compiler, *Stratemeyer Pseudonyms and Series Books: An Annotated Checklist of Stratemeyer and Stratemeyer Syndicate Publications,* Greenwood Press, 1982.

*   *   *

MARTIN, Tony   1942-

PERSONAL: Born February 21, 1942, in Port-of-Spain, Trinidad and Tobago; son of Claude G. and Vida (Scope) Martin. *Education:* Honourable Society of Gray's Inn, Barrister-at-Law, 1965; University of Hull, B.Sc. (with honors), 1968; Michigan State University, M.A., 1970, Ph.D., 1973.

ADDRESSES: Office—Department of Black Studies, Wellesley College, Wellesley, Mass. 02181.

CAREER: Called to English Bar, 1966, and to Trinidad Bar, 1969; accounts clerk in Water Department, Trinidad Public Service, 1961; accounts clerk, Office of the Prime Minister, Federal Government of the West Indies, Trinidad and Tobago, 1961-62; master of Latin, French, Spanish, English, history, and geography, St. Mary's College, Trinidad and Tobago, 1962-63; lecturer in economics and politics, Cipriani Labour College, Trinidad and Tobago, 1968-69; Michigan State University, East Lansing, instructor in history, 1970-71; University of Michigan—Flint, assistant professor of history and coordinator of African-Afro-American studies program, 1971-73; Wellesley College, Wellesley, Mass., associate professor, 1973-79, professor of black studies, 1979—, chairman of department, 1976-78, 1981-84, and 1985—. Visiting professor at Brandeis University, fall, 1974 and 1981, and at University of Minnesota, fall, 1975; visiting professor at Colorado College, 1985 and 1986.

MEMBER: Association for the Study of Afro-American Life and History, African Heritage Studies Association (member of executive board, 1982), Association of Caribbean Historians (member of executive board, 1985-86, 1986-87), National Council for Black Studies (vice-president of New England region, 1984-86), Organization of American Historians.

WRITINGS:

Race First: The Ideological and Organizational Struggles of Marcus Garvey and the Universal Negro Improvement Association, Greenwood Press, 1976.

(Co-author) *Rare Afro-Americana: A Reconstruction of the Adger Library,* G. K. Hall, 1981.

(Editor) *The Poetical Works of Marcus Garvey,* Majority Press, 1983.

Literary Garveyism: Garvey, Black Arts, and the Harlem Renaissance, Majority Press, 1983.

Marcus Garvey, Hero, Majority Press, 1983.

The Pan-African Connection: From Slavery to Garvey and Beyond, Majority Press, 1984.

(Editor) *In Nobody's Backyard: The Grenada Revolution in Its Own Words,* Majority Press, Volume I: *The Revolution at Home,* 1984, Volume II: *Facing the World,* 1985.

(Editor) Marcus Garvey, *Message to the People: The Course of African Philosophy,* Majority Press, 1986.

Amy Ashwood Garvey: Pan-Africanist, Feminist, and Wife Number One, Majority Press, 1988.

(Editor) *African Fundamentalism: A Literary Anthology of the Garvey Movement*, Majority Press, 1989.

Also author of pamphlets. Contributor of numerous articles and reviews to professional journals, including *Negro History Bulletin, American Historical Review, Journal of Modern African Studies, African Studies Review, Journal of Negro History, Mazungumzo, Race,* and *Journal of Human Relations.* Guest editor, *Pan-African Journal,* 1974.

WORK IN PROGRESS: African Fundamentalism; Audrey Jeffers, a biography; *Auntie Kay,* a biography.

*   *   *

MARVIN X
See El MUHAJIR

*   *   *

MASTERSON, J. B.
See EDMONDSON, G. C.

*   *   *

MATHES, W(illiam) Michael   1936-

PERSONAL: Born April 15, 1936, in Los Angeles, Calif.; son of William C. (a U.S. district judge) and Rilla (Moore) Mathes. *Education:* Loyola University, Los Angeles, Calif., B.S., 1957; University of Southern California, M.A., 1962; University of New Mexico, Ph.D., 1966. *Religion:* Roman Catholic.

ADDRESSES: Home—P.O. Box 1227, Sonoma, Calif. 95476. *Office*—Department of History, University of San Francisco, San Francisco, Calif. 94117.

CAREER: University of New Mexico, Albuquerque, special collections librarian in Coronado Room, 1963-65; University of San Francisco, San Francisco, Calif., assistant professor, 1966-71, associate professor, 1971-75, professor of history, 1975—. Taught course at Universidad Autonoma de Guadalajara, 1978; visiting professor at "First History Week" observance at Universidade Federal do Acre (Brazil), 1978, and at Colegio de Michoacan (Mexico), 1981. Academico supernumerario, Academia de la Historia de Occidente Guadalajara, and academico, Academia Sudcaliforniana de la Historia, La Paz, both 1982—; academico, El Colegio de Historia, Guadalajara, 1984—. Agente de canje, National Archives of Mexico, 1960-74; "Pablo L. Martinez" Historical Archives, La Paz, technical director, 1974-77, director of microfilming project, 1975-76; Commission of the Californias, archivist-historian, 1975—, and chairman of history committee, 1982—; Patronato para la Preservacion del Patromonio Historico-Cultural de Baja California Sur, assessor, 1975-77, secretary, 1977-78; cultural representative, Camara Nacional de Comercio, Ensenada, Baja California, 1977; special researcher, Centro de Investigaciones Historicas of Universidad Nacional Autonoma de Mexico and Universidad Autonoma de Baja California, 1977—; special representative to Archivo General de las Indias for Bancroft Library of University of California, 1981; honorary curator of Mexican collection of California State Library—Sutro Branch, 1981—; technical director, microfilm project in the Archivo Historico de Zacatecas, Bancroft Library, 1986—. California Historical Society, associate editor, 1967-69, review editor, 1981—, member of publications committee, 1982—; San Diego Historical Society, advisory editor, 1970-74, member of board of editors, 1981—; member of board of editors, Universidad de Baja California Sur, 1977—. Member of Serra bicentennial commission, 1984—; corresponding member, Academia Mexicana de la Historia, 1985—. Consultant, Oakland Museum, 1967-69; advisor-consultant, Automobile Club of Southern California, 1975-76; consultant, Depot Museum, Sonoma Valley Historical Society, Consejo Consultive del Archivo del Poder Ejecutivo, Estado de Baja California Sur, and Museo del Hombre, Naturaleza y Cultura, all 1982—, and National Geographic Society, California State Library, and Mundus Novus Foundation, 1984—.

MEMBER: American Historical Association, American Catholic Historical Association, Westerners International (member of executive board, 1978—), Western Historical Association, Asociacion Cultural de las Californias (representative, 1983—), California Historical Society, San Diego Historical Society, Sigma Delta Pi (honorary member), Phi Alpha Theta.

AWARDS, HONORS: Fulbright grant to Spain, 1962-63; Del Amo fellow in Spain, 1965-66; California Historical Society, award of merit, 1977, for contributions to California history, and Henry R. Wagner Memorial Award, 1979; Diploma de Merito, Universidade Federal do Acre (Brazil), 1978; certificate of award, Sonoma Valley Historical Society, and Medalla de Plata, Asociacion Espanola de Amigos de los Castillos, Madrid, both 1984; Condecoracion del Orden del Aguila Azteca, Secretaria de Relaciones Exteriores, Mexico, 1985.

WRITINGS:

(Editor) *Californiana* (in Spanish), seven volumes, J. Porrua Turanzas (Madrid), 1965-72.

(Editor) *Documentos para la historia de la demarcacion comercial de California, 1583-1632* (title means "Documents for the History of the Commercial Charting of California"), J. Porrua Turanzas, 1965.

(Transcriber, translator, and author of annotations) Juan Cavallero Carranco, *The Pearl Hunters in the Gulf of California, 1668,* Dawson's Book Shop, 1966.

Vizcaino and Spanish Expansion in the Pacific Ocean, 1580-1630, California Historical Society, 1968.

(Editor) *Documentos para la historia de la explotacion comercial de California, 1611-1679* (title means "Documents for the History of Commercial Exploitation of California"), J. Porrua Turzanas, 1968.

(Editor) Eusebio Francisco Kino, *First from the Gulf to the Pacific,* Dawson's Book Shop, 1969.

(Transcriber, translator, and author of annotations) *The Capture of "Santa Ana," Cabo San Lucas, November, 1587: The Accounts of Francis Pretty, Antonio de Sierra, and Tomas de Alzola,* Dawson's Book Shop, 1969.

Reparo a errores de la navegacion espanola (title means "Correction of Errors in Spanish Navigation"), J. Porrua Turanzas, 1970.

To Save a City: The Desague, Americas, 1970.

The Conquistador in California: The Voyage of Fernando Cortes to Baja California in Chronicles and Documents, 1535, Dawson's Book Shop, 1973.

A Brief History of the Land of Calafia: The Californias, 1533-1795, Gobierno del Territorio de Baja California Sur (La Paz, Mexico), 1974, 2nd edition, Patronato del estudiante sud-californiano, 1977.

Geographic and Hydrographic Descriptions of Many Northern and Southern Lands and Seas in the Indies: Specifically of the Discovery of the Kingdom of California (1632), Dawson's Book Shop, 1974.

Spanish Approaches to the Island of California, 1628-1632, Book Club of California, 1975.

(Contributor) *Some California Catholic Reminiscences for the United States Bicentennial,* Knights of Columbus (Los Angeles), 1976.

Piratas en la costa de Nueva Galicia en el siglo XVII (title means "Pirates on the Coast of New Galicia during the Seventeenth Century"), Libreria Font (Guadalajara), 1976.

Las misiones de Baja California—The Missions of Baja California: Una resena historica-fotografica—An Historical-Photographic Survey, Gobierno del Estado de Baja California Sur, 1977.

Cattle Brands of Baja California Sur, 1809-1885: Los registros de marcas de Baja California Sur, Dawson's Book Shop-Archivo Historico de Baja California Sur "Pablo L. Martinez," 1978.

Cortes en California, 1535, Universidad Autonoma de Baja California (Mexicali, Mexico), 1978.

Clemente Guillen: Explorer of the South, Dawson's Book Shop, 1979.

(Contributor) *Cabrillo and His Compatriots: The Explorers and Their Expeditions,* Cabrillo Historical Association, 1979.

Baja California cartografica: Catalogo de mapas, planos y disenos del siglo XIX que se encuentran en el Archivo Historico de Baja California Sur "Pablo L. Martinez" (title means "Cartographic Baja California: A Catalog of Maps, Plans, and Designs from the Nineteenth Century Found in the 'Pablo L. Martinez' Historical Archives of Baja California Sur"), Gobierno del Estado de Baja California Sur, 1979.

Missions, with photographs by Stanley Truman, California Historical Society, 1980.

Obras californianas del Padre Miguel Venegas, S.J., Universidad Autonoma de Baja California Sur, five volumes, 1980.

(Co-editor) Miguel del Barco, *The Natural History of Baja California,* Dawson's Book Shop, 1980.

(Author of prologue) Coronado, *Kino y Salvatierra en la Conquista de las Californias,* FONAPAS, 1981.

(With John H. R. Polt) *Vignettes of Early California: Childhood Reminiscences of Juan Bautista Alvarado,* Book Club of California, 1982.

(With J. Andres Cota Sandoval) *Importancia de Cabo San Lucas,* FONAPAS, 1982.

Santa Crus de Tlatelolco: La primera biblioteca academica de las Americas, Secretaria de relaciones exteriores, 1982, English translation published as *The America's First Academic Library: Santa Cruz de Tlatelolco,* California State Library Foundation, 1985.

(Author of prologue) Lopez, *Documentalia Novogalaica en los archivos de Espana,* Editorial Rocinante, 1982.

(Translator) Muria, *A Thumbnail History of Guadalajara,* Editorial Colomos, 1983.

Las defensas de Mexico en 1824 (monograph), Universidad Autonoma de Nuevo Leon, 1983.

Mexico on Stone: Lithography in Mexico, 1826-1900, Book Club of California, 1984.

La geografia mitologica de California: Origenes, desarrollo, concrecion y desaparicion (monograph), Academia Mexicana de la Historia, 1984.

Pensil Americano, edited by Ignacio Carrillo Perez, Edmundo

Avina Levy, 1985.

Un centro cultural novogalaico: La biblioteca del convento de San Francisco de Guadalajara en 1610, Instituto Cultural Cabanas, 1986.

Contributor of articles and reviews to journals, including *Pacific Historian, Journal of San Diego History, Hispanic American Historical Review, California Quarterly,* and *Western Historical Quarterly.* Member of board of editors, *Calafia,* 1977—, *Meyibo,* 1977—, and *California History,* 1982—; member of editorial committee, *The Californians,* 1982—. Editorial consultant, *The Journal of San Diego History,* 1975-80.

WORK IN PROGRESS: Research on the history of California in the seventeenth century, on the history of printing in colonial Mexico, and on the history of Russia in Mexican California.

* * *

MAURICE, Roger
  See ASSELINEAU, Roger (Maurice)

* * *

MAYFIELD, Jack
  See COOPER, Parley J(oseph)

* * *

MAYFIELD, Julian (Hudson)   1928-1984

PERSONAL: Born June 6, 1928, in Greer, S.C.; died of a heart ailment, October 20, 1984, in Tacoma Park, Md.; son of Hudson Peter and Annie Mae (Prince) Mayfield; married Ana Livia Cordero (a physician), 1954 (divorced); married Joan Cambridge, July 10, 1973; children: (first marriage) Rafael Ariel, Emiliano Kewsi. *Education:* Attended Lincoln University. *Politics:* Blackist-Marxist. *Religion:* Atheist.

ADDRESSES: Office—ObserVision Group, P.O. Box 63428, Washington, D.C. *Agent*—Ruth Aley, Maxwell Aley Associates, 145 East 35th St., New York, N.Y. 10016.

CAREER: Writer. Government of Ghana, communications aide to President Kwame Nkrumah, 1962-66; Government of Guyana, advisor to Prime Minister Forbes Burnbaum, 1971-75. Co-founder, editor and theatre reviewer, *World Journal,* Puerto Rico, 1954-58; founding editor, *African Review,* Accra, Ghana, 1964-66; editor, *New Nation International,* 1973. Cornell University, Ithaca, N.Y., Society for the Humanities Fellow, 1967-68, first W.E.B. DuBois Distinguished Visiting Fellow, 1970-71. Lecturer, Albert Schweitzer Program in the Humanities, New York University, New York City, 1969-70; Fulbright-Hays teaching fellow in West Germany, Austria, Denmark, Algeria, and Turkey, 1976-77; visiting professor of black culture and American literature, University of Maryland, 1977-78; writer in residence at Howard University, 1978-84. Participated in First Conference of Negro Writers, American Society for African Culture in New York, 1959. Former actor on and off Broadway, 1949-54, debuting in the Broadway production of the Maxwell Anderson-Kurt Weill musical, "Lost in the Stars," based on Alan Paton's *Cry, the Beloved Country;* actor in film "Uptight," 1969. Co-producer of Ossie Davis's first play, "Alice in Wonder," 1952. *Military service:* U.S. Army.

MEMBER: Actors Equity Association, Writers Guild of America East, Ghanian Association of Journalists and Writers, Harlem Writers Guild, Fulbright Alumni Association, Lincoln University Alumni Association.

WRITINGS:

NOVELS

The Hit (based on Mayfield's one-act play, "417"), Vanguard, 1957.
The Long Night, Vanguard, 1958.
The Grand Parade, Vanguard, 1961, published as *Nowhere Street,* Paperback Library, 1963.

PLAYS

"Fount of the Nation," first produced in Baltimore by Arena Players at Community Theatre, February 17, 1978.

Also author of one-act plays, "417," "The Other Foot," and "A World Full of Men," produced together with Ossie Davis's first play, "Alice in Wonder."

SCREENPLAYS

(With Ruby Dee and Jules Dassin) "Uptight," Paramount, 1968.
"Children of Anger," Irving Jacoby Associates, 1971.
(With Woodie King) "The Long Night" (based on Mayfield's novel of same title), Woodie King-St. Claire Bourne Production Company, 1976.

Also author of "The Hitch," 1969.

OTHER

(Contributor) *The American Negro Writer and His Roots,* American Society of African Culture (New York), 1960.
(Editor) *The World without the Bomb: The Papers of the Accra Assembly,* Ghana Government Press, 1963.
(Contributor) James A. Emanuel and Theodore L. Gross, editors, *Dark Symphony: Negro Literature in America,* Free Press, 1968.
"The History of the Black Man in the United States" (filmstrip), Educational Audio Visual, 1969.
"The Odyssey of W.E.B. DuBois" (filmstrip), Buckingham Enterprises, 1970.
(Contributor) Houston A. Baker, Jr., editor, *Black Literature in America,* McGraw-Hill, 1971.
(Editor and contributor) *Ten Times Black: Stories from the Black Experience,* Bantam, 1972.

Also contributor of political articles to *Nation, Commentary, New Republic,* and other periodicals.

SIDELIGHTS: Julian Mayfield's death in 1984 closed an extraordinarily varied career. His "life and career were themselves the stuff from which novels, plays, and films could conceivably be fashioned," wrote William B. Branch in the *Dictionary of Literary Biography Yearbook: 1984.* He was "a novelist, playwright, critical essayist, university teacher, Broadway and Hollywood actor, journalist, and adviser to the leaders of two Third-World governments," explained Estelle W. Taylor in a *Dictionary of Literary Biography* essay. The variety of Mayfield's experience allowed him to "articulate and interpret the black experience through an interesting array of media," said Taylor, indicating that despite the change in both "literary milieu and even the philosophical reach and direction that his first published works took," Mayfield's literary reputation still rests upon his first two novels, *The Hit* and *The Long Night.* "In these works he became a significant

part of a literary tradition," wrote Taylor, "one of a long line of writers who used Harlem as the vantage point from which to write about the black condition and the black experience."

After much acting experience both on and off Broadway, Mayfield debuted as a playwright with "417," which he expanded into the novel *The Hit.* It is the story of an impoverished but hard-working family in the Harlem ghetto. The father, James Lee Cooley, whose only hope is that "God will redeem Himself by letting him hit the numbers big," explained Taylor, borrows from the household money to support his numbers habit. Eventually Cooley's chosen number, 417, "hits" but the numbers writer absconds with the winnings. Called "well-plotted" and "extremely perceptive" by a *Kirkus Reviews* contributor, Langston Hughes wrote in the *New York Herald Tribune Book Review* that "as a fictional exploration into a comparatively new field of subject matter—the numbers game—'The Hit' is a first novel of unusual interest, treating as it does one phase of 'that most solid and persistent of all American phenomena—the dream.'" And Saunders Redding remarked that although "his characters are like reflections in a darkened mirror," the book represents "an intelligent, energetic foray into a complex milieux."

The Long Night, Mayfield's second Harlem novel, "tells the story of a young boy's fateful search for his father," wrote Branch; and according to Taylor, "Mayfield's Harlem shows signs of decay." A struggling father leaves his family in the charge of his ten year old son, Steely. Sent by his mother to retrieve the winnings from a numbers bet, Steely encounters a gang and is robbed. Taylor observed that, as in *The Hit,* Mayfield depicts "the variety of ways in which working-class blacks and those dependent upon them are systematically victimized by poverty and oppression, but the Harlem of Steely is much uglier than the Harlem of James Lee Cooley." In the *New York Herald Tribune Book Review,* Langston Hughes stated that the novel "is gentler and more poetic than many other such novels in its unfolding of a story that has been told before, and each time in the telling is too grim for tears."

"It was as an essayist that Mayfield's fertile mind found perhaps its most fulfilling utilization, however, as he turned out articles, editorials, academic papers, reviews, and other periodical and anthology contributions from among his earliest writings until just before his death," wrote Branch. Taylor indicated that Mayfield "had become deeply involved in and touched by not only the civil rights movement in the United States but also by movements for freedom from oppression throughout the world." Mayfield journeyed to Cuba after Castro's revolution, and expatriated to Ghana as a journalist, serving as as communications aide and speech writer for the Ghanian president, and later went to Guyana where he was advisor to the prime minister there. Taylor added that "Mayfield called for a separation of the Negro writer from the so-called mainstream. Following it could lead only to oblivion for blacks since the mainstreamers had isolated themselves from the 'great questions facing the peoples of the world.'" A black nationalist, Mayfield "prophetically cautioned black American writers—and, by implication, black Americans generally—to pause and reexamine the headlong push of the time for across-the-board integration into the mainstream of American life, literary or otherwise." In a tribute to Mayfield in the *Dictionary of Literary Biography Yearbook,* John Oliver Killens wrote that "he was a highly sensitive human being, and his art was consistently committed to the cause of freedom and justice and therefore always found itself aligned on the side of the angels."

"It will no doubt require time for the ultimate impact of Julian Mayfield's career and writings to be critically assessed," concluded Branch. "Suffice it to say here, however, that he was both black and American; both untiring in assailing injustice and unstinting in defending the rights of those he felt were being wronged; perspicacious in analyzing the world he lived in and prophetic in foretelling certain perils as well as opportunities which lay ahead. In his youth, he went forth, as he once put it, to 'engage the world.' And over the course of an extraordinary lifetime, engage it he did."

BIOGRAPHICAL/CRITICAL SOURCES:

BOOKS

Davis, Arthur P., *From the Dark Tower: Afro-American Writers, 1900-1960*, Howard University Press, 1981.
Dictionary of Literary Biography, Volume 33: *Afro-American Fiction Writers after 1955*, Gale, 1984.
Dictionary of Literary Biography Yearbook: 1984, Gale, 1984.

PERIODICALS

Ebony, November, 1968.
Freedomways, summer, 1961.
Interracial Review, May, 1962.
Kirkus Reviews, August 15, 1957, August 15, 1958.
New Directions, April, 1979.
New York Herald Tribune Book Review, October 20, 1957, October 26, 1958, July 9, 1961.
New York Times, December 29, 1957.
New York Times Book Review, June 18, 1961.
Saturday Review, October 19, 1957.
Time, October 20, 1958.
Times Literary Supplement, January 22, 1960.
Washington Post, July, 1975.

OBITUARIES:

PERIODICALS

Chicago Tribune, October 25, 1984.
Los Angeles Times, November 3, 1984.
New York Times, October 23, 1984.
Philadelphia Inquirer, October 24, 1984.
Washington Post, October 23, 1984.†

—*Sketch by Sharon Malinowski*

*   *   *

McCLURE, Larry 1941-

PERSONAL: Born March 18, 1941, in Union City, Tenn.; son of Joe David (an educator) and Ernestine (an educator; maiden name, Diggs) McClure; married Eleanor Carlson, December 26, 1967; children: Douglas, Jennifer, Andrew. *Education:* University of Washington, Seattle, B.A., 1963; Oregon State University, Ed.M., 1966; University of Oregon, Ph.D., 1971. *Politics:* Democrat. *Religion:* United Methodist.

ADDRESSES: Home—17760 Cheyenne Way, Tualatin, Ore. 97062. *Office*—Northwest Regional Educational Laboratory, 710 Southwest Second, Portland, Ore. 97204.

CAREER: Teacher in public schools in Portland, Ore., 1963-67; Oregon State Department of Education, Salem, administrative assistant, 1967-69; Northwest Regional Educational Laboratory, Portland, senior associate, 1971—. Chairperson of local community planning advisory committee.

MEMBER: National Association for Career Education (member of board of directors), Phi Delta Kappa, Lions Club.

WRITINGS:

(Editor with Carolyn Buan) *Essays on Career Education*, Northwest Regional Educational Laboratory, 1973.
Career Education Survival Manual, Olympus, 1975.
(With Sue Carol Cook and Virginia Thompson) *Experience-Based Learning: How to Make the Community Your Classroom*, Northwest Regional Educational Laboratory, 1977.
The Regional Laboratory Connection: Improving Educational Practices Through Systematic Research and Development, Northwest Regional Educational Laboratory, 1977.
(With Nancy Bridgeford and Marilyn Clark) *Directions in Career Education: Questions People Ask about Education and Work*, Department of Health, Education, and Welfare, National Institute of Learning, 1977.
(Editor) *Inside Experience-Based Career Education: Personal Reactions to Non-Traditional Learning*, Department of Health, Education, and Welfare, National Institute of Education, 1979.
(Editor with Ruth Nickse) *Competency-Based Education: Beyond Minimum Competency Testing*, Teachers College Press, Columbia University, 1981.

Contributor to education journals.

SIDELIGHTS: McClure writes that he is concerned about the "lack of an experiential base in schools today and how we can help learners rediscover the world as their classroom. Organizations like Northwest Regional Educational Laboratory are helping foster changes in education that are every bit as far reaching as medical and space research and development. I enjoy being at the 'cutting edge.' I also enjoy writing about what others are doing."†

*   *   *

McDONALD, Ian A(rchie) 1933-

PERSONAL: Born April 18, 1933, in Trinidad, West Indies; son of John Archie (a businessman) and Thelma (Seheult) McDonald; married Myrna Camille Foster, December 5, 1959 (divorced); married Mary Angela Callender, 1983; children: (first marriage) Keith Ian; (second marriage) Jamie. *Education:* Attended Queens Royal College, Trinidad, 1941-51; Cambridge University, B.A. (honors), 1955, M.A., 1959.

ADDRESSES: Home—16 Bel Air Gardens, East Coast, Demerara, Guyana, South America. *Office*—c/o Guyana Sugar Corp., 22 Church St., Georgetown, Guyana, South America.

CAREER: Bookers Group Committee, Georgetown, Guyana, secretary, 1955-59; Bookers Sugar Estates Ltd., Georgetown, Guyana, company secretary, 1959-64, administrative secretary, 1964-70; currently administrative director, Guyana Sugar Corp., Georgetown. Chairman of Demerara Sugar Terminals and of Demerara Publishers.

MEMBER: Royal Society of Literature (London; fellow).

AWARDS, HONORS: Winifred Holtby Memorial Prize of Royal Society of Literature, 1969, for best regional novel, *The Humming-Bird Tree*; Golden Arrow of Achievement.

WRITINGS:

The Humming-Bird Tree (novel), Heinemann, 1969.
Poems, [Georgetown, Guyana], 1971.
Selected Poems, Labour Advocate (Georgetown), 1983.

(Editor) *A. J. S. at 70: A Celebration on his 70th Birthday of the Life, Work, and Art of A. J. Seymour*, Autoprint (Georgetown), 1984.

Contributor of short stories and poems to *Penthouse, Bim, Outposts, Chicago Tribune, Greenfield Review*, and other publications. Joint editor, *Kyk-Over-Al* (literary magazine).

WORK IN PROGRESS: Two volumes of poems; a novel; short stories.

AVOCATIONAL INTERESTS: Tennis (captained the Cambridge University team and the West Indian Davis Cup team and has played at Wimbledon).

BIOGRAPHICAL/CRITICAL SOURCES:

PERIODICALS

Books and Bookmen, June, 1969.
Times Literary Supplement, March 6, 1969.

*   *   *

McGINNISS, Joe   1942-

PERSONAL: Born December 9, 1942, in New York, N.Y.; son of Joseph Aloysius (a travel agent) and Mary (Leonard) McGinniss; married Christine Cooke, September 25, 1965 (divorced); married Nancy Doherty (an editor and photographer), November 20, 1976; children: (first marriage) Christine, Suzanne, Joe; (second marriage) Matthew, James. *Education:* Holy Cross College, B.S., 1964.

ADDRESSES: Agent—Morton L. Janklow, 598 Madison Ave., New York, N.Y. 10022.

CAREER: Port Chester Daily Item, Port Chester, N.Y., reporter, 1964; *Worcester Telegram*, Worcester, Mass., reporter, 1965; *Philadelphia Bulletin*, Philadelphia, Pa., reporter, 1966; *Philadelphia Inquirer*, Philadelphia, columnist, 1967-68; free-lance writer, 1968—. Lecturer in writing at Bennington College.

WRITINGS:

The Selling of the President, 1968, Trident, 1969, reprinted with an introduction by the author, 1988.
The Dream Team (novel; Literary Guild alternate selection), Random House, 1972.
Heroes, Viking, 1976.
Going to Extremes (Book-of-the-Month Club selection), Knopf, 1980.
Fatal Vision (Book-of-the-Month Club selection), Putnam, 1983.
Blind Faith, Putnam, 1988.

Contributor of articles to *Harper's, Sports Illustrated, TV Guide*, and other periodicals.

SIDELIGHTS: Joe McGinniss is a noted nonfiction author whose works are characterized by an intense personal involvement with the topics at hand. For more than twenty years McGinniss, a former journalist, has concentrated on writing full-length books; his research has taken him to the upper reaches of Alaska as well as far and wide through the lower forty-eight states. Two of his titles—*The Selling of the President, 1968* and *Fatal Vision*—have been bestsellers in the nonfiction market and have proven controversial in both their subjects and their composition. These and other McGinniss works, including *The Dream Team, Heroes*, and *Going to Extremes*, have been praised for their insights and cogency of expression.

To quote *New York Times* contributor Jimmy Breslin, McGinniss's style produces "sentences that read so easily that one tends to forget he is reading."

McGinniss was born in New York City late in 1942. He grew up in Rye, New York, an imaginative youngster who was educated in parochial schools. In 1964 he received a Bachelor of Science degree from Holy Cross College and immediately went to work as a reporter for the *Port Chester Daily Item*. Within months he landed a job in Worcester, Massachusetts on the *Worcester Telegram*. McGinniss worked as a general assignment reporter at both newspapers, but he aspired to sportswriting. He finally achieved that goal at the *Philadelphia Bulletin* in 1966 and was so successful that the rival *Philadelphia Inquirer* offered him a sports column. After only a year with the *Bulletin* he went to the *Inquirer*, not as a sportswriter but as a general issues columnist—a coveted position, especially for a writer several years shy of thirty. According to *New Republic* reviewer John Osborne, McGinniss became known in Philadelphia as "something of a journalistic prodigy, a sharpshooter with minimal regard for reportorial niceties and a special appeal to young readers." McGinniss aimed at the biggest issues—the escalation of America's involvement in the Vietnam War, the assassinations of Dr. Martin Luther King, Jr., and Robert F. Kennedy, and the 1968 presidential primaries. The latter experience prepared him for his first book, *The Selling of the President, 1968*.

A chance conversation on a commuter train led McGinniss to an astonishing subject. McGinniss discovered that both 1968 presidential candidates, Hubert Humphrey and Richard Nixon, employed teams of advertising executives to create "images" that would make the candidates more palatable to television viewers. McGinniss's commuter train contact was with the "Humphrey account," but McGinniss could not persuade that camp to reveal its secrets. Instead he turned to the Nixon campaign, where the media advisors accorded him an unusually intimate view of the marketing of candidate Nixon. Quitting his job at the *Inquirer*, McGinniss travelled with the Nixon team for five months. "My great advantage was that I wasn't considered press," he told *Life* magazine. "I was the guy writing a book."

Publication of *The Selling of the President, 1968* caused a sensation. The book was on the bestseller list seven months and topped the list for four. McGinniss had the distinction of becoming the youngest author of nonfiction—excepting Anne Frank—ever to have penned such a blockbuster. Nixon's aides were shocked to discover that the innocuous young observer who had watched them at work had revealed their attempts to manipulate the electorate. Reviewers, on the other hand, have praised McGinniss for his revelations. *Christian Century* contributor Robert Miller writes: "Readers with illusions about the relationship of media and message in a large-scale political campaign will quickly be disillusioned by this book. McGinniss gives a behind-the-scenes look at a group of men and women using a very effective TV technique to help their client win the presidency of the U.S. At times this book will scare you." In the *New York Times*, Christopher Lehmann-Haupt calls the work "a series of smartly turned-out scenes from backstage at the 1968 Presidential turkey raffle" and adds that what McGinniss saw and heard "he has recorded artfully enough to simultaneously entertain us and make us fear for the future of the Republic."

National notoriety at age twenty-seven can be daunting. McGinniss's next two books, *The Dream Team* and *Heroes*, both explore the pleasures and perils of fame, premature and otherwise. In the novel *The Dream Team*, a bestselling author on tour promoting his book becomes sidetracked by horse racing, alcohol, and the attentions of a young television reporter. *Heroes*, a nonfiction work, consists of a series of interviews with prominent national figures from several walks of life; critics have contended that the book reveals as much about McGinniss's emotional turmoil as it does about the men he interviewed. McGinniss invested much time and effort in the projects, and both were modest successes. Then, in 1975, he opted for a complete change of environment and subject matter. Journeying to Alaska, he spent a year documenting life in that beautiful but inhospitable state. The resulting book, *Going to Extremes*, offers a glimpse at the underside of Alaska's economic expansion. *New Republic* correspondent Dan Cryer observes that in *Going to Extremes*, McGinniss "has succeeded well in capturing an Alaska on the verge of selling its soul to big oil. . . . He is a first-rate reporter whose stories graphically convey the culture shock wracking present-day Alaska." In the *Nation*, Mark Kramer concludes that the book "is fine reading. It is thick with whole people, exotic landscapes, the nervous and constant curiosity of an adventurer who knows that the essence of place is more likely found while chatting in barrooms than while viewing the wondrous works of man and nature."

McGinniss's next project consumed more than four years of his life. *Fatal Vision*, his 1983 bestseller, gives a comprehensive account of the murder conviction of Dr. Jeffrey MacDonald, who is serving time for the brutal slayings of his pregnant wife and two young daughters. When McGinniss met MacDonald in 1979, the infamous surgeon was facing trial after a series of legal delays and after having been exonerated in a shoddily-conducted Army hearing. MacDonald staunchly maintained his innocence in the 1970 triple murder, but as McGinniss began to piece together the evidence he became more and more convinced of the doctor's guilt. According to Joan Barthel in the *New York Times Book Review*, McGinniss "becomes a genuinely sympathetic character in [Fatal Vision]. . . . He confronts recurring questions of guilt and innocence and the ambivalence of love. . . . These things happen when reporters become involved in people's lives and deaths, when a writing project evolves into a kind of selective, if unforeseen and not entirely voluntary, human bondage. It is this involvement, finally, that makes 'Fatal Vison'—even beyond the fascination of the story it tells . . .—well worth reading."

Throughout his protracted legal battles to stay out of prison, MacDonald was convinced that McGinniss intended to portray him as an innocent victim of police harrassment. When *Fatal Vision* was published, MacDonald—who already was earning a percentage of the profits—sued McGinniss for wooing his further cooperation even though the author believed him to be guilty. A community of fellow writers came to McGinniss's aid in a court case that many felt would determine every nonfiction author's prerogative to formulate independent conclusions. McGinniss maintained that he never led MacDonald to believe the book would exonerate him and that it took many months of research and conversations to reach any conclusion at all. Lehmann-Haupt, for one reviewer, finds this attitude reflected in the book. McGinnis "makes it clear to the reader from the start that he was free to decide one way or another about Dr. MacDonald's claim of innocence, and he makes it clear, I think, that Dr. MacDonald knew he was taking his chances," Lehmann-Haupt writes. "'Fatal Vision' smells of

integrity, and that's one of the many things about it that make it irresistible to read, even if its vision of the human soul is somewhat bleak and frightening."

The celebrated court case ended with a deadlocked jury. MacDonald pursued a new trial, prompting McGinniss to agree to an out-of-court settlement without admission of liability. The author told the *Los Angeles Times* that he accepted the settlement—which he does not have to pay personally—because he wanted to reduce MacDonald's avenues for public attention. Also, he said, "I don't want to give MacDonald the satisfaction of taking me away from productive work again." That productive work includes new writing projects in Williamstown, Massachusetts, in a rural retreat where, he says, distractions are few. In the *Washington Post*, McGinniss observed that the craft of writing "is like looking for the perfect wave. You can't quit until you write the perfect book."

MEDIA ADAPTATIONS: The Selling of the President, 1968 was adapted for stage by Stuart Hample; *Fatal Vision* was filmed as a television miniseries that first aired in 1984; *Blind Faith* will be adapted as a television miniseries by National Broadcasting Company.

CA INTERVIEW

CA interviewed Joe McGinniss by telephone on March 17, 1988, at his home in Williamstown, Massachusetts.

CA: Fatal Vision, *your 1983 account of the trial of convicted murderer Jeffrey MacDonald, has been in the news recently with the lawsuit Dr. MacDonald brought against you for fraud—not libel—because he worked with you in the expectation of a book about his innocence, whereas you became convinced that he was guilty of killing his wife and two daughters and so portrayed him. What are your feelings now about the settlement you reached in November, 1987?*

McGINNISS: I'm glad it's over. I'm a writer; I want to write books. MacDonald is in prison for the rest of his life, and he has nothing else to do. This was becoming an exercise in gratifying his whims. There comes a point beyond which you don't want to continue with a thing like that. I'm better off pursuing new work. And in terms of the questions raised by that suit and the impact those questions might have had on me and other authors of nonfiction, the settlement disposed of those in a way that caused no harm to anyone. That, I think, was an appropriate outcome. And MacDonald's father-in-law has filed litigation which has tied up all the money from the settlement, so MacDonald didn't get that.

CA: Writers and publishers are having to spend more and more time in court defending what they do. Your case is just one example of that among many.

McGINNISS: These days it seems that there's a new stage in the process in writing nonfiction. There's the research, then there's the writing, then there's the publication, and then there's the litigation. That's the extra fourth step. If you look at the people who've been involved in suits on the basis of nonfiction books they've published in the past five years, the list is almost endless. It includes J. Anthony Lukas, Peter Matthiessen, Janet Malcolm, Joseph Wambaugh, myself—it goes on and on. It's really something which wasn't there ten years ago, and which has to give one pause in thinking about how to pursue writing as a career. Is it any longer possible to tell true stories about living people if there's any chance that the story will not be flattering? Are you restricted to writing only about those whom you admire?

This takes away from the writer a dimension that's always been there. I was very pleased to see the recent Supreme Court decision in favor of *Hustler* in the Jerry Falwell-*Hustler* case. Had it been made two years earlier, it would have eliminated seventy-five percent of MacDonald's complaints. We have libel and we have invasion of privacy, and they're vague enough and hard enough to deal with. When you start expanding the parameters so that a disgruntled subject can sue even over a story he admits to be true simply because it displeases him, then, I think, the writer has lost a lot of freedom.

CA: MacDonald still proclaims his innocence, and from some of what you've written about him, it seems almost as if he really believes himself innocent at times. Do you think he'll ever crack?

McGINNISS: No. There's no chance of that at all. I don't think it causes him any strain. To the extent that I understand the psychopathic mentality (and my understanding is far from perfect, but it's greater than it was five years ago), I don't think people who suffer from that kind of disorder have any connection between feeling and action or feeling and words. It doesn't bother him to say something untrue that might bother you or me. I don't think he has the capacity to feel guilt.

CA: In the last part of the book Fatal Vision, *and later also in* TV Guide *just before the airing of the TV version, you explained how your initial belief in MacDonald's innocence changed to a firm conviction of his guilt. Did this involve any major reshaping of material you'd already written?*

McGINNISS: I don't know that I ever had—or said that I had—a belief in his innocence. It's important to make the distinction between believing in someone's innocence and simply not knowing. When I met MacDonald, I was willing to presume innocence the way a juror would at the start of a trial, but that's different from believing in it. I believed nothing. I was an agnostic; I didn't know what the facts were. I had no particular reason to believe him or not to believe him. So it wasn't a question of going from belief to disbelief in his story. It was a question of starting from a neutral point of view and gradually coming to recognize that the story he told was not true. It didn't cause any reshaping because there was nothing to reshape. The book formed itself as my understanding of what probably happened formed itself.

CA: After two years of writing a column for the Philadelphia Inquirer, *you left to write a book that was both ambitious and extremely successful,* The Selling of the President, 1968, *an account of the media marketing of Richard Nixon. Had you grown up with a lively interest in politics and public figures?*

McGINNISS: In the sixties it was pretty hard to be writing anything and not feel interested in and connected to what was happening politically. It was very different from today, for example. I graduated from college in 1964, and the sixties really didn't start until the second half of the sixties; I don't think it was until Lyndon Johnson made the speech at Johns Hopkins that committed American troops to Vietnam in July, 1965, that what we think of as the sixties really began. So my professional writing career commenced at almost the same time that all that social and political upheaval began, and I think the two were naturally intertwined.

Writing about people in a newspaper column, as I was, it was impossible to avoid politics. It wasn't that I had grown up wondering how presidential campaigns were structured and had always wanted to write a book about an election or the campaign process; it was more serendipitous than that. On my way to catch a train I met somebody from Doyle Dane Bernbach, the advertising firm that was going to handle Hubert Humphrey in the campaign, and I thought it would be an interesting thing to observe the process. The Humphrey people didn't think it was such a good idea, and they refused to cooperate. But the Nixon people took a different view; they thought it would be a fine thing to have a book about the advertising campaign, and they cooperated completely.

It's interesting that twenty years later that book is about to be republished, and I just wrote the new introduction to it. The people I wrote about in that book were not harmed at all by it. Roger Ailes, who was probably the key figure in it, is now George Bush's media adviser. Both Doyle and Bush sought his services at the beginning of the campaign, and he chose Bush. And by choosing Bush, he quite possibly may have chosen the nominee. So the power that these guys continue to wield is really remarkable.

CA: What comparisons do you see in the campaign for the coming 1988 presidential election?

McGINNISS: Over twenty years, technology improves. But the principle is still the same: to try to create an image which may or may not have anything to do with the man behind it but which is palatable to the majority of the people who tune in to television. Television today, even more than twenty years ago, has become the sole means of our connecting with people who run for national office. And having had an actor, literally, in the White House for eight years, there seems nothing peculiar anymore about the process of people acting or performing under controlled circumstances on television. Twenty years ago the people involved in the process were somewhat ashamed of it or felt a little bit guilty about it, and therefore didn't want a whole lot of scrutiny. These days the first thing a candidate does when he announces that he's running for office is to hold a press conference to proclaim whom he's hired to be his media advisor. They've really come out of the closet.

CA: I notice that there aren't as many debates as there used to be, because the candidates who show up badly in them now simply refuse to debate.

McGINNISS: That's right. Their advisers know there are better ways to get the candidate across than to put him in a situation where debates are not controlled. You can certainly exercise control if you have the money to buy the time to do it, and that seems to be the goal of everyone's campaign today with the exception of Jesse Jackson's. I find it interesting that he's gone about it in a very different way, of necessity and maybe of principle too, and that he's gotten as far as he has.

CA: You were very young to have the success that came with The Selling of the President, 1968, *and in* Heroes, *published in 1976, you chronicled some of the down side of that success: the depression when your second book, the novel* The Dream Team, *didn't do as well; the breakup of your marriage; the long period when things just didn't seem to work in your writing. How do you feel about* Heroes *now, twelve years later?*

McGINNISS: I think that was an interesting little book. A lot of the apparently autobiographical content of that book was material which I inserted in there very consciously, attempting to create certain effects. It wasn't some sort of purgative; I wasn't just in a confessional mode where I thought the whole world would be interested in the details of my life. I was trying to set myself up as a character in that book who was representative of rootless man in the post-heroic age without calling a lot of attention to the process. I'm not sure that was entirely successful as a device, but that's what the connection between the autobiographical stuff and the journalistic portions of the book was about. It didn't sell well, but I still kind of like that book. And I wasn't as out of control, even during the period I was writing about, as the book makes it appear.

If your question was about success, I've had some years to reflect on this and I think the connection between success and subsequent dislocation in personal life is not a very strong one, at least in my case. I think things that are going to happen in your personal life are probably going to happen anyway, and I am very grateful for the success of *The Selling of the President.* I think it made the rest of my life a lot easier than it would have been otherwise.

CA: Your point about our having no heroes is an interesting one, and I think it's still valid. Teachers say that when they ask their students who their heroes are, they get in response names like singer Michael Jackson and TV star Don Johnson.

McGINNISS: Yes. The whole notion of the hero has almost disappeared, even from our unconscious. It hasn't entirely disappeared, but it's harder to access it, so that it's totally confused with the notion of celebrity, which is such an empty vessel. I think that just may be indicative of a culture that is running out of its energy. We're probably approaching the end of a fairly long cycle, and I'm not sure what's about to happen or what form it will take. But I think in periods of waning cultural energy, it's harder for individuals to achieve heroic stature because the energy on the part of the public just isn't there.

CA: Do you think one factor may be that our political figures, who were often our heroes in the past, don't seem admirable anymore?

McGINNISS: There are no secrets anymore, and there's no distance. Television has been a great leveler. Heroes exist in a mythic dimension, even up to the time of Franklin Delano Roosevelt, who was rarely glimpsed but occasionally his voice would come over the radio. There was a certain almost magical appeal about people like that. The power they wielded and their remoteness from us lent them more of an air of the legendary, even as they were functioning in public life. Today, with journalism and particularly the blinding lights of television eliminating shadows from all the dark corners, there's no place for these roots to take hold. Everybody is reduced to the level of what can fit inside a three-minute segment of a twenty-two minute broadcast every night. It may well be that Albert Gore or Michael Dukakis or Robert Dole is every bit as innately heroic as somebody from a hundred years ago, but the means by which we communicate with our leaders and they with us is so radically altered by the dominance of television that I don't think it's likely anyone will soon again achieve that status—at least until we come to a time of crisis. In a time of terrible crisis, there's a natural tendency to turn towards someone you hope is larger than life and can lead you out of it. We haven't had a national crisis that has gripped the imagination and touched the souls of the people for a long

time. And that's not a bad thing either. The more time we can pass through without a major crisis, the better off we are—but it's not as interesting.

CA: In Going to Exremes *you put down your experiences and observations from a long stay in Alaska that began in 1975. Some are funny, some very sad; some make the reader want to quit work today and go there to see first-hand the incredible beauty of the place. Have you been back since you wrote the book to see what changes have taken place?*

McGINNISS: The last time I was back was when the book came out in 1980, and I could see changes that had taken place. I've still got a lot of close friends in Alaska and some who have just left Alaska after a long time, and I think what's happened in recent years has been very much a function of the collapse of international oil prices and the whole boom period that *Going to Extremes* encompassed, when the pipeline was being built. We're at the tail-end of that now, where people are giving away their apartments in Anchorage and getting out as fast as they can because there's no money and no work.

But there's no place like Alaska—in America, certainly—and it still retains a lot of the frontier qualities that other parts of America have lost. I was very tempted to stay there, but I think it's a tough place to raise kids. You have a real problem with the public school system, a heavy influx of religious fundamentalists, a lot of crackpots. And most of the cities are jerry-built for maximum profit; they're boom-town-type cities. There are only two cities on the mainland, Anchorage and Fairbanks, and neither is a city that you'd be drawn to for its charm. If you get far outside, you're living a very remote, self-reliant sort of life, which is fine for a lot of people for some period of time, but it's only a very few people who can function happily like that forever.

But the book I've just finished is set in New Jersey, and if I had my choice, I'd write ten books about Alaska before I'd ever write another book about New Jersey. There couldn't be two places more different. All the things that make Alaska interesting, New Jersey has the opposite. I lived in New Jersey for ten years before moving up here, but it's all so much the same, all so drab.

CA: Can you tell me more about the new book?

McGINNISS: It's too soon to talk much about it, because I've just finished it. It's called *Blind Faith,* and it's a true story about two adolescent boys whose mother is murdered and whose father is eventually accused of having hired people to come up from Louisiana to commit the murder so that he would be free to continue an affair he was having with the woman across the street—and also to collect a million-and-a-half dollars in life insurance, which he needed to pay off debt he had fallen into as a result, probably, of his compulsive gambling in Atlantic City casinos. It's a true story, and it revolves around these two boys who were sixteen and eighteen when it happened. They go through the process of wanting so much to believe in their father but gradually coming to understand that he was guilty and that the whole happy home life they thought they'd had all their lives was just a sham and an illusion, then trying to rebuild their own lives out of those ashes.

CA: Even the reviewers who weren't ecstatic about The Dream Team *liked the horse racing part of it and recognized it as authoritative. Do you still find time to enjoy the races?*

McGINNISS: If I get to Saratoga once a year, I'm lucky. That was a phase of my life that I enjoyed very much when I was able to pursue it actively, but it's solely recreational now and I just don't have that much time. Also, I don't live near any race tracks; I'm probably two hundred miles from the nearest places where the horses are running today.

CA: Would you like to write another novel?

McGINNISS: I think so. I'm very interested in the boundary between fiction and nonfiction, which is constantly shifting and often very blurred. Many novels have so much nonfiction, straightforward narrative in them, and many works of nonfiction use techniques like scene-by-scene construction and dialogue which often is enhanced if not utterly invented. The difference between the two seems to be more a matter of marketing convenience in many cases than any true literary distinction.

I have a couple of ideas which I think I could start out explaining to a publisher as ideas for nonfiction, but once into the work I could tell the stories more effectively by incorporating fiction. Whenever I become interested in doing a piece of writing, I think about what the story is and what is the most effective way to tell it. In five cases out of six, it has been largely through nonfictive means—although, if you look back at *Heroes*, you see that a lot of what's in there could easily be called fiction. In *Going to Extremes* there are scenes and characters that are rearranged and enhanced for the sake of dramatic effect, which is a fictive technique. *Fatal Vision* is not an example of that, because it was really hard-core, rock-solid, old fashioned meticulous reporting, laying it down just as it was because of the kind of story it was. But I'm interested, I think, more consciously than ever before in trying to find that point out on the horizon where the two forms meet.

CA: Certainly there's a growing body of respectable work in which the lines are deliberately blurred.

McGINNISS: Sure. How much of Tom Wolfe's *The Bonfire of the Vanities* couldn't just as easily have been the basis for a work of nonfiction? And much of Wolfe's nonfiction, while meticulously reported, like *The Electric Kool-Aid Acid Test* and *The Right Stuff*, has been presented essentially in the form of a novel. There's *The Executioner's Song*, which Norman Mailer, for reasons that appear almost whimsical, decided to slap the word *novel* on at the very end, after a 700-page nonfiction account of a real person named Gary Gilmore and the real people he killed. I think I start off with the notion of a story that may have some basis in fact, and then pursue it to find the most effective way to tell it.

BIOGRAPHICAL/CRITICAL SOURCES:

BOOKS

Authors in the News, Volume 2, Gale, 1976.
Contemporary Literary Citicism, Volume 32, Gale, 1985.
McGinniss, Joe, *Heroes*, Viking, 1976.

PERIODICALS

Atlantic, July, 1976.
Chicago Tribune, August 22, 1987.
Christian Century, February 4, 1970.
Christian Science Monitor, November 13, 1969.
Commonweal, October 24, 1969.
Detroit News, May 30, 1972.

Globe & Mail (Toronto), November 17, 1984.
Harper's, October, 1983, August, 1985.
Life, October 10, 1969.
Listener, March 5, 1970.
Los Angeles Times, July 9, 1987, July 23, 1987, July 24, 1987, August 3, 1987, August 5, 1987, August 6, 1987, August 22, 1987, November 24, 1987, November 25, 1987.
Nation, September 27, 1980, November 12, 1983.
National Review, November 18, 1969.
New Republic, October 11, 1969, November 15, 1980, October 24, 1983.
New Statesman, March 6, 1970, June 1, 1973.
Newsweek, September 29, 1969, October 13, 1969, April 12, 1971, September 22, 1980, September 12, 1983.
New Yorker, December 27, 1969, October 3, 1983.
New York Post, October 8, 1969.
New York Times, August 6, 1969, October 3, 1969, January 30, 1972, March 5, 1972, May 9, 1972, April 27, 1976, September 21, 1983, November 16, 1984, August 22, 1987.
New York Times Book Review, October 5, 1969, April 30, 1972, April 18, 1976, September 14, 1980, September 25, 1983.
Publishers Weekly, April 27, 1984.
Saturday Review, September, 1980.
Spectator, March 14, 1970.
Time, September 26, 1983.
Times (London), November 25, 1987.
Times Literary Supplement, November 20, 1969, May 25, 1973, August 17, 1984.
TV Guide, November 17, 1984.
Village Voice, September 20, 1983.
Washington Post, December 2, 1980, October 20, 1983, August 21, 1987.
Washington Post Book World, April 18, 1976, September 14, 1980, December 2, 1980, August 28, 1983.
Writers Digest, March, 1976.

—*Sketch by Anne Janette Johnson*

—*Interview by Jean W. Ross*

*   *   *

McINTYRE, W(illiam) David 1932-

PERSONAL: Born September 4, 1932, in Hucknall, England; son of John (a clergyman) and Alice Muriel (Stallard) McIntyre; married Marion Jean Hillyard, December 14, 1957; children: Jefferson John, Benjamin James, Ruth Margaret, Marcus Edwin, James Maurice. *Education:* Peterhouse, Cambridge, B.A., 1955, M.A., 1959; University of Washington, Seattle, M.A., 1956; School of Oriental and African Studies, London, Ph.D., 1959. *Politics:* "Floating voter." *Religion:* Church of Jesus Christ of Latter-day Saints.

ADDRESSES: Home—54A Bryndur Rd., Christchurch, New Zealand. *Office*—University of Canterbury, Private Bag, Christchurch, New Zealand.

CAREER: University of Nottingham, Nottingham, England, assistant lecturer, 1959-61, lecturer in history, 1961-65; University of Canterbury, Christchurch, New Zealand, professor of history, 1966—. Occasional broadcaster and commentator on defense and foreign policy issues. Member of advisory committee, historical publications branch, New Zealand Department of Internal Affairs, 1967-73, 1988—. Member of executive committee, Paton Theological College, Nottingham, 1963-66. *Military service:* British Army, Royal Corps of Signals, 1950-52; became second lieutenant. Territorial Army, 1952-60; became lieutenant.

MEMBER: New Zealand Institute of International Affairs (vice-chairman, Christchurch branch, 1967-70), Canterbury Historical Association (president, 1967).

WRITINGS:

Colonies into Commonwealth, Blandford, 1966, 3rd edition, 1974, Walker, 1968.
The Imperial Frontier in the Tropics, 1865-1875, St. Martin's, 1967.
Britain, New Zealand and the Security of Southeast Asia in the 1970s, New Zealand Institute of International Affairs, 1969.
Neutralism, Non-Alignment and New Zealand, University of New Zealand Press, 1969.
Britain and the Commonwealth since 1907, Heinemann, 1970.
(With W. J. Gardner) *Speeches and Documents on New Zealand History*, Clarendon Press, 1971.
The Commonwealth of Nations, 1869-1971: Origins and Impact, University of Minnesota Press, 1977.
The Rise and Fall of the Singapore Naval Base, 1919-1942, Macmillan, 1979.
The Journal of Henry Sewell, 1853-1857, two volumes, Whitcoulls, 1980.
(With Len Richardson) *Provincial Perspectives*, University of Canterbury Press, 1981.
New Zealand Prepares for War, 1919-39, University of Canterbury Press, 1988.

CONTRIBUTOR

Wang Gungwu, editor, *Malaysia: A Survey*, Pall Mall, 1964.
Australia, New Zealand, and the South Pacific: A Handbook, Blond, 1970.
J. Jensen, editor, *The European Experience*, A. H. & A. W. Reed, Volume I, 1970, Volume IV, 1971.
K. Keith, editor, *Defence Perspectives*, Price, Milburn, 1972.
Mary Boyd, editor, *Pacific Horizons*, Price, Milburn, 1972.
The Commonwealth: Its Past, Present and Future, New Zealand Institute of International Affairs, 1973.
C. D. Cowan and O. W. Wolters, editors, *Southeast Asian History and Historiography*, Cornell University Press, 1976.
A. McIntosh and others, *New Zealand in World Affairs*, New Zealand Institute of International Affairs, 1977.
H. Gold, editor, *New Directions in New Zealand Foreign Policy*, Benton Ross, 1985.

OTHER

Contributor to history and American studies journals. Area organizer for the South Pacific, *Historical Abstracts*, 1966—.

WORK IN PROGRESS: What the Commonwealth Means to Its Members; Background to ANZRS.

AVOCATIONAL INTERESTS: Architectural history, photographing buildings and cities, reading detective stories.

*   *   *

McKINNEY, D. J.
See COOPER, Parley J(oseph)

McNAMARA, Eugene (Joseph)   1930-

PERSONAL: Born March 18, 1930, in Oak Park, Ill.; son of Martin Joseph (an office worker) and Anna (Ryan) McNamara; married Margaret Lindstrom, July 19, 1952; children: Michael, Mary, David, Brian, Christopher. *Education:* DePaul University, B.A., 1953, M.A., 1955; Northwestern University, Ph.D., 1964. *Politics:* New Democratic Party. *Religion:* Roman Catholic.

ADDRESSES: Home—166 Randolph Pl., Windsor, Ontario, Canada. *Office*—Department of English, University of Windsor, Windsor, Ontario N9B 3P4, Canada.

CAREER: Fenwick High School, Oak Park, Ill., English teacher, 1953-55; University of Illinois at Chicago Circle, instructor in English, 1955-59; University of Windsor, Windsor, Ontario, 1959—, began as associate professor, currently professor of English, director of graduate program in creative writing, 1967—.

MEMBER: National Council of Teachers of English, Canadian Association of American Studies, Canadian Association of University Teachers of English, League of Canadian Poets.

WRITINGS:

Discovery: Voyage of Exploration (twenty-four scripts of radio talks given over the Canadian Broadcasting Corp.), Assumption University Press, 1962.
(Editor) *The Interior Landscape: The Literary Criticism of Marshall McLuhan, 1934-1962*, McGraw, 1969.

POETRY

For the Mean Time, Gryphon Press (Windsor), 1965.
Outerings, Delta Canada, 1970.
Love Scene, Hellric House, 1970.
Dillinger Poems, Black Moss Press, 1971.
Hard Words, Fiddlehead, 1972.
Passages and Other Poems, Sono Nis Press, 1972.
Diving for the Body, Borealis Press, 1974.
In Transit, Pennyworth Press, 1975.
Screens, Coach House Press, 1977.
Forcing the Field, Sesame Press, 1981.
Call It a Day, blewointment press, 1984.
The Moving Light, Wolsak & Wynn, 1986.

FICTION

Salt: Short Stories, Sono Nis Press, 1975.
Search for Sarah Grace and Other Stories, Black Moss Press, 1977.
Spectral Evidence (short stories), Black Moss Press, 1986.

OTHER

Also author of a teleplay, "The Stranger," with James Hurley, for ABC-TV series "Johnny Ringo." Also contributor to anthologies, including *Best American Short Stories*, 1975, *Best Canadian Stories*, 1979 and 1986, and *Die Weite Reise*. Author of weekly column "Flicks" for *Windsor Star*. Contributor of poems, articles, and short stories to periodicals, including *America, Critic, Western Humanities Review, Midwestern University Quarterly, Vagabond, Films in Review, Canadian Forum*, and *Texas Quarterly*. Editor, *University of Windsor Review*, 1966—.

WORK IN PROGRESS: A novel, *Home in the Dark;* a study of the production of the film "Laura," entitled *Laura: The Face in the Misty Light;* poems; short stories.

SIDELIGHTS: Eugene McNamara once told *CA:* "I give forms to loss, grief, etc. I impose order on the chaos, the scattered pieces of my divided self." He added: "The poem is a tight-rope between the canyon of the trivial (uttering) and the abyss of the ego (self-celebration as an end in itself). A poet must of all men be reverent of others, otherwise he will use them as things in his self-dramatization. It's all been said: trees, rocks, clouds, autumn, women, God, horses, loss of youth, hair, love, hate, rage, lust, and politics. Ordinary must . . . be made fresh."

McNamara is interested in contemporary American literature and lists as influences Thomas Wolfe, Walt Whitman, William Carlos Williams, and Robinson Jeffers. Some of his stories have been read on the Canadian Broadcasting Corp. series "Anthology."

BIOGRAPHICAL/CRITICAL SOURCES:

PERIODICALS

Canadian Fiction Magazine, Volume 46, 1983.
Canadian Forum, July, 1971, August, 1973, June, 1975.
Globe and Mail (Toronto), February 22, 1986.

*   *   *

McWILLIAMS, Margaret (Ann Edgar) 1929-

PERSONAL: Born May 26, 1929, in Osage, Iowa; daughter of Alvin R. (a professor) and Mildred Irene (Lane) Edgar; married former husband, Don A. McWilliams (a physicist), September 20, 1953; children: Roger, Kathleen. *Education:* Iowa State University of Science and Technology, B.S., 1951, M.S., 1953; Oregon State University, Ph.D., 1968.

ADDRESSES: Home—P.O. Box 220, Redondo Beach, Calif. 90277. *Office*—California State University, 5151 State College Dr., Los Angeles, Calif. 90032.

CAREER: California State University, Los Angeles, assistant professor, 1961-66, associate professor, 1966-68, professor of home economics, 1968—, and chairman of department, 1968-76.

MEMBER: Institute of Food Technologists, College Teachers of Food and Nutrition, American Dietetic Association, Society for Nutrition Education, Phi Kappa Phi, Phi Upsilon Omicron (nation founders fellow, 1964, 1967), Omicron Nu, Iota Sigma Pi, Sigma Alpha Iota, Sigma Delta Epsilon.

AWARDS, HONORS: Iowa State University of Science and Technology, Alumni Centennial Award, 1971, and Professional Achievement Award, 1977; Outstanding Professor Award, California State University, Los Angeles, 1976.

WRITINGS:

Food Fundamentals, Wiley, 1966, 4th edition, 1985.
Nutrition for the Growing Years, Wiley, 1967, 4th edition, 1986.
(With Lendal Kotschevar) *Understanding Food,* Wiley, 1969.
(With Linda Davis) *Food for You,* Ginn, 1971, 2nd edition, 1972.
Illustrated Guide to Food Preparation, Plycon, 2nd edition, 1972, 5th edition, 1986.
(With Fredrick Stare) *Living Nutrition,* Wiley, 1973, 4th edition, 1984.
Meatless Cookbook, Plycon, 1973.
(With Stare) *Nutrition for Good Health,* Plycon, 1974, 2nd edition, 1982.

(With Harriett Paine) *Modern Food Preservation,* Plycon, 1977.
Experimental Foods Laboratory Manual, Plycon, 1977, 2nd edition, 1981.
Fundamentals of Meal Management, Plycon, 1978.
(With Holly Heller) *World of Nutrition,* Ginn, 1984.
Parents' Nutrition Book, Wiley, 1986.

WORK IN PROGRESS: Foods: Experimental Perspectives, for Macmillan.

*   *   *

MESA-LAGO, Carmelo 1934-

PERSONAL: Surname is pronounced "Mayseh-Lahgo"; born August 11, 1934, in Havana, Cuba; son of Rogelio (in legal field) and Ana Maria (Lago) Mesa; married Elena Gross, September 3, 1966; children: Elizabeth, Ingrid, Helena. *Education:* University of Havana, Master in Law, 1957; University of Madrid, LL.D., 1958; University of Miami, M.A. (economics), 1965; Cornell University, Ph.D., 1968. *Religion:* Roman Catholic.

ADDRESSES: Office—YE36 Forbes Quadrangle, University of Pittsburgh, Pittsburgh, Pa. 15260.

CAREER: University of Pittsburgh, Pittsburgh, Pa., assistant professor, 1967-70, associate professor, 1970-76, professor of economics, 1976-80, distinguished service professor, 1980—, assistant director of Center for Latin American Studies, 1967-70, associate director, beginning 1970, director, 1976-86. Consultant to Hispanic Foundation, Library of Congress, 1969, State Department, 1972, 1975, International Labour Organization, 1973, 1986-88, Organization of American States, 1981, 1982, 1983, World Bank, 1982, 1983, 1985-87, United Nations Economic Commission for Latin America, 1983, Inter-American Development Bank, 1985, and USAID, 1985-87.

MEMBER: International Association of Labor Law and Social Security, Association for Comparative Economic Studies, Latin American Studies Association (president, 1980), American Economic Association, Caribbean Studies Association (member of executive council, 1973).

AWARDS, HONORS: Arthur Whitaker Prize, 1982, for *The Economy of Socialist Cuba: A Two-Decade Appraisal;* Hoover Institution Prize, 1986, for best article on Latin America.

WRITINGS:

Planificacion de la seguridad social, Organizacion Iberoamericana de Seguridad Social (Madrid), 1959, 2nd edition, Editorial Libreria Marti (Havana), 1960.
(Co-author) *Labor Conditions in Communist Cuba,* University of Miami Press, 1963.
(Co-author) *Social Security in Cuba,* University of Miami, 1964.
The Labor Sector and Socialist Distribution in Cuba, Praeger, 1968.
(Editor) *Revolutionary Change in Cuba,* University of Pittsburgh Press, 1971.
Cuba in the 1970s: Pragmatism and Institutionalization, University of New Mexico Press, 1974.
Comparative Socialist Systems: Essays in Politics and Economics, Center for International Studies, University of Pittsburgh, 1975.
Social Security in Latin America: Pressure Groups, Stratification and Inequality, University of Pittsburgh Press, 1978.

The Economy of Socialist Cuba: A Two-Decade Appraisal, University of New Mexico Press, 1981.

(Editor) *Cuba in Africa,* University of Pittsburgh Press, 1982.

El desarrollo de la seguridad social en America Latina, CEPAL, 1985.

(Editor) *The Crisis of Social Security and Health Care,* University of Pittsburgh Press, 1985.

Contributor to journals.

WORK IN PROGRESS: Models of Economic Development and Performance: Chile, Costa Rica, and Cuba; Social Security in the English-Speaking Caribbean.

*   *   *

MIDELFORT, H(ans) C(hristian) Erik   1942-

PERSONAL: Born April 17, 1942, in Eau Claire, Wis.; son of Peter A. (a physician) and Gerd (Gjems) Midelfort; married Corelyn Senn, June 16, 1965 (divorced, 1981); married Cassandra Hughes, May 25, 1985; children: (first marriage) Katarina Christianna Senn, Kristian Nicholas Senn; (second marriage) Sanford M., Raphael N., Lucy Winona Lilly. *Education:* Yale University, B.A., 1964, M.Phil., 1967, Ph.D., 1970.

ADDRESSES: Home—1806 Rugby Place, Charlottesville, Va. 22903. *Office*—Department of History, University of Virginia, Charlottesville, Va. 22903.

CAREER: Stanford University, Stanford, Calif., instructor in history, 1968-70; University of Virginia, Charlottesville, assistant professor, 1970-72, associate professor, 1982-87, professor of history, 1987—.

MEMBER: American Philosophical Society (fellow), American Society for Reformation Research, Past and Present Society, Phi Beta Kappa.

AWARDS, HONORS: German Academic Exchange Service fellow, 1967-68; National Endowment for the Humanities summer stipend, 1971, and fellowship, 1987-88; Gustave O. Arlt Award from Council of Graduate Schools in the United States, 1973, for *Witch Hunting in Southwestern Germany 1562-1684: The Social and Intellectual Foundations;* Guggenheim Memorial Foundation fellowship, 1975-76.

WRITINGS:

(Translator and editor with Mark U. Edwards, Jr.) Bernd Moeller, *Imperial Cities and the Reformation,* Fortress, 1972.

Witch Hunting in Southwestern Germany 1562-1684: The Social and Intellectual Foundations, Stanford University Press, 1972.

(Contributor) *After the Reformation,* University of Pennsylvania, 1980.

(Translator with Thomas A. Brady) Peter Blickle, *The Revolution of 1525: The German Peasants' War from a New Perspective,* Johns Hopkins University Press, 1982.

Contributor to *Papers of the Bibliographical Society of America,* and *Archiv fur Reformationsgeschichte.* Member of board of editors and contributor, *Central European History,* 1978-87.

WORK IN PROGRESS: Research on the history of insanity in sixteenth-century Germany and on the vulgar Renaissance in Germany.

MIDWINTER, E(ric) C(lare)   1932-

PERSONAL: Born February 11, 1932, in Sale, Lancashire, England; son of Harold and Edna (Ashworth) Midwinter; married Margaret Eley, December 28, 1964; children: Matthew, Daniel, Catharine. *Education:* St. Catharine's College, Cambridge, B.A. (first class honors), 1955, M.A., 1958; University of London, Post-graduate Certificate in Education (with distinction), 1959; University of York, D.Phil., 1966; University of Liverpool, M.A.Ed., 1968.

ADDRESSES: Home—37 Bloomfield Rd., Harpenden, Hertshire, England. *Office*—Centre for Policy on Ageing, 25-31 Ironmonger Row, London EC1V 3QP, England. *Agent*—Murray Pollinger, 4 Garrick St., London WC2 9BH, England.

CAREER: Teacher, lecturer, and deputy principal at schools in Manchester, Newcastle, and Liverpool, England, 1956-68; Liverpool Educational Priority Area Project, Liverpool, project director of government action-research project in education for the socially disadvantaged, 1968-71; director of Priority, Centre for Urban Community Education, Liverpool, 1971-73; Liverpool Teachers' Centre, Liverpool, principal, 1973-75; head of public affairs unit, National Consumer Council, 1975-80; Centre for Policy on Ageing, London, England, director, 1980—. Chairman of Advisory Centre for Education, Cambridge, 1976-84, London Transport Users Consultative Committee, 1977-84, and London Regional Passengers' Committee, 1984—. *Military service:* British Army, National Service, 1950-52; became sergeant.

MEMBER: Savage Club.

WRITINGS:

Victorian Social Reform, Longmans, Green, 1968.

Law and Order in Early Victorian Lancashire, St. Anthony's Press, 1968.

Social Administration in Lancashire, 1830-1860, Barnes & Noble, 1969.

Nineteenth Century Education, Longmans, Green, 1970.

Old Liverpool, David & Charles, 1971.

(Editor) *Projections: An Education Priority Project at Work,* Ward, Lock, 1972.

Social Environment and the Urban School, Ward, Lock, 1972.

Priority Education: An Account of the Liverpool Project, Penguin, 1972.

Patterns of Community Education, Ward, Lock, 1973.

(Editor) *Pre-School Priorities,* Ward, Lock, 1974.

Education and the Community, Wiley, 1975.

Make 'em Laugh: Famous Comedians and Their Worlds, Allen & Unwin, 1979.

Schools in Society: The Evolution of English Education, Batsford, 1980.

W. C. Grace: His Life and Times, Allen & Unwin, 1981.

Age Is Opportunity: Education and Older People, Centre for Policy on Ageing, 1982.

(Editor) *Mutual Aid Universities: Radical Forum on Adult Education,* Croom Helm, 1984.

Wage of Retirement: Case for New Pensions Policy, Centre for Policy on Ageing, 1985.

Fair Game: Myth and Reality in Sport, Allen & Unwin, 1986.

Caring for Cash: The Issue of Private Domiciliary Care, Centre for Policy on Ageing, 1986.

(With June Armstrong and Deirdre Wynne-Harley) *Retired Leisure: Four Ventures in Post-Work Activity,* Centre for Policy on Ageing, 1987.

(With Susan Tester) *Polls Apart?: Older Voters and the 1987 General Election*, Centre for Policy on Ageing, 1987.
Re-defining Old Age, Centre for Policy on Ageing, 1987.
The Lost Seasons: Cricket in Wartime, 1939-1945, Methuen, 1987.
New Design for Old: Function, Style and Older People, Centre for Policy on Ageing, 1988.

CONTRIBUTOR

Ernest Walter, editor, *Comparative Developments in Social Welfare*, Allen & Unwin, 1972.
John Raynor and Jane Harden, editors, *Cities, Communities and the Young*, Routledge & Kegan Paul, 1973.
Leigh, editor, *Better Social Services*, National Council of Social Service, 1973.
K. Jones, editor, *Year Book of Social Policy, 1972*, Routledge & Kegan Paul, 1973.
Lees and Smith, editors, *Action-Research in Community Development*, Routledge & Kegan Paul, 1975.
Goodlad, editor, *Education and Social Action*, Allen & Unwin, 1975.

OTHER

Contributor to *Equality and City Schools* and *Fit to Teach*.

* * *

MIKLOWITZ, Gloria D. 1927-

PERSONAL: Surname is pronounced *Mick*-lo-witz; born May 18, 1927, in New York, N.Y.; daughter of Simon (president of a steamship company) and Ella (Goldberg) Dubov; married Julius Miklowitz (a college professor), August 28, 1948; children: Paul Stephen, David Jay. *Education:* Attended Hunter College (now Hunter College of the City University of New York), 1944-45; University of Michigan, B.A., 1948; New York University, graduate study, 1948. *Politics:* Democrat.

ADDRESSES: Home—5255 Vista Miguel Dr., La Canada, Calif. 91011.

CAREER: Writer. U.S. Naval Ordnance Test Station, Pasadena, Calif., scriptwriter, 1952-57; Pasadena City College, Pasadena, instructor, 1971—; instructor for Writers Digest School.

MEMBER: PEN International, Society of Children's Book Writers, California Writer's Guild (member of board of directors), Southern California Council of Literature for Children and Young People.

AWARDS, HONORS: Outstanding Science Books for Children Awards, 1977, for *Earthquake!*, and 1978, for *Save That Raccoon!;* Young Reader Trophy from Western Australia for *Did You Hear What Happened to Andrea?*

WRITINGS—All juveniles:

Barefoot Boy, Follett, 1964.
(Contributor) *The Old Fashioned Ice-Cream Freezer*, Science Research Associates, 1967.
The Zoo That Moved, Follett, 1968.
The Parade Starts at Noon, Putnam, 1969.
(With Wesley A. Young) *The Zoo That Was My World*, Dutton, 1969.
(Contributor) *Real and Fantastic*, Harper, 1970.
The Marshmallow Caper, Putnam, 1971.
Sad Song, Happy Song, Putnam, 1973.
Turning Off, Putnam, 1973.

A Time to Hurt, a Time to Heal, Tempo Books, 1974.
Harry Truman, Putnam, 1975.
Nadia Comaneci, Tempo Books, 1977.
Unwed Mother, Tempo Books, 1977.
Paramedics, Scholastic Book Services, 1977.
Earthquake!, Messner, 1977.
Ghastly Ghostly Riddles, Scholastic Book Services, 1977.
Tracy Austin, Tempo Books, 1978.
Martin Luther King., Jr., Tempo Books, 1978.
Steve Cauthen, Tempo Books, 1978.
Save That Raccoon!, Harcourt, 1978.
Did You Hear What Happened to Andrea?, Delacorte, 1979.
Natalie Dunn, Roller Skating Champion, Tempo Books, 1979.
Roller Skating, Tempo Books, 1979.
The Love Bombers, Delacorte, 1980.
Movie Stunts and the People Who Do Them, Harcourt, 1980.
The Young Tycoons, Harcourt, 1981.
Before Love, Tempo Books, 1982.
Close to the Edge, Delacorte, 1983.
The Day the Senior Class Got Married, Delacorte, 1983.
Carrie Loves Superman, Tempo Books, 1983.
After the Bomb, Scholastic Books, 1985.
The War between the Classes, Delacorte, 1985.
Love Story, Take Three, Delacorte, 1986.
After the Bomb, Week One, Scholastic Books, 1987.
The Emerson High Vigilantes, Delacorte, 1988.
Anything to Win, Delacorte, 1989.

Contributor of children's stories to anthologies. Also contributor to magazines, including *Sports Illustrated, Hadassah*, and *Writer*.

WORK IN PROGRESS: An untitled book for Bantam Books.

SIDELIGHTS: Gloria D. Miklowitz told *CA:* "I began writing for children when my own were very young. . . . My writing experience previous to that had been in writing documentary films on rockets and torpedoes for the Navy Department.

"In writing I can live hundreds of different lives. In real life I live quite a normal existence, but on paper I have been a boy on drugs, a runaway, unwed mother, paramedic, a rape victim, a Moonie, a would-be suicide, and more. In a typical book, I may enter the hearts and minds of many people. For example, in the rape novel, *Did You Hear What Happened to Andrea?*, I played the part of victim, rapist, mother, father, sister, brother, boyfriend, and school friends, as well as police officers and doctors. In each book, I enter lives I can never really live and try to bring to my readers compassion and understanding for those lives.

"I write for young adults because teenage years are difficult ones. . . . Teenage problems interest me. Young people are still malleable enough to be influenced to constructive change. I try to offer or suggest alternatives to destructive behavior in my books.

"I do extensive research for each book, including reading and interviewing. To write *The Love Bombers*, for example, I not only read a great deal and interviewed former Moonies and cult specialists, but I stayed with the Moonies for a short time. To write the rape novel, I served on a rape hotline for a year and interviewed victims, psychologists, police, and medical people. It isn't until I've thoroughly understood every aspect of a problem that I feel qualified to write with conviction." Miklowitz's books have been translated into Spanish, Swedish, Japanese, German, and Danish.

MEDIA ADAPTATIONS: Did You Hear What Happened to Andrea? has been adapted for an ABC-TV "Afterschool Special," aired in September, 1983.

BIOGRAPHICAL/CRITICAL SOURCES:

PERIODICALS

Los Angeles Times, June 6, 1987.

*   *   *

MILLAR, T(homas) B(ruce)

PERSONAL: Born in Western Australia. *Education:* Royal Military College, Duntroon, Australia, graduate, 1944; University of Western Australia, B.A., 1952; University of Melbourne, M.A., 1958; University of London, Ph.D., 1960.

ADDRESSES: Home—6/126 Long Acre, London WC2E 9PE, England. *Office*—Australian Studies Centre, University of London, 28 Russell Square, London WC1B 5DS, England.

CAREER: High school teacher, 1953-58; Australian National University, Canberra, research fellow, 1962-64, fellow, 1964-66, senior fellow, 1966-68, professorial fellow, 1968—; Australian Institute of International Affairs, Canberra, director, 1969-76; University of London, London, England, professor of Australian studies and head of Australian Studies Centre, 1985—. *Military service:* Australian Army, 1943-50.

WRITINGS:

Australia's Defence, Melbourne University Press, 1965, 2nd edition, 1969, published as *Australia's Defense,* Praeger, 1970.
The Commonwealth and the United Nations, University of Sydney Press, 1967.
(Editor) *Britain's Withdrawal from Asia,* Australian National University Press, 1967.
Australia's Foreign Policy, Angus & Robertson, 1968.
(Editor) *Australian-New Zealand Defence Cooperation,* Australian National University Press, 1968.
Foreign Policy: Some Australian Considerations, Georgian House, 1972.
(Editor) *Australian Foreign Minister: The Diaries of R. G. Casey, 1951-1960,* Collins, 1972.
Australia in Peace and War: External Relations, 1788-1977, Hurst, 1978.
Contemporary Alliances, Department of International Relations, Australian National University, 1981.
The East-West Strategic Balance, Allen & Unwin, 1981.
(Editor) *International Security in the Southeast Asian and Southwest Pacific Region,* University of Queensland Press, 1983.
(Editor with Robin Ward) *Current International Treaties,* Croom Helm, 1984.
South Africa and Regional Security, South African Institute of International Affairs, 1985.
South African Dilemmas, Department of International Relations, Australian National University, 1985.
(Editor) *Australia, Britain, and Antarctica,* Australian Studies Centre, University of London, 1986.
(Editor) *Higher Education Policy in Britain and Australia,* Australian Studies Centre, University of London, 1987.

CONTRIBUTOR

John Wilkes, editor, *Australian Defence and Foreign Policy,* Angus & Robertson, 1964.

Norman Harper, editor, *Ferment in Asia,* Australian Broadcasting Commission, 1966.
The Year Book of World Affairs, London Institute of World Affairs, 1967.
Gordon Greenwood and Harper, editors, *Australia in World Affairs, 1961-65,* F. W. Cheshire, 1968.
Roy Forward and Bob Reece, editors, *Conscription in Australia,* University of Queensland Press, 1968.
Harper, editor, *Pacific Orbit,* F. W. Cheshire, 1968.
Brassey's Annual: The Armed Forces Year Book 1968, Clowes, 1968.
J. D. B. Miller, editor, *India, Japan, Australia: Partners in Asia?,* Australian National University Press, 1968.
James N. Rosenau, editor, *International Politics and Foreign Policy,* Free Press, 1969.
Brassey's Annual: The Armed Forces Year Book 1969, Clowes, 1969.
Charles Osborne, editor, *Australia, New Zealand and the South Pacific,* Anthony Blond, 1970.
Marion W. Ward, editor, *The Politics of Melanesia,* Australian National University, 1970.
Carsten Holbraad, editor, *The Nuclear Non-Proliferation Treaty and Super-Power Condominium,* Australian National University Press, 1971.
Bruce Brown, editor, *Asia and the Pacific in the 1970's,* Australian National University Press, 1971.
Alvin J. Cottrell and R. M. Burrell, editors, *The Indian Ocean: Its Political, Economic and Military Importance,* Praeger, 1972.
Robert M. Lawrence and Joel Larus, editors, *Nuclear Proliferation Phase II,* University Press of Kansas, 1974.
George H. Quester, editor, *Seapower in the 1970's,* Dunellen, 1975.
Abbas Amirie, editor, *The Persian Gulf and Indian Ocean in International Politics,* International Institute for Political and Economic Studies (Tehran), 1975.

OTHER

Editor of *Canberra Papers on Strategy and Defence, 1966-70.* Contributor to journals. Editor, *Australian Outlook,* 1965, 1969-70.

*   *   *

MILLER, Alice P(atricia McCarthy)

PERSONAL: Born in Lynn, Mass.; daughter of William Henry and Julia (McCarthy); married Warren Hudson Miller (an insurance executive), April 3, 1942; children: Nancy, Jacqueline. *Education:* Hunter College (now Hunter College of the City University of New York), A.B.; New School for Social Research, M.S.S.; Columbia University, M.A., 1963.

CAREER: Former editor and staff writer for various publications, and substitute teacher in high schools; New York City Community College of Applied Arts and Sciences of the City University of New York, Brooklyn, N.Y., instructor in communication arts and skills, 1960-61; Pratt Institute, Brooklyn, instructor in psychology, 1961-65; Juilliard School of Music (now Juilliard School), New York City, instructor in sociology and psychology, 1965-66; writer. Free-lance writer, Harper & Row, New York City, 1969-70. Instructor in sociology, Helene Fuld School of Nursing, 1973; instructor in creative writing, Riverdale Community Center, 1977—. Founding trustee, Levittown Public Library, 1950-52.

MEMBER: American Psychological Association, Authors Guild, Phi Beta Kappa.

AWARDS, HONORS: Indiana University writing fellowship, 1958; merit award, *Woman's Day* Bicentennial Essay Contest, 1976.

WRITINGS:

The Heart of Camp Whippoorwill (young people), Lippincott, 1960.
Make Way for Peggy O'Brien (young people), Lippincott, 1961.
The Little Store on the Corner (young people), Abelard, 1961.
In Cold Red Ink: How Term Papers Are Graded and Why (adult), Allwyn, 1968.
It Happened in 1918 (adult), Allwyn, 1968.
A Kennedy Chronology, Allwyn, 1968.
(With husband, Warren Hudson Miller) *Who Shares Your Birthday?* (adult), Allwyn, 1970.
(With W. H. Miller) *The 1910-1919 Decade* (adult), Allwyn, 1972.
Edmund Burke: A Biography (young adult), Allwyn, 1976.
Edmund Burke and His World (adult), Devon-Adair, 1979.
The Mouse Family's Blueberry Pie (young people), Dandelion Press, 1980.
Prisoners of Childhood, Basic Books, 1981.
Melissa the Mouse, Children's Press, 1983.
For Your Own Good, Farrar, Straus, 1983.

Writer for Dave Garroway's "Today" television show, National Broadcasting Co., 1952-53. Contributor to magazines and anthologies.

SIDELIGHTS: Alice P. Miller once wrote *CA:* "I'm interested in current movements to eliminate prejudice from books for the young but not uncritical about some of the methods being used to eradicate such prejudice. We need greater representation of the various minority groups among those who decide which manuscripts shall be published and which published books shall be purchased by school and public library systems. We need greater encouragement of writing talent among persons from many backgrounds."†

*   *   *

MILLER, Richard (Connelly)   1925-

PERSONAL: Born September 17, 1925, in Cleveland, Ohio; son of Levi Lewis (a businessman) and Linda (Connelly) Miller; married Cora McCaughna, 1953; children: John, Lisa, Eric, Michael, Andrew, Kate. *Education:* Ohio State University, B.A., 1949; University of Paris, Certificat de Langue Francaise, 1951; Claremont Graduate School, M.A., 1956; University of California, Berkeley, Ph.D., 1961. *Politics:* Democrat.

ADDRESSES: Home—280 Grove Acre, Pacific Grove, Calif. 93950. *Office*—Box 621, Monterey, Calif. 93942. *Agent*—Joan Fulton, Harold Matson Co., 276 Fifth Ave., New York, N.Y. 10001.

CAREER: Merchant seaman, 1945-50; free-lance writer and photographer, 1950-53; Golden Gate College, San Francisco, Calif., faculty member, 1958; College of the San Francisco Art Institute, San Francisco, faculty member, 1959-80, chair of humanities department, 1972-74. Candidate for Democratic nomination to House of Representatives (12th Congressional District), 1964, 1966. Co-chairman, Monterey County Committee to End the War in Vietnam, 1965-67. *Military service:* U.S. Marine Corps, 1943-45.

MEMBER: Cousteau Society, National Writers Union.

AWARDS, HONORS: Honorable mention, Joseph Henry Jackson Awards (literary awards administered by San Francisco Foundation), 1957; John Randolph and Dora Haynes Fellow in History, 1959-60.

WRITINGS:

Amerloque (novel), Crown, 1966.
Bohemia: The Protoculture Then and Now (history), Nelson-Hall, 1977.
Snail (satiric fantasy), Holt, 1984.

Contributor to *Creative States* and other magazines and newspapers.

WORK IN PROGRESS: Canam: A Canadian/American Adventure, a novel; *Squed,* a "lively tale about death and the dead"; *Sowboy,* a novel of "life on a pig farm and beyond"; *The First Game,* a novel of "the genesis of the first intercollegiate football game"; *Zeugma,* a novel about "bad connections."

SIDELIGHTS: Richard Miller comments: "Some things are too serious to take seriously and too funny to be laughed at."

*   *   *

MILLER, Sally M.   1937-

PERSONAL: Born April 13, 1937, in Chicago, Ill.; daughter of Robert (a businessman) and Clara (Nixon) Miller. *Education:* University of Illinois, B.A., 1958; University of Chicago, A.M., 1963; University of Toronto, Ph.D., 1966. *Religion:* Jewish.

ADDRESSES: Home—2004 Franklin Ave., Stockton, Calif. 95204. *Office*—Department of History, University of the Pacific, 3601 Pacific Ave., Stockton, Calif. 95211.

CAREER: Michigan State University, East Lansing, instructor, 1965-66, assistant professor of American thought and language, 1966-67; University of the Pacific, Stockton, Calif., assistant professor, 1967-70, associate professor, 1970-75, professor of history, 1975—. Visiting senior lecturer in history, University of Warwick, 1978-79. Fulbright lecturer, University of Otago, 1986. Founder, Southwest Labor Studies Conference.

MEMBER: American Historical Association, Organization of American Historians, American Association of University Professors, Immigration History Group, European Labor and Working Class History Study Group, Western Association of Women Historians.

AWARDS, HONORS: American Philosophical Society travel grants, 1971, 1976; distinguished faculty award, University of the Pacific, 1976; American Council of Learned Societies travel grant, 1979; California Council for the Humanities grant, 1981.

WRITINGS:

Victor Berger and the Promise of Constructive Socialism, 1910-1920, Greenwood Press, 1973.
The Radical Immigrant, Twayne, 1974.
(Contributor) *Socialism and the Cities,* Kennikat, 1975.
(Editor) *Flawed Liberation: Socialism and Feminism,* Greenwood Press, 1981.
(Editor with Philip S. Foner) *Kate Richards O'Hare: Selected Writings and Speeches,* Louisiana State University Press, 1982.

The Ethnic Press in the United States, Greenwood Press, 1987.

Contributor of articles to history journals; during early 1960's contributed fiction to other periodicals.

WORK IN PROGRESS: Autobiographical sketches; fiction ("for own amusement").

* * *

MILLINGTON, Ada
   ### See DEYNEKA, Anita

* * *

MILNER, Clyde A. II   1948-

PERSONAL: Born October 19, 1948, in Durham, N.C.; son of Charles F. (a university administrator) and Eloyse (Sargent) Milner; married Carol O'Connor, August 14, 1977; children: Catherine Carol, Charles Clyde. *Education:* University of North Carolina, A.B., 1971; Yale University, M.A., 1973, M.Phil., 1974, Ph.D., 1979.

ADDRESSES: Home—203 Boulevard, Logan, Utah 84321. *Office*—Department of History, Utah State University, Logan, Utah 84322-0710.

CAREER: Guilford College, Greensboro, N.C., admissions counselor and assistant to the director of the Honors Program, 1968-70; Yale University, New Haven, Conn., instructor in history of the American West, 1974-75; Utah State University, Logan, instructor, 1976-79, assistant professor, 1979-82, associate professor of American history, 1982—, co-director of Western Writers' Conference, 1980-81, member of board of advisers to renamed Mountain West Writing Conference, 1985—. Reader and reviewer for Western and American Indian history, History Book Club, Inc., 1986—. Has participated in numerous professional meetings; has reviewed numerous proposals for National Endowment for the Humanities, periodicals, and publishing companies. Public speaker.

MEMBER: American Historical Association, American Studies Association, American Association for State and Local History, Organization of American Historians, American Folklore Society, Friends Historical Association, Western History Association, Phi Beta Kappa, Phi Alpha Theta.

AWARDS, HONORS: Danforth fellowship; faculty research grant, Utah State University, 1981-82, 1983-84; grant from National Endowment for the Humanities, 1981-82; Outstanding Researcher of the Year in the Social Sciences, Utah State University, 1983; resident fellowship, William Andrews Clark Memorial Library, University of California, Los Angeles, 1984; grant-in-aid, American Association for State and Local History, 1984-85, for research; James H. Bradley Memorial Fellowship, Montana Historical Society, 1985; Faculty Service Award, Associated Students of Utah State University, 1987; Vivian A. Paladin Award, board of editors of *Montana: The Magazine of Western History,* 1987, for best article of the year.

WRITINGS:

(Contributor) Howard R. Lamar and Leonard M. Thompson, editors, *The Frontier in History: North America and Southern Africa Compared,* Yale University Press, 1981.
With Good Intentions: Quaker Work among the Pawnees, Otos, and Omahas in the 1870s, University of Nebraska Press, 1982.

(Editor with Floyd A. O'Neil, and contributor) *Churchmen and the Western Indians, 1820-1920,* University of Oklahoma Press, 1985.
(Editor) *Major Problems in the History of the American West,* Heath, 1988.

Contributor to *Reader's Encyclopedia of the American West,* Crowell, 1977. Contributor to numerous periodicals, including *American Historical Review, Western Historical Quarterly, Montana: The Magazine of Western History, Journal of American History, Journal of the West, Quaker History,* and *Utah Historical Quarterly. Western Historical Quarterly,* associate editor, 1984-87, co-editor, 1987—.

WORK IN PROGRESS: Becoming Native: Western Identity and Personal Memory in Montana; Native and American: The Family La Flesche; contributing a chapter to *The Future of the Western Past,* William Cronon, George Miles, and Jay Gitlin, editors, for Norton.

SIDELIGHTS: Clyde A. Milner told *CA:* "My first book, *With Good Intentions,* and my second, co-edited work, *Churchmen and the Western Indians,* examined the efforts of well-meaning, religious peoples who wanted to aid American Indians in the 1800s. Each book showed that 'good intentions' are often not enough to assure success especially in complex cross-cultural settings. These two volumes helped me hone my skills as a writer and editor.

"My present interests now center on questions of identity and how it forms in a regional and cultural context. One of my writings, 'The Shared Memory of Montana's Pioneers' [article in *Montana: The Magazine of Western History*], considers the role of supposedly personal memories that become expressions of a shared historical identity. In Montana, the same basic stories of the Indian threat during the overland journey and the vigilante actions against the road agents in the early mining camps reappear in different 'personalized' versions. The Indian threat is highly exaggerated whereas the robberies and murders of the road agents are real. Nonetheless, both episodes became emblems of pioneer identity for Montanans by the turn of the twentieth century.

"I plan to expand my Montana research into a book that examines the role of personal memory in creating a form of cultural history. My major resources for this study will be the memoirs, reminiscences, and oral histories of Montanans from the mining camps of the 1860s to the present. At the same time, I'm also beginning research on another book that considers the establishment of a 'modern' mixed-heritage identity for one fascinating family of Omaha Indians—the La Flesches. In the late nineteenth century, three children of Joseph La Flesche (Inshtamaza of the Omahas) gained national recognition as examples of Indian 'success' in the dominant white world. One son, Francis La Flesche, became a noted anthropological writer who helped produce a massive study of his own native people. I hope to bring the story of this family up to the present day.

"My experience as an editor for a national scholarly journal has led me into some other projects, most especially the compiling and editing of a one-volume reader of documents and articles on the history of the American West. This book has allowed me to examine the major historical writings on the West that have been produced in the last two decades. I'm amazed at the vitality and productivity in the field despite its relative neglect at many major research universities.

"When my graduate students ask me about launching a career as a publishing scholar, I try to assure them that the most important commitment must be to 'doing history.' They should try to get involved in questions and research topics that excite them and enjoy the writing that they are able to do. If they overanticipate criticism or worry about historiographic debates they may never get started. We need more and more active minds reading, researching, teaching, and writing."

*   *   *

MITCHELL, Loften 1919-

PERSONAL: Born April 15, 1919, in Columbus, N.C.; married Helen March, 1948; children: two. *Education:* Attended City College (now of the City University of New York), 1937-38; Talladega College, B.A., 1943; Columbia University, M.A., 1951; additional study at Union Theological Seminary, and General Theological Seminary.

ADDRESSES: Home—88-45 163rd St., Jamaica, N.Y. 11432.

CAREER: Playwright, theatre historian, and novelist. Began as actor in New York City during the 1930s; social worker for City of New York Department of Welfare; publicity director for Jewish Federation of Welfare Services; assistant for special programs at Harlem Preparatory School; WNCY-Radio, New York City, writer of weekly program "The Later Years," 1950-62; WWRL-Radio, New York City, writer of daily program "Friendly Adviser," 1954; State University of New York at Binghamton, department of theatre and department of Afro-American studies, professor, 1971-85, professor emeritus, 1985—. Adjunct professor of English, Long Island University, 1969, and New York University, 1970. *Military service:* U.S. Navy; served during World War II.

AWARDS, HONORS: Guggenheim fellowship, 1958-59; Rockefeller Foundation grant, 1961; Harlem Cultural Council special award, 1969; playwriting award, Research Foundation, State University of New York, 1974; Outstanding Theatrical Pioneer Award, Audience Development Committee (AUDELCO), 1979.

WRITINGS:

Black Drama: The Story of the American Negro in the Theatre (essays), Hawthorn, 1967.
The Stubborn Old Lady Who Resisted Change (novel), Emerson Hall, 1973.
(Compiler and contributor) *Voices of the Black Theatre* (oral history), James T. White, 1975.

PLAYS

"Shattered Dreams" (originally entitled "Cocktails"), first produced in New York City by Pioneer Drama Group, 1938.
"Blood in the Night," first produced in New York City, 1946.
"The Bancroft Dynasty," first produced in New York City at 115th Street Peoples Theatre, 1948.
"The Cellar," first produced in New York City at Harlem Showcase Theatre, 1952.
A Land beyond the River (also see below; first produced off-Broadway at Greenwich Mews Theatre, March 28, 1957), Pioneer Drama Service, 1963.
(With Irving Burgie) "Ballad for Bimshire" (musical), first produced on Broadway at Mayfair Theatre, October 15, 1963, revised version produced in Cleveland, Ohio, 1964.
(With John Oliver Killens) "Ballad of the Winter Soldiers," first produced in New York City at Lincoln Center, 1964.

Star of the Morning: Scenes in the Life of Bert Williams (also see below; musical; music by brother, Louis D. Mitchell, lyrics by Romare Bearden and Clyde Fox; first produced as "Star of the Morning" in Cleveland, 1965, produced in New York City at American Folk Theatre, 1985), Free Press, 1965.
Tell Pharaoh (also see below; concert drama; first produced in New York City at Colden Theatre, Queens College, February 19, 1967), Negro Universities Press, 1970, revised edition, Broadway Play, 1987.
"The Phonograph," first produced off-Broadway at Maidman Playhouse, 1969.
"The Final Solution to the Black Problem in the United States; or, The Fall of the American Empire," first produced in New York City, 1970.
Bubbling Brown Sugar (musical; adapted from a concept by Rosetta LeNoire; music and lyrics by various artists; first produced off-Broadway at AMAS Repertory Theatre, 1975, produced on Broadway at ATNA Theatre, March 2, 1976), Broadway Play, 1984.
(Author of libretto) "And the Walls Came Tumbling Down" (opera; music by Willard Roosevelt), first produced in New York City at Lincoln Center, 1976.
"Cartoons for a Lunch Hour" (musical), first produced in New York City at Perry Street Theatre, 1978.
"A Gypsy Girl" (musical), first produced in Pine Bluff, Ark., 1982.
"Miss Ethel Waters" (musical), first produced off-Broadway at AMAS Repertory Theatre, 1983.

Also author of "Cross Roads" (1938); "Sojourn to the South of the Wall"; "The World of a Harlem Playwright"; and "The Afro-Philadelphian." Also author of musical, "Prelude to the Blues" (music by Wallace Pritchett).

SCREENPLAYS

"Young Man of Williamsburg," YM & YMHA of Brooklyn, 1954.
"Integration—Report One," Andover Productions, 1960.
"I'm Sorry," Courtney Hafela Productions, 1962.
"The Vampires of Harlem" Vanguard Productions, 1972.

CONTRIBUTOR

The American Negro Writer and His Roots, American Society of African Culture, 1960.
C.W.E. Bigsby, editor, *The Black American Writer*, two volumes, Penguin, 1969.
William Adams, Peter Conn, and Barry Slepian, editors, *Afro-American Literature: Drama* (contains "A Land beyond the River"), Houghton, 1970.
William R. Reardon and Thomas D. Pawley, editors, *The Black Teacher in the Dramatic Arts* (contains "A Land beyond the River" and "Tell Pharaoh"), Negro Universities Press, 1970.
Addison Gayle, Jr., editor, *The Black Aesthetic*, Doubleday, 1971.
Alice Childress, editor, *Black Scenes*, Doubleday, 1971.
Woodie King, Jr., and Ron Milner, editors, *Black Dream Anthology*, New American Library, 1971.
James V. Hatch and Ted Shine, editors, *Black Theatre U.S.A.: 1874-1974* (contains "Star of the Morning"), Free Press, 1974.

OTHER

Also author of *Harlem, My Harlem* (essay collection); also author of radio scripts. Contributor to *Oxford Companion to the Theatre* and *Encyclopedia della spetta colo* (Rome). Contributor to periodicals, including *Amsterdam News, Crisis, Freedomways, Negro Digest, New York Times,* and *Theatre Arts Monthly.* Editor of *Freedom Journal,* NAACP, 1964.

SIDELIGHTS: The contributions of playwright and theatre historian Loften Mitchell "to the black American theater—his plays and his essays—show his recognition of the contributions of those who preceded him," writes Ja A. Jahannes in *Dictionary of Literary Biography.* "He acknowledges throughout his work the belief that the black theater in America is the result of black artists' collective contributions of genius, talent, pioneering efforts, denials, sacrifices, sensitivity to black culture, race consciousness, and their view of theater as art." In a theatre career that spans over fifty years, Mitchell stands as "one of the chief chroniclers of the history of black theater in America," notes Jahannes. He "projects a holistic view of black culture in his plays and essays, . . . present[ing] his subject in the contexts of American development and the social, political, and economic histories of black people in America."

Mitchell began his theatre career while still a high school student in Harlem, where he wrote sketches for the Progressive Dramatizers Group at Salem Church and then worked as an actor for the Rose McClendon Players. In Harlem, Mitchell had exposure to a wide range of up-and-coming black theatrical performers, such as Ethel Waters, Ralph Cooper, and George Wiltshire. It was also in Harlem that Mitchell had the formulative experiences that taught him how blacks were discriminated against in America. He writes of an early experience: ". . . At age 10, I sold newspapers on the streets of New York—and got into a fist fight with a white boy who told me: 'This place belongs to us more than it does to youse.' Along with other newsboys I was later arrested for selling newspapers without a license. We were kept overnight in the Children's Society where we 'colored boys had to sleep on cots in the hallway.'" (Mitchell adds that "ironically, in 1983 the AMAS Repertory Theatre presented my musical 'Miss Ethel Waters' in this same building—and there was a standing ovation"). Mitchell also came to realize that racial discrimination carried over to theatre. According to Jahannes, "Mitchell also saw that black people had been maligned, misrepresented, and deliberately cast in negative stereotypes in American theater. He dedicated himself to shattering those negative images, to projecting real-life images of the noble people who had lived in his beloved Harlem, and to harnessing their history as the principal vehicle of his artistic campaign."

Finding opportunities for black actors limited and scarce in the 1930s, Mitchell decided to leave New York City and accepted a scholarship to Talladega College in Alabama. He recalls in a *Freedomways* interview, as Doris Abramson cites in *Negro Playwrights in the American Theatre, 1925-1959,* that although many blacks during the Depression were financially or academically ineligible to attend college, "Southern Negro colleges, offering athletic scholarships and grants-in-aid, rescued many from the despair into which they had been dumped." At Talladega, Mitchell wrote the paper which would later become the basis for his acclaimed essay collection, *Black Drama: The Story of the American Negro in the Theatre.*

The predominant themes in Mitchell's essays and plays, Jahannes notes, center on "the contributions and struggles of black people in America, the evils of racism, and the potential of black artists to enrich American theater and American life." In a 1965 article for *Crisis,* Mitchell spoke of inadequate black representation in the contemporary art scene. "Today—with

the Negro making headlines in a great revolution—our widely acclaimed writers are not fully represented on Broadway, in Hollywood, nor on television," he is quoted by Abramson. "Since the artist must seek the truth, communicate, educate, and entertain, I know that art is being distorted in these times. I know, too, that unless there is a sharp reversal, modern history will not be recorded in our plays and movies." *Black Drama: The Story of the American Negro in the Theatre* can be seen as an attempt to correct this situation. Isaiah Sheffer notes in *Nation* that "in an anecdotal and argumentative style, [*Black Drama*] traces the history of black theatre in this country from the West Indian slave, Mungo, who appears as a clown in a 1769 comedy, *The Padlock,* to the blackface minstrel shows of the pre-Civil War era, the Harlem theatre movements of the 1920s, and the struggles and problems of the fifties and sixties on and off Broadway." Jahannes adds that "more than anything else, [*Black Drama*] establishes the fact that there *is* a history of blacks in the American theater."

In 1975 Mitchell published a second book of history, *Voices of the Black Theatre,* which brought together first-hand testaments of seven important figures in American black drama: Ruby Dee, Abram Hill, Eddie Hunter, Dick Campbell, Vinnette Carroll, Frederick O'Neal, and Regina M. Andrews. Jahannes notes that each contributor "tells his or her story of a proud people determined to offer the best of theater to America; each attests to the indomitable will of black Americans to see their people portrayed in noble and realistic terms." Mitchell serves as commentator of this oral history, offering personal and historical insights to references made by the contributors. A reviewer in *Choice* calls the collection "readable, informative, and inspirational," adding that Mitchell's "writing reveals a warm and personal admiration for the standards set by these 'voices of the black theatre.'"

Among Mitchell's best-known theatrical works are the drama "A Land beyond the River" and the musical "Bubbling Brown Sugar." "A Land beyond the River" premiered in March of 1957 for a ten-week engagement at New York City's Greenwich Mews Theatre and was popular enough to be held over for a year. "Heavy with message, unashamedly didactic in purpose," according to Abramson, the play parallels the real-life story of Rev. Joseph A. DeLaine, who led a group from Clarendon County, South Carolina, on a legal battle for desegregation in schools and buses. Mitchell's play was especially praised for its vivid characters. In a review of the Greenwich Mews Theatre production, Brooks Atkinson of the *New York Times* writes that "Mitchell's craftsmanship is rough and ready—rough with theme, but ready with humor," a quality he attributes to "characters [that] are explosively emotional, quick to take offense from one another and quick to subside once they have let go with their fists or their tongues." This aspect contributes to what Jahannes identifies as one of the play's major themes, "the conflict between violence and nonviolence as a means to achieve full rights." Nearly twenty years later, Mitchell wrote the script for the popular Broadway musical "Bubbling Brown Sugar," a nostalgic tribute to the entertainers of Harlem from the early 1920s to the 1940s. In the musical, a modern black couple is transported back to "an earlier Harlem where they see the real sites, sounds, and dancing feet of that community's artistic side," notes Jahannes. The Broadway production was nominated for a Tony Award as best musical of 1976, while Mitchell's script won praise for providing illuminating historical background to the lively song and dance numbers. Jahannes writes that "Bubbling Brown Sugar" and "A Land beyond the River", in addition to the rest of Mitchell's plays, relate "the saga of black life in America."

Collections of Mitchell's papers are housed by the State University of New York at Binghamton, the New York City Library Schomberg Collection, Talladega College, and Boston University.

BIOGRAPHICAL/CRITICAL SOURCES:

BOOKS

Abramson, Doris E., *Negro Playwrights in the American Theatre, 1925-1959*, Columbia University Press, 1969.
Dictionary of Literary Biography, Volume 38: *Afro-American Writers after 1955: Dramatists and Prose Writers*, Gale, 1985.

PERIODICALS

Choice, January, 1976.
Contemporary Literature, winter, 1968.
Crisis, February, 1965.
Freedomways, summer, 1963, fall, 1964.
Nation, August 25, 1969.
Negro Digest, June, 1966.
New York Post, March 29, 1957.
New York Times, March 29, 1957.

—*Sketch by Michael E. Mueller*

*   *   *

MOLETTE, Barbara Jean 1940-

PERSONAL: Born January 31, 1940, in Los Angeles, Calif.; daughter of Baxter R. and Nora L. (Johnson) Roseburr; married Carlton W. Molette II (a college administrator and writer), June 15, 1960; children: Carla Evelyn, Andrea Rose. *Education:* Florida Agricultural and Mechanical University, B.A. (with highest honors), 1966; Florida State University, M.F.A., 1969.

ADDRESSES: Home—255 West Lanvale Park, Baltimore, Md. 21217.

CAREER: Spelman College, Atlanta, Ga., instructor in fine arts, 1969-72, instructor in drama, 1972-75; Texas Southern University, Houston, assistant professor in fine arts, 1975-87. Makeup artist and designer, costume designer, technical theatre worker at Tuskegee Institute, 1960-61, University of Iowa, 1961, Iowa City Community Theatre, 1962, Des Moines Community Playhouse, 1962-63, and Howard University, 1964; member of costume construction crew, designer, and wardrobe mistress, Asolo Theatre Festival, Sarasota, Fla., summer, 1968; drama coordinator for Upward Bound Program, Florida Agricultural and Mechanical University, summer, 1969; costumer, Morehouse-Spelman Players, 1969-75. Costumer for motion picture, "Together for Days," 1971.

MEMBER: Dramatists Guild, Authors League of America, National Association of Dramatic and Speech Arts, National Conference of African American Theatre.

AWARDS, HONORS: Faculty development grant, Spelman College, 1972; graduate fellowship, University of Missouri, 1986-87; 3rd place, WMAR-TV Drama Competition, 1987, for "Perfect Fifth."

WRITINGS:

WITH HUSBAND, CARLTON W. MOLETTE II

Rosalee Pritchett (also see below; play; first produced in Atlanta by Morehouse-Spelman Players, March 20, 1970; produced Off-Broadway at St. Mark's Playhouse, January 12, 1971), Dramatists Play Service, 1972.
"Booji Wooji" (also see below; play), first produced at Atlanta University Summer Theatre, July 8, 1971.
(Contributor) Richard Barksdale and Keneth Kinnamon, editors, *Black Writers of America: A Comprehensive Anthology* (contains "Rosalee Pritchett"), Macmillan, 1972.
(And with Charles Mann) "Doctor B. S. Black" (also see below; musical), first produced at Atlanta University Summer Theatre, July 20, 1972.
(Compilers) *Afro-American Theatre: A Bibliography*, privately printed, 1972.
(Contributor) Eileen J. Ostrow, editor, *Center Stage: An Anthology of Twenty-One Contemporary Black-American Plays* (contains "Noah's Ark"), Sea Urchin, 1983.
Black Theatre: Premise and Presentation, Wyndham Hall, 1986.

Also co-author of filmstrip, "Stage Makeup for Black Actors," Paramount Theatrical Supplies; screenplay adaptation of "Booji Wooji"; and non-musical version of "Dr. B. S. Black."

OTHER

"The Escape; or, A Leap to Freedom" (adapted from the play by William Wells Brown), first produced at Texas Southern University, 1976.

Also author of teleplay, "Perfect Fifth." Author of syndicated column, "Upstage/Downstage." Contributor to periodicals. Book review editor, *Encore*, 1970-72.

*   *   *

MOORE, Fenworth
[Collective pseudonym]

WRITINGS:

(Contributor) *Popular Stories for Boys* (includes *Wrecked on Cannibal Island;* also see below), Cupples & Leon, 1934.
Thrilling Stories for Boys (contains *Wrecked on Cannibal Island, Lost in the Caves of Gold, Cast Away in the Land of Snow,* and *Prisoners on the Pirate Ship;* also see below), Cupples & Leon, 1937.

"JERRY FORD WONDER STORIES"

Wrecked on Cannibal Island; or, Jerry Ford's Adventures among Savages, Cupples & Leon, 1931.
Lost in the Caves of Gold; or, Jerry Ford among the Mountains of Mystery, Cupples & Leon, 1931.
Cast Away in the Land of Snow; or, Jerry Ford among the Polar Bears, Cupples & Leon, 1931.
Prisoners on the Pirate Ship; or, Jerry Ford and the Yellow Men, Cupples & Leon, 1932.

SIDELIGHTS: For additional information see the entries for Harriet S. Adams, Edward L. Stratemeyer, and Andrew E. Svenson.

BIOGRAPHICAL/CRITICAL SOURCES:

BOOKS

Johnson, Deidre, editor and compiler, *Stratemeyer Pseudonyms and Series Books: An Annotated Checklist of Strat-*

emeyer and Stratemeyer Syndicate Publications, Greenwood Press, 1982.

PERIODICALS

Journal of Popular Culture, winter, 1974.

* * *

MOORE, John A(lexander) 1915-

PERSONAL: Born June 27, 1915, in Charles Town, W.Va.; son of George Douglas (a lawyer) and Louise Hammond (Blume) Moore; married Betty Clark (a research biologist), June 4, 1938; children: Sally (Mrs. W. Einar Gall), Nancy (deceased). *Education:* Columbia University, A.B., 1936. M.A., 1939, Ph.D., 1940.

ADDRESSES: Home—11522 Tulane Ave., Riverside, Calif. 92507. *Office*—Department of Biology, University of California, Riverside, Calif. 92521.

CAREER: Brooklyn College (now Brooklyn College of the City University of New York), New York City, tutor in biology, 1939-41; Queens College (now Queens College of the City University of New York), New York City, instructor in biology, 1941-43; Barnard College, New York City, assistant professor, 1943-47, associate professor, 1947-50, professor of biology, 1950-68, chairman of department, 1948-52, 1953-54, and 1960-66; University of California, Riverside, professor of biology, 1969-82, professor emeritus, 1982—. Research associate, American Museum of Natural History, 1942—. Columbia University, chairman of zoology department, 1949-52, professor of zoology, 1954-68; Walker-Ames professor at University of Washington, Seattle, 1966. Chairman of Commission on Science Education, 1971-72.

MEMBER: American Association for the Advancement of Science (fellow), Marine Biology Laboratory, American Society of Zoologists (president, 1974), Genetics Society of America, American Society of Naturalists (vice-president, 1970, president, 1972), Society for the Study of Evolution (president, 1963), National Academy of Sciences, American Academy of Arts and Sciences, American Society of Ichthyologists and Herpetologists, Harvey Society, Cosmos Club.

AWARDS, HONORS: Fulbright research scholar in Australia, 1952-53; Guggenheim fellowship, 1959.

WRITINGS:

Principles of Zoology, with laboratory workbook, Oxford University Press, 1957.
The Frogs of Eastern New South Wales, American Museum of Natural History, 1961.
The Wonder of Life, Home Library Press, 1961.
Heredity and Development, Oxford University Press, 1963, 2nd edition, 1972.
A Guide to Washington, National Academy of Sciences, 1963.
(Supervisor) *Biological Science: An Inquiry into Life*, Harcourt, 1963, 3rd edition, 1973.
(Editor) *Physiology of the Amphibia*, Academic Press, 1964.
(Editor) *Ideas in Modern Biology*, Natural History Press, 1965.
(Editor) *Ideas in Evolution and Behavior*, Natural History Press, 1970.
(With Norman Abraham and others) *Interaction of Man and the Biosphere*, Rand McNally, 1970, 3rd edition, 1979.
Science for Society: A Bibliography, American Association for the Advancement of Science, 1971, 2nd edition, 1972.

(Editor) *Readings in Heredity and Development*, Oxford University Press, 1972.
Academic Abbreviations and Acronyms, University of California, Riverside, 1981.
(Co-editor) *Dobzhansky's Genetics of Natural Populations*, Columbia University Press, 1981.

Author of "Science As a Way of Knowing" series, 1984-88. Contributor of numerous chapters to various books. Contributor to professional journals. Member of editorial board of *Ecology*, 1948-50, and *American Zoologist*, 1960-63; *Journal of Morphology*, member of editorial board, 1951-52, managing editor, 1955-60.

WORK IN PROGRESS: Scientific and popular books dealing with biology, especially with evolution; a study of academic libraries; additional volumes in the "Science As a Way of Knowing" series.

* * *

MOORE, P(eter) G(erald) 1928-

PERSONAL: Born April 5, 1928, in Richmond, England; son of Leonard J. and Ruby (Wilburn) Moore; married Margaret Gertrude Sonja Enevoldson Thomas, September 27, 1958; children: Penelope, Richard, Charles. *Education:* University College, London, B.Sc. (first-class honors), 1949, Ph.D., 1956; also studied at Princeton University, 1953-54.

ADDRESSES: Home—3 Chartway, Sevenoaks, Kent, England. *Office*—London Business School, Sussex Pl., Regents Park, London NW1 4SA, England.

CAREER: Reed Paper Corp., London, England, head of statistical and mathematical services, 1958-66; London Business School, London, professor of statistics, 1966-72, deputy principal, 1972-84, principal, 1984, member of grants committee, 1979—. Partner, Duncan C. Fraser, 1974-77. Member of board of directors of Shell Ltd., United Kingdom, 1969-72, Copeman Paterson Ltd., 1978—, and Martin Paterson Associates, 1984—. Consultant to Marketing Advisory Services. *Military service:* British Army, 1949-51; became major.

MEMBER: International Statistical Institute (member of council, 1985—), Royal Statistical Society (member of council, 1966-78; honorary secretary, 1968—), Institute of Actuaries (member of council, 1966—; vice-president, 1973-76; president, 1984—).

AWARDS, HONORS: Rosa Morison Memorial Medal, 1949; J. D. Scaife Medal, Institution of Production Engineers, 1964; Guy Medal, Royal Statistical Society, 1970; honorary D.Sc. from Heriot-Watt University.

WRITINGS:

Principles of Statistical Techniques, Cambridge University Press, 1958, 2nd edition, 1969.
(With D. E. Edwards) *Standard Statistical Calculations*, Pitman, 1965, 2nd edition, 1972.
Statistics and the Manager, Macdonald & Co., 1966.
Basic Operational Research, Pitman, 1968, 3rd edition, 1986.
(Editor with S. D. Hodges) *Programming for Optimal Decisions: Selected Readings in Mathematical Programming Techniques for Management Problems*, Penguin, 1970.
Risk in Business Decision, Longmans, Green, 1972.
(With Howard Thomas) *The Anatomy of Decisions*, Penguin, 1976.
(With others) *Case Studies in Decision Analysis*, Penguin, 1976.

Reason by Numbers, Penguin, 1980.
The Business of Risk, Cambridge University Press, 1983.

Editor for Penguin's series on operational management.

AVOCATIONAL INTERESTS: Travel, walking, golf, detective stories, French food and wine.

*   *   *

MORAY WILLIAMS, Ursula 1911-

PERSONAL: Born April 19, 1911, in Petersfield, Hampshire, England; daughter of Arthur (an archaeologist) and Mabel (a teacher; maiden name, Unwin) Moray Williams; married Peter Southey John (an aircraft engineer), September 28, 1935 (died, 1974); children: Andrew, Hugh, Robin, James. *Education:* Privately educated at home by governess; attending finishing school in France, 1927-28, and art school in Winchester, England, 1928-29. *Religion:* Church of England.

ADDRESSES: Home—Court Farm House, Beckford near Twekesbury, Gloucestershire, England. *Agent*—Curtis Brown Ltd., 162-168 Regent St., London W1R 5TA, England.

CAREER: Author of books for children, 1931—. Former Justice of the Peace, Worcestershire-Evesham bench; chairman of Evesham Juvenile Panel, 1972-75; deputy chairman of Adult Bench, 1975-81. Former governor of County High School, Evesham; former governor of Vale of Evesham School for Educationally Subnormal Children. President of Women's British Legion, 1974—; former presiding member of Mothers Union. Founder of children's writing competitions in Cheltenham, England, the Outer Hebrides, and New Zealand. Has given talks about books at school libraries in the United Kingdom, New Zealand, and Australia.

MEMBER: National Book League, West Country Writers Association, Cheltenham Literary Festival Society.

WRITINGS:

FOR CHILDREN

(Self-illustrated) *Jean-Pierre,* A. & C. Black, 1931.
(Self-illustrated) *For Brownies: Stories and Games for the Pack and Everybody Else,* Harrap, 1932.
(Self-illustrated) *Grandfather* (verse), Allen & Unwin, 1933.
(Self-illustrated) *Pettabomination* (also see below), Search Publishing, 1933, revised edition, Lane, 1948.
(Self-illustrated) *Autumn Sweepers, and Other Plays for Children,* A. & C. Black, 1933.
(Self-illustrated) *More for Brownies,* Harrap, 1934.
(Co-illustrated with twin sister, Barbara Moray Williams) *Kelpie, the Gipsies' Pony,* Harrap, 1934, Lippincott, 1935.
(Self-illustrated) *Sandy-on-the-Shore,* Harrap, 1936.
(Co-illustrated with B. Moray Williams) *Elaine of La Signe,* Harrap, 1937, published as *Elaine of the Mountains,* Lippincott, 1939.
(With husband Peter John) *Adventures of Boss and Dingbatt,* Harrap, 1937.
Adventures of the Little Wooden Horse, Harrap, 1938, Lippincott, 1939, reprinted, Puffin, 1982.
Adventures of Puffin, Harrap, 1939.
Peter and the Wanderlust, Harrap, 1939, Lippincott, 1940, revised edition published as *Peter on the Road,* Hamish Hamilton, 1963.
Pretenders' Island, Harrap, 1940, Knopf, 1942.

(Self-illustrated) *Gobbolino, the Witch's Cat,* Harrap, 1942, new edition, 1981, abridged edition, Puffin, 1965.
(Self-illustrated) *The Good Little Christmas Tree* (also see below), Harrap, 1943, reprinted with illustrations by Jane Paton, Hamish Hamilton, 1970.
The House of Happiness (also see below), Harrap, 1946.
(Self-illustrated) *The Three Toymakers,* Harrap, 1946, Thomas Nelson, 1971, reprinted with illustrations by Shirley Hughes, Hamish Hamilton, 1976.
(Self-illustrated) *Malkin's Mountain,* Harrap, 1948, Thomas Nelson, 1972, revised edition illustrated by S. Hughes, Hamish Hamilton, 1976.
(Self-illustrated) *The Story of Laughing Dandino,* Harrap, 1948.
Pettabomination (play; adapted from her book of same title), Samuel French, 1951.
The Good Little Christmas Tree (play; adapted from her book of same title), Samuel French, 1951.
The House of Happiness (play; adapted from her book of same title), Samuel French, 1951.
Jockin the Jester, illustrated by B. Moray Williams, Chatto & Windus, 1951, Thomas Nelson, 1973.
The Binklebys at Home, Harrap, 1951.
(Self-illustrated) *The Binklebys on the Farm,* Harrap, 1953.
(Self-illustrated) *Secrets of the Wood,* Harrap, 1955.
(Self-illustrated) *Grumpa,* Brockhampton Press, 1955.
(Self-illustrated) *Goodbody's Puppet Show,* Hamish Hamilton, 1956.
(Self-illustrated) *The Golden Horse with a Silver Tail,* Hamish Hamilton, 1957.
(Self-illustrated) *Hobbie,* Brockhampton Press, 1958.
(Self-illustrated) *The Moonball,* Hamish Hamilton, 1958, Morrow, 1960.
The Noble Hawks, Hamish Hamilton, 1959, published as *The Earl's Falconer,* Morrow, 1961.
The Nine Lives of Island Mackenzie, Chatto & Windus, 1959, reprinted, Transworld, 1980, published as *Island Mackenzie,* Morrow, 1960.
Beware of This Animal, Hamish Hamilton, 1964, Dial, 1965.
Johnnie Tigerskin, Harrap, 1964, Duell, Sloane, & Pearce, 1966.
(Self-illustrated) *O For a Mouseless House!,* Chatto & Windus, 1964.
High Adventure, Thomas Nelson, 1965.
The Cruise of the "Happy-Go-Gay", Hamish Hamilton, 1967, Meredith Press, 1968.
A Crown for a Queen, Meredith Press, 1968.
The Toymaker's Daughter, Hamish Hamilton, 1968, Meredith Press, 1969.
Mog, Allen & Unwin, 1969.
Boy in a Barn, Thomas Nelson, 1970.
Johnny Golightly and His Crocodile, Chatto, Boyd, & Oliver, 1970, Harvey House, 1971.
Hurricanes, Book 1: *Traffic Jam,* Book 2: *Man on a Steeple,* Book 3: *Mrs. Townsend's Robber,* Book 4: *Out of the Shadows,* Chatto & Windus, 1971.
Castle Merlin, Thomas Nelson, 1972.
A Picnic with the Aunts, Chatto & Windus, 1972.
The Kidnapping of My Grandmother, Heinemann, 1972.
Children's Parties, and Games for a Rainy Day, Corgi Books, 1972.
Tiger-Nanny, Brockhampton Press, 1973, reprinted, 1988, Thomas Nelson, 1974.
The Line, Puffin, 1974.
Grandpapa's Folly and the Woodworm-Bookworm, Chatto & Windus, 1974.

No Ponies for Miss Pobjoy, Thomas Nelson, 1975.
Bogwoppit, Thomas Nelson, 1978.
Jeffy, the Burglar's Cat, Andersen, 1981.
Bellabelinda and the No-Good Angel, Chatto & Windus, 1982.
The Further Adventures of Gobbolino and the Little Wooden Horse, Puffin, 1984.
Spid, Andersen Press, 1985.
Grandma and the Ghowlies, Andersen Press, 1986.
Paddy on the Island, Andersen Press, 1987.

"MILLY-MOLLY-MANDY" SERIES; FOR CHILDREN

(Self-illustrated) *Anders and Marta*, Harrap, 1935.
(Self-illustrated) *Adventures of Anne*, Harrap, 1935.
(Self-illustrated) *The Twins and Their Ponies*, Harrap, 1936.
(Self-illustrated) *Tales for the Sixes and Sevens*, Harrap, 1937.
(Self-illustrated) *Dumpling: The Story of a Pony*, Harrap, 1937.
Castle for John Peter, Harrap, 1941.

OTHER

Contributor to numerous anthologies and magazines, including *Puffin Post, Cricket, USA*, and *Lady*.

SIDELIGHTS: A number of critics note Ursula Moray Williams's ability to infuse her children's stories with a sense of authenticity. These reviewers find her characters and dialogue especially convincing, producing stories that combine fantasy or comedy with realism. For example, critic Zena Sutherland, writing for the *Saturday Review*, describes Moray Williams's *Moonball* as a story in which "realism and fantasy are skillfully blended by an author with a sure ear for dialogue and an ingenuous, direct style." It is "a tale for . . . readers of all ages," adds Jane Yolen in the *New York Times Book Review*.

Moray Williams told *CA:* "I began writing stories with my twin sister and produced a volume every birthday and Christmas. I was first published in 1931 at the age of twenty. I write for all ages of children. Children's books have changed a bit since the 1930s in that violence, divorce, and to a certain extent, sex are now tolerated—but children respond eternally to sincerity, a proportion of emotion or sentiment, excitement, and kindness—which makes them feel less vulnerable!"

Gobbolino, the Witch's Cat was buried in a time capsule in 1978 at Harmondsworth for the children of 2078 to disinter. Many of Moray Williams's books have been translated into foreign languages. And, as the author herself points out, "*The Little Wooden Horse* is [over] fifty years old . . . and still printing."

MEDIA ADAPTATIONS: Gobbolino, the Witch's Cat was recorded on Delyse Records, 1967, and on Storyteller Cassettes, 1982-83. *The Three Toymakers, Bogwoppit, The Nine Lives of Island Mackenzie, Gobbolino, the Witch's Cat, Paddy on the Island*, and *Jeffy, the Burglar's Cat* were adapted for the British Broadcasting Company children's program, "Jackanory."

BIOGRAPHICAL/CRITICAL SOURCES:

PERIODICALS

New York Times Book Review, May 7, 1967.
Saturday Review, May 13, 1967, June 15, 1968, August 16, 1969, January 23, 1971.
Times Literary Supplement, June 17, 1965, June 6, 1968, December 11, 1970, November 3, 1972, December 8, 1972, July 7, 1978.

MORRISON, Gertrude W.
[Collective pseudonym]

WRITINGS:

"GIRLS OF CENTRAL HIGH" SERIES

The Girls of Central High; or, Rivals for All Honors, Grosset & Dunlap, 1914.
. . . on Lake Luna; or, The Crew That Won, Grosset & Dunlap, 1914.
. . . at Basketball; or, The Great Gymnasium Mystery, Grosset & Dunlap, 1914.
. . . on the Stage; or, The Play That Took the Prize, Grosset & Dunlap, 1914.
. . . on Track and Field; or, The Girl Champions of the School League, Grosset & Dunlap, 1914.
. . . in Camp; or, The Old Professor's Secret, Grosset & Dunlap, 1915.
. . . Aiding the Red Cross; or, Amateur Theatricals for a Worthy Cause, Grosset & Dunlap, 1919.

SIDELIGHTS: "The Girls of Central High" series dealt with adventure and sport. For more information see the entries for Harriet S. Adams, Edward L. Stratemeyer, and Andrew E. Svenson.

BIOGRAPHICAL/CRITICAL SOURCES:

BOOKS

Johnson, Deidre, editor and compiler, *Stratemeyer Pseudonyms and Series Books: An Annotated Checklist of Stratemeyer and Stratemeyer Syndicate Publications*, Greenwood Press, 1982.

*   *   *

MOSKOS, Charles C.   1934-

PERSONAL: Born May 20, 1934, in Chicago, Ill.; son of Charles and Rita (Shukas) Moskos; married Ilca Hohn; children: Andrew, Peter. *Education:* Princeton University, B.A. (cum laude), 1956; University of California, Los Angeles, M.A., 1961, Ph.D., 1963.

ADDRESSES: Office—Department of Sociology, Northwestern University, Evanston, Ill. 60208.

CAREER: University of California, Los Angeles, research assistant with political change committee at Center for Advanced Study in the Behavioral Sciences, Palo Alto, 1963-64; University of Michigan, Ann Arbor, assistant professor of sociology, 1964-66; Northwestern University, Evanston, Ill., associate professor, 1966-70, professor of sociology, 1970—. External examiner in sociology, University of Guyana, Georgetown, 1966—. *Military service:* U.S. Army, Combat Engineers, 1956-58.

MEMBER: International Sociological Association (president, Research Committee on Armed Forces and Conflict Resolution, 1982-86), American Political Science Association, American Sociological Association, Inter-University Seminar on Armed Forces and Society (member of executive committee, 1967—, chairman, 1987—), Mid-West Sociological Society.

AWARDS, HONORS: Grants from Social Science Research Council for work in British Caribbean, 1961-63, Russell Sage Foundation for studies in military sociology, 1965-67, Council for Intersocietal Studies, Northwestern University, 1966-70, and Ford Foundation for study of United Nations peacekeeping in Cyprus, 1969-70; Ford Foundation senior faculty fellow, 1969-70; Woodrow Wilson International Center for Scholars fellow, 1980-81; Rockefeller Foundation Humanities fellow, 1983-84; S.L.A. Marshall Chair, Army Research Institute, 1987-88.

WRITINGS:

The Sociology of Political Independence: A Study of Nationalist Attitudes among West Indian Leaders, Schenkman, 1967.
The American Enlisted Man, Basic Books, 1970.
Public Opinion and the Military Establishment, Sage Publications, 1971.
Peace Soldiers, University of Chicago Press, 1976.
Greek Americans, Prentice-Hall, 1980.
The Modern Military—More Than Just a Job?, Pergamon, 1988.
National Service in America, Twentieth Century Fund, 1988.

CONTRIBUTOR

P. S. Kronenberg and F. N. Trager, editors, *National Security and American Society,* University Press of Kansas, 1973.
Brent Scowcroft, editor, *Military Service in the United States,* Prentice-Hall, 1982.
Donald J. Eberly and Michael W. Sherraden, editors, *National Service: Social, Economic, and Military Impacts,* Pergamon, 1982.
Lloyd H. Elliott and Andrew J. Goodpaster, editors, *Toward a Consensus on Military Service: Report of the Atlantic Council's Working Group on Military Service,* Pergamon, 1982.
Morris Janowitz and Stephen D. Westbrook, editors, *The Political Education of Soldiers,* Sage Publications, 1983.
Gerald Suttles and Mayer N. Zald, editors, *The Challenge of Social Control,* Ablex Publishing, 1985.
James F. Short, Jr., editor, *The Social Fabric,* Sage Publications, 1986.
Joseph Kreuzel, editor, *American Defense Annual,* Lexington, 1988.

Also contributor to numerous other books, including *Sociological Realities,* 1975.

OTHER

Contributor of articles to professional and popular periodicals, including *Atlantic, Foreign Affairs, New York Times Magazine, Public Interest, Washington Post,* and *Wilson Quarterly.*

*   *   *

MPHAHLELE, Es'kia
 See MPHAHLELE, Ezekiel

*   *   *

MPHAHLELE, Ezekiel   1919-
 (Es'kia Mphahlele; Bruno Eseki, a pseudonym)

PERSONAL: Born December 17, 1919, in Marabastad Township, Pretoria, South Africa; son of Moses (a messenger) and Eva (a domestic; maiden name, Mogale) Mphahlele; married Rebecca Mochadibane (a social worker), 1945; children: Anthony, Teresa Kefilwe, Motswiri, Chabi Robert, Puso. *Education:* Attended Adams Teachers Training College, Natal, 1939-40; University of South Africa, B.A. (with honors), 1949, M.A., 1956; University of Denver, Ph.D., 1968.

ADDRESSES: Office—African Studies Institute, University of the Witwatersrand, Johannesburg 2001, South Africa.

CAREER: Clerk for an institute for the blind, 1941-45; Orlando High School, Johannesburg, South Africa, teacher of English and Afrikaans, 1945-52; *Drum* magazine, Johannesburg, fiction editor, 1955-57; University of Ibadan, Ibadan, Nigeria, lecturer in English literature, 1957-61; International Association for Cultural Freedom, Paris, France, director of African programs, 1961-63; Chemchemi Creative Centre, Nairobi, Kenya, director, 1963-65; University College, Nairobi, lecturer, 1965-66; University of Denver, Denver, Colo., visiting lecturer, 1966-68, associate professor of English, 1970-74; University of Zambia, Lusaka, senior lecturer in English, 1968-70; University of Pennsylvania, Philadelphia, professor of English, 1974-77; University of Witwatersrand, Johannesburg, senior resident fellow, 1978—, professor of African literature, 1979—. Inspector of education, Lebowa, Transvaal, 1978-79.

AWARDS, HONORS: African Arts magazine prize, 1972, for *The Wanderers.*

WRITINGS:

Man Must Live and Other Stories, African Bookman, 1947.
(Contributor) Prudence Smith, editor, *Africa in Transition,* Reinhardt, 1958.
Down Second Avenue (autobiography), Faber, 1959, reprinted, 1985.
The Living and the Dead and Other Stories, Black Orpheus, 1961.
The African Image (essays), Faber, 1962, Praeger, 1964, revised edition, 1974.
(Editor with Ellis Ayitey Komey) *Modern African Stories,* Faber, 1964.
The Role of Education and Culture in Developing African Countries, Afro-Asian Institute for Labor Studies in Israel, 1965.
A Guide to Creative Writing, East African Literature Bureau, 1966.
In Corner B and Other Stories, Northwestern University Press, 1967.
(Editor and contributor) *African Writing Today,* Penguin, 1967.
The Wanderers (autobiographical novel), Macmillan, 1971.
Voices in the Whirlwind and Other Essays, Hill & Wang, 1972.
(Under name Es'kia Mphahlele) *Chirundu* (novel), Lawrence Hill, 1981.
(Under name Es'kia Mphahlele) *The Unbroken Song: Selected Writings of Es'kia Mphahlele,* Ravan Press, 1981.
(Under name Es'kia Mphahlele) *Afrika My Music: An Autobiography, 1957-83,* Ravan Press, 1984, Ohio University Press, 1986.
Father Come Home (juvenile), Ravan Press, 1984.
(Under name Es'kia Mphahlele) *Bury Me at the Marketplace: Selected Letters of Es'kia Mphahlele,* edited by N. Chabani Mangayani, Skotaville, 1984.
Let's Talk Writing: Prose, Skotaville, 1985.
Let's Talk Writing: Poetry, Skotaville, 1985.

CONTRIBUTOR TO ANTHOLOGIES

Langston Hughes, editor, *An African Treasury: Articles, Essays, Stories, Poems by Black Africans,* Crown, 1960.
Jacob Drachler, editor, *African Heritage: An Anthology of Black African Personality and Culture,* Crowell, 1962.

Leonard Sainville, editor, *Anthologie de la litterature negro-africaine: Romaciers et conteurs negro-africains*, Volume II, Presence Africaine, 1963.

Richard Rive, editor, *Modern African Prose*, Heinemann, 1964, reprinted, 1982.

Ulli Beier, editor, *Black Orpheus: An Anthology of New African and Afro-American Stories*, Longmans, 1964, McGraw-Hill, 1965.

W. H. Whiteley, compiler, *A Selection of African Prose*, Volume II, Oxford University Press, 1964.

Anne Tibble, editor, *African-English Literature: A Survey and Anthology*, October House, 1965.

Hughes, editor, *Poems from Black Africa*, Indiana University Press, 1966.

Denny Neville, editor, *Pan African Short Stories*, Humanities, 1966.

Paul Edwards, compiler, *Modern African Narrative: An Anthology*, Humanities, 1966.

Edwards, compiler, *Through African Eyes*, Volume I, Cambridge University Press, 1966.

Lilyan Kesteloot, editor, *Anthologie negro-africaine: Panorama critique des prosateurs, poetes et dramatourges noirs du XXeme siecle*, Gerard, 1967.

Nadine Gordimer and Lionel Abrahams, editors, *South African Writing Today*, Penguin, 1967.

Herbert I. Shore and Megchelina Shore-Bos, editors, *Come Back, Africa: Fourteen Stories from South Africa*, International Publishers, 1968.

Ime Ikiddeh, compiler, *Drum Beats: An Anthology of African Writing*, E. J. Arnold, 1968.

Oscar Ronald Dathorne and Willfried Feuser, editors, *Africa in Prose*, Penguin, 1969.

John P. Berry, editor, *Africa Speaks: A Prose Anthology with Comprehension and Summary Passages*, Evans, 1970.

Joseph O. Okpaku, editor, *New African Literature and the Arts*, Volumes I and II, Crowell, 1970.

Charles Larson, editor, *African Short Stories: A Collection of Contemporary African Writing*, Macmillan, 1970.

Bernth Lindfors, editor, *South African Voices*, African and Afro-American Studies Research Center, 1975.

OTHER

Contributor of essays, short stories and poems, sometimes under pseudonym Bruno Eseki, to *Drum, Africa South, Denver Quarterly, Journal of Modern African Studies, Black World, New Statesman*, and other periodicals. Editor, *Black Orpheus*, 1960-66; member of staff, *Presence Africaine*, 1961-63; member of editorial staff, *Journal of New African Literature and the Arts*.

WORK IN PROGRESS: A Critical Anthology of African Poetry.

SIDELIGHTS: "A writer who has been regarded as the most balanced literary critic of African literature," Ezekiel Mphahlele can also "be acknowledged as one of its most significant creators," writes Emile Snyder in the *Saturday Review*. Mphahlele's transition from life in the slums of South Africa to life as a professor of English at a large American university was an odyssey of struggle both intellectually and politically. He trained as a teacher in South Africa, but was banned from the classroom in 1952 as a result of his protest of the segregationist Bantu Education Act. Although he later returned to teaching, Mphahlele first turned to journalism, criticism, fiction, and essay writing.

During an exile that took him to France and the United States, Mphahlele was away from Africa for over a decade. Never-

theless, "no other author has ever earned the right to so much of Africa as has Ezekiel Mphahlele," says John Thompson in the *New York Review of Books*. "In the English language, he established the strength of African literature in our time." Some critics, however, feel that Mphahlele's absence from his homeland has harmed his work by separating him from its subject. Ursula Barnett, writing in the conclusion of her 1976 biography *Ezekiel Mphahlele*, asserts that Mphahlele's "creative talent can probably gain its full potential only if he returns to South Africa and resumes his function of teaching his discipline in his own setting, and of encouraging the different elements in South Africa to combine and interchange in producing a modern indigenous literature."

Mphahlele himself has agreed with this assessment, for after being officially silenced by the government of his homeland and living in self-imposed exile for twenty years, Mphahlele returned to South Africa in 1977. "I want to be part of the renaissance that is happening in the thinking of my people," he told *CA*. "I see education as playing a vital role in personal growth and in institutionalizing a way of life that a people chooses as its highest ideal. For the older people, it is a way of reestablishing the values they had to suspend along the way because of the force of political conditions. Another reason for returning, connected with the first, is that this is my ancestral home. An African cares very much where he dies and is buried. But I have not come to die. I want to reconnect with my ancestors while I am still active. I am also a captive of place, of setting. As long as I was abroad I continued to write on the South African scene. There is a force I call the tyranny of place; the kind of unrelenting hold a place has on a person that gives him the motivation to write and a style. The American setting in which I lived for nine years was too fragmented to give me these. I could only identify emotionally and intellectually with the African-American segment, which was not enough. Here I can feel the ancestral Presence. I know now what Vinoba Bhave of India meant when he said: 'Though action rages without, the heart can be tuned to produce unbroken music,' at this very hour when pain is raging and throbbing everywhere in African communities living in this country."

Chirundu, Mphahlele's first novel since his return to South Africa, "tells with quiet assurance this story of a man divided," says Rose Moss in a *World Literature Today* review. The novel "is clearly this writer's major work of fiction and, I suppose, in one sense, an oblique commentary on his own years of exile," observes Charles R. Larson in *World Literature Today*. Moss finds that in his story of a man torn between African tradition and English law, "the timbre of Mphahlele's own vision is not always clear"; nevertheless, the critic admits that "in the main his story presents the confused and wordless heart of his character with unpretentious mastery." "*Chirundu* is that rare breed of fiction—a novel of ideas, and a moving one at that," says Larson. "It has the capacity to involve the reader both intellectually and emotionally." The critic concludes by calling the work "the most satisfying African novel of the past several years."

On the subject of writing, Mphahlele commented: "In Southern Africa, the black writer talks best about the ghetto life he knows; the white writer about his own ghetto life. We see each other, black and white, as it were through a keyhole. Race relations are a major experience and concern for the writer. They are his constant beat. It is unfortunate no one can ever think it is healthy both mentally and physically to keep hacking at the social structure in overcharged language. A language that burns and brands, scorches and scalds. Language that is as a machete with a double edge—the one sharp, the other blunt, the one cutting, the other breaking. And yet there are levels of specifically black drama in the ghettoes that I cannot afford to ignore. I have got to stay with it. I bleed inside. My people bleed. But I must stay with it.''

BIOGRAPHICAL/CRITICAL SOURCES:

BOOKS

Barnett, Ursula A., *Ezekiel Mphahlele*, Twayne, 1976.
Contemporary Literary Criticism, Volume 25, Gale, 1983.
Durden, Dennis, editor, *African Writers Talking*, Heinemann, 1972.
Herdeck, Donald E., *African Writers: A Companion to Black African Writing, 1300-1973*, Black Orpheus, 1973.
Lindfors, Bernth, editor, *South African Voices*, African and Afro-American Studies Center, 1975.
Moore, Gerald, *Seven African Writers*, Oxford University Press, 1962.
Moore, Gerald, *The Chosen Tongue*, Longmans, Green, 1969.
Mphahlele, Es'kia, *Afrika My Music: An Autobiography, 1957-1983*, Ravan Press, 1984, Ohio University Press, 1986.
Mphahlele, Ezekiel, *Down Second Avenue*, Faber, 1959.

PERIODICALS

Modern African Studies, March, 1963.
Nation, March 20, 1972.
New Statesman, April 25, 1959.
New York Review of Books, September 23, 1971.
New York Times Book Review, October 22, 1972.
Saturday Review, June 19, 1971.
Times Literary Supplement, August 11, 1961, March 23, 1967, March 10, 1972.
World Literature Today, summer, 1983, winter, 1983, winter, 1987.

*   *   *

MUCHA, Jiri 1915-

PERSONAL: Born March 12, 1915, in Prague, Czechoslovakia; son of Alphonse Maria (an art noveau artist) and Maria (Chytilova) Mucha; married Vitezslava Kapralova (a composer), April 26, 1940; married second wife, Geraldine Thomson (a composer), July 5, 1941; children: (second marriage) John. *Education:* Attended Charles University, 1934-39. *Religion:* Protestant.

ADDRESSES: Home—Hradcanske namesti 6, Prague 1, Czechoslovakia. *Agent*—Dilia, Vysehradska 28, Prague 2, Czechoslovakia.

CAREER: British Broadcasting Corp. correspondent in North Africa, Middle East, Southeast Asia, and Northwestern Europe during the later years of World War II; writer in Prague, Czechoslovakia, 1946-51; arrested for alleged espionage and imprisoned, 1951-54; writer and translator in Prague, 1954—. *Military service:* French Army, 1939, served in Czech Division; evacuated to Britain, 1940; Royal Air Force, 1943-45, served as flight lieutenant.

MEMBER: PEN, Garrick Club (London).

AWARDS, HONORS: Order of Merit; Mlada Fronta Award, 1966, for *Cerny a bily New York;* Memorial Medal, 1968; Ph.D., Dundee University, 1969; Officer of the Order of Arts and Letters, France, 1982.

WRITINGS:

Most (title means ''The Bridge''), Lofox, 1943.
The Problems of Lieutenant Knap (short-story collection), Hogarth Press, 1945.
Ohen proti ohni (war diary; title means ''Fire Braves Fire''), Sfinx (Prague), 1947.
Sklenena Stena (title means ''The Glass Wall''), Prace, 1948.
Spalena Setba, Melantrich, 1948, translation published as *The Scorched Crop*, Hogarth Press, 1949.
Valka Pokracuje (title means ''The War Continues''), Knihovna Lidovych Novin, 1949.
Cim zraje cas (title means ''Maturing and Time''), Ceskoslovensky Spisovatel, 1958.
Provdepodobna tvar (novel; title means ''Probable Face''), Ceskoslovensky Spisovatel, 1963.
Cerny a bily New York (title means ''Black and White New York''), Mlada Fronta, 1965.
Alphonse Mucha: His Life and Art, Heinemann, 1966.
Alphonse Mucha: The Master of Art Nouveau, Hamlyn, 1966.
Living and Partly Living (prison diary), translated from the original Czech by Ewald Osers, Hogarth Press, 1967, McGraw, 1968.
Studene Slunce, Ceskoslovensky Spisovatel, 1968.
Kankan se svatozari (title means ''Cancan with a Halo''), Obelisk, 1968.
Marieta v noci (title means ''Marieta by Night''), Ceskoslovensky Spisovatel, 1969.
(With Marina Henderson and Aaron Scharf) *Mucha*, Academy Editions, 1971.
(With Henderson) *The Graphic Works of Alphonse Mucha*, Academy Editions, 1973.
Alfons Mucha, Mlada Fronta, 1982.
Lloyd's Head, Melantrich, 1987.
Strange Loves, Mlada Fronta, 1988.
Alphonse Mucha, Academy Editions (London), 1988.

CONTRIBUTOR

John Lehmann, *The Face of War Britain*, [London], 1946.
Desmond Hawkins and Donald Boyd, editors, *Invasion*, Sfinx, 1947.
Klaus Mann zum Gedaechtnis, Querido Verlag, 1950.
Cecil Woolf and John Bagguley, editors, *Authors Take Sides on Vietnam*, Owen, 1967.
Marianne Alexandre, editor, *Viva Che!*, Lorrimer Publishing, 1968.
A. J. Liehm, *Generation*, [Paris], 1969.
B. S. Johnson, editor, *You Always Remember the First Time*, Quartet Books, 1975.

Also contributor to *New Writing* by Lehmann.

TRANSLATOR OF BOOKS INTO CZECH

Jack Lindsay, *The Betrayed Spring*, Statni Nakladatelstvi Krasne Literatury, 1956.
Norman Mailer, *The Naked and the Dead*, Statni Nakladatelstvi Krasne Literatury, 1957.
Sinclair Lewis, *The Man Who Knew Coolidge*, Statni Nakladatelstvi Krasne Literatury, 1957.
Kingsley Amis, *Lucky Jim*, Statni Nakladatelstvi Krasne Literatury, 1959.

OTHER

Also author of produced plays: ''Zlaty vek,'' 1948; ''Broucci ve fraku,'' 1960; ''Tanec mezik stiny,'' 1966. Also author of filmscripts, including ''Roztrzka,'' ''Povoden,'' ''Prvna a posledni," "Vanice," "Kral kralu," "Kohout plasi smrt," "Thirty-nine in the Shade," and "Prazske noci." Also translator of plays into Czech: Edward Albee, *The Zoo Story;* Samuel Beckett, *Happy Days;* William Gibson, *Two for the Seesaw;* Frank Gillroy, *Who Will Save the Ploughboy;* Doris Lessing, *Play with a Tiger;* Brendan Behan, *The Hostage;* Keith Waterhouse and Willis Hall, *Billy Liar, The Long and the Short and the Tall;* Arnold Wesker, *Roots* (Orbis, 1961), and *Kitchen;* Monty Norman, Julian More, and David Heneker, *Irma La Douce;* Wolf Mankowitz, More, Heneker, and Norman, *Expresso Bongo;* Mankowitz and Norman, *Belle; or The Ballad of Dr. Crippen;* Mankowitz, Norman, and Heneker, *Make Me an Offer;* John Osborne and Anthony Creighton, *Epitaph for George Dillon;* Peter Shaffer, *The Private Eye, Royal Hunt of the Sun;* Noel Coward, *Nude with Violin;* Patrick Hamilton, *Gas Light;* Norman and More, *The Perils of Scobie Prilt;* Arthur Miller, *A Memory of Two Mondays;* Shelagh Delaney, *Taste of Honey;* Robert Bolt, *A Man for All Seasons* (Orbis, 1963); Peter Ustinov, *Photo Finish, Half Way Up the Tree,* and *The Unknown Soldier and His Wife.* Regular contributor to *Literarni Listy* (Czechoslovak weekly), 1968—, and *Nation;* also contributor to *New York Review of Books.*

SIDELIGHTS: Jiri Mucha was one of a group of young writers who helped launch the publication *Daylight* in London in the early days of World War II. He was sentenced to prison in Czechoslovakia for espionage for a term of six years in 1951. He served half of the sentence and recorded his thoughts and experiences in a prison diary, *Living and Partly Living.* He wrote the book secretly in the coal mine with pencil stubs by the light of a lamp that he had to dig up and then bury again every day.

Mucha told *CA:* "Even though my books made usually several editions with over 100,000 copies and were translated into various languages, I would have written more, had I not been most of my life prevented by political circumstances from publishing. On the other hand, this saved me probably from publishing a lot of nonsense. Hence—you never know what is good for you."

BIOGRAPHICAL/CRITICAL SOURCES:

BOOKS

Mucha, Jiri, *Living and Partly Living* (prison diary), translated from the original Czech by Ewald Osers, Hogarth Press, 1967, McGraw, 1968.
Mucha, Jiri, Marina Henderson, and Aaron Scharf, *Mucha,* Academy Editions, 1971.

PERIODICALS

Canadian Forum, August, 1968.
Kultura (Prague), December 8, 1946.
Kulturni Politika, September 9, 1950.
Lidora Kultura (Prague), February 5, 1947.
London Tribune, December 14, 1945.
Lud (Bratislava), January 1, 1950.
Mlada Fronta (Prague), February 26, 1947.
Month (London), May, 1967.
Narodni Osvobozeni (Prague), September 15, 1946.
New York Times, January 13, 1969, February 16, 1969.
Observer, February 2, 1950.
Observer Reviews, April 23, 1967.
Spectator, December 14, 1945.
Times Literary Supplement, June 22, 1967.
Tvorba, July 7, 1970.
Vyvoj (Prague), July 16, 1947.

MUHAJIR, Nazzam Al Fitnah
See El MUHAJIR

*   *   *

MULISCH, Harry 1927-

PERSONAL: Born July 29, 1927, in Haarlem, Netherlands; son of Kurt and Alice (Schwarz) Mulisch; married Sjoerdje Woudenberg; children: Anna, Frieda.

ADDRESSES: Home—103 Leidsekade, Amsterdam, Netherlands. *Agent*—De Bezige Bij, Van Miereveldstraat 1, Amsterdam, Netherlands.

CAREER: Writer. Participant in writer's congresses in Finland, Scotland, Romania, and Germany.

AWARDS, HONORS: Reina Prinsen Geerligs Prize, 1951, for *Archibald Strohalm;* Bijenkorf Literatuur Prize, 1957, for *Het Zwarte licht;* Anne Frank Prize, 1957; Visser Neerlandia Prize, 1960, for *Tanchelijn, kroniek van een ketter;* Athos Prize, 1961; State Prize, 1977; granted knighthood within the Order of Orange-Nassau, 1977.

WRITINGS:

Het mirakel: Episodes van troost en liederlijkheid uit het leven van der heer Tiennoppen, De Arbeiderspers, 1956.
Manifesten (aphorisms), Heinisz, 1958.
De sprong der paarden en de zoete zee, Meulenhoff, 1964.
Israel is zelf een mens: Onzakelijke noitities uit de zaak 40/61, Bakker, 1969.
(Contributor) E. W. Johnson, editor, *Short Stories International,* Houghton, 1969.
(With others) "Reconstructie" (opera libretto), Steim Recording, 1969.
De vogels, Polak & Van Gennep, 1974.
Tegenlicht (poetry), Polak & Van Gennep, 1975.
Het ironische van de ironie: Over het geval G. K. van het Reve, Manteau, 1976.
Vergrote raadsels: Verklaringen, paradoxen, mulischesken, Orion, 1976.
Verzamelde verhalen, 1947-1977 (title means "Collected Stories, 1947-1977"), Athènaeum/Polak & Van Gennep, 1977.
De taal is ein ei, Athenaeum/Polak & Van Gennep, 1979.
What Poetry Is (chapbook), translated by Claire Nicolas White, Cross-Cultural Communications, 1982.
Opus Gran, Harmonie (Amsterdam), 1982.
De gezochte spiegel, Ad ten Bosch, 1983.
(With others) *De Toekomst van het boek,* J. Nijsen, 1984.
Last Call, translated by Adrienne Dixon, Collins Harvill, 1987.

PUBLISHED BY DE BIZIGE BIJ (AMSTERDAM)

Archibald Strohalm (novel), 1952, reprinted, 1980.
Chantage op het leven (two stories; title means "Blackmailing Life"), 1953, reprinted, 1979.
De diamant (novel; title means "The Diamond"), 1954.
Het Zwarte licht (novel; title means "The Black Light"), 1956, reprinted, 1982.
De versierde mens (stories; title means "The Decorated Man"), 1957.
Het stenen bruidsbed (novel), 1959, reprinted, 1983, translation by Adrienne Dixon published as *The Stone Bridal Bed,* Abelard, 1962.
Tanchelijn, kroniek van een ketter (play), 1960.

De Knop (one-act play), 1960.

Voer voor psychologen (autobiographical; title means ''Fodder for Psychologists''), 1961, reprinted, 1983.

Wenken voor de bescherming van uw gezin en uzelf, tijdens de jongste dag, 1961.

De zaak 40/61: Een Reportage (about Eichmann Trial), 1962.

The Discovery of Moscou, 1964.

Nol Gregoor in gesprek met Harry Mulisch, 1965.

Bericht aan de rattenkoning (about Provo; title means ''Report to the King Rat''), 1966.

Wenken voor de jongste dag (political), 1967.

Het Woord bij de daad: Getuigenis van de revolutie op Cuba, 1968.

Paralipomena orphica (autobiographical), 1970.

De verteller (novel; title means ''The Storyteller''), 1970.

Oidipous, Oidipous, naar Sofokles, 1972.

Soep lepelen met een vork, 1972.

De toekomst van gisteren (title means ''Yesterday's Future''), 1972.

Wat gebeurde er met sergeant Massuro?, 1972.

Woorden, woorden, woorden, 1973.

Het seksuele bokwerk (title means ''Sexual Stronghold''), 1973.

Bezoekuur, 1974.

Volk en vaderliefde, 1975.

Twee vrouwen: Roman, 1975, translation by Els Early published as *Two Women*, Riverrun Press, 1980.

Mijn getijdenboek, 1975.

De wijn in drinkbaar dank zij het glas, 1976.

De verteller: Of een idioticon voor zegelbewaarders gevolgd door kommentaar, katalogus, duriosa en een katastrofestuk, 1978.

De aanslag (novel; title means ''The Assassination''), 1982, translation by Claire Nicolas White published as *The Assault*, Pantheon, 1985.

Egyptisch, 1983.

Aan het woord: Seven toespraken, 1986.

De pupil, 1987.

OTHER

Also author of *De verteller verteld* (title means ''The Storyteller Told''), 1971, *Oude lucht* (title means ''Antique Air''), 1977, *Paniek der onschuld* (essays), 1979, and *De compositie van de wereld* (philosophy; title means ''The Composition of the World''), 1980. Author of ''Axel,'' an opera libretto, and ''Quauhquauhtinchan in den vreemde,'' a libretto for a radiophonic opera by Ton de Kruyf. Mulisch's books have been translated into numerous languages, including Spanish, Hebrew, Welsh, Slovakian, French, Swedish, German, and Polish.

SIDELIGHTS: Dutch writer Harry Mulisch has written over forty-five books, including novels, poetry, and plays, and philosophical, political, and autobiographical works. Although he has long been considered one of the Netherlands' most respected writers, Mulisch is best known in the United States for his 1982 novel, *The Assault*, his first translated work published in America. *The Assault* was immensely popular in the Netherlands also, where it sold nearly 300,000 copies under the title *De aanslag* (''The Asassination''). *The Assault* was welcomed by American critics. John Updike, for example, writes in the *New Yorker* that Mulisch's ''debut . . . is a brilliant one,'' and *Christian Science Monitor* reviewer Bruce Allen notes that *The Assault* ''is overdue, for Mulisch emerges in this tense and fascinating novel . . . as a sophisticated and resourceful craftsman who has much to say about the lingering after effects of World War II on his homeland and his generation.''

Mulisch's interest in the Second World War is evident not only in *The Assault* but in several other of his books as well. As the son of a Jewish mother whose family died in the concentration camps, and a Hungarian father who was imprisoned after the war for collaborating with the Nazis, Mulisch has stated, ''It isn't so much that I went through the Second World War, I *am* the Second World War,'' relates Stephen Spender in the *New York Review of Books*. ''That heritage,'' writes *New York Times Book Reviewer* contributor Harold Beaver, ''made [Mulisch] a telling witness of the internal splits that still haunt such a prosperous, jovial-seeming community as that of the contemporary Netherlands.''

The Assault is set in Haarlem, Holland during the Nazi occupation of 1945. The story begins at Carefree, one of four homes situated on the quayside, the others being Hideaway, Bide-a-Wee, and Home-at-Last. Carefree is the residence of the Steenwijk family, who is spending a quiet evening reading, sewing, and playing board games. Without warning, the stillness of the evening is shattered by six gun shots. The Steenwijks rush to their window and see their chief of police Fake Ploeg, who is also a Nazi collaborator, fall dead outside their neighbors', the Kortewegs', home. To the Steenwijks' dismay, the Kortewegs move the body to their doorstep. Before the Steenwijks can react, Nazi troops arrive and kill all of the Steenwijks except twelve-year-old Anton, who, after spending the night in jail, is sent to live with an aunt and uncle in Amsterdam. The remainder of the novel ''is devoted to unraveling the consequences of that first fateful night,'' writes John Gross in the *New York Times*.

Anton, however, concentrates on putting the events of that night behind him. He eventually becomes an anaesthesiologist, which critics note is a symbolic choice of career. His attempts to repress these memories are unsuccessful; as Gross observes, ''In a series of episodes spaced over 35 years, we watch the experience he wants to forget reasserting itself.'' While attending a wedding in Haarlem, for example, Anton is disturbed by a political discussion and decides to take a walk. He finds himself near his childhood home where one of the original neighbors, Mrs. Beumer, recognizes him and invites him in to tea. From her he learns why the Kortewegs chose to move Ploeg's body to the Steenwijk's home, instead of the Aartses', a family no one liked. The second chance occurence takes place at the funeral of a former underground leader, where Anton overhears two men discussing a shooting. Jolted by its similarities to the shooting of Ploeg, he questions the men, one of whom turns out to be Cor Takes, Ploeg's assassin. Finally, thirty-five years after his traumatic experience, Anton is attending a nuclear demonstration with his college-aged daughter when he bumps into one of the Kortewegs, who explains why her family betrayed the Steenwijks, and at what cost.

Since the final piece of information about Anton's past is not put into place until the end of the novel, *The Assault* has been described by reviewers as being, at one level, a psychological thriller. Updike describes the novel as 'a kind of detective story emanating from a violent incident in the Second World War [that] combines the fascination of its swift, skillfully unfolded plot with that of a study in the psychology of repressed memory.'' Although Stephen Spender concurs with this assessment, he maintains in the *New York Review of Books* that the novel has deeper implications as a ''debate about politics, morality, and guilt.'' He writes: ''Mr. Mulisch's achievement is to make us concerned with the actions of his Dutch characters on that night of terror and, at the end of his book, to persuade us that the potential of evil as great as that of the Nazis still exists in our world of nuclear armaments and of leaders of demonstrations against them.''

Reviewers also praise the clarity and economy of Mulisch's prose. Updike notes, for instance, that while Mulisch is sometimes described as an absurdist, ''there is nothing absurd about this economically and thoughtfully worked-out novel except, perhaps, the wartime reality that serves as its premise. The surreal abruptness with which fateful events develop is stunningly rendered.'' Gross writes: ''Mr. Mulisch . . . brings exceptional skill and imagination to his task. Townscapes and interiors are firmly delineated—cliche or not, you can hardly help being reminded of the clarity of Dutch painting; characters are established with a deft economy. . . . As the story develops, a hundred small touches sustain the effect of psychological truthfulness.'' While *Los Angeles Times Book Review* contributor Herb Hain believes the book ''is weakened by Anton's passivity and by some rather far-fetched coincidences,'' he concedes that ''there are flashes of brilliance, mainly in three powerful confrontations in which Anton's past comes back to haunt him.'' Allen concludes, ''Harry Mulisch's subtle and resonant novel ranks with the finest European fiction of recent years.''

MEDIA ADAPTATIONS: The Assault was made into a motion picture in 1985.

BIOGRAPHICAL/CRITICAL SOURCES:

BOOKS

Contemporary Literary Criticism, Volume 42, Gale, 1987.

PERIODICALS

Christian Science Monitor, July 16, 1985.
Glasgow Herald, November 16, 1985.
Guardian, November 13, 1985.
Hudson Review, winter, 1963-64.
Listener, December 11, 1980.
London Review of Books, December 19, 1985.
Los Angeles Times Book Review, November 3, 1985.
Newsweek, July 8, 1985.
New Yorker, May 25, 1963, January 6, 1986.
New York Review of Books, December 5, 1985.
New York Times, May 31, 1985.
New York Times Book Review, June 16, 1985.
Observer, November 17, 1985.
Review of Contemporary Fiction, spring, 1982.
Times Literary Supplement, October 3, 1980, January 8-14, 1988.
World Literature Today, autumn, 1977.

—*Sketch by Melissa Gaiownik*

*   *   *

MULLARKY, Taylor 1922-
(Bob N. Holder)

PERSONAL: Born October 29, 1922, in Detroit, Mich.; daughter of Harris Tweed and Pearl (Singer) Mullarky; married Elias I. Lett, June 20, 1959 (died, 1982); married Ken Moore, September 20, 1985; children: Polly, Esther. *Education:* Attended girls' vocational school in Detroit, Mich. *Politics:* Democrat.

ADDRESSES: Home and office—9568 Columbia, Redford, Mich. 48239.

CAREER: Seagull's (clothing store), Detroit, Mich., seamstress in alterations department, 1940-42; American Cos-

tumes, Detroit, seamstress, 1945-46, designer, 1946-49; Detroit Theatre Group, Detroit, 1949-55, began as costume designer, became wardrobe supervisor; Querida's Bridal Salon, Detroit, owner, designer, and seamstress, 1955-59; freelance designer, 1959—; writer, 1974—. *Wartime service:* Sewed uniforms for U.S. Armed Forces and sewed bandages for Red Cross, 1942-45.

MEMBER: International Seamsters Union, Society of Embroidery Workers.

AWARDS, HONORS: Golden Thimble Award, Southeastern Michigan Seamsters Union, 1987.

WRITINGS:

One Thousand and One Halloween Costumes for Children, For Tomorrow Books, 1975.
Don't Needle Me! (autobiography), Boben, 1977.
Machine Embroidery to Keep You in Stitches, Zigzag Productions, 1978.
Thread Bear and Other Stories, (juvenile), Tapestry Books, 1978.
The Seamy Side of Life (novel), Boben, 1980.
Knitwit (juvenile novel), Tapestry Books, 1982.
(Editor) *Thimble Be Nimble: Sewing Tips for Beginners*, Bind Brothers, 1983.
(Under pseudonym Bob N. Holder) *Darts of Death* (suspense), Bludingutz, 1985.
Future Suture: How to Create Innovative Fashion Designs, Mid-Michigan Designers Clubs, 1986.
Gathering Calico (novel), Grimalkin, 1988.

WORK IN PROGRESS: Dashin' Fashion, a book of dressing tips for men; another suspense novel, *The Felling of Howe*.

SIDELIGHTS: Taylor Mullarky told *CA:* ''While sewing bandages for the Red Cross during World War II, I used to tell my co-workers stories to keep myself occupied. So I guess you could say that my love for sewing has always been connected with my ability to 'spin a good yarn.' I hadn't thought to publish my stories, though, until a friend, overhearing me tell bedtime stories to my granddaughter, Georgette, suggested that I try my luck. I thought even less of trying to write a full-length novel—my first attempts felt too fabricated. But since seeing that first book in print, my next efforts netted better results. Now I attempt to write stories that demonstrate the importance of values and morals—I feel today's society places too much emphasis on material goods. Writing still feels like sheer effort to me, but the rewards more than make up for it.''

*   *   *

MURPHY, Mario
See EDMONDSON, G. C.

*   *   *

MURRAY, Albert L. 1916-

PERSONAL: Born June 12, 1916, in Nokomis, Ala.; son of John Lee and Sudie (Graham) Young; married Mozelle Menefee, May 31, 1941; children: Michele. *Education:* Tuskegee Institute, B.S., 1939; New York University, M.A., 1948; postgraduate work at University of Michigan, 1940, Northwestern University, 1941, and University of Paris, 1950.

ADDRESSES: Home and office—45 West 132nd St., New York, N.Y. 10037.

CAREER: U.S. Air Force, 1943-62, retired as major. Instructor, Tuskegee Institute, 1940-43, 1946-51, director of College Little Theatre; lecturer, Graduate School of Journalism, Columbia University, 1968; Colgate University, O'Connor Professor of Literature, 1970, O'Connor Lecturer, 1973, professor of humanities, 1982; visiting professor of literature, University of Massachusetts, Boston, 1971; Paul Anthony Brick lecturer, University of Missouri, 1972; writer in residence, Emory University, 1978; adjunct associate professor of creative writing, Barnard College, 1981-83; lecturer and participant in symposia.

MEMBER: PEN International, Authors League of America, Authors Guild, Alpha Phi Alpha.

AWARDS, HONORS: Lillian Smith Award for fiction, 1974, for *Train Whistle Guitar;* Litt.D., Colgate University, 1975; ASCAP Deems Taylor Award for music criticism, 1976, for *Stomping the Blues.*

WRITINGS:

The Omni-Americans: New Perspectives on Black Experience and American Culture (essays), Outerbridge & Dientsfrey, 1970, published as *The Omni-Americans: Some Alternatives to the Folklore of White Supremacy,* Vintage Books, 1983.
South to a Very Old Place, McGraw, 1972.
The Hero and the Blues, University of Missouri Press, 1973.
Train Whistle Guitar (novel), McGraw, 1974.
Stomping the Blues, McGraw, 1976.
(With Count Basie) *Good Morning Blues: The Autobiography of Count Basie,* Random House, 1985.

WORK IN PROGRESS: The Spyglass Tree, a novel.

SIDELIGHTS: "As a writer, [Albert L. Murray] implicitly perceives himself as proceeding in the same fashion as he maintains legendary heroes, early Americans, and black Americans have always proceeded: by conceptualizing their lives out of chaos and against hostile forces," states *Dictionary of Literary Biography* contributor Elizabeth Schultz. Schultz declares that the "abiding concern of [Murray's] writing is the triumph, of Afro-American people, who, despite and, indeed, in Murray's view, because of centuries of difficulties, created a courageous, complex, life-sustaining, and life-enhancing culture—apparent in their language, religion, sports, fashions, food, dance, and above all in their music." Murray articulates these views in his collection of essays *The Omni-Americans: New Perspectives on Black Experience and American Culture,* in which he argues that black Americans have a distinctive identity of their own, developing a unique culture "which allows them to see themselves 'not as the substandard, abnormal *non-white* people of American social science surveys and the news media, but rather as if they were, so to speak, fundamental *extensions* of contemporary possibilities,'" says Schultz. "Like jam session musicians and blues singers," she

continues, "they have learned the skills of improvisation, not only translating white models of excellence into their own terms, but also transforming degrading conditions into culture."

Murray expresses an interest in jazz in other works, especially in *The Hero and the Blues* and *Stomping the Blues,* an attempt to redefine "the music and its connotations for American culture," according to Jason Berry of *Nation.* S. M. Fry, writing in *Library Journal,* points out that Murray "views the music not as a primitive musical expression of black suffering but as an antidote to the bad times—active good-time music, music to be danced to, music that because of its substance and talented exponents, has emerged the most significant American music." Murray, the reviewer says, also emphasizes the importance of the performance, "the performing style and the music itself over the lyrics and social or political connotations of the blues as significant factors in its expression as an art." These books have made him "one of the foremost literary interpreters of blues, jazz and improvisation," states Brent Staples in the *New York Times Book Review.*

AVOCATIONAL INTERESTS: Recordings, photography, cookbooks, and gourmet cooking.

BIOGRAPHICAL/CRITICAL SOURCES:

BOOKS

Dictionary of Literary Biography, Volume 38: *Afro-American Writers since 1955: Dramatists and Prose Writers,* Gale, 1985.

PERIODICALS

Chicago Tribune Book World, January 19, 1986.
Library Journal, February 1, 1977.
Los Angeles Times Book Review, March 26, 1986.
Nation, Janaury 15, 1977.
Newsweek, March 23, 1970, January 31, 1972, December 20, 1976.
New Yorker, October 17, 1970, January 8, 1972, July 22, 1974.
New York Review of Books, February 24, 1972, June 18, 1974, January 16, 1986.
New York Times, April 4, 1972, December 11, 1976.
New York Times Book Review, May 3, 1970, January 2, 1972, June 4, 1972, December 3, 1972, May 12, 1974, December 1, 1974, December 26, 1976, December 26, 1982, February 2, 1986.
Rolling Stone, January 13, 1977.
Saturday Review, January 22, 1972.
Time, January 10, 1972, March 10, 1986.
Times Literary Supplement, July 28, 1978, July 11, 1986.
Voice Literary Supplement, February, 1982.
Washington Post Book World, March 22, 1970, December 26, 1971, December 8, 1974, January 8, 1986.†

N

NAPIER, Mary
See WRIGHT, (Mary) Patricia

*   *   *

NEBRENSKY, Alex
See COOPER, Parley J(oseph)

*   *   *

NEHER, Andre   1914-

PERSONAL: Born October 22, 1914, in Obernai, France; son of Albert and Rosette (Strauss) Neher; married Renee Bernheim, December 25, 1947. *Education:* University of Strasbourg, Dr. es Lettres, 1947.

ADDRESSES: Home—14 Rehov Ussishkin, Jerusalem, Israel.

CAREER: Ordained rabbi, 1947; University of Strasbourg, Strasbourg, France, professor of Hebrew language and literature, 1948—, head of department, 1955-70. Visiting professor at University of Tel Aviv, 1968-74, member of board of governors, 1968—; member of board of governors of Haifa University, 1972—. Vice-president of ZF of France, 1949; member of central committee of Alliance Israelite Universelle, 1962—; chairman of Jewish Intellecutals in France, 1965-71.

MEMBER: International Union for Jewish Studies (member of executive committee, 1957), World Jewish Congress (chairman of French section and International Cultural Commission, 1965-71).

AWARDS, HONORS: Named Sage of Israel by Prime Minister Ben Gurion, 1957; Remembrance Award, World Federation of Bergen-Belsen Associations, 1975, for books and papers on the Holocaust; chevalier of French Legion of Honor.

WRITINGS:

L'Essence du prophetisme, Presses Universitaires de France, 1955, reprinted, Calmann-Levy, 1983, translation by William Wolf published as *The Prophetic Existence,* A. S. Barnes, 1969.
Moise et la vocation juive, Editions du Seuil, 1956, translation by Irene Marinoff published as *Moses and the Jewish Vocation,* Harper, 1959.
L'Exil de la parole: Du silence biblique au silence d'Auschwitz, Editions du Seuil, 1970, translation by David Maisel published as *The Exile of the Word: From the Silence of the Bible to the Silence of Auschwitz,* Jewish Publication Society, 1981.
David Gans, 1541-1613: Disciple du Maharal, assistant de Tycho Brahe et Jean Kepler, Klincksieck, 1975, translation by Maisel published as *Jewish Thought and the Scientific Revolution of the Sixteenth Century: David Gans (1541-1613) and His Times,* Oxford University Press, 1987.

IN FRENCH

Amos: Contribution a l'etude du prophetisme, J. Vrin, 1950, reprinted, 1981.
Notes sur Qohelet, Editions de Minuit, 1951.
Jeremie, Librairie Plon, 1960, reprinted, Stock, 1980.
L'Existence juive: Solitude et affrontements, Editions du Seuil, 1962.
(With wife, Renee Neher) *Histoire du peuple d'Israel,* Librairie d'Amerique et d'Orient Adrien-Maisonneuve, three volumes, Klincksieck, 1966-74.
Le Puits de l'exil: La Theologie dialectique du Maharal de Prague, A. Michel, 1966.
De l'hebreu au francais, Klincksieck, 1969.
Dans tes portes, Jerusalem, A. Michel, 1972.
Le dur bonheur d'etre juif, Le Centurion, 1978.
Ils ont refait leur ame, Stock, 1979.
Jerusalem, vecu juif et message, Le Rocher, 1984.
Faust et le Maharal de Prague, Presses Universitaires de France, 1987.

OTHER

Author of teleplay, ''To Be a Jew.'' Contributor to *Encyclopedie francaise* and *Hebrew Encyclopedia.* Contributor of about three hundred articles to magazines.

BIOGRAPHICAL/CRITICAL SOURCES:

PERIODICALS

Choice, January, 1988.
Jerusalem Post Literary Magazine, February 26, 1982.
Times Literary Supplement, December 25, 1981, June 5, 1987.

NEISSER, Ulric   1928-

PERSONAL: Surname is pronounced "nicer"; born December 8, 1928, in Kiel, Germany. *Education:* Harvard University, A.B. (summa cum laude), 1950, Ph.D., 1956; Swarthmore College, M.A., 1952; attended Massachusetts Institute of Technology, 1952-53.

ADDRESSES: Office—Department of Psychology, Emory University, Atlanta, Ga. 30322.

CAREER: Swarthmore College, Swarthmore, Pa., instructor in psychology, 1953-54; Harvard University, Cambridge, Mass., lecturer in psychology, 1956-57; Brandeis University, Waltham, Mass., assistant professor, 1957-61, associate professor of psychology, 1961-66; University of Pennsylvania, Philadelphia, associate professor of psychology, 1965-67; Cornell University, Ithaca, N.Y., professor of psychology, 1967-83; Emory University, Atlanta, Ga., Robert W. Woodruff Professor of Psychology, 1983—. Member of staff at Lincoln Laboratories, Massachusetts Institute of Technology, summers, 1958-63; senior research psychologist with Unit for Experimental Psychiatry, Institute of the Pennsylvania Hospital, 1965-67; fellow at Center for Advanced Studies in the Behavioral Sciences, Palo Alto, Calif., 1973-74.

MEMBER: American Association of University Professors, American Psychological Association, Cognitive Science Society, Psychonomic Society, Phi Beta Kappa, Sigma Xi.

AWARDS, HONORS: Grants from National Science Foundation, 1955-57, 1962-64, Carnegie Corp., 1965-66, National Institute of Mental Health, 1966-67, and Guggenheim Foundation, 1987-88; Honorary *Laurea*, University of Rome, 1988.

WRITINGS:

Cognitive Psychology, Appleton, 1967.
Cognition and Reality, W. H. Freeman, 1976.
Memory Observed, W. H. Freeman, 1982.
Concepts and Conceptual Development, Cambridge University Press, 1987.

Contributor to psychology journals and other magazines, including *Science* and *Scientific American*.

*   *   *

NELSON, R(adell) Faraday   1931-
(Ray Nelson; R. N. Elson, Jeffrey Lord, pseudonyms)

PERSONAL: Born October 3, 1931, in Schenectady, N.Y.; son of Walter Hughes (an electrical engineer) and Marie (a school teacher; maiden name, Reed) Nelson; married Perdita Lilly, 1951 (divorced,1955); married Lisa Mullikin, 1955 (divorced, 1958); married Kirsten Enge, October 4, 1958; children: Walter Trygvi. *Education:* Attended Art Institute of Chicago, 1954, Alliance Francaise, 1957-58, and the Sorbonne, Paris, 1958; University of Chicago, B.A., 1960; Automation Institute, Oakland Calif., programmer's certificate, 1961; attended Peralta College, 1978. *Religion:* "The Arts."

ADDRESSES: Home—333 Ramona Ave., El Cerrito, Calif. 94530.

CAREER: Worked various jobs in Michigan and Chicago, Ill., 1947-54; Northside Poster Co., Chicago, printer, 1954; Artcraft Poster Co., Oakland, Calif., printer and art director, 1955; Jean Linard, Vesoul, France, translator, 1959; University of

California Press, Berkeley, computer programmer and accounting assistant, 1961-62; free-lance writer and artist, 1962—; screenwriter, Universal Pictures, 1988—. Gag writer for cartoonist Grant Canfield. Co-director, Berkeley Free University, 1967-68; founder, Microcosm Fiction Workshop, later Ramona Street Regulars, 1967; teaching assistant, Adams Junior High School, El Cerrito, Calif., 1968-87.

MEMBER: Science Fiction Writers of America, Mystery Writers of America, California Writers Club (president, Berkeley branch, 1977-78, 1980-82, 1987-90).

AWARDS, HONORS: Hugo Award nomination for best short story, 1964, for "Turn Off the Sky"; Nebula Award nomination for best novel, 1976, for *Blake's Progress;* Ina Coolbrith Poetry Award, 1979, for *Dancing Masters;* Philip K. Dick citation, 1983, for *Prometheus Man;* Jack London Award, 1983; named to Old Beatniks Hall of Fame, 1987.

WRITINGS:

(Contributor) Avram Davidson, editor, *The Best from Fantasy and Science Fiction 13*, Doubleday, 1964.
(Contributor) Judith Merril, editor, *Year's Best Science Fiction*, Dial, 1965.
(With Philip K. Dick; under name Ray Nelson) *The Ganymede Takeover*, Ace Books, 1967.
(Under name Ray Nelson) *The Agony of Love*, Greenleaf Classics, 1969.
(Under name Ray Nelson) *Girl with the Hungry Eyes*, Greenleaf Classics, 1969.
(Contributor) Harlan Ellison, editor, *Again, Dangerous Visions*, Doubleday, 1972.
Blake's Progress, Laser Books, 1975.
Then Beggars Could Ride, Laser Books, 1977.
Revolt of the Unemployables, Anthelion Press, 1977.
(Under pseudonym Jeffrey Lord) *Dimension of Horror*, Pinnacle Books, 1978.
(Contributor) Lin Carter, editor, *Weird Tales 2*, Zebra Books, 1981.
(Contributor) Michael Bastraw, editor, *Fifty Extremely SF Stories*, Niekas, 1982.
The Prometheus Man, Donning, 1982.
The Branching Forks, Donning, 1984.
Timequest, Tor Books, 1985.

UNDER PSEUDONYM R. N. ELSON

How to Do It, Greenleaf Classics, 1970.
Sex Happy Hippy, Greenleaf Classics, 1970.
Black Pussy, Greenleaf Classics, 1970.
The DA's Wife, Greenleaf Classics, 1970.

OTHER

Contributor of short stories and articles to periodicals.

SIDELIGHTS: R. "Ray" Faraday Nelson, who says that his brand of science fiction "dispenses with a lot of the furniture of science fiction, and instead concentrates on ideas," told *CA:* "I work in the tradition of Jack London, combining adventure fiction with political and philosophical speculation. I see Jack London as the founder of American science fiction, predating Hugo Gernsback and providing a literary example I do not need to feel ashamed of; for me London's role is more important than that of H. G. Wells, Jules Verne, John Campbell or the modern Harlan Ellison. With time, I may become London's equal. This is my ambition."

AVOCATIONAL INTERESTS: Walking, gardening, hypnosis, songwriting, guitar playing, and collecting cats.

BIOGRAPHICAL/CRITICAL SOURCES:

PERIODICALS

Berkeley Gazette, December 29, 1975.
Northern Michigan Life, September 3, 1976.
San Francisco Chronicle, February 13, 1977.
Washington Post Book World, March 27, 1983.

*   *   *

NELSON, Ray
See NELSON, R(adell) Faraday

*   *   *

NESTOR, William P(rodromos) 1947-

PERSONAL: Born July 29, 1947, in Atlantic City, N.J.; son of George Peter and Sophie (Prodromos) Nestor; married Florence Karis (a teacher), November 1, 1970; children: W. Ryan. *Education:* Glassboro State College, B.A., 1970; Antioch Graduate School, Keene, N.H., M.S.T., 1975. *Religion:* Greek Orthodox.

ADDRESSES: Home—14 Greenleaf, Brattleboro, Vt. 05301.

CAREER: Elementary school teacher in Attleboro, Mass., 1970-72, and Millburn, N.J., 1972-74; New Hampshire Environmental Education Center, Hillsboro, director, 1974-75; New England College, Henniken, N.H., assistant professor of environmental studies, natural history, and education, 1975-80; Hitchcock Center for the Environment, Amherst, Mass., executive director, 1980-82; New England Solar Engery Association, Brattleboro, Vt., editor of *Northeast Sun,* 1982-84; Solar Vision, Peterborough, N.H., member of market and advertising staff of *Solar Age* and *Custom Building,* 1984—. Consultant on education and environmental studies.

MEMBER: National Science Teachers Association.

AWARDS, HONORS: Into Winter was named an outstanding science book for children by Children's Book Council of National Science Teachers Association, 1982.

WRITINGS:

Into Winter (juvenile), illustrations by Susan Banta, Houghton, 1982.
View from Wantastiquet, Millers River, 1988.

Contributor to newsletters.

WORK IN PROGRESS: A novel, based on his sailing trip from Key West, Fla., to Honduras in 1981.

SIDELIGHTS: William P. Nestor wrote: "Understanding the natural environment—its systems and cycles—fosters in each of us a reverence for our life support system.

"My experience with elementary-age students emphasized the wealth of opportunity for enhancing education through the natural curiosity inherent in human interaction with the natural environment. *Into Winter* provides natural history information about the winter season while fostering exploration and discovery through a variety of activities for experiencing the natural world in winter."

AVOCATIONAL INTERESTS: Bicycling, canoeing, snowshoeing, cross-country skiing, racquetball, wilderness travel.

NEWBIGIN, (James Edward) Lesslie 1909-

PERSONAL: Born December 8, 1909, in Newcastle upon Tyne, England; son of Edward Richmond and Ellen (Affleck) Newbigin; married Helen Stewart Henderson, August 20, 1936; children: Margaret (Mrs. David Beetham), Alison, Janet (Mrs. A. J. Williamson), John. *Education:* Queens' College, Cambridge, M.A., 1931; Westminster College, Cambridge, England, theological study, 1933-36. *Politics:* Labour.

ADDRESSES: Home—15, Fox Hill, Birmingham, England.

CAREER: Ordained minister, Church of Scotland, 1936. Missionary in India, 1936-59, and bishop of Church of South India in Madura, 1947-59; general secretary, International Missionary Council, 1959-61; World Council of Churches, Geneva, Switzerland, associate general secretary, 1961-65; bishop in Madras, India, 1965-74; Selly Oak Colleges, Birmingham, England, lecturer, 1974-79; United Reformed Church, Winson Green, Birmingham, minister, 1979—.

AWARDS, HONORS: D.D. from Chicago Theological Seminary, 1954, University of St. Andrews, 1958, and University of Hamburg, 1964.

WRITINGS:

Christian Freedom in the Modern World, S.C.M. Press, 1937.
The Reunion of the Church, S.C.M. Press, 1948.
South India Diary, S.C.M. Press, 1951, published as *That All May Be One,* Association Press, 1952.
The Household of God, S.C.M. Press, 1953.
Sin and Salvation, S.C.M. Press, 1956.
A Faith for This One World?, S.C.M. Press, 1961.
The Church: Local and Universal (booklet), World Dominion Press, 1962.
The Relevance of Trinitarian Doctrine for Today's Mission, Edinburgh House Press, 1963, published as *Trinitarian Faith and Today's Mission,* John Knox, 1964.
Honest Religion for Secular Man, Westminster Press, 1966.
Christ Our Eternal Contemporary, Christian Literature Society (Madras), 1968.
The Finality of Christ, John Knox, 1969.
Set Free to Be a Servant: Studies in Paul's Letter to the Galatians, Christian Literature Society, 1969.
The Holy Spirit and the Church, Christian Literature Society, 1972.
Journey into Joy, Eerdmans, 1973.
The Good Shepherd: Meditations on Christian Ministry in Today's World, Eerdmans, 1975.
Christian Witness in a Plural Society, British Council of Churches, 1977.
Context and Conversion, Church Missionary Society, 1979.
The Open Secret, Eerdmans, 1979.
Sign of the Kingdom, Eerdmans, 1981.
The Light Has Come, Eerdmans, 1982.
The Other Side of 1984, World Council of Churches, 1983.
Unfinished Agenda: An Autobiography, Eerdmans, 1985.
Foolishness to the Greeks, Eerdmans, 1986.

Editor, *International Review of Missions,* 1959.

BIOGRAPHICAL/CRITICAL SOURCES:

BOOKS

Newbigin, Lesslie, *Unfinished Agenda: An Autobiography,* Eerdmans, 1985.

NICHOLAS, Herbert George 1911-

PERSONAL: Born June 8, 1911, in Treharris, Wales; son of W. D. (a clergyman) Nicholas. *Education:* Attended Mill Hill School; attended Yale University, 1935-37; New College, Oxford, M.A., 1938.

ADDRESSES: Home—3 William Orchard Close, Old Headington, Oxford, England.

CAREER: Oxford University, Exeter College, Oxford, England, lecturer and fellow, 1938-51; Ministry of Information, American Division, and His Majesty's Embassy, Washington, D.C., civil servant, 1941-46; Oxford University, New College, fellow, 1951-78, reader in the comparative study of institutions, 1956-68, Rhodes Professor of American History and Institutions, 1968-78, emeritus, 1978—, honorary fellow, 1980—. Faculty fellow, Nuffield College, Oxford University, 1948-57. Visiting professor, Brookings Institution, Washington, D.C., 1960; Albert Shaw Lecturer in Diplomatic History, Johns Hopkins University, 1961; visiting fellow, Institute of Advanced Studies, Princeton University, 1964; visiting faculty fellow, Institute of Politics, Harvard University, 1968.

MEMBER: British Association for American Studies (chairman, 1959-62), British Academy (fellow; vice-president, 1975-76), Athenaeum Club (London).

AWARDS, HONORS: D.C.L., University of Pittsburgh, 1968.

WRITINGS:

The American Union, Chatto & Windus, 1948.
The British General Election of 1950, Macmillan, 1951, reprinted, Biblio Distribution Centre, 1968.
(Editor) *To the Hustings: Election Scenes from English Fiction,* Cassells, 1955.
The United Nations as a Political Institution, Oxford University Press, 1959, 5th edition, 1975.
Britain and the U.S.A., Johns Hopkins Press, 1963.
The American Past and the American Present, Clarendon Press, 1971.
(With William E. Leuchtenburg) "The New Deal" (phonotape), BFA Educational Media, 1974.
The United States and Britain, University of Chicago Press, 1975.
The Nature of American Politics, Oxford University Press, 1980, 2nd edition, 1986.
(Editor) Isaiah Berlin, *Washington Despatches, 1941-45: Weekly Political Reports from the British Embassy,* University of Chicago Press, 1981.

Also author of *Law and Government in the United States,* in Chinese, 1950. Editor of *De la Democratie en Amerique,* by Alexis de Tocqueville. Contributor to *Reporter, Yale Review, Times Literary Supplement, Economist, Listener, Observer,* and other journals.

SIDELIGHTS: A period of study at Yale University as well as five years spent in Washington, D.C., in the British diplomatic service have given Herbert George Nicholas an insight into the American political system that is rare for a foreign observer. Nicholas brings to his work "a profound and sympathetic . . . understanding of what makes the United States tick," remarks a reviewer in *Economist.* In a *Times Literary Supplement* review of *The Nature of American Politics,* Max Beloff likens Nicholas's work to that of other foreign scholars such as Tocqueville, Bryce, and Brogan. Although some critics have remarked that the author's work occasionally overlooks details and fails to comment on certain issues, many echo Beloff's assessment that "Mr. Nicholas has excellent and illuminating things to say" about American politics.

The Nature of American Politics has been translated into Spanish.

AVOCATIONAL INTERESTS: Gardening, listening to music.

BIOGRAPHICAL/CRITICAL SOURCES:

PERIODICALS

Economist, December 13, 1975.
New Republic, July 19, 1982.
New York Review of Books, December 17, 1981.
New York Times Book Review, October 4, 1981.
Times Literary Supplement, February 29, 1980, April 30, 1982.

* * *

NICHOLSON, Shirley J. 1925-

PERSONAL: Born January 8, 1925, in Little Rock, Ark.; daughter of Franc Irving (a salesman) and Shirley (Paris) Mullen; married William M. Nicholson (a psychologist), February 17, 1957; children: Carol, Patty. *Education:* University of California, Los Angeles, B.A., 1957; Newark State College, Teacher Certification, 1968; Montclair State College, Teacher Certification, 1977. *Religion:* Episcopalian.

ADDRESSES: Office—Theosophical Publishing House, 306 West Geneva Rd., Wheaton, Ill. 60187.

CAREER: Prospect Hill School, Newark, N.J., teacher of science, 1963-68; Newark Museum, Newark, giver of talks for children, 1968-74; Glen Ridge Schools, Glen Ridge, N.J., teacher of children with learning disabilities, 1974-78; Theosophical Publishing House, Wheaton, Ill., senior editor in charge of Quest Books, 1981—.

MEMBER: Theosophical Society, New Jersey Association of Independent Schools, Phi Beta Kappa.

WRITINGS:

Nature's Merry-Go-Round (juvenile), Theosophical Publishing, 1969.
Ancient Wisdom: Modern Insight, Theosophical Publishing, 1985.
Shamanism: An Expanded View of Reality, Theosophical Publishing, 1987.

Contributor to *Main Currents in Modern Thought.*

* * *

NICOL, Abioseh
See NICOL, Davidson (Sylvester Hector Willoughby)

* * *

NICOL, Davidson (Sylvester Hector Willoughby) 1924-
(Abioseh Nicol)

PERSONAL: Born September 14, 1924, in Freetown, Sierra Leone; married; children: three sons, two daughters. *Education:* Attended London University, 1943; Christ's College, Cambridge, B.A. (first class honors), 1946, M.D., 1958; also received M.A., Ph.D. *Religion:* Christian.

ADDRESSES: Office—World Federation of United Nations Associations, c/o Palais des Nations, CH-1211 Geneva 10,

Switzerland. *Agent*—Phyllis Westberg, Harold Ober Associates, 40 East 49th St., New York, N.Y. 10017; and David Higham Associates Ltd., 5-8 Lower John St., Golden Square, London W1R 4HA, England.

CAREER: University of London, London Hospital Medical College, London, England, house physician and research assistant, 1950-52; The Medical School, Ibadan, Nigeria, university lecturer, 1952-54; Cambridge University, Cambridge, England, Beit Memorial Fellow, 1954, fellow and supervisor in natural sciences and medicine at Christ's College, 1957-59; Sierra Leone Government, senior pathologist, 1958-60; Fourah Bay College, Freetown, Sierra Leone, principal, 1960-67; University of Sierra Leone, Freetown, first vice-chancellor, 1966-68; ambassador from Sierra Leone to United Nations, 1968-71, member of Economic and Social Council, 1969-70, chairman of Committee of 24 (decolonization), 1970, Security Council, member 1970-71, president, 1970; high commissioner of the Republic of Sierra Leone to United Kingdom, and ambassador to Denmark, Norway, Sweden, and Finland, 1971-72; United Nations, New York, New York, under-secretary and executive director of United Nations Institute for Training and Research (UNITAR), 1973-82; World Federation of United Nations Associations, Geneva, Switzerland, president, 1983—.

Member of West African Council for Medical Research, 1959-62; member of public service commission, Sierra Leone, 1960-68. Conference delegate to World Health Organization Assembly, 1960, United Nations Educational, Scientific, and Cultural Organization (UNESCO) Higher Education Conference, 1963, and Commonwealth Prime Ministers' Conference, 1965, 1969, and 1971. Chairman, United Nations Mission to Angola, 1976.

Member of executive council, Association of Universities of the British Commonwealth, 1960, 1966; member of commission for proposed University of Ghana, 1960; chairman, University of East Africa Visiting Committee, 1962; chairman, West African Exams Council, 1964-69. Visiting lecturer, University of Toronto, University of California—Berkeley, and Mayo Clinic, 1958. Aggrey-Fraser-Guggisberg memorial lecturer, University of Ghana, 1963; Danforth Fellowship lecturer in African affairs, Association of American Colleges, 1968-71. Visiting fellow, Johns Hopkins School of Advanced International Studies, 1983; visiting scholar, Woodrow Wilson International Center, 1983, and Hoover Institution, Stanford University, 1984. Member, governing body, Kumasi University, Ghana; member of board of trustees, African-American Institute and Fund for Peace. Chairman of Sierra Leone National Library Board, 1959-65. Former director, Central Bank of Sierra Leone, Consolidated African Selection Trust Ltd., and Davesme Corporation. Fellow, Christ's College, Cambridge, Royal College of Pathologists (London), West African College of Physicians, and West African College of Surgeons. Honorary consultant pathologist, Sierra Leone Government. Consultant to Ford Foundation.

MEMBER: Sierra Leone Red Cross Society (president, 1962-66), West Africa Science Association (president, 1964-66); Ghana Academy of Sciences (honorary member), United Oxford and Cambridge University, Royal Commonwealth Society, Senior Dinner (Freetown).

AWARDS, HONORS: Margaret Wrong Prize and Medal for Literature in Africa, 1951; Independence Medal, Government of Sierra Leone, 1961; D.Sc. from University of Newcastle on Tyne, and Kalamazoo College, both 1964, and Laurentian

(Ontario) College; named Companion of the Order of St. Michael and St. George, 1964; LL.D., University of Leeds, 1968, Barat College, 1980, University of the West Indies, 1981, and Tuskegee College, 1981; D.Litt., Davis-Elkins College, 1971; Grand Commander of the Order of Rokel, Sierra Leone, 1974; Star of Africa, Liberia, 1974; honorary special fellow, UNITAR, 1983.

WRITINGS:

Alienation: An Essay, MacGibbon & Kee, 1960.
(Contributor) *An African Treasury*, Crown, 1960.
(Contributor) *An Anthology of Commonwealth Verse*, Blackie, 1963.
(Contributor) Langston Hughes, editor, *Poems from Black Africa*, Indiana University Press, 1963.
Africa: A Subjective View, Longmans, Green, 1964.
(Contributor) *African Heritage*, Macmillan (London), 1964.
(Contributor) *A Book of African Verse*, Heinemann, 1964.
(Under pseudonym Abioseh Nicol) *The Truly Married Woman and Other Stories* (fiction), Oxford University Press, 1965.
(Under pseudonym Abioseh Nicol) *Two African Tales* (fiction), Cambridge University Press, 1965.
(Contributor) D. I. Nwoga, editor, *West African Verse*, Longmans, Green, 1967.
(Contributor) *African Writing Today*, Penguin, 1967.
(Contributor) *Commonwealth Poems of Today*, J. Murray, 1967.
(Contributor) *New Voices of the Commonwealth*, Evans Brothers, 1968.
(Editor and author of introduction) *Africanus Horton: The Dawn of Nationalism in Modern Africa*, Longmans, Green, 1969, published as *Black Nationalism in Africa, 1867*, Africana Publishing, 1969.
New and Modern Roles for the Empire and Commonwealth, Cambridge University Press, 1976.
(Editor) *Regionalism and the New International Economic Order*, Pergamon, 1981.
(Editor) *Paths to Peace: The U.N. Security Council and Its Presidency*, Pergamon, 1981.
(Editor with Luis Echeverria) *Regionalism and the New International Economic Order*, Pergamon, 1981.
(Editor with Pamela D'Onofrio) *Scientific-Technological Change and the Role of Women in Development*, Westview, 1981.
(With Margaret Crole and Babatunde Adeniran) *The United Nations Security Council: Towards Greater Effectiveness*, UNITAR, 1982.
(Editor with Torill Stokland and Mallica Vajrathon) *Creative Women in Changing Societies: A Quest for Alternatives*, Transnational, 1982.

Also author of *The United Nations and Decision-Making: The Role of Women*, 1978, and *Nigeria and the Future of Africa*, 1980. Contributor to *Malnutrition in African Mothers and Children*, 1954, *The Mechanism of the Action of Insulin*, 1960, *The Structure of Human Insulin*, 1960, *Conditions of World Order*, and *The Task of Universities in a Changing World*. Contributor to *Encyclopaedia Britannica*, 1974, and *International Encyclopedia of Higher Education*, 1976. Contributor of articles, short stories, and verse to anthologies and periodicals, including *Encounter*, *Blackwood's Magazine*, the London *Times*, *Guardian*, and *Economist*.

SIDELIGHTS: Although most of his career has been spent in the fields of medicine and diplomatic service, Davidson Nicol, writing as Abioseh Nicol, is "in the very forefront of African short story writers," comments Adrian A. Roscoe in *Mother Is Gold: A Study in West African Literature*. While critical attention to African literature has focused more on novels and novelists, Roscoe finds that "there is no novelist in Nigeria . . . whose creative flair and command of prose are superior to those of Abioseh Nicol." Roscoe also commends Nicol's consistency, observing that he is able to sustain quality writing in his stories where some novelists weaken after a strong beginning. Nicol's talent lies in his "taking a slice of real life and offering it to us in all its workaday detail, all its blending of the tragic and the absurd," says Roscoe. "The style that allows this effect must possess the translucence of crystal."

Nicol's fiction deals more with "workaday" African life, often setting Westernized middle-class characters against an African background. Seemingly in contrast to these everyday subjects is Nicol's poetry, which Martin Tucker in *Africa in Modern Literature* characterizes as dealing with "Africa as a symbolic entity related to a social cause." Nicol reconciles these apparent differences, writing that his fiction addresses social issues, not by using symbols but by presenting a different viewpoint. In a foreword to *Two African Tales*, the author writes that his stories of colonial Africa "owe something to European writers . . . who wrote about similar situations. However, being both black and African, I was then on the other side of the fence and perhaps saw things differently."

MEDIA ADAPTATIONS: Readings of Nicol's poetry have been broadcast by the British Broadcasting Corp. and the Voice of America.

AVOCATIONAL INTERESTS: Antiques, especially old maps and coins.

BIOGRAPHICAL/CRITICAL SOURCES:

BOOKS

Nicol, Abioseh, *Two African Tales*, Cambridge University Press, 1965.
Roscoe, Adrian A., *Mother Is Gold: A Study in West African Literature*, Cambridge University Press, 1971.
Tibble, Anne, *African-English Literature*, P. Owen, 1965.
Tucker, Martin, *Africa in Modern Literature*, Ungar, 1967.†

*　　*　　*

NIEVERGELT, Jurg 1938-

PERSONAL: Born June 6, 1938, in Lucerne, Switzerland; son of Albert and Hedwig Nievergelt; married Teresa Quiambao (a librarian), February 14, 1965; children: Mark, Derek. *Education:* Swiss Federal Institute of Technology, Diploma, 1962; University of Illinois, Ph.D., 1965.

ADDRESSES: Office—Department of Computer Science, University of North Carolina, Chapel Hill, N.C. 27514.

CAREER: University of Illinois at Urbana-Champaign, assistant professor, 1965-68, associate professor, 1968-72, professor of computer science and mathematics, 1972-77; Swiss Federal Institute of Technology, Zurich, Switzerland, professor, 1971-72, 1975-85; University of North Carolina, Chapel Hill, William Rand Kenan Professor of Computer Science and chairman of department, 1985—.

MEMBER: Association for Computing Machinery, Institute of Electrical and Electronics Engineers, Sigma Xi, Phi Kappa Phi.

WRITINGS:

(Editor with Don Secrest) *Conference on Emerging Concepts in Computer Graphics*, University of Illinois Press, 1967, published as *Emerging Concepts in Computer Graphics*, W. A. Benjamin, 1968.
(Editor with Michael Faiman) *Pertinent Concepts in Computer Graphics*, University of Illinois Press, 1969.
(With J. C. Farrar and E. M. Reingold) *Computer Approaches to Problems in Mathematics*, Prentice-Hall, 1974.
(With Reingold and N. Deo) *Combinational Algorithms: Theory and Practice*, Prentice-Hall, 1977.
(Editor) *Document Preparation Systems: A Collection of Survey Articles*, North-Holland Publishing, 1982.
(With Andrea Ventura) *Small Programs for Small Machines: Computers and Education*, Addison-Wesley, 1985.
(With others) *Interactive Computer Programs for Education: Philosophy, Techniques, and Examples*, Addison-Wesley, 1986.

*　　*　　*

NORMAN, Adrian R(oger) D(udley) 1938-

PERSONAL: Born October 10, 1938, in Alverstoke, Hampshire, England; son of Edward Dudley (a captain in the Royal Navy) and Aileen L. (Piper) Norman; married Katherine Redwood, September 22, 1962; children: Roger H., Fiona M. *Education:* Clare College, Cambridge, B.A., 1962, M.A., 1966; Columbia University, M.B.A., 1967. *Politics:* Tory. *Religion:* Atheist.

CAREER: Atomic Weapons Research Establishment, Aldermaston, England, engineer officer, 1957-63; International Business Machines Ltd., London, England, systems engineer, 1964-69; L. Messel & Co. (stockbrokers), London, computer manager, 1969-71; consultant, Interbank Research Organisation, 1971-73; Arthur D. Little Ltd., London, management sciences consultant, beginning 1973.

MEMBER: British Institute of Management (associate member), British Computer Society (fellow), Beta Gamma Sigma.

WRITINGS:

(With James Martin) *The Computerized Society: An Appraisal of the Impact of Computers on Society over the Next Fifteen Years*, Prentice-Hall, 1970.
(Editor with Peter Hamilton) *Handbook of Security*, Kluwer-Harrap, 1975.
Electronic Document Delivery: The Artemis Concept, Knowledge Industry Publications, 1981.
Electronic Document Delivery, Knowledge Industry Publications, 1981.
Computer Insecurity, Chapman and Hall, 1983.

Co-author of British Broadcasting Corp. television program, "The Invasion of Privacy."†

*　　*　　*

NORTHCOTE, Peter
See COTES, Peter

*　　*　　*

NOVAK, William (Arnold) 1948-

PERSONAL: Born August 1, 1948, in Toronto, Ontario, Canada; son of George (a stockbroker) and Esther (Brill) Novak;

married Linda Mali Manaly, June 19, 1977; children: Benjamin, Jesse. *Education:* York University, B.A., 1969; Brandeis University, M.A., 1972. *Religion:* Jewish.

ADDRESSES: Home—Newton, Mass. *Agent*—Steven Axelrod, 350 Fifth Ave., Suite 5805, New York, N.Y. 10118.

CAREER: Response, New York, N.Y., editor in New York and Boston, 1969-74; *Moment,* Boston, Mass., executive editor, 1975-77; writer.

WRITINGS:

High Culture: Marijuana in the Lives of Americans, Knopf, 1980.
(With Moshe Waldoks) *The Big Book of Jewish Humor,* Harper, 1981.
The Great American Man Shortage and Other Roadblocks to Romance, Rawson, Wade, 1983.
(With Lee Iacocca) *Iacocca: An Autobiography,* Bantam, 1984.
(With Sydney B. Barrows) *Mayflower Madam: The Secret Life of Sydney Biddle Barrows,* Arbor House, 1986.
(With Herbert Schmertz) *Goodbye to the Low Profile: The Art of Creative Confrontation,* Little, Brown, 1986.
(With Thomas P. O'Neill) *Man of the House: The Life and Political Memoirs of Speaker Tip O'Neill,* Random House, 1987.
(Co-editor) Natan Sharansky, *Fear No Evil,* Random House, 1988.

Contributor of articles and reviews to magazines and newspapers. Editor, *New Traditions,* 1984-86.

WORK IN PROGRESS: Co-writing former First Lady Nancy Reagan's memoirs, for Random House.

SIDELIGHTS: William Novak had almost given up on the writing profession when he was approached to help an unnamed businessman write his biography. "Well, I immediately knew who it was," Novak remarked to Garry Abrams of the *Los Angeles Times.* "Of course, it had to be Armand Hammer because he was the only businessman I had ever heard of." Novak was mistaken, for the man in question was Chrysler chairman Lee Iacocca and the ensuing collaboration, *Iacocca: An Autobiography,* sold over five million copies, becoming one of the most successful nonfiction books ever published. Since then, Novak has had his pick of numerous offers and has chosen to work with Herb Schmertz, former vice-president for public affairs for Mobil Oil; Sydney Biddle Bar-

rows, the "Mayflower Madam"; former Speaker of the House Tip O'Neill; and Soviet dissident Natan Sharansky. Novak's success in relating the stories of other people has led to his being recognized as "king of the ghosts" as well as increased respect for the profession itself.

Although Novak is able to adapt his writing style to each individual's story, his first attempts at "ghosting" were not so accomplished. When he submitted the initial draft of *Iacocca* to the publishers, they rejected it as being "too well written." As Novak told Lois Romano in the *Washington Post,* "what they meant was that it was my writing style and it didn't sound like Lee talking, so I had to go back and rewrite." In order to gain an accurate sense of his subject's style, Novak spends "as much time as possible with my coauthor, and I use a tape recorder," he explained to Risa Dickstein in *Interview.* "I listen carefully and ask a million questions. I read everything I can get my hands on. I also interview a few of my partner's colleagues who can elaborate on certain points that we want to cover in the book."

Some critics are not entirely comfortable with the idea of "ghostwriting"; Mark Starr, in a *Newsweek* article, cites William Safire as "lament[ing] the absence of deep reflection in these books." Novak disagrees with this criticism: "If the person is reflective, that'll be in the book," he told Starr. 'It's *their* book." As he commented to Dickstein, "My job is to help my partners put into writing their own versions of themselves." Novak still has several people in mind for future projects, even though he is also interested in writing about such topics as the Jewish community and the tofu industry. But when Dickstein asked him about writing fiction, Novak replied: "I'd love to write fiction, but I'm not sure I have the talent to do it. Besides, who could invent characters like Lee Iacocca and Sydney Biddle Barrows? When reality is that interesting, it can be difficult for fiction to compete."

BIOGRAPHICAL/CRITICAL SOURCES:

PERIODICALS

Detroit News, June 30, 1985.
Interview, March, 1987.
Los Angeles Times, July 17, 1987.
Maclean's, December 1, 1986.
Newsweek, January 25, 1988.
New York Times Book Review, September 13, 1987.
Washington Post, June 21, 1985.

O

OATES, Stephen B.   1936-

PERSONAL: Born January 5, 1936, in Pampa, Tex.; son of Steve Theodore and Florence (Baer) Oates. *Children:* Gregory Allen, Stephanie. *Education:* University of Texas at Austin, B.A. (magna cum laude), 1958, M.A., 1960, Ph.D., 1969.

ADDRESSES: Home—10 Bridle Path, Amherst, Mass. 01003. *Office*—Department of History, University of Massachusetts, Amherst, Mass. 01003.

CAREER: Arlington State College (now University of Texas at Arlington), instructor, 1964-67, assistant professor of history, 1967-68; University of Massachusetts, Amherst, assistant professor, 1968-70, associate professor, 1970-71, professor of history, 1971—, adjunct professor of English, 1980—, Paul Murray Kendall Professor of Biography, 1985—. Guest lecturer at numerous colleges, universities, societies and associations throughout the United States; has made numerous guest appearances on radio and television programs. Honorary member of board of directors, Abraham Lincoln Association. American history and biography consultant to various commercial and university presses, and consultant to National Endowment for the Humanities for various book, museum, television, and motion-picture projects.

MEMBER: Society of American Historians, American Antiquarian Society, Texas Institute of Letters, Phi Beta Kappa.

AWARDS, HONORS: Texas State Historical Association fellow, 1968; Texas Institute of Letters fellow, 1969; Guggenheim fellow, 1972; Chancellor's Medal for Outstanding Scholarship, University of Massachusetts, 1976; Christopher Award, 1977, and Barondess/Lincoln Award, New York Civil War Round Table, 1978, both for *With Malice toward None: The Life of Abraham Lincoln;* National Endowment for the Humanities senior summer fellow, 1978; Distinguished Teaching Award, University of Massachusetts, 1981; Litt.D., Lincoln College, 1981; graduate faculty fellowship, University of Massachusetts, 1981-82; Christopher Award, 1982, Robert F. Kennedy Memorial Book Award, 1983, and Chancellor's Certificate of Recognition, University of Massachusetts, 1983, all for *Let the Trumpet Sound: The Life of Martin Luther King, Jr.;* Institute for Advanced Studies in the Humanities fellow, 1984; Author's Award for best article of the year, *Civil War Times Illustrated,* 1984, for "Abraham Lincoln: Man and Myth"; University of Massachusetts Presidential Writers Award,

1985; Master Teacher Award, University of Hartford, 1985; Silver Medal winner and semi-finalist in national professor of the year competition, Council for Advancement and Support of Education, 1986 and 1987.

WRITINGS:

Confederate Cavalry West of the River, University of Texas Press, 1961.

(Editor and author of introduction and commentary) John Salmon Ford, *Rip Ford's Texas,* University of Texas Press, 1963, reprinted, 1987.

(General editor and contributor) *The Republic of Texas,* American West Publishing, 1968.

Visions of Glory: Texas on the Southwestern Frontier, University of Oklahoma Press, 1970.

To Purge This Land with Blood: A Biography of John Brown (Literary Guild selection), Harper, 1970, revised 2nd edition, University of Massachusetts Press, 1984.

(Editor) *Portrait of America,* Volume 1: *From the European Discovery to the End of Reconstruction,* Volume 2: *From Reconstruction to the Present,* Houghton, 1973, 4th revised editon, 1987.

The Fires of Jubilee: Nat Turner's Fierce Rebellion, Harper, 1975.

With Malice toward None: The Life of Abraham Lincoln (Book-of-the-Month Club selection), Harper, 1977.

Our Fiery Trial: Abraham Lincoln, John Brown, and the Civil War Era, University of Massachusetts Press, 1979.

Let the Trumpet Sound: The Life of Martin Luther King, Jr. (Literary Guild selection), Harper, 1982.

Abraham Lincoln: The Man behind the Myths (History Book Club selection), Harper, 1984.

(Editor, author of prologue, and contributor) *Biography as High Adventure: Life-Writers Speak on Their Art,* University of Massachusetts Press, 1986.

William Faulkner: The Man and the Artist; A Biography, Harper, 1987.

CONTRIBUTOR

Howard Quint, Milton Cantor, and Dean Albertson, editors, *Main Problems in American History,* Dorsey Press, 3rd edition, 1972.

Odie B. Faulk and Joseph A. Stout, Jr., editors, *The Mexican War: Changing Interpretations,* Swallow Press, 1973.

Richard Warch and Jonathan Fanton, editors, *John Brown*, Prentice-Hall, 1973.

C. Vann Woodward, editor, *Responses of the Presidents to Charges of Misconduct: An Authoritative History Requested by Counsel John Doar for the Impeachment Inquiry Staff Investigating Charges against Richard M. Nixon*, Delacorte, 1974, published in paperback as *White House under Fire*, 1974.

Stories of Great Crimes and Trials from American Heritage, American Heritage/McGraw-Hill, 1974.

John A. Garraty, editor, *Encyclopedia of American Biography*, Harper, 1974.

Robert P. Swierenga, editor, *Beyond the Civil War Synthesis*, Greenwood Press, 1975.

Allen Weinstein, editor, *Conflict in America: A History of Domestic Confrontations*, Forum Series (Washington, D.C.), 1976.

The Chancellor's Lectures, 1976, University of Massachusetts Press, 1976.

John J. Turner, Jr., and Roger Lane, editors, *Riot, Rout, and Tumult: Readings in American Social and Political Violence*, Greenwood Press, 1978.

Ralph A. Wooster and Robert A. Clavert, editors, *Texas Vistas: Selections from the Southwestern Historical Quarterly*, Texas State Historical Association, 1980.

David C. Roller and Robert W. T. Wyman, editors, *Encyclopedia of Southern History*, Louisiana State University Press, 1980.

Gary Gallagher, editor, *Essays on Southern History Written in Honor of Barnes F. Lathrop*, General Libraries, University of Texas at Austin, 1980.

Robert Jones and G. L. Sullivan, Jr., editors, *The Sweep of American History*, 3rd edition, John Wiley, 1981.

Garraty, editor, *Historical Viewpoints*, 4th edition, Harper, 1983.

Kenneth G. Alfers, editor, *America's Second Century: Topical Readings*, Kendall/Hunt Publishing, 1983.

Robert James Maddox, editor, *Annual Editions*, 7th edition, Dushkin, 1983.

James F. Veninga, editor, *The Biographer's Gift: Life Histories and Humanism*, Texas A & M University Press, 1983.

Abraham Lincoln, Eastern Acorn Press, 1984.

Byron Dobell, editor, *A Sense of History: The Best Writing from the Pages of American Heritage*, American Heritage Press, 1985.

Charles F. Fater, *Selma, 1965*, 2nd edition, Beacon Press, 1985.

Paul Murray Kendall, *The Art of Biography*, 2nd edition, Norton, 1985.

John L. Thomas, editor, *Abraham Lincoln and the American Political Tradition*, University of Massachusetts Press, 1986.

William C. Davis, editor, *Touched by Fire: A Photographic Portrait of the Civil War*, Little, Brown, 1986.

OTHER

Editor with Paul Mariani of the "Commonwealth Classics in Biography" series for University of Massachusetts Press, 1986—. Contributor to numerous periodicals, including *American Heritage, American History Illustrated, American West, Civil War History, Timeline*, and *Nation*. Former contributor of reviews to journals such as *American History Review, Journal of American History*, and *Southwestern Historical Quarterly*.

WORK IN PROGRESS: *Voices of the Storm: A Biographical History of the Civil War Era* for Harper, publication expected 1992; *RFK: A Life of Robert F. Kennedy* for Harper; essays for *Timeline, The Dictionary of American Biography—Supplement*, edited by John A. Garraty for Scribners, and *Lincoln—175*, edited by Gabor S. Boritt for University of Illinois Press.

SIDELIGHTS: Distinguished biographer and educator Stephen B. Oates links his lifelong dual interests in history and literature by not only assuming professorial posts in both disciplines, but by crafting biographies of historical and literary figures as well; and as the Paul Murray Kendall Professor of Biography at the University of Massachusetts, he guides others in that art. "Inevitably," Oates recalls in *Biography as High Adventure: Life-Writers Speak on Their Art*, "biography appealed to me as the form in which I wanted to write about the past, because the best biography—pure biography—was a storytelling art that brought people alive again, eliciting from the coldness of fact 'the warmth of a life being lived,' as Paul Murray Kendall expressed it." Oates explains that unlike other biographical approaches such as the critical study, with its "appropriate detachment and skepticism," or the scholarly chronicle, with its "straightforward recitation of facts," pure biography is the narration or "simulation" of an individual's life. Describing the pure biographer as "both a historian who is steeped in his material and an artist who wields a deft and vivid pen," Oates says that "by telling a story, the pure biographer hopes to engage our hearts as well as our minds."

Oates is especially recognized for what he refers to in *Biography as High Adventure* as "a biographical quartet on the Civil War era and its century-old legacies, a quartet that sought to humanize the monstrous moral paradox of slavery and racial oppression in a land based on the ideals of the Declaration of Independence." In these four biographies, *To Purge This Land with Blood: A Biography of John Brown, The Fires of Jubilee: Nat Turner's Fierce Rebellion, With Malice toward None: The Life of Abraham Lincoln*, and *Let the Trumpet Sound: The Life of Martin Luther King, Jr.*, Oates examines the lives of men profoundly committed to the struggle for equality. "All four were driven, visionary men, all were caught up in the issues of slavery and race, and all devised their own solutions to those inflammable problems," writes Oates. "And all perished, too, in the conflicts and hostilities that surrounded the quest for equality in their country." A former civil rights activist himself, Oates considers these men "martyrs of our racial hatred," states Genevieve Stuttaford in *Publishers Weekly*, "martyrs of what he describes as the hateful thing they hated." Complementing this biographical quartet of historical figures is Oates's *William Faulkner: The Man and the Artist; A Biography*, about one of America's most esteemed literary figures who was a voice in the turbulent South for the cause of equality of opportunity, and whose fiction frequently concerns the Civil War and its legacies. Based upon his own native Mississippi, the fictional world that Faulkner created spanned generations and microcosmically mirrored the South's changing landscape while exploring the capacity of the human spirit to not only "endure" but "prevail."

John Brown, the subject of *To Purge This Land with Blood*, Oates's first book in his biographical quartet, was a "white northerner who hated slavery from the outside," explains Oates in *Biography as High Adventure*. Resolved to forcefully abolish slavery by leading an armed insurrection, Brown seized the government's arsenal in Harpers Ferry, Virginia in 1859, but was ultimately captured, tried, and executed. In the *Saturday Review*, T. Harry Williams calls the book "a major work, based on research in a wide variety of sources . . . that treats in detail Brown's career before he went to Kansas and his actions in that territory, as well as the blazing climax at Harpers Ferry.'' Noting in the *New York Times Book Review* that ''Brown's activities and motivations . . . have been the subject of heated historiographical debate,'' Eric Foner observes that unlike previous biographers who have set out ''either to vindicate or demolish'' Brown's legend as an American folk hero, thereby losing ''sight of the man himself,'' Oates neither indicts nor eulogizes Brown. ''Brown's life was filled with drama,'' says Foner, ''and Oates tells his story in a manner so engrossing that the book reads like a novel, despite the fact that it is extensively documented and researched.''

While acknowledging the ''almost complete acceptance and much praise'' with which *To Purge This Land* has met, Truman Nelson suggests in a *Nation* review that Oates misunderstands and even maligns his subject by creating a portrait of ''a hate-filled man.'' Nelson disagrees with the premise that Brown's actions derive from his religious beliefs, and feels that to instill ''the false consciousness of orthodox Calvinism in Brown diminishes him as a revolutionary.'' Foner maintains, though, that while Oates's portrait of Brown is ''not wholly flattering,'' neither does it ''denigrate the genuinely heroic aspects of Brown's life,'' and that ''about all we can say with certainty is that Brown was fanatic about both his religious and antislavery convictions, but in this he was hardly alone.'' Willie Lee Rose points out in the *New York Review of Books* that ''biographers of men who lived in violent times have the special problem of dealing with the abstractions about means and ends that clutter the rhetoric of political systems in a state of polarization. When do men mean what they say?'' Rose also feels that Oates has examined the ''whole of John Brown's life as carefully and thoroughly as the end of it . . . and has given us the most objective and absorbing biography of John Brown ever written.''

Nat Turner, the subject of *The Fires of Jubilee*, Oates's second biography, was a ''victim of human bondage, a brilliant and brooding slave preacher blocked from his potential by an impregnable wall,'' writes Oates in *Biography as High Adventure*. Oates adds that he ''tried to narrate Nat's story as graphically and as accurately'' as he could, hoping to ''convey how the insurrection rocked the South to its foundations and pointed the way to civil war thirty years later.'' Assessed as ''vivid and convincing'' by a *Publishers Weekly* contributor, *The Fires of Jubilee* ''presents as complete a narrative account of this affair as we are likely to get,'' remarks Henry Mayer in the *New York Times Book Review*. Oates re-creates the violent and doomed 1831 uprising in which more than fifty whites ''were murdered by Turner's insurgents, a band that grew from its nucleus of six to more than forty black men,'' explains Mayer, adding that Oates also devotes much attention to the ''indiscriminate reprisals directed by vengeful whites against blacks'' in which almost two hundred blacks died during ''the several weeks' reign of terror that followed Turner's two-day uprising.''

Mayer argues, however, that the attempt ''to present a rational, secularized explanation of the deeply emotional and religious forces'' at work in Turner's ability to organize and lead the rebellion, ''makes Turner's claim of freedom depend more upon merit than right and does not lay adequate stress upon Nat Turner's role as an avenging Messiah.'' In a *Nation* essay about Turner, Oates deems him ''a complex and paradoxical man, a victim of a violent system who in the end struck back with retributive violence,'' and suggests that ''the historical Turner with all his strength and human frailty, his loves and hatreds, his family cares and Messianic posturings, his liberating visions and bloody doom, lived a life that affords

profound insight into the tragic consequences of man's inhumanity to his fellow man.''

Discussing the subject of his third biography, *With Malice toward None*, Oates indicates in *Biography as High Adventure* that ''one of the supreme ironies of Lincoln's life—and of my quartet—was that he who spurned violence, he who placed his reverence for the system above his loathing of slavery, ended up smashing the institution in a violent civil war, a war that began because southerners equated Lincoln with John Brown and Nat Turner and seceded from the very system that protected slavery from Lincoln's grasp.'' Reviewing *With Malice toward None* in the *Washingotn Post Book Review*, Bernard Weisberger asserts that ''what [Oates] has done in this admirable book is to synthesize basic source materials with an array of new scholarly writing on slavery, Republicanism, the Civil War and Lincoln,'' a synthesis that Luther Spoehr in *Saturday Review* refers to as ''both comprehensive and tightly focused.''

Translated into French, Spanish, and Polish, *With Malice toward None* ''is an impressive performance,'' David Herbert Donald comments in the *New York Times Book Review*. ''Full, fair and accurate, it does, as its author boasts, cover all significant aspects of Lincoln's life.'' Oates carefully probes the obfuscatory legends about Lincoln to reveal the man himself. Noting that the Lincoln of *With Malice toward None* is neither Carl Sandburg's ''hardscrabble folk-hero, voicing the soul of a lost frontier,'' nor is he the ''too overrated'' figure perceived by the revisionists, Weisberger thinks that Oates ''has made Lincoln recognizably human instead of homespun saint—moody, unusual, inner-directed, but very successful in the world at large.'' Donald observes that ''what most distinguishes Oates from all previous Lincoln biographers is the fact that he is consistently nonjudgmental.''

Although Donald believes that *With Malice toward None* represents ''the most objective biography of Lincoln ever written,'' he suggests that ''the most crippling consequence of Oates's objectivity is that he is prevented from reflecting about his materials, from raising interesting new questions and attempting fresh answers to old questions.'' Similarly, Esmond Wright declares in a *Times Literary Supplement* review, ''It is all here, without much pause for analysis or assessment, and without any new revelations or discoveries.'' In the *Spectator*, though, Hugh Brogan interprets Oates's method somewhat differently: ''Oates is content to state his own view of every point persuasively, and to move on. Nor does he provide an explicit analysis of Lincoln's character, policies, achievements and significance: he leaves all that to his reader. Of course, his view of Lincoln emerges; but it is not stated outright in any page or sentence. He seems to hold that the story, well-told, will interpret itself, itself fascinate the reader. He is right, of course; and he narrates the extraordinary saga very well.''

John Brown, Nat Turner, and Abraham Lincoln all ''embraced violent solutions to slavery and racial oppression,'' says Oates in *Biography as High Adventure*. ''Martin Luther King, by contrast, tried to combat such injustice through nonviolent resistance and the power of redemptive love.'' *Let the Trumpet Sound*, the last book in Oates's biographical quartet, examines King's life ''from Montgomery to Memphis,'' says Roger Wilkins in the *Washington Post Book World;* Oates traces King's development from the ''enormously bright . . . and sensitive'' child and the youthful ''serious scholar'' to an adulthood spent ''reshaping and refining against hard experience the moral and intellectual view of the world he had developed in his student days.'' In the *New York Times Book Review,* Foner finds that ''King emerges as a charismatic leader, a brilliant tactician of the civil rights struggle, but also a deeply troubled man, subject to periodic bouts of depression and indecisiveness and, like Lincoln, wracked by premonitions of his own death.'' Calling it ''by far the most complete examination of the progression of King's movement and of the crosscurrents that beset it,'' Harry S. Ashmore notes in a *Chicago Tribune Book World* review that Oates has ''remained faithful to his conviction that biography is a storytelling art'' by capturing ''the high drama and moving tragedy of King's brief passage through our time.''

Let the Trumpet Sound, which has been translated into French, German, and Arabic, ''succeeds very well in describing King's intellect'' and represents a ''good place to begin for the facts of King's own life,'' says Wilkins, a nephew of the late NAACP executive director Roy Wilkins, but it fails to adequately treat the movement's other prominent figures as more than ''shadows in King's play.'' Suspecting that the biography is too uncritical of its subject, Elliott Rudwick similarly suggests in *American Historical Review* that ''Oates pictures King as more heroic than he probably was and greatly overstates the importance of his role in the movement.'' However, Foner declares that it ''provides more than just a chronicle of King's life; as his story is unfolded, the roles of other prominent personalities of the period become clearer.'' Concerning such criticism, Oates indicates to Stuttaford, ''I never leave anything out. And I certainly showed King's warts, showed when he had hatred, when he was angry. He overcame all that, and he showed other blacks how to overcome.'' Ashmore thinks that ''as Oates portrays him, King was not only mortal but, for all his great gifts, essentially humble. It was this quality that allowed him to inspire the lowliest blacks and touch the conscience of guilt-ridden whites.''

Oates's examination of the Civil War and its legacies does not culminate in his ''biographical quartet,'' though. He recently told *CA* that while a physical disability prevents him from presently proceeding with a biography of Robert F. Kennedy, it permits him to write the ''magnum opus'' he has been contemplating for some thirty years. *Voices of the Storm: A Biographical History of the Civil War Era,* says Oates, will be a ''biographical history of the antebellum and Civil War era that tries to capture its human experiences, that presents the entire period through the perceptions and feelings of some twenty-three significant figures whose lives and destinies intersected on many levels.'' Oates hopes to reinfuse that fratricidal war with the passion that he thinks has been wrung out of it through ''dry, scholarly analysis.'' Oates discusses the two parts that comprise the book: the first part addresses the coming war and demonstrates ''in human terms, which is the strength of biography, America's tragic failure to find a peaceful solution to slavery''; and the second part addresses the war itself and explores ''what it was like, through various inividual perceptions, to fight and suffer in that conflict and to make the human decisions that determined the outcome.''

Suggesting that a more meaningful term for this genre might be ''*literary* biography,'' Oates explains in *Biography as High Adventure* that ''the term would encompass biographies that attempt to create a life through the magic of language, that seek to illuminate universal truths about humankind through the sufferings and triumphs of a single human being.'' Oates points out in a *Publishers Weekly* interview with William Goldstein that ''biography is an exercise in the art of omission,'' explaining that in his biography *William Faulkner: The*

Man and the Artist, he tried to suggest the writer's art as well as his life through ''the use of telling detail alone.'' He also expresses to Goldstein why he chose a literary figure as a biographical subject: ''I am attracted to figures who have [a profound] sense of history, and Faulkner shares this with the men I have already written about. Faulkner's imagination was fired to incandescence by the history of the South.''

Calling Oates's *William Faulkner* ''romantic and absorbing,'' *New York Times*'s Christopher Lehmann-Haupt likens reading it to ''racing through a streamlined verison'' of the more massive, two-volume, fact-filled, scholarly biography by Joseph Blotner: ''Suddenly, instead of being the sum of a million particles, Faulkner's life assumes terrific motion. His personality coalesces—the courtliness, the obdurate eyes, the impenetrable silences. There is action to his story.'' Liberating Faulkner from a ''marble block of information,'' says Lehmann-Haupt, enables him ''to live out his life at twice its normal rate and degree of drama.'' And praising Oates's ''streamlined storytelling techniques,'' John Blades concludes in the *Chicago Tribune Book World* that ''with considerable narrative skill, Oates navigates the muddy, turbulent currents of Faulkner's life, so that few readers will come away unmoved by his tragedy and his glory.''

Translated into French and German, *William Faulkner* is aimed at a broad audience; however, it has generated a somewhat mixed critical reception. Some critics who fault the biography feel that it suffers from a lack of critical commentary on Faulkner's life as well as his work; Louis D. Rubin, Jr., for instance, ponders in the *New York Times Book Review,* ''What *is* the point of literary biography . . . if not to illuminate the sources—historical, familial, geographical, social—of the author's literary imagination, and to interpret, as best possible, the ties between an author's life and what he or she wrote?'' However, in *Biography as High Adventure* Oates discusses the importance of restraint in the crafting of a biography, indicating that the pure biographer is ''careful not to lapse into critical commentary or psychoanalytical speculation'' lest the narrative itself be destroyed.

Other critics who fault Oates's *William Faulkner* tend to believe that Faulkner was not an autobiographical writer and that the life, therefore, does not inform the work; Jonathan Yardley, for example, suggests in the *Washington Post Book World* that although ''Faulkner was the great American novelist of the century . . . his life's story is essentially irrelevant to his work.'' Oates, however, finds ''Faulkner's inner life . . . illuminated by his fiction,'' and tells Goldstein that ''even an artist as reticent as Faulkner reveals a lot about his personal life and conflicts in his art.'' Moreover, Oates also thinks that ''the themes that troubled him in art and life are universal themes: man's suffering as well as his triumph, his trouble with alcohol, with depression, with feeling unloved, unappreciated, especially by the literary establishment. Toiling in loneliness and solitude, only partly by choice. He was the only American writer of his generation who chose to go back home and write about that.'' Faulkner wrote about the Mississippi of his birth ''because he knew its history,'' says Oates. ''he sensed [the] problems there were a microcosm of the human race.''

In *Biography as High Adventure,* Oates speaks about the current popularity of biography and offers a possible explanation for why it ''may now be the preferred form of reading'' in America. Aside from a certain natural curiosity about the lives of others, he says that in an increasingly complex and technical society like our own, biography's ability to personalize events, "demonstrates that the individual does count—which is reassuring to people . . . who often feel caught up in vast impersonal forces beyond their control." Oates indicates that for himself, biography has not only served as "high literary and historical adventure, but deep personal experience as well." Having lived vicariously through the several lives he has documented biographically, Oates believes that he has been enriched "beyond measure as a writer and a man," adding that the experience of writing biographies has "reenforced my lifelong conviction that the people of the past have never really died. For they enjoy a special immortality in biography, in our efforts to touch and understand them and so to help preserve the human continuum. Perhaps this is what Yeats meant when he said that 'nothing exists but a stream of souls, that all knowledge is biography.'"

CA INTERVIEW

CA interviewed Stephen B. Oates by telephone on October 23, 1987, at his home in Amherst, Massachusetts.

CA: You've taught history and biography at the University of Massachusetts, Amherst, and since 1985 have been Paul Murray Kendall Professor of Biography. Speaking to Publishers Weekly *of* William Faulkner: The Man and the Artist, *then still in progress, you said, "Literature is my early and original love, so in a sense, turning to Faulkner has been like going home." When did these three interests—history, literature, and biography—begin to merge?*

OATES: I've loved storytelling ever since I was a child, both hearing stories and telling them myself. I recall spending a good bit of my time in the early part of junior high school in the library reading biographies and novels, and, later on, narrative histories. I had a fantastic English teacher my senior year who is still living in my hometown of Pampa, Texas. We are still in touch with one another. He wrote his master's thesis on William Faulkner; we've enjoyed talking about these connections. He gave me a sense of language and a sense of the importance of literature. That same year I had a history teacher who turned me on to something I had loved for years, history itself. History and literature have been my twin loves since I've been old enough to remember.

CA: What techniques do you think biography can fairly borrow from fiction?

OATES: Let's talk first about what it can't borrow. It cannot borrow invention. Biography is a nonfiction art and therefore must rely on facts, on evidence. The biographer never has the license the fiction writer has to invent situations or to make up dialogue. I understand how wonderful that kind of freedom is, because in biography we run into gaps in the record, things that don't make sense, and conflicting evidence. But we can't invent to bridge those gaps. Like the fiction writer, though, we do engage in conception and depiction of character. We shape a life—plot how we're going to tell the life story—much as a novelist might do in terms of interior climaxes and interpersonal relationships and character development and scene painting, which helps bring the subject alive. The art of biography is to tease from the facts the warmth of a life being lived. It's a fabulous and challenging art, but at the same time it's restrictive because we are limited by facts. As Paul Murray Kendall said, the biographer uses his imagination on the facts to rub them until they glow with human life.

CA: Before Faulkner your biographical subjects were John Brown, Nat Turner, Abraham Lincoln, and Martin Luther King, Jr. Do you see common traits among them besides the Civil War and civil rights connection?

OATES: Oh yes. All four of those men were deeply spiritual. Two of them were ministers: Nat Turner was a slave preacher, and Martin Luther King, Jr., was a Baptist preacher. While Lincoln did not belong to any official church, he was deeply religious and deeply spiritual. John Brown, a Congregationalist Calvinist of the old style, truly believed himself an instrument of God called to Harpers Ferry to help put an end to slavery. There's that common theme with all of them. Too, they were all brooding men who worried to their roots about the injustice of slavery and racial discrimination in this country, about the country's failure to live up to the promise of the Declaration of Independence.

Certainly Nat Turner, King, and Lincoln were extraordinary human beings with a deep sense of history and a deep insight into what their lives might amount to. And I guess I would include old John Brown in that. Though he failed in most business enterprises he tried, he was spectacularly successful in igniting humanitarian and liberal communities and abolitionists in the North to contribute money and weapons to his cause, and he was able to attract a number of idealistic young men to follow him to Harpers Ferry—several of them young blacks.

CA: When you write a biography for the general educated reader as opposed to the academic audience, you must still set yourself the challenge of bringing something new to the subject. How do you feel you succeeded in doing that with the Faulkner book?

OATES: I got to use a private collection of Faulkner letters that no other writer and indeed no other biographer had been able to use, a cache of original evidence that let me probe more deeply into Faulkner's relationship with his wife and his extramarital affairs and his trouble with alcohol, all of which in one way or another either added to or detracted from his art. I think that enabled me to depict the sufferings of this extraordinarily gifted artist in some depth. And I tried to bring some original ideas to bear on the way he was able to transform his anguish into art.

In addition, I am a writer, too, and this, I think, gave me further insight into his anguish and triumph as an artist. Earlier in my career, I spent four years writing fiction—a novel, a novelette, and many short stories. None of my fiction was ever published, but writing it was excellent training for narrative biography. And it helped me immensely when it came to understanding Faulkner.

CA: Did you feel there were specific problems involved in going from more or less historical biography to literary biography—though obviously those categories overlap?

OATES: They do overlap. I have to be careful here, because I've made the mistake of saying that I've turned from public figures to a private one. Well, Faulkner became a Nobel Prize winner and went around the globe representing the United States as a kind of cultural ambassador. In his later years he became a public figure indeed. The difference between writing about a public figure and an artist like Faulkner, a literary figure, is in the problem of the writings: how do you deal with them without becoming a literary critic? The problem with a historical figure is how you write biography without lapsing into straight history and losing your subject for whole pages or even chapters at a time. With literary biography, the problem is to avoid slipping off into literary criticism and thus losing the subject for entire passages. You have to figure out how to interweave the literary output and the development of the artist with the artist's life so that there isn't a discordant critical voice creeping in to disrupt the narrative flow and throw readers completely off. I was quick to criticize literary biographies before I tried one myself! It's an extraordinary challenge to show the work and the life as an integrated whole.

CA: And presenting that integrated whole is a different problem with each writer; it can't be solved once and for all.

OATES: That's true. Before I got off on my Civil War figures, I had hoped to do something biographical about James Agee, and I still hope to do that someday. It would have been different with Agee, whose smaller literary output included a magnificent maverick work of nonfiction, plus movie and book criticism, and who died at age forty-five. Faulkner, by contrast, produced close to thirty-seven books, including nineteen novels, and also lived a long time for his day, almost sixty-five years. Their lives and literary output were quite different. What might work in a biography of one might not work in a biography of the other.

CA: Who are the biographers you most admire?

OATES: Mari Sandoz, for her biography of Crazy Horse. I think it is one of the finest biographies ever written by anybody anywhere. She pulled off what must be one of the great literary feats of the twentieth century, a white woman in the late 1930s writing a biography about a mythic Indian figure who belonged to a preliterate society. Her information could come only from interviews with surviving Indians who either were relatives of Crazy Horse or knew him and fought with him, and from the white reports about the Indian wars. Sometimes she had to use evidence I wouldn't use if I were writing about a figure such as Faulkner or Lincoln in a literate society with all its written records, but that's all she had to go on. She drew from the Indians' rich oral tradition and oral history about Crazy Horse to produce a beautifully written biography, one that radiates empathy from the first word to the last. It's a passion play, a monumental work which captures Crazy Horse's elusive spirit and imperiled world view.

Another book I deeply admire is Henri Troyat's *Tolstoy*. This is storytelling biography at its best. I like to call it the *War and Peace* of biography. It measures up to its subject. For another, Frank Vandiver's two-volume biography of General John Pershing is simply the best military biography yet written. Black Jack Pershing was not somebody I wanted to read even a hundred pages about, but I knew Vandiver's Civil War biographies and decided I should at least familiarize myself with his work on Pershing. I read the first ten pages and he had me. The text of that biography is more than two thousand pages long, but it was so vividly written, such a full presentation of a three-dimensional character, that it gripped me to the end. He brings Pershing back from the past, gives you a sense of the immediacy of the military man who saw action in all the U.S. military campaigns from the Indian Wars of the 1880s through World War I.

Of course I love Paul Murray Kendall's *Louis XI*. Kings are not my favorite people to read about either, but when I read

that book, it was difficult to put down because Kendall truly lived up to all his own injunctions about biography in his book *The Art of Biography*, which is the best thing ever written on the subject.

CA: There is sometimes the criticism that in following what you've called the "storytelling art" as a biographer, you have neglected critical analysis of the life. How do you respond to that charge?

OATES: Our current worship of the critical mode is so dominant that anything that doesn't run with the herd is automatically suspect. The charge that my kind of biography "lacks analysis" betrays a real ignorance of the narrative form. Every good narrative biography proceeds from an analytical premise. Every choice of detail, the way in which the life is told, the way relationships are depicted, the interpretation of character—all come from painstaking critical analysis, which begins when you start taking notes and continues as you interpret your character and decide exactly how to plot out his life story. There is no such thing as narrative without analysis. It may be that the narrative voice doesn't engage in a critical lecture. I always tell people, Look, if you want to get on stage and expound, then write a critical study. This is an entirely acceptable way to write about individuals; it's another biographical approach. I tried that myself with my second book on Lincoln, *The Man behind the Myths*. But this is a different genre of biographical writing from that in *With Malice toward None*, which belongs to what Kendall calls pure biography—that is, bringing somebody back from the mists of history and making him live again on the written page. It's impossible to bring the subject alive if the author keeps jumping into the story and delivering long and learned lectures on the significance of things.

In narrative biography, by contrast, the author's interpretations are woven into the very fabric of the story; they are unostentatious; they do not disrupt the simulation of a life unfolding. Alas, there are those today who refuse to understand this, who insist that the critical mode—*their* mode—is the only way to truth. Beware of anybody who tells you that.

CA: Have any of your subjects been particularly difficult to bring back to life?

OATES: They all posed difficulties, but the one I found the hardest was the one I didn't feel very close to. From my study of biography these past twenty-five years, I've found that biographies are best when the biographers felt real empathy for their subjects. I don't mean by that some blind, dog-like love; I mean empathy, the ability to walk in their footsteps, to take them warts and all, a real projection into their sensibilities. My first biography, on John Brown, was difficult because of his single-minded Calvinistic zeal and his humorlessness, his intolerance of others. I'm not like that, and I found him challenging and different. It was hard to find character traits in him that I could identify with and that would give me empathy for him. I wrote that book in the 1960s, at the height of the civil rights movement, in which I had been involved. Brown was one of the great ancestors in the sixties' debate over violence versus nonviolence to effect social change. I am not a violent man—I was one of King's followers in the early sixties; but I came to understand why Brown decided that only violence could remove the sin of slavery in his own embattled time. Certainly I could care about his cause, the abolition of slavery, and I wanted to understand him better. The historical literature on Brown, either for or against him, was so incredibly strident—almost hysterically so—that I set out to write a portrait in which I would try to understand him. I had a hard time with him—his day-to-day life, the way he treated his children, his single-minded zealotry about his Calvinist faith. But I took it seriously. People in our secular age refuse to take his religion seriously, but if you don't, you're blinded to what motivated the man.

Nat Turner was also a violent revolutionary. But I felt more empathy for Nat Turner, perhaps because he was a slave and so a direct victim of slavery. In my book about him, I tried to narrate his story as accurately and graphically as I could. I wanted readers to suffer with him and see the world of slavery and the Old South through his eyes. That way they might gain melancholy insight into what it was like to be a slave.

Once I got to Lincoln, I had nothing but total empathy for my subjects. I felt much closer to Lincoln, Martin Luther King, and William Faulkner. They have haunted me in my dreams and come to me in my reveries and musings during the day. Frank Vandiver points out that the unique thing about biography is the interaction of two humanities—the biographer and the subject. This whole process of biography allows one generation to touch another and so to preserve the human continuum. I felt that more in my last three biographies than in the first two. I may have felt it even more with Faulkner than with King and Lincoln, two men I felt great empathy for, who truly lived with me every day I worked on them.

CA: What was it about Faulkner that made you feel that way?

OATES: As I said, I tried writing fiction myself for four years and decided that wasn't the form for me. What Kendall calls pure biography was where I ended up. You'd be surprised how many biographers have come to life-writing that way. Mari Sandoz, Andre Maurois, Henri Troyat, and Mark Schorer, to name a few. Anyway, that I'd tried fiction was part of the reason I felt such empathy for Faulkner. But it was also because he told so much more about his interior self and his feelings in his letters—and indeed in his writings—than the two public figures did. Lincoln was really a closed individual; it was hard to get inside of him. With King I ran into the difficulty that biographers of recent public figures have: many of them stopped writing letters and used the telephone. Without the letters it becomes increasingly difficult to write biography—unless the FBI bugged your subject's telephone, as they did King's. But then you don't know what to believe in the FBI reports because Hoover had set out to destroy the man in the public eye. For the King biographer, for any biographer, FBI reports are loaded with evasions and duplicities, and must be used with extreme care.

CA: With Lincoln especially there was the biographer's work of separating truth from myth. Isn't this a problem that starts in grade school? We're taught so much mythical nonsense about our national figures, we find it hard to see them straight even after we're grown.

OATES: That's true. But I have a great regard for myth. It has its own truth. It doesn't tell us as much about the historical figures we mythologize, but it does tell us a great deal about us. It tells us about how we need mythic figures from our past, how they contribute to our own spiritual growth and understanding of ourselves. That's another area of study, and I would be the last person to want to deprive any culture of its my-

thologies. What amuses me is that we deny we're a myth-bound culture, but we're as myth-bound as any culture I know. But I do think maybe the process is all wrong. Maybe grade school and high school children should be given the historic truth first, given the facts so that they can try to see these figures as they really were, flawed human beings as we all are, and have them study the mythology when they have the thorough grounding in the facts. Then they could appreciate what the mythology is. But I wouldn't want to get rid of mythology; I would just reverse the order in which myth and history are taught.

CA: How do you feel about the teaching of history now generally, after the beating the subject took in the sixties? Does it attract bright and enthusiastic students on the undergraduate level?

OATES: Sure it does. I think bright students would have always been attracted to history had it been presented right. On the one hand you had history being taught that's largely myth—and I'm not knocking mythology, as I said before; I simply think it's not the right place to be teaching mythology. It's also misguided in the sense that it seems to assume that if we teach young people the truth about the past, they'll all become communists and traitors. I went into shock when I got into college and found out that much I had been told was actually mythical. Then I didn't know *who* was telling the truth, and it took me years to sort it all out.

The other problem is that too often these days historians, when confronted with an undergraduate class, tend to forget who the students are; historians seem to see not bright and eager laymen, but a gathering of the American Historical Association, and they fall into such technical professional history that it becomes boring to young people who don't necessarily want to become history majors. Historians should never give up their professional approach to research and their sophisticated concepts, but I've always suggested that they ought to dramatize history, too, by bringing to life the people and the times they talk about in the classroom. There is nothing wrong with enlivening all that learning with a little drama. The past is full of drama, and capturing that is, or should be, part of the historian's job. Alas, though, many historians now function as statisticians and sociologists, producing recondite studies aimed at fellow specialists. I worry that they are going to lose that large audience that historians once commanded, and become highly specialized social scientists who only write for each other. That would be a disaster to literate Americans everywhere.

CA: You seem to find teaching and writing mutually enriching activities.

OATES: I do, but I try to take the same approach in both. I've gone out to talk with students and teach them, and they've raised questions which I've then gone back to try to answer in writing my biographies. When I get them answered, I can take the books back to the students and see what they think. For me, teaching and writing are symbiotic—mutually beneficial and reinforcing. I might add that I teach a year-long graduate seminar in the art and technique of biography, the only course in the country, we think, which not only probes the extant literature, but tries to teach the principles of biographical research and narrative biographical writing. Many of my students have published books and articles that originated in the seminar. Several of us (myself and seminar graduates actively writing biography) also belong to the New England Creative Biography Group, whose monthly meetings are devoted to readings and constructive criticism by the members.

CA: Both the Faulkner biography and the King biography tapped you on the shoulder, you also told William Goldstein for Publishers Weekly *in 1985. Is there a subject tapping now? You mentioned James Agee earlier.*

OATES: James Agee has been tapping me on the shoulder for about twenty-five years. Someday, I keep telling him, I will answer that tapping. But there's someone else now. When I'm thinking about my next subject, I always make a list of the people who might interest me, for whom I could have empathy, and then I wait for some kind of connection to take place. Within a few weeks, maybe a couple of months, something usually does. This time it was dramatic. The first visitation came while I was sitting in my study, the lights dim, and I kept seeing Bobby Kennedy. I had thought about Robert Kennedy as a sequel biography after I had finished King, but shied away from him because, frankly, I didn't want to write about another figure who got assassinated. I began to worry about myself: two of my figures have been hanged, and two assassinated. What does that tell me about *me*? Besides that, when you do this kind of biography, you get not just intellectually but emotionally involved in the life, and it's wrenching when you have to get down to that end. Most biographers find the death traumatic, even if the figure lived a long and productive life and died in old age. You have to grieve through it as if somebody in your own family had died. I didn't want to grieve through another assassination; it hurts too much.

But I guess Kennedy had other ideas, because he kept nudging me on the shoulder. I already had a lot of notes on Kennedy because he was a major character in my life of King. When he came to me in my study, I closed my eyes, and damned if I didn't see him staring at me with a panorama of the world in back of him, including the Vietnamese War, Washington, the civil rights struggle, and on back into history. His whole life was spread before me in this incredible panorama, and Kennedy was looking at me and impatiently giving me a sign with his hand to come on. I thought, I'm losing my mind. I opened my eyes, then closed them, and saw it all again. It was an unmistakable sign.

So that is the book I'm working on now. It's going to be enormously hard. Here again is one of those driven figures of the modern era who relied on the telephone. He may have left a lot of letters, but they're not presently available to the public. Whether I can see them or not is a big question mark. But Kennedy is provocative; he's got not only a myth spun around him but a counter-myth. The counter-myth is the ruthless Bobby, a politician who never did anything for anybody—the Indians, the blacks—except for political reasons. Then there's the myth of the saintly Bobby who could have saved the world had he not been assassinated. I like the latter myth best, but I'm not going to write mythology. I'm going to try to wring the historical figure from the mists and make him live again through the art of biography. And what a figure! Full of so many contradictions, a man of great strengths as well as flaws. His is one of the great stories of our time. I only hope I can do it justice. One thing I do know for certain: the act of re-creating his life will enrich mine immeasurably.

BIOGRAPHICAL/CRITICAL SOURCES:

BOOKS

Oates, Stephen B., *Biography as High Adventure: Life-Writers Speak on Their Art,* University of Massachusetts Press, 1986.

PERIODICALS

American Historical Review, October, 1983.
American History Illustrated, January, 1986.
Antioch Review, summer, 1970, fall, 1984.
Atlantic, July, 1987.
Best Sellers, August 15, 1970.
Book Forum, Volume VII, number 4, 1986.
Chicago Tribune, July 26, 1987.
Chicago Tribune Book World, August 8, 1982, September 18, 1983, April 22, 1984.
Christian Science Monitor, February 28, 1977.
Chronicle of Higher Education, November 3, 1982.
Contemporary Review, January, 1983.
Globe and Mail (Toronto), August 23, 1986.
Library Journal, February 1, 1975.
Los Angeles Times Book Review, August 29, 1982.
Nation, March 29, 1971, May 31, 1975.
Newsweek, July 6, 1970.
New Republic, September 13, 1982.
New York Review of Books, December 3, 1970, October 27, 1983.
New York Times, March 12, 1977, August 25, 1982, August 3, 1987.
New York Times Book Review, November 1, 1970, October 5, 1975, March 13, 1977, September 12, 1982, October 28, 1984, September 20, 1987.
Publishers Weekly, January 13, 1975, August 27, 1982, June 28, 1985.
Saturday Review, August 22, 1970, February 5, 1977.
Spectator, February 25, 1978.
Times Literary Supplement, April 28, 1978.
Washington Post Book World, March 6, 1977, August 8, 1982, April 29, 1984, August 16, 1987.

—*Sketch by Sharon Malinowski*

—*Interview by Jean W. Ross*

*   *   *

OBERG, James E(dward)   1944-

PERSONAL: Born November 7, 1944, in New York, N.Y.; son of John Lincoln (an accountant) and Jean (a college registrar; maiden name, Grams) Oberg; married Alcestis Ritsos (an author), August 30, 1969; children: Gregory James, John Nicholas. *Education:* Ohio Wesleyan University, B.A. (summa cum laude), 1966; Northwestern University, M.S. in astrodynamics, 1969; University of New Mexico, M.S. in computing science, 1972. *Politics:* Libertarian/Conservative. *Religion:* None.

ADDRESSES: Home—Route 2, Box 350, Dickinson, Tex. 77539. *Office*—Johnson Space Center (code DM4), Houston, Tex. 77058.

CAREER: U.S. Air Force, 1970-78; weapons laboratory analyst at Kirtland Air Force Base, N.M., 1970-72, instructor at Department of Defense Computer Institute, Washington, D.C., 1972-75, flight controller at NASA Mission Control, Houston, Tex., 1975—; retired as captain.

MEMBER: British Interplanetary Society, American Institute of Aeronautics and Astronautics, National Association of Science Writers, Commmittee for the Scientific Investigation of Claims of the Paranormal, Phi Beta Kappa.

AWARDS, HONORS: National Space Club History Awards, 1975, for "Russia Meant to Win the Moon Race," and 1977, for "Korolev"; best essay award from Cutty Sark International for UFO essay "The Failure of the Science of UFOlogy," 1979; NASA-area Technical Man of the Year, 1985.

WRITINGS:

(Contributor) *Famous Spaceships of Fact and Fantasy,* edited by Harold A. Edmondson, Kalmbach, 1979.
Red Star in Orbit (Astronomy Book Club and Conservative Book Club selection), Random House, 1981.
New Earths: Transforming Other Planets for Humanity (Book of the Month Club alternate selection, Astronomy Book Club selection), Stackpole, 1981, published as *New Earths: Restructuring Earth and Other Planets,* New American Library, 1983.
UFOs and Outer Space Mysteries: A Sympathetic Skeptic's Report, edited by Hank Stine, Donning, 1982.
Mission to Mars: Plans and Concepts for the First Manned Landing, Stackpole, 1982.
The New Race for Space: The U.S. and Russia Leap to the Challenge for Unlimited Rewards, foreword by Ben Bova, Stackpole, 1984.
(With wife, Alcestis Oberg) *Pioneering Space: Living on the Next Frontier* (Astronomy Book Club alternate selection), foreword by Isaac Asimov, McGraw-Hill, 1986.
Space Shuttle Rendezvous Flight Procedures Handbook, NASA, 1987.
Uncovering Soviet Disasters: Exploring the Limits of Glasnost, Random House, 1988.

Also author of *The Great Galactic Ghoul and Other Space Legends,* 1986. Regular contributor to *Omni* and *Science Digest.* Associate editor of *Space World,* 1976—; consulting editor for *Skeptical Inquirer,* 1977—.

WORK IN PROGRESS: Research for a biography of Sergey Korolev, father of the Russian space program; a twelve-volume series on manned exploration of and expansion into the solar system in coming centuries; analysis of "space age folklore," including bimillenial apocalypsism; investigations into Soviet disinformation and strategic deception.

SIDELIGHTS: In *Red Star in Orbit,* James E. Oberg relates the history of the Russian space program. Not an easy task, Thomas Powers asserted in the *New York Times Book Review,* considering the Soviet "obsession with secrecy and prestige," their "horror of failure [that] sometimes results in grotesque extremes of denial," and their "bland house-organ history" that is filled with "omissions, distortions, and bald lies." In his history, Oberg recreates one particularly dramatic representative case concerning Field Marshal Mitrofan Nedelin, former commander of the Soviet Strategic Rocket Forces. Reportedly killed in a plane crash, Nedelin was actually annihilated along with scores of other key Soviet space scientists, technicians, and military officers when a rocket ready to launch (near Tyura Tam, October 23-24, 1960) toppled and ignited, along with its 500 tons of fuel. The accident was the Soviet space program's greatest catastrophe. "Only the barest details have been gathered in two decades," the reviewer noted. "Mr. Oberg's account of this incident and the program as a whole is a stunning *tour de force.*"

"*Red Star in Orbit* is an excellent book," Powers continued, "crisply written, full of surprises, at times both dramatic and touching. Researchers will find the many appendices invaluable. Ordinary readers would be hard put to find a better account in one volume of the extraordinary adventure involved in man's first steps beyond the planet. But at the same time James Oberg draws a disquieting portrait of Russia itself, a great power neurotically unsure of itself. It is a melancholy irony that this fair-minded history of Russia in space—its achievements as well as its failures—had to be written by an American."

James E. Oberg told *CA:* "I am a grown-up space nut, repaying with interest the childhood inspirations derived from the works of Jules Verne, Arthur Clarke, Wernher von Braun, Willy Ley, and other 'crackpots' who dared to dream great dreams. I wish to be perceived in that tradition."

BIOGRAPHICAL/CRITICAL SOURCES:

BOOKS

Clarke, Arthur C., *The Odyssey File,* Ballantine, 1984.

PERIODICALS

Booklist, October 15, 1982.
Choice, October, 1981, June, 1983.
Christian Science Monitor, July 13, 1981, December 3, 1982.
Nature, February 24, 1983.
New York Times Book Review, June 7, 1981, February 28, 1988.

*   *   *

OESTERREICHER, John M(aria)   1904-

PERSONAL: Born February 2, 1904, in Stadt Liebau, Austria (now in Czechoslovakia); naturalized U.S. citizen; son of Nathan and Ida (Zelenka) Oesterreicher. *Education:* University of Vienna, medical student, 1922-24, later theology student; University of Graz, Lic.theol., 1928, State Teaching Certificate of professorship, 1936.

ADDRESSES: Home—Seton Hall University, South Orange, N.J. 07079. *Office*—Institute of Judaeo-Christian Studies, Seton Hall University, South Orange, N.J. 07079.

CAREER: Jewish-Catholic scholar and Roman Catholic priest; appointed papal chamberlain with title of monsignor, 1961, appointed honorary prelate, 1967; Waehringer Maedchen Realgymnasium, Vienna, Austria, professor of religion, 1935-38; Manhattanville College of the Sacred Heart, New York, N.Y., research professor of scared theology, 1944-53; Seton Hall University, South Orange, N.J., distinguished university professor emeritus, director of Institute of Judaeo-Christian Studies, 1953—. Danforth lecturer at Columbia University, 1962, and University of Miami, 1963; also has lectured in Germany, Italy, England, and Austria. Consultor, Secretariat for Promotion of Christian Unity, Rome, 1961-68; contributing designer of the *Statement by the Second Vatican Council on the Church's Bond to the Jewish People,* chapter four of the declaration *Nostra Aetate;* advisor to the Secretariat for Catholic-Jewish Relations; member of subcommittee for Catholic-Jewish Concerns, Ecumenical and Interreligious Affairs of Archdiocese of Newark, N.J.

MEMBER: Catholic Biblical Association, Society of Biblical Literature, Catholic Theological Society, Catholic Commission on Intellectual and Cultural Affairs, Council on Religion and International Affairs, American Professors for Peace in the Middle East, National Committee for Foreign Affairs.

AWARDS, HONORS: Brotherhood Award of Congregation Agudath Achim, Taunton, Mass., 1963; LL.D., Incarnate Word College, 1967; D.H.L., Canisius College, 1968.

WRITINGS:

Racisme-Antisemitisme-Antichristianisme, Editions de la Maison Francaise (New York), 1943.
Walls Are Crumbling: Seven Jewish Philosophers Discover Christ, foreword by Jacques Maritain, Devin-Adair, 1952 (published in England as *Seven Jewish Philosophers Discover Christ,* Hollis & Carter, 1953), abridged edition published as *Five in Search of Wisdom,* University of Notre Dame Press, 1967.
(Translator) Richard Baumann, *To See Peter: A Lutheran Minister's Journey to the Eternal City,* McKay, 1953.
(With others) *The Gospel of Jesus the Christ,* Seton Hall University Press, 1962.
Der Papst und die Juden (booklet), Paulus Verlag, 1962.
The Israel of God: On the Old Testament Roots of the Church's Faith, Prentice-Hall, 1963.
(Editor and author of preface) Edward Flannery, *The Anguish of the Jews,* Macmillan, 1965.
(Editor and author of preface) Edward Synan, *The Popes and the Jews in the Middle Ages,* Macmillan, 1965.
Auschwitz, the Christian and the Council, Palm Publishers, 1965.
(Contributor) *Concilium,* Paulist Press, 1967.
(Contributor) *American Participation in the Second Vatican Council,* Sheed, 1967.
Der Baum und die Wurzel, Herder (Freiburg), 1968.
(Contributor) *Commentary on the Documents of Vatican II,* Herder & Herder, 1969.
The Rediscovery of Judaism, Institute of Judaeo-Christian Studies, Seton Hall University, 1971.
(Editor with L. Frizzell and A. Finkel) *Beginnings: The Master's Program in Judaeo-Christian Studies, 1975-1980,* Seton Hall University, 1980.
The Unfinished Dialogue: Martin Buber and the Christian Way, Philosophical Library, 1986.
The New Encounter: Between Christians and Jews, Philosophical Library, 1986.

AUTHOR OF PREFACE

Justus George Lawler, *The Christian Imagination,* Newman, 1955.
Rene Aigrain and Ome Englebert, *Prophecy Fulfilled,* McKay, 1958.
Claude Tresmontant, *Essay on Hebrew Thought* (translation of *Essai sur la pensee hebraique*), Desclee, 1960.

OTHER

General editor and contributor, *The Bridge: A Yearbook of Judaeo-Christian Studies,* Herder & Herder, for Institute of Judaeo-Christian Studies, Volume I, 1955, Volume II, 1957, Volume III, 1959, Volume IV, 1962, Volume V, 1970. Writer of other Institute publications; also author of four Institute Teshuvah papers, *Salute to Israel, Internationalization of Jerusalem?, Jerusalem the Free,* and *The Anatomy of Contempt.* Contributor to *Die Erfuellung, Dublin Review, Orate Fratres, Pax Romana, America, Today's Family,* and other theological and secular periodicals.

WORK IN PROGRESS: The Geneology of Hitler's Jew-hatred.

SIDELIGHTS: John M. Oesterreicher's *Walls Are Crumbling* has been published in six countries, with translations in French, Dutch, Spanish, and Japanese.†

*   *   *

OLIVER, Raymond (Davies) 1936-

PERSONAL: Born January 28, 1936, in Arlington, Mass.; son of Raymond Joseph and Bernice (Davis) Oliver; married Mary Anne McPherson (a professor and writer), August 28, 1959; children: Kathryn, Nathan. *Education* Oberlin College, B.A., 1957; University of Wisconsin—Madison, M.A., 1958; Stanford University, Ph.D., 1967. *Religion:* Anglican.

ADDRESSES: Office—322 Wheeler Hall, University of California, Berkeley, Calif. 94720.

CAREER: University of California, Berkeley, assistant professor, 1965-72, associate professor, 1972-85, professor of English, 1985—, director of Education Abroad Program at University of Bordeaux, 1982-84.

MEMBER: American Association of University Professors, Phi Beta Kappa.

WRITINGS:

Poems Without Names (criticism), University of California Press, 1970.
To Be Plain (verse translations), Robert L. Barth, 1981.
Entries (poems), David R. Godine, 1982.
Private Stock (poems), Robert L. Barth, 1982.
Other Times (poems), Robert L. Barth, 1985.
Fireflies in an Old Yard (poems), Red Candle Press, 1987.

WORK IN PROGRESS: A technical study of the short poem; a work in prose and verse on *Beowulf* and Anglo-Saxon culture.

SIDELIGHTS: Poet and translator Raymond Oliver's writings depict and illuminate the everyday world. "He is an avowed enemy of all gnostic and puritanical schemes that out of spiritual pride cut off the human being from devotion to the common earth and reality," explains John Finlay in the *Southern Review.* Finlay continues that Oliver's images correct "the excessively abstract and denatured modern mind that too often belongs nowhere." In *Chicago Tribune Book World,* Mary Kinzie comments, "Subdued as if by his own propriety, the poet makes a poetic and rhetorical virtue of his common humanity." Oliver's poems are traditional in form, and as the title of his collection of verse translations, *To Be Plain,* indicates, simple in style. Referring to the book in *PN Review 27,* Dick Davis writes, "Mr. Oliver is a good translator—he can manage with equal dexterity the lyrical and charming . . . the satiric epigram . . . and the epigram that has a serious moral point to make beneath its wit." Finlay agrees: "Oliver's translations are excellent. . . . Most rarely are the required talents for such a book to be found in a single person, for it combines the scholarly, the critical, and the creative, and in his mastery of all three Oliver recalls, strangely enough for his classicism, the achievement of Ezra Pound."

Oliver told *CA:* "I write poetry to make sense of experience, to celebrate it, and to fix it in memorable form. 'Form' is a key word. Everything I write is in strict metrical form—iambics, usually rhymed—because that, and that only, gives a sense of definitiveness, like the sense of things fitting exactly into position when you turn the right key in the lock. And strict form is easy to remember, therefore lends itself to being memorable; we still remember about Humpty Dumpty, even though he goes back to Indo-European times, because his career was preserved in rhyme and meter—a consideration not lost on song-writers even now.

"Every object (a road, a tree, a meal), every piece of bric-a-brac from my own daily life, any fragment of U.S. or European history, is potentially a window that opens up on human experience. I am not a poetic specialist; my theme is miscellany, on principle. Anything goes. A 'philosophy of life' will emerge as it emerges, over the years, inductively. Above all, I want the world, piece by piece, to enter into my poetry with a minimum of distortion.

"Because variety of experience is important, and because I am obsessed with language, especially in its aural aspect, I have learned French and German very thoroughly, and have lived for years in Germany, France, and England. I have also learned, with varying degrees of competence and for the same reasons, Latin, Portuguese, Russian, Greek, and Welsh."

AVOCATIONAL INTERESTS: "My principal hobby is food, which goes well with poetry and languages and travel. All in all I think that life, like God, is meant to be enjoyed, precisely and in depth."

BIOGRAPHICAL/CRITICAL SOURCES:

PERIODICALS

Chicago Tribune Book World, September 26, 1982.
Denver Quarterly, November, 1982.
Occident, fall, 1981.
PN Review 27, Volume 7, number 1, 1982.
Southern Review, winter, 1983.

*   *   *

OLSEN, Marvin E(lliott)   1936-

PERSONAL: Born April 18, 1936, Hamilton, N.Y.; son of Edward Gustave and Faith (Eliott) Olsen; married Katherine Melchiors (a social worker), September 8, 1956; children: Lawrence, Steven, David. *Education:* Grinnell College, B.A., 1957; University of Michigan, M.A., 1958, Ph.D., 1965.

CAREER: University of Michigan, Ann Arbor, instructor in sociology, 1963-65; Indiana University at Bloomington, assistant professor, 1965-69, associate professor, 1969-74, professor of sociology, 1974-75, director of Institute of Social Research, 1970-74; Battelle Human Affairs Research Centers, Seattle, Wash., senior research scientist, 1974-79. Affiliate professor, University of Washington, beginning 1975. Visiting summer professor at University of Oregon, 1967, and at University of Washington, 1970; visiting professor, Uppsala University, Uppsala, Sweden, 1971-72. *Military service:* U.S. Air Force, 1958-62; became captain.

MEMBER: International Sociological Association, American Sociological Association, World Future Society (president of Evergreen chapter, 1975-76), Society for the Study of Social Problems, Pacific Sociological Association, Western Washington Solar Energy Association (director), Phi Beta Kappa, Phi Kappa Phi.

WRITINGS:

The Process of Social Organization: Power in Social Systems, Holt, 1968, 2nd edition, 1978.
(Editor) *Power in Societies,* Macmillan, 1970.
Social Aspects of Energy Conservation, Northwest Energy Policy Project, 1977.

(With others) *Beluga Coal Field Development: Social Effects and Management Alternatives,* Battelle Human Affairs Research Centers, 1979.
(Editor with Michael Micklin) *Handbook of Applied Sociology: Frontiers of Contemporary Research,* Praeger, 1981.
Participatory Pluralism: Political Participation and Influence in the United States and Sweden, Nelson-Hall, 1982.
Consumer Energy Conservation Policies in the United States and the Pacific Northwest Region, International Institute for Environment and Society, 1982.

Contributor to sociology journals. Book review editor, *American Sociological Review,* 1968-71.†

*   *   *

O'NEILL, Judith (Beatrice)   1930-

PERSONAL: Born June 30, 1930, in Melbourne, Australia; daughter of John Ramsden (a school inspector) and Beatrice (a teacher; maiden name, McDonald) Lyall; married John Cochrane O'Neill (a professor), April 17, 1954; children: Rachel, Catherine, Philippa. *Education:* University of Melbourne, B.A. (with honors), 1950, M.A., 1952; Institute of Education, London, P.G.C.E., 1953.

ADDRESSES: Home—9 Lonsdale Terrace, Edinburgh EH3 9HN, Scotland. *Agent*—A. P. Watt Ltd., 20 John St., London WC1N 2DL, England.

CAREER: University of Melbourne, Victoria, Australia, tutor in English, 1954-55; Open University, Buckinghamshire, England, tutor and counselor, 1971-73; St. Mary's Convent, Cambridge, England, English teacher, 1974-82; free-lance writer, 1982—.

AWARDS, HONORS: Third prize, Rigby Anniversary Literary Contest (Australia), 1982, for *Jess and the River Kids.*

WRITINGS:

JUVENILES

Martin Luther, Cambridge University Press, 1975, Lerner Publications, 1978.
Transported to Van Diemen's Land: The Story of Two Convicts, Cambridge University Press, 1977.
Jess and the River Kids, Hamish Hamilton, 1984.
Stringybark Summer, Hamish Hamilton, 1985.
Deepwater, Hamish Hamilton, 1987.

EDITOR; "READINGS IN LITERARY CRITICISM" SERIES

Critics on Keats, Allen & Unwin, 1967, University of Miami Press, 1968.
Critics on Charlotte and Emily Bronte, Allen & Unwin, 1967, University of Miami Press, 1979.
Critics on Pope, University of Miami Press, 1968.
Critics on Marlowe, Allen & Unwin, 1969, University of Miami Press, 1970.
Critics on Blake, University of Miami Press, 1970.
Critics on Jane Austen, University of Miami Press, 1970.

WORK IN PROGRESS: Cry of the Currawong, publication expected in 1989.

SIDELIGHTS: Judith O'Neill told *CA:* "I am a third-generation Australian and, although I have lived in Britain for twenty-five years, my novels for young people are all set in Australia and all in the past. Now that I live in Scotland, I very much enjoy my visits to schools to talk with children about my writing and to encourage their writing."

P

PADFIELD, Peter 1932-

PERSONAL: Born April 3, 1932, in Calcutta, British India (now India); son of William L. N. (a British Army captain) and Annice Edna (Abbott) Padfield; married Dorothy Jean Yarwood, 1960; children: Deborah, Guy, Fiona. *Education:* Attended Christ's Hospital School, 1943-48, and Thames Nautical Training College, 1948-50. *Religion:* Church of England.

ADDRESSES: Home—Westmoreland Cottage, Drybridge Hill, Woodbridge, Suffolk, England. *Agent*—McIntosh & Otis, Inc., 475 Fifth Ave., New York, N.Y. 10017.

CAREER: Shaw Savill & Albion Shipping Line, London, England, cadet, 1950-53; Peninsular and Oriental Steam Navigation Co., London, officer, 1953-58; *Shipbuilding and Shipping Record,* London, editorial assistant, 1960; Angula Engineering Co. Ltd., London, director, 1960-63; writer, 1963—.

MEMBER: Society for Nautical Research.

WRITINGS:

NONFICTION

The Sea Is a Magic Carpet, P. Davies, 1960.
The "Titanic" and the "Californian," John Day, 1965.
An Agony of Collisions, Hodder & Stoughton, 1966.
Aim Straight: A Biography of Admiral Sir Percy Scott, Hodder & Stoughton, 1966.
Broke and the "Shannon": A Biography of Admiral Sir Philip Broke, Hodder & Stoughton, 1968.
The Battleship Era, McKay, 1972.
Guns at Sea: A History of Naval Gunnery, St. Martin's, 1973.
The Great Naval Race: Anglo-German Naval Rivalry, 1900-1914, McKay, 1974.
Nelson's War, Hart-Davis, 1976.
Tide of Empires: Decisive Naval Campaigns in the Rise of the West, Routledge & Kegan Paul, Volume I: *1481-1654,* 1979, Volume II: *1655-1763,* 1981.
Rule Britannia: The Victorian and Edwardian Navy, Routledge & Kegan Paul, 1981.
Beneath the Houseflag of the P & O, Hutchinson, 1981.
Doenitz: The Last Fuehrer, Gollancz, 1984.
Armada, Naval Institute Press, 1988.

Contributor to *Oxford Companion to Ships and the Sea* and *Purnell's History of the First World War.*

NOVELS

The Lion's Claw, Hutchinson, 1978.
The Unquiet Gods, Hutchinson, 1980.
Gold Chains of Empire, Hutchinson, 1982.
Salt and Steel, Century Hutchinson, 1986.

WORK IN PROGRESS: Tide of Empires: Decisive Naval Campaigns in the Rise of the West, Volumes III and IV, for Routledge & Kegan Paul; a biography of the Reichsfuehrer SS, Heinrich Himmler, for Macmillan.

SIDELIGHTS: Peter Padfield wrote: "I was fortunate to gain a berth as a mariner aboard *Mayflower II,* which sailed to Plymouth, Mass., in 1957, and subsequently to travel independently in the United States and the Pacific. The experiences provided material for my first book, which was an account of those travels and, as it were, set me on a writing course.

"Since then I have concentrated on naval history, which has become I fear a rather specialized subject. My concern now is to widen the scope and bring naval history back into the mainstream of general history where it belongs, and where it has for too long been neglected.

"My work *Tide of Empires: Decisive Naval Campaigns in the Rise of the West* places naval and mercantile struggles at the very center of the development of civilization, and indeed of future developments; the struggle for world markets continues as fiercely as ever, so does the struggle between the great territorial empires, now represented by Russia and China, and the market-acquisitive sea peoples, represented by the United States, Japan, and Western Europe. I believe that the struggle between these two different types of power (at present labeled communist and capitalist, but in reality the old 'centrally-controlled' and 'market-acquisitive' powers) will be decided, as it has been in the past, by trading power and the wealth and sophisticated banking systems that have always followed trading power. In short I believe that economic and mecantile and naval history are inseparably linked, and together these factors add up to the driving force in world history, which if studied in these terms yields much food for thought about the present global struggle."

BIOGRAPHICAL/CRITICAL SOURCES:

PERIODICALS

New York Times Book Review, September 23, 1984.
Times (London), March 1, 1984.
Times Literary Supplement, March 21, 1980, November 26, 1982, April 20, 1984.

*   *   *

PARFITT, George (Albert Ekins) 1939-

PERSONAL: Born November 7, 1939, in San Fernando, Trinidad; son of Albert Walter (a priest) and Sara (a nurse; maiden name, Ekins) Parfitt; married Margaret Anne King, April 15, 1962 (divorced, 1979); married Maureen Bell (a part-time lecturer), June 27, 1981; children: Stephen, Peter, Elisabeth, Catherine, Jessica. *Education:* University of Bristol, B.A., 1962, Ph.D., 1966. *Politics:* Socialist. *Religion:* Atheist.

ADDRESSES: Home—4 Elm Ave., Beeston, Nottingham, England. *Office*—School of English Studies, University of Nottingham, Nottingham, England.

CAREER: University of Nottingham, Nottingham, England, assistant lecturer, 1966-68, lecturer in English studies, 1968-86, reader, 1986—. Editor of Byron Press. Member of board of governors of Beeston Girls Secondary School, 1974-77. Member of Beeston Anti-Nuclear Group.

MEMBER: Association of University Teachers, University of Nottingham Staff Club.

WRITINGS:

(Editor with James Kinsley) *John Dryden: Selected Criticism,* Oxford University Press, 1970.
(Editor) *Silver Poets of the Seventeenth Century,* Dent, 1974.
(Editor) *Ben Jonson: The Complete Poems,* Penguin, 1975, Yale University Press, 1981.
Ben Jonson: Public Poet and Private Man, Dent, 1976.
(Editor) *The Plays of Cyril Tourneur,* Cambridge University Press, 1978.
English Poetry of the Seventeenth Century, Longman, 1985.
(Editor with Ralph Houlbrooke) *Leonard Wheatcroft,* Whiteknights Press, 1986.
Fiction of the First World War, Faber, 1987.
English Poetry of the First World War, Harvester Press, 1988.
(With M. Bell and S. Shepherd) *A Dictionary of Women Writers in Seventeenth Century England,* Harvester Press, 1988.

Editor of ''Nottingham Drama Texts,'' University of Nottingham, 1978—. Editor of *Renaissance and Modern Studies.*

SIDELIGHTS: Parfitt told *CA:* ''My writing springs, obviously enough, from my circumstances. Specifically, although I am not primarily a creative writer, my writing relates to creative questions: how have we, as a species, got where we now are, what does our past mean? In England, much of this has to go back to our 'revolution' in the seventeenth century—just as the United States has its revolt against Britain later. The first World War links, for me, with my seventeenth-century interests because that war was another crisis for Britain.

''My writings express my own views insofar as they are my writings. I do not write to please anyone else, although I do try to respond to what seem to me to be needs in the people I teach and speak to. But I try to avoid egocentric subjectivism; I listen, as best I can, to the authors I write about and write

about them to encourage others to listen to them also. That is what criticism, scholarship, and editing should be about.''

BIOGRAPHICAL/CRITICAL SOURCES:

PERIODICALS

Times Literary Supplement, February 11, 1977, October 28, 1983, December 13, 1985.
Washington Post Book World, July 11, 1982.

*   *   *

PARKER, Robert B(rown) 1932-

PERSONAL: Born September 17, 1932, in Springfield, Mass.; son of Carroll Snow (a telephone company executive) and Mary Pauline (Murphy) Parker; married Joan Hall (an education specialist), August 26, 1956; children: David F., Daniel T. *Education:* Colby College, B.A., 1954; Boston University, M.A., 1957, Ph.D., 1970.

ADDRESSES: Agent—The Helen Brann Agency, Inc., 157 West 57th St., New York, N.Y. 10019.

CAREER: Curtiss-Wright Co., Woodridge, N.J., management trainee, 1957; Raytheon, Co., Andover, Mass., technical writer, 1957-59; Prudential Insurance Co., Boston, Mass, advertising writer, 1959-62; Boston University, Boston, lecturer in English, 1962-64; Massachusetts State College at Lowell (now University of Lowell), instructor in English, 1964-66; Massachusetts State College at Bridgewater, instructor in English, 1966-68; Northeastern University, Boston, assistant professor, 1968-74, associate professor, 1974-76, professor of English, 1976-79; novelist, 1979—. Lecturer, Suffolk University, 1965-66. Co-chairman, Parker-Farman Co. (advertising agency), 1960-62. Film consultant to Arthur D. Little, 1962-64. *Military service:* U.S. Army, 1954-56.

AWARDS, HONORS: Edgar Allan Poe Award, Mystery Writers of America, 1976, for *Promised Land.*

WRITINGS:

(With others) *The Personal Response to Literature,* Houghton, 1970.
(With Peter L. Sandberg) *Order and Diversity: The Craft of Prose,* Wiley, 1973.
(With John R. Marsh) *Sports Illustrated Weight Training,* Lippincott, 1974.
(With wife, Joan Parker) *Three Weeks in Spring* (nonfiction), Houghton, 1978.
Wilderness (novel), Delacorte, 1979.
Love and Glory (novel), Delacorte, 1983.
The Private Eye in Hammett and Chandler, Lord John, 1984.
Parker on Writing, Lord John, 1985.

''SPENSER'' DETECTIVE SERIES

The Godwulf Manuscript, Houghton, 1974.
God Save the Child, Houghton, 1974.
Mortal Stakes, Houghton, 1975.
Promised Land, Houghton, 1976.
The Judas Goat, Houghton, 1978.
Looking for Rachel Wallace, Delacorte, 1980.
Early Autumn, Delacorte, 1981.
A Savage Place, Delacorte, 1981.
Surrogate: A Spenser Short Story, Lord John, 1982.
Ceremony, Delacorte, 1982.
The Widening Gyre, Delacorte, 1983.
Valediction, Delacorte, 1984.

A Catskill Eagle, Delacorte, 1985.
Taming a Sea-Horse, Delacorte, 1986.
Pale Kings and Princes, Delacorte, 1987.
Crimson Joy, Delacorte, 1988.
Playmates, Putnam, 1989.

OTHER

Also author with wife, Joan Parker, of several television scripts for series "Spenser: For Hire." Contributor to *Lock Haven Review* and *Revue des langues vivantes*. Contributor of restaurant reviews to *Boston Magazine*, 1976.

SIDELIGHTS: Robert B. Parker's "Spenser" series represents "the best American hardboiled detective fiction since Ross Macdonald and Raymond Chandler," according to *Armchair Detective* writer Anne Ponder. Parker's career as a novelist began only after he spent years producing ad copy and technical writing for various companies. At his wife's urging, he completed his Ph.D. and entered the teaching profession to gain more time for his own writing projects. "Being a professor and working are not the same thing," Parker explained to Wayne Warga in the *Los Angeles Times*. In a Toronto *Globe and Mail* interview with Ian Brown, Parker expressed his feelings about the university environment even more frankly: "The academic community is composed largely of nitwits. If I may generalize. People who don't know very much about what matters very much, who view life through literature rather than the other way around. . . . In my 14 or 16 years in the profession, I've met more people that I did not admire than at any other point in my life. Including two years in the infantry, where I was the only guy who could read."

It took two and a half years of writing in his spare time for Parker to complete his first fiction manuscript, but only three weeks for it to be accepted for publication. Parker's doctoral thesis had treated the classic detective fiction of Raymond Chandler and Dashiell Hammett, and his first novel, *The Godwulf Manuscript*, presented a detective in the tradition of Philip Marlowe and Sam Spade. A Boston policeman turned private eye after being fired for insubordination, Spenser is "a man's man, all six feet plus of him, a former professional fighter, a man who can take on any opposition," relates Newgate Callendar in the *New York Times Book Review*. The character's traditional toughness is balanced by his "honesty and his sensitivity," continues Callendar. "Spenser may be something of a smart aleck but only when he is faced with pomposity and pretension. Then he reacts, sometimes violently. He is educated and well read, though he never parades his knowledge. His girlfriend is the perfect woman, as smart as he is, and so he never has to chase around. Pushed as he is by his social conscience, he is sometimes dogged enough to seem quixotic."

Parker followed *The Godwulf Manuscript* with *God Save the Child, Mortal Stakes, Promised Land* and other Spenser novels. Their growing success soon enabled him to quit his teaching post and devote himself to writing full-time. The author now estimates that it takes him three to five months to write a Spenser adventure. Many critics point to Parker's plotting as his weakness, but he is widely praised for his evocative descriptions, for his sharp, witty dialogue, and for introducing a more human, emotional tone to the hard-boiled detective genre. H. R. F. Keating comments in the London *Times* that in the Spenser books "there is a concern with human beings that rises at times to compassion and perhaps falls at other times to that commonish complaint among American novelists 'psychology showing through.' But the seriousness that this indicates is always well-compensated for by Parker's dialogue.

Spenser is a wisecracking guy in the firm tradition of the Chandler shamus, and above and beyond this all the conversations in the books are splendidly swift and sharp." In her review of *Pale Kings and Princes*, *Washington Post Book World* writer Jean M. White concurs that "Parker . . . writes some of the snappiest and sauciest dialogue in the business," and calls the book "lean and taut and crisply told with moments of genuine humor and genuine poignancy."

One of Parker's most notable departures from the detective novelists before him is Spenser's monogamous commitment to his psychologist lover, Susan Silverman. "By all the unwritten rules of private-eye fiction, that [relationship] should have handicapped Spenser's future literary prospects disastrously," declares Derrick Murdoch in the Toronto *Globe and Mail*. "Instead it has allowed him to develop into the most fully rounded characterization of an intelligent human being in the literature—a mixture of idealism, passion, strength, frailty and unselfish tenacity." In his book *Sons of Sam Spade, The Private-Eye Novel in the 70s: Robert B. Parker, Roger L. Simon, Andrew Bergman*, David Geherin also states his belief that the Spenser character has "grown significantly, especially in the area of self-knowledge, thanks in part to the frequent confrontations between his ever-deepening relationship with Susan. Even when she is absent . . . her presence is felt. . . . Parker's handling of Spenser's relationship with Susan effectively disproves Chandler's assertion that the love story and the detective story cannot exist in the same book. Not only do they coexist in Parker's novels, the love story adds an element of tension by serving as a poignant reminder of the vast distance that separates the mean streets from the quiet ones." A *Time* reviewer emphasizes, however, that for all the intellectual and romantic dialogue, Parker's novels never lack "slambang action."

"Robert B. Parker's influence on the [detective] genre is unquestioned," summarizes Margaret Cannon in the Toronto *Globe and Mail*. "Spenser liberated the PI from California, gave him a whole new line of inquiry, and taught him to love." Furthermore, "With each novel Parker has exhibited growing independence from his predecessors, confidently developing his own themes, characters, and stylistic idiom," concludes Geherin. "However, despite his innovative efforts, he has remained faithful to the conventions of the genre, so effectively laid down by his predecessors. He has thus earned for himself the right to be designated *the* legitimate heir to the Hammett-Chandler-Macdonald tradition, which, thanks to the efforts of writers like Parker, shows no signs of diminishing."

MEDIA ADAPTATIONS: Film rights have been sold to many of the Spenser novels.

CA INTERVIEW

CA interviewed Robert B. Parker by telephone on May 8, 1987, at his home in Cambridge, Massachusetts.

CA: You've been asked a million times about Spenser's similarity to you, so I won't go into that again. I do wonder, though, if your own moods or problems during the writing of a book may affect Spencer's behavior.

PARKER: Writers use what they have, and what they have is who they are at the time they are working, so sure, that could happen. It probably does.

CA: Does he ever take off on his own, so to speak, and do something that surprises you?

PARKER: Absolutely not. I think that's voodoo. I make him up. He is the sole creation of my imagination, and he never does anything I don't want him to or haven't thought out. *Au contraire,* I have to work very hard to get him to do what he does.

CA: Many writers say their characters develop minds of their own and make their decisions. Your Spenser obviously isn't one of those characters.

PARKER: That's writer's talk to try to describe a process that they don't really understand either. Writers don't know how they do what they're doing, so they say a lot of dumb stuff in public. That business about the characters coming alive has always struck me as one of the dumbest things writers say in public. I don't know how that would work. It also tends to denigrate the effort and the imagination used to create the characters and make them seem as if they *were* alive. I don't subscribe to that whole theory.

CA: You were writing long before the Spenser books. Was it something you always wanted to do?

PARKER: I was writing in some sense. I had been writing advertising copy and speeches and things like that. I hadn't been writing fiction long before the Spenser books; *The Godwulf Manuscript* was my first piece of fiction. It was something I'd always wanted to do and perhaps would have done sooner if I hadn't married young and had children—before the movement; where was liberation when I really needed it? I had to support everybody and I didn't have time to write. But I had always wanted to, and I manipulated myself (and Joan helped me considerably in that) into a position of being a college professor so that I would have time to write, which I then did. As soon as I got the chance, I wrote the first book. Whether I'd have been able to write it ten years earlier under different circumstances, I have no idea.

CA: You've said you went for the Ph.D. as a part of that plan to secure the teaching career. Did the graduate study affect the writing in less precise and planned ways?

PARKER: It didn't teach me anything about how to write, in terms of the management of language—which word goes where and all of the nonsense they try to teach in composition courses about varying sentence structure and length. But I think the extended formal education—I have a Ph.D. in English and American literature and have read everything since Caxton—allows me to have a kind of allusiveness which I might otherwise not have. It's tempting to say the Ph.D. didn't have an effect, but it's not so. I think whatever resonance I may be able to achieve is in part simply from the amount of reading and learning that I acquired along the way. So it probably helps. I don't think that I would be writing differently if I didn't have it, in terms of style, but I think there's a dimension to my work that I wouldn't have if I'd had much less education.

CA: Were the early technical writing and the work in advertising valuable in any way to the later fiction writing?

PARKER: Not concretely in any way that I can tell. But I think if one is going to be a writer, one ought to be writing; and the more writing one does, I assume, the better one learns how to do it. So I can't imagine that it wasn't useful in the sense that I just kept practicing, practicing. It certainly helped me to learn early some of the things I *didn't* want to do—like writing advertising copy.

CA: Your place descriptions are very exact, very evocative. Can you do them sitting at your desk, or do you sometimes make notes at the actual site?

PARKER: I sit at my desk. I never even make notes, and I never use a tape recorder or any of that stuff. I think it was Marshall Brickman who was asked that once, and he quoted Woody Allen: he said, "Woody always says you never forget the good stuff." I think probably you never do. What I do is write about places I can write about without having to leave my desk, so I don't have to do research. If I'm going to set an extended sequence in New York City or Chicago or Los Angeles, cities that I know quite well, I may go there and walk around, or I may use a street map to remind me which way Michigan Avenue runs or something like that. But that's the extent of it. When I used to teach fiction writing, the kids would always be carrying notebooks and tape recorders to get "human speech" and study it. I would urge them not to do that, just as the great Yale art history professor Vincent Scully always starts his classes by forbidding anyone to take notes. I subscribe to that fully. That way you can listen and pay attention rather than sit there scribbling it all down. I think it's very good advice for writers as well.

CA: Lines from old popular songs occur frequently in your books, even as titles. Is that done for more than just setting the time and mood? Does music mean something special to you?

PARKER: I don't know. The allusions are never deliberated. They come from the context of what I'm talking about. I have that kind of mind. It's full of scraps of popular songs, names of forgotten baseball players, tag lines of poems. They come unbidden, by and large, except for the titles; the titles have something to do with the book, and also have something to do with getting people to pick the book up and read it—or at least buy it.

CA: How do you feel about the television series based on your character, "Spenser: For Hire"?

PARKER: It's in its second year, and we're looking for a third. My response to that is, the check comes every week.

CA: Do you have any sort of control in the series?

PARKER: Control, no. I have a lot of input. I'm a consultant on the project and they are solicitous of my views, but I do not have any control and can't imagine a circumstance in which I would. The network has control. The only way you can get even a semblance of control is if you're Bill Cosby. His show is so successful that he can tell the networks to stuff it if they don't like it. But unless you have one powerful central figure who is willing to fight the studio and the network every day, all day, and who has enough clout to pull it off, then you don't have any control. I'm not a television writer, I'm a novelist. I do not wish to spend my time screwing around with Standards and Practices about whether we can say "ragging" on the air or not, which is something we've been arguing about. I've written one script, and if we get picked up this year I'll write the opening script for the third season. I don't particularly enjoy it, but I think it is useful. And if we can get this thing into syndication, then we can all get rich, which is what you do television for.

CA: Do you have any idea how much, if at all, your readers and the television viewers overlap? Does one medium seem to bring people to the other?

PARKER: I don't really have much idea. The book sales increase with each new book so far, and have continued to do so since "Spenser: For Hire" went on the air. I don't know that it's been a quantum leap. Maybe. This last earnings statement was the biggest I've ever gotten, but the previous one was the second-biggest I'd ever gotten. It's hard to say. I don't get a lot of mail from people who came to the books from the series. I think people who read the books will look at the series, but they will see that it's somewhat dissimilar. Some like it very much and tell me that Robert Urich's a wonderful Spenser. Others say, "How dare you perpetrate this fraud upon us?" My guess, if I had to guess, is that most people who are avid television watchers are not avid readers, and vice versa.

CA: What about the movies that have been reported as in the works?

PARKER: There have been scripts written and projects underway, but neither *Early Autumn* nor *Wilderness* has yet actually exposed any film.

CA: The Spenser books are translated into many languages. Are there countries in which Spenser is outstandingly popular?

PARKER: Japan. He does great in Japan, better in Japan than any place but here. And he does almost as well there as he does here, if you take the population ratios into consideration. I'm sufficiently popular there through Spenser that the Massachusetts Tourist Bureau wants me to go to Japan to promote tourism in Massachusetts. They're doing a feature film in Japanese of *Valediction*, and I do commercial endorsements in Japan.

CA: There's a good bit of academic critical writing on your work. Do you keep up with it?

PARKER: No. I don't read anything about myself, not excluding this interview. It's not personal, I just don't think it does me any good to read about myself or about my books. I think it tends to exteriorize me. All of that is not for writers, it's for readers. I don't mean to denigrate the work, either. There may be some fine criticism being written on me, pro or con, which is useful in some other fashion. But criticism and reviews are not useful to writers, they're useful to other people. I have not read any of it in years.

CA: In Three Weeks in Spring, *you and Joan Parker wrote a very moving personal account of her discovery of breast cancer and subsequent surgery. Has that book brought a tremendous response from readers?*

PARKER: It's been out of print for a while; it came out in 1978. And it is not an upbeat topic, even though it is given a somewhat upbeat treatment. I don't think it would have had a long life. But I rarely go someplace that someone doesn't say they've read and responded to the book in some fashion; either they had a relative or knew someone who had gone through a

similar experience and found the book helpful. But "tremendous response" would be an overstatement.

CA: You've said you felt the problem with Love and Glory *was the weakness of Jennifer Grayle. In the Spenser books you have some very strong female characters. Have they attracted a feminist readership?*

PARKER: A little, I think. It's hard to say about these things; all you can do is judge by the fan mail or what people say to you at signings. So you're dealing with a very select group here. Most people don't write letters, and most people don't come to signings. But I have had some positive feedback from feminists, and after *Looking for Rachel Wallace*, from lesbian groups who endorsed my treatment of Rachel Wallace and said I must have known a lesbian woman like that. Which I didn't. Most people don't believe in imagination. They insist that you must have experienced something to write about it.

CA: The only trouble I have reading your books is that when I get to the food parts, I usually want to go straight to the kitchen and try them out. In the Los Angeles Times, *Jon Markham reported that a Spenser cookbook was in the works. Is that progressing?*

PARKER: Yes, it is. I don't have a hell of a lot to do with that; my job will be to cash the check when it's done. A woman here in Cambridge, Kate Mattes, who runs Kate's Mystery Books, is doing the actual preparation: collecting the recipes from the books, quantifying them, testing them out. I think probably next year, spring of 1988, it should be out. I will write an introduction and a few words here and there, but essentially it's Kate's work.

CA: What's the process of doing a book like for you, start to finish?

PARKER: I get up in the morning and have a couple of double martinis to get my heart going . . . No. I'm now in the process of finishing the fourth book on a four-book contract, so I don't sit around waiting for inspiration. When I finish one book, I have some TV and movie stuff that I fiddle around with. And after a couple of months, I sit down and think up the next book. It takes a few months, probably, or a few weeks; or sometimes, if I'm lucky, about five days. I make a two-or three-page treatment of the basic story idea, develop that into a chapter outline, and then I write the book. I write five pages a day each weekday. I don't revise in any significant degree. When it's done, I send it in and they print it and publish it. I get some help from my wife on ideas. She's not a writer, but she's a thinker, so we will in effect have a little story conference periodically as I go along. If I'm running dry or I've hit a dead end or I'm not sure what to do, she provides me with some suggestions. Other than that, I'm on my own.

CA: Have you ever started a Spenser book that just never worked out and finally had to be abandoned?

PARKER: No. They all work out. The story's always in there.

CA: Do you ever feel constrained by Spenser and the detective story format?

PARKER: No. It is, to the extent that I'm capable of it, my art. It's certainly what I'll be remembered for a hundred years from now—which I don't imagine will do me a whole lot of good. When I have something to say that doesn't fit into a Spenser book, then I write another book, like *Love and Glory* or *Wilderness*. And I will again. The publisher is never enthusiastic about it, but they'll do it anyway.

CA: Teaching obviously wasn't a labor of love for you. Do you ever go back long enough to do a single course or a workshop?

PARKER: It was not a labor of love. For several years I've done a workshop in London with a friend of mine, which provides a free trip to London for me and Joan. My contribution to that is one two-hour appearance during the week of teaching, and one appearance on a panel at the end of the workshop. That workshop is no longer in existence, so I won't be doing that. I won't be doing any others. No, I don't like to teach, and I'm not terribly happy with the academic world.

CA: How do you take to the promotion tours for the books when you have to do them?

PARKER: I do them well, if I may say so immodestly. I think they are necessary and important, and I think they have contributed mightily to my present position, whatever the hell that is. But I have hung it up on that this year; I'm not going to do a promotion tour. I've done thirteen of them, and they run typically eleven cities in two weeks. I think they are effective and I should probably be doing them all my life, but I can't stand them. My refusal to do them is not motivated by their worth, it's motivated by the fact that I can't stand to do them. I will do "Today" on television this June and do some individual appearances, such as a book-and-author lunch in Cleveland. As I said to my publisher, I'll do anything that they want me to do as long as I can come home at night instead of getting on a plane and going to another city. It gets gruelling. It's a way that books are sold, and if you are any good at it, it's a very effective way. And it's part of the writer's job. I think if you write it, then you ought to help sell it. If you don't help sell it, then you can't bitch at your publisher for not selling it. But the time has come for me to pass on that.

And everyone seems to agree that I have sufficient eminence that I don't need to do it too much any more. There are places where I may be a little overexposed, in fact; it's time to *not* do too many things in Boston or Chicago, or people might say, "Christ, it must be spring; here he comes again."

CA: Would you like to do more non-Spenser books, maybe something completely different from anything you've ever done?

PARKER: I don't think that way. It's perfectly conceivable that I might, if I have occasion to. But I don't have that kind of a master plan. I don't think ahead or think that I'd like to do something different. Joan and I are playing around with television and motion picture stuff, partly because she finds it very interesting and has all the skills that one needs in it to do the things that I can't stand to do, like go to story meetings, talk to producers. Bill Goldman said it as well as anyone could: you have to understand that the cardinal rule in Hollywood is that nobody knows anything. Never has a truer word been spoken. I can't stand that, and Joan can. We have two sons, one is an actor and one is a dancer, who would be kind of interesting to include in this. So we play around a little bit with the family business in the film and entertainment world and see where that leads us. I'll probably do something entirely unlike what I'm doing one of these days. But I don't have a master plan.

CA: You seem to regard writing as simply your job, without glamorizing it in any way. It's just what you do every day.

PARKER: Right. And it gives me autonomy. I can stay here and do what I want to. When I finish something, I send it in and they publish it; they don't tell me to rewrite it. It is freedom. It's a craft and I'm good at it and it pleases me to do it.

BIOGRAPHICAL/CRITICAL SOURCES:

BOOKS

Carr, John C., *Craft of Crime*, Houghton, 1983.
Contemporary Literary Criticism, Volume 27, Gale, 1984.
Geherin, David, *Sons of Sam Spade, The Private-Eye Novel in the 70s: Robert B. Parker, Roger L. Simon, Andrew Bergman*, Ungar, 1980.
Parker, Robert B., *Three Weeks in Spring*, Houghton, 1978.

PERIODICALS

Armchair Detective, fall, 1984.
Chicago Tribune, September 20, 1985.
Chicago Tribune Book World, June 28, 1987.
Clues: A Journal of Detection, fall/winter, 1980, spring/summer, 1984.
Critique, fall, 1984.
Globe and Mail (Toronto), May 12, 1984, June 6, 1984, June 15, 1985, June 21, 1986.
Los Angeles Times, January 26, 1981, March 20, 1981, June 21, 1982, January 17, 1984, February 16, 1986.
Los Angeles Times Book Review, July 6, 1986, May 10, 1987.
New Republic, March 19, 1977, November 4, 1978.
Newsweek, June 7, 1982, June 17, 1985, July 7, 1986.
New Yorker, July 13, 1987.
New York Times, January 21, 1981, September 20, 1985, July 2, 1987.
New York Times Book Review, January 13, 1974, December 15, 1974, November 11, 1979, August 2, 1981, May 1, 1983, May 20, 1984, June 30, 1985, June 22, 1986, May 31, 1987.
People, May 7, 1984.
Southwest Review, autumn, 1974.
Time, July 1, 1985, July 7, 1986, July 27, 1987.
Times (London), November 4, 1978, May 4, 1987.
USA Today, March 20, 1987.
Washington Post, May 17, 1983, March 7, 1984.
Washington Post Book World, April 15, 1984, June 15, 1986, June 21, 1987.

—Sketch by Joan Goldsworthy

—Interview by Jean W. Ross

*   *   *

PARKS, Gordon (Alexander Buchanan) 1912-

PERSONAL: Born November 30, 1912, in Fort Scott, Kan.; son of Andrew Jackson and Sarah (Ross) Parks; married Sally Alvis, 1933 (divorced, 1961); married Elizabeth Campbell, December, 1962 (divorced, 1973); married Genevieve Young (a book editor), August 26, 1973; children: (first marriage) Gordon, Jr. (deceased), Toni (Mrs. Jean-Luc Brouillaud), David; (second marriage) Leslie. *Education:* Attended high school in St. Paul, Minn. *Politics:* Democrat. *Religion:* Methodist.

ADDRESSES: Home—860 United Nations Plaza, New York, N.Y. 10017. *Agent*—(Film) Ben Benjamin, Creative Management Associates, 9255 Sunset Blvd., Los Angeles, Calif. 90069.

CAREER: Photographer, writer, film director, and composer. Worked at various jobs prior to 1937; free-lance fashion photographer in Minneapolis, 1937-42; photographer with Farm Security Administration, 1942-43, with Office of War Information, 1944, and with Standard Oil Co. of New Jersey, 1945-48; *Life,* New York City, photo-journalist, 1948-72; *Essence* (magazine), New York City, editorial director, 1970-73. President of Winger Corp. Film director, 1968—, directing motion pictures for Warner Brothers-Seven Arts, Metro-Goldwyn-Mayer (M.G.M.), and Paramount Pictures, including "The Learning Tree," Warner Brothers, 1968, "Shaft," M.G.M., 1972, "Shaft's Big Score," M.G.M., 1972, "The Super Cops," M.G.M., 1974, and "Leadbelly," Paramount, 1975, as well as several documentaries. Composer of concertos and sonatas performed by symphony orchestras in the United States and Europe.

MEMBER: Authors Guild (member of council, 1973-74), Authors League of America, Black Academy of Arts and Letters (fellow), Directors Guild of America (member of national council, 1973-76), Newspaper Guild, American Society of Magazine Photographers, Association of Composers and Directors, American Society of Composers, Authors, and Publishers, American Federation of Television and Radio Artists, National Association for the Advancement of Colored People, Directors Guild of New York (member of council), Urban League, Players Club (New York), Kappa Alpha Mu.

AWARDS, HONORS: Rosenwald Foundation fellow, 1942; once chosen Photographer of the Year, Association of Magazine Photographers; Frederic W. Brehm award, 1962; Mass Media Award, National Conference of Christians and Jews, for outstanding contributions to better human relations, 1964; Carr Van Adna Journalism Award, University of Miami, 1964, Ohio University, 1970; named photographer-writer who had done the most to promote understanding among nations of the world in an international vote conducted by the makers of Nikon photographic equipment, 1967; A.F.D., Maryland Institute of Fine Arts, 1968; Litt.D., University of Connecticut, 1969, and Kansas State University, 1970; Spingarn Medal from National Association for the Advancement of Colored People, 1972; H.H.D., St. Olaf College, 1973, Rutgers University, 1980, and Pratt Institute, 1981; Christopher Award, 1980, for *Flavio;* President's Fellow award, Rhode Island School of Design, 1984; named Kansan of the Year, Native Sons and Daughters of Kansas, 1986; additional awards include honorary degrees from Fairfield University, 1969, Boston University, 1969, Macalaster College, 1974, Colby College, 1974, Lincoln University, 1975, and awards from Syracuse University School of Journalism, 1963, University of Miami, 1964, Philadelphia Museum of Art, 1964, and Art Directors Club, 1964, 1968.

WRITINGS:

Flash Photography, [New York], 1947.
Camera Portraits: The Techniques and Principles of Documentary Portraiture, F. Watts, 1948.
The Learning Tree (novel; also see below), Harper, 1963.
A Choice of Weapons (autobiography), Harper, 1966, reprinted, Minnesota Historical Society, 1986.
A Poet and His Camera, self-illustrated with photographs, Viking, 1968.
(And composer of musical score) "The Learning Tree" (screenplay; based on novel of same title), produced by Warner Brothers-Seven Arts, 1968.
Gordon Parks: Whispers of Intimate Things (poems), self-illustrated with photographs, Viking, 1971.

Born Black (essays), self-illustrated with photographs, Lippincott, 1971.
In Love (poems), self-illustrated with photographs, Lippincott, 1971.
Moments without Proper Names (poems), self-illustrated with photographs, Viking, 1975.
Flavio, Norton, 1978.
To Smile in Autumn: A Memoir, Norton, 1979.
Shannon (novel), Little, Brown, 1981.

Also author of several television documentaries produced by National Educational Television, including "Flavio" and "Mean Streets." Contributor to *Show, Vogue, Venture,* and other periodicals.

SIDELIGHTS: Gordon Parks's "life constitutes an American success story of almost mythic proportions," Andy Grundberg once commented in the *New York Times.* A high school dropout who had to fend for himself at the age of sixteen, Parks overcame the difficulties of being black, uneducated, and poor to become a *Life* magazine photographer; a writer of fiction, nonfiction, and poetry; a composer; and a film director and producer. The wide scope of Parks's expertise is all the more impressive when viewed in its historical context, for many of the fields he succeeded in formerly had been closed to blacks. Parks was the first black to work at *Life* magazine, *Vogue,* the Office of War Information, and the Federal Security Administration. He was also the first black to write, direct, produce, and score a film, "The Learning Tree," based on his 1963 novel. Parks maintains that his drive to succeed in such a variety of professions was motivated by fear. "I was so frightened I might fail that I figured if one thing didn't work out I could fall back on another," Parks stated in the *Detroit News.*

Parks's first professional endeavor was photography, a craft he practiced as a free-lance fashion photographer in Minneapolis and later as a Rosenwald Foundation fellow in 1942. In 1948 he was hired as a *Life* magazine photographer, and throughout his over twenty-year affiliation with that publication photographed world events, celebrities, musicians, artists, and politicians. In addition to his work for *Life,* Parks has exhibited his photography and illustrated his books with photos. In a *New York Times* review of one of Parks's photography exhibitions, Hilton Kramer notes that while Parks is a versatile photographer, "it is in the pictures where his 'black childhood of confusion and poverty' still makes itself felt that he moves us most deeply." Grundberg similarly notes that Parks's "most memorable pictures, and the most vividly felt sections of the exhibition, deal specifically with the conditions and social fabric of black Americans."

Parks found, however, that despite his love of and expertise in photography, he needed to express in words the intense feelings about his childhood. This need resulted in his first novel, *The Learning Tree,* which in some ways parallels Parks's youth. The novel concerns the Wingers, a black family living in a small town in Kansas during the 1920s, and focuses in particular on Newt, the Wingers' adolescent son. "On one level, it is the story of a particular Negro family who manages to maintain its dignity and self-respect as citizens and decent human beings in a border Southern town," writes *Dictionary of Literary Biography* contributor Jane Ball. "On another, it is a symbolic tale of the black man's struggle against social, economic, and natural forces, sometimes winning, sometimes losing." A *Time* reviewer comments: "[Parks's] unabashed nostalgia for what was good there, blended with sharp recollections of staggering violence and fear, makes an immensely readable, sometimes unsettling book.''

Parks explores his life further in two autobiographical volumes, *A Choice of Weapons* and *To Smile in Autumn*. The first volume begins when Parks is sixteen and describes how, after his mother's death and an unsuccessful stint living with relatives in Minneapolis, Parks found himself out on the street. For a decade, Parks struggled to feed and clothe himself, all the while cultivating his ambition to be a photographer. The book's theme, according to *Washington Post* contributor Christopher Schemering, is that "one's choice of weapons must be dignity and hard work over the self-destructive, if perhaps understandable, emotions of hate and violence.'' Alluding to the unfortunate circumstances of his youth, Parks expressed a similar view in the *Detroit News*. "I have a right to be bitter, but I would not let bitterness destroy me. As I tell young black people, you can fight back, but do it in a way to help yourself and not destroy yourself.''

Saturday Review contributor Edwin M. Yoder, Jr., writes: "[*A Choice of Weapons*] is an excellent introduction to what it must have been like to be black and ambitious—and poor—in the America of a generation ago, when nearly every door was sealed to Negroes as never before or since in American history.'' Observing that "what [Parks] has refused to accept is the popular definition of what being black is and the limitations that the definition automatically imposes,'' Saunders Redding concludes in the *New York Times Book Review:* "'A Choice of Weapons' is . . . a perceptive narrative of one man's struggle to realize the values (defined as democratic and especially American) he has been taught to respect.''

To Smile in Autumn, Parks's second autobiographical volume, covers the years from 1943 to 1979. Here Parks celebrates "the triumph of achievement, the abundance and glamour of a productive life,'' writes *New York Times Book Review* contributor Mel Watkins. Parks also acknowledges, however, that his success was not without a price. Ralph Tyler comments in the *Chicago Tribune Book World:* "Although this third memoir doesn't have the drama inherent in a fight for survival, it has a drama of its own: the conflict confronting a black American who succeeds in the white world.'' As Parks writes in *To Smile in Autumn:* "In escaping the mire, I had lost friends along the way. . . . In one world I was a social oddity. In the other world I was almost a stranger.''

Schemering notes that the book contains material "recast'' from Parks's earlier work, *Born Black*, and is in this respect somewhat disappointing. He writes: "It's unfortunate to see a major talent and cultural force coast on former successes. Yet, even at half-mast, Parks manages a sporadic eloquence, as in the last few pages when he pays tribute to his son Gordon Parks Jr., who died in a plane crash.'' Watkins offers this view: "Gordon Parks emerges here as a Renaissance man who has resolutely pursued success in several fields. His memoir is sustained and enlivened by his urbanity and generosity.''

BIOGRAPHICAL/CRITICAL SOURCES:

BOOKS

Authors in the News, Volume 2, Gale, 1976.
Contemporary Literary Criticism, Gale, Volume 1, 1973, Volume 16, 1981.
Dictionary of Literary Biography, Volume 33: *Afro-American Fiction Writers after 1955*, Gale, 1984.
Harnan, Terry, *Gordon Parks: Black Photographer and Film Maker*, Garrard, 1972.

Monaco, James, *American Film Now: The People, the Power, the Money, the Movies*, New American Library, 1979.
Parks, Gordon, *A Choice of Weapons*, Harper, 1966, reprinted, Minnesota Historical Society, 1986.
Parks, Gordon, *To Smile in Autumn: A Memoir*, Norton, 1979.
Rolansky, John D., editor, *Creativity*, North-Holland Publishing, 1970.
Turk, Midge, *Gordon Parks*, Crowell, 1971.

PERIODICALS

Best Sellers, April 1, 1971.
Black World, August, 1973.
Chicago Tribune Book World, December 30, 1979.
Commonweal, September 5, 1969.
Cue, August 9, 1969.
Detroit News, February 1, 1976.
Films in Review, October, 1972.
Horn Book, April, 1971, August, 1971.
Newsweek, April 29, 1968, August 11, 1969, April 19, 1976.
New York, June 14, 1976.
New Yorker, November 2, 1963, February 13, 1966.
New York Times, October 4, 1975, December 3, 1975, March 1, 1986.
New York Times Book Review, September 15, 1963, February 13, 1966, December 23, 1979.
Saturday Review, February 12, 1966, August 9, 1969.
Show Business, August 2, 1969.
Time, September 6, 1963, September 29, 1969, May 24, 1976.
Variety, November 6, 1968, June 25, 1969.
Vogue, October 1, 1968.
Washington Post, October 20, 1978, January 24, 1980.†

—*Sketch by Melissa Gaiownik*

*   *   *

PARTRIDGE, Jenny (Lilian)   1947-

PERSONAL: Born July 25, 1947, in Romford, England; daughter of Frank Munden and Dorothy (Miles) Partridge; married Nigel Casseldine (a painter and illustrator), April 16, 1971; children: Alice, Nicholas. *Education:* Attended South East Essex Technical College, 1963-68. *Religion:* Church of England.

ADDRESSES: Home and office—Mount Cottage, St. Mary's, Chalford, Gloucestershire, England.

CAREER: Presentation Colour Ltd. (photographic processors), London, England, retoucher, 1967-72; Romany Studio Workshop, Ebley, England, founder and artist, 1972—.

AWARDS, HONORS: Critici in Erba Award from Bologna Children's Book Fair, 1981, for *Mr. Squint*.

WRITINGS:

FOR CHILDREN; SELF ILLUSTRATED

Mr. Squint, World's Work, 1980.
Colonel Grunt, World's Work, 1980.
Peterkin Pollensnuff, World's Work, 1980.
Hopfellow, World's Work, 1980.
Grandma Snuffles, World's Work, 1981.
Dominic Sly, World's Work, 1981.
Harriet Plume, World's Work, 1981.
Lop-Ear, World's Work, 1981.
Oakapple Wood Stories, World's Work, 1982.
A Tale of Oakapple Wood, World's Work, 1983.
Four Friends in Oakapple Wood, World's Work, 1984.

Clara Quince, Heinemann, 1986.
Jack Flax, Heinemann, 1986.
Rafferty's Return, Heinemann, 1986.
Rifkins, Heinemann, 1986.

SIDELIGHTS: Jenny Partridge told *CA:* "Writing the Oakapple Wood books was a secondary response, as I had been illustrating for some time before it was put to me to try to write stories around my illustrations. At first I found the idea daunting but after several false starts I discovered that the very way I felt about my drawings seemed to add credence to the characters. They existed, and with them the legend of Oakapple Wood, all from the very first pen and ink sketches springing into animated life. I saw the stories take form before me, and in this way the characters almost told their own tales, using me as a willing medium. Oakapple Wood is a real place to me, and there is a warmth of feeling each time I visit it and its many inhabitants, who have become my very good friends since their creation some years ago."

AVOCATIONAL INTERESTS: Wildlife.

*   *   *

PELL, Arthur R.   1920-

PERSONAL: Born January 22, 1920, in New York, N.Y.; son of Harry and Rae (Meyers) Pell; married Erica Frost (a music teacher), May 19, 1946; children: Douglas, Hilary. *Education:* New York University, B.A., 1939, M.A., 1944; Cornell University, Professional Diploma, 1943; California Coast University, Ph.D., 1977.

ADDRESSES: Home and office—111 Dietz St., Hempstead, N.Y. 11550.

CAREER: Eagle Electric Manufacturing Co., Long Island, N.Y., personnel manager, 1946-50; North Atlantic Construction Co., New York City, personnel manager, 1950-53; Harper Associates (personnel consultants), New York City, vice-president, 1953-73; consultant in human resources management in Long Island, 1975—. Professor of management in evening classes, City College of the City University of New York, 1947-67. Adjunct professor of management, New York University, 1960-81, and St. John's University, 1971-77. *Military service:* U.S. Army, 1942-46; became warrant officer.

MEMBER: American Society for Personnel Administration, American Society for Training and Development, National Association of Personnel Consultants.

WRITINGS:

Placing Salesmen, Impact Publishers, 1963.
(With Walter Patterson) *Fire Officers Guide to Leadership,* privately printed, 1963.
Placing Executives, Impact Publishers, 1964.
Police Leadership, C. C Thomas, 1967.
(With Maxwell Harper) *How to Get the Job You Want after Forty,* Pilot Books, 1967.
Recruiting and Selecting Personnel, Simon & Schuster, 1969.
(With Harper) *Starting and Managing an Employment Agency,* U.S. Small Business Administration, 1971.
Advancing Your Career (home study program), Management Games Institute, 1971.
Recruiting, Training and Motivating Volunteer Workers, Pilot Books, 1973.
Interviewing and Selecting Sales, Advertising and Marketing Personnel, Personnel Publications, 1974, revised edition, 1981.

Be a Better Employment Interviewer, Personnel Publications, 1974, revised edition, 1976.
(With Wilma Rogalin) *Women's Guide to Management Positions,* Simon & Schuster, 1975.
(With Albert Furbay) *The College Student Guide to Career Planning,* Simon & Schuster, 1975.
Managing through People, Simon & Schuster, 1975.
Choosing a College Major: Business, McKay, 1978.
Enrich Your Life the Dale Carnegie Way, Dale Carnegie & Associates, 1979.
Interviewing and Selecting Engineering and Computer Personnel, Personnel Publications, 1980.
(Editor) Dale Carnegie, *How to Win Friends and Influence People,* revised edition (Pell was not associated with previous edition), Simon & Schuster, 1981.
(With George Sadek) *Resumes for Engineers,* Simon & Schuster, 1982.
Interviewing and Selecting Financial and Data Processing Personnel, Personnel Publications, 1982.
How to Sell Yourself on an Interview, Simon & Schuster, 1982.
(With Sadek) *Resumes for Computer Professionals,* Simon & Schuster, 1984.
The Part-Time Job Book, Simon & Schuster, 1984.
Making the Most of Medicare, Prentice-Hall, 1987.
How to Be a Successful Supervisor, Dun & Bradstreet, 1988.

Also author of "Career Aid Pamphlets" series for Personnel Publications. Author of syndicated monthly feature "The Human Side," published in eighty periodicals. Contributor of more than one hundred articles to trade and professional magazines, including syndicated newspaper series, "When Your Husband Loses His Job," 1971.

SIDELIGHTS: Arthur R. Pell told *CA:* "The mission of my writing is to utilize my God-given talents to help others identify, develop and make the most of their capabilities in their work and in their lives."

*   *   *

PERRY, George   1935-

PERSONAL: Born January 7, 1935, in London, England; son of George Cox (a civil servant) and Irene (Sadler) Perry; married Susanne Puddefoot, March 25, 1959 (divorced, 1976); married Frances Nicola Murray-Scott (a magazine executive), July 1, 1976; children: Matthew Richard Scott. *Education:* Trinity College, Cambridge, B.A., 1957, M.A., 1961.

ADDRESSES: Home—4 Swan Pl., Barnes, London SW13 9LT, England. *Office*—*Sunday Times,* 1 Pennington St., London, England. *Agent*—Deborah Rogers Ltd., 49 Blenheim Crescent, London W11 2EF, England.

CAREER: Sphere, London, England, member of editorial staff, 1957-58; J. Walter Thompson Co., London, advertising copywriter, 1958-62; *Sunday Times,* London, projects editor, 1965-70, assistant editor, 1970-77, senior editor of *Sunday Times Magazine,* 1977—. Managing editor of *Crossbow,* 1966-70. External examiner, Harrow College of Higher Education, 1980-83, and London College of Printing, 1984—. Director of Cinema City, an exhibition and film festival, 1970. Organizer of exhibition at National Portrait Gallery, 1979. Member of advisory committee of Minnesota Symposium of Visual Communication, 1974-77.

MEMBER: British Film Institute, American Film Institute, Cambridge Society (external examiner).

WRITINGS:

The Films of Alfred Hitchcock, Dutton, 1965.
(With Terence Kelly and Graham Norton) *A Competitive Cinema*, Institute of Economic Affairs, 1966.
(With Alan Aldridge) *The Penguin Book of Comics*, Penguin, 1967, 3rd edition, 1975.
The Great British Picture Show, Hill & Wang, 1974, revised edition, Little, Brown, 1985.
The Moviemakers: Hitchcock, Doubleday, 1975.
Movies from the Mansion: A History of Pinewood Studios, Elm Tree, 1976.
Forever Ealing, Pavilion, 1981.
Diana: A Celebration, Windward Publishing, 1982.
Life of Python, Little, Brown, 1983.
(With Alfred Bestall) *Rupert: A Bear's Life*, Pavilion, 1985.
Bluebell, Pavilion, 1986.
The Complete Phantom of the Opera, Holt, 1988.

EDITOR

The Book of the Great Western, Times Books, 1970.
King Steam, Times Books, 1971.
Wheels of London, Times Books, 1972.
(With Nicholas Mason) *The Victorians: A World Built to Last*, Viking, 1974 (published in England as *Rule Britannia: The Victorian World*, Times Books, 1974).
The Great British, New York Graphic Society, 1979.
Give My Regards to Broad Street, Pavilion, 1984.

CONTRIBUTOR

One Thousand Makers of the Twentieth Century, David & Charles, 1971.
Eureka, Thames & Hudson, 1973.
John Lennon: The Life and Legend, Times Newspapers, 1980.
Twentieth-Century Genius, Exeter, 1981 (published in England as *Twentieth-Century Makers*).
(Of film commentary) Derek Jewell, *Frank Sinatra: A Celebration*, Pavilion, 1985.

OTHER

Writer for British Broadcasting Corp. (BBC) radio and television programs; film critic for *Illustrated London News*, 1982—. Contributor to periodicals, including *Radio Times* and *Los Angeles Times*.

WORK IN PROGRESS: A biography.

SIDELIGHTS: George Perry wrote to *CA:* "Since 1981 most of my books have been published by Pavilion, which was founded in that year by my friend Colin Webb with the aim of producing books devoted to the pleasures of life, be they esthetic, sporting, or merely trivial. Moreover, Webb believes that the visual appearance of a book is as important as its words, and I support that view totally.

"In the 1960s the book I was most pleased to produce was *The Penguin Book of Comics*, which owed its handsome appearance to the design of Alan Aldridge, and helped to kindle an interest in Britain in comic strips, never before taken seriously there. I have recently returned to that subject with a book on Rupert, a famous bear, and his longtime illustrator, Alfred Bestall. It is a hope that I can do more books about specific characters and artists.

"I have always had a tremendous passion for the cinema and have been fortunate in being able to travel the world to interview filmmakers. That experience will, I suspect, be the foundation for further books in the time I have left."

AVOCATIONAL INTERESTS: Travel, photography, video, film, word processing.

BIOGRAPHICAL/CRITICAL SOURCES:

PERIODICALS

Los Angeles Times Book Review, October 27, 1985.
Times Literary Supplement, December 20, 1985.

*   *   *

PERTSCHUK, Michael 1933-

PERSONAL: Born January 12, 1933, in London, England; American citizen born abroad; son of David and Sarah (Baumander) Pertschuk; married Carleen Joyce Dooley, September, 1954 (divorced December, 1976); married Anna Phillips Sofaer (an artist), April, 1977; children: (first marriage) Mark, Amy. *Education:* Yale University, B.A., 1954, J.D., 1959. *Politics:* "Progressive Democrat." *Religion:* Jewish.

ADDRESSES: *Home*—3411 Rodman St. N.W., Washington, D.C. 20008. *Office*—Advocacy Institute, 1730 M St., N.W., Suite 600, Washington, D.C. 20036.

CAREER: Law clerk to U.S. District Court Judge Gus O. Solomon, Portland, Ore., 1959; Hart, Rockwood, Davies, Biggs & Strayer (law firm), Portland, associate, 1960-62; legislative assistant to Senator Maurine B. Neuberger of Oregon, 1962-64; U.S. Senate Commerce Committee, Washington, D.C., trade relations counsel, 1964-68, chief counsel and staff director, 1968-77; Federal Trade Commission, Washington, D.C., chairman, 1977-81; Advocacy Institute, Washington, D.C., co-director, 1984—. Adjunct professor of law, New York University Law School, 1986—; adjunct professor at Georgetown University; professorial lecturer at American University; lecturer at Brookings Institution. Public member of National Interagency Council on Smoking and Health, 1973-76; member of National Commission on Product Safety, 1967-70, and National Commission for Review of Antitrust Laws and Procedures; member of council of Administrative Conference of the United States. *Military service:* U.S. Army, 1954-56.

MEMBER: National Academy of Public Administration.

AWARDS, HONORS: LL.D. from Yale University, 1959.

WRITINGS:

Revolt Against Revolution: The Rise and Pause of the Consumer Movement, University of California Press, 1982.
Giant Killers, Norton, 1986.

SIDELIGHTS: In *Revolt Against Revolution*, former Federal Trade Commission (FTC) chairman Michael Pertschuk recounts a partial history of the U.S. consumer movement and discusses the movement's possible future. Prior to his affiliation with the FTC, Pertschuk served as chief counsel of the Senate Commerce Committee, where he worked "hand in glove with [Ralph] Nader creating much of the important regulatory legislation of the 1960s and '70s," notes Peter H. Schuck in the *Washington Post Book World*. After joining the FTC, Pertschuk "quickly became white-hatted hero to the consumer movement and black-hatted villain to conservatives and the business community," explains Norman Ornstein, also writing in the *Washington Post Book World*.

In his laudatory review of *Revolt Against Revolution*, Schuck applauds Pertschuk for "writing with grace, humor and scrupulous honesty." Pertschuk draws upon "his own experiences as a Washington insider and . . . maintains that corporate dominance of the social agenda is virtually inevitable.'' Schuck concludes by praising the author's ''candid, moving epilogue,'' in which Pertschuk ''acknowledges, and then seeks to reconcile, the dogged contradictions between populism and politics, possibility and pessimism, that he has so engagingly laid bare.''

Pertschuk's second book, *Giant Killers,* recounts some of the lobbying victories of the Advocacy Institute, which he co-founded with David Cohen. The consumer-oriented group trains public-interest lobbyists as well as arranges for lawyers to take on under-financed causes. "With all of the headlines about national security, portentous events, sounding brass and brass sounding off, it is refreshing to read a book about how hard work, imagination and good humor can deflect and deflate juggernauts,'' writes *New York Times Book Review* contributor David Murray. Ornstein labels Pertschuk ''a darn good yarn-spinner,'' and continues, ''Pertschuk makes no bones about his subjectivity in this book; there are heroes and villains, although . . . the designation is not immutable. In some cases, the villains are public-interest types who simply disagree. The author's biases, even if one does not share them, actually add to the enjoyment of reading the book—Pertschuk is clearly into it, and his own enthusiasm rubs off. The political novice will enjoy the stories and may root along with the author. The political sophisticate will enjoy the insider perspective and the nuances, even if one has to make one's own generalizations. For both, *Giant Killers* is a fun and interesting read.''

BIOGRAPHICAL/CRITICAL SOURCES:

PERIODICALS

New York Times Book Review, December 28, 1986.
Washington Post Book World, December 12, 1982, October 12, 1986.

* * *

PETERSON, Levi S(avage)   1933-

PERSONAL: Born December 13, 1933, in Snowflake, Ariz.; son of Joseph (a teacher of English) and Lydia Jane (an elementary school teacher; maiden name, Savage) Peterson; married Althea Sand, (a teacher of Spanish), August 31, 1958; children: Karrin. *Education:* Brigham Young University, B.A., 1958, M.A., 1960; University of Utah, Ph.D., 1965. *Politics:* Democrat. *Religion:* Church of Jesus Christ of Latter-day Saints (Mormons).

ADDRESSES: Home—1561 25th St., Ogden, Utah 84401. *Office*—Department of English, Weber State College, 3750 Harrison Blvd., Ogden, Utah 84408.

CAREER: Weber State College, Ogden, Utah, assistant professor, 1965-68, associate professor, 1968-72, professor of English, 1972—, chairman of department, 1970-73, director of honors program, 1973-82. President of Utah Trails Council, 1977-79.

MEMBER: Association for Mormon Letters (member of board of directors, 1978-82; president, 1981), Western Literature Association (member of executive council, 1973-75), Rocky Mountain Modern Language Association, Utah Academy of Sciences, Arts and Letters (member of board of directors, 1973-81), Phi Kappa Phi, Kiwanis International.

AWARDS, HONORS: First prize from Utah Art Council, 1978, for collection of stories ''The Confessions of Augustine,''

published as *The Canyons of Grace;* first prize from Association for Mormon Letters, 1978, for stories ''The Confessions of Augustine'' and ''Road to Damascus,'' and 1986, for novel *The Backslider;* first prize from Center for the Study of Christian Values in Literature, 1981, for story ''The Gift''; distinguished service award from Utah Academy of Sciences, Arts, and Letters, 1984; first prize from Sunstone Foundation, 1985, for story ''Sunswath''; second prize from Utah Art Council, 1985, for manuscript novel *The Backslider;* editorial award from Association for Mormon Letters, 1986, for *Greening Wheat;* second prize from *Dialogue* magazine, 1986, for story ''The Third Nephite.''

WRITINGS:

The Canyons of Grace (stories), University of Illinois Press, 1982.
(Editor) *Greening Wheat: Fifteen Mormon Short Stories* (anthology), Signature Books, 1983.
The Backslider (novel), Signature Books, 1986.
Juanita Brooks: A Biography, University of Utah Press, 1988.

Contributor to history and western American literature journals. Editor of *Encyclia: Journal of the Utah Academy of Sciences, Arts, and Letters,* 1977-81.

WORK IN PROGRESS: A collection of short stories about Utah Mormons.

SIDELIGHTS: Levi S. Peterson told *CA:* ''I grew up in a Mormon village in northern Arizona. I was a Mormon missionary in Switzerland and Belgium from 1954 to 1957; as a result, I speak French. Intellectually I believe I am a humanist and a citizen of the world; emotionally I still live in the stern ambiance of a frontier Mormon town.

''One of my fictional purposes is to explore the penitential impulse in human beings. Although my characters, as Mormons with rural roots, are fundamental Christians, I hope to reveal universal preoccupations and themes through them. I hope, through a carefully modulated narrative voice, to avoid moralizing or preachment. I am not personally interested in doctrinal or ideological issues; rather I am interested in the tensions which arise among characters who rationalize their lives in doctrinal terms.''

BIOGRAPHICAL/CRITICAL SOURCES:

PERIODICALS

Chicago Tribune, February 6, 1983.
Western American Literature, Volume 19, spring, 1984.

* * *

PETERSON, Owen M.   1924-

PERSONAL: Born February 17, 1924, in Parker, S.D.; son of Arthur A. and Grace (Radley) Peterson. *Education:* University of Iowa, B.A., 1946, M.A., 1949, Ph.D., 1952.

ADDRESSES: Home—2100 College Dr., #47, Baton Rouge, La. 70808. *Office*—Department of Speech Communication, Louisiana State University, Baton Rouge, La. 70803.

CAREER: DePauw University, Greencastle, Ind., assistant professor of speech, 1952-54; Louisiana State University, Baton Rouge, 1954—, began as instructor, became assistant professor, then associate professor, currently professor of speech communication. Visiting lecturer at Michigan State University, summers, 1952-53, and Wichita State University, summer, 1954.

MEMBER: Speech Communication Association (executive secretary, 1957-60), English Speaking Union, Hansard Society, Southern Speech Communication Association, Delta Sigma Rho.

WRITINGS:

(With Robert C. Jeffrey) *Speech: A Text with Adapted Readings,* Harper, 1971, 3rd edition, 1980.
(With Jeffrey) *Speech: A Basic Text,* Harper, 1976, 2nd edition, 1982.
(Editor) *Representative American Speeches,* H. W. Wilson, Volume 53: *1980-81,* 1981, Volume 54: *1981-82,* 1982, Volume 55: *1982-83,* 1983, Volume 56: *1983-84,* 1984, Volume 57: *1984-85,* 1985, Volume 58: *1985-86,* 1986, Volume 59: *1986-87,* 1987.
A Divine Discontent: The Life of Nathan S. S. Beman, Mercer University Press, 1986.

CONTRIBUTOR

James Silver, editor, *Mississippi in the Confederacy as Seen in Retrospect,* Louisiana State University Press, 1961.
W. W. Braden, editor, *Oratory in the Old South, 1828-1860,* Louisiana State University Press, 1971.

OTHER

Contributor to communication and history journals. Editor of *Southern Speech Communication Journal,* 1961-66; associate editor of *Speech Teacher,* 1967-70, and *Speech Monographs,* 1968-71.

WORK IN PROGRESS: Research on prominent British political, literary, religious, and theatrical speakers who have made lecture tours of the United States and Canada.

SIDELIGHTS: Owen M. Peterson told *CA:* "For many years I have been interested in the effective use of speech by British leaders. I have been particularly impressed by the speaking activities of the British Labour Party in its rise from virtual obscurity at the beginning of this century to its formation of a government in less than twenty-five years. That initial interest led me to a study of the ways that the Fabian Society sought to influence public opinion and promote the new Labour Party through debates, lectures, and pamphlets. From there, it was a short step to consideration of how prominent British speakers have sought to influence public opinion abroad, especially in America."

*   *   *

PETROV, Victor P. 1907-

PERSONAL: Born March 22, 1907, in Harbin, China; naturalized U.S. citizen; son of Porfiry Nicholas (a priest of Russian Orthodox Church) and Catherine (Ryazanov) Petrov; married Elizabeth Onufrieff (a reference librarian), February 6, 1942 (died October 1, 1981); stepchildren: Tatiana B. Tontarski (died August 8, 1986). *Education:* Institute of Jurisprudence, Harbin, China, student, 1925-29; American University, B.S., 1951, M.A., 1952, Ph.D., 1954. *Religion:* Russian Orthodox.

ADDRESSES: Home—15524 Pennyroyal Ln., Rockville, Md. 20853.

CAREER: U.S. Navy School of Oriental Languages, Boulder, Colo., instructor, 1945-46; U.S. Naval Language School, Washington, D.C., assistant professor, 1946-50, associate professor, 1950-57, professor of languages andgeography, 1957-

63; Defense Language Institute, Washington, D.C., professor of languages and geography, 1963-65; Shippensburg State College, Shippensburg, Pa., professor of geography, 1965-67; National Science Foundation, Washington,D.C., assistant program director, foreign science information program, 1967-70; California State University, Los Angeles, professor of geography, 1970-74, Professorial lecturer in geography, George Washington University, 1962-65; visiting professor, University of Victoria, Victoria, British Columbia, 1974-75.

MEMBER: Association of American Geographers, Association for Asian Studies, American Association of Teachers of Slavic and East European Languages.

WRITINGS:

Albazinians in China, Kamkin, 1956.
Geography of the Soviet Union, Kamkin, Part IV-B: *Electric Power,* 1959, Part IV: *Soviet Industry,* 1960, Part IV-A: *Energy Resources,* 1962, Part I: *Physical Features,* 1964, Part II: *Geographic Zone,* 1964, Part III: *Population,* 1964, Part V: *Transportation,* 1967.
100th Aniversary of the Arrival of Russian Naval Squadrons to America, Kamkin, 1963.
China: Emerging World Power, Van Nostrand, 1967, 2nd edition, 1976.
History of Russian Ecclesiastical Mission in China, Kamkin, 1968.
Mongolia: A Profile, Praeger, 1970.

IN RUSSIAN

Pod Amerikanskim Flagom (title means "Under American Flag"), Malyk & Kamkin (Shanghai), 1933.
Lola (novel), Malyk & Kamkin, 1934.
V Manchzhurii (title means "In Manchuria"), Slovo (Shanghai), 1937.
Saga Forta Ross (title means "Saga of Fort Ross"), Kamkin (Washington, D.C.), Book I: *Printsessa Elena* (title means "Princess Elena"), 1961, Book II: *Konets Mechtam* (title means "End of Dreams"), 1963.
Kitayskie Rasskazy (title means "Chinese Stories"), Kamkin, 1962.
Kolumby Rossiyskie (title means "Russian Columbuses"), Kamkin, 1971.
Kamerger Dvora (title means "Grand Chamberlain of the Court"), Kamkin, 1973.
Zavershenie Tsikla (title means "Completion of a Cycle"), Rodnye Dali, 1975.
Russkaia Amerika (title means "Russian America"), Friends of Fort Ross, 1975, 2nd edition, 1981.
Fort Ross i Ego Kul'turnoe Nasledie (title means "Fort Ross and Its Cultural Heritage"), Friends of Fort Ross, 1977, 2nd edition, 1980.
Kataklizm (title means "Cataclysm"), Russian-American Historical Society, 1982.
Gorod na Sungari (title means "A City on the Sungari"), Russian-American Historical Society, 1984.
Shanhai na Vampu (title means "Shanghai on the Whangpoo"), Russian-American Historical Society, 1985.
Po Sviatoy Zemle (title means "In the Holy Land"), Russian-American Historical Society, 1986.
Po Sledam Inka i Maya (title means "Following the Steps of Inca and Maya"), Russian-American Historical Society, 1987.
Russkie v Istorii Ameriki (title means "Russians in American History"), Russian-American Historical Society, 1988.

OTHER

Contributing editor, *Dictionary of Political Science*, 1964; contributor to *Encyclopedia Britannica*, 1981. Contributor of about fifty articles on geography of the Soviet Union and China and on astrogeography to professional journals. Also contributor of four articles in Japanese to *Tokyo Kaiho*, and more than three hundred articles to Russian language newspapers in the United States and Australia.

SIDELIGHTS: Victor P. Petrov is competent in German, Russian, and Chinese and gets along well in several other Slavic languages.

* * *

PHELPS, Gilbert (Henry, Jr.) 1915-

PERSONAL: Born January 23, 1915, in Gloucester, England; son of Gilbert Henry (a clerk) and Mary (Wilks) Phelps; married Dorothy Elizabeth Coad, April 11, 1939 (divorced); married Dorothy Kathleen Batchelor, 1972; children: (first marriage) John David, Jean Hazel; (second marriage) Sebastian Barnes, Bartholomew Barnes, Julian Wesley (stepsons). *Education:* Fitzwilliam College, Cambridge, B.A. (first class honors), 1937, St. John's College, Cambridge, M.A., 1941. *Politics:* Progressive. *Religion:* Anglican.

ADDRESSES: Home—The Cottage, School Rd., Finstock, Oxford OX7 3DJ, England. *Agent*—Elaine Green Ltd., 31 Newington Green, Islington, London N16 9PU, England.

CAREER: British Institute, Lisbon, Portugal, British Council lecturer in English, 1940-42; Blundell's School, Tiverton, Devon, England, senior English master, 1943-45; British Broadcasting Corp., producer in Bristol, England, 1945-50, supervisor of educational talks in London, England, 1950-52, chief instructor of staff training, 1953-60; full-time writer, lecturer, and broadcaster on travel, history, and literature. Lecturer to British Armed Forces, 1943-50. Guest lecturer at numerous universities and colleges throughout Great Britain and the United States. Has made numerous appearances on BBC network for Home, World, European, and Far Eastern Services. Judge for various literary awards. *Military service:* Royal Air Force, 1940-43.

MEMBER: International PEN, Royal Society of Literature (fellow), Society of Authors, Royal Commonwealth Society, Southern Arts Association (former chairman of literature panel).

AWARDS, HONORS: Poetry award, University of Pennsylvania, 1950; Arts Council Award, 1965; Arts Council bursary, 1968.

WRITINGS:

The Dry Stone (novel), Barker, 1953, published as *The Heart in the Desert*, John Day, 1954.
A Man in His Prime (novel), John Day, 1955.
The Russian Novel in English Fiction, Hutchinson, 1956, reprinted, Scholarly Press, 1971.
Latin America, British Broadcasting Corp., 1956.
The Centenarians (novel), Heinemann, 1958.
The Love before the First, Heinemann, 1960.
The Winter People (novel), Bodley Head, 1962, Simon & Schuster, 1964, abridged edition, Chatto & Windus, 1965.
A Short History of English Literature, Folio, 1962, revised and enlarged edition published as *A Survey of English Literature: Some of the Main Themes and Developments from Beowulf to 1939*, Pan Books, 1965.

The Green Horizons: Travels in Brazil, Simon & Schuster, 1964 (published in England as *The Last Horizon: Travels in Brazil*, Bodley Head, 1964, 2nd edition published as *The Last Horizon: A Brazilian Journey*, Knight, 1971).
The Tenants of the House (novel), Barrie & Jenkins, 1971.
Mortal Flesh (novel), Random House, 1973 (published in England as *The Old Believer*, Barrie & Jenkins, 1973).
The Low Roads (novel), Barrie & Jenkins, 1975.
The Tragedy of Paraguay, St. Martin's, 1975.
Squire Waterton (biography), EP Publishing, 1976.
Story of the British Monarchy, Nile & Mackenzie, 1977.
A Reader's Guide to Fifty British Novels, 1600-1900, Barnes & Noble, 1979 (published in England as *An Introduction to Fifty British Novels, 1600-1900*, Pan Books, 1979).
From Myth to Modernism: A Short Survey of World Fiction, Folio, 1987.

EDITOR

Living Writers, Sylvan Press, 1950.
Question and Response: A Critical Anthology of English and American Poetry, Cambridge University Press, 1969.
The Byronic Byron: A Selection from the Poems of Lord Byron, Longman, 1971.
(And author of introduction) Charles Waterton, *Wanderings in South America, the North-West of the United States, and the Antilles in the Years 1812, 1816, 1820, 1824*, abridged edition, Knight, 1973, Transatlantic, 1974.
(And author of introduction) *The Rare Adventures and Painful Peregrinations of William Lithgow*, Folio, 1974.
(And author of introduction) *Byron: An Autobiographical Anthology*, Grasshopper Press, 1974.
Arlott and Trueman on Cricket, British Broadcasting Corp., 1977.
(With son, John Phelps) James Herriot and others, *Animals Tame and Wild*, Sterling, 1979.

Also editor of an edition of William Shakespeare's *Romeo and Juliet*.

EDITOR AND AUTHOR OF INTRODUCTION AND NOTES

William Makepeace Thackery, *Vanity Fair*, Pan Books, 1967.
Laurence Sterne, *Tristram Shandy*, Folio, 1970.
H. G. Wells, *Tono-Bungay*, Pan Books, 1972.
Charlotte Bronte, *Villette*, Pan Books, 1973.
E. M. Forster, *Howard's End*, Folio, 1973.
William Makepeace Thackeray, *Henry Esmond*, Pan Books, 1974.
Samuel Johnson, *The History of Rasselas*, Folio, 1975.
Stendhal, *The Charterhouse of Parma*, Folio, 1977.
Henry James, *The Europeans*, Folio, 1982.
Virginia Woolf, *To the Lighthouse*, Folio, 1988.

CONTRIBUTOR

Life under the Tudors, Falcon Press, 1950.
Life under the Stuarts, Falcon Press, 1951.
Explorers Remember, Hodder & Stoughton, 1967.
Collected Articles on George Gissing, Cassell, 1967.
Notes on Literature, British Council, 1973.
John D. Jump, editor, *A Byron Symposium*, Macmillan, 1975.
Pelican Guide to English Literature, eight volumes, Penguin, 1981-82.
A History of British Culture, nine volumes, Folio, 1988.

Also contributor to *A Guide to English Literature*, Cassell.

WORK REPRESENTED IN ANTHOLOGIES

Malcolm Elwin, editor, *Faber Book of West County Stories; Book of Ghost Stories; The Pleasureground*, Macdonald & Co., 1947.
Poetry Awards, University of Pennsylvania Press, 1950.
PEN New Poems, M. Joseph, 1953.

OTHER

Author of radio plays, including "The Tide Comes In," 1960, "The Spanish Cave" (based on novel by Geoffrey Household), 1960, "The Winter People" (based on Phelps's novel of same title), 1964, "Deliberate Adventure," 1968, and "The Tankerdown Skull"; also author of television features. Contributor of fiction, poetry, and articles on education to London periodicals, including *Observer, Spectator, Listener, New Statesman*, and *Poetry Review*.

BIOGRAPHICAL/CRITICAL SOURCES:

PERIODICALS

Atlantic, October, 1964.
Books, October, 1971.
Book Week, December 6, 1964.
Commonweal, June 18, 1954.
New York Times, May 16, 1954, May 16, 1955.
Saturday Review, May 22, 1954, June 4, 1955, October 10, 1964.
Spectator, March 11, 1955.
Times Literary Supplement, March 25, 1955.

* * *

PHILLIPS-JONES, Linda 1943-

PERSONAL: Born March 3, 1943, in South Bend, Ind.; daughter of Robert M. (a civil servant and chemical analyst) and Priscilla (an executive secretary; maiden name, Tancy) Phillips; married G. Brian Jones (a psychologist and author), February 16, 1980; children: (stepdaughters) Laurie, Tracy. *Education:* University of Nevada, B.S., 1964; Stanford University, A.M., 1965; University of California, Los Angeles, Ph.D. 1977. *Religion:* Christian.

ADDRESSES: Home—Los Gatos, Calif. *Office*—SRI International, 333 Ravenswood Ave., Menlo Park, Calif. 94025.

CAREER: International Training Consultants, Saigon, Vietnam, trainer and curriculum specialist, 1966-71; private career and personal development consultant, 1972—. Research scientist for American Institutes for Research, 1979-83. Counselor/psychologist at Coalition of Counseling Centers (Christian organization), 1981—.

MEMBER: American Psychological Association, American Society for Training and Development.

WRITINGS:

(With husband, G. Brian Jones, and H. N. Drier) *Developing Competencies for Training Career Guidance Personnel* (monograph), American Vocational Association and National Vocational Guidance Association, 1981.
Mentors and Proteges: How to Establish, Strengthen, and Get the Most from a Mentor-Protege Relationship, Arbor House, 1982.
(With G. B. Jones) *Men Have Feelings, Too!*, Victor Books, 1988.
(With G. B. Jones) *Where Do We Agree? How to Resolve Conflicts and Still Enjoy People*, Victor Books, in press.

Contributor to magazines, including *Glamour, New Woman, Woman*, and *Business WOMAN*.

WORK IN PROGRESS: Continuing research on mentoring relationships, structured mentoring programs, stress management, building of self-esteem, marriage improvement, and effective counseling strategies.

SIDELIGHTS: Linda Phillips-Jones wrote: "Unlike many of my colleagues in research and psychology, I prefer to write for the layperson. I like to translate what experts find into everyday strategies that will help my readers face Monday morning at the office or Friday night dinner with a new friend.

"A *Library Journal* review of *Mentors and Proteges* recommended the book for public libraries, stating that 'the case examples and step-by-step approach appear to make what is often an important factor in career success a more rational and accessible pursuit.'

"That is exactly what I intended. I approached this book from the point of view of the prospective protege, who is very much like the client I see in counseling. What does he or she need to feel and know to tackle the somewhat mysterious task of finding the right mentor—not only for a career, but for any important area of life? What do mentors know that proteges don't? Assuming that proteges are in a somewhat vulnerable position to start with, what can I give them that will provide a detour around some errors and pain and save time in the process?

"Not everyone has favored my approach. One reviewer called the book 'misleading' and took me to task for thinking that 'programming' of mentor-protege relationships is possible.

"In the personal counseling I do, mostly with women who range in age from fifteen through their fifties, I find that once feelings are explored and shared, I am asked to be more specific in offering how-to's, and my clients do better. They appreciate steps, examples, demonstrations, even sample 'scripts' to use in their interpersonal problem solving. Of course, they modify these to fit their own language, personalities, and situations, but the specifics give them a concrete 'rough draft' with which to begin. We 'program' together. I attempt to carry this philosophy over into my writing.

"As I write this, I just celebrated my forty-fifth birthday, a major milestone for me. My life has been rich with travel and change (the years in Vietnam, numerous vacation journeys, thirty-seven residences since I was a child), unusual work, some successes, and intriguing, loving friends. The glue that has held this together has been my Christian faith. My husband and I are now co-authoring books with a spiritual dimension. This is what we both plan to do for the next many years. I intend to be a better mentor to many—through my personal contacts and through the words I write."

BIOGRAPHICAL/CRITICAL SOURCES:

PERIODICALS

Calgary Herald, September 9, 1982.
Executive Educator, April, 1983.
Kansas City Times, September 14, 1982.
Los Angeles Times, December 17, 1982.

* * *

PIERCE, Meredith Ann 1958-

PERSONAL: Born July 5, 1958, in Seattle, Wash.; daughter

of Frank N. (in advertising; a professor) and Jo Ann (an agriculture editor and professor; maiden name, Bell) Pierce. *Education:* University of Florida, B.A., 1978, M.A., 1980.

ADDRESSES: Home—703 Northwest 19th St., Gainesville, Fla. 32603.

CAREER: Bookland, Gainesville, Fla., clerk, 1981; Waldenbooks, Gainesville, clerk, 1981-87; Alachua County (Fla.) Library District, library assistant, 1987—.

AWARDS, HONORS: First prize in junior division, *Scholastic/Hallmark Cards* creative writing contest, 1973, for short story "The Snail"; Children's Book Award, International Reading Association, 1982, for *The Darkangel; The Darkangel* was named to the American Library Association's Best Books for Young Adults and Best of the Best Books 1970-1982 lists, the *New York Times* Notable Children's Book list, and the Parents' Choice Award Superbook list, all 1982; Jane Tinkham Broughton Fellow in writing for children, Bread Loaf Writers' Conference, 1984; Best Books for Young Adults semifinalist, American Library Association, 1985, for *A Gathering of Gargoyles; The Woman Who Loved Reindeer* was named to the American Library Association's Best Books for Young Adults list, 1985, the Parents' Choice Award for Literature list, 1985, and the New York Public Library's Books for the Teenage exhibit list, 1986; California Young Reader Medal, 1986, for *The Darkangel;* Individual Artist Fellowship Special Award for Children's Literature, Florida Department of State, Division of Cultural Affairs, 1987.

WRITINGS:

FOR YOUNG ADULTS

The Darkangel (fantasy; first novel in "Darkangel" trilogy), Little, Brown, 1982.
A Gathering of Gargoyles (fantasy; second novel in "Darkangel" trilogy), Little, Brown, 1984.
Birth of the Firebringer (fantasy; first novel in "Firebringer" trilogy), Macmillan, 1985.
The Woman Who Loved Reindeer (fantasy), Little, Brown, 1985.
Where the Wild Geese Go (picturebook), Dutton, 1988.

OTHER

Contributor to *Mythlore, Horn Book, ALAN Review,* and *New Advocate.*

WORK IN PROGRESS: The Pearl of the Soul of the World, the third novel in the "Darkangel" trilogy; *Dark Moon,* the second novel in the "Firebringer" trilogy; *The Wonder Hound,* a picture book.

SIDELIGHTS: Meredith Ann Pierce's fairy tale, *The Darkangel,* was inspired by a dream recorded in Jung's *Memories, Dreams, and Reflections.* "It is the story of a servant girl, Aeriel," recounts Nancy Willard in the *New York Times Book Review,* "and her struggle to destroy the handsome vampire who has kidnapped her mistress and to keep his evil power from taking over the world. It is also the story of Aeriel's journey from innocence to experience, involving love's power to heal and evil's terrible attractiveness."

Willard finds that Pierce's tale is "written with plenty of skill and elfish craft." She also comments that while the story was without illustrations, "Miss Pierce makes her own word pictures." "It was one of the best fantasies I've read in a long time," concludes the critic. "Like the best of fairy tales, *The Darkangel* will last and be loved by readers of all ages."

A Gathering of Gargoyles, the next novel in the "Darkangel" trilogy, continues the tale of Aeriel and the darkangel Irrylath. It is about "Aeriel's search for the lost lons of Irrylath, great ugly animals . . . that she had once befriended," summarizes Eleanor Cameron in the *New York Times Book Review.* Similar to other praise of Pierce's writing, Cameron finds the author "intensely visual, even poetic in her descriptions and imaginative in her surprising plot turns." The critic adds that Pierce's work reminds her of Ursula K. Le Guin's *A Wizard of Earthsea;* it also contains "echoes of other outstanding fantasies . . . [such as] the cycles of Susan Cooper and Jane Louise Curry." Pierce "is strong in her overall conception" of the "Darkangel" series, concludes Cameron.

Meredith Pierce told *CA:* "When I am constructing a story, image always comes first. I am a primary-process thinker. I have to *see* what happened, understand the 'how' of it before I can figure out the 'why.' So images come, string themselves into a plot. Once I've got plot, then I have to start devising the second component—what I mentally refer to as 'the excuse'—that is, some sort of theme. As for the third thing, style (I'm a scrutable Occidental: I like things to come in threes), one simply hopes as a writer that one has read enough, practiced at writing enough, to be able to use language intelligently, even beautifully. (From time to time, all of us have our moments.)

"Like good baklava, a work of fiction should be multilayered. If it doesn't have its components properly situated in correct proportion, the taste and texture will be off. Plot is like the pastry: The body and support. Theme is the nut: The kernel and the heart. Style is the savor, blending honey and spice. Nothing is more delicious either to fashion or to devour."

BIOGRAPHICAL/CRITICAL SOURCES:

PERIODICALS

New York Times Book Review, April 25, 1982, December 30, 1984.

*   *   *

PIRTLE, Caleb (Jackson) III 1941-

PERSONAL: Born December 30, 1941, in Kilgore, Tex.; son of Caleb Jackson, Jr. (an oil field worker) and Mary Eunice (Price) Pirtle; married Linda Sue Greer (a legal secretary), August 31, 1963; children: Joshua Jackson. *Education:* Kilgore College, A.A., 1961; University of Texas, B.J., 1963.

ADDRESSES: Home—401 East Marvin, Waxahachie, Tex. 75165. *Office*—TraveLink Publishing, Waxahachie, Tex. 75165.

CAREER: Plainfield Daily Herald, Plainview, Tex., reporter, 1963; *Fort Worth Star-Telegram,* Fort Worth, Tex., feature writer, 1963-65; Texas Tourist Development Agency, Austin, press chief, 1965-68; *Southern Living,* Birmingham, Ala., travel editor, 1968—; Crawford, Pirtle & Lynn, Waxahachie, Tex., partner, 1977-83; Calan Enterprises, Waxahachie, partner, 1983—; TraveLink Publishing, executive editor, 1988—.

MEMBER: Society of American Travel Writers (past vice-president of Central States chapter), Discover America Travel Organizations.

AWARDS, HONORS: Award from Southwest Journalism

Forum, 1963, for feature writing; William Randolph Hearst Award, 1963; feature writing award from Texas Associated Press, 1964, and from Texas Headliners, 1964; awards from Discover America Travel Organizations, 1969, 1971, 1973, for magazine coverage of travel; named headliner of the year by local chapter of Texas Women's Press Association, 1975; award from Southeastern Library Association, 1973, for *Callaway Gardens: The Unending Season,* and 1975, for *XIT: The American Cowboy.*

WRITINGS:

(With Gerald Crawford) *Callaway Gardens: The Unending Season,* Oxmore, 1973.
XIT: The American Cowboy, Oxmore, 1975.
(With Texas Cowboy Artists Association) *American Cowboy,* Oxmoor, 1977.
The Grandest Day, Opryland, 1979.
Fort Worth: The Civilized West, Continental Heritage, 1980.
M.L.M.: A Shortcut to Financial Freedom, Synergetic Publishing, 1982.
This Great Land, Rand McNally, 1983.
Texas: Its Lore and Its Lure, Turtle Creek Galleries, 1984.
(With Michael F. Cusack) *The Lonely Sentinel: Fort Clark on Texas's Western Frontier,* Eakin Press, 1985.
The Texas Outback, McLennan House, 1986.
From the Dark Side of the Rainbow, McLennan House, 1986.
Trail of Broken Promises, Eakin Press, 1986.
Last Deadly Lie, PaperJacks, 1988.
Friday Night Heat, PaperJacks, 1988.

Contributor to magazines, including *Westward, Travel and Leisure, Travel, Sky, Holiday Inn Companion, Atlanta Weekly, Washingtonian,* and *Rotarian.*

WORK IN PROGRESS: "The Portrait of America Travel Series."

SIDELIGHTS: Caleb Pirtle III told *CA* that some of his writing assignments have included interviews with former president Lyndon Johnson, former vice-president John Nance Garner, former governor John Connally, the world's strongest man, country-western performers Tom T. Hall, Minnie Pearl, Porter Waggoner, Dolly Parton, Jimmy Driftwood, Dottie West, Jerry Clower, the world champion tobacco spitter, the world champion muleshoe pitcher, champion cowboys, and professional golfers and tennis players.

He comments: "I believe in people. And I'm convinced that what happens is not nearly as important as the people who make it happen. And that has been my approach to travel writing. Most simply tell you where to go, how to get there, and how much it's going to cost. I like to add a new dimension. I like to tell you the kind of people you're going to meet when you get there. And these include tobacco spitters, muleshoe pitchers, story tellers, chili cookers, domino players, and guitar pickers. I've been fortunate enough to travel throughout the United States, Mexico, Europe and Russia. And when I get home I find I remember the people I've talked with long after I've forgotten the sights I've seen. I write for one reason. I'm curious and like to find out what's going on. . . . Then I can't wait to tell someone."

BIOGRAPHICAL/CRITICAL SOURCES:

PERIODICALS

Southwest Review, spring, 1986.

PITTOCK, Joan (Hornby) 1930-
(Joan Wesson)

PERSONAL: Born May 1, 1930, in Purston Jaglin, England; daughter of George Hornby (an inspector of horses in mines) and Dorothy Muriel (a secretary; maiden name, Poyner) Mould; married Malcolm Pittock (a lecturer), August 21, 1955 (divorced, 1973); married Harry Chamberlain Wesson (an industrial consultant), July 23, 1974 (died July 22, 1983); children (first marriage) Murray George. *Education:* Victoria University of Manchester, B.A. (with first class honors), 1951, M.A., 1952, Ph.D., 1960. *Politics:* "Radical conservative." *Religion:* Church of England.

ADDRESSES: Home—144 Bon Accord St., Aberdeen AB1 2TX, Scotland. *Office*—Department of English, University of Aberdeen, Taylor Building, King's College, Old Aberdeen AB9 2UB, Scotland.

CAREER: University of Keele, Keele, England, lecturer in English, 1957; teacher of extra-mural and adult education classes in Cumberland, England, 1955-57; University of Aberdeen, Old Aberdeen, Scotland, assistant lecturer, 1964-66, lecturer, 1966-78, senior lecturer in English, 1978—, convener and L Course (M.A. degree) organizer, Cultural History Group, 1985—. Visiting research fellow, Magdalen College, Oxford University, 1986; fellow, Institute for Advanced Studies in the Humanities, Edinburgh University, 1986. International Society for Eighteenth-Century Studies (British delegate to executive committee, 1980—), British Society for Eighteenth-Century Studies (president, 1980-82), Modern Humanities Research Association, Association of Scottish Literary Studies, Scottish Georgian Society.

AWARDS, HONORS: British Academy grant, 1982.

WRITINGS:

The Ascendancy of Taste, Routledge & Kegan Paul, 1973.
(Editor) *Joseph Warton: Odes on Various Subjects, 1746,* Scholar Press, 1977.
(Editor) *George Hardinge: Rowley and Chatterton in the Shades,* Augustan Reprint Society, 1979.
(Editor with J. J. Carter) *Aberdeen and the Enlightenment,* Aberdeen University Press, 1987.
(Editor with A. Wear) *New Directions in Cultural History,* Princeton University Press, in press.

Contributor of poems to periodicals, under name Joan Wesson. Editor of newsletter of British Society for Eighteenth Century Studies, 1976-78—; founder and editor of *British Journal for Eighteenth-Century Studies,* 1978-80.

WORK IN PROGRESS: History of the Oxford Chair of Poetry in the Eighteenth Century; research on politics and literature in the late eighteenth century, Scottish writers of the eighteenth century (including Beattie, Macpherson, and Gerard), and the literature of childhood.

SIDELIGHTS: Joan Pittock told *CA:* "My career has been dominated by domestic circumstances. I followed my first husband's career, taking part-time appointments wherever he happened to work from 1955 onward, and with him was an active member of the Campaign for Nuclear Disarmament and Bertrand Russell's Committee of One Hundred until the birth of my son in 1962. My second marriage has been affected by the serious ill health of my husband, who died in 1983.

"Throughout my teaching career I have been concerned with the importance of multidisciplinary approaches to the teaching of literature. I have now convened a group of colleagues who have established the first undergraduate honours course in Cultural History in a British university.''

BIOGRAPHICAL/CRITICAL SOURCES:

PERIODICALS

New Statesman, April 20, 1973.
Times Literary Supplement, October 5, 1973.

* * *

POOLE, Josephine
See HELYAR, Jane Penelope Josephine

* * *

PRICE, R(onald) F(rancis) 1926-

PERSONAL: Born June 24, 1926, in Hondon, Wales; son of John and Marguerite E. M. Price; married Erika R. Flack (an art teacher in a training college), 1960. *Education:* Attended University College of South West, Exeter (now University of Exeter), 1948-52; University of London, External B.Sc., 1951, Ph.D., 1969.

ADDRESSES: Home—13 Glenard Dr., Heidelberg, Victoria 3083, Australia. *Office*—School of Education, La Trobe University, Bundoora, Victoria 3083, Australia.

CAREER: Teacher, 1953-67; taught biology in a technical college, physics at an English-language school in Sofia, Bulgaria, educational psychology at University College of Cape Coast, Cape Coast, Ghana, and then English at a foreign language institute in Peking, China; La Trobe University, Bundoora, Victoria, Australia, 1970—, began as lecturer, currently senior lecturer in comparative and international education. *Military service:* British Army, 1944-48; served in Mideast Command.

MEMBER: Institute of Biology, Comparative Education Society in Europe (British section).

WRITINGS:

A Reference Book of English Words and Phrases for Foreign Science Students, Pergamon, 1966.
Education in Communist China, Praeger, 1970, 3rd edition published as *Education in Modern China,* Routledge & Kegan Paul, 1979.
What Chinese Children Read About: Serial Picture Books and Foreigners, School of Education, La Trobe University, 1976.
(Under name Ronald F. Price) *Marx and Education in Russia and China,* Roman & Littlefield, 1977.
(Editor) *The Anti-Confucius Campaign in China,* Centre for Comparative and International Studies in Education, La Trobe University, 1977.
(Editor) *English for China: Papers for Discussion,* Committee for Australia-China Relations, 1984.
Marx and Eduction in Late Capitalism, Croom Helm, 1986.
(Editor) *Chinese Writers on Education in China,* Centre for Comparative and International Studies in Education, La Trobe University, 1987.

WORK IN PROGRESS: Currently working on the problems of teaching science in China.

AVOCATIONAL INTERESTS: Swimming, table tennis, listening to all kinds of music other than ''pop.''

PRINCE, Alison (Mary) 1931-

PERSONAL: Born March 26, 1931, in Kent, England; daughter of Charles (a bank official) and Louise (David) Prince; married Goronwy Siriol Parry (a teacher), December 26, 1957; children: Samantha, Andrew, Benjamin. *Education:* Slade School of Art, London, Diploma in Fine Art, 1952; Goldsmiths' College, London, Art Teacher's Diploma, 1954. *Politics:* None. *Religion:* Agnostic.

ADDRESSES: Home—28 Hawes Rd., Bromley, Kent, England.

CAREER: Free-lance writer and illustrator. Head of school art department in London, England, 1954-58; adult education art teacher in Bromley, Kent, England, 1960—.

MEMBER: International PEN, Royal Society of Painter-Etchers and Engravers.

AWARDS, HONORS: The Turkey's Nest was chosen one of American Library Association's best books for young adults, 1980.

WRITINGS:

FOR CHILDREN

The Joe Annual, Polystyle Publications, 1968, 1969, 1970, 1971.
Joe and the Horse, and Other Short Stories about Joe from ''Watch with Mother,'' British Broadcasting Corp., 1969.
(Self-illustrated) *The House on the Common,* Methuen, 1969, Farrar, Straus, 1970.
(Self-illustrated) *The Red Alfa,* Methuen, 1971, published as *The Red Jaguar,* Atheneum, 1972.
(With Joan Hickson) *Joe and the Nursery School,* British Broadcasting Corp., 1972.
(With Hickson) *Joe Moves House,* British Broadcasting Corp., 1972.
(With Chris Connor) *Ben's Fish,* illustrated by Connor, Benn, 1972.
Whosaurus? Dinosaurus!, Studio Vista, 1976.
Who Wants Pets?, Methuen, 1980.
Willow Farm, Ace Books, 1981.
(Self-illustrated) *The Good Pets Guide,* Armada, 1981.
Haunted Children, illustrated by Michael Bragg, Methuen, 1982.
The Sinister Airfield, Methuen, 1982.
Goodbye Summer, Methuen, 1983.
Night Landings, Methuen, 1983, Morrow, 1984.
The Ghost Within, Methuen, 1984.
Scramble!, Methuen, 1984.
Nick's October, Methuen, 1986.
The Others, Methuen, 1986.
(Self-illustrated) *How's Business,* Deutsch, 1987.
(Self-illustrated) *The Type One Super Robot,* Deutsch, 1987.
A Haunting Refrain, Methuen, 1988.

''MILL GREEN'' CHILDREN'S SERIES

Mill Green on Fire, Armada, 1982.
Mill Green on Stage, Fontana, 1982.
A Spy at Mill Green, Armada, 1985.
Rock On, Mill Green, Armada, 1985.

FOR YOUNG ADULTS

The Doubting Kind, Methuen, 1975, Morrow, 1977, published

as *The Doubting Kind,* Volume 1: *A Friend in Need,* Volume 2: *All Who Love Us,* Macmillan, 1977.
The Night I Sold My Boots, Heinemann, 1979.
The Turkey's Nest, Methuen, 1979, Morrow, 1980.

ILLUSTRATOR

(With Samantha Parry) Audrey Coppard, *Don't Panic!,* Heinemann, 1975.
Coppard, *Get Well Soon,* Heinemann, 1978.
Jane Allen and Mary Danby, *Hello to Ponies,* Heinemann, 1979.
Allen and Danby, *Hello to Riding,* Heinemann, 1980.

Also illustrator of *Let's Explore Mathematics* and *Jessica on Her Own.*

OTHER

Television series for British Broadcasting Corp. include "Joe," with a second film series of that name started in 1971, and five war stories for the "Jackanory" series. Contributor to *Times Educattonal Supplement.*

SIDELIGHTS: Alison Prince's interests embrace everything related to her work—films, music, art, children, schools, and animals. She likes writing for children "because they are honest and they read a book because they want to read it, not because they want to be seen reading it." She told *CA* that she is interested in farming ("rearing calves commerically") as well as writing.

BIOGRAPHICAL/CRITICAL SOURCES:

BOOKS

Micklethwait, Lucy, and Brigid Peppin, *Book Illustrators of the Twentieth Century,* Arco, 1984.†

PULKINGHAM, Betty (Jane)   1928-

PERSONAL: Born August 25, 1928, in Burlington, N.C.; daughter of Leo (a lawyer and judge) and Betty (Knott) Carr; married William Graham Pulkingham (an Episcopalian priest), September 1, 1951; children: William Graham III, Mary Graham, Nathan Carr, Elizabeth Jane, Martha Louise, David Earle. *Education:* University of North Carolina at Greensboro, B.S. (magna cum laude), 1949; graduate study at Eastman School of Music. *Religion:* Episcopalian.

ADDRESSES: Home—Community of Celebration, Aliquippa, Pa. *Office*—Celebration, P.O. Box 309, Aliquippa, Pa. 15001.

CAREER: Music theory instructor at University of Texas, 1949-52; Austin High School, Austin, Tex., choral music teacher, 1956-57; private piano teacher in Galveston, Tex., 1958-60; Church of the Redeemer, Houston, Tex., choir director, 1964-71; currently director of research and development, Celebration.

WRITINGS:

(Arranger and compiler with Oressa Wise) *Songs of Fellowship,* privately printed, 1972, Net Music Co., 1975.
(Compiler with Jeanne Harper) *Sound of Living Waters: Songs of Renewal* (also see below), Eerdmans, 1974.
(Compiler with Harper) *Fresh Sounds* (also see below), Hodder & Stoughton, 1976.
Mustard Seeds, Hodder & Stoughton, 1977.
(Compiler with Harper) *Sound of Living Waters* [and] *Fresh Sounds,* Hodder & Stoughton, 1977.
Little Things in the Hands of a Big God, Word Publishers, 1977.
(Editor) *Hosanna in the Highest: Collection of Descants for Traditional Hymns,* Celebration, 1978.
(Editor with Mimi Farra) *Cry Hosanna,* Hope Publishing, 1980.
Sing God a Simple Song: Exploring in Worship for the Eighties, Morgan and Scott Marshall Publications, 1986.

Q-R

QUEEN, Ellery
   See DAVIDSON, Avram

       *   *   *

RABASSA, Gregory   1922-

PERSONAL: Born March 9, 1922, in Yonkers, N.Y.; son of Miguel and Clara (Macfarland) Rabassa; married Roney Edelstein, July 14, 1956 (marriage ended, 1966); married Clementine C. Christos (a teacher and critic), May 29, 1966; children: Catherine, Clara. *Education:* Dartmouth College, A.B., 1945; Columbia University, M.A., 1947, Ph.D., 1954. *Politics:* Democrat. *Religion:* None.

ADDRESSES: Home—136 East 76th St., New York, N.Y. 10021. *Office*—Department of Romance Languages, Queens College of the City University of New York, 65-30 Kissena Blvd., Flushing, N.Y. 11367.

CAREER: Columbia University, New York City, assistant professor, 1948-64, associate professor of Spanish and Portuguese, 1964-68; City University of New York, Queens College, Flushing, N.Y., and Graduate School and University Center, New York City, professor, 1968-85, distinguished professor of Romance languages and comparative literature, 1985—. Democratic committeeman, New York County, 1956-60. *Military service:* U.S. Army, Office of Strategic Services, 1942-45; became staff sergeant; received Croce al Merito di Guerra (Italy), and special citation from Allied Forces Headquarters, both 1945.

MEMBER: Modern Language Association of America, PEN American Center (member of executive board, 1972-77), American Association of Teachers of Spanish and Portuguese, American Association of University Professors, Latin American Studies Association, American Literature Translators Association, Hispanic Society of America, Renaissance Society of America, Congreso Internacional de Literatura Iberoamerica, Phi Beta Kappa.

AWARDS, HONORS: Fulbright-Hays fellow, Brazil, 1965-66; National Book Award for translation, 1967, for *Hopscotch;* National Book Award nominations for translations, 1971, for *One Hundred Years of Solitude,* and 1977, for *The Autumn of the Patriarch;* American PEN translation prize, 1977, for *The Autumn of the Patriarch;* National Endowment for the Hu-

manities grant, 1980; Alexander Gode Medal, American Translators Association, 1980; Gulbenkian Award, 1981, for translation of *Avalovara;* PEN Medal for Translation, 1982; Litt.D., Dartmouth College, 1982; Professional Staff Congress/City University of New York grant, 1983; New York Governor's Arts Award, 1985; Order of San Carlos, Republic of Colombia, 1985; Guggenheim fellow, 1988-89; Wheatland Prize for Translation, 1988.

WRITINGS:

O Negro na ficcao brasileira (title means "The Negro in Brazilian Fiction"), Tempo Brasileiro, 1965.
(Author of introduction) *The World of Translation,* PEN American Center, 1987.

TRANSLATOR

Julio Cortazar, *Hopscotch,* Pantheon, 1966.
Clarice Lispector, *The Apple in the Dark,* Knopf, 1967, reprinted, University of Texas Press, 1986.
Miguel Asturias, *Mulata,* Delacorte, 1967 (published in England as *The Mulatta and Mr. Fly,* P. Owen, 1967).
Mario Vargas Llosa, *The Green House,* Harper, 1969.
Juan Goytisolo, *Marks of Identity,* Grove, 1969.
Afranio Coutinho, *An Introduction to Literature in Brazil,* Columbia University Press, 1969.
Asturias, *Strong Wind,* Delacorte, 1969.
Manuel Mujica-Lainez, *Bomarzo,* Simon & Schuster, 1969.
Gabriel Garcia Marquez, *One Hundred Years of Solitude,* Harper, 1970.
Asturias, *The Green Pope,* Delacorte, 1971.
Garcia Marquez, *Leaf Storm and Other Stories,* Harper, 1972.
Cortazar, *Sixty-Two: A Model Kit,* Pantheon, 1973.
Dalton Trevisan, *The Vampire of Curitiba,* Knopf, 1973.
Asturias, *The Eyes of the Interred,* Delacorte, 1973.
Jose Lezama Lima, *Paradiso,* Farrar, Straus, 1974.
Vargas Llosa, *Conversation in the Cathedral,* Harper, 1975.
Garcia Marquez, *The Autumn of the Patriarch,* Harper, 1976.
Garcia Marquez, *Innocent Erendira and Other Stories,* Harper, 1978.
Cortazar, *A Manual for Manuel,* Pantheon, 1978.
Demetrio Aguilera-Malta, *Seven Serpents and Seven Moons,* University of Texas Press, 1979.
Garcia Marquez, *In Evil Hour,* Harper, 1979.
Osman Lins, *Avalovara,* Knopf, 1980.

Cortazar, *A Change of Light and Other Stories,* Knopf, 1980.
Luis Rafael Sanchez, *Macho Camacho's Beat,* Pantheon, 1981.
Vinicius de Moraes, *The Girl from Ipanema,* Cross-Cultural Communications, 1982.
Juan Benet, *A Meditation,* Persea Books, 1983.
Cortazar, *We Love Glenda So Much and Other Tales,* Knopf, 1983.
Garcia Marquez, *Chronicle of a Death Foretold,* Knopf, 1983.
Luisa Valenzuela, *The Lizard's Tail,* Farrar, Straus, 1983.
Jorge Amado, *Sea of Death,* Avon, 1984.
Cortazar, *A Certain Lucas,* Knopf, 1984.
(With B. J. Bernstein) Garcia Marquez, *Collected Stories,* Harper, 1984.
Benet, *Return to Region,* Columbia University Press, 1985.
Oswald Franca, Jr., *The Man in the Monkey Suit,* Ballantine, 1986.
Amado, *Captains of the Sands,* Avon, 1988.
Amado, *Showdown,* Bantam, 1988.

Contributor of translations, articles, and reviews to *Playboy, Esquire, Nation, New York Times Book Review, New Yorker, Atlantic, Saturday Review,* and other periodicals, and to professional journals. Associate editor, *Odyssey Review,* 1961-63. Latin American editor, *Kenyon Review,* 1978—.

WORK IN PROGRESS: An anthology of Antonio Vieira; a book on the craft of translation for Yale University Press; a translation of Volodia Teitelboim's *Internal War.*

SIDELIGHTS: Translator of over thirty works, Gregory Rabassa is "a one-man conveyor belt" bringing Latin American fiction to the English speaking world, according to Patrick Breslin in the *Washington Post Book World.* A professor of Romance languages with the City University of New York, Rabassa never had the intention of becoming a professional translator. In the early 1960s, however, Rabassa began translating short fiction as part of his work with *Odyssey Review,* a literary quarterly. Shortly after the magazine folded, Rabassa was contacted about writing an English version of Julio Cortazar's *Hopscotch.* "An editor called me up and we had lunch," Rabassa recalled to Edwin McDowell in *Americas.* "I looked through the novel, liked it and gave her a couple of sample chapters. . . . She chose me, and I went to work on it immediately in my spare time. It took about a year working in spurts, and I've been translating ever since."

Cortazar so approved of Rabassa's manuscript that he recommended his work to Gabriel Garcia Marquez, a Colombian writer. Rabassa's rendition of *One Hundred Years of Solitude,* published in 1970, gained widespread attention in the U.S. for both Garcia Marquez's work and that of other Latin American writers. The work also gained attention for Rabassa when Garcia Marquez, the 1982 Nobel laureate, remarked that he preferred the translation to his own work; "Rabassa's *One Hundred Years of Solitude* improved the original," the author remarked to *Time* contributor R. Z. Sheppard. Rabassa comments, however, that the work lent itself to translation because of its quality: "A very good book in its own language goes over more easily into another language than a book that's not so good," he told Jason Weiss in the *Los Angeles Times.* "Part of the quality of the well-written book is that it's easy to translate."

Rabassa takes a reader's approach to his writing, almost always choosing to work with manuscripts that interest him. His translating methods also reflect this interest; in working with *Hopscotch,* "I read it as I translated it," Rabassa remarked to McDowell. "I do that with many books because it's more fun

that way, and because translation should be the closest possible reading of the book." Although he commented to Weiss that translation is "lazy man's writing," he sees it as creative work in its own right. "One of the great advantages of translation," he told McDowell, "is that your plots and characters are already written, all you have to do is breathe life into them."

BIOGRAPHICAL/CRITICAL SOURCES:

PERIODICALS

Americas, July-August, 1986.
Los Angeles Times, August 12, 1982.
Time, March 7, 1983.
Washington Post Book World, December 19, 1984.

*   *   *

RACHLIN, Harvey (Brant) 1951-

PERSONAL: Born June 23, 1951, in Philadelphia, Pa.; son of Philip (a business broker) and Mazie (Drucker) Rachlin; married Marla Sivak Goldwert, June 28, 1987. *Education:* Hofstra University, B.A., 1973.

ADDRESSES: Home—252 Robby Lane, Manhasset Hills, N.Y. 11040.

CAREER: Western Hemisphere Music Co., Manhasset Hills, N.Y., owner, 1975—. Instructor at Five Towns College, 1978-83; Ellipsis Management Co. (a rock 'n' roll music artists management firm), president, 1984—. Vice-president of Clone Records, 1981—.

MEMBER: American Guild of Composers and Authors, American Society of Composers, Authors and Publishers, Long Island Songwriters Workshop (member of board of directors).

AWARDS, HONORS: The Songwriter's Handbook was selected as one of the New York Public Library's "Books for the Teenage," 1979-85; *The Encyclopedia of the Music Business* was named outstanding reference book of the year by the American Library Association, 1981; *The Money Encyclopedia* was named outstanding reference book of the year by *Library Journal,* 1984.

WRITINGS:

The Songwriter's Handbook, Funk, 1977.
The Encyclopedia of the Music Business, Harper, 1981.
Love Grams: Seventy-five Hilarious Do-It-Yourself Love Letters to Fill In and Send Out, Putnam, 1983.
(Editor) *The Money Encyclopedia,* Harper, 1984.
The Kennedys: A Chronological History, 1823-Present, World Almanac, 1986.
The Songwriter's and Musician's Guide to Making Great Demos, Writers Digest Books, 1988.

Contributor to *Songwriter's Market 1987,* edited by Julie Wesling Whaley. Contributor to magazines, including *High Fidelity* and *Songwriter.*

WORK IN PROGRESS: A book on the movie business for Harmony/Crown.

SIDELIGHTS: Harvey Rachlin's 1977 book, *The Songwriter's Handbook,* was called "the most comprehensive book on the business available to songwriters today," by *High Fidelity's* Susan Elliott. The handbook details every aspect of songwriting, from lyrics and melody composing to copyrights, producing, and recording. Rachlin explains contracts, publishing, and commercial writing to the would-be songwriter as well.

Good Times deemed the book an "unusually useful guide to the music biz." *The Instrumentalist* proclaimed the handbook "straightforward and thorough in its explanations" and added, "the book can be valuable to both amateur and professional songwriters." Rachlin, according to *Sheet Music*, "has made what otherwise could have been a very dry subject, a sparkling and entertaining one." *The Encyclopedia of the Music Business,* Rachlin's 1981 book, was equally well received by critics. The encyclopedia's more than four hundred fifty entries were judged by *Los Angeles Times Book Review* critic Robert Hilburn to constitute "an impressive, extremely comprehensive reference work." Rachlin indicated to *CA* that "following the 1984 Grammy Awards show, Henry Mancini recommended *The Encyclopedia of the Music Business* on behalf of the CBS television network and the Library of Congress."

"After a relatively very short amount of working experience in the music field," Rachlin once told *CA*, "I have written two books that have come to be regarded as standard reference works in the fields of songwriting and music business. Ordinarily, it takes a lifetime of working experience in a field to write even one authoritative reference work on a subject, but I believe my lack of experience gave me a fresh perspective—any and every detail was of interest for me to explore in my writing. I try to take intricate subjects and write everything there is to know about them in extremely simple language.

"I believe the song is the focal point of the music business. While the industry has undergone profound changes through the years, both technologically and creatively, it is my opinion that the general public wants to hear a song that is catchy and has a lyric they can relate to. All the gimmicks, sound effects, and other studio production techniques cannot sell an unattractive song. The music business, which spends millions of dollars annually developing technology, might be better off using that money to hone the talents of its most important creative pioneer, the songwriter.

"As for book writing, I think it can, in one sense, be frustrating, because you know you're not going to finish your work today or tomorrow, next month or even next year. And since it takes a good deal of time to edit and manufacture the book, you may not even see the fruits of your labor for two years. It's hard to put everything you have into something that's so far away; and, if one major thing goes wrong during that wide space of time you may never even see your work come to fruition. You may get sick or get into an accident, someone in your family might die, someone else might come out with a very similar book before yours, your editor might leave the company and the company might lose interest in the work, the company might get sold or go out of business, or it might just cancel the contract for what will inevitably seem a preposterous excuse. Worse yet, your manuscript may be rejected for any of a multitude of reasons. This is a tension, an anxiety all writers have to live with. Writing is a lonely and often depressing profession to begin with, so this added apprehension only compounds the situation. Being fully aware of this makes the process of writing like dreaming because it is that much of a fantasy. The actual end product, if and when you ever see it, is like a dream come true, that you relish and cherish and constantly look at and touch, just to make sure that you're not still living in that dream.

"People often write differently from the way they talk. This holds true even for many professional writers. Their written vocabulary often consists of colorful, intricate words while their speech comprises simplicity. The immediate reasons for this are that the writer gives more thought to his choice of words and has more time to select such colorful vocabulary; speaking is spontaneous and immediate. It leaves no or little time for the talker to search his mind for ten-dollar words.

"I submit, however, that many polished writers go into a state of semi-consciousness when working at their trade or this practice. The writer's mind goes 'soft' and may be likened to a 'grab-bag'—a vessel containing a large assortment of words from which he can draw. Often words will come to him that he could not consciously define with accuracy but he knows they are appropriate for a certain situation or they fit the context in which he needs a word and thinks it could be used. This is because his senses and faculties are in a subconscious state, where the mind is a reservoir waiting to be tapped."

Rachlin recently wrote: "At thirty-five years of age I am completing my seventh book. The past ten years of writing have been intense and from my experience, albeit limited, I would like to offer the following observations. Why do I write? There are many reasons. One is that it is a passport—a passport to opportunity, respect, and recognition. I don't want to be an undistinguished grain of sand on the beach of humanity. Some of my most creative ideas come to me in the period when I get into bed and fall asleep. This is a creatively fruitful period for me, in a work sense. Everytime the going gets rough or I am overly excited about a project or take myself too seriously, I try to put life in perspective: I'm just a dot on a dot. That is, I'm just a single organism on a planet that is a speck in the universe.

"As a nonfiction writer, I've sometimes written books on subjects I've known little about. I believe the vantage point of having little knowledge on a subject allows or forces me to be completely unassuming and to present explanations that are extremely basic and lucid. When I understand a complex subject, I can explain it in a way that almost anyone can grasp. Writing is much safer than speaking. You can't stutter with the written word. What worries me about publishing is that you're entrusting your work, indeed, a meaningful portion of your life to a bunch of people who aren't even smart enough to do what you're doing! With every book I write there's always a few months of sheer misery. This is brought on by the necessity to hibernate in a world unto myself, whereby I will not go outside, inhale fresh air, see the sun or the blue sky or the green grass, or walk on the concrete of a street. With every book I usually wear through a pair of pants and a sweatshirt. The holes come at the knees and the elbows.

"My favorite word in the English language is a mere two letters but represents the fruition of tremendous imagination, thought, physical labor, emotional stress, concern, diligence, spiritual immersion, indeed, obsession: 'by'."

BIOGRAPHICAL/CRITICAL SOURCES:

PERIODICALS

American Reference Book Annual, 1982, 1985.
ASCAP in Action, winter, 1982.
Booklist, January 1, 1982, November, 1984.
Choice, November, 1984.
Fayetteville Observer-Times, June 10, 1984.
Good Times, November 29-December 7, 1977.
High Fidelity, March, 1978.
Instrumentalist, December, 1977.
Library Journal, January 1, 1982, May 15, 1982, April 15, 1984, April 15, 1985.
Los Angeles Herald Examiner, June 24, 1984.

Los Angeles Times Book Review, December 20, 1981, July 29, 1984.
Mirror (Gilmer, Texas), August 15, 1984.
Money, October, 1984.
Monitor (McAllen, Texas), September 16, 1984.
Musical Merchandise Review, January, 1978.
Nashville Banner, October 15, 1977.
New York Daily News, December 21, 1987.
New York Times, May 30, 1982.
On Music and Media, August, 1982.
Performance, July 16, 1982.
Popular Music and Society, Volume VIII, 1982.
Rocking Chair, February, 1978, February, 1982.
RQ, spring, 1982.
Sheet Music, February, 1978.
Stereo Review, March, 1978.
Variety, February 1, 1978.

*   *   *

RADZINOWICZ, Leon 1906-

PERSONAL: Born August 15, 1906, in Lodz, Poland; naturalized British subject, 1947; son of David (a physician) and Maria (Braude) Radzinowicz; married third wife, Isolde (Doernenburg) Klarmann, 1979; children: (second marriage) Ann Stacy, Willam Francis Henry. *Education:* University of Paris, LL.D., 1925; University of Geneva, LL.D., 1927; University of Rome, LL.D. (cum laude), 1928, and recipient of diploma from Criminological Institute; University of Cracow, LL.D., 1929; Cambridge University, M.A., 1949, LL.D., 1951.

ADDRESSES: Home—Rittenhouse Claridge, No. 2416, Rittenhouse Square, Philadelphia, Pa. 19103. *Office*—Trinity College, Cambridge CB2 1TQ, England.

CAREER: University of Geneva, Geneva, Switzerland, assistant professor, 1929-31; Free University of Warsaw, Warsaw, Poland, 1932-36; went to England in 1936 on behalf of the Polish Ministry of Justice to report on the English penal system; Cambridge University, Cambridge, England, helped establish criminological studies, beginning 1937, assistant director of research, 1946-49, director of department of criminal science, 1949-59, first Wolfson Professor of Criminology, 1959-73, founder and first director of Institute of Criminology, 1960-73.

Fellow of Trinity College, Cambridge, 1948—; Yale University, Yale Law School, Walter E. Meyer Visiting Professor, 1962-63, Silliman College, associate fellow, 1966—; Lionel Cohen Lecturer, Jerusalem University, 1963; Columbia Law School, Carpentier Lecturer, 1965, adjunct professor of law and criminology, 1966-77; distinguished visiting professor, Rutgers University, 1968-72, 1979-81; visiting professor, University of Virginia Law School, 1968-69, 1970-74; visiting fellow, Princeton Institute of Advanced Studies and Rockefeller Foundation Center at Belagio, 1975; Law Alumni Chair for Distinguished Professors, University of Minnesota Law School, 1977; distinguished visiting professor of criminology, Wichita State University, 1977, 1980; distinguished visiting professor, Pennsylvania State University, 1977, 1979, 1981; distinguished visiting professor of law, Benjamin N. Cardozo Law School, Yeshiva University, New York, 1978-79; distinguished visiting professor of criminal justice, John Jay College of Criminal Justice, City University of New York, 1978-79; overseer of the University of Pennsylvania Law School and associate trustee of the University, 1979-84; visiting lecturer,

Criminological Center, Toronto University, 1982; visiting lecturer at numerous universities in Europe and South America.

Member of the Royal Commission on Capital Punishment, 1949-68; Home Office Advisory Council on the Treatment of Offenders, member, 1950-68, chairman of subcommittee on maximum security in prisons, 1967-68; member of the Royal Commission on the Penal System in England and Wales, 1964-66. Head of the social defense section of the United Nations, 1947; joint vice-president of the Second United Nations International Congress on Crime, 1955, general rapporteur of the Fourth United Nations Congress on Crime, 1970, and honorary vice-chairman of the Fifth United Nations Congress on Crime, 1975; first chairman of the Criminological Council of the Council of Europe, 1963-70; rapporteur on penal systems at International Mental Association Congress, Vancouver, British Columbia, 1968.

Consultant, Bar Association of the City of New York, 1965, Ford Foundation on the promotion of criminological research and teaching, 1965, President Johnson's Commission of the Causes and Prevention of Violence, 1968-69, Ministry of Justice of New South Wales, Australia, 1973, National Institute of Criminology, Canberra, Australia, 1973, and United States Law Enforcement Assistance Administration, 1976-77.

MEMBER: British Academy of Forensic Sciences (fellow; first president, 1960-61), Australian Academy of Forensic Sciences (honorary foreign member), American Academy of Forensic Sciences (honorary foreign member), American Academy of Arts and Sciences (honorary foreign member), American Law Institute (honorary foreign member).

AWARDS, HONORS: Chevalier de l'Ordre de Leopold of Belgium, 1930; James Barr Ames Prize and medal of the Harvard Law School, 1950, for *History of English Criminal Law and Its Administration from 1750*, Volume I: *The Movement for Reform*; Coronation Medal, 1953; LL.D., University of Leicester, 1965; honorary fellow, Police College at Bramshill, 1968; knighted by Queen Elizabeth II, 1970; Bruce Smith, Sr., Award, 1976, for outstanding contributions to criminal justice science in the United States; Sellin-Glueck Award, American Society of Criminology, 1976; Joseph L. Andrews Award, American Association of Law Libraries.

WRITINGS:

(Editor with J.W.C. Turner, and contributor) *The Modern Approach to Criminal Law*, Macmillan, 1945.
A History of English Criminal Law and Its Administration From 1750, Stevens, Volume I: *The Movement for Reform*, 1948, Volume II: *The Clash Between Private Initiative and Public Interest in the Enforcement of the Law*, 1956, Volume III: *Cross-Currents in the Movement for the Reform of the Police*, 1956, Volume IV: *Grappling for Control*, 1968, Volume V: (with Roger Hood) *The Emergence of Penal Policy*, 1986.
(Contributor) *Studi in memoria de Arturo Rocco*, Juffre, 1952.
Sir James Fitzjames Stephen, 1828-1894, and His Contribution to the Development of Criminal Law, Quaritch, 1957.
(Editor with Marc Ancel) *Introduction au droit criminel de l'Angleterre*, Editions de l'Epargne, 1959.
In Search of Criminology, Heinemann, 1961, Harvard University Press, 1962.
(Author of introduction) Sidney Webb and Beatrice Webb, *English Prisons Under Local Government*, Cass, 1963.
(Contributor) *Estratto dagli atti del Convegno Internazionale su Cesare Beccarie*, Vincenzo Bona, 1964.

Criminology and the Climate of Social Responsibility, Heffer, 1964.

The Need for Criminology, Heinemann, 1965.

Ideology and Crime, Columbia University Press, 1966.

(Contributor) Marvin E. Wolfgang, editor, *Crime and Culture: Essays in Honor of Thorsten Sellin*, Wiley, 1968.

(Compiler) *Crime, Violence, and Disorder: An Election Issue*, [Charlottesville, Va.], 1968.

(Contributor) J. P. Buhl and other editors, *Liber Amicorum in Honour of Professor Stephen Hurwitz, LL.D.*, Juristforbundets Forlag, 1971.

(Editor with Wolfgang) *Crime and Justice*, Volume I: *The Criminal and Society*, Volume II: *The Criminal in the Arms of the Law*, Volume III: *The Criminal in Confinement*, Basic Books, 1971, revised edition, 1977.

(With Hood) *Criminology and the Administration of Criminal Justice: A Bibliography*, Mansell, 1976.

(With Joan F. S. King) *The Growth of Crime: The International Experience*, Basic Books, 1977.

Co-editor of "English Studies in Criminal Science," Macmillan; editor of "Cambridge Studies in Criminology," fifty-two volumes, Macmillan, Heinemann. Contributor of articles to law and social science journals, newspapers, and other periodicals.

WORK IN PROGRESS: Cambridge Institute of Criminology: Background and Scope.

SIDELIGHTS: One of the world's most distinguished criminologists, Leon Radzinowicz has long emphasized the interdependence of all aspects of the study of crime: the legal, sociological, psychiatric, and biological, as well as questions of enforcement and penal policy. He is particularly concerned about criminology's role in the analysis of public policy, noting in his book *In Search of Criminology* that "to rob it of this practical function is to divorce criminology from reality and render it sterile." In seeking to realize his conception of the role of criminology, Radzinowicz has been active in public life as well as in academic affairs, lending his expertise to governments and international bodies such as the United Nations and the Council of Europe. He was the first director of the Institute of Criminology at Cambridge University, where his leadership helped to establish criminology as an academic discipline in England and elsewhere.

Radzinowicz developed his interdisciplinary approach to criminal science early, taking four doctorates by the age of twenty-three, studying sociology, political theory, and history as well as law and criminology. Under the influence of Enrico Ferri of the University of Rome, Radzinowicz became a proponent of the positivist school of criminology, which stressed both economic inequality and innate personality as causes of crime and advocated indeterminate sentences and other then-innovative approaches to punishment and rehabilitation.

During the 1930s, Radzinowicz traveled widely in Europe, studying the penal systems of several countries. Because of what he observed, he became less doctrinaire in his positivism, stressing an empirical, historical attitude toward the study of crime rather than an ideological one. When he traveled to England in 1936, he was impressed with the "humane and rational" character of the English prison system, which was then having considerable success with a liberal, reformative approach that stressed probation and aftercare rather than confinement for most offenders. Radzinowicz endorsed the principle that imprisonment is to be avoided, except for violent and dangerous criminals. This is a belief to which he still

adheres: "The best prison reform is to send as few people there as possible," he told *People* magazine in 1979.

When World War II broke out, Radzinowicz remained in England, living in Cambridge and pursuing his research and writing. After the war, he joined the faculty of Cambridge University and began his major work, *A History of English Criminal Law and Its Administration From 1750*. This five-volume work is the first to explore its subject in such a comprehensive manner, drawing on vast, untapped archives of British government records. The first volume, which focuses on the role of capital punishment, "compels a kind of awed admiration," writes Norman Birkett in *Spectator*. The subsequent two volumes examine the development of government's role in peacekeeping and law enforcement and the ideas of various reformers. R. A. Eastwood, in the *Manchester Guardian*, called the work "exceptionally good. It is readable and based on prodigious and expert research."

The merit of Radzinowicz's *History*, according to a *Times Literary Supplement* critic, is not that "of scale and comprehensiveness alone. [It has an] originality in the conception of a study of the Criminal Law (and of its enforcement) within its total social situation." The same critic says of the fourth volume that although it "does not meet the exceptional standards that Profesor Radzinowicz has set himself . . . the volume is competent enough: with its excellent indexes and bibliography it is a valuable piece of scholarly machinery." Volume Five continues Radzinowicz's thorough investigation of penal policy; it is "administrative history at its best," comments Phillip Thurmond Smith in the *American Historical Review*. "Like the previous volumes, it is fascinating and well written and of course uniquely comprehensive."

Radzinowicz's views have evolved considerably since he entered the field; he is less optimistic than he once was about the effectiveness of criminology in preventing crime. He wrote in 1961's *In Search of Criminology* that crime is an integral part of society, not a narrow problem to be solved by the application of scientific expertise, and suggested that criminology's role should be to provide "descriptive analytic accounts . . . of all the matters which come within the orbit of penal policy and penology." He noted further that "public morality, social expediency," and "the subtle but vital balance between the rights of the individual and the protection of the community" are as important in formulating policy as are the findings of scientists. Radzinowicz attributes the worldwide increase in crime in recent years to several factors, including increased availability of goods and the breakdown of such institutions as religion and the family, but he has expressed skepticism about the value of searching for the ultimate causes of crime. Nor does he believe that harsher punishments are likely to prove an effective solution: he is opposed to capital punishment.

BIOGRAPHICAL/CRITICAL SOURCES:

BOOKS

Hood, Roger, editor, *Crime, Criminology, and Public Policy: Essays in Honor of Sir Leon Radzinowicz*, Free Press, 1975.

Radzinowicz, Leon, *In Search of Criminology*, Heinemann, 1961, Harvard University Press, 1962.

PERIODICALS

American Historical Review, June, 1987.

Manchester Guardian, March 1, 1957.

New Statesman, July 8, 1966.
People, March 12, 1979.
Spectator, January 7, 1949.
Times Literary Supplement, November 10, 1961, April 24, 1969.

*   *   *

RAKEL, Robert E(dwin)   1932-

PERSONAL: Born July 13, 1932, in Cincinnati, Ohio; son of Edwin J. (a laundry driver) and Elsie (a secretary; maiden name, Machino) Rakel; married Peggy A. Klare; children: Barbara, Cindy Zajicek, Linda, David. *Education:* University of Cincinnati, B.S., 1954, M.D., 1958. *Politics:* Independent. *Religion:* Roman Catholic.

ADDRESSES: Home—2420 Underwood, Houston, Texas 77030. *Office*—Family Practice Center, 5510 Greenbriar, Houston, Texas 77005.

CAREER: St. Mary's Hospital, Cincinnati, Ohio, intern, 1958-59; U.S. Public Health Service Hospital, Seattle, Wash., resident in internal medicine, 1959-61; Monterey County Hospital, Salinas, Calif., resident in general practice, 1961-62; private practice of medicine in Newport Beach, Calif., 1962-69; University of California, Irvine, assistant professor, 1969-71, associate professor of family practice, 1971, chairman of family practice program, 1969-71; University of Iowa, Iowa City, professor of family practice and head of department, 1971-85; Baylor College of Medicine, Houston, Texas, associate dean for academic and clinical affairs, Richard M. Kleberg, Sr., professor, and chairman of department of family medicine, 1985—. First Angus Memorial Lecturer, University of Toronto, 1984. Chairman of department of general practice at Orange County Medical Center, 1968-71; member of executive committee at Hoag Memorial Hospital, 1967-70, director of family practice residency program, 1969-71; member of medical staff of Mercy Hospital, Iowa City, 1971-85; chief of family practice service, St. Luke's Episcopal Hospital, Houston, Texas, 1985—. Member of advisory council of Patient Care Systems, 1970-76; member of organizing board of directors of Costa Mesa Memorial Hospital, 1968-69; member of board of trustees, New Age Hospice of Houston, Inc., 1986—; member of board of trustees, Institute of Religion, Texas Medical Center, Houston, 1986—. People to People Family Practice Delegation leader, Peoples Republic of China, 1983. Consultant to Bureau of Health Manpower, Department of Health and Human Services, National Heart, Lung and Blood Institute, and Health Learning Systems, Inc.

MEMBER: World Organization of National Colleges, Academies, and Academic Associations of General Practice, American Board of Family Practice (charter diplomate; member of board of directors, 1973-79; vice-president, 1977-79; chairman of research and development committee, 1971-79, and examination committee, 1974-79), American Board of Medical Specialties (member of specialty evaluation committee, 1978-81), American Medical Association (member of governing council of section on medical schools, 1986—), Texas Medical Association, Society of Teachers of Family Medicine (member of board of directors, 1971-79), Council of Academic Societies, National Board of Medical Examiners (member of board of directors, 1975-79), Association of American Medical Colleges, American Academy of Family Physicians (fellow; president of Orange County California Chapter, 1969; member of board of directors of California Academy of Family Physicians, 1970-72), History of Medi-

cine Society (founder and chairman at University of Iowa, 1978-85, and at Baylor College of Medicine, 1986—), American Osler Society, Cosmos Club.

AWARDS, HONORS: Mead-Johnson scholarship from American Academy of Family Physicians, 1971; Thomas W. Johnson Award from American Academy of Family Physicians, 1973, for outstanding contribution to family practice and education; Wade and Harold Mack Chair in Family Medicine from Ogden Surgical Society, 1983.

WRITINGS:

(Editor) *Selected References in Family Medicine,* Society of Teachers of Family Medicine, 1973.
(Editor with H. F. Conn and T. W. Johnson) *Family Practice* (textbook), Saunders, 1973, 2nd edition (editor with Conn), 1978, 3rd edition (sole editor), 1984.
(Author of foreword) R. J. Cadoret and L. J. King, *Psychiatry in Primary Care,* Mosby, 1974.
(Contributor) I. M. Smith, S. T. Donta, and Sergio Rabinovich, editors, *Antibiotics and Infection,* Spectrum, 1974.
Principles of Family Medicine (textbook), Saunders, 1977.
(Editor) *Year Book of Family Practice,* Year Book Medical Publishers, 1977-87.
(Author of foreword) Adrian E. Flatt, *The Care of Minor Hand Injuries,* 4th edition (Rakel was not associated with earlier editions), Mosby, 1979.
(Author of foreword) L. R. Mercier and F. J. Pettid, *Practical Orthopedics,* Year Book Medical Publishers, 1980.
(Contributor) J. S. Lloyd and D. G. Langsley, editors, *Evaluating the Skills of Medical Specialists,* American Board of Specialties, 1983.
(Editor) *Conn's Current Therapy,* Saunders, 1984-88.
(Contributor) M. Kaufman, S. Galishoff, and T. L. Savitt, editors, *Dictionary of American Medical Biography,* Volumes I and II, Greenwood Press, 1984.
(Author of foreword) R. G. Feldman, *Neurology for the Everyday Practice of Medicine,* Thieme-Stratton, 1984.

FILMS

"The Office Record: Making It Work for Your Practice," released by Network for Continuing Medical Education and Sleep Center at Pennsylvania State University, 1979.
"Disturbed Sleep: Five Case Problems," released by Network for Continuing Medical Education, 1980.

OTHER

Also editor and coordinator of Volume 18 of series "Procedures for Your Practice Patient Care." Contributor to *Encyclopaedia Britannica.* Contributor of articles and reviews to journals. Associate editor of *Female Patient,* 1978—, associate editor-in-chief, 1981-85; associate editor of *Emergency Department News,* 1979-81. Member of editorial board of *Update International,* 1973-74; *Continuing Education for the Family Physician,* 1974—, *Infectious Disease,* 1978—, *Primary Cardiology,* 1978—, *Archives of Internal Medicine,* 1979—, *Journal of Clinical Psychopharmacology,* 1980—, *Consultant,* 1981—, and *Journal of the American Medical Association,* 1982—.

WORK IN PROGRESS: Research on patient satisfaction and compliance; 4th edition of *Family Practice.*

SIDELIGHTS: Robert E. Rakel told *CA:* "As a bibliophile since youth, I welcomed the opportunity to become involved in editing medical texts after ten years in practice, followed by three years in teaching. In the past nine years I have edited nine books and written one textbook. Although the written text still excites me, I enjoy writing most because it is a stimulus to learn.''

*   *   *

RAMAZANI, Rouhollah K(aregar) 1928-

PERSONAL: Born March 21, 1928, in Tehran, Iran; came to United States in 1952, naturalized U.S. citizen in 1961; son of Ali K. (an architect) and Azam (Sultani) Ramazani; married Nesta Shahrokh, February 22, 1952; children: Vaheed, David, Jahan, Sima. *Education:* University of Tehran, LL.M., 1951; University of Georgia, additional study, 1952; University of Virginia, S.J.D., 1954.

ADDRESSES: Office—232 Cabell Hall, University of Virginia, Charlottesville, Va. 22903.

CAREER: University of Virginia, Charlottesville, lecturer in foreign affairs, 1954-57, research associate, Soviet Foreign Relations Economic Project, 1956-59, assistant professor of foreign affairs, 1957-60, associate professor, 1960-64, professor, 1964-72, Edward R. Stettinius, Jr., Professor of Government and Foreign Affairs, 1972—, Woodrow Wilson Department of Government and Foreign Affairs, acting chariman, 1976, chairman, 1977-82. Aga Khan Visiting Professor of Islamic Studies, American University of Beirut, 1967-68; visiting professor of Middle East studies at School of Advanced International Studies, Johns Hopkins University, 1967, 1970-71, 1972-73, 1975, 1977, and Kings College, Cambridge University, spring, 1975. Former vice-president and trustee, Ameican Institute of Iranian Studies. Member of executive committee, Council on Foreign Relations, 1965-67. Appeared as a featured guest on ''Meet the Press,'' NBC-TV, December 16, 1979. Consultant to Rockefeller Foundation, Institute of Foreign Policy Analysis, Pan America International Oil Co., Research Analysis Corp., U.S. Departments of State and Defense, White House, United Nations Secretariat, American Institutes for Research, and Energy Policy Studies Center.

MEMBER: Shaybani Society of International Law (executive officer), American Political Science Association, American Society of International Law, Middle East Institute, British Institute of International and Comparative Law, Southern Political Science Association, Phi Beta Kappa, Raven Society.

AWARDS, HONORS: Recipient of grants from Old Dominion Foundation Fund, 1961, Social Science Research Council, 1967, Fulbright Research Program, 1968, Washington Center for Foreign Policy Research, School of Advanced International Studies, Johns Hopkins University, 1979-80, and Energy Policy Studies Center, University of Virginia, 1979-82; American Association for Middle East Studies prize, 1964, for manuscript of *The Foreign Policy of Iran, 1500-1941: A Developing Nation in World Affairs;* Distinguished Professor Award, University of Virginia, 1974.

WRITINGS:

The Middle East and the European Common Market, University Press of Virginia, 1964.
The Foreign Policy of Iran, 1500-1941: A Developing Nation in World Affairs, University of Virginia Press, 1966.
The Northern Tier: Afghanistan, Iran and Turkey, Van Nostrand, 1966.
The Persian Gulf: Iran's Role, University Press of Virginia, 1972.

Iran's Foreign Policy, 1941-73: A Study of Foreign Policy in Modernizing Nations, University Press of Virginia, 1975.
Beyond the Arab-Israeli Settlement: New Directions for U.S. Policy in the Middle East (monograph), Institute of Foreign Policy Analysis, 1977.
The Persian Gulf and the Strait of Hormuz, Sijthoff & Noordhoff International, 1979.
The United States and Iran: The Patterns of Influence, Praeger, 1982.
Security of Access to Persian Gulf Oil Supplies in the 1980s, The Energy Policy Studies Center, University of Virginia, 1982.
Revolutionary Iran: Challenge and Response in the Middle East, Johns Hopkins Univesity Press, 1986, paperback edition published with new epilogue, 1988.
(With Joseph A. Kechichian) *The Gulf Cooperation Council: Record and Analysis,* University Press of Virginia, 1988.

CONTRIBUTOR

Thomas T. Hammond, editor, *Soviet Foreign Relations and World Communism,* Princeton University Press, 1965.
Albert Lepawsky, Edward H. Buehrig, and Harold D. Laswell, editors, *The Search for World Security: Studies by Students and Colleagues of Quincy Wright,* Appleton-Century-Crofts, 1971.
Mehdi Heravi, editor, *Concise Encyclopaedia of the Middle East,* Public Affairs Press, 1973.
Hammond, editor, *The Anatomy of Communist Takeovers,* Yale University Press, 1975.
Iran: Past Present and Future, Aspen Institute for Humanistic Studies, 1975.
Mason Willrich, editor, *Energy and World Politics,* Free Press, 1975.
Colin Legum and Haim Shaked, editors, *The Middle East Contemporary Survey,* Holmes & Meier, Volume I, 1976-77, Volume II, 1977-78.
Environments for U.S. Naval Strategy in the Pacific-Indian Ocean Area, 1985-1995, Institute for Foreign Policy Analysis, 1977.
Itamar Rabinovich and Shaked, editors, *From June to October: The Middle East between 1967 and 1973,* Transaction Books, 1978.
Abbas Amirie and Hamilton A. Twitchell, editors, *Iran in the 1980s,* Institute for Political and Economic Studies (Tehran), 1978.
Robert Freedman, editor, *World Politics and the Arab-Israeli Conflicts,* Pergamon, 1979.
Z. Michael Zsaz, project director, *The Impact of the Iranian Events upon Persian Gulf and United States Security,* American Foreign Policy Institute, 1979.
The Revolution in Iran: Its Character and Political-Economic Implications, Joint Economic Committee of the United States Congress, 1980.
(With James P. Piscatori) Werne J. Feld and Gavin Boyd, editors, *Comparative Regional Systems,* Pergamon, 1980.
Waris Shere, editor, *In Search of Peace,* Exposition Press, 1980.
George S. Wise and Charles Issawi, editors, *Middle East Perspectives: The Next Twenty Years,* Darwin Press, 1981.
Larry W. Bowman and Ian Clark, editors, *The Indian Ocean and Global Politics,* Westview Press, 1981.
Robert D. Steele, editor, *The Iran Crisis and International Law: Proceedings of the John Bassett Moore Society of International Law,* University of Virginia School of Law, 1981.

Phillip H. Stoddard, David G. Cuthell, and Margaret W. Sullivan, editors, *Change and the Muslim World*, Syracuse University Press, 1981.

Enver M. Khoury and Charles G. MacDonald, editors, *The Revolution in Iran: A Reappraisal*, Institute of Middle Eastern and North African Affairs, 1982.

James Finn, editor, *Global Economics and Religion*, Transaction Books, 1983.

Adeed Dawisha, editor, *Islam in Foreign Policy*, Cambridge University Press, 1983.

Shere, editor, *Arm, Disarm for Peace: The Nuclear Threat and East-West Relations*, Hyperion Press, 1984.

(Author of foreword) Majid Khadduri, *The Islamic Conception of Justice*, Johns Hopkins University Press, 1984.

Hafeez Malik, editor, *International Security in Southwest Asia*, Praeger, 1984.

William L. Dowdy and Russell B. Trood, editors, *The Indian Ocean: Perspectives on a Strategic Arena*, Duke University Press, 1986.

Juan R. I. Cole and Nikki R. Keddie, editors, *Shi'ism and Social Protest*, Yale University Press, 1986.

Robert O. Freedman, editor, *The Middle East After the Israeli Invasion of Lebanon*, Syracuse University Press, 1986.

Richard F. Staar, editor, *1987 Yearbook on International Communist Affairs*, Hoover Institution, 1988.

OTHER

Contributor of numerous articles to journals, including *Middle East Journal, Foreign Affairs, Foreign Policy, International Affairs* (London), *Current History*, and *American Behavioral Scientist*.

SIDELIGHTS: Born in Iran and a resident there until 1952, Rouhollah K. Ramazani was personally affected by the Iranian revolution when a close relative was executed by the Khomeini regime. Ramazani brings this native's awareness to his book *Revolutionary Iran: Challenge and Response in the Middle East;* it is written "with intimacy and knowledge and a measure of sympathy," comments Fouad Ajami in *Washington Post Book World*. Ramazani's "ambitious and thorough book is about the consequences of the Iranian revolution for Iran's neighbors . . . [and] the mix of cunning and ferocity that has characterized the conduct of the Iranian state in foreign affairs since the clerics smashed the old order in 1979." Ajami praises Ramazani's book as "judicious and excellent . . . it sifts through the record of Iran's revolutionaries, and we are able to see both the passion, and then, the method and caution of Iran's clerical rulers."

Edward Mortimer, writing for the *New York Times Book Review*, presents a different assessment of Ramazani's work. He finds that "at its worst it suffers from . . . an unwillingness to accept that there are some situations that America *cannot* make any better." The critic remarks, however, that "at its best it is quite persuasive . . . [with] plenty of evidence." In the *New York Review of Books* Shaul Bakhash praises Ramazani's handling of his topic, declaring that he writes "with sparking clarity on a difficult subject, and with both passion and objectivity on an issue which, for both Iranians and Americans, is still laden with much emotional baggage. The book went to press before revelations of American arms transfers to Iran . . . but it provides the perspective from which one can make better sense of recent developments."

Ramazani told *CA:* "I write to improve the quality of my teaching, to promote understanding of the Middle East, and because I enjoy it."

BIOGRAPHICAL/CRITICAL SOURCES:

PERIODICALS

Los Angeles Times Book Review, January 31, 1988.
New York Review of Books, January 15, 1987.
New York Times Book Review, December 28, 1986.
Washington Post Book World, February 8, 1987.

*   *   *

RAWLYK, George Alexander 1935-

PERSONAL: Born May 19, 1935, in Thorold, Ontario, Canada; son of Samuel and Mary (Kautesk) Rawlyk; married, August 18, 1959; children: two. *Education:* McMaster University, B.A., 1957; University of Rochester, M.A., 1962, Ph.D., 1966.

ADDRESSES: Office—Department of History, Queen's University, Kingston, Ontario, Canada K7L 3N6.

CAREER: Mount Allison University, Sackville, New Brunswick, Canada, lecturer in history, 1959-61; Dalhousie University, Halifax, Nova Scotia, Canada, assistant professor of history, 1963-66; Queen's University, Kingston, Ontario, Canada, associate professor, 1966-69, professor of history, 1969—. W. P. Bell Professor, Mount Allison University, 1987-88. Scholar in residence, Harvard University, 1982-83 and 1985-86. Researcher for Royal Commission on Bilingualism and Biculturalism, 1965-67.

MEMBER: Canadian Historical Association, Canadian Political Science Association, Organization of Canadian Historians, American Historical Association, Champlain Society.

AWARDS, HONORS: Canada Council fellowship, 1967, senior fellowships, 1971-72, 1981-82.

WRITINGS:

(Editor and author of introduction) *Historical Essays on the Atlantic Provinces*, McClelland & Stewart, 1967.

(Editor) *Joseph Howe: Opportunist? Man of Vision? Frustrated Politician?*, Copp Clark, 1967.

Yankees at Louisbourg, University of Maine Press, 1967.

Revolution Rejected, 1775-1776, Prentice-Hall, 1968.

(With Ruth Hafter) *Acadian Education in Nova Scotia: An Historical Survey to 1965*, Information Canada, 1970.

(Contributor) *Colonists and Canadians*, Macmillan, 1971.

(Contributor) *Essays on the Left*, McClelland & Stewart, 1971.

(With Gordon Stewart) *A People Highly Favored of God*, Archon Books, 1972.

Nova Scotia's Massachusetts: A Study of Massachusetts-Nova Scotia Relations, 1630-1784, McGill-Queen's University Press, 1973.

(Editor) *The Atlantic Provinces and the Problems of Confederation*, Breakwater Press, 1979.

(With Bruce W. Hodgins and Richard P. Bowles) *Regionalism in Canada: Flexible Federalism or Fractured Nation?*, Prentice-Hall, 1979.

Streets of Gold, Peter Martin Associates, 1981.

(With Kevin Quinn) *The Redeemed of the Lord Say So*, QTC (Kingston, Ontario, Canada), 1981.

(With M. A. Downie) *Acadian pour de bon* (title means "A Proper Acadian"), Kids Can Press, 1982.

The New Light Letters and Spiritual Songs, Hantsport, 1983.

Ravished By the Spirit, McGill-Queen's University Press, 1984.

Henry Alline, Paulist Press, 1987.

(Editor) *Canadian Baptists and Christian Higher Education,* McGill-Queen's University Press, 1988.

Contributor to magazines, including *Queen's Quarterly.*

SIDELIGHTS: George Alexander Rawlyk once told *CA:* "I am now particularly interested in the ways in which Evangelical religion influences English-Canadian culture, especially during the period 1776 to 1843."

*   *   *

RAY, N(ancy) L(ouise) 1918-
(Nan Hunt)

PERSONAL: Born September 16, 1918, in Bathurst, New South Wales, Australia; daughter of Edwin (an orchardist) and Katie (a stenographer; maiden name, Hazlewood) Ray; married Walter Gibbs Hunt (a grazier), November 18, 1967 (died December 8, 1975); children: three (stepchildren). *Education:* Educated in Australia. *Religion:* Christian.

ADDRESSES: *Home and office*—219 Peel St., Bathurst, New South Wales 2795, Australia. *Agent*—A. B. Ingram, 4/6 Boronia St., Wollstonecraft, New South Wales 2065, Australia.

CAREER: Western Stores & Edgleys Ltd., Bathurst, New South Wales, Australia, stenographer, 1935-43; Aeronautical Supply Co. Pty. Ltd., Mascot, Australia, secretary, 1947-48; Briginshow Brothers Pty Ltd., Milsons Point, Australia, secretary, 1948-50; Bowes & Craig (chartered accountants), Sydney, Australia, secretary, 1950-67; writer. *Military service:* Women's Australian Auxiliary Air Force, 1943-46; became sergeant.

MEMBER: Australian Society of Authors, Children's Book Council of Australia.

AWARDS, HONORS: Premier's Literary Award for best children's book from the state of New South Wales, 1982, for *Whistle Up the Chimney,* and 1987, for *A Rabbit Named Harris.*

WRITINGS:

JUVENILE NOVELS

Roma Mercedes and Fred, Collins (Sydney, Australia), 1978.
The Everywhere Dog, Collins, 1978.
The Pow Toe, Collins, 1979.
There Was This Man Running, Collins, 1979, Macmillan, 1981.
Nightmare to Nowhere, Collins, 1980.

JUVENILE PICTURE BOOKS; UNDER PSEUDONYM NAN HUNT

Whistle Up the Chimney, illustrations by Craig Smith, Collins, 1981.
An Eye Full of Soot and an Ear Full of Steam, illustrations by Smith, Collins, 1983.
Wild and Woolly, illustrations by Noela Hills, Lothian, 1983.
Rain, Hail, or Shine, illustrations by Smith, Collins, 1984.
When Ollie Spat on the Ball, illustrations by Mark David, Collins, 1985.
Prisoner of the Mulligrubs, illustrations by Hills, Collins, 1985.
The Junk Eaters, illustrations by Peter Viska, Macmillan, 1987.
A Rabbit Named Harris, illustrations by Bettina Ogden, Collins, 1987.
The Show, illustrations by Ogden, Collins, 1988.
We Got Wheels, Man and Other Things, illustrations by David, Collins, 1988.

CONTRIBUTOR TO ANTHOLOGIES

Beneath the Sun, edited by Patricia Wrightson, Collins, 1972.

Too True, compiled by Anne Bower Ingram, Collins, 1974.
Emu Stew, edited by Wrightson, Kestrel Books, 1976.
The Pickled Boeing, edited by Ingram, Children's Medical Research Foundation, 1982.
Someone Is Flying Balloons, compiled by Jill Heylen and Cleia Jellett, Omnibus Press, 1983.
The All-Australian Ha-ha Book, Oxford University Press, 1983.
The All-Australian Ho-ho Book, Oxford University Press, 1983.
Incredible Book of Almost Everything, edited by Roland Harvey, Five Mile Press, 1984.
Writing and Illustrating for Children, edited by Eleanor Stodart, Children's Book Council of the A.C.T., 1985.
A Teddy Bear's Picnic, Oxford University Press, 1986.
Vile Verse, compiled by Jane Covernton, Omnibus Press, 1988.
After Dark, edited by Penny Matthews, Omnibus Press, 1988.

WORK IN PROGRESS: Juvenile novel, *A Nice Pair of Legs.*

SIDELIGHTS: N. L. Ray told *CA:* "I try to give children 'a good read' with dashes of humor. I make no apology for trying to stretch their imaginations, challenge them with the feelings and limitations of adults, or open their eyes to situations of fear and grief, which all come suddenly to many children. I try to be honest.

"Picture-book texts are a difficult discipline. To leave all the adjectives to the artist is the hardest thing I know in writing. Each word must be right."

*   *   *

REDDING, (Jay) Saunders 1906-1988

PERSONAL: Born October 13, 1906, in Wilmington, Del.; died of heart failure, March 2, 1988, in Ithaca, N.Y.; son of Lewis Alfred (a post office employee) and Mary Ann (Holmes) Redding; married Esther Elizabeth James, August 19, 1929; children: Conway Holmes, Lewis Alfred II. *Education:* Attended Lincoln University, 1923-24; Brown University, Ph.B., 1928, M.A., 1932; Columbia University, graduate study, 1933-34. *Politics:* Independent Democrat. *Religion:* Episcopalian.

ADDRESSES: *Home*—310 Winthrop Dr., Ithaca, N.Y. 14850. *Office*—Department of English, Cornell University, Ithaca, N.Y. 14850. *Agent*—Harold Matson Co., Inc., 276 Fifth Ave., New York, N.Y. 10001.`

CAREER: Morehouse College, Atlanta, Ga., instructor in English, 1928-31; Louisville Municipal College, Louisville, Ky., instructor in English, 1934-36; Southern University, Baton Rouge, La., head of English department, 1936-38; Hampton Institute, Hampton, Va., professor of English and American literature, 1943-55, Johnson Professor of Literature and Creative Writing, 1955-66; National Endowment for the Humanities, Washington, D.C., director of Division of Research and Publication, 1966-70, conservator, 1970-88; Cornell University, Ithaca, N.Y., Ernest I. White Professor of American Studies, 1970-75; professor emeritus, 1975-88. Visiting professor at Brown University, 1949-50; lecturer at several universities and colleges in India, Africa, and South America under auspices of U.S. Department of State, 1952, 1962, and 1977. Member of board of fellows, Brown University, 1969-81; member of board of directors, American Council of Learned Societies, 1976-88; trustee, Fund for Research and Education, American Civil Liberties Union. Consultant on graduate scholarships, U.S. Department of Health, Education, and Welfare, 1958-59; special consultant, National Endowment for the Humanities, 1970-88; member of advisory board, Center for Advanced Study, University of Virginia, 1977-88.

MEMBER: College English Association, Phi Beta Kappa, Sigma Pi Phi.

AWARDS, HONORS: Rockefeller Foundation fellow, 1939-40; Guggenheim fellow, 1944-45, 1959-60; Mayflower Award for distinguished writing, North Carolina Historical Society, 1944, for *No Day of Triumph;* New York Public Library citation for outstanding contribution to interracial understanding, 1945, 1946; National Urban League citation for outstanding achievement, 1950; Ford Foundation fellow at Duke University, 1964-65, and at University of North Carolina; honorary degrees from Virginia State College, 1963, Hobart College, 1964, University of Portland, 1970, and Wittinberg University, 1977, and from Dickinson College, Brown University, and University of Delaware; honorary conservator of American culture, Library of Congress, 1973-77.

WRITINGS:

To Make a Poet Black (criticism), University of North Carolina Press, 1939, reprinted, Core Collection Books, 1978, new edition, Cornell University Press, 1986.
No Day of Triumph, Harper, 1942.
Stranger and Alone (novel), Harcourt, 1950.
They Came in Chains: Americans from Africa, Lippincott, 1950, revised edition, 1973.
On Being Negro in America, Bobbs-Merrill, 1951.
An American in India: A Personal Report on the Indian Dilemma and the Nature of Her Conflicts, Bobbs-Merrill, 1954.
The Lonesome Road: The Story of the Negro's Part in America, Doubleday, 1958, reprinted, 1973.
The Negro, Potomac, 1967.
Of Men and the Writing of Books, Vail Memorial Library, Lincoln University, 1969.
Negro Writing and the Political Climate, Vail Memorial Library, Lincoln University, 1970.

CONTRIBUTOR

The American Negro Writer and His Roots, American Society of African Culture, 1960.
Herbert Hill, editor, *Soon, One Morning: New Writing by American Negroes 1940-1962,* Knopf, 1964.
(With Hill, Horace Cayton, and Arna Bontemps) Hill, editor, *Anger and Beyond: The Negro Writer in the United States,* Harper, 1966.
John Henrik Clarke, Esther Jackson, Ernest Kaiser, and J. H. O'Dell, editors, *Black Titan: W. E. B. DuBois, An Anthology by the Editors of Freedomways,* Beacon Press, 1970.
Jay Martin, editor, *A Singer in the Dawn: Reinterpretations of Paul Laurence Dunbar,* Dodd, 1975.

OTHER

(Editor with Ivan E. Taylor) *Reading for Writing,* Ronald Press, 1952.
(Author of introduction) W. E. B. DuBois, *The Souls of Black Folk: Essays and Sketches,* Peter Smith, 1963.
(Editor with Arthur P. Davis) *Cavalcade: Negro American Writing from 1760 to the Present,* Houghton, 1971.
(Author of introduction) Faith Berry, editor, *Good Morning Revolution: The Uncollected Social Protest Writings by Langston Hughes,* Lawrence Hill, 1973.

Member of editorial board, *American Scholar,* 1950-62, 1968-74. Contributor of numerous articles to publications, including *North American Review, American Mercury, Atlantic Monthly, American Scholar, Saturday Review, Nation,* and *American Heritage.*

WORK IN PROGRESS: A monograph to be included in the book, *History in Our Time.*

SIDELIGHTS: Saunders Redding has been called an outstanding figure in an older generation of black American writers. His works are recognized as having been instrumental in the education of white America in the areas of race relations and the problems of black existence in a white society. Redding's first book, *To Make a Poet Black,* published in 1939, is a unique appraisal of black literature from the point of view of a black scholar and creative writer. E. V. Stonequist in the *American Sociological Review* calls the book "an interpretation of the literary development of his race, marked by a very high degree of sympathetic understanding combined with intellectual honesty and fairness in criticism, and by pithy, original comments upon particular writers and their writings, situating them in their particular cultural backgrounds." In *Commonweal,* Theophilus Lewis writes: "There is more than a slight probability that future literary archeologists will refer to this book as a landmark of Negro literature. Not that it is even remotely a work of monumental significance. But it does mark a new departure. The Negro author has already won acceptance in the field of creative writing. In this volume he breaks new ground, emerges as critic and appraiser of the works of his fellow craftsmen."

Redding's second book, *No Day of Triumph,* was the result of a commission by the University of North Carolina in which he was told to report on black life in the South. The author added a good deal of autobiography and personal comment to his findings and the result was, according to Wallace Stegner in the *Atlantic,* "an angry and honest and compassionate book; a better book than the University of North Carolina and the Rockefeller Foundation, who financed it, had any right to expect; perhaps the sanest and most eloquent study of the Negro American that has appeared." And *Springfield Republican* contributor S. R. Harlow suggests that "Mr. Redding's book ought to be read by every Negro of the middle class in America and by all of 'the talented tenth.' They need not agree with all that the author says as he flays the pessimism and self-indulgence of some of their class, but it will prove a healthy stimulant against falling into similar habits of thought and action. Members of the white group who read the book need to be warned that this is not a complete picture of the Negro in America today, but it is a revelation of much that goes on in the shadow of democracy."

Redding's novel *Stranger and Alone* is the story of Shelton Howden, who is the son of a white father and a black mother. He despises his black heritage and eventually betrays his black friends to the white politicians of his Southern town. In a *New York Times* review of the book, Ralph Ellison writes: "If in his novel Mr. Redding has selected a protagonist too limited in personal appeal, and if his writing lacks the high quality that marked his autobiographical *No Day of Triumph,* he has done, nevertheless, a vastly important job of reporting the little known role of those Negro 'leaders' who by collaborating with the despoilers of the South do insidious damage to us all." The book was described as controversial at the time of its publication in 1950, and S. C. Watkins, writing in the *Chicago Sunday Tribune,* calls it "a story that few can read without having rather strong feelings aroused. It can be strongly liked or just as strongly disliked." *New York Herald Tribune Book Review* contributor Coleman Rosenberger says: "It is an angry book, but one in which the anger is controlled and made purposeful. It is written with both insight and skill. There is the ring of truth about it. It is as if the author were writing a biography of the man which he might easily have been, if he had yielded to the ever present pressures about him, some crude and massively direct, some very subtle.'' Finally, Paul Pickrel in the *Yale Review* concludes that ''this book adds more to our understanding of Negro life than many more sensational books; it is, in a sense, more shocking than the shockers, because it shows the critically weak points in those very institutions which most of us look to as the solution—in part, at least—of the problem of the Negro.''

With *They Came in Chains: Americans from Africa*, Redding took on the task of compiling a history of the black race in America, which a reviewer for the *Springfield Republican* called ''a project often attempted but rarely carried out in a fully satisfactory manner. The historian either is white and a trifle condescending or black and too emotional. *They Came in Chains* by a Negro educator, is as good an in-between job as could be asked.'' L. P. Stavisky of *Survey* notes that ''the paucity of footnote documentation, including the omission of periodical literature, is certain to elicit a hue and cry that some of the broad generalizations are based upon insufficient evidence. Yet the book has considerable merit. Seldom have the chroniclers of American Negro history possessed the literary talents which Mr. Redding demonstrates throughout the volume. This is no dry recital of events. In a fluid and imaginative style, the author has given us a vivid commentary on the story of the Negro people in America.''

In another book of history, *The Lonesome Road: The Story of the Negro's Part in America*, Redding uses biographical sketches of twelve famous black Americans to trace the struggle from slavery to equal rights. In a review of the book appearing in *Library Journal*, M. S. Byam writes: ''The history of the Negro has been well-covered both verbally and pictorially in both scholarly and colloquial language by Negroes and others. Here is another; yet it is so dynamic a presentation, so true to itself in both subject and technique that its addition must be recommended. This is no mere angry or shrieking picture of the poor Negro's plight but rather a documentation of his complete belongingness to America historically and culturally.'' *New Republic* reviewer Paula Snelling, however, finds that although Redding's subject is most important, ''his book is not. This is due to no lack of literary skill or erudition on the author's part, but to his unwillingness to engage himself here on a deeply creative or philosophic level.'' Snelling feels that not enough space is devoted to recent developments or to the impact that black artists have had on our culture. ''But the contribution Mr. Redding neglects most (and this, I think, reveals an unverbalized bias) is that of Negro leaders who have kept their home base in the South and sought ways of communicating with white Southerners without relinquishing personal dignity or the aspirations of their race.''

Saunders Redding once remarked: ''Things bothered me, and I set out to write them away—beginning with adolescent love, I suppose. And things still bother me—life, the quality and purpose of it; the myths that fail to explain it; the general and specifics of the American experience and particularly the black American experience; and I'm still trying to write them away.... My first obligation is to truth—factual and emotional truth. Since life is short, there is only so much truth that one can know and experience in the deeply personal and intimate way that is necessary to the writer, and even the little truth that one can know and experience in this way is often

painful—and 'painful' is a term frequently used to define anger. I think I am what is called a realist, but some of my critics say that I am an idealist. All I really know is that I'm obliged to tell, to write about, the little truth I know.''

BIOGRAPHICAL/CRITICAL SOURCES:

BOOKS

Davis, Arthur P., *From the Dark Tower: Afro-American Writers, 1900-1960*, Howard University Press, 1974.
Dictionary of Literary Biography, Volume 63: *Modern American Critics, 1920-1955*, Gale, 1988.
Wagner, Jean, *Black Poets of the United States: From Paul Laurence Dunbar to Langston Hughes*, University of Illinois Press, 1973.

PERIODICALS

American Sociological Review, June, 1939.
Atlantic, December, 1942.
Booklist, April 15, 1939, December 15, 1942.
Books, October 11, 1942.
Chicago Sunday Tribune, February 19, 1950.
Choice, April, 1968.
Christian Science Monitor, February 17, 1950, September 18, 1950, May 7, 1958.
Commonweal, May 12, 1939.
Library Journal, March 1, 1958.
Nation, November 17, 1951.
Negro Digest, January, 1968.
New Republic, October 12, 1942, June 23, 1958.
New Yorker, February 18, 1950, November 3, 1951.
New York Herald Tribune Book Review, February 19, 1950, July 16, 1950, November 11, 1951, March 3, 1958.
New York Times, October 25, 1942, February 19, 1950, July 30, 1950, October 21, 1951, April 20, 1958.
Saturday Review, February 16, 1952, March 22, 1969.
Saturday Review of Literature, November 21, 1942, February 25, 1950.
Springfield Republican, November 8, 1942, July 23, 1950, June 15, 1958.
Social Forces, March, 1952.
Survey, March, 1950, November, 1950.
Yale Review, spring, 1950.

OBITUARIES:

PERIODICALS

New York Times, March 5, 1988.†

*   *   *

REDEKOP, Calvin Wall 1925-

PERSONAL: Born September 19, 1925, in Volt, Mont.; son of Jacob Kasper and Katherine (Wall) Redekop; married Freda Pellman; children: William Charles, Benjamin Wall, Frederick Jacob. *Education:* Goshen College, B.A., 1949; University of Minnesota, M.A., 1955; University of Chicago, Ph.D., 1959. *Politics:* ''Liberal, uncommitted though normally Democratic.'' *Religion:* Mennonite.

ADDRESSES: Office—Department of Sociology, Conrad Grebel College, University of Waterloo, Waterloo, Ontario, Canada N2L 3G6.

CAREER: Hesston College, Hesston, Kan., professor of sociology, 1954-62; Earlham College, School of Religion, Richmond, Ind., associate professor, 1962-67; Goshen College,

Goshen, Ind., professor of sociology and anthropology, 1967-76; Tabor College, Hillsboro, Kan., dean, 1976-79; University of Waterloo, Waterloo, Ontario, professor of sociology, 1979—. President, Wayne County (Ind.) Anti-Poverty Program, 1962-67; secretary, Richmond Industrial Ministry, 1964-67. *Wartime service:* Conscientious objector doing civilian peace work, 1950-52.

MEMBER: American Sociological Association, Society for the Scientific Study of Religion, Religious Research Association, Society for the Sociology of Religion.

WRITINGS:

The Old Colony Mennonites: Dilemmas of Ethnic Minority Life, Johns Hopkins Press, 1969.
The Free Church and Seductive Culture, Herald Press, 1970.
(With J. R. Burkholder) *Kingdom, Cross, and Community,* Herald Press, 1976.
Reader in Sociology, Herald Press, 1980.
Strangers Become Neighbors, Herald Press, 1980.
(With Urie A. Bender) *Who Am I? What Am I? A Christian View of Work,* Zondervan, 1988.
(Editor with Samuel Steiner) *Mennonite Identity: Historical and Contemporary Perspectives,* University Press of America, 1988.
North American Mennonites: A Social Analysis, Johns Hopkins Press, 1988.

Also author of several pamphlets published by Mennonites. Contributor to professional and denominational journals.

WORK IN PROGRESS: Research on entrepreneurialism and religion; research on work, and volunteerism and work.

SIDELIGHTS: Calvin Redekop told *CA:* "Living (aging) brings with it interest in the past. I am now writing up some experiences [I had] growing up on the Montana prairies, 'Life on the Prairies.'" *Avocational interests:* Travel, music (piano and flute), inventions.

* * *

REES, (George) Leslie (Clarence) 1905-

PERSONAL: Born December 28, 1905, in Perth, Western Australia, Australia; married Coralie Clarke (a writer), 1931 (died, 1972); children: Megan, Dymphna. *Education:* University of Western Australia, B.A., 1929; graduate study at University College, London, 1930.

ADDRESSES: Home—4/5 The Esplanade, Balmoral Beach 2088, New South Wales, Australia.

CAREER: Writer, editor, and drama critic. *Era,* London, England, senior drama critic, 1931-35; Playwrights Advisory Board, Sydney, New South Wales, Australia, co-founder, 1937, continuing honorary chairman; Australian Broadcasting Commission, Sydney, chief drama editor, 1937-57, assistant director of drama, 1957-66. Mt. Lawley College of Advanced Education, Perth, Western Australia, Australia, writer in residence, 1975.

MEMBER: International PEN (president of Sydney Centre, 1968-76).

AWARDS, HONORS: Australian Children's Book-of-the-Year Award, 1946, for *The Story of Karrawingi, the Emu;* award from Townsville Literary Foundation, 1978, for *A History of Australian Drama;* named member of the Order of Australia, 1981.

WRITINGS:

JUVENILES

Digit Dick on the Barrier Reef, John Sands, 1942, published as *Digit Dick on the Great Barrier Reef,* Hamlyn, 1969.
Gecko: The Lizard Who Lost His Tail (also see below), John Sands, 1944.
The Story of Shy, the Platypus (also see below), illustrations by Walter Cunningham, John Sands, 1945, reprinted, Lansdowne Press, 1984.
Digit Dick and the Tasmanian Devil, John Sands, 1946.
The Story of Karrwingi, the Emu, illustrations by Cunningham, John Sands, 1946.
The Story of Sarli, the Barrier Reef Turtle (also see below), John Sands, 1947, reprinted, Lansdowne Press, 1984.
Bluecap and Bimbi (also see below), Trinity House, 1948.
Mates of the Kurlalong, illustrations by Alfred Wood, John Sands, 1948.
The Story of Kurri Kurri, the Kookaburra, illustrations by Margaret Senior, John Sands, 1950, reprinted, Lansdowne Press, 1984.
Quokka Island, illustrations by Arthur Horowicz, Collins, 1951.
Danger Patrol: A Young Patrol Officer's Adventures in New Guinea, Collins, 1954.
Two Thumbs: The Story of a Koala, illustrations by Senior, Ryerson Press, 1954.
The Story of Koonaworra, the Black Swan, illustrations by Senior, John Sands, 1957.
The Story of Aroora, the Red Kangaroo (also see below), illustrations by John Singleton, John Sands, 1958.
Australian Nature Tales (contains *The Story of Aroora, the Red Kangaroo, The Story of Shy, the Platypus,* and *The Story of Sarli, the Barrier Reef Turtle*), John Sands, 1958.
The Story of Wy-Lah, the Cockatoo, illustrations by Cunningham, John Sands, 1960.
The Story of Russ, the Australian Tree Kangaroo, illustrations by Cunningham, John Sands, 1964.
Boy Lost on a Tropic Coast: Adventure With Dexter Hardy, Ure Smith, 1968.
Digit Dick in Black Swan Land, Hamlyn, 1972.
Mokee, the White Possum (also see below), illustrations by Tony Oliver, Hamlyn, 1973.
Panic in the Cattle Country, Rigby, 1974.
Bluecap and Bimbi, Gecko, and Mokee (contains *Mokee, the White Possum, Gecko, the Lizard Who Lost His Tail,* and *Bluecap and Bimbi*), illustrations by Oliver, Hamlyn, 1975.

Also author of *The Story of Shadow, the Rock Wallaby,* and *Here's to Shane: The Story of a Boy Born Deaf.*

OTHER

(Editor) *Australian Radio Plays,* Angus & Robertson, 1946.
(Editor) *Modern Short Plays,* Angus & Robertson, 1951.
(With wife, Coralie Rees) *Spinifex Walkabout: Hitch-Hiking in Remote Australia,* Harrap, 1953.
Towards an Australian Drama, Angus & Robertson, 1953, revised edition published as *The Making of Australian Drama: A Historical and Critical Survey From the 1830's to the 1970's* (also see below), 1973.
(With C. Rees) *Westward from Cocos: Indian Ocean Travels,* Harrap, 1956.
(With C. Rees) *Coasts of Cape York: Travels Around Australia's Pearl-Tipped Peninsula,* Angus & Robertson, 1960.
(Editor) *Mask and Microphone* (plays), Angus & Robertson, 1963.

(With C. Rees) *People of the Big Sky Country*, Ure Smith, 1970.

Australian Drama in the 1970's: A Historical and Critical Survey (also see below), Angus & Robertson, 1978, revised edition published as *Australian Drama 1970-85*, 1986.

A History of Australian Drama (contains a revised version of *The Making of Australian Drama: A Historical and Critical Survey From the 1830's to the 1970's* and *Australian Drama in the 1970's: A Historical and Critical Survey*), Angus & Robertson, 1978.

Hold Fast to Dreams: Fifty Years in Theatre, Radio, Television, and Books (memoirs), Alternative Publishing Cooperative, Ltd. (APCOL), 1982.

SIDELIGHTS: Some of Leslie Rees's popular children's books are based on his childhood experiences near Perth, Australia. Rees spent many holidays exploring about the countryside and often camped along the Swan River or on coastal islands. *Digit Dick in Black Swan Land*, *Quokka Island*, and *Kurri Kurri, the Kookaburra* recapture the scenes of these adventures. His love and knowledge of Australian wildlife is also reflected in his many other books, but especially in *The Story of Shy, the Platypus*, *The Story of Karrawingi, the Emu*, and *The Story of Koonaworra, the Black Swan*.

*   *   *

REICHARD, Gary Warren   1943-

PERSONAL: Born November 23, 1943, in Philadelphia, Pa.; son of David Carl (a salesman) and Gabrielle (Doane) Reichard; married Marcia Ann King (a research specialist), August 7, 1965 (divorced); children: Jennifer Doane, James Jeffrey. *Education:* College of Wooster, B.A., 1965; Vanderbilt University, M.A., 1966; Cornell University, Ph.D., 1971.

ADDRESSES: Office—Department of History, University of Maryland, College Park, Md. 20742.

CAREER: College of Wooster, Wooster, Ohio, instructor in history, 1967-69; Ohio State University, Columbus, assistant professor, 1971-77, associate professor of history and chairman of department, 1977-82; University of Delaware, Newark, associate professor of history and director of honors program, 1983-85; University of Maryland, College Park, associate professor and assistant to associate vice-president for academic affairs for Central Administration, 1985—.

MEMBER: American Historical Association, Organization of American Historians, Southern Historical Association, Phi Beta Kappa.

AWARDS, HONORS: Danforth associate, 1974.

WRITINGS:

The Reaffirmation of Republicanism: Eisenhower and the Eighty-Third Congress, University of Tennessee Press, 1975.

(With Charles M. Dollar and others) *America: Changing Times*, Wiley, 1979, revised edition, 1982.

(Editor with Robert H. Bremner) *Reshaping America: Society and Institutions, 1945-1960*, Ohio State University Press, 1982.

(Editor with Bremner and Richard J. Hopkins) *American Choices: Social Dilemmas and Public Policy since 1960*, Ohio State University Press, 1986.

Politics as Usual: The Age of Truman and Eisenhower, Harlan Davidson, 1988.

(Editor with Dollar) *American Issues: A Documentary Reader*, Random House, 1988.

WORK IN PROGRESS: Liberal in the Middle: Hubert H. Humphrey, for Twayne; *The Politics of American Foreign Policy, 1950-1960*.

*   *   *

REINHOLD, Meyer   1909-

PERSONAL: Born September 1, 1909, in New York, N.Y.; son of Joseph and Ethel (Rosen) Reinhold; married Diane Roth (an executive medical secretary), September 29, 1939; children: Robert, Helen. *Education:* City College (now City College of the City University of New York), A.B., 1929; Columbia University, A.M., 1930, Ph.D., 1933; American Academy in Rome, F.A.A.R., 1935.

ADDRESSES: Home—63 Sparks St., Cambridge, Mass. 02138.

CAREER: Brooklyn College (now Brooklyn College of the City University of New York), Brooklyn, N.Y., 1938-55, began as instructor, became associate professor of classical languages and literature; Richmond Advertising Service, Inc., Brooklyn, vice-president, 1955-65; Southern Illinois University at Carbondale, associate professor of Greek, Latin, and ancient history, 1965-67; University of Missouri—Columbia, professor of classical studies, 1967-80, Byler Distinguished Professor of Classical Studies, 1976-80, professor emeritus, 1980—; Boston University, Boston, Mass., visiting professor, 1980—, interim chairman of department of classical studies, 1985-86, director, Institute for the Classical Tradition.

MEMBER: American Philological Association, American Association of Ancient Historians, Vergil Society, Classical Association of New England, Phi Beta Kappa.

WRITINGS:

Marcus Agrippa: A Biography, G. F. Humphrey, 1933, reprinted, L'Erma di Bretschneider (Rome), 1965.

Greek and Roman Classics, 1946, revised edition published as *Essentials of Greek and Roman Classics: A Guide to the Humanities*, Barron's, 1971.

(Editor with Naphtali Lewis) *Roman Civilization*, Columbia University Press, 1951, revised edition, Harper, 1965.

The Classical Drama, Barron's, 1959.

Barron's Teen-Age Summer Guide, Barron's, 1960, 3rd edition, 1965.

A Simplified Approach to Plato and Aristotle, Barron's, 1964.

Barron's Simplified Approach to Ten Greek Tragedies, Barron's, 1965.

Barron's Simplified Approach to Vergil: Eclogues, Georgics, Aeneid, Barron's, 1966.

Barron's Simplified Approach to "The Iliad": Homer, Barron's, 1967.

Barron's Simplified Approach to "The Odyssey": Homer, Barron's, 1967, revised edition, 1987.

History of Purple as a Status Symbol in Antiquity, Latomus, 1970.

Usurpation of Status and Status Symbols in the Roman Empire, Historia, 1970.

Past and Present: The Continuity of Classical Myths, Hakkert, 1972.

(Contributor) *Hellas and Rome: The Story of Greco-Roman Civilization*, New American Library, 1972.

(Editor) *The Classick pages: Classical Readings of Eighteenth-Century Americans*, American Philological Association, 1975, reprinted, Scholars Press, 1985.

The Classics and the Quest for Virtue in Eighteenth-Century America, American Philological Association, 1977.

(Editor and translator) *The Golden Age of Augustus*, Samuel/Stevens, 1978.

(Contributor) *Classical Influences on Western Education, Philosophy and Social Theory, 1650-1870*, Cambridge University Press, 1978.

(Editor and translator) *The Jewish Diaspora among Greeks and Romans*, Samuel/Stevens, 1981.

Classica Americana: The Greek and Roman Heritage in the United States, Wayne State University Press, 1984.

(Contributor) *The Craft of the Ancient Historian: Essays in Honor of Chester G. Starr*, AMF Press, 1985.

Bibliography of the Classical Tradition for 1980-1982, Classical and Modern Literature, 1985.

(Contributor) Merrill D. Peterson, editor, *Thomas Jefferson: A Reference Biography*, Scribner, 1986.

From Republic to Principate: An Historical Commentary on Cassius Dio's "Roman History" Books 49-52, American Philological Association, 1988.

Contributor to *Parents' Magazine, Science and Society*, and professional journals.

WORK IN PROGRESS: Co-editing, with J. Rufus Fears, *The Classical Tradition and the Founding Fathers, 1700-1828;* co-editing, with Fears and Wolfgang Haase, *The Classical Tradition and the Americas*, in six volumes; revising, with N. Lewis, a new edition of *Roman Civilization;* writing *The Rise of Augustus: An Historical Commentary on Cassius Dio's "Roman History" Books 45-48.*

*   *   *

RENKIEWICZ, Frank   1935-

PERSONAL: Born May 16, 1935, in New York, N.Y.; son of Frank and Estelle (Uszkowska) Renkiewicz. *Education:* St. Peter's College, Jersey City, N.J., B.S., 1956; University of Notre Dame, M.A., 1958, Ph.D., 1967; post-graduate study in India, 1967, Poland, 1969, and Europe, 1970, 1975, 1979, and 1986. *Politics:* Democrat. *Religion:* Roman Catholic.

ADDRESSES: Home—2846 Dudley Ave., Bronx, N.Y., 10461.

CAREER: College of St. Teresa, Winona, Minn., instructor, 1962-67, assistant professor, 1967-71, associate professor of history and chairman of department, 1971-75; research associate, Immigration History Research Center, University of Minnesota, 1975-77; College of St. Teresa, professor of history, 1977-81; St. John Fisher College, Rochester, N.Y., associate professor of history and director of Polish studies, 1981-83; St. Mary's College, Orchard Lake, Mich., dean of students, 1983-85, director of Orchard Lake Center for Polish Studies, and professor of history, 1983-87. Commentator or panelist at academic conferences, including the Congress of Polish Scientists and Scholars in America, 1971, Conference on Ethnic Fraternal Archives, University of Minnesota, 1979, the Conference on East European Experience in America, University of Wisconsin-Milwaukee, 1979, the Upper Midwest History Conference, 1980, and Research Conferences on Polish Immigration, Jagiellonian University, 1975, 1979, and 1986; speaker to community and ethnic associations, including Missouri Valley History Conference, 1972 and 1973, Organization of American Historians, 1973, Society of American Archi-

vists, 1976, Midwest Slavic Conference, 1976 and 1979, Polish American Historical Association, 1969, 1970, and 1985, and American Catholic Historical Association, spring conference, 1985. Consultant in American ethnic studies, 1977—.

MEMBER: American Historical Association, Organization of American Historians, Polish American Historical Association (president, 1976).

AWARDS, HONORS: Kosciuszko Foundation Doctoral Dissertation Award, 1969; Haiman Award, 1977, for contributions to field of Polish American history, and Halecki Award, 1986, for monographic publication, both from Polish American Historical Association.

WRITINGS:

(Editor) *The Poles in America, 1608-1972: A Chronology and Factbook*, Oceana, 1973.

(Contributor) Scott Cummings, editor, *Self Help in Urban America: Patterns of Minority Economic Development*, Kennikat, 1980.

(Contributor) Charles A. Ward and others, editors, *Studies in Ethnicity: The East European Experience in America*, East European Monographs, 1980.

(Contributor) June Holmquist, editor, *They Chose Minnesota: A Survey of the State's Ethnic Groups*, Minnesota Historical Society, 1981.

(Editor and author of introduction) *The Polish Presence in Canada and America*, Multicultural History Society of Ontario, 1982.

(Contributor) Stanislaus A. Blejwas and Mieczyslaw B. Biskupsi, editors, *Pastor of the Poles*, Polish Studies Program, Central Connecticut State College, 1982.

(Contributor) John S. Wozniak, editor, *Historic Lifestyles in the Upper Mississippi River Valley*, University Press of America, 1983.

For God, Country and Polonia: One Hundred Years of the Orchard Lake Schools, Center for Polish Studies and Culture, Orchard Lake Schools, 1985.

Also contributor to *Catholic Encyclopedia for School and Home*, 1965. Contributor of book reviews to *American Historical Review, Polish American Studies, Catholic Historical Review, Polish Review*, and *Journal of American Ethnic History*. Editor, *Polish American Studies* (publication of Polish American Historical Association), 1971-81.

*   *   *

REVELL, J(ohn) R(obert) S(tephen)   1920-
(Jack Revell)

PERSONAL: Born April 15, 1920, in Tunbridge Wells, Kent, England; son of Clifford Walter (a shopkeeper) and Edith (Wren) Revell; married Patricia M. B. Hiatt, February 23, 1946; children: Barbara, Alison, David John. *Education:* London School of Economics and Political Science, B.Sc., 1950; Cambridge University, M.A., 1960.

ADDRESSES: Home—12 Rustat Road, Cambridge, CB1 3QT England. *Office*—University College of North Wales, Bangor, Gwynedd, LL57 2DG Wales.

CAREER: Cambridge University, Cambridge, England, senior research officer in department of applied economics, 1957-68, fellow and senior tutor of Fitzwilliam College, 1965-68; University College of North Wales, Bangor, professor of economics, 1969-83; Institute of European Finance, Bangor, director,

1973-85, consultant director, 1985—. *Military service:* British Army, 1940-46; became staff sergeant.

MEMBER: Royal Economic Society, Societe Universitaire Europeenne de Recherche Financiere.

WRITINGS:

(With John Moyle) *The Owners of Quoted Ordinary Shares: A Survey for 1963*, Chapman & Hall, 1966.

The Wealth of the Nation: The National Balance Sheet of the United Kingdom, 1957-1961, Cambridge University Press, 1967.

Changes in British Banking: The Growth of a Secondary Banking System, Hill, Samuel & Co., 1968.

The British Financial System, Macmillan, 1973.

(With C. R. Tomkins) *Personal Wealth and Finance in Wales*, Welsh Office, 1974.

Flexibility in Housing Finance, Organization for Economic Cooperation and Development, 1975.

Solvency and Regulation of Banks, University of Wales Press, 1975.

Savings Flows in Europe: Personal Saving and Borrowing, Financial Times, 1976.

(Editor) *Competition and Regulation of Banks*, University of Wales Press, 1978.

Inflation and Financial Institutions, Financial Times, 1979.

Costs and Margins in Banking: An International Survey, Organization for Economic Cooperation and Development, 1980.

A Study of the Spanish Banking System, Banco de Vizcaya, 1980.

Banking and Electronic Fund Transfers, Organization for Economic Cooperation and Development, 1983.

Mergers and the Role of Large Banks, Institute of European Finance, 1987.

Also author of *Changes in Spanish Banking*, 1984. Contributor of more than fifty articles to economic and banking journals.

WORK IN PROGRESS: Research on the future shape of the British financial system; research on the structure of financial systems and the operation of financial institutions.

*   *   *

REVELL, Jack
      See REVELL, J(ohn) R(obert) S(tephen)

*   *   *

REYNOLDS, Ann
      See BLY, Carol(yn)

*   *   *

RICARDO-CAMPBELL, Rita

PERSONAL: Surname cited in some sources as Campbell; born in Boston, Mass.; daughter of David and Elizabeth (Jones) Ricardo; married Wesley Green Campbell (director of the Hoover Institution), September 15, 1946; children: Barbara Lee, Diane Rita, Nancy Elizabeth. *Education:* Simmons College, B.S., 1941; Harvard University-Radcliffe College, M.A., 1945, Ph.D., 1946.

ADDRESSES—Home—26915 Alejandro Dr., Los Altos Hills, Calif. 94022. *Office*—Hoover Institution, Stanford University, Stanford, Calif. 94305.

CAREER: Harvard University, Cambridge, Mass., instructor, 1947-48; Tufts University, Medford, Mass., assistant professor, 1948-51; Wage Stabilization Board, Washington, D.C., labor economist, 1951-53; U.S. House of Representatives, Ways and Means Committee, Washington, D.C., economist, 1953; consulting economist, 1957-60; Stanford University, Hoover Institution, Stanford, Calif., archivist and research associate, 1961-68, senior fellow, 1968—, lecturer in health services at Stanford Medical School, 1973-78. Visiting professor at San Jose State College (now University), 1960-61. Member of board of directors of Independent Colleges of Northern California, 1971-87, Watkins-Johnson Co., 1974—, Simmons College, 1974-80, and Gillette Co., 1978—. Member of President's Economic Policy Advisory Board, 1981—; appointed to National Council on the Humanities, 1982.

MEMBER: American Economic Association, Mount Pelerin Society, Phi Beta Kappa.

AWARDS, HONORS: National Endowment for the Humanities senior fellowship, 1971; Alumnae Achievement Award, Simmons College, 1972.

WRITINGS:

(With husband, Wesley Glenn Campbell) *Economics of Mobilization and War*, Irwin, 1952.

Economics of Health and Public Policy, American Enterprise Institute for Public Research, 1971.

Food Safety Regulation: A Study of the Use and Limitations of Cost-Benefit Analysis, American Enterprise Institute—Hoover Institution Joint Study, 1974.

Drug Lag: Federal Government Decision Making, Hoover Institution, 1976.

Social Security: Promise and Reality, Hoover Institution, 1977.

The Economics and Politics of Health, University of North Carolina Press, 1982, 2nd edition, 1985.

Health Care Policy Update, Hoover Institution, 1983.

(Editor with Kingsley Davis and Mikhail Bernstam) *Below-Replacement Fertility in Industrial Societies*, Cambridge University Press, 1987.

(Editor with Edward Lazear) *Issues in Contemporary Retirement*, Hoover Institution, 1988.

Contributor of articles and reviews to numerous journals.

*   *   *

RICHARDS, R(onald) C(harles) W(illiam)   1923-
      (Allen Saddler, K. Allen Saddler)

PERSONAL: Born April 15, 1923, in England; son of Charles James (a shopkeeper) and Alice (Bloomfield) Richards; married Doris Edmondson, September 9, 1945; children: Richard Samuel. *Education:* Attended elementary school in South London, England. *Politics:* Labour. *Religion:* Agnostic.

ADDRESSES: Home—5, St. John's Hall, Station Rd., Totnes, Devon TQ9 5HW, England. *Agent:* Serafina Clarke, 98, Tunis Rd., London W12 7EY, England.

CAREER: Writer and theatre critic. Former printer in London, England; *Guardian*, London, west country theatre critic, 1972—.

MEMBER: National Union of Journalists, Writers' Guild.

WRITINGS:

UNDER PSEUDONYM K. ALLEN SADDLER

The Great Brain Robbery (novel), Elek, 1965.

Gilt Edge (novel), Elek, 1966.
Talking Turkey (novel), M. Joseph, 1968.
Betty (novel), Sphere Books, 1974.

JUVENILES; UNDER PSEUDONYM ALLEN SADDLER

The Clockwork Monster, Hodder & Stoughton, 1981.
Mr. Whizz, Blackie & Son, 1982.
Smudger's Seaside Spectacular, Blackie & Son, 1986.
The Relay Race, Methuen, 1986.
Jerry and the Monsters, Methuen, 1986.
Smudger's Saturday Special, Blackie & Son, 1988.
Jerry and the Inventions, Methuen, 1988.

"THE KING & QUEEN" SERIES

The Archery Contest, Oxford University Press, 1982.
The King Gets Fit, Oxford University Press, 1982.
The King at Christmas, Oxford University Press, 1983.
The Queen's Painting, Oxford University Press, 1983.

RADIO PLAYS FOR BRITISH BROADCASTING CORP.

"The Penstone Commune," 1973.
"Willie Banks and the Technological Revolution," 1973.
"Who Needs Money?," 1974.
"The Road," 1974.
"Willie Banks and the Administrative Machine," 1977.
"Penstone Revisited," 1977.
"Ahead of the Game," 1978.
"Archie's Watergate," 1979.
"Revolution at the Palace," 1979.
"The Giveaway," 1979.
"The Price Strike," 1981.
"Daddy Good" 1982.
"Old and Blue," 1982.
"Undesirable Alien," 1982.
"Arson in Berlin," 1983.
"The Day War Breaks Out," 1984.
"Working the System," 1984.
"Up against the Wall," 1985.
"Man of the People," 1986.
"I Should Say So" (series of comedy monologues), 1986-88.
"Spring," 1987.
"Second Chance," 1988.

Also author of television documentary script "The Concert Party," 1980, and, with Doris Richards, a television comedy for Barnet BBC-TV; also author of stage plays "Them," 1976, "All Basic Comforts," 1977, "Naf," 1979, "The Puppet Man," 1981, and "Kindly Leave the Stage," 1981. Contributor of reviews and features to periodicals, including *Guardian, Plays & Players, Stage, Sunday Times, Observer,* and *Radio Times.*

WORK IN PROGRESS: Children's fiction; television comedy; children's stage plays; radio comedy.

SIDELIGHTS: R.C.W. Richards told *CA,* "I am a working writer, willing to tackle anything between masterpieces and matchbox labels."

*   *   *

RICHARDSON, Joanna

PERSONAL: Born in London, England; daughter of Frederick and Charlotte (Benjamin) Richardson. *Education:* St. Anne's College, Oxford, B.A. (with honors), M.A. *Politics:* Conservative.

ADDRESSES: Home—55 Flask Walk, London N. W. 3, England. *Agent*—Curtis Brown, 162-168 Regent St., London W1R 5TA, England.

CAREER: Biographer and critic.

MEMBER: Royal Society of Literature (fellow; member of council, 1961-86).

AWARDS, HONORS: Chevalier de l'Ordre des Arts et des Lettres, 1987.

WRITINGS:

Fanny Brawne: A Biography, Vanguard, 1952.
Rachel, Reinhardt, 1956, Putnam, 1957.
Theophile Gautier: His Life and Times, Reinhardt, 1958, Coward, 1959.
Sarah Bernhardt, Reinhardt, 1959.
Edward Fitzgerald, Longmans, Green, 1960.
The Disastrous Marriage: A Study of George IV and Caroline of Brunswick, J. Cape, 1960.
My Dearest Uncle: A Life of Leopold I of the Belgians, J. Cape, 1961.
The Pre-Eminent Victorian: A Study of Tennyson, J. Cape, 1962.
(Editor) *Fitzgerald: Selected Works,* Hart-Davis, 1962.
The Everlasting Spell: A Study of Keats and His Friends, J. Cape, 1963.
(Editor) *Essays by Divers Hands: The Transactions of the Royal Society of Literature,* Oxford University Press, 1963.
(Author of introduction) Victor Hugo, *Things Seen,* Oxford University Press, 1964.
Edward Lear, Longmans, Green, 1965.
George the Magnificent: A Portrait of King George IV, Harcourt, 1966.
The Courtesans: The Demi-Monde in Nineteenth-Century France, World Publishing Co., 1967.
The Bohemians: La Vie de Boheme in Paris, 1830-1914, Macmillan (London), 1969, A. S. Barnes, 1971.
Princess Mathilde, Scribner, 1969.
Verlaine, Viking, 1971.
La Vie Parisienne, 1852-1870, Viking, 1971.
Enid Starkie, Macmillan, 1973.
The Regency, Collins, 1973.
Stendhal, Gollancz, 1974.
Louis XIV, Weidenfeld & Nicholson, 1974.
(Translator) *Verlaine: Selected Poems,* Penguin, 1974.
Baudelaire: Selected Poems, Penguin, 1975.
Victor Hugo, St. Martin's, 1976.
Sarah Bernhardt and Her World, Putnam, 1977.
Zola, St. Martin's, 1978.
Keats and His Circle: An Album of Portraits, Cassell, 1980.
Gustave Dore: A Biography, Cassell, 1980.
The Life and Letters of John Keats, Folio Society, 1981.
(Translator) Theophile Gautier, *Mademoiselle de Maupin,* Penguin, 1981.
(Editor) *Letters from Lambeth: The Correspondence of the Reynolds Family with J.F.M. Dovaston,* Royal Society of Literature, 1981.
Colette, F. Watts, 1983.
Judith Gautier, F. Watts, 1987.

SIDELIGHTS: Biographer Joanna Richardson has received critical attention for her life-accounts of some of nineteenth-century France's most noted and notorious writers. Included among these are her portraits of poet Paul Verlaine and France's famous woman of letters, Colette.

When Verlaine died in 1896, he was a highly celebrated poet in Europe. For various reasons, his reputation has since diminished, but his life story remains fascinating material. For the most part, reviewers of Richardson's *Verlaine* consider the work adept at exposing the poet's double nature—on the one hand Verlaine was an irascible, violent sort but on the other he was endearing and compassionate. As a *Times Literary Supplement* critic maintains, "with this double nature [Richardson] deals competently. For the most part she is sympathetic without hiding or condoning the vices, and she rightly sees that [Verlaine's] love for Rimbaud . . . was the one great inspiring passion of his life. She has amassed a vast amount of documentation, and is for the most part accurate and level-headed in her use of it without adding any important discoveries of her own. . . . But when it comes to examining Verlaine's qualities as a poet . . . Richardson is content to admire and describe. . . . [She] gives the impression that his poetry just happened to spin itself out of his entrails." Anna Balakian, a *Saturday Review* contributor, expresses a similar opinion: "Richardson . . . has written a lively, detailed, and factually precise biography of Paul Verlaine. Her materials are not new, her revelations not earthshaking; but out of the medley of confessions, letters, critical and personal comments by Verlaine's contemporaries, she has fashioned a vivid account of the quick rise and protracted degradation of the saturnalian vagabond, who in his last years was designated 'prince of poets'. . . . This is not, however, a critical biography. I have always believed that in order to qualify as such, a biography must illuminate the creative achievements of its subject. In this instance, Miss Richardson does the exact opposite; one often has the impression that the poems appear from time to time to fill in and substantiate the life pattern, their content serving to document Verlaine's notoriety as a person." *New York Times Book Review* commentator William Beauchamp also believes Richardson has relegated Verlaine's poetry a minor place in her biography, but his belief is that "the fascination, the drama, the tumult and paradox, the pathos . . . is where . . . Richardson's book excels. . . . The resulting portrait is terrifying and unforgettable. . . . It is probably the best, the most convenient introduction to the poet's life now available in either English or French."

In turning from Verlaine, Richardson's account of Colette entitled simply *Colette* is commended by Anatole Broyard in the *New York Times* for concentrating on this scandalous woman without being scandalous itself. According to Broyard, Richardson "approaches the author of 'Cheri' with something like Colette's own cosmopolitanism. She is as tasteful as she is thorough, giving us the facts dispassionately, usually in someone else's words. Because almost every writer in Paris seems to have commented on Colette before she died in 1954 at the age of 81, Miss Richardson's book is a ripe and witty anthology of contemporary French criticism." Richardson's objectivity is also what *New York Review of Books* contributor Gabriele Annan values in *Colette*: "The most unexpected and reassuring thing about . . . Richardson's biography is that she does not appear to love Colette unduly. She slots in concise and lucid accounts of the major works, dismissing some, excusing others, admiring most, and not going overboard for any of them. . . . Richardson can be critical . . . but on the whole she remains uninvolved and simply assembles the facts." Even though Broyard and Annan congratulate Richardson for keeping a distance between herself and her subject, complaints about the work arise for this very reason. In the *Detroit News*, Peter Ross claims "Richardson evinces little feel for Colette, and her prose is frankly arid. She is not an unqualified ad-

mirer," and Isa Kapp writes in her *New Republic* review: "The very least we expect of a Colette biography are high spirits, but starting with its introduction . . . Richardson's book is mystifyingly schoolmarmish and matter-of-fact. She states that it is the first 'full-scale' biography of Colette in English, but its substance is slight and its ambition meager. Many readers would certainly like to know something of what was going on in French literary and artistic circles outside the immediate radius of Colette's sensibility. . . . Reliable enough on chronology, Richardson is erratic about covering Colette's works." Here, as with the Verlaine biography and a number of Richardson's other biographies, Richardson's critical capabilities are called into question. Finally, although Ross is of the opinion that Richardson lacks feel for Colette and that she concentrates too heavily some of the "less-admirable aspects of Colette's life, the overall impression given is of a woman with a genius for appreciation. Anyone who has read Colette on a sunset, on flowers, food, wine, or the delicate love between pet and owner will find enough in this book to increase their joy."

BIOGRAPHICAL/CRITICAL SOURCES:

PERIODICALS

Book World, November 21, 1971.
Detroit News, February 26, 1984.
Nation, February 21, 1972.
New Republic, June 4, 1984.
New Yorker, January 27, 1975.
New York Review of Books, July 18, 1974, April 26, 1984.
New York Times, December 25, 1978, February 25, 1983.
New York Times Book Review, December 11, 1966, October 26, 1969, October 31, 1971, August 18, 1974, April 26, 1987.
Saturday Review, September 25, 1971.
Spectator, September 1, 1973, August 1, 1981, June 25, 1983, March 7, 1987.
Times, (London), March 5, 1987.
Times Literary Supplement, June 19, 1969, January 15, 1970, June 4, 1971, August 31, 1973, February 21, 1975, March 21, 1980, March 6, 1987.
Washington Post Book World, June 2, 1974, June 16, 1974, February 20, 1977, February 6, 1979, May 31, 1981.

—*Sketch by Cheryl Gottler*

*   *   *

RICHARDSON, Joe M(artin)   1934-

PERSONAL: Born December 17, 1934, in Stella, Mo.; son of Jesse Martin and Twyla (Cox) Richardson; married Patricia Jean Lively, October 28, 1966; children: Leslie Ann, Joseph Martin. Education: Southwest Missouri State College, B.S., 1958; Florida State University, M.S., 1959, Ph.D., 1963.

ADDRESSES: Home—1806 Lenora Dr., Tallahassee, Fla. 32304. *Office*—Department of History, Florida State University, Tallahassee, Fla. 32306.

CAREER: University of Mississippi, Oxford, assistant professor of history, 1962-64; Florida State University, Tallahassee, assistant professor, 1964-68; associate professor, 1968-71, professor of history, 1972—. Senior fellow, Institute of Southern and Negro History, Johns Hopkins University, 1968-69. *Military service:* U.S. Army, 1954-56.

MEMBER: Association for the Study of Negro Life and History, Southern Historical Association, Florida Historical Association, Phi Alpha Theta.

WRITINGS:

The Negro in the Reconstruction of Florida, Florida State University Press, 1965.
(Editor and author of introduction) *Trial and Imprisonment of Jonathan Walker,* University of Florida Press, 1974.
A History of Fisk University, 1865-1946, University of Alabama Press, 1980.
Christian Reconstruction: The American Missionary Association and Southern Blacks, 1861-1890, University of Georgia Press, 1986.

Contributor of articles and book reviews to *Florida Historical Quarterly, Journal of Negro Education, Tequesta, Tennessee Historical Quarterly, Journal of Negro History, Apalachee, Journal of Southern History, Southern Studies, Journal of Ethnic Studies, Civil War History,* and numerous other periodicals.

WORK IN PROGRESS: Research on the American Missionary Association in the twentieth century.

*   *   *

RIDGWAY, Judith   1939-
(Judy Ridgway)

PERSONAL: Born November 10, 1939, in Stalybridge, Cheshire, England; daughter of Leslie Randal (a company director) and Lavinia (Bottomley) Ridgway. *Education:* University of Keele, B.A., 1962; studied at the Verge School of Cookery, Cannes, France.

ADDRESSES: Home and office—124 Queens Court, Queensway, London W2 4QS, England. *Agent*—Gloria Mosesson, 290 West End Ave., New York, N.Y. 10023.

CAREER: Northwestern Gas Board, Manchester, England, public relations executive, 1963-68; Thompson Yellow Pages Ltd., London, England, public relations manager, 1969-73; Welbeck Public Relations, London, associate director, 1973-79. Director of London Cooks (caterers). Cooking demonstrator at Ludlow festival, 1981. Has appeared on numerous television programs and radio shows.

MEMBER: Society of Authors, Guild of Food Writers, Circle of Wine Writers (committee member), National Union of Journalists.

WRITINGS—Under name Judy Ridgway:

ADULT COOKBOOKS

The Vegetarian Gourmet, Ward, Lock, 1979, Prentice-Hall, 1981.
Salad Days, Foulsham, 1979.
Home Preserving, Teach Yourself Books, 1980.
The Seafood Kitchen, Ward, Lock, 1980.
(Editor) *The Colour Book of Chocolate Cookery,* Hamlyn, 1981.
Mixer, Blender, and Processor Cookery, Teach Yourself Books, 1981.
The Breville Book of Toasted Sandwiches, Martin Books, 1982.
Waitrose Book of Pasta, Rice and Pulses, Hamlyn, 1982.
The Little Lemon Book, Piatkus Books, 1983.
Barbecues, Ward, Lock, 1983.
The Little Bean Book, Piatkus Books, 1983.
The German Food Book, Martin Books, 1983.

Frying Tonight, Piatkus Books, 1984.
The Little Rice Book, Piatkus Books, 1984.
Sprouting Beans and Seeds, Century Publshing, 1984.
(With Alan Curthoys) *Man in the Kitchen,* Piatkus Books, 1984.
Cooking with Nuts and Cereals, Century Publishing, 1985.
The Vegetable Year Cook Book, Piatkus Books, 1985.
Wining and Dining at Home, Kingswood Press, 1985.
Wheat and Gluten Free Cookery: Over 100 Recipes for Allergy Sufferers, Century Arrow, 1986.
Vegetarian Wok Cookery, Century Arrow, 1986.
Complete Cheese Cook Book, Piatkus Books, 1986.
101 Ways with Chicken Pieces, Piatkus Books, 1987.

"MAKING THE MOST OF" SERIES

Making the Most of Rice, David & Charles, 1983.
. . . *Pasta,* David & Charles, 1983.
. . . *Potatoes,* David & Charles, 1983.
. . . *Bread,* David & Charles, 1983.
. . . *Cheese,* David & Charles, 1983.
. . . *Eggs,* David & Charles, 1983.

CHILDREN'S COOKBOOKS

101 Fun Foods to Make, Hamlyn Children's Books, 1982.
Cooking around the World, Macmillan Educational, 1983.
Festive Occasions, Oxford University Press, 1986.
(With Jenny Ridgwell) *Food Around the World,* Oxford University Press, 1987.
(Co-author) *Investigations and Recipes for Healthy Eating,* Oxford University Press, 1988.

OTHER

Home Cooking for Money, Piatkus Books, 1983.
Running Your Own Wine Bar, Kogan Page, 1984.
(Co-author) *Running Your Own Catering Company,* Kogan Page, 1984.
Successful Media Relations, Gower Press, 1984.

Contributor of features on food, wine, cookery, catering, and travel to numerous magazines, including *Woman and Home, Living,* and *Winepress.* Cookery editor, *Woman's Weekly.*

WORK IN PROGRESS: High Vitality Cookbook, for Pharsons; *Investigations into Healthy Eating.*

SIDELIGHTS: Judy Ridgway's career as a culinary writer and caterer grew out of her hobby of cooking and experimenting with recipes. Her cookbooks now number more than two dozen, and, according to *Daily Telegraph* writer Avril Groom, her "success is all the more remarkable because she had no cookery training." "One of her great strengths as a cookery writer is that, as a working woman, she understands working women's culinary problems very well," Groom comments, adding that Ridgway's recipes often call for inexpensive and easy-to-find ingredients.

Ridgway told *CA:* "I have specialized in food and cooking, but am now looking to expand my writing into other fields."

AVOCATIONAL INTERESTS: Classical music, opera, reading, and visiting the countryside.

BIOGRAPHICAL/CRITICAL SOURCES:

PERIODICALS

Daily Telegraph, May 15, 1980.

RIDGWAY, Judy
See RIDGWAY, Judith

* * *

RIDLEY, Nat, Jr.
[Collective pseudonym]

WRITINGS:

"NAT RIDLEY RAPID FIRE DETECTIVE STORIES"

Guilty or Not Guilty? or, Nat Ridley's Great Race Track Case, Garden City, 1926.
Tracked to the West; or, Nat Ridley at the Magnet Mine, Garden City, 1926.
In the Nick of Time; or, Nat Ridley Saving a Life, Garden City, 1926.
The Crime on the Limited; or, Nat Ridley in the Follies, Garden City, 1926.
A Daring Abduction; or, Nat Ridley's Biggest Fight, Garden City, 1926.
The Stolen Nuggets of Gold; or, Nat Ridley on the Yukon, Garden City, 1926.
A Secret of the Stage; or, Nat Ridley and the Bouquet of Death, Garden City, 1926.
The Great Circus Mystery; or, Nat Ridley on a Crooked Trail, Garden City, 1926.
A Scream in the Dark; or, Nat Ridley's Crimson Clue, Garden City, 1926.
The Race Track Crooks; or, Nat Ridley's Queerest Puzzle, Garden City, 1926.
The Stolen Liberty Bonds; or, Nat Ridley's Circle of Clues, Garden City, 1926.
In the Grip of the Kidnappers; or, Nat Ridley in High Society, Garden City, 1926.
The Double Dagger; or, Nat Ridley's Mexican Trail, Garden City, 1926.
The Mountain Inn Mystery; or, Nat Ridley with the Forest Rangers, Garden City, 1927.
The Western Express Robbery; or, Nat Ridley and the Mail Thieves, Garden City, 1927.
Struck Down at Midnight; or, Nat Ridley and His Rivals, Garden City, 1927.
Detective against Detective; or, Nat Ridley Showing His Nerve, Garden City, 1927.

SIDELIGHTS: When Canadian author Leslie McFarlane first began to write for the Stratemeyer Syndicate, he was offered the chance to work on the ''Nat Ridley Rapid Fire Detective Stories'' series. He recounts in his autobiography *Ghost of the Hardy Boys* his impressions of the detective: ''When Nat Ridley came up against a mystery, he didn't spend much time thinking his way through its mazes. He just went out and did something about it. A man of action.'' This series was released only in paperback. For additional information see the entries for Harriet S. Adams, Edward L. Stratemeyer, and Andrew E. Svenson.

BIOGRAPHICAL/CRITICAL SOURCES:

BOOKS

Johnson, Deidre, editor and compiler, *Stratemeyer Pseudonyms and Series Books: An Annotated Checklist of Stratemeyer and Stratemeyer Syndicate Publications,* Greenwood Press, 1982.

McFarlane, Leslie, *Ghost of the Hardy Boys,* Two Continents, 1976.

* * *

RINVOLUCRI, Mario (Francesco Giuseppe)   1940-

PERSONAL: Surname is pronounced Rin-*vo*-luke-ree; born June 9, 1940, in Cardiff, Wales; son of Giuseppe and Mina (Moore) Rinvolucri; married Sophie Laure Gabrielle Leyris; children: Lola-Agnes, Martin, Bruno. *Education:* Queen's College, Oxford, B.A., 1961. *Politics:* Labour Party. *Religion:* Agnostic (''ex-Roman Catholic'').

ADDRESSES: Home—33 Kinnaird Way, Cambridge, England.

CAREER: Reuters (news agency), London, England, journalist, 1961-62; magazine correspondent in Athens, Greece, 1962-65, and part-time teacher of English in Athens; teacher of English and part-time writer, Cambridge, England, 1965-70; University of Valdivia, Valdivia, Chile, teacher of English, 1971-73; Pilgrims Language Courses, Canterbury, England, involved with teaching, training teachers, and developing materials in the field of English as a foreign language, 1974—.

WRITINGS:

Anatomy of a Church: Greek Orthodoxy Today, Burns & Oates, 1966.
(Translator) Sotiris Spatharis, *Behind the White Screen,* London Magazine Editions, 1967.
(With James Dixey) *Well Said,* Pilgrims, 1977.
(With Dixey) *Get Up and Do It,* Longman, 1977.
(With Maggie Melville, Lou Spaventa, and Langenheim) *Towards the Creative Teaching of English,* Heinemann, 1980.
(With Margaret Berer) *Mazes,* Heinemann, 1981.
(With Berer and M. Frank) *Challenge to Think,* Oxford University Press, 1982.
(Contributor) P. Early, editor, *ELT Documents 113-Humanistic Approaches: An Empirical View,* Prentice-Hall, 1982.
(With Frank) *Grammar in Action,* Prentice-Hall, 1983.
(With John Morgan) *Once upon a Time,* Cambridge University Press, 1983.
(Contributor) J. W. Oller, editor, *Methods that Work,* Newbury House, 1983.
Grammar Games, Cambridge University Press, 1984.
(Contributor) C. Sion, editor, *Recipes for Tired Teachers,* Addison-Wesley, 1985.
(With Morgan) *Vocabulary,* Oxford University Press, 1986.
(Contributor) V. Kilian and V. Borbein, editors, *Fremdsprachen in der Weiterbildung,* Lexika Verlag, 1987.
(With Paul Davis) *Dictation,* Cambridge University Press, 1988.
(With Morgan) *The Q Book,* Longman, 1988.

Also author of *Hitch-Hiking,* 1975.

SIDELIGHTS: Mario Rinvolucri told *CA:* ''I belong to a team of people, associated with *Pilgrims Language Courses,* Canterbury, U.K., who are determined to make the learning of foreign languages a pleasureable and energetic business. We believe in offering the student 'frames' in which she can learn a language, rather than imposing a set progression on all students. All the language books I have co-authored see the student as a person first and a technical learner second.''

* * *

RISKIND, Mary   1944-

PERSONAL: Born August 2, 1944, in Elmira, N.Y. *Educa-*

tion: Elmira College, B.A., 1966; doctoral study at University of Michigan, 1966-73.

ADDRESSES: Home—223 Brookside Ave., Ridgewood, N.J. 07450.

CAREER: Writer; children's librarian, 1985—.

AWARDS, HONORS: Apple Is My Sign was named a notable children's trade book in field of social studies by American Library Association, 1981.

WRITINGS:

Apple Is My Sign (juvenile), Houghton, 1981.
Wildcat Summer (juvenile), Houghton, 1985.
Follow That Mom! (juvenile), Houghton, 1987.

SIDELIGHTS: Mary Riskind told *CA:* "I began my adult life with plans to teach social psychology to undergraduates, but a bleak academic job market and a young child that I was unwilling to turn over to indifferent childcare led in the end to a writing career. I believed it was a temporary measure but I enjoyed such an enormous sense of 'coming home,' of finally having reached the place where I belong, that I gave up all thought of returning to social psychology.

"My identity as a writer is very much tied up with my identity as a deaf person, though I am, in fact, hearing. Both my parents were deaf. I grew up signing and still think of my origins as being in the deaf community in much the same way that other people think of themselves as Italian-Americans or Polish-Americans. Many of the same skills that are important to communicating in sign are important in writing. And, like the hearing person in the deaf world, as a writer you are simultaneously outsider, observer, and translator.

"I started writing first for adults, but eventually began writing for my son who was curious about the grandfather Harry he had never known. I wrote down an anecdote that my father loved to tell, hoping to give him something of my father. Much later this became the chapter 'Harrry's Joke' in *Apple Is My Sign. Wildcat Summer* grew out of my affection for cats and my son's curiosity about a bobcat that we saw at our local wildlife center. We did a lot of reading about bobcats. *Wildcat* started as an early reader, went through *many* revisions, and was completed as a book for older children. Though it has never been as successful as *Apple Is My Sign*, I felt I had made great strides as a writer with it, particularly in plotting. *Follow That Mom!* was my response to the children who asked for a funny book. Maxine is the brash, rebellious child I wish I had dared to be!

"I continue to write for children because books were so important to me as a young person. I still remember evenings spent wriggling with impatience, waiting for my father to finish reading the next chapter in *Log Cabin Days,* the next Grimm tale, or the next adventure of Thumper the Rabbit. Finally the book would be put down—my cue that the story was about to unfold on his hands. Books for me erased the boundaries between hearing and not hearing. There I found courage, I found humor, I found possibility."

*   *   *

ROBBINS, Harold   1916-

PERSONAL: Original name, Francis Kane; took name Harold Rubin (some sources list as Rubins) when adopted in 1927; name legally changed to Harold Robbins; born May 21, 1916, in New York, N.Y.; married Lillian Machnivitz, 1937 (divorced, 1962); married Grace Palermo; children: Caryn, Adreana. *Education:* Attended public high school in New York City.

ADDRESSES: Home—Le Cannet, Cannes, France. *Office*—c/o Simon & Schuster, 1230 Avenue of the Americas, New York, N.Y. 10020.

CAREER: Novelist. Worked as a grocery clerk, cook, cashier, errand boy, and bookies' runner, 1927-31; in food factoring business during 1930s; Universal Pictures, New York City, shipping clerk in warehouse, 1940-41, executive director of budget and planning, 1942-57.

WRITINGS:

NOVELS

Never Love a Stranger, Knopf, 1948, reprinted, Pocket Books, 1985.
The Dream Merchants, Knopf, 1949, reprinted, Pocket Books, 1987.
A Stone for Danny Fisher, Knopf, 1952, reprinted, Pocket Books, 1985.
Never Leave Me, Knopf, 1953, reprinted, Pocket Books, 1978.
79 Park Avenue, Knopf, 1953, reprinted, Pocket Books, 1982.
Stiletto, Dell, 1960, reprinted, 1982.
The Carpetbaggers, Trident Press, 1961, reprinted, Pocket Books, 1987.
Where Love Has Gone, Trident Press, 1962, reprinted, Pocket Books, 1987.
The Adventurers, Simon & Schuster, 1966, reprinted, Pocket Books, 1987.
The Inheritors, Trident Press, 1969, reprinted, Pocket Books, 1985.
The Betsy, Trident Press, 1971.
The Pirate, Simon & Schuster, 1974.
The Lonely Lady, Simon & Schuster, 1976.
Dreams Die First, Simon & Schuster, 1977.
Memories of Another Day, Simon & Schuster, 1979.
Goodbye, Janette, Simon & Schuster, 1981.
Spellbinder, Simon & Schuster, 1982.
Descent from Xanadu, Simon & Schuster, 1984.
The Storyteller, Simon & Schuster, 1985.
Piranha, Simon & Schuster, 1986.

OTHER

Also author of "The Survivors," a television series for American Broadcasting Co., 1969-70.

SIDELIGHTS: Each day, some 40,000 people buy a Harold Robbins novel, while total sales of his twenty books is over 250 million copies worldwide. Sales figures for individual titles are also phenomenal. *The Carpetbaggers* has gone through more than seventy printings and sold over eight million copies; *79 Park Avenue* has sold more than five and a half million copies; *Never Love a Stranger* and *Dreams Die First* have each topped three million in sales. None of Robbins's novels have sold less than 600,000 copies. The books have also been translated into thirty-nine languages and are on sale in sixty-three countries around the world. Many have been made into popular films as well.

Because of these impressive statistics, Robbins calls himself the best novelist alive. "There's not another writer being published today," he tells Leslie Hanscom of the *Pittsburgh Press,* "whose every book—every book he's ever written—is always on sale everywhere, and that's gotta mean something. . . . You can find my books anywhere in the world in any language.''

The typical Robbins novel is a long, intricately-plotted story loaded with illicit sex, graphic violence, and powerful conflicts between members of the international jet set. Often they are also exposes of a sort, taking the reader behind the scenes of a glamorous and respected industry to reveal the secret corruption there. Often, too, the characters are thinly veiled versions of famous people in business and high society. The best of Robbins's novels are ''fun to read, full of outrageous people and complicated plot lines, not to mention lots of supposedly sizzling sex,'' as Joy Fielding writes in the Toronto *Globe and Mail*.

Robbins divides his books into two categories. The first are the adventure novels like *The Carpetbaggers* which focus on the Machiavellian power plays of unscrupulous captains of industry. The second type is what Robbins calls his Depression novels. These are, Dick Lochte explains in the *Los Angeles Times Book Review*, ''close in style and substance to the hard-boiled novels of the '30s in which tough street kids fight their way out of the proletarian jungle to achieve wealth and power.'' These latter books are largely based on Robbins's own life story, which in many ways sounds fantastic enough to be fiction.

Robbins began life as Francis Kane, an abandoned infant whose parents were unknown. Raised in a Roman Catholic orphanage in New York's tough Hell's Kitchen area, Robbins was placed in a series of foster homes as a youth. When the last of his foster parents, a Manhattan pharmacist, adopted him in 1927, he was given the name of Harold Rubin. He used the name of Harold Robbins when he turned to writing in the 1940s and has since made it his legal name.

At the age of fifteen, Robbins left home to begin a series of low-paying jobs in New York City. He worked as a bookies' runner, a cook, a clerk, and an errand boy, yet none of these jobs in the Depression years of the 1930s provided much opportunity for the ambitious Robbins. But while working as an inventory clerk in a grocery store, Robbins noted that fresh produce was difficult to find. The food distribution system of the time was so bad that some crops were rotting in the fields while store shelves were empty. Robbins got into the food factoring business, buying options on farmers' crops that were in demand in the city and selling the options to canning companies and wholesale grocers. By the time he was twenty, Robbins was a millionaire.

But in 1939, with war looming in the public mind, Robbins speculated in crop futures and lost. Reasoning that a major war would cut off or sharply reduce shipments of sugar, thus sending prices upward, Robbins invested his fortune in sugar at $4.85 per hundred pounds. Unfortunately, the Roosevelt administration chose to freeze food prices, and sugar was frozen at $4.65 per hundred pounds. Robbins went bankrupt. He took a job with the Universal Pictures warehouse in New York City as a shipping clerk. When he uncovered overcharges made to the company in excess of $30,000, Robbins was promoted, eventually becoming the executive director of budget and planning.

It was while working for Universal Pictures that Robbins first began to write. A vice-president of the company overheard Robbins complain about a novel that the studio had bought for filming. He challenged him to write a better book himself, and Robbins took him up on it. The resulting six-hundred-page novel was sent to an agent and within three weeks, the

publishing house of Alfred Knopf accepted the book for publication.

Never Love a Stranger, still Robbins's personal favorite of his novels, appeared in 1948. Although the book's candid approach to sex caused the police in Philadelphia to confiscate copies, many reviewers found it a realistic portrayal of a tough New York City orphan coming of age. Drawing heavily on Robbins's own experiences on the streets of Manhattan, the story revolves around the hustlers and racketeers of that city and recounts the protagonist's efforts to find his place in the world. N. L. Rothman of the *Saturday Review of Literature* notes that ''Robbins' writing is strong, his pace varied, and his invention admirable.''

Robbins followed his initial success with *The Dream Merchants*, a novel set in the Hollywood film world and telling of the rise of Johnny Edge, a movie entrepreneur. The novel also traces the rise of Hollywood itself. Budd Schulberg of the *Saturday Review of Literature* finds that ''the upward climb of immigrant shopkeepers to positions of power in the industry of mass entertainment makes colorful history and entertaining reading, [but] Mr. Robbins never quite succeeds in re-creating them as vital fictional characters.'' Citing Robbins's daring sex scenes, the reviewer for the *Christian Science Monitor*, M. W. Stoer, complains that ''it is regrettable that a book with so much in it that is otherwise entertaining and tempered with warm humanity should have been allowed to lapse into such tastelessness.'' But the *New York Post*'s Lewis Gannett judges the novel more favorably. ''Robbins,'' Gannett writes, ''knows the great Hollywood art: he keeps his story moving, shifting expertly from tears to laughter and from desperation to triumph.''

Perhaps the most critically praised of Robbins's novels is *A Stone for Danny Fisher*, the story of a poor Jewish boy's struggle to succeed in the New York of the 1930s and 1940s. James B. Lane, writing in the *Journal of Popular Culture*, claims that the book ''recorded the epic battle of ethnic groups against inconsequentialness, and the disintegration of their rigid moral, ethical, and cultural standards under the stress and strain of survival.'' James Kelly of the *New York Times*, despite some reservations about the novel's believability, praises Robbins's ''vivid characterization'' and ''feeling for individual scenes.'' Thomas Thompson of *Life* speculates that had Robbins ended his career with *A Stone for Danny Fisher*, the novel ''would have reserved him a small place in literature.''

Unfortunately, Robbins went on to write many more bestselling novels, few of which have received a sympathetic hearing from the critics. Evan Hunter of the *New York Times Book Review*, for instance, argues that ''in true pulp style Mr. Robbins never tries to evoke anything except through cliche. . . . His people never simply say anything. They say it 'shortly' or 'darkly,' or they 'growl' or 'grunt' it.'' Reviewing *Spellbinder* for the *Chicago Tribune Book World*, Frederick Busch states that ''the book is the paginated equivalent of television: shallow, semiliterate, made of cliches and stereotypes, full of violence and heavy breathing. People who love TV love such books.'' Reviewing *The Betsy* for *Books and Bookmen*, Roger Baker calls it ''about as realistic and pungent as Batman. . . . The superficiality of the characters is beyond belief; the mechanical setting-up of the sexual bouts is crude; and the fact that everyone in the saga seems either vicious or bats or both doesn't help at all.'' Fielding even claims that Robbins's work has gotten worse over time: ''Robbins keeps churning them out, seemingly oblivious to the fact that his already cardboard characters have turned to paper, that his plots have virtually disappeared, and that . . . his sex scenes [are] not only silly but downright pathetic.''

But not all critics are so harsh with Robbins. In his review of *The Storyteller*, for instance, Lochte admits that "in describing the art of economic survival in the 1940s—how deals were cut with Brooklyn crime bosses, Manhattan publishers and Hollywood studio heads—Robbins shows how good a writer he is. His prose is lean and straightforward, with a keen, cynical edge." Robert Graecen of *Books and Bookmen* points out that "nobody can accuse Harold Robbins of not telling a story. He knows how to handle narrative and keep the novel on the move." Lane argues that "Robbins, the bestselling American novelist, has been spurned and overlooked by literary critics because of the alleged mediocrity of his work. Nevertheless, he has won public affection by portraying identifiable life-situations in a realistic and titillating manner. His characters resemble the common man even as their bizarre exploits, fascinating sex lives and heroic struggles exude an air of Walter Mitty.''

Despite the usual scorn his work receives from the critics, Robbins has fared quite well with the reading public. His books have set phenomenal sales records, while his *The Carpetbaggers* is estimated to be the fourth most-read book in history. The profits from such overwhelming popularity have assuaged some of the critical barbs. As a writer for the *Pittsburgh Press* notes, "all Robbins has to show for it is a style of living that might serve as a model for an oil sheik. His 85-foot yacht is moored in the Mediterranean not far from his Riviera villa. In Beverly Hills, he lives in Gloria Swanson's old mansion." Robbins tells Hascom how he feels about his success: "I know it hurts some of the others to admit I am the best. I couldn't care less about their feelings. I'll make it very simple. I've been writing books now for almost 30 years, and my books have lasted.''

MEDIA ADAPTATIONS: Never Love a Stranger was filmed by Allied Artists in 1957; *A Stone for Danny Fisher* was filmed as "King Creole" by Paramount in 1958; *The Carpetbaggers* was filmed by Paramount in 1963; *Where Love Has Gone* was filmed by Paramount in 1964; "Nevada Smith," based on a character in *The Carpetbaggers*, was filmed by Paramount in 1966; *The Adventurers* was filmed by Paramount in 1968; *Stiletto* was filmed by Avco-Embassy in 1970; *The Betsy* was filmed by Allied Artists in 1978; *Dreams Die First* was filmed by American International in 1979.

BIOGRAPHICAL/CRITICAL SOURCES:

BOOKS

Biography News, Gale, 1975.
Contemporary Literary Criticism, Volume 5, Gale, 1976.

PERIODICALS

Books and Bookmen, April, 1971.
Chicago Tribune Book World, February 3, 1980, January 2, 1983.
Christian Science Monitor, October 28, 1949.
Coronet, February, 1970.
Globe and Mail (Toronto), January 25, 1986.
Journal of Popular Culture, fall, 1974.
Life, December 8, 1967.
Los Angeles Times Book Review, September 12, 1982, February 16, 1986.
Newsday, April 16, 1966.
Newsweek, June 6, 1966.

New Yorker, March 15, 1952, June 17, 1961, November 29, 1969.
New York Post, March 31, 1966, February 4, 1967, September 6, 1969, June 24, 1972.
New York Times, March 7, 1948, March 9, 1952, June 25, 1961, February 28, 1965.
New York Times Book Review, June 25, 1961, November 18, 1979, June 7, 1981, September 5, 1982, April 29, 1984, January 26, 1986.
People, July 19, 1976.
Pittsburgh Press, March 16, 1975.
Punch, June 12, 1974.
Saturday Review of Literature, May 22, 1948, October 29, 1949.
Time, December 13, 1971, November 11, 1974.
TV Guide, April 11, 1970.
Variety, November 5, 1969.
Washington Post, November 29, 1979, October 5, 1983.
Washington Post Book World, July 5, 1981.

OTHER

"I'm the World's Best Writer—There's Nothing More to Say" (television documentary), ITV Network, 1971.†

—*Sketch by Thomas Wiloch*

* * *

ROBERTS, Ellen Elizabeth Mayhew 1946-

PERSONAL: Born October 5, 1946, in Knoxville, Tenn.; daughter of Elliott P. (a political scientist) and Sue (a lawyer; maiden name, Abraham) Roberts. *Education:* Reed College, B.A., 1969; attended Columbia University, 1980-81. *Religion:* Protestant.

ADDRESSES: Office—414 West 121st St., #64, New York, N.Y. 10027.

CAREER: St. Martin's Press, Inc., New York City, assistant editor, 1969-70; Lothrop, Lee & Shepard Co., New York City, assistant editor, 1970-71; Prentice-Hall, Inc., Englewood Cliffs, N.J., associate editor, 1971-73, editor-in-chief of children's books, 1973-82; Columbia University Press, New York City, marketing coordinator, 1982-84.

MEMBER: Association for Childhood Education International, American Library Association, American Institute of Graphic Arts, American Printing History Association, American Association of School Librarians, Children's Book Council, Printing Women of New York.

WRITINGS:

The Children's Picture Book: How to Write It, How to Sell It, Writer's Digest, 1981.
(Editor) *The Prentice-Hall Encyclopedia of Mathematics*, Prentice-Hall, 1982.
Nonfiction for Children, Funk, 1986.
How to Write and Sell Your Children's Book, Writer's Audio Shop (Austin, Tex.), 1987.

WORK IN PROGRESS: An illustrated how-to series, including *Christmas, Fit to Sit, Family Business, How to Write Clearly, and How to Keep Your House from Falling In; The Commerce of Childhood: Three Centuries of American Children's Books*, based on a lecture series at Armington Foundation, Case-Western Reserve University.

SIDELIGHTS: Ellen E.M. Roberts told *CA:* "I never thought of becoming a writer myself. I was a poor reader, preferring picture books long after my friends had graduated to novels. But I was always interested in other people's writing: at age nine, I established the *Pearl Post* at the James F. Oyster School in Washington, D.C., and I enjoyed editing and selecting the contributions.

"I was then, as I am now, always torn between my interest in words and my interest in pictures. When a family friend suggested that I try children's book publishing as a career that would satisfy both needs, I leaped at the opportunity. My first job paid eighty-five dollars a week, and I would have worked for half that for the opportunity to make books.

"The war between words and pictures still rages in my mind. When I was forty, I had the opportunity to take a drug that resolved a neurological problem that had plagued me all my life. I agonized over whether I should take it or not because the doctor warned me it is murder on the eyes. I chose to take it, a decision that I am glad of.

"My eyes are still good enough to read and draw, but I no longer take vision for granted. Long a staple in children's literature, illustrations are helpful to anyone of any age who is trying to 'see' something for the first time. The group of books that I am working on now uses words to see and pictures to amplify: I mean them as a testament to my faith in print, its pictures, its words, the touch of paper, the smell of new ink—and its marvelous message of portability, first as a book, then as images and ideas that become the reader's own.

"My first big break came when Prentice-Hall offered me a job as an acquisitions editor. There I pored over the slush pile, travelled across the country and Europe, too, looking for new talent and new approaches to books. My discoveries included Henry Allard, Shirley Hughes, Guy Billout, and Dennis Nolan. What an exciting ten years that was!

"But nothing can last forever, and I felt it was time for a change. I took a leave of absence to attend Columbia's Business School, and there became acquainted with the importance of marketing books effectively. At Columbia University Press I tried to sell the books that people write, and it was very exciting to meet readers as well as writers.

"While I was concentrating on my career, I was asked if I wanted to write a book about picture books. Faced with the isolation of going to school, I thought, 'This is *the* opportunity!' I immersed myself in libraries, reading all the old classic children's books and reviewing the offerings of the post-War period. It seemed to me that something had been lost as illustrators took the lead and writers fell behind. Since I believe firmly that success begins with the words, I enjoyed producing a work about writing.

"I am glad for the opportunity to write and draw as well as edit and publish; I feel that my publishing career is well-rounded, even though there are times that I would prefer to do anything but write. The writer's life is the scariest yet the most satisfying. I wouldn't change it for anything."

*   *   *

ROBERTS, Philip Davies   1938-

PERSONAL: Born October 9, 1938, in Sherbrooke, Quebec, Canada; son of Geoffrey Davies and Mary (Williams) Roberts; married Carol Lynn Berney, 1978 (divorced, 1984); children:

Rachael Ann, Megan Leah. *Education:* Acadia University, B.A., 1959; Oxford University, B.A. (with honors), 1962, M.A., 1966; University of Sydney, B.Mus., 1980.

ADDRESSES: Home—144 St. George St., Annapolis Royal, Nova Scotia, Canada B0S 1A0. *Agent*—Juri Gabriel, 35 Camberwell Grove, London SE5 8JA, England.

CAREER: British Institute, Madrid, Spain, English teacher, 1962; Reuters News Agency, London, England, sub-editor, 1963-66; Peters/Bishop & Partners, London, public relations consultant, 1966-67; University of Sydney, Sydney, Australia, lecturer, 1967-74, senior lecturer in English, 1974-79; freelance writer, 1980—; *Tico Times,* San Jose, Costa Rica, staff writer, 1982-83. Founder and editor of Island Press, 1970-79.

AWARDS, HONORS: Rhodes scholar at Oxford University, 1959-62; Chapman Memorial Prize for poetry, Oxford University, 1962.

WRITINGS:

Just Passing Through (poems), Ladysmith Press, 1969.
(With Geoff Page) *Two Poets,* University of Queensland Press, 1971.
(Editor with J. C. Bright and P. M. Bright) *Models of English Style,* Science Press, 1971.
Crux (poems), Island Press, 1973.
Will's Dream (poems), University of Queensland Press, 1975.
Selected Poems, Island Press, 1978.
How Poetry Works, Penguin Books, 1986.
Plain English: A User's Guide, Penguin Books, 1987.
Letters Home (poems), Broken Jaw Press, 1988.

Contributor to *Times Educational Supplement, English Studies,* and *Semiotica.* Poetry editor of *Sydney Morning Herald,* 1970-74.

SIDELIGHTS: Philip Davies Roberts told *CA:* "I write to communicate at least one possible way of looking at things. My writing habits are irregular—I am at the opposite end of the spectrum from those who write regularly every day a painstaking couple of pages. Apart from my poetry, the books I have written have so far been quite didactic, a step away from school books, though I hope not altogether humorless.

"I was much influenced at the start of my writing career by Robert Graves, who gave enthusiastic advice and criticism for a number of years. Since then, I have been most influenced by foreign poets: the Greeks Seferis and Kavafis, the Czech Holub, the Russian Pasternak, the French St. John Perse, to mention a few. English poets I particularly admire are Skelton, Donne, Herbert, Blake, Whitman, and Berryman. I treat poetry as being closer to music than to 'meaningful' speech.

"In the near future I hope to write books dealing with how music works, choosing a musical instrument, and the arts scene in Canada."

*   *   *

RODD, Kylie Tennant   1912-1988
(Kylie Tennant)

PERSONAL: First name originally Kathleen; born March 12, 1912, in Manly, New South Wales, Australia; died February 28, 1988, in Sydney, Australia; daughter of Thomas Walter and Kathleen (Tolhurst) Tennant; married Lewis Charles Rodd (a schoolteacher and headmaster), November 21, 1932 (died, 1979); children: Benison (daughter), John Laurence (died, 1978).

Education: Attended Brighton College and University of Sydney. *Religion:* Church of England.

ADDRESSES: Home—Cliff View Orchard, Blackheath, New South Wales, Australia. *Agent*—Judy Barry, 25 Yarranabbe Rd., Darling Point, Sydney, New South Wales, Australia.

CAREER: Worked at various jobs, c. 1928-32; full-time writer, 1935-59; in addition to writing, worked as journalist, editor, and publishing adviser, 1959-69; full-time writer, 1969-88. Commonwealth Literary Fund, lecturer, 1957-58, member of advisory board, 1961-73. Member of board, Australian Aborigines Cooperatives. Made appearances on Australian television and radio.

MEMBER: Australian Fellowship of Writers (life patron), Australian Journalists Association.

AWARDS, HONORS: S. H. Prior Memorial Prize, 1935, for *Tiburon,* and 1941, for *The Battlers;* gold medal, Australian Literary Society, 1941, for *The Battlers;* fellowship from Commonwealth Literary Fund, 1951; Commonwealth Jubilee Stage Play Award, 1952, for *Tether a Dragon;* Children's Book of the Year Award, Australian Children's Book Council, 1960, for *All the Proud Tribesmen;* Officer of the Order of Australia, 1980.

WRITINGS—Under name Kylie Tennant:

NOVELS

Tiburon (originally serialized in *Bulletin,* 1935), Endeavor Press, 1935, reprinted, Angus & Robertson, 1981.
Foveaux, Gollancz, 1939, reprinted, Angus & Robertson, 1981.
The Battlers, Macmillan, 1941, reprinted, Salem House, 1986.
Ride on, Stranger, Macmillan, 1943, reprinted, Angus & Robertson, 1980.
Time Enough Later, Macmillan, 1943.
Lost Haven, Macmillan, 1946, reprinted, 1968.
The Joyful Condemned, St. Martin's, 1953, complete version published as *Tell Morning This,* Angus & Robertson, 1968.
The Honey Flow, St. Martin's, 1956, reprinted, Angus & Robertson, 1973.
Tantavallon, Macmillan, 1983.

SHORT STORIES

(Contributor) Edith M. Fry, editor, *Tales by Australians,* British Authors' Press, 1939.
(Contributor) Cecil Mann, editor, *Coast to Coast 1941,* Angus & Robertson, 1941.
(Contributor) T. Inglis Moore, editor, *Australia Writes,* Cheshire, 1953.
(Contributor) H. P. Heseltine, editor, *Australian Idiom,* Cheshire, 1963.
(General editor; also contributor) *Great Stories of Australia,* seven volumes, St. Martin's, 1963-66.
(General editor; also contributor) *Summer's Tales,* two volumes, St. Martin's, 1964-65.
Ma Jones and the Little White Cannnibals (collection), St. Martin's, 1967.
(Contributor) *The Cool Man and Other Contemporary Stories by Australian Authors,* Angus & Robertson, 1973.

NONFICTION

Australia: Her Story; Notes on a Nation (history), St. Martin's, 1953, revised edition, Pan Books, 1964.
Speak You So Gently (travelogue), Gollancz, 1959.
(With husband, Lewis C. Rodd) *The Australian Essay,* Cheshire, 1968.

Evatt: Politics and Justice (biography of Herbert Vere Evatt), Angus & Robertson, 1970.
The Missing Heir: The Autobiography of Kylie Tennant, Macmillan, 1986.

JUVENILES

John o' the Forest and Other Plays, Macmillan, 1950.
The Bells of the City and Other Plays, Macmillan, 1955.
The Bushrangers' Christmas Eve and Other Plays, Macmillan, 1959.
All the Proud Tribesmen (story), illustrated by Clem Seale, St. Martin's, 1959.
Trail Blazers of the Air (stories), St. Martin's 1966.

OTHER

Tether a Dragon (play), Associated General Publications, 1952.
Long John Silver: The Story of the Film; Adapted by K. Tennant from the . . . Screenplay by Martin Rackin, Associated General Publications, 1954.
The Man on the Headland (fictionalized biography), Angus & Robertson, 1971.

Critic for *Sydney Morning Herald.* Australian literary advisor to Macmillan & Co.

Manuscript collection at Australian National Library in Canberra.

SIDELIGHTS: A noted Australian author of social-realist fiction, Kylie Tennant wrote novels offering spirited and authentic portrayals of Australian life. Her award-winning 1935 first novel *Tiburon,* profiling a small town during the Depression, launched a prolific writing career that, in addition to nine more novels, saw her produce short stories, nonfiction, plays, and criticism. Noted for emphasizing the externals of human experience, Tennant's fiction abounds with authentic place descriptions, colorful characters, and fast-paced, witty dialogue. Although she often emerges as a reformer—Tennant's writings display an affinity for characters besieged by modern societal ills—at the same time she demonstrates a good-natured acceptance of some of life's harsher conditions. The obituary writer for the London *Times* noted that Tennant's "desire to improve society was at odds in her with her almost Brechtian celebration of its rougher elements and her conviction that human nature was not likely to change."

Originally named Kathleen, Tennant acquired the name "Kylie"—an Australian aborigine word for boomerang—during childhood, and kept it all of her life. Tennant left school at the age of sixteen, after which she took on a variety of jobs, including work for the Australian Broadcasting Commission, work as a salesgirl, and operating a chicken farm. For a year she attended the University of Sydney as a psychology student. In 1932, she hitchhiked and jumped trains throughout New South Wales, eventually ending up in the northern city of Coonabarabran where she married her husband. Three years later *Tiburon* appeared, garnering critical praise for its authentic and lively depiction of the residents of a small New South Wales village living on handouts during the Great Depression. *Tiburon* won for its twenty-three-year-old author the S. H. Prior Memorial Prize and, as the *Times* obituary writer notes, "a certain notoriety amongst the polite readership for its many swipes at things they held sacred, such as local politics and bureaucracy."

Throughout her writing career, Tennant was noted for the rigorous and thorough research invested in her novels—often gained through first-hand experience. For *The Battlers* she camped with vagabonds and migrant laborers, travelling across Australia in a cart. For *The Joyful Condemned*, Tennant lived among prostitutes and the slum inhabitants of Sydney—even managing to get herself thrown into jail. For other novels, she turned to technical tasks. Preparing for *Lost Haven*, she studied ship-building, and for *The Honey Flow*, accompanied beekeepers on their annual migrations through the blossoming eucalyptus trees of Australia. Tennant once commented that her preference was for people who existed on the margins of modern industrial society.

Critics praised Tennant's ability to authentically portray, with understanding and honesty, a spectrum of unordinary characters, locales, and situations. Regarding *The Battlers*, which profiles the lives of hobos, vagrants, and migrant workers, Lionel Bridge commented in *Commonweal*: "Here is a combination of the most unusual events happening to the most original characters in the strangest setting the American fiction audience is likely to be offered again." J. S. Southron in the *New York Times* praised both Tennant's control of her subject matter and its integrity: "There are enough stories in 'The Battlers' to have filled a novel twice the size in the hands of a less concise, less artistic writer. And there is the curious affection aroused in us for characters as unglamorous and devoid of showmanship as they are genuine. It is a book whose outstanding feature is the sort of strength that compels admiration." Klaus Lambrecht in the *Saturday Review of Literature* called *The Battlers* "a most appealing book" in that "there is humor in it and a bitter realism, tragedy and love, warmth and cruelty, and sensitive conception of a peculiar form of life." Tennant's third novel won her another S. H. Prior Memorial Prize, in addition to a gold medal from the Australian Literary Society.

Like *The Battlers*, Tennant's other novels were noted for empathetic and vigorous characterizations. In *Ride on, Stranger*, she tells the story of an Australian girl who leaves her family of seven "on a career of moderately healthy disillusionment among faith-healers, occultists, left-wings, aesthetes and others," according to a reviewer for the *Times Literary Supplement*. John Hampon in *Spectator* called Tennant a "lively gifted writer," who, in *Ride on, Stranger*, "handles the seamy side of life with robust vigour." The *Times Literary Supplement* reviewer added: "There is a good deal of fun in this sprawling, crowded story of uncultivated types in the Australian wilds and of excessively cultivated or freakish types in Sydney, and with the fun goes a certain hard honesty of sentiment that is frequently telling." Regarding the 1946 novel *Lost Haven*, Robert Traver noted in *Book Week* that Tennant displayed "a remarkable facility for figurative expression, the evocative phrase." He added that, although such "occasionally gets a trifle out of hand" and that "at times she pelts the reader with words," when Tennant "wants to—which is most of the time—she can write like an inspired demon."

One of Tennant's most praised works is the 1953 novel *The Joyful Condemned*, initially published in abridged form due to a paper shortage and fears of censorship backlash, and reissued fifteen years later in its entirety as *Tell Morning This*. Tennant's longest novel, *The Joyful Condemned* traces the lives of several working-class girls in wartime Sydney who indulge themselves in the worlds of the slums. Tennant "is remarkably skilful in conveying the helpless ignorance of such girls in [the] face of authority and their eagerness to escape from the gentility of middle-class life into the riotous freedom of their own world," noted a reviewer for the *Times Literary Supplement*. Sylvia Stallings wrote in the *New York Herald Tribune Book Review* that Tennant's "quick ear and eye bring home

both the raciness of underworld speech and the curious beauty of the city at night, the searchlights 'working through the clouds like the fingers of a wool-classer through fleeces.' Her novel comes as a great wash of fresh air after the thin-blooded elegance of so many of her peers." Upon the novel's reissue as *Tell Morning This*, a reviewer for the *Times Literary Supplement* commented that the book was "told with clarity and honesty, and even, despite the bumpiness of much of the writing, a degree of poetic sensitivity."

In addition to her celebrated fiction, Tennant wrote in other genres, continuing to demonstrate thorough and thoughtful treatment of subject matter. *Australia: Her Story; Notes on a Nation* was praised by Fritz Stern in the *Saturday Review* as an "excellent example of popular history, an art which nowadays is too often neglected in favor of specialized treatises or historical novels which mistake life for lust." Tennant's 1970 biography of Herbert Vere Evatt entitled *Evatt: Politics and Justice* "goes a long way towards doing justice to the most fascinating figure in the Australian labour movement since W. M. Hughes," according to a *Times Literary Supplement* reviewer, who singled out both Tennant's "control of complex material and events," in addition to "the insight into Evatt's character." And in her 1959 children's book *All the Proud Tribesmen*, Tennant relates the lifestyles and history of Australia's aborigines. P. D. Beard noted in *Library Journal* that Tennant's story "reveal[s] keen insight into the minds of a people and a fine sense of local atmosphere." Howard Boston likewise commented in the *New York Times Book Review* that in *All the Proud Tribesmen*, Tennant's "characterization is deft and sure, and she is adept at juggling several themes simultaneously." "The story's real strength, though," added Boston, "lies in its sensitive and appealing portrayal of the island folk."

Tennant's last novel *Tantavallon*, published in 1983, displays the complexion of her earlier novels, offering a panorama of varied characters and situations. Featured in *Tantavallon*, notes Ken Goodwin in *A History of Australian Literature*, are "Vietnamese migrants mining uranium, a churchwarden attempting suicide in Sydney Harbour, a fire, a suburban street battle, a spectacular car accident, and a cancer scare." *Tantavallon* "illustrates well [Tennant's] belief that life in general is 'a thin layer of ice over a raging human volcano', full of 'absurdity and chaos,'" according to Goodwin; however, as in Tennant's other novels, "there is always vigour, entertainment, and comedy in her depiction." The *Times* obituary writer comments on a lasting impression of Tennant's work: "Her often noted slapdash writing and lack of psychological penetration . . . are compensated for, in her best books, by her zest for life, humour and, above all, by her affection for the human race."

AVOCATIONAL INTERESTS: The welfare of Australian aborigines.

BIOGRAPHICAL/CRITICAL SOURCES:

BOOKS

Dick, Margaret, *The Novels of Kylie Tennant*, Rigby, 1966.
Goodwin, Ken, *A History of Australian Literature*, St. Martin's, 1986.
Tennant, Kylie, *The Joyful Condemned*, reissued as *Tell Morning This*, Angus & Robertson, 1968.
Tennant, Kylie, *The Missing Heir: The Autobiography of Kylie Tennant*, Macmillan, 1986.

PERIODICALS

Books, August 10, 1941.
Book Week, September 5, 1943, March 31, 1946.
Christian Science Monitor, November 5, 1953.
Commonweal, October 10, 1941.
Listener, March 23, 1943.
Meanjin Quarterly, number 4, 1953.
New Republic, August 25, 1941.
New Statesman and Nation, January 25, 1941.
New Yorker, August 28, 1943, March 30, 1946, October 2, 1954.
New York Herald Tribune Book Review, May 10, 1953.
New York Times, August 10, 1941, November 8, 1941, February 14, 1943, September 12, 1943, April 7, 1946, May 10, 1953.
New York Times Book Review, August 21, 1960.
Saturday Review, October 17, 1953.
Saturday Review of Literature, August 9, 1941, May 18, 1946.
Spectator, April 9, 1943.
Times Literary Supplement, January 4, 1941, March 20, 1943, February 27, 1953, June 26, 1953, February 8, 1968, July 30, 1971.
Weekly Book Review, April 4, 1943, September 12, 1943, March 31, 1946.
Yale Review, autumn, 1941.

OBITUARIES:

PERIODICALS

Times (London), March 10, 1988. †

—*Sketch by Michael E. Mueller*

* * *

ROE, Harry Mason
[Collective pseudonym]

WRITINGS:

"LANKY LAWSON" SERIES

Lanky Lawson, the Boy from Nowhere: How He Arrived at Beanville, What Beanville Did to Him, and What He Did to Beanville, Barse & Co., 1929.
. . . with the One-Ring Circus: How He Joined the Show, What He Did to the Wild Animals, What Happened When the Circus Collapsed, Barse & Co., 1929.
. . . and His Trained Zebra: How He Happened to Get the Beast, How the Cantankerous Animal Performed, and What Happened at the County Fair, Barse & Co., 1930.

SIDELIGHTS: The Lanky Lawson series was unusual compared to other Stratemeyer Syndicate volumes in that it was written in the first person. An orphan, Lawson was, in the publishers' words, "always willing to aid a friend and equally willing to give an enemy what he deserves, but often in a laughable way." For additional information, see the entries for Harriet S. Adams, Edward L. Stratemeyer, and Andrew E. Svenson.

BIOGRAPHICAL/CRITICAL SOURCES:

BOOKS

Johnson, Deidre, editor and compiler, *Stratemeyer Pseudonyms and Series Books: An Annotated Checklist of Stratemeyer and Stratemeyer Syndicate Publications,* Greenwood Press, 1982.

ROGERS, Pattiann   1940-

PERSONAL: Born March 23, 1940, in Joplin, Mo.; daughter of William Elmer and Irene (Keiter) Tall; married John Robert Rogers (a geophysicist), September 3, 1960; children: John Ashley, Arthur William. *Education:* University of Missouri, B.A., 1961; University of Houston, M.A., 1981.

ADDRESSES: Home—11502 Brookmeadows Lane, Stafford, Tex. 77477.

CAREER: Poet. High school English teacher in Auxvasse, Mo., 1961-62, and St. Charles, Mo., 1962-63; kindergarten teacher in St. James, Mo., 1963-67; School for Little Children, Sugar Land, Tex., teacher, 1978-79. Poetry workshop instructor, Southwest Writers Conference, 1982 and 1986. Visiting assistant professor, Southern Methodist University, spring, 1985, and University of Houston, spring, 1986; faculty member, Vermont College of Norwich University, 1986—; senior lecturer, University of Texas, fall, 1987. Poet-in-residence, Robert Frost Place, summer, 1987; Richard Hugo Poet-in-Residence, University of Montana, spring, 1988. Poetry readings throughout the United States, 1981—; has also conducted workshops and lectures in conjunction with poetry readings. Director of Poetry Readings for Children, 1974-76.

MEMBER: PEN, Associated Writing Programs, Modern Poetry Association, Poets and Writers, Texas Institute of Letters, Phi Beta Kappa.

AWARDS, HONORS: Young Poet's Prize, 1980, and Theodore Roethke Prize, 1981, both from *Poetry Northwest;* Eunice Tietjens Prize, 1981, and Bess Hokin Prize, 1982, both from *Poetry;* grants from National Endowment for the Arts, 1982 and 1988; Voertmann Poetry Award from Texas Institute of Letters, 1982, for *The Expectations of Light;* Pushcart Prizes, 1984 and 1985; Guggenheim fellowship, 1984-85.

WRITINGS:

POETRY

The Expectations of Light, Princeton University Press, 1981.
The Ark River Review: Three Poet Issue (chapbook), Ark River Review, 1981.
The Only Holy Window (chapbook), Trilobite Press, 1984.
The Tattooed Lady in the Garden, Wesleyan University Press, 1986.
Legendary Performance, Ion Press, 1987.

CONTRIBUTOR OF POETRY

Pushcart Prize, 9: Best of the Small Presses, Avon, 1984.
The Morrow Anthology of Younger American Poets, Morrow, 1984.
Jack Myers and Roger Weingarten, editors, *New American Poets of the Eighties,* Wampeter Press, 1985.
Pushcart Prize, 10: Best of the Small Presses, Avon, 1985.
Leon Stokesbury, editor, *The Made Thing: An Anthology of Contemporary Southern Poetry,* University of Arkansas Press, 1986.
Frances Mayes, editor, *The Discovery of Poetry* (textbook), Harcourt, 1987.
From Sight to Insight: Stages in the Writing Process (textbook), Holt, 1987.
Mirrors: An Introduction to Literature (textbook), 3rd edition, Harper, 1987.
Elaine Dallman and others, editors, *Woman Poet: The South,* Women-in-Literature, 1988.

Also contributor to *Contemporary American Poetry from the University Presses*, University of Wisconsin Press. Contributor to numerous periodicals, including *American Poetry Review, Poetry, Poetry Northwest, Iowa Review, New Yorker, Georgia Review, Virginia Quarterly Review, Southern Review, Prairie Schooner, Chicago Review, Massachusetts Review, Yale Review, Michigan Quarterly Review, Missouri Review, Kenyon Review,* and *Nimrod.*

WORK IN PROGRESS: A fourth collection of poetry, tentatively titled *The Next Story;* an anthology of contemporary poems using the garden as setting, symbol, or image.

SIDELIGHTS: In her first book of poems, *Expectations of Light,* Pattiann Rogers explores the implications that modern science holds for humankind's perception of itself. As she explains to Richard McCann in the *Iowa Review:* "I wanted to express the kind of wonder and exhilaration that I felt was contained in much of what science has been discovering and also to reflect in my poetry how some of these discoveries affect our ways of seeing ourselves. I felt that somehow poetry was going to have to deal with the process of science and what science is saying." Writing in the *Georgia Review,* Peter Stitt calls *Expectations of Light* "an unusually original first book, surprising for its sophisticated incorporation of modern scientific thinking into poetry. Every poem manages somehow to present accurate knowledge of the physical universe, often in a multifaceted plethora of detail." Stitt later adds: "That Rogers is able to achieve lyrical beauty through this material is truly a testament to the century in which we live."

Rogers once told *CA:* "Circumstances important to my writing are leisure time and the ability to work within a family environment of economic and emotional security, within a country which permits and supports free expression and intellectual investigation."

AVOCATIONAL INTERESTS: Travel (including England).

BIOGRAPHICAL/CRITICAL SOURCES:

PERIODICALS

Georgia Review, summer, 1982.
Iowa Review, Volume 17, number 2, 1987.
Poetry, December, 1983, January, 1988.
Yale Review, autumn, 1982.

*   *   *

ROLLINS, Peter C(ushing) 1942-

PERSONAL: Born April 1, 1942, in Boston, Mass.; son of Daniel G. (a lawyer) and Selma (a lawyer; maiden name, Fox) Rollins; children: Michael Bradford. *Education:* Attended Dartmouth College, 1959-61; Harvard University, B.A. (with high honors), 1972. *Politics:* "Mugwump."

ADDRESSES: Office—Department of English, Oklahoma State University, Stillwater, Okla. 74078-0135.

CAREER: Harvard University, Cambridge, Mass., teaching assistant, 1967-72; Oklahoma State University, Stillwater, 1972-88, began as assistant professor, became professor; currently working in film and television studies/production. Fellow of National Humanities Institute at Yale University, 1976-77; Kellogg National fellow, 1980-83. *Military service:* U.S. Marine Corps, 1963-66; served in Vietnam; became captain.

MEMBER: American Studies Association (chairman of film committee), Popular Culture Association (national and regional president), University Film and Video Association, Society for Cinema Studies, Brookline (Mass.) Historical Society, Stillwater (Okla.) Historical Society, Blue Sky Film Consortium (executive board).

AWARDS, HONORS: Bronze Hugo Award from Chicago International Film Festival, 1977, Golden Eagle Certificate from Council on International Nontheatrical Events, 1977, Hemisfilm Medallion from International Fine Arts Center for the southwest, 1978, and "Best Film by an Oklahoman" citation from Governor of Oklahoma, 1978, all for film "Will Rogers' 1920s: A Cowboy's Guide to the Times."

WRITINGS:

"Will Rogers' 1920s: A Cowboy's Guide to the Times," Churchill Films, 1976.
Benjamin Lee Whorf: Lost Generation Theories of Mind, Language, and Religion, University Microfilms, 1980.
Will Rogers: A Biobibliography, Greenwood Press, 1982.
Hollywood As Historian: American Film in a Cultural Context, University Press of Kentucky, 1983.
"Television's Vietnam: The Real Story," Public Broadcasting System (PBS-TV), 1985.
"Television's Vietnam: The Impact of Media," PBS-TV, 1986.

Also author of conference video "New Ways of Escaping Poverty" for Ethics and Public Policy Center, Washington, D.C. Contributor to numerous journals in the fields of film and American studies, including *Journal of Popular Culture, American Quarterly, Proceedings of the 1972 Mid-America Linguistics Conference, Journal of Popular Film, Film and History, Literature/Film Quarterly, Proceedings of the Brookline Historical Society for 1970,* and *Proceedings of the Brookline Historical Society for 1972.*

SIDELIGHTS: Peter C. Rollins explained his work with visual media in *Harvard and Radcliffe College Class of 1963:* "It has been my mission," he wrote, "to teach what is called 'visual literacy.' Our students and fellow citizens need some familiarity with the lexicon of the visual media so that they can weigh and evaluate the messages aimed at them by self-interested politicians, corporations, interest groups. It has been my experience that students aware of the seductions and perils of visual communications gain a perspective on varying uses for words and image. The constant complaint of our students is that we have 'ruined' television for them."

Rollins recently told *CA:* "My work with Vietnam as a subject has had both positive and negative aspects. On the positive side, I have been pleased that I could gain a forum to correct the malicious and destructive stereotypes about Vietnam, the Vietnamese, and the Vietnam veteran. For my work in this effort, I have received numerous letters and awards; I was especially gratified by the special honors given by the Vietnamese communities of Arlington, Virginia, New Orleans, Louisiana, and Orange County, California. Since the programs have been on the air, I have run into a number of veterans who are happy that someone spoke up for them. On the negative side, many academics have not liked my programs. The shows have been assailed in professional meetings and in the press. *TV Guide,* the *New York Times,* and the *Wall Street Journal* all gave the shows positive reviews; kudos from such dominant media have helped. The truth is that Vietnam is still a very hot topic; furthermore, those who avoided serving their country have a vested interest in *not* learning from the experiences of Vietnam and Cambodia about the real tragedy caused by our departure from the region. My task has been to deliver an unpleasant message to my fellow intellectuals.''

Speaking of his work in television, Rollins told *CA:* ''Television is such a powerful medium today that humanists should be involved in the production of stimulating programs. If we do not contribute our talents, the task will be taken up by journalists and those who have only a surface familiarity with our cultural heritage; as teachers, we will later suffer the consequences in our classrooms.''

BIOGRAPHICAL/CRITICAL SOURCES:

BOOKS

Harvard and Radcliffe College Class of 1963: Fifteenth Anniversary Report, Crimson Printing Co., 1978.

PERIODICALS

Los Angeles Times Book Review, May 22, 1983.

* * *

ROOKMAAKER, Hendrik Roelof 1922-1977

PERSONAL: Born February 27, 1922; died 1977; son of Henderik and Dora (Heytink) Rookmaaker; married Anna Maria Huitker, August 1, 1949; children: Henderik R., Leendert C., Maria H. *Education:* University of Amsterdam, Drs., 1952, Dr., 1959. *Religion:* ''Christian—orthodox protestant.''

ADDRESSES: Home—23 Dr. Guerinweg, Ommeren, Netherlands. *Office*—Free University, Bolelaan, Amsterdam, Netherlands.

CAREER: Trouw (daily newspaper), Amsterdam, Netherlands, art critic, 1948-58; teacher in secondary school, Amsterdam, Netherlands, 1952-58; University of Leyden, Leyden, Netherlands, assistant professor of history of art, 1958-64; Free University, Amsterdam, Netherlands, professor of history of art, beginning 1965. Lecturer at colleges and universities in the United States and England. Member, programming committee of Dutch Radio NOS, Dutch film censor board, and L'Abri Fellowship Foundation. *Military service:* Dutch Royal Navy, 1939-45.

MEMBER: International Association of Art Critics, Society for Calvinistic Philosophy.

WRITINGS:

Synthetist Art Theories: Genesis and Nature of the Ideas on Art of Gauguin and His Circle, Swets & Zeitlinger, 1959, published as *Gauguin and 19th Century Art Theory,* 1972.
Jazz, Blues, Spirituals (in Dutch), Zomer & Keuning, 1960.
Kunst en amusement, J. H. Kok, 1962.
De kunstenaar een profect? (booklet), J. H. Kok, 1965.
Art and the Public Today, L'Abri, 1968, 2nd edition, 1969.
Modern Art and the Death of a Culture, Inter-Varsity Press, 1970.
Art Needs No Justification, Inter-Varsity Press, 1978.
The Creative Gift: Essays on Art and the Christian Life, Good News, 1981.

Contributor of articles to *Philosophia Reformata, Christianity Today,* and other journals.

WORK IN PROGRESS: Research on contemporary problems and modern art, spirituals and gospel songs, rock music, art theory, and the history of painting, particularly since the fifteenth century.

BIOGRAPHICAL/CRITICAL SOURCES:

BOOKS

Martin, Linette, *Hans Rookmaaker: A Biography,* Inter-Varsity Press, 1979.

PERIODICALS

Books and Bookmen, February, 1971.
Choice, July-August, 1973.
Philosophia Reformata, Volume 36, 1971. †

* * *

ROTBLAT, Joseph 1908-

PERSONAL: Born November 4, 1908, in Warsaw, Poland. *Education:* Received M.A. from University of Warsaw; received Ph.D. from University of Liverpool.

ADDRESSES: Home—8 Asmara Rd., London NW2 3ST, England. *Office*—Medical College, St. Bartholomew's Hospital, University of London, Charterhouse Sq., London E.C.1, England.

CAREER: Scientific Society of Warsaw, Warsaw, Poland, research fellow at radiological laboratory, 1933-39; University of Liverpool, Liverpool, England, Oliver Lodge fellow, 1939-40, lecturer, beginning in 1940, became senior lecturer in physics, ending 1949, director of research in nuclear physics, 1945-49; University of London, St. Bartholomew's Hospital, Medical College, London, England, professor of physics, 1950-76, vice-dean of faculty of science. Secretary-general of Pugwash Conferences on Science and World Affairs; assistant director of Atomic Physics Institute, Free University of Poland, 1937-39; work on atom bomb in Liverpool and Los Alamos, 1940-44. President of international Youth Science Fortnight.

MEMBER: British Institute of Radiology (president), Hospital Physicists Association (president), Polish Academy of Sciences, American Academy of Arts and Sciences.

AWARDS, HONORS: Commander of Order of the British Empire; D.Sc. from University of Bradford, 1973, University of Warsaw, and University of London; Order of Merit, Polish People's Republic, 1987.

WRITINGS:

(With Sir James Chadwick) *Radioactivity and Radioactive Substances,* Pitman & Sons, 1953.
Atomic Energy: A Survey, Taylor & Francis, 1954.
(With G. O. Jones and G. J. Whitrow) *Atoms and the Universe,* 1956, third revised edition, Penguin Books (England), 1973.
Science and World Affairs: History of the Pugwash Conferences, Dawsons of Pall Mall, 1962, published as *History of the Pugwash Conferences,* Taylor & Francis, 1962.
(Contributor) Charles Henry Dobinson, editor, *The Uses and Effects of Nuclear Energy,* Harrap & Co., 1964.
(Editor) *Aspects of Medical Physics,* Taylor & Francis, 1966.
Pugwash: The First Ten Years, Heinemann, 1967, Humanities, 1968.
Scientists in the Quest for Peace: A History of the Pugwash Conferences, MIT Press, 1972.
(Editor) *Nuclear Reactors: To Breed or Not to Breed?,* Taylor & Francis, 1977.
Nuclear Radiation in Warfare, Taylor & Francis, 1981.
Scientists, the Arms Race, and Disarmament, Oelgeschlager, 1982.

The Arms Race at a Time of Decision, Macmillan, 1984.
Nuclear Strategy and World Security, Macmillan, 1985.
World Peace and the Developing Countries, Macmillan, 1986.
Strategic Defence and the Future of the Arms Race, Macmillan, 1987.

Editor of *Physics in Medicine and Biology,* 1960-72.

* * *

ROTH, John K(ing) 1940-

PERSONAL: Born September 3, 1940, in Grand Haven, Mich.; son of Josiah V. (a Presbyterian minister) and Doris (King) Roth; married Evelyn Austin, June 25, 1964; children: Andrew Lee, Sarah Austin. *Education:* Pomona College, B.A. (magna cum laude), 1962; Yale University, attended Divinity School, 1962-63, M.A., 1965, Ph.D., 1966.

ADDRESSES: Home—1648 Kenyon Pl., Claremont, Calif. 91711. *Office*—Department of Philosophy, Pitzer Hall, Claremont McKenna College, Claremont, Calif. 91711.

CAREER: Claremont McKenna College, Claremont, Calif., assistant professor, 1966-71, associate professor, 1971-76, Russell K. Pitzer Professor of Philosophy, 1976—. Graves fellow in humanities, Harvard University, 1970-71; visiting professor of philosophy, Franklin College, Lugano, Switzerland, spring, 1973; Fulbright lecturer in American studies, University of Innsbruck, 1973-74; fellow, National Humanities Institute, Yale University, 1976-77; visiting professor of philosophy, Doshiva University, 1981-82; fellow, Japan-U.S. Friendship Commission, 1981-83; visiting professor of Holocaust studies, University of Haifa, 1982.

MEMBER: American Philosophical Association, American Studies Association, American Academy of Religion, Phi Beta Kappa.

WRITINGS:

Freedom and the Moral Life: The Ethics of William James, Westminster, 1969.
(Editor and author of introduction) *The Moral Philosophy of William James,* Crowell, 1969.
Problems of the Philosophy of Religion, Chandler Publishing, 1971.
(Editor and author of introduction) *The Philosophy of Josiah Royce,* Crowell, 1971.
(Editor and author of introduction) *The Moral Equivalent of War and Other Essays,* Harper Torchbooks, 1971.
(With Frederick Sontag) *The American Religious Experience,* Harper, 1972.
American Dreams, Chandler & Sharp, 1976.
(With Sontag) *God and America's Future,* Consortium, 1977.
A Consuming Fire, John Knox, 1979.
(With Robert H. Fossum) *The American Dream,* British Association for American Studies, 1981.
(Editor with Sontag) *The Defense of God,* Paragon, 1985.
(Editor with Robert C. Whittemore) *Ideology and American Experience,* Washington Institute for Values in Public Policy, 1986.
(With Richard L. Rubenstein) *Approaches to Auschwitz,* John Knox, 1987.
(With Sontag) *The Questions of Philosophy,* Wadsworth Publishing, 1988.
(Editor with Fossum) *American Ground,* Paragon, 1988.

WORK IN PROGRESS: With Richard L. Rubenstein, *The Politics of Liberation Theology;* with Michael Berenbaum, *Holocaust Questions.*

* * *

ROYKO, Mike 1932-

PERSONAL: Born September 19, 1932, in Chicago, Ill.; son of Michael (a saloon keeper) and Helen (a saloon keeper; maiden name, Zak) Royko; married Carol Joyce Duckman, November 6, 1954 (died, 1979); children: M. David, Robert F. *Education:* Attended Wright Junior College, 1951-52.

ADDRESSES: Home—6657 North Sioux Ave., Chicago, Ill. 60646. *Office*—*Chicago Tribune,* 435 N. Michigan Ave., Chicago, Ill. 60611.

CAREER: Chicago North Side Newspapers, Chicago, Ill., reporter, 1956; Chicago City News Bureau, Chicago, reporter and assistant city editor, 1956-59; *Chicago Daily News,* Chicago, reporter and columnist, 1959-78, associate editor, 1977-78; *Chicago Sun-Times,* Chicago, columnist, 1978-84; *Chicago Tribune,* Chicago, syndicated columnist, 1984—. *Military service:* U.S. Air Force, 1952-56.

MEMBER: Chicago Newspaper Reporters Association, La Salle Street Rod and Gun Club.

AWARDS, HONORS: Heywood Brown Award, 1968; Pulitzer Prize, 1972, for commentary; Man of the Year Award from City of Hope Medical Center and medal for service to journalism from University of Missouri School of Journalism, both 1979; named to Chicago Press Club Journalism Hall of Fame, 1980.

WRITINGS:

Up Against It (collection of columns), introduction by Bill Mauldin, Regenery, 1967.
I May Be Wrong, but I Doubt It (collection of columns), Regnery, 1968.
Boss: Richard J. Daley of Chicago, Dutton, 1971.
Slats Grobnik and Some Other Friends (collection of columns), Dutton, 1973.
Sez Who? Sez Me (collection of columns), Dutton, 1982.
Like I Was Sayin' (collection of columns), Dutton, 1984.

SIDELIGHTS: For more than two decades, Mike Royko has reigned as Chicago's most prominent journalist. Royko is an acknowledged master of the daily column; his topics range widely from political commentary to musings on modern romance, technology, sports, and day-to-day living. *Los Angeles Times Book Review* contributor Jerry Griswold notes that Royko's beat is his hometown of Chicago, and "he knows more about barroom hangouts, backroom politics and bureaucratic pettiness than any palooka on the street. He has a heart of gold, a ready hand for the Little Guy and the love of a whole city." In the *Nation,* Saul D. Alinski describes the columnist's singular hold on his readership: "Many a Chicagoan's daily conversation starts with, 'Jesus, did you see Mike's column today? Christ! I'll bet they're ready to kill him!'" "They," Alinski explains, often range from "His Honor through bankers and utilities and department store executives to our Police Department, better known as the 'Burglars in Blue.'" Although Royko's is "the most eloquent, bitterly ironic voice in Chicago," to quote *Book World* correspondent Clarence Peterson, the author—whose work is syndicated nationwide—tempers his indignation with humor. "Royko is almost always as entertaining as he is thoughtful," writes David Shaw in the *Los Angeles Times Book Review,* "and unlike virtually every other newspaper columnist . . . there is always something to make you think or laugh (or both)."

Royko grew up in a Polish neighborhood on Chicago's northwest side. The son of two saloonkeepers, he was a tough youth, accustomed to barroom brawls and street fights. Only when he joined the Air Force in 1951 did he discover his calling; having lied about prior journalism experience, he was given a reporting job with the base newspaper. No other line of work has deterred Royko since then. In 1956 he returned to Chicago as a reporter for North Side Newspapers, and within three years he was hired as a columnist for the *Chicago Daily News.* From 1959 until the newspaper folded in 1978, he used his column to expose the broad spectrum of life in his native city—its corridors of power as well as its neighborhood heroes—and gradually drew a national audience for his work. Politicians and sycophants have often served as targets for his ironic wrath, but equally common are short essays on the ordinary folk of Chicago's working class, most notably his fictitious alter ego Slats Grobnik. According to *Washington Post* reviewer Jonathan Yardley, Royko "loathes people who abuse their power, whether they be presidents who drop bombs in Asia or bus drivers who harass their passengers; he admires people who try to make the most of what little they've been given, who keep an eye alert for the welfare of others and who are able to laugh at the lumps that life delivers." In 1972 Royko earned the Pulitzer Prize for commentary.

Most of Royko's books are collections of his newspaper columns. An exception is *Boss: Richard J. Daley of Chicago,* published in 1971 when the controversial mayor was beginning his fifth term. *Saturday Review* contributor Dan Walker calls *Boss* "a well-directed, devastating attack on the mayor and his machine. But the criticism is never overstated; instead, the evidence builds and builds." Roy M. Fisher expresses a similar opinion in the *New Republic.* Fisher believes that Royko's portrait of Daley "adds much to one's understanding of why urban politics is played as it is. . . . Daley himself emerges as a complex mixture of integrity and debasement, of wisdom and stupidity, of vision and blindness, of compassion and brutality." But *Book World* reviewer Charles Monaghan finds fault with Royko for a "thorough, steely contempt for his subject" that renders Daley "a two-dimensional villain, a man of bad will, bad manners, bad grammar, and—one feels certain by the end—bad breath." Conversely, a *Saturday Review* correspondent feels that *Boss* "paints a tough, shrewd politician against a background of urban corruption and brutality. But Daley is not without humanity." A *Times Literary Supplement* reviewer likewise notes that Royko's portrait is "unsympathetic," but adds: "Biased as it is, his book is a marvellously detailed analysis of what makes a boss tick; his strengths and weaknesses." Walker concludes that by avoiding "the sensationalizing of Chicago's problems, Royko has come up with a classic study of a big-city political machine and why we can do without it."

As his readership has expanded beyond the borders of Chicago, Royko has also expanded the subject matter he explores. Shaw states that the columnist "writes about every human activity from dieting to driving, about every social phenomenon from digital watches to draft evasion and about every issue from feminism to racism." *Washington Post Book World* contributor William Howarth describes Royko's tone as "barroom banter, with all the subtlety of an ad for Lite Beer." Howarth explains, however, that the style never masks the substance

and that Royko "is only mock macho; he likes to pound his readers both left and right." Yardley characterizes Royko as a moral writer with a deep sense of righteous indignation. "Royko is funny," Yardley concludes, "but he rarely writes merely to amuse. Ridicule is his most effective weapon, which he uses to harpoon all those persons or institutions—and there are many of both—that violate his notions of decency and civility. . . . Sometimes his stance as the salt of the Chicago earth seems to become a pose, but more often than not his humor and his anger are absolutely genuine; he has been at his trade for a long time now, yet he remains remarkably fresh and original."

BIOGRAPHICAL/CRITICAL SOURCES:

PERIODICALS

Best Sellers, April 1, 1971.
Book World, March 28, 1971, September 19, 1971.
Chicago Tribune Book World, September 23, 1984.
Christian Science Monitor, April 29, 1971.
Commentary, September, 1971.
Detroit Free Press, July 9, 1979.
Detroit News, October 17, 1982.
Esquire, July, 1971, March, 1972, May 8, 1979.
Harper's, November, 1982.
Life, April 2, 1971.
Los Angeles Times Book Review, January 2, 1983, September 23, 1984.
McCall's, February, 1972.
Nation, April 19, 1971.
National Review, June 1, 1971.
New Republic, April 17, 1971.
New York Times, March 31, 1971.
New York Times Book Review, April 4, 1971, June 6, 1971.
Saturday Review, April 24, 1971, October 23, 1971.
Time, April 19, 1971.
Times Literary Supplement, November 12, 1971.
Village Voice, January 10, 1974.
Washington Post, November 10, 1982.
Washington Post Book World, February 3, 1974, May 26, 1974, October 14, 1984.†

—*Sketch by Anne Janette Johnson*

*   *   *

ROZMAN, Gilbert Friedell 1943-

PERSONAL: Born February 18, 1943, in Minneapolis, Minn.; son of David (an accountant) and Celia (a teacher; maiden name, Friedell) Rozman; married Masha Dwosh (a lawyer), June 25, 1968; children: Thea Dwosh, Noah Dwosh. *Education:* Carleton College, B.A., 1965; Princeton University, Ph.D., 1971.

ADDRESSES: Office—Princeton University, 2-N-2 Green Hall, Princeton, N.J. 08540.

CAREER: Princeton University, Princeton, N.J., assistant professor, 1970-75, associate professor, 1975-79, professor of sociology, 1979—, bicentennial preceptor, 1972-75. Member of U.S.-U.S.S.R. Binational Commission on Humanities and Social Sciences, 1978-85.

MEMBER: American Sociological Association, Association for Asian Studies, American Association for the Advancement of Slavic Studies.

AWARDS, HONORS: Woodrow Wilson fellow, 1965-66; Foreign Area fellow, 1968-69; grants from National Science

Foundation, 1976-79, National Endowment for the Humanities, 1976-79, Social Science Research Council, 1980, 1984-85, 1986-88, National Council on East European and Soviet Research, 1981-83, and Committee on Scholarly Communication with the People's Republic of China, 1984-85; Guggenheim fellow, 1979-80.

WRITINGS:

Urban Networks in Ch'ing China and Tokugawa Japan, Princeton University Press, 1973.
(With C. E. Black and others) *The Modernization of Japan and Russia,* Free Press, 1975.
Urban Networks in Russia, 1750-1800, and Premodern Periodization, Princeton University Press, 1976.
(Editor) *The Modernization of China,* Free Press, 1981.
Population and Marketing Settlements in Ch'ing China, Cambridge University Press, 1982.
(Editor) *Soviet Studies of China: Assessments of Recent Scholarship,* Michigan Publications on China, 1984.
A Mirror for Socialism: Soviet Criticisms of China, Princeton University Press, 1985.
(Editor with Marius B. Jansen) *Japan in Transition: From Tukugawa to Meiji,* Princeton University Press, 1986.
The Chinese Debate about Soviet Socialism, 1978-85, Princeton University Press, 1987.

WORK IN PROGRESS: Editing *The East Asian Region: Confucian Heritage and Modern Dynamism;* editing *Soviet-Japanese Mutual Perceptions.*

SIDELIGHTS: Gilbert Friedell Rozman commented: "I chose to approach international affairs as a sociologist able to use the languages of the major countries, concerned about the histories of their peoples, and eager to apply the comparative method of analysis. I often advise students with an interest in international affairs to concentrate on language skills early and to identify an unconventional specialization that is worth pursuing.

"I became interested in foreign areas in high school, when I was a winner in the *Minneapolis Star's* world affairs contest. In college and graduate school I chose to study societies that were likely to be of greatest importance during the decades ahead. Because scholarship aid was available, I could attend intensive language courses every summer and accelerate my studies. Increasingly, I realized that my background on three countries gave me unique opportunities to study major aspects of social change, including premodern urbanization, modernization, and the impact of communism. In addition, I found that there is a need to examine how people in one country view another country and its people. This new field might be called mutual perceptions among the great powers."

BIOGRAPHICAL/CRITICAL SOURCES:

PERIODICALS

Times Literary Supplement, June 27, 1986.

*   *   *

RUKEYSER, Muriel 1913-1980

PERSONAL: Born December 15, 1913, in New York, N.Y.; died February 12, 1980, in New York, N.Y.; daughter of Lawrence B. and Myra (Lyons) Rukeyser; married briefly; children: William L. *Education:* Attended Vassar College and Columbia University, 1930-32; briefly attended Roosevelt Aviation School.

ADDRESSES: Home—463 West St., New York, N.Y. 10014. *Agent*—Monica McCall, Inc., 677 Madison Ave., New York, N.Y.

CAREER: Poet, social activist, teacher, biographer, screenwriter, dramatist, translator, and author of children's books. Before World War II, worked for theaters and theater magazines and did office work; after the war, she read poetry and taught; Sarah Lawrence College, Bronxville, N.Y., member of faculty, 1946, 1956-67. House of Photography, vice-president, 1946-60. Sometime between 1930 and 1933, co-founded with Elizabeth Bishop, Mary McCarthy, and Eleanor Clark a literary magazine, *Student Review,* to protest the policies of the *Vassar Review;* later, the two magazines consolidated.

MEMBER: PEN American Center (president, 1975-76), Society of American Historians, American Association of University Professors, National Institute of Arts and Letters, Teachers-Writers Collaborative (member of board of directors, 1967-80).

AWARDS, HONORS: Yale Younger Poets Prize, 1935, for *Theory of Flight;* Oscar Blumenthal Prize for poetry, 1940; Harriet Monroe Poetry Award, 1941; grant from National Institute of Arts and Letters, 1942; Guggenheim fellowship, 1943; Levinson Prize for poetry, 1947; D.Litt., Rutgers University, 1961; American Council of Learned Societies fellowship, 1963, for work on biography of Thomas Hariot; translation award (shared with Leif Sjoeberg) of the Swedish Academy in Stockholm, 1967, for *Selected Poems of Gunnar Ekeloef;* Copernicus Award, 1977, in recognition of lifetime contribution to poetry; Shelley Memorial Award, 1977; in 1979, Rukeyser was honored at the annual New York Quarterly Poetry Day for her outstanding contribution to contemporary poetry.

WRITINGS:

POETRY

Theory of Flight, foreword by Stephen Vincent Benet, Yale University Press, 1935, reprinted, AMS Press, 1971.
Mediterranean, Writers and Artists Committee, Medical Bureau to Aid Spanish Democracy, 1938.
U.S. One, Covici, Friede, 1938.
A Turning Wind: Poems, Viking, 1939.
The Soul and Body of John Brown, privately printed, 1940.
Wake Island, Doubleday, 1942.
Beast in View, Doubleday, 1944.
The Green Wave (contains a section of translated poems of Octavio Paz and Rari), Doubleday, 1948.
Orpheus (with the drawing "Orpheus," by Picasso), Centaur Press, 1949.
Elegies, New Directions, 1949.
Selected Poems, New Directions, 1951.
Body of Waking (contains a section of translated poems of Paz), Harper, 1958.
Waterlily Fire: Poems 1935-1962 (including the group of poems entitled "The Speaking Tree"), Macmillan, 1962.
The Outer Banks, Unicorn Press, 1967, 2nd revised edition, 1980.
The Speed of Darkness, Random, 1968.
Mazes, photography by Milton Charles, Simon & Schuster, 1970.
Twenty-nine Poems, Rapp & Whiting, 1972.
Breaking Open: New Poems (contains translations of Eskimo songs), Random House, 1973.
The Gates: Poems, McGraw, 1976.
The Collected Poems of Muriel Rukeyser, McGraw, 1978.

BIOGRAPHY

Willard Gibbs, Doubleday, 1942.
One Life (biography of Wendell Willkie in poetry, prose, and documents), Simon & Schuster, 1957.
The Traces of Thomas Hariot, Random House, 1971.

CHILDREN'S BOOKS

(Self-illustrated) *Come Back, Paul*, Harper, 1955.
I Go Out, pictures by Leonard Kessler, Harper, 1962.
Bubbles, edited by Donald Barr, illustrated by Jeri Quinn, Harcourt, 1967.
More Night, illustrated by Symeon Shimin, Harper, 1981.

UNPUBLISHED PLAYS

"The Middle of the Air," produced in Iowa City, Iowa, 1945.
"The Colors of the Day," produced in Poughkeepsie, N.Y., at Vassar College, June 10, 1961.
"Houdini," produced in Lenox, Mass., at Lenox Arts Center, July 3, 1973.

TRANSLATOR

(From the Spanish; with others) Paz, *Selected Poems of Octavio Paz*, Indiana University Press, 1963, revised edition published as *Early Poems 1935-1955*, New Directions, 1973.
Paz, *Sun Stone*, New Directions, 1963.
(With Leif Sjoeberg) Gunnar Ekeloef, *Selected Poems of Gunnar Ekeloef*, Twayne, 1967.
Ekeloef, *Three Poems*, T. Williams, 1967.
(With Sjoeberg) Ekeloef, *A Molna Elegy: Metamorphoses*, two volumes, Unicorn Press, 1984.

Also translator of Bertolt Brecht's *Uncle Eddie's Moustache*, 1974.

OTHER

The Life of Poetry, Current Books, 1949, reprinted, Morrow, 1974.
The Orgy (a three-day journal), Coward, 1965.
The Poetry and Voice of Muriel Rukeyser (recording), Caedmon, 1977.

Also author of film scripts "A Place to Live" and "All the Way Home." Contributor to periodicals, including *Nation*, *New Republic*, *Poetry*, and *Saturday Review*.

SIDELIGHTS: Although poet Muriel Rukeyser often provoked a varying critical response to her work, there was never any doubt during her five-decade literary career that a resounding passion was on display. Of her first book, the award-winning collection *Theory of Flight*, W. R. Benet remarked in the *Saturday Review of Literature:* "She is a radical politically, but she writes as a poet not a propagandist. When you hold this book in your hand you hold a living thing." Some forty-five years later, *Gramercy Review* contributor Jascha Kessler labeled Rukeyser "the heroic, the bardic, the romantic. . . . Poets who are bardic . . . take on mankind and the whole cosmos as the field of their utterance, . . . [and] try to carry whole nations forward through the urgency of their message. . . . Wherever there are hot spots that journalists blow up on the front page—strikes, massacres, revolutions, tortures, wars, prisoners and marches—there is Rukeyser, in the very front line, a spokesperson, or spokespoet perhaps, speaking up loudly for freedom in the world." Though her outspoken nature obviously displeased certain critics, Rukeyser remained a "spokespoet" all of her adult life.

In the critical commentary on Rukeyser's more than a dozen poetry collections, such phrases as "social activist" or "poet of social protest" are common. Alberta Turner explains in the *Dictionary of Literary Biography* that Rukeyser was a native of New York City and "by her own choice her life was not bland or sheltered." In the 1930s Rukeyser attended Vassar College and became literary editor of the leftist undergraduate journal *Student Review*. As a reporter for this journal, Rukeyser covered the 1932 Scottsboro trial in Alabama in which nine black youths were accused of raping two white girls. According to Wolfgang Saxon in his *New York Times* obituary of Rukeyser, the Scottsboro incident was the basis of Rukeyser's poem "The Trial" and "may have been the genesis of her commitment to the cause of the underdog and the unjustly condemned."

Following the Scottsboro trial, Rukeyser moved within very broad social circles for the remainder of her years. Among other things, she supported the Spanish Loyalists during the Spanish Civil War; she was once jailed in Washington for her protest of the Vietnam War; and, as president of the American Center for PEN, she travelled to South Korea in the 1970s to rally against the death sentence of poet Kim Chi-Ha, the incident which later became the framework of one of Rukeyser's last poems, "The Gates." Since she aligned her creative capacities so closely with the current events of her day, a number of reviewers believe the history of the United States for several decades can be culled from Rukeyser's poetry.

Though frequently incensed by worldly injustices—as is apparent in both the subject matter and tone of her writing—Rukeyser had an optimism that at times surprised her critics. According to Roy B. Hoffman in his *Village Voice* review of *The Collected Poems of Muriel Rukeyser*, Rukeyser's distress with injustice was "mingled with a romantic's belief in the perfectibility of the universe, and a young patriot's belief in the perfectibility of her nation. . . . Perhaps it is this belief of Rukeyser's—in a radiant epiphany behind the pain of conflict—that both dates her and makes her refreshing to read. Her idealism is unmarked by heavy irony, cynicism, or an intricacy of wit that characterizes much contemporary poetry." Because of her optimism, reviewers compared Rukeyser's style to that of nineteenth-century American poet Walt Whitman. In an assessment of *Waterlily Fire: Poems, 1935-1962*, a *Virginia Quarterly Review* critic explained that "like Whitman, Muriel Rukeyser has so much joy that it is not to be contained in regular verse but comes out in lines that are rugged and soaring." In much the same vein, *New York Times Book Review*'s Richard Eberhart judged Rukeyser's poems in general to be "primordial and torrential. They pour out excitements of a large emotional force, taking in a great deal of life and giving out profound realizations of the significance of being. . . . She belongs to the Whitman school of large confrontations and outpourings."

In opposition to those who appreciated this poet's ability to merge her outrage with hope, some reviewers considered Rukeyser's optimism a weakness or a mere posturing. For instance, Thomas Stumpf in the *Carolina Quarterly* found that Rukeyser's later collection *Breaking Open* contains an "indefatigable optimism, hand-clasping brotherhood, and love for all ethnic groups . . . [which] feed[s] a poetry that is without muscle. . . . It is poetry that is fatally in love with exhortations and public promises, with first person posturings." What Stumpf ultimately detected in this particular collection was "the stuff of bathos." In turn, Louise Bogan criticized Rukeyser for creating a world in her poetry that, in reality, "could not last overnight." In her book *Selected Criticism: Prose, Poetry,* Bogan described the world in Rukeyser's *A Turning Wind* as "deficient in a sense of human life. . . . Her world is at once too nightmare and too noble. . . . She does not realize that such a world could not last overnight, that the sense of injustice is only relevant when applied to living human beings. . . . [There] is something hideously oversimplified in crude oppositions and blind idealism." Apart from complaints such as these, many reviewers fondly supported Rukeyser's optimism, an optimism grounded in what Kenneth Rexroth had labeled in a *Los Angeles Times* essay "the Community of Love."

In accordance with her impassioned nature, many of Rukeyser's earlier poems contain an intrepidness and exhortative voice that will surely be remembered. "Her intense tone, angry but also tender, jubilant, even exalted, which was to be dominant throughout her career, [was] already apparent in her first book," stated Turner; in it "she makes little use of silence." Some critics were inspired by this vigor. *Poetry* contributor John Malcolm Brinnin explained that with the publication of *Theory of Flight*, winner of the Yale Younger Poets Prize, "American poetry found its first full-blown expression of the rebellious temper that prevailed on American campuses and among the younger intellectuals. Its success was immediate. . . . Rukeyser was praised for the ruggedness of her technique, her experimentalism, and for the powerful utterance which, from a woman, seemed unique." Other critics could do without her brashness. "This passionate, innocent young woman . . . talks so noisily and so hurriedly that it never occurs to her that other people have seen these things before, and have learned to speak more calmly," wrote Michael Roberts in his *Spectator* review of *Theory of Flight*. When Turner remarked in her *Dictionary of Literary Biography* essay that Rukeyser would probably *not* be remembered as one of this century's greatest American poets, she based this statement, at least in part, on her belief that Rukeyser "wrote too much that was intense but fuzzy, trusting intensity to create a magic rather than selecting and juxtaposing fresh powerful words or images. But at times she was able to find the right image." Other critics of Rukeyser's early collections felt stimulated by her energy but, like Turner, professed that Rukeyser's methods needed perfecting. As one *Kirkus Reviews* contributor put it, "[Rukeyser] has achieved considerable reputation among those to whom lucidity is not a necessary factor."

Although Rukeyser's early poetic voice tended toward that of a sloganist, most critics sense that with time Rukeyser was able to develop greater sophistication and control in her poetry. Whereas Anne Stevenson commented in her *New York Times Book Review* critique of *The Collected Poems* that Rukeyser "seems to have been born poetically full-grown," others considered various developments in Rukeyser's craft important enough to analyze in their reviews. Brinnin, for instance, explains that "one of the most interesting phases of the transformation of the social poet in years of stress is the change in his use of language. In the case of Muriel Rukeyser, it moves from that of simple declarative exhortation, in the common phrases of the city man, to that of a gnarled, intellectual, almost private observation. In her earlier usage, images are apt to be simple and few; the whole approach is apt to be through the medium of urban speech. In the latter work, images become those of the psychologist, or of the surrealist, charged with meaning and prevalent everywhere." Albeit, her conviction was still strong, Brinnin added. Along the same lines, Turner found the later Rukeyser more relaxed, less rhetorical, "and though the poems still end firmly with clearly

stated, strong opinions, they are less likely to pummel their readers."

Another change involved the movement toward shorter poems in contrast to the cluster poems, or collage poems, that were somewhat of a trademark for Rukeyser, poems centered on a single theme but developed in "separate, autonomous bits, [and] varied in line length and stanza form[,] . . . the parts of each book roll[ing] toward the reader in a series of waves, each of which crashes firmly," explained Turner. This movement toward more concrete images and shorter poems coincided rather closely with Rukeyser's increased devotion to the personal as well as to the political in her poetry.

Even though Rukeyser would continue to write poems that attempted to "carry whole nations forward through the urgency of their message," political poetry was not the be-all and end-all for Rukeyser, who explored a myriad of topics during her literary career. Many of her poems, particularly after her first few collections, were very personal, speaking on her role as a mother and daughter, speaking on sexuality, on creativity, on the poetic process, speaking also on illness and death. One of her poems from *The Gates,* "Resurrection of the Right Side," details the human body's slow recovery after a debilitating stroke: "I begin to climb the mountain on my mouth, / word by stammer, walk stammered, the lurching deck of earth. / Left-right with none of my own rhythms." In her book *Beast in View,* the poem "Ajanta" is "purportedly" a poem about painted caves in India, "but when she wrote it," noted Rexroth, "Muriel had never been to India. . . . 'Ajanta' is an exploration . . . of her own interior—in every sense. It is the interior of her mind as a human being, as a poet, and as a woman. It is the interior of her self as her own flesh. It is her womb." Virginia R. Terris goes to some length in her *American Poetry Review* article to chronicle Rukeyser's movement from the social to the personal, or from theory to actual experience. Regarding Rukeyser's biography of business magnate Wendell Willkie entitled *One Life* and comprised partly of poems, Terris felt Rukeyser was "able to focus singlemindedly on what she [had] only tenatively explored in earlier volumes. . . . Although Rukeyser [was] exploring many of the themes she had earlier explored—family tensions, social and technological issues and women exploited—she [moved] into experiences that [were] hers uniquely."

In the same way that Rukeyser's poetry was one of variety— for it could be labeled many things: romantic, political, feminist, erotic, Whitmanesque—her oeuvre explored a variety of genres. Although known particularly for her poetry, Rukeyser wrote biographical material (which was sometimes in the form of poetry), children's books, plays, and television scripts, and she also translated poetry from the Swedish, French, German, Spanish, and Italian. In addition, she taught and read her poetry at institutions nationwide.

Poetry aside, Rukeyser's biographical work received the most critical attention. As Jane Cooper noted in the *Washington Post Book World,* Rukeyser "loved science and history and modern technology, enjoying their puzzles and solvings much as she enjoyed the puzzles and solvings of poetic form." Thus, the fact that Rukeyser wrote about individuals other than the literary and artistic should not be too suprising. While it is true that Rukeyser wrote memorable poems about the German lithographer Kaethe Kollwitz, American composer Charles Ives, and mythological figures like Orpheus, at the same time she profiled New England eccentric Lord Timothy Dexter; nineteenth-century mathematician Willard Gibbs; English mathematician and scientist Thomas Hariot; and, as previously noted, lawyer and business executive Wendell Willkie, who ran for president on the 1940 Republican party ticket. Indeed, Rukeyser wrote full-length biographies of the latter three men.

According to Terris, one of Rukeyser's intentions behind writing biographies of nonliterary persons was to find a meeting place between science and poetry. In an analysis of Rukeyser's expository work *The Life of Poetry,* Terris notes that Rukeyser was of the opinion that in the West, poetry and science are wrongly considered to be in opposition to one another. Thus, writes Terris, "Rukeyser [set] forth her theoretical acceptance of science . . . [and pointed] out the many parallels between [poetry and science]—unity within themselves, symbolic language, selectivity, the use of the imagination in formulating concepts and in execution. Both, she believe[d], ultimately contribute to one another."

Some critics were skeptical of this poet's attempts at interpreting history, but for others Rukeyser's poetic angle brought something more to the reader than could be expected from a biography in the strict sense. Regarding Rukeyser's account entitled *The Traces of Thomas Hariot,* *Washington Post Book World* critic Vincent Cronin stated: "By her carefully controlled imaginative sympathy, by the dazzling range of her learning, and above all by the poetry of her style she leads the reader further than he is ever likely to go into the speculative seventeenth century, where daring men were trying, on half-a-dozen fronts, to break through into what was to become the modern world. . . . From now on, thanks to this highly enjoyable trail-blazing book, Thomas Hariot will never be 'just another minor Elizabethan.'" *Commonweal* reviewer E. L. Keyes viewed Rukeyser's biography of Willard Gibbs as an "intelligible collation of a mountain of mysteries."

Impassioned, self-confident, eclectic, a poet of powerful expression, a poet of the political and the personal—these and similar phrases have characterized the life and work of Muriel Rukeyser for decades. Although the critics in Rukeyser's earlier, more prolific decades seldom agreed on the value of her achievements, a new generation of reviewers had come along by the time Rukeyser published *The Collected Poems;* and in looking at the totality of her accomplishments, these critics found cause for rejoicing. A year before Rukeyser's death, Hoffman concluded that "poems like 'The Poem as Mask' make me wonder if Muriel Rukeyser is not our greatest living American poet. *The Collected Poems* . . . enable us to see a breadth of history, energy, and experience rarely matched in American letters." As for Kessler, "any reading of [Rukeyser's] poems will excite the best and most ingenious impulses of . . . people everywhere, who want goodness and freedom and love in the world and in their own personal lives. Rukeyser remained faithful and consistent with her own youthful visions, and all this work [in *The Collected Poems*]. . . testifies to that."

BIOGRAPHICAL/CRITICAL SOURCES:

BOOKS

Bogan, Louise, *Selected Criticism: Prose, Poetry,* Noonday Press, 1955.
Contemporary Literary Criticism, Gale, Volume VI, 1976, Volume X, 1979, Volume XV, 1980, Volume XXVII, 1986.
Dictionary of Literary Biography, Volume XLVIII: *American Poets, 1880-1945, Second Series,* Gale, 1986.
Gould, Jean, *Modern American Women Poets,* Dodd, 1985.
Jarrell, Randall, *Poetry and the Age,* Knopf, 1953.
Kertesz, Louise, *The Poetic Vision of Muriel Rukeyser,* Louisiana State University Press, 1979.
Laughlin, James, editor, *New Directions in Prose and Poetry,* New Directions (Connecticut), 1953.
Rukeyser, Muriel, *The Gates: Poems,* McGraw, 1976.

PERIODICALS

American Poetry Review, May-June, 1974, May-June, 1978.
Best Sellers, April, 1977.
Books of the Times, August, 1979.
Book World, April 4, 1971.
Carolina Quarterly, spring, 1974.
Feminist Studies, fall, 1975.
Gramercy Review, autumn-winter, 1979-80.
Harper's, February, 1971.
Kirkus Reviews, December 15, 1947.
Los Angeles Times, March 2, 1980.
Ms., April, 1974.
Nation, February 23, 1963, March 15, 1965.
Newsweek, March 29, 1971.
New York Times, August 22, 1979.
New York Times Book Review, February 28, 1965, June 23, 1968, April 18, 1971, February 11, 1979.
Parnassus: Poetry in Review, spring-summer, 1979.
Partisan Review, Volume XLVII, number 4, 1980.
Poetry, May, 1936, January, 1943.
Saturday Review of Literature, December 7, 1935, August 10, 1940, March 11, 1950.
Spectator, May 1, 1936.
Times Literary Supplement, May 19, 1972.
Village Voice, November 22, 1976, February 26, 1979.
Virginia Quarterly Review, winter, 1963.
Washington Post Book World, January 21, 1979.

OBITUARIES:

PERIODICALS

Chicago Tribune, February 15, 1980.
Newsweek, February 25, 1980.
New York Times, February 14, 1980.
Time, February 25, 1980.†

—*Sketch by Cheryl Gottler*

*   *   *

RULFO, Juan   1918-1986

PERSONAL: Born May 16, 1918, in Sayula, Jalisco, Mexico; died January 7, 1986, of a heart attack in Mexico City, Mexico; married in 1948; wife's name, Clara; children: four.

ADDRESSES: Home—Mexico City, Mexico. *Office*—Centro Mexicano de Escritores, Luis G. Inclan, no. 2709, Col Villa da Cortes, 03130 Mexico 13, D. F., Mexico.

CAREER: Worked as an accountant and in several clerical positions; on staff of Mexican Immigration Department, beginning 1935, processed the crews of impounded German ships during World War II; member of sales staff, B. F. Goodrich Rubber Co., 1947-54; member of Papaloapan Commission, 1955; National Institute for Indigenous Studies, Mexico City, Mexico, beginning 1962, became director of editorial department. Adviser to writers at Centro Mexicano de Escritores.

MEMBER: Centro Mexicano de Escritores (fellow).

AWARDS, HONORS: Rockefeller grants, 1953 and 1954; Guggenheim fellowship, 1968; National Prize for Letters (Mexico), 1970; Principe de Asturias award (Spain), 1983.

WRITINGS:

FICTION

El llano en llamas y otros cuentos, Fondo de Cultura Economica, 1953, translation by George D. Schade published as *The Burning Plain and Other Stories,* University of Texas Press, 1967, 2nd Spanish edition, corrected and enlarged, Fondo de Cultura Economica, 1970.
Pedro Paramo (novel), Fondo de Cultura Economica, 1955, translation by Lysander Kemp published as *Pedro Paramo: A Novel of Mexico,* Grove, 1959.
El gallo de oro y otros textos para cine, Ediciones Era, 1980.

OMNIBUS VOLUMES

Obra completa, Biblioteca Ayacucho, 1977.
Antologia personal, Nueva Imagen, 1978.

CONTRIBUTOR

Aberlardo Gomez Benoit, editor, *Antologia contemporanea del cuento hispano-americano* (title means "A Contemporary Anthology of the Hispanic-American Story"), Instituto Latinoamericano de Vinculacion Cultural, 1964.
Cronicas de Latinoamericano, Editorial Jorge Alvarez, 1968.

OTHER

Juan Rulfo: Autobiografia armada, compiled by Reina Roffe, Ediciones Corregidor, 1973.
(With others) *Juan Rulfo: Homenaje nacional,* with photographs by Rulfo, Instituto Nacional de Bellas Artes (Mexico City), 1980, 2nd edition published as *Inframundo: El Mexico de Juan Rulfo,* Ediciones del Norte (Hanover, N.H.), 1983, translation by Jo Anne Engelbert published as *Inframundo: The Mexico of Juan Rulfo,* Ediciones del Norte, 1983.

Also author of television scripts and film adaptations, beginning 1954. Collaborator with Juan Arreola on the review *Pan.*

WORK IN PROGRESS: *La cordillera* (title means "The Mountain Range"), a novel.

SIDELIGHTS: The late Mexican novelist Juan Rulfo is included in what Alan Riding called in the *New York Times Magazine* "the contemporary Latin American literary boom." Rulfo and such writers as Jorge Luis Borges, Julio Cortazar, and Carlos Fuentes wrote imaginative fiction that was made available through translation to readers in the United States during the fifties, sixties, and early seventies. Unlike the other writers, who prolifically turned out stories and novels, Rulfo established his reputation with a solitary collection of stories, *El llano en llamas y otros cuentos*—translated as *The Burning Plain and Other Stories*—and one novel, *Pedro Paramo.*

Two characteristics of these Latin American writers were their special affinity for innovative narrative techniques and their style of interweaving the historical with the marvelous, called magic realism; both qualities are often mentioned by reviewers of Rulfo's work. In his introduction to *The Burning Plain and Other Stories,* George D. Schade used the story "Macario"—included in the collection—as an example of Rulfo's narrative style. "In 'Macario,'" Schade observed, "the past and present mingle chaotically, and frequently the most startling associations of ideas are juxtaposed, strung together by conjunctions which help to paralyze the action and stop the flow

of time in the present." In *Into the Mainstream: Conversations with Latin-American Writers,* Luis Harss and Barbara Dohmann comment on the story "The Man," noting the multiple points of view and foreshadowing used to heighten the reader's identification with the protagonist.

The narrative devices mentioned by Schade, Harss and Dohmann are also found in Rulfo's *Pedro Paramo,* a novel which Schade called "a bold excursion into modern techniques of writing." Using flashbacks, interior monologues and dialogues, and atemporal time-sequences, Rulfo creates what Enrique Anderson-Imbert claimed in *Spanish-American Literature: A History* is a "story . . . told in loops, forward, backward, [and] to the sides." The narrative technique demands a lot of the reader, but the story in itself is difficult. Half-way through the novel, for example, the reader realizes that all the characters are dead; the story all along has been the remembered history of ghosts conversing from their graves.

Startling as this revelation is, the mingling of death and life is typical of Mexican culture. Commenting in a *Nation* essay, Earl Shorris noted: "Everywhere in the novel, death is present: not the hidden, feared death we know in the United States but Mexican death, the death that is neither the beginning nor the end, the death that comes and goes in the round of time." Shorris observed that the constant reminders of death in Mexican life destroy "the distinction between [this] life" and the next. This hazy line between life and death accentuates the author's deliberately ambiguous delineation of scenes, narrators, and past and present time. The technical difficulties with which Rulfo confronts the reader become the framework for what Kessel Schwartz called in *A New History of Spanish-American Fiction* "an ambiguous and magical world, a kind of timeless fable of life and death" where historical facts—references to actual events in Mexican history—and fictive details are fused.

In his analysis of *Pedro Paramo* appearing in *Tradition and Renewal: Essays on Twentieth-Century Latin American Literature and Culture,* Luis Leal observed that while Rulfo's style was experimental, it was also firmly rooted in the historical reality of Mexico. Leal wrote: "The scenes are juxtaposed, united only by the central theme and lyrical motifs. . . . The novel, a mixture of realism and fantasy . . . has been created through the use of images, which, although poetic, are structured in a language that is characteristic of the countryside."

Rulfo's sparse, dry prose reflects the parched, stark Mexican landscape. Harss and Dohmann remarked: "His language is as frugal as his world, reduced almost to pure heartbeat. . . . He sings the swan song of blighted regions gangrened by age, where misery has opened wounds that burn under an eternal midday sun, where a pestilent fate has turned areas that were once rolling meadows and grasslands into fetid open graves. . . . He writes with a sharp edge, carving each word out of hard rock, like an inscription on a tombstone." According to Irving A. Leonard in the *Saturday Review,* "the bleak, harsh surroundings" Rulfo described with his "bare phrases" reflected his "pessimistic view of man's condition. Murder, incest, adultery, death overpowering life, violence in varied forms are predominant themes, unrelieved by humor or love."

Although Rulfo published a collection of film scripts and worked on the manuscript for another novel, *La cordillera,* for the rest of his life, further success as a writer eluded him. While a London *Times* reporter noted that *Pedro Paramo* "will be remembered as a unique achievement,'' the same writer believed that Rulfo himself seemed content to be known merely as ''the master who could not write a second masterpiece.''

MEDIA ADAPTATIONS: Pedro Paramo was made into a film in the 1960s.

BIOGRAPHICAL/CRITICAL SOURCES:

BOOKS

Anderson-Imbert, Enrique, *Spanish-American Literature: A History,* Volume II: *1910-1963,* 2nd edition, revised and updated by Elaine Malley, Wayne State University Press, 1969.
Contemporary Literary Criticism, Volume VIII, Gale, 1978.
Forster, Merlin H., editor, *Tradition and Renewal: Essays on Twentieth-Century Latin American Literature and Culture,* University of Illinois Press, 1975.
Harss, Luis, and Barbara Dohmann, *Into the Mainstream: Conversations with Latin-American Writers,* Harper, 1967.
Rulfo, Juan, *The Burning Plain and Other Stories,* translation by George D. Schade, University of Texas Press, 1967.
Schwartz, Kessel, *A New History of Spanish-American Fiction,* Volume II, University of Miami Press, 1971.

PERIODICALS

Christian Science Monitor, January 4, 1968.
English Journal, January, 1974.
Hispania, December, 1971, September, 1974, March, 1975.
Nation, May 15, 1982.
National Observer, March 24, 1973.
New York Herald Tribune Book Review, August 2, 1959.
New York Times Book Review, June 7, 1959.
New York Times Magazine, March 13, 1983.
San Francisco Chronicle, August 30, 1959.
Saturday Review, June 22, 1968.
Times (London), January 10, 1986.
Times Literary Supplement, February 5, 1960.

OBITUARIES:

PERIODICALS

AB Bookman's Weekly, February 17, 1986.
Los Angeles Times, January 9, 1986.
New York Times, January 9, 1986.
Times (London), January 10, 1986.
Washington Post, January 11, 1986.†

—*Sketch by Marian Gonsior*

*   *   *

RUMBERGER, Russell W(illiam) 1949-

PERSONAL: Born September 16, 1949, in Kansas City, Mo.; son of Allen B. and Ellen Rumberger. *Education:* Carnegie-Mellon University, B.S., 1971; Stanford University, M.S., 1978, Ph.D., 1978.

ADDRESSES: Office—Department of Education, University of California, Santa Barbara, Calif. 93106.

CAREER: Ohio State University, Columbus, research associate, 1979-80; Stanford University, Stanford, Calif., research associate, 1981-87; University of California, Santa Barbara, associate professor, 1988—.

WRITINGS:

Overeducation in the Labor Market, Praeger, 1981.
(With Martin Carney and Derek Sheaver) *The New Social Contract,* Harper, 1983.
(Editor with Gerald Burke) *The Future Impact of Technology on Work and Education,* Falmer Press, 1987.

Contributor to scholarly journals.

WORK IN PROGRESS: Research on technology, work, and education; school dropouts; education policy.

SIDELIGHTS: Russell W. Rumberger told *CA:* ''My interest in overeducation was spurred by my own observations of the relationship between education and jobs. During the 1970s, I increasingly witnessed cases of college graduates taking jobs incommensurate with their education. The more obvious cases were persons with bachelor degrees taking jobs as secretaries and waiters, or Ph.D.s taking jobs driving cabs and working in bars. The less obvious were graduates taking jobs that appeared commensurate, but were not. My own experiences as an engineer illustrated this. Students learn much more in school than they ever have the opportunity to apply in their work. It makes work unrewarding, workers often perform poorly, and there are a variety of adverse social consequences. I've become increasingly interested in the organization of work and the barriers to making work more demanding and stimulating.''

*   *   *

RUNES, Dagobert D(avid) 1902-1982

PERSONAL: Born January 6, 1902, in Bucovena, Rumania; came to United States in 1926, naturalized in 1936; died after a long illness, September 24, 1982, in New York, N.Y.; son of Isidore and Adele (Sussman) Runes; married Mary Theresa Gronich, October 18, 1936 (deceased); married Rose Morse, April 13, 1978; children: (first marriage) Regeen Lenore (Mrs. Thomas P. Kiernan), Richard Norton. *Education:* University of Vienna, Ph.D., 1924. *Religion:* Jewish.

ADDRESSES: Home—401 West End Ave., New York, N.Y. 10024. *Office*—Philosophical Library, Inc., 200 West 57th St, New York, N.Y. 10019.

CAREER: Lecturer and free-lance writer, 1926-31; Institute for Advanced Education, New York City, director, 1931-34; *Modern Thinker,* New York City, editor, 1923-36; *Current Digest,* New York City, editor, 1936-40; Philosophical Library, Inc., New York City, founder, editor in chief, and director, beginning 1941. *Military service:* Group Commander, Red Cross Military Legion, Vienna, 1918.

MEMBER: Vienna Academic Society Platonica (president, 1924), American Society of Aesthetics, American Association for the Advancement of Science.

WRITINGS:

Der Wahre Jesus, Rudolf Cerny (Vienna), 1927.
Jordan Lieder: Fruehe Gedichte, Philosophical Library, 1948.
Letters to My Son, Philosophical Library, 1949.
Of God, the Devil and the Jews, Philosophical Library, 1952.
The Societ Impact on Society: A Recollection, Philosophical Library, 1953.
Letters to My Daughter, Philosophical Library, 1954.
On the Nature of Man, Philosophical Library, 1956.
A Book of Contemplation, Philosophical Library, 1957, pub-

lished as *A Dictionary of Thought: From My Writings and from My Evenings*, 1959.
Letters to My God, Philosophical Library, 1958.
Pictorial History of Philosophy, Philosophical Library, 1959.
Lost Legends of Israel, Philosophical Library, 1961.
Letters to My Teacher, Philosophical Library, 1961.
The Art of Thinking, Philosophical Library, 1961.
Despotism: A Pictorial History of Tyranny, Philosophical Library, 1963, abridged edition published as *Crosscuts through History*, 1965.
The Disinherited and the Law, Philosophical Library, 1964.
The Jew and the Cross, Philosophical Library, 1965, 2nd edition, 1966.
Treasury of Thought: Observations over Half a Century, Philosophical Library, 1966.
The War against the Jews, Philosophical Library, 1967.
Philosophy for Everyman, Philosophical Library, 1968, paperback published as *Philosophy for Everyman: From Socrates to Sartre*, Littlefield, 1974.
Handbook of Reason, Philosophical Library, 1972.

EDITOR

(And contributor) *Goethe: A Symposium*, Roerick Museum Press, 1932.
Dictionary of Philosophy, Philosophical Library, 1942, revised and enlarged edition, Rowman & Allanheld, 1984.
Who's Who in Philosophy, Philosophical Library, 1942.
Twentieth Century Philosophy, Philosophical Library, 1943, subsequent editions published as *Living Schools of Philosophy*.
Franklin D. Roosevelt, *American Way: Selections from Public Addresses and Papers*, Philosophical Library, 1944.
(With Harry G. Schrickel) *Art in a Post War World*, Ayer Co., 1944.
Bible for the Liberal, foreword by Lin Yutang, Philosophical Library, 1946.
(With Schrickel) *Encyclopedia of the Arts*, Philosophical Library, 1946, reprinted, Gale, 1982.
Benjamin Rush, *Selected Writings*, Philosophical Library, 1947.
The Diary and Sundry Observations of Thomas Alva Edison, Philosophical Library, 1948, published as *The Diary and Observations of Thomas Alva Edison*, 1983.
Spinoza Dictionary, foreword by Albert Einstein, Philosophical Library, 1951, reprinted, Greenwood Press, 1976.
The Hebrew Impact on Western Civilization, Philosophical Library, 1951, abridged edition, Citadel, 1965, reprinted 1951 edition, Greenwood Press, 1975.
Treasury of Philosophy, Philosophical Library, 1955, subsequent editions published as *Treasury of World Philosophy*.
Benedictus de Spinoza, *How to Improve Your Mind*, Philosophical Library, 1956.
Wisdom of the Torah, Philosophical Library, 1956.
Treasury of World Literature, Philosophical Library, 1956.
The Wisdom of the Kabbalah, Philosophical Library, 1957.
Concise Dictionary of Judaism, Philosophical Library, 1959.
A Treasury of World Science, introduction by Wernher von Braun, Philosophical Library, 1962.
Classics in Logic, Philosophical Library, 1962.
Spinoza, *Reflections and Maxims*, Philosophical Library, 1965.
(And translator) Martin Heidegger, *German Existentialism*, Philosophical Library, 1965.
Spninoza, *Letters to Friend and Foe*, Philosophical Library, 1966.
The Gospel According to St. John, Philosophical Library, 1967.
Let My People Live!: An Indictment, Philosophical Library, 1974.

OTHER

Editor, *Philosophic Abstracts*, 1939-54, and *Journal of Aesthetics and Art Criticism*, beginning 1941.

[Sketch reviewed by wife, Rose Morse]

*   *   *

RUSSELL, Andy 1915-

PERSONAL: Born December 8, 1915, in Lethbridge, Alberta, Canada; son of Harold George (a rancher) and Lorenda Scarlett (McTavish) Russell; married Anna Kathleen Riggall, October 1, 1939; children: Richard Herbert, Charles Andrew, Harold John, Gordon Riggall, Lorenda Anna Raabe. *Education:* Educated at public schools in Alberta, Canada. *Politics:* Liberal.

ADDRESSES: Home—Box 790, Turner Valley, Alberta, Canada T0L 2A0.

CAREER: Professional outdoorsman and writer. Trapper, 1933-46; mountaineering guide and outfitter in Rocky Mountains and bronco-buster in Alberta, 1939-60; professional photographer, 1940—; cinematographer, 1954—; rancher in Alberta, 1964-72; associated with Andy Russell & Sons Production Ltd., Waterton Lakes National Park, Alberta, 1979. Lecturer on wildlife and mountaineering throughout Canada and in the United States. Writer and narrator of "Heritage" radio series for Calgary Power Co.; field director and photographer for television documentary films. Director of camera safari to Kenya for Air Canada, 1977; member of board of trustees, National Sportsman Fund; member of scientific advisory committee to Minister of the Environment, Ottawa.

MEMBER: Wildlife Federation, Writers Guild, Explorers Club, Foothills Protective Association (president, 1974-77).

AWARDS, HONORS: Awards for best nonfiction, 1974 and 1977; received Order of Canada; Julian T. Crandall Award, 1976, for conservation work; honorary doctor of laws degrees, 1977, from University of Lethbridge and from University of Calgary; Winchester Outdoorsman of the Year Award, 1978; Jerry Potts Award, 1979, for contribution to Canadian tourism.

WRITINGS:

(Illustrated with own photographs) *Grizzly Country*, Knopf, 1967, Douglas & McIntyre, 1986.
Trails of a Wilderness Wanderer, Knopf, 1971.
Horns in the High Country, Knopf, 1973, Douglas & McIntyre, 1987.
(With Ted Blacklock) *The High West*, Viking, 1974.
The Rockies, Hurtig Publishers, 1975.
(With Ted Grant) *Men of the Saddle*, Van Nostrand, 1978.
Adventures with Wild Animals, Knopf, 1978.
(With Janis Kraulis) *Alpine Canada*, Hurtig, 1979.
Memoirs of a Mountain Man, Macmillan, 1984.
Great Bear Adventures, Key Porter Books, 1987.
The Life of a River, McClelland & Stewart, 1987.

Also author of scripts for radio commercials. Contributor of articles and photographs to magazines.

WORK IN PROGRESS: Yellow Horse (working title), a historical novel about the training and early life of a Blackfoot brave.

SIDELIGHTS: "Andy Russell has worked as a trapper, grizzly hunter, bronc-buster and trail guide. Eventually, through writing, film-making and lecturing he became one of the most dedicated defenders of wildlife habitat in Canada,'' writes Erling Friis-Baastad in the *Globe and Mail*. Russell's autobiography, *Memoirs of a Mountain Man* tells of his childhood in Alberta, Canada, through his career as a trail guide for outdoor enthusiasts, including writers, politicians, and gangsters. *Memoirs of a Mountain Man* ''recounts so many near disasters that it would seem to be a miracle that the author survived to tell the tales,'' Friis-Baastad comments. He adds, ''Russell's writing shares the informality of a campfire chat; he is obviously fond of his audience and usually proud of his material.''

''If there is any such thing as a compulsive writer, I guess then I am one,'' Andy Russell once told *CA*. ''Ever since I was a very small boy, I have loved to read and have always been an admirer of those authors displaying craftsmanship and the art of storytelling.

''Living in itself is an adventure, but living, observing, and telling about it is satisfaction equal to no other. Being a survivor, successful in staying alive under sometimes trying conditions in all kinds of circumstances in wild and so-called civilized surroundings, I try to beam my writing to wake people up to the vital features of habitat in a world being wastefully plundered without thought.

''Occasionally the need for illumination is so huge and pressing that the job seems almost impossible, but dealing with it as a raconteur, historian, and naturalist does generate some satisfaction in the effort.

''I find it a bit discouraging sometimes when aspiring writers come to me asking advice. There is no substitute for work and unending reading. One is essentially dependent on the other. At least for me. Certainly there are no short-cuts to success; one has to be prepared to sweat and sometimes weep in frustration, but never quit until the objective is reached.

''Through much reading, I have been influenced by other writers, particularly those who obviously have done their homework in research.

''There was a time when no amount of work could earn anyone a living as a free-lance writer in Canada, but this has changed considerably for the better in the last couple of decades. Being one of the very few Canadian authors who make a decent living from their writing, I can assure any aspiring writer that there is a lot of room at the top.

''Writing is a craft and an art wherein the author must develop the ability to be at once informative and entertaining, if not always colorful. The manipulation of words can be fascinating for the author, but it must also be the same for the reader. Simplicity and forthrightness are the key.

''But no matter how skilled [the author] and regardless of the high quality of the end product, it can be very frustrating for a writer to find himself or herself on the receiving end of a bad contract. Writing is about fifty percent skill and art, and an equal amount of salesmanship and business principle. Do not be unreasonable, but take the time and find the help to make that contract right. A good agent can be a livesaver and save a lot of hours. A knowledgeable agent will more than earn the percentage of royalty required as a fee for his or her services.

''It has been said that laws are made for the direction of wise men and the edification of fools. The same can be applied to advice for writrs. There is no patent formula for all; each author must work out his own shape, his blueprint, perfect it and apply it with unending diligence.''

From 1961 to 1963, Russell and two of his sons covered over 25,000 miles of wild country in northwestern North America, making the first intimate film study of the grizzly bear. During that time, the Russells made 204 close range approaches to the bears, which, says Russell, ''will probably never be duplicated for the simple reason that there is nobody left alive with the background training.'' Russell has toured North America with the film.

BIOGRAPHICAL/CRITICAL SOURCES:

PERIODICALS

Globe and Mail, April 20, 1985, January 30, 1988.

*   *   *

RUSSELL, Roy 1918-
(Anthony Gresham)

PERSONAL: Born August 7, 1918, in Blackpool, England; son of William Thomas (a theatrical manager) and Beatrice (Warburton) Russell; married Barbara Mary Reynolds Chard, March 7, 1945. *Education:* Attended school in Kirkham, Lancashire, England.

ADDRESSES: Home—57 Lower Rd., Fetcham Park, near Leatherhead, Surrey KT22 9HD, England. *Agent*—Harvey Unna & Stephen Durbridge Ltd., 24 Pottery Lane, Holland Park, London W11 4LL, England.

CAREER: Television and radio playwright. Midland Bank Ltd., Overseas Branch, London, England, bank officer, 1946-58; Wyndsor Recording Co., London, England, general manager, 1958-63; writer, 1963—. *Military service:* British Army, Royal Signals, 1939-45; became lieutenant.

MEMBER: Writers Guild of Great Britain (council member, 1964-77), American Film Institute, Society of Authors.

AWARDS, HONORS: Laurel Award, Writers Guild of Great Britain, 1978, for ''distinguished service to writers.''

WRITINGS:

STAGE PLAYS

Return to Bedlam: A Comedy in Three Acts (first produced on the West End at Garrick Theatre, 1947), H.F.W. Deane, 1947.
Sawdust and Shuttlecocks: A Comedy in One Act (first produced in London, England, by Southgate Theatre Guild, 1947), Walter H. Baker, 1947.
Rope Enough: A Play (three-act; first produced in London by Southgate Theatre Guild, 1947), Walter H. Baker, 1949.
''Thanksgiving Day'' (also see below; three-act), first produced in London by Southgate Theatre Guild, 1952.
Women on View: A Play (one-act; first produced in Bookham, Surrey, England, at The Barn Theatre, 1972), Samuel French, 1973.
The Eleventh Commandment: A Play (three-act; first produced in Pirbright, Surrey, England), Samuel Frnech, 1976.
Chez Claudine: A Play (one-act; first produced in Ryde, Isle of Wight, England, at Seaview Theatre, 1975), Kenyon-Deane, 1978.

TELEVISION PLAYS

''Thanksgiving Day'' (adapted from stage play of same title), first broadcast by British Broadcasting Corp. (BBC-TV), 1952.

"A House in Regent Place" (a quartet of plays), first broadcast by Southern Television, 1973.
"Are You Stone Cold, Santa Claus?," first broadcast by Associated Television Ltd. (ATV), 1977.
"The Magic Poltergeist," first broadcast by BBC-TV, 1978.
"The Princess and the Inventor," first broadcast by BBC-TV, 1982.
"Skeleton Key," first broadcast by Anglia Television, 1982.
"The Winner," first broadcast by BBC-TV, 1982.
"The Reconciliation," first broadcast by Anglia Television, 1983.

Also author of "The Woodcutter Operation" (adapted from book of same title by Kenneth Royce), and of "Last Video and Testament," 1982.

RADIO PLAYS

"Wine in the Afternoon," first broadcast by BBC-Radio, 1964.
"The Respectable Men," first broadcast by BBC-Radio, 1965.
"I'll See You Next Friday," first broadcast by BBC-Radio, 1976.
"Chequemates," first broadcast by BBC-Radio, 1979.

Also author of two plays for "Ten Commandments" anthology, first broadast by BBC-World Service, 1982.

TELEVISION SERIALS

"Fothergale Company Ltd." (sixteen parts), first broadcast by BBC-TV, 1965.
"The Queen Street Gang" (nine parts), first broadcast by Thames Television, 1968.
"Fly into Danger" (seven parts), first broadcast by ATV, 1972.
"A Place to Hide" (six parts), first broadcast by ATV, 1975.
"Midnight Is a Place" (thirteen parts; adapted from book of same title by Joan Aiken), first broadcast by Southern Television, 1976.
"Together" (six parts), first broadcast by Southern Television, 1981.
"The Witches and the Grinnygog" (six parts; adapted from book of same title by Dorothy Edwards), first broadcast by Southern Television, 1982.
"Henry's Leg" (six parts; adapted from book by Ann Pilling), first broadcast by Southern Television, 1986.

Also author of individual scripts for more than thirty television series, including "A Family at War," broadcast by Granada Television; "Crime of Passion," broadcast by ATV; "Intimate Strangers," broadcast by London Weekend Television (LWT); "Doomwatch," "The Troubleshooters," and "The Onedin Line," all broadcast by BBC-TV.

RADIO SERIALS

"London Royal" (twelve parts), first broadcast by BBC-World Service, 1982.

DOCUMENTARY FILMS

"The Lonely Sea and the Sky," produced by Trade Winds, 1970.
"Be a Cargoman," produced by British Airways, 1971.
"Pilots Royal: Prince Bernhard," produced by Trade Winds, 1974.
"Pilots Royal: Prince Charles," produced by Paradine, 1975.
"Test-Match Special," produced Hawkshead Communications, 1982.

OTHER

A Family at War: Towards Victory (novel), Mayflower, 1972.

Drama critic for *City Press*, 1953-56; television critic (under pseudonym Anthony Gresham), 1954-56.

SIDELIGHTS: Roy Russell once told *CA:* "I am a storyteller. I try to create fascinating characters in intriguing, real-life situations and see how they make out or don't make out. Characters who are desperately trying to find their way out of problems generate action, tension, and suspense—the essentials of good storytelling. I see no conflict between writing to say something and writing to entertain. There is no reason why there should not be a serious underlying point in each episode of a highly popular television series, whether contemporary or historcal. For example, at the time when the concern was not yet a public issue, I wrote an episode of the 'Doomwatch' series involving the characters in the threat of pollution in the Mediterranean Sea.

"Several of the top-rated series I have written for have been shown around the world, and the film 'Pilots Royal: Prince Charles' achieved the second highest rating ever on BBC's second channel. My lecture 'Writing Television Drama' is well known for its combination of sound guidance and humor, making serious points while entertaining, like my writing—I hope."

*   *   *

RUTHERFORD, Michael (Andrew) 1946-

PERSONAL: Born December 22, 1946, in Albany, N.Y.; son of Robert Alexander (a lawyer) and Eugenia (Ogonowski) Rutherford. *Education:* Attended Hamilton College, 1963-64, and Junior College of Albany, 1964-65; State University of New York at Albany, B.A., 1968, M.L.S., 1973. *Politics:* None. *Religion:* "Pantheist."

ADDRESSES: Home—1 Indian Ledge Rd., Voorheesville, N.Y. 12186. *Office*—Harmanus Bleecker Library, 19 Dove St., Albany, N.Y.

CAREER: Poet. Albany Public Library, Albany, N.Y., librarian at Harmanus Bleecker Library, and teacher, 1969—. Regional coordinator of Poets in the Schools program, 1973—. Teaches poetry in schools, and teaches video and film-making; established Albany's "Dial-a-Poem" service, 1969. Publisher and editor of Conspiracy Press, 1972—.

AWARDS, HONORS: Lovenheim Poetry Prize from State University of New York at Albany, 1969; New York State Council on the Arts grants, 1971-74.

WRITINGS:

(Translator) Catullus, *Lesbia-Catullus*, Carnal Press, 1972.
Meat Is My Business (poems), Conspiracy Press, 1973.
The Tale and Its Master, Spring Harbor, 1986.

WORK IN PROGRESS: A book of poems on the sculptor Rodin; a collection of random poems. †

*   *   *

RUTHVEN, K(enneth) K(nowles) 1936-

PERSONAL: First syllable of surname rhymes with "doth";

born May 26, 1936, in Bradford, England; son of Thomas Knowles (a mining deputy) and Freda (Bennett) Ruthven; married Rachel Mary Bainbridge (a secondary school teacher), December 26, 1960; children: Simon, Guy, Patrick. *Education:* University of Manchester, B.A. (honors), 1958, M.A., 1959, Ph.D., 1965. *Politics:* None. *Religion:* None.

ADDRESSES: Office—English Department, University of Melbourne, Parkville, Victoria 3052, Australia.

CAREER: University of Canterbury, Christchurch, New Zealand, assistant lecturer, 1961-64, lecturer, 1965-69, senior lecturer, 1969-72, professor of English, 1972-79; University of Adelaide, Adelaide, Australia, professor of English, 1980-85; University of Melbourne, Parkville, Australia, professor of English, 1985—.

WRITINGS:

The Conceit, Methuen, 1969.
A Guide to Ezra Pound's Personae (1926), University of California Press, 1969.
Myth, Methuen, 1975, Barnes & Noble, 1976.
Critical Assumptions, Cambridge University Press, 1979.
Feminist Literary Studies: An Introduction, Cambridge University Press, 1984.

Contributor to learned journals.

WORK IN PROGRESS: Book on Ezra Pound as a literary critic, for Croom Helm.

BIOGRAPHICAL/CRITICAL SOURCES:

PERIODICALS

Times Literary Supplement, February 22, 1980.

S

SACKS, Karen 1941-

PERSONAL: Born November 21, 1941, in New York, N.Y.; daughter of Jacob (a teacher) and Sylvia (a teacher; maiden name, Schechter) Brodkin; married William Sacks (divorced, 1987); children: Benjamin, Daniel. *Education:* Brandeis University, A.B., 1963; Harvard University, M.A., 1964; University of Michigan, Ph.D., 1971.

ADDRESSES: Home—Venice, Calif. 90291. *Office*—Women's Studies Program, University of California, Los Angeles, Calif. 90024.

CAREER: Wayne State University, Detroit, Mich., part-time instructor in anthropology, 1968; Oakland University, Rochester, Mich., instructor, 1968-70, assistant professor of sociology and anthropology, 1970-75; Fordham University at Lincoln Center, New York, N.Y., visiting assistant professor of social sciences, 1975-76; University of Minnesota, Minneapolis, visiting assistant professor of anthropology, 1976; Clark University, Worcester, Mass., assistant professor of sociology and anthropology, 1976-80; American University, Washington, D.C., lecturer in anthropology, 1981; Business and Professional Women's Foundation, Washington, D.C., director of research and information services, 1981-85; University of California, Los Angeles, associate professor of anthropology and director of women's studies, 1987—. Center for the Study of the Family and the State, Institute for Public Policy, Duke University fellow, 1978-80, visiting scholar, 1980-82, research associate in anthropology, 1982-84. Conducted field work in Puerto Rico, 1965; public speaker; organizer of conferences on women and work.

MEMBER: American Anthropological Association, National Women's Studies Association, National Writers Union.

AWARDS, HONORS: Ford Foundation grant, 1967-68; National Science Foundation grant, 1982-84.

WRITINGS:

Sisters and Wives: The Past and Future of Sexual Equality, Greenwood Press, 1979.
(Editor with Dorothy Remy) *My Troubles Are Going to Have Trouble with Me,* Rutgers University Press, 1984.
Caring by the Hour, University of Illinois Press, 1988.

CONTRIBUTOR

Robin Morgan, editor, *Sisterhood Is Powerful,* Random House, 1970.
Michelle Rosaldo and Louise Lamphere, editors, *Women, Culture, and Society,* Stanford University Press, 1974.
Larry Reynolds and James Henselin, editors, *Social Problems in American Society,* 3rd edition, Allyn & Bacon, 1978.
Jean O'Barr, editor, *Perspectives on Power: Women in Asia, Africa, and Latin America,* Center for International Studies, Duke University, 1982.

OTHER

Contributor of articles and reviews to anthropology journals and popular magazines, including *Ms., Monthly Review, Radical Teacher,* and *Jewish Currents.*

WORK IN PROGRESS: A video on urban fishing.

SIDELIGHTS: Karen Sacks told *CA:* "I'm interested in women workers, both their family and work lives. The average woman today is doing two jobs and getting paid for less than one. I write about (and conduct research on) the ways women cope creatively with and prevail against the odds against them. As an activist and an academic, I want my writing to help women organize for equity and change."

*   *   *

SADDLER, Allen
See RICHARDS, R(onald) C(harles) W(illiam)

*   *   *

SADDLER, K. Allen
See RICHARDS, R(onald) C(harles) W(illiam)

*   *   *

SANDBERG, (Karin) Inger 1930-

PERSONAL: Born August 2, 1930, in Karlstad, Sweden; daughter of Johan and Hanna (a teacher; maiden name, Carlstedt) Erikson; married Lasse Sandberg (an artist), April 27, 1950; children: Lena, Niklas, Mathias. *Education:* Swedish Training College for Teachers, teacher's certificate, 1954.

ADDRESSES: Home—Muraregatan 9, 65228 Karlstad, Sweden; and Alvsbackov, Sweden (summer).

CAREER: Teacher in Karlstad, Sweden public schools, 1957-63; writer of books and of television and radio productions for children, 1963—.

MEMBER: Swedish Union of Writers, Swedish PEN Club, Zonta International.

AWARDS, HONORS: Swedish Author's Fund award, 1963; Karlstad culture prize, 1965; Hans Christian Andersen honorable mention and International Board on Books for Young People (IBBY) honorable mention, both 1966, and Leipzig International Book Exhibit award, 1971, all for *Niklas roeda dag;* Heffaklump award from *Expressen* newspaper (Sweden), 1969, for *Pappa, kom ut!;* Nils Holgersson Medal, 1973; Astrid Lindgren Prize, 1974; Varmlands Landstings Kulturstipendium, 1976; Wettergrens Bokollon, 1987, for *Sandberg's ABCD.*

WRITINGS:

Mina glada trojor (title means "Happy Knitting!"), Raben & Sjoegren, 1987, 2nd edition, 1988.

ILLUSTRATED BY HUSBAND, LASSE SANDBERG

Faaret Ullrik Faar medalj (title means "Woolrik the Sheep Gets a Medal"), Eklund, 1953.
Jag maalar en . . . (title means "I Paint a . . ."), Eklund, 1955.
Jonas bilen och aeventyret (title means "Jonas the Car and the Adventure"), Geber, 1959.
Godnattsagor paa rullgardinen (title means "Bedtime Stories on the Blind"), Geber, 1960.
Filuren paa aeventyr (title means "The Adventure of the Little Filur"), Geber, 1961.
Hemma hos mej (title means "At My Place"), Geber, 1962.
Lena beraettar, Geber, 1963, 3rd edition, 1971, translation by Patricia Crampton published as *Here's Lena,* Methuen, 1970.
Trollen i Lill-Skogen (title means "The Trolls in the Little Wood"), Karlstad Town, 1963.
Niklas roeda dag, Geber, 1964, 3rd edition, 1985, translation of second edition published as *Nicholas' Red Day,* Delacorte, 1967.
Barnens bildordlista (title means "Children's Wordbook"), Skrivrit, 1965.
Den musikaliska myran (title means "The Musical Ant"), Geber, 1965, 2nd edition, 1970.
En morgon i varuhuset (title means "One Morning in the Department Store"), [Stockholm], 1965.
Johan, Raben & Sjoegren, 1965, 3rd edition, 1970, translation by Crampton published as *Johan's Year,* Methuen, 1971.
Pojken med de Hundra bilarna, Raben & Sjoegren, 1966, 2nd edition, 1980, translation of first edition published as *The Boy with 100 Cars,* Delacorte, 1967.
Tomtens stadsresa (title means "The Tomten Goes to Town"), General Post Office (Sweden), 1966.
En konstig foersta maj, Raben & Sjoegren, 1967.
Niklas oenskedjur, Raben & Sjoegren, 1967, translation by R. Sadler published as *Nicholas' Ideal Pet,* Sadler & Brown, 1968, published as *Nicholas' Favorite Pet,* Delacorte, 1969.
Pojken med de maanga husen, Raben & Sjoegren, 1968, translation published as *The Boy with Many Houses,* Delacorte, 1969.
Vi passar oss sjaelva (title means "We Look after Ourselves"), Geber, 1968.

Pappa, kom ut!, Raben & Sjoegren, 1969, 2nd edition, 1986, translation of first edition published as *Daddy Come Out!,* Sadler & Brown, 1970, published as *Come On Out, Daddy,* Delacorte, 1971.
Johan i2:an, Raben & Sjoegren, 1969, 2nd edition, 1970, translation by Crampton published as *Johan at School,* Methuen, 1972.
Filurstjaernan (title means "The Filurstar"), Geber, 1969.
Buffalo Bengt och indianerna, Raben & Sjoegren, 1970, translation published as *Buffalo Bengt and the Indians,* Sadler & Brown, 1971.
Lena staar i koe (title means "Lena Lines Up"), Geber, 1970.
Stora Tokboken (title means "The Big Crazybook"), Geber, 1970.
Vad aer det som ryker?, Raben & Sjoegren, 1971, translation by Merloyd Lawrence published as *Where Does All That Smoke Come From?,* Delacorte, 1972.
Fred Strid krymper (title means "Mr. Fred Strid Shrinks"), Raben & Sjoegren, 1972.
Vi leker oeken, Froeken, Raber & Sjoegren, 1973, translation published as *Let's Play Desert,* Delacorte, 1974 (published in England as *The Desert Game,* Methuen, 1974).
Hej, vaelkommen till mej!, Raben & Sjoegren, 1974, translation published as *Let's Be Friends,* Methuen, 1975.
Perry och osynlige Wrolf (title means "Perry and the Invisible Wrolf"), Raben & Sjoegren, 1975.
Var aer laanga farbrorns hatt? (title means "Where's Tall Uncle's Hat?"), Raben & Sjoegren, 1976.
Tummens resa, Raben & Sjoegren, 1978.
Tummen tittar pa natten, Raben & Sjoegren, 1980.
Tummen far en vaen, Raben & Sjoegren, 1980.
Tummens mamma slutar roeka, Raben & Sjoegren, 1980.
En fin dag foer Johan, Raben & Sjoegren, 1981.
Tummen och Tossingarna, Raben & Sjoegren, 1982.
Titta daer, sa Pulvret, Raben & Sjoegren, 1983.
Hjaelpa till, sa Pulvret, Raben & Sjoegren, 1983, translation by Judy Abbott Maurer published as *Dusty Wants to Help,* ROS Books/Farrar, Straus, 1987.
Lana den, sa Pulvret, Raben & Sjoegren, 1984, translation by Maurer published as *Dusty Wants to Borrow Everything,* ROS Books/Farrar, Straus, 1988.
Radd for, sa Pulvret, Raben & Sjoegren, 1984.
Tummesagor, Raben & Sjoegren, 1984.
Mera macka, sa Pulvret, Raben & Sjoegren, 1985.
Lilla Nollan och dom andra, Carlsen Lit., 1985.
Hitta den, sa Pulvret, Raben & Sjoegren, 1986.
Vit och Svart och alla dom andra, Raben & Sjoegren, 1986.
Sandberg's ABCD, Raben & Sjoegren, 1987.
Pojken, prinsessan och gront, Raben & Sjoegren, 1988.

"LITTLE ANNA" SERIES; ILLUSTRATED BY L. SANDBERG

Vad Anna fick se, Raben & Sjoegren, 1964, 8th edition, 1987, translation published as *What Anna Saw,* Lothrop, 1964.
Lilla Anna och trollerihatten, Raben & Sjoegren, 1965, 8th edition, 1987, translation published as *Little Anna and the Magic Hat,* Lothrop, 1965 (published in England as *Anna and the Magic Hat,* Sadler & Brown, 1965).
Vad lilla Anna sparade paa, Raben & Sjoegren, 1965, 8th edition, 1987, translation published as *What Little Anna Saved,* Lothrop, 1965 (published in England as *What Anna Saved,* Sadler & Brown, 1965).
Lilla Annas mamma fyller aar, Raben & Sjoegren, 1966, 8th edition, 1987, translation published as *Little Anna's Mama Has a Birthday,* Sadler & Brown, 1965, Lothrop, 1966.

Naer lilla Anna var foerkyld, Raben & Sjoegren, 1966, 8th edition, 1987, translation published as *When Little Anna Had a Cold*, Lothrop, 1966 (published in England as *When Anna Had a Cold*, Sadler & Brown, 1966).

Lilla Anna och Laanga Farbrorn paa havet, Raben & Sjoegren, 1971, translation published as *Little Anna and the Tall Uncle*, Methuen, 1973.

Var aer lilla Annas hund?, Raben & Sjoegren, 1972, translation published as *Where Is Little Anna's Dog?*, Methuen, 1974.

Lilla Annas julklapp, Raben & Sjoegren, 1972, 5th edition, 1987, translation published as *Kate's Christmas Present*, A. & C. Black, 1974.

Lilla Anna flyttar saker, Raben & Sjoegren, 1972, 5th edition, 1987, translation published as *Kate's Upside Down Day*, A. & C. Black, 1974.

Lilla Anna leker med bollar, Raben & Sjoegren, 1973, 5th edition, 1987, translation published as *Kate's Bouncy Ball*, A. & C. Black, 1974.

Lilla Anna kom och hjaelp!, Raben & Sjoegren, 1972, 5th edition, 1987, translation published as *Kate, Kate Come and Help!*, A. & C. Black, 1974.

Lilla Anna i glada skolan (title means "Little Anna in the Happy School"), Raben & Sjoegren, 1975.

Lilla Anna och de mystiska froena, Raben & Sjoegren, 1979.

Lilla Anna reser till Landet Mittemot, Raben & Sjoegren, 1982.

"LITTLE SPOOK" SERIES; ILLUSTRATED BY L. SANDBERG

Lilla spoeket Laban, Geber, 1965, 3rd edition, 1976, translation by Nancy S. Leupold published as *Little Ghost Godfrey*, Delacorte, 1968, translation by Kertsi French published as *Little Spook*, Methuen, 1969.

Lilla spoeket Laban far en lillasyster, Raben & Sjoegren, 1977, translation published as *Little Spook's Baby Sister*, Methuen, 1978.

Labolinas Lina, Raben & Sjoegren, 1977, translation published as *Tiny Spook's Tugging Game*, Methuen, 1978.

Labolinas snubbeldag, Raben & Sjoegrens, 1977, translation published as *Tiny Spook's Tumbles*, Methuen, 1978.

Gissa vem jag aer idag? sa Labolina, Raben & Sjoegren, 1977, translation published as *Tiny Spook's Guessing Game*, Methuen, 1978.

Kommer snart, sa Laban och Labolina, Raben & Sjoegren, 1977, translation published as *Little Spook's Grubby Day*, Methuen, 1978.

Pappa aer sjuk, sa lilla spoeket Laban, Raben & Sjoegren, 1977, translation published as *Little Spook Haunts Again*, Methuen, 1978.

Var aer Labolinas Millimina?, Raben & Sjoegren, 1979, translation puiblished as *Little Spook and the Lost Doll*, Methuen, 1980.

"MATHIAS" SERIES

Mathias bakar kakor, Raben & Sjoegren, 1968, 3rd edition, 1974, trnaslation published as *Daniel and the Coconut Cakes*, A. & C. Black, 1973.

Mathias och trollet, Raben & Sjoegren, 1968, translation published as *Daniel's Mysterious Monster*, A. & C. Black, 1973.

Mathias maalar en . . ., Raben & Sjoegren, 1969, translation published as *Daniel Paints a Picture*, A. & C. Black, 1973.

Mathias hjaelper till, Raben & Sjoegren, 1969, 2nd edition, 1974, translation published as *Daniel's Helping Hand*, A. & C. Black, 1973.

OTHER

Writer, with husband, of over 180 children's television and radio programs broadcast in Sweden. Contributor to Swedish journals and magazines.

WORK IN PROGRESS: "The books of the future are secret. Exhibitions containing my 'wearable art'."

SIDELIGHTS: "The big challenge," Inger Sandberg told *CA*, "is to write books which make tiny little holes, from one year of age, happy and make them laugh and also expand their emotions and artistic and linguistic ability. One must *know* a lot about children, and above all, one must know what one wants and where one's loyalties are.

"The environment, the life of the modern city, means a lot to our work, both in the fifties when we lived in a tall block of flats, and now when we live in a modern terrace house. What we see and experience, we use, just like other writers use their own special environment. [Ours] is an environment where the big and the small play together and work together; an environment in which the little ones are rightful citizens with rights and responsibilities. We want to be on the side of the children in what we are doing, in our books and for people living in the world today.

"I don't think that any book for children can explain our complex, mad world to a child—hopefully the *good* book can explain a bit of what's going on—and make the world—the everyday life—more understandable."

*   *   *

SANDYS, Elspeth (Somerville)   1940-

PERSONAL: Born March 18, 1940, in Timaru, New Zealand; daughter of Thomas Sandilands (a printer and publisher) and Alice (a nurse; maiden name, Alley) Somerville; married Fraser Jefcoate Harbutt, December 17, 1960 (divorced December, 1969); married William Reginald Bruce Purchase (an actor), February 11, 1970 (separated, 1984); children: (first marriage) Josephine Jefcoate; (second marriage) Reuben Thomas William. *Education:* Trinity College of Music, L.T.C.L., 1959, F.T.C.L., 1960; University of Otago, B.A., 1960; University of Auckland, M.A. (with first class honors), 1967.

ADDRESSES: Home—2 Union St., Stow-on-the-Wold, Gloucester GL54 1BU, England. *Agent*—Diana Tyler, MBA Literary Agents Ltd., 45 Fitzroy St., London W1P 5HR, England.

CAREER: Writer. Teacher of English and history at schools in London, England, 1962-63, and Auckland, New Zealand, 1967-69; editorial work, London and Oxford, England, 1977—. Actress in London and Auckland, 1962-69.

WRITINGS:

Catch a Falling Star (novel), Blond & Briggs, 1978.

The Burning Dawn (novel), Dell, 1981 (published in England as *The Broken Tree*, Hutchinson, 1981).

Love and War (novel), Secker & Warburg, 1982.

The Chateau (novel), Secker & Warburg, 1983.

"The Body Politic" (two-act play), first produced in Oxford, England, at Oxford Playhouse, 1983.

"Consequences," produced by Oxford Playhouse, 1984.

RADIO PLAYS

"The Weather in the Streets," first broadcast by BBC-Radio, June, 1979.

"The Echoing Grove," first broadcast by BBC-Radio, May, 1981.

"No Fixed Address," first broadcast by BBC-Radio, November 30, 1982.

"Riding to Jerusalem," first broadcast by BBC-Radio, November, 1984.

"In a Summer Season," first broadcast by BBC-Radio, summer, 1988.

SIDELIGHTS: Elspeth Sandys told *CA:* "I became a writer largely in response to the realities of being married to an actor and having young children to care for—that is, long hours of isolation, insecurity, and a constant change of home. My novels tend to reflect a yearning for my home country of New Zealand, a love of the past, a tendency towards romanticism, and fascination with moral questions. My plays reflect more of my political nature, in particular my involvement with nuclear disarmament and the politics of the Left."

AVOCATIONAL INTERESTS: Music, politics, reading, travel (especially Greece), going to the theatre.

*   *   *

SARNAT, Marshall   1929-

PERSONAL: Surname originally Sarnatzky; born August 1, 1929, in Chicago, Ill.; son of Maurice (a pharmacist) and Dena (Lew) Sarnatzky; married Carmela Shainker (a botanist), January 17, 1956; children: Don, Iddo, Tamar. *Education:* Hebrew University of Jerusalem, B.A., 1955; Northwestern University, M.B.A., 1957, Ph.D., 1965. *Religion:* Jewish.

ADDRESSES: Home—Nayot 34, Jerusalem, Israel. *Office*—School of Business, Hebrew University, Jerusalem, Israel.

CAREER: Hebrew University of Jerusalem, Jerusalem, Israel, instructor, 1959-65, School of Business Administration, lecturer, 1965-67, senior lecturer, 1967-72, associate professor, 1972-76, professor of finance, 1976-85, Albertson and Waltuch Professor of Finance, 1985—, director of Institute of Business Research, 1973—. Visiting professor, New York University, 1967-68, University of California, Berkeley, 1973, University of Toronto, 1973, University of California, Los Angeles, 1979, and New University of Lisbon, 1982. Director, Israel Financial Research Institute, 1964—; member, National Council for Insurance, 1965-68.

MEMBER: American Economic Association, European Finance Association (president, 1983), American Finance Association, Beta Gamma Sigma.

AWARDS, HONORS: International Institute of Management research fellow, Berlin, 1975.

WRITINGS:

The Development of Securities Market in Israel, J. C. B. Mohr, 1966.

Saving and Investment through Retirement Funds in Israel, Maurice Falk Institute, 1966.

(With H. Levy) *Investment and Portfolio Analysis,* Wiley, 1972.

(Co-author) *Decision-Making under Uncertainty,* Academic Press, 1976.

(Co-author) *Capital Investment and Financing Decision,* Prentice-Hall, 1978, 3rd edition, 1986.

Inflation and Capital Markets, Ballinger, 1978.

(Co-author) *The Bank and the Economy: Seventy-Five Years of Bank Levmi Le'yisrael,* Shikmona Press, 1980.

(Co-author) *International Finance and Trade,* Ballinger, 1980.

(Co-author) *Portfolio and Investment Selection: Theory and Practice,* Prentice-Hall, 1984.

(Co-author) *Principles of Financial Management,* Prentice-Hall, 1988.

Contributor to finance and economics journals. Editor, *Journal of Banking and Finance,* 1977—.

*   *   *

SAVORY, Hubert Newman   1911-

PERSONAL: Born August 7, 1911, in Lowestoft, Suffolk, England; son of William Charles Newman (an engineer) and Amelia Alice (Minns) Savory; married Priscilla Valerie Thirkell, 1949; children: Bernard William, Caroline Anne, Catherine Elizabeth, Matthew Newman, Peter John, Daniel Iwan. *Education:* Oxford University, B.A. (with first class honors), 1934, D.Phil., 1937. *Religion:* Church of England.

ADDRESSES: Home—Lady Mary Rd., Cardiff, South Wales.

CAREER: National Museum of Wales, Cardiff, assistant, 1938-39, assistant keeper in department of archaeology, 1939-56, keeper of archaeology, 1956-76. Secretary of archaeology committee of Board of Celtic Studies, University of Wales; member of Ancient Monuments Board for Wales, Ministry of Public Building and Works, 1956-82; Glamorgan-Gwent Archaeological Trust, Ltd., trustee, 1975—, chairman, 1975-84. *Military service:* British Army, Royal Artillery and Intelligence Corps, 1940-45; became sergeant major.

MEMBER: Society of Antiquaries (London; fellow), Royal Commission on Ancient and Historical Monuments in Wales (chairman, 1979-83), Cambrian Archaeological Association (president, 1975-76), Cardiff Naturalists' Society (president, 1960-61).

AWARDS, HONORS: MacIver research grant, 1936-38; G. T. Clark Prize in Prehistory for 1956-1964, Cambrian Archaeological Association.

WRITINGS:

(With Willoughby Gardner) *Dinorben, a Hill-Fort Occupied in Iron Age and Roman Times,* National Museum of Wales, 1964.

Early Iron Age Art in Wales, National Museum of Wales, 1964.

Spain and Portugal: A Survey of the Prehistory, Praeger, 1968.

Excavations at Dinorben, 1965-69, National Museum of Wales, 1971.

(Contributor) P. M. Duval and C.F.C. Hawkes, editors, *Celtic Art in Ancient Europe,* Seminar Press, 1976.

Guide Catalog of the Early Iron Age Collections, National Museum of Wales, 1976.

(Contributor) D. Harding, editor, *Hillforts,* Academic Press, 1976.

(Contributor) V. Markotic, editor, *Ancient Europe and the Mediterranean,* Aris & Phillips, 1977.

Guide Catalogue to the Bronze Age Collections, National Museum of Wales, 1980.

(Contributor) J. A. Taylor, editor, *Culture and Environment in Prehistoric Wales,* British Archaeological Reports, 1980.

(Editor and co-author) *Glamorgan County History,* Volume II, Glamorgan County History Trust, 1984.

OTHER

Contributor to professional journals. Editor, *Transactions of* the *Cardiff Naturalists Society,* 1948-62; editor of archaeology section, *Bulletin* of the Board of Celtic Studies, 1956-68.

WORK IN PROGRESS: A revision of the archaeological aspects of the early chapters of a new edition of J. E. Lloyd's *History of Wales,* for Golden Grove Book Company.

* * *

SCHATT, Stanley 1943-

PERSONAL: Born September 14, 1943, in New York, N.Y.; son of Maurice (a businessman) and Lilyan (Goldman) Schatt; married Jane Abrams (a reading specialist), April 7, 1966; children: Daniel Brian. *Education:* Arizona State University, B.A., 1964, M.A., 1966; University of Southern California, Ph.D., 1970; American Graduate School of International Management, M.I.M., 1976.

ADDRESSES: Office—Honeywell Process Control Division, MS 144, 2222 West Peoria, Phoenix, Ariz. 85029.

CAREER: University of Southern California, Los Angeles, instructor in English, 1969-70; University of Houston, Houston, Tex., assistant professor of English, 1970-74; Fulbright professor of American literature in Japan at universities in Tokyo, Keio, and Hiroshima, 1974-75; administrative assistant for the city of Phoenix, Ariz., 1976; Honeywell Process Control Division, Phoenix, software instructor, 1977—. Professor of management at Institute for Professional Development, 1977—.

MEMBER: Modern Language Association of America, American Chemical Society, Philology Association of the Pacific Coast.

WRITINGS:

(Editor) *Bartleby the Scrivener: A Casebook for Research,* W. C. Brown, 1971.
(With Peter Mandelik) *A Concordance to the Poems of Langston Hughes,* Gale, 1975.
Kurt Vonnegut, Jr., G. K. Hall, 1976.
Understanding Modern American Literature: Cultural and Historical Perspectives, Bunkahvoron, 1977.
(With Thomas J. Agnos) *The Practical Law Enforcement Guide to Writing Field Reports, Grant Proposals, Memos, and Resumes,* C. C Thomas, 1980.
(With wife, Jane A. Schatt) *Projects and Peripherals for Kids and the VIC-20,* Dilithium, 1984.
(With J. A. Schatt) *Bank Street Writing with Your Apple,* SYBEX, 1984.
Navigating CompuServe, S & S Press, 1985.
Navigating the Source, S & S Press, 1985.
Business and Home Applications for the Macintosh Using Microsoft BASIC, Brady Communications, 1985.

Contributor to literature journals and to *Southwest Review.*

WORK IN PROGRESS: A study of polygraphy; a novel about an adolescent boy; *Software Applications to Reading;* science fiction stories.

SIDELIGHTS: Stanley Schatt once wrote *CA:* "Two men who influenced me significantly are Gene Montague and Max Schulz. With a background in literature, chemistry, and computer science, I am very much interested in the relationship between science and the humanities. I have also become interested in the psychological dimension of effective management. I remain fascinated by ethnic differences and languages—particularly Spanish and Japanese. I would like to travel in the future

and do some cross-cultural studies involving both management technique and popular culture." †

* * *

SCHLAFLY, Phyllis 1924-

PERSONAL: Born August 15, 1924, in St. Louis, Mo.; daughter of John Bruce (an engineer) and Odille (Dodge) Stewart; married John Fred Schlafly (a lawyer), October 20, 1949; children: John F., Bruce S., Roger S., P. Liza Forshaw, Andrew L., Anne V. *Education:* Attended Maryville College of the Sacred Heart for two years; Washington University, St. Louis, Mo., A.B., 1944, J.D., 1978; Radcliffe College, M.A., 1945.

ADDRESSES: Home—68 Fairmount, Alton, Ill. 62002. *Office*—Eagle Forum, 316 Pennsylvania Ave. S.E., Washington, D.C. 20003.

CAREER: Lawyer, 1979—. First National Bank and St. Louis Union Trust Company, St. Louis, Mo., librarian and researcher, 1946-49; homemaker, 1949—. Delegate to Republican national conventions; candidate for Congress, 1952, 1970; president, Illinois Federation of Republican Women, 1960-64; first vice-president, National Federation of Republican Women, 1965-67; national chairman, Stop ERA, 1972—; member, Illinois Commission on the Status of Women, 1975-85; founder and president, Eagle Forum, 1975—. Member, Administrative Conference of the United States, 1983—, and Commission on the Bicentennial of the United States Constitution, 1985—. Commentator on "Matters of Opinion," WBBM Radio, Chicago, Ill., 1973-75, on "Spectrum," CBS Radio Network, 1973-78, and on CNN Cable Television Network, 1980-83.

MEMBER: Authors Guild, Authors League of America, American Conservative Union, Daughters of the American Revolution (national chairman of American history committee, 1965-68; member of bicentennial committee, 1967-70, and of national defense committee, 1977-80, 1983—), Junior League of St. Louis, Phi Beta Kappa, Pi Sigma Alpha.

AWARDS, HONORS: Named woman of achievement in public affairs by *St. Louis Globe-Democrat,* 1963; named Woman of the Year by Illinois Federation of Republican Women, 1969; awarded ten George Washington Honor Medals by Freedoms Foundation; Brotherhood Award, National Conference of Christians and Jews, 1975; LL.D., Niagara University, 1976; named one of the ten "most admired women in the world" by *Good Housekeeping* magazine, 1977—.

WRITINGS:

A Choice Not an Echo, Pere Marquette, 1964.
(With Chester C. Ward) *The Gravediggers,* Pere Marquette, 1964.
(With Ward) *Strike from Space,* Pere Marquette, 1965.
Safe—Not Sorry, Pere Marquette, 1967.
(With Ward) *The Betrayers,* Pere Marquette, 1968.
Mindszenty the Man, Cardinal Mindszenty Foundation, 1972.
(With Ward) *Kissinger on the Couch,* Arlington House, 1975.
Ambush at Vladivostok, Pere Marquette, 1976.
The Power of the Positive Woman, Arlington House, 1977.
The Power of the Christian Woman, Standard Publishing, 1981.
(Editor) *Equal Pay for UNequal Work,* Eagle Forum Education and Legal Defense Fund, 1984.
Child Abuse in the Classroom, Pere Marquette, 1984.
Pornography's Victims, Pere Marquette, 1987.

Also author of *The Phyllis Schlafly Report* (monthly national newsletter), 1967—. Contributor of syndicated column to newspapers through Copley News Service.

SIDELIGHTS: Phyllis Schlafly, a housewife turned political activist, is a leading spokeswoman for the conservative, pro-family viewpoint on issues such as women's rights, national defense, education, the law, and politics. Schlafly's organizational techniques and outspoken personal leadership are widely cited as the forces that defeated the Equal Rights Amendment in 1982 after a ten-year battle; her nationwide Eagle Forum continues to represent the concerns of families and political conservatives. A tireless worker known for her unflappable demeanor, Schlafly is "one of the best loved and the most loathed women in the country," according to *New York Review of Books* contributor Frances FitzGerald. Opinion is indeed sharply divided on Schlafly and her goals. In the *Washington Post*, Sally Quinn notes that on the podium Schlafly "comes on like a female George Wallace. She is tough and aggressive, totally unlike the role she espouses for most women." Conversely, a *National Review* correspondent calls her "one of the most remarkable women in American history," a dynamo who "has triumphed over the major media, the bureaucrats (and bureaucrettes), and the 'women's movement,' almost singlehandedly." Supporters and detractors alike concede, however, that Schlafly is enormously successful at galvanizing support and influencing public policy. In the *New York Times Magazine*, Joseph Lelyveld observes that she "has become one of the most relentless and accomplished platform debaters of any gender to be found on any side of any issue."

Schlafly was born Phyllis Stewart in St. Louis, Missouri on August 15, 1924. Her conservatism was nurtured from earliest childhood by her parents. Even when her father lost his job in the Depression, forcing the family into dire financial straits, he continued to champion the free enterprise system and traditional values. Family circumstances forced Phyllis's mother to work outside the home, and she was the head librarian at the St. Louis Art Museum for 25 years. The young Miss Stewart rewarded her mother's diligence by graduating first in her Catholic school class and earning a college scholarship. She began her undergraduate education at Maryville College of the Sacred Heart, but transferred to Washington University, graduating Phi Beta Kappa in three years. While attending Washington University during World War II, she worked the night shift at a federal factory where she tested both rifles and machine guns for ammunition accuracy from midnight until eight in the morning, and then attended her classes during the day. "It was a strictly budgeted, time-managed life," Schlafly told the *New York Times*. In 1944 she won yet another scholarship, for graduate work at Radcliffe College. A year later she had earned her master's degree in political science. Deciding against a career in academia she served briefly as a researcher for several Washington congressmen, then helped to run the successful campaign of Republican Congressman Claude I. Bakewell of St. Louis. In 1946 she took a job as a researcher and librarian in a St. Louis bank and continued her Republican political activities in her spare time.

The newsletter that Phyllis Stewart helped to write for the bank brought her to the attention of Fred Schlafly, a successful lawyer from Alton, Illinois, who had similar conservative views. Fred and Phyllis Schlafly were married on October 20, 1949, and the bride quit her job to become a homemaker and a mother. Although she soon had six children, Schlafly continued to take an interest in politics and community volunteer work. She ran for Congress unsuccessfully in 1952 and has served as a delegate to Republican national conventions since the 1950s.

A new avenue of expression opened to Schlafly in 1964 when she published her first book, *A Choice Not an Echo*. The paperback, published by a company she and her husband created, championed Senator Barry M. Goldwater for the Republican presidential nomination. Over three million copies of *A Choice Not an Echo* were sold; political analysts contend that the work helped Goldwater to secure his party's nomination. Thereafter Schlafly teamed with a retired military man, Admiral Chester Ward, to coauthor more titles on the subjects of national defense policy and nuclear strategy. In works such as *The Gravediggers*, *Strike from Space*, *The Betrayers*, and *Kissinger on the Couch*, Schlafly and Ward find fault with a series of presidential advisors who, in their view, weakened the United States' defenses and paved the way for Soviet nuclear superiority. FitzGerald explains: "The central thesis of these books was that certain powerful government officials were plotting the unilateral disarmament of the United States." In 1980, Schlafly served on the Defense Policy Advisory Group; her work brought praise from President Ronald Reagan.

In 1965 Schlafly was elected first vice-president of the National Federation of Republican Women. She ran for president of the organization in 1967 but was narrowly defeated by a more liberal candidate. That same year she began the Eagles Trust Fund to support conservative political candidates and founded her monthly newsletter, *The Phyllis Schlafly Report*, in which she outlined the concerns of the Republican right. In 1970 she ran for Congress again in Illinois's twenty-third district, but she lost to a Democratic incumbent. Ironically, her campaign slogan, "A woman's place is in the House," was used the same year by another candidate, feminist Bella Abzug. Having lost her bid for Congress, Schlafly returned to her writing, concentrating on exposing the communist menace and calling for more vigilant national defense. Indeed, *Newsweek* quotes Schlafly as calling the atomic bomb "a marvelous gift that was given to our country by a wise God."

Schlafly's first blast against the Equal Rights Amendment was printed in the February, 1972 issue of *The Phyllis Schlafly Report*. She told *Newsweek* that she "didn't set out to confront the whole women's lib movement. These tasks were thrust upon me." Once convinced that the ERA would undermine family life, take away the legal rights of wives, and thrust women into military combat, however, Schlafly turned her full attention to a crusade to quash the amendment. She founded Stop ERA in 1972 and the Eagle Forum in 1975, both of which became sophisticated grass-roots lobby organizations with the goal of defeating ERA. She also testified against the amendment in 30 state legislatures. *New Republic* contributor Morton Kondracke observes that when state-by-state ratification of the amendment began to slow down, "it was caught up to and walloped by anti-feminist firebrand Phyllis Schlafly, one of the most gifted practitioners of political diatribe in the country today. Most of Schlafly's major arguments against ERA [were] outrageous fabrications, but they [were] so artful and so brazenly repeated that Schlafly . . . put ERA proponents on the defensive in state after state." Although polls showed that a majority of Americans favored ERA, Schlafly and her corps of trained volunteers "made the ERA so controversial that legislators preferred to avoid it—thus turning the weight of inertia against the amendment," according to FitzGerald. Schlafly's pro-family movement pooled forces with the burgeoning American Conservative Union, the Moral Majority, and the Catholic, Baptist, Orthodox Jewish, and Mormon churches to reach state legislators individually. She made speeches against ERA repeatedly, often driving hostile audiences to hysteria with her calmly-expressed and unshakeable convictions. *Newsweek* quotes Chicago feminist Diann Smith, who said, "The only way to debate Phyllis Schlafly is to jump up and down and shout 'Liar, liar, liar!'"

The Power of the Positive Woman, Schlafly's 1977 book, outlines her views on the status of American women. The Positive Woman, she writes, "rejoices in the creative capability within her body and the power potential of her mind and spirit. She understands that men and women are different, and that those very differences provide the key to her success as a person and fulfillment as a woman." The Women's Liberation Movement, she contends, is peopled by "a bunch of bitter women seeking a constitutional cure for their personal problems" and "Typhoid Marys carrying a germ called lost identity." In the *New York Times*, Gail Sheehy reacts to Schlafly's thesis: "Phyllis Schlafly's formula for the better life, then, is based on marrying a rich professional, climbing the pedestal to lady of leisure, and pulling up the rope behind her, thereby breaking any painful identifications with women who are still powerless, women who didn't have the wits to find a high-status male or the initiative to bind him legally into taking 'beautiful' care of them." FitzGerald also finds *The Power of the Positive Woman* a "guerrilla attack" on the feminist movement, "where the enemy has a fixed position but the attacker does not.... Schlafly must know better, but she consistently assumes that all American women are rich enough so that they don't have to go to work." Kondracke comments that Schlafly "has clearly tapped elemental currents of resentment, fear and anger running beneath the surface of American society.... Though she is hardly one of them, Schlafly represents the stay-at-homes who look at women's liberation and the working lifestyle as a threat and a rebuke. The old rules decreed that women got married and had babies, and millions of women dutifully followed the pattern. Now the rules are suddenly being changed, and these women are being told they have wasted their lives. They won't sit for it ... and Schlafly is leading the way." Such comments about her views, Schlafly tells *CA*, "are ridiculous and have no relation to my life or writings."

Despite Congressional extension of the ratification deadline, ERA was defeated in 1982. Since then, Schlafly and her Eagle Forum have been actively involved in other political issues including aid to Nicaragua's *contra* rebels, support for the Strategic Defense Initiative and for parental rights in public schools, lobbies to revise public school curricula, and aids conservative political candidates. Schlafly still conducts most of her business from her home in Alton, Illinois, where she lives with her husband. Sheehy characterizes the well-groomed activist as a "moral boss" who is "unencumbered by empathy on a personal level or by the democratic process on a political level." Other observers are not as critical; at a 1982 post-ERA dinner, Schlafly was lauded by John Lofton, editor of *Conservative Digest*, the Reverend Jerry Falwell, Morton Blackwell, a special assistant to President Reagan, and others, who praised her work on a wide variety of national concerns. She has also received ten George Washington Honor Medals from the Freedoms Foundation and citations from *Good Housekeeping* magazine. When asked about her own accomplishments, Schlafly usually speaks with pride of her six grown children, and thanks her husband for allowing her to pursue her causes. In *People* magazine, former National Organization of Women chief Karen DeCrow put Schlafly's achievements

in perspective. "If I had a daughter," DeCrow commented, "I'd like her to be a housewife just like Phyllis Schlafly."

BIOGRAPHICAL/CRITICAL SOURCES:

BOOKS

Authors in the News, Volume 1, Gale, 1976.
Contemporary Issues Criticism, Volume 1, Gale, 1982.
Felsenthal, Carol, *The Sweetheart of the Silent Majority: The Biography of Phyllis Schlafly*, Doubleday, 1981.
Schlafly, Phyllis, *The Power of the Positive Woman*, Arlington House, 1977.

PERIODICALS

Christian Century, April 24, 1985.
Modern Age, winter, 1977.
Ms., March, 1974, May, 1981, January, 1982, September, 1982.
National NOW Times, December, 1977.
National Review, June 6, 1975, February 3, 1978, May 15, 1981, August 6, 1982.
New Republic, April 30, 1977.
Newsweek, July 25, 1977, February 28, 1983, December 23, 1985.
New York Daily News, November 22, 1977.
New York Review of Books, November 19, 1981.
New York Times, December 15, 1975, October 14, 1977, January 24, 1980.
New York Times Book Review, October 30, 1977.
New York Times Magazine, April 17, 1977.
People, March 30, 1981.
Rolling Stone, November 26, 1981.
Time, July 3, 1978, May 4, 1981, July 12, 1982.
Washington Post, July 11, 1974.

*   *   *

SCHREINER, Samuel A(gnew), Jr. 1921-

PERSONAL: Born June 6, 1921, in Mt. Lebanon, Pa.; son of Samuel Agnew (a lawyer) and Mary (Cort) Schreiner; married Doris Moon (an artist and antique dealer and appraiser), September 22, 1945; children: Beverly Ann (Mrs. Jonathan S. Carroll), Carolyn Cort (Mrs. Scott Calder). *Education:* Princeton University, A.B., 1942. *Politics:* Republican. *Religion:* Presbyterian.

ADDRESSES: Home and office—111 Old Kings Highway S., Darien, Conn. 06820. *Agent*—Harold Ober Associates, Inc., 40 East 49th St., New York, N.Y. 10017.

CAREER: McKeesport Daily News, McKeesport, Pa., reporter, 1946; *Pittsburgh Sun-Telegraph*, Pittsburgh, Pa., reporter, 1946-51; *Parade*, New York, N.Y., writer and assistant managing editor, 1951-55; *Reader's Digest*, Pleasantville, N.Y., associate editor, 1955-68, senior editor, 1968-74; full-time writer, 1974—. President of Schreiner Associates. Elder, Noroton Presbyterian Church; secretary, Darien Library Association; former chairman, Darien Youth Advisory Committee and Centre Store. *Military service:* U.S. Army, Office of Strategic Services, cryptographer, 1942-45; served in China-Burma-India theater; became first lieutenant; received Bronze Star and Presidential unit citation.

MEMBER: Authors Guild, Authors League of America, Overseas Press Club, Princeton Club of New York, Noroton Yacht Club.

WRITINGS:

Urban Planning and Public Opinion, Bureau of Urban Research, Princeton University, 1942.
Thine Is the Glory (novel), Arbor House, 1975.
Pleasant Places (novel), Arbor House, 1976.
The Condensed World of the Reader's Digest, Stein, 1977.
Angelica (novel), Arbor House, 1977.
The Possessors and the Possessed (novel), Arbor House, 1980.
The Van Alens (novel), Arbor House, 1981.
A Place Called Princeton, Arbor House, 1984.
The Trials of Mrs. Lincoln (nonfiction), Donald I. Fine, 1987.

Contributor of articles and stories to popular magazines, including *McCall's, Saturday Evening Post, Collier's, Redbook, Reader's Digest*, and *National Geographic*.

SIDELIGHTS: Samuel A. Schreiner, Jr., wrote to *CA:* "Still going strong on the far side of sixty-five, I would recommend a free-lance writing career as the answer to the 'problem' of retirement; you can't afford to retire. Seriously, if you can do without the act of writing as an essential part of daily life, you shouldn't be writing for a living in the first place. The true rewards of writing come from the process not the profits, and there are very few human endeavors of which this can be said."

BIOGRAPHICAL/CRITICAL SOURCES:

PERIODICALS

Los Angeles Times, August 7, 1987.
Tribune Books (Chicago), August 9, 1987.

*   *   *

SCHWARZ, Ted
   See SCHWARZ, Theodore R., Jr.

*   *   *

SCHWARZ, Theodore R., Jr.   **1945-**
   (Ted Schwarz)

PERSONAL: Born October 12, 1945, in Cleveland, Ohio; son of Theodore (a salesman) and Ruth (a home economist; maiden name, Stern) Schwarz; married Nancy Clark (a civil servant), December 17, 1966 (divorced, 1978); married Leslie Carroll (a bookkeeper), August 17, 1979. *Education:* Attended Case Western Reserve University, 1964-66, and New York Institute of Photography, 1965.

ADDRESSES: Office—Bradley Building, 1220 West 6th St., Suite 800, Cleveland, Ohio 44113. *Agent*—Bob Tabian, International Creative Management, 40 West 57th St., New York, N.Y. 10019.

CAREER: Free-lance writer, 1964—. Radio writer for National Broadcasting Co., Inc., 1966, Storer Broadcasting Co., 1966-74, and Westinghouse Broadcasting Co., 1967; *Akron Beacon Journal*, Akron, Ohio, reporter, 1967-68, general assignment recorder, 1968-69; free-lance commercial photographer, 1969-73. Part-time instructor in writing at Pima College, 1976-87, and Yavapi College, 1982-87. Adjunct professor, Northern Arizona University, 1984-87. Teacher for Writer's Digest School. *Wartime service:* Worked as heart research technician at Akron City Hospital, as an alternative to military service, 1966-67.

MEMBER: Authors Guild, Authors League of America, Writers Guild of America West, Numismatic Literary Guild, Mystery Writers of America.

WRITINGS:

Coins as Living History, Arco, 1976.

UNDER NAME TED SCHWARZ

The Successful Promoter, Regnery, 1977.
(With Henry Hawksworth) *The Five of Me*, Regnery, 1977.
(With Christina Peters) *Tell Me Who I Am before I Die*, Rawson Associates, 1978.
(With Ralph Allison) *Mind in Many Pieces: The Making of a Very Special Doctor*, Rawson Associates, 1980.
Beginner's Guide to Coin Collecting, Doubleday, 1980.
The History of United States Coinage, A. S. Barnes, 1981.
The Hillside Strangler, Doubleday, 1981.
How to Protect Yourself, Your Home and Your Family, Arco, 1983.
Beginner's Guide to Stamp Collecting, Arco, 1983.
Arnold Friberg: The Passion of a Modern Master, Northland Press, 1985.
(With John DeLorean) *DeLorean*, Zondervan, 1985.
(With Parichehr Yomtoob) *A Gift of Life*, St. Martin's, 1985.
(Ghostwriter for Florence Henderson) *A Little Cooking, a Little Talking, and a Whole Lot of Fun with Florence Henderson and Friends from Her Krazy Kountry Kitchen*, Panorama, 1988.
(With Duane Empey) *That Other Church down Your Block*, Zondervan, 1988.
Time Management for Writers, Writer's Digest, 1988.

PHOTOGRAPHY BOOKS; UNDER NAME TED SCHWARZ

The Business Side of Photography, American Photographic Book Publishing Co., 1969.
How to Make Money with Your Camera, H. P. Books, 1974.
How to Start a Professional Photography Business, Regnery, 1977.
(Contributor) *The Encyclopedia of Practical Photography*, Amphoto, 1978.
Amphoto Guide to Modeling, Amphoto, 1979.
How to Be a Freelance Photographer, Contemporary Books, 1980.
Consumer Guide to Model Photography, Consumer Guide, 1980.
Careers in Photography, Contemporary Books, 1981.
The Complete Business Guide for the Freelance and Professional Photographer, Focal Press, 1983.
The Professional Photographer's Handbook, McGraw, 1983.
(With Brian Stoppee) *The Photographer's Guide to Using Light*, Amphoto, 1986.

Also co-author of *The Photographer's Business Handbook*, for McGraw-Hill.

OTHER

Ghostwriter of a business guide and several books about drug addiction and childhood health, for a number of publishers, including St. Martin's, McGraw, and Bobbs-Merrill. Author of columns, "Tips by Ted," *Rangefinder*, 1970—, and "Civil War Postal History," *Stamp News*, 1976—; also author of syndicated cartoon, "The Badge Guys," Newspaper Enterprise Association, 1971-73. Contributor of approximately two thousand articles to magazines, including *Family Circle, Writer's Market*, and *Studio Photography*. Contributing editor of *Stamp News*, 1976—, and *Physician's Management*.

WORK IN PROGRESS: Book on California history tentatively titled *The Secret History of California* for Northland Press; biography of Peter Lawford for Sidgwich & Jackson; book with Leslie McRay tentatively titled *Kept Women* for Morrow; book with Allen Friedman on the history of the Teamster's Union for F. Watts; mystery books entitled *Death Song Singing*, *Stalker in the Shadows*, *Dirty Little Secrets*, and *A Perfect Little Murder*; book with Sherry Brown on Ernest Blumenschein and the Taos Society of Artists; several film projects, including "Salons" with Joe Felice, and "The Godson."

SIDELIGHTS: Ted Schwarz told *CA* that he began writing during his childhood, compelled by an introvert's need to communicate with a larger number of people than he would "otherwise have the courage to face." After experiencing his first success at age fifteen with the sale of an article to a hobby publication, he concentrated on improving his style and ability, often neglecting his schoolwork in the process. A firm believer that a writer is only as good as his or her next work, he constantly lives with "a very mild case of nervous tension" and feels guilty when away from the typewriter for any length of time.

With perseverance, anyone can become a professional writer, maintains Schwarz: "It is often said that new writers have no chance. This has been said so long that, if it were true, all writing would have stopped after Matthew, Mark, Luke and John died and the Bible was published. There is great opportunity in this field that many writers fear to take advantage of. Other writers worry about talent. Writing is a growth field. I have no idea what talent is or if I have it. A new writer should write, try to understand where mistakes were made, and then write again. If the individual can keep writing, not repeating past mistakes but improving a little each time, at some point that person will be selling. No one succeeds in this field without sitting down and doing the work."

Schwarz additionally wrote to *CA:* "I am getting more involved with fiction, both in developing projects for television and in writing novels. I will probably try to spend between a quarter and a third of my time writing fiction. I not only like the freedom it provides to not have to travel quite so much, I also enjoy the challenge of creating a world which has never existed before, populating it with people no one knew until I created them, then making them all come so alive that the reader wants to spend a couple of hours in that world."

*   *   *

SCOTT, Justin
(J. S. Blazer)

PERSONAL: Son of Leslie (a writer) and Lily K. (a writer) Scott.

ADDRESSES: Home—New Town, Conn. *Agent*—Henry Morrison Inc., Box 235, Bedford Hills, N.Y. 10507.

CAREER: Writer.

AWARDS, HONORS: Nomination for best first novel of the year from Mystery Writers of America, 1973, for *Many Happy Returns*.

WRITINGS:

Many Happy Returns, McKay, 1973.
(Under pseudonym J. S. Blazer) *Deal Me Out*, Bobbs-Merrill, 1973.
Treasure for Treasure, McKay, 1974.

(Under pseudonym J. S. Blazer) *Lend a Hand*, Bobbs-Merrill, 1975.
The Turning, Dell, 1978.
The Shipkiller (alternate selection of Book-of-the-Month Club, Playboy Book Club, Dolphin Book Club, and Nautical Book Club), Dial, 1978.
Normandie Triangle (alternate Literary Guild selection), Arbor House, 1981.
A Pride of Royals (alternate Book-of-the-Month Club selection), Arbor House, 1983.
Rampage (Literary Guild selection), Simon & Schuster, 1986.

SIDELIGHTS: Justin Scott wrote to *CA:* "The advantage of being born into a family of writers is that the people you love and admire agree that writing fiction is a reasonable, even respectable, way to earn a living. If there's a disadvantage, it's that because fewer people write for a living in twentieth-century America than carve gargoyles, children of writers grow up a little disconnected from the real world that writers are supposed to write about."

Scott's first book, a humorous crime novel entitled *Many Happy Returns*, fared well with critics and received a nomination from the Mystery Writers of America for best first novel of the year in 1973. Although Scott's subsequent comic novels have been similarly well received, he observed a decline in the market for humorous fiction and began writing thrillers instead. His first, *The Turning*, is a psychological chiller about a fanatical religious cult that takes over a small town in the Adirondacks.

The Turning was followed by Scott's best-selling novel, *The Shipkiller*. It is the story of a modern-day Captain Ahab who sets out to destroy an immense oil tanker that had capsized his sailboat, killing his wife and leaving him for dead. After arming his thirty-eight-foot sloop with an antitank missile, Scott's protagonist relentlessly pursues the monster ship through the Atlantic Ocean and the Persian Gulf, seeking to avenge his wife's death. Like his other books, *The Shipkiller* has proved popular with critics, who note that Scott's careful research and skillfull writing result in an authentically detailed and exciting suspense novel.

Scott adds: "*Rampage* is my ninth published novel, though I've written fifteen or so. I've resisted repeating myself, so I sit down to each new novel an amateur. I believe variety helps a young writer grow, even at the sacrifice of brand name recognition, which is increasingly important in the marketplace. Commercial publishing demands competing qualities of a novelist: familiarity and originality. To convince a publisher to support your work, your novels should fit a recognizable market slot, yet you, the author, must remain unique. When in doubt, I turn to the advice of the singer Tony Bennett: 'To be different, be yourself.'"

BIOGRAPHICAL/CRITICAL SOURCES:

PERIODICALS

Best Sellers, July 1, 1974.
New York Times Book Review, May 6, 1973, October 7, 1973, July 21, 1974, October 19, 1975.
Publishers Weekly, September 12, 1977.
Time, November 10, 1978.

*   *   *

SCOTT, Kenneth   1900-

PERSONAL: Born May 4, 1900, in Waterbury, Conn.; son of

John Linus (a manufacturer) and Julie (Cooke) Scott; married Aurelia Grether (a professor of English), June 17, 1926; children: Jean Helen, Kenneth John. *Education:* Williams College, A.B., 1921; attended American School of Classical Studies, Athens, Greece, 1921-22; University of Wisconsin—Madison, M.A., 1923, Ph.D., 1925. *Politics:* Republican. *Religion:* Episcopalian.

ADDRESSES: Home—42-05 243 St., Douglaston, N.Y. 11363.

CAREER: University of Wisconsin—Madison, instructor in Latin, 1923-24, assistant professor of classics, 1925-27; Yale University, New Haven, Conn., assistant professor of Latin, 1927-29; Western Reserve University (now Case Western Reserve University), Cleveland, Ohio, professor of classics, 1929-42; master of classics and modern languages at private school in Concord, N.H., 1942-47, and of modern languages at a private school in Simsbury, Conn., 1947-48; Upsala College, East Orange, N.J., professor of classical languages, 1948-49; Wagner College, Staten Island, N.Y., professor of modern languages, 1949-59, chairman of department, 1950-59; Queensborough Community College of the City University of New York, Bayside, N.Y., assistant professor, 1960-61, associate professor, 1961-62, professor of foreign languages and chairman of department, 1962-65; Queens College of the City University of New York, Flushing, N.Y., professor of history, 1965-70, professor emeritus, 1970—.

MEMBER: American Society of Genealogists (fellow), American Philological Association, National Genealogical Society (fellow), New York Historical Society, New York Genealogical and Biographical Society, Holland Society of New York (fellow).

AWARDS, HONORS: Markham traveling fellowship, University of Berlin, 1926-1927; Guggenheim fellowship, 1934; commander of the Order of St. Agatha (San Marino), 1937; knight of the Order of the Crown (Italy), 1938.

WRITINGS:

(With Karl P. Harrington) *Selections from Latin Prose and Poetry*, Ginn, 1933.
(With R. S. Rogers and Margaret Ward) *Caesaris Augusti Res Gestae et Fragmenta* (title means "Deeds and Fragments of Caesar Augustus"), Heath, 1935.
The Imperial Cult under the Flavians, W. Kohlhammer Verlag, 1936.
Notes on the Bowman, Harter, and Sauer Families, Warner Press, 1948.
Counterfeiting in Colonial New York, American Numismatic Society, 1953.
Counterfeiting in Colonial Pennsylvania, American Numismatic Society, 1955.
Counterfeiting in Colonial America, Oxford University Press, 1957.
Counterfeiting in Colonial Connecticut, American Numismatic Society, 1957.
Counterfeiting in Colonial Rhode Island, Rhode Island Historical Society, 1960.
(With Julius Bloch, Leo Hershkowitz, and Constance Sherman) *An Account of Her Majesty's Revenue in the Province of New York, 1701-1709*, Gregg, 1967.
Genealogical Data from New York Administration Bonds, 1753-1799, New York Genealogical and Biographical Society, 1969.
Jasper Danckaert's Diary of Our Second Trip from Holland to New Netherlands, Gregg, 1969.

Genealogical Data from the New York Post-Boy, 1743-1773, National Geographical Society, 1970.
The Voyages and Travels of Francis Goelet, 1746-1758, Gregg, 1970.
(With James Owre) *Genealogical Data from Inventories of New York Estates, 1666-1825*, New York Genealogical Society, 1970.
Genealogical Data from Further New York Administration Bonds, New York Genealogical and Biographical Society, 1971.
Genealogical Data from the Pennsylvania Chronicle, 1767-1774, National Genealogical Society, 1971.
Records of the Chancery Court of New York—Guardianships, 1691-1815, Holland Society of New York, 1971.
Calendar of New York Colonial Commissions Book, Volume IV: 1770-1776, National Society of Colonial Dames in the State of New York, 1972.
Genealogical Data from Administration Papers from the New York State Court of Appeals in Albany, National Society of Colonial Dames in the State of New York, 1972.
The Slave Insurrection in New York in 1712, Bobbs-Merrill, 1972.
New York Marriage Bonds, 1753-1783, St. Nicholas Society in the City of New York, 1972.
Rivington's New York Newspaper: Excerpts from a Loyalist Press, 1773-1783, New York Historical Society, 1973.
Genealogical Abstracts from the American Weekly Mercury, 1719-1746, Genealogical Publishing, 1974.
Abstracts from Ben Franklin's Pennsylvania Gazette, 1728-1748, Genealogical Publishing, 1975.
New York: State Census of Albany County Towns in 1790, Genealogical Publishing, 1975.
(With Kenn Stryker-Rodda) *Denizations, Naturalizations and Oaths of Allegiance in Colonial New York*, Genealogical Publishing, 1975.
(With Kristin L. Gibbons) *The New York Magazine: Marriages and Deaths, 1790-1797*, Polyanthos, 1975.
(With Susan E. Klaffky) *A History of the Joseph Lloyd Manor House*, Society for the Preservation of Long Island Antiquities, 1976.
(Editor with Stryker-Rodda) E. B. O'Callaghan, *The Minutes of the Orphanmasters of New Amsterdam, 1663-1668*, Genealogical Publishing, 1976.
Abstracts (Mainly Deaths) from the Pennsylvania Gazette, 1775-1783, Genealogical Publishing, 1976.
Joseph Gavit's American Deaths and Marriages, 1784-1829: An Index to Non-Principal Names, Polyanthos, 1976.
(Editor with Styrker-Rodda) O'Callaghan, translator, *The Register of Solomon Lachaire: Notary Public of New Amsterdam, 1661-1662*, Genealogical Publishing, 1977.
Genealogical Data from Colonial New York Newspapers, Genealogical Publishing, 1977.
(With Stryker-Rodda) *Varied Genealogical Data: A Complete List of Addressed Letters Left in the Post Offices of Philadelphia, Lancaster, Chester, Trenton and Wilmington between 1748-1780*, Genealogical Publishing, 1977.
(With Janet R. Clarke) *Abstracts from the Pennsylvania Gazette, 1748-1755*, Genealogical Publishing, 1977.
(Editor with Rosanne K. Conway) *Abstracts from Colonial Connecticut Newspapers: New Haven, 1755-1775*, Genealogical Publishing, 1977.
(With Rosanne Conway) *New York Alien Residents, 1825-1848*, Genealogical Publishing, 1978.
British Aliens in the United States during the War of 1812, Genealogical Publishing, 1979.

Marriages and Deaths from "The New Yorker," (Double Quarto Edition), 1836-1841, National Genealogical Society, 1980.

Early New York Naturalizations, Genealogical Publishing, 1981.

New York City Court Records, 1684-1760, National Genealogical Society, 1982.

Minutes of the Mayors Court of New York, 1674-1675, Genealogical Publishing, 1983.

New York City Court Records, 1760-1797, National Genealogical Society, 1983.

Petitions for Name Changes in New York City, 1848-1899, National Genealogical Society, 1984.

Nineteenth Century Apprentices in New York City, National Genealogical Society, 1986.

New York City Court Records, 1797-1801, National Genealogical Society, 1988.

New York City Court Records, 1801-1804, National Genealogical Society, 1988.

WORK IN PROGRESS: A book on early New Jersey tavern licenses.

SIDELIGHTS: Kenneth Scott reads Latin and Greek and speaks Italian, French, German, Spanish, modern Greek, Danish, and Turkish.

*　　*　　*

SEARLE, John R(ogers)　1932-

PERSONAL: Born July 31, 1932, in Denver, Colo.; son of George W. (an electrical engineer) and Hester (a physician; maiden name, Beck) Searle; married Dagmar Carboch (a lawyer), December 24, 1959; children: Thomas R., Mark R. *Education:* University of Wisconsin, student, 1949-52; Oxford University, B.A. (with first class honors), 1955, M.A. and D.Phil., 1959.

ADDRESSES: Home—1900 Yosemite Rd., Berkeley, Calif. 94707. *Office*—Department of Philosophy, University of California, Berkeley, Calif. 94720.

CAREER: Oxford University, Christ Church, Oxford, England, lecturer in philosophy, 1956-59; University of California, Berkeley, assistant professor, 1959-64, associate professor, 1964-67, professor of philosophy, 1967—, special assistant to the chancellor, 1965-67, chairman of philosophy department, 1973-75. Visiting professor at University of Michigan, 1961-62, University of Washington, Seattle, 1963, Brasenose College, Oxford, 1967-68, State University of New York at Buffalo, 1971, University of Oslo, 1971, University of Colorado, 1980, University of Frankfurt-am-Main, summer, 1985, Rutgers University, 1986, and University of Venice, 1986; member of visiting committee for linguistics and philosophy, Massachusetts Institute of Technology, 1971-77. Regular panelist, 1970-77, moderator, 1972-74, of "World Press" weekly program for National Educational Television Network; secretary of treasury, Hanzell Vineyards Ltd., 1975—.

MEMBER: American Philosophical Association, American Council of Education, American Council of Learned Societies (member of board of directors, 1979-87), American Academy of Arts and Sciences, National Humanities Center (member of board of trustees, 1976—), American Civil Liberties Union (member of board of directors of California chapter, 1968-71), Aristotelian Society (England), Council on Philosophical Studies (member of board of directors, 1975-80).

AWARDS, HONORS: Rhodes scholar at Oxford University; American Council of Learned Societies research grant, 1963-64; Guggenheim fellowship, 1975-76.

WRITINGS:

Speech Acts: An Essay in the Philosophy of Language, Cambridge University Press, 1969, reprinted, 1985.

The Campus War: A Sympathetic Look at the University in Agony, World Publications, 1971.

(Editor and author of introduction) *The Philosophy of Language*, Oxford University Press, 1971.

Expression and Meaning: Studies in the Theory of Speech Acts, Cambridge University Press, 1979.

(Editor with Ferenc Kiefer and Manfred Bierwisch) *Speech Act Theory and Pragmatics*, D. Reidel, 1980.

Intentionality: An Essay in the Philosophy of Mind, Cambridge University Press, 1983.

Meaning: Protocol of the Fourty-fourth Colloquy, 3 October, 1982, edited by Julian Boyd, Center for Hermeneutical Studies in Hellenistic and Modern Culture, 1983.

Minds, Brains, and Science, BBC Publications, 1984, Harvard University Press, 1985.

(With Daniel Vanderveken) *Foundations of Illocutionary Logic*, Cambridge University Press, 1985.

Contributor of articles on philosophy, skiing, student unrest, and academic freedom to periodicals.

SIDELIGHTS: Some of John R. Searle's books have been translated into French, German, Italian, Spanish, Portuguese, Dutch, Korean, and Japanese.

BIOGRAPHICAL/CRITICAL SOURCES:

BOOKS

Devine, Elizabeth and others, editors, *Thinkers of the Twentieth Century: A Biographical, Bibliographical and Critical Dictionary*, Gale, 1983.

Nolte, Reinhard B., *Einfuhrung in die Sprechakttheorie John R. Searle*, Verlag Karl Alber, 1978.

PERIODICALS

Best Sellers, June 15, 1971.

New York Times Book Review, May 12, 1985.

Spectator, July 12, 1969.

Times Literary Supplement, March 7, 1980, March 2, 1984, December 14, 1984.

*　　*　　*

SEED, Cecile Eugenie　1930-
(Jenny Seed)

PERSONAL: Born May 18, 1930, in Cape Town, South Africa; daughter of Ivan Washington (a draftsman) and Bessie (Dickerson) Booysen; married Edward Robert Seed (a railway employee), October 30, 1953; children: Anne, Dick, Alan, Robbie. *Education:* Educated in Cape Town, South Africa.

ADDRESSES: Home—10 Pioneer Cres., Northdene, Queensburgh, Natal, South Africa.

CAREER: Before marriage, worked as draftsman in Roads Department and Town Planning Department, Pietermaritzburg, South Africa; free-lance writer, mainly for children.

WRITINGS:

ALL UNDER NAME JENNY SEED

The Dancing Mule, Thomas Nelson, 1964.

The Always-Late Train, Nasionale Boekhandel, 1965.

Small House, Big Garden, Hamish Hamilton, 1965.

Peter the Gardener, Hamish Hamilton, 1966.
Tombi's Song, Hamish Hamilton, 1966, Rand McNally, 1968.
To the Rescue, Hamish Hamilton, 1966.
Stop Those Children, Hamish Hamilton, 1966.
Timothy and Tinker, Hamish Hamilton, 1967.
The Red Dust Soldiers, Heinemann, 1968.
The River Man, Hamish Hamilton, 1968.
The Voice of the Great Elephant, Hamish Hamilton, 1968, Pantheon, 1969.
Kulumi the Brave, Hamish Hamilton, 1970.
The Prince of the Bay, Hamish Hamilton, 1970.
The Great Thirst, Hamish Hamilton, 1971.
The Broken Spear, Hamish Hamilton, 1972.
The Sly Green Lizard, Hamish Hamilton, 1973.
The Bushman's Dream, Hamish Hamilton, 1974.
Warriors on the Hills, Abelard Schuman, 1975.
The Unknown Land, Heineman, 1976.
Strangers in the Land, Hamish Hamilton, 1977.
The Year One, Hamish Hamilton, 1980.
The Policeman's Button, Human & Rousseau (Cape Town), 1981.
Gold Dust, Hamish Hamilton, 1982.
The New Fire, Human & Rousseau, 1983.
The Spy Hill, Human & Rousseau, 1984.
Place among the Stones, Tafelberg (Cape Town), 1987.
The Far-away Valley, Daan Retief (Pretoria), 1987.

WORK IN PROGRESS: Research in South African history.

SIDELIGHTS: Cecile Eugenie Seed told *CA:*"I began writing, I remember, at the age of eight, trying to express what I saw, thought, and felt in words. This desire remained dormant at times as I grew up, then in 1964 it took a definite direction with the publication of my first children's book. I now knew what I wanted to write. I wanted to write for children. It was not long before my interest in history led me into fascinating journeys back into the past of my own country, South Africa—journeys that opened my eyes and my understanding to some of the complexities of the present day. At the same time this restless seeking after knowledge became slowly also a quest for truth, which came to an end (or rather a beginning) when I became a Christian in 1974. This has a noticeable effect on my writing. For one thing, I was so involved (willingly) in Christian work that there was less time for scribbling. But the desire to write is still there—not to use books as a camouflage for 'preaching' but, in some small way perhaps, to turn the thoughts of young readers toward reality."

Seed's children's stories have been republished and prepared for broadcasting in Canada, England, Zimbabwe, New Zealand, and Australia.

*   *   *

SEED, Jenny
  See SEED, Cecile Eugenie

*   *   *

SERFATY, Simon   1940-

PERSONAL: Born May 18, 1940, in Casablanca, Morocco; son of Leon A. and Hilda (Cohen) Serfaty. *Education:* Lycee Lyautey, Casablanca, Morocco, Baccalaureats, 1956, 1957; Hautes Etudes Commerciales, Paris, France, Certificate of Business Administration, 1960; Hunter College of the City University of New York, B.A., 1963; Johns Hopkins School

of Advanced International Studies, Washington, D.C., M.A., 1964; Johns Hopkins University, Ph.D., 1967.

ADDRESSES: Office—Johns Hopkins School of Advanced International Studies, 1740 Massachusetts Ave. N.W., Washington, D.C. 20036.

CAREER: University of California, Los Angeles, assistant professor of political science, 1968-72; Johns Hopkins University, School of Advanced International Studies, Washington, D.C., director of Bologna Center of Advanced International Studies, Bologna, Italy, 1972-76, associate professor of U.S. foreign policy, 1976-82, director of Washington Center for Foreign Policy Research, 1977-81, adjunct professor of U.S. foreign policy and director of special programs, 1982-84, research professor of U.S. foreign policy and executive director of Foreign Policy Institute, 1984—. Guest lecturer in more than thirty countries in Europe, Africa, and Asia. American chairman, U.S.-Soviet binational commission on Europe.

AWARDS, HONORS: Albert Camus Prize from New School for Social Research, 1961.

WRITINGS:

France, de Gaulle and Europe: The Policy of the Fourth and Fifth Republics toward the Continent, Johns Hopkins Press, 1968.
The Elusive Enemy: American Foreign Policy since World War II, Little, Brown, 1972.
(Contributor) Morton A. Kaplan, editor, *Great Issues of International Politics*, Aldine, 1974.
(Contributor) George Ginsburgs and Alvin Z. Rubinstein, editors, *Soviet Foreign Policy toward Western Europe*, Praeger, 1978.
Fading Partnership: America and Europe after Thirty Years, Praeger, 1979.
(Editor and contributor) *The Foreign Policies of the French Left*, Westview, 1979.
The United States, Western Europe and the Third World: Allies and Adversaries, Center for Strategic and International Studies, 1980.
(Co-editor and contributor) *The Italian Communist Party: Yesterday, Today and Tomorrow*, Greenwood, 1980.
(Co-editor and contributor) *Portugal since the Revolution: Political and Economic Perspectives*, Westview, 1980.
(Co-author) *A Socialist France and Western Security*, Johns Hopkins School of Advanced International Studies Occasional Paper, 1981.
(Contributor) Helene Carrere d'Encausse and Francois de Rose, editors, *Apres la detente*, Hachette, 1982.
(Contributor) Robert W. Tucker and Linda Wrigley, editors, *The Atlantic Alliance and Its Critics*, Praeger, 1983.
American Foreign Policy in a Hostile World: Dangerous Years, Praeger, 1984.
(Contributor) Richard Ullman and Mario Zucconi, editors, *Western Europe and the Crisis in U.S.-Soviet Relations*, Praeger, 1987.
Les annees difficiles, Presses Universitaires de France, 1987.

Also contributor of papers to numerous professional journals in the United States, Western Europe, and Africa.

*   *   *

SEULING, Barbara   1937-

PERSONAL: Surname pronounced Soo-ling; born July 22, 1937, in Brooklyn, N.Y.; daughter of Kaspar Joseph (a postman) and Helen Veronica (Gadie) Seuling. *Education:* Attended Hunter College (now Hunter College of the City University of New York), 1955-57, Columbia University, 1957-59, and School of Visual Arts.

ADDRESSES: Home and office—320 Central Park W., New York, N.Y. 10025.

CAREER: Freelance writer and illustrator, 1968—. Has worked for an investment firm, a university, and at the General Electric Co. exhibit at the New York World's Fair; Dell Publishing Co., New York City, children's book editor, 1965-71; J. B. Lippincott Co., New York City, children's book editor, 1971-73. Lecturer, teacher, and consultant on children's books and writing for children.

MEMBER: Society of Children's Book Writers (member of board of directors).

AWARDS, HONORS: Award from American Institute of Graphic Arts, 1979, for *The Teeny Tiny Woman;* Christopher Award, The Christophers, 1979, for *The New York Kids' Book;* first place, Harold Marshall Solstad Prize, Cameron University Children's Short Story Competition, 1982.

WRITINGS:

JUVENILES

The Last Legal Spitball and Other Little Known Facts about Sports, Doubleday, 1975.
Abracadabra!: Creating Your Own Magic Show from Beginning to End, Messner, 1975.
You Can't Eat Peanuts in Church and Other Little Known Laws, Doubleday, 1975.
The Teeny Tiny Woman: An Old English Ghost Story, Viking, 1976.
The Loudest Screen Kiss and Other Little Known Facts about the Movies, Doubleday, 1976.
The Great Big Elephant and the Very Small Elephant, Crown, 1977.
The Last Cow on the White House Lawn and Other Little Known Facts about the Presidency, Doubleday, 1978.
You Can't Count a Billion Dollars and Other Little Known Facts about Money, Doubleday, 1979.
The New York Kids' Book, Doubleday, 1979.
The Triplets, Clarion, 1980.
Just Me, Harcourt, 1982.
You Can't Show Kids in Underwear and Other Little Known Facts about T.V., Doubleday, 1982.
Elephants Can't Jump and Other Freaky Facts about Animals, Lodestar, 1984.
Stay Safe, Play Safe: A Book about Safety Rules, Western Publishing, 1985.
You Can't Sneeze with Your Eyes Open and Other Freaky Facts about the Human Body, Lodestar, 1985.
What Kind of Family Is This?, Western Publishing, 1985.
I'm Not So Different: A Book about Handicaps, Western Publishing, 1986.
Who's the Boss Here?: A Book about Parental Authority, Western Publishing, 1986.

ILLUSTRATOR

Wilma Thompson, *That Barbara!*, Delacorte, 1969.
Nan Hayden Agle, *Tarr of Belway Smith*, Seabury Press, 1969.
Stella Pevsner, *Break a Leg!*, Crown, 1969.
Antonia Barber, *The Affair of the Rockerbye Baby*, Delacorte, 1970.
Pevsner, *Footsteps on the Stairs*, Crown, 1970.

Moses Howard, *The Ostrich Chase*, Holt, 1974.
Melinda Green, *Bembelman's Bakery*, Parents' Magazine Press, 1978.

OTHER

How to Write a Children's Book and Get It Published, Scribner, 1984.

Contributor to books for and about children. Also contributor to journals for and about children, including *Cricket*.

WORK IN PROGRESS: Picture books for children; a sequel to *You Can't Eat Peanuts in Church* (untitled); a biography.

SIDELIGHTS: "I love both writing and illustrating, but I find that writing takes much more discipline and a different sort of mental energy," Barbara Seuling told *CA*. "After an hour or two of steady writing, I am truly tired. With drawing, I can go on all day and tune in to my favorite radio station at the same time. Someone can interrupt me, talk to me, and I am still involved in my drawing without losing ground. A distraction when I'm writing, however, is serious, and often I cannot go back to work once this happens. I know a lot of it has to do with concentration, but I also wonder if a large part of it isn't the security I feel with drawing, which came naturally and was recognized early, and writing, which I discovered later, and with which I feel less on solid ground.

"My purpose is different for each book I create. With my novel I mean to share an emotional experience. I like to think of picture books as tools for growing—growing in some way to understand the world better and to find a way to fit into it—and yet all this must be kept carefully hidden so that it doesn't frighten children away. So, on the surface, I want to make children laugh, to entertain them, tell them a good story. My fact books are meant purely as entertainment because I feel there is a real need for fun. That doesn't mean one cannot learn from them, but that is not their purpose.

"This is a very exciting time to be writing for children. Never before have so many areas opened up for exploration through writing. With few exceptions (and they are decreasing), writers are free to write about whatever they choose. Young people want to know more and more about the life around them, about people and relationships and feelings, and, at last, we [writers] can feel a direct line to them, since [young people] are buying their own books.

"My advice to new writers is: be persistent. The saddest part of writing is the defeatism that is felt so early by writers. One's first work rarely gets published, but that is when our hopes and ideals are so high that they are easily dashed by rejection. It is a rough process, and if one can weather the first years, and keep writing in spite of the obstacles, the chances of success keep growing. A writer is a growing thing; we grow with each page we write, and therefore the more we write the more we learn and the better we become."

AVOCATIONAL INTERESTS: Movies (silent to modern).

*   *   *

SHUCARD, Alan R(obert) 1935-

PERSONAL: Born December 2, 1935, in Brooklyn, N.Y.; son of Jack Donald and Dorothy (Weber) Shucard; married Maureen O'Higgins (an executive secretary), June 23, 1962; children: Sarah Elizabeth Scheck. *Education:* Attended University of St. Andrews, 1955-56; Union College, Schenectady, N.Y.,

A.B., 1957; University of Connecticut, M.A., 1963; University of Arizona, Ph.D., 1971. *Politics:* "Less naive than formerly." *Religion:* "Corned beef and egg roll worship."

ADDRESSES: Home—72 Woodfield Court, Racine, Wis. 53402. *Office*—Department of English, University of Wisconsin—Parkside, Box 2000, Kenosha, Wis. 53141.

CAREER: Pratt & Whitney Aircraft, East Hartford, Conn., technical writer, 1962-63; University of British Columbia, Vancouver, instructor in English, 1965-70; University of Wisconsin—Parkside, Kenosha, assistant professor, 1970-73, associate professor, 1973-86, professor of English, 1986—. Consultant to American Motors, National Endowment for the Humanities, and Holt, Rinehart, Winston, Inc. *Military service:* U.S. Army, Security Agency, 1959-62.

MEMBER: Modern Language Association of America, Society for Values in Higher Education (fellow), American Studies Association, Wisconsin Fellowship of Poets.

AWARDS, HONORS: Fellow of the Canada Council, 1969; Wisconsin Alumni Research Foundation grant, 1972; Fulbright fellow, 1980-81.

WRITINGS:

The Gorgon Bag (poetry), Ladysmith Press, 1970.
The Louse on the Head of a Yawning Lord (poetry), Ladysmith Press, 1972.
Guidebook on Ernest Hemingway, University of Wisconsin Extension, 1978.
(Author of introduction) Carl Lindner, *Shooting Baskets in a Dark Gymnasium,* Linwood, 1984.
Countee Cullen, Twayne, 1984.

Also contributor to *Dictionary of Literary Biography,* 1987; contributing editor, *Contemporary Authors,* 1988. Contributor to *Contemporary Poets, Contemporary Novelists,* and *Writers in English.* Contributor to English and poetry journals, including *Arizona Quarterly, Hawk and Whipoorwill Recalled, Beloit Poetry Journal, Kansas Quarterly, English Quarterly, Library Journal,* and *American Literature.*

WORK IN PROGRESS: Leaping at Masada and Other Poems; Silent Running, a book of poems for Pterodactyl Press; a two-volume study of American poetry for Twayne.

SIDELIGHTS: Alan R. Shucard told *CA:* "My critical writing is motivated by my wish to understand my culture and others as they are illuminated by their literatures; my poetry is motivated by a determination to survive."

*   *   *

SHULMAN, Neil B(arnett) 1945-

PERSONAL: Born March 18, 1945, in Washington, D.C. *Education:* George Washington University, B.S., 1967; Emory University, M.D., 1971; also attended Harvard University, 1974, and Georgetown University, summer, 1976.

ADDRESSES: Home—2272 Vistamont Dr., Decatur, Ga. 30033. *Office*—Division of Hypertension, Department of Medicine, Emory University School of Medicine, 69 Butler St. S.E., Atlanta, Ga. 30303.

CAREER: Intern at Emory University Hospital, Veterans Administration Hospital, and Grady Memorial Hospital, all Atlanta, Ga., all 1971-72; Grady Memorial Hospital, fellow in nephrology and associate in department of medicine, 1972-74;

Emory University School of Medicine, Atlanta, assistant professor of nephrology, 1974-80, associate professor in Division of Hypertension, 1981—, co-director of First and Second International Interdisciplinary Conferences on Hypertension in Blacks, 1986, 1987; Pine Knoll Nursing Home, Carrollton, Ga., medical director, 1976—; Georgia Department of Human Resources, Atlanta, staff member in Division of Physical Health, 1977-78, primary and rural health care developer, 1977—.

American Heart Association-Georgia affiliate, chairman of state high blood pressure education program, 1973, member of hypertension task force, 1974, member of health education in the young committee, 1975; National Institutes of Health, conferee for national patient education task force on hypertension, 1973, member of community consultation team for national high blood pressure education program, 1975; member of technical review board, California Regional Medical Program, 1974-76; member of task force to review health care delivery in state prisons, Georgia Department of Human Resources, 1976; reviewer of grants for hypertension education and research, National Heart, Lung and Blood Institute, 1977—; chairman of statewide information sharing committee on primary health care, 1977-80; member of board of directors, Georgia Association of Primary Health Care, 1979-81. Investigator or project director of more than a dozen studies on hypertension. Host of daily television program "Health Care U.S.A.," WATL, Atlanta, 1976; host of medical humor shorts, Cable News Network, 1981. Chairman, Georgia 2000 (citizens' health and environmental group), 1977-80; member of board of directors and chairman, Village Writers Group, 1978-84, and Windward Bound, Inc., 1978—; member of board of directors, American Minor Emergency Enterprises, 1980—, and LaRosh Productions, Inc., 1985; member of consumer advisory board, Georgia Power Co., 1979-82. Consultant, Inner City Community Health Center, 1980.

MEMBER: American Heart Association.

AWARDS, HONORS: National Voluntary Action Award from American Heart Association-Georgia affiliate, 1975, for health education in the young; Bronze Medallion for Meritorious Service from American Heart Association-Georgia affiliate, 1976; Inner City Award of Recognition, 1981, for assisting with the development of the Atlanta Inner City Community Health Center; Georgia State Legislature Recognition, 1983, for community work in the control of high blood pressure in Georgia; chairman emeritus, Village Writers Group, 1985.

WRITINGS:

(With B. Corns and S. Heymsfield) *Up and Down: All about Blood Pressure,* Emory University, 1973.
(Contributor) Fisher, Croole, and McCombs, editors, *Hypertension: Assessment and Management,* Drew Medical-Dental Center, Stanford University, 1975.
Finally . . . I'm a Doctor, Scribner, 1976.
What? Dead Again?, Legacy Publishing, 1979.
(Contributor) J. Willis Hurst, *Medicine for the Practicing Physician,* Butterworth Publishing, 1983, 2nd edition, 1988.
(Editor with W. D. Hall and E. Saunders, and contributor) *Hypertension in Blacks: Epidemiology, Pathophysiology and Treatment,* Year Book Medical Publishers, 1985.
(With Hall and Saunders) *High Blood Pressure,* MacMillan, 1987.

Also contributor to *Hypertension Management,* edited by Hall and G. L. Wollam, Year Book Medical Publishers.

Contributor to medical journals, including *American Journal of Public Health, Journal of Clinical Hypertension, Journal of the American Medical Association, American Journal of Epidemiology,* and *Journal of Community Health.* Member of editorial board, *Forum* (publication of American College of Physicians), 1979-80, and *Emory Magazine,* 1981-83.

WORK IN PROGRESS: Novels on inner-city and rural health care; research on hypertension.

BIOGRAPHICAL/CRITICAL SOURCES:

PERIODICALS

Atlanta, June, 1976.
Atlanta Journal and Constitution, September 9, 1976.
Chicago Tribune, August 16, 1976.
Philadelphia Inquirer, August 23, 1976.

*   *   *

SHURA, Mary Francis
   See CRAIG, Mary (Francis) S(hura)

*   *   *

SILLITOE, Alan   1928-

PERSONAL: Born March 4, 1928, in Nottingham, England; son of Christopher Archibald (a tannery laborer) and Sylvina (Burton) Sillitoe; married Ruth Esther Fainlight (a poet, writer, and translator), November 19, 1959; children: David Nimrod, Susan (adopted). *Education:* Left school at the age of fourteen.

ADDRESSES: Home—c/o Savage Club, 9 Fitzmaurice Pl., London S.W. 1, England. *Agent*—Tessa Sayle, 11 Jubilee Pl., London SW3 3TE, England.

CAREER: Worked in a bicycle plant, in a plywood mill, and as a capstan-lathe operator; air traffic control assistant, 1945-46; free-lance writer, 1948—. *Military service:* Royal Air Force, radio operator in Malaya, 1946-49.

MEMBER: Society of Authors, Royal Geographical Society (fellow), Writers Action Group, Savage Club.

AWARDS, HONORS: Author's Club prize, 1958, for *Saturday Night and Sunday Morning;* Hawthornden Prize for Literature, 1960, for *The Loneliness of the Long-Distance Runner;* honorary fellow, Manchester Polytechnic, 1977.

WRITINGS:

POEMS

Without Beer or Bread, Outpost Publications (London), 1957.
The Rats and Other Poems, W. H. Allen, 1960.
A Falling Out of Love and Other Poems, W. H. Allen, 1964.
Shaman and Other Poems, Turret Books, 1968.
Love in the Environs of Voronezh and Other Poems, Macmillan (London), 1968, Doubleday, 1969.
(Contributor) *Poems* [by] *Ruth Fainlight, Ted Hughes, Alan Sillitoe,* Rainbow Press, 1971.
Storm and Other Poems, W. H. Allen, 1974.
Barbarians and Other Poems, Turret Books, 1974.
Snow on the North Side of Lucifer, W. H. Allen, 1979.
Sun before Departure, Grafton & Co., 1984.
Tides and Stone Walls, Grafton & Co., 1986.

NOVELS

Saturday Night and Sunday Morning (also see below), W. H. Allen, 1958, Knopf, 1959, revised edition, with an intro-

duction by the author and commentary and notes by David Craig, Longmans, Green, 1968.
The General (also see below), W. H. Allen, 1960, Knopf, 1961.
Key to the Door, W. H. Allen, 1961, Knopf, 1962.
The Death of William Posters (first volume of trilogy), Knopf, 1965.
A Tree on Fire (second volume of trilogy), Macmillan (London), 1967, Doubleday, 1968.
A Start in Life, W. H. Allen, 1970, Scribner, 1971.
Travel in Nihilon, W. H. Allen, 1971, Scribner, 1972.
The Flame of Life (third volume of trilogy), W. H. Allen, 1974.
The Widower's Son, W. H. Allen, 1976, Harper, 1977.
The Storyteller, W. H. Allen, 1979, Simon & Schuster, 1980.
Her Victory, F. Watts, 1982.
The Lost Flying Boat, Little, Brown, 1983.
Down from the Hill, Granada, 1984.
Life Goes On (sequel to *A Start in Life*), Grafton & Co., 1985.
Out of the Whirlpool, Hutchinson, 1987.

SHORT STORIES

The Loneliness of the Long-Distance Runner (also see below), W. H. Allen, 1959, Knopf, 1960, bound with *Sanctuary,* by Theodore Dreiser, and related poems, edited by Roy Bentley, Book Society of Canada, 1967.
The Ragman's Daughter and Other Stories, W. H. Allen, 1961, Knopf, 1964.
Guzman Go Home and Other Stories, Macmillan (London), 1968, Doubleday, 1969.
A Sillitoe Selection, Longmans, Green, 1968.
Men, Women and Children, W. H. Allen, 1973, Scribner, 1974.
The Second Chance and Other Stories, Simon & Schuster, 1981.

PLAYS

''Saturday Night and Sunday Morning'' (screenplay; based on novel of same title), Continental, 1960.
''The Loneliness of the Long-Distance Runner'' (screenplay; based on short story of same title), Continental, 1961.
''Counterpoint'' (screenplay, based on novel *The General*), Universal, 1968.
(Translator and adapter with Ruth Fainlight) Lope de Vega, *All Citizens Are Soldiers* (two acts; first produced at Theatre Royal, Stratford, London, 1967), Macmillan (London), 1969, Dufour, 1970.
Three Plays: The Slot Machine, The Interview, Pit Strike (''The Slot Machine,'' first produced as ''This Foreign Field'' in London at Round House, 1970; ''Pit Strike,'' produced by British Broadcasting Corporation, 1977; ''The Interview,'' produced at the Almost Free Theatre, 1978), W. H. Allen, 1978.

OTHER

Road to Volgograd (travel), Knopf, 1964.
(Author of introduction) Arnold Bennett, *Riceyman Steps,* Pan Books, 1964.
(Author of introduction) Bennett, *The Old Wives' Tale,* Pan Books, 1964.
The City Adventures of Marmalade Jim (juvenile), Macmillan, 1967.
Raw Material (memoir), W. H. Allen, 1972, Scribner, 1973.
Mountains and Caverns: Selected Essays, W. H. Allen, 1975.
Big John and the Stars (juvenile), Robson Books, 1977.

The Incredible Fencing Fleas (juvenile), Robson Books, 1978.
Marmalade Jim on the Farm (juvenile), Robson Books, 1979.
The Saxon Shore Way (travel), Hutchinson, 1983.
Marmalade Jim and the Fox (juvenile), Robson Books, 1985.
Nottinghamshire (travel; photography by David Sillitoe), Grafton, 1987.

Also author of film script "Che Guevara," 1968.

WORK IN PROGRESS: A novel; a new collection of poems.

SIDELIGHTS: "I was twenty years old when I first tried to write, and it took ten years before I learned how to do it," remarked Alan Sillitoe in reference to *Saturday Night and Sunday Morning,* the novel that catapulted the thirty-year-old self-educated Briton into the literary limelight. Described by the *New Yorker's* Anthony West as a "brilliant first book," *Saturday Night and Sunday Morning* broke new ground with its portrayal of "the true robust and earthy quality characteristic of English working-class life." Only one year later, Sillitoe was again the center of critical attention, this time for "The Loneliness of the Long-Distance Runner," the title novella in a collection of short stories which also contained some frank representations of working-class life in Britain. Although he has since written numerous novels and short stories, as well as several poems and plays, Sillitoe has almost always been evaluated in terms of these first two works. Both, in fact, are the focus of a debate that has yet to be resolved: is Alan Sillitoe a traditionalist, a sentimental throwback to writers of an earlier age, or is he a genuine "revolutionary," an Angry Young Man of the modern age?

On a thematic level, Sillitoe seems to draw inspiration from both the old and the new. As is true of many contemporary writers, he often centers his stories around an individual isolated from society, studying what the *Guardians's* Roy Perrot calls "the spirit of the outsider, the dissenter, the man apart." But instead of limiting himself strictly to the psychological confines of this one person and allowing the rest of the world to remain somewhat shadowy, Sillitoe places his rebellious outsider in a gritty, distinctive milieu—Nottingham, an English industrial town (and the author's birthplace) where, as Charles Champlin explains in the *Los Angeles Times,* "the lower-middle and working classes rub, where breaking even looks like victory, and London is a long way South." This strong regionalism, reminiscent of the regionalism common in nineteenth-century British fiction, is one of the most striking features of Sillitoe's writing.

Sillitoe populates his rather grim world with factory workers, shop girls, and other types not often depicted from the inside in English literature. Whether they are at home, at work, or relaxing in the pubs, these characters reveal themselves to be "unfamiliar with the great world of London or country houses or what is called high culture," says the *Chicago Tribune Book World's* Kendall Mitchell. "And they don't care—they have their lives to live, their marriages to make and wreck, their passions to pursue." "The cumulative impression of Sillitoe's people," notes Champlin, "is of their strength and will to survive, however forces beyond their control blunt their prospects."

These "forces beyond their control" play a major role in the author's fiction; Sillitoe's conception of fate, however, differs from the classical one in that economic and social factors, not the whim of the gods, determine one's destiny. As James Gindin writes in *Postwar British Fiction: New Accents and Attitudes:* "Nothing really changes Sillitoe's jungle world. A man may win or lose, depending on the wheel of chance, but he cannot control the wheel or change his position. Often, too, the wheel is rigged, for the same numbers keep coming up as privilege and power keep reinforcing themselves." In short, comments Saul Maloff in *Contemporary British Novelists,* "for Sillitoe, class is fate."

John W. Aldridge expands on this idea in the book *Time to Murder and Create: The Contemporary Novel in Crisis,* but suggests that Sillitoe's belief in the power of fate hinders rather than helps the reader to understand his characters and their motivations. States the critic: "To the extent that his people are the victims of their economic situation, they are people without the power of moral freedom. And to the extent that they are unfree, and lack even the opportunity to be enticed to choose freedom and to be damned by it, they are grossly oversimplified as fictional characters, pawns in a chess game in which every move is necessary and therefore none is possible." Aldridge continues, "Hence, nothing they think is interesting, nothing they do is finally worth doing, and nothing they want will in the end be of any value whatever to them. There can be no doubt that one may be impressed by this and frequently moved to compassion. But one is emphatically not moved to understanding."

Yet as even Aldridge admits, Sillitoe is a master at presenting his material in such a way that compassion, and not disgust, is what most readers feel for his rough-edged characters. Several critics, including the *Washington Post's* Daniel O'Neill, credit the author with an "ability to blend cold-blooded rendering of the exterior world with insightful and sensitive representation of the inner workings of the characters' minds." According to Max Cosman of *Commonweal,* "such is Mr. Sillitoe's interest in his fellow man and such his skill in compelling attention, that ignoble, or subnormal as his Nottinghamites are, they can [bring] forth compassion even in the midst of disapproval."

Others, however, feel that this emphasis on compassion makes Sillitoe less an Angry Young Man with a special talent for describing the plight of the proletariat than a sentimentalist who idealizes the lives of his working-class heroes. Though the *New Republic's* Irving Howe is pleased by the lack of romanticization, "moral nagging [and] political exhortation" in *Saturday Night and Sunday Morning,* for instance, he nevertheless concludes that "in its hard-headed and undeluded way it is not quite free from sentimentality." *New York Review of Books* contributor Stanley Kauffmann is especially critical of what he feels is Sillitoe's mishandling of pathos, pointing out that "often he appeals for sympathy with music-hall blatancy." David Boroff of the *Saturday Review* agrees that Sillitoe is "sometimes betrayed by his own sentimentality," as does a *Times Literary Supplement* critic, who suggests that such lapses may stem not from the author's attitude toward his subject but from "the difficulties presented by the use of a fictitious narrator who is not supposed to be as articulate or as sophisticated as the writer himself."

Sillitoe's practice of speaking through a narrator who is less articulate and sophisticated than himself has resulted in a style many critics have trouble classifying. As Champlin notes, "at times the essayist, social historian and social reporter in Sillitoe seems simply to have chosen fiction as the best carrier of impressions he wants to leave and points he wants to make." Consequently, remarks Kauffmann, his writing "fluctuates from straight hard prose to Nottingham slang to the most literary effusions, often all on the same page." In most other respects, comment a number of reviewers, including the *Times Literary Supplement's* John Lucas, Sillitoe's style is "peculiarly artless" in that "even the best of [the stories] work in a manner that is unusual or unorthodox." There is, for example, no particularly strong emphasis on plot in a Sillitoe story, no "half hidden thread that can be traced," no sudden flash or insight that makes everything clear; as Lucas states, "nothing happens: there is no revelation, the story hardly seems to be a story at all." West also notices that Sillitoe's stories are "so firmly rooted in experience, and so ably handled, that they do not seem to have been written at all; they seem to be occurrences of a most engrossing and absorbing kind." Gene Baro agrees with this assessment of the author, writing in the *New York Herald Tribune Book Review* that "Sillitoe exhibits . . . lucid design, pace, a gift for salty vernacular, an unerring eye for the telling gesture, a robust and yet a restrained sense of the comic. . . . All is achieved simply, matter-of-factly, without apparent striving for effect."

A *Times Literary Supplement* critic is especially impressed by Sillitoe's "integrity of style that never falsifies the writer's role—which is why, for instance, he refuses to go on 'like a penny-a-liner to force an ending' if inspiration stops before he knows what to do with the character he has created. There may not even *be* an ending to a Sillitoe story." John Updike notices this same feature in Sillitoe's writing, pointing out in a *New Republic* article that his stories "have a wonderful way of going on, of not stopping short . . . that lifts us twice, and shows enviable assurance and abundance in the writer."

P. H. Johnson of the *New Statesman* also regards Sillitoe as "highly gifted technically: he is an excellent story-teller, and his style is perfectly adapted to his subject-matter; he has literary tact and a sense of design." The *Saturday Review's* James Yaffe reports that among Sillitoe's "many wonderful qualities" are "a fluent, often brilliant command of language, an acute ear for dialect, [and] a virtuoso ability to describe the sight, sound, and smell of things."

What reviewers cannot agree upon in their evaluations of Sillitoe's work is whether he writes in the tradition of an earlier age (notably the American proletarian novelists of the 1930s) or in the tradition of certain British authors of the 1950s and 1960s whose bitter attacks on the political and social establishment earned them the name "Angry Young Men." Kauffmann, for one, feels Sillitoe is a victim of the cultural "time-lag" that exists between the United States and England and is therefore merely rediscovering the themes that once preoccupied American writers such as John Steinbeck, Erskine Caldwell, Theodore Dreiser, and John Dos Passos. Maloff shares this view, commenting: "Sillitoe is a throwback, an old-fashioned realist—in fact, a regionalist. He has attempted to make viable as art what was called, without embarrassment or sneering, the 'proletarian novel' in the 1930's. His protagonists are profoundly rooted in their class, and draw such strengths as they possess—or come finally to possess—from that identification." This, he adds, makes Sillitoe very different from other post-war writers. "[He] is a historical surprise. In the utterly changed circumstances of the fifties and sixties, he has partially validated as art the 'proletarian novel' of the thirties; and standing eccentrically against the current driven by his defter contemporaries, he has made possible a working-class novel."

Aldridge suggests that part of Sillitoe's inspiration may date back even earlier than the 1930s. States the critic: "Sillitoe stands as a comforting reminder to the English that the grand old roistering 'low life' tradition of Fielding and Dickens may have lost its sting, but is not yet dead. . . . Although [the author] does have his grievances, he seems basically content to keep the working man in his place, and as a writer he evidently wants to remain a working man." Aldridge indicates, however, that other writers "did all that he has done first and better than he. It might be objected that working-class life is, after all, Sillitoe's material, and that he ought to have a perfect right to use it if he so chooses. But there is little virtue in repeating the discoveries or the mistakes of one's predecessors, or in trying to make literature out of a cultural lag that merely social reform and the payment of some money can rectify."

Allen R. Penner of *Contemporary Literature* also sees traces of an old-fashioned literary tradition in Sillitoe's works—but with a modern twist. Explains Penner: "'The Loneliness of the Long-Distance Runner' . . . is written in a tradition in English fiction which dates at least from Elizabethan times, in . . . the rogue's tale, or thief's autobiography." In his opinion Sillitoe "has reversed the formula of the popular crime tale of fiction, wherein the reader enjoys vicariously witnessing the exploits of the outlaw and then has the morally reassuring pleasure of seeing the doors of the prison close upon him in the conclusion. Sillitoe begins his tale in prison, and he ends it before the doors have opened again, leaving us with the unsettling realization that the doors will indeed open and that the criminal will be released unreformed." This emphasis on unrepentant rebellion, says Penner, proves that "Sillitoe was never, really, simply an 'angry young man.' His hostility was not a transitory emotion of youth, but a permanent rancor well grounded in class hatred. 'The Loneliness of the Long-Distance Runner' contains the seeds of the revolutionary philosophy which would eventually attain full growth in his works."

On the other hand, some critics see nothing but youthful anger in Sillitoe's writings. Commenting in the *New York Times Book Review,* Malcolm Bradbury notes that "if the heroes of some . . . English novels are angry young men, Mr. Sillitoe is raging; and though he doesn't know it, he is raging for much the same reasons." Champlin remarks that Sillitoe's emergence was "a sharp signaling of an end to quiet acceptance of the way things are. It was a protest, fueled by the war, against the stratified status quo. . . . Unlike some of Britain's angry young men who have matured and prospered into more conservative postures, Sillitoe remains the poet of the anonymous millions in the council flats and the cold-water attached houses, noting the ignored, remembering the half-forgotten."

Though John R. Clark of the *Saturday Review* also sees Sillitoe as an Angry Young Man, he feels that "his anger and fictions have altered with time. In [his] early work there was something single-minded and intense in the actions and scenes, particularly in the shorter novels." On the other hand, "Later novels reveal a broader social and political horizon. Sillitoe's characters not only privately rebel but become dedicated to larger 'movements.'"

Prairie Schooner's Robert S. Haller rejects the notion that Sillitoe is an Angry Young Man. "If this title is justified for any writers," he begins, "it would be so for [those] men with university training who wanted room at the top but who resented the moral and aesthetic cost of getting there. But it hardly applies to Sillitoe [and others] who are authentically of the working class, self-educated, and uninterested in the matter of rising to the upper classes. . . . Anger is the resentment of frustrated ambition; neither Sillitoe nor his early heroes see in established values and styles anything to aspire to.''

Nor is Sillitoe's style based on that of any grand literary tradition, Haller goes on to state. In fact, declares the critic, the author's ''commitment to his [Nottinghamite] people has been an expression of a refusal to mimic the educated literary man.'' Consequently, books like *Saturday Night and Sunday Morning* and *The Loneliness of the Long-Distance Runner* ''have been continuous best sellers because they provide a mirror for working-class readers and a window for others into a culture with its own richness of circumstance and its own integrity.''

Sillitoe himself sees little merit in arguing about whether he is traditional or modern, sentimental or angry. As he told Igor Hajek in a *Nation* interview: ''I cannot understand why people are always looking for trends and movements. Writers work just as all others: miners, engineers, psychologists. From their point [of view] trends do not exist. Why should they exist in writing? Although I admit that looking from a distance some similarities may appear, the writer himself usually does not realize it.''

In this same interview, Sillitoe reveals that he is not at all dismayed by the fact that he is best known for his earliest works, especially ''The Loneliness of the Long-Distance Runner.'' ''I think those people [who remember me primarily as the author of 'The Loneliness of the Long-Distance Runner'] are absolutely right,'' he says. ''This story of a working-class youth is at the same time the statement of my artistic integrity. I shall never write anything to uphold this Establishment and this society. And I'm ready to stick to my principles even to a self-damaging extent.''

Continues the author: ''Whatever I have against [English society] I say through my characters: every character in my books has an opinion, and they are all mine. On the other hand, it is very difficult to write about something you hate, you have to try to understand and even show some sympathies. That is why people, who consider writers from a political rather than artistic viewpoint, accuse them of being treacherous: they take this for sympathizing with enemy. . . . If they ask me what I am, a Communist or Socialist, etc., I can only answer that I'm on the Left, beyond that I can't say much.'' In his opinion, ''A writer never stands still. When you are young, everything is simple, but I am not young any more, [which] means that I am leaving a lot of simplicities behind. Basic beliefs stay, but things now look more complex.''

In short, concludes Sillitoe, ''Each individual has to make a choice: either to accept this society or stand up against it. . . . In this country, as in any other, a writer is liked if he is loyal to the system. But it is the writer's duty in a sense to be disloyal. In the modern world, he is one of the few people who are listened to, and his primary loyalty should be to his integrity and to his talent. He can speak up in many ways; the best way is to write a book.''

BIOGRAPHICAL/CRITICAL SOURCES:

BOOKS

Aldridge, John W., *Time to Murder and Create: The Contemporary Novel in Crisis*, McKay, 1966.
Authors in the News, Volume I, Gale, 1976.
Contemporary Authors Autobiography Series, Volume II, Gale, 1985.
Contemporary Literary Criticism, Gale, Volume I, 1973, Volume III, 1975, Volume VI, 1976, Volume X, 1979, Volume XIX, 1981.
Dictionary of Literary Biography, Volume XIV: *British Novelists since 1960*, Gale, 1983.
Gindin, James, *Postwar British Fiction: New Accents and Attitudes*, University of California Press, 1962.
Shapiro, Charles, editor, *Contemporary British Novelists*, Southern Illinois University Press, 1965.

PERIODICALS

Chicago Tribune Book World, October 26, 1980, August 31, 1981.
Commonweal, September 4, 1959, April 29, 1960, March 27, 1964.
Contemporary Literature, Volume X, number 2, 1969.
Globe and Mail (Toronto), September 7, 1985.
Guardian, September 25, 1959.
Los Angeles Times, October 1, 1980, April 21, 1981.
Los Angeles Times Book Review, November 21, 1982.
Milwaukee Journal, November 10, 1974.
Nation, January 27, 1969.
New Republic, August 24, 1959, May 9, 1960.
New Statesman, October 3, 1959.
New Yorker, September 5, 1959, June 11, 1960.
New York Herald Tribune Book Review, August 16, 1959, May 29, 1960.
New York Review of Books, March 5, 1964.
New York Times Book Review, August 16, 1959, April 10, 1960, September 28, 1980, April 19, 1981, December 12, 1982.
Prairie Schooner, winter, 1974/75.
San Francisco Chronicle, November 29, 1959, May 1, 1960.
Saturday Review, September 5, 1959, April 16, 1960, January 25, 1964, October 16, 1971.
Sewanee Review, summer, 1975.
Spectator, September 25, 1959.
Time, April 18, 1960.
Times (London), November 10, 1983, November 15, 1984, October 10, 1985.
Times Literary Supplement, October 2, 1959, October 19, 1973, January 15, 1981, January 23, 1981, October 15, 1982, November 11, 1983, June 7, 1985.
Washington Post, June 2, 1981, December 10, 1982.
Washington Post Book World, October 26, 1980.
Yale Review, September, 1959.

*   *   *

SIMMONS, Marc   1937-

PERSONAL: Born May 15, 1937, in Dallas, Tex.; son of Julian Marion and Lois (Skielvig) Simmons. *Education:* University of Texas, B.A., 1958; University of New Mexico, M.A., 1961, Ph.D., 1965; University of Guanajuato, Spanish study; North Texas Farrier's School, certificate, 1969.

ADDRESSES: Home—P.O. Box 51, Cerrillos, N.M. 87010.

CAREER: Writer. Former ranch hand in Wyoming, horseshoer in Arizona, movie extra at Warner Brothers, and adobe maker and plasterer; University of New Mexico, Albuquerque, visiting assistant professor of history, 1965-66, 1967-68; St. John's College, Santa Fe, N.M., director of Latin American area studies in Peace Corps training program, 1968; Colorado College, Colorado Springs, visiting professor of history, spring, 1975. Expert on eighteenth-century Spanish documents.

MEMBER: Authors Guild, Authors League of America, Western Writers of America, Phi Beta Kappa.

AWARDS, HONORS: Woodrow Wilson fellowship; Guggenheim fellowship.

WRITINGS:

(Translator from the Spanish and editor) *Border Comanches*, Stagecoach Press, 1967.

Turquoise and Six Guns: The Story of Cerrillos, Galisteo Press, 1968.

Spanish Government in New Mexico, University of New Mexico Press, 1968.

Two Southwesterners: Charles Lummis and Amado Chaves, San Marcos Press, 1968.

Yesterday in Santa Fe: Episodes in a Turbulent History, San Marcos Press, 1969.

The Little Lion of the Southwest: A Life of Manuel Antonio Chaves, Swallow Press, 1974.

Witchcraft in the Southwest: Spanish and Indian Supernaturalism on the Rio Grande, Northland Press, 1974.

New Mexico: A Bicentennial History, Norton, 1977.

(Contributor) Alfonso Ortiz, editor, *Handbook of American Indians North of Mexico*, Smithsonian Institution Press, 1979.

People of the Sun, University of New Mexico Press, 1979.

(With Frank Turley) *Southwestern Colonial Ironwork*, Museum of New Mexico Press, 1980.

Albuquerque: A Narrative History, University of New Mexico Press, 1982.

Along the Santa Fe Trail, University of New Mexico Press, 1986.

Murder on the Santa Fe Trail, Texas Western Press, 1987.

The Last Conquistador: Juan de Onate and the Settling of the Far Southwest, University of Oklahoma Press, in press.

Assisted in cataloging the Spanish archives of New Mexico for a guide published by the State Records Center. Contributor to *Encyclopedia Americana*. Contributor to periodicals, including *National Geographic*, *Journal of the West*, and *El Palacio*.

SIDELIGHTS: Marc Simmons built his own adobe home at a cost of $135.00 in Cerrillos, N.M., now technically a ghost town. He then added a second building for his library. Research projects have taken him to Mexico, Colombia, Ecuador, Peru, and other parts of South and Central America; he also has visited Europe and North Africa.

BIOGRAPHICAL/CRITCIAL SOURCES:

PERIODICALS

Christian Science Monitor, February 11, 1980.
Santa Fe New Mexican, November 3, 1968.

*   *   *

SIMON, (Marvin) Neil 1927-

PERSONAL: Born July 4, 1927, in Bronx, N.Y.; son of Irving (a garment salesman) and Mamie Simon; married Joan Baim (a dancer), September 30, 1953 (died, 1973); married Marsha Mason (an actress), 1973 (separated, 1983); married Diana Lander, 1986; children (first marriage) Ellen, Nancy. *Education:* Attended New York University, 1946, and University of Denver.

ADDRESSES: *Office*—c/o Albert Da Silva, Esq., Da Silva & Da Silva, 502 Park Ave., New York, N.Y. 10022.

CAREER: Playwright. Owner of the Eugene O'Neill Theatre, New York City. Warner Brothers, Inc., New York City, mail room clerk, 1946; Columbia Broadcasting System, New York City, comedy writer for Goodman Ace, late 1940s; comedy writer for "The Phil Silvers Arrow Show," NBC-TV, 1948, "The Tallulah Bankhead Show," NBC-TV, 1951, "The Sid Caesar Show," NBC-TV, 1956-57, "The Phil Silvers Show," CBS-TV, 1958-59, "The Garry Moore Show," CBS-TV, 1959-60, for "The Jackie Gleason Show" and "The Red Buttons Show," both CBS-TV, and for NBC-TV specials. *Military service:* U.S. Army Air Force Reserve; sports editor of *Rev-Meter*, the Lowry Field (Colorado) base newspaper, 1946.

MEMBER: Dramatists Guild, Writers Guild of America.

AWARDS, HONORS: Academy of Television Arts and Sciences Award (Emmy), 1957, for "The Sid Caesar Show," and 1959, for "The Phil Silvers Show"; Antoinette Perry Award (Tony) nomination, 1963, for "Little Me" and "Barefoot in the Park," 1968, for "Plaza Suite," 1969, for "Promises, Promises," 1970, for "Last of the Red Hot Lovers," 1972, for "The Prisoner of Second Avenue," and 1987, for "Broadway Bound"; Tony Award, 1965, for best playwright, and 1985, for "Biloxi Blues"; Writers Guild Award nomination, 1967, for "Barefoot in the Park"; *Evening Standard* Drama Award, 1967, for "Sweet Charity"; Sam S. Shubert Foundation Award, 1968; Academy of Motion Picture Arts and Sciences Award (Oscar) nomination, 1968, for "The Odd Couple"; Writers Guild Award, 1969, for "The Odd Couple," 1970, for "Last of the Red Hot Lovers," 1971, for "The Out-of-Towners," and 1972, for "The Trouble with People"; named Entertainer of the Year, *Cue* magazine, 1972; L.H.D., Hofstra University, 1981; New York Drama Critics Circle Award, 1983, for "Brighton Beach Memoirs"; elected to the Theater Hall of Fame, Uris Theater, 1983; a Neil Simon tribute show was held at the Shubert Theater, March 1, 1987; the Neil Simon Endowment for the Dramatic Arts has been established at Duke University.

WRITINGS:

PUBLISHED PLAYS

(With William Friedberg) *Adventures of Marco Polo: A Musical Fantasy* (music by Clay Warnick and Mel Pahl), Samuel French, 1959.

(Adaptor with Friedberg) *Heidi* (based on the novel by Johanna Spyri; music by Warnick), Samuel French, 1959.

(With brother, Danny Simon) *Come Blow Your Horn* (also see below; first produced in New Hope, Pa., at the Bucks County Playhouse, August, 1960; produced on Broadway at the Brooks Atkinson Theatre, February 22, 1961; produced on the West End at the Prince of Wales Theatre, February 17, 1962), Doubleday, 1963.

Barefoot in the Park (also see below; first produced, under title "Nobody Loves Me," in New Hope, Pa., at the Bucks County Playhouse, 1962; produced on Broadway at the Biltmore Theatre, October 23, 1963; produced on the West End, 1965), Random House, 1964.

The Odd Couple (also see below; first produced on Broadway at the Plymouth Theatre, March 10, 1965; produced on the West End at the Queen's Theatre, October 12, 1966; revised version first produced in Los Angeles at the Ahmanson Theatre, April 6, 1985; produced on Broadway at the Broadhurst Theatre, June, 1985), Random House, 1966.

Sweet Charity (musical; based on the screenplay "The Nights of Cabiria" by Federico Fellini; music and lyrics by Cy Coleman and Dorothy Fields; first produced on Broadway at the Palace Theatre, January 29, 1966; produced on the

West End at the Prince of Wales Theatre, October 11, 1967), Random House, 1966.

The Star-Spangled Girl (also see below; first produced on Broadway at the Plymouth Theatre, December 21, 1966), Random House, 1967.

Plaza Suite (also see below; three one-acts entitled "Visitor from Hollywood," "Visitor from Mamaroneck," and "Visitor from Forest Hills"; first produced on Broadway at the Plymouth Theatre, February 14, 1968; produced on the West End at the Lyric Theatre, February 18, 1969), Random House, 1969.

Promises, Promises (also see below; musical; based on the screenplay "The Apartment" by Billy Wilder and I.A.L. Diamond; music by Burt Bacharach; lyrics by Hal David; first produced on Broadway at the Shubert Theatre, December 1, 1968; produced on the West End at the Prince of Wales Theatre, October 2, 1969), Random House, 1969.

Last of the Red Hot Lovers (also see below; three-act; first produced in New Haven at the Shubert Theatre, November 26, 1969; produced on Broadway at the Eugene O'Neill Theatre, December 28, 1969; produced in London, 1979), Random House, 1970.

The Gingerbread Lady (also see below; first produced in New Haven at the Shubert Theatre, November 4, 1970; produced on Broadway at the Plymouth Theatre, December 13, 1970; produced in London, 1974), Random House, 1971.

The Prisoner of Second Avenue (also see below; first produced in New Haven at the Shubert Theatre, October 12, 1971; produced on Broadway at the Eugene O'Neill Theatre, November 11, 1971), Random House, 1972.

The Sunshine Boys (also see below; first produced in New Haven at the Shubert Theatre, November 21, 1972; produced on Broadway at the Broadhurst Theatre, December 20, 1972; produced in London, 1975), Random House, 1973.

The Good Doctor (also see below; musical; adapted from stories by Anton Chekhov; music by Peter Link; lyrics by Simon; first produced on Broadway at the Eugene O'Neill Theatre, November 27, 1973), Random House, 1974.

God's Favorite (also see below; first produced on Broadway at the Eugene O'Neill Theatre, December 11, 1974), Random House, 1975.

California Suite (also see below; first produced in Los Angeles, April, 1976; produced on Broadway at the Eugene O'Neill Theatre, June 30, 1976; produced in London, 1976), Random House, 1977.

Chapter Two (also see below; first produced in Los Angeles, 1977; produced on Broadway at the Imperial Theatre, December 4, 1977; produced in London, 1981), Random House, 1979.

They're Playing Our Song (musical; music by Marvin Hamlisch; lyrics by Carol Bayer Sager; first produced in Los Angeles, 1978; produced on Broadway at the Imperial Theatre, February 11, 1979; produced in London, 1980), Random House, 1980.

I Ought to Be in Pictures (also see below; first produced in Los Angeles, 1980; produced on Broadway at the Eugene O'Neill Theatre, April 3, 1980; produced in London at the Offstage Downstairs, December, 1986), Random House, 1981.

Fools (first produced on Broadway at the Eugene O'Neill Theatre, April, 1981), Random House, 1982.

Brighton Beach Memoirs (also see below; first produced in Los Angeles at the Ahmanson Theatre, December, 1982; produced on Broadway at the Alvin Theatre, March 27, 1983), Random House, 1984.

Biloxi Blues (also see below; first produced in Los Angeles at the Ahmanson Theatre, December, 1984; produced on Broadway at the Neil Simon Theatre, March, 1985), Random House, 1986.

Broadway Bound (first produced at Duke University, October, 1986; produced on Broadway at the Broadhurst Theatre, December, 1986), Random House, 1987.

OMNIBUS COLLECTIONS

The Comedy of Neil Simon (contains *Come Blow Your Horn, Barefoot in the Park, The Odd Couple, The Star-Spangled Girl, Promises, Promises, Plaza Suite,* and *Last of the Red Hot Lovers*), Random House, 1971, published as *The Collected Plays of Neil Simon,* Volume 1, New American Library, 1986.

The Collected Plays of Neil Simon, Volume 2 (contains *The Sunshine Boys, Little Me* [also see below], *The Gingerbread Lady, The Prisoner of Second Avenue, The Good Doctor, God's Favorite, California Suite,* and *Chapter Two*), Random House, 1979.

UNPUBLISHED PLAYS

(Contributor of sketches) "Tamiment Revue," first produced in Tamiment, Pa., 1952-53.

(Contributor of sketches, with D. Simon) "Catch a Star!" (musical revue), first produced on Broadway at the Plymouth Theatre, November 6, 1955.

(Contributor of sketches, with D. Simon) "New Faces of 1956," first produced on Broadway at the Ethel Barrymore Theatre, June 14, 1956.

(Adaptor) "Little Me" (musical; based on the novel by Patrick Dennis), music by Coleman, first produced on Broadway at the Lunt-Fontanne Theatre, November 17, 1962, produced on the West End at the Cambridge Theatre, November 18, 1964.

(Contributor of sketch) "Broadway Revue" (satirical musical revue), first produced in New York City at the Karmit Bloomgarden Theatre, November, 1968.

(Editor of book for musical) "Seesaw" (based on "Two for the Seesaw" by William Gibson), first produced on Broadway, March 18, 1973.

"Rumors," first produced in San Diego at the Old Globe Theater, 1988, produced on Broadway, November, 1988.

SCREENPLAYS

(With Cesare Zavattini) "After the Fox," United Artists, 1966.

"Barefoot in the Park" (based on Simon's play of the same title), Paramount, 1967.

"The Odd Couple" (based on Simon's play of the same title), Paramount, 1968.

"The Out-of-Towners," Paramount, 1970.

"Plaza Suite" (based on Simon's play of the same title), Paramount, 1971.

"Last of the Red Hot Lovers" (based on Simon's play of the same title), Paramount, 1972.

"The Heartbreak Kid" (based on short story by Bruce Jay Friedman), Twentieth Century-Fox, 1972.

"The Sunshine Boys" (based on Simon's play of the same title), Metro-Goldwyn-Mayer, 1974.

"The Prisoner of Second Avenue" (based on Simon's play of the same title), Warner Bros., 1975.

"Murder by Death," Columbia, 1976.

"The Goodbye Girl," Warner Bros., 1977.

"The Cheap Detective," Columbia, 1978.

"California Suite" (based on Simon's play of the same title), Columbia, 1978.

"Chapter Two" (based on Simon's play of the same title), Columbia, 1979.

"Seems Like Old Times," Columbia, 1980.

"Only When I Laugh," Columbia, 1981.

"I Ought to Be in Pictures" (based on Simon's play of the same title), Twentieth Century-Fox, 1982.

"Max Dugan Returns," Twentieth Century-Fox, 1983.

(With Ed. Weinberger and Stan Daniels) "The Lonely Guy," Universal, 1984.

"The Slugger's Wife," Columbia, 1985.

"Brighton Beach Memoirs" (based on Simon's play of the same title), Universal, 1986.

"Biloxi Blues" (based on Simon's play of the same title), Universal, 1988.

TELEVISION SCRIPTS

"The Trouble with People," National Broadcasting Co., 1972.

(Co-author) "Happy Endings," 1975.

WORK IN PROGRESS: "A Foggy Day," a musical incorporating music and lyrics written by the late Ira and George Gershwin; "Jake's Women."

SIDELIGHTS: "When I was a kid," playwright Neil Simon tells Tom Prideaux of *Life,* "I climbed up on a stone ledge to watch an outdoor movie of Charlie Chaplin. I laughed so hard I fell off, cut my head open and was taken to the doctor, bleeding and laughing.... My idea of the ultimate achievement in a comedy is to make a whole audience fall onto the floor, writhing and laughing so hard that some of them pass out." In his own comedies Simon has often come close to realizing this ideal. "At *The Odd Couple,*" Prideaux notes, "at least two people a week do—literally—fall out of their seats laughing."

For some thirty years Simon's comedies have dominated the Broadway stage and have been adapted as popular Hollywood films as well. As David Richards explains in the *Washington Post,* Simon's comedies have always run "forever on Broadway and made him pots of money, after which they were turned into movies that made him pots more." Such plays as "Barefoot in the Park," "The Odd Couple," "Plaza Suite," "The Prisoner of Second Avenue," "The Sunshine Boys," and the autobiographical trilogy of "Brighton Beach Memoirs," Biloxi Blues," and "Broadway Bound," have ensured Simon a position as "one of America's most popular and prolific playwrights" and "the most formidable comedy writer in American theatre," as Sheila Ennis Geitner reports in the *Dictionary of Literary Biography.*

Even though Simon's plays are often "detonatingly funny," as a critic for *Time* claims, in recent years they have grown more serious too, confronting issues of importance, the humor developing naturally from the characters and their interactions. With these plays, Simon has gained a new respect for his work. "Simon's mature theatre work," Robert K. Johnson writes in his *Neil Simon,* "combines comedy with moments of poignance and insight." Speaking of the Tony Award-winning "Biloxi Blues," Frank Rich of the *New York Times* argues that in this play Simon "at last begins to examine himself honestly, without compromises, and the result is his most persuasively serious effort to date." In his review of the same play, Clive Barnes of the *New York Post* calls it "a realistic comedy of the heart" and allows that it "is funny, often heart-rendingly funny, but nowadays Simon will not compromise character for a laugh."

Simon began his career as a radio writer in the 1940s. He and his brother Danny Simon worked as a team, writing comedy sketches for radio personality Goodman Ace. In the 1950s the pair graduated to television, working with such popular entertainers as Sid Caesar, Phil Silvers, and Jackie Gleason, and with such other writers as Mel Brooks and Woody Allen. But after some ten years in the business, Simon wanted out. "I hated the idea of working in television and having conferences with network executives and advertising executives who told you what audiences wanted and in what region they wanted it," Simon tells the *New York Times Magazine.* With the success of his play "Come Blow Your Horn," written with Danny, Simon was finally able to leave television and devote his efforts to the stage. He has never regretted the move. As he tells Richards, "I would rather spend my nights writing for an audience of 1,000, than an audience of 14 million."

Since the initial success of "Come Blow Your Horn," which ran for eighty-four weeks on Broadway, Simon has seldom had a disappointing reception to his work. His second play, "Barefoot in the Park," ran for over 1,500 performances on Broadway; "The Odd Couple" for over 900 performances; "Plaza Suite" for over 1,000 performances; and "Last of the Red Hot Lovers" and "The Prisoner of Second Avenue" ran for over 700 performances each. Richards notes that "all but a handful of Simon's plays" have made a profit, while Simon is reputedly "the richest playwright alive and arguably the richest ever in the history of the theater." "Most of Simon's plays . . . ," Richard Christiansen remarks in the *Chicago Tribune,* "have been good box office. [And] he still holds the record for having the most plays running simultaneously on Broadway (four)." Speaking of Simon's phenomenal career, Christine Arnold of the *Chicago Tribune* calls him "America's most successful playwright, more prolific and far less troubled than Tennessee Williams, more popular than Eugene O'Neill or Lanford Wilson or Sam Shepard. Critics may dismiss or embrace his work, but they cannot dispute his genius for creating plays that resonate for vast audiences."

Although Simon's plays have dealt with a wide range of situations and characters, certain elements recur in all of them. The setting is usually Simon's hometown of New York, the characters are often native New Yorkers, and their problems are similar to those experienced by Simon himself. "Come Blow Your Horn," for instance, is a thinly-disguised version of Simon and brother Danny coming of age and leaving home. "The Odd Couple" stems from Danny's experience of sharing an apartment with a divorced friend. And "Chapter Two" concerns Simon's recovery following the death of his first wife in 1973. Simon tells Leslie Bennetts of the *New York Times* about how he has incorporated events from his own life into his plays: "The theme is me, my outlook on life. If you spread [my career] out like a map, you can chart my emotional life: some of the growth, some of the changes, some of the side trips."

Critics often point out that Simon has an admirable ability to accurately depict American domestic life. "Simon has a gift for sketching America in small-scale situations," states Joe Brown of the *Washington Post.* Writing in the *Humanist,* Julius Novick claims that Simon immerses "himself in the minutiae of modern American upper-middle-class existence, which no one conveys with more authority—or, anyhow, more assiduity—than he."

Simon's plays usually focus on the members of one family or on a small group of friends, and often concern the more disruptive problems of modern life: divorce, urban crime and congestion, conflicts between children and parents, infidelity. These conflicts occur in a closed environment: an apartment or the family home. "Many of my plays [deal] with people being dumped together in a confined space, physically and emotionally," Bennetts quotes Simon as explaining. He uses this confined space with expert skill. David Kehr of the *Chicago Tribune* claims that Simon has "a kind of genius—a genius for stagecraft, the art of getting characters on and off a stage as unobtrusively as possible and of finding plausible, natural excuses for restricting a whole range of dramatic action to the confines of a single set. As a master of logistics, Simon is without peer."

Although Simon's plays are often concerned with domestic troubles, they nonetheless find humor in these painful situations. In his critique of "The Odd Couple" for the *Saturday Review*, Henry Hewes explains that Simon "makes comic cadenzas out of our bleats of agony." Simon's characters, Hewes maintains, "are blissfully unhappy but the pain of what they do to each other and to themselves is exploded into fierce humor." In his analysis of what makes Simon's plays funny, T. E. Kalem of *Time* finds that "the central aspect of his plays is that the central characters are not funny at all. They never laugh, and they are frequently utterly miserable. . . . Why does the audience laugh? Two reasons suggest themselves. The first is the catharsis of relief—thank God, this hasn't happened to me. The second is to ward off and suppress anxiety—by God, this might happen to me." Speaking to Paul D. Zimmerman of *Newsweek*, Simon explains: "My view is 'how sad and funny life is.' I can't think of a humorous situation that does not involve some pain. I used to ask, 'What is a funny situation?' Now I ask, 'What is a sad situation and how can I tell it humorously?'"

This fusion of the sad and funny in Simon's work is noted by several critics who see it as a central reason for his theatrical success. Marilyn Stasio writes in her review of "Last of the Red Hot Lovers": "There is nothing at all funny about the painfully neurotic and really quite profoundly unhappy characters in this play, which is actually about the disintegration of our moral codes and the chaos which such a breakdown has made of our emotional lives. What makes the play so wildly funny is not its author's vision, for Simon's is close to tragedy, but his conceptualization of that vision as high comedy-of-manners. It is neither the personae of the characters nor the situations of their drama which Simon treats humorously, but only the superficial foibles which they have erected as elaborate defenses against their own anxieties." Prideaux argues that Simon's comic characters—who, like his audience, are usually from the middle class—offer something more than simple entertainment. "By making a modern audience feel that its foibles and vices are not too serious because he makes them seem so funny," Prideaux writes, "Simon is also selling a sort of forgiveness: absolution by laughter."

In her *Neil Simon: A Critical Study*, Edythe M. McGovern argues that in his early plays Simon also advocates compromise and moderation. In "Barefoot in the Park," for instance, a newly-married couple are opposites: she is spontaneous; he is overly-careful. Their different outlooks on life threaten to pull them apart. But by play's end, they have moderated their behavior so that they can live comfortably together. "Simon," McGovern writes, "has made a point here regarding the desirability of following a middle course in order to live plea-

surably without boredom, but with a sensible regard for responsibility."

The same theme is returned to in "The Odd Couple," in which two divorced male friends share an apartment, only to find that the disagreeable personality traits which led them to get divorces also make their living together impossible. They are "two rather nice human beings who will never be able to communicate with one another simply because each man has a completely different way of viewing the world and is committed to what amounts to an extreme position with no intention of compromise," as McGovern explains. Their unyielding attitudes lead to an angry confrontation and eventual break. In showing the consequences of their inability to compromise, Simon again argues for "a middle course rather than an extremely polarized position," McGovern writes. Speaking of Simon's handling of such important themes in his comedies, McGovern claims that "to Neil Simon, . . . the comic form provides a means to present serious subjects so that audiences may laugh to avoid weeping."

But not all critics have been kind to Simon. Some believe his long string of hit comedies to be filled with funny one-liners and little else. Jack Kroll of *Newsweek* refers to Simon's image as "Gagman Laureate." Writing in his *Uneasy Stages: A Chronicle of the New York Theater, 1963-73*, John Simon claims that "the basic unit of [Simon's] playmaking is the joke. Not the word, the idea, the character, or even the situation, but the gag. It kills him if here and there a monosyllable resists funnying up, if now and then someone has to make a move that won't fracture the audience." According to Gerald M. Berkowitz, writing in *Players*, "Simon is a critical embarrassment. . . . A Neil Simon comedy makes the audience laugh. . . . [But] the secret of his special comic talent is a matter of pure technique; . . . it is not the content of his plays, but the manner in which the content is presented that generates most of the laughter."

For many years, Simon was taken less than seriously even by critics who enjoyed his work. A *Time* reviewer, for example, once claimed that "Santa Claus is just an alias for Neil Simon. Every year just before Christmas, he loads up packets of goodies and tosses two unbridled hours of laughter to Broadway audiences." Johnson notes that many people saw Simon as "a sausage grinder turning out the same pleasing 'product' over and over again. The 'product' is a play or movie realistic in style and featuring New Yorkers who spout a lot of funny lines." Geitner remarks that Simon's reputation as "the most formidable comedy writer in American theatre . . . prevented his being considered a serious dramatist by many critics."

With the production of the trilogy "Brighton Beach Memoirs," "Biloxi Blues," and "Broadway Bound" in the 1980s, however, critical opinion about Simon's work has improved enormously. Speaking of the critical reception of "Brighton Beach Memoirs," Richards explains that "the critics, who have sometimes begrudged the playwright his ability to coin more funny lines per minute than seems humanly possible, have now decided that he has a very warm heart." And "Biloxi Blues," his twenty-first Broadway play, won Simon in 1985 his first Tony Award for best drama. (He had twenty years earlier won the Tony for best playwright.)

The trilogy is based on Simon's own childhood and youth in the 1930s and 1940s, although he tells Charles Champlin of the *Los Angeles Times*: "I hate to call it autobiographical, because things didn't necessarily happen, or happen to me. It's an Impressionist painting of that era and that place. But there are bits and pieces of me in several of the characters.'' ''Broadway Bound'' is close enough to the truth, however, for William A. Henry III of *Time* to report that both Simon ''and his brother Danny have wept openly while watching it in performance.''

''Brighton Beach Memoirs'' is set in the Brooklyn of 1937 and tells of a Jewish family, the Jeromes, and their financial troubles during the Depression. When an aunt loses her job, she and her son move in with the Jeromes, and the family, now seven people in a cramped house, must survive their financial crisis and the aggravatingly close proximity to each other. Rich explains that ''Simon uses the family's miseries to raise such enduring issues as sibling resentments, guilt-ridden parent-child relationships and the hunger for dignity in a poverty-stricken world.'' Simon's alter ego is the family's teenage son, Eugene, who comments on his family's problems in asides to the audience. Eugene, Richards explains, ''serves as the play's narrator and [his] cockeyed slant on the family's tribulations keeps the play in comic perspective.''

The play has earned Simon some of the best reviews of his career. Brown writes that ''Brighton Beach Memoirs'' has ''plenty of laughs,'' but ''Simon avoids the glib, tenderly probing the often-awkward moments where confused emotions cause unconscious hurts.... Simon's at his best, finding the natural wit, wisecracking and hyperbole in the words and wisdom of everyday people.'' Barnes finds ''Brighton Beach Memoirs'' to be ''a very lovely play.'' He continues: ''I am certain—if the kids of our academic establishment can get off their pinnacles and start taking Simon as seriously as he deserves—*Brighton Beach Memoirs* will become a standard part of American dramatic literature.''

Eugene Jerome joins the Army in ''Biloxi Blues,'' the second play of the trilogy. The story follows Eugene through his ten weeks of basic training in Biloxi, Mississippi. During this training, one recruit is jailed for his homosexuality; one comes into constant conflict with his superior officers; and Eugene faces anti-Semitic insults from another soldier. Eugene, an aspiring writer, records these events faithfully in his diary, learning to examine his life and the lives of his friends honestly, and developing personal values in the process. Eugene's dream of becoming a writer is greatly furthered when he is assigned to work on an Army newspaper instead of being sent to the front, a fortunate turn of events that nonetheless makes him feel guilty.

Eugene's Army career is virtually identical to Simon's own stint in the military. Simon explains to Michiko Kakutani of the *New York Times* that writing the play was an act of self-discovery: ''I wanted to know how this extremely shy, not enormously well-educated boy came to do what I consider a very hard thing to do—write plays. I wanted to see how I became the person I am. I seem to be, in my own mind, a very unlikely candidate for success.''

This self-examination has been well received by the critics, who find that Simon realistically presents life in the Army. ''For all the familiarity of its set pieces,'' Dan Sullivan of the *Los Angeles Times* says of ''Biloxi Blues,'' ''it feels like life, not 'Gomer Pyle.''' Critics have also been impressed with how Simon subordinates the play's humor to its more serious concerns. As Howard Kissel writes in *Women's Wear Daily*, ''Biloxi Blues'' ''is certainly Simon's best play, to my mind the first in which he has had the courage to suggest there are things that matter more to him than the reassuring sound of the audience's laughter. My admiration for the play is deep

and unqualified.'' Richards claims that ''Biloxi Blues'' ''may be the most touching play ever written about the rigors of basic training.''

The story of Eugene Jerome continues in ''Broadway Bound,'' in which Eugene and his older brother, Simon, become comedy writers, leave home, and take jobs with a major network radio show. The breakup of their parents' marriage, the family's resistance to their new profession, and Eugene's realization that life does not enjoy the happy endings found in art form the basis of the plot. Danny Simon tells Nina Darnton of the *New York Times* that ''Broadway Bound'' ''is the closest in accuracy'' of the three autobiographical plays.

Eugene's mother is the primary character in ''Broadway Bound.'' ''Through much of the comedy,'' Christiansen notes, ''she has been the needling, nagging Jewish mother who gets the old, familiar laughs. But by the end of the play, with her personal life a shambles, she has turned into a creature of great sorrow and weariness, as well.'' After recounting to Eugene the story of how she once danced with actor George Raft—an exhilerating and romantic moment she still recalls fondly—Eugene asks his mother to dance with him. ''In this,'' Kroll observes, ''perhaps the most delicate and highly charged moment in any Simon play, we feel the waste of a woman's unlived life and the shock of a young man who feels in his arms the repressed rhythm of that life.'' Eugene ''sees that behind his mother's depressed exterior,'' Mel Gussow comments in the *New York Times*, ''is the heart of a once vibrant and hopeful young woman; she is someone who has been defeated by the limits she has imposed on her life.''

According to Sylvie Drake of the *Los Angeles Times*, ''Broadway Bound'' is the third and best and final segment of Simon's semiautobiographical trilogy.... There is plenty of comedy left, but of a different order. The one-liners are gone, replaced by a well-timed visceral humor that is coated in melancholy.'' Drake concludes that ''Broadway Bound'' is Simon ''not only at his finest, but at his most personal and complex.'' Similarly, although he sees some flaws in ''Broadway Bound,'' Rich admits that it ''contains some of its author's most accomplished writing to date—passages that dramatize the timeless, unresolvable bloodlettings of familial existence as well as the humorous conflicts one expects.''And Holly Hill, writing for the London *Times*, believes that Eugene's mother ''is the most masterful portrait Neil Simon has ever drawn.''

Although primarily known for his plays, Simon also has written a score of popular films. These include the screen adaptations of many of his own hit plays—including ''Barefoot in the Park,'' ''The Odd Couple,'' and ''The Sunshine Boys''—as well as such original screenplays as ''The Cheap Detective,'' ''Murder by Death,'' and ''The Goodbye Girl.'' Simon's best screen work is found in films where he creates a desperate situation, Vincent Canby argues in the *New York Times*. Simon's ''wisecracks define a world of mighty desperation,'' Canby writes, ''in which every confrontation, be it with a lover, a child, a husband, a friend or a taxi driver, becomes a last chance for survival. When he writes a work in which the desperation is built into the situations, Mr. Simon can be both immensely funny and surprisingly moving.''

But not all critics appreciate Simon's film work. Gene Siskel of the *Chicago Tribune*, for one, declares: ''I dread going to see a movie of Neil Simon's. In fact, I would see anything but a Disney live-action film rather than a Neil Simon movie. Anything. Even a mad-slasher movie.'' Simon's adaptations of his own plays, while often good box office, have sometimes been criticized for being too stagey, like "photographed plays," as Johnson puts it. Yet, most of Simon's films, especially "The Heartbreak Kid" and "Only When I Laugh," have been extremely popular with audiences and critics alike.

"The Heartbreak Kid" concerns a young couple who get divorced during their honeymoon in Florida after the husband meets another woman. Simon creates humor in this film, as Johnson allows, "out of situations which are not basically surefire comedy material." It is this blend of the humorous and the essentially tragic—with the humor emerging naturally from the actions and speech of the characters—which makes "The Heartbreak Kid" "the best film created thus far from a Neil Simon script," Johnson believes.

"Only When I Laugh" was also a critical success for Simon. It tells the story of Georgia Hines, an alcoholic Broadway actress who, despite rehabilitation, cannot beat her dependence. Georgia "is one of the most interesting, complicated characters that Mr. Simon, the master of the sometimes self-defeating one-liner, has ever written," according to Canby. Johnson finds "Only When I Laugh" "one of the most absorbing pieces of work that Simon has written."

"Writing is an escape from a world that crowds me," Simon tells John Corry of the *New York Times*. "I like being alone in a room. It's almost a form of meditation—an investigation of my own life." He explains to Henry how he begins a play: "There's no blueprint per se. You just go through the tunnels of your mind, and you come out someplace." Simon admits to Zimmerman that the writing process still frightens him. "Every time I start a play," he explains, "I panic because I feel I don't know how to do it. . . . I keep wishing I had a grownup in the room who would tell me how to begin." Accepting his success as a writer has also been difficult. "I was depressed for a number of years," Simon tells Corry. The opening of a new play always filled him with guilt. It took psychoanalysis, and a consultation with his second wife's swami, before Simon learned to enjoy his accomplishments.

Simon writes on a daily basis, although much of his work is never completed. Richards reports that "Simon's desk overflows with the plays he's begun over the years. On an average, for every one he finishes, there are 10 he abandons after 15 or 20 pages." Generally, if Simon gets past page thirty-five he will finish the play, a process that takes four months for a first draft, longer for the final draft. "Come Blow Your Horn," for example, was rewritten twenty times before Simon was satisfied with it. In "Broadway Bound," Simon has his alter ego, Eugene, say: "I love *being* a writer. It's the writing that's hard."

Despite the difficulty involved in writing, Simon has managed to produce an impressive body of work. A new Simon comedy every theatrical season has been a Broadway staple for three decades. Henry calls him "America's foremost stage comedist" and places Simon "in the top rank of American playwrights." Rich calls him "not just a show business success but an institution." After surveying Simon's many achievements during his long career as a writer for the stage and screen, Johnson concludes by calling him "one of the finest writers of comedy in American literary history."

MEDIA ADAPTATIONS: "Come Blow Your Horn" was filmed by Paramount in 1963; "Sweet Charity" was filmed by Universal in 1969; "The Star-Spangled Girl" was filmed by Paramount in 1971; "Barefoot in the Park" was adapted as a television series by American Broadcasting Co. in 1970; "The Odd Couple" was adapted as a television series by ABC in 1970-75, and as "The New Odd Couple," ABC, in 1982-83.

BIOGRAPHICAL/CRITICAL SOURCES:

BOOKS

Authors in the News, Volume 1, Gale, 1976.
Contemporary Literary Criticism, Gale, Volume 6, 1976, Volume 9, 1979, Volume 31, 1985, Volume 39, 1986.
Dictionary of Literary Biography, Volume 7: *Twentieth-Century American Dramatists,* Gale, 1981.
Johnson, Robert K., *Neil Simon,* Twayne, 1983.
Kerr, Walter, *Thirty Plays Hath November,* Simon & Schuster, 1969.
McGovern, Edythe M., *Neil Simon: A Critical Study,* Ungar, 1979.
Monaco, James, *American Film Now,* Oxford University Press, 1979.
Simon, John, *Uneasy Stages: A Chronicle of the New York Theater, 1963-73,* Random House, 1975.
Simon, Neil, *Broadway Bound,* Random House, 1987.

PERIODICALS

America, May 20, 1961, May 29, 1965.
American Film, March, 1978.
Chicago Tribune, March 26, 1982, April 7, 1986, November 2, 1986, December 31, 1986.
Christian Science Monitor, January 17, 1970, November 11, 1970.
Commonweal, November 15, 1963, April 2, 1965.
Critic's Choice, December, 1969.
Cue, January 3, 1970, January 15, 1972.
Daily News (New York), April 4, 1980, April 7, 1981, March 29, 1985.
Horizon, January, 1978.
Hudson Review, spring, 1978.
Humanist, September/October, 1976.
Life, April 9, 1965, March 6, 1970, May 7, 1971.
Los Angeles Times, December 5, 1982, December 11, 1982, August 24, 1984, December 15, 1984, April 6, 1985, April 8, 1985, December 6, 1986, December 25, 1986, March 25, 1988.
Nation, March 4, 1968, July 3, 1976.
National Observer, November 20, 1971.
New Republic, January 16, 1971.
New Statesman, November 1, 1974.
Newsweek, January 9, 1967, February 26, 1968, February 2, 1970, November 23, 1970, December 10, 1973, April 26, 1976, February 26, 1979, April 14, 1980, April 20, 1981, December 15, 1986.
New York, January 13, 1975, April 11, 1983.
New Yorker, January 10, 1970, December 23, 1974.
New York Post, December 22, 1966, November 12, 1971, April 7, 1981, March 28, 1983, March 29, 1985.
New York Times, August 4, 1968, December 2, 1968, December 31, 1969, November 17, 1971, December 9, 1973, December 12, 1974, December 22, 1974, December 1, 1977, June 23, 1978, December 22, 1978, December 19, 1980, March 23, 1981, April 5, 1981, April 7, 1981, April 12, 1981, September 23, 1981, March 25, 1983, March 27, 1983, March 28, 1983, April 3, 1983, March 29, 1985, April 1, 1985, April 7, 1985, April 16, 1985, June 9, 1985, August 29, 1986, November 30, 1986, December 5, 1986, December 14, 1986, December 25, 1986, December 26, 1986, January 8, 1987, January 25,

1987, August 17, 1987, December 9, 1987, March 25, 1988, April 15, 1988.
New York Times Magazine, March 7, 1965, March 22, 1970, May 26, 1985.
Philadelphia Inquirer, March 27, 1988.
Playbill, January, 1969.
Playboy, February, 1979.
Players, February/March, 1972, September, 1977.
Plays and Players, February, 1975, July, 1975, September, 1977.
Saturday Review, March 27, 1965.
Seventeen, November, 1979.
Show Business, January 10, 1970.
Spectator, November 2, 1974.
Time, November 1, 1963, January 12, 1970, January 15, 1973, December 23, 1974, April 8, 1985, December 15, 1986.
Times (London), April 20, 1983, April 10, 1985, December 4, 1986, January 3, 1987, June 4, 1987.
TV Guide, November 4, 1972.
Variety, December 24, 1969, February 25, 1970, November 4, 1970, September 8, 1971, December 27, 1972, December 5, 1973.
Village Voice, January 8, 1970.
Vogue, April 1, 1968, October 1, 1968, January 1, 1970.
Washington Post, January 13, 1970, February 9, 1971, April 10, 1983, December 14, 1984, April 6, 1985, July 16, 1985, June 12, 1986, September 12, 1986, October 19, 1986, December 25, 1986, December 26, 1986, March 25, 1988.
Women's Wear Daily, November 15, 1971, April 4, 1980, March 29, 1985.
World Journal Tribune, December 22, 1966.

—*Sketch by Thomas Wiloch*

*   *   *

SIMON, Sheldon W(eiss)   1937-

PERSONAL: Born January 31, 1937, in St. Paul, Minn.; son of Blair S. and Jennie (Dim) Simon; married Charlann Scheid (a speech therapist), April 23, 1962; children: Alex Russell. *Education:* University of Minnesota, B.A. (summa cum laude), 1958, Ph.D., 1964; Princeton University, M.A., 1960; additional study at Graduate Institute for International Studies, Geneva, Switzerland, 1962-63. *Politics:* Democrat.

ADDRESSES: Home—5630 South Rocky Point, Tempe, Ariz. 85282. *Office*—Center for Asian Studies, Arizona State University, Tempe, Ariz. 85281.

CAREER: University of Minnesota, Minneapolis, assistant director of Center for International Relations, 1961-62; U.S. Government, Washington, D.C., foreign affairs analyst, 1963-66; University of Kentucky, Lexington, assistant professor, 1966-69, associate professor, 1969-74, professor of political science, 1974-75; Arizona State University, Tempe, professor of political science and chairman of department, 1975-79, director of Center for Asian Studies, 1980—. George Washington University, lecturer, 1965-66, research associate of Institute of Sino-Soviet Studies, 1967; visiting professor, University of Hawaii, 1968, University of British Columbia, 1972-73, 1979-80, and Carleton University, 1976. Visiting lecturer in Asia for the United States Information Service, 1973, 1980-82, 1984, 1986. Acting director, Patterson School of Diplomacy, 1970-71; research associate, American Enterprise Institute for Public Policy Research, 1974. Consultant to Agency for International Development, 1966—, Research Analysis Corp., Bendix Research Corp., and Orkand Corp.

MEMBER: International Studies Association, American Political Science Association, Association for Asian Studies, Asia Society, American Association of University Professors, Phi Beta Kappa.

WRITINGS:

The Broken Triangle: Peking, Djakarta, and the PKI, Johns Hopkins Press, 1969.
A Systems Approach to Security in the Indian Ocean Arc, Research Analysis Corp., 1970.
War and Politics in Cambodia, Duke University Press, 1974.
Asian Neutralism and U.S. Policy, American Enterprise Institute for Public Policy Research, 1975.
(Editor and contributor) *The Military and Security in the Third World,* Westview, 1978.
The ASEAN States and Regional Security, Hoover Institution, 1982.
The Future of Asian-Pacific Security Collaboration, Lexington Books, 1988.

CONTRIBUTOR

R. Frost, editor, *Cases in State and Local Government,* Prentice-Hall, 1961.
Zacher and Milne, editors, *Conflict and Stability in Southeast Asia,* Doubleday, 1974.
Zasloff and Brown, editors, *Communism in Indo-China,* Lexington Books, 1975.
Rosenau, Boyd, and Thompson, *World Politics,* Free Press, 1976.
W. Raymond Duncan, editor, *Soviet Policy in the Third World,* Pergamon, 1980.
Kolodjiez and Harkavy, editors, *The Security Policies of Developing States,* Heath, 1982.
Ramon Myers, editor, *Conflict or Peace: An American Foreign Policy for Asia,* Hoover Institution, 1982.
Donald Zagoria, editor, *Soviet Policy in East Asia,* Yale University Press, 1982.
Raju Thomas, editor, *The Great Power Triangle and Asian Security,* Heath, 1983.
T. B. Millar, editor, *Security in Southeast Asia and the Southwest Pacific,* University of Queensland Press, 1983.
James Hsiung, editor, *Beyond China's Independent Foreign Policy,* Praeger, 1985.
Donald Weatherbee, editor, *Southeast Asia Divided: The ASEAN-Indochina Crisis,* Westview, 1985.
Edward Olson and Stephen Junka, Jr., editors, *The Armed Forces in Contemporary Asian Societies,* Westview, 1986.
Russell Trood and William Dowdy, editors, *The Indian Ocean: Perspectives on a Strategic Region,* Duke University Press, 1986.
Stephen Walker, editor, *Role Theory and Foreign Policy Analyses,* Duke University Press, 1987.

OTHER

Contributor to journals of Asian studies.

WORK IN PROGRESS: An assessment of U.S. naval strategy in the Pacific.

AVOCATIONAL INTERESTS: Theater and music as a performer (has about eight years of semiprofessional musical theater experience).

SIMS, Naomi (Ruth) 1949-

PERSONAL: Born March 30, 1949, in Oxford, Miss.; daughter of John and Elizabeth (Parham) Sims; married Michael Alastair Findlay (an art dealer), August 4, 1973; children: John Phillip Sims. *Education:* Attended New York University and Fashion Institute of Technology, 1966-67. *Religion:* Roman Catholic.

ADDRESSES: Naomi Sims Beauty Products Ltd., 435 West 57th St., New York, N.Y. 10019.

CAREER: Ford Modeling Agency, New York City, fashion model, 1967-73; free-lance writer and lecturer, 1970—; Naomi Sims Collection, New York City, founder, owner, and chief executive officer, 1972—; co-developer of new hair fiber for wigs, 1972-73; Naomi Sims Inc., New York City, owner, 1979—. Volunteer teacher of remedial reading in New York City public schools, 1973-75. Member of board of directors, Northside Center for Child Development, Harlem, N.Y., Sickle Cell Anemia Drive, New York State Drug Rehabilitation Program, Play Schools Association of New York. Member, Women's Forum, Inc., 1977.

MEMBER: National Association for the Advancement of Colored People (NAACP).

AWARDS, HONORS: Model of the Year award, International Famous Mannequins, 1969 and 1970; New York City Board of Education award, 1970, for teaching underprivileged children in Bedfor Stuyvesant; Woman of Achievement medal, *Ladies Home Journal,* 1970; awarded the key to the city of Cleveland, 1971; named to the International Best Dressed List, 1971-73, 1976-77; Woman of Achievement award, American Cancer Society, 1972; September 20, 1973, was proclaimed "Naomi Sims Day" by the governor of Illinois; Top Hat Award, *Pittsburgh Courier,* 1974; named to the Modeling Hall of Fame, International Mannequins, 1977; named Woman of the Century, International Mannequins, 1977; named to the *Ebony* Success Library.

WRITINGS:

All about Health and Beauty for the Black Woman, Doubleday, 1976, revised and expanded edition, 1986.
How to Be a Top Model, Doubleday, 1979.
All about Hair Care for the Black Woman, Doubleday, 1982.
All about Success for the Black Woman, Doubleday, 1982.

Contributor of articles on fashion and beauty to popular magazines, including *Redbook, Essence,* and *Encore.* Columnist, *Right On.*

SIDELIGHTS: During the height of the civil rights movement in 1967, Naomi Sims became the first black woman to enter the world of high fashion. She landed on the cover of the *New York Times* fashion section on her first job and went on to become the first black model to appear in a television commercial, the first to land the cover of a major women's magazine (*Ladies Home Journal* in 1969), and the first to be featured in *Vogue.* Nevertheless, at 24 Sims quit the modeling profession to start her own business, manufacturing wigs for black women. In conjunction with an existing firm, Sims researched and developed a new hair fiber for her wigs. The Naomi Sims Collection was launched in 1973, and within four years Sims's company was grossing five million dollars. Sims has since expanded her business to include perfume and other beauty products, and in conjunction has published two books geared especially to the beauty needs of black women. In addition to her work, Sims also lectures and volunteers her time to charitable causes. In 1982 she wrote *All about Success for the Black Woman,* a book of tips for working women; it was a book she wrote because as she traveled and lectured, she encountered many black women who felt dissatisfied. As she remarks in the introduction to her book, "I met hundreds of Black women in a very great variety of jobs. . . . The majority of them were intelligent and hardworking, yet in one way or another they all told me that they were being exploited—overworked, underpaid, and not appreciated."

BIOGRAPHICAL/CRITICAL SOURCES:

BOOKS

Sims, Naomi, *All about Success for the Black Woman,* Doubleday, 1982.

PERIODICALS

Ladies Home Journal, November, 1968.
Life, October 17, 1969.
People, August 22, 1977.†

*   *   *

SINCLAIR, Olga 1923-
(Ellen Clare; Olga Daniels)

PERSONAL: Born January 23, 1923, in Watton, England; daughter of Daniel Robert and Betty (Sapey) Waters; married Stanley George Sinclair (a headmaster), April 1, 1945; children: Michael, Alistair, Jeremy. *Education:* Educated in Norfolk, England. *Religion:* None.

ADDRESSES: Home and office—Dove House Farm, Potter Heigham, Norfolk NR29 5LJ, England.

CAREER: Writer. Justice of the peace in county of Norfolk, England. *Wartime service:* Auxiliary Territorial Service, pay-clerk, 1942-45.

MEMBER: Society of Authors, Society of Women Writers and Journalists, Romantic Novelists Association.

AWARDS, HONORS: Margaret Rhonda Award from Society of Authors, 1972, for research on Lithuanian immigrants.

WRITINGS:

Children's Games (children's nonfiction), Basil Blackwell, 1961.
Gypsies (children's nonfiction), Basil Blackwell, 1967.
Night of the Black Tower, Lancer Books, 1968.
Man of the River, R. Hale, 1968.
Dancing in Britain, Basil Blackwell, 1970.
The Man at the Manor, Dell, 1972.
Bitter Sweet Summer, Simon & Schuster, 1972.
Wild Dreams, R. Hale, 1973.
Toys and Toymaking (children's nonfiction), Basil Blackwell, 1975.
My Dear Fugitive, R. Hale, 1976.
Never Fall in Love, R. Hale, 1977.
Master of Melthorpe, R. Hale, 1979.
Gypsy Girl, Collins, 1981.
Orchids from the Orient, R. Hale, 1986.
When Wherries Sailed By, Poppyland, 1987.

UNDER PSEUDONYM ELLEN CLARE

Ripening Vine Mills, Mills & Boon, 1981.

UNDER PSEUDONYM OLGA DANIELS

Lord of Leet Castle, Mills & Boon, 1984.

The Gretna Bride, Mills & Boon, 1985.
The Bride from Far Away, Mills & Boon, 1987.
The Untamed Bride, Mills & Boon, 1988.

WORK IN PROGRESS: "Still researching the history of runaway marriages at Gretna Green, Scotland. Also working on another children's book."

SIDELIGHTS: Olga Sinclair writes *CA:* "[My] novel *Bitter Sweet Summer* was based on a camping holiday with my family in the summer of 1968, through East Germany to Czechoslovakia, that fateful summer when Czechoslovakia was invaded. Whilst in Prague the sound of machine gun fire in Wenceslas Square made us hasten for the Austrian border.

"[My] continuing interest in the Romany race has resulted in another children's book *Gypsy Girl*. Based on fact, this highlights the problems and pleasures of these fascinating nomadic people.

"I have a continuing urge to write and cannot now imagine being without it. Although I have had a very happy life, my writing still has an element of escapism in it—and I hope it also takes my readers away to a land where dreams can come true. I particularly enjoy writing historical romance. *The Bride from Far Away* was very special to me because I drew on the real-life background of Lithuanian immigrants to Scotland in the early years of this century—using personal reminiscences from my husband's forebears.

"Most of my books have been translated into foreign languages, and I have one recorded on casette. Editors are as unpredictable now as they were when I sent out my first pieces thirty years ago. The main thing I have learned is that rejections need not be final. You have to keep on and on. Writing is a constant challenge."

*   *   *

SKYRMS, Brian   1938-

PERSONAL: Born March 11, 1938, in Pittsburgh, Pa.; married Pauline Jenkins, December 4, 1973. *Education:* Lehigh University, B.A. (economics), 1960, B.A. (philosophy), 1961; University of Pittsburgh, M.A., 1962, Ph.D., 1964.

ADDRESSES: Office—Department of Philosophy, University of California, Irvine, Calif. 92717.

CAREER: San Fernando Valley State College (now California State University, Northridge), Northridge, Calif., assistant professor of philosophy, 1964-65; University of Delaware, Newark, assistant professor of philosophy, 1965-66; University of Michigan, Ann Arbor, visiting assistant professor of philosophy, 1966-67; University of Illinois at Chicago Circle, Chicago, assistant professor, 1967-68, associate professor, 1968-70, professor of philosophy, 1970-80; University of California, Irvine, professor of philosophy, 1980—. Member of visiting faculty at University of California, Santa Barbara, 1971, University of California, Berkeley, 1974, 1975, 1978, 1979, University of North Carolina, 1977, LaTrobe University, 1977, and University of Queensland, summer, 1981.

MEMBER: American Philosophical Association, Association for Symbolic Logic, Philosophy of Science Association, National Audubon Society, American Museum of Natural History, Art Institute of Chicago, Sierra Club, Society for Exact Philosophy, Evanston Art Center.

AWARDS, HONORS: National Science Foundation fellowship, 1968, 1969, 1980, 1984-87; distinguished alumnus award for excellence, 1986; Humanities Council visiting senior fellow and Old Dominion fellow, Princeton University, 1987; Guggenheim fellow, 1987-88.

WRITINGS:

Choice and Chance: An Introduction to Inductive Logic, Dickenson, 1966, 3rd edition, Wadsworth Publishing, 1986.
Causal Necessity: A Pragmatic Investigation of the Necessity of Laws, Yale University Press, 1980.
Pragmatics and Empiricism, Yale University Press, 1984.

CONTRIBUTOR

Davis, Hockney, and Wilson, editors, *Philosophical Logic*, Reidel (Dordrecht, Netherlands), 1968.
Michael D. Roth and Leon Galis, editors, *Knowing: Essays in the Analysis of Knowledge*, Random House, 1970.
R. Martin, editor, *The Liar*, Yale University Press, 1971.
Feigl, Sellars, and Lehrer, editors, *Readings in Philosophical Analysis*, Appleton-Century-Crofts, 1972.
Maxwell and Anderson, editors, *Minnesota Studies in the Philosophy of Science*, Volume 6, University of Minnesota Press, 1975.
Harper and others, editors, *IFs*, Reidel, 1980.
D. H. Mellor, editor, *Prospects for Pragmatism: Essays in Honor of F. P. Ramsey*, Cambridge University Press, 1980.
R. Cohen and others, editors, *Philosophy, Physics and Psychoanalysis*, Reidel, 1983.
John Earman, editor, *Testing Scientific Theories*, University of Minnesota Press, 1983.
Martin, editor, *Recent Essays on Truth and the Liar*, Oxford University Press, 1984.
H. Wettstein, editor, *Causation and Causal Theories*, University of Minnesota Press, 1984.
N. Rescher, editor, *The Heritage of Logical Positivism*, University Press of America, 1985.
P. Lakki and P. Mittlestadt, editors, *Symposium on the Foundations of Modern Physics: Fifty Years of the EPR Gadanken Experiment*, World Scientific Publishing (Singapore), 1986.
Rescher, editor, *Scientific Inquiry in Philosophical Perspective*, University of Pittsburgh Press, 1987.
I. B. MacNeill and G. Umphrey, editors, *Advances in the Statistical Sciences*, Volume 2: *Foundations of Statistical Inference*, Reidel, 1987.

OTHER

Contributor of articles and reviews to philosophy journals, including *Philosophy of Science*, *Journal of Philosophy*, *American Philosophical Quarterly*, and *Australasian Journal of Philosophy*. Member of editorial board, *Australasian Journal of Philosophy*, and *Philosophy of Science*.

WORK IN PROGRESS: Editor, with Harper, of *Probability and Causation*.

*   *   *

SMITH, Ruth Schluchter   1917-

PERSONAL: Born October 18, 1917, in Detroit, Mich.; daughter of Clayton John and Gertrude (Kastler) Schluchter; married Thomas Guilford Smith (a manufacturers' representative and engineer), September 28, 1946; children: Pemberton III. *Education:* Wayne University (now Wayne State University), A.B., 1939; University of Michigan, A.B. in L.S., 1942. *Politics:* Republican. *Religion:* Methodist.

ADDRESSES: Home—5304 Glenwood Rd., Bethesda, Md. 20014. *Office*—National Technical Information Service, 5285 Port Royal Rd., Springfield, Va. 22161.

CAREER: Detroit Public Library, Detroit, Mich., junior librarian, 1936-43; University of Pennsylvania, Moore School of Electrical Engineering, Philadelphia, research assistant, 1946-47; Bethesda Methodist Church Library, Bethesda, Md., librarian, 1955-61; Institute for Defense Analyses, Arlington, Va., reference librarian and chief of reader services, 1961-65, chief of unclassified library section, 1965-67, head librarian, 1967-75, manager of technical information services, 1975-81; National Technical Information Service, Springfield, Va., chief of office of customer services, 1981-88, director of liaison programs, 1988—. *Military service:* U.S. Naval Reserve, Women Accepted for Volunteer Emergency Service (WAVES), 1943-46; became lieutenant, junior grade.

MEMBER: Church and Synagogue Library Association (founding member and president, 1967-68; member of executive board, 1967-77), Special Libraries Association (chairman of aerospace division, 1975-76, library management division, 1978-79, and division cabinet, 1980-81; member of board of directors, 1981-83), American Society for Information Science.

AWARDS, HONORS: John Cotton Dana Award, Special Library Association, 1979, fellow, 1987, Hall of Fame, 1988.

WRITINGS:

Outline for Building Vitality in Your Church Library, Church Library Council, 1961.
(With Robert Collins) *Lasers* (bibliography), Institute for Defense Analyses, 1963.
(With Jay Schwartz, J. Kaiser, and Joseph Aein) *Multiple Access to a Common Radio Repeater* (bibliography), Institute for Defense Analyses, 1964.
Publicity for a Church Library, Zondervan, 1966.
(Contributor) Allen Kent and Harold Lancour, editors, *Encyclopedia of Library and Information Science*, Volume IV, Dekker, 1970.
Workshop Planning, Church and Synagogue Library Association, 1972.
Getting the Books off the Shelves, Hawthorn, 1975, revised edition published as *Getting the Books Off the Shelves: Making the Most of Your Congregation's Library*, Church and Synagogue Library Association, 1985.
(With Claudia Hannaford) *Promotion Planning*, Church and Synagogue Library Association, 1975.
Cataloging Books Step-by-Step, Church and Synagogue Library Association, 1977.
Cataloging Made Easy, Seabury, 1978, revised edition published as *Cataloguing Made Easy: How to Organize Your Congregation's Library*, Church and Synagogue Library Association, 1987.
Running a Library, Seabury, 1982.
Setting Up a Library: How to Begin or Begin Again, Church and Synagogue Library Association, 1987.

Author of scripts for video presentations. Contributor to *Special Libraries, Library Journal, New Christian Advocate*, and other periodicals.

SIDELIGHTS: Ruth Schluchter Smith told *CA:* "A lifelong enthusiasm for libraries, seasoned by an early interest in journalism, just naturally gave birth to writing—most of it interpretive reporting based on experience in the library field. As an administrator of a scientific research library, I have dealt with the problems of coping with federal government information sources and services, organizing user feedback groups, and participating in cooperative library networks. As the chairman of a church library committee and formerly a church librarian, I have described the challenges of organizing and administering a church library ministry, promoting and publicizing its services, and inspiring or training volunteer workers through workshops and interfaith library fellowship activities."

*   *   *

SMYTH, Alice M.
   See HADFIELD, Alice M(ary)

*   *   *

SOUTHAM, B(rian) C(harles)   1931-

PERSONAL: Born September 15, 1931, in London, England. *Education:* Lincoln College, Oxford, B.A., 1956, M.A., 1960, B.Litt., 1961.

ADDRESSES: Office—Athlone Press, 44 Bedford Row, London WC1, England.

CAREER: University of London, Westfield College, London, England, lecturer in English literature, 1961-63; Routledge & Kegan Paul Ltd. (publishers), London, editorial director, 1963-75; Concord Books, London, managing director, 1977-79; Athlone Press, London, managing director, 1979—.

WRITINGS:

Jane Austen's Literary Manuscripts: A Study of the Novelist's Development through the Surviving Papers, Oxford University Press, 1964.
A Student's Guide to the Selected Poems of T. S. Eliot, Faber, 1968, published as *A Guide to the Selected Poems of T. S. Eliot*, Harcourt, 1969, revised edition published as *A Student's Guide to the Selected Poems of T. S. Eliot*, Faber, 1974, 4th edition, 1981.
(Contributor) G. Watson, editor, *The New Cambridge Bibliography of English Literature*, Volume III: *1800-1900*, Cambridge University Press, 1969.
Tennyson, Longman, 1971.
(Contributor) A. E. Dyson, *The English Novel: Selected Bibliographic Guides*, Oxford University Press, 1974.
Jane Austen, edited by Ian Scott-Kilvert, Longman, 1975.
(Contributor) Juliet McMaster, editor, *Jane Austen's Achievement*, Macmillan (London), 1976, Harper, 1977.

EDITOR

Jane Austen, *Volume the Second*, Clarendon Press, 1963.
(And author of introduction and notes) Alfred Tennyson, *Selected Poems*, Chatto & Windus, 1964.
Critical Essays on Jane Austen, Routledge & Kegan Paul, 1968, Barnes & Noble, 1969.
Austen, *Minor Works*, revised edition, Oxford University Press, 1969.
(And author of introduction) Austen, *Sanditon: An Unfinished Novel*, Clarendon Press, 1975.
Minor Works of Jane Austen, revised edition, Oxford University Press, 1975.
(And contributor) *Jane Austen: "Northanger Abbey" and "Persuasion"* (casebook), Macmillan (London), 1976, State Mutual Book, 1981.
Jane Austen: "Sense and Sensibility," "Pride and Prejudice," and "Mansfield Park" (casebook), Macmillan (London), 1976, State Mutual Book, 1981.

T. S. Eliot: "Prufrock," "Gerontion," "Ash Wednesday" and Other Shorter Poems (casebook), Macmillan (London), 1978, State Mutual Book, 1981.
(Transcriber and author of introduction) *Jane Austen's "Sir Charles Grandison"* (play), foreword by David Cecil, Oxford University Press, 1981.
(With J. David Grey and A. Walton Litz; and contributor) *The Jane Austen Companion*, Scribner, 1986.

EDITOR; "CRITICAL HERITAGE" SERIES

Jane Austen: The Critical Heritage 1812-1870, Routledge & Kegan Paul, 1968, revised edition, 1987.
. . . *1870-1940*, Routledge & Kegan Paul, 1987.

OTHER

Also general editor of "Routledge Critics" and "Social History of the English Novel" series. Contributor of entry on Jane Austen to *Encyclopaedia Britannica*, 15th edition, 1974. Contributor of articles and reviews to periodicals, including *Essays in Criticism, Nineteenth-Century Fiction, Library, Notes and Queries, Times Literary Supplement, Ariel, Twentieth-Century Literature, Explicator, Shakespeare Quarterly, Keats-Shelley Journal, Southern Review, Review of English Studies,* and *Year's Work in English Studies.*

WORK IN PROGRESS: The Culture and Civilization of Jane Austen's World: A Study of the Novel, the Novelist, and Society; Julia Margaret Cameron, Tennyson and G. F. Watts.

BIOGRAPHICAL/CRITICAL SOURCES:

PERIODICALS

New York Times, August 2, 1986.
Times Literary Supplement, April 3, 1981, November 6-12, 1987.

*   *   *

SOWELL, Thomas 1930-

PERSONAL: Born June 30, 1930, in Gastonia, N.C.; married Alma Jean Parr; children: two. *Education:* Harvard University, A.B. (magna cum laude), 1958; Columbia University, A.M., 1959; University of Chicago, Ph.D., 1968.

ADDRESSES: Office—Hoover Institution, Stanford, Calif. 94305.

CAREER: U.S. Department of Labor, Washington, D.C., economist, 1961-62; Rutgers University, Douglass College, New Brunswick, N.J., instructor in economics, 1962-63; Howard University, Washington, D.C., lecturer in economics, 1963-64; American Telephone & Telegraph Co., New York, N.Y., economic analyst, 1964-65; Cornell University, Ithaca, N.Y., assistant professor of economics, 1965-69; director of Summer Intensive Training Program in Economic Theory, 1968; Brandeis University, Waltham, Mass., associate professor of economics, 1969-70; University of California, Los Angeles, associate professor, 1970-74, professor of economics, 1974-80; Urban Institute, Washington, D.C., project director, 1972-74; Center for Advanced Study in the Behavioral Sciences, Stanford, Calif., fellow, 1976-77; Hoover Institution, Stanford, senior fellow, 1977, 1980—. Visiting professor, Amherst College, 1977. *Military service:* U.S. Marine Corps, 1951-53.

WRITINGS:

(Contributor) I. H. Rima, editor, *Readings in the History of Economic Thought*, Holt, 1970.

Economics: Analysis and Issues, Scott, Foresman, 1971.
Black Education: Myths and Tragedies, McKay, 1972.
Say's Law: An Historical Analysis, Princeton University Press, 1972.
Classical Economics Reconsidered, Princeton University Press, 1974.
Affirmative Action: Was It Necessary in Academia?, American Enterprise Institute for Public Policy Research, 1975.
Race and Economics, McKay, 1975.
Patterns of Black Excellence, Ethics and Public Policy Center, Georgetown University, 1977.
(Editor) *American Ethnic Groups*, Urban Institute, 1978.
(Editor) *Essays and Data on American Ethnic Groups*, Urban Institute, 1978.
Markets and Minorities, Basic Books, 1981.
(Editor with others) *The Fairmont Papers: Black Alternatives Conference, December, 1980*, ICS Press, 1981.
Pink and Brown People, and Other Controversial Essays, Hoover Institution, 1981.
(Contributor) W. E. Block and M. A. Walker, editors, *Discrimination, Affirmative Action and Equal Opportunity: An Economic and Social Perspective*, Fraser Institute, 1982.
Knowledge and Decision, Basic Books, 1982.
Ethnic America: A History, Basic Books, 1983.
The Economics and Politics of Race: An International Perspective, Morrow, 1983.
Marxism: Philosophy and Economics, Morrow, 1985.
Civil Rights: Rhetoric or Reality?, Morrow, 1985.
Education: Assumptions versus History, Hoover Institution, 1986.
Compassion versus Guilt, and Other Essays, Morrow, 1987.
A Conflict of Visions: Ideological Origins of Political Struggles, Morrow, 1987.

Contributor to numerous periodicals, including *New York Times Magazine, Ethics, American Economic Review, Social Research, Education Digest, Western Review, University of Chicago Magazine, Oxford Economic Papers,* and *Economica.*

SIDELIGHTS: Called "a free-market economist and perhaps the leading black scholar among conservatives" by Fred Barnes of the *New York Times Book Review*, Thomas Sowell has written a score of controversial books about economics, race, and ethnic groups. His support for a laissez-faire economic system with few government constraints and his vocal opposition to most of the social programs and judicial actions favored by most other black spokesmen have made him a target for much criticism. Yet, Steven E. Plaut of *Commentary* calls Sowell "one of America's most trenchant and perceptive commentators on the subject of race relations and ethnicity." Davis Holmstrom, writing in the *Los Angeles Times*, maintains that "in the writing of economist Thomas Sowell, scholarship, clarity and genuine information come together as nicely and perfectly as a timeless quote."

Sowell has done extensive research into the economic performance of racial and ethnic groups throughout the world, trying to determine the factors which make some groups more successful than others. He has presented his research findings and the conclusions he has drawn from it in such books as *Race and Economics, American Ethnic Groups, Markets and Minorities, Ethnic America: A History, The Economics and Politics of Race: An International Perspective,* and *Civil Rights: Rhetoric or Reality?* These books have disproven a number of popularly held beliefs while bringing new and potentially valuable information to light. As George M. Fredrickson notes in the *New York Times Book Review*, "Sowell is engaged in a continuing polemic against the basic assumptions of liberals, radicals and civil rights leaders. But the quality of his evidence and reasoning requires that he be taken seriously. His ideological opponents will have to meet his arguments squarely and incisively to justify the kind of policies currently identified with the pursuit of racial equality and social justice.''

One of Sowell's most controversial contentions is that a racial or ethnic group's economic success is not seriously hindered by discrimination from society at large. In *The Economics and Politics of Race,* for instance, he gives several examples of minority groups who have fared well despite prejudice against them, and of other groups with little discrimination to overcome who have done poorly. The Chinese minorities in Southeast Asian countries, despite intense resistance from the native populations, have done very well economically. They often dominate their local economies. European Jews have also faced opposition from majority population groups. Yet they too have performed outstandingly well and enjoy a high level of economic success. On the other hand, Plaut gives an example of underachievement from Sowell's *The Economics and Politics of Race:* ''In Brazil and other parts of South America blacks face less racism than do American blacks. . . . Yet for all this tolerance, Brazil shows a larger gap in black-white earnings, social position, and education than does the United States.''

The key factor in an ethnic group's economic success, Sowell argues, is ''something economists refer to as human capital—values, attitudes and skills embodied in a culture,'' as Stanley O. Williford explains it in the *Los Angeles Times Book Review.* An ethnic or racial group which emphasizes hard work, saving money, and acquiring an education will generally do well whatever the political or social climate. *Newsweek*'s David Gelman notes that Sowell ''has a conservative message to impart. Essentially, it is that diligence, discipline and entrepreneurial drive can overthrow the most formidable barriers of poverty and bigotry.''

Because of this belief, Sowell argues against continued efforts by the federal government to end racial discrimination, a problem he believes was largely eliminated during the civil rights struggle, and calls instead for a greater emphasis on free market economics. A healthy, growing economy, Sowell believes, does the most good for minority groups who suffer from poverty. As Aaron Wildavsky writes in the *National Review,* ''When labor is scarce and the markets for it are competitive, wages go up regardless of the prejudices of employers.'' Sowell points out in *Civil Rights: Rhetoric or Reality?* that ''the economic rise of minorities preceded by many years passage of the Civil Rights Act . . . [and] that this trend was not accelerated either by that legislation or by the quotas introduced during the seventies,'' as Tony Eastland reports in the *American Spectator.* Sowell believes that minority groups, Chris Wall writes in the *Los Angeles Times Book Review,* are ''crying racism at every turn to divert attention from the fact that their cultures or subcultures may be economically unproductive.''

Sowell dismisses much of what black civil rights leaders believe necessary for the betterment of American blacks. He questions, for example, the value for black students of integrated public schools, called for by the Warren Court in the case Brown vs. Board of Education. Joseph Sobran of *National Review* reports that Sowell finds that the court's contention ''that segregated schools produced inferior black education . . . expresses and justifies a destructively paternalistic attitude, according to which a black child can't learn anything except in close proximity to a white one. With forced busing,

[Sowell] reflects ironically, the white man's burden has become 'the white *child's* burden—to go forth and civilize the heathen.' ''

Other government programs, including affirmative action racial quotas and public welfare, are also attacked by Sowell. Sowell is convinced, Nathan Glazer writes in the *New Republic,* ''that hardly anything government will do can help blacks and other minorities with high levels of poverty and low levels of educational and economic achievement, and that almost anything government will do will only make matters worse.'' In a *Choice* review of *Civil Rights,* R. J. Steamer admits that ''Sowell's revolutionary view—that government programs such as affirmative action, forced busing, and food stamps will not bring the disadvantaged black minority into the economic and social mainstream and might better be abandoned—will anger many.'' One such angered critic is Gelman, who claims that Sowell ''seems to fault blacks for resting on their grievances instead of climbing aboard the success wagon.'' But Sowell sees government programs and those who call for them as part of a self-destructive mind-set. The black civil rights establishment, Sowell believes, ''represents a thin layer of privileged blacks who have risen socially by echoing liberal ideology, with its view of blacks in general as helpless victims who depend on political favors for whatever gains they can make,'' Sobran explains.

Sowell's own life story seems to illustrate many of the values he now expounds. Born in North Carolina, Sowell attended a segregated high school where he was at the top of his class. ''We never wondered why there weren't any white kids there,'' he tells Sobran. ''We never thought we'd be learning more if there *had* been white kids there. In fact, we never *thought* about white kids.'' A graduate of Harvard University, Columbia University, and the University of Chicago, Sowell went on to hold a number of positions in government and academia before joining the Hoover Institution in 1980. Through it all, Sobran remarks, Sowell has been ''matter-of-fact about his race and its bearing on his intellectual life.''

The consistent differences between Sowell's views and those of other black commentators, and the differences between those of the political left and right, moved Sowell to examine the underlying assumptions that create this dichotomy. In *A Conflict of Visions: Ideological Origins of Political Struggle,* he describes ''two divergent views of man and society that he convincingly contends underlie many of the political, economic and social clashes of the last two centuries and remain very much with us today,'' as Walter Goodman of the *New York Times* explains. Sowell posits the unconstrained and the constrained views of man. ''The unconstrained see human beings as perfectible,'' Otto Friedrich of *Time* writes, ''the constrained as forever flawed.'' Sowell writes in the book that ''the constrained vision is a tragic vision of the human condition. The unconstrained vision is a moral vision of human intentions.''

These two visions are, Daniel Seligman writes in *Fortune,* ''the mind-sets that originally made [intellectuals] gravitate to some ideas instead of others.'' Those with an unconstrained view of man, for example, tend to believe that social problems can be ultimately solved, and that man will usually act rationally. Such beliefs can lead to social engineering efforts to correct perceived societal ills. Those with a constrained view of man see him as imperfect and human nature as unchanging. They often call for a limited government, a strong defense, and strict criminal penalties.

Sowell admits that not all people hold to one or the other vision consistently. And such ideologies as Marxism and fascism are compounds of both the constrained and unconstrained visions. Yet, critics see much of value in Sowell's plan. "Right or wrong in his main thesis," Sobran states, "he is full of stunning insights." "The split between the constrained and the unconstrained," Barnes notes, "works as a framework for understanding social theories and politics." Goodman finds that *A Conflict of Visions* "does lay out styles of thinking that we can readily recognize today in the divisions between left and right." And Michael Harrington, who explains in his *Washington Post Book World* review that "I reject the basic assumptions and the very inellectual framework" of the book, nonetheless concludes that "its insights and *apercus* reveal a serious mind honestly and fairly . . . trying to grapple with those visionary premises on which our supposedly objective data are so often based and ordered."

During his career as a leading black economist, Sowell "has spoken out often, with considerable force and eloquence, against many of the assumptions about black life in the United States that are widely held by the black leadership and its white allies," Jonathan Yardley reports in the *Washington Post Book World*. His arguments are beginning to attract converts in the black community. As Glazer notes, "One has the impression that increasingly he is heeded, that this unbending analyst is having a greater influence on the discussion of matters of race and ethnicity than any other writer of the past ten years." Harrington, a socialist who admits that he is "utterly at odds" with Sowell's political beliefs, still calls him "one of the few conservative thinkers in America today who is interesting as a theorist."

BIOGRAPHICAL/CRITICAL SOURCES:

BOOKS

Sowell, Thomas, *Civil Rights: Rhetoric or Reality?*, Morrow, 1985.
Sowell, Thomas, *A Conflict of Visions: Ideological Origins of Political Struggles*, Morrow, 1987.

PERIODICALS

American Spectator, July, 1984.
Choice, September, 1984.
Commentary, December, 1983.
Fortune, March 16, 1987.
Los Angeles Times, March 22, 1985.
Los Angeles Times Book Review, September 6, 1981, January 8, 1984.
National Review, October 16, 1981, February 13, 1987.
New Republic, November 21, 1983, June 11, 1984.
Newsweek, August 24, 1981.
New York Times, January 24, 1987.
New York Times Book Review, October 16, 1983, January 25, 1987.
Time, March 16, 1987.
Washington Post Book World, April 29, 1984, January 4, 1987.

—*Sketch by Thomas Wiloch*

*   *   *

SPALDING, Frances 1950-

PERSONAL: Born July 16, 1950, in Surrey, England; daughter of Hedley Stinston (an aeronautical engineer) and Margaret (Holiday) Crabtree; married Julian Spalding (an art gallery director), April 20, 1974. *Education:* University of Nottingham, B.A. (with first class honors), 1972, Ph.D., 1978.

ADDRESSES: Home and office—74 Ashland Rd., Sheffield S7 1RJ, England.

CAREER: Sheffield City Polytechnic, Sheffield, England, part-time lecturer in art history, 1978—. Guest lecturer at University of San Francisco, summer, 1977.

MEMBER: PEN, Royal Society of Literature (fellow), Society of Authors.

WRITINGS:

Magnificent Dreams: Burne-Jones and the Late Victorians, Phaidon, 1978.
Whistler, Phaidon, 1979.
Roger Fry: Art and Life, University of California Press, 1980.
Vanessa Bell, Tickner & Fields, 1984.
British Art since 1900, Thames & Hudson, 1986.

Contributor to art journals and to periodicals, including *Times Literary Supplement*.

WORK IN PROGRESS: Stevie Smith: A Biography.

SIDELIGHTS: In *Vanessa Bell*, art historian Frances Spalding presents the first biography of this British painter, who was also the older sister of Virginia Woolf. According to *New York Times Book Review* critic Samuel Hynes, "Insofar as [Bell] is known at all, it is as a supporting character in other people's lives, and especially in the drama of Virginia Woolf's life and death. . . . So it is good to have . . . Spalding's careful and comprehensive biography that takes [Bell's] art seriously and keeps Virginia Woolf in the background. . . . If it is only partly a painter's life, that is because the painter was a woman: It is therefore also a mother's life, a housekeeper's life, a wife's and a lover's life."

In general, reviewers find *Vanessa Bell* an interesting, sensitive, responsible, and serious work. Richard Shone explains in the *Spectator* that "Bell's total dedication to painting still stands as a monolithic example when seen in the light of her life's vicissitudes. If this alone emerges for the reader as the central statement of . . . Spalding's ruminative and thought-provoking book, her subject might be pleased and pacified." However, Shone later questions what he calls Spalding's "psychological reading" of Bell's paintings and points to what he sees as the biography's major flaw—Spalding's portrayal of the homosexual man in Bell's life, painter Duncan Grant. As Shone maintains, Spalding "tries hard to be understanding, to be swayed, as almost everyone was, by [Grant's] charm. But the result is cardboard. . . . Spalding misses the finer shades of Grant's emotional, as opposed to purely sexual, needs." As for Walter Kendrick in the *Partisan Review*, he claims that Spalding "has too little perspective on her subject, too little awareness of the social and professional contexts in which, despite her retiring habits, Vanessa moved. Paragraph after paragraph of *Vanessa Bell* looks like cut-and-pasted snippets of letters translated into indirect discourse. . . . The minutiae of anyone's life can be interesting, in a mindless sort of way; but when that life is proclaimed significant, even a model, one expects details to be planned according to their value, not just rattled off as if all were equal. It is by no means self-evident that we should take heed of Vanessa Bell, and Spalding is unpersuasive." In contrast, although London *Times* reviewer Fiona MacCarthy believes "no one will agree with all interpretations of all the minor characters, or even the major ones . . .

the central portrait of Vanessa Bell is full and generous and it rings wonderfully true.''

Spalding wrote to *CA:* "Like most biographers, I realized as a child that there was more going on in books than in the world around me. I admired the achievement of Michael Holroyd and was given a boost of self-confidence by an invitation to lecture on Robert Fry at the University of San Francisco. My touchstone is Rainer Maria Kilke's 'Letters to a Young Poet.' Biography is a combination of diligence, diplomacy and luck. It's something one keeps in one's pocket and tinkers with obsessively. Working on Stevie Smith, I've come to share her admiration for biographies that are creative, compassionate and comical.''

BIOGRAPHICAL/CRITICAL SOURCES:

PERIODICALS

American Scholar, winter, 1980-81.
Burlington, July, 1980.
Globe and Mail (Toronto), February 25, 1984.
Los Angeles Times, November 13, 1980, October 20, 1983.
Ms., December, 1983.
Nation, November 19, 1983.
Newsweek, October 24, 1983.
New York Review of Books, December 22, 1983.
New York Times Book Review, October 5, 1980, October 23, 1983.
Partisan Review, fall, 1985.
Spectator, August 27, 1983, May 17, 1986.
Times (London), May 28, 1980, September 1, 1983.
Times Literary Supplement, March 21, 1980, February 6, 1987.

* * *

SPARSHOTT, F. E.
   See SPARSHOTT, Francis (Edward)

* * *

SPARSHOTT, Francis (Edward)   1926-
   (F. E. Sparshott; Cromwell Kent, a pseudonym)

PERSONAL: Born May 19, 1926, in Chatham, England; son of Frank Brownley (a teacher) and Gladwys Winifred (Head) Sparshott; married Kathleen Elizabeth Vaughan, February 7, 1953; children: Pumpkin Margaret Elizabeth. *Education:* Corpus Christi College, Oxford, B.A. and M.A., with first-class honors, 1950.

ADDRESSES: Home—50 Crescentwood Rd., Scarborough, Ontario, Canada M1N 1E4. *Office*—Department of Philosophy, Victoria College, University of Toronto, 73 Queen's Park Crescent E., Toronto, Ontario, Canada M5S 1K7.

CAREER: University of Toronto, Toronto, Ontario, lecturer in philosophy, 1950-55, Victoria College, assistant professor, 1955-62, associate professor, 1962-64, professor of philosophy, 1964—, chairman of department, 1965-70, university professor, 1982—. Visiting associate professor, Northwestern University, 1958-59; visiting professor, University of Illinois, 1966. *Military service:* British Army, 1944-47; served in Palestine, became sergeant.

MEMBER: American Philosophical Association, American Society for Aesthetics (trustee, 1971-73, 1976-78, president, 1981-82), Aristotelian Society, Canadian Classical Association, Canadian Philosophical Association (president, 1975-76),

League of Canadian Poets (president, 1977-78), Royal Society of Canada (fellow, 1977).

AWARDS, HONORS: American Council of Learned Societies fellowship, 1961-62; Canada Council fellowship, 1970-71; Killam research fellowship, 1977-78; first prize for poetry, CBC Radio Literary Competition, 1981; Centennial Medal, Royal Society of Canada, 1982; Connaught senior fellowship in the humanities, 1984-85.

WRITINGS:

(Under name F. E. Sparshott) *An Enquiry into Goodness and Related Concepts,* University of Toronto Press, 1958.
The Structure of Aesthetics, University of Toronto Press, 1963.
(Under name F. E. Sparshott) *The Concept of Criticism: An Essay,* Oxford University Press, 1967.
(Under pseudonym Cromwell Kent) *A Book,* privately printed, 1970.
(Under name F. E. Sparshott) *Looking for Philosophy,* McGill Queens University Press, 1972.
(Author of introduction) John Stuart Mill, *Collected Works,* Volume XI: *Essays in Philosophy and the Classics,* University of Toronto Press, 1978.
The Theory of the Arts, three volumes, Princeton University Press, 1982.
Off the Ground, Princeton University Press, 1988.

POETRY

A Divided Voice, Oxford University Press, 1965.
A Cardboard Garage, Clarke, Irwin, 1969.
(Contributor) John Robert Columbo, editor, *How Do I Love Thee: Sixty Poets of Canada Select and Introduce Their Favourite Poems from Their Own Work,* Hurtig, 1970.
The Rainy Hills: Verses after a Japanese Fashion, privately printed by Porcupine's Quill, 1979.
The Naming of the Beasts, Black Moss, 1979.
New Fingers for Old Dikes, League of Canadian Poets, 1980.
The Cave of Trophonius and Other Poems, Brick Books, 1983.
The Hanging Gardens of Etobicoke, Childe Thursday, 1983.
Storms and Screens, Childe Thursday, 1986.

CONTRIBUTOR

Paul Hernadi, editor, *What Is Literature?,* Indiana University Press, 1978.
Stanley G. French, editor, *Philosophers Look at Canadian Confederation,* Canadian Philosophical Association, 1979.
New Grove Dictionary of Music and Musicians, Macmillan, 1980.
Hernadi, editor, *What Is Criticism?,* Indiana University Press, 1981.
Denis Dutton and Michael Krausz, editors, *The Concept of Creativity in Science and Art,* Nijhoff, 1981.
Eleanor Cook and Julian Patrick, editors, *Centre and Labyrinth: Essays in Honour of Northrop Frye,* University of Toronto Press, 1983.

OTHER

Contributor of essays to periodicals, including *Ethics, Journal of Aesthetic Education,* and *Philosophy and Literature;* contributor of poetry to periodicals, including *Poetry, Nation, Canadian Forum, Literary Review, Fiddlehead,* and *West Coast Review.*

WORK IN PROGRESS: Finality, a study of Aristotelian ethics.

SIDELIGHTS: ''Philosopher, critical theorist, and poet, Francis Edward Sparshott has written on a wide range of moral, aesthetic, and intellectual issues," says Wendy Robbins Keitner in a *Dictionary of Literary Biography* essay. Sparshott's reputation as a philosopher and critical theorist is confirmed by "his series of enquiries into aesthetics, *The Theory of the Arts . . .* a massive, 726-page survey," says Keitner, who believes that his versatility as a poet is beginning to be recognized as well. Describing Sparshott's verse as "traditional and impersonal," Keitner adds that "critics have commented on Sparshott's cerebral poetic style, and his subjects, too, suggest the academic and the thinker: the nature of reality, memory, perception, change, and unmerited pain."

"I've always thought of myself as primarily a poet, secondarily a writer of miscellaneous prose, and a teacher by necessity," Sparshott once told *CA.* "Unfortunately my poetry is not as good as my prose, and my miscellaneous prose tends to be esoteric and hence uneconomic, so that I seem to be turned into a purveyor of academic philosophy. But I fight on."

The E. J. Pratt Library at the Victoria College of the University of Toronto houses a collection of Sparshott's manuscripts.

BIOGRAPHICAL/CRITICAL SOURCES:

BOOKS

Dictionary of Literary Biography, Volume 60: *Canadian Writers since 1960; Second Series,* Gale, 1987.
Heath, Jeffrey M., editor, *Profiles in Canadian Literature,* Dundurn Press, 1986.

PERIODICALS

Canadian Forum, July, 1969.

*   *   *

SPERBER, Philip   1944-

PERSONAL: Born February 29, 1944, in New York, N.Y.; son of Sol and Sally (Dolsky) Sperber; married Doreen Strachman, December 27, 1969; children: Shoshana, Ryan, Sara. *Education:* New Jersey Institute of Technology, B.S.E.E., 1965; University of Maryland, J.D., 1969.

ADDRESSES: Home—30 Normandy Heights Rd., Convent Station, N.J. 07961. *Office*—REFAC International Ltd., 122 East 42nd St., New York, N.Y. 10168.

CAREER: Blair, Olcutt & Sperber, Washington, D.C., partner, 1968-71; Cavitron Corp., New York City, division counsel, 1971-72, manager of legal department, 1972-74, vice-president, 1974-77; International Telephone & Telegraph Corp. (ITT), Harmon Cove, N.J., group executive, 1977-79; REFAC International Ltd., New York City, general manager, 1979-81, vice-president, 1981-82, president, 1982—. Lecturer at universities. Member, New Jersey Inventors Congress and Hall of Fame (chairman of board of trustees, 1987—), New Jersey Literary Hall of Fame (chairman of board of trustees, 1986—), and New Jersey Institute of Technology Alumni Association (chairman of alumni council, 1986—).

MEMBER: International Executives Association, International Platform Association, Licensing Executives Society (trustee, 1977-79), Ultrasonic Industry Association (vice-president, 1975-77), American Institute of Chemical Engineers, Sales Executives Club, American Bar Association (chairman of corporation, banking, and business committee, 1976-78), Institute of Electrical and Electronics Engineers (senior member), American Society for Testing and Materials (section chairman, 1976-

66), National Council of Patent Law Associations (councilman, 1985-87), Association for the Advancement of Medical Instrumentation (standards industry co-chairman, 1976-77), New Jersey State Bar Association (councilman, 1976-79), New York State Bar Association (legislation committee chairman, 1975-76), New Jersey Patent Law Association (president), New Jersey Jaycees (director, 1965-66), Maryland Lions International (director, 1970-71), National Engineering Honor Society.

AWARDS, HONORS: Award from U.S. Jaycees, 1966, for service as outstanding U.S. Jaycee; certificate from American Law Institute, 1976, for contributions to legal education; citation from American Marketing Association, 1977, for contributions to marketing education; award from American Arbitration Association, 1977, for service as a judge; certificate from Graduate School of Business Administration at Rutgers University, 1977, for contributions as an educator; award from American Management Associations, 1978, for contributions to management education; award from New Jersey Institute of Technology, 1981, for contributions to industry and to society in general; named Estrin Alumni Scholar by New Jersey Institute of Technology, 1981, for achievements in journalism; Eminent Engineer Award from Tau Beta Pi, 1986; citations from New Jersey Writers Conference, 1986, for *A Negotiator's Views on How to Avoid Nuclear War* and six prior books; dubbed a Knight of Malta, order of St. John of Jerusalem (1040), 1986.

WRITINGS:

Intellectual Property Management: Law-Business-Strategy, two volumes, Boardman, 1974, third edition, 1982.
(Associate editor) Joseph L. Tramutola, editor, *Patent Manual,* Fairleigh Dickinson University Press, 1974.
(Contributor) Jack Stuart Ott, editor, *Les Nouvelles* (title means "The Innovations"), Licensing Executives Society, 1976.
Negotiating in Day-to-Day Business, American Negotiating Institute, 1976.
(Contributor) J. C. Ross and Kenneth Ross, editors, *Products Liability of Manufacturers: Prevention and Defense,* Practicing Law Institute, 1977.
(Editor) *The Consumer Clearinghouse,* PDS Industries, 1977.
(Contributor) Robert Goldscheider, *Licensing in Foreign and Domestic Operations,* Boardman, 1978.
The Science of Business Negotiation, Pilot Books, 1979.
(Editor and contributor) *Corporation Law Department Manual,* American Bar Association, 1980.
(Contributor) Paul D. Rheingold, editor, *Drug Litigation,* Practicing Law Institute, 1981.
Fail-Safe Business Negotiating: Strategies and Tactics for Success, Prentice-Hall, 1983.
Closing the Deal, Negotiating Group, 1985.
The Attorney's Practice Guide to Negotiations, Callaghan, 1985.
International Transactions, Negotiating Group, 1986.
A Negotiator's Views on How to Avoid Nuclear War, Hillside, 1986.

Also author of *Counseling Your Medical Device Client: Law, Business, Strategy,* 1981. Also contributor to *Ultrasonic Proceedings,* Institute of Electric and Electronics Engineers, 1976.

Editor in chief of *Jaycee News,* 1965-66, *Lion's Den,* 1970-71, *ABA Legislative News,* 1976-77, *FDCL News,* 1979-80, and *NJPLA News,* 1979-80; associate editor, *Vector,* 1964-65, *Justinian,* 1966, and *Advocate,* 1969.

SIDELIGHTS: Philip Sperber told *CA:* "The common thread linking the one hundred published papers and books I have written (covering the fields of law, business, technology, medicine, government, and consumerism) is my deep motivation to aid others in the intricacies of their occupations and lives in general.

"There is nothing magical about conducting fail-safe negotiation as long as one is willing to change his thinking, behavior, and actions after learning the fundamentals of prenegotiation planning, bottom-line strategy, prenegotiation maneuvers, positioning, presentation, subconscious suggestion, personality-dependent communication, proxemics, body language, power dressing, ego states, life scripts, communicating styles, negotiation tactics, techniques of obtaining acceptance, breaking deadlocks, closings, and many other considerations.

"Even a 5 percent improvement in company-wide negotiating results can produce massive dollar savings through increased morale and productivity, better advertising messages, decreased purchasing costs, smaller dealer margins, fewer lawsuits, and more sales closings."

*   *   *

SPERRY, Raymond, Jr.
[Collective pseudonym]

WRITINGS:

"WHITE RIBBON BOYS" SERIES

The White Ribbon Boys of Chester; or, The Old Tavern Keeper's Secret, Cupples & Leon, 1915.

OTHER

Also author of *The White Ribbon Boys at Long Shore; or, To the Rescue of Dan Bates*, Cupples & Leon.

SIDELIGHTS: The "White Ribbon Boys" books were the only series attempted under this pseudonym, and they dealt with "the great modern movement for temperence," according to the publisher. A reviewer for *Fortune* magazine described these volumes as the series books' "worst failure." For more information see the entries for Harriet S. Adams, Edward L. Stratemeyer, and Andrew E. Svenson.

BIOGRAPHICAL/CRITICAL SOURCES:

BOOKS

Johnson, Deidre, editor and compiler, *Stratemeyer Pseudonyms and Series Books: An Annotated Checklist of Stratemeyer and Stratemeyer Syndicate Publications*, Greenwood Press, 1982.

PERIODICALS

Fortune, April, 1934.

*   *   *

STASHEFF, Christopher   1944-

PERSONAL: Born in January, 1944, in Mt. Vernon, N.Y.; son of Edward (a professor) and Evelyn (a teacher; maiden name, Maher) Stasheff; married Mary Miller, June 9, 1973; children: Isobel Marie, Edward James, Genevieve Elizabeth, Eleanor Theresa. *Education:* University of Michigan, B.A., 1965, M.A., 1966; University of Nebraska, Ph.D., 1972. *Politics:* Democrat. *Religion:* Roman Catholic.

ADDRESSES: Home—P.O. Box 2189, Station A, Champaign, Ill. 61875.

CAREER: University of Michigan, Ann Arbor, member of television floor crew, 1961-67; University of Nebraska, Lincoln, administrative assistant for CCTV-Nebraska Television Council for Higher Education, 1967-68; Montclair State College, Upper Montclair, N.J., beginning 1972, began as instructor, became assistant professor of radio and television.

MEMBER: Science Fiction Writers of America.

WRITINGS:

SCIENCE FANTASY

The Warlock in Spite of Himself, Ace Books, 1969.
King Kobold, Ace Books, 1970.
A Wizard in Bedlam, Doubleday, 1979.
The Warlock Unlocked, Ace Books, 1982.
Escape Velocity, Ace Books, 1983.
King Kobold Revived, Ace Books, 1984.
The Warlock Enraged, Ace Books, 1985.
The Warlock Wandering, Ace Books, 1986.
The Warlock Is Missing, Ace Books, 1986.
Her Majesty's Wizard, Del Rey Books, 1986.
The Warlock Heretical, Ace Books, 1987.

PLAYS

"The Three-Legged Man," first produced in Lincoln, Neb., May 11, 1970.
"Cotton-Eye Joe," first produced in Lincoln, Neb., December 16, 1970.
"Joey Winn," first produced in Lincoln, Neb., March 21, 1971.

WORK IN PROGRESS: Conventionalism for the Playwright; eight novels, *Golem in Limbo, The Closing of the Weird, The Wizard Who Wasn't, The Wizard Who Was, The Warlock's Companion, The Warlock's Insane, The Wizard Who Would Be King,* and *Star Troupe;* research on the differences in kinds of dramatic media.

SIDELIGHTS: Christopher Stasheff told *CA:* "In my boyhood, I was a puppeteer; I began to write my own scripts. In high school, I began writing for radio and did my first original script, which I adapted to short-story form. I submitted it to *Fantasy and Science Fiction* and got back a note explaining that it was very good but too long for a first publication. Could they see something shorter? Oh, they certainly could!

"Even if I never made another sale, I would keep writing anyway—it sustains my belief in myself and provides a much-needed escape into worlds I can control (usually). Also, I need the money, and my wife tells me I get nasty when I'm away from the typewriter too long. Even more, I need the illusion to keep me going. . . . A man without dreams loses youth and must constantly fight off bitterness—which is why society needs fantasy and science fiction, yes, and even the junk you see on prime-time television.

"I like SF—because it's the playground of ideas, one of the last places where a man can play with concepts for their own sake, without someone demanding he prove the validity of what he has written. Such a place is very important; a man must have a place to try a hypothesis per se. . . . In politics and culture, I'm a middle-of-the-road liberal—I look forward to new cultural aspects, but don't want to forsake the old ones."

Several of Stasheff's books have been translated into German, Italian, and Japanese.

AVOCATIONAL INTERESTS: Reading, "playing with my children (occasionally)."

BIOGRAPHICAL/CRITICAL SOURCES:

BOOKS

del Rey, Lester, *Science Fiction: A Critical History*, Garland, 1975.

* * *

STAYER, James M(entzer)   1935-

PERSONAL: Born March 15, 1935, in Lancaster, Pa.; naturalized Canadian citizen in 1977; son of Raymond R. (a dentist) and Helen (Mentzer) Stayer; married Marcia Sweet (a professional librarian), June 1, 1958; children: Elizabeth, William, James. *Education:* Juniata College, B.A., 1957; University of Virginia, M.A., 1958; University of Freiburg, graduate study, 1961-62; Cornell University, Ph.D., 1964. *Politics:* New Democratic Party.

ADDRESSES: Home—132 Welborne Ave., Kingston, Ontario, Canada. *Office*—Department of History, Queen's University, Kingston, Ontario, Canada K7L 3N6.

CAREER: Ithaca College, Ithaca, N.Y., instructor in history, 1959-61; Bridgewater College, Bridgewater, Va., assistant professor of history, 1962-65; Bucknell University, Lewisburg, Pa., assistant professor of history, 1965-68; Queen's University, Kingston, Ontario, assistant professor, 1968-72, associate professor, 1972-78, professor of history, 1978—.

MEMBER: Canadian Association of University Teachers, American Society for Reformation Research, Sixteenth Century Studies Conference (member of council, 1977—).

AWARDS, HONORS: Grants from American Philosophical Society, 1967-68, and Alexander von Humboldt Foundation, 1967, 1979-80; Canadian Council leave fellow, 1974-75.

WRITINGS:

Anabaptists and the Sword, Coronado Press, 1972, 2nd revised edition, 1976.
(Contributor) *Umstrittenes Taufertums, 1525-1975*, Vandenhoeck & Ruprecht, 1975.
(With Werner O. Packull) *The Anabaptists and Thomas Muntzer*, Kendall-Hunt, 1980.

Contributor to *Journal of the History of Ideas, Archiv fuer Reformationsgeschichte, Mennonite Quarterly Review, Church History, Sixteenth Century Journal, Mennonitische Geschichtsblaetter, Doopsgezinde Bijdragen, Blaetter fuer wuerttembergische Kirchengeschichte*, and *Brethren Life and Thought*.

* * *

STEELE, Chester K.
[Collective pseudonym]

WRITINGS:

The Mansion of Mystery: Being a Certain Case of Importance, Taken from the Notebook of Adam Adams, Investigator and Detective, Cupples & Leon, 1911.
The Diamond Cross Mystery: Being a Somewhat Different Detective Story, G. Sully, 1918.
The Golf Course Mystery: Being a Somewhat Different Detective Story, G. Sully, 1919.

The Crime at Red Towers, E. J. Clode, 1927.
The House of Disappearances: A Detective Story, Chelsea House, 1927.
The Great Radio Mystery: A Detective Story, Chelsea House, 1928.

SIDELIGHTS: For more information see the entries for Harriet S. Adams, Edward L. Stratemeyer, and Andrew E. Svenson.

BIOGRAPHICAL/CRITICAL SOURCES:

BOOKS

Johnson, Deidre, editor and compiler, *Stratemeyer Pseudonyms and Series Books: An Annotated Checklist of Stratemeyer and Stratemeyer Syndicate Publications*, Greenwood Press, 1982.

* * *

STEINMANN, Martin, Jr.   1915-

PERSONAL: Born March 3, 1915, in Minneapolis, Minn.; son of Martin and Grace (Dockery) Steinmann; married Jane Tyack, 1958; children: John Edward, Joan Margaret, Catherine Ann. *Education:* University of Minnesota, B.A., 1937, M.A., 1946, Ph.D., 1954.

ADDRESSES: Office—Martin Steinmann & Associates, 525 Grove St., Evanston, Ill. 60201.

CAREER: University of Minnesota, Minneapolis, instructor, 1946-54, assistant professor, 1954-57, associate professor, 1957-60, professor of English, 1960-79, director of freshman English, 1950-64, director of Minnesota Center for Advanced Studies in Language, Style, and Literary Theory, 1972-74, 1977-79, director of composition, 1978-79; University of Illinois at Chicago Circle, Chicago, professor of English, beginning 1979; currently director, Martin Steinmann & Associates (writing and language consultants), Evanston, Ill. Advisory editor, Charles Scribner's Sons, New York, N.Y., 1961-67. *Military service:* U.S. Naval Reserve, 1943-45; became lieutenant junior grade.

MEMBER: American Society for Aesthetics, American Business Communication Association, Linguistic Society of America, Rhetoric Society of America, Victorian Society in America, Association of Professional Writing Consultants, New Society for Language and Rhetoric.

AWARDS, HONORS: American Philosophical Society grant, 1957-58; Louis W. and Maud Hill Family Foundation grant, 1957-58; Putnam D. Macmillan Fund grant, 1964-65; Rockefeller Foundation grant, 1964-65; National Endowment for the Humanities grant, 1980.

WRITINGS:

Words in Action: A Rhetoric-Reader, Harcourt, 1979.

EDITOR

(With William M. Sale, Jr., and James Hall) *Short Stories: Tradition and Direction*, New Directions, 1949.
(With Hall) *The Permanence of Yeats: Selected Criticism*, Macmillan, 1950.
(With Robert C. Rathburn) *From Jane Austen to Joseph Conrad*, University of Minnesota Press, 1958.
(With Rathburn) *75 Prose Pieces*, Scribner, 1961, 2nd edition, 1967.
(With Gerald Willen) *Literature for Writing*, Wadsworth Publishing, 1962, 2nd edition, 1966.

New Rhetorics, Scribner, 1967.
(With Robert L. Brown, Jr.) *Rhetoric 78: Proceedings of Theory of Rhetoric—An Interdisciplinary Conference,* Center for Advanced Studies in Language, Style, and Literary Theory, University of Minnesota Press, 1979.

CONTRIBUTOR

Wolfgang Bernard Fleischmann, editor, *Encyclopedia of World Literature in the Twentieth Century,* Ungar, 1969.
Roger W. Shuy and Charles-James N. Bailey, editors, *Toward Tomorrow's Linguistics,* Georgetown University Press, 1974.
Hassan Sharifi, editor, *From Meaning to Sound,* University of Nebraska Press, 1975.
Ralph W. Fasold and Shuy, editors, *Analyzing Variation in Language,* Georgetown University Press, 1975.
Salilko S. Mufwene and others, editors, *Papers from the Twelfth Regional Meeting of the Chicago Linguistic Society,* Chicago Linguistic Society, 1976.
Frances Ingemann, editor, *1975 Mid-America Linguistics Conference Papers,* University Press of Kansas, 1976.
Profession 78, Modern Language Association of America, 1978.
Proceedings of the 1977 Mid-America Linguistics Conference, University of Missouri Press, 1978.
Paul Hernadi, editor, *What Is Literature?,* Indiana University Press, 1978.
Richard Beach and P. David Pearson, editors, *Perspectives on Literacy: Proceedings of the 1977 Perspectives on Literacy Conference,* College of Education, University of Minnesota Press, 1978.
Turner S. Kobler, William E. Tanner, and J. Dean Bishop, editors, *Retrospectives and Perspectives: A Symposium in Rhetoric,* Texas Woman's University Press, 1978.
David Sankoff and Henrietta Cedergren, editors, *Variation Omnibus,* Linguistic Research (Edmondon), 1981.
Martin Nystrand, editor, *What Writers Know: The Language and Structure of Written Discourse,* Academic Press (New York, N.Y.), 1982.
Tanner and Bishop, editors, *Rhetoric and Change,* Ide, 1982.

OTHER

General editor, Scribner Research Anthologies, 1961-70. Contributor to encyclopedias. Contributor to professional journals, such as *Essays in Criticism* and *College English.* Editor, *Centrum,* 1972-74.

AVOCATIONAL INTERESTS: Painting; collecting paintings, prints, and sculpture.

*   *   *

STEPTOE, John (Lewis) 1950-

PERSONAL: Born September 14, 1950, in Brooklyn, N.Y.; son of John Oliver (a transit worker) and Elesteen (Hill) Steptoe; children: Bweela (daughter), Javaka (son). *Education:* Attended New York School of Art and Design, 1964-67.

ADDRESSES: Home—840 Monroe St., Brooklyn, N.Y. 11221. *Agent*—Alice Bach, 222 East 75th St., New York, N.Y.

CAREER: Artist and author of children's books. Teacher at Brooklyn Music School, summer, 1970.

MEMBER: Amnesty International.

AWARDS, HONORS: John Steptoe Library dedicated in Brooklyn, New York, 1970; Gold Medal, Society of Illustrators, 1970, and Lewis Carrol Shelf Award, 1978, both for *Stevie,* which was also named an American Library Association notable children's book; *The Story of Jumping Mouse: A Native American Legend* was named a Caldecott Honor Book, and was named to *Horn Book* Fanfare List, both 1985; Coretta Scott King Award, 1988, for *Mufaro's Beautiful Daughters: An African Tale,* which was also named a Caldecott Honor Book, 1988.

WRITINGS:

SELF-ILLUSTRATED; FOR CHILDREN

Stevie, Harper, 1969, published with cassette and guide, Live Oak Media, 1987.
Uptown, Harper, 1970.
Train Ride, Harper, 1971.
Birthday, Holt, 1972.
My Special Best Words, Viking, 1974.
Marcia, Viking, 1976.
Daddy Is a Monster . . . Sometimes, Lippincott, 1980.
Jeffrey Bear Cleans Up His Act, Lothrop, 1983.
The Story of Jumping Mouse: A Native American Legend, Lothrop, 1984.
Mufaro's Beautiful Daughters: An African Tale, Lothrop, 1987.
Baby Says, Lothrop, 1988.

ILLUSTRATOR; FOR CHILDREN

Lucille B. Clifton, *All Us Come Cross the Water,* Holt, 1972.
Eloise Greenfield, *She Come Bringing Me That Little Baby Girl,* Lippincott, 1974.
Arnold Adoff, *OUTside INside Poems,* Lothrop, 1981.
Birago Diop, *Mother Crocodile = Maman-Caiman,* Delacorte, 1981.
Adoff, *All the Colors of the Race: Poems,* Lothrop, 1982.

SIDELIGHTS: John Steptoe once commented: "One of my incentives for getting into writing children's books was the great and disastrous need for books that black children could honestly relate to. I ignorantly created precedents by writing such a book. I was amazed to find that no one had successfully written a book in the dialogue which black children speak."

Written when the author was sixteen, Steptoe's widely acclaimed *Stevie* recounts a child's experience with overcoming peer jealousy. The book is called "an honest and touching story, with stunning illustrations" by a *Saturday Review* contributor, and critics generally consider *Stevie* somewhat of a landmark book, in that it represents a very early example of an author's treatment of black life using a ghetto setting with black characters and dialogue. "I wrote the book for black children," Steptoe tells a *New York Times Book Review* contributor, "therefore the language reflects it. I think black children need this. I wrote it this way because they are never spoken to. They always read about themselves as the 'Negro'—something outside, not included." Pointing out that the book's "modified black English" is really "more a transcription of pronunciation than a different grammatical system," Ellen Tremper adds in *Lion and the Unicorn* that "the non-black reader certainly does not feel he is in a different language system, and the story line has universal appeal as well." Similarly, Barbara Novak O'Doherty suggests in the *New York Times Book Review* that while the story "certainly stems from black culture," it speaks to a "common experience."

In his books for children, Steptoe explores the common experiences or concerns of children and young adults. *Uptown,* for instance, is a story of two boys who ponder their future, wondering what they will be when they become adults; *Train Ride* tells the story about a subway ride two boys take without parental permission and the punishment they both receive as a result; and *Daddy Is a Monster . . . Sometimes* explores the inherent tensions between parents and their children, showing how interrelated their behavior often is, with parents responding in kind to the "monster" behavior of their offspring.

Critics note that Steptoe also speaks to an issue that many books for and about children neglect—sex education. "Most books for young children concerned with sex education describe the birth process," writes Marsha Kabakow Rudman in her *Children's Literature: An Issues Approach.* "They rarely take into consideration the other aspects of sexuality in a child's life." Steptoe's *My Best Special Words,* however, depicts a young girl's attempts to toilet train her brother. "The two children romp together in the bathroom," says Rudman. "They are comfortable with their bodies. The illustrations help to convey the sense of joy and comfort with themselves and each other. As usual, Steptoe is educational at the same that that he is disturbing the complacency of some of the reading public." And *Marcia,* Steptoe's first young adult novel, explores the responsibilities involved in becoming sexually active; and "for urban Black teen-age girls, this book deals frankly with male 'machismo,' responsible sex, and contraception," says Joan Scherer Brewer in *School Library Journal.* Concurring that the story "is appealing, and its concerns are common ones for young people," Denise M. Wilms adds in *Booklist* that "Steptoe hasn't flinched from dealing with the issue head on."

More recently, though, Steptoe has departed from creating books that speak directly to the experiences of children in urban environments, and has reworked older tales or legends. *The Story of Jumping Mouse: A Native American Legend,* for example, which is described in *Kirkus Reviews* as a story about "a seeking, selfless mouse who turns into an eagle," retells an American Indian explanation of the origin of the eagle. Not only is the story itself a departure for Steptoe, the artwork has changed as well. Donnarae MacCann and Olga Richard note in *Wilson Library Bulletin* that Steptoe is "moving in an entirely new direction. He creates mixtures of black and white, and is able to animate the surfaces and depict a rich environment with more success than most artists can achieve with a full range of color. He also designs arrangements that are handsome, asymmetrical, and unusual in their intricate weaving of negative and positive spaces." Steptoe's illustrations in *Mufaro's Beautiful Daughters: An African Tale* are described by Paulette Childress White in the *New York Times Book Review* as having "a muted brilliance and luminosity." White adds that "Steptoe weaves tribal culture and history, magic and mystery in this version of the timeless moral lesson of pride going before a fall" in his retelling of the "fates of two very beautiful and very different daughters." Describing the illustrations, Tim Wynne-Jones suggests in the Toronto *Globe and Mail* that "the lavish form of the book perfectly reflects the noble content of the story." And a *Los Angeles Times Book Review* contributor writes, "While this beautiful picture book is dedicated to the children of South Africa, its story will touch youngsters of any culture."

Critics respond favorably to the candor, optimism, and universality of themes in Steptoe's books for children. Although some may feel that at times the work is not as strongly constructed as it could be, they nonetheless praise the authenticity and innovation in its presentation; and they continue to appreciate Steptoe's development as an artist. From the "icon-like intensity" of Steptoe's bold and colorful illustrations in *Stevie,*

as described by Barbara Bader in her *American Picture Books from Noah's Ark to the Beast Within,* and the renderings in "black, white, and shades of gray like a full palette, with subtle gradations and nuances" in *The Story of Jumping Mouse,* as described by Ethel L. Heins in *Horn Book,* to the lushness that several critics believe distinguishes *Mufaro's Beautiful Daughters,* Steptoe's illustrations have earned several honors.

BIOGRAPHICAL/CRITICAL SOURCES:

BOOKS

Bader, Barbara, *American Picture Books from Noah's Ark to the Beast Within,* Macmillan, 1976.
Children's Literature Review, Gale, Volume 2, 1976, Volume 12, 1987.
Rudman, Marsha Kabakow, *Children's Literature: An Issues Approach,* D. C. Heath, 1976.

PERIODICALS

Booklist, May 1, 1976, June 15, 1984.
Children's Book Review Service, September, 1976.
Globe and Mail (Toronto), May 30, 1987.
Horn Book, August, 1984.
Interracial Books for Children Bulletin, Volume 12, numbers 7 and 8, 1981.
Kirkus Reviews, April 15, 1976, April 1, 1980.
Life, August 29, 1969.
Lion and the Unicorn, winter, 1979/80.
Los Angeles Times Book Review, May 17, 1987.
New York Times Book Review, October 10, 1969, November 30, 1969, November 11, 1970, June 28, 1987.
Saturday Review, September 13, 1969.
School Library Journal, May, 1976, February, 1981.
Times Literary Supplement, July 2, 1970.
Washington Post, December 18, 1987.
Wilson Library Bulletin, September, 1984.†

—*Sketch by Sharon Malinowski*

*   *   *

STERNLICHT, Sanford 1931-

PERSONAL: Born September 20, 1931, in New York, N.Y.; son of Irving Stanley (a food manager) and Sylvia (Hilsenroth) Sternlicht; married Dorothy Hilkert, June 7, 1956 (died, 1977); children: David, Daniel. *Education:* State University College of Education (now State University of New York College at Oswego), B.S., 1953; Colgate University, M.A. (with distinction), 1955; Syracuse University, Ph.D., 1962.

ADDRESSES: Home—100 Buckingham Ave., Syracuse, N.Y. 13210 *Office*—Department of English, Syracuse University, Syracuse, N.Y. 13244.

CAREER: Colgate University, Hamilton, N.Y., instructor in remedial reading, 1953-55; State University of New York College at Oswego, instructor, 1959-60, assistant professor, 1960-62, associate professor, 1962, professor of English, 1962-72, professor of theatre, 1972-86, chairman of department, 1973-85; Syracuse University, lecturer in English, 1986—. Leverhulme Foundation visiting fellow, University of York, York, England, 1965-66. Has worked in professional theater, radio, and television. *Military service:* U.S. Navy, active duty with Atlantic and Mediterranean fleets, 1955-59; became lieutenant junior grade. U.S. Navy Reserve, retired as commander.

MEMBER: PEN, Modern Language Association of America, Poetry Society of America (fellow), Shakespeare Association of America.

AWARDS, HONORS: Six prizes from Poetry Society of Norfolk (Va.), 1959-64; *Writer* magazine's annual award for a new poet, 1960; State University of New York Research Foundation fellowships for writing, 1963, 1965, 1969, 1970, and grant, 1964.

WRITINGS:

(Contributor of poetry) *Avalon Anthology,* Different Press, 1960.
(Contributor) *Anthologie de la poesie contemporaine aux Etats-Unis,* Revue Moderne (Paris), 1961.
Gull's Way (poetry), Richard R. Smith, 1961.
Uriah Philips Levy: The Blue Star Commodore (biography), Bloch Publishing, 1961.
Love in Pompeii (poetry), South and West, 1967.
(With E. M. Jameson) *The Black Devil of the Bayous: The Life and Times of the United States Steam-Sloop Hartford* (history), Gregg, 1971.
John Webster's Imagery and the Webster Canon, University of Salzburg, 1972.
McKinley's Bulldog: The Battleship Oregon (history), Nelson-Hall, 1977.
John Masefield (criticism), Twayne, 1977.
C. S. Forester (criticism), Twayne, 1981.
(With Jameson) *U.S.F. Constellation: Yankee Racehorse* (history), Liberty Publishing, 1981.
Padraic Colum (criticism), Twayne, 1985.
(Editor) *Selected Short Stories of Padraic Colum,* Syracuse University Press, 1985.
John Galsworthy (criticism), Twayne, 1986.
(Editor) *Selected Plays of Padraic Colum,* Syracuse University Press, 1986.

Contributor of articles, reviews, more than two hundred poems, and more than thirty articles and short stories to periodicals, including *Quartet, Canadian Forum, Gent, Fiddlehead, Poetry Review,* and *New York Times.*

WORK IN PROGRESS: R. F. Delderfield, for Twayne.

SIDELIGHTS: Sanford Sternlicht told *CA:* "I cut my literary teeth on the poetry of John Masefield and the history of Samuel Eliot Morison. Melville, Conrad, the Navy, and the sea have shaped me."

BIOGRAPHICAL/CRITICAL SOURCES:

PERIODICALS

New York Times Book Review, February 24, 1985.
Times Literary Supplement, September 6, 1985.

*   *   *

STEVENSON, Elizabeth   1919-

PERSONAL: Born June 13, 1919, in Ancon, Panama; daughter of John Thurman (an oil company executive) and Bernice (Upshaw) Stevenson. *Education:* Agnes Scott College, B.A. (magna cum laude), 1941. *Politics:* Democrat.

ADDRESSES: Home—532 Daniel Ave., Decatur, Ga. 30032. *Office*—Graduate Institute of Liberal Arts, Emory University, Atlanta, Ga. 30322.

CAREER: Writer. Audit clerk, U.S. Government, Atlanta, Ga., 1942-47; Atlanta Public Library, Atlanta, library assistant in

order department, 1948-56; Emory University, Atlanta, assistant to the dean, 1960-74, associate professor of American studies, 1974—.

MEMBER: American Studies Association, Authors Guild, Authors League of America, National Association of Olmsted Parks (member of advisory board of directors, 1980—), Frederick Law Olmsted Association (member of board of directors, 1968—), Georgia Writers Association, Common Cause, Audubon Society, Wilderness Society, Phi Beta Kappa.

AWARDS, HONORS: Guggenheim fellow, 1950-51, 1955-56; Bancroft Prize from Columbia University, 1956, for *Henry James: A Biography;* Rockefeller Foundation fellow, 1956-57; summer stipend from National Endowment for the Humanities, 1974; grant from American Council of Learned Societies, 1975; recipient of Faculty Research Fund awards from Emory University.

WRITINGS:

The Crooked Corridor: A Study of Henry James, Macmillan, 1949, reprinted, Octagon, 1981.
Henry Adams: A Biography, Macmillan, 1955, reprinted, Octagon, 1977.
(Editor) *A Henry Adams Reader,* Doubleday, 1958.
Lafcadio Hearn: A Biography, Macmillan, 1961, reprinted, Octagon, 1979.
(Author of introduction) Jane Austen, *Pride and Prejudice,* Collier Books, 1962.
Babbitts and Bohemians: The American 1920s, Macmillan, 1967, revised edition published as *The American 1920s: Babbitts and Bohemians,* Collier Books, 1970.
Park Maker: A Life of Frederick Law Olmsted, Macmillan, 1977.

Contributor of articles and reviews to *Commentary, Nation, South Atlantic Quarterly,* and other magazines.

SIDELIGHTS: Elizabeth Stevenson wrote to *CA:* "I am interested in writing biography and history that has integrity of fact and also validity of form. Travel to all of the places concerned is necessary to me. Research in libraries is pure fun for me, but giving the book finish and shape is even more important. I have traveled to Quincy, Massachusetts, for Henry Adams, to Matsue, Japan, for Lafcadio Hearn, and to the sites of Olmsted's parks. I consider such travel vocation and avocation."

BIOGRAPHICAL/CRITICAL SOURCES:

PERIODICALS

Book World, September 24, 1967.
Christian Science Monitor, November 30, 1967.
New York Times Book Review, September 17, 1967, August 7, 1977.
Saturday Review, May 14, 1977.
Washington Post Book World, June 12, 1977.

*   *   *

STILL, James   1906-

PERSONAL: Born July 16, 1906, in LaFayette, Ala.; son of J. Alex (a veterinarian) and Lonie (Lindsey) Still. *Education:* Lincoln Memorial University, A.B., 1929; Vanderbilt University, M.A., 1930; University of Illinois, B.S., 1931.

ADDRESSES: Home—Wolfpen Creek, Mallie, Ky. 41836. *Office*—Box 865, Hindman, Ky. 41822. *Agent*—Mitch Douglas, International Creative Management, 40 West 57th St., New York, N.Y. 10019.

CAREER: Hindman Settlement School, Hindman, Ky., librarian, 1932-39; free-lance writer, 1939-41, 1945-52; Hindman Settlement School, librarian, 1952-62; Morehead State University, Morehead, Ky., associate professor of English, 1962-71; free-lance writer, 1971—. Visiting professor, Ohio University, 1970, and Berea College, 1972. Speaker, Lilyan Cohen Lecture Series, Clinch Valley College, 1987. Member of board of directors, Kentucky Humanities Council, 1980—; commentator for radio show, "All Things Considered," National Public Radio. *Military service:* U.S. Army Air Forces, 1941-45; served in Africa and the Middle East; became technical sergeant.

MEMBER: Phi Beta Kappa.

AWARDS, HONORS: MacDowell Colony fellowship, 1938; O. Henry Memorial Prize, 1939, for short story "Bat Flight"; Southern Authors Award from Southern Women's National Democratic Organization, 1940, for *River of Earth;* Guggenheim fellowships, 1941-42, 1946-47; fiction award from American Academy of Arts and Letters, 1947; Litt.D. from Berea College, 1973, and University of Kentucky, 1979; L.H.D. from Lincoln Memorial University, 1974; Weatherford Award, 1978, for Appalachian writing; Marjorie Peabody Waite Award, American Academy and Institute of Arts and Letters, 1979; Milne Award for service to the arts, Kentucky Arts Council, 1981; Book of the Year citation, Appalachian Writers Association, 1987. The James Still Room at Johnson-Camden Library, Morehead State University, was dedicated in 1961; James Still fellowships for advanced studies for the humanities, social science, and Appalachian studies were established at the University of Kentucky in 1980.

WRITINGS:

Hounds on the Mountain (poems), Viking, 1937, reprinted, Anvil Press, 1968.
River of Earth (novel), Viking, 1940, reprinted, University Press of Kentucky, 1977.
On Troublesome Creek (stories), Viking, 1941.
Way Down Yonder on Troublesome Creek: Appalachian Riddles and Rusties (juvenile), Putnam, 1974.
The Wolfpen Rusties: Appalachian Riddles and Gee-Haw Whimmy-Diddles (juvenile), Putnam, 1975.
Pattern of a Man (stories), Gnomon Press, 1976.
Jack and the Wonder Beans (juvenile), Putnam, 1976.
Sporty Creek: A Novel about an Appalachian Boyhood, Putnam, 1977.
The Run for the Elbertas (short stories), University Press of Kentucky, 1983.
River of Earth: A Poem and Other Poems, King Press, 1983.
The Wolfpen Poems, Berea College Press, 1986.
The Man in the Bushes: The Notebooks of James Still, 1935-1987, University Press of Kentucky, 1988.

CONTRIBUTOR TO ANTHOLOGIES

Harry Hanson, editor, *O. Henry Memorial Prize Stories,* Doubleday, 1939.
Hershall Brickell, editor, *O. Henry Memorial Prize Stories,* Doubleday, 1941.
Wilbur Cross and Helen MacAfee, editors, *The Yale Review Anthology,* Yale University Press, 1942.
Martha Foley, editor, *The Best American Short Stories,* Houghton, 1946, 1950, 1952.

Barbara Howes, editor, *Twenty-Three Modern Stories,* Random House, 1963.
C. B. Levitas, editor, *The World of Psychoanalysis,* Braziller, 1966.
Helen White and Redding S. Sugg, Jr., *From the Mountain,* Memphis State University Press, 1972.

OTHER

Contributor of stories and poems to popular magazines and literary journals, including *Atlantic, Esquire, Nation, New Republic, Saturday Evening Post, Yale Review, Poetry, Virginia Quarterly Review,* and *Sewanee Review.*

SIDELIGHTS: "With his friends Jesse Stuart and Harriette Simpson Arnow, James Still is perhaps the best known and most respected of Appalachian writers," says Leon V. Driskell in the *Dictionary of Literary Biography: American Novelists, 1910-1945.* Still has been a librarian at the Hindman School and resident in Eastern Kentucky for nearly sixty years; accordingly, his poems and books chronicle Appalachian life. His first book of poems, *Hounds on the Mountain,* was called "very simple and direct, but also natural and authentic," by W. R. Benet in the *Saturday Review of Literature.* This sense of authenticity has characterized Still's style throughout his writing career.

The author's first novel, *River of Earth,* tells the story of a boy's life in the hills and coal camps of Kentucky. "It is rich with sights, sounds and smells, with the feel and taste of things," comments S. V. Benet in *Books,* "[and] it is rich, as well, with salty and earthy speech, the soil of ballad and legend and tall story." And W. J. Gold notes in *Saturday Review of Literature:* "Its material is drawn from the mountains of Kentucky, and the story is told with the same clarity and strength born of restraint that characterized [*Hounds on the Mountain*].... The economy of its style and the directness of its aim give evidence of a mature and intelligently used talent." In his preface to the 1977 edition of *River of Earth,* Dean Cadle compares the novel to John Steinbeck's *The Grapes of Wrath,* saying that these are "the only books chronicling the demoralizing Depression years that have continued to gain readers in more affluent ones."

"'The Wolfpen Poems' seem to me to establish Still as the truest and most remarkable poet that the mountain culture has produced," suggests William Dickey in the *Los Angeles Times Book Review.* In his opinion, the poems "bring home, among other good and painful things, the necessity of Appalachia and the things it stands for, even to those who have never seen it. From the curves of his land, Still has more than the right to ask for all of us, as the fox goes and the dulcimer, as we destroy the natural world and its traditional cultures, 'is there no pardon anywhere?'"

BIOGRAPHICAL/CRITICAL SOURCES:

BOOKS

Dictionary of Literary Biography, Volume 9: *American Novelists, 1910-1945,* Gale, 1981.
Ford, Thomas S., editor, *Southern Appalachian Region,* University of Kentucky Press, 1962.
MacGill, Frank N., editor, *Cyclopedia of Literary Characters,* Harper, 1963.
Still, James, *Hounds on the Mountain,* Anvil Press, 1968.
Still, James, *River of Earth,* University Press of Kentucky, 1977.
Still, James, *The Wolfpen Poems,* Berea College Press, 1986.

PERIODICALS

Appalachian Journal, winter, 1979.
Books, February 4, 1940.
Commonweal, February 23, 1940.
Los Angeles Times Book Review, December 7, 1986.
Saturday Review of Literature, June 19, 1937, February 3, 1940.
Southwest Review, summer, 1977.
Yale Review, winter, 1968.

*   *   *

STOKES, Roy Eliot
[Collective pseudonym]

WRITINGS:

"UNIVERSITY" SERIES

Andy at Yale; or, The Great Quadrangle Mystery, Sully & Kleinteich, 1914.
Chet at Harvard; or, A Young Freshman's Triumph, Sully & Kleinteich, 1914.

SIDELIGHTS: For more information see the entries for Harriet S. Adams, Edward L. Stratemeyer, and Andrew E. Svenson.

BIOGRAPHICAL/CRITICAL SOURCES:

BOOKS

Johnson, Deidre, editor and compiler, *Stratemeyer Pseudonyms and Series Books: An Annotated Checklist of Stratemeyer and Stratemeyer Syndicate Publications,* Greenwood Press, 1982.

*   *   *

STONE, Raymond
[Collective pseudonym]

WRITINGS:

"TOMMY TIPTOP" SERIES

Tommy Tiptop and His Baseball Nine; or, The Boys of Riverdale and Their Good Times, Graham & Matlack, 1912.
. . . and His Football Eleven; or, A Great Victory and How It Was Won, Graham & Matlack, 1912.
. . . and His Winter Sports; or, Jolly Times on the Ice and in Camp, Graham & Matlack, 1912.
. . . and His Boat Club; or, The Young Hunters of Hemlock Island, Graham & Matlack, 1914.
. . . and His Boy Scouts; or, The Doings of the Silver Fox Patrol, Graham & Matlack, 1915.
. . . and His Great Show; or, Raising Some Money That Was Needed, C. E. Graham Co., 1917.

SIDELIGHTS: Tommy Tiptop was a young organizer and leader of boys. This series was described by the publisher as being "A new series for outdoor boys, that fairly bristles with boyish humanness." For more information see the entries for Harriet S. Adams, Edward L. Stratemeyer, and Andrew E. Svenson.

BIOGRAPHICAL/CRITICAL SOURCES:

BOOKS

Johnson, Deidre, editor and compiler, *Stratemeyer Pseudonyms and Series Books: An Annotated Checklist of Stratemeyer and Stratemeyer Syndicate Publications,* Greenwood Press, 1982.

*   *   *

STONE, Richard H.
[Collective pseudonym]

WRITINGS:

(Contributor) *Popular Stories for Boys* (includes *Sky Riders of the Atlantic;* also see below), Cupples & Leon, 1934.
Aviation Stories for Boys (contains *Sky Riders of the Atlantic, Lost over Greenland, An Air Cargo of Gold,* and *Adrift over Hudson Bay;* also see below), Cupples & Leon, 1936.

"SLIM TYLER" AIR STORIES

Sky Riders of the Atlantic; or, Slim Tyler's First Trip in the Clouds, Cupples & Leon, 1930.
Lost over Greenland; or, Slim Tyler's Search for Dave Boyd, Cupples & Leon, 1930.
An Air Cargo of Gold; or, Slim Tyler, Special Bank Messenger, Cupples & Leon, 1930.
Adrift over Hudson Bay; or, Slim Tyler in the Land of Ice, Cupples & Leon, 1931.
An Airplane Mystery; or, Slim Tyler on the Trail, Cupples & Leon, 1931.
Secret Sky Express; or, Slim Tyler Saving a Fortune, Cupples & Leon, 1932.

SIDELIGHTS: The Slim Tyler Air Stories featured a young man who wanted to become a flyer and overcame many obstacles to reach his goal. For more information, see the entries for Harriet S. Adams, Edward L. Stratemeyer, and Andrew E. Svenson.

BIOGRAPHICAL/CRITICAL SOURCES:

BOOKS

Johnson, Deidre, editor and compiler, *Stratemeyer Pseudonyms and Series Books: An Annotated Checklist of Stratemeyer and Stratemeyer Syndicate Publications,* Greenwood Press, 1982.

*   *   *

STRELKA, Joseph P(eter)   1927-

PERSONAL: Listed in some sources as Josef Strelka; born May 3, 1927, in Wiener Neustadt, Austria; came to United States, 1964; son of Josef and Maria (Lisetz) Strelka; married Lucy Zambal, 1951 (divorced, 1957); married Brigitte Vollmer, July 13, 1963; children: Alexandra. *Education:* University of Vienna, Ph.D., 1950.

ADDRESSES: *Home*—Hope Falls, Northville, N.Y. 12134. *Office*—Department of German, State University of New York, 1400 Washington Ave., Albany, N.Y. 12222.

CAREER: Municipal Office of Cultural Activities, Wiener Neustadt, Austria, director, 1950-51; free-lance critic in Vienna, Austria, 1951-64; University of Southern California, Los Angeles, visiting associate professor, 1964, assistant director of program at University of Vienna, 1964-65, professor of German literature, 1965-66; Pennsylvania State University, University Park, professor of German, 1966-71; State University of New York at Albany, professor of German and comparative literature, 1971—. Visiting professor at Free University of Berlin, 1980, University of Augsburg, 1981, University of the Witwatersrand, 1981, and University of Parma, 1983.

MEMBER: International Robert Musil Society, International Association of Germanic Studies, PEN, American Comparative Literature Association, Humboldt Society, Austrian Writers Association (honorary member), Vienna Goethe Society.

AWARDS, HONORS: Theodor Koerner Foundation award, 1955-57; City of Vienna award, 1958; Austrian Institute of Cultural Affairs research fellowship (Paris), 1958-59; Austrian Cross of Honor for the Arts and Sciences, First Class, 1978; Medal of Honor, University of Parma, 1983.

WRITINGS:

Georg Forsters literarhistorische Bedeutung (title means "Georg Forster's Literary-Historical Significance"), F. Berger, 1955.

Der burgundische Renaissancehof Margarethes von Oesterreich und seine literarhistoriche Bedeutung (title means "The Burgundian Renaissance Court of Margaret of Austria and Its Literary-Historical Significance"), A. Sexl, 1957.

Kafka, Musil, Broch und die Entwicklung des modernen Romans (title means "Kafka, Musil, Broch, and the Development of the Modern Novel"), Forum Verlag, 1959.

Rilke, Benn, Schoenwiese und die Entwicklung der modernen Lyrik (title means "Rilke, Benn, Schoenwiese, and the Development of Modern Poetry"), Forum Verlag, 1960.

Brecht, Horvath, Duerrenmatt: Wege und Abwege des modernen Dramas (title means "Brecht, Horvarth, Duerrenmatt: Paths and Deviations of Modern Drama"), Forum Verlag, 1962.

Bruecke zu vielen Ufern (title means "Bridges to Many Shores"), Europe Verlag, 1966.

(With Harold von Hofe) *Luegendichtung* (title means "Tall Tales"), Scribner, 1966.

(With von Hofe) *Vorboten der Gegenwart: Marx, Nietzsche, Freud, Einstein* (title means "Precursers to the Present: Marx, Nietzsche, Freud, Einstein"), Holt, 1967.

Vergleichende Literaturkritik (title means "Comparative Literary Criticism"), Francke, 1970.

Die gelenkten Musen (title means "The Bound Muses"), Europa Verlag, 1971.

Auf der Suche nach dem verlorenen Selbst, Francke Verlag, 1977.

Werk, Werkverstaendnis, Wertung, Francks Verlag, 1978.

Methodologie der Literaturwissenschaft, Niemayer, 1978.

Esoterik bei Goethe, Niemayer, 1980.

Stefan Zweig: Freier Geist der Menschlichkeit, Osterreichischer Bundersverlag, 1981.

Exilliteratur, Peter Lang Verlag, 1983.

EDITOR OR COMPILER

Gedichte Margarethe's von Oesterreich (title means "Poems of Margaret of Austria"), A. Sexl, 1954.

(And author of introduction) Felix Grafe, *Dichtungen* (title means "Collected Works"), Bergland Verlag, 1961.

(And author of introduction) *Das zeitlose Wort: Eine Anthologie oesterreichischer Lyrik von Peter Altenberg bis zur Gegenwart* (title means "The Timeless Word: An Anthology of Austrian Verse from Peter Attenberg Up to the Present"), Stiasny Verlag, 1964.

(With Robert Stauffer and Paul Wimmer) *Aufruf zur Wende: Eine Anthologie neuer Dichtung, Ernst Schoenwiese zum 60* (title means "A Call to Change: An Anthology of Modern Literature"), Oesterreichische Verlaganstalt, 1965.

(And author of introduction) Gustav Meyrink, *Der Engel vom westlichen Fenster* (title means "Angel of the Western Window"), Stiasny Verlag, 1966.

(With Walter Hinderer) *Moderne amerikanische Literaturtheorien* (title means "Modern American Theories of Literature"), S. Fischer Verlag, 1970.

Broch heute, Francke Verlag, 1978.

Der Weg war schon das Ziel: Festschrift fuer Friedrich Torberg, Langen-Mueller, 1978.

(With Robert F. Bell and Eugene Dobson) *Protest, Form, Tradition: Essays on German Exile Literature*, University of Alabama Press, 1979.

(With Joerg Jungmayr) *Virtus und Fortuns: Festschrift fuer Hans Gert Roloff*, Peter Lang Verlag, 1983.

Heinrich Heine, *Deutschland: Ein Wintermaerchen*, Insel-Taschenbuch Verlag, 1983.

Internationales Georg Trakl Symposium, Peter Lang Verlag, 1983.

Bruno Petzhold, *Goethe und der Mahayana-Buddhismus*, Octobus Verlag, 1983.

(With Marguerite Schlueter) *Versunken in den Traum: Poems of Ernst Schoenwiese*, Limes Verlag, 1984.

Alt-Wiener Geschichten, Insel Taschenbuch Verlag, 1984.

Literary Theory and Criticism: Festschrift fuer Rene Wellek, two volumes, Peter Lang Verlag, 1984.

Ernst Schoenwise: Sein geistigrs Profil und seine literarische Bedeutung, Peter Lang Verlag, 1986.

Psalm und Hawdalah: Zum Werk Paul Celans, Peter Lang Verlag, 1987.

OTHER

Editor of "Yearbook of Comparative Criticism" series, 1968—, and "Penn State Series in German Literature," 1971—, both for Pennsylvania State University Press; editor of "New Yorker Beitraege zur Vergleichenden Literaturwissenschaft" series and "New Yorker Studien zur Neueren Deutschen Literaturgeschichte" series, both 1982—, both for Peter Lang Verlag. Contributor of articles to journals, including *Wort in Zeit* and *German Quarterly*. Co-editor, *Deutsche Exilliteratur*, 1976—; member of editorial board, *Colloquia Germanica*, 1971—, *North Carolina Studies in Comparative Literature*, 1972—, *Michigan Germanic Studies*, 1975—, *Modern Austrian Literature*, 1981—, and *Comparative Literature Studies*, 1987—.

WORK IN PROGRESS: Zwischen Traum und Wirklichkeit; Literarische Textanalyse.

SIDELIGHTS: Joseph P. Strelka told *CA* that his reasons for writing include a "search for new information, search for truth, [and] establishing ethical, aesthetic, and religious values in the sense of a universal humanism."

*   *   *

STUBBS, Harry C(lement)   1922-
(Hal Clement)

PERSONAL: Born May 30, 1922, in Somerville, Mass.; son of Harry Clarence (an accountant) and Marjorie (a teacher; maiden name, White) Stubbs; married Mary Elizabeth Myers, July 19, 1952; children: George Clement, Richard Myers, Christine. *Education:* Harvard University, B.S., 1943; Boston University, M.Ed., 1947; Simmons College, M.S., 1963. *Politics:* Republican. *Religion:* Episcopalian.

ADDRESSES: Home—12 Thompson Ln., Milton, Mass. 02187.

CAREER: Milton Academy, Milton, Mass., teacher of science, 1949-87. Science fiction writer. Member of Milton Warrant Committee (finance), 1962-65. *Military service:* U.S. Army Air Forces, World War II; bomber pilot with 8th U.S. Air Force; received Air Medal and four oak leaf clusters. U.S. Air Force, technical instructor at Sandia Base, N.M., 1952-53. U.S. Air Force Reserve, 1953-76; retired as colonel.

MEMBER: American Association for the Advancement of Science, New England Association of Chemistry Teachers (division chairman, 1961-62; president, 1981-83), New England Science Fiction Association, Meteoritical Society.

AWARDS, HONORS: International Fantasy Award, second place, 1955, for *Mission of Gravity;* Hugo Award nomination, 1971, for *Star Light.*

WRITINGS:

SCIENCE FICTION NOVELS; UNDER NAME HAL CLEMENT

Needle (first serialized in *Astounding Science Fiction,* May-June, 1949), Doubleday, 1950, reprinted, Avon, 1976, published as *From Outer Space,* Avon, 1957.
Iceworld, Gnome Press, 1953, reprinted, Ballantine, 1977.
Mission of Gravity, Doubleday, 1954, reprinted with an essay, "Whirligig World," by Clement and an introduction by Poul Anderson, Gregg Press, 1978.
The Ranger Boys in Space (juvenile), L. C. Page & Co., 1956.
Cycle of Fire, Ballantine, 1957, reprinted, 1981.
Close to Critical, Ballantine, 1964.
Star Light (sequel to *Mission of Gravity*), Ballantine, 1971.
Ocean on Top, DAW Books, 1973.
Through the Eye of a Needle (sequel to *Needle*), Ballantine, 1978.
The Nitrogen Fix, Ace Books, 1980.
Still River, Del Rey, 1987.

UNDER NAME HAL CLEMENT; CONTRIBUTOR

Reginald Bretnor, editor, *Science Fiction Today and Tomorrow* (nonfiction), Harper, 1974.
Bretnor, editor, *The Craft of Science Fiction* (nonfiction), Harper, 1976.
Bretnor, editor, *The Future at War,* Volume 3: *Orion's Sword* (nonfiction), Ace Books, 1980.
Harlan Ellison, editor, *Medea,* Bantam, 1985.

OTHER

Some Notes on Xi Bootes (nonfiction), Advent, 1959.
(Under name Hal Clement) *Natives of Space* (short stories), Ballantine, 1965.
(Under name Hal Clement) *Small Changes* (short stories), Doubleday, 1969, published as *Space Lash,* Dell, 1969.
(Editor under name Hal Clement) *First Flights to the Moon,* introduction by Isaac Asimov, Doubleday, 1970.
(Editor) George Gamow, *The Moon,* introduction by Isaac Asimov, Abelard-Schumann, 1971.
(Under name Hal Clement) *Left of Africa* (juvenile historical fiction), Aurian Society Press, 1976.
(Under name Hal Clement) *The Best of Hal Clement,* edited by Lester Del Rey, Ballantine, 1979.

Contributor to periodicals, including *Astounding Science Fiction, Satellite Magazine,* and *Sky and Telescope.* Also author of column on children's science books, under name Harry C. Stubbs, in *Horn Book Magazine,* 1969-84.

WORK IN PROGRESS: A sequel to *Still River,* tentatively entitled *Outspread.*

SIDELIGHTS: Harry C. Stubbs, who writes as Hal Clement, is "one of the most exactingly scientific of science-fiction writers," according to *Dictionary of Literary Biography* contributor Bruce Herzberg. "Most of his novels and stories," Herzberg continues, "work out in minute detail the physical conditions for life on other worlds, from the astrophysical characteristics of the planet and its system to the chemical composition of its seas and atmosphere and the physiological adaptations of its inhabitants." In novels such as *Mission of Gravity, Needle, Iceworld,* and *The Nitrogen Fix,* say Daryl Lane, William Vernon, and David Carson in the introduction to their interview with Clement in *The Sound of Wonder: Interviews from "The Science Fiction Radio Show,"* Volume 1, the author "is a classic in the true sense of the term . . . he epitomizes the hard science fiction writer."

Although his work first appeared in book form in 1950, Clement is considered one of the Golden Age science fiction writers, a member of the select group of authors—including Isaac Asimov, Robert Heinlein, A. E. van Vogt, and Theodore Sturgeon—discovered and encouraged by John W. Campbell, editor of *Astounding Science Fiction* during the 1930s and 1940s. Lane, Vernon, and Carson, in *The Sound of Wonder,* explain that Campbell "required certain kinds of stories from his authors and demanded scientific accuracy." "While we didn't always agree," says Clement of Campbell in *The Sound of Wonder,* "we both felt that there were rules [to writing science fiction] and that they ought to be followed. . . . We were both materialists, I guess; we felt that the universe does run by rules. We felt that a story was most believable when it matched those rules, at least as we—'we' meaning humanity in general—currently understood them."

Clement's fidelity to these universal rules is characteristic of his work. "The ideal reader of his books is very likely a science buff who would be moved to verify the astronomical accuracy of Buck Rogers's adventures," declares Herzberg. "Each novel is a puzzle that requires lessons in physical science and in scientific method for its solution." He calls *Mission of Gravity* "very much a joyful science-class romp." Clement's novels are not totally didactic, however; knowledge of science and the scientific method is crucial for the author's characters as well as the reader. Donald M. Hassler, in his study *Hal Clement,* contends that "wide and accurate knowledge about the variability of nature—what will happen given certain conditions—is the answer" to the problems Clement's protagonists face.

"In addition to his reputation as a writer of scientific science fiction, Clement is noted for his realistic aliens and for the realistic worlds he constructs for them," comment Lane, Vernon, and Carson in *The Sound of Wonder.* Among the most famous of the aliens are the Hunter, the alien symbiont in *Needle* and its sequel, *Through the Eye of a Needle;* Sallman Ken, the high school science teacher protagonist of *Iceworld;* and Barlennan, leader of the caterpillar-like Mesklinites in *Mission of Gravity* and *Star Light.* Clement's planets include Abyormen, a planet orbiting a double star system in *Cycle of Fire;* Tenebra, a place in *Close to Critical* whose surface temperature, atmospheric pressure, and gravity cause massive daily variations in its climate; and Mesklin, the gigantic variable-gravity planet of *Mission of Gravity.*

Hal Clement told *CA:* "Science fiction is to me essentially a hobby. I regard the 'real' ('hard') science fiction as having much higher standards of realism than ordinary literature, and most of the time needed for me to prepare a novel goes into calculation of the scientific probabilities, as currently understood, of the background situation and events which take place. To me, the chief problems faced by an intelligent being are supplied by an environment which is not in the least bit interested in his, her, or its survival as an individual; conflict *between* intelligent beings, while certainly not trivial, is far more difficult for me to understand and portray. I doubt that I could ever produce fast enough to make a living from science fiction or any other form of writing.''

BIOGRAPHICAL/CRITICAL SOURCES:

BOOKS

Benson, Gordon, Jr., *Hal Clement (Harry Clement Stubbs)*, Galactic Central, 1985.
Clareson, Thomas D., editor, *Many Futures, Many Worlds*, Kent State University Press, 1977.
Dictionary of Literary Biography, Volume 8: *Twentieth-Century American Science Fiction Writers*, Gale, 1981.
Hassler, D. M., *Hal Clement*, Starmont, 1982.
Lane, Daryl, William Vernon, and David Carson, *The Sound of Wonder: Interviews from "The Science Fiction Radio Show,"* Volume 1, Orynx Press, 1985.
Schweitzer, Darrell, *Science Fiction #1*, Borgo Press, 1979.

PERIODICALS

Algol, spring, 1980.
Amazing Science Fiction, March, 1977.
Chicago Sunday Tribune, April 2, 1950.
Fantasy Review, May, 1986.
New York Herald Tribune Book Review, July 19, 1953, March 28, 1954.
New York Times, June 14, 1953, May 23, 1954.
New York Times Book Review, August 2, 1987.
Saturday Review of Literature, June 17, 1950.
Science & Technology, May, 1969.
Times Literary Supplement, June 23, 1966.
Washington Post Book World, March 30, 1975, March 5, 1978, September 23, 1979, July 29, 1984.

*   *   *

SULLIVAN, J(ohn) P(atrick)   1930-

PERSONAL: Born July 13, 1930, in Liverpool, England; son of Daniel and Alice (Long) Sullivan; married Mary Frances Rock, July 20, 1954 (divorced, 1963); married Judith Patrice Eldridge, April 7, 1967 (divorced, 1971); married Judith Lee Godfrey. *Education:* Attended St. Francis Xavier's College, Liverpool, 1941-49; St. John's College, Cambridge, B.A. (with honors), 1953, M.A., 1957; Oxford University, B.A., 1954, M.A., 1957. *Politics:* Liberal. *Religion:* None.

ADDRESSES: Home—1020 Palermo Dr., Santa Barbara, Calif. 93105. *Office*—Department of Classics, University of California, Santa Barbara, Calif. 93106. *Agent*—Harold Ober Associates, Inc., 40 East 49th St., New York, N.Y. 10017; and David Higham Associates Ltd., 5-8 Lower John St., London W1R 4HA, England.

CAREER: Oxford University, Oxford, England, research fellow, Queen's College, 1954-55, fellow and tutor in classics, Lincoln College, 1955-62, dean of Lincoln College, 1960-61; University of Texas at Austin, visiting professor, 1961-62, associate professor, 1962-63, professor of classics, 1963-69, chairman of department, 1963-65; State University of New York at Buffalo, faculty professor of arts and letters, 1969-78, provost of Faculty of Arts and Letters, 1973-75; University of California, Santa Barbara, professor of classics, 1978—. Visiting summer professor, University of Victoria, 1964; visiting professor, University of Hawaii, 1977; distinguished visiting Hill Professor, University of Minnesota, 1982; visiting fellow, Clare Hall, Cambridge University, 1975-76, and Wolfson College, Oxford University, 1981. Martin Classical Lecturer, Oberlin College, 1976; Grey Lecturer, Cambridge University, 1978. *Military service:* British Army, Royal Army Education Corps, 1949-50; became sergeant.

MEMBER: American Philological Association, United Oxford and Cambridge Club.

AWARDS, HONORS: Bromberg Award for teaching, University of Texas, 1962, and university research grants, 1963, 1965-66, 1968; American Council of Learned Societies travel grant, 1963; Redditt Award, 1965, for *Ezra Pound and Sextus Propertius*, 1965; National Endowment for the Arts and Humanities senior fellowship, 1967-68, translation grant, 1980; Guggenheim fellowship, 1984.

WRITINGS:

(Editor and author of introduction) *Critical Essays on Roman Literature: Elegy and Lyric*, Harvard University Press, 1962.
(Editor, author of introduction, and contributor) *Critical Essays on Roman Literature: Satire*, Routledge & Kegan Paul, 1963, Indiana University Press, 1968.
Ezra Pound and Sextus Propertius: A Study in Creative Translation, University of Texas Press, 1964.
(Translator and author of introduction) *The Satyricon of Petronius*, Penguin, 1965.
The Satyricon of Petronius: A Literary Study, Indiana University Press, 1968.
(Editor and author of introduction) *Ezra Pound: A Critical Anthology*, Penguin, 1970.
Propertius: A Critical Introduction, Cambridge University Press, 1976.
(Editor with J. Peradotto) *Women in the Ancient World: The Arethusa Papers*, State University of New York Press, 1984.
Literature and Politics in the Age of Nero, Cornell University Press, 1985.
(Editor with P. Whigham) *Martial Englished by Divers Hands Sixteenth to Twentieth Century*, University of California Press, 1987.

CONTRIBUTOR

Walter Sutton, editor, *Ezra Pound: A Collection of Critical Essays*, Prentice-Hall, 1963.
Frederic Will, editor, *Seven Essays on the Modern Experience of the Classical*, University of Texas Press, 1964.
Ezra Pound: 22 Versuche ueber einen Dichter, Athenaeum Verlag, 1967.
Christopher Ricks, editor, *A. E. Housmen: A Collection of Critical Essays*, Prentice-Hall, 1968.
Eva Hess, editor, *New Approaches to Ezra Pound*, University of California Press, 1969.
David Daiches and others, editors, *The Literature of the Western World*, 1974.
D. R. Dudley, editor, *Studies in Latin Literature*, Routledge & Kegan Paul, 1974.
S. Kresic, editor, *Contemporary Literary Hermeneutics and Interpretation of Classical Texts*, [Ottawa, Canada], 1981.

K. Baker, editor, *I Have No Gun, but I Can Spit*, Methuen, 1981.

T. J. Luce, editor, *Ancient Writers: Greece and Rome*, Scribner, 1982.

H. D. Evjen, editor, *Mnemai: Classical Studies in Memory of Karl K. Hulley*, Scholar's Press, 1984.

M. Grant, editor, *Civilization of the Ancient Mediterranean*, Scribner, 1987.

W. Radice, editor, *The Translator's Art: Essays in Memory of Betty Radice*, Penguin, 1987.

P. Hardy and M. White, editors, *Homo Viator: Essays in Honor of John Bramble*, Bristol Classical Press, 1987.

Also author of *Two-Eyed Jacks* (poems). Contributor of poetry to *Cambridge New Writing, Khayyam, Granta, The Eagle*, and other periodicals in the early 1950s; contributor of articles, reviews, and translations to *Wiener Studien, Kenyon Review, Classical World, Times Literary Supplement, Texas Quarterly*, and other publications. Editor, *Arion: A Journal of Humanities and the Classics*, 1961-69, and *Arethusa*, 1972-75.

WORK IN PROGRESS: Martial, the Unexpected Classic; Gulliver's Last Voyage to the Americas (a satirical novel); *The Complete Epigrams of Martial Translated by Various Hands;* (with A. J. Boyle, editor) *Early Imperial Latin Poetry;* (with G. Schmeling) *Petronii Arbitri Satyricon* (text, commentary, introduction); *The Birth and Death of Roman Love Elegy.*

SIDELIGHTS: "'Scribble, scribble, eh, Mr. Sullivan?' Lord Chesterfield might have remarked of me," J. P. Sullivan told *CA*. "I like the activity of writing my own prose or verse, or translating that of others. The keenest pleasure is in honing the style. For scholarly subjects, I prefer the challenges presented by neglected or misunderstood authors or works, such as Petronius, Martial, and Ezra Pound's *Homage to Sextus Propertius*. Since I believe most American poetry is self-indulgent, rich in imagery and poverty-stricken in thought and form, I tend there to look backwards for my models; but since most literary scholarship in classics nowadays tends to be arid and narrow, 'settling *hoti's* dash, firmly basing *oun*,' I try to open some louvers to fresh winds blowing from new directions and disciplines. Consequently I like editing and encouraging younger scholars who will tackle once taboo subjects."

BIOGRAPHICAL/CRITICAL SOURCES:

PERIODICALS

New Statesman, June 7, 1968.
Times Literary Supplement, July 5, 1985.

*　　*　　*

SULTAN, Stanley 1928-

PERSONAL: Born July 18, 1928, in Brooklyn, N.Y.; son of Jack (a merchant) and Bess (Leinwand) Sultan; married Betty Hillman; children: James Lehman, Sonia Elizabeth. *Education:* Cornell University, A.B., 1949; Boston University, M.A., 1950; Yale University, Ph.D., 1955. *Politics:* "Democratic Socialists of America." *Religion:* Secularist.

ADDRESSES: Home—25 Hardwick St., Brighton, Mass. 02135. *Office*—Department of English, Clark University, Worcester, Mass. 01610.

CAREER: National Lexicographic Board Ltd., New York, N.Y., assistant editor, 1952-55; Smith College, Northampton, Mass., instructor in English, 1955-59; Clark University, Worcester, Mass., assistant professor, 1959-62, associate professor, 1962-

68, professor of English literature, 1968—. Lecturer at University of Trier, 1980. Director of National Defense Education Institute in English, 1965.

MEMBER: International Association for the Study of Anglo-Irish Literature, Democratic Socialists of America (founding member), Malone Society.

AWARDS, HONORS: Yaddo fellowship.

WRITINGS:

The Argument of Ulysses, Ohio State University Press, 1965, 2nd edition, Wesleyan University Press, 1987.

(Contributor) Maurice Harmon, editor, *The Celtic Master*, Dolmen Press, 1969.

(Editor) John Millington Synge, *The Playboy of the Western World*, Imprint Society, 1970.

Yeats at His Last, Dolmen Press, 1975.

"Ulysses," "The Waste Land," and Modernism, Kennikat, 1977.

Rabbi: A Tale of the Waning Year, Morning Star Press, 1978.

Eliot, Joyce and Company, Oxford University Press, 1987.

(Contributor) Weldon Thornton and Robert Newman, editors, *Ulysses: The Larger Perspective*, University of Delaware Press, 1987.

Also contributor, *Best American Short Stories*, 1953; also contributor, Shyamal Bagchee, editor, *(First) T. S. Eliot Annual*, Macmillan (London), 1988.

WORK IN PROGRESS: Eloquent Form in Modernist Drama.

SIDELIGHTS: "Fiction," Stanley Sultan told *CA*, "is fundamentally different from our great technological art (screen and tube), to which it has lost so many former readers. It may share with that art a common subject—happenings to human beings. But reading a novel or story is experiencing *written language*. The language conveys what happened; but some things can be achieved only by words saying their say. *The Gospel According to Saint John* repeats in Greek the first phrase (a word in Hebrew) of *The Book of Genesis*, then explains the Creation: 'In the Beginning was The Word.' Language is the root of human existence, of the consciousness/mind/soul that distinguishes us from other species: for no dolphin or chimpanzee can be taught to comprehend a *new* metaphor. And literature, the art made out of written words, is the flower of language. Maybe that's why some people write fiction though other people think they ought to have their heads examined."

*　　*　　*

SUPRANER, Robyn 1930-
(Olive Blake, Erica Frost, Elizabeth Warren)

PERSONAL: Surname is pronounced Soo-*pray*-ner; born September 14, 1930, in New York N.Y.; daughter of Mortimer (an insurance broker) and Dorothy (Kalmanowitz) Rubenstein; married Leon Supraner (a photographer), December 16, 1950; children: Keith, Scott, Dennis, Lauren. *Education:* Attended Pratt Institute and Parson's School of Design, 1944-48, and Adelphi University, 1948-51. *Politics:* "Feminist."

ADDRESSES: Home—420 Bryant Ave., Roslyn Harbor, N.Y. 11576. *Agent*—McIntosh & Otis, Inc., 310 Madison Ave., New York, N.Y. 10017.

CAREER: Free-lance song writer, 1962-72 (songs have been recorded by popular recording artists, including Chubby Checker, Mel Torme, and Johnny Winter); writer, 1970—.

Taught creative dramatics at Roslyn Creative Arts Workshop, 1973-74. Conducts numerous speaking engagements as a children's book author; gives public poetry readings at various locations in New York.

MEMBER: Authors Guild, Authors League of America, Poetry Society of America.

AWARDS, HONORS: Giggly, Wiggly, Snickety Snick was selected book of the year by Child Study Association, 1978; poetry award from Pen and Brush Club, 1980; *It's Not Fair* was selected classroom choice by International Reading Association.

WRITINGS:

FOR CHILDREN

Draw Me a Circle, illustrated by Evelyn Kelbish, Simon & Schuster, 1970.
Draw Me a Square, illustrated by Kelbish, Simon & Schuster, 1970.
Draw Me a Triangle, illustrated by Kelbish, Simon & Schuster, 1970.
Would You Rather Be a Tiger?, illustrated by Barbara Cooney, Houghton, 1973.
Think about It, You Might Learn Something, illustrated by Sanford Kossin, Houghton, 1973.
It's Not Fair! (Junior Literary Guild selection), illustrated by Randall Enos, Warne, 1976.
Giggly, Wiggly, Snickety-Snick, pictures by Stan Tusan, Parents' Magazine Press, 1978.
Sam Sunday and the Strange Disappearance of Chester Cats, pictures by Robert Tallon, Parents' Magazine Press, 1979.
(Contributor) *Language Basics Plus*, Harper, 1979.

FOR CHILDREN; PUBLISHED BY TROLL

I Can Read about Witches, 1975.
I Can Read about Weather, 1975.
I Can Read about Baseball, 1975.
I Can Read about Seasons, 1975.
I Can Read about Homonyms: The Mystery of the Hidden Treasure, 1977.
I Can Read about Synonyms and Antonyms: The Case of Strange Aunt Pickles, 1977.
Mrs. Wiggleworth's Secret, illustrated by Paul Harvey, 1979.
Mystery at the Zoo, illustrated by Bert Dodson, 1979.
Mystery of the Witch's Shoes, illustrated by Margot Apple, 1979.
The Case of the Missing Canary, illustrated by Robbie Stillerman, 1979.
The Ghost in the Attic, illustrated by Eulala Conner, 1979.
The Second Troll Talking Dictionary, 1979.
Fun-to-Make Nature Crafts, illustrated by Renzo Barto, 1981.
Fun with Paper, illustrated by Barto, 1981.
Great Masks to Make, illustrated by Barto, 1981.
Happy Halloween: Things to Make and Do, illustrated by Barto, 1981.
Magic Tricks You Can Do!, illustrated by Barto, 1981.
Merry Christmas!: Things to Make and Do, illustrated by Barto, 1981.
(With daughter, Lauren Supraner) *Plenty of Puppets to Make*, illustrated by Barto, 1981.
Quick and Easy Cookbook, illustrated by Barto, 1981.
Rainy Day Surprises You Can Make, illustrated by Barto, 1981.
Science Secrets, illustrated by Barto, 1981.
Stop and Look!: Illusions, illustrated by Barto, 1981.

Valentine's Day: Things to Make and Do, illustrated by Barto, 1981.
Case of the Missing Rattles, illustrated by Joan E. Goodman, 1982.
Mystery of the Lost Ring (with Two Hearts), illustrated by Marsha Winborn, 1982.
The Amazing Mark, 1986.
The Cat Who Wanted to Fly, 1986.
Kitty: A Cat's Diary, 1986.
Molly's Special Wish, 1986.
No Room for a Sneeze!, 1986.

UNDER PSEUDONYM OLIVE BLAKE; FOR CHILDREN

The Grape Jelly Mystery, illustrated by Goodman, Troll, 1979.
The Mystery of the Lost Letter, illustrated by Kossin, Troll, 1979.
The Mystery of the Lost Pearl, illustrated by Ed Parker, Troll, 1979.

UNDER PSEUDONYM ERICA FROST; FOR CHILDREN

I Can Read about Ballet, Troll, 1975.
I Can Read about Good Manners, Troll, 1975.
I Can Read about Ghosts, Troll, 1975.
Harold and the Dinosaur Mystery, illustrated by Deborah Sims, Troll, 1979.
The Mystery of the Runaway Sled, illustrated by Leigh Grant, Troll, 1979.
The Mystery of the Midnight Visitors, illustrated by Ann Gamache, Troll, 1979.
The Case of the Missing Chick, illustrated by Harvey, Troll, 1979.
(With Lauren Supraner) *The Littlest Pig Troll*, Troll, 1986.
The Story of Matt and Mary, Troll, 1986.
A Kitten for Rosie, Troll, 1986.
Mr. Lion Goes to Lunch, Troll, 1986.
Jonathan's Amazing Adventure, Troll, 1986.

UNDER PSEUDONYM ELIZABETH WARREN; FOR CHILDREN

I Can Read about Trees and Plants, Troll, 1975.
I Can Read about Bats, Troll, 1975.
I Can Read about Indians, Troll, 1975.
I Can Read about Baby Animals, Troll, 1975.

OTHER

(Contributor) Norbert Krapf, editor, *Under Open Sky: Poets on William Cullen Bryant*, Fordham University Press, 1986.

Author of twelve single-concept learning books for Columbia Broadcasting System (CBS), published by Shelley Graphics, 1971; author of other learning books published by Shelley Graphics, 1972, and of a sixteen-volume dictionary for children and other learning books, published by Educational Reading Service, 1972—; also author of books with cassette tapes, under pseudonyms Erica Frost and Elizabeth Warren, for Educational Reading Service, 1975. Contributor of over forty poems to American and Canadian literary journals, including *Prairie Schooner, Ploughshares, Unicorn, Xanadu, Beloit Poetry Journal,* and *Queen's Quarterly.*

WORK IN PROGRESS: Poetry collection under the working title *Carrying On.*

SIDELIGHTS: Robyn Supraner told *CA:* "Since I was little, I have tried to understand my life by writing things down. Many of my books spring from the bewilderments of my childhood. I was a bewildered child, and now, as a parent, I am a bewildered adult.

"I was almost six when my sister was born. I had wanted a brother. When, in spite of my injunctions, my sister was born, I wept for my lost place and my parents' cruel disregard. It wasn't fair. Some thirty odd years later, still smarting, I wrote *It's Not Fair!*

"Now, I live on a wooded hillside in Roslyn Harbor. My house is large and rambling and has slowly emptied itself of children who are grown."

AVOCATIONAL INTERESTS: Gardening, rock polishing, gathering shells, snorkeling.

*   *   *

SUTHERLAND, Daniel E(llyson) 1946-

PERSONAL: Born March 5, 1946, in Detroit, Mich.; son of Monte Henry Milliron (stepfather; a carpenter) and Dorothy Nell Parrish; married Diane Kim Bowman (a linguist), September 1, 1978; children: Christopher Michael. *Education:* Wayne State University, B.A., 1968, M.A., 1973, Ph.D., 1976.

ADDRESSES: Office—Department of History, McNeese State University, Lake Charles, La. 70609.

CAREER: McNeese State University, Lake Charles, La., assistant professor, 1977-82, associate professor, 1982-86, professor of American history, 1986—, head of department, 1983—. *Military service:* U.S. Naval Reserve, 1964-72; active duty, 1968-70; became petty officer second class.

MEMBER: Organization of American Historians, Southern Historical Association, Louisiana Historical Association, Virginia Historical Society, Society of Civil War Historians.

AWARDS, HONORS: Research grants from Society of Colonial Dames, 1975, National Endowment for the Humanities, 1978, and Association for State and Local History, 1984; Shearman research fellow, 1988.

WRITINGS:

Americans and Their Servants: Domestic Service in the United States From 1800 to 1920, Louisiana State University, 1981.
The Confederate Carpetbaggers (History Book Club selection), Louisiana State University Press, 1988.
Everyday Life during the Civil War and Reconstruction, Harper, 1988.

Contributor of articles to history and humanities journals. Member of editorial board of *The McNeese Review,* 1981—.

WORK IN PROGRESS: A social/military history of Culpeper County, Virginia, during the Civil War.

SIDELIGHTS: Americans and Their Servants: Domestic Service in the United States From 1800 to 1920 is an account of how changing economic structures in America affected the status of domestic servants. According to Sutherland, jobs that involved waiting on others came to be regarded as lesser tasks, and the persons who performed these duties were looked down upon by their employers and others as Americans became more affluent. Relations between employers and domestic employees became strained, so people began to perform their own household duties, thus increasing demand for mechanized means of performing such duties and rendering the role of the domestic servant obsolete.

The Confederate Carpetbaggers examines another little-known aspect of American history. This book, according to Sutherland, traces the histories of various Southerners who moved north after the Civil War, seeing in the industrial northeastern and midwestern cities a means of rebuilding their fortunes. This is the first time, Sutherland suggests, that this subject has been examined in any detail by American historians.

Daniel E. Sutherland told *CA:* "My professional writing career has been conducted under a melancholy cloud. Academic historians, with a few notable exceptions, have long borne the stigma of being dull, plodding, unexciting writers. Current trends toward statistical and quantitative history have tended to solidify this unflattering reputation. The door has been left wide open to the 'popular' historian, i.e., the writer whose training is primarily journalistic. Some popular historians (Bruce Catton and Barbara Tuchman come to mind) are exceptional, both as scholars and writers. However, too many others produce history that is facile, inaccurate, and wrongheaded (academic historians do, too, but not, I fancy, as frequently). Thus the strongest stimulus to my writing has been the belief that academic historians have a responsibility to write for the public rather than for themselves. General readers will not tolerate the inane, esoteric subject matter and style so often found in professional journals, and there is no reason why they should. There is no reason why academic historians cannot produce histories that are at once scholarly and entertaining, histories that offer something to professionals and laymen alike."

BIOGRAPHICAL/CRITICAL SOURCES:

PERIODICALS

New Yorker, November 30, 1981.
Washington Post Book World, May 15, 1988.

*   *   *

SWEETMAN, Jack 1940-

PERSONAL: Born January 5, 1940, in Orlando, Fla.; son of Jack and Bertha (Michael) Sweetman; married Gisela Tetzel, 1963; children: Jeanne Jacqueline. *Education:* Stetson University, B.A., 1961; Emory University, M.A., 1970, Ph.D., 1973. *Religion:* Episcopalian.

ADDRESSES: Home—884 Mallard Circle, Arnold, Md. 21012. *Office*—Department of History, U.S. Naval Academy, Annapolis, Md. 21402.

CAREER: Sweetman-Herb Construction & Realty, Inc., Orlando, Fla., vice-president, 1965-68; Indiana University at Bloomington, visiting assistant lecturer, 1972-73; U.S. Naval Academy, Annapolis, Md., 1973—, began as assistant professor, currently associate professor of history. *Military service:* U.S. Army Reserves, 1962-66; served in Europe as company commander; became captain.

MEMBER: Commission International d'Histoire Militaire, North American Society of Oceanic Historians, United States Naval Institute, American Historical Association, American Military Institute, Orders and Medals Society of America, Marine Corps Historical Foundation, German Studies Association.

AWARDS, HONORS: Ford Foundation fellow, 1968-72.

WRITINGS:

The Landing at Vera Cruz, 1914, U.S. Naval Institute, 1968.
(Contributor) Gerald Jordan, editor, *Naval Warfare in the Twentieth Century,* Crane, Russak, 1977.

The U.S. Naval Academy: An Illustrated History, U.S. Naval Institute, 1979.

(Editor with R. W. Love, Jr.) *Changing Interpretations and New Sources in Naval History*, Garland Publishing, 1980.

(Translator) Burkard von Muellenheim-Rechberg, *Battleship Bismark: A Survivor's Story*, U.S. Naval Institute, 1980.

(Contributor) Michael Barrett, editor, *Proceedings of the Citadel Conference on Hitler and the National Socialist Era*, Citadel, 1982.

(Contributor) Donald R. Whitnah, editor, *Government Agencies*, Greenwood Press, 1983.

American Naval History: An Illustrated Chronology of the U.S. Navy and Marine Corps, 1775-Present, U.S. Naval Institute, 1984.

(Editor) Rear Admiral Charles E. Clark, *My Fifty Years in the Navy*, U.S. Naval Institute, 1984.

(Contributor) *Above and Beyond: A History of the Medal of Honor from the Civil War to Vietnam*, Boston Publishing, 1985.

(Contributor) *Flags into Battle*, Boston Publishing, 1987.

Associate editor, U.S. Naval Institute *Proceedings*, 1975-80. Series editor, "Classics of Naval Literature," Naval Institute Press, 1984—. Consulting editor, *Naval History*, 1987—.

WORK IN PROGRESS: From Knowledge, Sea Power: A History of Research at the U.S. Naval Academy, The Great Admirals: Centuries of Command at Sea, The U.S. Marine Corps: An Illustrated History with Lieutenant Colonel Merrill L. Bartlett, USMC (retired), and *The Last Powder Monkey* with Captain Roy C. Smith III, USNR (retired), all for U.S. Naval Institute.

*   *   *

SYMONS, Leslie John   1926-

PERSONAL: Born November 8, 1926, in Reading, England; son of Edward John (an organ builder) and Gertrude (Mainwaring) Symons; married Gloria Colville, March 24, 1954; children: Alison Heather, Jennifer Rosalind. *Education:* London School of Economics and Political Science, London, B.Sc., 1953, Ph.D., 1958.

ADDRESSES: Home—Squirrels Jump, 17 Wychwood Close, Langland, Swansea SA3 4PH, Wales, United Kingdom. *Office*—Department of Geography, University College of Swansea, University of Wales, Swansea SA2 8PP, Wales, United Kingdom.

CAREER: Queen's University, Belfast, Northern Ireland, lecturer in geography, 1953-63; University of Canterbury, Canterbury, New Zealand, senior lecturer in geography, 1963-70; University of Wales, University College of Swansea, Swansea, senior lecturer, 1970-73, reader, 1973-80, professor of geography, 1980—. Simon senior research fellow at University of Manchester, 1967-68. *Military service:* British Army, Royal Engineers, 1944-48.

MEMBER: Institute of British Geographers, British Association of Soviet and East European Studies, Royal Aeronautical Society.

WRITINGS:

(Editor and contributor) *Land Use in Northern Ireland*, University of London Press, 1963.

Agricultural Geography, G. Bell, 1967, 2nd edition, 1978.

(With Lewis Hanna) *Northern Ireland: A Geographical Introduction*, University of London Press, 1967.

Russian Agriculture: A Geographical Survey, G. Bell, 1972.

(Editor with Colin White, and contributor) *Russian Transport: An Historical and Geographical Survey*, Bell & Hyman, 1975.

(Editor and contributor) *The Soviet Union: A Systematic Geography*, Hodder & Stoughton, 1982.

(Editor with J. Ambler and D. J. Shaw, and contributor) *Soviet and East European Transport Problems*, Croom Helm, 1985.

(Editor with J. F. Tismer and Ambler, and contributor) *Transport and Economic Development: Soviet Union and Eastern Europe*, Duncker & Humblol, 1987.

General editor of "Geography of the U.S.S.R." series, Hicks-Smith & Son, 1968-70.

WORK IN PROGRESS: Research on prediction, impact, and effects of snowfall, on Soviet transport, especially air transport, and on applications of aerial work to agriculture.

SIDELIGHTS: Leslie John Symons told *CA:* "My interest in the U.S.S.R. evolved from the feeling that this was a country that we in the West knew far too little about and that geographers, especially, had a duty to study objectively—the character of both the people and the country itself, its economy and resources, and its achievements in harnessing these resources. I was especially curious about the collective system of agriculture which was widely studied by economists and political scientists but had been neglected in geographical circles. It appeared that judgments on the virgin lands campaign of the 1950s, advanced by people who were neither agriculturalists nor natural scientists, needed reevaluating—or at least updating—as Soviet thinking became more attuned to the needs of the environment for conservation. I was also anxious to add another language to my capabilities to improve my knowledge of the work of geographers in regions with which most of us were unfamiliar. I traveled as widely as possible in Siberia, Central Asia, and the Caucasus regions as well as European Russia while writing my books on agriculture and, later, transport in the U.S.S.R. Meanwhile I was appointed to the Centre of Russian and East European Studies at Swansea and became involved with wider aspects of the study of the Soviet Union in conjunction with other specialists. The study of Russian transport was a joint undertaking with other geographers and economic historians to fill some gaps in Western knowledge about this facet of the development of Russia and the U.S.S.R.

"My present research project concerning snowfall evolved out of work on agricultural aviation, which is widely used on the Soviet scene. While I was carrying out work on aerial application, severe blizzards in Britain led to a major deployment of helicopters for rescue work. After writing this up with a colleague I began to think in terms of a wider study of the disruption caused by snowfall, and after the severe snowstorms of January, 1982, Dr. A. H. Perry and I were approached by the Welsh Office to study the problem and make recommendations on measures which might be undertaken to reduce the economic and social impact of winter weather in the future. As a result of this work we received a contract from the Welsh Office to plan a system of ice detectors on highways throughout Wales, to oversee their installation, and to introduce a system of 24-hour monitoring of climate conditions throughout the winter, a service which was unique in its coverage in the British Isles when introduced in 1986-87."

AVOCATIONAL INTERESTS: Mountaineering, aviation, railways, philately, music, travel (including the U.S.S.R., Asia, Australia, and New Zealand).

T

TAFURI, Manfredo 1935-

PERSONAL: Born November 4, 1935, in Rome, Italy; son of Simmaco (an engineer) and Elena (Trevi) Tafuri; married Guiseppina Rapisarda (a professor), June 15, 1966; children: Dafne. *Education:* University of Rome, M. Arch., 1960. *Politics:* Partito Comunista Italiano.

CAREER: Instituto Universitario di Architettura di Venezia, Tolentini, Italy, professor of history of architecture, 1968—. Director, Institute of History, Instituto Universitario di Architettura, Venice, 1968—; member of board of directors, Centro Internazionale di Studi di Architettura "Andrea Palladio," 1974—; member of board of directors of architectural magazine, *Casabella,* 1977—. Lecturer.

WRITINGS:

L'Architettura moderna in Giappone, Cappelli (Bologna), 1964.
Ludovico Quaroni e lo sviluppo dell' architettura moderna in Italia, Edizioni di Comunita, 1964.
Teorie e Storia dell' architettura, Laterza, 1968, translation by Giorgio Verrecchia published as *Theories and History of Architecture,* Harper, 1980.
Jacopo Sansovino e l'architettura dell '500 a Venezia, Marsilio, 1969.
L'Architettura dell'umanesimo, Laterza, 1969, 4th edition, 1980.
(With Luigi Salerno and Luigi Spezzaferro) *Via Giulia: Un'Utopia urbana del '500,* Staderini, 1973.
Progetto e utopia, Laterza, 1973, translation by Barbara Luigi La Penta published as *Architecture and Utopia: Design and Capitalist Development,* MIT Press, 1976.
(With Giorgio Ciucci, Francesco Dal Co, and Mario Manieri-Elia) *La Citta Americana,* Laterza, 1973.
(With Dal Co) *Architettura Contemporanea,* Electa (Milano), two volumes, 1976, translation by Robert Erich Wolf published as *Modern Architecture,* Abrams, 1979.
(With Dal Co) *Architektur der Gegenwart,* Electa, 1977.
Projet et utopie: De l'avant-garde a la metropole, Dunod (Paris), 1979.
Vienna rossa: La politica residenziale nella Vienna socialista, 1919-1933, Electa, 1980.
Five Architects N.Y., Officina (Rome), 1981.
Vittorio Gregotti: Buildings and Projects, Rizzoli International, 1982.

(With Antonio Foscari) *L'armonia e i conflitti: La Chiesa di San Francesco della Vigna nella Venezia del '500,* Einaudi, 1983.
Venezia e il Rinascimento: Religione, scienza, archittetura, Einaudi, 1983.
The Sphere and the Labyrinth: Avant-Gardes and Architecture from Piranesi to the 1970s, translated by Pellegrino D'Acierno and Robert Connolly, MIT Press, 1987.

Contributor of articles on architecture to *Casabella, Contropiano, Oppositions, Lotus, Archithese,* and other periodicals.

WORK IN PROGRESS: Research on architecture and planning in the New Deal age in the U.S.

SIDELIGHTS: Manfredo Tafuri told *CA:* "My historical research is based on a Marxist methodology, for the criticism of the modern and contemporaries ideologies. In this sense the history of art, of the architecture, of the urban planning, is, for me, an approach to the discovery of the most advanced Capitalist strategies, in relationship to the utopias of the intellectual work. The crisis of the avant-gardes and of the contemporary architecture are at the center of my interests. I am convinced that the history cannot change, alone, the present social and economical establishment: but it may aid the architects to understand the real situation of their work, in the perspective of a general and radical devlopment."

BIOGRAPHICAL/CRITICAL SOURCES:

PERIODICALS

Times Literary Supplement, July 25, 1980. †

*   *   *

TANNEHILL, Robert C(ooper) 1934-

PERSONAL: Born May 6, 1934, in Clay Center, Kan.; son of Francis V. (a clergyman) and Cecelia (Cooper) Tannehill; married Alice Hunter (a nursery school teacher), August 13, 1955; children: Grace, Celia, Paul. *Education:* Hamline University, B.A., 1956; Yale University, B.D., 1959, M.A., 1960, Ph.D., 1963; also studied at University of Tuebingen, 1960-61.

ADDRESSES: Home—3 Mason Ct., Delaware, Ohio 43015. *Office*—Methodist Theological School, Delaware, Ohio 43015.

CAREER: Ordained Methodist clergyman, 1965; Oberlin School of Theology, Oberlin, Ohio, instructor in New Testament, 1963-66; Methodist Theological School, Delaware, Ohio, assistant professor, 1966-69, associate professor, 1969-74, professor of New Testament, 1974—.

MEMBER: Society of Biblical Literature, Studiorum Novi Testamenti Societas, Eastern Great Lakes Biblical Society (president, 1978-79).

AWARDS, HONORS: Danforth fellowship, 1956-63; Association of Theological Schools faculty fellowship, 1969-70, research award, 1975-76; Claremont fellow, Society of Biblical Literature, 1982.

WRITINGS:

Dying and Rising with Christ: A Study in Pauline Theology, Toepelmann, 1967.
(Contributor) *Jesus in Nazareth,* edited by Walther Eltester, de Gruyter, 1972.
The Sword of His Mouth: Forceful and Imaginative Language in Synoptic Sayings, Scholars Press, 1975.
A Mirror for Disciples: Following Jesus through Mark, Discipleship Resources, 1977.
(Contributor) *Studies in Literary Criticism and Biblical Literary Criticism in Honor of William A. Beardslee,* edited by Richarrd A. Spencer, Pickwick, 1980.
(Contributor) *Der Erzaehler des Evangeliums: Methodische Neuansaetze in der Markusforschung,* edited by Ferdinand Hahn, Verlag Katholisches Bibelwerk, 1985.
(Contributor) *The Interpretation of Mark,* edited by William Telford, Fortress, 1985.
The Narrative Unity of Luke-Acts: A Literary Interpretation, Fortress, Vol. 1: *The Gospel According to Luke,* 1986.

Associate editor of "Society of Biblical Literature Monograph Series," 1979-85. Also contributor to *Harper's Bible Dictionary.* Contributor to *Anglican Theological Review, Interpretation, Journal of Religion, Journal of Biblical Literature, Semeia, Aufstieg und Niedergang der roemischen Welt.*

*   *   *

TASCA, Jules 1938-

PERSONAL: Born December 10, 1938, in Philadelphia, Pa.; son of Edward Michael (an electrician) and Mary (Zaccaria) Tasca; married Beatrice Marie Hartranft (a tennis player), January 29, 1962; children: Edward, Jennifer, Joel. *Education:* Pennsylvania State University, B.A., 1961; Villanova University, M.A., 1963.; Heed University, D.A., 1985.

ADDRESSES: Home and office—313 Heston Ave., Norristown, Pa. 19401. *Agent*—Lois Berman, 250 West 57th St., New York, N.Y. 10019.

CAREER: Gwynedd Mercy College, Gwynedd Valley, Pa., associate professor of drama, 1963—, chairman of department, 1982—. Visiting professor at Beaver College, Glenside, Pa., 1965, 1982, Villanova University, Villanova, Pa., 1966, and Pennsylvania State University, Abington, Pa., 1966; director of public relations for Philadelphia Playhouse in the Park, 1969.

MEMBER: Dramatists Guild, Authors League of America, Writer's Guild East, Dramatists Guild (New York).

AWARDS, HONORS: First Prize Award, Performing Arts Repertory Theater, 1983, for *The Amazing Einstein;* Lindback Award for Outstanding Teaching, 1985.

WRITINGS:

PLAYS

Subject to Change (three-act; first produced in Chicago at Pheasant Run Theatre, April, 1971), Samuel French, 1970.
The Mind With the Dirty Man (two-act; first produced in Los Angeles at Mark Taper Forum, March, 1973), Samuel French, 1971.
Tear Along the Dotted Line (three-act; first produced in Gwynedd Valley, Pa., at Julia Ball Auditorium, 1965), Dramatic Publishing, 1973.
Tadpole (three-act; first produced in Los Angeles at Mark Taper Forum, 1973), Dramatists Play Service, 1974.
Chop Off Olympus (three-act; first produced in New York City at Triangle Theatre), Samuel French, 1974.
Five One-Act Plays By Mark Twain (adaptation; first produced in Gwynedd Valley, Pa., at Julia Ball Auditorium, 1975), Samuel French, 1976.
Susan B! (one-act; first produced in New York City at Town Hall, 1981), Dramatic Publishing, 1982.
The Amazing Einstein (libretto), Dramatic Publishing, 1983.
Romeo and Juliet Are Lovers, Aran Press, 1984.
Alive and Kicking, Dramatic Publishing, 1984.
The Necklace and Other Plays (adapted from stories of Guy de Maupassant), Samuel French, 1984.
Sire DeMaletroit's Door (adapted from Robert Louis Stevenson story), Dramatic Publishing, 1985.
Will (adapted from Stevenson story), Baker's Plays, 1985.
Women in Congress (modernization of Aristophanes' *Ecclesiazusae*), Samuel French, 1985.
(With Thomas Tierney and Ted Drachman) *Narnia* (adaptation of *The Lion, The Witch and the Wardrobe* by C. S. Lewis; produced in New York at Christ and St. Stephen's Church, October, 1986), Dramatic Publishing, 1987.
The God's Honest: An Evening of Lies (eight one-acts), Samuel French, 1988.

Also author of screenplay, "Frisbee." Author of "Nip'n Tuck," "Party of the First Part," "One Act by Art Smythe, Full Length Play by Joe Jones," "The Last Damned Witch in Salem," and "Goody One Shoe."

OTHER

(Contributor) Howard Teichmann, *George S. Kaufman: An Intimate Portrait,* Atheneum, 1972.
(Co-author) "Hal Linden Special," first broadcast by Columbia Broadcasting System, Inc. (CBS-TV), April, 1979.

SIDELIGHTS: In "The Mind With the Dirty Man," the longest running straight play in Las Vegas history, the leader of a small town's censorship board is challenged when his son, an underground filmmaker, plans to show his X-rated work in the local theatre. The plot is complicated by the son's love for the star of his movie and his plan to marry her on opening night in front of the theatre.

In a review of the play's Los Angeles production, a *Variety* critic notes that Tasca "has no particular axe to grind and writes only for entertainment." Tasca verifies this estimate in a *Philadelphia Bulletin* article when he states, "Okay, it's a situation comedy, like on TV. . . . It's meant to entertain. If people start thinking about it later, and decide that censorship is really kind of silly, so much the better. But there's no sense in satirizing an attitude if you turn off the types that may hold it. Acting superior to your audience is no good. The Greeks, Shakespeare, Moliere—they were all very popular entertainment in their own times."

Tasca told *CA:* "I am still writing. Every step is as hard to take as the last. The march is still on. The road is still called Hope. The end of the road is achievement. It is a land of few dwellers. If I get there, perhaps I can hide out until they find me and tell me I can't stay."

BIOGRAPHICAL/CRITICAL SOURCES:

BOOKS

Authors in the News, Volume 1, Gale, 1976.

PERIODICALS

New York Times, October 5, 1986.
Philadelphia Bulletin, June 23, 1974.
Variety, April 4, 1973.

*   *   *

TAYLOR, Karen
    See MALPEDE, Karen (Sophia)

*   *   *

TAYLOR, L(ester) B(arbour), Jr.   1932-

PERSONAL: Born November 9, 1932, in Lynchburg, Va.; son of Lester B. (a salesman) and Ruth (Hanna) Taylor; married Norma Billings, September 6, 1958; children: Cynthia, Chris, Tony. *Education:* Florida State University, B.S., 1955.

ADDRESSES: Home—5405 E. Lane Place Dr., Williamsburg, Va. 23185. *Office*—BASF Corp., Route 60, Williamsburg, Va. 23185.

CAREER: Pan-American Airlines, Kennedy Space Center, Cape Kennedy, Fla., public relations representative, 1957-62; Radio Corporation of America (now RCA Corp.), Kennedy Space Center, writer and editor, 1963-64; Ling, Temco, Vought (LTV), Kennedy Space Center, writer and editor, 1964-66; National Aeronautics and Space Administration, Kennedy Space Center, public information officer, 1966-68; Rockwell International, Pittsburgh, Pa., manager of publications, 1968-74; BASF Corp., Williamsburg, Va., public relations director, 1974—. *Military service:* U.S. Army, 1955-57.

MEMBER: Public Relations Society of America.

AWARDS, HONORS: Special citation from Aviation and Space Writers Association, 1975, for *For All Mankind: America's Space Programs of the Seventies and Beyond.*

WRITINGS:

Pieces of Eight: Recovering the Riches of a Lost Spanish Treasure Fleet, Dutton, 1966.
That Others Might Live: The Aerospace Rescue and Recovery Service, Dutton, 1967.
Liftoff: The Story of America's Spaceport, Dutton, 1968.
For All Mankind: America's Space Programs of the Seventies and Beyond, Dutton, 1974.
Gifts from Space: How Space Technology Is Improving Life on Earth (Junior Literary Guild selection), Crowell, 1977.
Chemistry Careers, F. Watts, 1978.
Rescue: True Stories of Heroism, F. Watts, 1979.
Emergency Squads, F. Watts, 1979.
Shoplifting, F. Watts, 1979.
Space Shuttle, Crowell, 1980.
The Draft: A Necessary Evil?, F. Watts, 1981.
Southeast Africa, F. Watts, 1981.

The New Right, F. Watts, 1981.
The Nuclear Arms Race, F. Watts, 1982.
The Military in Space, F. Watts, 1982.
Teenage Idols, Simon & Schuster, 1982.
Haunted Houses, Simon & Schuster, 1983.
Driving High, F. Watts, 1983.
Chemical and Biological Warfare, F. Watts, 1984.
The Commercialization of Space, F. Watts, 1986.
Electronic Surveillance, F. Watts, 1987.
Space: The New Battleground, F. Watts, 1988.
Manufacture in Space, F. Watts, 1990.
Hostage Taking, F. Watts, 1990.

Contributor of more than three hundred articles to national magazines, including *Ladies' Home Journal, Reader's Digest, Saturday Evening Post, True, Parade,* and *Family Weekly.*

SIDELIGHTS: L. B. Taylor, Jr. told *CA:* "I enjoy writing books and magazine articles because it exposes me to such a variety of intriguing subject matter and introduces me to so many interesting people. My book topics, for example, have included treasure hunting, the space shuttle, teenage heroes, haunted houses, and such celebrities as Scott Baio and John Schneider. I view writing, or at least my type of writing, as a craft at which you must work hard to master. The rewards from such effort can be very self-satisfying."

AVOCATIONAL INTERESTS: More writing, golf, gin rummy.

*   *   *

TAYLOR, Ronald (Jack)   1924-

PERSONAL: Born May 19, 1924, in London, England; son of J. Arthur (a banker) and Mary (Biggar) Taylor; children: Mark, Diana. *Education:* Royal Academy of Music, L.R.A.M., 1942; King's College, London, B.A., 1949, M.A., 1951, Ph.D., 1956.

ADDRESSES: Office—Arts Building, University of Sussex, Brighton, England.

CAREER: University instructor in English language and culture in Germersheim, West Germany, 1947, 1948; University of Wales, University College of Swansea, assistant lecturer, 1950-52, lecturer, 1952-59, senior lecturer in German, 1959-62; Northwestern University, Evanston, Ill., visiting professor of German, 1963-64; University of Sussex, Brighton, England, professor of German, 1965-85. Visiting professor at University of Chicago, 1960, and University of British Columbia, 1974, 1976. Member of panel of judges for the Schlegel-Tieck Translation Prize.

WRITINGS:

(With Arthur T. Hatto) *The Songs of Neidhart von Reuental,* Manchester University Press, 1958.
(Editor) E.T.A. Hoffmann, *Das Fraeulein von Scuderi,* Thomas Nelson, 1959, 2nd edition, 1962.
(With Walter Gottschalk) *A German-English Dictionary of Idioms,* Hueber Verlag, 1960, 6th edition, 1983.
Die Melodien der weltlichen Lieder des Mittelalters (title means "The Melodies of the Secular Songs of the Middle Ages"), two volumes, Metzler Verlag, 1964.
E.T.A. Hoffmann, Bowes, 1964.
The Art of the Minnesinger, two volumes, University of Wales Press, 1968.
The Romantic Tradition in Germany, Methuen, 1970.
The Intellectual Tradition of Modern Germany, two volumes, Bell & Sons, 1973.

(Translation editor) *Aesthetics and Politics: Debates Between Ernst Bloch, Georg Lukacs, Berthold Brecht, Walter Benjamin, Theodor Adorno,* New Left Books, 1977.
Richard Wagner: His Life, Art, and Thought, Taplinger, 1979.
Literature and Society in Germany, 1918-1945, Harvester, 1980.
Robert Schumann: His Life and Work, Granada Publishing, 1982.
Franz Liszt: The Man and the Musician, Granada Publishing, 1985.

TRANSLATOR

Hoffmann, *The Devil's Elixirs,* J. Calder, 1963.
Gottfried Keller, *A Village Romeo and Juliet,* J. Calder, 1966.
Theodor Storm, *Immensee,* J. Calder, 1966.
Eichendorff, *Memoirs of a Good-for-Nothing,* J. Calder, 1966.
Bruno Boesch, editor, *German Literature: A Critical Survey,* Methuen, 1971.
Herbert von Einem, *Michelangelo,* Methuen, 1973.
Konrad Lorenz, *Behind the Mirror: A Search for a Natural History of Human Knowledge,* Methuen, 1977.
Hanne Levy-Hass, *Inside Belsen,* Barnes & Noble, 1982.
(And author of introduction) Heinrich von Kleist, Ludwig Tieck, and Hoffmann, *Six Romantic German Tales,* Angel Books, 1985.

CONTRIBUTOR

Raghavan Iyer, editor, *The Glass Curtain Between Europe and Asia,* Oxford University Press, 1965.
Frederick Norman, editor, *Essays in German Literature,* Volume I, Institute of Germanic Studies, University of London, 1965.
Studies Presented to F. Norman, Institute of Germanic Studies, University of London, 1965.
Siegbert S. Prawer, editor, *The Romantic Period in German Literature,* Weidenfeld & Nicolson, 1970.
J. Malcolm S. Pasley, editor, *Germany: A Companion to German Studies,* Methuen, 1972.
Festschrift fuer Erich Heller, Stiehm, 1976.
Keith Bullivant, editor, *Society and Culture in the Weimar Republic,* Manchester University Press, 1977.

Contributor to *Penguin Companion to European Literature* and *Encyclopaedia Britannica.* Contributor of more than thirty articles and reviews to literature and music journals.

WORK IN PROGRESS: The Philosophical and Political Thought of Richard Wagner; Music and Politics: The Life and Career of Kurt Weill.

SIDELIGHTS: In *Literature and Society in Germany: 1918-1945,* Ronald Taylor investigates an artistically prolific time in recent German history and connects socio-political events with simultaneous trends in literature. While *Times Literary Supplement* contributor Michael Butler finds "Taylor's book does tell a fascinating, at times horrifying, story," he believes "the author's empirical approach works well enough in the drive of historical narrative, carried along as it is on a basis of well-documented fact and sources, but a similar pace in covering a very large number of minor and major literary figures, far from integrating them into the social fabric, is more likely to leave the reader breathless and with an impression of bittiness." Butler concludes, "The most successful pages of the book, in fact, document society and culture in Hitler's Germany.... Taylor's description of how the Nazis created their own canon of literature is chillingly instructive."

Taylor commented to *CA,* "I am by nature and by training as much a musician as a writer on literature, and I have pursued the relationship between the two areas in various historical periods. Further, I am concerned to study all art in its historical and social setting as a manifestation of human creativity." Taylor's biography, *Robert Schumann: His Life and Work,* analyzes the composer's life and his music. According to April FitzLyon in the *Times Literary Supplement,* Taylor "is at his best on the literary aspects of Schumann's life and work." *Washington Post Book World* contributor Joseph McLellan states that Taylor "has not tried to produce a definitive study but rather a fresh, readable one, based on a new examination of the abundant source material and distinguished primarily by the focus of his particular background and interests." FitzLyon concludes that Taylor "retells the sad story soberly and clearly, sets Schumann against the intellectual background of his time, and is at pains to avoid the sentimental excess which have marred some biographies of the composer." Taylor's subsequent volume, *Franz Liszt: The Man and the Musician,* also takes a literary approach to the composer, which provides "a wider context than many a purely musical approach," says Andrew Clements in the *New Statesman.* Clements also finds the book "compact and sensible," written with "control and breadth." J. E. Johnson in *Choice* likes the span of Taylor's work, and claims that "'Moving' is the key word to describe this portrait of Franz Lizst, the artist and the human being, in all his dimensions."

Taylor also told *CA:* "My earliest publications dealt with the medieval German lyric, especially the relationship between words and music. This is an analytical and highly specialized field of research in which the intellect is paramount, but the emotions barely touched. After a few years I felt my satisfaction in this work growing less and less. Hence I moved, still via the combination of literature and music, to the Romantic nineteenth century, to the philosophy of Romanticism, and to the problems of the relationship between art and life that it poses. This in turn led to my book, *The Intellectual Tradition of Modern Germany,* with its attempt to show, through the writings of leading German thinkers through the ages, the dominant strands in the German personality.

"My concern with present-day Germany, both as teacher and writer, has led me to spend a good deal of time in East Germany also, where I did a series of English language programmes on television. Some of my conclusions on the East-West problem have found their way into newspapers, including the London *Daily Telegraph.*

"In all of this activity I am concerned above all with what might be called intellectual and cultural continuity as it shows itself in different periods of German and European history (my book on literature and society in Germany between 1918 and 1945 is another part of this picture). Perhaps this is a natural interest for one whose activity centers on Germany, a country whose tortured history through the centuries seems to me to make it almost inevitable, if one is to seek a blend of mind and spirit, that one's net should be cast wide in the attempt to understand the subject more fully."

BIOGRAPHICAL/CRITICAL SOURCES:

PERIODICALS

Choice, October, 1986.
New Statesman, November 21, 1986.
Times Literary Supplement, May 15, 1981, December 17, 1982.
Washington Post Book World, December 31, 1982.

TENNANT, Kylie
See RODD, Kylie Tennant

*   *   *

THAYER, Charles Wheeler   1910-1969

PERSONAL: Born February 9, 1910, in Villanova, Pa.; died of a heart attack August 27, 1969, in Salzburg, Austria; buried in Bryn Mawr, Pa.; son of George Chapman and Gertrude May (Wheeler) Thayer; married Cynthia Dunn Cochrane, 1950; children: James Dunn, Diana Cochrane (stepdaughter). *Education:* United States Military Academy at West Point, B.S., 1933; attended National War College, 1946.

ADDRESSES: Agent—Brandt & Brandt, 101 Park Ave., New York, N.Y. 10017.

CAREER: U.S. Foreign Service, held various posts in Germany, 1937-38, Hamburg, 1939-40, Kabul, Afghanistan, 1942-43, and London, England, 1943-44. Served as political commissioner on U.S.-U.S.S.R. Commission for Korea, 1946; chief of division of international broadcasting, Voice of America, 1947-49; U.S. political liaison officer to German government at Bonn, 1949-52, and consul general and land commissioner to Bavaria, 1952-53. *Military service:* U.S. Army, Cavalry, 1933; became lieutenant; active duty, 1943-45; became lieutenant colonel; served as chief, U.S. Military Mission to Marshall Tito in Yugoslavia, 1944-45, and chief, Office of Strategic Services Mission to Austria, 1945.

AWARDS, HONORS: Legion of Merit.

MEMBER: Metropolitan Club, Overseas Writers Club (both Washington, D.C.), Travelers Club (Paris).

WRITINGS:

Bears in the Caviar, Lippincott, 1949.
Hands across the Caviar, Lippincott, 1950.
The Unquiet Germans, Harper, 1957.
Diplomat, Harper, 1959, Greenwood, 1974.
(With others) *Russia,* Time, Inc., 1960.
Moscow Interlude, Harper, 1962.
Natasha, M. Joseph, 1962.
Guerilla, Harper, 1963.
Checkpoint, Harper, 1964.
Muzzy, Harper, 1966.

Contributor to *Atlantic, Life, Look, New Yorker, Saturday Evening Post, Sports Illustrated,* and other national magazines.

SIDELIGHTS: Once referred to in the *Washington Post* as "one of the country's leading experts on Russia," American diplomat Charles Wheeler Thayer was fluent in Russian, German, French, Spanish, Italian, and Serbo-Croatian. *Bears in the Caviar* was translated into German; *Russia* was translated into French and Spanish.

BIOGRAPHICAL/CRITICAL SOURCES:

PERIODICALS

America, August 24, 1957.
Harper's, December, 1959.
Nation, September 14, 1957.
Reader's Digest, April, 1959.
Saturday Evening Post, March 31, 1956, April 7, 1956, April 14, 1956.
Saturday Review, September 28, 1957.
Washington Post, August 29, 1969.

OBITUARIES:

PERIODICALS

Washington Post, August 29, 1969.†

*   *   *

THOMPSON, Eugene Allen   1924-
(Gene Thompson)

PERSONAL: Born June 28, 1924, in San Francisco, Calif.; son of Andrew A. (a naval officer) and Rose (Gleenblat) Thompson; married Sylvia Vaughn Thompson (a writer), June 15, 1955; children: David Oxley, Benjamin Stuart, Dinah Vaughan, Amanda Greenleaf. *Education:* University of California, Berkeley, B.A., 1949; independent graduate study abroad, 1950-54.

ADDRESSES: Home—P.O. Box 145, Idyllwild, Calif. 92349. *Agent*—Robert Lescher, 155 East 71st St., New York, N.Y. 10021.

CAREER: Writer for radio programs "The Groucho Marx Show," and "Duffy's Tavern," 1943-45; free-lance writer in Europe, 1950; director of publications for U.S. Army Corps of Engineers, and teacher of literature for U.S. Army, Heidelberg, West Germany, 1950-54; copywriter for C. J. La Roche in New York, N.Y., and later director of radio and television for BBD & O in San Francisco, Calif., 1955-64; writer for comedy and dramatic shows, including "Baretta," "Columbo," "Cannon," "Harry-O," "Marcus Welby, M.D.," "The Lucille Ball Show," "Love, American Style," "My Three Sons," "The Beverly Hillbillies," and "Bob Newhart," in Hollywood, Calif., 1965-76; novelist, 1977—.

MEMBER: Writers Guild of America (West), Authors League of America.

WRITINGS:

UNDER NAME GENE THOMPSON

Lupe, Random House, 1977.
Murder Mystery, Random House, 1980.
Nobody Cared for Kate (Literary Guild selection), Random House, 1982.
A Cup of Death, Random House, 1988.

SIDELIGHTS: Gene Thompson told *CA:* "My writing has been greatly influenced by the fact that my earlier work was written for radio and television and performed before an audience." Thompson's work has been translated into French, German, Spanish, Dutch, and Italian.

BIOGRAPHICAL/CRITICAL SOURCES:

PERIODICALS

Globe and Mail (Toronto), January 2, 1988.
Los Angeles Times, November 21, 1980.
Newsweek, July 25, 1977.
New Yorker, March 2, 1981, September 12, 1983.
New York Times Book Review, August 7, 1977, January 18, 1981, September 4, 1983.
Time, July 4, 1983.
Times Literary Supplement, August 14, 1981.
Washington Post Book World, November 16, 1980.

*   *   *

THOMPSON, Gene
See THOMPSON, Eugene Allen

THOMPSON, Sylvia
  See THOMPSON, Sylvia Vaughn (Sheekman)

* * *

THOMPSON, Sylvia Vaughn (Sheekman)   1935-
  (Sylvia Thompson)

PERSONAL: Born June 19, 1935, in Santa Monica, Calif.; daughter of Arthur (a screenwriter) and Gloria (a film star; maiden name, Stuart) Sheekman; married Gene Thompson (a free-lance writer and novelist), June 15, 1955; children: David Oxley, Benjamin Stuart, Dinah Vaughan, Amanda Greenleaf. *Education:* Attended University of California, Berkeley, 1952-55, and Sorbonne, 1954.

ADDRESSES: Home—P.O. Box 145, Idyllwild, Calif. 92349. *Agent*—Susan Lescher, 67 Irving Pl., New York, N.Y. 10003.

CAREER: Writer. Lord & Taylor, New York, N.Y., copywriter, 1955-56.

WRITINGS:

Economy Gastronomy: A Gourmet Cookbook for the Budget-Minded, Atheneum, 1963.
The Budget Gourmet, Random House, 1975.
Woman's Day Crockery Cuisine: Slow-Cooking Recipes for Family and Entertainment, Random House, 1977.
(Under name Sylvia Thompson) *Feasts and Friends: The Education of a Cook,* North Point Press, 1988.

Contributor of articles to *Vogue, House Beautiful, Gourmet, Woman's Day, Holiday, Family Circle, Travel & Leisure, Good Housekeeping, Harrowsmith,* and *Sphere.*

BIOGRAPHICAL/CRITICAL SOURCES:

PERIODICALS

Money, May, 1976.
New York Times, May 9, 1978.
Publishers Weekly, March 10, 1975, October 17, 1977, May 22, 1978.
Village Voice, December 22, 1975.
Washington Post Book World, December 4, 1977.

* * *

THULSTRUP, Niels   1924-

PERSONAL: Born May 6, 1924, in Aalborg, Denmark; son of C. C. and J. M. E. Thulstrup; married Marie Mikulova, 1950; children: Johannes. *Education:* University of Copenhagen, Th.M., 1950, D.Th., 1968; graduate study at University of Zurich, University of Rome, Oxford University and Cambridge University, 1950-66.

CAREER: University of Copenhagen, Copenhagen, Denmark, assistant professor of systematic theology, 1950-59, university librarian, 1958-60; pastor, Evangelical-Lutheran Church of Denmark, 1959-68; University of Copenhagen, associate professor, 1963-68, senior professor of systematic theology, 1968-86, director of Soeren Kierkegaard Library, 1965-86. Visiting lecturer, 1965-87, at University of Groningen, University of Helsinki, Princeton University, Drew University, Central Michigan University, University of Rome, University of Freiburg, University of Basel, Harvard University, Yale University, and Cambridge University. Member of advisory board for Kierkegaard's writings, 1972-76.

MEMBER: Soeren Kierkegaard Society (founder, 1948; secretary, 1948-66; vice-president, 1967-81), Kierkegaard Academy (co-founder and editor, 1976—), Danish Humanistic Literature Society.

AWARDS, HONORS: Silver medal, University of Copenhagen, 1948, for a treatise on Hegel's *Philosophy of Right;* Swenson-Kierkegaard Memorial fellowship, 1951; Knight of the Dannebrog, 1976; Great Cross of Merit, Federal Republic of Germany, 1984; grants from University of Copenhagen, the Carlsberg Foundation, and the Danish Research Council for Humanities.

WRITINGS:

Soeren Kierkegaard: Bidrag til en Bibliografi (title means "Soeren Kierkegaard: Contributions Towards a Bibliography"), Munksgaard (Copenhagen), 1951.
(Editor and contributor) *Jubilaeumsausgabe,* Jakob Hegner, (Cologne), Volumes I-IV, 1951-60.
(Author of introduction) *Augustins Bekendelser,* Haase (Copenhagen), 1952.
(Editor and contributor) *Soeren Kierkegaard: Breve og Akstykker vedrorende,* Munksgaard, Volume I, 1953, Volume II, 1954, published together with commentaries as *Letters and Documents,* Princeton University Press, 1978.
(Editor and contributor) *Soeren Kierkegaard: Philosophiske Smuler med Indledning og Kommentar,* Munksgaard, 1955, 2nd revised edition, 1977, translation by Howard V. Hong published as *Philosophical Fragments with Introduction and Commentary,* Princeton University Press, 1962.
(Editor) *Kierkegaardiana,* eleven volumes, Munksgaard, 1955-80.
Introduceret Udgave af: Katalog over Soeren Kierkegaard's Bibliotek (title means "Catalogue of Soeren Kierkegaard's Library with Introduction"), Munksgaard, 1957.
(Editor and author of introduction and notes) *Soeren Kierkegaard: Frygt og Baeven* (title means "Soeren Kierkegaard: Fear and Trembling"), Gyldendal, 1961, 12th revised edition, 1983.
(Editor and author of introduction and notes) *Soeren Kierkegaard: Afsluttende uvidenskabelig Efterskrift* (title means "Soeren Kierkegaard: Concluding Unscientific Postscript"), Gyldendal, Volume I, 1962, Volume II, 1962, revised edition, translated by Robert J. Widenmann, published as *Commentary on Kierkegaard's Concluding Unscientific Postscript,* Princeton University Press, 1984.
(Editor with Howard A. Johnson) *A Kierkegaard Critique,* Harper, 1962.
Kierkegaard's Forhold til Hegel, Gyldendal, 1967, translation published as *Kierkegaard's Relation to Hegel,* Princeton University Press, 1980.
(Editor) *Soeren Kierkegaard's Papirer,* 25 volumes, 2nd enlarged edition, Munksgaard, 1968-78.
(Editor with Soeren Holm) *Ethisk Antologi* (title means "Anthology of Ethics"), [Copenhagen], 1972.
(Editor) *Fra Platon til Hegel: Religionsfilosotisk Antologi* (title means "From Plato to Hegel: Anthology of the Philosophy of Religion"), three volumes, [Copenhagen], 1976, 2nd revised edition, 1980.
(Co-editor) *Bibliotheca Kierkegaardiana,* Volumes 1-16, C. A. Reitzel (Copenhagen), 1978-88.
Akcept og Protest: Artikler i Udvalg (title means "Acceptance and Protest: Selected Essays"), two volumes, [Copenhagen], 1981.

Kierkegaard and the Church in Denmark, C. A. Reitzel, 1984.
(Contributor) G. L. Stengren, editor, *Faith, Knowledge, and Action*, C. A. Reitzel, 1984.
The Copenhagen of Kierkegaard, C. A. Reitzel, 1986.

SIDELIGHTS: Niels Thulstrup's *Commentary on Kierkegaard's Concluding Unscientific Postscript* "provides a useful historical outline of previous developments in the philosophy of religion," observes Patrick Gardiner in the *Times Literary Supplement*, "many of which are certainly relevant to the interpretation of Kierkegaard's work and its aims." Gardiner notes that one of the features of Thulstrup's work is that "it helps to illuminate the Danish context of Kierkegaard's work." The critic concludes by commending Thulstrup's book as "undoubtedly [being] of great value to those who wish to find a path through [the *Postscript*'s] elusive and allusive complexities."

BIOGRAPHICAL/CRITICAL SOURCES:

PERIODICALS

Times Literary Supplement, April 12, 1985.

*   *   *

TIERNEY, Kevin (Hugh)   1942-

PERSONAL: Born September 22, 1942, in Bristol, England; came to United States in 1966, naturalized in 1979; son of Hugh John (a chartered accountant) and Margaret Ellis (Davies) Tierney. *Education:* St. John's College, Cambridge, B.A., 1964, LL.B., 1965; Yale University, LL.M., 1967, M.A., 1968.

ADDRESSES: Office—Department of Law, Hastings College of the Law, 200 Mcallister St., San Francisco, Calif. 94102.

CAREER: Called to the bar, England, 1966; admitted to the State Bar of Michigan, 1977, the Bar of the U.S. District Court, Eastern District of Michigan, 1978, and the Bar of the U.S. Court of Appeals, 9th Circuit, 1984; Donovan, Leisure, Newton & Irvine (law firm), New York, N.Y., associate lawyer, 1969-70; Wayne State University Law School, Detroit, Mich., associate professor, 1971-75, professor, 1975-79; University of California, Hastings College of Law, San Francisco, visiting professor, 1979-80, professor, 1980—; writer. Reporter, Michigan Standard Jury Instruction Committee, 1975-79; member of executive committee, Institute for Continuing Legal Education, Ann Arbor, Mich., 1977-80.

MEMBER: American Law Institute, State Bar of Michigan, Order of Coif, Lincoln's Inn (London), University Club (San Francisco).

AWARDS, HONORS: Lord Mansfield scholar, 1966; Sterling fellow, 1967.

WRITINGS:

Courtroom Testimony: A Policeman's Guide, Funk, 1970.
How to Be a Witness, Oceana, 1971.
Darrow: A Biography, Crowell, 1979.

Contributor of articles to encyclopedias and journals, including *New Law Journal* and *New Republic*.

WORK IN PROGRESS: A biography of the poet Robert Graves (1895-1985).

SIDELIGHTS: In his 1979 biography of famed attorney Clarence Darrow, the first published since 1941, Kevin Tierney

"marshals the evidence as counsel for the defense and also as prosecutor, then figuratively takes the bench as judge and renders a fair verdict" on Darrow's life, writes W. A. Swanberg in the *New York Times Book Review*. Presenting a thorough picture of the lawyer's life, *Darrow: A Biography* is based on comprehensive research, including public manuscript collections and Darrow's own writings. "Tierney has done enormous reading about Darrow," comments *Chicago Tribune Book World* contributor Leon M. Despres, "and he presents the facts of Darrow's life in a steady, orderly progression." Although the critic faults the book's style and the occasional error, he commends Tierney's treatment of his subject, remarking that the author "does not spare Darrow." Swanberg also finds the work equitable: "[Tierney's] own knowledge of the law, supported by extensive research and a point of view that is scrupulously fair, makes this the best Darrow biography yet, an engrossing portrayal of a man utterly original and all too human."

Tierney wrote *CA:* "Above all, I value clarity and precision in language; the greatest literary sin is incomprehensibility. In both fact and fiction, I favor a spare, uncluttered style. I try to avoid mere word-spinning and am brutal in editing my own rough drafts.

"I used to work best at a typewriter (on which I am self-taught and very inaccurate) but have now 'graduated' to a word-processing computer, and have often wondered if I should be reincarnated as a journalist. I work well to a deadline, but it must be absolutely hard and fast with no possibility of extension. I admire both Henry Mencken and Malcolm Muggeridge as stylists and gadflies, though I profoundly disagree with the former's opinion that there is (or ought to be) an 'American' language distinct from English; for myself, I rejoice in the commonality of the Anglo-American literary tradition."

BIOGRAPHICAL/CRITICAL SOURCES:

PERIODICALS

Chicago Tribune Book World, June 24, 1979.
Los Angeles Times, June 18, 1979.
New Yorker, July 16, 1979.
New York Times Book Review, May 27, 1979.
Washington Post, June 14, 1979.

*   *   *

TILLINGHAST, Richard (Williford)   1940-

PERSONAL: Born November 25, 1940, in Memphis, Tenn.; son of Raymond Charles (a mechanical engineer) and Martha (Williford) Tillinghast; married Nancy Walton Pringle, 1965 (divorced, 1970); married Mary Graves, April 22, 1973; children: (second marriage) three sons, one daughter. *Education:* University of the South, Sewanee, Tenn., A.B., 1962; Harvard University, A.M., 1963, Ph.D., 1970.

ADDRESSES: Home—1317 Granger Ave., Ann Arbor, Mich. 48104. *Office*—Department of English, University of Michigan, Haven Hall, Ann Arbor, Mich. 48109.

CAREER: University of California, Berkeley, assistant professor of English, 1968-73; University of the South, Sewanee, Tenn., visiting assistant professor, 1979-80; Harvard University, Cambridge, Mass., Briggs-Copeland lecturer, 1980-83; University of Michigan, Ann Arbor, associate professor of English, 1983—; formerly affiliated with College of Marin and the college program at San Quentin State Prison. Associate, Michigan Institute for the Humanities, 1988-89.

AWARDS, HONORS: Woodrow Wilson fellow, 1962-63; Sinclair-Kennedy travel grant, Harvard University, 1966-67; Creative Arts Institute grant, University of California, Berkeley, 1970; National Endowment for the Humanities grant, 1980; Bread Loaf fellowship, 1982; Michigan Arts Council grant, 1985; Millay Colony residency, 1985; residency, Yaddo Writers' Retreat, 1986.

WRITINGS:

POETRY

Sleep Watch, Wesleyan University Press, 1969.
(Contributor) *Ten American Poets,* Carcanet Press, 1974.
The Knife and Other Poems, Wesleyan University Press, 1980.
Sewanee in Ruins (also see below), drawings by Edward Carlos, University of the South, 1981.
Fossils, Metal, and the Blue Limit, White Creek Press, 1982.
Our Flag Was Still There (contains *Sewanee in Ruins*), Wesleyan University Press, 1984.

OTHER

Contributor to *Antaeus, Atlantic Monthly, Boston Globe, Boston Review, Crazy Horse, Critical Quarterly, Georgia Review, Harper's Bazaar, Harvard Advocate, New Republic, New York Times Book Review, Paris Review, Partisan Review, Ploughshares, Poetry, Sewanee Review, Shenandoah, Southern Review, Washington Post,* and *Yale Review.*

SIDELIGHTS: Richard Tillinghast's speech "is quiet, modest, witty, while he talks about the oddness of the ordinary experiences of life," observes *Poetry* contributor Robert Watson. The critic remarks that "the title of this collection, *Sleep Watch,* is very accurate, for a large number of his poems are about sleeping and waking, about the operation of the mind. The experiences he presents have the quality of a collage or surrealistic film: waking states of mind shift to dream states, to memories, memories seem to merge with fantasy or vision." Tillinghast's second collection, *The Knife and Other Poems,* addresses "the experience of outliving the 1960s . . . ," says Alan Williamson in *Parnassus: Poetry in Review,* "one from which my generation never fully recovered." Williamson thinks that the author's work "is poetry carefully made, phrase by phrase, so that it often succeeds in incising itself on one's memory. If it also lacks something, a darting speed, a playfulness with language, when compared with Tillinghast's first volume . . . well, that too is part of the plot. Indeed, one of the things I admire about the Tillinghast of *The Knife* is his flat acknowledgment of dispirited and even rather nasty feelings." Concludes the critic: "This tone is rare in poetry though more mannered, more romanticized, self-condemnations are not."

In *Our Flag Was Still There,* Tillinghast's 1984 collection, the author "writes with a new confidence, direction, and stylistic maturity," comments Thomas Swiss in the *Sewanee Review.* The focal point of the book is "Sewanee in Ruins," a long poem that combines journals, biographical sources, letters, and Tillinghast's own experiences to deliver a broad portrait of the University of the South. "The poem evolves into an elaborate meditation, beginning with the destruction of the University of the South during the Civil War and finally projecting a vision of a future after nuclear war in the same setting," summarizes Swiss. While *New York Times Book Review* contributor Paul Breslin remarks that the author occasionally "rambles on too long" and "runs the risk . . . of writing an alumni-magazine piece," he observes that Tillinghast "escapes that fate by combining his documentary sources to establish a cu-

mulative portrait of a way of life." Swiss also notes, similar to previous criticism of Tillinghast's work, a slow deliberateness to the poet's language: "Tillinghast's habitual listing of images and his linking of adjectives slows the poem, but not often and not in a way that detracts from its impact." The critic continues: "Tillinghast creates a complex system of rhythm and sound with his careful lineation, finding unusual and dynamic verbs. [He] has learned . . . a particular kind of phrasal style that is carefully crafted and yet seemingly colloquial."

BIOGRAPHICAL/CRITICAL SOURCES:

BOOKS

Contemporary Literary Criticism, Volume 29, Gale, 1984.

PERIODICALS

New York Times Book Review, May 10, 1981, July 22, 1984.
Parnassus: Poetry in Review, fall-winter, 1981.
Poetry, December, 1970.
Sewanee Review, October, 1985.

*   *   *

TODD, Burbank L.
[Collective pseudonym]

WRITINGS:

"BACK TO THE SOIL" SERIES

Hiram, the Young Farmer; or, Making the Soil Pay, Sully & Kleinteich, 1914.
Hiram in the Middle West; or, A Young Farmer's Upward Struggle, Sully & Kleinteich, 1915.

SIDELIGHTS: For more information see the entries for Harriet S. Adams, Edward L. Stratemeyer, and Andrew E. Svenson.

BIOGRAPHICAL/CRITICAL SOURCES:

BOOKS

Johnson, Deidre, editor and compiler, *Stratemeyer Pseudonyms and Series Books: An Annotated Checklist of Stratemeyer and Stratemeyer Syndicate Publications,* Greenwood Press, 1982.

*   *   *

TRAFZER, Clifford Earl   1949-

PERSONAL: Born March 1, 1949, in Mansfield, Ohio; son of Donald W. (an upholsterer) and Mary Lou (a businesswoman; maiden name, Henry) Trafzer; married Lee Ann Smith (a lawyer), January 31, 1982. *Education:* Northern Arizona University, B.A., 1970, M.A., 1971; Oklahoma State University, Ph.D., 1973. *Politics:* Democrat.

ADDRESSES: Home—3543 Quailview St., Spring Valley, Calif. 92077. *Office*—American Indian Studies, San Diego State University, San Diego, Calif. 92124.

CAREER: Arizona Historical Society, Yuma, museum curator, 1973-76; Navajo Community College, Tsaile, Ariz., instructor in American Indian history, 1976-77; Washington State University, Pullman, assistant professor, 1977-82, associate professor of American Indian history, 1982; San Diego State University, San Diego, Calif., associate professor of American Indian studies, 1982-83, professor, 1983—, department chair, 1983—. Consultant on racism, academics, and Indian history to Colville Confederated Tribe and Shoalwater Bay Indian tribe. Member of board, San Diego American Indian Health Clinic.

MEMBER: American Historical Association, Organization of American Historians, American Indian Historical Association, Western History Association.

AWARDS, HONORS: Best nonfiction award nomination, Western Writers of America and the National Cowboy Hall of Fame, 1982, for *The Kit Carson Campaign: The Last Great Navajo War;* Governor's Award for best nonfiction on Northwest history, State of Washington, 1986, for *Renegade Tribe.*

WRITINGS:

(Contributor) Albert H. Shroeder, editor, *The Changing Ways of Southwestern Indians: A Historical Perspective,* Rio Grande, 1973.
The Judge: The Life of Robert A. Hefner, University of Oklahoma Press, 1975.
Navajo Raiders and Anglo Expansionists: A Conflict of Interest, Navajo Community College Press, 1978.
Navajos and Spaniards, Navajo Community College Press, 1978.
(With Richard D. Scheuerman) *The Volga Germans: Pioneers of the Northwest,* University Press of Idaho, 1980.
The Kit Carson Campaign: The Last Great Navajo War, University of Oklahoma Press, 1982.
(Editor) *Indians, Superintendents, and Councils,* University Press of America, 1983.
(Editor) *American Indian Prophets,* Sierra Oaks, 1986.
(With Scheuerman) *Renegade Tribe: The Palouse Indians and the Invasion of the Inland Pacific Northwest,* Washington State University Press, 1986.
(With Scheuerman) *Chief Joseph's Allies: The Palouse Indians and the Nez Perce War of 1877,* Sierra Oaks, 1987.

Contributor to history journals, including *Journal of American History, Pacific Historian, American West, Journal of Arizona History, Chronicles of Oklahoma,* and *Montana.*

WORK IN PROGRESS: The Yakima Reservation, 1855-1930, a study using the many statistics regarding births, deaths, disease, agriculture, and law and order on the reservation.

SIDELIGHTS: Clifford Earl Trafzer once told *CA:* "I became interested in American Indian history because of my own Indian ancestry, the interest my mother gave me in history, and the need for a new dimension in the historical writings of Indians. American Indian history must be approached through Indian sources as well as white sources and with an understanding of the oral tradition, religious beliefs, language, and other aspects of the specific Indian group one studies."

*   *   *

TROUGHTON, Joanna (Margaret) 1947-

PERSONAL: Born September 9, 1947, in London, England; daughter of Patrick (an actor) and Margaret Troughton; married Brian Melling (an illustrator), 1986; children: Jack. *Education:* Hornsey College of Art, N.D.A.D. (with first class honors), 1969.

ADDRESSES: Home—London, England. *Agent*—B. L. Kearley Ltd., 13 Chiltern St., London W1M 1HF, England.

CAREER: Free-lance illustrator for advertising, magazines, and books, 1969—. Part-time teacher, Harrow School of Art, Middlesex, England, 1975-81, Barnet College of Art, 1979-86, Watford College of Art, 1982-85, and Croyden College of Art, 1985-86. Speaker at schools and libraries throughout Britain on her work.

AWARDS, HONORS: Kate Greenaway Medal commendation, 1976, for *How the Birds Changed Their Feathers.*

WRITINGS:

FOR CHILDREN

(Reteller) *Sir Gawain and the Loathly Damsel,* illustrated by Troughton, Dutton, 1972.
Soldier, Soldier, Won't You Marry Me?, Blackie & Son, 1972.
Spotted Horse, Blackie & Son, 1972.
(Reteller) *Why Flies Buzz: A Nigerian Folk Tale,* Blackie & Son, 1974.
(Adapter) *The Story of Rama and Sita,* Blackie & Son, 1975.
(Reteller) *How the Birds Changed Their Feathers,* Blackie & Son, 1976, published as *How the Birds Changed Their Feathers: A South American Folk Tale,* Peter Bedrick, 1986.
(Reteller) *What Made Tiddalik Laugh,* Blackie & Son, 1977, published as *What Made Tiddalik Laugh: An Australian Aborigine Folk Tale,* Peter Bedrick, 1986.
How Rabbit Stole the Fire, Blackie & Son, 1979, published as *How Rabbit Stole the Fire: A North American Indian Folk Tale,* Peter Bedrick, 1986.
Tortoise's Dream, Blackie & Son, 1980, published as *Tortoise's Dream: An African Folk Tale,* Peter Bedrick, 1986.
The Magic Mill, Blackie & Son, 1981.
(Reteller) *The Wizard Punchkin,* Blackie & Son, 1982.
Blue-Jay and Robin, Blackie & Son, 1983.
Mouse-Deer's Market: A Folk Tale from Borneo, illustrated by Troughton, Peter Bedrick, 1984.
Who Will Be the Sun?: A North American Indian Folk Tale, illustrated by Troughton, Peter Bedrick, 1986.
How Night Came: A Folk Tale from the Amazon, illustrated by Troughton, Peter Bedrick, 1986.
The Quail's Egg, illustrated by Troughton, Peter Bedrick, 1988.

ILLUSTRATOR

Greta James, *The Bodhi Tree,* Geoffrey Chapman, 1971.
The Little Mohee: An Appalachian Ballad, Dutton, 1971.
Kevin Crossley-Holland, *The Sea Stranger,* Heinemann, 1972.
Barbara S. Briggs, *Cookery Corner Cards,* Mills & Boon, 1973.
Geoffrey Trease, *Days to Remember: A Garland of Historic Anniversaries,* Heinemann, 1973.
(With Andrew Sier and Barry Wilkinson) Jenny Taylor and Terry Ingleby, *The Scope Storybook,* Longman, 1974.
Crossley-Holland, *The Fire-Brother,* Seabury, 1975.
Elizabeth Kyle (pseudonym of Agnes Mary Robertson Dunlop), *The Key of the Castle,* Heinemann, 1976.
Crossley-Holland, *The Earth-Father,* Heinemann, 1976.
Sheila K. McCullagh, *The Kingdom under the Sea,* Hulton, 1976.
James Reeves, reteller, *Quest and Conquest: "Pilgrim's Progress" Retold,* Blackie & Son, 1976, published as *Pilgrim's Progress Retold,* Bedrick/Blackie, 1987.
(With Fiona French) Richard Blythe, *Fabulous Beasts,* Mac-

donald Educational, 1977, published as *Dragons and Other Fabulous Beasts,* Grosset, 1980.

Julia Dobson, *The Smallest Man in England,* Heinemann, 1977.

John D. Lincoln, *Montezuma,* Cambridge University Press, 1977.

Lincoln, *The Fair-Skinner Strangers,* Cambridge University Press, 1977.

Robert Nye, *Out of the World and Back Again,* Collins, 1979.

Wendy Body, *Clay Horses,* Longman, 1979.

Adele Geras, *A Thousand Yards of Sea,* Hodder & Stoughton, 1979.

Gillian Wrobel, reteller, *Ali Baba and the Forty Thieves,* Macdonald Educational, 1979.

(With Kim Blundell) Michael Pollard, *My World,* Macdonald Educational, 1979.

Taylor and Ingleby, *Ganpat's Long Ride* [and] *Shanti and the Snake,* Longman, 1979.

Anna Sproule, reteller, *Warriors,* Macdonald Educational, 1980.

Sproule, reteller, *Villains,* Macdonald Educational, 1980.

(With Peter Dennis and Sara Cole) Jenny Vaughan, *The Easter Book,* Grosset, 1980.

Patricia Daniels, reteller, *Ali Baba and the Forty Thieves,* Raintree, 1980.

Gail Robinson, *Raven the Trickster,* Chatto & Windus, 1981.

Jamilia Gavin, *Stories from the Hindu World,* Silver Burdett, 1986.

SIDELIGHTS: Joanna Troughton told *CA:* "Although I retell myths and legends from all around the world, my favorite areas for stories are North and South America. I'm not sure if this is because the myths were collected in these areas at just the right time, that is before they became too 'civilized,' or whether it is simply that the Indians' stories are so good! They also have the best 'trickster' stories in the world—a group of myths that particularly fascinates me. I suppose that mythology inspires me because it is made up of 'archetypes.' And the study of mythology leads to other areas that interest me—ethnology, ethology, anthropology, etc. I am also very inspired by 'primitive' art.

"The medium I work in is watercolor; I may use other bits and pieces with this (for example, crayon and gouache), but watercolor is my favorite. For line work, I use pen and change the nib size to suit the illustration."

MEDIA ADAPTATIONS: What Made Tiddalik Laugh was made into a film for the British Broadcasting Corporation's "Words and Pictures" series.

*   *   *

TWITCHETT, Carol Cosgrove 1943-
(Carol Ann Cosgrove)

PERSONAL: Born May 7, 1943, in Slough, Buckinghamshire, England; daughter of Thomas Jack (an engineer) and Gay (Killick) Cosgrove; married Kenneth Joseph Twitchett (a university lecturer), July 16, 1966; children: Robin, Andrew. *Education:* London School of Economics, B.Sc. (honors), 1965, M.Sc., 1966, Ph.D., 1976. *Politics:* "Vaguely liberal." *Religion:* Christian.

ADDRESSES: Home—154 Craven Rd., Newbury, Berkshire, England. *Office*—University of Surrey, Guildford, Surrey GU2 5XH, England.

CAREER: University of Reading, Berkshire, England, lecturer in politics, 1966-68; Aberdeen College of Education, Aberdeen, Scotland, lecturer in politics, 1968-72; University of Surrey, Guildford, Surrey, England, associate professor, 1976—. Lecturer for European Communities' Information Service.

WRITINGS:

(Under name Carol Ann Cosgrove; editor with husband, Kenneth J. Twitchett) *The New International Actors: The United Nations and the European Economic Community,* St. Martin's, 1970.

(Under name Carol Ann Cosgrove) *A Reader's Guide to Britain and the European Communities,* Chatham House, 1970.

Europe and Africa: From Association to Partnership, Gower, 1978.

Harmonisation in the EEC, St. Martin's, 1981.

(Editor with K. J. Twitchett) *Building Europe: Britain's Partners in the EEC,* Europa, 1981.

A Framework for Development, Allen and Unwin, 1981.

Contributor to *International Relations, World Today, Journal of Contemporary History, European Community, Europa-Archiv,* and other journals. Literary editor, *Journal of Common Market Studies.*†

U

ULAM, Adam B(runo) 1922-

PERSONAL: Born April 8, 1922, in Lwow, Poland; son of Jozef and Anna (Auerbach) Ulam; married Mary Hamilton Burgwin, 1963; children: Alexander Stanislaw, Joseph Howard. *Education:* Brown University, A.B., 1943; Harvard University, Ph.D., 1947. *Politics.* Democrat.

ADDRESSES: Office—Littauer Center, Harvard University, Cambridge, Mass. 02138.

CAREER: Harvard University, Cambridge, Mass., began as teaching fellow, 1947, professor of government, 1959-79, Gurney Professor of History and Political Science, 1979—, Russian Research Center, research associate, 1948—, director, 1973-76, 1980—. Research associate, Center for International Studies, Massachusetts Institute of Technology, 1953-55.

MEMBER: Signet Club (Cambridge).

AWARDS, HONORS: Guggenheim fellow, 1956; Rockefeller fellow, 1957, 1960.

WRITINGS:

Philosophical Foundations of English Socialism, Harvard University Press, 1951.
Titoism and the Cominform, Harvard University Press, 1952.
(Editor with Samuel Hutchinson Beer) *Patterns of Government*, Random House, 1958, revised edition, 1979.
The Unfinished Revolution, Random House, 1960.
The New Face of Soviet Totalitarianism, Harvard University Press, 1963.
The Bolsheviks: The Intellectual and Political History of the Triumph of Communism in Russia, Macmillan, 1965.
Expansion and Coexistence: The History of Soviet Foreign Policy, 1917-1967, Praeger, 1968, 2nd edition published as *Expansion and Coexistence: Soviet Foreign Policy, 1917 to 1973*, Holt, 1974.
The Rivals: America and Russia since World War II, Viking, 1971.
The Fall of the American University, Library Press, 1972.
Stalin: The Man and His Era, Viking, 1973.
Russian Political System, Random House, 1974.
A History of Soviet Russia, Praeger, 1976.
Ideologies and Illusions: Revolutionary Thought from Herzen to Solzhenitsyn, Harvard University Press, 1976.

In the Name of the People: Prophets and Conspirators in Prerevolutionary Russia, Viking, 1977.
Russia's Failed Revolution: From the Decembrists to the Dissidents, Basic Books, 1981.
Dangerous Relations: The Soviet Union in World Politics, 1970-1982 (sequel to *Expansion and Coexistence: The History of Soviet Foreign Policy, 1917-1967*), Oxford University Press, 1983.
The Kirov Affair (novel), Harcourt, 1988.

Contributor to professional journals.

SIDELIGHTS: Adam B. Ulam's studies of Russian politics and society have focused on the revolutionary currents within Russian history. In the *New York Times Book Review*, Paul Avrich comments on *Stalin: The Man and His Era:* "The character of Stalin's dictatorship is admirably described and analyzed in Ulam's impressive book. . . . But it is much more than a biography of Stalin: it is also a history of the Bolshevik Party, of the Russian Revolution and of the Soviet regime up to Stalin's death in 1953. . . . It is the fullest and most up-to-date biography of Stalin now available, and will make instructive reading for specialist and layman alike."

Ulam's *In the Name of the People: Prophets and Conspirators in Prerevolutionary Russia* traces, as Theodore Shabad observes in the *New York Times*, "the seeming political inertness of the masses and the conviction of a small minority, whether revolutionary terrorists or Communist functionaries, that it has the right to speak and act for the people 'because history has so ordered'. . . . Ulam has now pulled together the many strands into a coherent, detailed story of the radicals, dissenters, writers and students who sought the overthrow of czarism from the 1860's into the 1880's." "Benjamin DeMott writes in the *New Republic:* "The book is a solid and illuminating work of historical research. . . . *In the Name of the People* never raises its voice or departs from the honorable norms of its discipline. Yet it does become in its course—movingly, irrefutably, invaluably—a command: *judge the means.* This book is better than history, in a word; it is a shield."

Dangerous Relations: The Soviet Union in World Politics, 1970-1982 is considered a continuation of Ulam's now-classic *Expansion and Coexistence.* In the *New Republic*, David E. Kaiser comments that "*Dangerous Relations* continues Ulam's history of Soviet-American relations. . . . Three themes dominate the book: the changing preoccupations of the Soviet leadership, the gains and losses of detente, and the significance of recent Soviet advances in the third world. Although . . . Ulam regards the Soviet leaders as prisoners of an expansionist dynamic that they cannot escape, he does not believe that they seek world rule or that they regard nuclear war as a rational means of extending their power.'' According to Kaiser and *New York Times Book Review* contributor Alexander Dallin, Ulam detects shortcomings in American leadership responses to the Soviet Union during the 1970 to 1982 period. As Kaiser maintains, ''*Dangerous Relations,* like [Ulam's] *The Rivals,* reflects poorly upon American leaders, none of whom in the author's opinion have ever consistently demonstrated the patience, courage, and singleness of purpose necessry to deal effectively with Moscow. Frequently sheer inadvertence has cost Washington dearly.'' Dallin similarly responds that 'Ulam's picture of American policy is damning. He sees ignorance, impatience and naivete, combined with a failure of American intelligence 'in both senses of the word.' On the other side, the Russians' superior negotiating skills, he argues, make up for the inherent weakness of their system. Time and again he sees Western failure as the central condition for Soviet success. . . . While . . . Ulam understandably deplores the growing inability of the West to implement a concerted policy toward the Soviet Union, he does not tell us how he would restore Western unity of interest and purpose.'' In the end, *Los Angeles Times Book Review* critic Karel Kovanda does not feel Ulam has thoroughly analyzed his subject but rather that he has merely provided a strict, albeit useful, chronology of the years in question, whereas Dallin concludes: ''There are . . . many tantalizing, controversial and unanswered questions in this book. They deserve to be discussed. But even where the book is a bit frustrating, it is always stimulating.''

BIOGRAPHICAL/CRITICAL SOURCES:

PERIODICALS

Commentary, August, 1981.
Harper's, February, 1974.
Los Angeles Times, April 30, 1981, April 13, 1988.
Los Angeles Times Book Review, Mayy 22, 1983, May 22, 1988.
National Review, May 15, 1981.
New Republic, November 2, 1968, June 4, 1977, April 14, 1983.
Newsweek, November 26, 1973, April 11, 1977.
New York Review of Books, November 18, 1971, January 24, 1974, June 23, 1977.
New York Times, July 28, 1974, July 6, 1977.
New York Times Book Review, December 26, 1965, February 23, 1969, January 27, 1974, March 22, 1981, March 27, 1983, June 12, 1988.
Saturday Review, November 20, 1965, November 20, 1971, September 4, 1976.
Times Literary Supplement, January 12, 1967, April 3, 1969, February 2, 1973, November 30, 1973, June 14, 1974, October 2, 1981.
Washington Post, June 10, 1988.
Washington Post Book World, November 25, 1973, June 26, 1977, April 19, 1981, April 13, 1983.

*   *   *

UNDERDOWN, David (Edward) 1925-

PERSONAL: Born August 19, 1925, in Wells, Somerset, England; son of John Percival and Ethel (Gell) Underdown; married Mary Ebba Ingholt, 1954; children: Harold D., Peter C., Philip J. *Education:* Exeter College, Oxford, B.A., 1950, M.A., 1951, B.Litt., 1953; Yale University, M.A., 1952.

ADDRESSES: Office—Department of History, Yale University, P.O. Box 1504A Yale Station, New Haven, Conn. 06520-7425.

CAREER: Royal Holloway College, London, England, tutorial fellow, 1952-53; University of the South, Sewanee, Tenn., assistant professor, 1953-58, associate professor of history, 1958-62; University of Virginia, Charlottesville, associate professor of history, 1962-68; Brown University, Providence, R.I., professor of history, 1968-85; Yale University, New Haven, Conn., professor of history, 1986—. Director, Yale Center for Parliamentary History. *Military service:* Royal Air Force, 1944-47; became sergeant.

MEMBER: American Historical Association, Conference on British Studies, Royal Historical Society (fellow).

AWARDS, HONORS: Guggenheim fellow, 1964-65; American Council of Learned Societies fellow, 1973-74; National Endowment for the Humanities fellow, 1980-81; D.Litt., University of the South, 1981.

WRITINGS:

Royalist Conspiracy in England, 1649-1660, Yale University Press, 1960.
Pride's Purge: Politics in the Puritan Revolution, Oxford University Press, 1971.
Somerset in the Civil War and Interregnum, Shoe String, 1973.
Revel, Riot and Rebellion: Popular Politics and Culture in England, 1603-1660, Oxford University Press, 1985.

Contributor of articles and reviews to professional journals.

SIDELIGHTS: Revel, Riot and Rebellion: Popular Politics and Culture in England, 1603-1660 by British historian David Underdown presents the 1650s in England ''as a period when . . . moralizing Puritans of the middling sort tried to impose their values and culture upon a resistant majority which clung to their traditional festive culture of the alehouse and the Maypole,'' notes Lawrence Stone in the *New York Review of Books.* ''At the same time,'' relates Stone, ''both groups ferociously persecuted the extreme libertarian radicals of the 'inner light' on the left, like the Quakers and Ranters. The 1650s were therefore marked by acute cultural conflict between a zealous, moralistic self-appointed Puritan minority, now in full political control of local government, and an increasingly hostile population.'' Stone finds Underdown's argument very persuasive given the ''powerful reinforcement'' available in studies of late seventeenth-century village life. *Times Literary Supplement* contributor John Wilders concurs that Underdown's ''admirably undogmatic conclusions are supported by a vast quantity of specific, detailed, fully documented evidence, much of it original, the fruit of exhaustive research into parish records, sermons, memoirs, legal documents, popular ballads and the work of his fellow historians. . . . Indeed, one of his most remarkable achievements is to have assembled so firmly all this multifarious and at times contradictory information.'' In Stone's view, *Revel, Riot and Rebellion* ''greatly helps our understanding of the divisions in society from 1640 to 1660. It allows us to get away from unconvincing Marxist social explanations of particular class allegiances in the Revolution, and to shift our attention to cultural aspects.''

BIOGRAPHICAL/CRITICAL SOURCES:

PERIODICALS

American Historical Review, December, 1987.
English Historical Review, January, 1987.
History Today, August, 1987.
Journal of Interdisciplinary History, summer, 1987.
New York Review of Books, February 26, 1987.
Seventeenth-Century News, spring, 1987.
Sewanee Review, October, 1987.
Times Literary Supplement, July 18, 1986.

*   *   *

URQUHART, Brian (Edward)   1919-

PERSONAL: Born February 28, 1919, in Bridport, England; son of Murray and Bertha (Rendall) Urquhart; married Alfreda Huntington, March 31, 1944 (marriage ended, 1963); married Sidney Damrosch Howard, April 29, 1963; children: (first marriage) Thomas, Katharine, Robert; (second marriage) Rachel, Charles. *Education:* Attended Christ Church, Oxford, 1937-39.

ADDRESSES: Home—131 East 66th St., New York, N.Y. 10021. *Office*—Ford Foundation, New York, N.Y. 10017.

CAREER: United Nations, New York City, personal assistant to executive secretary of Preparatory Commission in London, England, 1945-46, personal assistant to secretary-general, 1945-49, secretary of collective measures committee, 1951-53, member of Office of Undersecretary for special political affairs, 1954-71, assistant secretary-general, 1972-74, undersecretary-general for special political affairs, 1974-86, executive secretary of conferences on peaceful use of atomic energy, 1955 and 1958, worked with emergency force in the Middle East, 1956, deputy executive secretary of Preparatory Commission of International Atomic Energy Agency, 1957, assistant to special representative in the Congo, 1960, representative in Katanga, Congo, 1961-62; Ford Foundation, New York City, scholar-in-residence, 1986—. *Military service:* British Army, Dorset Regiment and Airborne Forces, 1939-45; served in North Africa, Sicily, and Europe; became major; mentioned in dispatches.

MEMBER: Century Association.

AWARDS, HONORS: Member of Order of the British Empire, 1945; Knight Commander of St. Michael and St. George, 1986.

WRITINGS:

Hammarskjold (biography), Knopf, 1972.
A Life in Peace and War (memoir), Harper, 1987.

Contributor of articles and reviews to magazines.

SIDELIGHTS: As a memoir, *A Life in Peace and War* focuses most of its attention on Brian Urquhart's four decades with the United Nations. *Times Literary Supplement* reviewer Richard Falk claims "Urquhart's book is particularly welcome because it so convincingly develops the positive case for the UN's role in world affairs. . . . What emerges from this highly readable and persuasive account is Urquhart's deep respect for the government and military establishments entrusted with [peacekeeping] missions, often carried out at great risk and under pressure of harsh criticism or unrealistic expectation. . . . More than this, Urquhart shows how valuable peacekeeping has been in saving lives, and in bringing a minimum stability in circumstances that would otherwise be likely to produce extensive bloodshed and devastation. . . . Urquhart is at his best when concentrating on the development of the [United Nations]." Many critics express interest in Urquhart's portrayals of the United Nations's five leaders thus far. As Charles William Maynes remarks in the *New York Times Book Review*, "most readers will turn quickly to Mr. Urquhart's assessments of the five Secretaries General he served, particularly Kurt Waldheim, now President of Austria. Mr. Urquhart concludes that Mr. Waldheim, 'emerging as a living lie,' did 'immense damage' to the world body. The portraits are skillfully drawn and honest enough to reveal the strengths of Mr. Urquhart's villains and the weaknesses of his heroes."

Overall, Urquhart's memoir has been warmly received—the book is described as "witty," "colorful," and "hilarious." However, some reviewers detect a degree of caution and reticence on Urquhart's part. According to *Washington Post Book World* contributor Bernard D. Nossiter, "Urquhart has been a professional diplomat too long and is teasingly reticent on some subjects." Additionally, *Los Angeles Times* critic Jonathan Kirsch finds that Urquhart is "oblique in his reminiscences about the great men and women with whom he has contended, and he is guarded about his private life. Thus, for example, Urquhart treats the former secretary-generals whom he served with restraint. He downplays the notion that the plane crash in which Dag Hammarskjold [the United Nations's second secretary general] died was an assassination. . . . Even when he confesses his own passions and prejudices, Urquhart is meticulously indirect. . . . Still, Urquhart's perspective on history is compelling, if also sometimes aggravating, and the book is full of fascinating anecdotes and asides." In a more positive light, Clyde Sanger concludes in the Toronto *Globe and Mail* that *A Life in Peace and War* "is a book of fine style and well-argued opinions. . . . It is full of lively descriptions and sharply drawn portraits. . . . [Urquhart's] judgements may be too straightforward and not sufficiently analytical. But he has been in the forefront of world events since 1945. He has a historian's understanding of complex situations, a politician's eye for the essentials and a reporter's gift for storing up the memorable phrase. . . . This experience and these talents are an unbeatable combination."

BIOGRAPHICAL/CRITICAL SOURCES:

PERIODICALS

Globe and Mail (Toronto), February 27, 1988.
Los Angeles Times, November 6, 1987, December 31, 1987.
New Republic, March 3, 1973.
New York Times Book Review, September 27, 1987.
Time, November 16, 1987.
Times Literary Supplement, April 20, 1973, March 11-17, 1988.
Washington Post Book World, February 4, 1973, September 27, 1987.

V

VALENCY, Maurice 1903-

PERSONAL: Born March 22, 1903, in New York, N.Y.; son of Jacques and Mathilde (Solesme) Valency; married Janet Cornell (an artist), December 25, 1936. *Education:* City College (now City College of the City University of New York), A.B., 1923; Columbia University, A.M., 1924, LL.B., 1927, Ph.D., 1938.

ADDRESSES: Home—404 Riverside Dr., New York, N.Y. 10025. *Agent*—International Creative Management, 40 West 57th St., New York, N.Y. 10019.

CAREER: Admitted to New York Bar, 1928; City College of New York (now City College of the City University of New York), New York City, instructor in philosophy, 1931-33; Brooklyn College (now Brooklyn College of the City University of New York), Brooklyn, N.Y., instructor, 1933-42, assistant professor of English, 1942-46; Columbia University, New York City, associate professor, 1946-54, professor of comparative literature, 1954-69, Brander Matthews Professor of Dramatic Literature, 1968-71, professor emeritus, 1971—; Juilliard School, New York City, director of academic studies, 1971-85. Visiting professor at Graduate Center of the City University of New York, 1985, 1986, and at Hunter College of the City University of New York, 1987. Member of board of directors, Dramatists Play Service, Inc., 1960-66; overall advisor, Film-Text Division, McGraw-Hill Book Co., 1966-72; senior faculty member, Future Resources and Development, Inc., 1968-73.

MEMBER: Modern Language Association of America, American Comparative Literature Association, American Association of University Professors, Dramatists Guild of the Authors League of America (member of council, 1950-72; vice-president of Guild Fund, 1962-82; vice-president of Authors League, 1966-68; secretary of League, 1968-75), American Society of Composers, Authors and Publishers (ASCAP), Renaissance Society of America, Dante Society of America, Asia Society of America, Century Association.

AWARDS, HONORS: New York Drama Critics Circle Award for best foreign play, 1949, for his adaptation of "The Madwoman of Chaillot," 1954, for his adaptation of "Ondine," and 1959, for his adaptation of "The Visit"; Ford Foundation fellowship, 1958; Guggenheim fellowships, 1961, 1965; American Society of Composers, Authors and Publishers awards, 1965—; Litt.D., Long Island University, 1975.

WRITINGS:

"Whirlpool," first produced in Moylan, Pa., at Hedgerow Theatre, 1928.
The Writings of Herod and Mariamne, Columbia University Press, 1939.
The Thracian Horses (first produced in Cleveland, Ohio, at Cleveland Play House, 1941, produced on the West End at Lyric Theatre, May 8, 1946, produced Off-Broadway at Orpheum Theatre, September 27, 1961), Dramatists Play Service, 1963.
"The Reluctant Virgin," first produced in Cleveland at Cain Park Theatre, 1947.
In Praise of Love, Macmillan, 1958.
(Editor and translator) Jean Giradoux, *Four Plays,* Hill & Wang, 1958.
(Editor with Harry Levtow and author of introduction) *Palace of Pleasure: An Anthology of the Novella,* Putnam, 1960.
The Flower and the Castle: An Introduction to Modern Drama, Macmillan, 1963.
"The Long Night," first produced in Tallahassee, Fla., at Florida State University, 1963.
Feathertop (also see below), Dramatists Play Service, 1963.
The Breaking String: The Plays of Anton Chekhov, Oxford University Press, 1966.
The Cart and the Trumpet: The Plays of George Bernard Shaw, Oxford University Press, 1973.
Regarding Electra, Dramatists Play Service, 1976.
The End of the World: An Introduction to Contemporary Drama, Oxford University Press, 1980.
Conversation with a Sphinx, Dramatists Play Service, 1980.
Ashby (novel), Schocken, 1984.
Julie (novel), Amsterdam Books, 1988.

ADAPTATIONS OF PLAYS

Jean Giraudoux, *The Madwoman of Chaillot* (first produced on Broadway at Belasco Theatre, December 27, 1948), Random House, 1949.
Giraudoux, *The Enchanted* (first produced on Broadway at Lyceum Theatre, January 18, 1950), Random House, 1950.
Giraudoux, *Ondine* (first produced on Broadway at Forty-Sixth Street Theatre, February 18, 1954), Random House, 1954.

Augustin Eugene Scribe, *The Queen's Gambit*, Samuel French, 1954.

Giraudoux, *The Apollo of Bellac* (also see below; first produced Off-Broadway with "The Virtuous Island" at Carnegie Hall Playhouse, April 9, 1957), Samuel French, 1954.

Giraudoux, *The Virtuous Island* (also see below; first produced Off-Broadway with "The Apollo of Bellac" at Carnegie Hall Playhouse, April 9, 1957), Samuel French, 1956.

Frederick Duerenmatt, *The Visit* (first produced on Broadway at Lunt-Fontanne Theatre, May 5, 1958), Samuel French, 1958.

LIBRETTOS

(Author of English version, with musical adaptation by Jean Morel and Ignace Strasfogel) Jacques Offenbach, *La Perichole* (first produced by Metropolitan Opera Co., November 25, 1958), Boosey & Hawkes, 1957.

"The Gypsy Baron," first produced by Metropolitan Opera Co., December 15, 1960.

"The Reluctant King," first produced by American Opera Center at the Julliard School, 1980.

TELEVISION PLAYS

"Battleship Bismarck," Columbia Broadcasting System (CBS-TV), 1951.

"Toine" (for "Omnibus" series), CBS-TV, 1953.

"The Man without a Country" (for "Omnibus" series), CBS-TV, 1953.

(Adaptor) "The Apollo of Bellac" (for "Omnibus" series), CBS-TV, 1954.

(Adaptor) "She Stoops to Conquer" (for "Omnibus" series), CBS-TV, 1955.

(Adaptor) "The Virtuous Island" (for "Omnibus" series), American Broadcasting Companies (ABC-TV), 1956.

"The Second Stranger" (for "General Electric Theatre"), CBS-TV, 1957.

"Feathertop" (for "General Electric Theatre"), CBS-TV, 1957.

OTHER

Also author of a play, "Savonarola," 1973. Contributor of articles and reviews to periodicals. Advisory editor *Encyclopedia Americana*, 1968—.

BIOGRAPHICAL/CRITICAL SOURCES:

PERIODICALS

Economist, July 14, 1973.
Los Angeles Times Book Review, December 9, 1984.
Nation, July 30, 1973.
New York Times, November 30, 1984.
New York Times Book Review, December 30, 1984.
Spectator, September 1, 1967.
Times Literary Supplement, October 26, 1973.

*   *   *

van APPLEDORN, Mary Jeanne   1927-

PERSONAL: Born October 2, 1927, in Holland, Mich.; daughter of John (an insurance man and organist) and Elizabeth (Rinck) van Appledorn. *Education:* University of Rochester, B.M., 1948, M.M., 1950, Ph.D., 1966.

ADDRESSES: Home—1629 16th St., Apt. 216, Lubbock, Tex. 79401. *Office*—Department of Composition and Music Theory, Texas Tech University, P.O. Box 4239, Lubbock, Tex. 79409.

CAREER: Texas Tech University, Lubbock, 1950—, began as instructor, professor of music, 1966—, chairman of department of composition and music theory, 1969—. Had piano debut at Carnegie Hall, New York City, 1957. Founder and chairman, Symposium of Contemporary Music.

MEMBER: National Association for American Composers and Conductors, American Association of University Professors, College Music Society, Mu Phi Epsilon, Alpha Chi Omega, Delta Kappa Gamma.

AWARDS, HONORS: First awards in Mu Phi Epsilon national composition contest, 1951, 1953; selected one of three most outstanding Texas women composers, 1971; named to Hall of Fame of Texas Composers, 1973; Premier Prix, World Carillon Federation, 1980, for *Suite for Carillon*; Texas Composers Guild Award, 1980, for *Matrices*; Standard Panel Award, American Society of Composers, Authors, and Publishers, 1980-82; Virginia College Band Directors National Association awards, 1981, 1982; Outstanding Researcher Award, Texas Tech University, 1982; First Prize, Texas Composers Guild, 1987, for "Four Duos."

WRITINGS:

BOOKS

Keyboard, Singing and Dictation Manual, W. C. Brown, 1968.

MUSICAL COMPOSITIONS

Sonnet for Organ, Galaxy Music Corportion, 1974, recorded by Opus One Records.

Scenes from Pecos County (for piano), Carl Fischer, 1976.

"West Texas Suite" (for chorus, symphonic band and percussion ensemble), performed at Lubbock Bicentennial choral concert, 1976.

Concerto Brevis (for piano and orchestra), Carl Fischer, 1977.

Set of Five (for piano), Oxford University Press, 1978, recorded by Northeastern Records, 1982, and by Opus One Records.

Darest Thou Now, O Soul (for women's choir and organ; text by Walt Whitman), Carl Fischer, 1978.

Cantata: Rising Night after Night (for chorus and orchestra), Carl Fischer, 1979.

Matrices (for alto saxophone and piano), Dorn, 1979, recorded by Golden Crest Records.

Suite for Carillon, Association Bourguignonne Culturelle, La Federation Mondiale de Carillon, 1980.

"Cacophony" (for wind ensemble, percussion, and toys), performed by Spring High School Band at Midwest Band and Orchestra Clinic, 1980, recorded by Golden Crest Records.

"Lux: Legend of Sankta Lucia" (for symphonic band), performed by National Intercollegiate Band at College-Conservatory of Music, University of Cincinnati, 1981, recorded by Century Records.

Elegy for Pepe, Galaxy Music Corporation, 1982.

Liquid Gold (for alto saxophone and piano), Dorn, 1982.

Concerto for Trumpet and Band (first performed by International Trumpet Guild, Albuquerque, N.M.), Molenaar's Muziekcentrale (The Netherlands), 1985.

"Missa Brevis" (for trumpet and organ), world premiere by Anatoly Selianin, Saratov State Conservatoire, Saratov, U.S.S.R., 1987, American premiere by Robert M. Birch in Washington, D.C.

"Sonic Mutation" (for harp solo), premiered by NACUSA, New York, 1987.

Also author of musical composition "A Celestial Clockwork," 1983, and "Four Duos," for viola and violoncello.

OTHER

Also contributor to *New Scribner Music Library*, 1960. Contributor of articles to *College Music Society Journal*.

WORK IN PROGRESS: Form, Style and Analysis, a book for graduate classes.

AVOCATIONAL INTERESTS: Sports.

*   *   *

van den HAAG, Ernest 1914-

PERSONAL: Born September 15, 1914, in The Hague, Netherlands; came to United States in 1940; naturalized citizen in 1947; son of Max (an attorney) and Flora van den Haag. *Education:* Attended University of Naples, University of Florence, and Sorbonne, University of Paris, 1938-40; State University of Iowa, M.A., 1942; New York University, Ph.D., 1952.

ADDRESSES: Home—118 West 79th St., New York, N.Y. 10024.

CAREER: Practicing psychoanalyst. New York University, New York City, adjunct professor of social philosophy, 1946-75; New School for Social Research, New York City, lecturer in sociology and psychology, 1946-80; currently John M. Olin Professor of Jurisprudence and Public Policy at Fordham University, New York City. Visiting professor of criminal justice, State University of New York at Albany; visiting distinguished service professor at Queens College of the City University of New York. Lecturer at City College of the City University of New York, Brooklyn College of the City University of New York, Columbia University, Yale University, Harvard University, and other universities. Distinguished scholar, Heritage Foundation. National Endowment for the Humanities senior fellow, 1973.

MEMBER: American Sociological Association (fellow), Royal Economic Society (fellow), New York Academy of Sciences.

AWARDS, HONORS: Guggenheim fellow, 1967, Christopher Book Award, Christophers, 1973, for *Political Violence and Civil Disobedience*.

WRITINGS:

Education as an Industry, Augustus Kelley, 1956, reprinted, 1972.
(With Ralph Gilbert Ross) *The Fabric of Society*, Harcourt, 1957.
(With Ross) *Passion and Social Constraint*, Stein & Day, 1963.
Symbols and Civilization, Harcourt, 1963.
The Jewish Mystique, Stein & Day, 1969, revised edition, 1977.
Political Violence and Civil Disobedience, Harper, 1972.
Punishing Criminals: Concerning a Very Old and Painful Question, Basic Books, 1975.
Capitalism: Sources of Hostility, Heritage Foundation, 1979.
(With John P. Conrad) *The Death Penalty: A Debate*, Plenum, 1983.
(With Conrad) *The U.N.: In or Out?*, Plenum, 1987.

CONTRIBUTOR

David White and Bernard Rosenberg, editors, *Mass Culture*, Free Press, 1957.
Sidney Hook, editor, *Psychoanalysis: Scientific Method and Philosophy*, New York University Press, 1959.
The American Scholar Reader, Atheneum, 1960.
Hook, editor, *Religious Experience and Truth*, New York University Press, 1961.
Norman Jacobs, editor, *Culture for the Millions*, Van Nostrand, 1961.
H. Ruitenbeek, editor, *Psychoanalysis and the Social Sciences*, Dutton, 1962.
Hook, editor, *History and Philosophy*, New York University Press, 1963.
John Chandos, editor, *To Deprave and Corrupt*, Association Press, 1963.
Ruitenbeek, editor, *Varieties of Modern Social Theory*, Dutton, 1963.

OTHER

Also author with Robert Martinson, *Crime Deterrence and Offender Career*, 1975. Contributor of more than two hundred articles to *Harper's, Commonweal, Partisan Review, Modern Age, National Review, Commentary*, and other magazines and sociology journals in the United States, England, France and Italy.

SIDELIGHTS: In *The U.N.: In or Out?*, Ernest van den Haag and John P. Conrad debate the purpose and efficacy of the United Nations, along with the United States' role in its future. "The tone of their exchanges [is] friendly but sharp, sometimes acerbic, frequently witty," writes James Finn in the *Los Angeles Times Book Review*. However, Conor Cruise O'Brien, *Times Literary Supplement* contributor, claims "the debate is rather uneven, because Mr. Conrad concedes the many imperfections of the United Nations, and many failures on its record, while Mr. van den Haag concedes absolutely nothing. For him, the United Nations serves no useful purpose, never will serve any useful purpose, and ought to be scrapped forthwith. Van den Haag throughout treats his adversary's careful, courteous and often rather tentative argument with off-hand contempt." On the other hand, Finn adds that "each reader will decide for him or herself which of these debaters presents the better arguments and whether they are finally persuasive." He continues, "[I] found that Van den Haag's arguments were frequently more firmly grounded in reality and more persuasive than were those of Conrad's. Those of us who continue to support the United Nations must acknowledge the force and accuracy of many of the criticisms made by observers as acute and cogent as Van den Haag."

BIOGRAPHICAL/CRITICAL SOURCES:

PERIODICALS

Los Angeles Times Book Review, October 25, 1987.
Times Literary Supplement, November 6-12, 1987.

*   *   *

VANDERWALL, Francis W(illiam) 1946-

PERSONAL: Born April 24, 1946, in Colombo, Ceylon (now Sri Lanka); came to the United States in 1964, naturalized citizen, 1976; son of William Samuel (a hospital administrator) and Pearl (a Montessori teacher and school director; maiden name, D'Oliveira) Vanderwall. *Education:* St. Louis University, B.A., 1967, M.A., 1970, Ph.L., 1971; Graduate Theological Union, Berkeley, Calif., M.Div., 1976, postgraduate study, 1987—; also studied at Oxford University and Kino Institute.

ADDRESSES: Home—2091 California St., #227, Berkeley, Calif. 94703.

CAREER: Entered Society of Jesus, 1967, ordained Roman Catholic priest, 1976; Strake Jesuit Preparatory School, Houston, Tex., teacher of English, history, and theology, 1971-73; Our Lady of the Oaks Retreat House, Grand Coteau, La., associate director, 1976-78, 1986-87; Spring Hill College, Mobile, Ala., instructor of theology, 1979-86. Visiting spiritual director of Jesuit Spirituality Center, Grand Coteau, 1973-82.

AWARDS, HONORS: Research fellow at Yale University, 1979.

WRITINGS:

Spiritual Direction: An Invitation to Abundant Life, Paulist/ Newman, 1981.
Water in the Wilderness: Paths of Prayers Springs for Life, Paulist Press, 1985.
Paths of Prayers (video and audio), Teleketics (Franciscan Communications), 1986.

Contributor to magazines.

WORK IN PROGRESS: Research in the area of Reconciliation and in "methods of effecting 'healing and wholeness' in the human being who wants it."

SIDELIGHTS: Francis W. Vanderwall told *CA:* "Anyone intent on a life of perduring happiness has to embark on an inward journey of self-awareness that takes time, courage, and determination. The fruits are many and the rewards multifoliate. One begins to arrive at an inward peace and enduring love that transcends the struggles of daily living. In a harsh and often frightening world this interior journey becomes an indispensable tool for all who seek personal wholeness. When the invitation is accepted, the quality of one's life can be changed for the better for the rest of one's days."

*   *   *

van KAAM, Adrian (L.) 1920-

PERSONAL: Born April 19, 1920, in The Hague, Netherlands; son of Charles L. van Kaam. *Education:* Studied philosophy and theology at Gemert, Netherlands, 1940-47, and psychology of personality and education at Hoogveld Institute, Nijmegen, Netherlands, 1950-51; Dutch Study Center, Gulemborg, M.O., 1954, University of Chicago and Alfred Adler Institute, training in psychotherapy, 1956-57; Western Reserve University (now Case Western Reserve University), Ph.D., 1958.

ADDRESSES: Office—Institute of Formative Spirituality, Duquesne University, Pittsburgh, Pa. 15282.

CAREER: Roman Catholic priest, member of Congregation of the Spiritans. Psychological consultant to life schools for young adults in Netherlands, 1949-52; counselor in psychological observation center for juvenile delinquents, Veenendaal, Netherlands, 1952-54; Duquesne University, Pittsburgh, Pa., instructor, 1957; Brandeis University, Waltham, Mass., visiting professor of psychology, 1958-59; Duquesne University, assistant professor, 1959-60, associate professor, 1961-65, professor of psychology, 1965—, founder and director of Institute of Man (now Institute of Formative Spirituality), 1963-80, director emeritus and professor of foundational formation,

1980—. Visiting professor, University of Heidelberg, summer, 1966. Lecturer at Universities of Heidelberg and Oslo, 1963; lecturer throughout United States with Institute of Man workshop, and on radio and television. Honorary chaplain, U.S. Navy, 1987—.

MEMBER: American Psychological Association, Epiphany Association (founding member, 1979—).

AWARDS, HONORS: William C. Bier Award, American Psychological Association, 1982; President's Award for excellence in scholarship, Duquesne University, 1983.

WRITINGS:

Light to the Gentiles (translation of *De Jood Van Saverne;* biography of Frances Libermann, Jewish-born founder of Congregation of the Spiritans), Duquesne University Press, 1959, new edition, University of America Press, 1985.
The Third Force in European Psychology, Psychosynthesis Research Foundation, 1960.
The Vocational Director and Counseling, St. Paul Publications, 1962.
Religion and Personality, Prentice-Hall, 1964.
Personality Fulfillment in the Spiritual Life, Dimension Books, 1966.
Existential Foundations of Psychology, Duquesne University Press, 1966.
The Art of Existential Counseling, Dimension Books, 1966.
Personality Fulfillment in Religious Life, Volume I: *Religious Life in a Time of Transition,* Dimension Books, 1967.
(With Kathleen Healy) *The Demon and the Dove,* Duquesne University Press, 1967.
The Vowed Life, Dimension Books, 1968.
(With Bert van Crooenburg and Susan Annette Muto) *The Emergent Self,* four volumes, Dimension Books, 1968.
(With van Crooenburg and Muto) *The Participant Self,* two volumes, Dimension Books, 1969.
On Being Involved, Dimension Books, 1970.
On Being Yourself, Dimension Books, 1972.
Envy and Originality, Doubleday, 1972.
Spirituality and the Gentle Life, Dimension Books, 1974.
In Search of Spiritual Identity, Dimension Books, 1975.
The Dynamics of Spiritual Self Direction, Dimension Books, 1976.
The Woman at the Well, Dimension Books, 1976.
(Co-author) *Tell Me Who I Am,* Dimension Books, 1977.
Looking for Jesus, Dimension Books, 1978.
Living Creatively, Dimension Books, 1978.
(With Muto) *Am I Living a Spiritual Life?,* Dimension Books, 1978.
The Transcendent Self: Formative Spirituality of the Middle, Early, and Late Years of Life, Dimension Books, 1979.
Religion and Personality, Dimension Books, 1980.
(Co-author) *Practicing the Prayer of Presence,* Dimension Books, 1980.
The Mystery of Transforming Love, Dimension Books, 1982.
Foundations for Personality Study: An Adrian van Kaam Reader, Dimension Books, 1983.
Roots of Christian Joy, Dimension Books, 1985.
(With Muto) *Adult Christian Formation,* Paulist Press, 1988.

CONTRIBUTOR

Modern Myths and Popular Fancies, Duquesne University Press, 1961.

Lloyd-Jones and Westervelt, editors, *Behavioral Science and Guidance*, Teachers College, Columbia University Press, 1963.
Samuel Hazo, editor, *The Christian Intellectual*, Duquesne University Press, 1963.
Guidance: An Examination, Harcourt, 1965.
Erwin W. Straus and Richard M. Griffith, *Phenomenology of Will and Action*, Duquesne University Press, 1965.
J. M. Lee and L. J. Putz, editors, *Seminary Education in a Time of Change*, Fides, 1965.
K. T. Hargrove, editor, *Star and the Cross*, Bruce, 1966.
Herbert C. Otto, editor, *Explorations in Human Potentialities*, C. C Thomas, 1966.
Alvin R. Mahrer, editor, *The Goals of Psychotherapy*, Appleton-Century-Crofts, 1966.
Nathaniel Lawrence and Daniel O'Connor, editors, *Readings in Existential Phenomenology*, [New Jersey], 1967.
D. S. Arbuckle, editor, *Counseling and Psychotherapy: An Overview*, McGraw, 1967.
Duane P. Schultz, editor, *The Science of Psychology: Critical Reflections*, Appleton-Century-Crofts, 1970.
Psychologia Pedagogica Sursum, University Publishers and Bookseller (South Africa), 1970.
Raymond J. Corsini, editor, *Handbook of Innovative Psychotherapies*, Wiley, 1981.

OTHER

Contributor to *Jahrbuch fuer Psychologie und Medizinische Anthropologie*, 1966, *Wiley Encyclopedia of Psychology*, 1984, *Dictionary of Pastoral Care and Counseling*, 1986, *New Catholic Encyclopedia*, and *International Encyclopedia of Psychiatry, Psychoanalysis, and Psychology*. Contributor of more than thirty articles to scientific periodicals in the Netherlands, 1952-54; also contributor to *Journal of Individual Psychology, American Journal of Nursing, Review of Existential Psychology and Psychiatry, Current Psychiatric Therapies*, and *Journal of Humanistic Psychology*. Consulting editor, *Journal of Individual Psychology*, 1958—, and *Journal of Humanistic Psychology*, 1963—; editor of *Studies in Formative Spirituality* (formerly *Humanitas*) and of *Envoy* (publications of the Institute of Formative Spirituality), 1965—; former editor of *Review of Existential Psychology and Psychiatry*.

*   *   *

Van WOERKOM, Dorothy (O'Brien)   1924-

PERSONAL: Born June 26, 1924, in Buffalo, N.Y.; daughter of Peter S. (a refinery superintendent) and Helen (Miller) O'Brien; married John W. Van Woerkom (a retired U.S. Army lieutenant colonel), February 22, 1961. *Education:* Graduate of Mount Mercy Academy and Bryant and Stratton Business College. *Politics:* "To me the candidate, not the party, matters." *Religion:* Roman Catholic.

ADDRESSES: Home and office—8826 McAvoy Dr., Houston, Tex. 77074.

CAREER: Free-lance writer. U.S. Army Corps of Engineers, Buffalo, N.Y., secretary, 1943-47, 1951-61; elementary school teacher in parochial schools, Buffalo, 1947-51.

MEMBER: Authors League of America, Authors Guild, Mystery Writers of America, American Library Association.

AWARDS, HONORS: Stepka and the Magic Fire was named best religious children's book of 1974 by Catholic Press Association; *Harry and Shellburt* was named a notable book by American Library Association in 1977.

WRITINGS:

JUVENILES

Stepka and the Magic Fire, Concordia, 1974.
Journeys to Bethlehem, Concordia, 1974.
The Dove and the Messiah, Concordia, 1975.
The Queen Who Couldn't Bake Gingerbread (Junior Literary Guild selection), Knopf, 1975.
Becky and the Bear (Junior Literary Guild selection), Putnam, 1975.
Sea Frog, City Frog, Macmillan, 1975.
Abu Ali: Three Tales of the Middle East, Macmillan, 1976.
The Rat, the Ox, and the Zodiac, Crown, 1976.
Meat Pies and Sausages, Greenwillow, 1976.
Let Us Go to Bethlehem!, Concordia, 1976.
Wake Up and Listen, Concordia, 1976.
A Hundred Angels Singing, Concordia, 1976.
Tit for Tat, Greenwillow, 1977.
Harry and Shellburt, Macmillan, 1977.
Donkey Ysabel, Macmillan, 1978.
Alexandra the Rock-Eater, Knopf, 1978.
Friends of Abu Ali: Three More Tales of the Middle East, Macmillan, 1978.
Hidden Messages, Crown, 1979.
When All the World Was Waiting, Concordia, 1979.
Lands of Fire and Ice, Concordia, 1980.
Pearl in the Egg, Crowell, 1980.
(With Mary Blount Christian) *Bible Heroes, Kings and Prophets*, Concordia, 1981.
Something to Crow About, Whitman Publishing, 1982.
Old Devil Is Waiting, Harcourt, 1985.
Tall Corn, Milliken, 1987.

WORK IN PROGRESS: Several books for beginning readers; a fantasy novel for middle readers; short stories for children's textbook readers.

SIDELIGHTS: Dorothy Van Woerkom's book *Pearl in the Egg* is the story of an eleven-year-old serf girl who becomes a minstrel at the court of King Edward I. "What is truly memorable" about *Pearl in the Egg*, writes Jean Fritz in the *New York Times Book Review*, "is the thirteenth century, . . . which springs to life on the first page and never languishes. . . . [It] takes skill and grace, as well as scholarship, to re-create that time with such apparent ease—in language, detail, texture and color."

Van Woerkom told *CA:* "After publishing in the children's field for over fourteen years, I still find this field of writing and reading the most exciting and versatile in literature." She adds: "One must be an adult or nearly so to become involved in adult reading/writing. But even adults can enjoy, learn from and profit by good children's literature!"

AVOCATIONAL INTERESTS: Needlework, travel to historic places; sheltering homeless cats.

BIOGRAPHICAL/CRITICAL SOURCES:

PERIODICALS

New York Times Book Review, January 11, 1982.

*   *   *

VECOLI, Rudolph J(ohn)   1927-

PERSONAL: Born March 2, 1927, in Wallingford, Conn.; son

of Giovanni B. (a laborer) and Settima (Palmerini) Vecoli; married Jill Cherrington, June 27, 1959; children: Christopher, Lisa, Jeremy. *Education:* University of Connecticut, B.A., 1950; University of Pennsylvania, M.A., 1951; University of Wisconsin, Ph.D., 1963.

ADDRESSES: Office—Department of History, University of Minnesota, Minneapolis, Minn.

CAREER: U.S. Department of State, Washington, D.C., foreign affairs officer, 1951-54; instructor in history at Ohio State University, Columbus, 1957-59, and Pennsylvania State University, State College, 1960-61; Rutgers University, New Brunswick, N.J., lecturer and assistant professor of history, 1961-65; University of Illinois at Urbana-Champaign, associate professor of history, 1965-67; University of Minnesota, Minneapolis, professor of history and director of Immigration History Research Center, 1967—. Visiting professor, Uppsala University, spring, 1970, University of Amsterdam, spring, 1988. Commentator at University of Bremen Conference on American Labor and Immigration History; chair of history committee, Statue of Liberty-Ellis Island Foundation; speaker at various ethnic meetings and festivals. Director, National Endowment for the Humanities Summer Seminars for College Teachers, 1980, and 1983; member, Minnesota Humanities commission, 1983-86. Participant in Project '87 seminar for faculty in immigrants and the Constitution. Member, national committee for preservation of Ellis Island, advisory committee of Ethnic Cultural Center, Minnesota Public Schools, advisory board of Oral History of the American Left, Tamiment Library, New York University, and national advisors group of Ethnic Millions Political Action Committee. Member of board of directors, American Immigration and Citizenship Conference, and American Council for Nationalities Service. Member of executive council, National Ethnic Studies Assembly. *Military service:* U.S. Navy, 1945-46.

MEMBER: American Historical Association (member of research division, 1984-87), Organization of American Historians, American Association of University Professors, American Italian Historical Association (president, 1966-70; member of council, 1979—), Immigration History Society (vice-president, executive council, 1979—; president, 1982-85).

AWARDS, HONORS: Social Science Research Council fellow, 1959-60; Newberry Library fellow, 1964; Rutgers Research Council faculty fellow, 1964-65; American-Scandinavian Foundation fellow, 1970; American Philosophical Society grant, 1970; Medaglia d'oro, 1971; senior Fulbright-Hays research scholar in Italy, 1973-74; American Council of Learned Societies grant, 1974; U.S. Department of State travel grant, 1977; New Jersey Historical Commission research grant, 1978; City of Ljubljana (Yugoslavia) Medallion, for contributions to the study of the Slovene immigration to the U.S., 1981; made Cavaliere Ufficiale nell 'Ordine al Merito della Reppublica Italiana, 1982; Marraro Prizes in Italian history, American Historical Association, 1984-87; National Endowment for the Humanities fellowship for independent study and research, 1985-86; American Council of Learned Societies grant-in-aid for research, 1986.

WRITINGS:

The People of New Jersey, Van Nostrand, 1965.
(Editor with Keith Dyrud and Michael Novak, and contributor) *The Other Catholics,* Arno, 1978.
(Editor and contributor) *Italian Immigrants in Rural and Small Town America,* American Italian Historical Association, 1987.

CONTRIBUTOR

Herbert J. Bass, editor, *The State of American History,* Quadrangle, 1970.
Murray Friedman, editor, *Overcoming Middle Class Rage,* [Philadelphia], 1971.
William H. Cartwright and Richard L. Watson, Jr., editors, *The Reinterpretation of American History and Culture,* National Council for the Social Studies, 1973.
Sallie TeSelle, editor, *The Rediscovery of Ethnicity,* Harper, 1974.
S. I. Kutler, editor, *Looking for America,* Canfield Press, 1976.
R. M. Miller and T. D. Marzik, editors, *Immigrants and Religion in Urban America,* Temple University Press, 1977.
Barbara Cunningham, editor, *The New Jersey Ethnic Experience,* [Union City, N.J.], 1977.
L. Dinnerstein and F. C. Jaher, editors, *Uncertain Americans,* Oxford University Press, 1977.
S. M. Tomasi, editor, *Perspectives in Italian Immigration and Ethnicity,* [New York], 1977.
George E. Pozzetta, editor, *Pane e Lavoro,* Multicultural History Society of Ontario, 1980.
Janez Stanonik, editor, *Proceedings of the International Symposium on Louis Adamic,* Edvard Kardelj University, 1981.
June Holmquist, editor, *They Chose Minnesota,* Minnesota Historical Society, 1981.
Lydio Tomasi, *Italian Americans,* Center for Migration Studies, 1983.
Bruno Bezza, editor, *Gli Italiani fuori Italia,* Franco Angeli Editore, 1983.
Jefferson B. Kellogg and Robert H. Walker, editors, *Sources for American Studies,* Greenwood Press, 1983.
J. H. M. Laslett and S. M. Lipset, editors, *Failure of a Dream?,* University of California Press, 1984.
Ira Glazier and Luigi de Rosa, editors, *Migration across Time and Nations,* Holmes & Meier, 1986.
Raymond A. Mohl, editor, *The Making of Urban America,* Scholarly Resources, 1988.

AUTHOR OF INTRODUCTION

Marie Hall Ets, *Rosa: The Life of an Italian Immigrant,* University of Minnesota Press, 1970.
Jacob A. Riis, *The Children of the Poor,* Johnson Reprint Corp., 1970.
N.C. Burckel and J. D. Buenker, editors, *Immigration and Ethnicity,* Gale, 1977.
Carl Ross, *The Finn Factor in American Labor, Culture, and Society,* New York Mills (Minnesota), 1977.

OTHER

Also contributor to *The Aliens,* edited by Dinnerstein and Jaher, *The Enduring Ghetto,* edited by David R. Goldfield and James B. Lane, and *Many Pasts,* edited by Herbert G. Gutman and Gregory S. Kealey. General editor of Research Collections on Immigration History, University Publications of America, Inc. Contributor to *Dictionary of American Biography Supplement III, 1941-1945,* and to proceedings of the annual conference of the American Italian Historical Association, 1969, and 1974. Contributor to journals. Advisory editor of *International Migration Review* (formerly *International Migration Digest*); member of editorial boards, *Ethnicity, American History and Life, Studi Emigrazione* (Rome),*Estudios Migratorios Latinoamericanos* (Buenos Aires), *Italian Americana, Revue Francaise d'Etudes Americaines,* and *Journal of American Ethnic History.*

WORK IN PROGRESS: A history of the Italian-American labor and radical movements.

*   *   *

VESEY, Paul
   See ALLEN, Samuel W(ashington)

*   *   *

VINCENT, John J(ames)   1929-

PERSONAL: Born December 29, 1929, in Sunderland, England; son of David and Ethel Beatrice Vincent; married Grace Johnston Stafford, December 4, 1958; children: Christopher John, Helen Faith, James Stafford. *Education:* Richmond College, London, B.D. (with first class honors), 1954; Drew University, S.T.M. (summa cum laude), 1955; University of Basel, Dr.Theol. (insigni cum laude), 1960.

ADDRESSES: Home—239 Abbeyfield Rd., Sheffield S4 7AW, England. *Office*—Pitsmoor Study House, 210 Abbeyfield Rd., Sheffield S4 7AZ, England.

CAREER: Clergyman of Methodist Church; minister in Manchester, England, 1956-62, and at Rochdale Mission, 1962-69; Pitsmoor Study House, Urban Theology Unit, Sheffield, England, director, 1970—; Sheffield Inner-City Ecumenical Mission, superintendent minister, 1970—. Harris Franklin Rall Lecturer at Garrett Theological Seminary, spring, 1969; visiting professor at Boston University, autumn, 1969, New York Theological Seminary, spring, 1970, and Drew University, spring, 1977.

MEMBER: British Council of Churches (member of Commission on Defense and Disarmament, 1963-65, 1969-74), Studiorum Novi Testamenti Societas, Campaign for Nuclear Disarmament (member of national executive committee, 1957-69), Alliance of Radical Methodists (founding member; chairman, 1971-75), Ashram Community Trust (leader, 1967—), Urban Mission Training Association (chairman, 1982—), Association of Centres of Adult Theological Education (member of executive committee, 1984—), Pitsmoor Action Group (chairman, 1970—).

WRITINGS:

Christ in a Nuclear World, Crux Press, 1962, 2nd edition, 1963.
Christ and Our Stewardship: Six Bible Studies, Epworth Press, 1963.
Christian Nuclear Perspective, Epworth Press, 1964.
Christ and Methodism: Towards a New Christianity for a New Age, Abingdon, 1965, 2nd edition, Epworth Press, 1966.
Here I Stand: The Faith of a Radical, Epworth Press, 1967.
Secular Christ: A Contemporary Interpretation of Jesus, Abingdon, 1968.
The Working Christ: Christ's Ministries through His Church in the New Testament and in the Modern City, Epworth Press, 1968.
The Race Race, Friendship Press, 1970.
The Jesus Thing, Abingdon, 1973.
Stirrings: Essays Christian and Radical, Epworth Press, 1975.
Alternative Church, Christian Journals, 1976.
Starting All over Again, World Council of Churches, 1981.
Into the City, Epworth Press, 1982.
OK, Let's Be Methodists, Epworth Press, 1984.
Radical Jesus, Zondervan, 1986.

(With J. D. Davies) *Mark at Work,* Bible Reading Fellowship, 1986.

WORK IN PROGRESS: Dynamics of Christ: A Radical Dogmatics; Urban Problems and Christian Theology.

SIDELIGHTS: John J. Vincent wrote that he is "committed to academic writing within the context of personal lifestyle commitment with deprived inner-city communities and small experimental Christian groups." Vincent also told *CA* that in the 1980s he "sees such communities and groups as prophetic for the coming post-technological small-scale society."

BIOGRAPHICAL/CRITICAL SOURCES:

PERIODICALS

Books and Bookmen, March, 1968.
Christian Century, June 19, 1968.
Encounter, spring, 1969.

*   *   *

VIORST, Judith   1931-

PERSONAL: Born February 2, 1931, in Newark, N.J.; daughter of Martin Leonard (an accountant) and Ruth June (Ehrenkranz) Stahl; married Milton Viorst (a political reporter and writer), January 30, 1960; children: Anthony Jacob, Nicholas Nathan, Alexander Noah. *Education:* Rutgers University, B.A. (with honors), 1952; Washington Psychoanalytic Institute, graduate, 1981. *Religion:* Jewish.

ADDRESSES: Home—3432 Ashley Terrace N.W., Washington, D.C. 20008. *Agent*—Robert Lescher, 67 Irving Pl., New York, N.Y. 10003.

CAREER: Poet, journalist, and writer of books for adults and children. Contributing editor, *Redbook* magazine.

MEMBER: Phi Beta Kappa.

AWARDS, HONORS: Emmy Award, 1970, for poetic monologs written for CBS special, "Annie: The Women in the Life of a Man"; Silver Pencil Award, 1973, for *The Tenth Good Thing About Barney;* Penney-Missouri Award, 1974, for article in *Redbook;* American Academy of Pediatrics Award, 1977, for article in *Redbook;* American Association of University Women Award, 1980, for article in *Redbook.*

WRITINGS:

The Village Square (poems), Coward, 1965.
It's Hard to Be Hip over Thirty and Other Tragedies of Married Life (poems), World Publishing, 1968.
(With husband, Milton Viorst) *The Washington, D.C. Underground Gourmet,* Simon & Schuster, 1970.
People and Other Aggravations (poems), World Publishing, 1971.
Yes, Married: A Saga of Love and Complaint (collected prose pieces), Saturday Review Press, 1972.
How Did I Get to Be Forty and Other Atrocities (poems), Simon & Schuster, 1976.
Love and Guilt and the Meaning of Life, Etc., Simon & Schuster, 1979.
A Visit from St. Nicholas (To a Liberated Household), Simon & Schuster, 1979.
If I Were in Charge of the World and Other Worries: Poems for Children and Their Parents, Atheneum, 1981.
Necessary Loses, Simon & Schuster, 1986.
When Did I Stop Being Twenty and Other Injustices: Selected Poems from Single to Mid-Life, Simon & Schuster, 1987.

JUVENILE FICTION

Sunday Morning, Harper, 1968.

I'll Fix Anthony, Harper, 1969, reprinted, Macmillan, 1988.

Try It Again, Sam: Safety When You Walk, Lothrop, 1970.

The Tenth Good Thing about Barney (Junior Literary Guild selection), Atheneum, 1971, reprinted, Macmillan, 1988.

Alexander and the Terrible, Horrible, No Good, Very Bad Day (Junior Literary Guild selection), Atheneum, 1972, reprinted, Macmillan, 1987.

My Mama Says There Aren't Any Zombies, Ghosts, Vampires, Creatures, Demons, Monsters, Fiends, Goblins, or Things, Atheneum, 1973, reprinted, Macmillan, 1988.

Rosie and Michael, Atheneum, 1974.

(Contributor) *Free to Be . . . You and Me,* McGraw, 1974.

Alexander, Who Used to Be Rich Last Sunday, Atheneum, 1978.

The Good-bye Book, Atheneum, 1988.

JUVENILE NONFICTION

(Editor with Shirley Moore) *Wonderful World of Science,* Science Service, 1961.

Projects: Space, Washington Square Press, 1962.

One Hundred and Fifty Science Experiments, Step-by-Step, Bantam, 1963.

Natural World, Bantam, 1965.

The Changing Earth, Bantam, 1967.

OTHER

Also author of musical play, "Happy Birthday and Other Humiliations." Author of syndicated column for Washington Star Syndicate, 1970-72, and of regular column for *Redbook,* 1968—. Author of poetic monologs for television, including "Annie: The Women in the Life of a Man." Contributor of poems and articles to *New York, New York Times, Holiday, Venture, Washingtonian,* and other periodicals.

WORK IN PROGRESS: A book of poetry.

SIDELIGHTS: A wryly humorous poet as well as the author of several well-received children's books, Judith Viorst has been described by a reviewer for *Booklist* as "part Ann Landers, part Ogden Nash." Much of the success that Viorst has achieved in her writings, whether it be her very popular books irreverently describing her life and family, her monthly column in *Redbook,* her contributions to numerous other periodicals, or her works for children, is due, Barbara Karlin explains in *Los Angeles Times Book Review,* to the fact that Viorst "holds up a mirror to our lives so we can reflect and understand."

Viorst admits that a writing career is something she has had her eye on since the age of seven. "I always, always, always wanted to be a writer," Viorst stated in an interview with Beth Austin published in the *Chicago Tribune.* "I never wanted to be anything else—never. It never entered my mind that I was going to earn a living at it or be well-known as a result of it." Her first efforts, neatly printed poems mailed to various magazines, were promptly returned. Recalls Viorst, "[They were] terrible poems—about dead dogs, mostly." Her later works fared little better, meeting with what she describes as a "spectacular lack of success." All of them, she notes, were "deadly serious things. . . . Very grim. The meaning of life. Death. Pain. Lust. Suicide. That sort of thing."

One of Viorst first "official" writing assignments came when she was hired as a stringer by the *New York Herald Tribune* to report on parties in Washington, D.C. However, she re-

veals, "I could never recognize anyone famous. Milton [her husband] had to go everywhere with me." Eventually, she began contributing poems to the newspaper's Sunday magazine section. In 1965 these poems were collected to form her first book, *The Village Square.* When her second collection of poetry, *It's Hard to Be Hip over Thirty and Other Tragedies of Married Life,* was published in 1968, the book was an instant bestseller establishing Viorst as one of the country's most popular writers of light verse.

While her verse may be termed "light," Viorst disputes the notion that writing poems such as hers is as effortless as it appears. "I slave over them," she told *CA.* "It always makes me feel embarrassed to say how hard I work on them because they are 'light verse' and yet it took me four years to write the twenty four poems in *How Did I Get to Be Forty and Other Atrocities.*"

Readers have come to appreciate her labor, and reviewers point to Viorst's dedication to accurately portraying her thoughts as one of the major reasons for her success, especially in her books detailing the humorous side to everyday life. C. K. Carey writes in a *Library Journal* review of *How Did I Get to Be Forty and Other Atrocities:* "Is there a reader . . . out there so self-assured, so together that she can't identify with Viorst's heroine? I doubt it. No one does it quite like Viorst; no one better expresses our daily discontents and unfulfilled fantasies." Carol Kleiman remarks in the *Chicago Tribune* that "as a poet, [Viorst] has a wonderful gift for convincing us in her first few stanzas that she always is cool and in charge of her life—then she wryly gets down to the truth, making us laugh aloud at the dichotomy."

Viorst gives much of the credit for her success to her husband and children, who usually serve as inspirations for her witty reflections on contemporary marriage and family life. Husband Milton Viorst is on the receiving end of most of that praise. Says Judith: "Someone once remarked to me that if I hadn't gotten married, I might have written the great American novel, but I think if I hadn't gotten married, maybe I wouldn't have written anything. Milton and my life with him have given me the encouragement I needed to pursue writing. . . . I don't think it's a coincidence that I never had anything published before I was married to Milton." Recalling that early lack of self-confidence, Viorst remarks, "there was a time in my life when I was incapable of sending anything out until Milton said it was ready."

Viorst continued to remark to *CA:* "Married life is the rock on which I sit and do my work and the kids' role in this should not be dismissed. It is possible to find delight in just hanging around the kitchen while one kid is making a chicken sandwich and the other is tossing a napkin into the trash and missing. Milton and I are two people who know that is good, that it is better than most things going on in the universe."

Viorst's children have, of course, inspired their mother in more concrete ways. Many of the characters in her children's books are based on her three children and their experiences and problems. She explains: "Most of my children's books are for or about my own children, and mostly they're written to meet certain needs. For instance, when Anthony was mercilessly persecuting his younger brother I decided to write *I'll Fix Anthony* to cheer up Nick. When a lot of questions about death were being raised around our house, my struggle for a way to respond to those questions resulted in the Barney book. I observed that the concept of 'I'm having a bad day' seemed to help adults get through those bad days a little better and so I wrote about such a day for Alexander, who ws having a lot of them. For Nick, who used to be scared of monsters and doubtful of his mother's infallibility (he's recovered from the former but not the latter), I wrote *My Mama Says*."

It is books such as *I'll Fix Anthony* and *My Mama Says There Aren't Any Zombies, Ghosts, Vampires, Creatures, Demons, Monsters, Fiends, Goblins, or Things*, in addition to other favorites as *Alexander and the Terrible, Horrible, No Good, Very Bad Day, Rosie and Michael, The Tenth Good Thing about Barney* that have provided her readers with sensitive, tender, yet realistic stories that consistently thrilled her loyal audience. "Viorst is an author who can enter imaginatively into a child's difficulties without being either tactless or disablingly sympathetic," writes a review for the *Times Literary Supplement*.

In *Dictionary of Literary Biography*, Douglas Street states that "Viorst has shown herself to be a writer of talent and insight who has successfully combined entertainment and enrichment in her creations for the child audience. . . . Stories of her young sons, Anthony, Nicholas, and Alexander, show the sensitivity, humor, and timeliness readily accessible to American children today." And Barbara Karlin comments in the *Los Angeles Times Book Review* that the gifted and talented Viorst "deftly zeroes in on the minor traumas and neuroses of childhood and lets us laugh at them."

In 1981 after her youngest son entered college, Viorst enrolled in classes at the Washington Psychoanalytic Institute. She explained in the *Chicago Tribune* interview: "I really wanted to keep doing what I was doing, which was writing about what goes on between people and inside people's heads. I wanted to pick up another source for writing about that. I wanted to expand the resources in my life. . . . Going back to school was really one of the great thrilling experiences in my life. Viorst continued: "I had originally thought that I would just take everything I was learning and keep doing the same kind of writing I was doing and the writing would change somehow as a result of it. . . . [However,] psychoanalytic theory made me realize that everything I heard and saw could be better understood with it. And than I knew that I wanted to write more directly about it." As a result of these feelings, Viorst started thinking about writing about dealing with losses and in 1986 *Necessary Losses* was published.

Vic Sussman writes in the *Washington Post Book World* that Viorst "brings an unsual perspective to *Necessary Losses*, a book that explores the painful separations we must continually undergo. . . . Yet while *Necessary Losses* glides above a landscape of heartache, it's never clinical or depressing. Viorst is, after all, a poet with a wonderful sense of humor and insight. She skillfully combines psychoanalytic theory, poetry (her own and others), interviews, anecdotes, and her personal experiences into an instructive yet warm survey of the human journey." And Elinor Lenz states in the *Los Angeles Times Book Review* that "there is much of value in this book—in Viorst's respect for the individual, in her emphatic detailing of the ways in which various people deal with the necessary losses in their lives, in her often poignant sketches of her own family relationships, and, though it may leave some readers unsatisfied, in her faith that self-understanding is better than self-delusion."

The ability to express her feelings on a variety of topics and in a number of different genres is one of the reasons Viorst considers herself to be a very lucky woman. Commenting on her career, she remarked to *CA*: "It's a dream come true, exactly what I've always wanted to do. I have the freedom,

the independence, the flexibility—following no one's schedule but my own, being able to tailor my schedule to the needs of my household and three children. . . . My experiences have exceeded my expectations, and I do think these are the best years of my life. I know what I love. I have what I love and I love what I have."

CA INTERVIEW

CA interviewed Judith Viorst by telephone on August 7, 1987, at her home in Washington, D.C.

CA: Since the mid-1960s you've been comforting people with your writing—witty and wise poems, articles, and books for all ages. The latest book, Necessary Losses, *is a very serious consideration of the processes of loss we must go through in order to attain growth. Was the book already in mind when you entered the Washington Psychoanalytic Institute?*

VIORST: No, it was not. What was in mind was my wish at that particular time in my life to deepen and enlarge upon my resources for writing about what I always write about—which is, basically, the state of people's inner emotional lives and their relationships with each other. I'm interested in people's fears and dreams and hopes and love lives and jealousies and pleasures and motivations—the struggles of grown-ups and kids to live with themselves and with other people. What I was doing by going to the Washington Psychoanalytic Institute was trying to add another dimension to the information I drew upon to write about these subjects. I had been drawing upon my own experience, the experience of my friends, the books I had read, the eavesdropped conversations I had listened to—I'm a very outrageous eavesdropper—and I wanted to add to all that the clinical theory, the theories that psychoanalysis has to offer on who we are and why we do what we do, theories which, though imperfect, are in my view the best available to help us understand ourselves. I went back to school to acquire a new resource, and, while I knew I would use it in my writing in some way, I had no particular plan to write *Necessary Losses*. I knew that I would be using my studies in some way for the rest of my life.

CA: How much did you know of the literature of psychoanalysis when you entered the Institute?

VIORST: I probably knew a little bit more than the average educated person, because I've always been interested in it. I've had friends in the field and have talked with them about it, and I've always found it a useful point of view.

CA: Were you to some extent already a Freudian in orientation when you began your study?

VIORST: Only in a very broad sense, as I still am. I would describe myself as a Freudian exactly as I say it in the book. I believe that there is an unconscious, and I believe that what happens to us in our present is powerfully influenced by what has happened to us in the past. But I really like to view theories of mental functioning as complementary rather than exclusionary, so I was interested, in my book, in putting together ideas from other sources. I think, however, that Freud was a genius who laid the groundwork for what all other people have had to say about human psychology. I also think that if he were around he'd still be evolving and transforming his theories.

CA: Necessary Losses has been both a critical and a popular success. You must have heard from thousands of people who've found help in the book. Is there such a thing as a typical reader response?

VIORST: One pattern in the responses was the sense of relief that people seem to feel in finding themselves to be part of the human condition and not singled out for some particular rotten fate, finding that struggles in marriage, struggles with their children, struggles with growing older, struggles with loss were struggles that everybody shared. People did take comfort in that and talked a lot, in their letters, about finding themselves in the book. Another frequent response, which I found fascinating, had to do with people's willingness to work at changing themselves. You know, there are no answers in the book, no *Here are twelve ways to survive loss and live happily ever after.* It's a book that invites you to think about your life and to use that understanding, that greater insight that you have struggled towards, to make changes. I love the fact that people wrote me letters which showed them wrestling with this information, that people were willing to work so hard, to struggle so much.

CA: Necessary Losses deals with many kinds of loss, from the child's separation from the mother through the loss of youth and the youthful image to the final loss, death. Is it possible to say that any one loss or stage is hardest for most people, or is that very much an individual matter?

VIORST: It is very much an individual matter, though it does seem that the loss people find hardest to get over is the death of a child. Mid-life also seems to hit large numbers of people very hard, because of their confrontation—at that stage—with non-negotiable limits and with mortality.

CA: One of the hard things about getting old is that old people so often aren't well regarded by others. Do you think that's changing, or likely to change?

VIORST: I think that what's changing is, first of all, our definition of what "old" is. (Doesn't sixty-five sound a lot younger to you than it used to?) I also think that looking good, enjoying sex, working productively are becoming perceived as options that more and more "old" people will avail themselves of. These changes may very well make the difference in how old people are regarded.

CA: Would you advise analysis for people who aren't visibly troubled, just as a means of getting to know themselves better?

VIORST: I think it is a remarkable voyage of self-discovery, and if somebody has the time and money and interest, psychoanalysis is probably one of the great graduate-school educations available to mankind. But that doesn't mean everybody should do it or even that everybody could benefit from doing it. Psychoanalysis really invites you to dive down and confront things that some people who are feeling pretty good just don't want to mess with in their lives—and fair enough.

I also want to add that although psychoanalysis is a remarkable form of therapy for trouble people, I don't think there is any such thing as *one* form of therapy that is right for everybody. There are all kinds of appropriate matches, from group therapy to short-term psychotherapy to supportive psychotherapy.

CA: Was your decision to undergo analysis a part of or outgrowth of your study at the Institute?

VIORST: Yes, it is required. You cannot go to an analytic institute if you're not analyzed. Your studies would be too abstract. And when you're in analysis, you're in analysis; you're not a student being analyzed, looking on it as an interesting phenomenon. You're really in there.

CA: Will there be more writing as a result of your study at the Psychoanalytic Institute, perhaps a book related to Necessary Losses?

VIORST: I like to think that everything I write will be informed by that education, but I don't have anything specifically planned right now. I'm having a book come out in October, a collection based on four previous books of poems, and I'm working on a book of poems about being in my fifties, which is not due until a year from December. I think that book will also benefit very much from the psychoanalytic training.

CA: According to an article by Victoria Dawson in the Washington Post, *you began writing—and sending your work out—when you were seven and eight. And in* Necessary Losses *you referred to the Girl Scout leader who made you feel you could be a writer. Were you writing steadily, in some form or other, until you began to be published?*

VIORST: Steadily in some form or other, yes. Steadily but unpublished. I worked for a confessions magazine, I wrote a confessions story; I worked for a fashion magazine, I wrote a fashion story; I worked in a children's books publishing house, I wrote a children's book. Everything got turned down. I was also sending out science fictions stories and poems. I was a very busy little bee, but I was a total flop.

CA: My first acquaintance with your work was through your funny, wistful, absolutely on-target poems collected in such books as It's Hard To Be Hip Over Thirty and Other Tragedies of Married Life. *Was being a poet the first ambition?*

VIORST: Yes. I really wanted to get my poetry published, but that started feeling more like a daydream than a real goal. Still, when I started writing poems for *The Village Square,* I began to get positive rejection slips, which was very encouraging. Then, finally, I got my first poems published in what is now *New York Magazine.* That was really the beginning of great opportunities to get poetry published.

CA: As you've said previously, "light verse" isn't something that can be tossed off in a few spare minutes. Were there other poets who served as inspirations, light verse writers or not so light?

VIORST: I have always been a reader of serious poetry—I love Eliot, Yeats, Hopkins—but it seems outrageous to claim that they inspired me.

CA: You've given your family the lion's share of the credit for helping you become a writer—your sons for providing the situations and problems that figure in the writing for children, and your husband, also a writer, for inspiration and encouragement from the start. It seems to work very well having two writers in your house.

VIORST: It works very well. We've been married now for twenty-seven years, and we've both been writing at home for twenty-five years. We read each other's work, help each other think of synonyms when we can't think of a word, and all the rest of it. Of course we have the great advantage of writing about very different areas. I don't know how wonderful it would be if we were in a competitive situation, both writing children's books or both writing on politics. My husband is a political specialist, probably one of the country's leading experts on the Middle East, and not madly informed about poetry, as I am not madly informed about the Middle East. So it works out very well.

CA: Do you write every day or otherwise keep a definite schedule for the work?

VIORST: I pretty much get up in the morning and write. I organize my life very efficiently. As we speak, I am boiling the water for some pasta, chopping scallions, and slicing steak to make a steak-and-scallion pasta. I never talk on the phone without keeping my hands busy. I have a certain quota for myself in the writing. For the book of poems I'm currently writing, my general quota is a poem a month. I write a *Redbook* column nine times a year, and that's on a fixed schedule. I'm very disciplined by nature, so it isn't a big psychological achievement for me to get my work done in an orderly fashion. It would be a big psychological achievement for me to hang loose.

CA: Since your sons are no longer—I assume—waking up with gum in their hair or worrying about vampires, do you have much contact with very young people who read your books for children?

VIORST: Yes. I have friends of all different ages, including friends with little kids and friends who are grandparents of little kids. So I do have a lot of contact with them. I'm going to have a visit from a one-year-old and a three-year-old tomorrow. And people tell me stories about their kids because they know I'm interested. I have a very good memory for everybody's kid stories.

CA: What are your three sons up to now?

VIORST: My oldest son, Anthony, just graduated from law school and took the bar exam. He's going to work for a judge in Washington for a year. My middle son, Nicholas, is getting a Ph.D. in political theory at the University of Chicago. He's spending the summer at home delivering pizza. My youngest son, Alexander, is going into his third year at Georgetown University in the School of Foreign Service. They're terrific kids.

CA: In a recent issue of Publishers Weekly *you and other writers were quoted on your feelings about Washington. Do you have a great deal of contact with writers there?*

VIORST: I know a lot of writers, but I don't live in a writers' scene; I live in a family scene. Many of my friends at this point are people who've been married twenty-five or thirty years, and we've been involved with each other's lives, and children, for a long time.

CA: You seem to be very happy with your career, your life in general, and the way life and career dovetail. Is there anything you'd like to change, anything new you'd like to try in the work?

VIORST: I've just tried something new—I wrote a musical which finished a three-week run in East Hampton last week.

That was a lot of fun to do. It starred Bonnie Franklin. It's called "Happy Birthday and Other Humiliations."

CA: Is it going to be produced somewhere else now?

VIORST: There are no plans at the moment, but we'll see.

BIOGRAPHICAL/CRITICAL SOURCES:

BOOKS

Children's Literature Review, Volume 3, Gale, 1978.
Dictionary of Literary Biography, Volume 52: *American Writers for Children since 1960: Fiction,* Gale, 1986.
Lanes, Selma G., *Down the Rabbit Hole,* Atheneum, 1971.

PERIODICALS

Booklist, January 1, 1973, November 15, 1976, March 1, 1986.
Chicago Tribune, March 29, 1987, November 15, 1987, December 8, 1987.
Children's Book Review, April, 1973.
House Beautiful, October, 1972.
Junior Literary Guild Catalogue, September, 1972, September, 1973.
Kirkus Reviews, September 15, 1972, July 15, 1974.
Library Journal, January 15, 1969, November 15, 1976, July, 1986.
Life, December 17, 1971.
Los Angeles Times, January 7, 1988.
Los Angeles Times Book Review, September 16, 1984, April 27, 1986, March 27, 1988.
McCall's, September, 1969.
New Yorker, December 4, 1971.
New York Times Book Review, November 9, 1969, September 26, 1971, October 22, 1972, December 30, 1973, February 2, 1975, November 15, 1981, March 10, 1985, March 23, 1986, May 8, 1988.
People, February 18, 1980.
Publishers Weekly, January 8, 1979.
Saturday Review, November 30, 1968.
Saturday Review/World, December 4, 1973.
School Library Journal, January, 1969, February, 1971, September, 1973, January, 1982.
Times Literary Supplement, November 23, 1973.
Washington Post, May 31, 1979, June 8, 1986.
Washington Post Book World, December 29, 1968, November 5, 1972, December 5, 1976, May 14, 1978, May 11, 1986, April 5, 1987.

—*Sketch by Margaret Mazurkiewicz*

—*Interview by Jean W. Ross*

*   *   *

VIORST, Milton 1930-

PERSONAL: Born February 18, 1930, in Paterson, N.J.; son of Louis and Betty (LeVine) Viorst; married Judith Stahl (a poet, journalist, and writer of books for adults and children), January 30, 1960; children: Anthony Jacob, Nicholas Nathan, Alexander Noah. *Education:* Rutgers University, B.A., 1951; Harvard University, M.A., 1954; Columbia University, M.S., 1955; postgraduate study at University of Lyon.

ADDRESSES: Home—3432 Ashley Terrace N.W., Washington, D.C. 20008.

CAREER: Political reporter and writer. Reporter for *Bergen Record,* 1955-56, *Newark Star Ledger,* 1956-57, and *Wash-*

ington Post, 1957-61; *New York Post,* Washington correspondent, 1961-64; *Washington Star,* Washington, D.C., syndicated political columnist, 1970-75. Woodrow Wilson senior fellow, 1975—; Alicia Patterson fellow, 1979-80. *Military service:* U.S. Air Foce, Intelligence, 1952-54; became first lieutenant.

MEMBER: Fund for Investigative Journalism (member of board, 1968—; chairman of board, 1968-78).

WRITINGS:

Liberalism: A Guide to Its Past, Present and Future in American Politics, introduction by Hubert H. Humphrey, Avon, 1963.
Hostile Allies: F.D.R. and Charles de Gaulle, Macmillan, 1965.
The Great Documents of Western Civilization, Chilton, 1965.
Fall from Grace: The Republican Party and the Puritan Ethic, New American Library, 1968.
(With wife, Judith Viorst) *The Washington, D.C. Underground Gourmet,* Simon & Schuster, 1970.
(With Clinton P. Anderson) *Outsider in the Senate: Senator Clinton Anderson's Memoirs,* World Publishing, 1970.
Hustlers and Heroes, Simon & Schuster, 1971.
Fire in the Streets: America in the 1960's, Simon & Schuster, 1980.
(Editor) *Making a Difference: The Peace Corps at Twenty-five,* Weidenfeld & Nicholson, 1986.
Sands of Sorrow: Israel's Journey from Independence, Harper, 1987.

Regular contributor to *New Yorker;* contributor to *Harper's, Nation, Esquire, New York Times Magazine,* and *Figaro Citteraire.*

SIDELIGHTS: Once described by Robert Murphy in the *New York Times Book Review* as an author "of undoubted talent—even brilliance—and verve," Milton Viorst is an influential and well-respected political journalist. Besides his books profiling famous politicians, recounting the history of the Republican Party, and studying the political mood in the United States during the turbulent '60s, Viorst has brought his political thoughts and theories to his readers through his nationally syndicated newspaper column and his contributions to such respected periodicals as the *New Yorker, Nation, Esquire,* and *Harpers.*

In 1965, although he was the Washington correspondent for the *New York Post* and had already written *Liberalism: A Guide to Its Past, Present and Future in American Politics,* Viorst seemed to capture national public attention when his book, *Hostile Allies: FDR and Charles de Gaulle* was published. In this book, Viost explores the dislike and rivalry that developed between the two world leaders Franklin D. Roosevelt and Charles de Gaulle and examines the impact their drive for political power had on world events. B. B. Fall writes in the *New Republic* that a reader "would learn more from *Hostile Allies* about what is wrong with American-French relations that he can learn from reading miles of official background briefings.... Viorst documents the tragic difference which to this day affect American-French relations." Robert Murphy remarks in the *New York Times Book Review:* "I felt that the author ... demonstrates hardy courage in undertaking an analysis of the wartime relations between the two men at the center of this narrative.... [*Hostile Allies*] is a tribute to the author's industry and ability as a writer."

Reviewers of *Hostile Allies* have praised Viorst for his painstaking research and detailed attention to such material as previously published materials, government documents, and interviews. Malcolm Muggeridge comments in the *New York Review of Books* that *Hostile Allies* "is clear, readable, full of apposite quotations and references.... Mr. Viorst's careful account ... makes fascinating reading."

Viorst's *Fall from Grace: The Republican Party and the Puritan Ethic* has also been praised for the quality of research and attention to historical detail. In this book, Viorst recounts the history of the *Republican Party* detailing its beginnings, citing its high and low periods, and tracing its development to its present state. Viorst examines the links within the Republican Party between party members, big business, and Puritanism. Of *Fall from Grace,* Grant McConnell writes in the *New York Times Book Review* that "Viorst, in a lively account claims that the Republican party is heavily committed to a particular ideology. That party, he maintains, is the political arm of the Yankee, the Puritan who moved out of his original base in New England to the Middle West and has used the party ever since to preserve his own power and his own principles."

"Viorst has rummaged through GOP history and found a guiding thread that tries to make polemic sense of the Republican Party's fall from grace and power," states a reviewer for *Newsweek.* "The Republicans, for Viorst, are not primarily politicians, but priestly ideologues evangelizing for the Protestant ethic, Yankee morality and Brahmin supremacy." And I. F. Stone comments in the *New York Review of Books* that *Fall from Grace* "is a short and lively, a swift and engaging synthesis of the work in the field,... but with many fresh insights—Viorst shows real gifts as an historian." Stone continues: "Viorst depicts the Republicans as the party of business and of the Wasp [and] tries to make the story a little more interesting by linking the party with the Puritan ethic, though it is hard to tell where Puritanism ends and plain acquisitiveness begins."

Another of his books to receive national attention is Viorst's account of the political climate during the nineteen-sixties, *Fire in the Streets: America in the 1960's.* Viorst looks at this turbulent period in American history by presenting portraits of fourteen men who played key roles in influencing the political atmosphere. Included in *Fire in the Streets* are profiles of such people as Allen Ginsberg, Tom Hayden, Stokely Carmichael, and Jerry Rubin.

A reviewer for the *New Yorker* writes that *Fire in the Streets* is "a solid, though informal, history of the nineteen-sixties. The author, a reporter and political journalist, has done a first-rate job of synthesis in giving some coherence to the dizzying array of ideas, personalities, mass rages, and explosive confrontations that marked the era: the Mississippi Summer, Berkeley, Watts, Selma, Birmingham, Kent State." J. Anthony Lukas of the *New York Times Book Review* notes: "In [*Fire in the Streets*], Milton Viorst has marshaled ... dramatic elements into a lively, readable account of the decade's most tumultuous moments.... The book makes good reading. It is the work of a professional reporter who knows how to gather facts, how to shape them into coherent patterns, how to write with style and pace." And Joyce Milton suggests in *Saturday Review* that "this strong and compassionate history is a welcome reminder of how rewarding, and how perilous, it can be to live in more interesting times."

In 1987, Viorst's *Sands of Sorrow: Israel's Journey from Independence* was published. Calling his book "part journalism, part historical and political commentary, part personal odyssey," Viorst believes *Sands of Sorrow* should be a signal to defenders of Israel "to grasp the limits of what armed might can achieve."

James Feron comments in the *New York Times Book Review* that Viorst's book "is a valuable examination of the competing values of religious and secular Jews, of rival Ashkenazi and Sephardic interests and of a mainstream Zionism whose struggle with revisionists remains a factor. [*Sands of Sorrow*] is valuable not only for the linear examination that carries us from the 1948 War of Independence to the debilitating invasion of Lebanon, but for the study of rival domestic forces that continue to bear on Israel's relations with Washington and with its neighbors." J. Robert Moskin remarks in *Washington Post* that *Sands of Sorrow* "contends that the United States has done Israel a major disservice by making it a clients." Moskin goes on to write that Viorst believes "the only way to have peace between Arab and Jew in the Middle East is to set up a Palestinian state on the West Bank. As Viorst knows, this is not the common wisdom in the American Jewish community."

Finally, Charles Chi Halevi states in *Chicago Tribune* that in *Sands of Sorrow* "Viorst contends that Israel is being killed with kindness by the United States, its best friend and ally, which has armed it out of proportion to its size in order for Israel to serve as America's surrogate spearhead in this arena of the Cold War." Halevi concludes: "This influx of weapons, Viorst argues, not only has created a new Sparta, it has also created obstacles to peace because it froze the diplomatic process and took away Israel's incentives to negotiate."

BIOGRAPHICAL/CRITICAL SOURCES:

BOOKS

Viorst, Milton, *Sands of Sorrow: Israel's Journey from Independence*, Haper, 1987.

PERIODICALS

Chicago Tribune, May 12, 1987.
Christian Science Monitor, March 25, 1965, September 14, 1968.
Library Journal, December 1, 1979.
New Republic, March 13, 1965.
Newsweek, May 20, 1968.
New York, January 19, 1970.
New Yorker, April 17, 1965, March 31, 1980.
New York Review of Books, February 25, 1965, June 20, 1968.
New York Times Book Review, February 21, 1965, August 4, 1968, January 13, 1980, October 19, 1986, August 2, 1987.
Saturday Review, March 19, 1966, January 19, 1980.
Washington Post, May 21, 1968, May 18, 1987.
Washington Post Book World, January 20, 1980.

—*Sketch by Margaret Mazurkiewicz*

*   *   *

VISCOTT, David S(teven)   1938-

PERSONAL: Born May 24, 1938, in Boston, Mass.; son of Hiram (a pharmacist) and Shirley (Levy) Viscott; married Judith Ann Finn (a figure skater), July 12, 1959 (divorced); married Katherine Random (a designer); children: (first mar-riage) Elizabeth, Penelope, Jonathan. *Education:* Dartmouth College, A.B., 1959; Tufts University, M.D., 1963.

ADDRESSES: c/o Pocket Books, 1230 Avenue of the Americas, New York, N.Y. 10020.

CAREER: Barnes Hospital, St. Louis, Mo., intern, 1963-64; University Hospital, Boston, Mass., resident in psychiatry, 1964-67; Boston University, School of Medicine, Boston, instructor in psychiatry, beginning 1967. President of Sensitivity Games, Boston, 1970—. Radio host, ABC Talkradio network.

MEMBER: American Psychiatric Association, Authors Guild, Authors League of America, Royal Society for Health, New York Academy of Science (fellow), Massachusetts Medical Society, Phi Sigma Delta.

AWARDS, HONORS: Mosby Book Award, 1963, for research as a medical student; Law Medicine Institute fellow, 1967-68.

WRITINGS:

Labyrinth of Silence (novel), Norton, 1970.
Feel Free, Peter H. Wyden, 1971.
Winning, Peter H. Wyden, 1972, reprinted, Pocket Books, 1987.
The Making of a Psychiatrist (autobiography), Arbor House, 1973.
Dorchester Boy: Portrait of a Psychiatrist as a Very Young Man (autobiography), Arbor House, 1973.
How to Live with Another Person, Arbor House, 1974.
The Language of Feelings, Arbor House, 1976.
(With Jonah Kalb) *What Every Kid Should Know*, Houghton, 1976.
Risking: How to Take Chances and Win, Simon & Schuster, 1977.
The Viscott Method, Houghton, 1984.
Taking Care of Business: A Psychiatrist's Guide to Success, Morrow, 1985.
I Love You, Let's Work It Out, Simon & Schuster, 1987.

Contributor of articles to *Psychiatry, Archives of General Psychiatry, Bulletin of Tufts New England Medical Center, Cosmopolitan, Marketing Age, New Woman*, and *Today's Health*.

WORK IN PROGRESS: The Making of a Psychiatrist II: Natural Therapy; a collection of essays; an art book on Oriental rugs, filmscripts, poetry, and a novel.

SIDELIGHTS: David Viscott told *CA:* "I first began writing when I was about eight. . . . Throughout grade and secondary school I experimented with different forms, always attracted to dialogue, the drama, musical settings for spoken voice and the short story. My artistic interest was mainly music and perhaps the greatest influence on my writing is still music. I am most concerned with the sound of the spoken word. I read aloud everything I write to myself and always have. At Dartmouth I was in English Honors and edited the literary magazine. Honors English was closely copied from the Cambridge Don system and for two years I studied the English language from Beowulf to Virginia Woolf and became steeped in the English tradition. With this background I entered Tufts medical school and of course quickly published, wrote scientific papers on my own cancer research and eventually drifted into psychiatry. . . .

"I write sporadically, but I am always gathering material. I have day books in which I keep a running account of ideas. When I am working on a book the day book will contain first draft material. Often it contains lists of errands. When I write

I can sit at the typewriter 6 to 10 hours a day, the highest output I have is around 20,000 words per day. There are months when I don't write at all.''

Viscott's book *The Language of Feelings* has been translated into Spanish.

BIOGRAPHICAL/CRITICAL SOURCES:

PERIODICALS

People, August 18, 1986.

SOUND RECORDINGS

Your Mental Health (interview), The Christophers, 1979. †

*   *   *

VOSE, Ruth Hurst   1944-

PERSONAL: Born February 10, 1944, in Southport, England; daughter of Thomas (a farmer) and Helena Mary (a teacher; maiden name, Molyneux) Hurst; married James Edward Vose (a farmer), September 19, 1969. *Education:* University of Liverpool, B.A. (with honors), 1966; Diploma of the Museums Association, 1971; Blythe College, D.H.P., 1981.

ADDRESSES: Home and office—Moorfield Lane, Scarisbrick, Nr. Ormskirk, Lancashire L40 9JD, England.

CAREER: Pilkington Glass Museum, St. Helens, Merseyside, England, assistant curator, 1966-72; *Ormskirk Advertiser* (group of newspapers), Lancashire, England, senior journalist, 1973-77; free-lance writer, lecturer, and broadcaster, 1978—. Edge Hill College of Higher Education, Ormskirk, Lancashire, publicity consultant, governor, 1978-82, and vice-chairman, 1982.

MEMBER: L'Association Internationale pour l'Histoire du Verre, National Union of Journalists, Society of Authors, Glass Association, Museums Association (associate member), Society for Post-Medieval Archaeology, Association of Hypnotists and Psychotherapists, Graduates Society for Psychotherapists and Counsellors (honorary member), Historical Society of Lancashire and Cheshire, Glass Circle (London).

WRITINGS:

Glass, The Connoisseur, 1975.
Glass, Collins, 1980.
Agoraphobia, Faber, 1981, revised edition, 1986.
(Contributor) Ward Lloyd and Dan Klein, editors, *The History of Glass,* Orbis Publishing, Ltd., 1983.
(Contributor) Alan Bullock and R. B. Woodings, editors, *The Fontana Biographical Companion to Modern Thought,* Fontana, 1983.
The International Dictionary of Glass, Country Life, 1984.
Torture Chamber (novel), Piatkus Books, 1986.
Omskirk Town and Country Trails, The Omskirk Book Shop, 1987.

Also author of scripts for ''The Sparkling Stream'' and ''Old Wives' Remedies and All That,'' both British Broadcasting Corp. (BBC-Radio) series. Contributor of articles and reviews to magazines, newspapers, and journals. Book reviewer for *Museum Journal.*

WORK IN PROGRESS: Archaeological reports on glass and glasshouse sites for *Post-Medieval Archaeology* and the *Greater Manchester Archaeology Journal; History of Omskirk,* for The Omskirk Book Shop, due in 1991; a book on the physical contribution to psychological problems.

SIDELIGHTS: Initially, Ruth Hurst Vose wrote to fill gaps in the literature of her profession, although she is currently branching out into other literary interests. ''All my books,'' she explains, ''have been written with a view to the sort of publications that I needed at various points in my career but that simply did not exist at the time.'' *Glass,* a volume of ''The Connoisseur Illustrated Guides,'' approaches the problems involved in collecting glass. In the book, Vose develops a cataloguing system whereby the techniques of glassmaking are classified historically. Thus a sample can be identified quickly and easily. According to H. W. Woodward's *Museum Journal* review, ''The book is a fine pioneer effort, a useful reference work, full of factual information, neatly abbreviated, assembled and illustrated, to help in the identification of a wide range of glass.''

Her second book, also titled *Glass,* investigates the archaeology of four thousand years of glassmaking as well as the origins and evolution of the process. 'I was able to write this since I had been professionally studying and excavating glassmaking sites for six years,'' comments Vose. ''The insight this gave me allowed me to add a genuine enthusiasm and practical understanding of the subject.'' ''It must be said right off,'' remarks Paul Hollister in the *Glass Club Bulletin,* ''that Ruth Hurst Vose nearly always knows precisely what she is writing about, and knows whom to call upon when she is not 100% sure—a tribute to any writer.'' ''Her enthusiasm for the subject,'' writes Ada Polak in the *British Book News,* ''shines through the soberly professional narrative.''

Other critics have noticed the author's competence, calling *Glass* ''a good general work'' that, in the words of R. J. Hunter's *Times Literary Supplement* review, ''provides an excellent background to the subject.'' Continuing the praise of the book, Philip Whatmoor notes in *Post-Medieval Archaeology* that *Glass* ''lives up to the editor's intention to take the reader to the frontiers of knowledge. The general reader will find it readable and stimulating, the specialist will find it indispensable as the first reference book to combine history and archaeology.'' And Woodward adds: ''*Glass* is the first book to deal in a comprehensive way with all important aspects of glass history and archaeology.''

Since the publication of her first book on glass, Vose has taken up journalism and explored the subject of agoraphobia, from which she suffered. ''Using her own experiences and those of other sufferers, she gives great insight into the terrible impact this condition can have on its victims, their families and friends,'' observes Pauline A. Stewart in the *Nursing Times.* In producing ''a rare and informative book, valuable to therapist and sufferer,'' says Caroline Ridley in *Therapy,* Vose relied on her personal situation to lobby for the understanding of agoraphobia whether the reader is a physician or a patient. As Henry R. Rollin states in the *British Medical Journal,* ''The medical practitioner need not consider it beneath his dignity to read in particular Ruth Hurst Vose's book, which is a most valuable aid to the understanding and treatment of this dreaded complaint.''

Agoraphobia has given Vose a very personal insight into terror, and she has used this insight in creating *Torture Chamber,* her first horror novel. ''Truth can be stranger than fiction,'' comments reviewer Alan Burgess of the *Lancashire Evening Post,* ''and in Ruth Hurst Vose's first novel the fiction is never far from the truth—horrible as it may be.'' Since the success of *Torture Chamber,* Vose has remarked that she intends ''to remain in fiction writing for some time, since it has been my most enjoyable literary experience to date.''

Vose told *CA:* ''As one of Britain's leading experts on the history and archaeology of glass, I have had the opportunity of lecturing to specialized university, museum, and society organizations both in the United Kingdom and abroad, including the U.S.A. and Canada. I have appeared on both British and American television in the course of my studies. Professional pressures were finally to take their toll, and after a back-breaking excavation in Manchester and a whistle-stop tour of the U.S.A. and Canada in 1971, I developed the first symptoms of agoraphobia (the phobic fear of public places), which finally led to my having to give up my job.

''In the end I have to be grateful to my agoraphobia, from which I suffered severely for five years, for inadvertently bringing me to a writing career that I now much prefer to my original profession and that has brought me a much greater understanding of humankind. Unable to travel anywhere, at last I had the time to accept commissions to write books on glass, and with a large dictionary of glass and other contributions to publications on the subject in the pipeline, I feel I have made a worthwhile contribution in at least one field of human study. I still keep my hand in my writing reports on excavated glass for archaeologists, which is far less arduous than actually running a dig!

''At the same time I was training to become a journalist. I completed my traineeship in record time, becoming a senior journalist within the Associated Newspaper Group in eighteen months instead of the usual two years. The discipline of journalism, added to my industrial and academic training, made me into a very efficient in-depth researcher for specialized features for newspapers, magazines, and radio series. By this time I had conquered my agoraphobia with the help of a new treatment. With my peculiar talents I decided to write a book on agoraphobia, since I had found much ignorance and even fear of the subject among ordinary people, doctors, and even psychiatrists. I think my two proudest moments were reading good reviews of *Agoraphobia* in the *British Medical Journal*, where it is rare indeed for a lay person's view to be noticed, and one on *Glass* in the Collins series in the *Times Literary Supplement*.''

BIOGRAPHICAL/CRITICAL SOURCES:

PERIODICALS

British Book News, November, 1980.
British Medical Journal, November 28, 1980.
Glass Club Bulletin, number 137, 1982.
Lancashire Evening Post, January 27, 1979, October 5, 1981, April 4, 1986.
Museum Journal, March, 1976, March, 1981.
Nursing Times, February 10, 1982.
Post-Medieval Archaeology, volume 15, 1981.
Therapy, September 30, 1982.
Times Literary Supplement, November 7, 1980.

W

WAGENHEIM, Kal 1935-

PERSONAL: Born April 21, 1935, in Newark, N.J.; son of Harold and Rozlon (Heller) Wagenheim; married Olga Jimenez, June 10, 1961; children: David, Marie-Dolores. *Education:* Rutgers University, student, 1953-54, 1956, 1959; State University of New York at Buffalo, M.A., 1975. *Religion:* Jewish.

ADDRESSES: Home—52 Maple Ave., Maplewood, N.J. 07040.

CAREER: Newark Star-Ledger, Newark, N.J., part-time sports reporter, 1953-54, 1956-58; Prudential Insurance Co., Newark, copywriter, 1956-60; Keuffel & Esser Engineering Products, Hoboken, N.J., technical writer, 1960-61; reporter for weekly periodicals and radio announcer for WKYN, San Juan, Puerto Rico, 1961-63; free-lance writer on Caribbean affairs, also translator and researcher, Puerto Rico, 1963-68; University of Puerto Rico, Rio Piedras, editor of scientific publications for Nuclear Center, 1968-70; *Buffalo Evening News,* Buffalo, N.Y., reporter, 1970-71; Columbia University, New York, N.Y., lecturer, 1978-80; free-lance writer. Co-founder and co-editor of *San Juan Review* (monthly), 1963-66, and *Caribbean Review* (quarterly), 1968-70; part-time correspondent for *New York Times,* 1967-70; editorial and research assistant, U.S. Atomic Energy Commission, 1968-70, U.S. Commission on Civil Rights, 1975, U.S. Information Agency, 1977; worked in public relations and advertising for U.S. Environmental Protection Agency, 1973, and government of Puerto Rico Tourism Bureau, 1976. *Military service:* U.S. Army, 1954-56.

MEMBER: Authors Guild, American Newspaper Guild, Overseas Press Club of Puerto Rico (member of board of directors, 1968-70).

AWARDS, HONORS: Overseas Press Club of Puerto Rico Award, 1969, for best story published off-island (in *New York Times*); recipient with Barry Bernard Levine of grant from the Plumstock Foundation to support publication of *Caribbean Review,* 1969.

WRITINGS:

Puerto Rico: A Profile, Praeger, 1971, revised edition, 1976.
(Editor) *Cuentos: An Anthology of Puerto Rican Short Stories,* Institute of Puerto Rican Culture, 1971, published as *Cuentos: An Anthology of Short Stories from Puerto Rico,* Schocken, 1979.
(Translator) Ricardo Alegria, *Discovery, Conquest and Colonialization of Puerto Rico,* Institute of Puerto Rican Culture, 1971.
(Editor with wife, Olga Jimenez de Wagenheim) *The Puerto Ricans: A Documentary History,* Praeger, 1973.
Clemente!, foreword by Wilfrid Sheed, Praeger, 1973, 2nd edition published as *Clemente!: The Life of Roberto Clemente,* Waterfront Press (Maplewood, N.J.), 1984.
Babe Ruth: His Life and Legend, Praeger, 1974.
A Survey of Puerto Ricans on the U.S. Mainland in the 1970's, Praeger, 1975.
Reading Exercises on the History and Culture of Puerto Rico, Continental Press, 1975.
Paper Gold: How to Hedge against Inflation by Investing in Postage Stamps, Peter H. Wyden, 1976.
Puerto Ricans in the Continental United States: An Uncertain Future, Commission on Civil Rights, 1976.
(Translator) Manuel Zeno-Gandia, *The Pond,* Waterfront Press (Maplewood, N.J.), 1983.
Beating the Races: Seven Easy Steps to Becoming a Consistent Winner, Waterfront Press (Maplewood, N.J.), 1985.

Contributor of more than one hundred news articles to *New York Times* and other articles to *Nation, New Leader, New Republic,* and *Liberation.* Has sold cartoon ideas to *New Yorker, Playboy,* and other magazines.

WORK IN PROGRESS: Translating and researching for Oscar Lewis, for his forthcoming book *Six Women.*

BIOGRAPHICAL/CRITICAL SOURCES:

PERIODICALS

New Republic, November 23, 1974.
New York Times Book Review, October 7, 1973, October 13, 1974. †

*   *   *

WAGNER, Walter F(rederick), Jr. 1926-1985

PERSONAL: Born October 28, 1926, in Yonkers, N.Y.; died July 6, 1985, of heart disease in Weston, Conn.; son of Walter Frederick (a designer) and Georgia (Lamoreaux) Wagner; married Barbara Jane Alden (a town selectman), March 2, 1952;

children: Jonathan, Jennifer Ann, Daniel Seth, Margaret Ann. *Education:* Massachusetts Institute of Technology, S.B., 1949, S.M., 1950.

ADDRESSES: Home—131 Goodhill Rd., Weston, Conn. 06880. *Office*—*Architectural Record,* McGraw-Hill Publishing Co., 1220 Avenue of the Americas, New York, N.Y. 10020.

CAREER: Factory Management and Maintenance, New York City, 1950-57, began as assistant editor, became assistant managing editor; *House and Home,* New York City, assistant managing editor, 1957-65; *Popular Boating,* New York City, editor, 1963-65; *Architectural Record,* New York City, executive editor, 1965-68, editor in chief, 1969—. Member of local planning, zoning, and conservation commissions; past president of Weston-Westport Community Theater; consultant to National Endowment for the Arts and American Institute of Architects. *Military service:* U.S. Naval Reserve, active duty, 1945-46.

MEMBER: American Institute of Architects (fellow), Cedar Point Yacht Club.

AWARDS, HONORS: National Magazine Award from American Society of Magazine Editors and Magazine Publishers Association, 1971, for "New Life for Old Buildings."

WRITINGS:

(Editor) *Houses Architects Design for Themselves,* McGraw, 1974.
(Editor) *Great Houses for View Sites, Beach Sites, Sites in the Woods, Meadow Sites, Sloping Sites, Steep Sites, and Flat Sites,* McGraw, 1976.
By Design: A Ten-Year Report by the Architecture and Environmental Arts Program 1966-1976, Publishing Center for Cultural Resources, 1977.
(Editor) *A Treasury of Contemporary Houses,* McGraw, 1978.
(Editor) *Energy-Efficient Buildings,* McGraw, 1980.
(Editor) *More Houses Architects Design for Themselves,* McGraw, 1981.

OBITUARIES:

PERIODICALS

Architectural Record, August, 1985.
New York Times, July 9, 1985. †

*   *   *

WALCOTT, Derek (Alton) 1930-

PERSONAL: Born January 23, 1930, in Castries, St. Lucia, West Indies; son of Warwick (a civil servant) and Alix (a teacher) Walcott; married Fay Moston, 1954 (divorced, 1959); married Margaret Ruth Maillard, 1962 (divorced); married Norline Metivier (actress and dancer); children: one son (first marriage), two daughters (second marriage). *Education:* St. Mary's College, St. Lucia, B.A., 1953; attended University of the West Indies, Kingston, Jamaica.

ADDRESSES: Home—165 Duke of Edinburgh Ave., Diego Martin, Trinidad and Tobago, (summers); 71 St. Mary's, Brookline, Mass. 02146 (winters). *Office*—Creative Writing Department, Boston University, 236 Bay State Rd., Boston, Mass. 02215. *Agent*—Bridget Aschenberg, International Famous Agency, 1301 Avenue of the Americas, New York, N.Y. 10019.

CAREER: Poet and playwright. Teacher at St. Mary's College, St. Lucia, at Boys' Secondary School, Grenada, and at Kings-ton College, Jamaica. Founding director of Trinidad Theatre Workshop, 1959—. Visiting professor at Columbia University, 1981, and Harvard University, 1982; visiting professor in Creative Writing Department of Boston University, 1985—. Also lecturer at Rutgers and Yale Universities.

AWARDS, HONORS: Rockefeller fellowship, 1957; Jamaica Drama Festival prize, 1958, for "Drums and Colours"; Guinness Award, 1961; Heinemann Award, Royal Society of Literature, 1966, for *The Castaway,* and, 1983, for *The Fortunate Traveller;* Cholmondeley Award, 1969, for *The Gulf;* Eugene O'Neill Foundation-Wesleyan University fellowship, 1969; Order of the Humming Bird, Trinidad and Tobago, 1969; Obie Award, 1971, for "Dream On Monkey Mountain"; honorary doctorate of letters, University of the West Indies, 1972; Jock Campbell/*New Statesman* Prize, 1974, for *Another Life;* John D. and Catherine T. MacArthur Foundation grant, 1981; *Los Angeles Times Book Review* Prize in poetry, 1986, for *Collected Poems, 1948-1984;* National Writer's Council Prize, Welsh Arts Council.

WRITINGS:

POETRY

Twenty-Five Poems, Guardian Commercial Printery, 1948.
Epitaph for the Young: A Poem in XII Cantos, Advocate (Bridgetown, Barbados), 1949.
Poems, Kingston City Printery (Jamaica), 1953.
In a Green Night: Poems, 1948-1960 (also see below), J. Cape, 1962.
Selected Poems (includes poems from *In a Green Night: Poems, 1948-1960*), Farrar, Straus, 1964.
The Castaway and Other Poems (also see below), J. Cape, 1965.
The Gulf and Other Poems, J. Cape, 1969, published with selections from *The Castaway and Other Poems* as *The Gulf: Poems,* Farrar, Straus, 1970.
Another Life (long poem), Farrar, Straus, 1973, 2nd edition published with introduction, chronology and selected bibliography by Robert D. Hammer, Three Continents Press, 1982.
Sea Grapes, J. Cape, 1976, slightly revised edition, Farrar, Straus, 1976.
Selected Verse, Heinemann, 1976.
The Star-Apple Kingdom, Farrar, Straus, 1979.
The Fortunate Traveller, Farrar, Straus, 1981.
Selected Poetry, selected, annotated and introduced by Wayne Brown, Heinemann, 1981.
The Caribbean Poetry of Derek Walcott, and the Art of Romare Beardon, Limited Editions Club (New York), 1983.
Midsummer, Farrar, Straus, 1984.
Collected Poems, 1948-1984, Farrar, Straus, 1986.
The Arkansas Testament, Farrar, Straus, 1987.

PLAYS

Henri Christophe: A Chronicle in Seven Scenes (first produced in Castries, St. Lucia, West Indies, 1950, produced in London, England, 1951), Advocate (Bridgetown, Barbados), 1950.
Harry Dernier: A Play for Radio Production, Advocate, 1951.
Wine of the Country, University College of the West Indies (Mona, Jamaica), 1953.
The Sea at Dauphin: A Play in One Act (first produced in Mona, Jamaica, 1953, produced in London, 1960; also see below), Extra-Mural Department, University College of the West Indies, 1954.

Ione: A Play with Music (first produced in Port of Spain, Trinidad, 1957), Extra-Mural Department, University College of the West Indies, 1957.

"Drums and Colours: An Epic Drama" (published in *Caribbean Quarterly,* March-June, 1961), first produced in Kingston, Trinidad, April 23, 1958.

"In a Fine Castle," first produced in Jamaica, 1970, produced in Los Angeles, Calif., 1972.

"Ti-Jean and His Brothers" (also see below), first produced in Port of Spain, Trinidad, 1958, produced Off-Broadway at Delacorte Theatre, July 20, 1972.

Malcochon; or, Six in the Rain (one-act; first produced as "Malcochon" in Castries, St. Lucia, 1959, produced in London under title "Six in the Rain," 1960, produced Off-Broadway at St. Mark's Playhouse, March 25, 1969; also see below), Extra-Mural Department, University of West Indies, 1966.

"Dream on Monkey Mountain" (also see below), first produced in Toronto, Ontario, Canada, 1967, produced Off-Broadway at St. Mark's Playhouse, March 9, 1971.

Dream on Monkey Mountain and Other Plays (contains "Dream on Monkey Mountain," "Sea at Dauphin," "Malcochon; or, Six in the Rain," "Ti-Jean and His Brothers," and the essay "What the Twilight Says: An Overture"; also see below), Farrar, Straus, 1970.

"The Joker of Seville" (musical; also see below), first produced in Port of Spain, Trinidad, 1974.

"The Charlatan," first produced in Los Angeles, 1974.

"O Babylon!" (also see below), first produced in Port of Spain, Trinidad, 1976.

"Remembrance" (three-act; also see below), first produced in St. Croix, Virgin Islands, December, 1977, produced Off-Broadway at The Other Stage, May 9, 1979.

"Pantomime" (also see below), Port of Spain, Trinidad, 1978, produced at the Hudson Guild Theater, 1986.

The Joker of Seville & O Babylon!: Two Plays, Farrar, Straus, 1978.

Remembrance & Pantomime: Two Plays, Farrar, Straus, 1980.

"The Isle Is Full of Noises," first produced at the John W. Huntington Theater, in Hartford, Conn., April, 1982.

Three Plays (contains "The Last Carnival," "Beef, No Chicken," and "A Branch of the Blue Nile"), Farrar, Straus, 1986.

Also author of "Franklin, a Tale of the Islands," "Jourmard," and "To Die for Grenada."

CONTRIBUTOR

John Figueroa, editor, *Caribbean Voices,* Evans, 1966.

Barbara Howes, editor, *From the Green Antilles,* Macmillan, 1966.

Howard Sergeant, editor, *Commonwealth Poems of Today,* Murray, 1967.

O. R. Dathorne, editor, *Caribbean Verse,* Heinemann, 1968.

Anne Walmsley, compiler, *The Sun's Eye: West Indian Writing for Young Readers,* Longmans, 1968.

Orde Coombs, editor, *Is Massa Day Dead?,* Doubleday, 1974.

D. J. Enright, editor, *Oxford Book of Contemporary Verse, 1945-80,* Oxford University Press, 1980.

Errol Hill, editor, *Plays for Today,* Longman, 1985.

Also contributor to *Caribbean Literature,* edited by George Robert Coulthard; *New Voices of the Commonwealth,* edited by Sergeant; and, *Young Commonwealth Poetry,* edited by Peter Ludwig Brent.

OTHER

Art and literature critic for *Trinidad Guardian;* feature writer for *Public Opinion* (Jamaica). Contributor of poems to numerous periodicals, including *New Statesman, London Magazine, Encounter, Evergreen Review, Caribbean Quarterly, Tamarack Review,* and *Bim.*

SIDELIGHTS: Although born of mixed racial and ethnic heritage on St. Lucia, a West Indian island where a French/English patois is spoken, poet and playwright Derek Walcott was educated as a British subject. Taught to speak English as a second language, he grew to be a skilled craftsman in his adopted tongue. His use of the language has drawn praise from critics including British poet and novelist Robert Graves who, according to *Times Literary Supplement* contributor Vicki Feaver, "has gone as far to state that [Walcott] handles English with a closer understanding of its inner magic than most (if not all) of his English-born contemporaries."

Walcott's major theme is the dichotomy between black and white, subject and ruler, Caribbean and Western civilization present in his culture and ancestry. In "What the Twilight Says," the introduction to *Dream on Monkey Mountain and Other Plays,* Walcott refers to his "schizophrenic boyhood" in which he led "two lives: the interior life of poetry [and] the outward life of action and dialect." In *Derek Walcott* Robert D. Hamner notes that this schizophrenia is common among West Indians and comments further that "since [Walcott] is descended from a white grandfather and a black grandmother on both paternal and maternal sides, he is a living example of the divided loyalties and hatreds that keep his society suspended between two worlds."

"As a West Indian . . . writing in English, with Africa and England in his blood," Alan Shapiro writes in the *Chicago Tribune Book World,* "Walcott is inescapably the victim and beneficiary of the colonial society in which he was reared. He is a kind of a Caribbean Orestes . . . unable to satisfy his allegiance to one side of his nature without at the same time betraying the other." Caryl Phillips describes Walcott's work in much the same way in her *Los Angeles Times Book Review* essay. The critic notes that Walcott's poetry is "steeped in an ambivalence toward the outside world and its relationship to his own native land of St. Lucia."

One often-quoted poem, "A Far Cry from Africa," from *In a Green Night,* deals directly with Walcott's sense of cultural confusion. "Where shall I turn, divided to the vein? / I who have cursed / the drunken officer of British rule, how choose / Between this Africa and the English tongue I love? / Betray them both, or give back what they give?"

In another poem, "The Schooner *Flight,*" from his second collection, *The Star-Apple Kingdom,* the poet uses a Trinidadian sailor named Shabine to appraise his own place as a person of mixed blood in a world divided into whites and blacks. According to the mariner: "The first chain my hands and apologise, 'History'; / the next said I wasn't black enough for their pride." Not white enough for whites, not black enough for blacks, Shabine sums up the complexity of his situation near the beginning of the poem saying: "I had a sound colonial education, / I have Dutch, nigger and English in me, / and either I'm nobody or I'm a nation."

It is Walcott, of course, who is speaking, and *New York Review of Books* contributor Thomas R. Edwards notes how the poet suffers the same fate as his poetic alter-ego, Shabine. Edwards writes, "Walcott is a cultivated cosmopolitan poet who is black, and as such he risks irrelevant praise as well as blame, whites finding it clever of him to be able to sound so much like other sophisticated poets, blacks feeling that he's sold his soul by practicing white arts.''

Although pained by the contrasts in his background, Walcott has chosen to embrace both his island and colonial heritage. His love of both sides of his psyche is apparent in an analysis of his work. As Hamner notes: ''Nurtured on oral tales of gods, devils, and cunning tricksters passed down by generations of slaves, Walcott should retell folk stories; and he does. On the other hand, since he has an affinity for and is educated in Western classics, he should retell the traditional themes of European experience; and he does. As inheritor of two vitally rich cultures, he utilizes one, then the other, and finally creates out of the two his own personalized style.''

Walcott seems closest to his island roots in his plays. For the most part, he has reserved his native language—patois or creole—to them. They also feature Caribbean settings and themes. According to *Literary Review* contributor David Mason, through Walcott's plays he hopes to create a ''catalytic theater responsible for social change or at least social identity.''

Although a volume of poems was his first published work, Walcott originally concentrated his efforts on the theater. In the fifties, he wrote a series of plays in verse, including *Henri Christophe: A Chronicle*, *The Sea at Dauphin*, and *Ione*. The first play deals with an episode in Caribbean history: ex-slave Henri Christophe's rise to kingship of Haiti in the early 1800s. The second marks Walcott's first use of the mixed French/English language of his native island in a play.

In *Dictionary of Literary Biography Yearbook: 1981* Dennis Jones notes that while Walcott uses the folk idiom of the islands in the play, the speech of the characters is not strictly imitative. It is instead ''made eloquent, as the common folk represented in the work are made noble, by the magic of the artist.''

In ''What the Twilight Says'' Walcott describes his use of language in his plays. In particular, he expresses the desire to mold ''a language that went beyond mimicry, . . . one which finally settled on its own mode of inflection, and which begins to create an oral culture, of chants, jokes, folk-songs, and fables.''

The presence of ''chants, jokes, and fables'' in Walcott's plays causes critics such as Jones and the *Los Angeles Times*'s Juana Duty Kennedy to call the playwright's best pieces for theater folk dramas. In *Books and Bookmen* Romilly Cavan observes the numerous folk elements in Walcott's plays: ''The laments of superstitious fishermen, charcoal-burners and prisoners are quickly counter-pointed by talking crickets, frogs, and birds. Demons are raised, dreams take actual shape, [and] supernatural voices mingle with the natural lilting elliptical speech rhythms of downtrodden natives.'' Animals who speak and a folk-representation of the devil are characters, for example, in the play, ''Ti-Jean and His Brothers.''

Walcott's most highly praised play, *Dream on Monkey Mountain*, is also a folk drama. It was awarded a 1971 Obie Award and deemed ''a poem in dramatic form'' by Edith Oliver in the *New Yorker*. The play's title is itself enough to immediately transport the viewer into the superstitious legend-filled world of the Caribbean backcountry.

In the play, Walcott draws a parallel between the hallucinations of an old charcoal vendor and the colonial reality of the Caribbean. Islanders subjected to the imposition of a colonial culture over their own eventually question the validity of both cultures. Ultimately, they may determine that their island culture—because it has no official status other than as an enticement for tourists—is nothing but a sterile hallucination. Or, as Jones notes, they may reach the conclusion at which Walcott wishes his audience to arrive: the charcoal vendor's ''dreams connect to the past, and that it is in that past kept alive in the dreams of the folk that an element of freedom is maintained in the colonized world.''

Perhaps because of critics' unfamiliarity with the Caribbean reality which Walcott describes in his plays, the author's work for theater has received only mixed reviews in this country. For example, while Walter Goodman writes in the *New York Times* that Walcott's ''Pantomime'' ''stays with you as a fresh and funny work filled with thoughtful insights and illuminated by bright performances,'' the *New York Times*'s Frank Rich's comments on the same play are not as favorable. ''Walcott's best writing has always been as a poet . . . ,'' Rich observes, ''and that judgment remains unaltered by 'Pantomime.' For some reason, [he] refuses to bring the same esthetic rigor to his playwriting that he does to his powerfully dense verse.''

In James Atlas's *New York Times Magazine* biographical/critical essay on Walcott, the critic confronts Rich's remarks head on, asserting that the poet would respond to Rich by commenting ''that he doesn't conceive of his plays as finished works but as provisional effects to address his own people. 'The great challenge to me,' he says, 'was to write as powerfully as I could without writing down to the audience, so that the large emotions could be taken in by a fisherman or a guy on the street, even if he didn't understand every line.'''

If Walcott's plays reveal what is most Caribbean about him, his poetry reveals what is most English. If he hopes to reach the common man in his plays, the same cannot be said of his poetry. His poems are based on the traditional forms of English poetry, filled with classical allusions, elaborate metaphors, complex rhyme schemes, and other poetic devices.

In the *New York Times Book Review*, Selden Rodman calls Walcott's poems ''almost Elizabethan in their richness.'' The *New York Times*'s Michiko Kakutani agrees, noting that ''from England, [Walcott] appropriated an old-fashioned love of eloquence, an Elizabethan richness of words and a penchant for complicated, formal rhymes. In fact, in a day when more and more poets have adopted a grudging, minimalist style, [his] verse remains dense and elaborate, filled with dazzling complexities of style.''

Some critics object that Walcott's attention to style sometimes detracts from his poetry, either by being unsuitable for his Caribbean themes or by becoming more important than the poems' content. Denis Donoghue, for example, remarks in the *New York Times Book Review*, ''It is my impression that his standard English style [is] dangerously high for nearly every purpose except that of Jacobean tragedy.'' In Steve Ratiner's *Christian Science Monitor* review of *Midsummer*, the critic observes that ''after a time, we are so awash in sparkling language and intricate metaphor, the subject of the poem is all but obscured.'' In her *New York Review of Books* essay, Helen Vendler finds an ''unhappy disjunction between [Walcott's] explosive subject . . . and his harmonious pentameters, his lyrical allusions, his stately rhymes, [and] his Yeatsian meditations.''

More criticism comes from those who maintain that the influence of other poets on Walcott's work have drowned out his authentic voice. While Vendler, for instance, describes Walcott as a "man of great sensibility and talent," she dismisses much of his poetry as "ventriloquism" and maintains that in Walcott's 1982 collection of poems, *The Fortunate Traveller,* he seems "at the mercy of influence, this time the influence of Robert Lowell."

Poet J. D. McClatchy also notices Lowell's influence in *The Fortunate Traveller* as well as two other Walcott poetry collections: *The Star-Apple Kingdom* and *Midsummer.* In his *New Republic* review McClatchy not only finds similarities in the two men's styles but also a similar pattern of development in their poetry. "Like Lowell," the critic notes, "Walcott's mode has . . . shifted from the mythological to the historical, from fictions to facts, and his voice has gotten more clipped and severe. There are times when the influence is almost too direct, as in 'Old New England,' [a poem from *The Fortunate Traveller,*] where he paces off Lowell's own territory."

Both major criticisms of Walcott's poetry are answered in Sven Birkerts's *New Republic* essay. Birkerts observes: "Walcott writes a strongly accented, densely packed line that seldom slackens and yet never loses conversational intimacy. He works in form, but he is not formal. His agitated phonetic surfaces can at times recall Lowell's, but the two are quite different. In Lowell, one feels the torque of mind; in Walcott, the senses predominate. And Walcott's lines ring with a spontaneity that Lowell's often lack."

Other critics defend the integrity of Walcott's poems. Poet James Dickey notes in the *New York Times Book Review,* "Fortunately, for him and for us,. . . Walcott has the energy and the exuberant strength to break through his literary influences into a highly colored, pulsating realm of his own." In his *Poetry* review of *Midsummer* Paul Breslin writes: "For the most part,. . . Walcott's voice remains as distinctive as ever, and the occasional echoes of Lowell register as homage rather than unwitting imitation."

Hamner maintains that when dealing with Walcott's poetry the term assimilation rather than imitation should be used. The critic observes: "Walcott passed through his youthful apprenticeship phase wherein he consciously traced the models of established masters. He was humble enough to learn from example and honest enough to disclose his intention to appropriate whatever stores he found useful in the canon of world literature. . . . But Walcott does not stop with imitation. Assimilation means to ingest into the mind and thoroughly comprehend; it also means to merge into or become one with a cultural tradition."

The uniqueness of Walcott's work stems from his ability to interweave British and island influences, to express what McClatchy calls "his mixed state" and do so "without indulging in either ethnic chic or imperial drag." His plays offer pictures of the common Caribbean folk and comment on the ills bred by colonialism. His poetry combines native patois and English rhetorical devices in a constant struggle to force an allegiance between the two halves of his split heritage.

According to *Los Angeles Times Book Review* contributor Arthur Vogelsang, "These continuing polarities shoot an electricity to each other which is questioning and beautiful and which helps form a vision all together Caribbean and inter-

national, personal (him to you, you to him), independent, and essential for readers of contemporary literature on all the continents."

BIOGRAPHICAL/CRITICAL SOURCES:

BOOKS

Contemporary Literary Criticism, Gale, Volume 2, 1974, Volume 4, 1975, Volume 9, 1978, Volume 42, 1987.
Dictionary of Literary Biography Yearbook: 1981, Gale, 1982.
Goldstraw, Irma, *Derek Walcott: An Annotated Bibliography of His Works,* Garland Publishing, 1984.
Hamner, Robert D., *Derek Walcott,* Twayne, 1981.
Walcott, Derek, *Collected Poems, 1948-1984,* Farrar, Straus, 1986.
Walcott, Derek, *Dream on Monkey Mountain and Other Plays,* Farrar, Straus, 1970.

PERIODICALS

Books and Bookmen, April, 1972.
Book World, December 13, 1970.
Chicago Tribune Book World, May 2, 1982, September 9, 1984, March 9, 1986.
Christian Science Monitor, March 19, 1982, April 6, 1984.
Georgia Review, summer, 1984.
Hudson Review, summer, 1984.
Literary Review, spring, 1986.
London Magazine, December, 1973-January, 1974, February-March, 1977.
Los Angeles Times, November 12, 1986.
Los Angeles Times Book Review, April 4, 1982, May 21, 1985, April 6, 1986, October 26, 1986, September 6, 1987.
Nation, February 12, 1977, May 19, 1979, February 27, 1982.
National Review, November 3, 1970, June 20, 1986.
New Republic, November 20, 1976, March 17, 1982, January 23, 1984, March 24, 1986.
New Statesman, March 19, 1982.
New Yorker, March 27, 1971, June 26, 1971.
New York Magazine, August 14, 1972.
New York Review of Books, December 31, 1964, May 6, 1971, June 13, 1974, October 14, 1976, May 31, 1979, March 4, 1982.
New York Times, March 21, 1979, August 21, 1979, May 30, 1981, May 2, 1982, January 15, 1986, December 17, 1986.
New York Times Book Review, September 13, 1964, October 11, 1970, May 6, 1973, October 31, 1976, May 13, 1979, January 3, 1982, April 8, 1984, February 2, 1986, December 20, 1987.
New York Times Magazine, May 23, 1982.
Poetry, February, 1972, December, 1973, July, 1977, December, 1984, June, 1986.
Review, winter, 1974.
Spectator, May 10, 1980.
Time, March 15, 1982.
Times Literary Supplement, December 25, 1969, August 3, 1973, July 23, 1976, August 8, 1980, September 8, 1980, September 24, 1982, November 9, 1984, October 24, 1986.
Tribune Books (Chicago), November 8, 1987.
TriQuarterly, winter, 1986.
Village Voice, April 11, 1974.
Virginia Quarterly Review, winter, 1974, summer, 1984.
Washington Post Book World, February 21, 1982, April 13, 1986.
Western Humanities Review, spring, 1977.

World Literature Today, spring, 1977, summer, 1979, summer, 1981, winter, 1985, summer, 1986, winter, 1987.
Yale Review, October, 1973.†

—*Sketch by Marian Gonsior*

* * *

WALDMAN, Diane 1936-

PERSONAL: Born February 24, 1936, in New York, N.Y.; daughter of Robert and Beatrice Rose (Albert) Deleson; married Paul Waldman (an artist), 1957. *Education:* Hunter College (now Hunter College of the City University of New York), B.F.A., 1956; New York University, M.A., 1965; Columbia University, supplementary studies in art history, 1961 and 1963; Institute of Fine Arts, Certificate in Museum Training, 1965.

ADDRESSES: Home—38 West 26th St., New York, N.Y. 10010. *Office*—Guggenheim Museum, 1071 Fifth Ave., New York, N.Y. 10028.

CAREER: Guggenheim Museum, New York, N.Y., staff member, 1965-71, curator of exhibitions, beginning 1971, deputy director, 1982—. American Commissioner for the Biennale of Sydney, 1988. Organized exhibition of Laslo Maholy-Nagy for the Thirty-fifth Venice Biennale; has also organized free-lance exhibition for the School of Visual Arts, exhibitions on winners of the Theodoron Awards, exhibition on Selected Sculpture and Works on Paper from the Guggenheim Collection, and exhibitions in conjunction with the Stedelijk Museum, Amsterdam, the Centre National d'Art Moderne, Paris, and the Kunsthalle, Duesseldorf.

WRITINGS:

(Contributor) *Chryssa: Selected Works, 1955-1967,* Pace Gallery, 1968.
Roy Lichtenstein: Drawings and Prints (monograph), Chelsea House, 1969.
Ellsworth Kelly: Drawings, Collages, and Prints, New York Graphic Society, 1971.
Roy Lichtenstein (monograph), Thames & Hudson, 1971.
(Contributor) *Roy Lichtenstein,* edited by John Coplans, Praeger, 1972.
Joseph Cornell, Braziller, 1977.
Anthony Caro, Abbeville Press, 1982.
Willem de Kooning, Abrams, 1988.

EXHIBITION CATALOGUES

Joseph Cornell, Guggenheim Museum, 1967.
(With Robert Doty) *Adolph Gottlieb,* Praeger, 1968.
Roy Lichtenstein, Guggenheim Foundation, 1969.
Arshile Gorky, 1904-1948: A Retrospective, Abrams, 1981.
Italian Art Now, an American Perspective: 1982 Exxon International Exhibition, Guggenheim Foundation, 1982.

Also author of *Carl Andre,* 1970, (with Fry) *Guggenheim International Exhibition, 1971* (survey), 1971, *Robert Mangold,* 1971, *John Chamberlain: A Retrospective Exhibition,* 1971, *Robert Ryman,* 1972, *Max Ernst,* 1975, *Twentieth-Century American Drawing: Three Avant-Garde Generations,* 1976, *Kenneth Noland: A Retrospective,* 1977, *Willem de Kooning in East Hampton,* 1978, *Mark Rothko: A Retrospective,* 1978, *British Art Now, an American Perspective: 1980 Exxon International Exhibition,* 1980, *New Perspectives in American Art: 1983 Exxon National Exhibition,* 1983, *Charles Simonds* (brochure), 1983, *Michael Singer,* 1984, *Australian Visions: 1984 Exxon International Exhibition,* 1984, *Transformations in

Sculpture: Four Decades of American and European Art, 1985, *Jack Youngerman,* 1986, *Enzo Cucchi,* 1986, *Emerging Artists, 1978-1986: Selections from the Exxon Series,* 1987. Contributor to *Art International, Arts Magazine, Art News, Art Press,* and *Art in America.*

BIOGRAPHICAL/CRITICAL SOURCES:

BOOKS

New York Times Book Review, June 21, 1981.
Times Literary Supplement, June 4, 1982.

* * *

WALKER, Alan 1911-

PERSONAL: Born June 4, 1911, in Sydney, Australia; son of Alfred Edgar (a clergyman) and Louise (Lavis) Walker; married Winifred Channon, March 26, 1938; children: Lynette, Bruce, David, Christopher. *Education:* Attended Leigh Theological College, Sydney, Australia, 1929-32; University of Sydney, B.A., 1936, M.A., 1943.

ADDRESSES: Home—14 Owen Stanley Ave., Beacon Hill 2100, Australia. *Office*—Number One Angel Pl., Sydney 2000, Australia.

CAREER: Ordained Methodist minister in Australia, 1934; associate director of New South Wales Methodist Youth Department, 1936-38; minister in Cessnock, Australia, 1939-44; Waverley Methodist Mission, Sydney, Australia, superintendent, 1944-54; director of Australian Mission (Methodist) to the Nation, 1955-56; leader of mission to the United States and Canada, 1956-57; Boston University School of Theology, Boston, Mass., visiting professor of evangelism, 1957-58; Central Methodist Mission, Sydney, superintendent, 1958-78; World Evangelism for the World Methodist Council, Sydney, director, 1978—. Founder of Sydney Life Line Centre, 1963; president of Life Line International, 1966—. Participant in foreign missions to Fiji, 1962, South Africa, 1963, South America, 1967, Singapore, 1972, Malaysia, 1972, and Sri Lanka, 1975; New South Wales Methodist Conference, secretary, 1970, president, 1971; visiting professor of evangelism and preaching at Claremont School of Theology, 1973; former conductor of Australian television program, "I Challenge the Minister." Adviser to Australian delegation to the United Nations, 1949, to Third Assembly of World Council of Churches, 1962, and to Fourth Assembly of World Council of Churches, 1968.

AWARDS, HONORS: Officer, Order of the Birtish Empire, 1955; Institute de la Vie Award, 1978, for his work with Life Line; created Knight Bachelor by Queen Elizabeth II, 1981; joint receiver with wife, Lady Winifred Walker, of World Methodist Peace Award, 1986.

WRITINGS:

There Is Always God, Epworth Press, 1938.
Everybody's Calvary, Epworth Press, 1943.
Coal-Town: A Sociological Survey, Oxford University Press, 1945.
Heritage without End, Methodist Publishing House, 1953.
The Whole Gospel for the Whole World, Abingdon, 1957.
A New Mind for a New Age, Abingdon, 1958.
God Is Where You Are, Lutterworth, 1961.
The Many-Sided Cross of Jesus, Epworth Press, 1962, new edition, Christian Journals, 1980.
How Jesus Helped People, Abingdon, 1964.

A Ringing Call to Mission, Abingdon, 1966.

As Close as the Telephone: The Dramatic Story of the Australian Life Line Movement, Abingdon, 1967 (published in England as *The Life Line Story*, Collins, 1967).

Breakthrough: Rediscovering the Holy Spirit, Abingdon, 1969, revised edition, Collins, 1979.

God, the Disturber, Word, Inc., 1973.

Jesus, the Liberator, Abingdon, 1973.

The New Evangelism, Abingdon, 1974.

Love in Action, Collins, 1977.

Life Begins at Christ, Discipleship Resources, 1979.

Caring for the World: The Continuing Story of the Life Line Christian Telephone Ministries, Collins, 1979.

(Editor) *See How They Grow: The Story of Twelve Growing Churches around the World*, Collins, 1979.

Life Grows with Christ, Discipleship Resources, 1981.

Life Ends in Christ, Discipleship Resources, 1983.

Standing Up to Preach, Discipleship Resources, 1983.

Your Life Can Be Changed, Discipleship Resources, 1985.

Life in the Holy Spirit, Discipleship Resources, 1986.

Whither Australia, Albatross Books (Sydney), 1987.

Also author of *Making Disciples*, 1980.

BIOGRAPHICAL/CRITICAL SOURCES:

BOOKS

Harold Henderson, *Reach for the World: The Alan Walker Story*, Discipleship Resources, 1981.

*   *   *

WALKER, Joseph A.   1935-

PERSONAL: Born February 23, 1935, in Washington, D.C.; son of Joseph (a house painter) and Florine Walker; married Barbara Brown (divorced, 1965); married Dorothy A. Dinroe, 1970. *Education:* Howard University, B.A., 1956; Catholic University of America, M.F.A., 1970; New York University, Ph.D.

ADDRESSES: Home—New York, N.Y. *Office*—Department of Speech and Theatre, City College of the City University of New York, New York, N.Y. 10031.

CAREER: Educator, actor, director, playwright, choreographer, producer. Worked as taxi driver, shoe and cosmetics salesman, and postal clerk; English teacher at junior high and high schools in Washington, D.C., and New York City; actor, set designer, and playwright, in New York City, beginning 1967; Negro Ensemble Co., New York City, playwright, director and choreographer, beginning 1969; Yale University, New Haven, Conn., playwright-in-residence, 1970-71; City College of the City University of New York, New York City, currently instructor; Howard University, Washington, D.C., currently instructor of advanced acting and playwrighting. Actor in stage productions, including "The Believers," 1967, "Cities of Beziques," 1969, "Once in a Lifetime," "A Raisin in the Sun," and "Purlie Victorious," in motion pictures, including "April Fools," 1969, and "Bananas," 1971, and in television program "N.Y.P.D." (ABC-TV); narrator of "In Black America" (CBS-TV). Co-founder and artistic director of The Demi-Gods (dance-music theatre repertory company). *Military service:* U.S. Air Force; became second lieutenant.

AWARDS, HONORS: Guggenheim fellowship, 1973; Obie Award, 1971, Antoinette Perry (Tony) Award, 1973, Elizabeth Hull-Kate Award from Dramatist Guild, First Annual

Audelco Award, John Gassner Award from Outer Circle, Drama Desk Award, Black Rose, all for "The River Niger"; Rockefeller Foundation grant, 1979.

WRITINGS:

PLAYS

(With Josephine Jackson) *The Believers* (first produced Off-Broadway at the Garrick Theatre, May 9, 1968), published in *The Best Plays of 1967-1968*, edited by Otis L. Guernsey, Dodd, 1968.

"The Harangues" (two one-act plays), first produced Off-Broadway at St. Mark's Playhouse, December 30, 1969.

Ododo (title means "The Truth"; first produced Off-Broadway at St. Mark's Playhouse, November 24, 1970), published in *Black Drama Anthology*, edited by Woodie King and Ron Milner, Columbia University Press, 1972.

"Yin Yang," first produced Off-Off-Broadway at the Afro-American Studio, June 30, 1972, produced Off-Broadway at St. Mark's Playhouse, May 30, 1973.

The River Niger (three-act; first produced Off-Broadway at St. Mark's Playhouse, December 5, 1972; also see below), Hill & Wang, 1973.

"Antigone Africanus," first produced in New York, 1975.

"The Lion Is a Soul Brother," first produced in New York, 1976.

"District Line," first produced Off-Broadway at Theatre Four, December, 1984.

Also author of "Themes of the Black Struggle" and "The Hiss."

OTHER

"The River Niger" (screenplay; based on play of the same title), Cine Artists, 1976.

Contributor to periodicals, including the *New York Times*.

SIDELIGHTS: When Joseph A. Walker's first solo effort, "The Harangues," was produced by the Negro Ensemble Company in 1970, Walter Kerr wrote in the *New York Times:* "The company has come upon a playwright whose theatrical instincts are strong even when he is letting them gallop along a little bit ahead of him; that is better than playing it shy, or tentative, or safe."

Certainly, Walker does not play it safe. Alan Bunce of the *Christian Science Monitor* describes "The Harangues" as "an unabashed polemic whose impact on the stage is ultimately stirring." The play consists of two main segments sandwiched between a tribal prologue and interlude. In the first main act, a black man, engaged to a pregnant white woman, intends to murder his fiancee's millionaire father; the other of the two long segments concerns another pregnant white woman, her "liberal" brother, and her black fiance, all of whom are confronted by a gun-wielding black intruder who talks them into confessing their true racial attitudes. Likening the entire performance to the films of Luis Bunuel, Martin Washburn writes in the *Village Voice:* "Walker's play is strong because he has the courage to speak directly from his tradition instead of disguising it."

After seeing "Ododo," *New York Times* contributor Clive Barnes was prompted to observe that the Negro Ensemble Company seemed to have become more "separatist, militant and black" than it had previously been. The play is a musical, tracing the background and history of the North American black from the African jungle through slave ships, American slavery, Lincoln, and reconstruction to the ghetto and contemporary black consciousness. While John Simon of *New York* magazine dismisses "Ododo" as "a black supremist, racist show," Barnes concedes that, though propaganda, it is "beautifully-written propaganda" nevertheless.

With *The River Niger* Walker achieved his first true critical success. Grace Cooper in the *Dictionary of Literary Biography* claims the play "shows [Walker's] full growth as a playwright." She continues, "While it expresses many of the same strong feelings of the earlier plays, *The River Niger* is more subtle, therefore allowing him to make his points acceptable to a larger audience. The play has been widely recognized as a realistic depiction of black life." Mel Gussow says in *Time* that Walker "has a distinct voice and his own sensitive awareness of what makes people different. The play is rich with character, atmosphere, and nuance." In the *New York Times*, Kerr describes the dialogue as "exemplary, knife sharp when adrenalin is meant to flow and gently rhetorical whenever the father of a Harlem family remembers that he meant to be a poet." Dedicated "to my mother and father and to highly underrated Black daddies everywhere," the play is semi-autobiographical and centers on the father's struggle and sacrifice for his family amidst the violent world they live in. Reviewing the play in the *Washington Post*, Anthony Astrachan says, "It is unquestionable black theater: Its characters could only be black. But it is also universal theater: It speaks to audiences of all colors." Barnes also believes *The River Niger* can speak to a multi-racial audience. "This strong family drama eludes simple labels such as black," he affirms in the *New York Times*. "Broadway audiences, whether they be black, white, or sky-blue pink, will assuredly react to the strength of its melodrama and the pulse of its language.... It is a testimony to man's unending fight for survival."

MEDIA ADAPTATIONS:

The River Niger was made into a film starring Cicely Tyson and James Earl Jones.

BIOGRAPHICAL/CRITICAL SOURCES:

BOOKS

Contemporary Literary Criticism, Volume 19, Gale, 1981.
Dictionary of Literary Biography, Volume 38: *Afro-American Writers after 1955: Dramatists and Prose Writers*, Gale, 1985.

PERIODICALS

Black World, April, 1971.
Christian Science Monitor, January 23, 1970.
Cue, December 5, 1970.
Modern Drama, December, 1976.
Nation, February 2, 1970, December 25, 1972.
New Republic, September 29, 1973.
New York, December 14, 1970.
New Yorker, January 24, 1970, December 16, 1972.
New York Times, May 10, 1968, January 14, 1970, January 25, 1970, November 25, 1970, December 6, 1970, December 14, 1970, December 6, 1972, December 17, 1972, March 28, 1973, May 31, 1973, December 5, 1984.
Saturday Review, February 14, 1970.
Show Business, November 28, 1970.
Time, January 1, 1973.
Variety, December 9, 1970.
Village Voice, January 22, 1970.
Washington Post, April 13, 1973.†

WALKER, Margaret Abigail   1915-

PERSONAL: Born July 7, 1915, in Birmingham, Ala.; daughter of Sigismund C. (a Methodist minister) and Marion (Dozier) Walker (a music teacher); married Firnist James Alexander, June 13, 1943 (deceased); children: Marion Elizabeth, Firnist James, Sigismund Walker, Margaret Elvira. *Education:* Northwestern University, A.B., 1935; University of Iowa, M.A., 1940, Ph.D., 1965. *Religion:* Methodist.

ADDRESSES: Home—2205 Guynes St., Jackson, Miss. 39213. *Office*—Department of English, Jackson State College, Jackson, Miss. 39217.

CAREER: Worked as a social worker, newspaper reporter, and magazine editor; Livingstone College, Salisbury, N.C., member of faculty, 1941-42; West Virginia State College, Institute, W.Va., instructor in English, 1942-43; Livingstone College, professor of English, 1945-46; Jackson State College, Jackson, Miss., professor of English, 1949—, director of Institute for the Study of the History, Life, and Culture of Black Peoples, 1968—. Lecturer, National Concert and Artists Corp. Lecture Bureau, 1943-48. Visiting professor in creative writing, Northwestern University, spring, 1969. Staff member, Cape Cod Writers Conference, Craigville, Mass., 1967 and 1969. Participant, Library of Congress Conference on the Teaching of Creative Writing, 1973.

MEMBER: National Council of Teachers of English, Modern Language Association, Poetry Society of America, American Association of University Professors, National Education Association, Alpha Kappa Alpha.

AWARDS, HONORS: Yale Series of Younger Poets Award, 1942, for *For My People;* named to Honor Roll of Race Relations, a national poll conducted by the New York Public Library, 1942; Rosenthal fellowship, 1944; Ford fellowship for study at Yale University, 1954; Houghton Mifflin Literary Fellowship, 1966; Fulbright fellowship, 1971; National Endowment for the Humanities, 1972; Doctor of Literature, Northwestern University, 1974; Doctor of Letters, Rust College, 1974; Doctor of Fine Arts, Dennison University, 1974; Doctor of Humane Letters, Morgan State University, 1976.

WRITINGS:

POETRY

For My People, Yale University Press, 1942, reprinted, Ayer Co., 1969.
Ballad of the Free, Broadside Press, 1966.
Prophets for a New Day, Broadside Press, 1970.
October Journey, Broadside Press, 1973.

Also author of *This Is My Century.*

PROSE

Jubilee (novel), Houghton, 1965, Bantam, 1981.
How I Wrote "Jubilee," Third World Press, 1972.
(With Nikki Giovanni) *A Poetic Equation: Conversations between Nikki Giovanni and Margaret Walker*, Howard University Press, 1974, reprinted with new postscript, 1983.
Richard Wright: Daemonic Genius, Dodd, 1987.

CONTRIBUTOR

Addison Gayle, editor, *Black Expression*, Weybright & Tally, 1969.

Stanton L. Wormley and Lewis H. Fenderson, editors, *Many Shades of Black*, Morrow, 1969.

Henderson, Stephen, *Understanding the New Black Poetry: Black Speech and Black Music as Poetic References*, Morrow, 1973.

Also contributor to numerous anthologies, including Adoff's *Black Out Loud*, Weisman and Wright's *Black Poetry for All Americans*, and Williams's *Beyond the Angry Black*.

OTHER

Contributor to *Yale Review, Negro Digest, Poetry, Opportunity, Phylon, Saturday Review,* and *Virginia Quarterly.*

WORK IN PROGRESS: Minna and Jim, a sequel to *Jubilee; Mother Broyer,* a novel; an autobiography, for Howard University Press.

SIDELIGHTS: When *For My People* by Margaret Walker won the Yale Younger Poets Series Award in 1942, "she became one of the youngest Black writers ever to have published a volume of poetry in this century," as well as "the first Black woman in American literary history to be so honored in a prestigious national competition," notes Richard K. Barksdale in *Black American Poets between Worlds, 1940-1960.* Walker's first novel, *Jubilee,* is notable for being "the first truly historical black American novel," according to University of Maryland professor Joyce Anne Joyce, reports *Washington Post* contributor Crispin Y. Campbell. It was also the first work by a black writer to speak out for the liberation of the black woman. The cornerstones of a literature that affirms the African folk roots of black American life, these two books have also been called visionary for looking toward a new cultural unity for black Americans that will be built on that foundation.

The title of Walker's first book, *For My People,* denotes the subject matter of "poems in which the body and spirit of a great group of people are revealed with vigor and undeviating integrity," says Louis Untermeyer in the *Yale Review.* Here, in long ballads, Walker draws sympathetic portraits of characters such as the New Orleans sorceress Molly Means; Kissie Lee, a tough young woman who dies "with her boots on switching blades;" and Poppa Chicken, an urban drug dealer and pimp. Other ballads give a new dignity to John Henry, killed by a ten-pound hammer, and Stagolee, who kills a white officer but eludes a lynch mob. In an essay for *Black Women Writers (1950-1980): A Critical Evaluation,* Eugenia Collier notes, "Using . . . the language of the grass-roots people, Walker spins yarns of folk heroes and heroines: those who, faced with the terrible obstacles which haunt Black people's very existence, not only survive but prevail—with style." Soon after it appeared, the book of ballads, sonnets and free verse found a surprisingly large number of readers, requiring publishers to authorize three printings to satisfy popular demand.

Some critics found fault with the sonnets in the book, but others deemed it generally impressive, R. Baxter Miller summarizes in *Black American Poets between Worlds.* "The title poem is itself a singular and unique literary achievement," Barksdale claims. In *Black American Literature: A Critical History,* Roger Whitlow elaborates, "The poem, written in free verse, rhythmically catalogues the progress of black American experience, from the rural folkways, religious practices, and exhausting labor of the South, through the cramped and confusing conditions of the northern urban centers, to what she hopes will be a racial awakening, blacks militantly rising up to take control of their own destinies." Collier relates, "The final stanza is a reverberating cry for redress. It demands

a new beginning. Our music then will be martial music; our peace will be hard-won, but it will be 'written in the sky.' And after the agony, the people whose misery spawned strength will control our world. This poem is the hallmark of Margaret Walker's works. It echoes in her subsequent poetry and even in her monumental novel *Jubilee.* It speaks to us, in our words and rhythms, of our history, and it radiates the promise of our future. It is the quintessential example of myth and ritual shaped by artistic genius."

Reviewers especially praise Walker's control of poetic technique in the poem. Dudley Randall writes in Addison Gayle's *The Black Aesthetic,* "The poem gains its force . . . by the sheer overpowering accumulation of a mass of details delivered in rhythmical parallel phrases." To cite Barksdale,"it is magnificently wrought oral poetry. . . . In reading it aloud, one must be able to breathe and pause, pause and breathe preacher-style. One must be able to sense the ebb and flow of the intonations. . . . This is the kind of verbal music found in a well-delivered down-home folk sermon." By giving the poem a musical rhythm, Walker underscores the poem's message, observes Barksdale: "The poet here is writing about the source of the Black peoples' blues, for out of their troubled past and turbulent present came the Black peoples' song." In this case, Walker steps forward to remind her people of the strength to be found in their cultural tradition as she calls for a new, hopeful literature that can inspire social action.

"If the test of a great poem is the universality of statement, then 'For My People' is a great poem," remarks Barksdale. The critic explains in Donald B. Gibson's *Modern Black Poets: A Collection of Critical Essays* that the poem was written when "world-wide pain, sorrow, and affliction were tangibly evident, and few could isolate the Black man's dilemma from humanity's dilemma during the depression years or during the war years." Thus, the power of resilience presented in the poem is a hope Walker holds out not only to black people, but to all people, to "all the adams and eves." As she once remarked, "Writers should not write exclusively for black or white audiences, but most inclusively. After all, it is the business of all writers to write about the human condition, and all humanity must be involved in both the writing and in the reading."

Jubilee, a historical novel, is the second book on which Walker's literary reputation rests. It is the story of a slave family during and after the civil war, and took her thirty years to write. During these years, she married a disabled veteran, raised four children, taught full time at Jackson State College in Mississippi, and earned a Ph.D. from the University of Iowa. The lengthy gestation, she believes, partly accounts for the book's quality. As she told Claudia Tate in *Black Women Writers at Work,* "Living with the book over a long period of time was agonizing. Despite all of that, *Jubilee* is the product of a mature person," one whose own difficult pregnancies and economic struggles could lend authenticity to the lives of her characters. "There's a difference between writing about something and living through it," she said in the interview; "I did both."

The story of *Jubilee'*s main characters Vyry and Randall Ware was an important part of Walker's life even before she began to write it down. As she explains in *How I Wrote "Jubilee,"* she first heard about the "slavery time" in bedtime stories told by her maternal grandmother. When old enough to recognize the value of her family history, Walker took initiative, "prodding" her grandmother for more details, and promising to set down on paper the story that had taken shape in her mind. Later on, she completed extensive research on every aspect of the black experience touching the Civil War, from obscure birth records to information on the history of tin cans. "Most of my life I have been involved with writing this story about my great-grandmother, and even if *Jubilee* were never considered an artistic or commercial success I would still be happy just to have finished it," she claims.

Soon after *Jubilee* was published in 1966, Walker was given a Fellowship award from Houghton-Mifflin, and a mixed reception from critics. Granting that the novel is "ambitious," *New York Times Book Review* contributor Wilma Dykeman deemed it "uneven." Arthur P. Davis, writing in *From the Dark Tower: Afro-American Writers, 1900-1960*, suggests that the author "has crowded too much into her novel." Even so, say reviewers, the novel merits praise. Abraham Chapman of the *Saturday Review* appreciates the author's "fidelity to fact and detail" as she "presents the little-known everyday life of the slaves," their music, and their folkways. In the *Christian Science Monitor*, Henrietta Buckmaster comments, "In Vyry, Miss Walker has found a remarkable woman who suffered one outrage after the other and yet emerged with a humility and a mortal fortitude that reflected a spiritual wholeness." Dykeman concurs, "In its best episodes, and in Vyry, 'Jubilee' chronicles the triumph of a free spirit over many kinds of bondages." Later critical studies of the book emphasize the importance of its themes and its position as the prototype for novels that present black history from a black perspective. Claims Whitlow, "It serves especially well as a response to white 'nostalgia' fiction about the antebellum and Reconstruction South."

Walker's next book to be highly acclaimed was *Prophets for a New Day*, a slim volume of poems. Unlike the poems in *For My People*, which, in a Marxist fashion, names religion an enemy of revolution, says Collier, *Prophets for a New Day* "reflects a profound religious faith. The heroes of the sixties are named for the prophets of the Bible: Martin Luther King is Amos, Medgar Evars is Micah, and so on. The people and events of the sixties are paralleled with Biblical characters and occurrences. . . . The religious references are important. Whether one espouses the Christianity in which they are couched is not the issue. For the fact is that Black people from ancient Africa to now have always been a spiritual people, believing in an existence beyond the flesh." One poem in *Prophets* that harks back to African spiritism is "Ballad of Hoppy Toad" with its hexes that turn a murderous conjurer into a toad. Though Collier feels that Walker's "vision of the African past is fairly dim and romantic," the critic goes on to say that this poetry "emanates from a deeper area of the psyche, one which touches the mythic area of a collective being and reenacts the rituals which define a Black collective self." Perhaps more importantly, in all the poems, says Collier, Walker depicts "a people striking back at oppression and emerging triumphant."

Walker disclosed in *A Poetic Equation: Conversations between Nikki Giovanni and Margaret Walker* that the poem "Ballad of the Free" in *Prophets* articulates "better than even 'For My People' so much of what I [feel] about black people and the whole movement toward freedom." Davis calls the book "the best poetical comment to come from the civil rights movement—the movement which came to a climax with the march on Washington and which began thereafter to change into a more militant type of liberation effort." Barksdale shares this view; as he comments in *Black American Poets between Worlds*, "Because of her experience, background, and train-

ing—her familial gift of word power, her intensive apprenticeship in Chicago's literary workshop in the 1930s, and her mastery of Black orature—her *Prophets* . . . stands out as the premier poetic statement of the death-riddled decade of the 1960s. The poems of this small volume reflect the full range of the Black protest during the time—the sit-ins, the jailings, the snarling dogs, the . . . lynching of the three Civil Rights workers in Mississippi. All of the poems in the volume touch the sensitive nerve of racial memory and bring back, in sharply etched detail, the trauma and tension and triumphs of that period."

In the same essay, Barksdale relates that Walker's books owe little to her academic life and much to a rich cultural sensibility gained in her youth. "There was . . . New Orleans with its . . . folk mythology, its music, . . . and its assortment of racial experiences to be remembered and recalled." And there was the shaping influence of Walker's parents. Born in Jamaica but educated at Atlanta's Gammon Theological Institute, her father Sigismond was a Methodist preacher. Her mother, Marion (nee Dozier), was a musician. "So [the poet] grew up in a household ruled by the power of the word, for undoubtedly few have a greater gift for articulate word power than an educated Jamaican trained to preach the doctrine of salvation in the Black South," Barksdale remarks. In such a home, survival "without mastery of words and language was impossible," he adds, citing Walker's comment. And, given her family background, Walker felt destined for an academic career.

That career was characterized by opposition and difficulty. In the interview with Tate, Walker reflects, "I'm a third-generation college graduate. Society doesn't want to recognize that there's this kind of black writer. I'm the Ph.D. black woman. That's horrible. That is to be despised. I didn't know how bad it was until I went back to school [to teaching] and found out." With her older children nearing college age, Walker had taken leave from her position at Jackson State University to earn an advanced degree in hope that afterward she would be given more pay. She returned only to be slighted by the administration. Eventually, she developed the school's black studies program, attaining personal fulfillment only during the last years of her career as an educator.

Discouragements of many kinds have not kept Walker from producing works that have encouraged many. *For My People, Jubilee*, and *Prophets for a New Day* are valued for their relation to social movements of twentieth century America. In 1937, the poem "For My People" called for a new generation to gather strength from a militant literature, and the black literature of the 1960s—including the autobiographies of Malcolm X, Eldridge Cleaver, Huey Newton, and Angela Davis, to name just a few—answered that challenge, suggests C.W.E. Bigsby in *The Second Black Renaissance: Essays in Black Literature*. Her example over the years has also proved to be instructive. This summary of Walker's achievement closes the epilogue of *How I Wrote "Jubilee"*: "She has revealed the creative ways in which methods and materials of the social science scholar may be joined with the craft and viewpoint of the poet/novelist to create authentic black literature. She has reaffirmed for us the critical importance of oral tradition in the creation of our history. . . . Finally, she has made awesomely clear to us the tremendous costs which must be paid in stubborn, persistent work and commitment if we are indeed to write our own history and create our own literature."

BIOGRAPHICAL/CRITICAL SOURCES:

BOOKS

Bankier, Joanna and Dierdre Lashgari, editors, *Women Poets of the World*, Macmillan, 1983.

Baraka, Amiri, *The Black Nation*, Getting Together Publications, 1982.

Bigsby, C.W.E., editor, *The Second Black Renaissance: Essays in Black Literature*, Greenwood Press, 1980.

Contemporary Literary Criticism, Gale, Volume 1, 1973, Volume 2, 1976.

Davis, Arthur P., *From the Dark Tower: Afro-American Writers, 1900 to 1960*, Howard University Press, 1974.

Emanuel, James A., and Theodore L. Gross, editors, *Dark Symphony: Negro Literature in America*, Free Press, 1968.

Evans, Mari, editor, *Black Women Writers (1950-1980): A Critical Evaluation*, Anchor/Doubleday, 1982.

Gayle, Addison, editor, *The Black Aesthetic*, Doubleday, 1971.

Gibson, Donald B., editor, *Modern Black Poets: A Collection of Critical Essays*, Prentice-Hall, 1983.

Jackson, Blyden and Louis D. Rubin, Jr., *Black Poetry in America: Two Essays in Historical Interpretation*, Louisiana State University Press, 1974.

Jones, John Griffith, in *Mississippi Writers Talking*, Volume II, University of Mississippi Press, 1983.

Kent, George E., *Blackness and the Adventure of Western Culture*, Third World Press, 1972.

Lee, Don L., *Dynamite Voices I: Black Poets of the 1960s*, Broadside Press, 1971.

Miller, R. Baxter, editor, *Black American Poets between Worlds, 1940-1960*, University of Tennessee Press, 1986.

Redmond, Eugene B., *Drumvoices: The Mission of Afro-American Poetry—A Critical Evaluation*, Doubleday, 1976.

Tate, Claudia, editor, *Black Women Writers at Work*, Continuum, 1983.

Walker, Margaret, *For My People*, Yale University Press, 1942, reprinted, Ayer Co., 1969.

Walker, Margaret, *How I Wrote "Jubilee,"* Third World Press, 1972.

Walker, Margaret, and Nikki Giovanni, *A Poetic Equation: Conversations between Nikki Giovanni and Margaret Walker*, Howard University Press, 1974, reprinted with a new postscript, 1983.

Walker, Margaret, *Prophets for a New Day*, Broadside Press, 1970.

Whitlow, Roger, *Black American Literature: A Critical History*, NelsonHall, 1973.

PERIODICALS

Atlantic, December, 1942.
Best Sellers, October 1, 1966.
Black World, December, 1971, December, 1975.
Books, January 3, 1973.
Book Week, October 2, 1966.
Callaloo, May, 1979.
Christian Science Monitor, November 14, 1942, September 29, 1966, June 19, 1974.
Common Ground, autumn, 1943.
Ebony, February, 1949.
Freedomways, Volume 2, number 3, summer, 1967.
National Review, October 4, 1966.
Negro Digest, February, 1967, January, 1968.
New Republic, November 23, 1942.
New York Times, November 4, 1942.

New York Times Book Review, August 2, 1942, September 25, 1966.
Opportunity, December, 1942.
Publishers Weekly, April 15, 1944, March 24, 1945.
Saturday Review, September 24, 1966.
Times Literary Supplement, June 29, 1967.
Washington Post, February 9, 1983.
Yale Review, winter, 1943.†

—*Sketch by Marilyn K. Basel*

*   *   *

WALLACE, Ruby Ann 1923(?)- (Ruby Dee)

PERSONAL: Professionally known as Ruby Dee; born October 27, 1923 (some sources say 1924), in Cleveland, Ohio; daughter of Marshall Edward (a railroad porter and waiter) and Emma (a teacher; maiden name, Benson) Wallace; married Ossie Davis (an actor, writer, director, and producer of stage and motion picture productions), December 9, 1948; children: Nora, Guy, La Verne. *Education:* Hunter College (now of the City University of New York), B.A., 1945; also attended Actors Workshop during 1950s, Fairfield University, Iona College, and Virginia State University.

ADDRESSES: Agent—Artists Agency, 10000 Santa Monica Blvd., Suite 305, Los Angeles, Calif. 90067.

CAREER: Actress and writer. American Negro Theatre, apprentice, 1941-44. Actress in numerous Broadway productions, including "South Pacific," 1943, "Jeb," 1946, "A Raisin in the Sun," 1959, "Purlie Victorious," 1961, and "Boesman and Lena," 1970. Actress in motion pictures, including "No Way Out," 1950, "The Jackie Robinson Story," 1950, "Edge of the City," 1957, "St. Louis Blues," 1958, "A Raisin in the Sun," 1961, and "Gone Are the Days" (also released as "Purlie Victorious" and "The Man from C.O.T.T.O.N."), 1963. Actress in television productions, including "Black Monday," 1961. Co-host of radio program "Ossie Davis and Ruby Dee Story Hour," 1974-78, and of television series "With Ossie and Ruby," Public Broadcasting System (PBS-TV), 1981. Performer on recordings for Caedmon, Folkways Records, and Newbery Award Records. Civil rights activist.

MEMBER: American Federation of Television and Radio Artists, Screen Actors Guild, Actors Equity Association, National Association for the Advancement of Colored People, Negro American Labor Council, Southern Christian Leadership Conference, Students for Non-Violence (member of coordinating committee).

AWARDS, HONORS: Emmy Award nomination for outstanding single performance by an actress in a leading role, Academy of Television Arts and Sciences, 1964, for "Express Stop from Lenox Avenue"; with husband Ossie Davis, Frederick Douglass Award from New York Urban League, 1970; Obie Award, 1971, for "Boseman and Lena"; Martin Luther King, Jr., Award from Operation PUSH, 1972; Drama Desk Award, 1974.

WRITINGS—Under name Ruby Dee:

(With Jules Dassin and Julian Mayfield) "Up Tight" (screenplay; adapted from Liam O'Flaherty's novel *The Informer*), Paramount, 1968.

(Editor) *Glowchild, and Other Poems*, Third Press, 1972.

(And director) "Take It from the Top" (stage musical), first produced Off-Broadway at New Federal Theatre, January 19, 1979 (revised as "Twin Bit Gardens," 1979).
My One Good Nerve: Rhythms, Rhymes, Reasons (stories, poems, and essays), Third World Press, 1987.
Two Ways to Count to Ten, Holt, 1988.

Former columnist for *New York Amsterdam News;* associate editor, *Freedomways.*

SIDELIGHTS: Ruby Dee is among America's most prominent black performers. While studying at Hunter College in the early 1940s, Dee became involved with the American Negro Theatre. With fellow artists such as Sidney Poitier and Harry Belafonte, Dee contributed to all facets of the group's productions, mopping floors and selling tickets when not appearing in works such as "Natural Man" and "Starlight." She also participated in radio plays and acted in the Broadway production "South Pacific" (not the musical by Rodger and Hammerstein). In 1946 she appeared in Robert Ardrey's "Jeb," the drama of a black veteran's efforts to secure employment in the South, and eventually married the work's principal performer, Ossie Davis.

In the 1950s Dee continued working on the stage while expanding into television and film. Among her most acclaimed roles in this period were stirring performances as the wife of a young black working on the docks of New York in the film "Edge of the City" and as the daughter-in-law in Lorraine Hansberry's heralded play "A Raisin in the Sun." Dee repeated her performance in the film adaptation of the play in 1961, then worked in husband Davis's satirical play "Purlie Victorious." Dee played Lutiebelle Gussie Mae Jenkins, a young woman who helps Purlie, an eloquent itinerant preacher, bilk five hundred dollars from a bigoted plantation owner in order to establish an integrated church.

Throughout her career, Dee has appeared in a wide range of works, from Shakespearean productions to television series. She also co-authored the screenplay for the motion picture "Up Tight," which details the dilemma of a black man who betrays his friends after one of them murders a guard during a robbery. Vincent Canby, writing in the *New York Times,* called "Up Tight" "such an intense and furious movie that it's impossible not to take it seriously" and credited the screenplay by Dee, director Jules Dassin, and Julian Mayfield as possessing "the sound of authenticity." In addition to the musical stage production "Take It from the Top," in which she played the leading role of an angel who returns to earth to recruit good people to thwart an evil capitalist, Dee's other writing ventures include collections of poetry, stories, and essays.

BIOGRAPHICAL/CRITICAL SOURCES:

PERIODICALS

Book World, March 8, 1987.
Ebony, December, 1979.
Essence, May, 1987.
New Yorker, April 8, 1961.
New York Times, December 19, 1968, January 20, 1979.
New York Times Book Review, November 5, 1972.†

*   *   *

WALLACH, Michael A(rthur)   1933-

PERSONAL: Born April 8, 1933, in New York, N.Y.; son of Max and Wilma (Cheiker) Wallach; married Lise Wertheimer (a psychologist), July 26, 1959; children: Rachel Paula. *Education:* Swarthmore College, B.A. (with highest honors), 1954; Harvard University, Ph.D., 1958; Cambridge University, Westengard traveling fellow from Harvard, 1955-56.

ADDRESSES: Office—Department of Psychology, Duke University, Durham, N.C. 27706.

CAREER: Harvard University, Cambridge, Mass., instructor in social psychology, 1958-59; Massachusetts Institute of Technology, Cambridge, assistant professor of psychology, 1959-62; Duke University, Durham, N.C., associate professor, 1962-66, professor of psychology, 1966-72; University of Chicago, Chicago, Ill., William S. Gray Professor of Education, 1972-73; Duke University, professor of psychology, 1973—. Principal or co-principal investigator in research projects for National Institute of Mental Health, 1958-61, U.S. Office of Education, 1961-65, and National Science Foundation, 1961-63, 1964-67.

AWARDS, HONORS: Social Science Research Council research grant, 1962.

WRITINGS:

(With Nathan Kogan) *Risk Taking: A Study in Cognition and Personality,* Holt, 1964.
(With N. Kogan) *Modes of Thinking in Young Children: A Study of the Creativity-Intelligence Distinction,* Holt, 1965.
(With C. W. Wing, Jr.) *The Talented Student: A Validation of the Creativity-Intelligence Distinction,* Holt, 1969.
(With C. W. Wing) *College Admission and the Psychology of Talent,* Holt, 1971.
The Intelligence/Creativity Distinction, General Learning Press, 1971.
(With wife Lise Wallach) *Teaching All Children to Read,* University of Chicago Press, 1976.
(With L. Wallach) *The Teaching All Children to Read Kit,* University of Chicago Press, 1976.
Letter Tracing and Drawing Spirit Masters, University of Chicago Press, 1976.
(With L. Wallach) *Psychology's Sanction for Selfishness,* W. H. Freeman, 1983.

CONTRIBUTOR

P. H. Hoch and J. Zubin, editors, *Psychopathology of Aging,* Grune, 1961.
L. C. Crow and A. Crow, editors, *Readings in Child and Adolescent Psychology,* Longmans, Green, 1961.
S. Messick and J. Ross, editors, *Measurement in Personality and Cognition,* Wiley, 1962.
H. W. Stevenson, editor, *Child Psychology: The Sixty-Second Yearbook of the National Society for the Study of Education,* University of Chicago Press, 1963.
R.J.C. Harper, C. C. Anderson, C. M. Christensen, and S. M. Hunka, editors, *The Cognitive Processes: Readings,* Prentice-Hall, 1964.
M. Kornrich, editor, *Underachievement,* C. C Thomas, 1965.
M. Schwebel, editor, *Behavioral Science and Human Survival,* Science and Behavior Books, 1965.
A. H. Rubenstein and C. J. Haberstroh, editors, *Some Theories of Organization,* Dorsey, 1966.
R. Jessor and S. Feshbach, editors, *Cognition, Personality, and Clinical Psychology,* Jossey-Bass, 1967.
J. Hagan, editor, *Creativity and Learning,* Houghton, 1967.
New Directions in Psychology III, Holt, 1967.

D. Cartwright and A. Zander, editors, *Group Dynamics: Research and Theory*, 3rd edition, Harper, 1968.

B. L. Neugarten, editor, *Middle Ages and Aging: A Reader in Social Psychology*, University of Chicago Press, 1968.

C. C. Spielberger, R. Fox, and B. Masterton, editors, *Contributions to General Psychology*, Ronald, 1968.

R. K. Parker, editor, *Readings in Educational Psychology*, Allyn & Bacon, 1968.

Rogers, editor, *Readings in Child Psychology*, Brooks/Cole, 1969.

J. C. Mancuso, editor, *Readings for a Cognitive Theory of Personality*, Holt, 1970.

M. Wertheimer, editor, *Confrontation: Psychology and the Problems of Today*, Scott, Foreman, 1970.

P. H. Mussen, editor, *Carmichael's Manual of Child Psychology*, 3rd edition, Wiley, 1970.

R. D. Strom, editor, *Teachers and the Learning Process*, Prentice-Hall, 1971.

J. L. Freedman, J. M. Carlsmith, and D. O. Sears, editors, *Readings in Social Psychology*, Prentice-Hall, 1971.

M. Berbaum and G. Stricker, editors, *Search for Human Understanding*, Holt, 1971.

J. J. Eysenck, editor, *Readings in Extraversion-Introversion*, Halsted, Volume II: *Fields of Application*, 1971, Volume III: *Bearings on Basic Psychological Processes*, 1971.

R. A. Baron and R. M. Liebert, editors, *Human Social Behavior*, Dorsey, 1971.

J. McV. Hunt, editor, *Human Intelligence*, Transaction Books, 1972.

C. A. Insko and J. Schople, editors, *Experimental Social Psychology: Text with Illustrative Readings*, Academic Press, 1972.

A. R. Binter and S. H. Frey, editors, *The Psychology of the Elementary School Child*, Rand McNally, 1972.

R. J. Ofshe, editor, *Interpersonal Behavior in Small Groups*, Prentice-Hall, 1973.

M. Bloomberg, editor, *Creativity: Theory and Research*, College & University Press, 1973.

H. Z. Lopata, editor, *Marriages and Families*, Van Nostrand, 1973.

Eysenck, editor, *The Measurement of Personality*, University Park Press, 1976.

A. Rothenberg and C. R. Hausman, editors, *The Creativity Question*, Duke University Press, 1976.

N. S. Endler and D. Magnusson, editors, *Interactional Psychology and Personality*, Halsted, 1976.

Messick and others, editors, *Individuality in Learning: Implications of Cognitive Styles and Creativity for Human Development*, Jossey-Bass, 1976.

I. L. Janis, editor, *Current Trends in Psychology: Readings from American Scientists*, William Kaufmann, 1977.

Wertheimer and L. Rappoport, editors, *Psychology and the Problems of Today*, Scott, Foresman, 1978.

L. B. Resnick and P. A. Weaver, editors, *Theory and Practice of Early Reading*, Lawrence Erlbaum Associates, 1979.

W. M. Cruickshank and J. W. Lerner, editors, *Coming of Age*, Syracuse University Press, 1982.

R. S. Albert, editor, *Genius and Eminence*, Pergamon, 1983.

F. D. Horowitz and M. O'Brien, editors, *The Gifted and Talented: Developmental Perspectives*, American Psychological Association, 1985.

N. J. Smelser, editor, *Contemporary Classics in the Social and Behavioral Sciences*, ISI Press, 1987.

Contributor of numerous articles to various journals, including *Journal of Personality and Social Psychology, Journal of Social and Clinical Psychology, Developmental Psychology, Psychological Review, Journal of Abnormal and Social Psychology, Psychological Reports, Journal of Consulting Psychology, Journal of Aesthetics and Art Criticism, American Journal of Psychology, American Journal of Psychiatry, American Scientist, Washington Monthly,* and *Harvard Educational Review.* Editor of *Journal of Personality,* 1963-72.

*   *   *

WALTERS, A(lan) A(rthur)   1926-

PERSONAL: Born June 17, 1926, in Leicester, England; son of James Arthur and Clarabel (Heywood) Walters; married Audrey Elizabeth Claxton, March 30, 1950; children: Louise. *Education:* University College, Leicester (now University of Leicester), B.Sc. (London), 1951; Nuffield College, Oxford, further study, 1951-52; Oxford University, M.A., 1981.

ADDRESSES: Home—2820 P St. N.W., Washington, D.C. 20007. *Office*—American Enterprise Institute, 1150 17th St. N.W., Washington, D.C. 20036.

CAREER: University of Birmingham, Birmingham, England, lecturer in econometrics, 1952-61, professor and head of department of econometrics and social statistics, 1961-68; University of London, London School of Economics and Political Science, London, England, Cassel Professor of Economics, 1968-75; Johns Hopkins University, Baltimore, Md., professor of economics, 1975—. Visiting professor of economics, Northwestern University, 1958-59, University of Virginia, 1966-67, Massachusetts Institute of Technology, 1967-68, and Monash University, Clayton, Australia, 1971; resident scholar, American Enterprise Institute, 1983-84. Economic advisor, Secretary of State for Health and Social Security, 1970—, and World Bank, 1976-80; advisor to Prime Minister of the United Kingdom, 1981-83, consultant, 1983—. Consultant to various central banks and to the governments of Israel, Singapore, and Malaysia. Governor, Centre for Environmental Studies, 1971—. Director, Economists Bookshop. Member, Commission on London's Third Airport, 1968-70.

MEMBER: Econometric Society (fellow).

AWARDS, HONORS: D.Litt., University of Leicester, 1981; Francis Boyer Lecture award, American Enterprise Institute, 1983; D.Soc.Sc., University of Birmingham, 1984; Gerstenberg prize; knight of the Order of the British Empire.

WRITINGS:

The Theory and Measurement of Private and Social Cost of Highway Congestion, Faculty of Commerce and Social Science, University of Birmingham, 1959.

A Survey of Statistical Production and Cost Functions, Faculty of Commerce and Social Science, University of Birmingham, 1959.

(With N. J. Kavanagh) *Demand for Money in the U.K., 1877-1962*, Faculty of Commerce and Social Science, University of Birmingham, 1964.

(With Mitchell Harwitz, George Dalton, and R. W. Clower) *Growth Without Development*, Northwestern University Press, 1966.

Integration in Freight Transport, Transatlantic, 1968.

The Economics of Road User Charges, Johns Hopkins Press, for International Bank for Reconstruction, 1968.

An Introduction to Econometrics, Macmillan (London), 1968, 2nd edition, Norton, 1970.

(With Esra Bennathan) *Economics of Ocean Freight Rates*, Praeger, 1969.

Money in Boom and Slump: An Empirical Inquiry into British Experience Since the 1880s, Transatlantic, 1969, 3rd edition, Institute of Economic Affairs (London), 1971.

(Editor) *Money and Banking: Selected Readings*, Penguin, 1973.

(With others) *Government and the Land*, Institute of Economic Affairs, 1974.

Noise and Prices, Clarendon Press, 1975.

(With J. H. Wood) *Commercial Bank Loan and Investment Behavior*, Wiley, 1975.

(With P. R. G. Layard) *Microeconomic Theory*, McGraw-Hill, 1978.

(With Bennathan) *Port Pricing and Investment Policy for Developing Countries*, Oxford University Press for the World Bank, 1979.

Economic Advisor's Role: Scope and Limitations, Centre for Policy Studies (London), 1981.

Britain's Economic Renaissance: Margaret Thatcher's Reforms, 1979-84, Oxford University Press, 1986.

Author or co-author of a number of pamphlets on money, inflation, and transportation economics. Contributor of articles to *American Economic Review*, *Econometrica*, *Economic Journal*, *Economica*, and *Journal of Political Economy*. Managing editor, *Review of Economic Studies*, 1971; member of editorial board of *Journal of Money Credit and Banking* and *Urban Economics*.

BIOGRAPHICAL/CRITICAL SOURCES:

PERIODICALS

Times Literary Supplement, May 23, 1975, May 30, 1986. †

*　　*　　*

WALTHAM, Antony Clive 1942-

PERSONAL: Born June 18, 1942, in Birmingham, England; son of Clive (a surveyor) and Mary (Platts) Waltham; married former wife, Janet Gore, December 16, 1963; married Janet Myles, February 20, 1979; children: (first marriage) Sam, Megan. *Education:* B.Sc., D.I.C., and Ph.D. from Imperial College of Science and Technology, London.

ADDRESSES: Office—Department of Civil Engineering, Trent Polytechnic, Nottingham NG1 4BU, England.

CAREER: Trent Polytechnic, Nottingham, England, lecturer in geology, 1968—. Lecturer, department of adult education, University of Nottingham, 1971—; part-time tutor in geology, Open University, Milton Keynes, England, 1973-76.

MEMBER: Royal Geographical Society (fellow), British Cave Research Association.

AWARDS, HONORS: Travel fellowship, Winston Churchill Memorial Trust, 1970; Cuthbert Peek Award, Royal Geographical Society, 1981.

WRITINGS:

(Editor) *Limestone and Caves of Northwest England*, David & Charles, 1974.
Caves, Crown, 1974.
The World of Caves, Putnam, 1976.
Catastrophe—The Violent Earth, Crown, 1978.
Caves, Crags and Gorges, Constable, 1984.
China Caves, Royal Geographical Society, 1986.
Yorkshire Dales National Park, Webb and Bower, 1987.

Contributor to a number of encyclopedias. Contributor to geology, geography and cave research journals and magazines.

WORK IN PROGRESS: Research on the geomorphology and hydrology of limestone caves and the engineering geology of ground engineering.

SIDELIGHTS: Antony Clive Waltham writes: "From schooldays, I was interested in geography and travel but then went to study geology because it seemed more promising careerwise than geography. While at University, I was persuaded to go caving, on the principle of trying anything, but I got hooked on the sport of underground exploration. I drifted into teaching because it was the only occupation to give long summer vacations for travel, but then found teaching was my true vocation anyway, and I have developed it along the lines of practical and applied geology, well away from remote academic principles. My parallel interest in caving has developed to include geological research into cave development.

"Caves may appear to be a bit obscure and even unpleasant to many people, but they have kept me occupied for years. I started off exploring them just for the adventure, but once I could be happy and confident in the cave environment, I started to develop my caving. First I was mapping the caves, then studying their geology, and then photographing them more. Now I like to find some application in my cave work, whether it is to contribute to broader landscape studies or to locate useable underground water supplies. I've been to caves almost all around the world, and their variety and contrasts never cease to fascinate me. There's still plenty to see above and below the ground."

AVOCATIONAL INTERESTS: Travel (has led or joined cave expeditions in Nepal, Iran, Canada, Jamaica, Malaysia, Indonesia, and China, in addition to having visited nearly every country in Europe).

BIOGRAPHICAL/CRITICAL SOURCES:

PERIODICALS

Los Angeles Times Book Review, August 23, 1987.

*　　*　　*

WALTON, Ortiz Montaigne 1933-

PERSONAL: Born 1933, in Chicago, Ill.; son of Peter Leon (a civil service administrator) and Gladys (Porche) Walton; married Carol A. Dozier (a doctoral candidate), June 29, 1957; children: Omar Kwame. *Education:* Attended University of Hartford, 1951-54, Mannes School of Music, 1954, and Loyola University, Chicago, 1964; Roosevelt University, B.S., 1965; University of California, Berkeley, M.A., 1970, Ph.D., 1973.

ADDRESSES: Home—242 West 123rd St., New York, N.Y. 10027.

CAREER: Affiliated with Buffalo Philharmonic, Buffalo, N.Y., 1954-57; Boston Symphony Orchestra, Boston, Mass., double bassist, 1957-62; Cairo Symphony Orchestra, Cairo, Egypt, principal, 1963-64; University of California, Berkeley, member of faculty of ethnic studies, 1969-70, 1974-76; principal investigator of a study of adolescent drinking patterns sponsored by National Institute of Alcohol Abuse and Alcoholism. Recorded "The Walton Statement" (for solo contrabass and orchestra) by Arthur Cunningham and "Per Oquesta Obellamand" by Mozart with National Philharmonic Orchestra; debut, Merkin Concert Hall, New York City, January, 1987; performance with David Tigner, Carnegie Hall, 1987.

MEMBER: American Sociological Association.

WRITINGS:

Coronation of the King: Contributions by Duke Ellington to Black Culture, University of California, Extension Division, 1969.
A Comparative Analysis of the African and Western Aesthetic, Doubleday, 1970.
Music: Black, White and Blue, Morrow, 1972.
(Contributor) Ishmael Reed, editor, *Yardbird Reader* (semi-annual publication), Yardbird Cooperative (Berkeley), 1972.

* * *

WARD-THOMAS, Evelyn Bridget Patricia Stephens 1928-
(Evelyn Anthony, Anthony Evelyn)

PERSONAL: Born July 3, 1928, in London, England; daughter of Henry Christian (an inventor) and Elizabeth (Sharkey) Stephens; married Michael Ward-Thomas (director of a diamond mining company), April 16, 1955; children: Susan Ileana Mary, Anthony Christian, Ewan Fitzgerald, Katharine Maria, Christian Rupert Francis, Luke Richard. *Education:* Attended Convent of Sacred Heart, Roehampton, London, England. *Religion:* Roman Catholic.

ADDRESSES: Agent—A. P. Watt Ltd., 26-28 Bedford Row, London WC1R 4HL, England.

CAREER: Writer, 1952—.

WRITINGS:

UNDER PSEUDONYM EVELYN ANTHONY

Rebel Princess (first novel of trilogy), Crowell, 1953 (published in England as *Imperial Highness,* Museum Press, 1953).
Royal Intrigue (second novel of trilogy), Crowell, 1954 (published in England as *Curse Not the King,* Museum Press, 1954).
Far Flies the Eagle (third novel of trilogy), Crowell, 1955.
Anne Boleyn (Literary Guild and Dollar Book Club selections), Crowell, 1957.
Victoria and Albert (novel; Literary Guild selection), Crowell, 1958 (published in England as *Victoria,* Museum Press, 1959).
All the Queen's Men (novel), Crowell, 1960 (published in England as *Elizabeth,* Museum Press, 1960).
Charles the King (novel), Doubleday, 1961, reprinted, Queens House, 1976.
Clandara, Doubleday, 1963.
The Heiress (sequel to *Clandara*), Doubleday, 1964.
The French Bride, Doubleday, 1964.
Valentina, Doubleday, 1966.
The Legend, Hutchinson, 1967, Coward, 1969.
The Rendezvous, Coward, 1968.
The Cardinal and the Queen, Coward, 1968 (published in England as *Anne of Austria,* Hurst & Blackett, 1968).
The Assassin, Coward, 1970.
The Tamarind Seed, Coward, 1971.
The Poellenberg Inheritance, Coward, 1972.
Stranger at the Gates, Coward, 1973 (published in England as *The Occupying Power,* Hutchinson, 1973).

Mission to Malaspiga, Coward, 1974 (published in England as *The Malaspiga Exit,* Hutchinson, 1974).
The Persian Price, Coward, 1975 (published in England as *The Persian Ransom,* Hutchinson, 1975).
The Silver Falcon, Coward, 1977.
The Return, Coward, 1978.
The Grave of Truth, Hutchinson, 1979.
The Janus Imperative, Coward, 1980.
The Defector, Coward, 1981.
The Avenue of the Dead, Hutchinson, 1981.
Albatross, Hutchinson, 1982, Putnam, 1983.
The Company of Saints, Putnam, 1984.
Voices on the Wind, Putnam, 1985.
A Place to Hide, Putnam, 1986.

OTHER

Contributor of short stories to British periodicals under pseudonym Anthony Evelyn.

SIDELIGHTS: Evelyn Bridget Patricia Stephens Ward-Thomas reversed her original pseudonym used in magazine writing ("thought [a] man's name more acceptable") when her first historical novel was published. Her first three novels form a trilogy based on Catherine the Great, her son, Paul I, and his son, Alexander I. She classifies her first seven novels as "animated history"—based on real people with an endeavor to give a new slant on their contemporary relations and motives. She began writing pure historical fiction with *Clandara* and its sequel, *The Heiress;* but feeling that historical novels "were in the doldrums," she changed over to "contemporary thrillers."

About her literary and private life, the novelist says that she moved to Ireland in 1976 to take advantage of the "generous" tax laws; and she writes for money, "which is always useful."

MEDIA ADAPTATIONS: The Tamarind Seed was adapted for the screen by Blake Edwards and filmed by Avco-Embassy in 1974, starring Julie Andrews and Omar Sharif. †

* * *

WARNER, Frank A.
[Collective pseudonym]

WRITINGS:

"BOB CHASE BIG GAME" SERIES

Bob Chase with the Big Moose Hunters, Barse & Co., 1929.
. . . after Grizzly Bears, Barse & Co., 1929.
. . . in the Tiger's Lair, Barse & Co., 1929.
. . . with the Lion Hunters, Barse & Co., 1930.

"BOBBY BLAKE" SERIES

Bobby Blake at Rockledge School; or, Winning the Medal of Honor, Barse & Hopkins, 1915.
. . . at Bass Cove; or, The Hunt for the Motor Boat Gem, Barse & Hopkins, 1915.
. . . on a Cruise; or, The Castaways of Volcano Island, Barse & Hopkins, 1915.
. . . and His School Chums; or, The Rivals of Rockledge, Barse & Hopkins, 1916.
. . . at Snowtop Camp; or, Winter Holidays in the Big Woods, Barse & Hopkins, 1916.
. . . on the School Nine; or, The Champions of Monotook Lake League, Barse & Hopkins, 1917.
. . . on a Ranch; or, The Secret of the Mountain Cave, Barse & Hopkins, 1918.

. . . *on an Auto Tour; or, The Mystery of the Deserted House*, Barse & Hopkins, 1920.

. . . *on the School Eleven; or, Winning the Banner of Blue and Gold*, Barse & Hopkins, 1921.

. . . *on a Plantation; or, Lost in the Great Swamp*, Barse & Hopkins, 1922.

. . . *in the Frozen North; or, The Old Eskimo's Last Message*, Barse & Hopkins, 1923.

. . . *on Mystery Mountain*, Barse & Hopkins, 1926.

SIDELIGHTS: Two Stratemeyer Syndicate series were released under this pseudonym. Bob Chase, according to the publisher's advertisements, was "a young lumberjack who is a crack shot. While tracking game in the wilds of Maine he does some rich hunters a great service," and he becomes their companion, travelling around the world with them on hunting expeditions. The stories contained "much valuable data on animal life as lived in the wilderness." The Bobby Blake books were intended for boys from eight to twelve years old. They were advertised as "true stories of life at a modern American boarding school." For more information see the entries for Harriet S. Adams, Edward L. Stratemeyer, and Andrew E. Svenson.

BIOGRAPHICAL/CRITICAL SOURCES:

BOOKS

Johnson, Deidre, editor and compiler, *Stratemeyer Pseudonyms and Series Books: An Annotated Checklist of Stratemeyer and Stratemeyer Syndicate Publications*, Greenwood Press, 1982.

*   *   *

WARREN, Elizabeth
See SUPRANER, Robyn

*   *   *

WARREN, Roland L(eslie)   1915-

PERSONAL: Born June 24, 1915, in Islip, N.Y.; son of Ruy Waverly and Jenny (Simonds) Warren; married Margaret Hodges (a violin maker), June 17, 1938; children: Ursula Washburn, David Hardy, Margaret Robin. *Education:* New York University, B.S., 1935; University of Heidelberg, Ph.D., 1937.

ADDRESSES: Home—R.D. 1, Andover, N.Y. 14806.

CAREER: Hofstra College (now Hofstra University), Hempstead, N.Y., instructor, 1937-39, assistant professor of social science, 1939-41; Alfred University, Alfred, N.Y., associate professor, 1941-43, professor of sociology, 1945-58; co-director of Area Study, 1949-58; State Charities Aid Association, New York, N.Y., director of Social Research Service, 1958-62; American Friends Service Committee, Philadelphia, Pa., Quaker international affairs representative for Germany, 1962-64; Brandeis University, Waltham, Mass., professor of community theory, 1964-80. National Institute of Mental Health Problems Review Committee, member, 1969-74, chairman, 1972-74. *Military service:* U.S. Naval Reserve, 1943-45.

MEMBER: International Society for Community Development, American Sociological Association (fellow; chairman of community section, 1973—), Society for the Study of Social Problems (chairman of community research and development committee, 1955-56), Community Development Society.

AWARDS, HONORS: Guggenheim fellowship, 1956-57, to study voluntary citizen participation in community affairs in Stuttgart, Germany; Russell Sage Foundation fellowship, 1958-62; research science award, National Institute of Mental Health, 1964-74; Community Section Award, American Sociological Association, 1982, for outstanding achievements and inspiring contributions to the study of community.

WRITINGS:

Studying Your Community, Russell Sage, 1955.

(With Joseph S. Roucek) *Sociology: An Introduction*, Rowman, 1957, revised edition, Littlefield, 1976.

The Community in America, Rand McNally, 1963, 3rd edition, 1978.

Social Research Consultation: An Experiment in Health and Welfare Planning, Russell Sage Foundation, 1963.

(Editor) *Perspectives on the American Community: A Book of Readings*, Rand McNally, 1966, 3rd edition published as *New Perspectives on the American Community: A Book of Readings*, 1977, 5th edition, (with Larry Lyon), 1987.

(Editor) *Politics and the Ghettos*, Atherton, 1969.

Truth, Love, and Social Change: And Other Essays on Community Change, Rand McNally, 1971.

(With Stephen M. Rose and Ann F. Burgunder) *The Structure of Urban Reform: Community Decision Organizations in Stability and Change*, Heath, 1974.

Social Change and Human Purpose: Toward Understanding and Action, Rand McNally, 1977.

(With Robert Perlman) *Families in the Energy Crisis: Impacts and Implications for Theory and Policy*, Ballinger, 1977.

An Old Feud and a New House (drama), Nantucket Historical Association, 1986.

Mary Coffin Starbuck and the Early History of Nantucket, Pingoy Press, 1987.

CONTRIBUTOR

Herman D. Stein and Richard A. Cloward, editors, *Social Perspectives on Behavior: A Reader in Social Science for Social Work and Related Professions*, Free Press, 1958.

Terry N. Clark, editor, *Community Structure and Decision Making: Comparative Analyses*, Science Research Associates, 1968.

Peter K. Manning, editor, *Research and Theories in Social Deviance*, Lippincott, 1969.

Robert Mills French, editor, *The Community: A Comparative Perspective*, F. E. Peacock, 1969.

Arthur Dunham, editor, *The New Community Organization*, Crowell, 1969.

Ralph M. Kramer and Harry Specht, editors, *Readings in Community Organization*, Prentice-Hall, 1969.

Paul White and George Vlasak, editors, *Inter-Organizational Research in Health: Conference Proceedings*, National Center for Health Services Reaserch and Development, Johns Hopkins University, 1970.

Lee J. Cary, editor, *Community Development as a Process*, University of Missouri Press, 1970.

Robert W. Klenk and Robert M. Ryan, editors, *The Practice of Social Work*, Wadsworth, 1970.

Fred M. Cox and others, editors, *Strategies of Community Organization*, F. E. Peacock, 1970.

The Social Welfare Forum, Columbia University Press, 1971.

Charles M. Bonjean, Clark, and Robert L. Lineberry, editors, *Community Politics: A Behavioral Approach*, Free Press, 1971.

R. Serge Denisoff and Richard A. Peterson, editors, *Sounds of Social Change: Studies in Popular Culture*, Rand McNally, 1972.

William O'Neill, editor, *Problems and Issues in American Social History*, Burgess, 1972.

Melvin B. Brinkerhoff and Phillip R. Kunz, editors, *Complex Organizations and Their Environments*, W. C. Brown, 1972.

Matthew Tuite, Robert Chisolm, and Michael Radnor, editors, *Interorganizational Decision-Making*, Aldine, 1972.

Sandor Halebsky, editor, *The Sociology of the City*, Scribner, 1973.

Bruce Denner and Richard H. Price, editors, *Community Mental Health*, Holt, 1973.

Donald N. Rothblatt, editor, *National Policy for Urban and Regional Development*, Heath, 1974.

Hans B.C. Spiegel, editor, *Citizen Participation in Urban Development*, National Institute for Applied Behavioral Science, 1974.

William C. Sze and June G. Hopps, editors, *Evaluation and Accountability of Human Service Programs*, Schenkman, 1974.

Steven A. Waldhorn and Joseph Sneed, editors, *Restructuring the Federal System: Approaches to Accountability in Post-Categorical Programs*, Crane, Russack, 1975.

John W. McDonald, Jr., and Diane B. Bendahmane, editors, *Conflict Resolution: Track Two Diplomacy*, Foreign Service Institute, U.S. Department of State, 1987.

OTHER

Correspondent for *Community Development Journal International*. Contributor of more than forty articles to journals, including *Yankee, Community Development Journal, Social Problems, Social Science Quarterly, Community Mental Health Journal, American Sociological Review,* and *Journal of the American Institute of Planners*. Associate editor of *Journal of Voluntary Action Research;* member of editorial committee of *Journal of the Community Development Society;* member of editorial board of *Urban Affairs Quarterly.*

SIDELIGHTS: Roland L. Warren told *CA:* "Why the sudden change in nontechnical writing, such as the biography of a nineteenth-century woman? The answer, though easy, is perhaps unusual. I have always felt, to paraphrase a more widely known author, that there was more to life than my sociology. So I retired a few years early and used the time to engage in many activities that were not new, but that had been eclipsed by my major occupation: working in stained glass, composing poetry and music, clarifying my own thoughts about what I believe in the area of religion and what I do not believe. Along the way I became intrigued with the story of the early settlement of Nantucket and with the so-called 'great woman' of that island, Mary Coffin Starbuck: hence the biography, play and *Yankee* article.

"Sociology, like other social and natural sciences, affords a set of concepts and theories (a kit of tools, a pair of glasses) with which to understand *aspects* of reality. It helps to change glasses once in a while and come to participate in other equally fascinating aspects of reality that we might otherwise miss."

The Community in America has been published in German.

*   *   *

WARREN, Vernon

See CHAPMAN, G(eorge) W(arren) Vernon

WASHINGTON, Mary Helen 1941-

PERSONAL: Born January 21, 1941, in Cleveland, Ohio; daughter of David C. and Mary Catherine (Dalton) Washington. *Education:* Notre Dame College, B.A., 1962; University of Detroit, M.A., 1966, Ph.D., 1976.

ADDRESSES: Office—Department of English, Boston Harbor College, University of Massachusetts, Boston, Mass. 02125.

CAREER: High school teacher of English in the public schools of Cleveland, Ohio, 1962-64; St. John College, Cleveland, instructor in English, 1966-68; University of Detroit, Detroit, Mich., assistant professor of English, 1972-75, director of Center for Black Studies, beginning 1975; currently associate professor of English, Boston Harbor College, University of Massachusetts, Boston. Bunting fellow, Radcliffe College.

MEMBER: National Council of Teachers of English, College Language Association, Michigan Black Studies Association.

AWARDS, HONORS: Richard Wright Award for Literary Criticism from *Black World*, 1974.

WRITINGS:

(Editor and author of introduction) *Black-Eyed Susans: Classic Stories By and About Black Women*, Doubleday, 1975.

(Editor and author of introduction and critical notes) *Midnight Birds: Stories by Contemporary Black Women Writers*, Doubleday, 1980 (published in England as *Any Woman's Blues: Stories by Black Women Writers*, Virago Press, 1980).

(Editor and author of introduction and critical notes) *Invented Lives: Narratives of Black Women, 1860-1960*, Doubleday, 1987.

Contributor of articles and reviews to *Negro Digest* and *Black World*.

SIDELIGHTS: Mary Helen Washington is the editor and author of introduction and critical notes of three valued anthologies containing the work of some of the best black women writers. In reviews of all three books, *Black-Eyed Susans: Classic Stories By and About Black Women, Midnight Birds: Stories by Contemporary Black Women Writers,* and *Invented Lives: Narratives of Black Women, 1860-1960*, reviewers have praised Washington for expertly assembling unique and sensitive stories describing the life and plight of black women.

Black-Eyed Susans, Washington's first anthology, presents the writing of such authors as Toni Cade Bambara, Gwendolyn Brooks, Louise Meriwether, Toni Morrison, Jean Wheeler Smith, and Alice Walker. Joyce Carol Oates writes in *Ms.* that *Black-Eyed Susans* "constitutes an indictment of stereotyped thinking." Oates goes on to state that "no one has been so misunderstood, perhaps, as the black woman: she has been defined by others, whether white writers or black men writers, always seen from the outside, ringed in by convenient stereotypes. . . . What strikes the reader who comes to most of these stories for the first time is the wide range of their humanity. All the protagonists are black women: they are *black* women, black *women,* and fiercely individualistic *persons.* And the fiction that presents them is of a high order, the product of painstaking craftsmanship. There is much anger, and no little despair and heartbreak, but emotion has been kept under control; each of the stories is a work of art, moving and convincing."

Marlene Veach writes in *Best Sellers* that Washington's second book, *Midnight Birds,* ''is a collection of stories that revolt against ideologies and attitudes that impress women into servitude. It deals with the real lives and actual experiences of black women, in the hope of demolishing racial and sexual stereotypes.'' And Margaret Atwood writes in a *Harvard Review* of *Midnight Birds* that ''this is American writing at its finest, by turns earthy, sinuous, thoughtful, and full of power.'' Atwood continues to explain that the writers included in this collection, Toni Cade Bambara, Alexis De Veaux, Gayl Jones, Toni Morrison, Ntozake Shange, Alice Walker, and others, ''know exactly whom they are writing for. They are writing for other black American women, and they believe in the power of their words. They see themselves as giving a voice to the voiceless. They perceive writing as the forging of saving myths, the naming of forgotten pasts, the telling of truths.''

According to publicity material released by the publisher, Anchor Press, each contribution to *Midnight Birds* was ''chosen to reflect the efforts of black women to liberate themselves from the structures and constraints of the past. These are not stories about victims but positive stories of and by those women who have provided models of how to live.''

In *Invented Lives* Washington chose to highlight the work of ten women, including Harriet Jacobs, Frances E.W. Harper, Zora Neale Hurston, and Dorothy West, who wrote between the years of 1860 and 1960. Washington stated in a *New York Times Book Review* interview conducted by Rosemary L. Bray that ''a lot of people think the tradition of black women writing began in the last 20 years. In fact, black women have been writing about their experiences in America for more than 200 years.... I found black women working as domestics, writers, migrant farmers, artists, secretaries—and having economic and personal problems centering around these jobs.''

Henry Louis Gates, Jr. comments in the *New York Times Book Review* that in each author's selection ''we hear a black woman *testifying* about what the twin scourges of sexism and racism, merged into one oppressive entity, actually *do* to a human being, how the combination confines the imagination, puzzles the will and delimits free choice. What unites these essays, short stories and novel excerpts is their common themes: 'Their literature is about black women; it takes the trouble to record the thoughts, words, feelings, and deeds of black women, experiences that make the realities of being black in America look very different from what men have written.'''

Although the contributors to Washington's anthologies are all of black heritage, their tales can be understood and felt by all women. For example, calling Washington's second book, *Midnight Birds,* ''a book that is difficult to fault,'' Buchi Emecheta remarks in the *Washington Post* that this book ''speaks through its admirable selection of stories to black women in particular and to all women in general. The message is clear: it is about time we women start to talking to each other, the white to the black, the black American to her African sister, ironing out our differences. For as Toni Morrison said, 'Because when you don't have a woman to really talk to, whether it be an aunt or a sister or a friend, that is the real loneliness.'''

BIOGRAPHICAL/CRITICAL SOURCES:

PERIODICALS

America, January 31, 1981.
Best Sellers, August, 1980.
Harvard Review, February, 1981.
Library Journal, January 15, 1980.

Ms., March, 1976, July, 1980.
New York Times Book Review, October 4, 1987.
Publishers Weekly, December 3, 1979.
Times Literary Supplement, October 30, 1981.
Washington Post, June 3, 1980.†

*   *   *

WATKIN, David (John) 1941-

PERSONAL: Born April 7, 1941, in Salisbury, England; son of Thomas Charles and Vera Mary Watkin. *Education:* Trinity Hall, Cambridge, B.A. (with first class honors), 1963, Ph.D., 1967.

ADDRESSES: Home—67 Charlwood St., London SW1, England. *Office*—Department of Art History, Cambridge University, Cambridge, England.

CAREER: Cambridge University, Cambridge, England, fellow of Peterhouse, 1970—, lecturer in history of art, 1972—, librarian of the Faculty of Architecture and History of Art, 1967-72. Member, Historic Buildings Council for England, 1980-84; member, Historic Buildings Advisory Committee of the Historic Buildings and Monuments Commission for England, 1984—.

MEMBER: Society of Antiquaries (fellow), Beefsteak Club, Travellers Club, University Pitt Club.

AWARDS, HONORS: Alice Davis Hitchcock Medallion, Society of Architectural Historians of Great Britain, 1975, for *The Life and Work of C. R. Cockerell, R.A.*

WRITINGS:

Thomas Hope, 1769-1831, and the Neo-Classical Idea, J. Murray, 1968, Transatlantic, 1970.
(Editor and author of introduction) *Sale Catalogues of Libraries of Eminent Persons,* Volume 4: *Architects,* Mansell, 1972.
The Life and Work of C. R. Cockerell, R.A., A. Zwemmer, 1974.
Morality and Architecture: The Development of a Theme in Architectural History and Theory from the Gothic Revival to the Modern Movement, Oxford University Press, 1977.
The Triumph of the Classical, Cambridge Architecture, 1804-34, Cambridge University Press, 1977.
English Architecture: A Concise History, Thames & Hudson, 1979.
The Rise of Architectural History, Eastview Editions, 1980.
(With Robin Middleton) *Neo-Classical and Nineteenth-Century Architecture,* Abrams, 1980.
(With Hugh Montgomery-Massingberd) *The London Ritz: A Social and Architectural History,* Aurum, 1980.
The English Vision: The Picturesque in Architecture, Landscape and Garden Design, Harper, 1982.
Athenian Stuart: Pioneer of the Greek Revival, Allen & Unwin, 1982.
Regency: A Guide and Gazetteer, Barrie & Jenkins, 1982.
The Royal Interiors of Regency England: From Watercolors First Published by W. H. Pyne in 1817-1820, Vendome, 1984.
(With J. D'Ormesson, Montgomery-Massingberd, P. J. Remy, F. Grendel, and M. Walter) *Grand Hotel: The Golden Age of Palace Hotels—An Architectural and Social History,* Vendome, 1984.

(With A. Ratcliff, N. Thompson, and J. Mills) *A House in Town, 22 Arlington Street: Its Owners and Builders*, Batsford, 1984.

Peterhouse, 1284-1984: An Architectural Record, Peterhouse, 1984.

A History of Western Architecture, Thames & Hudson, 1986.

(With Tilman Mellinghoff) *German Architecture and the Classical Ideal, 1740-1840*, MIT Press, 1987.

Also coauthor of *Burke's and Savill's Guide to Country Houses*, Volume 3: *East Anglia*, 1981.

BIOGRAPHICAL/CRITICAL SOURCES:

PERIODICALS

New York Times Book Review, December 4, 1969.
Spectator, December 31, 1977, November 13, 1982.
Times Literary Supplement, August 1, 1975, February 17, 1978, July 25, 1980, January 7, 1983, February 13, 1987.

*   *   *

WEAVER, Gordon (Allison) 1937-

PERSONAL: Born February 2, 1937, in Moline, Ill.; son of Noble Rodel and Inez (Nelson) Weaver; married Judith Gosnell, September 14, 1961; children: Kristina Katherine, Anna Lynne, Jessica Merle. *Education:* University of Wisconsin—Milwaukee, B.A., 1961; University of Illinois, M.A., 1962; University of Denver, Ph.D., 1970. *Politics:* None. *Religion:* None.

ADDRESSES: Home—2018 West Sunset Dr., Stillwater, Okla. 74074. *Office*—Department of English, Oklahoma State University, Stillwater, Okla. 74078.

CAREER: Siena College, Loudonville, N.Y., instructor in English, 1963-65; Marietta College, Marietta, Ohio, assistant professor of English, 1965-68; University of Southern Mississippi, Hattiesburg, assistant professor, 1970-72, associate professor of English and director, Center for Writers, 1972-75; Oklahoma State University, Stillwater, professor of English, 1975—, chairman of English department, 1975-84. *Military service:* U.S. Army, 1955-58.

AWARDS, HONORS: Woodrow Wilson national fellowship, 1961-62; Poetry Prize, Mississippi State Arts Committee, 1971; Star Award, Kansas City Poetry Contest, 1972; St. Lawrence Award for Fiction, 1973; National Endowment for the Arts fellowship in creative writing, 1974; O. Henry first prize, 1979; Sherwood Anderson prize, 1982; *Quarterly West* Novella Prize, 1983.

WRITINGS:

Count a Lonely Cadence (novel), Regnery, 1968.
The Entombed Man of Thule (short stories), Louisiana State University Press, 1972.
(Editor and author of introduction) Abram Joseph Ryan, *Selected Poems*, University Press of Mississippi, 1973.
(Co-editor) Robert Frost, *Frost: Centennial Essays*, University Press of Mississippi, 1974.
Such Waltzing Was Not Easy (short stories), University of Illinois Press, 1975.
Give Him a Stone (novel), Crown, 1975.
Getting Serious (short stories), Louisiana State University Press, 1980.
Circling Byzantium (novel), Louisiana State University Press, 1980.

(Editor) *The American Short Story: A Critical History, 1945-1980*, G. K. Hall, 1983.
Morality Play (short stories), Chariton Review, 1985.
A World Quite Round (short stories), Louisiana State University Press, 1986.
The Eight Corners of the World (novel), Chelsea Green, 1988.

Contributor to *Epoch, North American Review, Prism International*, and other literary quarterlies.

WORK IN PROGRESS: Various short stories; editing an anthology.

BIOGRAPHICAL/CRITICAL SOURCES:

PERIODICALS

New York Times Book Review, July 6, 1986.
Times Literary Supplement, January 30, 1981.

*   *   *

WEIGLE, Marta 1944-

PERSONAL: Original name, Mary Martha; born July 3, 1944, in Janesville, Wis.; daughter of Richard Daniel (a college president) and Mary (Day) Weigle. *Education:* Attended St. John's College, Annapolis, Md., 1961-62; Radcliffe College, A.B., 1965; University of Pennsylvania, M.A., 1968, Ph.D., 1971.

ADDRESSES: Office—Department of American Studies, University of New Mexico, Albuquerque, N.M. 87131.

CAREER: University of New Mexico, Albuquerque, assistant professor, 1972-77, associate professor of folklore, 1977-83, professor of anthropology, English, and American studies, 1983—, chair, department of American studies, 1984—. Secretary and editor of Ancient City Press, 1981—. Trustee, American Folklife Center, Library of Congress, 1987-92.

MEMBER: American Folklore Society, New Mexico Folklore Society, Texas Folklore Society.

AWARDS, HONORS: Award of honor from New Mexico Cultural Properties Review Committee, 1976; Zia Award from New Mexico Press Women, 1977; fellowship from American Folklore Society, 1988.

WRITINGS:

Follow My Fancy: The Book of Jacks and Jack Games, Dover, 1970.
The Penitentes of the Southwest, Ancient City Press, 1970.
Brothers of Light, Brothers of Blood: The Penitentes of the Southwest, University of New Mexico Press, 1976.
(With Kyle Fiore) *Santa Fe and Taos: The Writer's Era, 1916-1941*, Ancient City Press, 1982.
Spiders & Spinsters: Women and Mythology, University of New Mexico Press, 1982.
(With Peter White) *The Lore of New Mexico*, University of New Mexico Press, 1988.
Creation and Procreation: Feminist Reflections on Mythologies of Cosmogony and Parturition, University of Pennsylvania Press, in press.

EDITOR

Lorenzo de Cordova, *Echoes of the Flute*, Ancient City Press, 1972.
Hispanic Villages of Northern New Mexico, Lightning Tree, 1975.

The Lightning Tree Bicentennial Southwestern Reader for 1976: An Anthology of Folklore with Weekly Calendar, Lightning Tree, 1975.

The Annual Lightning Tree Southwestern Reader with Weekly Calendar for 1977, Lightning Tree, 1976.

(And compiler) *A Penitente Bibliography*, University of New Mexico Press, 1976.

Hispano Folklife of New Mexico, University of New Mexico Press, 1978.

Hispanic Arts and Ethnohistory in the Southwest, Ancient City Press, 1983.

New Mexicans in Cameo and Camera, University of New Mexico Press, 1985.

Two Guadalupes: Hispanic Legends and Magic Tales from Northern New Mexico, Ancient City Press, 1987.

OTHER

Contributor to history, anthropology, and folklore journals.

SIDELIGHTS: Marta Weigle told *CA* that she is "working on women and oral tradition and various aspects of the Southwest, especially tourism and Hispanic folk culture there."

BIOGRAPHICAL/CRITICAL SOURCES:

PERIODICALS

Los Angeles Times Book Review, October 3, 1982.

*   *   *

WEINSTEIN, Allen   1937-

PERSONAL: Born September 1, 1937, in New York, N.Y.; son of Samuel (a storekeeper) and Sarah (Popkoff) Weinstein; married Diane Gilbert, June 14, 1969; children: Andrew Samuel, David Meyer. *Education:* College of the City of New York (now City College of the City University of New York), B.A., 1960; Yale University, M.A., 1962, Ph.D., 1967. *Politics:* Democrat. *Religion:* Jewish.

ADDRESSES: Home—2022 Columbia Rd. N.W., No. 601, Washington, D.C. 20009. *Office*—Center for Democracy, 1155 15th St. N.W., Washington, D.C. 20005.

CAREER: University of Maryland, College Park, lecturer in history, 1964-66; Smith College, Northampton, Mass., 1966-81, began as assistant professor, professor of history, 1974—, director of American studies, 1972-77; Georgetown University, Washington, D.C., professor of history, 1981-83; Boston University, Boston, Mass., professor of history, 1985—. President, R. M. Hutchins Center for the Study of Democratic Institutions, 1984; president, Center for Democracy, 1985—. Senior Fulbright lecturer at Australian universities, 1971. Director of project on access and privacy, Twentieth-Century Fund, 1977-78. Member of humanities advisory council, Massachusetts Council on the Arts, 1975-77. Executive director, The Democracy Program, 1982-83; acting president, National Endowment for Democracy, 1983-84; member-designate, U.S. Institute for Peace, 1985. Member of editorial board, Foreign Policy Association, 1982.

MEMBER: Society of American Historians, American Historical Association, Organization of American Historians, Columbia University Seminar in American Civilization (associate).

AWARDS, HONORS: National Endowment for the Humanities research grant, 1968; Binkley-Stephenson Prize for best article in *Journal of American History*, 1968; American Council of Learned Societies fellow, 1975; Harry S Truman Library In-

stitute award, 1975; National Endowment for the Humanities fellow, Hoover Institution, 1977-78; American Book Award nomination, 1980, for *Perjury: The Hiss-Chambers Case;* Woodrow Wilson Center fellow, 1981; United Nations Peace Medal, 1986.

WRITINGS:

(Editor with F. O. Gatell) *American Themes: Essays in Historiography*, Oxford University Press, 1968.

(Editor with Gatell) *American Negro Slavery: A Modern Reader*, Oxford University Press, 1968, 3rd revised edition, 1978.

(Editor with Gatell) *The Segregation Era: A Modern Reader*, Oxford University Press, 1969.

Prelude to Populism: Origins of the Silver Issue, Yale University Press, 1970.

(General editor) *Random House Readings in American History*, six volumes, Random House, 1970.

Origins of Modern America, 1865-1900, Random House, 1970.

(With R. J. Wilson) *Freedom and Crisis: An American History*, Random House, 1974, 2nd edition, 1978.

Perjury: The Hiss-Chambers Case, Knopf, 1978.

(Editor with Moshe Ma'Oz) *Harry S. Truman and the Founding of Israel*, Hebrew University Press, 1981.

Contributor of articles to numerous publications, including *American Historical Review, American Scholar, Commentary, Journal of American History, Journal of American Studies, Nation, New York Times Book Review, TransAction, Business History Review, Esquire, New York Times*, and *New Republic*. Member of editorial board, *Washington Post*, 1981. Executive editor, *Washington Quarterly*, 1981-83.

WORK IN PROGRESS: The Assault on Secrecy; The Haunted Wood; The Pursuit of Subversion in America, 1940-1960; Theft of the Bomb?: The Rosenberg Case and Soviet Atomic Espionage.

SIDELIGHTS: In 1950, Alger Hiss, former U.S. State Department aide, was convicted on two counts of perjury: one for denying that he met with *Time* editor Whittaker Chambers in February or March of 1938, and the second for testifying that he did not provide Chambers, an admitted Communist spy, with classified documents. For more than thirty years Hiss has maintained his innocence. He insists that Chambers was a pathological liar, that he was an early victim of Communist witch-hunt tactics, and that his case was used by certain ruthless politicians to further their own careers. Hiss's grand jury testimony and the outcome of the trial came to represent far more than the guilt or innocence of an individual. As *Commonweal* contributor Peter Steinfels puts it: "A lot of symbolism was pumped into the Hiss case. Hiss represented the New Deal. Hiss represented the 'best people,' the Ivy League crowd with pin-stripes and pinko sympathies. Hiss represented the victim of anti-Communist hysteria, of HUAC [House Unamerican Activities Committee] and McCarthyism."

Allen Weinstein began research on the Hiss-Chambers case in 1969, convinced, he said, that Alger Hiss was innocent. "My first article on the case," he told a *Publishers Weekly* interviewer, "indicates my sympathy for Hiss." In 1972, representatives of the American Civil Liberties Union convinced him to sue, under the Freedom of Information Act, for access to the FBI files on the case. In November, 1973, Weinstein was given the files which were to change his opinion of Hiss. He says, "I thought the suit would go on for years. But then came Watergate and then Elliot Richardson as Attorney General, and suddenly there were the Hiss files." Weinstein and several research assistants studied 40,000 pages of documents; he traveled 125,000 miles and interviewed hundreds of people who had been involved with the case, including forty who supposedly had never been questioned before; he interviewed Alger Hiss and his wife. The book which resulted from this extensive research, *Perjury: The Hiss-Chambers Case*, concluded that the jury "made no mistake in finding Alger Hiss guilty as charged."

Weinstein's work on the controversial case provoked immediate and intense controversy itself. The book was hailed by conservatives as the definitive treatise on the subject and denounced by liberals as one more card in a deck stacked against Alger Hiss. George F. Will writes in *Newsweek:* "Occasionally a work of history is a historic event. This is one such. It is stunningly meticulous, and a monument to the intellectual ideal of truth stalked to its hiding place." He continues, "It is based on 40,000 pages of previously classified material, and meetings with forty people involved but never before interviewed, including retired Soviet agents who confirm Whittaker Chambers's testimony. The myth of Hiss's innocence suffers the death of a thousand cuts, delicate destruction by a scholar's scalpel."

One of Weinstein's earliest and most vocal critics was Victor Navasky. Navasky believes in the *Nation* that a review of Weinstein's writings "reveals no commitment to the innocence of Alger Hiss. Whatever his original motives and aspirations, Professor Weinstein is now an embattled partisan, hopelessly mired in the perspective of one side," the reviewer continues. "[Weinstein's] conversion from scholar to partisan, along with a rhetoric and methodology that confuse his beliefs with his data, make it impossible for the nonspecialist to render an honest verdict on the case. This condition, however, should not inhibit us from rendering a necessarily negative verdict on the scholarship itself."

Victor Navasky checked with seven of Weinstein's key sources to confirm the accuracy of statements attributed to them. Six of them claimed that Weinstein had distorted some or all of their quotes. According to a *Newsweek* article, Weinstein replied by showing reporters "a mass of tape recordings and interview transcripts that he said confirmed his account. The reasons for the attack on his research, he asserted, was simply that liberals feel 'betrayed' by his affirmation of Hiss's guilt." Navasky's conclusion: "Whatever new data Weinstein may have gathered are fatally tainted by his unprofessionalism, his apparent intolerance for ambiguity, especially when it gets in the way of his thesis." Finally, he states, "The target of *Perjury* is Alger Hiss and his claim of innocence, but its temporary victim is historical truth."

John Chabot Smith, author of *Alger Hiss: The True Story*, in which he asserted Hiss's innocence, and reporter at the trial in 1949-50, also questions the seriousness of Weinstein's scholarship in *Perjury*. He calls the book in a *Harper's* review "a sadly disjointed work, in which research reports seem to have been pasted together without sufficient context or interpretation on the professor's part to make them useful. There is little or no critical analysis of the validity of the material quoted or the reliability of the sources; Weinstein's technique is to argue with every statement that seems to support Hiss, and accept every pro-Chambers statement without question." Smith believes that Weinstein relies too heavily on interviews with prejudicial parties rather than concentrating on the newly released FBI files. He writes: "Weinstein pays less attention to these documents than to other material he got from former

associates of Whittaker Chambers and alleged members of various Communist underground groups and Soviet spy organizations, though none of these people had anything useful to tell him about Hiss, and only one of them even claimed to have met him."

Smith's own study of the documents revealed that "it was not only Chambers the perjurer and Nixon the popularity-seeker who contrived the miscarriage of justice by which Hiss was convicted. Groundwork had been laid for them by the self-serving actions of J. Edgar Hoover and James F. Byrnes, not to mention the personal resentments of the respected 'adviser to Presidents,' Bernard Baruch. By condemning Hiss unheard, without revealing his accuser or the accusations against him, they sealed his fate before he or the public knew anything about it. This is not a 'conspiracy theory,' as Weinstein likes to say; it is an observation of the way this bit of history happened. It is based on documents Weinstein evidently overlooked, part of a huge volume of new documentation that deserves further study, from scholars less committed to their own theory of the Hiss-Chambers case, and better qualified to study it."

The battle over the guilt or innocence of Alger Hiss is being fought as vigorously today as it was in 1950 when the verdict was handed down. And, if the reaction to *Perjury* is any indication, the battle will continue. The lines were drawn at the time of the trial and sides are still being chosen: liberals, New Dealers, anti-McCarthyites, anti-Nixonites, and "anti-anti-Communists" on the left; and conservatives, anti-Communists, anti-Liberal Press, "witch-hunters" on the right. As Smith puts it, the controversy revolves around two men, "one convicted of perjury and the other a confessed perjurer whose testimony helped convict the other. . . ." Weinstein, in a *Time* interview, states his case simply: "In the end, Chambers's version turned out to be truthful, and Hiss's version did not. Alger Hiss is a victim of the facts." In truth, the case may be so complicated and the arguments so involved and so far removed from what actually occurred, that nothing short of a monumental revelation could hope to resolve the debate.

BIOGRAPHICAL/CRITICAL SOURCES:

PERIODICALS

Booklist, April 15, 1978.
Christian Science Monitor, April 19, 1978.
Commonweal, May 26, 1978, July 7, 1978.
Harper's, June, 1978.
Nation, April 8, 1978, April 28, 1978.
National Review, April 28, 1978, May 12, 1978.
Newsweek, March 20, 1978, April 3, 1978, April 17, 1978.
New Yorker, May 22, 1978.
New York Review of Books, April 20, 1978.
New York Times, April 7, 1978.
New York Times Book Review, April 9, 1978.
Publishers Weekly, February 20, 1978.
Saturday Review, April 1, 1978.
Time, February 13, 1978.
Village Voice, April 17, 1978.
Wall Street Journal, May 3, 1978.
Washington Post Book World, April 16, 1978.

*   *   *

WEINSTEIN, Grace W(ohlner) 1935-

PERSONAL: Born November 19, 1935, in New York, N.Y.; daughter of David (chief of property department of New York

State Insurance Bureau) and Esther (Lobel) Wohlner; married Stephen D. Weinstein (an architect), February 24, 1957; children: Lawrence, Janet. *Education:* Cornell University, B.A., 1957.

ADDRESSES: Home—283 Maitland Ave., Teaneck, N.J. 07666. *Agent*—Claire Smith, Harold Ober Associates, 40 East 49th St., New York, N.Y. 10017.

CAREER: Equitable Life Assurance Society, New York City, member of group annuity department, involved in interpreting contract provisions, 1957-60; *Party Line* (weekly public relations newsletter), New York City, editorial associate, 1961-86; free-lance writer, 1967—. Appears frequently on radio and television, including regular weekly "Daytime" show on Hearst/ABC Video Network (cable) as money expert. Editorial researcher and ghostwriter, 1962-68. Instructor at Bergen Community College, 1974-75. Lecturer and consultant on financial topics, including children and money and pre-retirement planning.

MEMBER: Society of Magazine Writers (now American Society of Journalists and Authors; vice-president, 1978-79; president, 1979-80, 1980-81), Authors Guild, Authors League of America, Council of Writers Organizations (co-founder; first president, 1979-82), League of Women Voters (director of New York chapter, 1969-70; director of Teaneck chapter, 1971-73; second vice-president of Teaneck chapter, 1972-75).

AWARDS, HONORS: Honorable mention in National Media Awards, American Psychological Foundation, 1975, for *Children and Money: A Guide for Parents;* Science Writer of the Year, American Dental Association, 1979.

WRITINGS:

Children and Money: A Guide for Parents, Charterhouse, 1975, revised edition published as *Children and Money: A Parents' Guide,* New American Library/Plume, 1985.
Retire Tomorrow—Plan Today, Dell, 1976.
A Teacher's World, McGraw, 1977.
Money of Your Own, Dutton, 1977.
People Study People: The Story of Psychology, Dutton, 1979.
Life Plans: Looking forward to Retirement, Holt, 1979.
The Lifetime Book of Money Management (a Book-of-the-Month Club alternate selection), New American Library, 1983, revised edition, New American Library/Plume, 1987.
Men, Women and Money: New Roles, New Rules, New American Library/Plume, 1986.
The Bottom Line: Inside Accounting Today, New American Library, 1987.

Author of monthly columns, "You and Retirement," *Elks Magazine,* 1975-87, and "Your Money," *Good Housekeeping,* 1979-88; syndicated newspaper columnist, "Grace Weinstein on Your Money," 3 times weekly, Universal Press Syndicate, 1987—. Contributor of articles to numerous magazines, including *McCall's, Self, Money, House Beautiful, Ladies' Home Journal, Consumer Reports,* and *Parents' Magazine.*

BIOGRAPHICAL/CRITICAL SOURCES:

PERIODICALS

New York Times, September 29, 1985.
Washington Post Book World, August 26, 1979.

* * *

WEINTRAUB, Sidney 1922-

PERSONAL: Born May 18, 1922, in New York, N.Y.; son of Reuben and Anna (Litwin) Weintraub; married Gladys Katz, August 11, 1946; children: Jeffrey, Marcia Weintraub Plunkett, Deborah. *Education:* City College (now City College of the City University of New York), B.B.A., 1943; University of Missouri, M.A. (journalism), 1948, Yale University, M.A. (economics), 1958; American University, Ph.D., 1966.

ADDRESSES: Home—Washington, D.C. *Office*—Lyndon B. Johnson School of Public Affairs, Drawer Y, University Station, Austin, Tex. 78712.

CAREER: U.S. Department of State, Washington, D.C., foreign service officer in Madagascar, Mexico, Japan, and Chile, beginning in 1949, deputy assistant secretary for international finance and development, 1969-74, interagency development coordination, assistant administrator, 1974-75, executive director of committee, 1974-75; University of Texas at Austin, Lyndon B. Johnson School of Public Affairs, Dean Rusk professor, 1976—. Senior fellow, Brookings Institution, 1978-79. Member of advisory board, Institute of Latin American Studies and Office of Mexican Studies. International economic consultant, 1981-82. *Military service:* U.S. Army, 1943-46.

MEMBER: Society for International Development, American Economic Association, American Foreign Service Association, Cosmos Club (Washington, D.C.).

WRITINGS:

Mexican Slay Ride (novel), Abelard, 1962.
The Siamese Coup Affair (novel), T. V. Boardman, 1963.
The Foreign Exchange Gap of the Developing Countries, Princeton University Press, 1965.
Trade Preferences for Less-Developed Countries, Praeger, 1967.
The Illegal Alien from Mexico, University of Texas Press, 1980.
(Editor with William R. Cline) *Economic Stabilization Policies in Developing Countries,* Brookings Institution, 1981.
Free Trade between Mexico and the United States, Brookings Institution, 1984.
Industrial Strategy and Planning in Mexico and the United States, Westview, 1986.

WORK IN PROGRESS: Relations between Mexico and the United States (working title).

* * *

WEISS, Nicki 1954-

PERSONAL: Born January 25, 1954, in New York, N.Y.; daughter of Harry (a textile importer) and Lyla (a sculptress; maiden name, Gutman) Weiss. *Education:* Union College, B.A., 1976.

ADDRESSES: Home—New York, N.Y.; and Jerusalem, Israel.

CAREER: Scheck-Rosenblum Textiles, Inc., New York City, textile designer, 1977-79; free-lance textile designer, 1979-81; free-lance author/illustrator, 1981—. Pre-school teacher at Walden School in New York City, 1983.

WRITINGS:

ALL SELF-ILLUSTRATED JUVENILES

Menj!, Greenwillow, 1981.
Waiting, Greenwillow, 1981.
Chuckie, Greenwillow, 1982.
Hawk and Oogie, Greenwillow, 1982.
Maude and Sally, Greenwillow, 1983.

Weekend at Muskrat Lake, Greenwillow, 1984.
Battle Day at Camp Delmont, Greenwillow, 1985.
Princess Pearl, Greenwillow, 1986.
A Family Story, Greenwillow, 1987.
If You're Happy and You Know It, Greenwillow, 1987.
Barney Is Big, Greenwillow, 1988.
Where Does the Brown Bear Go?, Greenwillow, 1988.

WORK IN PROGRESS: A book about the Jewish Holocaust, concerning collective dreaming among concentration camp prisoners.

BIOGRAPHICAL/CRITICAL SOURCES:

PERIODICALS

New York Times Book Review, April 25, 1982.

* * *

WELLS, John Jay
See COULSON, Juanita (Ruth)

* * *

WENDER, Paul H. 1934-

PERSONAL: Born May 12, 1934, in New York, N.Y.; son of Louis (a physician) and Luba (Kibrick) Wender; married Dorothea Schmidt (divorced); children: Leslie and Jocelyn (twins), Melissa. *Education:* Harvard University, A.B., 1955; Columbia University, M.D., 1959.

ADDRESSES: *Office*—Department of Psychiatry, University of Utah, College of Medicine, Salt Lake City, Utah 84132.

CAREER: Barnes Hospital, St. Louis, Mo., intern, 1959-60; Massachusetts Mental Health Center, Boston, resident in adult psychiatry, 1960-62; St. Elizabeth's Hospital, Washington, D.C., resident, 1962-63; Johns Hopkins University, Baltimore, Md., fellow in child psychiatry at Johns Hopkins Hospital, 1962-63, instructor in child psychiatry, 1967-68, assistant professor of pediatrics and psychiatry, 1968-73; University of Utah, Salt Lake City, professor of psychiatry, 1973—. Served as a senior surgeon in the U.S. Public Health Service, 1962-64. Research psychiatrist at National Institutes of Health, 1967-73.

MEMBER: American Psychiatric Association, American Academy of Child Psychiatry, American Psychopathological Association, American College of Neuropsychopharmacology, Psychiatric Research Society (president, 1977-78), Utah Psychiatric Association, Phi Beta Kappa, Alpha Omega Alpha.

AWARDS, HONORS: National Institute of Mental Health fellowship, 1964-66; Hofheimer Award from the American Psychiatric Association, 1974, for psychiatric research.

WRITINGS:

Minimal Brain Dysfunction in Children, Wiley, 1971.
The Hyperactive Child, Crown, 1973, revised and enlarged edition (with Esther H. Wender) published as *The Hyperactive Child and the Learning Disabled Child: A Handbook for Parents*, 1978.
(With Donald F. Klein) *Mind, Mood, and Medicine: A guide to the New Biopsychiatry*, Farrar, Straus, 1981.
The Hyperactive Child, Adolescent and Adult: Attention Deficit Disorder through the Lifespan, Oxford University Press, 1987.
(With Klein) *Do You Have a Depressive Illness?*, Plume Press, 1988.

CONTRIBUTOR

D. Rosenthal and Seymour S. Kety, editors, *The Transmission of Schizophrenia*, Pergamon, 1968.
S. A. Mednick, F. Schulsinger, J. Higgins, and B. Bell, editors, *Genetics, Environment and Psychopathology*, Elsevier-North Holland, 1974.
J. Gordon Millichap, editor, *Learning Disabilities and Related Disorders*, Year Book Medical Publishers, 1974.
Rachel Gittelman-Klein, editor, *Recent Advances in Child Psychopharmacology*, Human Sciences, 1974.
R. Fieve, H. Brill, and Rosenthal, editors, *Genetics and Psychopathology*, Johns Hopkins University Press, 1976.
Robert M. Knights and D. Bakker, editors, *The Neuropsychology of Learning Disorders*, University Park Press, 1976.
Lyman C. Wynne, R. L. Cromwell, and Steven Matthysse, editors, *The Nature of Schizophrenia*, Wiley, 1977.
Peter Hartocollis, editor, *Borderline Personality Disorders*, International Universities Press, 1977.
Vivian M. Rackoff, Harvey C. Stancer, and Henry B. Kedard, editors, *Psychiatric Diagnosis*, Brunner, 1977.
Stella Chess and Alexander Thomas, editors, *Annual Progress in Child Psychiatry and Child Development*, Brunner, 1977.
Morris A. Lipton, Alberto Dimascio, and Keith F. Killam, editors, *Psychopharmacology: A Generation of Progress*, Raven Press, 1978.
Wynne and others, editors, *The Nature of Schizophrenia: New Approaches to Research and Treatment*, Wiley, 1978.
Leopold Bellak, editor, *Psychiatric Aspects of Minimal Brain Dysfunction in Adults*, Grune, 1979.
M. Schou and E. Stromgren, editors, *Origin, Prevention and Treatment of Affective Disorders*, Academic Press, 1979.
James E. Barrett, Robert M. Rose, and Gerald L. Klerman, editors, *Stress and Mental Disorder*, Raven Press, 1979.
Lasagna Louis, editor, *Controversies in Therapeutics*, Saunders, 1980.
Matthysse, editor, *Psychiatry and the Biology of the Human Brain: A Symposium Dedicated to Seymour S. Kety*, Elsevier-North Holland, 1981.
John G. Howells, *Modern Perspectives in Clinical Psychiatry*, Brunner/Mazel, 1988.
Harold I. Kaplan and Benjamin J. Sadock, *Comprehensive Textbook of Psychiatry V*, William & Wilkins, 1988.

OTHER

Contributor of articles to numerous journals, including *International Journal of Mental Health*, *American Journal of Psychiatry*, *American Journal of Orthopsychiatry*, *Child Development*, *Medical Opinion*, *Life Sciences*, and *Pediatric News*. Member of editorial board of *Psychiatry* and *Psychiatry Research*.

WORK IN PROGRESS: Research on the role of genetics in the development of psychiatric illnesses and on the mechanism and utilization of drugs for the treatment of psychiatric conditions.

SIDELIGHTS: In *Mind, Mood and Medicine* Wender and Klein support the contention that many forms of mental illness have a biological base and should therefore be treated with medication rather than relying exclusively on psychotherapy. Among the treatments advocated by the authors is the administration of anti-depressant drugs to people suffering from depression and separation anxiety. In *New Republic*, British psychoanalyst Anthony Storr observed that Wender and Klein's position "illustrates an approach to mental illness which, though familiar in Great Britain, is less so in the U.S." "In the U.S.," explained Storr, "psychoanalysis has been the dominant force in psychiatry for over 40 years." In praise of the authors' balanced presentation, Storr commented: "It is one of the virtues of this book that the authors recognize that one or another form of psychotherapy may be the treatment of choice in certain types of mental distress. Moreover, even in those conditions that are best treated initially with drugs, the authors recognize that psychotherapy may and should play an important subsidiary role."

Wender told *CA:* "Klein and I were prompted to write *Mind, Mood, and Medicine* by a number of motivations, one of which was our awareness of the vast discrepancy between the knowledge of the psychiatric cognoscenti and intelligent laymen, regarding the roll of biological factors in psychological distress. The well-read layman has been led to believe that most human unhappiness results from wrong attitudes, wrong values, and wrong behavior, which in turn are the derivatives of the manner in which he or she was raised. Not so!

"Current evidence suggests that between 15 and 30 percent of the population has psychological disorders that have genetic contributions and are probably caused through abnormalities in biochemistry. The differences between illnesses so produced and those produced by faulty learning and realistic unhappiness (existential problems) are not widely recognized. As a result, suffering individuals receive inappropriate treatment.

"Our intention in writing the book was to present the intelligent layman with the very powerful evidence that much psychological distress is genetic in origin and biochemically mediated. We wish not only to inform the individual of the status of the field, but, perhaps, to allow him to discriminate between disorder, dislearning, and realistic problems. In addition, we wish him or her to develop a feeling for the way biopsychiatrists think, how their thinking leads to hard scientific experiments, and how this differs from much of the airy philosophical speculation that has beclouded the field."

AVOCATIONAL INTERESTS: Reading, skiing, flute, piano, chess.

BIOGRAPHICAL/CRITICAL SOURCES:

PERIODICALS

New Republic, October 31, 1981.
Voice Literary Supplement, October, 1981.

*   *   *

WESSON, Joan
   See PITTOCK, Joan (Hornby)

*   *   *

WETTENHALL, Roger (Llewellyn)   1931-

PERSONAL: Born February 4, 1931, in Hobart, Australia; son of Ralph Henry (a shipping clerk) and Dorothy Mabel (a dental nurse; maiden name, Rumbold) Wettenhall; married, 1955 (divorced, 1974); remarried; children: Irene, Lynn, Dean. *Education:* University of Tasmania, Diploma in Public Administration, 1955, M.A., 1959; Australian National University, Ph.D., 1962.

ADDRESSES: Home—12 Carmichael St., Deakin, Australian Capital Territory 2600, Australia. *Office*—Canberra College

of Advanced Education, Belconnen, Australian Capital Territory 2616, Australia.

CAREER: Australian Commonwealth Public Service, personnel cadet in Hobart, 1948-51, personnel officer in Adelaide and Hobart, 1952-59; Australian National University, Canberra, research scholar, 1959-61; University of Tasmania, Hobart, lecturer, 1961-65, senior lecturer, 1966-69, reader in political science, 1969-71; Canberra College of Advanced Education, Belconnen, Australia, head of School of Administrative Studies, 1971-85, College Fellow in Administrative Studies, 1985—. Hallsworth research fellow at University of Manchester, 1964-65; visiting scholar at State University of New York at Albany, autumn, 1978, and University of Southern California, autumn, 1985. Consultant to Advisory Council of Intergovernment Relations and Royal Commission on Australian Government Administration.

MEMBER: International Association of Schools and Institutes of Administration, Royal Institute of Public Administration (national fellow; president of Australian Capital Territory Group, 1973-75), Royal Australian Institutes.

AWARDS, HONORS: Haldane Silver Medal from Royal Institute of Public Administration, 1965, for essay "The Recoup Concept in Public Enterprise."

WRITINGS:

Railway Management and Politics in Victoria, 1856-1906, Australian Capital Territory Group, Royal Institute of Public Administration, 1961.
A Guide to Tasmania Government Administration, Platypus Publications, 1968.
The Iron Road and the State: W. M. Acworth as Scholar, Critic, and Reformer, University of Tasmania, 1970.
Bushfire Disaster: An Australian Community in Crisis, Angus & Robertson, 1975.
(Editor with Martin Painter) *The First Thousand Days of Labor,* Canberra College of Advanced Education, 1975.
(Editor with G. R. Curnow) *Understanding Public Administration,* Allen & Unwin, 1981.
(Editor with J. M. Power and J. A. Halligan) *Local Government Systems of Australia,* Australian Government Publishing Service, 1981.
(Editor with A. Kouzmin and J. R. Nethercote) *Australian Commonwealth Administration: Essays in Review,* Canberra College of Advanced Education, 1984.
Organising Government: The Problem of Ministries and Departments, Croom Helm, 1986.
Public Enterprise and National Development: Selected Essays, Australian Capital Territory Group, Royal Australian Institute of Public Administration, 1987.
(Editor with C. O Nvallain) *Getting Together in Public Enterprise,* International Institute of Administrative Sciences, 1988.
Public Enterprise: The Management Challenge, International Institute of Administrative Sciences, 1988.

Contributor to political science, public administration, and current affairs journals. Co-editor of *Australian Journal of Public Administration;* member of editorial committee of *International Review of Administrative Sciences* and *Governance.*

SIDELIGHTS: Roger Wettenhall told *CA,* "As a former public servant with academic preparation mainly in political science, I have been concerned to further the systematic study of public administration, which I believe has too long been relegated to a position of minor importance by the older academic disciplines.''

* * *

WHEELER, Janet D.
[Collective pseudonym]

WRITINGS:

"BILLIE BRADLEY" SERIES

Billie Bradley and Her Inheritance; or, The Queer Homestead at Cherry Corners (also see below), G. Sully, 1920.
. . . at Three-Towers Hall; or, Leading a Needed Rebellion, G. Sully, 1920.
. . . on Lighthouse Island; or, The Mystery of the Wreck, G. Sully, 1920.
. . . and Her Classmates; or, The Secret of the Locked Tower, G. Sully, 1921.
. . . at Twin Lakes; or, Jolly Schoolgirls Afloat and Ashore, G. Sully, 1922.
. . . at Treasure Cove; or, The Old Sailor's Secret, Cupples & Leon, 1928.
. . . at Sun Dial Lodge; or, School Chums Solving a Mystery, Cupples & Leon, 1929.
. . . and the School Mystery; or, The Girl from Oklahoma, Cupples & Leon, 1930.
. . . Winning the Trophy; or, Scoring against Big Odds, Cupples & Leon, 1932.

OTHER

(Contributor) *Popular Stories for Girls* (includes *Billie Bradley and Her Inheritance*), Cupples & Leon, 1934.

SIDELIGHTS: The ''Billie Bradley'' books were a humorous adventure series for girls. For additional information, see the entries for Harriet S. Adams, Edward L. Stratemeyer, and Andrew E. Svenson.

BIOGRAPHICAL/CRITICAL SOURCES:

BOOKS

Johnson, Deidre, editor and compiler, *Stratemeyer Pseudonyms and Series Books: An Annotated Checklist of Stratemeyer and Stratemeyer Syndicate Publications,* Greenwood Press, 1982.

* * *

WHITE, Ramy Allison
[Collective pseudonym]

WRITINGS:

"SUNNY BOY" SERIES

Sunny Boy in the Country, Barse & Hopkins, 1920.
. . . at the Seashore, Barse & Hopkins, 1920.
. . . in the Big City, Barse & Hopkins, 1920.
. . . in School and Out, Barse & Hopkins, 1921.
. . . and His Playmates, Barse & Hopkins, 1922.
. . . and His Games, Barse & Hopkins, 1923.
. . . in the Far West, Barse & Hopkins, 1924.
. . . on the Ocean, Barse & Hopkins, 1925.
. . . with the Circus, Barse & Hopkins, 1926.
. . . and His Big Dog, Barse & Hopkins, 1927.
. . . in the Snow, Barse & Co., 1929.

. . . at Willow Farm, Barse & Co., 1929.
. . . and His Cave, Barse & Co., 1930.
. . . at Rainbow Lake, Grosset & Dunlap, 1931.

SIDELIGHTS: The ''Sunny Boy'' series, intended for young children, chronicled the adventures of Sunny, described by the publishers as ''a little fellow with big eyes and an inquiring disposition.'' For additional information, see the entries for Harriet S. Adams, Edward L. Stratemeyer, and Andrew E. Svenson.

BIOGRAPHICAL/CRITICAL SOURCES:

BOOKS

Johnson, Deidre, editor and compiler, *Stratemeyer Pseudonyms and Series Books: An Annotated Checklist of Stratemeyer and Stratemeyer Syndicate Publications,* Greenwood Press, 1982.
Mason, Bobbie Ann, *The Girl Sleuth: A Feminist Guide,* Feminist Press, 1975.

PERIODICALS

Journal of Popular Culture, winter, 1974.

* * *

WHITEFORD, Andrew H(unter)　　1913-

PERSONAL: Born September 1, 1913, in Winnipeg, Manitoba, Canada; came to United States, 1923, naturalized citizen, 1928; son of John (a bricklayer) and Janet (Hunter) Whiteford; married Marion Bonneville Salmon, September 2, 1939; children: John Hunter, Michael Bonneville, Linda McMillan Uzell, Laurie Andrea Richards. *Education:* Beloit College, B.A., 1937; University of Chicago, M.A., 1943, Ph.D., 1950. *Religion:* Unitarian.

ADDRESSES: Home—447 Camino Monte Vista, Santa Fe, N.M. 87501.

CAREER: Works Progress Administration, research supervisor of laboratory of anthropology at University of Tennessee, Knoxville, 1938-42; Beloit College, Beloit, Wis., 1942-74, began as instructor, became professor of anthropology, George L. Collie Professor of Anthropology, 1955-74, professor emeritus, 1974—, chairman of department, 1944-73, director of Logan Museum of Anthropology, 1946-74. Visiting professor, Michigan State University, 1975, 1976, 1979; visiting professor of art history, University of New Mexico, 1980; Faye Laverne Bumpass Lecturer, Texas Tech University, 1981; Research Curator, School of American Research, 1981-84; Wheelwright Museum of the American Indian, research associate, and member of board of trustees, 1982-84; research associate, New Mexico Museum of Indian Art and Culture; member of board of directors, Wisconsin Archaeological Survey. Member of advisory board, American Indian Art Magazine, Ellis Museum, and Ghost Ranch, New Mexico.

MEMBER: American Anthropological Association (fellow), Phi Beta Kappa, Sigma Xi, Omicron Delta Kappa, Pi Epsilon Delta, Beta Theta Pi.

AWARDS, HONORS: Research grants from Wenner-Gren Foundation, 1950, 1969-70, 1974, Social Science Research Council, 1951, American Council of Learned Societies-Social Science Research Council, 1962, Cullister Foundation, 1965, and National Institute of Mental Health, 1970; National Science Foundation faculty fellow, 1961, research grant, 1966; L.L.D. from Beloit College, 1981.

WRITINGS:

(With wife, Marion Whiteford) *How Sandy Squirrel Got His Tail* (juvenile), Follett, 1945.

Two Cities of Latin America: A Comparative Description of Social Classes (first published as bulletin of Logan Museum of Anthropology), Doubleday, 1964.

(Editor) *Reappraisal of Economic Development: Perspectives for Cooperative Research*, Aldine, 1967.

North American Indian Arts (young adult book), Western Publishing, 1970.

An Andean City at Mid-Century: A Traditional Urban Society, Michigan State University, 1977.

(With Susan Brown McGreevy) *Translating Tradition: Basketry Arts of the San Juan Paiutes*, Wheelwright Museum of the American Indian, 1985.

Southwestern Indian Baskets: Their History and Their Makers, School of American Research (Santa Fe, New Mexico), 1988.

CONTRIBUTOR

James Griffin, editor, *Archaeology of the Eastern United States*, University of Chicago Press, 1952.

Arthur Field, editor, *Town and Country in the Third World*, Schenkman, 1970.

American Indian Art: Form and Tradition, Dutton, for Walker Art Center and Minneapolis Institute of Arts, 1972.

Barbara Butler and Diane M. Turner, editors, *Children and Anthropological Research*, Plenum, 1987.

John Ware, editor, *Treasures of the Laboratory of Anthropology*, Museum of New Mexico Press, 1988.

Albert Schroeder, editor, *Festschrift in Honor of Charles Lange*, Archaeological Society of New Mexico, 1988.

OTHER

Contributor to *American Antiquity, Americas, Choice, Christian Century, American Indian Art, American Anthropoligist*, and other journals.

*   *   *

WILDE, Larry   1928-

PERSONAL: Surname originally Wildman; born February 6, 1928, in Jersey City, N.J.; son of Selig and Gertrude (Schwartzwald) Wildman; married Maryruth Poulos, June 2, 1974. *Education:* University of Miami, Coral Gables, Fla., B.A., 1952. *Politics:* Liberal. *Religion:* Jewish.

ADDRESSES: Office—P.O. Box 86, The Sea Ranch, Calif. 95497-0086. *Agent*—Jane Jordan Browne, 410 South Michigan Ave., Chicago, Ill. 60605.

CAREER: Comedian, performing in night clubs, on stage, and in television. Made professional appearances while attending the University of Miami, has since performed in more than eight hundred cities in forty-eight states, sharing the bill with such stars as Vikki Carr, Jack Jones, Diahann Carroll, Ann-Margaret, Debbie Reynolds, Pat Boone, and Andy Williams; night club engagements include the Copacabana in New York, Harrah's at Lake Tahoe, Desert Inn in Las Vegas, and Latin Casino in Philadelphia. Has appeared on stage in the revue, ''One Damn Thing After Another,'' a comedy play, ''Send Me No Flowers,'' the musical, ''Of Thee I Sing,'' and the musical drama, 'Candide.'' On television makes frequent appearances on the Mike Douglas, Merv Griffin, and Johnny Carson shows, and on many situation comedies such as ''The Mary Tyler Moore Show'' and ''Sanford and Son.'' Has also done commercials for State Farm Insurance, Exxon, Chevrolet, Wrigley gum, and others. Lecturer on comedy at universities, including University of Southern California, University of California, University of Miami, and New York University. Conducts humor workshops for corporate executives and public speakers. Founder of National Humor Month. *Military service:* U.S. Marine Corps, Special Services, 1946-48; mainly writer, director, and actor in service musicals and variety shows.

MEMBER: P.E.N. (president, Los Angeles Center, 1981-83), Screen Actors Guild, American Federation of Television and Radio Artists.

WRITINGS:

The Great Comedians Talk about Comedy (compendium of taped interviews), Citadel, 1968, revised edition published as *The Great Comedians*, 1973.

How the Great Comedy Writers Create Laughter, Nelson-Hall, 1976.

The Larry Wilde Library of Laughter, Jester Press, 1988.

PUBLISHED BY PINNACLE

The Official Polish/Italian Joke Book, 1973.
The Official Jewish/Irish Joke Book, 1974.
The Official Virgins/Sex Maniacs Joke Book, 1975.
The Official Black Folks/White Folks Joke Book, 1975.
More of the Official Polish/Italian Joke Book, 1975.
The Official Democrat/Republican Joke Book, 1976.
The Official Religious/Not So Religious Joke Book, 1976.
The Official Ethnic Calendar for 1977, 1977.
The Official Smart Kids/Dumb Parents Joke Book, 1977.
The Official Golfers Joke Book, 1977.
The Last Official Polish Joke Book, 1977.
The Official Dirty Joke Book, 1977.
The Official Cat Lovers/Dog Lovers Joke Book, 1978.
The Last Official Italian Joke Book, 1978.
More of the Official Jewish/Irish Joke Book, 1978.
The Complete Book of Ethnic Humor, 1978.
The Official Book of Sick Jokes, 1979.
More of the Official Smart Kids/Dumb Parents Joke Book, 1979.
More of the Official Democrat/Republican Joke Book, 1979.
The Official Bedroom/Bathroom Joke Book, 1980.

PUBLISHED BY BANTAM

The Last Official Jewish Joke Book, 1980.
More of the Official Sex Maniacs Joke Book, 1981.
The Official Doctors Joke Book, 1981.
The Official Lawyers Joke Book, 1982.
The Larry Wilde Book of Limericks, 1982.
The Last Official Sex Maniacs Joke Book, 1982.
The Last Official Irish Joke Book, 1983.
The Absolutely Last Official Polish Joke Book, 1983.
The Last Official Smart Kids Joke Book, 1983.
The Official Rednecks Joke Book, 1984.
The Official Politicians Joke Book, 1984.
The Official Book of John Jokes, 1985.
The Official Sports Maniacs Joke Book, 1985.
The Absolutely Last Official Sex Maniacs Joke Book, 1985.
The Official Executive Joke Book, 1986.
More of the Official Doctors Joke Book, 1986.
The Ultimate Jewish Joke Book, 1986.
The Ultimate Lawyers Joke Book, 1987.
The Official All-America Joke Book, 1988.
The Official W.A.S.P. Joke Book, 1988.

OTHER

Has recorded albums including "The Joker Is Wilde," for Dot Records, and "The Official Polish/Italian Comedy Album," for Samada Records. Contributor to *Equity* and other trade periodicals; contributor of articles to *Coronet, Gallery, Genesis,* and *Penthouse.*

WORK IN PROGRESS: A novel; more comedy books.

SIDELIGHTS: "You can hardly walk into a bookstore these days without coming upon a new collection of jokes by Larry Wilde," writes Clarence Peterson in the *Chicago Tribune.* Wilde's books have sold over nine million copies and are available in fifty-three countries. In a *Publishers Weekly* article, Wilde explains his popularity: "Really offensive ethnic jokes may not be exactly tasteful, but from time immemorial this sort of comedy has met a primal need, whether it be for the pure fun of it or because it releases some basic tension and fear in man. The ethnic joke has become America's most popular form of wisecracking." While ethnic humor often comes under attack, Wilde feels it will survive. "Ethnic humor will stay with us in spite of those who think of it as being 'sick, mean-spirited and sacreligious,'" he adds. "We are a nation of many peoples from many lands, and if we have learned anything about the human spirit it is that in order to survive we must laugh at ourselves."

Wilde once told *CA:* 'I love comedy. Making people laugh has been a significant part of my life for over thirty years. I like hearing that a hospital patient enjoyed one of my joke books or that someone needing a lift got big giggles from some of my gags. When I learn that an aspiring comedian or comedy writer was motivated or influenced by having read one of my serious works on humor it makes me proud. I feel I've made some small contribution to the potential of future professionals."

Wilde's *The Great Comedians Talk about Comedy* has been serialized in *TV Guide* and in newspapers; his National Humor Month commences each April to "spotlight the importance of laughter in our lives."

AVOCATIONAL INTERESTS: Golf, skiing, cooking (with salads as the specialty of the house).

BIOGRAPHICAL/CRITICAL SOURCES:

PERIODICALS

Chicago Tribune, July 7, 1987.
Publishers Weekly, November 25, 1983.

*   *   *

WILKINSON, Brenda   1946-

PERSONAL: Born January 1, 1946, in Moultrie, Ga.; daughter of Malcolm (in construction) and Ethel (a nurse; maiden name, Anderson) Scott; separated; children: Kim, Lori. *Education:* Attended Hunter College of the City University of New York.

ADDRESSES: Home—210 West 230th St., Bronx, N.Y. 10463. *Office*—Board of Global Ministries, 475 Riverside Dr., New York, N.Y.

CAREER: Poet and author of books for children. Conducts poetry readings.

MEMBER: Authors Guild of Authors League of America.

AWARDS, HONORS: National Book Award nominee, 1976, for *Ludell; Ludell and Willie* was named one of the outstanding children's books of the year by the *New York Times* and a best book for young adults by the American Library Association, both 1977.

WRITINGS:

BOOKS FOR CHILDREN

Ludell (first book in trilogy), Harper, 1975.
Ludell and Willie (second book in trilogy), Harper, 1976.
Ludell's New York Time (third book in trilogy), Harper, 1980.
Not Separate, Not Equal, Harper, 1987.

OTHER

Also author of poetry and short stories.

SIDELIGHTS: Brenda Wilkinson's Ludell trilogy has been praised for its accurate, yet sensitive and compassionate portrayal of rural black life. These books, *Ludell, Ludell and Willie,* and *Ludell's New York Time* follow the life of a poor, young, black child growing up in Waycross, Georgia, in the mid-fifties to early sixties.

In the first volume of this trilogy, Ludell Wilson is left in the care of her grandmother after her mother moves to New York City in search of a better life. L. W. Lindsay writes in the *Christian Science Monitor* that *Ludell* is a "beautiful little novel about a sensitive young girl whose individuality and talent blossom in spite of the abysmal circumstances under which she has to live and go to school." Addison Gayle notes in *Nation* that "the universe of this novel is alive with innocence, which emanates from the community . . . and it is highlighted by the love and care that each black person exhibits toward the other—characteristics of black life from the days of slavery until the present time."

"Unlike many novels of the South, 'Ludell' is not a tragedy in any sense, not any angry book, nor is it soft-centered," remarks Cynthia King in the *New York Times Book Review.* "By the end of the book I liked Ludell. I was glad to have known her and her friends."

Wilkinson's second book, *Ludell and Willie,* tells the story of Ludell's teenage years when she falls in love, starts to plan for the future, and experiences the death of her grandmother. Ludell must leave her love, Willie, and her home in Georgia and live with her mother in New York City. *Publishers Weekly* calls *Ludell and Willie* "a brilliant novel." In the *New York Times Book Review* Georgess McHargue comments that "we should be grateful to Ludell and Willie, their families and friends, for living and talking like themselves, thus transcending weighty generalizations about black teen-agers, Southern mores or social justice. I'm looking forward to the next book about Ludell."

Ludell's New York Time, the last book in Wilkinson's trilogy, finds Ludell unhappily trying to cope with her separation from her love, while getting reacquainted with her mother, and adjusting to her vastly different life in New York City. "Wilkinson has crafted a special kind of love story with wideranging appeal," believes Jerrie Norris. Writing in the *Christian Science Monitor* Norris comments that "the clash of Ludell's Waycross background with the Harlem of the '60s reveals the social fabric of both places. [Wilkinson writes] with a keen eye for detail and a carefully paced presentation of events to totally involve us with Ludell and her life."

BIOGRAPHICAL/CRITICAL SOURCES:

PERIODICALS

Christian Science Monitor, November 5, 1975, April 14, 1980.
Ms., August, 1980.
Nation, April 17, 1976.
New York Times Book Review, February 22, 1976, August 3, 1980.
Publishers Weekly, February 7, 1977.†

*   *   *

WILKINSON, Winifred
See HAUSMANN, Winifred

*   *   *

WILLIAMS, David Ricardo   1923-

PERSONAL: Born February 28, 1923, in Kamloops, British Columbia, Canada; son of Humphrey David (a banker) and Mary Elizabeth (Cassady) Williams; married Laura Ella-Belle Bapty, May 29, 1948; children: Bruce, Suzanne, Harry, Owen, Jonathan. *Education:* University of British Columbia, B.A., 1948, LL.B., 1949. *Politics:* Conservative. *Religion:* Anglican.

ADDRESSES: Home—3355 Gibbins Rd., Duncan, British Columbia, Canada. *Office*—170 Craig St., Duncan, British Columbia, Canada V9L 1W1.

CAREER: Author-researcher in Duncan, British Columbia, 1949—. Writer-in-residence at University of Victoria, 1980-90. Became member of Queen's Counsel, 1969. Member of board of governors of Queen Margaret's School; past member of board of governors of University of British Columbia. Past president of Duncan Chamber of Commerce; past chairman of British Columbia Forest Museum and King's Daughters' Hospital. *Military service:* Canadian Army, 1943-45; became lieutenant.

MEMBER: Writers Union of Canada, Foundation for Legal Research (fellow), Association for Canadian Studies, Oregon Historical Society.

AWARDS, HONORS: Medal for Canadian biography from University of British Columbia, 1978, for *The Man for a New Country;* biography award from Association for Canadian Studies, 1979; British Columbia Book Prize, 1986, for *Duff: A Life in the Law.*

WRITINGS:

One Hundred Years at St. Peter's Quamichan, Cowichan Leader, 1966, 2nd edition, 1977.
The Man for a New Country: Sir Matthew Baillie Begbie, Gray's Publishing, 1977.
Matthew Baillie Begbie, Fitzhenry & Whiteside, 1980.
Trapline Outlaw: Simon Peter Gunanoot, Sono Nis Press, 1982.
Duff: A Life in the Law, U. B. C. Press, 1984.
Mayor Gerry: The Remarkable Gerald Grattan McGeer, Douglas & McIntyre, 1986.
(Contributor) *Law and Justice in a New Land*, edited by Louis Knafla, Carswell, 1986.

Contributor to *Biographical Dictionary of the Common Law*, Butterworths, 1984. Contributor to various periodicals.

WORK IN PROGRESS: Trial and Error? Eight Controversial Canadian Criminal Trials; The Ace of Pentacles, a novel.

SIDELIGHTS: Lawyer and historian David Ricardo Williams often chronicles the lives of famous Canadians. In *Mayor Gerry: The Remarkable Gerald Grattan McGeer*, he relates the career of the early twentieth-century Vancouver mayor who Williams calls "perhaps the most successful failed politician of his time." Using sources culled from McGeer's private papers, including letters to his wife, Williams "has written a well-researched and entertaining book," praises Allan Levine in the *Globe and Mail*. He continues, "His prose is readable and concise, accompanied by the right amount of analysis.... The author is generally sympathetic to his subject, but is critical when a tough judgment of McGeer is warranted. In short, Williams' account of Gerry McGeer's unusual career is popular history at its best."

Williams once told *CA:* "My field of interest is biography and history, related in some way to law, lawyers or judges. You might say I am a legal biographer. My experience as a practising lawyer has been helpful when it comes to researching material for biographies (lawyers, after all, are supposed to deal in facts). Assembling the facts in a readable fashion is another matter. I find writing to be extremely hard work. I tend to write on impulse rather than by adhering to a fixed schedule of so many words a day, but impulsiveness in writing may lead to unevenness of style. It is also rather difficult in writing in a rather esoteric field to reach the general reader, which is what I try to do. However ... I firmly intend on continuing."

BIOGRAPHICAL/CRITICAL SOURCES:

BOOKS

Mayor Gerry: The Remarkable Gerald Grattan McGeer, Douglas & McIntyre, 1986.

PERIODICALS

Canadian Studies, July, 1978.
Globe and Mail, February 21, 1987.
University of British Columbia Alumni Chronicle, winter, 1978.

*   *   *

WILLIAMS, John A(lfred)   1925-
(J. Dennis Gregory)

PERSONAL: Born December 5, 1925, in Jackson, Miss.; son of John Henry (a laborer) and Ola Mae Williams; married Carolyn Clopton, 1947 (divorced); married Lorrain Isaac, October 5, 1965; children: (first marriage) Gregory D., Dennis A.; (second marriage) Adam J. *Education:* Syracuse University, A.B., 1950, graduate study, 1950-51.

ADDRESSES: Home—Teaneck, N.J. *Office*—Department of English, Rutgers University, Newark, N.J. 07102.

CAREER: Writer. Case worker for county welfare department, Syracuse, N.Y.; public relations man with Doug Johnson Associates, Syracuse, N.Y., 1952-54, and later with Arthur P. Jacobs Co.; Columbia Broadcasting System (CBS), Hollywood, Calif. and New York City, staff member for radio and television special events programs, 1954-55; Comet Press Books, New York City, publicity director, 1955-56; *Negro Market Newsletter*, New York City, publisher and editor, 1956-57; Abelard-Schuman Ltd., New York City, assistant to the publisher, 1957-58; American Committee on Africa, New York City, director of information, 1958; European correspondent for *Ebony* and *Jet* (magazines), New York City, 1958-59; Station WOV, New York, special events announcer, 1959; *News-*

week, New York City, correspondent in Africa, 1964-65. Lecturer in writing, City College of the City University of New York, 1968; lecturer in Afro-American literature, College of the Virgin Islands, summer, 1968; guest writer at Sarah Lawrence College, Bronxville, N.Y., 1972; regents lecturer, University of California, Santa Barbara, 1972; distinguished professor of English, La Guardia Community College, 1973-74, 1974-75; visiting professor, University of Hawaii, summer, 1974, and Boston University, 1978-79; professor of English, Rutgers University, 1979—; Exxon Professor of English, New York University, 1986-87. National Education Television, narrator and co-producer of programs, 1965-66, interviewer on "Newsfront" program, 1968. Special assignments writer and stringer for about fifteen American newspapers. Has given lectures or readings at more than twenty major colleges and universities in the United States. *Military service:* U.S. Naval Reserve, pharmacist's mate, active duty, 1943-46; served in the Pacific.

MEMBER: Authors Guild, Authors League of America, New York State Council on the Arts (member of board of directors), Rabinowitz Foundation (member of board of directors), Coordinating Council of Literary Magazines (chair, 1984).

AWARDS, HONORS: Award from National Institute of Arts and Letters, 1962; centennial medal for outstanding achievement from Syracuse University, 1970; LL.D. from Southeastern Massachusetts University, 1978, Lindback Award, Rutgers University 1982, for distinguished teaching; American Book Award, Before Columbus Foundation, 1983, for *!Click Song*.

WRITINGS:

NOVELS

The Angry Ones, Ace Books, 1960, published as *One for New York*, Chatham Bookseller, 1975.
Night Song, Farrar, Straus, 1961.
Sissie, Farrar, Straus, 1963 (published in England as *Journey out of Anger*, Eyre & Spottiswoode, 1965).
The Man Who Cried I Am, Little, Brown, 1967.
Sons of Darkness, Sons of Light: A Novel of Some Probability, Little, Brown, 1969.
Captain Blackman, Doubleday, 1972.
Mothersill and the Foxes, Doubleday, 1975.
The Junior Bachelor Society, Doubleday, 1976.
!Click Song, Houghton, 1982.
The Berhama Account, New Horizon Press, 1985.
Jacob's Ladder, Thunder's Mouth, 1987.

NONFICTION

Africa: Her History, Lands, and People, Cooper Square, 1962, 3rd edition, 1969.
(Under pseudonym J. Dennis Gregory, with Harry J. Anslinger) *The Protectors: The Heroic Story of the Narcotics Agents, Citizens and Officials in Their Unending, Unsung Battles against Organized Crime in America and Abroad*, Farrar, Straus, 1964.
This Is My Country Too, New American Library, 1965.
The Most Native of Sons: A Biography of Richard Wright, Doubleday, 1970.
The King God Didn't Save: Reflections on the Life and Death of Martin Luther King, Jr., Coward, 1970.
Flashbacks: A Twenty-Year Diary of Article Writing, Doubleday, 1973.
(Author of introduction) *Romare Bearden*, Abrams, 1973.
Minorities in the City, Harper, 1975.

EDITOR

The Angry Black (anthology), Lancer Books, 1962, 2nd edition published as *Beyond the Angry Black*, Cooper Square, 1966.
(With Charles F. Harris) *Amistad I*, Knopf, 1970.
(With Harris) *Amistad II*, Knopf, 1971.
Yardbird No. 1, Reed & Young, 1979.
The McGraw-Hill Introduction to Literature, McGraw-Hill, 1985.

CONTRIBUTOR TO ANTHOLOGIES

Harlem: A Community in Transition, Citadel, 1964.
Best Short Stories of Negro Writers, Little, Brown, 1967.
Black on Black, Macmillan, 1968.
Thirty-four by Schwartze Lieb, Barmier & Nickel, 1968.
How We Live, Macmillan, 1968.
Dark Symphony, Free Press, 1968.
John Henrik Clarke, editor, *Nat Turner: Ten Black Writers Respond*, Beacon Press, 1968.
The Now Reader, Scott, Foresman, 1969.
The New Black Poetry, International, 1969.
Black Literature in America, Crowell, 1970.
The Black Novelist, C. E. Merrill, 1970.
Black Identity, Holt, 1970.
A Native Sons Reader, Lippincott, 1970.
The New Lively Rhetoric, Holt, 1970.
Brothers and Sisters, Macmillan, 1970.
Nineteen Necromancers from Now, Doubleday, 1970.
Black Insights, Ginn, 1971.
The Immigrant Experience, Dial, 1971.
Cavalcade, Houghton, 1971.
Racism, Crowell, 1971.
An Introduction to Poetry, St. Martin's, 1972.
Different Drummers, Random House, 1973.

OTHER

"The History of the Negro People: Omwale—The Child Returns Home" (for television; filmed in Nigeria), National Education Television, 1965.
"The Creative Person: Henry Roth" (for television; filmed in Spain), National Education Television, 1966.
"Sweet Love, Bitter" (screenplay), Film 2 Associates, 1967.
Last Flight from Ambo Ber (play; first produced in Boston, 1981), American Association of Ethiopian Jews, 1984.

Contributor of numerous stories and articles to newspapers and magazines, including *Negro Digest*, *Yardbird*, *Holiday*, *Saturday Review*, *Ebony*, and *New York*. Member of editorial board, *Audience*, 1970-72; contributing editor, *American Journal*, 1972—.

SIDELIGHTS: John A. Williams, says *Dictionary of Literary Biography* contributor James L. de Jongh, is "arguably the finest Afro-American novelist of his generation," although he "has been denied the full degree of support and acceptance some critics think his work deserves." Part of the reason for this, Williams believes, may be because of racial discrimination. In 1961, for instance, he was awarded a grant to the American Academy in Rome based on the quality of his novel *Night Song*, but the grant was rescinded by the awarding panel. Williams felt that this happened because he was black and because of rumors that he was about to marry a white woman, which he later did. However, Alan Dugan, "the poet who eventually was awarded the prize, courageously made public the issue at the presentation ceremony," explains Jeffrey Helterman, another *Dictionary of Literary Biography* commentator, and the resulting scandal caused the American Academy to discontinue its prize for literature for a time.

Williams's first three novels trace the problems facing blacks in a white society. The books *The Angry Ones, Night Song,* and *Sissie* relate attempts of black men and women to come to terms with a nation that discriminates against them. In *The Angry Ones,* for instance, the protagonist Steve Hill ''struggles with various kinds of racial prejudice in housing and employment, but the focus [of the novel] is on his growing realization of the way his employers at Rocket Press destroy the dreams of would-be authors,'' explains Helterman. Like Williams himself, Hill perceives that he is being exploited by a white-dominated industry in which a black artist has no place. Williams has said that ''the plain, unspoken fact is that the Negro is superfluous in American society as it is now constructed. Society must undergo a restructuring to make a place for him, or it will be called upon to get rid of him.''

The Man Who Cried I Am, a novel that brought Williams international recognition, further explores the exploitation of blacks by a white society. The protagonist, Max Reddick, is a black writer living in Europe, as did Williams for a time. Max is married to a Dutch woman, and he is dying of colon cancer. His chief literary rival and mentor is one Harry Ames, a fellow black author, but one who ''packages racial anger and sells it in his books,'' according to Helterman. While in Paris to attend Harry's funeral Max learns that Harry has in fact been murdered because he had uncovered a plot by the Western nations to prevent the unification of black Africa. Max himself unearths another conspiracy: America's genocidal solution to the race problem—code-named ''King Alfred''—which closely resembles Hitler's ''Final Solution.'' Finally Max, and a Malcolm X-like figure called Minister Q, are captured by the opposing forces and put to death.

The Man Who Cried I Am escapes the protest novel format of most black literature by putting the situation on an epic scale. Jerry H. Bryant describes the book in *Critique: Studies in Modern Fiction* as ''Williams's adaptation of the rhetoric of black power to his own needs as a novelist,'' calling it ''in a sense Williams's *Huckleberry Finn.* It reflects his deep skepticism over the capacity of America to live up to its professed ideals, and a development of deep pessimism about whites in particular and man in general.'' ''What purpose does the King Alfred portion of the novel serve?'' asks Robert E. Fleming in *Contemporary Literature.* ''In one sense, black people have been systematically killed off in the United States since their first introduction to its shores. Malnutrition, disease, poverty, psychological conditioning, and spiritual starvation have been the tools, rather than military operations and gas chambers, but the result has often been the same. King Alfred is not only a prophetic warning of what might happen here but a fictional metaphor for what has been happening and is happening still,'' he concludes.

Williams states in his *Contemporary Authors Autobiography Series* entry that he considers *!Click Song* to be his ''very best novel.'' Like *The Man Who Cried I Am,* the book details the careers of two writers, in this case Paul Cummings and Cato Caldwell Douglass, friends who attended school on the GI Bill after World War II. Cummings is Jewish; it is his reaffirmation of his Jewishness that provides the theme for his novels, and his suicide opens the book. Douglass, on the other hand, is black; his problem, as Jervis Anderson in the *New York Times Book Review* indicates, is to overcome racism in the publishing industry. *Chicago Tribune Book World* contributor Seymour

Krim compares the two characters: Cummings ''was a more successful competitor, a novelist who had won a National Book Award and all the attention that goes with it, while Cato was forced to lecture for peanuts before Black Studies groups. A further irony is the fact that Cummings was a 'passed' Jew who had only recently declared his real name, Kaminsky, in an effort to purge himself. Purge or not, his writing has gone downhill since his born-again declaration, while his earnings have gone up.'' Roy Hoffman, writing for the *Washington Post Book World* points out, however, that ''as Paul's career skyrockets, his private life goes to shambles. As Cato's career runs into brick walls, his personal life grows ever more fulfilled, ever more radiant.''

''*!Click Song* is at least the equal of Williams's other masterpiece, *The Man Who Cried I Am,''* states de Jongh. ''The emotional power, the fluid structuring of time, the resonant synthesis of fiction and history are similar. But the novelist's mastery is greater, for Williams's technique here is seamless and invisible,'' the reviewer concludes. Other critics also celebrate Williams's work; says Krim, ''Unlike a James Baldwin or an Amiri Baraka, Williams is primarily a storyteller, which is what makes the reality of Black Rage become something other than a polemic in his hands. . . . Before [Cato Douglass's] odyssey is ended, we know in our bones what it is like to be a gifted black survivor in America today; we change skins as we read, so to speak, and the journey of living inside another is so intense that no white reader will ever again be able to plead ignorance.''

MEDIA ADAPTATIONS: The Junior Bachelor Society was filmed for television and broadcast by NBC as ''Sophisticated Gents'' in 1981.

AVOCATIONAL INTERESTS: Travel (has visited Belgium, Cameroon, the Caribbean, Congo, Cyprus, Denmark, Egypt, Ethiopia, France, Germany, Ghana, Great Britain, Greece, Israel, Italy, Mexico, the Netherlands, Nigeria, Portugal, Senegal, Spain, the Sudan, Sweden).

BIOGRAPHICAL/CRITICAL SOURCES:

BOOKS

Cash, Earl A., *Evolution of a Black Writer,* Third Press, 1975.
Contemporary Authors Autobiography Series, Volume 3, Gale, 1986.
Contemporary Literary Criticism, Gale, Volume 5, 1976, Volume 13, 1980.
Dictionary of Literary Biography, Gale, Volume 2: *American Novelists since World War II,* 1978, Volume 23: *Afro-American Fiction Writers after 1955,* 1984.
Muller, Gilbert H., *John A. Williams,* Twayne, 1984.

PERIODICALS

Black World, June, 1975.
Chicago Tribune Book World, April 18, 1982, November 17, 1985.
Contemporary Literature, spring, 1973.
Critic, April, 1963.
Critique: Studies in Modern Fiction, Volume 16, number 3, 1975.
Detroit News, June 6, 1982.
Library Journal, November 1, 1961, September 15, 1967.
Los Angeles Times Book Review, May 9, 1982, November 29, 1987.
Nation, September 18, 1976.
New Yorker, August 16, 1976.

New York Times Book Review, July 11, 1976, April 4, 1982, October 18, 1987, November 15, 1987.
Prairie Schooner, spring, 1976.
Publishers Weekly, November 11, 1974.
Time, April 12, 1982.
Washington Post Book World, March 23, 1982, October 4, 1987.

—*Sketch by Kenneth R. Shepherd*

*   *   *

WIRTH, John D(avis)   1936-

PERSONAL: Born June 17, 1936, in Dawson, N.M.; son of Cecil W. (a school administrator) and Virginia (Davis) Wirth; married Nancy Farwell Meem, June 22, 1960; children: Peter Farwell, Timothy Corbin, Nicholas Newhall. *Education:* Harvard University, B.A., 1958; Stanford University, Ph.D., 1966. *Politics:* Democrat. *Religion:* Episcopalian.

ADDRESSES: Home—37 Park Dr., Atherton, Calif. 94025. *Office*—Department of History, Stanford University, Stanford, Calif. 94305.

CAREER: Stanford University, Stanford, Calif., assistant professor, 1966-72, associate professor, 1971-77, professor of history, 1977—, director of Center for Latin American Studies, 1975-83, chairman of department of Spanish and Portuguese, 1985-87, vice-provost for academic planning and development, 1988—. *Military service:* U.S. Army Reserve, 1958-64.

MEMBER: American Historical Association, Conference on Latin American History, Latin American Studies Association.

AWARDS, HONORS: Social Science Research Council fellowship, 1969-70, 1972; Bolton Memorial Prize, 1971; Pacific Coast Council on Latin American Studies Prize, 1971; Fulbright scholar, 1980.

WRITINGS:

The Politics of Brazilian Development, 1930-1954, Stanford University Press, 1970.
Minas Gerais in the Brazilian Federation, 1889-1937, Stanford University Press, 1977.
(Editor with Robert L. Jones) *Manchester and Sao Paulo: Problems of Rapid Urban Growth,* Stanford University Press, 1978.
The Inca and Aztec States, 1400-1800, Academic Press, 1982.
(Editor) *Latin American Oil Companies and the Politics of Energy,* University of Nebraska Press, 1985.
State and Society in Brazil: Continuity and Change, Westview, 1987.

WORK IN PROGRESS: Working Together: Three Core Studies of Interdependence in the Western Hemisphere.

SIDELIGHTS: John D. Wirth once told *CA,* "With my first book translated into Portuguese, I am proud to be one of the Brazilianists, a small group which is privileged to interpret one of the world's most fascinating societies, contemporary Brazil."

*   *   *

WITTE, Ann Dryden   1942-

PERSONAL: Surname is pronounced *Wit*-tee; born August 28, 1942, in Oceanside, N.Y.; daughter of Harry Clifford (in business) and Frances (an office manager; maiden name, Ferguson) Dryden; married Charles Leo Witte (a manager), June 2, 1969; children: Jeffrey Dryden. *Education:* University of Florida, B.A., (with highest honors), 1963; Columbia University, M.A., 1965; North Carolina State University, Ph.D., 1971.

ADDRESSES: Office—Department of Economics, Wellesley College, Wellesley, Mass. 02181.

CAREER: U.S. Government, Washington, D.C., economic analyst, 1963-66, systems analyst, 1966-67; Tougaloo College, Tougaloo, Miss., instructor in economics, 1967-68; North Carolina State University, Raleigh, instructor in economics, 1970-72; University of North Carolina, Chapel Hill, visiting assistant professor, 1972-74, assistant professor, 1974-79, associate professor, 1979-83, professor of economics, 1983-85; Wellesley College, Wellesley, Mass., professor of economics, 1985—. Visiting professor of economics, Wellesley College, 1984-85; research associate, National Bureau of Economic Research, 1984—; fellow in law and economics, Harvard University, 1987-88. Fulbright lecturer at Federal University of Pernambuco, Recife, Brazil, 1981, and at Federal University of Ceara, Fortaleza, Brazil, 1984. Trustee, Law and Society Association, 1981-82; resident scholar, Rockefeller Foundation's Study and Conference Center, Bellagio, Italy, 1983; invited participant, "The Unofficial Economy: Consequences and Policies in the West and East" conference, Trento, Italy, 1984. Testified before U.S. House of Representatives and U.S. Senate; consultant to U.S. Department of Justice, U.S. Department of Housing and Urban Development, U.S. Department of Labor, Internal Revenue Service, and National Science Foundation, and to other national, state, and local bodies.

MEMBER: American Economic Association (chairperson of census advisory committee, 1981), American Statistical Association, National Tax Association (member of program committee, 1985), American Society of Criminology, Law and Society Association (member of board of trustees, 1981-83; member of program committee, 1984), Phi Beta Kappa.

AWARDS, HONORS: Grants from University Research Council, 1973-75, 1975-77, 1982-84, from North Carolina Department of Correction, 1975-76, 1977-78, 1979, from Federal Bureau of Prisons, 1975-76, 1979-82, from National Institute of Law Enforcement and Criminal Justice, 1978-79, from National Institute of Justice, 1980-81, 1981-87, from National Institute of Mental Health, 1982-85, from National Institute of Child Health and Human Development, 1980-82, from National Science Foundation, 1984—, from United Way, 1987, and from Massachusetts Office for Children, Department of Social Services, 1987.

WRITINGS:

Work Release in North Carolina: The Program and the Process, Institute of Government, University of North Carolina, 1973.
Work Release in North Carolina: An Evaluation of Its Effects after Release from Incarceration, North Carolina Department of Correction, 1975, revised edition published as *Work Release in North Carolina: An Evaluation of Its Post-Release Effects,* Institute for Research in Social Science, University of North Carolina, 1975.
(With Gloria A. Grizzle, Jeffrey S. Bass, and others) *Measuring Corrections Performance,* U.S. Government Printing Office, 1982.
(With Carl Simon) *Beating the System: The Underground Economy,* Auburn House, 1982.

(With Peter Schmidt) *An Economic Analysis of Crime and Justice: Theory, Methods, and Applications*, Academic Press, 1984.
(Editor with V. Kerry Smith, and contributor) *Advances in Applied Micro-Economics*, Volume III, JAI Press, 1984.
Economics, Volume III, JAI Press, 1984.
(With Schmidt) *Predicting Recidivism Using Survival Models*, Springer-Verlag, 1988.

CONTRIBUTOR

Lee Sechrest, Susan White, and Elizabeth Brown, editors, *The Rehabilitation of Criminal Offenders: Problems and Prospects*, National Academy of Sciences, 1979.
(With Schmidt and Robin Sickles) *Proceedings of the Summer 1978 Conference of the Criminal Justice Statistics Association*, Criminal Justice Statistics Association, 1979.
(With Richard Hofler) Charles M. Gray, editor, *The Costs of Crime*, Sage, 1979.
(With Seymour Halleck) Martin D. Schwartz, Todd L. Clear, and Lawrence F. Travis III, editors, *Corrections: An Issues Approach*, Anderson Publishing, 1980.
(With James Bachman) Irving Leveson, editor, *Quantitative Explorations in Drug Abuse Policy*, Spectrum, 1980.
(With Grizzle) Malcolm W. Klein and Katherine S. Teilmann, editors, *Handbook of Criminal Justice Evaluation*, Sage, 1980.
(With Sharon K. Long) J. Thomas Black and James E. Hoben, editors, *Urban Land Markets: Price Indices, Supply Measures and Public Policy Effects*, Urban Institute, 1980.
(With Simon) *Government Regulation: Achieving Social and Economic Balance*, U.S. Government Printing Office, 1980.
(With Schmidt) Joel Garner and Victoria Jaycox, editors, *The First National Conference on Criminal Justice Evaluation: Selected Papers*, U.S. Government Printing Office, 1981.
(With Long) Kevin N. Wright, editor, *Crime and Criminal Justice in a Declining Economy*, Oelgeschlager, Gunn and Hain, 1981.
Unemployment and Crime, U.S. Government Printing Office, 1982.
(With Simon) Saul H. Hymans, editor, *The Economic Outlook for 1983*, Research in Quantitative Economics, Department of Economics, University of Michigan, 1982.
Sanford H. Kadish, editor, *Encyclopedia of Crime and Criminal Justice*, Free Press, 1983.
(With Simon) Richard R. Nelson and Felicity Skidmore, editors, *American Families and the Economy: The High Cost of Living*, National Academy of Sciences, 1983.
(With Grizzle) Gordon L. Whitaker and Charles Phillips, editors, *Evaluating Performance of Criminal Justice Agencies*, Sage, 1983.
(With Diane F. Woodbury) Phillip Sawicki, editor, *Income Tax Compliance: A Report of the ABA Section of Taxation Invitational Conference on Income Tax Compliance*, American Bar Association, 1983.
(With Jeffrey Roth) Internal Revenue Service, *Conference on Tax Administration Research Volume I*, Office of the Assistant Commissioner, Planning Finance and Research, 1985.
Neil O. Alper and Daryl Hellman, editors, *Economics of Crime*, Northeastern University Press, 1986.
(With Helen Tauchen) *1985 Proceedings of the Seventy-Eighth Annual Conference of the National Tax Association—Tax*

Institute of America, NTA-TIA, National Tax Association, 1986.
(With Pamela K. Lattimore) D. B. Cornish and R. V. Clarke, editors, *The Reasoning Criminal: Rational Choice Perspectives on Offending*, Springer-Verlag, 1986.
Sergio Alessandrini and Bruno Dallago, editors, *Real Estate Market Analysis: Methods and Applications*, Greenwood Press, 1987.
Richard W. Lindhold, editor, *The Income Tax Debacle*, Praeger, 1987.

OTHER

Contributor to scholarly journals, including *Southern Economic Journal, Journal of Economics and Business, Law and Society Review, Journal of Public and International Affairs*, and many others. Referee for journals, including *American Economic Review, Demography, Econometrica, Land Economics, Journal of Political Economy*, and many others. Member of editorial board, *Review of Regional Studies*, 1976-79, and *Law and Society Review*, 1985—. Advisory editor, *Evaluation Review*, 1982—.

WORK IN PROGRESS: The Affordability of Daycare; The Impact of Law and Administrative Rules on Compliance: The Case of the Federal Income Tax.

SIDELIGHTS: Anne Witte told *CA:* "My major interest is the application of social science research and statistical methods. Most problems do not lend themselves well to the perspectives of a single discipline, so much of my research is interdisciplinary. I am particularly interested in the way individuals react to institutional structures, laws, and regulations.

"Another concern is cross-cultural research; I have worked with researchers in Brazil and Denmark, and am hoping to work in Poland and New Zealand. I have traveled extensively in North and South America, Europe, and India."

AVOCATIONAL INTERESTS: Swimming, hiking, biking, racquetball, reading (particularly modern American, European, Japanese, and South American literature), music.

*   *   *

WITTE, Glenna Finley   1925-
(Glenna Finley)

PERSONAL: Born June 12, 1925, in Puyallup, Wash.; daughter of John Ford (a biologist) and Gladys de F. (Winters) Finley; married Donald Macleod Witte (a corporation official), May 19, 1951 (died March 19, 1987); children: Duncan. *Education:* Stanford University, B.A. (cum laude), 1945. *Religion:* Episcopalian.

ADDRESSES: Home—P.O. Box 866182, Plano, Tex. 75086. *Agent*—Ann Elmo Agency, Inc., 52 Vanderbilt Ave., New York, N.Y. 10017.

CAREER: National Broadcasting Co., New York City, producer in International Division, 1945-47; Time, Inc., New York City, member of staff, *Life* (magazine), news bureau, 1947, film librarian for "March of Time," 1948-50; publicity and copywriter in Seattle, Wash., 1950-51; free-lance writer, currently under contract with New American Library, Signet Books Division.

MEMBER: Romance Writers of America, Free-lancers Association, Women's University Club, Stanford Club.

WRITINGS—Under name Glenna Finley:

Death Strikes Out, Arcadia House, 1957.
Career Wife, Arcadia House, 1964.
Nurse Pro Tem, Arcadia House, 1967.
A Tycoon for Ann, Lancer, 1968.

PUBLISHED BY SIGNET

Journey to Love, 1970.
Love's Hidden Fire, 1971.
Treasure of the Heart, 1971.
Love Lies North, 1972.
Bridal Affair, 1972.
Kiss a Stranger, 1972.
Love in Danger, 1973.
When Love Speaks, 1973.
The Romantic Spirit, 1973.
Surrender My Love, 1974.
A Promising Affair, 1974.
Love's Magic Spell, 1974.
The Reluctant Maiden, 1975.
The Captured Heart, 1975.
Holiday for Love, 1976.
Love for a Rogue, 1976.
Storm of Desire, 1977.
Dare to Love, 1977.
To Catch a Bride, 1977.
Master of Love, 1978.
Beware My Heart, 1978.
The Marriage Merger, 1978.
Wildfire of Love, 1979.
Timed for Love, 1979.
Love's Temptation, 1979.
Stateroom for Two, 1980.
Affairs of Love, 1980.
Midnight Encounter, 1981.
Return Engagement, 1981.
Taken by Storm, 1982.
One Way to Love, 1982.
A Business Affair, 1983.
Wanted for Love, 1983.
A Weekend for Love, 1984.
Love's Waiting Game, 1985.
A Touch of Love, 1985.
Diamonds for My Love, 1986.
Secret of Love, 1987.

SIDELIGHTS: Glenna Finley Witte has travelled throughout the world researching settings and plots for her novels.

BIOGRAPHICAL/CRITICAL SOURCES:

BOOKS

Authors in the News, Volume 1, Gale, 1976.

PERIODICALS

Seattle Post-Intelligencer, March 17, 1974.

*   *   *

WOLF, William B. 1920-

PERSONAL: Born June 9, 1920, in Chicago, Ill.; son of Meyer and Mabel (Cohen) Wolf; married Anne Peters, December 22, 1951 (died August 4, 1968). *Education:* University of California, Berkeley, A.B., 1942; Northwestern University, M.B.A., 1945; University of Chicago, Ph.D., 1954.

ADDRESSES: Home—435 Hilledge Dr., Laguna Beach, Calif. 92651.

CAREER: Union Asbestos & Rubber Co., Chicago, Ill., supervisor of industrial engineering, 1942-48; University of Chicago, Chicago, instructor in business administration, 1949-54; University of Washington, Seattle, associate professor of personnel and production, 1954-58; University of Southern California, Los Angeles, professor of management, 1958-69; Cornell University, New York State School of Industrial and Labor Relations, Ithaca, N.Y., professor of industrial relations, 1969-82. Visiting professor at University of Hawaii, 1962, University of New South Wales, 1964, Hiroshima University, 1964, University of California, Los Angeles, 1982-85, Zhongshan University, 1985-86, Kyoto University, 1986, and Graduate School of Management, University of California, Irvine, 1986—. Consultant to business and government agencies.

MEMBER: Academy of Management (president, Western division, 1965; national president, 1971; chairman of Division of International Management, 1973), American Arbitration Association, Phi Beta Kappa, Alpha Phi Omega.

AWARDS, HONORS: Carnegie Foundation fellowship, 1949.

WRITINGS:

Wage Incentives as a Managerial Tool, Columbia University Press, 1957.
Merit Rating as a Managerial Tool, Bureau of Business Research, University of Washington, 1958.
The Management of Personnel, Wadsworth, 1961.
Cases and Exercises in the Management of Personnel, Wadsworth, 1962.
(Editor) *Management: Readings Toward a General Theory*, Wadsworth, 1964.
Conversations with Chester I. Barnard, New York State School of Industrial and Labor Relations, Cornell University, 1973.
The Basic Barnard: An Introduction to Chester I. Barnard and His Theories of Organization and Management, New York State School of Industrial and Labor Relations, Cornell University, 1974.
Management and Consulting: An Introduction to James O. McKinsey, New York State School of Industrial and Labor Relations, Cornell University, 1978.
(Editor) *Top Management of the Personnel Function: Current Issues and Practices*, New York State School of Industrial and Labor Relations, Cornell University, 1979.
(Editor) *The Golden Book of Management*, Amacom, 1982, expanded edition, with Lyn Urwick, 1985.
(With Haruki Iino) *Philosophy for Managers: Selected Papers of Chester I. Barnard*, New York State School of Industrial and Labor Relations, Cornell University, 1986.

Contributor of articles to periodicals.

WORK IN PROGRESS: The Management of Quality of Work Life; Corporate Level Management of Human Resources; Business Ethics.

*   *   *

WOOD, Fred M. 1921-

PERSONAL: Born April 1, 1921, in Memphis, Tenn.; son of Claude Wayne and Florence (Cox) Wood; married Lillie Belle Johnson, December 19, 1943; children: Mitchell, David. *Education:* Union University, A.B., 1944; Southern Baptist Theological Seminary, B.D., 1947, Th.M., 1948, Th.D., 1949.

ADDRESSES: Home and office—726 Forest Lake Dr., Memphis, Tenn. 38117.

CAREER: Southern Baptist minister. Eudora Baptist Church, Memphis, Tenn., pastor, 1952-83, pastor emeritus, 1983—; Fred M. Wood Preach Teach Ministries, Memphis, founding president, 1983—. Evangelist, Bible conference speaker, lecturer, and Sunday School lesson writer. President of Memphis Pastor's Conference, 1970; president of Tennessee Baptist Convention, 1972-73; member of board of managers of Tennessee Baptist Children's Homes and of board of trustees of Union University. Member of Board of Solicitations for the City of Memphis.

AWARDS, HONORS: D.D., Union University, 1962.

WRITINGS:

Fire in My Bones, Broadman, 1959.
Bible Truth in Person, Broadman, 1965.
Yesterday's Voice for Today's World, Broadman, 1967.
Instant Bible, Zondervan, 1968.
The Glory of Galatians, Broadman, 1972.
(Contributor) *Teacher's Bible Commentary*, Broadman, 1972.
Dynamic Living for Difficult Days, Broadman, 1973.
Growing a Life Together, Broadman, 1975.
Hosea: Prophet of Reconciliation, Southern Baptist Convention Press, 1975.
Great Questions of the Bible, Broadman, 1977.
(Contributor) *Award Winning Sermons of the Southern Baptist Convention*, Broadman, 1980.
God of Grace, God of Glory, Broadman, 1982.
Songs of Life, Southern Baptist Convention Press, 1984.
The Sunnier Side of Doubt, Broadman, 1984.
The Dilemma of Daniel, Broadman, 1985.
Coming Home, Broadman, 1987.
(Contributor) *The Holy Spirit in the Minister's Life Changes*, Southern Baptist Convention Press, 1988.
(Contributing editor) *Holman Study Bible*, Broadman, 1989.

Contributor to religious periodicals, including *Pastor's Annual, Brotherhood Journal*, and *Royal Ambassador*.

SIDELIGHTS: Fred M. Wood is a student of Hebrew and Greek. *Instant Bible* has been translated into Chinese.

AVOCATIONAL INTERESTS: Golf.

*   *   *

WOOD, Kenneth   1922-

PERSONAL: Born September 13, 1922, in Sheffield, England; son of Thomas Pashley and Mary Winifred (Horsfield) Wood; married Patricia O'Donnell, April 29, 1962; children: John Michael, Julia. *Education:* University of Sheffield, B.A., 1948, diploma in education, 1949, M.A., 1950. *Politics:* "Inconsistent."

ADDRESSES: Home—7 Church Howle Crescent, Marske-by-the-Sea, Redcar, Cleveland, England. *Agent*—David Higham Associates Ltd., 5-8 Lower John St., London W1R 4HA, England.

CAREER: Teacher in Blackpool, England, 1951-52, Briancon, France, 1952-53, Manchester, England, 1953-55, and Middlesbrough, England, 1955-87.

WRITINGS:

"The Wheel" (radio play), British Broadcasting Corp., 1971.

Gulls (juvenile), Dobson, 1974.
A Period of Violence (juvenile), Dobson, 1977.
Shadows (juvenile), Dobson, 1979.
(Contributor) *Love You, Hate You, Just Don't Know* (anthology of stories), Evans Brothers, 1980.
Shining Armour, Julia MacRae, 1982.

Contributor of a short story to *Punch*. Contributor of articles on education theory and practice to periodicals, including *Exercise Exchange*.

WORK IN PROGRESS: Domes, a science fiction novel.

SIDELIGHTS: "I spent the first ten years of my life in a small village near Sheffield, England," writes Kenneth Wood, "and I think this fact has coloured my outlook: I am by nature inclined to be introverted, disliking large social gatherings and preferring to have a few close friends. I did a great deal of reading as a child, but I have no recollection of attempting to write fiction. I was middle-aged when I began to write. I regret this: I have many things I would like to say which will probably never be said. As a writer, I try to express something real and meaningful in language that would really be used by the people involved. I am concerned about the plight of individuals trapped in systems—teenagers in large, impersonal schools, for example. I think education offered in schools often fails to meet the needs of today's young people.

"I have always had an interest in educational theory and practice and have written articles on this. My writing is always hard work, as I seek precision of expression. . . . I fuss interminably over details of dialogue. The characters about which I write appear very real to me. I once did a radio interview about my writing, and found that I could remember the names of the fictional characters but forgot that of the man to whom I was speaking!

"I wrote very little between 1982-88. However I retired [from teaching] at the end of 1987 and have now resumed with considerable enthusiasm. I think that perhaps being retired is a great asset to a writer!"

AVOCATIONAL INTERESTS: Ornithology, games, walks by the sea and in the countryside.

BIOGRAPHICAL/CRITICAL SOURCES:

BOOKS

Foster, John L., editor, *Reluctant to Read?*, Ward, Lock Educational, 1977.

PERIODICALS

Books across the Sea, winter, 1978.
Evening News Magazine, December, 1979.
Times Literary Supplement, March 26, 1982.

*   *   *

WOOD, Leon J(ames)   1918-1976

PERSONAL: Born October 6, 1918, in Middleville, Mich.; died March 2, 1976; son of Clyde Earl (a minister) and Effa (Porter) Wood; married Helen Allison DeNise, August 21, 1942; children: James Lee, Carol Joan, Marilyn Ruth. *Education:* Calvin College, A.B., 1941; Calvin Theological Seminary, Th.B., 1943, Th.M., 1949; Michigan State University, Ph.D., 1963.

ADDRESSES: Home—2722 Durham Ave. N.E., Grand Rapids, Mich. 49505. *Office*—Grand Rapids Baptist Bible College and Seminary, 1001 East Beltline Ave. N.E., Grand Rapids, Mich. 49505.

CAREER: Ordained to ministry of Baptist Church, 1943; pastor in Paw Paw, Mich., 1943-45; Grand Rapids Baptist Bible College and Seminary, Grand Rapids, Mich., professor of Old Testament, beginning 1945, dean of education, 1950-61, dean of seminary, 1961-73.

MEMBER: Evangelical Theological Society.

WRITINGS:

Is the Rapture Next?, Zondervan, 1956.
Elijah: Prophet of God, Regular Baptist Press, 1968.
A Survey of Israel's History, Zondervan, 1970, revised edition, 1986.
A Commentary on Daniel, Zondervan, 1973.
The Bible and Future Events, Zondervan, 1973.
Distressing Days of the Judges, Zondervan, 1975.
Daniel: A Study Guide, Zondervan, 1975.
Genesis: A Bible Study Commentary, Zondervan, 1975.
The Holy Spirit and the Old Testament, Zondervan, 1976.
Israel's United Monarchy, Baker Book, 1979.
The Prophets of Israel, Baker Book, 1979.

Also author of two study guides on Old Testament readings.†

*   *   *

WOSMEK, Frances 1917-
(Frances Brailsford)

PERSONAL: Born December 16, 1917, in Popple, Minn.; daughter of Frank J. (a farmer) and Rebecca Mabel (Fenton) Wosmek; married Paul Brailsford, November 18, 1949 (divorced); children: Brian, Robin. *Education:* Attended Wadena Teachers Training College, Wadena, Minn., and Meinzinger's Art School, Detroit, Mich. *Religion:* "Somewhere outside the limitations of any special creed."

ADDRESSES: Home—44 Lexington Ave., Magnolia, Mass. 01930.

CAREER: School teacher in rural Minnesota; designer of greeting cards for American Greetings, Cleveland, Ohio, and Rustcraft, Boston, Mass.; teacher of creative writing classes; also has done layout and advertising art; presently free-lance designer of toys, children's products, and textiles; teacher of creative writing and writer.

AWARDS, HONORS: A Brown Bird Singing was named a Notable Book in the Social Sciences by the Children's Book Council of New York, 1986, was on the Sequoyah Book Award Committee's MasterList in Okalahoma, 1988-89, and was nominated for the South Carolina Book Award by the South Carolina Association of School Librarians, 1988-89; three first prizes for adult short stories; special Edgar Allen Poe Award, Mystery Writers of America, for *Mystery of the Eagle's Claw*.

WRITINGS:

SELF-ILLUSTRATED JUVENILES

Sky High, John Martin's House, 1949.
Twinkle Tot Tales, Lowe, 1949.
Cuddles and His Friends, Lowe, 1949.
A Bowl of Sun, Children's Press, 1976.
The ABC of Ecology, May Davenport, 1981.
It's Nice to Be Nice, Kiddie Products, 1983.

JUVENILES

Little Dog, Little Dog, Rand McNally, 1963.
(Under name Frances Brailsford) *In the Space of a Wink*, illustrations by Ati Forberg, Follet, 1969.
Never Mind Murder, Westminster, 1977.
Mystery of the Eagle's Claw, Westminster, 1979.
Let's Make Music, Houghton, 1981.
A Brown Bird Singing, Lothrop, 1986.

ILLUSTRATOR

Edith May Lowe, *Throughout the Day*, John Martin's House, 1949.
Rosemary Smith Fitzgerald, *Bobby and Buttons*, Garden City Books, 1949.
Josephine Van Dolzen Pease, *One, Two, Cock-a-doodle-do*, Rand McNally, 1950.
Helen Earle Gilbert, *Go to Sleep Book*, Rand McNally, 1969.

OTHER

Acknowledge the Wonder (adult), Theosophical Publishing House, 1988.

Contributor of poems to *Christian Science Monitor* and *North Shore Examiner*.

WORK IN PROGRESS: Children's books.

SIDELIGHTS: "My career has been an attempt to be as true to who I am in as honest an expression as I am able," Frances Wosmek told *CA*. "It has not always been easy. We live in a materialistic society that believes itself to be a practical and 'down-to-earth' one, impatient with those who persist in straying beyond the bounds of the proven and provable. However, some of us remain convinced that even the rigid forms of a generally accepted reality are produced and supported from within by the same living spirit that is the source of an artist's inspiration. Science seems about ready to confirm that 'poetry' and pattern may be, in the final count, the true reality."

*   *   *

WRIGHT, Charles Stevenson 1932-

PERSONAL: Born June 4, 1932, in New Franklin, Mo.; son of Stevenson (a laborer) and Dorthey (Hughes) Wright. *Education:* Attended public schools in New Franklin and Sedalia, Mo., left high school in his junior year; studied writing intermittently at Lowney Handy's Writers Colony in Marshall, Ill. *Religion:* Protestant.

ADDRESSES: c/o Farrar, Straus & Giroux, 19 Union Square W., New York, N.Y. 10003.

CAREER: Free-lance writer. Began his writing career as a teenager with a regular column in *Kansas City Call*, a weekly Negro paper in Kansas City, Mo., and received one dollar from this paper for his first published short story; has worked as a messenger and at various other jobs in New York City. *Military service:* U.S. Army, 1952-54; served in Korea.

WRITINGS:

The Messenger, Farrar, Straus, 1963.
The Wig: A Mirror Image, Farrar, Straus, 1966.
(Contributor) Langston Hughes, editor, *Best Short Stories by Negro Writers*, Little, Brown, 1967.
Absolutely Nothing to Get Alarmed About, Farrar, Straus, 1973.

Also author of short story collection, *Erotic Landslide;* author of "Madam on the Veranda," a play as yet neither published nor produced. Author of column "Wright's World," in *Village Voice*.

WORK IN PROGRESS: A novel based on the life of Jean Rhys.

SIDELIGHTS: Charles Stevenson Wright "has, with some justification, been called a satirist, a black humorist, a surrealist, an experimentalist—even a phenomenologist," remarks Joe Weixlmann in a *Dictionary of Literary Biography* essay. "By virtue of [his] probing examinations of contemporary America . . . Wright has earned an intense literary following." Jerome Klinkowitz, in *Literary Disruptions: The Making of a Post-Contemporary American Fiction,* says that "of young black fictionists, Charles Wright was one of the first to shatter the old conventions, presenting the usual 'search for meaning' theme in a radical new form: imaginative literature, and ultimately fantasy." *The Messenger,* his first novel, draws so heavily on Wright's own experiences as a messenger in New York City that some critics find it difficult to distinguish divisions between fact and fiction. The novel is a portrait of a young black New Yorker whose increasing awareness of the futility of his situation "individualizes issues of general, not just personal, significance—most saliently, the isolation and alienation produced in persons who fall prey to America's social, economic, and racial caste systems," relates Weixlmann.

Similar to Wright's first novel, *The Wig: A Mirror Image* is a "farcical novel blending reality and fantasy in the story of a young Harlemite's vain attempt at economic and personal self-realization during the Johnson era," says Eberhard Kreutzer in *The Afro-American Novel Since 1960*. The novel follows the attempts of another black New Yorker, Lester Jefferson, to gain financial and social success in the world of the "Great Society." In order to facilitate his entry into "mainstream" society, Lester uses a hair relaxer to make his "wig" straight and silky. He then "sets out on a series of picaresque adventures," summarizes a *Times Literary Supplement* reviewer, in which he meets some of "the most messed-up people imaginable—the fear-ridden products of the Great Society." Victor Navasky, writing in the *New York Times Book Review,* finds most of these characters "pass by . . . without really engaging the reader or each other"; nevertheless, the critic observes that "the varying guises adopted by his people suggest the ambiguous relationship man's social masks bear to his true identity."

Wright's sharply satiric style has led some critics to characterize him as a "black black humorist"; in *The Wig,* this element of satire accentuates the bleak situation facing many young blacks. The novel "is a tale of bitterness told with malice, alleviated only by satiric relief," comments Navasky. "[It] is a disturbing book by a man with a vicious, significant talent." Conrad Knickerbocker remarks in the *New York Times* that "Mr. Wright's style, as mean and vicious a weapon as a rusty hacksaw, is the perfect vehicle for his zany pessimism." Wright's satire incorporates elements of horror and comedy which are both bitter and realistic, leading the *Times Literary Supplement* critic to observe that the work "rings sickeningly true." "Like all good satirists, he sees no hope," notes Knickerbocker. "His jibes confirm the wounds no Great Society will ever salve, and his laughter has no healing powers. 'The Wig' is a brutal, exciting, and necessary book."

In *Absolutely Nothing to Get Alarmed About,* Wright breaks down "the artificial barriers between the personal essay and fiction," says Clarence Major in the *American Poetry Review*. As in his previous works, Wright weaves his own experiences into the fabric of the novel. Remarks David Freeman in the

New York Times Book Review, "one of the pleasures of this book . . . is that one is never certain what is fact and what is fiction." As reflected in Wright's original title, *Black Studies: A Journal,* the work is a "journal-novel, an act of self-definition [which] appears at first to be more an act of the will than of the imagination," according to Freeman. "But at its best, the two worlds—private imagination and harsh reality—merge and hover between gentle evocation of the sad eccentricity of street life and canny social and political views."

"There is plenty to get alarmed about in Charles Wright's literary world," says Weixlmann. "On the one hand, it records, in excruciating detail, the result of deferred and destroyed black dreams. On the other hand, it warns of the consequences that await the destroyers." *Absolutely Nothing to Get Alarmed About* is perhaps more pessimistic than Wright's first two novels, for it relates all the disillusionment and none of the hope that Wright's previous characters had for the "Great Society." Freeman describes the work as "about a lost passion, and a weariness that envelops. . . . [It] feels like the rough draft of a suicide note." In assessing Wright's work, however, Major emphasizes its quality rather than its content: "[Wright's] language has the power to suddenly illuminate the dullest moment. . . . He has worked out a language and a landscape that is a kaleidoscope of mystery and simplicity, filled with miracles and puzzles." Although there may be despair and disillusionment in Wright's work, Major also notes that "there is humor and a kind of unholy wisdom."

MEDIA ADAPTATIONS: The U.S. Information Agency broadcast *The Messenger* overseas.

AVOCATIONAL INTERESTS: Jazz, good books, good people, travel.

BIOGRAPHICAL/CRITICAL SOURCES:

BOOKS

Bruck, Peter, and Wolfgang Kaarer, editors, *The Afro-American Novel Since 1960,* Gruener, 1982.
Dictionary of Literary Biography, Volume 33: *Afro-American Fiction Writers after 1955,* Gale, 1984.
Klinkowitz, Jerome, *Literary Disruptions: The Making of a Post-Contemporary American Fiction,* University of Illinois Press, 1975.
O'Brien, John, *Interviews with Black Writers,* Liveright, 1973.
Black Humor Fiction of the Sixties: A Pluralistic Definition of Man and His World, Ohio University Press, 1973.

PERIODICALS

American Poetry Review, May, 1976.
Books and Bookmen, May, 1967.
New York Times, March 5, 1966.
New York Times Book Review, February 27, 1966, March 11, 1973.
Times Literary Supplement, March 9, 1967.†

*   *   *

WRIGHT, (Mary) Patricia   1932-
(Mary Napier)

PERSONAL: Born May 10, 1932, in Surrey, England; daughter of Roy (a company chairman) and Violet Mary (Wilkinson) Matthews; married Richard M. Wright (an engineer), April 25, 1959; children: Katherine Mary, Penelope Diana. *Educa-*

tion: Royal Institution of Chartered Surveyors, A.R.I.C.S., 1957; Chartered Land Agents' Society, Q.A.L.A.S., 1958; University of London, degree (with first class honors), 1966. *Politics:* "A liberal if the liberals were any good, which they aren't, so usually a conservative." *Religion:* "Church of-England—up to a point."

ADDRESSES: Home—Whitehill House, Frant, Sussex, England. *Agent*—Vanessa Holt, John Farquharson Ltd., 162-168 Regent St., London W1R 5TB, England.

CAREER: Writer, 1959—. Hughes & Wilbraham, Exeter, England, agricultural surveyor and agent, 1955-57; Alsop & Co., London, England, saleswoman, 1957-59; Turnbridge Wells Grammar School for Girls, Turnbridge Wells, England, part-time teacher of history and economics, 1966-80. Elected county councillor of Sussex, 1981, re-elected, 1985.

AWARDS, HONORS: Georgette Heyer Historical Novel Prize, 1987, for *I Am England.*

WRITINGS:

NOVELS

Space of the Heart, Doubleday, 1976, new edition published as *Ilena,* Fontana, 1978.
Journey into Fire, Doubleday, 1977.
Shadow of the Rock, Doubleday, 1979.
Storm Harvest, Collins, 1979, published as *Heart of the Storm,* Doubleday, 1980.
This, My City, Collins, 1981.
The Storms of Fate, Doubleday, 1981.
While Paris Danced, Doubleday, 1982.

I Am England, St. Martin's, 1987.
That Near and Distant Place, St. Martin's, 1988.

UNDER PSEUDONYM MARY NAPIER

Women's Estate (humor), Hat-Davis, 1959.
The Waiting (romantic thriller), Bantam, 1979.
Blind Chance, Collins, 1980.
Forbidden Places (romantic thriller), Coward, 1981.
State of Fear, Hutchinson, 1984.
Heartsearch, Fawcett, 1988.

OTHER

Conflict on the Nile (study of the Fashoda incident, 1898-1901), Heinemann, 1971.

Contributor to *History Today.*

SIDELIGHTS: Patricia Wright comments: "Although no die-hard in politics—in fact rather sceptical of all politicians and in favour of pragmatic approach to problems—I am very concerned about all issues of personal freedom and how easily it can be lost. I am also concerned about how easily we can destroy our most precious possessions of beauty and continuity. This has been the chief motive for my writings over the past several years."

AVOCATIONAL INTERESTS: Travel (Western Europe and the Soviet Union), local government, environment.

BIOGRAPHICAL/CRITICAL SOURCES:

PERIODICALS

Washington Post Book World, December 11, 1987.

Y

YOUNG, Al(bert James) 1939-

PERSONAL: Born May 31, 1939, in Ocean Springs, Miss.; son of Albert James (a professional musician and auto worker) and Mary (Campbell) Young; married Arline June Belch (a free-lance artist), October 8, 1963; children: Michael James. *Education:* Attended University of Michigan, 1957-61; University of California, Berkeley, B.A., 1969. *Politics:* Independent. *Religion:* "Free Thinker."

ADDRESSES: Home—514 Bryant St., Palo Alto, Calif. 94301. *Agent*—Lynn Nesbit, International Creative Management, 40 West 57th St., New York, N.Y. 10019.

CAREER: Free-lance musician playing guitar and flute, and singing professionally throughout the United States, 1957-64; KJAZ-FM, Alameda, Calif., disc jockey, 1961-65; San Francisco Museum of Art, San Francisco, Calif., writing instructor, 1967-69; Berkeley Neighborhood Youth Corps, Berkeley, Calif., writing instructor and language consultant, 1968-69; Stanford University, Stanford, Calif., Edward H. Jones Lecturer in creative writing, 1969-74; screenwriter for Laser Films, New York City, 1972, Stigwood Corporation, London, England, and New York City, 1972, Verdon Productions, Hollywood, Calif., 1976, First Artists Ltd., Burbank, Calif., 1976-77, and Universal Studios, Hollywood, Calif., 1979; director, Associated Writing Programs, 1979—. Writer in residence, University of Washington, Seattle, 1981-82. Vice-president, Yardbird Publishing Cooperative. Lecturer and speaker at numerous universities throughout the country.

MEMBER: American Association of University Professors, Authors League of America, Authors Guild, Writers Guild of America, Committee of Small Magazine Editors and Publishers, Sigma Delta Pi.

AWARDS, HONORS: Wallace E. Stegner fellowship in creative writing, Stanford University, 1966-67; National Endowment for the Arts grants, 1968, 1969, 1975; Joseph Henry Jackson Award, San Francisco Foundation, 1969, for *Dancing: Poems;* National Arts Council awards for poetry and editing, 1968-70; California Association of Teachers of English special award, 1973; Guggenheim fellowship, 1974; Outstanding Book of the Year citation, *New York Times,* 1980, for *Ask Me Now;* Pushcart Prize, Pushcart Press, 1980; Before Columbus Foundation award, 1982.

WRITINGS:

NOVELS

Snakes: A Novel, Holt, 1970.
Who Is Angelina?, Holt, 1975.
Sitting Pretty, Holt, 1976.
Ask Me Now, McGraw-Hill, 1980.

POETRY

Dancing: Poems, Corinth Books, 1969.
The Song Turning Back into Itself, Holt, 1971.
Some Recent Fiction, San Francisco Book Company, 1974.
Geography of the Near Past, Holt, 1976.
The Blues Don't Change: New and Selected Poems, Louisiana State University Press, 1982.

EDITOR

James P. Girard, *Changing All Those Changes,* Yardbird Wing, 1976.
William Lawson, *Zeppelin Coming Down,* Yardbird Wing, 1976.
(With Ishmael Reed) *Yardbird Lives!,* Grove Press, 1978.
(And contributor) Ishmael Reed, editor, *Calafia: The California Poetry,* Y'Bird Books, 1979.

CONTRIBUTOR

Wallace Stegner and Richard Scowcroft, editors, *Stanford Short Stories 1968,* Stanford University Press, 1968.
The Heath Introduction to Poetry, Heath, 1975.
John Ciardi and Miller Williams, editors, *How Does a Poem Mean?,* Houghton, 1976.

OTHER

Bodies and Soul: Musical Memoirs, Creative Arts Book Co., 1981.
Kinds of Blue: Musical Memoirs, Creative Arts Book Co., 1984.
Things Ain't What They Used to Be: Musical Memoirs, Creative Arts Book Co., 1987.

Also author of screenplays, *Nigger,* and *Sparkle,* both 1972. Contributor of articles, short stories, and reviews to *Audience, California Living, New Times, Rolling Stone, Evergreen Review, Encore, Journal of Black Poetry,* and others. Founding editor, *Loveletter,* 1966-68; co-editor, *Yardbird Reader,* 1972-

76; contributing editor, *Changes*, 1972—, and *Umoja*, 1973—; co-editor and co-publisher, *Quilt*, 1981—.

SIDELIGHTS: American poet and novelist Al Young's art destroys "glib stereotypes of black Americans," states William J. Harris in the *Dictionary of Literary Biography*, presenting an image of the black person in "the American tradition of the singular individual." "Not surprisingly," the contributor continues, "his work illustrates the complexity and richness of contemporary Afro-American life through a cast of highly individualized black characters. Since he is a gifted stylist and a keen observer of the human comedy, he manages to be both a serious and an entertaining author." In his oeuvre, says Harris, Young explores themes of "the beauty of black music and speech, the importance of family love, the dignity and romance of vocation, the quest for identity and the need to come to terms with one's life."

Snakes, Young's first novel, is the story of MC, a young musician whose successful jazz single, called "Snakes," meets with a modest success in Detroit, his home town. Eventually, he leaves home for New York in order to start a career as a jazz musician. Like many of Young's characters MC is black, but the author's interest in him lies not only in his blackness, but also in his humanity; as Harris declares, "although it is important that MC . . . is undeniably black, it is equally important that he is young and trying to come to terms with who he is." MC faces, among other problems, the bleakness of his Detroit environment, but, as L. E. Sissman points out in the *New Yorker*, *Snakes* "offers some alternative to hopelessness." Sissman suggests that MC's pursuit of jazz as a vocation "gives his life purpose; it palliates the terrors and disjunctures of the ghetto; it restores his adolescence to a semblance of normal adolescent joy and hope." And Douglass Bolling of *Negro American Literature Forum* concludes that "*Snakes* is clearly a work which seeks to reach out for the universals of human experience rather than to restrict itself to Black protest or Black aesthetic considerations."

Similar statements are made about the main characters of *Who Is Angelina?* and *Sitting Pretty;* according to Jacqueline Adams in the *Christian Science Monitor*, Angelina "represents that classical Everyman figure struggling against conformity, commercialized sentiments, crime, life's insanities and riddles to find peace, happiness, security, honesty, love, beauty, soul." Sidney J. Prettymon, the philosophical janitor and protagonist of *Sitting Pretty*, is, in the opinion of Mel Watkins in the *New York Times Book Review*, "the natural man, with no pretenses, just trying to live with as little chaos as possible and to enjoy the simple pleasures of growing old." Even Durwood Knight, the ex-basketball player hero of *Ask Me Now*, says James A. Steck in the *San Francisco Review of Books*, discovers "how 'you learn everything there is to know about life no matter what line of endeavour you take up.'"

In his early career Young performed as a jazz musician, and his fascination with these musical rhythms permeates his writing. Harris states that "dancing and music figure as central metaphors in [Young's] poetry," and his novels, which are also "rich in black language." Not only is music the subject of *Snakes*, notes *Paunch*'s Neil Schmitz, but "the music heard in [the novel] is the music of voices speaking." "It is this elusive sound," he continues, "which hangs Grail-like before MC's imagination throughout *Snakes*, which figures finally as the novel's unifying theme." He concludes,"MC's quest for the right language in his music is a reflection of Young's discovery of the music in his language." Dean Flower remarks in the *Hudson Review*, "I don't know of any other black novel where the vernacular is used so well [as in *Sitting Pretty*], unless it be in Young's own *Snakes* and *Who Is Angelina?*" He is persuaded that "the beauty of Young's vernacular method is that it brings alive a thoroughly engaging human being"; and Sheldon Frank of the *National Observer* notices that *Sitting Pretty* "talks music all the time." "In sum," concludes Harris, "Al Young has captured much of the beauty and complexity of black life and black speech in his impressive and extensive oeuvre."

BIOGRAPHICAL/CRITICAL SOURCES:

BOOKS

Chapman, Abraham, editor, *New Black Voices*, New American Library, 1972.
Contemporary Literary Criticism, Volume 19, Gale, 1981.
Dictionary of Literary Biography, Volume 33: *Afro-American Fiction Writers after 1955*, Gale, 1984.
O'Brien, John, editor, *Interviews with Black Writers*, Liveright, 1973.
Rush, Theresa Gunnels, Carol Fairbanks Myers, and Esther Spring Arata, *Black American Writers Past and Present: A Biographical and Bibliographical Dictionary*, Scarecrow Press, 1975.

PERIODICALS

California Living (Sunday Supplement of *San Francisco Chronicle/Examiner*), May 3, 1970.
Christian Science Monitor, March 6, 1975, December 7, 1984.
Greenfield Review, summer/fall, 1982.
Hudson Review, summer, 1976.
Kite, June 9, 1976.
MELUS, winter, 1978.
National Observer, July 24, 1976.
Negro American Literature Forum, summer, 1974.
New Yorker, July 11, 1970, August 4, 1980.
New York Times, January 23, 1975.
New York Times Book Review, May 17, 1970, February 9, 1975, May 23, 1976, July 6, 1980, January 24, 1987.
Paunch, February, 1972.
Peninsula Magazine, June, 1976.
Poetry, May, 1977.
San Francisco Review of Books, August, 1979, September, 1980.
Saturday Review, August 22, 1970, March 20, 1976.
Stanford Observer, March, 1970.
Time, June 29, 1970.
Times Literary Supplement, July 30, 1971.
Washington Post Book World, May 17, 1970.
Yale Review, June, 1970.†

Z

ZEITLIN, Maurice 1935-

PERSONAL: Born February 24, 1935, in Detroit, Mich.; son of Albert Joseph and Rose (Goldberg) Zeitlin; married Marilyn Geller, March 1, 1959; children: Michelle, Carla, Erica. *Education:* Wayne State University, B.A. (cum laude), 1957; University of California, Berkeley, M.A., 1960, Ph.D., 1964. *Politics:* Democrat. *Religion:* Jewish.

ADDRESSES: Home—Los Angeles, Calif. *Office*—Department of Sociology, University of California, Los Angeles, Calif. 90024.

CAREER: Princeton University, Princeton, N.J., instructor in sociology and anthropology, 1961-64, research associate at Center of International Studies, 1962-64; University of Wisconsin—Madison, assistant professor, 1964-67, associate professor, 1967-70, professor of sociology, 1970-77, director of Center for Social Organization, 1974-76; University of California, Los Angeles, professor of sociology, 1977—, research associate at Institute of Industrial Relations, 1979—. Visiting professor, University of California, Santa Barbara, 1970-71, and Hebrew University of Jerusalem, 1971-72. Member of editorial board, New Critics Press, 1969-73. Madison Citizens for a Vote on Vietnam, founder, chairman 1967-68; American Committee for Chile, founder, chairman 1973-75; member of executive board, U.S. Committee for Justice to Latin American Political Prisoners, 1977—; member of executive board, California Campaign for Economic Democracy, 1983—; founder, Faculty for Peace.

MEMBER: American Sociological Association (member of council, 1977-80), Latin American Studies Association, Monthly Review Associates, American Historical Association, American Civil Liberties Union.

AWARDS, HONORS: Woodrow Wilson Foundation fellowship in sociology, 1959-61; Ford Foundation postdoctoral fellowship in Latin American studies, 1965-67; Louis M. Rabinowitz Foundation grant, 1969-70; Ford Foundation research fellowship and American Philosophical Society grant, 1970-71; article "Who Owns America? The Same Old Gang" received National Media Project award, Sonoma State University, and was named one of the "ten best censored stories of 1978" by a prominent print media panel; article "How We Got into this [Economic] Mess, and How to Get Out" was named the top censored story of 1981 by a prominent print media panel; Guggenheim fellowship, 1981-82; National Science Foundation grant, 1981-82.

WRITINGS:

(With Robert Scheer) *Cuba: Tragedy in Our Hemisphere,* Grove, 1963, revised edition published as *Cuba: An American Tragedy,* Penguin, 1964.

Revolutionary Politics and the Cuban Working Class, Princeton University Press, 1967, augmented edition, Harper, 1970.

(Editor and translator with James Petras) *Latin America: Reform or Revolution?,* Fawcett, 1968.

(With Petras) *El radicalismo politico de la clase trabajadora chilena,* Centro Editor de America Latina, 1969, revised edition, 1970.

(Editor and author of introduction) *American Society, Inc.: Studies of the Social Structure and Political Economy of the United States,* Markham, 1970, 2nd revised edition, Rand McNally, 1977.

(Editor and author of introduction) *Father Camilo Torres: Revolutionary Writings,* Harper, 1972.

Propiedad y control: La Gran corporacion y la clase capitalista, edited and translated by Lluis Argemi and Luis Rodriguez Zuniga, Editorial Anagrama, 1976.

(Editor and author of introduction) *Classes, Class Conflict, and the State: Empirical Studies in Class Analysis,* Little, Brown, 1980.

(Editor) *How Mighty A Force? Workers' Consciousness and Organization in the United States,* University of California, 1983.

The Civil Wars in Chile (or the Bourgeois Revolutions that Never Were), Princeton University Press, 1984.

(Editor and author of introduction) *Insurgent Workers: The Origins of Industrial Unionism in the United States,* University of California, 1987.

(With Richard E. Ratliff) *Landlords and Capitalists: The Dominant Class of Chile,* Princeton University Press, 1988.

CONTRIBUTOR

Ramon Eduardo Ruiz, editor, *Source Readings in Latin American History,* Holt, 1969.

Rodolfo Stavenhagen, editor, *Agrarian Problems and Peasant Movements in Latin America,* Doubleday, 1969.

I. L. Horowitz, editor, *Cuban Communism,* Aldine, 1969.

W. LeFeber, editor, *America in the Cold War*, Wiley, 1969.

R. Bonachea and N. Valdes, editors, *Che: Selected Works of Ernesto Guevara*, MIT Press, 1969.

E. O. Lauman, P. Siegel, and R. W. Hodge, editors, *The Logic of Social Hierarchies*, Markham, 1970.

Giancario Santarelli, editor, *Il Nuovo Marxismo Latino Americano*, Giangiacomo Feltrinelli, 1970.

A. Desai, editor, *Essays on the Modernization of Underdeveloped Societies*, Volume II, Thacker, 1971.

A. H. Richmond, editor, *Readings in Race and Ethnic Relations*, Pergamon, 1972.

H. Shapiro and R. Gliner, editors, *Human Perspectives: Introductory Readings for Sociology*, Free Press, 1972.

Ada Finifter, editor, *Alienation and the Social System*, Wiley, 1972.

S. Davis and L. W. Goodman, editors, *Workers and Managers in Latin America*, Heath, 1972.

A. David Hill and others, editors, *The Quality of Life in America*, Holt, 1972.

D. Gordon, editor, *Problems in Political Economy*, Heath, 1972.

Salvatore Sechi, editor, *Dependenza e Sottoviluppo in America Latina*, Fondazione Luigi Einaudi, 1972.

J. C. Leggett, editor, *Taking State Power*, Harper, 1973.

W. J. Chambliss, editor, *Sociological Readings in the Conflict Perspective*, Addison-Wesley, 1973.

A. R. Wilcox, editor, *Public Opinion and Political Attitudes*, Wiley, 1973.

L. Kaplan, editor, *Revolutions: A Comparative Study*, Random House, 1973.

A. Valenzuela and S. Valenzuela, editors, *Chile: Politics and Society*, Transaction Books, 1976.

K. Ellis, editor, *External Dependence and Problems of Development in Latin America and the Caribbean*, University of Toronto Press, 1976.

Richard Quinney, editor, *Capitalist Society: Readings for a Critical Sociology*, Dorsey, 1979.

John Perry and Edna Perry, editors, *Contemporary Society*, Harper, 1980.

Peter Blau and Robert K. Merton, editors, *Continuities in Structural Inquiry*, Sage, 1981.

Daniel Carrier and others, editors, *Social Problems 81/82, Annual Editions*, Dushkin, 1981.

Mark Kann, editor, *The Future of American Democracy: Views from the Left*, Temple University Press, 1983.

M. Mizruchi and M. Schwartz, editors, *Intercorporate Relations: The Structural Analysis of Business*, Cambridge University Press, in press.

OTHER

Member of editorial board of Bobbs-Merrill series of studies in sociology, 1969-75, and International Sociological Association's "Sage" series in international sociology, 1977-81; editor of research annuals, *Political Power and Social Theory*, Volumes I-VI, 1980-86.

Contributor of numerous articles and reviews to periodicals, including *American Journal of Sociology*, *Politics and Society*, *American Sociological Review*, *Nation*, *Ramparts*, and *Progressive*. Contributing editor, *Canadian Dimension*, 1966-69; *Ramparts*, contributing editor, 1967-68, Latin American editor, 1971-73; associate editor, *American Sociologist*, 1968-71, and *Journal of Political and Military Sociology*, 1975-87; member of board of advisors, *Third World Review*, 1974-76.

WORK IN PROGRESS: The Large Corporation and Contemporary Classes, a collection of previously published articles, for Polity Press.

SIDELIGHTS: As founder and chairman of the American Committee for Chile, Maurice Zeitlin spent much of 1973 and 1974 in rescue and relief work for imprisoned and exiled Chilean scholars. Zeitlin recently told *CA:* "I think I write not to praise history but to make it, if not just as I please, as much as I can. But scholarly works don't usually have an immediate impact on their times. All my writings—whether journalistic, sociological, or historical—are meant to be socially relevant, to contribute not only to understanding society but to changing it.

"That was the explicit aim of my first book, a critique of U.S. foreign policy toward Cuba. But it is also the underlying premise of my work on the left voting of Chilean workers, on the role of landlords and capitalists in Chile's development, on the large corporation under advanced capitalism, and on the phenomenology of workers' consciousness in the midst of the Cuban revolution, etc."

Some of Zeitlin's work has been translated into Japanese, Spanish, Swedish, German, Portuguese, Arabic, and other languages.

*   *   *

ZELAZNY, Roger (Joseph) 1937-
(Harrison Denmark)

PERSONAL: Born May 13, 1937, in Cleveland, Ohio; son of Joseph Frank and Josephine (Sweet) Zelazny; married Sharon Steberl, December 5, 1964 (divorced, June 27, 1966); married Judith Alene Callahan, August 20, 1966; children: (second marriage) Devin, Trent (sons), Shannon (daughter). *Education:* Western Reserve University (now Case Western Reserve University), B.A., 1959; Columbia University, M.A., 1962.

ADDRESSES: Home—Santa Fe, N.M. *Agent*—Kirby McCauley, 432 Park Ave. S., Suite 1509, New York, N.Y. 10016.

CAREER: Writer, 1969—. U.S. Social Security Administration, claims representative in Cleveland, Ohio, 1962-65, claims policy specialist in Baltimore, Md., 1965-69. Lecturer at colleges, universities, and at writing workshops and conferences. *Military service:* U.S. Army Reserve, 1960-66.

MEMBER: Authors Guild, Authors League of America, School of American Research, Science Fiction Oral History Association, Science Fiction Research Association, Science Fiction Writers of America (secretary-treasurer, 1967-68), Ohioana Library Association, Santa Fe Chamber of Commerce.

AWARDS, HONORS: Nebula Award, Science Fiction Writers of America, 1965, for best novella, "He Who Shapes," 1965, for best novelette, "The Doors of His Face, the Lamps of His Mouth," and 1975, for best novella, "Home Is the Hangman"; Hugo Award, World Science Fiction Convention, 1966, for best novel, *This Immortal*, 1968, for best novel, *Lord of Light*, 1975, for best novella, "Home Is the Hangman," 1983, for best novelette, "Unicorn Variations," 1986, for best novella, "Twenty-Four Views of Mount Fuji by Hokusai," and 1987, for best novelette, "Permafrost"; Prix Apollo, 1972, for French edition of *Isle of the Dead*; Guest of Honor, World Science Fiction Convention, 1974, Australian National Science Fiction Convention, 1978, and at numerous regional and local science fiction conventions; *Doorways in the Sand* named one of the best young adult books of the year, 1976, American Library Association; Balrog Award, 1980, for best story, "The Last Defender of Camelot," and 1984, for best collection, *Unicorn Variations; Locus* Award, 1984, for collection *Unicorn Variations*, and 1986, for novel *Trumps of Doom*.

WRITINGS:

SCIENCE FICTION NOVELS

This Immortal, Ace Books, 1966.
The Dream Master, Ace Books, 1966, reprinted, 1982.
Lord of Light, Doubleday, 1967.
Isle of the Dead, Ace Books, 1969, reprinted, 1985.
Creatures of Light and Darkness, Doubleday, 1969.
Damnation Alley, Putnam, 1969, reprinted, Tor Books, 1984.
Jack of Shadows, Walker & Co., 1971.
Today We Choose Faces, Signet, 1973.
To Die in Italbar, Doubleday, 1973.
Doorways in the Sand, Harper, 1976.
Bridge of Ashes, New American Library, 1976.
(With Philip K. Dick) *Deus Irae*, Doubleday, 1976.
Roadmarks, Ballantine, 1979.
Changeling, Ace Books, 1980.
The Changing Land, Ballantine, 1981.
Madwand, Ace Books, 1981.
(With Fred Saberhagen) *Coils*, Simon & Schuster, 1982.
Eye of Cat, Ultramarine, 1982.
Dilvish, the Damned, Ballantine, 1983.
(With others) *Berserker Base*, Tor Books, 1985.
A Dark Traveling, Walker & Co., 1987.

"AMBER" SERIES

Nine Princes in Amber (also see below), Doubleday, 1970.
The Guns of Avalon (also see below), Doubleday, 1972.
Sign of the Unicorn (also see below), Doubleday, 1975.
The Hand of Oberon (also see below), Doubleday, 1976.
The Courts of Chaos (also see below), Doubleday, 1978.
The Chronicles of Amber (contains *Nine Princes in Amber, The Guns of Avalon, Sign of the Unicorn, The Hand of Oberon,* and *The Courts of Chaos*), Doubleday, 1979.
A Rhapsody in Amber (chapbook), Cheap Street, 1981.
Trumps of Doom, Arbor House, 1985.
Blood of Amber, Arbor House, 1986.
Sign of Chaos, Arbor House, 1987.

STORY COLLECTIONS

Four for Tomorrow, Ace Books, 1967 (published in England as *A Rose for Ecclesiastes*, Hart Davis, 1969).
The Doors of His Face, The Lamps of His Mouth, and Other Stories, Doubleday, 1971.
My Name Is Legion, Ballantine, 1976.
The Last Defender of Camelot, Pocket Books, 1980.
Unicorn Variations, Pocket Books, 1983.

OTHER

(Author of introduction) Harlan Ellison, *From the Land of Fear*, Belmont/Tower, 1967.
(Author of introduction) Philip Jose Farmer, *A Private Cosmos*, Ace Books, 1968.
(Editor) *Nebula Award Stories 3*, Doubleday, 1968.
Poems, Discon, 1974.
(Author of introduction) Bruce Gillespie, editor, *Philip K. Dick: Electric Shepherd*, Norstrilia Press, 1975.
(With Gray Morrow) *The Illustrated Roger Zelazny*, Baronet, 1978.
The Bells of Shoredan (booklet), Underwood/Miller, 1979.

When Pussywillows Last in the Catyard Bloomed (poems), Norstrilia Press, 1980.
For a Breath I Tarry, Underwood/Miller, 1980.
To Spin Is Miracle Cat (poems), Underwood/Miller, 1982.

CONTRIBUTOR

Avram Davidson, editor, *The Best from Fantasy and Science Fiction*, Doubleday, 1965.
Harlan Ellison, editor, *Dangerous Visions: 33 Original Stories*, Doubleday, 1967.
Terry Carr, editor, *New Worlds of Fantasy #2*, Ace Books, 1970.
Robert Silverberg, editor, *The Science Fiction Hall of Fame*, Doubleday, 1970.
Robert Silverberg, editor, *Great Short Novels of SF*, Ballantine, 1970.
Ted White, editor, *The Best from Amazing*, Manor Books, 1973.
Ted White, editor, *The Best from Fantastic*, Manor Books, 1973.
Isaac Asimov, Martin Henry Greenberg, and Joseph T. Olander, editors, *100 Great Science Fiction Short Short Stories*, Doubleday, 1978.
Ben Bova, editor, *The Best of Analog*, Baronet, 1978.

Also contributor to other books. Contributor of over 100 stories, sometimes under pseudonym Harrison Denmark, to *New Worlds, Omni, Magazine of Fantasy and Science Fiction, Fantastic Stories, Amazing Stories,* and *Galaxy.*

SIDELIGHTS: Known for his colorful prose style and innovative adaptations of ancient myth, Roger Zelazny is one of the most popular of contemporary science fiction writers. His early works, first published in the 1960s, feature characters derived from Egyptian and Hindu mythology, while his more recent "Amber" series concerns a world existing in all times and places at once, and of which the Earth and other worlds are mere reflections. Speaking of the wide range of interests and approaches to be found in his work, Michael Vance of *Fantasy Newsletter* claims that Zelazny is "not easily categorized. He seems at home swimming with or against the main currents of science fiction. . . . [But] Zelazny wins awards and sells books because he weaves wordspells that transport readers into the farthest reaches of space or the darkest mysteries of magic with equal ease."

Zelazny burst on the science fiction scene in the early 1960s. At that time working for the Social Security Administration, a position he was to hold until 1969, Zelazny began to write short stories during his spare time in the evenings and on weekends. "Zelazny's procedure," Joseph L. Sanders explains in his *Roger Zelazny: A Primary and Secondary Bibliography,* " . . . was to write one story an evening and to polish it the following night." He submitted these stories to the major science fiction magazines, working his way down an alphabetical list he compiled. After a short time the editor of *Amazing Stories* began to show an interest in his work, jotting down encouraging comments on Zelazny's manuscripts. "Slightly more than a month after Zelazny began sending stories around," Sanders notes, his first story was accepted for publication in *Amazing.* He published another seventeen stories in his first year as a science fiction writer. And between 1962 and 1969, Zelazny "was nominated for the Hugo and Nebula awards sixteen times," Carl B. Yoke reports in the *Dictionary of Literary Biography.*

Zelazny's most important writings from this period are novellas, stories of between 20,000 and 40,000 words in length.

"A Rose for Ecclesiastes" and "The Doors of His Face, the Lamps of His Mouth" have been especially cited by critics as among the best of his early work. Zelazny's novellas, George Warren writes in the *Los Angeles Times Book Review*, are "full of fantastic imagery and soaring, even overblown, poetry." Writing in *Voices for the Future: Essays on Major Science Fiction Writers*, Thomas D. Clareson claims that "A Rose for Ecclesiastes" "revitalized science fiction.... Zelazny introduced color, poetry, metaphor, and a deeper psychological dimension into science fiction." The story concerns an Earth man, Gallinger, who works on Mars as a translator of ancient religious texts. The Martian race is sterile and dying out. When Gallinger impregnates Braxa, a Martian woman with whom he has fallen in love, it promises a continuance of the Martian race. But Gallinger soon realizes that Braxa has never loved him, has only had his child to fulfill an old religious prophecy, and his ego is shattered. Gallinger attempts suicide. This painful episode leads him to undergo a dramatic personality change. Yoke remarks that "in 'A Rose for Ecclesiastes' Zelazny brilliantly explores man's capability to grow from his experience."

Zelazny again borrows from biblical precedents for the title of "The Doors of His Face, the Lamps of His Mouth," which is taken from the Book of Job. The protagonist of this story, Carlton Davits, is similar to the biblical Job as well. Both are wealthy, self-centered men. Davits is undone when he travels to Venus in quest of a giant sea creature never before caught by Earthlings. The creature wrecks his ship and kills six of his crew, and Davits is reduced to bankruptcy and alcoholism. But during a later trip in search of the creature, this time with his ex-wife, Davits succeeds in capturing and killing the monster. This triumph brings him to a new maturity. Like Gallinger in "A Rose for Ecclesiastes," Davits undergoes a personality change. In an article for *Extrapolation*, Yoke notes that "in the pattern of his development, Davits mirrors the psychological evolution of many Zelazny protagonists." Acknowledging the story's popularity among science fiction readers, Douglas Barbour of *Riverside Quarterly* refers to "The Doors of His Face, the Lamps of His Mouth" as "the now famous" story. Zelazny won a Nebula Award for the work.

Zelazny's early stories, with their dazzling prose style and audacious mix of myth, allusions, and high technology, quickly made him a major figure in the science fiction field. Speaking of these early writings, Sidney Coleman of the *Magazine of Fantasy and Science Fiction* states: "In an important sense Zelazny really was without fear and without blame; he would try the most daring tricks, and bring them off. Zelazny's famous skill as a culture-magpie is an outstanding instance: He would cast a computer as both Faust and Adam, mix grail legend with electric psychotherapy, work a line from the *Cantos* into a story whose basic plot was the old pulp chestnut about the white hunter and Miss Richbitch.... [and] he made it work." Algis Budrys of the *Magazine of Fantasy and Science Fiction*, writing of Zelazny's early career, claims that those were "the days when each new Zelazny story was like nothing that had been done before."

By 1969, having established himself in the science fiction field, Zelazny left his job with the Social Security Administration to become a full-time writer. The career move entailed one major change in his writing. While employed with the government, Zelazny had been obliged to write relatively short works, stories he could finish in his spare time. But once he relied on science fiction for his livelihood, he relegated the shorter, less profitable works to secondary status and focused his attention

on the writing of novels. As George R. R. Martin explains in the *Washington Post Book World*, "it was in the shorter forms that he first made a name for himself. Like many other writers, however, Zelazny was soon seduced away from his first love by the greater glory and riches of the novel."

Zelazny's first novel, *This Immortal*, is inspired in part by the author's experiences while serving in the Army's Arts, Monuments, and Archives unit, a department which preserves important historical and cultural landmarks in occupied foreign countries. In the novel, the alien Myshtigo is on a tour of Earth's cultural monuments, guided by the immortal Earthling Conrad. Myshtigo has bought the planet, long before devastated by nuclear war and conquered by the Vegans, and is now interested in learning something about his property. His unspoken desire is to determine whether Conrad is fit to lead the massive restoration effort Myshtigo plans for the ruined Earth.

The novel's focus is on Conrad's ability to overcome his long-standing antagonism to the aliens and see where both he and Myshtigo share common goals and concerns. His immortality has enabled Conrad to experience widely divergent aspects of life. Through this process he has learned that "things, places, people are real; judgments that might have applied to reality in the past, though, cannot be trusted," as Sanders remarks in *Death and the Serpent: Immortality in Science Fiction and Fantasy*. By suppressing his strong aversion to the aliens and allowing himself to learn about Myshtigo, Conrad is eventually given leadership of the effort to restore the Earth, an effort that even the most persistent opponents of the Vegans support. "Conrad," Joseph V. Francavilla writes in *Extrapolation*, "passes from being a destroyer, disrupter, and fighter to being a creator, restorer, and peacemaker." "The main thing Zelazny shows about immortality in *This Immortal*," Sanders writes, "is that the successful immortal, such as Conrad, who not only stays alive but does something satisfying with his life, does so by avoiding confinement within a set of rules or preconceptions." Writing in the *Dictionary of Literary Biography*, Yoke maintains that "the striking originality of the story and its characterization make [*This Immortal*] well worth reading." *This Immortal* won a Hugo Award in 1966.

Lord of Light is concerned with many of the same themes introduced in *This Immortal*, including personality growth, immortality, and the renewal of a planet. It is set on a far future world where technologically advanced human beings have set themselves up as gods over the less advanced populace. Taking the Hindu deities as their models, they have enhanced their mental powers through neurosurgery, hypnosis, and drugs to achieve a semblance of actual godlike ability. One of their number has succeeded in reaching inner perfection. When it becomes clear to him that his companions have become tyrants, he overthrows their system and frees the native population. *Lord of Light*, Yoke explains in the *Dictionary of Literary Biography*, "was hailed as a science-fiction classic" when it first appeared, and won Zelazny a Hugo Award.

Later Zelazny novels are also fashioned from a blend of ancient myths and futuristic science. *Creatures of Light and Darkness* features the gods of Egyptian mythology, while the plot borrows elements from several different mythologies. As Pauline F. Micciche of *Library Journal* notes, it is "a warp of Christian, Greek, Egyptian and Norse myths spun into one thread." *Isle of the Dead* concerns a battle between a wealthy, sardonic immortal and his enemy, who is a personification of a god. Writing in the *New York Times Book Review*, Gerald Jonas notes that "Zelazny is a playful writer, but there is nothing lighthearted about his play. He plays with myths—archetypes and themes borrowed from the ancestral store-houses of different cultures.''

A continuing theme in these novels is the nature of divinity. Often, Zelazny writes of immortal characters with enormous technological powers who must grow to godlike stature to deal with overwhelming situations. ''Immortality, or near-immortality, is a persistent theme in Zelazny's writing,'' Yoke acknowledges in *The Mechanical God: Machines in Science Fiction,* ''and it is a key factor in raising man or humanoid to the god level.'' ''To live forever,'' Francavilla explains, ''means simply to have time enough to experience, learn, develop, and to increase one's self-awareness—to define oneself. In his quest for self-definition . . . , the immortal hero in Zelazny's works defines what it means to be human by expanding man's potential and by boldly extending the boundaries of the human into the region of the divine.''

Perhaps Zelazny's most ambitious project has been the series of books set in the imaginary world of Amber; the series consists of a five-novel sequence, three novels in a new, ongoing sequence, and a chapbook. The world of Amber transcends normal time and space limitations. It exists in all times at once, and its inhabitants are immortals who can time travel as they please between an endless multitude of alternate worlds. These alternate worlds, one of which is the Earth, are mere reflections of the one true world of Amber. As Edwin Morgan of the *Times Literary Supplement* maintains, ''Amber is a place, a city, a state, a 'world'. . . . Amber is the perfect place, the Substance to which everything else is Shadow. It is not in our space and time, and its inhabitants, although they talk and act for the most part in human ways, are not human. Since they have enormous powers, they appear at times like gods.''

The series follows the machinations among Amber's ruling family as they vie for power over multiple worlds. The first five novels form one complete story in which Corwin seeks the throne during a demonic invasion that threatens to reduce Amber and her shadow worlds to chaos. He begins the first novel with amnesia, his memory wiped clean by his rivals, and ends the fifth book as the ruler of Amber. ''In the Amber series, as Corwin finally comes to understand,'' Sanders writes in his Zelazny bibliography, ''life exists between two poles, Pattern and Chaos. Neither 'wins'. The difficult, creative tension between them continues, just as life continues.'' Lester Del Rey, writing in *Analog: Science Fiction/Science Fact,* warns that the Amber ''books have to be read from first to last. They form a single novel, not a series of novels.'' He concludes with the comment that the five novels would have been a better story if written as a single book.''Had that been done,'' Del Rey writes, ''this could well have been a genuinely superb piece of fantasy. As it is, it's a good story—no more.'' But Marshall B. Tymm, Kenneth J. Zoharski, and Robert H. Boyer have a more positive reaction to the five-novel Amber sequence in their *Fantasy Literature: A Core Collection and Reference Guide.* These books are, they claim, ''on the whole excellent, both for their unusually original fantasy elements and for their literary qualities,'' and they judge Amber to be ''one of the more ingeniously conceived secondary worlds in fantasy literature.''

The three most recent Amber novels concern the adventures of Corwin's son, Merlin, who is being stalked through alternate worlds by an unknown group of assassins. Speaking of *Blood of Amber,* H. J. Kirchhoff of the Toronto *Globe and Mail* states: ''As usual in the Amber books, Zelazny parlays

hip dialogue, quirky characters and an anything-is-possible multiple universe into a winning swords-and-sorcery adventure.'' *Trumps of Doom,* the first in the new Amber series, won a *Locus* Award in 1986.

Speaking to Vance about his conception of science fiction, Zelazny explains: ''It is, for me, a special way of looking at anything, really—by pulling it out of context and into a different situation. . . . Sometimes you just ask yourself, 'What If?' And you make up something that's considered unlikely to happen, just to take a look at it.'' When writing science fiction, Zelazny prefers a spontaneous technique. In an article for *Science Fiction Chronicle* about how he writes, Zelazny claims: ''Generally, I do not like knowing beforehand how I will end a novel. My ideal method of composition is to begin writing once I know my major character and a few of the situations in which he or she will be functioning—*i.e.,* about thirty percent of the story. . . . I enjoy relying upon a subconscious plotting mechanism and discovering its operation as I work.''

Zelazny's work has explored a range of genre types during his career, moving from strict science fiction based on mythological models to an alternate world fantasy of castles, kings, and sword-wielding heroes. Charles Platt of the *Washington Post Book World* notes that ''in his early work, . . . closely observed characters interacted with advanced technology; today, Zelazny deals more with sorcery than science, in fanciful mythic landscapes, laconically described. He still writes more fluently and with more authority than nine-tenths of his contemporaries.'' Lew Wolkoff of *Best Sellers* believes that Zelazny can handle both types of fiction well. ''He can take a reader,'' Wolkoff writes, ''on tour across a radiation-scarred America in one story and show him/her a wizards' duel in the next, swinging easily from hard science to dark fantasy.''

Not all critics have been satisfied with the changes in Zelazny's writing. Some prefer his earlier, more flamboyantly poetic work. Coleman, for example, complains that Zelazny ''put away his magician's tricks and turned his gold into lead. . . . We once had something unique and wonderful, and it is gone, and what we have in its place is only a superior writer of preposterous adventures.'' Although Nick Totton of the *Observer* calls Zelazny ''a skilled and fluent writer with both powerful ideas and a grasp of their broader reference,'' he also finds that Zelazny ''generally prefers playing cosily within a familiar convention to exploring fresh territory.'' Sanders notes in his Zelazny bibliogrraphy that some critics of the author ''have voiced irritation when Zelazny has not done exactly *what they expected.*''

Despite such criticism, Zelazny enjoys a prominent position in contemporary science fiction. Martin places the book *The Doors of His Face, the Lamps of His Mouth, and Other Stories* ''among the three best story collections of the last decade,'' and calls Zelazny ''one of the most important contemporary science-fiction writers.'' ''There is no question of his stature,'' Yoke maintains in the *Dictionary of Literary Biography.* ''He has contributed major works to the field, and perhaps more than any other writer has brought the techniques, style, and language of serious literature to science fiction. His greatest contribution, however, may be that he has brought to a literature famous for its cardboard figures, characters who are psychologically credible, who are sympathetic, who have scope and dimension.'' Clareson concludes that ''Zelazny has dealt intelligently, lightly, and good-humoredly with a number of serious questions about the ways in which our fantasies mesh with our realities.'' Although holding some reservations about Zelazny's work, Clareson nevertheless believes he is ''a story teller, an entertainer in the best sense,'' and praises his ''exemplary craftsmanship, which has continued with few hiatuses throughout his career.''

BIOGRAPHICAL/CRITICAL SOURCES:

BOOKS

Clareson, Thomas D., *Voices for the Future: Essays on Major Science Fiction Writers*, Bowling Green State University, 1979.
Collins, R. A., editor, *Scope of the Fantastic: Culture, Biography, Themes in Children's Literature*, Greenwood Press, 1985.
Contemporary Literary Criticism, Volume 21, Gale, 1982.
Dictionary of Literary Biography, Volume 8: *Twentieth Century American Science Fiction Writers*, Gale, 1981.
Dunn, Thomas P. and Richard D. Erlich, editors, *The Mechanical God: Machines in Science Fiction*, Greenwood Press, 1982.
Krulik, Theodore, *Roger Zelazny*, Ungar, 1986.
Levack, Daniel J. H., *Amber Dreams: A Roger Zelazny Bibliography*, Underwood/Miller, 1983.
Reilly, Robert, editor, *The Transcendent Adventure*, Greenwood Press, 1984.
Sanders, Joseph L., *Roger Zelazny: A Primary and Secondary Bibliography*, G. K. Hall, 1980.
Science Fiction and Fantasy Authors: A Bibliography of First Printings of Their Science Fiction and Selected Nonfiction, G. K. Hall, 1979.
Staicar, Tom, editor, *Critical Encounters II*, Ungar, 1982.
Tymm, Marshall B., Kenneth J. Zoharski, and Robert H. Boyer, *Fantasy Literature: A Core Collection and Reference Guide*, Bowker, 1979.
Walker, Paul, *Speaking of Science Fiction*, Luna Publications, 1978.
Yoke, Carl B., *Roger Zelazny and Andre Norton: Proponents of Individualism*, State Library of Ohio, 1979.
Yoke, Carl B., *A Reader's Guide to Roger Zelazny*, Starmont, 1979.
Yoke, Carl B., and Donald M. Hassler, editors, *Death and the Serpent: Immortality in Science Fiction and Fantasy*, Greenwood Press, 1985.

PERIODICALS

Algol, summer, 1976.
Amazing Stories, July, 1984.
Analog: Science Fiction/Science Fact, February, 1979, March 2, 1981, March, 1983.
Baltimore Sun, January 29, 1967.
Best Sellers, September, 1976, June, 1978.
Extrapolation, December, 1973, summer, 1980, spring, 1984.
Fantasy Newsletter, October 1980, January 1983, September, 1983.
Foundation, March, 1977.
Future Life, March, 1981.
Globe and Mail (Toronto), February 14, 1987, November 14, 1987.
Journal of American Culture, summer, 1979.
Library Journal, September 15, 1969.
Locus, October, 1983.
Los Angeles Times Book Review, January 11, 1981.
Magazine of Fantasy and Science Fiction, May, 1971, August, 1974, February, 1982.
Media Sight, summer, 1984.

Mosaic, winter, 1981.
New Scientist, February 23, 1978.
New York Review of Books, October 2, 1975.
New York Times Book Review, May 23, 1976, December 19, 1982.
Observer, June 24, 1979.
Riverside Quarterly, June, 1970, August, 1973.
Science Fiction: A Review of Speculative Literature, June, 1978, December, 1979.
Science Fiction Chronicle, January, 1985.
Science Fiction Review, May, 1980, August, 1980.
SF Commentary, November, 1978.
Times Literary Supplement, February 29, 1968, March 28, 1968, February 13, 1981.
Washington Post Book World, December 23, 1979, January 25, 1981, December 25, 1983.

—*Sketch by Thomas Wiloch*

*   *   *

ZIEMER, Gregor (Athalwin)   1899-198(?)

PERSONAL: Born May 24, 1899, in Columbia, Mich.; son of Robert (a minister) and Adele (Grabau) Ziemer; married Edna Wilson (a teacher), May 30, 1926; children: Patricia Erika (Mrs. William Eadie). *Education:* University of Illinois, B.A., 1922; University of Minnesota, M.A., 1923; University of Berlin, Ph.D., 1934. *Politics:* Independent. *Religion:* Lutheran.

CAREER: Teacher and superintendent at government schools, Philippine Islands, 1926-28; American School, Berlin, Germany, founder and headmaster, 1928-39; WLW-Radio, Cincinnati, Ohio, newscaster, 1942-44; Town Hall, New York City, director of education, 1945-60; WRVA-Radio, Richmond, Va., newscaster, 1948-50; International Enterprises, Inc., Philadelphia, Pa., vice-president for public relations, 1949-50; American Foundation for the Blind, Inc., New York City, director of public education, 1952-64; Institute of Lifetime Learning, Long Beach, Calif., director, 1966-71; free-lance writer, beginning 1971. Berlin correspondent, *Chicago Tribune*, 1928-34, *New York Herald*, 1934-39, and *London Daily Mail*, 1934-39. Writer and producer of radio and television shows. Public lecturer on international affairs and other topics, sometimes appearing in dialogue lectures with wife, Edna Ziemer. Member of Lake City (Minn.) Chamber of Commerce bicentennial committee. *Military service:* U.S. Army, lieutenant colonel with Fourth Armored Division of Third Army in Europe, 1945; military government work in Bavaria with Supreme Headquarters, Allied Expeditionary Force.

MEMBER: Public Relations Society of America (president, New York chapter, 1960), Overseas Press Club (member of board, 1950), Association of Radio-Television News Analysts (secretary, 1948), Council of National Organizations, American Legion, Cuvier Press Club, Tau Kappa Alpha, Kappa Delta Pi, Beta Sigma Psi.

AWARDS, HONORS: American Public Relations Association, Silver Anvil Award, 1956, 1958, 1960, and Paul Revere Citation, 1958; Westinghouse citation, 1958; named Man of the Year, 1960, for work with the blind; award from Freedoms Foundation for work on ''American Heritage'' series, 1969.

WRITINGS:

(With daughter, Patsy Ziemer) *Two Thousand and Ten Days of Hitler*, Harper, 1941.

Education for Death: The Making of the Nazi (also see below), Oxford University Press, 1941, reprinted, Octagon, 1972.

"Hitler's Children" (screenplay adaptation of one of his books), RKO General Productions, 1943.

(With wife, Edna Ziemer) *Whirlaway Hopper*, Bobbs-Merrill, 1962.

Also author of *Should Hitler's Children Live?*, 1946, *Too Old for What?*, 1968, *Witness on Water Skis*, 1975, *Let'm Eat Grass*, 1975, and *Brigand of Monserrat*, 1979. Author of "Education for Death" (screenplay), "Torchbearers" (screenplay), "Let's Listen to Lifetime Learning" (radio script), "Giant Step Forward" (television script), and "One Empty Rocking Chair" (television script). Contributor to *Reader's Digest, Collier's, Saturday Evening Post, Good Housekeeping, Mademoiselle, Look, Liberty, Town and Country*, and *American Mercury*.

WORK IN PROGRESS: A humorous novel on experiences with Fourth Armored Division in World War II; *The Halfbreed*, a historical novel.

SIDELIGHTS: Gregor Ziemer's *Education for Death: The Making of a Nazi* has been translated into Spanish.

AVOCATIONAL INTERESTS: Traveling. †